ALSO BY WILLIAM I. HITCHCOCK

The Age of Eisenhower: America and the World in the 1950s

The Bitter Road to Freedom: A New History of the Liberation of Europe

The Struggle for Europe: The Turbulent History of a Divided Continent, 1945–Present

France Restored: Cold War Diplomacy and the Quest for Leadership in Europe

The Human Rights Revolution: An International History (coedited with Petra Goedde and Akira Iriye)

Shaper Nations: Strategies for a Changing World (coedited with Melvyn P. Leffler and Jeffrey W. Legro)

From War to Peace: Altered Strategic Landscapes in the 20th Century (coedited with Paul Kennedy)

A SHADOW OVER THE WORLD

FRANKLIN D. ROOSEVELT, THE RISE OF FASCISM, AND THE MAKING OF AMERICA'S WORLD WAR II

WILLIAM I. HITCHCOCK

SIMON & SCHUSTER

New York Amsterdam/Antwerp London
Toronto Sydney/Melbourne New Delhi

Simon & Schuster
1230 Avenue of the Americas
New York, NY 10020

The authorized representative in the EEA is Simon & Schuster Nederland B.V., Herculesplein 96, 3584 AA Utrecht, Netherlands. info@simonandschuster.nl

First Simon & Schuster hardcover edition September 2026

Interior design by Carly Loman

Manufactured in the United States of America

1 3 5 7 9 10 8 6 4 2

Library of Congress Control Number: 2026934295

ISBN 978-1-9821-5772-2
ISBN 978-1-9821-5774-6 (ebook)

For my sisters

Lucinda Lee Hitchcock and Evelyn Taylor Hitchcock

Today is far from Childhood
But up and down the hills,
I held her hand the tighter
Which shortened all the miles.

—EMILY DICKINSON

"I should like to be able to offer the hope that the shadow over the world might swiftly pass. I cannot. The facts compel my stating, with candor, that darker periods may lie ahead."

—FRANKLIN D. ROOSEVELT, SEPTEMBER 21, 1939

CONTENTS

A SHADOW OVER THE WORLD

Vincenzo Laviosa

PROLOGUE

NO LONE ISLAND

"The future of the nation and of the American people is at stake."

—FRANKLIN D. ROOSEVELT

I

The Memorial Gymnasium at the University of Virginia—a large Beaux-Arts building of brick, white plaster pillars, and tall, vaulted windows—opened in 1924 as a tribute to the graduates of the school who had died in the Great War. The largest gym in the South at the time, it could comfortably hold 2,500 spectators for boxing matches, basketball games, swimming competitions, and track meets. On the afternoon of Monday, June 10, 1940, as a light rain fell outside, three times that number had crammed into the large stuffy central hall to observe the commencement ceremonies of the class of 1940—and to hear remarks from the day's distinguished speaker, Franklin D. Roosevelt.

The president and Mrs. Roosevelt had a particular reason to attend this ceremony: their son Franklin D. Roosevelt Jr. would receive his law degree that day. Knowing this, the university's president, John Lloyd Newcomb, had invited FDR to address the graduating class. The Roosevelts rode down to Charlottesville by train and then motored the short distance from the train station to the packed gymnasium. Although the legions of journalists there did not mention it, FDR was helped from his car and into his steel leg braces by his senior military aide, General Edwin "Pa" Watson; his naval aide, Captain Daniel J. Callaghan; and his physician, Admiral Ross T. McIntire. They supported him as he entered the hall and lurched toward the rostrum. There he stood, cloaked in the traditional gown and crimson academic hood of a Harvard man, while the university band struck up "Hail to the Chief." The crowd gave the president a thundering ovation, punctuated with shouts and rebel yells. Under normal circumstances, President Roosevelt might have amused his audience with a few lighthearted anecdotes about his own college days. But he had arrived in Charlottesville at a moment of extreme tension and anxiety in world affairs. He came not to entertain his listeners, but to awaken them.[1]

The war in Europe, which began in September 1939 with Germany's invasion of Poland, reached new intensity on May 10, 1940, when the German army launched a swift and devastating invasion of France and the Low Countries. In World War I, France and Germany struggled for four terrible years over every inch of this same landscape, with the battle lines rarely moving. Not this time. In a few weeks of fighting, Hitler's forces penetrated the defensive positions of the British, French, Dutch, and Belgian armies. German divisions cleverly maneuvered through the hilly wooded terrain of the Ardennes Forest in Belgium, totally surprising and surrounding the outmatched Anglo-French troops. In the first days of June, 330,000 British and French soldiers undertook a daring but humiliating retreat from the shrapnel-strewn beaches of Dunkirk, boarding a flotilla of ships that ferried them toward safety across the foaming English Channel. By the time FDR began his journey to Charlottesville, the Netherlands and Belgium had surrendered, the French government had fled Paris, and the Germans were just three days away from entering France's capital.

As his train rolled southward through the rolling green countryside of central Virginia on the morning of June 10, President Roosevelt received more disheartening news: Fascist Italy declared war on France and sent troops across the Alps, eager to scoop up territory from its mortally wounded neighbor. Italy's decision to join Germany as an allied combatant seemed inevitable, given the close affinity of Mussolini and Hitler and the "pact of steel" the two had concluded in May 1939. But for months in the spring of 1940, Roosevelt had been in touch with the Italians, trying to keep them out of the war. He hoped his diplomacy might avoid a widening of the European conflict. The news from Europe shattered those illusions.

Suddenly the world seemed headed toward a terrible, almost inconceivable fate. Mussolini's decision to attack France officially aligned Fascist Italy with Nazi Germany and completed the formation of an imposing bloc of the world's dictatorships. The August 1939 Hitler-Stalin Pact had already linked Germany and the Soviet Union into a tacit alliance, while Japan, aligned with Germany's ambitions, was rapidly subduing China and seemed poised to strike at Southeast Asia. The American press often lumped these aggressive states together under the term "totalitarian." They combined military, technological, and industrial power with fanatical ideologies that welcomed war as the means to bring about the destruction of a world order that had stymied their ambitions. The aggressive militarist states stood shoulder to shoulder, determined to build a New Order on the ashes of the old. By the time Roosevelt reached Charlottesville, Hitler was on the cusp of absolute victory, and America looked ever more cut off and alone.

When Roosevelt began to speak to the university graduates in the packed hall, with his rhythmic cadences and his familiar patrician accent, it became clear this would not be an ordinary commencement address. The president knew that the moment called for a sobering message of forceful determination. After years of drift and uncertainty, he wished to strike a new note. The young men arrayed before him in gowns and mortarboards had a right to know "what the future holds for all peoples and all nations that have been living under democratic forms of Government—under the free institutions of a free people." Should America be drawn into this war, the president knew, the lives of these students would be unalterably changed. These young men might soon find themselves in uniform, and in harm's way.

Roosevelt did not try to assuage the anxieties of the students and their families. Instead, he drew an alarming picture. Democracy was dying before their very eyes. "The ideal of individual liberty," the president said, "the ideal of free franchise, the ideal of peace through justice," these had been called "decadent" by Europe's dictators. The fascists, determined to rule with an iron fist, had "abandoned with deliberate contempt all the moral values to which even this young country for more than three hundred years has been accustomed and dedicated." Italy's attack on France that very day only illustrated the treachery of Europe's thuggish leaders. In a much-quoted phrase, borrowed from the French prime minister Paul Reynaud, FDR rebuked Italy's aggression: "The hand that held the dagger has struck it into the back of its neighbor." He laid out the hard facts: The fascists were on the march and democracy was losing the war.

What, Roosevelt asked, will America do? With a confidence and determination all too often lacking during his first two terms, he firmly and clearly rejected a policy of isolation or appeasement. He expressed his contempt for those who "still hold to the now somewhat obvious delusion that we of the United States can safely permit the United States to become a lone island, a lone island in a world dominated by the philosophy of force." In chilling imagery, he depicted America alone, chained up, and forgotten. "Such an island may be the dream of those who still talk and vote as isolationists. Such an island represents to me and to the overwhelming majority of Americans today a helpless nightmare of a people without freedom—the nightmare of a people lodged in prison, handcuffed, hungry, and fed through the bars from day to day by the contemptuous, unpitying masters of other continents."

Instead of isolation, Roosevelt promised action on behalf of the democracies. "In our American unity, we will pursue two obvious and simultaneous courses. We will extend to the opponents of force the material resources of this nation; and, at the same time, we will harness and speed up the use of those resources in order that we ourselves in the Americas may have equipment and training equal to the task of any emergency and every defense." FDR was promising military aid to the anti-fascist forces overseas, and a rapid rearmament program at home. It wasn't war yet, but it was perilously close. The president acknowledged that the country had been divided over how to respond to the rise of the dictators. "But in recent months," he said, "the principal question has been somewhat simplified." The dictators threatened democracy not just in Europe and Asia but at home. A world war had begun, one that might soon engulf the United States. Concluding with an ominous send-off, he said, "The future of the nation and of the American people is at stake."

The speech at Charlottesville marked Roosevelt's boldest, most powerful statement yet about how the United States would respond to the fascist onslaught. In fact, the policies that flowed from this address marked a turning point in the history of the Second World War and of the subsequent "American Century." Robert Sherwood, the celebrated playwright who joined the administration as a speechwriter and later wrote a sympathetic biography of Roosevelt, called the commitment made at the University of Virginia to arm the European democracies "the most important and most courageous decision of his entire career." From this point on, the United States engaged its economic resources, and soon its military might, in a struggle for the survival of democracy in the world. As German, Italian, Soviet, and Japanese armies rolled across the world map with ever more force and confidence, the isolationism that had appealed to so many Americans in the 1930s lost its allure. Well before the Japanese attack on Pearl Harbor on December 7, 1941, that would bring the United States into World War II, Franklin Roosevelt positioned America as the world's guarantor of democracy against authoritarian rule.[2]

II

But this declaration of June 10, 1940, which was met with an outpouring of praise by the press and the public, had been a long time coming. Though some historians like to portray Roosevelt as a secret internationalist who long expected war with the fascist powers but was constrained by public opinion from doing anything to prepare for it, this book presents a more complex portrait of the president than we have seen before. It is a picture of a man who remained unsure for many years just what kind of threat fascism posed to the United States. Though he instinctively hated fascism, he did not have a strategy for confronting it, nor did he fully grasp its potential dangers. He came only slowly and quite grudgingly to the realization that fascism and American democracy could not coexist in the world.[3]

From the start of his presidency in 1933 and through his first two terms, Franklin Roosevelt sought to avoid war, urged world disarmament, and even signed legislation banning U.S. arms sales to any nation at war. His administration faced the collapse of democratic capitalism at home, and the immense effort to restore basic economic security to the American people dominated his first years in office. Pushing international affairs to the back burner, he proposed the policy of nonintervention and the "good neighbor" in 1933 and reaffirmed it in 1936. Even as Hitler repudiated the Versailles peace agreements that had ended World War I; even as he launched a vast, illegal rearmament program; even as Italy invaded Ethiopia and both the Nazis and Italians poured soldiers and weapons into Spain to support the fascists in the civil war there; even as the German concentration camps began to fill up—Roosevelt insisted on neutrality, not conflict. He signed the Neutrality Acts of 1935, 1936, and 1937, refusing to fight Congress over them because he largely supported the measures. "We shun political commitments which might entangle us in foreign wars," he said in August 1936. "We seek to isolate ourselves completely from war." The "conflicting economic and political fanaticisms" of Europe would not, he said, stir America from its neutrality. "I have seen war," he said darkly. "I hate war." There is no reason to doubt that he spoke from the heart.

By 1937, as Japan intensified its brutal conquest of China and committed unspeakable atrocities across that war-scarred country, FDR began to speak out about what America's responsibilities in the world should be. Yet his calls for negotiation, moral leadership, peace, and collective security were cautious, even passive. "The epidemic of world lawlessness is spreading," he said in Chicago in October 1937, and "when an epidemic of physical disease starts to spread, the community approves and joins in a quarantine of the patients in order to protect the health of the community against the spread of the disease." Despite a surprisingly welcome reception for this speech, and its implied "quarantine" of lawless militarists, little action followed. Vague schemes for using naval power to hem in the Japanese Empire evaporated quickly. Roosevelt certainly expressed anxiety about trends in world affairs; but as of 1937, he saw no role for the United States in altering them.

Following Hitler's bellicose demands for a revision of the map of Europe, Roosevelt fell in line with British and French appeasement policy. Hitler swallowed Austria; FDR did nothing. To be sure, in 1938 he made a worthy effort to ease the plight of Europe's Jews by convening a conference about sheltering refugees right after Hitler's troops marched into Vienna, but it brought no solutions. Roosevelt knew Hitler would take aim at Czechoslovakia next, but remained passive. When British prime minister Neville Chamberlain flew across the English Channel not once but three separate times to beg Hitler to negotiate the peaceful dismembering of Czechoslovakia and avoid war, FDR encouraged him with a one-line telegram: "Good man." He also wrote numerous public letters to the dictators, urging them to pursue peace and negotiation. He spoke and acted like a pacifist, and in fact he described himself as a pacifist. Though he certainly loathed fascism, he did not commit American power to contain it or fight it. Even his effort to cultivate the Soviet Union as a bid to keep pressure on Germany crumbled into ashes when Stalin and Hitler agreed to a nonaggression pact and a trade deal in August 1939. When war came the following month, Roosevelt insisted that America would remain neutral. He wanted to keep America out of war, and that meant staying free from foreign entanglements of any kind.[4]

III

What happened to change Roosevelt's mind so completely that by the time of his speech in Charlottesville he seemed ready to commit America to aid Britain in its desperate struggle with Nazi Germany, even at the risk of war? This is the most fundamental question that scholars of the Roosevelt years must ask. Because FDR is often elusive, and because he left so little in writing about his own thoughts and intentions, the answer is not immediately apparent. Without access to a Roosevelt presidential memoir or a detailed diary, scholars must knit together fragments from his presidency, drawing from government papers, the writings of those around him, as well as the letters and press conferences in which Roosevelt revealed pieces of himself to friends and to reporters (usually off the record). Placing these materials alongside the roiling, turbulent events of the 1930s, we can begin to make sense of Roosevelt's evolution from an anti-war pacifist, a nationalist, and an American exceptionalist to a man who embraced a stunningly ambitious global task:

the safeguarding of democracy in a world that had fallen under the shadow of fascism.[5]

At least three major forces propelled Roosevelt's transformation and brought him to that speech in Charlottesville. The first was the immediate problem: In June 1940 Hitler was winning the war. Roosevelt's policies of neutrality and mediation had failed to have any impact whatsoever on the course of world affairs. If he did not act quickly and use American power to assist the anti-fascist states in stemming the Nazi tide, the war would end with Hitler triumphant. Once France and Britain had been subdued by the Nazis, all of Eurasia, from Japan to the Irish Sea, would be entirely dominated by dictatorships. The oceans would be closed to American trade and commerce and organized around new militarist empires bent on war and conquest. In such a dystopian scenario, America would have to transform itself into a garrison state, always on alert, always fearful of a possible attack. Democracy itself might be snuffed out forever. No president likes to admit failure; to his great credit, FDR understood that he needed to change course quickly. With his words in Charlottesville, he announced a new direction.

The second reason for Roosevelt's move from neutrality to confrontation lies in American domestic politics. Like most presidents, Roosevelt initially saw foreign policy as a distraction from his domestic priorities. He feared that his New Deal coalition would be rent apart by any adventures overseas, and he remained neutral and passive on the world stage because he was so active at home. During his second term in office, however, from 1936 to 1940, Roosevelt faced a major backlash against the New Deal. Most Republicans disliked it from the start and some members of Roosevelt's own Democratic Party turned against it, especially conservative Southerners, who feared the New Deal's support for labor unions and its promise of greater economic and political opportunity for African Americans. And some American demagogues and charlatans—the Detroit priest Father Charles Coughlin being the most effective—claimed that Roosevelt and his New Deal policies were un-American, and part of a Jewish-Communist conspiracy to undermine America from within.

In defending his transformational domestic achievements, Roosevelt embraced a rhetorical strategy that emphasized the New Deal as a triumph of American democracy—a practice of government that gave power back to the people. FDR talked about democracy often. It became the keyword of his presidency. And from late 1937 on, as part of his defense of the New Deal, he used the threat of fascism *in the world* to raise the stakes of his program for strengthening democracy at home. Opponents of the New Deal in America, he implied, were part of a *global* reaction against democracy. Brownshirts and Blackshirts in Europe were in league with American fascist sympathizers as well as oligarchs and "economic royalists" who feared the great democratic experiment of the New Deal. Since the danger to democracy was a global one, the defense of democracy must also become global in its scope. Roosevelt developed his most powerful argument by linking democracy at home with anti-fascism in the world.

In 1940, as he sought an unprecedented third term in office, FDR accelerated this strategy and painted his domestic opponents as lackeys of the world's dictators. He hinted that Republican standard-bearer Wendell Willkie was a type of American fascist, seeking to impose Mussolini's model of a "corporate state" on America. His Democratic surrogates in the campaign regularly asserted that Willkie was the man the dictators wanted as president. If Americans wished to save their democracy, Roosevelt argued, they would have to beat back fascism wherever it reared its menacing head. In this way, FDR domesticated the global fascist threat and used it to explain why Americans could not remain isolated from the wars of the dictators.[6]

The third explanation for Roosevelt's remarkable shift from neutrality to intervention in the world can be found in the changing patterns of American public opinion, a process that started much earlier than the emergencies of 1940. Although historians have devoted extensive attention to the "isolationists" of this era, they have tended to overlook the simultaneous growth—and ultimate victory—of internationalism.[7] This book shows that, for all the importance of neutrality, pacifism, and the widespread reluctance to intervene in the world's troubles, Americans during the 1930s became increasingly hostile to the world's dictators. The crises of this era—from the early assaults on Jews in Germany to the Italian invasion of Ethiopia, the fascist war on democracy in Spain, Japan's brutal invasion of China, and the Nazi assault on Austria, Czechoslovakia, Poland, and Western Europe—engaged and enraged the American public. In the pages of countless publications, on radio airwaves, and in public meetings of every kind, Americans argued about how to stem the rising tide of fascism and how to halt the drift of the world toward the abyss of war and tyranny.[8]

Of course, Americans did not want to enter another war, so soon after the Great War ended. But they did not wish to remain passive accomplices in the death of democracy, either. Was there a path for them between these two alternatives, between doing nothing and entering another world war? Roosevelt strove to find it. He, too, wished to keep American soldiers out of European trenches and Asian jungles. In 1940, he developed a robust and ambitious program of "methods short of war" that he hoped would play a decisive role in helping Britain and China stave off their attackers. These policies carried the risk that America might be drawn into war, and by the start of 1941, both he and the country were willing to run that risk. This was a sea change in America's world outlook, and it emerged not from Roosevelt alone but from a prolonged national debate about the proper role for America in the world. This book will show that the daring ambition Roosevelt revealed in the Charlottesville speech was largely a product, not a catalyst, of American hostility toward the ideology of fascism. While Roosevelt is central to this story of an American awakening, he was by no means its only author. His gradual embrace of an active world role for the country reflected the transformation of American values and ideas that took place in these years.

Taken together, these three developments—Roosevelt's immediate fear of a Nazi victory; his political defense of the New Deal during his second term; and the decade-long growth of anti-fascist sentiment in the country—set America on a new course, toward a tragic but necessary and just war for the survival of democracy in the world. How Americans chose that path and accepted that heavy responsibility is the subject of this book.

IV

To mobilize a people for war, leaders must first mobilize ideas. Ideas mattered to Roosevelt, and he regularly framed his major policy plans, foreign and domestic, in a distinctive language of progress, economic justice, and democracy—principles that he believed comprised the American tradition. To follow Roosevelt as he grew from a cautious pacifist and nationalist focused strictly on domestic economic problems into a militant defender of democracy in the world, we need to understand the network of people and ideas that animated him and spurred his transformation.

Roosevelt sat at the center of at least three large concentric circles between which ideas, information, and policy flowed. Though the people inside these circles differed in their political beliefs and policy prescriptions, they helped to prompt in Roosevelt's mind the conclusion that American democracy could not thrive or even survive in a world dominated by barbarism, mass murder, fascism, and war. Democracy was worth saving, even if that meant fighting for it.

In the inner ring, closest to the president, we find those who worked with FDR almost daily—the cabinet officers, "brain trust" policy advisers, family members, and trusted friends of the president. Among the most important was First Lady Eleanor Roosevelt. A champion of liberal causes and especially African American civil and economic rights, her influence on FDR's domestic policy is well-known. Yet by 1938, particularly in response to the death struggle of democracy in the Spanish Civil War, she developed a language of her own to justify a bolder world role for America—a language of humanitarian concern, Christian charity, and defiance in the face of evil. She used "My Day," her enormously popular syndicated daily newspaper column, to inject these ideas into public discourse and to undercut the central claim of isolationism: that the world's problems were not America's to solve. Though Roosevelt did not often credit Eleanor's influence, he valued her instincts and respected the immense prestige she had accumulated in the country.

Alongside the First Lady, Roosevelt relied on a chorus of intimate advisers who helped him build a case for confronting fascism in the world. Treasury Secretary Henry Morgenthau Jr., Interior Secretary Harold Ickes, Commerce Secretary (and later FDR's closest counselor on national security matters) Harry Hopkins, associate justice of the Supreme Court Felix Frankfurter, the lawyer Samuel Rosenman, the playwright Robert Sherwood, the librarian of Congress Archibald MacLeish, among others formed a phalanx of trusted counselors that became crucial in helping Roosevelt to articulate a new American resolve to meet the fascist threat.[9]

In a second ring around the president, there gathered the diplomatic officials and envoys who provided FDR with a perspective on the wider world as it descended into chaos and disorder. From this group, Roosevelt received wildly mixed messages, which may explain in part his long delay in awakening to the foreign danger. Secretary of State Cordell Hull shared Roosevelt's internationalist instincts, yet his innately cautious and territorial nature undermined his influence in the White House. Sumner Welles, Hull's deputy, knew Roosevelt well and relied on his personal connection to encourage Roosevelt to break away from the restraints of isolationism. William C. Bullitt, the ambassador to the Soviet Union and later to France, was tricky and manipulative, but he, like FDR, shifted from advocating appeasement to urging a muscular confrontation with Hitler by 1940. In London, Ambassador Joseph P. Kennedy, appeasement-prone, ambitious, and self-centered, was a disastrous appointment whose defeatism became a major obstacle to Roosevelt at the height of the world crisis; after replacing this difficult envoy at the end of 1940, however, Roosevelt took more personal control of American relations with Britain.

From Berlin, William Dodd—a history professor turned diplomat who was much maligned for his lack of ambassadorial flair and his provincial ways—

sent Roosevelt ever-more alarming memos about the true nature of the Third Reich. Though FDR did not welcome Dodd's foreboding letters, he drew from them undeniable evidence of the malevolent intent of the Nazis. George Messersmith, consul in Berlin and ambassador in Vienna from 1934 until 1937, sent reams of long, detailed, and portentous missives to the State Department and the president about Nazi outrages. Claude Bowers, a Democratic Party strategist awarded with the embassy in Madrid, became an ardent anti-fascist and, like Dodd, sent Roosevelt thousands of pages of anxious cables warning about the spread of aggressive fascism in Spain and Europe.

And two formidable Republican leaders, Henry Stimson, a former secretary of both state and war, and Frank Knox, a newspaper publisher, former army officer, and 1936 vice presidential candidate, were outspoken advocates of confrontation with fascist powers. Stimson in particular penned numerous open public letters and speeches from 1937 onward calling for robust action by the democracies against the dictatorships in Europe and Asia. FDR brought both men into his cabinet in June 1940. Cumulatively, these and many other presidential envoys persuaded FDR that only the United States had the power, and the moral standing, to rally the world in an anti-fascist coalition. Failing this, Hitler and the other dictators would determine the fate of the world.[10]

In the outer ring of influence around the president, there circulated what we might call the witnesses of the world's descent to war: the enormously influential journalists, writers, editors, lobbyists, religious leaders, and public figures who sounded the alarm about fascism from its earliest days. Roosevelt, it is well-known, paid close attention to newspaper editorials and foreign reporting; he read about a dozen papers every day. In the morning, in bed with his breakfast, he riffled through the *New York Times*, the *New York Herald Tribune*, the *Baltimore Sun*, the *Chicago Tribune*, the *Washington Post*, and the *Washington Times-Herald*. In the evening, he looked at the *Washington Evening Star*, the *Washington Daily News*, the *New York World-Telegram*, the *New York Journal American* (published by arch-isolationist and Hitler admirer William Randolph Hearst), and the *New York Sun*. He also paid attention to a tabloid, the *New York Daily News*, which was one of the nation's most-read papers. And he spent a great deal of time with reporters, holding press conferences twice a week, usually Tuesday afternoons and Friday mornings. He made every effort to shape press coverage of his presidency, and to stay abreast of the editorial pages. Newspapers conveyed to him the temper of the nation.[11]

Foreign correspondents were especially valuable because Roosevelt's ambassadors were unreliable, while the State Department was excessively legalistic and procedure-bound. And unlike presidents today, FDR had only a limited intelligence service, located in the armed services, to give him timely information about the intentions of potential adversaries. The overseas reporters whose work he read painted a portrait of a darkening world. They sought to alert their readers to the grave danger of fascism to human liberty and to American security. Many of these writers went to Europe in search of sophistication and liberation, and perhaps to leave behind a dull, provincial, and rapidly commercializing America—the land Sinclair Lewis brutally satirized in his 1922 novel *Babbitt*. Instead, they found in Europe a political culture in profound crisis, unable to defend itself from internal enemies. Observing the sinister methods of fascism up close, they advocated American engagement in the world because they believed America must become a bulwark against this dangerous ideology. In pushing Roosevelt to embrace this global vision of America's responsibilities, they helped him develop the language and the intellectual arguments he would use to mobilize the nation for the coming clash.[12]

No one made the case for confrontation more forcefully than Dorothy Thompson, a woman of extraordinary gifts who acted as a powerful counterweight to the neutralism and disengagement of the 1930s. Thompson appears often in the pages that follow, almost Roosevelt's alter ego. Brash, uncompromising, often self-righteous, a Republican, and an acute critic of the New Deal, Thompson was also an anti-fascist of the first hour. An active suffragist in her youth, she became the Central European correspondent of a Philadelphia newspaper in the 1920s and knew European politics better than anyone in the insular State Department. In 1931, she interviewed Hitler and chronicled the alarming rise of the Nazis to power. Through her syndicated, thrice-weekly column in the *New York Herald Tribune*, which she wrote from 1936 to 1941, Thompson became a national sensation, putting hundreds of thousands of words of warning into circulation.

She was regularly referred to as the "First Lady of American Journalism" and the most influential woman in America after Eleanor Roosevelt. Her friend John Gunther called her "a blue-eyed tornado," though others were less charitable and considered her an alarmist and warmonger. Her fellow columnist and rival at the *Herald Tribune*, Walter Lippmann, uncharitably likened her to the Statue of Liberty: "made of brass; visible at all times to all the world; holding the light aloft but always the same light." But Lippmann could only have dreamed of possessing the power and influence Thompson enjoyed in these years. Her consistent hatred of fascism and dictatorship, her clear-eyed understanding of the nature of the threat they posed, and her enormous public reach through her columns, radio broadcasts, books, and lectures (as well the notoriety of her marriage to novelist Sinclair Lewis) made her the most compelling and consequential analyst of world affairs in this dark decade.[13]

Of course, these years formed the high-water mark of the foreign correspondent. "Ours is the age of the reporter," Thompson believed. Events were moving too fast for historians or academics to study them carefully. Snap judgments were needed, and America's newspapers and airwaves were full of sharp, well-informed, and ever-more ominous reports from dozens of brilliant journalists who watched with dread as fascism took hold and metastasized across Europe. Many of them appear here, including the brainy, uncompromising Edgar Mowrer of the *Chicago Daily News*, who ran afoul of both Mussolini and Hitler; the sparkling, fiery Martha Gellhorn, who covered the civil war in Spain and passed on heartbreaking reports to Eleanor Roosevelt; and the dogged, skillful chief of the *Chicago Tribune*'s Berlin bureau, Sigrid Schultz, who despite the deeply anti-Roosevelt and isolationist views of her boss, the *Tribune*'s owner, Robert McCormick, pulled no punches in her careful reporting on the rise of the Nazis.[14]

The *New York Times*, though not yet the national newspaper it later became, carried particular influence in the White House. That made the work of its most well-respected foreign correspondent, Anne O'Hare McCormick, especially important. A rather aloof, independent-minded woman who did not join the boys at the local watering holes, but traveled in the company of her devoted husband, McCormick won a Pulitzer Prize in 1937 in the category of "correspondence." Across the entire two decades of the 1920s and 1930s, she demonstrated her gifts as a portraitist of foreign leaders—and became an occasional apologist for dictators, who she tried to humanize in her essays.[15]

It was an age of words, millions of them, on pages and airwaves, too. Radio correspondents like William Shirer and Edward R. Murrow joined print journalists in informing Americans about world affairs as Europe slipped into fascism. Influential editors on the home front did their part to promote the anti-fascist cause. Freda Kirchwey of *The Nation*; Henry Luce, publisher of *Time*, *Life*, and *Fortune*; and Hamilton Fish Armstrong of *Foreign Affairs* were wholly different in their politics, but fully committed to stopping the advance of fascism. A lively and popular Black press, owned by African Americans and written chiefly for Black readers in cities like Pittsburgh, Baltimore, Chicago, New York, and Atlanta, kept a watchful eye on world events. In these pages could be found the reflections of travelers like

W. E. B. Du Bois and Langston Hughes or policy advice from activists like A. Philip Randolph and Adam Clayton Powell Jr. And Jewish weekly papers carried a stream of worried editorials about the rise of Nazism and fascism in the world. These were years when journalists, publishers, and intellectuals formed a powerful advocacy bloc that valiantly fought back against what they perceived as an irresponsible, reflexive neutralism and passivity in America.[16]

Lobbying committees also popped up with almost weekly regularity in the 1930s, dedicated to countless causes and beleaguered peoples around the globe. These groups were visible, well funded, and capable of enrolling leading public figures from the churches, universities, law firms, the military, industry, and the entertainment world. The most influential included interventionist organizations like the Committee to Defend America by Aiding the Allies, led by the Kansas Republican newspaper editor William Allen White; the Fight for Freedom organization that in 1941 made the explicit case for war against Nazi Germany and Fascist Italy; and the small, discreet Century Group, composed of powerful, well-connected, civic-minded elites who helped design both the first peacetime conscription law and the framework for getting military aid to Britain in 1940 and 1941. These public voices mattered. In fact, they helped Roosevelt capture the public arena from the advocates of American neutrality. In the fall of 1939, with the help of these able publicists and activists, Roosevelt broke the choke hold of the Neutrality Act on his freedom of action; from that point on, he moved with greater confidence and certainty to guide the country toward the confrontation with fascism he now expected.[17]

To help him slip free of the neutrality strictures, FDR drew upon ideas that had been hammered out in the public sphere during the previous decade to explain to an apprehensive public what was at stake. No longer, Roosevelt said at Charlottesville, could America think of itself as a "lone island" of democracy in a world of tyranny. Should fascism and dictatorship triumph in Europe and Asia, Americans would find themselves not safely shielded from the world's troubles, but imprisoned and isolated by ruthless tyrants. Such vivid images sprang from a vocabulary honed over the years by advocates for aid to the European democracies, who led a relentless and highly effective campaign against appeasement and neutrality. In fact, by late 1940, Dorothy Thompson herself was involved in writing some of Roosevelt's most powerful speeches.

In placing Roosevelt onto a broad canvas populated with many dynamic, compelling characters, this book moves beyond earlier works on Roosevelt and American foreign policy. Although FDR has attracted excellent biographers, their concern, naturally enough, is on the daily doings of the president in the White House or at presidential retreats in Hyde Park, New York, and Warm Springs, Georgia. Such accounts typically do not reach out into the public arena to capture the tumult in America at this time.[18] Similarly, studies of FDR's foreign policy often give too little attention to nonofficial actors and analysts, the very people whose voices shaped American public opinion; while others race past the great arguments that unfolded in the years before 1939.[19] Some popular works about America and the world in the 1930s compress the era into a verbal duel between Roosevelt and the young aviator and outspoken isolationist Charles Lindbergh, as if the arm's-length sparring of those two in 1940 and 1941 could adequately summarize the full and prolonged national debate about the fascist threat that gripped the country from 1922 until Pearl Harbor.[20]

When we widen the lens to capture a fuller picture of society, we can see that Americans were never "isolated" from global events in the 1930s. The combined shocks of a worldwide depression and the rise of fascism prompted one of the greatest periods of introspection and self-diagnosis that Americans had ever experienced. In newspapers and journals, on nationwide radio broadcasts, in town halls, mass meetings, rallies, auditoriums, college classrooms, street corners and, of course, during election time, Americans anxiously asked complex, unsettling questions: What kind of society did they want to build? Could they revive and defend their own distinctly American way of life in the shadow of war? Was capitalism even worth saving? Was democracy still viable in the modern world, and did it possess the strength and endurance to meet the ideological challenge of fascism? Could a world of law and justice supplant a world built on war, empire, and force—and did America have a responsibility to bring that world into being? These questions animated millions of Americans across the interwar years, shaping domestic politics as much as foreign policy.[21]

Roosevelt, too, wrestled with these questions, but only in late 1938 at the earliest did he begin to develop the idea—so crucial to later U.S. and world history—that to save democratic capitalism at home, he would have to ensure the survival of democracy in the world. And that could mean war. In coming to that conclusion, Roosevelt listened to, and learned from, a remarkable assortment of people who saw, much sooner than he did, that the forces of fascism, race war, and autarkic imperialism presented a mortal danger to America's security and prosperity. They would help Roosevelt, and indeed an entire generation, find the words to legitimate the coming struggle between democracy and fascism in the world.[22]

By adopting this method, by seeing him within the colorful, angry, tumultuous years of the 1930s, a time when chaos, fear, and profound human insecurity ruled, we will see FDR in a new light. We will observe that, as the dictators tightened their grip, Roosevelt initially temporized, equivocated, and deferred decisions. The renowned "juggler," he dropped more than a few balls. Like many Americans, he expressed a certain admiration for fascism of the kind Mussolini imposed on Italy, while feeling quiet revulsion at Hitler and Nazism. In due course, however, he grew into the century's most fervent champion of democracy at home and in the world. This is a story of a great leader becoming great over time, searching in the darkness until finally lighting the way forward with his own sense of certainty and courage. Even the great presidents are not born so; they must test themselves in the heat of battle, as Franklin Roosevelt certainly did.[23]

But that battle was not fought alone, nor did it begin only in 1940. The effort to define America's response to the crisis of democracy started immediately in 1922, when Mussolini's Blackshirts bullied their way to power in Rome; it carried on until the Japanese attack on December 7, 1941. In these two decades, Americans ceaselessly debated how to respond to democracy's alarming collapse, and fascism's alarming success. Over time, the public view of the fascist challenge shifted from smug indifference to a grim determination to face the dictators. FDR's leadership had something to do with this, of course, but so, too, did the innate sense of indignation the American public felt toward the naked brutality of the dictators and their open, aggravated assault on the foundations of modern civilization. Well before the Japanese torpedo bombers took to the air for the fateful attack on Pearl Harbor, Americans had come to accept what many commentators often called their "destiny" to fight fascism, to sustain the ideas of political liberty and self-determination, and to establish what they saw as the liberating power of democratic capitalism. As Roosevelt put it in his "Four Freedoms" address in January 1941, almost a year before taking the country to war, Americans would use their strength not only to defend their shores and to protect their form of government, but so that freedom of speech and religion, and freedom from want and fear, might flourish "everywhere in the world."

V

This inspiring story of America gathering itself to take on the dictators comes with a sting in the tail: As we will discover throughout this book, in preparing to wage a war for democracy, the United States frequently betrayed the values it claimed to embody. The country throughout these years remained committed to racial segregation not just in society generally, but specifically in the U.S. armed forces—the very instrument through which the nation would seek to roll back fascism. The racial apartheid of Jim Crow deprived millions of African Americans of their rights. Roosevelt himself led a political party composed of some of the most virulent racists in American history, and because he needed their political support in Congress to pass his ambitious domestic priorities, he rarely tangled with his Southern supporters on issues of race. Furthermore, from the late 1930s on through the war, Roosevelt and many of his closest policy advisers all too willingly trampled on civil liberties at home. Long before the United States entered the war, FDR ordered wiretapping and surveillance of suspected spies, aliens, and political rivals. On the eve of war, he spoke frequently of a dangerous "fifth column" in America and urged the public to be alert to any un-American activities in their neighborhoods. The decision to incarcerate Japanese Americans almost immediately after the war began sprang from this long public effort to demonize German and Japanese Americans as subversive and threatening.

Throughout the late 1930s, FDR also joined with many other politicians to stigmatize Communists, and he lumped them together with Nazis and fascists as America's "totalitarian" enemies. The Smith Act, or Alien Registration Act of 1940, made it possible for the government to prosecute anyone—chiefly Communists—who might "advocate, abet, advise, or teach" the violent destruction of the U.S. government. And perhaps most consequential in the long run, the language that FDR deployed to awaken the country to the fascist threat legitimated the unprecedented expansion of what scholars would later call "the warfare state"—a massive and permanent structure of military power at the heart of American life.[24]

This bitter paradox compels us to confront what we might call "the progressive origins of the American empire." In the name of saving democracy, Roosevelt made tactical alliances with segregationists as well as J. Edgar Hoover's FBI. He deployed Christian rhetoric of human rights while demonizing his and the nation's enemies as less than human. In 1940 and 1941, he characterized the European and Asian conflicts as wars between the free and the enslaved, between democracy and tyranny, between God-fearing individualists and the unchristian monolith of Nazism. In waging a war to protect democracy, he projected U.S. military power across the globe, supplanting the old order of European empires with a new form of hegemony.[25]

After FDR's death in April 1945, a new generation of leaders turned to Roosevelt's storehouse of arresting phrases and images; they borrowed freely from it as they moved toward a new ideological contest with the Soviet Union in the emerging Cold War. FDR served as an example to later leaders: When they chose to attack Communists, left-wing radicals, labor activists, agrarian rebels, anti-colonial freedom fighters, Black nationalists, and eventually Islamist extremists, they used many of the concepts Roosevelt developed in the early 1940s. Like a genie let out of its glowing lantern, the idea of an American war for democracy, so luminous and hopeful when the enemy was Nazism, took on malevolent force when it was repurposed against new foes long after the Second World War had ended. After 1945, across Asia, Latin America, and the Middle East, the United States justified wars using many of the tropes Roosevelt had articulated.[26]

Does such misuse of power by FDR and many later U.S. leaders compel us to repudiate the larger purpose—the defeat of fascism in the world—for which Roosevelt strived? Surely not, and for two reasons. First, America's cause in the Second World War was undoubtedly a just one, and the innumerable half-truths and hypocrisies that Roosevelt accepted ought not to obscure the larger purpose of this anti-fascist war. Second, Roosevelt came to believe that the war would genuinely help secure and advance democracy at home. The New Deal, he felt, was his chief legacy and for much of the 1930s, he feared that war would be its undoing, allowing conservatives to mount a counterattack against its signature measures. But by 1939, he came to see that the only way to ensure the future of democracy at home was to confront, and defeat, fascism in the world. Progress and reform, so hard-won against the vested interests of American capitalism, required Roosevelt to turn back the forces of reaction and tyranny abroad.

In these pages, then, we will see an imperfect nation and an imperfect leader strive to do good after a long stretch of doing nothing in the face of fascist persecution. In the 1930s, in the shadow of the greatest economic *and* ideological upheaval the country had ever known, American citizens from across the social and political spectrum—men and women, Republicans and Democrats, Southerners and Northerners, Catholics and Protestants, African Americans and Jews—wove their voices together with the cries of millions of anguished people around the world—Ethiopians, Spaniards, Austrians, Czechs, Poles, British, French, Chinese, Finns, among many others—and shaped a call to fight for freedom from fascist tyranny. The crusading internationalists we will encounter may have promised a future they could not deliver. They sometimes fell short in living up to the idealism they regularly deployed in public debate.

Knowing this, however, we must still take heart from this story, when a president, in tandem with an extraordinary cast of talented counselors and advocates, brought the country to accept that America had a moral and national interest in fighting for democracy against the inhuman, monstrous wrong of the fascist New Order. After all, no one now would look back at those crisis-filled days at the start of history's most terrible war—as German, Italian, Soviet, and Japanese forces moved from triumph to triumph, as more and more people filled up the concentration camps, as ever-greater swaths of the globe fell to jackbooted columns—and wish that Americans had turned away, and closed their ears and their hearts to the torment of others. Fortunately, rather than stay silent, they stood up and threw themselves into a great battle for a better world. We are fighting for it still.

CHAPTER I

THE MOST MAGNETIC PERSONALITY

"His voice was strong and true and vigorous."

—FRANCES PERKINS

I

Just a short walk.

That's all, maybe thirty feet from his chair on the stage in Madison Square Garden to the podium from which he would deliver a speech nominating Governor Al Smith of New York as the Democratic Party's candidate for president. It was June 26, 1924, and the magnificent arena was packed with over ten thousand delegates and officials. The lights blazed down on Franklin D. Roosevelt as the hall grew quiet. Determined to show the huge crowd that his legs still functioned, Roosevelt, his strong hands gripping a pair of crutches, set out across that deceptively short length of floor, uncertain but determined. He knew he must succeed. His career, and perhaps the fate of the country, depended on it.

It had been a difficult two days at the convention, with the Democratic Party deeply split. One camp gathered around Al Smith, the colorful and charismatic son of New York City's Lower East Side who had risen to become a forceful, much-loved progressive governor of New York. Smith had grown up working in the Fulton Fish Market and had little formal education. A Catholic who represented the urban Democratic Party, mainly working people and recent immigrants, Smith was a working-class hero who now aimed for the biggest prize of them all: the presidency. Athwart Smith's path to the Democratic nomination stood William G. McAdoo, a frosty Episcopalian Southerner who had made a career as a lawyer and businessman in New York City before becoming the treasury secretary under President Woodrow Wilson. He later moved to California and made money in the burgeoning film industry. Like Wilson, McAdoo was a progressive; he favored a shorter workweek, unemployment insurance for workers, and a federal minimum wage. Like Wilson, too, he was a zealous segregationist and had eagerly imposed racial segregation in all offices of the Treasury Department. McAdoo was also a "dry" who favored the prohibition of alcohol as enacted in the Eighteenth Amendment; Smith, a "wet," wanted the amendment repealed. The two factions of the party—urban vs. rural, Northeast vs. West and South, Catholic vs. Protestant, wet vs. dry, workers vs. business elites—were split down the middle along an uncrossable divide. Deadlocked, the convention seemed likely to end in disaster.

For Franklin Roosevelt, too, the convention posed a moment of testing. He was a political thoroughbred who had burst forth from Harvard and Columbia Law School to win a seat in the New York State Senate in 1910, when he was just twenty-eight years old. Blessed with handsome looks, a tall, athletic build, a large (and wealthy) family, and a famous last name, he swiftly became a national figure and served throughout the Wilson administration as assistant secretary of the navy. In 1920, he accepted the Democratic nomination for vice president and campaigned across the country as the sturdy lieutenant of presidential candidate James M. Cox of Ohio. Though the ticket lost to the dull, pro-business Republican Warren G. Harding, FDR seemed poised on the edge of greater national success.

But in the late summer of 1921, at the age of thirty-nine, he fell ill from what was then called infantile paralysis, or poliomyelitis, a viral infection that strikes at the central nervous system. It is still unknown when he contracted the dreaded disease—perhaps during a late July tour of a Boy Scout encampment, one of his many duties as president of the Boy Scout Foundation of Greater New York. On August 10, while at his beloved summer home on Campobello Island, off the coast of Maine, he began to feel chills and fatigue; by the next day, he experienced a high fever, and his legs began to grow numb and then ceased moving. For a time, he even lost feeling in his hands and had difficulty breathing. His skin became agonizingly sensitive. Not until two weeks passed did a specialist diagnose Roosevelt with polio.

In constant pain, racked by fever, he spent a month in bed before taking a private railway car back to his home in New York City. On September 16, the *New York Herald* made the illness public with a story under the ill-informed headline "F. D. Roosevelt Has Infant Paralysis; Condition Is Not Serious." At Presbyterian Hospital, Dr. George Draper gave out a mendacious statement to the press: "There was no cause for alarm. . . . [Roosevelt] temporarily lost control of both legs below the knees." According to the *Herald*, "Dr. Draper asserted that the acute attack had passed and that from now on, Mr. Roosevelt should get better." In fact, though Draper was a noted specialist, his early prognosis was wildly off the mark: "I can say definitely," Draper told the public, "that he will not be crippled, and no one need have any fear of permanent injury in any way from this attack." This was a remarkably casual statement, given that there had been 269 cases of polio in New York that year, of which 53 had been fatal. And just a few years earlier, in 1916, a major polio epidemic swept through American cities, killing thousands.[1]

Draper's blithe optimism, combined with Roosevelt's own courage and will, fueled his determination to regain the use of his legs. Released from the hospital, Roosevelt began an intensive regimen of exercise with the aim of strengthening his upper body as well as his hips and legs. His arms and chest grew large and well muscled; but his legs withered and remained inert. At his mother's home in Hyde Park, where he had spent a blessed childhood among the forests and fields, collecting birds, riding horses, and sailing on the Hudson River, Roosevelt now worked daily to master the use of crutches so that he could at least appear to walk. This required the strapping on of large, heavy steel braces that had to be locked into place; only with the greatest effort could he swing one leg forward, and then the other, while staying upright. It was exhausting, draining work, and his legs showed no signs of recovery.[2]

Alongside this grueling physical regimen, Roosevelt remained determined not to lose the political connections he had worked so hard to build. He kept up correspondence with leading Democrats and signaled his desire to assist Al Smith in seeking the presidency in 1924. The two men had been allies, if not friends, in their earlier days in Albany. Smith needed Roosevelt's upstate, Protestant pedigree on his team; Roosevelt needed to stay active in politics. When Smith asked him to manage his 1924 presidential campaign, Roosevelt accepted with pleasure. While Roosevelt could do most of the campaign work on the telephone or by letter-writing, there was one thing he would have to do in person: give a speech nominating Smith at the Democratic convention. And he would have to do it standing up.

Just before the convention opened, speculation began to mount. The *Washington Post* wrote that "if Mr. Roosevelt is to be the man [to nominate Smith], he will mount the speaker's stand on crutches, for he is only beginning to recover the use of his lower limbs." It had been over three years since he had been seen in such a vast public setting. There was no way to hide his disability, but Roosevelt felt certain it could be effectively diminished with a certain amount of legerdemain. He enrolled his son James to assist him in arriving on the floor of the convention hall by a side entrance, closest to the seats reserved for the New York delegation. With his left hand gripping James's arm and his right firmly holding a crutch, he could just get himself seated in a chair, where James could lower him down and assist with unlocking his braces.[3]

But walking to the podium on the raised dais in front of thousands of expectant viewers would be another matter. To prepare for it, Roosevelt planned carefully. In the second-floor hallway of his New York City townhouse, he marked off the precise distance he would have to cover, and he rehearsed the agonizing performance. Over many days, he practiced, slowly gaining the confidence that he could do it. Just after noon on June 26, the moment came for his speech. A watching journalist described the scene:

> [Roosevelt] was helped up the steps to the platform and was given a cheer from the floor and the galleries. There was a touch of pathos reflected in the faces of many delegates who had not seen him since the San Francisco convention of four years ago, when he was nominated for the vice-presidency. Then he was among the most active of all the delegates, a central figure in several demonstrations, and a vigorous, athletic man in the prime of his life. Today, after months of suffering from paralysis, he literally had to be lifted up the staircase by two strong men, and his face was drawn and deeply lined.

Having reached his chair on the platform, Roosevelt now had to make his way to the rostrum as thousands of delegates, journalists, and politicians anxiously watched. His crutches wedged under his arms, he slowly swung each steel-braced leg forward in a herky-jerky walking motion, as he had rehearsed. Frances Perkins, a Smith ally and leading labor reformer, was present on the platform; she saw just how much exertion this effort demanded. "When he came to the platform to make the nomination," she said, "a change came from the whole convention assembly. There was a hush, and everybody was holding their breath. Everybody was sort of weeping inwardly. The old-line politicians remembered him as a very vigorous young man at the previous convention." The few minutes it took him to move toward the podium seemed "a long hour," a friend recalled. Step by agonizing step, he lurched across the stage, his strong hands and arms doing most of the work, his face turned up and outward. At last, he made it. Grasping for the edges of the podium to steady himself, he thrust out his chin and beamed his dazzling smile. The hall erupted in cheers of admiration mixed with sighs of relief. According to one witness, "it was five minutes before the cheering stopped, and he began his speech."[4]

If that poignant scene softened the hearts of the observers, the speech that came next fired their enthusiasm. Perkins saw the effect: "Here was this terribly crippled person operating on a crutch and an arm and getting himself to the platform somehow, looking so pale, so thin, so delicate that it was a surprise to hear him begin to speak and see that his voice was strong and true and vigorous." Roosevelt nominated Smith in a good-humored, roaring, partisan address, indelibly labeling him the "happy warrior" while singing his praises in a magnificent voice that cascaded down over the smiling delegates. Standing erect in what was surely a painful exercise, and showing great poise, courage, and warmth of spirit, Roosevelt made Democrats feel proud of their progressive policies and their party, whose deep divisions briefly seemed to fade under the sunshine of Roosevelt's character. The *New York Herald Tribune* thought his name "would stampede the convention were he put in nomination." He was "easily the foremost figure on floor or platform."[5]

Roosevelt makes his return to public life, nominating Al Smith for president, June 26, 1924.
FDR Library

Perkins, though, saw through that cheerful, smiling face: "The hand that was on the paper was literally shaking, because of the extreme pain and tenseness with which he held himself up to make that speech." Afterward, when Roosevelt had been helped offstage, various leaders including Smith came to congratulate him. "He was just shaking almost like a leaf," Perkins remembered. He was "wringing wet, perspiration streaming off his face," and "weak as a rag." But the effect of his speech was "electrical," she said, "a tour de force." Above all, his smile revealed the triumph he felt within. "It proved to him that he could do it and it roused his interest and ambition again." Watching him overcome his disability to rally the fractious party with a stirring, noble address, the cigar-chewing Kansas City political boss Tom Pendergast remarked that Roosevelt "has the most magnetic personality of any individual I have ever met." Despite and perhaps because of his disability, Franklin Roosevelt left the delegates in no doubt: The Democratic Party, and the country, had a new star.[6]

II

Franklin Roosevelt's rise to national prominence as a leader of the progressive wing of the Democratic Party demanded more than fortitude in facing polio. It also required him to construct a political identity that could transcend his origins as the scion of a wealthy aristocratic family whose fortune had been made in various still-unregulated industries from banking to railroads, sugar refining, and even opium trafficking. Who was Franklin Roosevelt, and what did he stand for? He would later dismiss the idea that he was guided by some kind of fixed intellectual system. "Philosophy?" he replied quizzically to a reporter who asked him if he had one. "I am a Christian and a Democrat—that's all." And in later years, it suited him to act like a political shape-shifter, one day a conservative budget balancer, the next a generous spender, moving pragmatically from problem to problem, reaching for whatever tool might work. Nonetheless, if he never articulated a systematic ideology, there were recurring themes that ran through his long public life the way a melody returns throughout a symphony. These ideas—about democracy, about America's place in the world, and about the role of the state in governing America—took shape in his mind by the late 1920s, and Roosevelt proved his political genius by braiding them together into a coherent whole.[7]

Born in a handsome mansion situated on a high bank above the Hudson River in Hyde Park, New York, Roosevelt grew up in gracious comfort, surrounded by a family and kinship network that included some of America's oldest and wealthiest families. He traced his ancestry back to the immigration of Calvinist Dutch settlers to New York (then New Amsterdam) in the 1640s. His great-grandfather Jacobus Roosevelt earned a considerable fortune in the sugar trade and banking; he also went into politics, serving in the New York State Assembly in the late eighteenth century. FDR's father, James Roosevelt, was born in Hyde Park, attended Union College in Schenectady and then the Harvard Law School. He pursued a career in law, banking, coal, and railroads, and supported New York's Democratic governor Grover Cleveland in his successful 1884 run for the presidency. James, like Cleveland, adhered to the doctrine of the old Democratic Party (sometimes called the Bourbon Democrats), favoring pro-business, low-tariff, small-government, laissez-faire ideals. On a one-thousand-acre tract of land in Hyde Park with stunning river views, he built a large, comfortable veranda-wrapped home for his family that he called Springwood, and he obliged his neighbors by serving in local government and at his church, St. James Episcopal. With his first wife, Rebecca, James bore a namesake son, James "Rosy" Roosevelt. Four years after Rebecca's untimely death from heart failure in 1876, James married a distant cousin, Sara Ann Delano, whose father, Warren Delano Jr., had made a fortune in the China tea and opium trade. Sara was twenty-six years old; James was fifty-two.[8]

On January 30, 1882, Sara, after a prolonged and difficult labor, gave birth to a baby boy, Franklin Delano; the doctor advised her afterward that because of complications during childbirth, she should not attempt to bear more children. The small family lived happily at Springwood, riding horses through the well-tended fields, planting trees and improving the estate, and spending long summers at Campobello, where young Roosevelt honed his sailing skills in the tricky waters of the Bay of Fundy. Sara raised her only child in a close and at times smothering embrace, mixing devotion and love with a carefully refined sense of privilege and duty. The family took extended trips to Europe, where Franklin learned German and French; the boy was homeschooled by governesses until the age of fourteen, when he was tearfully packed off to the Groton School for Boys. There, under the stern tuition of its headmaster, the Episcopal priest Endicott Peabody, Franklin received a thorough grounding in a certain kind of muscular Christianity and what Peabody considered the manly virtues of competitive athletics, classical languages, and public service. FDR had a rather unserious passage through Harvard College, where he enrolled in 1900. With flair and condescending charm, he pursued social influence among the prestigious fraternities and threw himself into editing the *Harvard Crimson* newspaper. He took a degree in history in 1903, went on to law school at Columbia briefly, but dropped his legal studies for lack of interest.

When James Roosevelt died in December 1900, while Franklin was at Harvard, his considerable fortune (worth perhaps $20 million today) was divided among his wife; his first son, Rosy; and young Franklin, who set out in the world as a rich, well-educated, well-connected country squire with no particular skills. Sara, however, who already possessed significant wealth from her Delano inheritance, now owned Springwood, too. Franklin therefore remained dependent on her for his home in Hyde Park. Ensconced in a world of wealth, taste, and achievement, pampered by a watchful mother, bewitched by the natural beauty of the Hudson Valley and the family's estate, FDR had developed a strong sense of place and belonging. He also bore the burden of the family name, one of the oldest and most prestigious in America. His mother made it clear that he would have to live up to his distinguished forebears.

In 1905, he married his fifth cousin, Anna Eleanor Roosevelt, against the wishes of his mother, who felt the rather shy, self-effacing young woman insufficiently impressive for her perfect son. In a rare case of defiance, Franklin persisted, and at a wedding presided over by Reverend Peabody, the president of the United States, Theodore Roosevelt—Eleanor's uncle—gave the bride away. It was the start of a difficult, even tragic marriage—and an extraordinary partnership. Sara Roosevelt offered the newlyweds a generous if double-edged wedding present: a townhouse at 47–49 East Sixty-Fifth Street in Manhattan, designed with twin living quarters for both the young couple and Sara herself. Mrs. James Roosevelt had no plans to part from her golden boy. Over the course of eleven years, Eleanor bore six children, one of whom—named Franklin—died at seven months. The growing family continued to depend on Sara's wealth to pay for some of the costs of their lifestyle, and Sara in return insisted on remaining at the center of her son's life. Franklin serenely ignored his wife's increasing distress at being treated like a third wheel in the marriage.

In 1908, Roosevelt took a position in the New York law firm of Carter Ledyard & Milburn, but the work bored him, and he allowed himself to be talked into running on the Democratic ticket for an open seat in the state senate, representing a district that included his own (strongly Republican) home of Dutchess County. Using his own money and his own automobile and happily benefiting from the name of his popular presidential cousin, Roosevelt campaigned aggressively and cheerfully for the seat and won a narrow victory in November 1910. Though in Albany he gave the appearance of being an upper-class dilettante and having too little gravitas for politics, Roosevelt soon developed a reputation as a pro-reform, anti-machine politician who because of his family wealth could afford to take the risk of speaking out against the entrenched Democratic Party bosses in New York City. His haughty self-confidence and immaturity turned off many seasoned pols, but gradually FDR earned plaudits for his embrace of progressive issues like conservation and clean government. It was a modest start, but anyone who found solid footing in New York, then the nation's most populous state, could fairly aim for larger things.

In Albany, FDR also won the devotion of a wizened, savvy local reporter named Louis McHenry Howe, who soon became his full-time aide and trusted confidant. For twenty-six years, until his death in 1936, Howe served FDR with fanatical loyalty as a chief of staff, live-in assistant, publicity man, and adviser. A master of detail and a tactician with a keen sense of retail politics, Howe became FDR's most important personal relationship other than his mother, a fact not lost on Eleanor, who once again found herself outmaneuvered in the contest to win the attention of the rising political star.[9]

In these early days of his career, Roosevelt sought to define himself as a reform-minded Democrat who wished to use government to advance the common good. The man he most admired in public life was his cousin Theodore Roosevelt (TR), who as president from 1901 to 1909 dominated American politics. A Republican and a figure of boundless energy, progressive ideals, and physical courage, TR championed many of the policies that Franklin would eventually make his own, such as curtailing the power of corporate monopolies, conservation of natural resources, and the robust defense of the Monroe Doctrine with a big navy. Yet the Republican Party held no appeal for Franklin. Its high-tariff, pro-business, corporate-friendly leaders had turned a deaf ear to the needs of farmers and rural people, of the kind FDR knew in the Hudson Valley. Nor did the Bourbon Democrats, with their close ties to business and banking, attract him. FDR might have followed in the steps of the populist William Jennings Bryan, a Democratic presidential nominee in 1896, 1900, and 1908, who adopted the label of "the great commoner." Bryan spoke for the farmers and the blue-collar workers who struggled to make a living in the years of Republican high-tariff and tight-money policies. He was able to pull together Northern farmers, Southern cotton growers, Western progressives, and ethnic voters in the cities to make his bid for national office. He failed, and in any case his fundamentalist Christianity and prohibitionism was not to FDR's tastes. Yet Bryan helped sketch out a future coalition-building strategy that FDR would one day make his own.[10]

It was neither the old Democrats of Grover Cleveland nor the agrarian Democrats of Bryan that Roosevelt finally chose as his political lodestar. He reached for the historical figure of Thomas Jefferson, a more useful and elastic figure than TR or Bryan. Of course, the gentleman farmer and Sage of Monticello had long been a figure of veneration for Democrats, a spiritual forefather among the founding generation. A Virginia planter and slave owner, Jefferson exalted the idea of a Republic in which white men could transcend the class and religious divisions so prominent in the Old World and instead create an egalitarian society joined together by a certain idea of freedom, limited government, and, of course, white supremacy. This last element of Jeffersonian ideology—the racial solidarity of white people in a slaveholding Republic—was a crucial feature of Jefferson's utopia and explains why his legacy remained so strong in the American South.[11]

In identifying himself with Jefferson, then, FDR signaled his commitment to progressive government, religious toleration, and the interests of the little man, particularly the farmer, while also upholding the racial order of the South. Though he himself may have been less concerned than some of his fellow Democrats with policing the boundaries of race, Roosevelt understood that a successful Democratic coalition would run through the Southern states; invoking Jefferson's political legacy made clear to Southern leaders that Roosevelt, an aristocratic Yankee, would not challenge the institution of Jim Crow segregation. This commitment to white supremacy was embedded in the very name "Jefferson" and did not need to be spelled out. Instead, Roosevelt's Jefferson stood for certain core beliefs about class and democracy: the idea that virtue resided in the humble tillers of the soil, not the captains of industry or the mercantile class; that democracy required religious toleration rather than the dominance of an organized church hierarchy; that monarchical Britain and its empire was America's natural enemy, while revolutionary France was America's spiritual twin; and that the states must be allowed to govern themselves based on local customs and traditions, free from overweening federal centralization. Above all, FDR adopted Jefferson's view that Providence had assigned America a duty to populate, subdue, and tame the "virgin" lands of the continent and create not a European empire of exploitation and oligarchy but, in Jefferson's words, an "empire of liberty" in which the individual (white) pioneer could shape democracy in his own image.

Such Jeffersonian ideas—one might better call them Jeffersonian myths—were refreshed and popularized in 1925 by Claude G. Bowers, an Indiana journalist and Democratic Party speechwriter, in a wildly successful book called *Jefferson and Hamilton: The Struggle for Democracy in America*. FDR not only read this book but reviewed it in the *New York World*—the only book review he ever wrote. Bowers powerfully reinforced the idea of an elemental conflict in American life between popular democracy and the antidemocratic aristocracy of wealth and privilege. Bowers caught the moment just right, as the United States in 1926 would celebrate the 150th anniversary of American independence as well as the centennial of Jefferson's death. Bowers later helped revive Monticello as a national shrine where the cult of Jefferson would never fade. Meanwhile, FDR seized on Bowers's simple thesis of ongoing "struggle" in America between the oligarchy and ordinary working people. He described himself as "breathless" after reading the book, claiming that the "the same contending forces" of the eighteenth century were still locked in a fight for supremacy at the start of the twentieth. Bankers and industrialists had their armies at the ready. But who would take up the banner of the common people? "Is a Jefferson on the horizon?" Roosevelt asked. There is no doubt that he imagined himself in that role.[12]

In 1912, FDR rightly anticipated a Democratic victory in the presidential contest. A feud among the Republicans between Theodore Roosevelt, who was hoping to make a political comeback by running as an independent progressive, and incumbent president William Howard Taft left the GOP vulnerable. Franklin came out early in his support of Woodrow Wilson, the progressive governor of New Jersey, as the Democratic nominee. He worked hard to swing the New York State delegation into Wilson's column at the Democratic Party convention, and this earned him a valuable credit with Wilson. After defeating both Taft and TR in the national contest (though winning only 42 percent of the vote), Wilson offered FDR a plum: an appointment as assistant secretary of the navy, the very job that had served his illustrious cousin as a springboard to national fame. Roosevelt had just turned thirty-one years old.

An ambitious assistant secretary of the navy. *Library of Congress*

With the loyal Louis Howe by his side, FDR flourished in his new position at the Navy Department. The job entailed supervising the infrastructure of the navy: the yards and docks, the naval bases, the construction crews, and the flow of raw materials necessary to sustain the fleet. Though he had no executive experience, his enthusiasm for naval history and his skill as an amateur yachtsman made him a natural ally of senior naval officers, who welcomed his support for naval expansion. In particular, he knew the work of Rear Admiral Alfred Thayer Mahan, whose 1890 book, *The Influence of Sea Power upon History*, argued that America's future prosperity as a trading and industrial nation depended upon seaborne access to markets around the world. Mahan asserted that lines of communication to such markets required a large navy and naval bases to supply them. FDR, following Mahan, supported the expansion of U.S. naval power to serve America's industrial growth and future prosperity.[13]

Roosevelt gained invaluable bureaucratic experience in Washington during eight years in the Navy Department. He won large appropriations for the navy from Congress; he improved the navy's contracting procedures; he developed relationships with labor leaders whose workforce manned the navy dockyards; and he took advantage of the patronage possibilities that his supervision of federal navy yards gave him, installing allies in key posts and expanding his political network. Yet he grew frustrated with his boss, Secretary of the Navy Josephus Daniels. A North Carolina newspaper publisher, a populist, a pacifist, and a champion of prohibition, Daniels embodied the combination of progressivism and racism that characterized the Democratic Party across the South in these years. In addition to his support for white women's suffrage, improved transportation, schools, and regulation of railroads, Daniels was an eager white supremacist who used his newspaper, the Raleigh *News and Observer*, to stir up race hatred against African Americans and conjure up the specter of "Negro Rule" in the South. Daniels was quite anti-British and opposed to any entanglement in European rivalries; he had little interest in expanding the navy, even as the war in Europe seemed ever more likely to impact the United States.[14]

Roosevelt disagreed with Daniels. After such outrages as the sinking of the *Lusitania*, with 128 Americans among the 1,198 killed by a German torpedo, as well as repeated attacks on American shipping, Roosevelt voiced his concern in *Scribner's Magazine* about what he termed "the Great Inertia"—that is, the army's and navy's lack of readiness for a possible war. The explanation for inaction, he asserted, was "an inability to visualize our position in the world." While the United States did not want "to subjugate foreign nations" or "grab territory," the nation did aim "to develop a growing foreign trade, to build up a merchant marine, to take a very leading place in the general affairs of the world." Given the growing threat from Germany to America's seaborne power, Roosevelt wrote, the country needed "an adequate defense" to protect its interests. "This adequate defense does not now exist," he declared. Not only had there been no industrial planning to gather raw materials and harness industry to produce armaments, there had been no serious national training and recruitment effort. These words constituted a direct rebuke of Daniels as well as the president. More striking, the article appeared in April 1917, the very month that Wilson, at long last and against his strong preference for neutrality, asked Congress to declare war on Germany in response to Germany's sinking of neutral American vessels on the seas. Though Roosevelt's article got lost in the rush to war, it revealed the powerful influence of Mahan on the future president, and his firm belief in America's need to project global power in defense of the national interest.[15]

As an active participant in the American war effort, FDR came to appreciate President Wilson's skill, both as a war leader who now moved swiftly to mobilize the country, and as an adroit communicator who shaped a compelling intellectual argument for why America must fight Imperial Germany. In his address to Congress of April 2, 1917, Wilson provided Americans with a war aim consistent with their own idea of themselves: They were not conquerors or imperialists, but champions of democracy. "The world must be made safe for democracy," Wilson said in words that would influence Roosevelt's own war leadership. "We have no selfish ends to serve. We desire no conquest, no dominion. . . . We are but one of the champions of the rights of mankind." One can hear the future Roosevelt in Wilson's ringing concluding words to Congress: "We shall fight for the things which we have always carried nearest our hearts, for democracy, for the right of those who submit to authority to have a voice in their own Governments, for the rights and liberties of small nations, for a universal dominion of right by such a concert of free peoples as shall bring peace and safety to all nations and make the world itself at last free." For such a world of peace, rights, and security, Wilson believed, Americans could justly fight.[16]

Wilson also provided Roosevelt with an example of how to use the federal government not just for war but for social reform. If Thomas Jefferson's ideas of agrarian democracy appealed to FDR's farmer-citizen self-image, and Admiral Mahan fired his enthusiasm for expanding America's global reach, Wilson showed Roosevelt how to push progressive reform through the bureaucracy. Wilson aimed to transform America from a chaotic place of rough-and-tumble political strife and unfettered, unregulated capitalism into an efficient, balanced, well-ordered industrial society. In his first term, Wilson had focused on an ambitious domestic agenda of regulation and reform that he labeled the "New Freedom." He positioned the Democratic Party as the inheritor of the Jeffersonian legacy, a leader who would use government to protect citizens from rapacious oligarchs and giant corporations. Wilson sought tariff reductions, regulations over banking, new antitrust laws, an end to child labor, better working hours and conditions, and easier credit for farmers. Here lay the seeds of some of the progressive policies Roosevelt would later adopt and extend. There can be little doubt that Roosevelt embraced both Wilson's domestic progressive program and his vision of a world order in which America's moral example might bring the great powers into a shared, orderly peace.[17]

Yet along with Wilson's success there came a tragic cautionary tale. In leading the country into war, he found himself forced to abandon his progressive domestic agenda. Instead, the federal government grew rapidly, taking the reins of the economy, nationalizing many sectors of industry and services, controlling labor, raw materials, transport, and production, all in the interest of war. These measures were surely necessary for the huge military effort America undertook in France. But liberals and progressives grew disheartened by Wilson's crackdown on civil liberties, and by the loss of focus on curbing the power of industry and banking. Many progressives drew the lesson from World War I that war contained within it the seeds of reaction and would always lead to the repression of civil and social progress at home. From such views sprang much liberal opposition to FDR's later efforts to join the fight against fascism.

Even more significant, Wilson's failure to secure the lasting peace he sought impressed, and worried, Roosevelt. When the war ended in November 1918, Wilson occupied a position of immense prestige and power, the leader of the nation that had tipped the balance toward victory for the allies, and which had bankrolled much of the British and French war effort. Wilson traveled to Paris at the start of 1919 to oversee a peace treaty with Germany into which the president inserted his signature idea: the League of Nations, which would substitute collective security and arbitration for Europe's constant quarrels. The scheme echoed Wilson's vision of government as a buffer and shield against corporate tyrants; the League would ameliorate the selfish, ideological nationalism that had set the continent ablaze in 1914. Wilson believed that with a peaceful and enduring security settlement, Europeans could at last construct truly liberal democratic institutions, allowing America to rescue Europe from its ancient hatreds.

FDR accepted Wilson's argument that the League would open the Old World to the benevolent influence of American power. Still, he could not go so far as Wilson in pledging the United States to defend European security without a clear statement that it remained the role of the U.S. Congress, not the president or foreign nations, to decide when and where the nation would commit overseas forces. No League, however well-intended, could usurp that right. For this reason, he privately accepted the argument of some Republicans, led by Massachusetts senator Henry Cabot Lodge, that Wilson's design for the League must be altered to ensure that America could not be dragged into war unwillingly. Wilson refused to compromise, instead heading out to the country in September for a grueling speaking tour in favor of the League. But his health failed him, and soon after he returned to Washington in a state of collapse, he suffered a massive stroke that left him nearly mute and lifeless.

To add to his misery, the Senate twice failed to pass the Treaty of Versailles by the required two-thirds margin, thus dooming Wilson's brainchild. A group of senators called "the irreconcilables," hostile to U.S. membership in the League under any circumstances, managed to shatter Wilson's internationalist dream. Some of those same men would, fifteen years hence, attempt to frustrate Roosevelt's global ambitions, too. By the spring of 1920, Wilson's shrunken, crippled body mirrored his destroyed presidency. An invalid, isolated, out of touch, Wilson had fallen from the pinnacle of success to the depths of failure. For lack of compromise with his critics, for want of pragmatism, and for his failure to read the domestic politics of foreign policy, Wilson destroyed his presidency. Roosevelt never forgot the lesson.[18]

As Wilson's star dimmed, Roosevelt's grew brighter still. In the summer of 1920, his party nominated him by acclamation for the vice presidency, to run alongside James Cox of Ohio. FDR was thirty-eight years old, just barely able to clear the constitutional threshold of thirty-five to hold the office. Cox and Roosevelt carried Wilson's banner in the election, supporting the League of Nations and progressive policies in government. But the headwinds created by Wilson's unpopularity, the collapse of the wartime economic boom, nationwide strikes in key industries, and the appeal of Senator Warren G. Harding's call for a "return to normalcy" swept away the Democrats. Cox and Roosevelt got whipped soundly, winning barely 34 percent of the vote to 60 percent for Harding. Democrats got trounced in the congressional elections, too, as Republicans ended up with a 303–131 majority in the House of Representatives and a 59–37 advantage in the Senate. A dozen years of Republican dominance lay ahead, while Democrats skulked, rudderless and forlorn.

Yet for Franklin Roosevelt, the experience of running for vice president lifted him into view as the young hope of the Democratic Party. Charismatic, handsome, now a seasoned administrator, Roosevelt had also acquired a political identity. A Jeffersonian Democrat armed with Mahanian ideas of world power and Wilson's theory of the state as an agent of progressive social policy, FDR stepped out of the war years with a strong sense of himself and his ambitions. He may have lost big in 1920, but Franklin Roosevelt stood on the cusp of greatness.

III

The story of Roosevelt's rise to national prominence, as well as his tragic illness that cut him down in August 1921, hung about him during that hot, humid week in late June 1924 as the delegates to the Democratic convention gathered in Madison Square Garden. Even the crusty pols and cynical insiders cheered on FDR's courageous effort to speak at the convention and nominate Al Smith for president. He also sought to demonstrate his own fitness for high office. He performed brilliantly, though he failed in persuading the Democratic Party to accept the Catholic Smith as its standard-bearer. After an interminable stalemate during which the delegates went through 102 rounds of balloting, neither Smith nor McAdoo could amass two-thirds of the delegates, as required by Democratic Party rules, and so the convention, exhausted and embittered, turned to a bland moderate named John W. Davis of West Virginia, giving him the nod on the 103rd ballot. A lawyer and former ambassador to Britain, Davis was duly crushed by Calvin Coolidge in November, winning only 28.8 percent of the national vote.

FDR in 1924 did not yet possess the stature to unite the fractious Democrats around his vision of a progressive party. He tried speaking with gusto about putting limits on the power of big corporations, improving working conditions for laborers, and making "progress for humanity." Taking on the anti-Catholic animus so widely directed at Smith, he also admonished the delegates to reject prejudice and bigotry. In this, too, he demonstrably failed. In fact, the 1924 Democratic convention fell apart in ugly, spectacular fashion over this very issue: whether or not the party could rouse itself to condemn the principal agent of bigotry and nativism in America, the Ku Klux Klan. The party that Roosevelt hoped one day to lead simply could not make up its mind: Was it an inclusive multiethnic coalition with a base in America's big cities, or a rigidly anti-Catholic rural party with an appeal largely limited to the Deep South? The argument in 1924 over the Klan shows how strong bigotry and racism remained inside the Democratic Party, and how far the party would have to travel before it would confront such evils, both at home and abroad.

In its first iteration, the "invisible empire" of the KKK launched a reign of terror across the South in the years immediately following the Civil War, using intimidation, violence, and murder to reassert white supremacy and crush any hopes of Black political power in the era of Reconstruction. The Enforcement Acts of 1870 and 1871 gave the president the power to use federal troops to suppress the Klan and its racial violence. Even though the Klan thereafter went dormant, it spawned many imitators; threats, violence, and lynching became common methods to suppress Black voting and sustain white rule across the South. In 1915, a somewhat-deranged Methodist preacher named William Simmons, inspired by the blockbuster film of that year, *The Birth of a Nation*, decided to revive the Klan as a fraternal organization. On a windy Thanksgiving night, he and a dozen friends hiked to the top of Stone Mountain, Georgia, swore various oaths on an open Bible and a drawn sword, burned a cross, and declared the new Klan open for business.

Simmons, a racist dunderhead with no particular talent for leadership, appointed himself Imperial Wizard and developed a number of sinister rituals (the white robes and conical headgear in particular). But the Klan stagnated until Simmons turned to the Southern Publicity Association for marketing advice. Appealing to the anti-immigrant xenophobia and anti-Communism that had been stimulated—and indeed welcomed—by the U.S. government during World War I, the marketing team for the Klan repositioned the once-invisible empire into a highly visible social movement. From 1920 on, the Klan began to cast itself not simply as a fraternal organization for negrophobic Southerners, but as the nationwide agent of resistance against the mongrelization of America by immigrants, Jews, Catholics, socialists and syndicalists, Black people, jazz, sexual promiscuity, alcohol, and secularism.

To stem these mortal threats, the Klan advocated prohibition of alcohol, evangelical Protestantism, the banishing from public life of moneylenders (a code word for Jews) and Catholics (thought loyal only to the "despotic" foreign pope); a halt to immigration and miscegenation, and the purification of the citizenry through selective breeding known by a newly popular term, "eugenics." Under the new leadership of a gifted charlatan named Hiram Wesley Evans, the Ku Klux Klan after 1922 became a nationwide organization, holding countless rallies of white-robed members in placid suburbs and village greens, bundling all the racial, religious, and class grievances of white Protestants into one powerful and attractive term: "100% Americanism."

Klan members parade in Washington, D.C., on September 13, 1926.
Library of Congress

It spread like wildfire. By 1924, the Klan could boast more than 4 million members, among them 16 U.S. senators, 75 congressmen, a dozen governors, and many more state and municipal officials. It had a national newspaper, the *Fiery Cross*, and developed strength both in rural villages and big cities, most notably Atlanta, Birmingham, Dallas, Los Angeles, Denver, Chicago, Detroit, Indianapolis, and Philadelphia. By the time the Democratic convention of 1924 convened in New York, the Klan could already take some credit for the passage of the most sweeping anti-immigration law in U.S. history, the Johnson-Reed Act (or the Immigration Act of 1924), which imposed a racist national-origins quota on would-be immigrants, drastically curtailed immigration from Eastern and southern Europe, and virtually halted all immigration from Asia. The act sped through Congress with enormous bipartisan support and President Coolidge signed it into law in May 1924.[19]

To tangle with the Klan, then, meant going up against a political lobbying organization of real power. But at the Democratic convention, the forces behind Al Smith felt it was essential to include in the Democratic Party platform a statement condemning the Klan for its anti-Catholic bigotry. They put it plainly: How could the Democratic Party tolerate a cultlike secretive society that sought to cast out Americans from the nation merely on the grounds of religion? The *Pittsburgh Courier*, one of the nation's leading African American papers, applauded the Democrats for "taking the bit between their teeth" and making a bid for the support of those most persecuted by the Klan, namely, "the Jew, the Negro, and the Catholic."[20]

By contrast, William McAdoo, supportive of prohibition and a white Protestant Southerner, quietly welcomed the backing of the Klan and had no intention of turning on it now. His delegates showed real sympathy for the religious zeal of the KKK—"are we to condemn and execute a million men who are professed followers of the Lord?" asked North Carolina governor Cameron Morrison. William Jennings Bryan, three-time presidential nominee of the party, gave a windy address to the delegates in which he argued that publicly shaming the Klan would only give it more attention; "it doesn't deserve the advertising," he said. "What the country needs," he preached from the rostrum, "was to get back to God." And that meant, apparently, avoiding a confrontation with the Klan.

Amid pandemonium, the police had to be called to suppress fights on the convention floor, while Smith supporters taunted their opponents by crying, "Ku, Ku, McAdoo!" from the galleries. The anti-Klan resolution went down to defeat by one vote, a perfect encapsulation of the deep cleft dividing the party that Roosevelt had hoped to unite. "Anti-Klan Plankers Lose!" crowed the *Fiery Cross*. Not far from the convention, 20,000 Klansmen staged a huge "Klorero" on July 4 at Long Beach, New Jersey, where an effigy of Al Smith was beaten to a pulp. The same day, 1,500 Klansmen marched through Binghamton, New York, bearing among other displays a float depicting robed Klansmen tarring and feathering a Black man. In Greensburg, Pennsylvania, 5,000 men nominated a local judge and Klan leader as a candidate for president from the American Party, a Klan front. Down in Little Rock, Arkansas, 10,000 robed Klansmen staged what they called a "kommemoration" of Independence Day, after which many new recruits were registered into the local Klan chapter. In light of these and many similar Klan rallies, the NAACP issued a statement castigating the Democrats for failing to condemn "the secret fomenter of religious intolerance, race-hate, and midnight murder." The *New York Times* editorialized that "the Klan has become in some states a thing bigger than parties, more influential than candidates." It had "thrust a sword into the very vitals of the Democratic Party."[21]

The baleful influence of the Klan upon the 1924 Democratic convention stands out as the defining feature of that gathering, a sad testament to the unwillingness of the Democrats to unite in denunciation of religious bigotry. Yet it ought not to obscure the power of the moment when a paraplegic man nominated a Catholic as the party's candidate for president of the United States. Of course, Smith did not win the nomination in 1924, in part because he was a New York City machine politician, a son of immigrants, opposed to prohibition, and because he was a Catholic. But he remained governor of the nation's most important state, and in 1928 his party would set aside its anti-Catholic bigotry and nominate him as its candidate for president.

IV

The 1924 convention proved that Franklin Roosevelt's disability need not derail his political ambitions, provided he could disguise its severity. But why hide his malady? After all, polio sufferers abounded in this era, as did disfigured veterans of the Great War. Yet in the late nineteenth and early twentieth century, a man who could not walk or even stand unaided would not normally be considered fit for high public office—or even for American citizenship. Since 1882, American immigration law had prohibited the entry into the country of anyone "likely to become a public charge" due to some kind of impairment; in 1907, the statutes were updated to ban entry of anyone "mentally or physically defective."

These laws reflected the growing American enthusiasm for the popular "science" of eugenics, which held that the selective breeding of human beings, like plants and animals, could improve the caliber of the national "stock." By the 1920s, eugenics had become a widely praised approach for the improvement of the American "race." The nation's elites embraced this quackery; in fact, former president Theodore Roosevelt was one of its most ardent advocates. "Society," he wrote in 1913, must not allow "degenerates to reproduce their kind." The United States, he feared, "permits unlimited breeding from the worst stocks. . . . We have no business permitting the perpetuation of citizens of the wrong type." Many states wrote these sentiments into statute. In 1907, Indiana adopted a law allowing the state to sterilize citizens deemed unworthy of the privilege of procreation. Eventually, thirty-two states followed suit and as many as seventy thousand people were sterilized under these codes.[22]

The authority of the states to carry out such invasive procedures was taken up by the Supreme Court in 1927. In the case of *Buck v. Bell*, an 8–1 majority supported the measures, with Justice Oliver Wendell Holmes Jr. declaring that society must "prevent those who are manifestly unfit from continuing their kind. . . . The principle that sustains compulsory vaccination is broad enough to cover cutting the Fallopian tubes. Three generations of imbeciles are enough." This contempt for fellow human beings who were deemed, in the language of the day, "degenerate" or "defective" proliferated among elites in academia, medicine, and government. The Carnegie Institution and the Rockefeller Foundation larded the practitioners of this phony science with grant money. The idea that imperfect humans were an impediment to national progress became the dogma of the day.[23]

These prevailing attitudes provide the backdrop to FDR's arduous effort to conceal, or at least to minimize, his inability to walk. Naturally, Roosevelt, an elite, white aristocrat and the scion of one of America's oldest, most prestigious families would never be called "degenerate"—eugenicists claimed to be more concerned with hereditary defects than with diseases like polio. Nonetheless, polio was often associated with immigrant communities; a major polio epidemic in 1916 had killed over 2,300 people in New York City, mostly "Italians living in crowded tenements" in Brooklyn, the *New York Times* reported. And polio was also an "infantile" disease, something that inherently suggested weakness and frailty. Whatever the cause of his disability, the stigma attached to any "cripple" was so great that Roosevelt, when in public, sought to give the appearance of a man overcoming a temporary illness. He insisted on telling a cheerful, optimistic story of steady progress and improvement, of his unceasing efforts to strengthen himself and "throw away" his crutches. In Warm Springs, Georgia, FDR found the perfect setting to dramatize his ongoing and "gallant fight," as the press often put it, to regain the use of his legs.[24]

He had already experimented with swimming as a therapeutic treatment. In a pool on the estate of his Hyde Park neighbor Vincent Astor, Roosevelt had spent many afternoons exercising and trying to bring life back to his withered legs. But it was warm water that seemed to provide the greatest relief. In February 1923 he chartered a sixty-five-foot houseboat, invited his intimate friends aboard, and cruised up and down the Florida Keys for two months of swimming in tropical waters, sunbathing, and fishing—all of which improved his health generally and made him feel as if he were gaining strength in his legs. "I am convinced that there is a vast improvement in the leg muscles," he wrote to his Boston physician, Robert Lovett, in April 1923. Pleased with the results, he bought his own houseboat later that year and set out for another cruise in early 1924.[25]

He was therefore primed to receive a letter that summer from George Foster Peabody, a banker and longtime financial supporter of the Democratic Party, who wrote to Roosevelt about the remarkable healing properties of the warm springs in Bullochville, Georgia, where he had recently purchased a dilapidated but storied old Victorian hotel. In the pool of the Meriwether Inn, guests bobbed about in naturally heated mineral water that gushed from the rocks of Pine Mountain. Peabody reported the case of a polio victim whose mobility had been much improved by regular swimming in the buoyant, eighty-nine-degree water. Intrigued, FDR and Eleanor sped south by train, arriving on October 3 at the tiny remote village, eager to take the cure.

Half a century earlier, wealthy Georgians had come to the Meriwether Inn to enjoy the warm baths, but now the place looked worn and threadbare. The small cottages in which guests stayed had no running water and daylight sliced through the cracks in the walls. Mice and squirrels had taken up residence. Eleanor was quietly appalled at the squalid scene, the rural poverty, and the glaring racial divide of the Deep South; she returned to New York after a few days. FDR, by contrast, was delighted. "We shall be quite comfortable," he wrote to his mother, and he spent three weeks there, swimming for hours daily, and enjoying the feeling of "walking" while suspended in water.[26]

When the *Atlanta Journal* reported that the 1920 Democratic nominee for vice president planned on coming regularly to Georgia to "swim to health," as the headline put it, polio patients from around the country began to arrive in Bullochville, whose name was soon officially changed to Warm Springs. FDR saw in the hotel a glittering future as a treatment center for polio patients, and in the summer of 1925, he returned for a prolonged stay, supervising the addition of ramps for wheelchairs and the general improvement of the property. In the spring of 1926, he drew upon his personal fortune to purchase the place outright for $200,000, and in subsequent years he bought over one thousand surrounding acres. He established the Georgia Warm Springs Foundation in 1927 as a nonprofit and tax-sheltered institution, built himself a private cottage there, and came to think of Warm Springs as a second home. During the next twenty years, Roosevelt visited Georgia over forty times, often for prolonged stays at Warm Springs. He died there in April 1945.[27]

Warm Springs became more than a country retreat for Roosevelt; he used his ties to Georgia to enhance his political appeal in the South. By inviting state and local politicians to come visit him at Warm Springs, Roosevelt soon developed a network of Southern Democratic friends who he knew would be useful to him in the future. Yet to cultivate those ties, FDR had to make it clear that he had no desire to question or destabilize the basic racial order of the South, which to an outsider was its most glaring feature. In passing this assurance to his Georgia friends, Roosevelt deliberately chose to remain silent on matters of race. As one sympathetic account of his time in Georgia put it, "Roosevelt never undertook to remonstrate with his white Georgian neighbors about the evils of the racist arrangement of their society. . . . Georgia was a place for *relaxing*."[28]

Yet Georgia's racial divide was impossible to ignore. In 1930, it had a population just under 3 million residents, 37 percent of whom were Black and whose lives were bound by a racial caste system that had been deliberately constructed by white politicians over many years. The state legislature had segregated schools as far back as 1872 and imposed poll taxes in 1877 to bar Black voting. When the U.S. Supreme Court in 1896 gave its sanction in *Plessy v. Ferguson* to the doctrine of "separate but equal"—concluding that public accommodations could be segregated by race provided that equal facilities such as schools, streetcars, and parks were made available to both races—segregation became the legal framework of Southern society.[29]

As Atlanta boomed in the early years of the century, drawing in both Black and white laborers, racial tensions flared along the color line. In September 1906, a race riot triggered by lurid accounts in Atlanta's newspapers of rapes allegedly inflicted by Black men on white women left twenty-five African Americans dead and scores wounded. Such forms of mob violence proliferated in the early years of the twentieth century. To enforce their system of white supremacy, white Georgians resorted to lynching—that is, the public hanging, beating, knifing, burning, castration, and mutilation of Black men (and occasionally women) who had been implicated (often groundlessly) in the murder or rape of white persons. "Between 1882 and 1930," the data reveal, "Georgia's toll of 458 lynch victims was exceeded only by Mississippi's 538." Between 1890 and 1900, there was at least one mob killing of a Black person every month in Georgia, all duly reported in the state's newspapers.[30]

Although lynchings in Georgia decreased in the mid-1920s, scholars believe this may have been due to the impact of a rigid and well-policed system of racial segregation in all walks of life, from restaurants to theaters, workplaces, schools, churches, and parks. By the time FDR came to Warm Springs, this caste system had been in place for years; as one scholar put it, "the region's codes of deference transformed daily life into a theater of racial rituals, where every encounter, exchange, and gesture reinforced Black inferiority." And the lynch mob always stood ready to enforce the color line. In February 1930, 150 miles south of Warm Springs, a mob launched a manhunt for James Irwin, who stood accused of murdering a white girl. An all-night search with bloodhounds ended with Irwin bound by wires, his toes and fingers cut off, his torso and mouth stabbed through with sharp sticks, and his still-moving body set alight with gasoline.[31]

Segregation ruled this world that Franklin Roosevelt adopted as his own when he became a property owner, employer, and local political celebrity in rural Georgia. In 1930, about 385 people called Warm Springs home, and 220 of them were Black. The town was of course strictly segregated by race, as was the Meriwether Inn and its warm swimming pool. The town's Black residents lived in dire poverty in unheated shacks along rutted red-clay lanes, and they had no facilities for education; a 1934 survey found that among the African Americans in Warm Springs, only two men and six women had completed the seventh grade. Farmwork was done by manual labor, often by hired Black men, whose wages ran about a dollar a day. In one nostalgic memoir of FDR's time in Georgia, written in the early 1950s by fellow polio sufferer Turnley Walker, Black workers at the spa were depicted as happy "Negroes" who "bob their heads in greeting," emerging at dawn from their "sagging lean-to shanties" to hasten along worn paths through pinewoods to their day's labor at the inn. The Warm Springs Foundation, as it grew, employed over forty Black workers as stewards, maids, laundresses, waiters, and groundskeepers. But none ever enjoyed the soothing warm water of the pool, and the foundation never accepted any Black polio patients during FDR's life.[32]

V

Between 1926 and 1928, Roosevelt spent a great deal of time—349 days—at Warm Springs, attempting to improve his legs and build the foundation into a well-equipped institution for the treatment of polio patients. He did not regain the ability to walk, as he had once hoped he might, but through countless hours of agonizing therapy, he learned to stand unaided, using leg braces and a cane; over short distances he could propel himself just enough to give the appearance of limited mobility. In 1926, he fended off attempts by New York Democrats to enlist him to run for the U.S. Senate. He declined, pleading for more time to improve his legs. By August 1927, in a public statement designed to promote the Warm Springs Foundation and its healing properties, Roosevelt referred to his own "astounding" progress. By the start of 1928, newspapers reported (quite incorrectly) that Roosevelt "has almost completely recovered from the infantile paralysis which attacked him five years ago."[33]

This came as welcome news to Al Smith, who in 1928 was plotting another run at the presidency. The people of New York had elected Smith to four two-year terms as governor (1918, 1922, 1924, and 1926). Though the U.S. economy was booming under the hands-off presidency of Calvin Coolidge, and the Republican Party seemed likely to nominate the pro-business engineer and commerce secretary Herbert Hoover for president, Smith thought if he could win the solid South, hold New York, win a few states in the Northeast and Midwest, he had a shot to take the White House. But to pull it off, he needed every Democrat working hard for his cause. In 1928, Smith, knowing FDR's value as a speaker and popular party leader, asked him once again to place his name in nomination for the presidency as he had done in 1924.[34]

FDR thought it highly unlikely any Democrat could win in 1928, but dutifully accepted the invitation to extol Al Smith's virtues at the sweltering Democratic National Convention in Houston in June. The keynote of the convention was given by none other than Claude Bowers, the hagiographer of Jefferson, who began by calling for "a war of extermination against privilege" and lambasted the Republicans as the party of Hamilton. "We go forth to battle for the principles of Thomas Jefferson," Bowers proclaimed, taking up the age-old contest of aristocracy against democracy. To an audience of Southern Democrats gathered in Houston, Bowers also offered many political dog whistles that conjured up the specter of Reconstruction, when a powerful federal Republican administration allegedly imposed Black rule on the South and destroyed states' rights. Bowers's description of the enemy as "the Black Horse Cavalry of privilege and pillage" might have referred not just to Morgan bankers in New York but to federal troops occupying the South and endangering the racial order of white supremacy. The assembled delegates roared their approval again and again as Bowers linked the Democratic Party with Jefferson, states' rights, and opposition to centralized power in Washington.[35]

FDR, as was his wont, struck a happier note. Now using only a cane and the arm of his stout seventeen-year-old son, Elliott, to steady himself as he stood or briefly walked, he came to the convention stage and met with the same acclaim that he had won in 1924. Unlike that contentious meeting, the

1928 convention featured little drama; Smith had already clinched two-thirds of the delegates to assure him the nomination. Roosevelt's speech, therefore, could make the case for progressive principles against the Republican Party. Carefully prepared and pre-circulated to national newspapers, the speech also went out over the radio, bringing FDR's charm, humor, accent, and eloquence into millions of homes. He spoke about the characteristics demanded by the presidency—leadership ability, experience, honesty, and a willingness to draw citizens into the daily functioning of democratic self-government—and many listeners began to see Roosevelt himself in the role. The country needed more than a mere banker as president, he insisted; it needed a leader who "understands the human side of life . . . the needs of the individual, the farmer, the wage earner—the great mass of average citizens who make up the backbone of our nation." The country, FDR concluded, yearned for a "pathfinder, a blazer of the trail to the high road that will avoid the crass materialism that has engulfed so many of the great civilizations of the past." These words, though written for Smith, laid out a theme that Roosevelt would soon make his own.[36]

Smith's 1928 campaign stumbled out of the gate. In a controversial move, he named the millionaire General Motors executive John J. Raskob as chairman of the Democratic National Committee. Raskob, one of the richest men in America and a donor to Calvin Coolidge's campaign in 1924, professed no party affiliation. In fact, he possessed no experience in politics at all. He had become close to Smith through a common network of New York Catholic political leaders and businessmen who opposed prohibition. Smith, who liked Raskob's rags-to-riches story, hoped he would help lure business leaders and other titans of finance to support the Democrats. But with two Catholic New Yorkers at the helm of the party, Smith's campaign immediately risked alienating a key constituency: Protestant (and often deeply anti-Catholic) Democratic voters in the Southern and Western states.[37]

And Smith did face a barrage of anti-Catholic bigotry, a good deal of it from within his party. Alabama's notoriously racist senator, Thomas Heflin, a Democrat and Klan member, denounced the Smith candidacy on the floor of the Senate, saying "the Roman Catholics of every country on the earth are backing his campaign. . . . The Roman Catholic edict has gone forth in secret articles, 'Al Smith is to be made President. . . .' They will lay the heavy hand of a Catholic state upon you and crush the life out of Protestantism in America." In cities where Smith campaigned, handbills circulated claiming that, if elected, Smith would annul Protestant marriages, among other calumnies. In September, when Smith's campaign train rolled into Wichita, Kansas, it was met by a burning cross on the track. Smith courageously called out the bigots in a smoldering speech in Oklahoma City—deep in Klan country. Guarded by a phalanx of police, he declared that the world "knows no greater mockery" than the use of the cross "upon which Christ died" to instill fear and hate into the hearts of people. But his valiant struggle did little to build electoral support.[38]

Desperate to shore up his crumbling campaign, Smith asked Roosevelt to do him yet another service. To win the presidency, he knew he must win New York's forty-five electoral votes. A good way to do this was to put Franklin Roosevelt, a popular, well-known, progressive upstate Protestant, on the ticket as a candidate to succeed him as governor of New York. Turnout for Roosevelt would help him, Smith calculated. But when Smith sent an intermediary to sound out Roosevelt about running for governor, FDR gave a firm refusal. Roosevelt and his chief political adviser, Louis Howe, believed that 1928 would be a Republican year, one that FDR should sit out while laying the groundwork for a gubernatorial run in 1932 and a presidential bid in 1936. To run now and be dragged down to defeat by Smith's sinking campaign might deal a fatal blow to Roosevelt's greater ambitions.

But Smith persisted, calling Roosevelt directly on an unreliable and static-filled line to rural Georgia and pleading for his presence on the New York ballot. FDR again declined, going so far as to send a telegram he knew would reach the press stating that his efforts to recover the use of his legs must take precedence over a run for office. As the delegates to the New York Democratic Party gathered in Rochester on October 1 to select a candidate for governor, Smith frantically tried again, now adding inducements. FDR would be assisted in Albany by the talented and enormously wealthy investment banker Herbert Lehman of Lehman Brothers, who had agreed to run for lieutenant governor; and John Raskob also offered to provide a very substantial gift to the Warm Springs Foundation, which badly needed the money. Against the stern advice of Howe and of his intimate friend and personal secretary, Missy LeHand, Roosevelt relented, concerned that if he refused and Smith lost New York, he would be saddled with the blame. He reluctantly allowed his name to be presented to the Democratic state convention, and on October 3, he was nominated by acclamation.[39]

However unwilling he had been about running, FDR flourished as a candidate for governor, leaning into the campaign and delighting in the daily combat of politics. He had only four weeks to present his case to the voters of New York, but in those few days he began to voice ideas that would in due course form the foundation of the New Deal. Rejecting the laissez-faire philosophy of the Harding-Coolidge-Hoover Republicans, Roosevelt summed up his credo: "[I]t is the duty of the State to concern itself with the health, welfare, and general education of the people of the State." That meant active, innovative social programs. "Progress means change," he insisted, in a phrase that would characterize his political career.[40]

To help him take this message to the people of New York, Roosevelt turned to Samuel Rosenman, then a thirty-two-year-old lawyer, World War I veteran, and a former New York State assemblyman, to research and write speeches on a battery of urgent policy issues. Rosenman, who had worked on Al Smith's staff, knew only of Roosevelt's "aristocratic" pedigree and his education at exclusive schools, and upon meeting him for the first time thought he looked like a "country squire," complete with tweed suit, floppy hat, soft collar, and distinct highborn accent. Rosenman had heard FDR characterized as a "playboy and idler." But upon meeting him, Rosenman saw that "the broad jaw and upthrust chin, the piercing, flashing eyes, the firm hands—they did not fit the description." FDR possessed "an unspoken dignity," Rosenman found. And the speechwriter's admiration grew when, in his first major address of the campaign, Roosevelt denounced religious bigotry as "an assault on one of the most fundamental principles on which our country was founded." As a Jew, Rosenman thrilled to FDR's words.[41]

Rosenman, who gathered thick files of research on dozens of topics to support Roosevelt's speeches, was struck by the scope and ambition of FDR's liberalism. When Herbert Hoover denounced Al Smith as a "socialist," Roosevelt retorted that "anybody in public life who goes ahead and advocates improvements is called a radical." But, he went on, if being a socialist meant favoring reduced working hours for women, improved public health and education, more public parks, cheap electricity and public utilities, assistance to farmers facing low prices, prison reform, workers' compensation, better housing, and more hospitals, "then we are all socialists."[42]

Roosevelt poked fun at the rumors launched by Republicans that he was too ill to serve as governor. After regaling his audiences with the details of his day on the hustings, which often involved a dozen speeches and hundreds of miles of driving across New York, he chortled: "Too bad about this unfortunate sick man, isn't it?" Yet this kind of nonchalance hid what Rosenman called the candidate's "strenuous physical ordeal." Just getting into a standing position from the back of his open car and speaking at every small town and crossroads took a toll. "He could not climb stairs," Rosenman said, "and often we had to carry him up some back stairs of a hall and down again. He always went through this harrowing experience smiling."

Frances Perkins, who campaigned for Roosevelt in 1928, saw how his disability had steeled him. "I began to see," she said after a month of watching Roosevelt's physical courage, "what the great teachers of religion meant when they said that humility is the greatest of virtues." The handsome young athlete of 1920 now had to be carried by assistants up and down stairs and through awkward back entrances of the buildings in which he spoke. Yet Perkins believed that FDR's handicap "made it possible for the common people to trust him," for he knew what it was like to face adversity. And his close aides knew that he had chosen to mask his suffering with inexhaustible cordiality and grace. Roosevelt possessed an "infectious sense of humor," Rosenman wrote. "He knew how to laugh, and he loved to laugh. . . . He made people feel he was deeply interested in their own lives and in their families. . . . Only a person who really loved human beings could give that impression."[43]

At times, it seemed that FDR was running for president in 1928 rather than governor of New York. Making human welfare the theme of the campaign and ignoring his real opponent, State Attorney General Albert Ottinger, Roosevelt took aim at the Republican presidential candidate. The son of a Quaker blacksmith who studied engineering at Stanford and went on to make a fortune in the mining business in China, Australia, and Europe, Herbert Hoover became an immensely well-regarded humanitarian during the Great War. He served admirably as head of the Commission for Relief in Belgium, feeding hungry Belgians whose country had been overrun by the Germans; he would go on to head the American Relief Administration, which shipped millions of tons of food and supplies to war-torn Europe during and after the conflict. Rewarded with the job of commerce secretary in the Harding administration, he demonstrated tenacious bureaucratic skill and became an evangelist for modern American capitalism.

Hoover was a formidable political opponent, and FDR had the luxury of not facing him in the gubernatorial election. Yet on November 1, five days before the election, Roosevelt delivered a searing attack on Hoover, contrasting Al Smith's progressive principles with Hoover's theories of government as expressed in a short book Hoover had written titled *American Individualism*. In this curious pamphlet, about eighty pages long and published in 1922, Hoover set out to evaluate the "great social philosophies" that were contending for ascendancy in the postwar world. Rejecting communism, socialism, syndicalism, and autocracy, he held up American individualism—with its emphasis on ambition, innovation, and competition—as the purest and most successful creed of human development, "the only safe avenue to further human progress."[44]

Roosevelt used Hoover's little essay as the epitome of Republican contempt for ordinary people—what Hoover dismissively called "the crowd." As the commerce secretary put it, the crowd "only feels, it has no mind of its own which can plan. The crowd is credulous, it destroys, it hates, and it dreams, but it never builds." Hoover, said Roosevelt, seemed to believe that "there exists at the top of our social system a very limited group of highly able, highly educated people, through whom all progress in this land must originate." Echoing the attack on the Hamiltonian philosophy that Democrats had long made popular, Roosevelt alleged that in Hoover's worldview, America should be run by the rich and the few, the "little tin gods on wheels up at the top who have got some kind of heavenly right to rule." FDR rejected this theory and insisted that many of the great progressive reforms that he and Al Smith championed had arisen from below. The "mass of humanity does think," he retorted, "it can make up its own mind." The people demanded cheap electricity provided by public utilities, public parks, old-age pensions, workplace safety, as well as limited working hours for women and children in industry. Government must respond to the needs of the people. For Roosevelt, that was the meaning of democracy.[45]

Hoover's campaign did not have to rely on ideas. It could simply point to indices of economic growth as evidence that Republican policies had worked. The U.S. economy grew 42 percent during the 1920s, and the United States produced almost half the world's output by the end of the decade. After a brief recession following the end of World War I, unemployment in the twenties remained steady at about 4 percent. Three times during the decade, Republican administrations cut income taxes, especially for earners in the highest tax brackets. Per capita GDP rose from $6,460 to $8,016 per person, and that meant more cash on hand to buy new cars, new household appliances, and new suburban homes. Across the 1920s, Americans purchased new radios, electric iceboxes, irons, fans, indoor lighting, vacuum cleaners, and other laborsaving household appliances. The electricity needed to power these devices was distributed by the ever-growing electric utility companies, whose stock value soared, along with many other sectors. The Dow Jones Industrial Average rose 39 percent in 1928 alone—a good omen for the political party that had presided over this growth.[46]

In August 1928, Hoover could assert to a roaring crowd of seventy thousand people in Stanford University Stadium that "we in America today are nearer to the final triumph over poverty than ever before in the history of any land. . . . We shall soon, with the help of God, be in sight of the day when poverty will be banished from this nation." This belief that Republican policies had engineered permanent abundance underpinned one of the most memorable campaign slogans of the twentieth century: broadside sheets in national newspapers carried the phrase "Chicken for Every Pot," accompanied by a list of all the ways Americans had got richer in the 1920s.[47]

It worked. American voters preferred Hoover's brand of technocratic, moralizing prosperity to Al Smith's multiethnic, urban progressivism. On November 6, 1928, Hoover simply clobbered Smith, winning 58 percent of the vote and forty of forty-eight states. Smith could not even win the solid South, losing five normally reliable Democratic (and former Confederate) states: Texas, Florida, North Carolina, Tennessee, and Virginia. The GOP picked up eight seats in the U.S. Senate and thirty-two in the House of Representatives, consolidating control of both chambers. For the third time in a row, the Republicans had won the presidential race in a landslide. Perhaps most bitterly, Al Smith could not even hold his home state, losing New York by 103,000 votes. The Democratic Party looked set to become a permanent minority party, a home for a few rural states in the South and no one else.

Despite a dismal night for Democrats nationally, though, something quite remarkable happened in New York. As the tallies in the governor's race came in from the upstate counties, slowly mounting through the night and into the early morning, it seemed that the Democratic candidate had eked out a victory, by a final margin of 25,564 votes out of over 4.2 million cast. Al Smith's career was finished. Franklin Roosevelt's had just begun.

CHAPTER 2

FALLING FOR FASCISM

"He is the perfect dictator."

—ANNE O'HARE MCCORMICK

I

Seated anxiously in the anteroom of the prime minister's office in the Chigi Palace, awaiting her appointment with Italy's fascist leader, the American journalist Ida Tarbell faced a vast carved mantelpiece in the center of the room, its tall mirror surrounded by sphinxes and dolphins. High above her, the elaborate gilded ceiling featured painted panels depicting the life of Pope Clement VIII—a cunning and ruthless leader who some three centuries earlier had brought Henry IV of France into the Catholic Church, vigorously persecuted Italy's Jews, and ordered the Dominican friar and cosmologist Giordano Bruno to be burned alive in the central Roman marketplace on charges of heresy.

It was 1926, and Tarbell had come to Rome on behalf of *McCall's*, a monthly magazine aimed chiefly at affluent American women. Its pages normally carried poetry, fiction, and colored drawings of the latest fashions from Paris. But Tarbell had little interest in such matters. She had earned a reputation as a muckraker—one of the progressive, reform-minded investigative journalists who, at the start of the century, had exposed the mercenary practices of America's chief monopolists and titans of industry. Her unsparing articles on John D. Rockefeller and the monopoly practices of Standard Oil had caused a sensation when they appeared in 1904, eventually leading to the breakup of the oil giant for violating the Sherman Anti-Trust Act. Tarbell, now sixty-nine years old, had been offered a colossal sum—$25,000—to go to Italy and investigate the rise of fascism and its charismatic founder, Benito Mussolini. She leaped at the chance. What was happening in Italy, she believed, was "the greatest story in the world today."[1]

During her passage to Italy, Tarbell stopped to visit friends in Paris and was sternly cautioned about traveling into the lair of fascism. The customs officials, she was warned, would search her belongings, and read her notebooks and letters. She was sure to be followed by the fascist secret police, and anyone she interviewed could never speak candidly. In preparation for blending in among the obedient citizens, she practiced the fascist salute in her Paris bedroom, shooting her right arm out in a stiff-armed greeting. Yet Tarbell did not discover an imprisoned Italy. "None of the dire prophecies of interference to which I had listened," she wrote later, "came true."

In fact, Tarbell fell in love with Italy under fascism. During a stay of nearly five months, she traveled up and down the peninsula, interviewing workers, farmhands, shopkeepers, schoolteachers, writers and hoteliers, café owners and street sweepers. Tarbell found a country in the midst of what she took to be a profound transformation. The anarchy of the years right after World War I, with its parliamentary stalemate, its economic collapse, work stoppages, and the threat of Communism and anarchism—all this had been swept away. She sought an explanation for this remarkable change. And at every turn, the people gave her only one answer: Mussolini.

Benito Mussolini in the early days of his rule.
Bettmann / Getty Images

At the urging of the American ambassador, she made an appointment to see the man himself, who held office hours from 9 a.m. until noon every day at the Chigi Palace. As she waited in the busy anteroom, she saw many others in line before her, ordinary people coming to ask their leader to address their particular concerns. All were received with sincerity and fairness; all went away certain that Mussolini would help them. And then at last her turn came. She entered the prime minister's office, and behind a desk, a smiling gentleman stood to greet her. Tarbell was thunderstruck. As she would later put it, "he has one of the loveliest smiles I ever saw—it is not only on his lips but in his eyes." More than that, "he has a dimple!" Mussolini greeted his visitor in English, apologizing for keeping her waiting. Then switching to French, the two chatted amiably. Mussolini was affable and sweet, "like a friend you come across at a tea party."

Yes, she acknowledged in the four-part story she would later publish about him, Mussolini "is a dictator." But the times had called for decisive action and Mussolini had brought it. Tarbell extolled his alleged achievements: He had balanced the budget, ended class conflict, and brought about national unity. He suppressed the Communists and encouraged a cult of spiritual values rather than crass materialism. Mussolini got the trains running on time, overhauled the tax system, created millions of jobs, drained the malarial swamps, and brought "cleanliness and order in the large cities." Above all, he encouraged hard work for the nation. "No schoolmaster in the world," Tarbell wrote, "ever preached work as he is doing." And not just work, but recreation, too. "He is a brilliant fencer," she learned, an excellent horseman, "an omnivorous reader of books," and "plays the violin rather well." His "terrific energy and absolute power" were the twin engines driving Italy's transformation. He even swept the Mafia out of Sicily, Tarbell claimed. "The methods were medieval," she duly noted, but in no time, the rural villages of Italy "became as safe and orderly as an American countryside."

When her thirty-minute visit to the prime minister's office ended, Tarbell stood to leave. Mussolini "kissed my hand in the gallant Italian fashion," his smile flashing. Mussolini's charm offensive clearly worked. Upon returning home to Connecticut, Tarbell would declare Mussolini "the most interesting and enigmatic of living men." She concluded her long series for *McCall's* with undisguised admiration: "It would be hard to find in all the world a more active and versatile mind, and more sustained energy, than in Benito Mussolini." The benevolent Italian dictator desired only "the betterment of the lives of everyday men, women, and children." The fortunate Italians, she concluded, "had found their Moses!"[2]

II

It seems astonishing that a leading American writer, especially one known for her keen investigative talents, would fall so hard for fascism. Yet during the 1920s, American writers, journalists, diplomats, and politicians found Italian fascism, and Mussolini in particular, alluring. They praised his creed of discipline, unity, and authoritarian rule as the solution to Europe's postwar malaise and drift. Watching Mussolini sweep into power in 1922 at the head of columns of handsome young men wielding heavy sticks and wearing sleek black shirts, American observers experienced the frisson of fascism—and they liked it.

This warm reception for fascism stemmed from the perception among Americans that Italy in the years just after World War I teetered on the brink of anarchy. To journalist Anne O'Hare McCormick, a former writer for the *Catholic World* who toured Italy in late 1920 on a monthlong freelance assignment, postwar Europe appeared "unsettled, uncertain, dazed and staggering." Arriving from America by ship at the Italian port of Naples, she encountered "dust, disorder and discomfort," and a "surliness that was almost hostility." Italy, in McCormick's words, felt like "a country smoldering and seething toward a terrible eruption." The people she interviewed remained mired in bitterness, frustration, and despair. The war had cost Italy dearly, and everyone asked: "What did Italy get out of the war? Nothing but cemeteries choked with dead, and a debt that will keep us poor forever."[3]

Some of the anguish McCormick encountered stemmed from Italy's profound sense of betrayal at the hands of its World War I allies, and especially the American president Woodrow Wilson. Italy had entered the war in 1915 on the side of the British and French, having pocketed a promise that, should the allies win, Italy could snap up a large slice of territory from the Austro-Hungarian Empire. The Italians proved themselves inept cobelligerents, suffering a humiliating defeat at the hands of the Austrians at Caporetto in November 1917. Even so, Italy lost 650,000 young men in the war, enduring four years of hunger, disease, and economic collapse. With this sacrifice in mind, the Italian government presented its bill to the great powers at the postwar Paris Peace Conference. Italy demanded a chunk of the mountainous Austrian Tyrol and a swath of the Adriatic coastline, including the deepwater port of Fiume—a sleepy town of fifty thousand residents located forty-five miles south of Trieste.

In Paris, where the victors had gathered to carve up the defeated empires and share the spoils, the British and French governments were willing to meet Italy's demands. After all, half of Fiume's residents spoke Italian; the rest were ethnically Croatian and Slovenian. But President Wilson, the latecomer to the war who nonetheless felt empowered to adjudicate these petty squabbles like a self-appointed Solomon, insisted the town be allocated to the newly created Kingdom of Yugoslavia. In a condescending public memorandum, Wilson instructed the Italians that the Istrian peninsula, with Fiume, lay beyond Italy's reach. "Fiume," opined the American president, "is by situation and by all the circumstances of its development not an Italian, but an international, port serving the countries to the east and north of the Gulf of Fiume." It could not be handed over to Italy. Wilson acknowledged that the peace settlement would place some Italian-speaking peoples along the Adriatic under a foreign flag. But, he breezily asserted, the League of Nations "will abundantly safeguard the liberty, the development and all the just rights of national and racial minorities." Upon receiving this ex cathedra announcement from Wilson, the Italian delegation led by Prime Minister Vittorio Orlando stormed out of the peace conference and boarded the next train for Rome.[4]

The Italians were determined not to sign the peace treaty without securing control of Fiume. Upon arriving in Rome, Orlando received a hero's welcome, and cheering crowds expressed unwavering support for Italy's claim to the disputed town. Demonstrators howled "Fiume or Death!" and the press carried bitter denunciations of the "dictator" Wilson. Some U.S. citizens in Italy endured stone throwing and jeers from irate mobs, while the American embassy in Rome had to be ringed with armed guards. The phrase *figlio di Wilson*—"son of Wilson"—became the foulest epithet one could throw at an enemy. Throughout the month of May 1919, the world waited as the conference stalled—Wilson rigid and uncompromising, Orlando backed by an enraged nation. In the end, the parties agreed to place Fiume under international control as a free city and postpone any final adjudication of its fate. Prime Minister Orlando, who regretfully returned to Paris and put his name to the peace treaties with Germany and Austria, knew he had failed to meet his people's expectations, and resigned.[5]

This obscure border dispute, which ought to have slipped away into the mists of time, in fact became a significant episode in the history of fascism. For although the great powers thought they had finished with this minor quarrel, the Italian people were not mollified. And on September 12, 1919, about two thousand lightly armed Italian irregular troops, acting without official sanction, marched into Fiume and declared it liberated. The leader of this bold and provocative action was an aristocratic journalist, poet, and former army officer named Gabriele D'Annunzio. Probably Italy's best-known living novelist and man of letters, and a narcissistic libertine to boot, D'Annunzio had served with distinction as a fighter pilot in the war, as well as a member of the elite force of shock troops known as the Arditi—the daring ones. His speechmaking over Fiume in the spring of 1919 had kept the nation in a frenzy, and when Orlando failed to bring home this prize from the negotiations at Paris, D'Annunzio decided to force the government's hand. He marched into Fiume, pitched out a bemused garrison of French soldiers, and sat down to await the annexation of the port by Italy.

But it never came. For fifteen months, with the delighted Italian public cheering him on, D'Annunzio presided over the town in the guise of a charismatic (and frequently debauched) dictator, pioneering many of the rituals that Mussolini would later adopt. He called himself Il Duce (the leader). He used the stiff-armed Roman salute and the rallying cry "*Eja Eja Alala!*" that would later ring through fascist formations. His followers wore black shirts and black fezzes as well as badges featuring flaming skulls. The song "Giovinezza" (Youth), adopted during the war by the Arditi shock troops, could be heard cascading down the cobbled streets of Fiume; it would later be taken up as the official hymn of the Fascist Party.

Above all, D'Annunzio popularized action, violence, and the coup d'état as the means to defy a slumbering, ineffectual government and unleash Italy's restive spirit. He was finally run out of Fiume by the Italian armed forces in December 1920 when his antics threatened to trigger a full-on war with Yugoslavia that the government wished to avoid. Yet his defiance and daring, his ability to inflame and to inspire young men who felt the great sacrifices of the war had never yet been repaid, all served as a sharp contrast to the stalemated parliamentary democracy in Rome. The moment seemed ripe for a man of action to emerge and apply these same tactics to the nation as a whole.[6]

III

These years just after the war saw unprecedented challenges to the old order erupt from one end of Europe to the other. The Bolshevik Revolution in early November 1917, followed by the murder of the Russian royal family in July 1918, helped inspire the German revolution in November 1918 and the abdication of Kaiser Wilhelm II. In March 1919, Communists in Hungary set up a short-lived, and particularly bloodthirsty, Hungarian Soviet Republic. The Irish War of Independence erupted in January 1919 as Irish Republicans sought independence from Britain. It was a moment when radicals and revolutionaries felt themselves closer than ever to overturning the aristocratic and capitalist order, once and for all.

In the same months as the Fiume controversy erupted, Italy slipped into a prolonged economic and social crisis. With millions of demobilized soldiers returning home after the war, unemployment spiked. Shortages of goods triggered price increases of basic foods, and the government, saddled by enormous war debts, could do little to improve the lot of the people. In the elections of November 1919, Italy, too, moved sharply to the left: the Italian Socialist Party, openly dedicated to Marxist doctrine, won a smashing victory. Polling one-third of the vote, the Socialists became the largest party in the Chamber of Deputies. Workers felt themselves in command of events, and there now opened a period of industrial unrest in Italy that would come to be known as the *biennio rosso*—the two "red" years.

Over 1 million workers went on strike in 1919, and these actions spread to the countryside, where peasants seized land from large estates. While the leaders of the Socialist Party remained committed to working within the parliamentary system, anarchist and Communist factions organized vast, rolling strikes, bringing the nation's trains, workshops, and marketplaces to a halt. In September 1920, half a million workers seized control of the factories in the industrial cities of Milan, Turin, and Genoa, and set up workers' councils, or "soviets." Red flags with the hammer and sickle fluttered above the grimy factories. Italy looked ready to follow Russia into open rebellion against the bourgeoisie. In this atmosphere of ideological upheaval, economic and social crisis, of thwarted nationalism and revolutionary dreams, Fascism was born.[7]

Benito Mussolini did not create these circumstances, but he instinctively knew how to exploit them. He had been born and raised in Predappio, a small northeastern town in the Emilia-Romagna region. His father—the village blacksmith—deeply believed in the struggle of the working class for dignity and equality, and he named his son after Benito Juárez, the Mexican revolutionary. While hammering away at his forge, he rehearsed the ideological arguments of the left in the presence of his boy. A pugnacious, rebellious, quick-witted young child, Mussolini struggled with the discipline of school, but managed to complete his studies in 1901 and, at age eighteen, he left his provincial hometown for broader horizons.

Penniless, adrift, Mussolini moved first to Switzerland, then Austria, then back to Italy, surviving as a manual laborer, a part-time teacher, and occasionally as a writer of fiery left-wing essays for local newspapers. He frequently tangled with the law, and was arrested a dozen times for vagrancy, fighting, forgery, as well as incitement to violence—his published screeds against the Catholic Church and the Italian monarchy caught the eyes of the authorities. He developed a reputation as a magnetic speaker, and his threadbare clothes, haunting eyes, and vagabond look only enhanced the effect. After taking over the editorship of a small Socialist weekly called the *Class Struggle*, he won the notice of the Italian Socialist Party executive committee and in 1912, began to edit the party's national daily paper, *Avanti!* (Forward!). Based in Milan, Mussolini proved a gifted propagandist for the Socialist cause, and the paper's circulation spiked dramatically.

When war broke out in the summer of 1914, Italy remained neutral, not wishing to choose sides in the gigantic conflagration. The Italian Socialists welcomed this pacifism, but Mussolini did not. He felt certain that the war would lead to the collapse of the rotten empires of Europe. The French and British socialists supported the war against Germany and Austria; why should Italians let the workers of Europe do their fighting for them? Mussolini became an outspoken interventionist, breaking with his party. When the Italian government did enter the war in 1915, Mussolini was delighted. He served two years in uniform. Wounded by a mortar blast in February 1917, he spent months in the hospital and never returned to the front. The war transformed him from a revolutionary leftist into a chest-thumping nationalist, a man who still loathed the oligarchs and elites, but who disavowed socialism. He founded a newspaper called *Il Popolo d'Italia*, and charted a new course for himself as an activist and political leader. He felt the working class would respond to a doctrine of nationalism combined with economic benefits like an eight-hour day and heavy taxation on the rich. Mussolini espoused what would later be called populism: an appeal to workers and the lower middle classes, whose hearts still beat for their nation, who wanted protection both from the oligarchs as well as the revolutionary left, and who demanded that their heroic sacrifices in the war be honored.

In March 1919, Mussolini made his first attempt to form a political movement around these ideas. He held a sparsely attended meeting of what he styled "fighting leagues," or *fasci di combattimento*, in a hall on the Piazza San Sepolcro in Milan, and attracted mostly right-wing war veterans to his cause. The main theme of the gathering was that socialism had turned its back on the nation in its hour of need, and that the *fasci* must confront the left in a struggle to protect the nation from Bolshevism. Ideologically, the movement was a concoction of reactionary and revolutionary impulses, drawn to heroic action and hostile to deliberative democracy. Like D'Annunzio in Fiume, Mussolini trafficked in demagoguery, romantic irredentism, nationalism, anti-parliamentarism, and sheer audacity. He had invented a potent cocktail that would inebriate millions across Europe in the coming years.

If he could not yet create a disciplined party, he could at least fan the flames of crisis. In 1920 to 1921, as massive strikes and factory shutdowns rocked Italy, the *fasci di combattimento* acted simply as terrorists, rampaging through the countryside in trucks and buses, inflicting murder and mayhem on Socialist and Communist activists. The fascists found friends among the army and police, who looked the other way or even helped arm these roving gangs. Meanwhile, leading industrialists and financiers secretly bankrolled Mussolini's newspaper. Fascism, then, had no program other than bloody confrontation with the left, fueled by the martial values of unity, loyalty to comrades in arms, and a desire for revenge.[8]

IV

"Looking back on the two years immediately following the war," recalled the writer Lilian Mowrer about her time in Rome, "I seem to remember them as one long strike." With her husband, Edgar, the Rome correspondent for the *Chicago Daily News*, Lilian watched Italy emerge from the war in a state of shock and distress. "Telephones did not work, letters went astray, trains failed to reach their destination, and gas and electricity mysteriously disappeared." Trash collectors regularly left mountains of garbage rotting in the streets. The Socialists "did everything they could to fan discontent among the workers. Strike after strike broke out like a rash on a fevered body." Defiant workers spat on anyone in uniform, soldier or policeman. The national flag became an emblem of scorn. "It was wildly exciting. Bolshevism might have been right round the corner."

At the start of 1921, Lilian began to notice bands of young men in black shirts belligerently walking the streets of Rome. "They called themselves *fascisti*—Fascists," she recalled. "The word was not new. It referred to the *fasces*—a bundle of rods carried before the Roman victors, signifying authority." Organized spontaneously in groups of a few dozen and even a few hundred, these young toughs, often armed with truncheons and clubs, staged spectacular attacks on Socialist newspapers and meeting halls. Lilian remembered that they "carried carbines and revolvers and walked with tremendous swagger." She heard their "ringing challenge as they strode about the capital: 'A-yah, A-yah, ah lah lah,' like a college yell."[9]

In 1921, almost daily reports from across the country depicted Italy in a state of anarchy and civil war. "Like wildfire is spreading the merciless crusade of devastation started by the Nationalist faction in reaction against the communistic excesses during the last 18 months," declared the *New York Times* in January. In the telling of Walter Littlefield, an experienced European correspondent who knew Italy well, the fascists sought "to preserve the solidarity of the nation" against the threat of Communism; stirred by the Fiume example, they now sought to "save Italy from Lenin."[10]

The riots grew ugly and lethal. In March, dozens were killed in Florence as fascists burned down labor meeting halls and beat up left-wingers in public, often in especially humiliating fashion: compelling them to sign a resignation from the Socialist Party, stripping them naked, forcing them to gulp down pints of castor oil—a powerful laxative that ended in terrible illness and dehydration. Open conflict featuring pistols, hand grenades, and bombs thrown in cafés and public streetcars left hundreds dead and wounded across 1921.

"Civil War Raging in Italian Cities," the newspapers blared. "A cyclone of bloodshed" had crashed over northern and central Italy.[11]

To some Americans, though, the very violence of fascism carried with it a powerful appeal. In the eyes of Anne McCormick, back in Italy in mid-1921 for another assessment of the scene, Fascist rallies were "almost as exciting as a horse-race," with the handsome Blackshirts racing down the Roman boulevards, "the lines in excellent order, the runners brandishing their thick canes and singing at the top of their voices." Watching their "joyous and vivid energy, I experienced a thrill," she confided to her readers. "'How young they are!' I kept saying to myself." To McCormick, these "battalions of fighting, singing, scornful, unrelenting boys" promised to reinvigorate the sclerotic Italian political class. That they used brutal methods seemed not to bother McCormick, for they were only trying to preserve order from the revolutionary left—or so she told her readers. She was sure they would go far in Italy, and beyond: "One need not be a prophet to foresee that the flame will spread to other countries."[12]

This form of violent score settling with the left proved quite popular among shopkeepers, large-scale farmers, factory owners, and the middle classes. "The *Fascisti* movement is gaining ground in every town and village of Italy," reported the *New York Times*. "Their chief object is to fight socialism, communism and anarchism," and to "free the country from her internal enemies." Edgar Mowrer, reporting for the *Daily News*, confirmed that "public opinion was now largely on the side of the Fascists," while some police and army officers participated in fascist assaults "without even bothering to remove their uniforms." But could this surge of violence be channeled into a political party? That was Mussolini's ambition, and he managed to win election to parliament in the elections of May 1921.[13]

Hoping to give some meaning to this mass movement beyond simple hooliganism, Mussolini stressed that Fascism stood for order, hierarchy, national unity, and respect for property. Such order, he claimed, would redeem the sacrifices the nation had made in the war. Indeed, the language and styling of fascism deliberately borrowed the militarism of wartime to send a message: The victory of 1918 was incomplete, the struggle against the Communists must continue, and the suffering nation must be reborn. Initially, Mussolini met with resistance from the leaders of the *squadristi*—the gangs who had been so effective in shattering the left's hold in the countryside. A Fascist Party, they feared, would replicate the boring, antiquated politics that they rejected.

In early November 1921, fifteen thousand Fascists poured into Rome for a congress that featured "overgrown youths armed with sticks, revolvers, hand grenades and knives" bullying their way through the streets, according to Edgar Mowrer. Running battles with communists left five dead and scores wounded. In retaliation, all the workers in the city went on strike, shutting down the trains and plunging Rome into darkness. Amid the chaos, fascist delegates gathered inside the Augusteo—the mausoleum of Emperor Augustus that had been converted into a magnificent concert hall—and while the Blackshirts nosily defiled the place, carving their names on the walls and slashing the velvet seats, Mussolini firmly guided his followers to adopt his proposal for the creation of a National Fascist Party. This proved a masterstroke. He would use his gangs to ignite a national crisis and then present himself as the only man who could master it.[14]

V

"Italy has a Frankenstein and his name is Benito Mussolini." That was the assessment at the start of 1922 of T. R. "Tommy" Ybarra, the Venezuelan-born, Harvard-educated *New York Times* European correspondent. And Mussolini, like the fictional doctor, had lost control of his monster—"*Fascismo*." Now in parliament at the head of a political party and in search of respectability, Mussolini would be "happier and less apprehensive if the unruly youths who elected him would behave better," Ybarra thought. His followers had used brutal methods to defeat Communism and "uphold law and order and conservatism." The lads had been "prepared to go to any lengths to save Italy from the radicals." But having reached high office, Mussolini was "constantly calling upon his violent followers to calm themselves." He "certainly seems embarrassed by the doings of the more violent *Fascisti*."[15]

In fact, Mussolini had not lost control of the creature he brought to life; in 1922, he used it to sow chaos and attack the left, all the while leaving open the possibility that Fascism could take power legally. Edgar Mowrer observed the fascist method. In May, he reported that "the coming of hot weather has brought a recrudescence of those factional battles, street fights, and murders which have wasted much of the best energy of Italy in the last three years." With the obvious support of "former aristocracy, large capitalists, employers, professional men, and many well-dressed women of the leisure classes," the Fascists stormed into Socialist strongholds, threw out mayors and union officials, and gunned down anyone who defied them.

In June 1922, Mowrer saw sixty thousand armed Blackshirts seize the town of Bologna and eject the "Red" city government. In Rome, the government spoke of banning the *fascisti* squads, and Mussolini dared them. "We have numerous disciplined, well-organized forces. We will react with extreme violence against any attempt to oppress us," he shouted in the Italian Chamber of Deputies. "To any reaction, we will answer with insurrection." In early August, bloody clashes broke out in all the major cities as fascist squads went on the offensive against Socialist newspapers, meeting halls, and politicians. On August 4, fascists entered Milan, a longtime stronghold of the organized left, and unleashed a reign of terror, seizing the town hall and leaving over fifty people wounded. Similar acts of violence took place in Ancona, Genoa, Naples, and the port of Civitavecchia, with dozens killed. The body count rose: By October, some three thousand people had been killed since 1919 in such street battles.[16]

The bloodshed did not diminish the appeal of this movement. Anne McCormick helped define the American attitude toward fascism: Yes, it was violent, she admitted, but Italy was a wild country that needed a firm hand. The parliament had become a ludicrous circus, featuring "howling and growling in the ring, cheers and groans in the galleries, wildly waving arms, pouncing back and forth, deafening din, enraged Deputies, impotent Ministers." To McCormick, "the Italy of today seems almost ungovernable." There was something about these people that made them incapable of self-rule: Democracy had failed here because "the Italians are far too democratic to make a success of it." Factions, splinter parties, and ideologies had riven politics into a thousand pieces and this "nation of individualists had no reverence for authority." Though not openly choosing sides, McCormick could not contain her enthusiasm for fascism. "Youth is in the saddle," she gushed, full of admiration for one "sleek and perfectly groomed" fascist squad leader who, she wrote, was "burnished as a blooded racehorse." Deploring their violent means, she could not hide her excitement for their vigor: "It is rather inspiriting to see youth rampant in the great-grandmother of civilization."[17]

McCormick was not wrong about the political stalemate. The chamber was divided between the Socialists, the Catholic People's Party, and various conservative factions. An uneasy coalition, led by a moderate Socialist, held power for ten months, only to collapse and be replaced at the start of 1922 by an even less secure coalition of the right, led by Luigi Facta of the Liberal Party. In the midst of fascist terror, and with an insecure hold on power, the Facta government proved too feeble for decisive action. Mussolini believed his moment was near. His shock troops were seizing power in the towns; he might follow suit in Rome.

At the start of October, Mussolini turned up the temperature, declaring that Italy now had two governments: the "fictitious" one in Rome and the "real one run by the Fascists." One of them had to go. He called for new nationwide elections and expected to win them. Failing that, he threatened to seize power. And increasingly the politicians of the right were ready to give Mussolini his chance; he might impose much-needed order—albeit at the end of a revolver. A reporter for the *Chicago Tribune* heard right-wing parliamentarians privately say: "The country might as well get it over with and bring about necessary radical changes in the political system so that the nation may find social peace again." A *New York Times* editorial claimed "there is much that is good and much that is evil" in fascism, yet hailed the "artistic impulse" behind the movement—"a throwback to the Renaissance." This kind of colorful description transformed Mussolini into a charming swordsman one might find in Shakespeare's Padua, complete with billowing shirtsleeves, satin doublet, and silk hose.[18]

There was nothing comic or lighthearted about the giant fascist rally Mussolini staged in Naples in the last week of October, however. Designed deliberately to create the impression of an unstoppable wave, the rally gathered forty thousand men dressed head to toe in black for a mass demonstration with a single purpose: to point a dagger at Italian democracy. Speaking to a frenzied audience in the elaborately gilded San Carlo Theater in Naples on October 24, Mussolini declared "the moment has arrived, in fact, when the arrow must leave the bow; or the cord, too far stretched, will break." His rousing peroration elicited thunderous approval from the audience. "I say to you with all the solemnity that the moment requires: either we will be given the government or else we must take it by marching on Rome." Across the country, fascist squads began to marshal their forces, eager to move on the Eternal City.[19]

Saturday, October 28, dawned cold and wet. Lilian Mowrer looked out the window of her apartment in the Palazzo Galitzin, just a block from the pale green river that runs through central Rome. "The Tiber was rushing along, swift and high, and sheets of drenching rain almost hid the great dome of St. Peter's from view." Her cook reported that "the roads were blocked" by soldiers; the telephone was cut, too. A friend arrived in the afternoon to say that disorganized and ragged columns of Blackshirts, soaked to the bone, had gathered idly near the Quirinal Palace, the royal residence, unsure of what to do. A whiff of grapeshot might have frightened them off, and Prime Minister Luigi Facta begged King Victor Emmanuel III to declare martial law. He refused, fearing the soldiers might not obey and perhaps showing a bit of sympathy for the fascist cause. Facta resigned.

By the late afternoon, the rain stopped, and the fascist battalions grew. They sang their anthem, "Giovinezza," as they quick-marched through the streets. There was little violence, just boisterous carousing all night long in the public parks, where the Blackshirts camped under the stars. The next morning, a Sunday, "the houses were decorated with flags, and crowds were gayly parading through the main thoroughfares," awaiting the arrival of the man of the moment, Mussolini.[20]

Mussolini had not marched alongside his rain-soaked loyalists as they gathered in Rome. He remained in Milan, awaiting a call from the king that finally came: an invitation to form a government at the head of a coalition to include all parties except the Socialists and Communists. His bluff had worked. A delighted Mussolini boarded a night train for Rome, arriving on Monday morning to cheering throngs. He called on the king, wearing the black shirt of his movement. By noon on October 30, the ironworker's son, erstwhile scofflaw, radical journalist, and rabble-rouser had become Italy's prime minister. He would remain in power for the next twenty-three years.[21]

VI

Although fascist mythology would forever hail this moment as "the March on Rome," Mussolini had not seized power in a coup d'état; he had instead created a national crisis, fueled it for three years with political terrorism, egged on angry young men as they brutalized and bullied their way across the country, and then—at the point of a gun—demanded an invitation to the traditional and entirely constitutional procedure of forming a government. This clever preservation of norms gave Mussolini a dual mandate: While his followers could praise his muscular seizure of the reins of power, foreign observers held tight to the idea that Mussolini had been asked by the king to save Italy from chaos and communism.

The whitewashing of Mussolini's Blackshirts began immediately in the American press. Describing the scenes in Rome on October 31, the day Mussolini and his cabinet returned to the royal palace in morning coats and silk top hats for their formal swearing in, journalists surrendered to the grandeur of the moment. "Romans Hail Fascisti!" declared the *Baltimore Sun*. Italians "wept for joy," as "Italy has been saved from Bolshevism." The endless marching of "dark-visaged youths with set, determined faces" moved many observers, and "every window was filled with Romans cheering, some showering flowers upon the passing Blackshirts." The *New York Tribune* described Mussolini as "an exceptional type . . . a born leader," while Arthur Brisbane, whose syndicated column "Today" was seen by millions across America, rejoiced at the arrival of determined leadership in Rome. Mussolini, Brisbane said, had turned his back on the utopian pipe dreams of his youth. He now leads "a REAL government, giving REAL orders to REAL people." Brisbane assured his readers that Mussolini "has taken over the country on behalf of the middle-class people that have little and want to keep it."[22]

A new thesis took hold in conservative media outlets like the *Chicago Tribune* that fascism was a "revolution against revolution." The communists, by seizing "private property," had inflamed the former soldiers of the Great War, who "fought for Italy, not for Lenin." Mussolini did not intend "to overthrow the existing order but to save it." Fascism represented the "successful effort of the middle class to meet the tide of revolutionary socialism." This analysis, that fascism signaled the return to power of the middle class and "white collar men," was picked up by the United Press's Europe expert, J. W. T. Mason. The middle class had lost ground during the war and once-secure men were now "wearing the same old clothes, concealing their poverty as best they can. . . . The Fascisti movement represents to them the possibility of successful self-assertion." Walter Littlefield, the dean of the *New York Times* overseas correspondents, confirmed that fascism was "the middle class in revolt." He approvingly called Mussolini "a severe disciplinarian, but no dictator."[23]

Journalists also lavished attention on Mussolini's commanding presence and masculinity. He had "the broad shoulders of an athlete" and a "Napoleon-like profile," one wrote. Alice Rohe, who had spent the war years in Rome reporting for the United Press, nabbed one of the first personal interviews with the premier. She breathlessly praised his "indomitable will, personal fearlessness, powerful intellect, profound learning, straight thinking and direct action." His dark eyes were "piercing, commanding, blazing," but also "brooding and melancholy." Rohe dwelt on Mussolini's features: His mouth was "strong, determined, domineering, uncompromising." His lips revealed "an unmistakable sensuousness. His teeth are white and even. His nose is large, well-formed, suggestive of power." Asked to describe the first goal of his government, Mussolini replied briskly: "discipline."[24]

As Mussolini tightened his grip on power—in mid-November 1922 he demanded and received from the parliament full powers for one year to reform Italy's electoral laws and finances—his stock rose in America. The *Chicago Tribune* even justified his use of terror on his path to power. "The backbone of Fascism is youth, and youth is violent. But we have no respect for the fuss made over Fascist violence. . . . It is easy for American ideologues and parlor pinks to condemn the Fascisti for the use of illegal force." But Italy faced communist subversion, claimed the *Tribune*, and "it was the task of Fascism to defend Italy. . . . Italy was slipping into the Red morass. Fascism has stopped the descent."[25]

Edgar Mowrer remained unmoved by all this froth. One of the few writers to cast doubt on the story of fascism rescuing Italy from Red revolution, Mowrer described Mussolini's assumption of power as "brutally illegal." Italian Socialism, he claimed, had been fatally weakened by internal squabbling well before Mussolini took power; it posed no serious threat to the country. Fascism simply took advantage of anti-communist paranoia "to overthrow the weak and senile, pseudo-democratic politicians of the old regime." Mowrer prophesied a bleak future for Italy. The country was now led by men who had passed through the "brutalizing influence of three years in the trenches." They retained martial values, showed "contempt for democracy," welcomed conflict, and were driven by "blind nationalism." All they wanted was power, and the chance to mete out rough justice to their enemies. At the end of 1923, Mowrer and his wife, Lilian, fed up with the increasing militarization of the Fascist regime in Rome, accepted a new assignment that offered the chance to cover politics in a freer, more democratic city: Berlin.[26]

But such dissenting voices were rare in American coverage of fascism. Instead, Anne McCormick wrote an astonishing essay for the Sunday *New York Times* in July 1923 that was embellished with a drawing of a grim-faced, muscular Mussolini seated atop a powerful steed. She praised "Mussolini the Autocrat" for shining a light on the "dark and stabbing doubts of democracy that secretly assail all who have tried it." Mussolini had found Italy in paralysis and set it all running again, showing that "one-man power is less dangerous than the powerlessness of many men." As for dictatorship, Italians loved the "swashbuckling" style and "impudence" of their new leader, whose very vulgarity bespoke honesty. "They adore a masterful man," McCormick wrote. *Time* magazine put a charcoal sketch of a glowering Mussolini on its cover in August 1923, while inside its pages, an essay marveled at the leader's "remarkable self-control, rare judgment, and efficient application of his ideas to existing problems."[27]

In October, an American journalist named Isaac Marcosson returned from a four-month tour in Europe and described Mussolini in the *New York Times* as "a Latin Roosevelt," referring to the late president Theodore, "who first acts and then inquires if it is legal." This caught on: At the start of 1924, the popular monthly magazine *McClure's* also called Mussolini an "exceptionally able" politician who resembled "[Teddy] Roosevelt and Henry Ford" in his combination of efficiency, pragmatism, charisma, his anti-communism and love for a managed or disciplined brand of capitalism.[28]

In the pages of the *Saturday Evening Post*, with a circulation of over 2 million a week, readers encountered the glowing testimonials of a man who knew Mussolini personally and could vouch for his heroic character. Richard Washburn Child, the U.S. ambassador to Italy from 1921 to 1924, became one of Mussolini's most fawning admirers. Educated at Harvard, Child started his career as a journalist covering Washington, D.C., politics for *Ridgway's* magazine and writing short stories for *McClure's*, *Collier's*, and the *Saturday Evening Post*. He found a minor role in the 1912 presidential campaign of Theodore Roosevelt, who was then hoping to stage a comeback as the Progressive Party candidate running against Woodrow Wilson and William Howard Taft. Child stayed active in Republican circles and, in 1920, offered his speechwriting talents to the Republican candidate for president, Warren G. Harding. Following Harding's victory, Child was rewarded with a plum: the ambassadorship to Rome. It was thought to be a quiet, luxurious sinecure. Instead, Child had a front-row seat to the violent pageantry of Mussolini's rise to power.

Child saw in Mussolini the same kind of masculine, patriotic dash and daring as in his hero Teddy Roosevelt. When his three-year tour came to an end in 1924, Child began writing extensively about Mussolini and Italy for the *Saturday Evening Post*. Not only did he publish his own enthusiastic essays about Il Duce, later collected in his 1925 book, *A Diplomat Looks at Europe*, Child also helped write Mussolini's made-for-export political testament, *My Autobiography*, which appeared in serialized form in the *Post* before coming out as a book in 1928. Child became Mussolini's most able and zealous American publicist.

In his popular writing, Child echoed the thesis that Mussolini was no dictator, but an immensely popular leader who had brought "discipline, work, and justice" back to Italy. Child followed Anne McCormick's idea that Italy had suffered from too much democracy and too little leadership. "It was so liberal a state that it could not maintain order," he declared. In the postwar years, as Italy faced strikes, Communists, and corruption, "everything was cynicism and drifting. There was a ravenous yearning to begin a new day." Before Mussolini, Italy was wallowing in what Child called "a sentimental jelly of misnamed democracy."

More than that, Child claimed, Mussolini's Fascist movement had restored grandeur and romance to politics. Fascism, he wrote, had a "lyric and epic quality. Let its opponents damn it if they will; they cannot deny that it had gladness, hope, [and] loyal service" at its core. Indeed, Mussolini "had the whole country singing, and the song was not a song of battle and conflict, of class against class. It was a song of unity." Was the march on Rome undemocratic? A silly question. "The people of Italy were too hungry for action, for strength, for leadership out of the wilderness, to make fine distinctions between constitutional legal action and direct action."

In a telling dismissal of liberalism, Child asserted that "*Fascismo* is a philosophy and an emotion running counter to the recent stream of thought which centers mankind's attention on rights. Mussolini . . . has organized political unity not around rights but around duties." He had responded to a yearning in people for "order, organization, service," even submission. In a modern world of atomized individuals unmoored from religious faith and clamoring for a spiritual cause, Child felt that fascism provided an answer: "There is something mystical and religious in the Fascist conception of the nation." Fascism and its bold leader, Child believed, offered a secular religion to a people who had lost faith in the old gods but hungered for a new one.[29]

VII

Most American writers did not see, or did not wish to report, the realities behind the shimmering novelty of fascism. Soon after taking office, Mussolini privately deployed the Fascist Party militia to silence the opposition. Three members of parliament were killed by fascists and fifty others were attacked and beaten. Mussolini took personal control of the police and had thousands of political opponents arrested and jailed. He conspired in the kidnapping and murder of a leading critic, the secretary of the Socialist Party, Giacomo Matteotti, in June 1924. That crisis nearly led to an early downfall, but Mussolini weathered the storm. And he took particular care in muzzling the free press. A former journalist and editor, he knew how vital it was to control information. He put every newspaper under careful watch and had some directly taken over by fascists. If Americans failed to grasp the essential danger of Mussolini's movement, it was in part because the regime carefully hid the truth. In the next two years, he consolidated his control of Italy's governing machinery, closing all opposition parties, filling the police with obedient loyalists, abolishing trade unions, and imposing fascist control of the economy. His new "corporate state" mandated cooperation between labor and management, banned strikes, and compelled all Italians to pledge their loyalty to the state. Mussolini transformed Italy's illiberal democracy into a full-fledged dictatorship. By the end of 1926, he served not only as prime minister and foreign minister, but he directed the interior, war, navy, and air ministries.[30]

And influential Americans eagerly and gladly closed ranks behind the dictator. In late May 1925, Thomas Lamont, a director of the banking house J. P. Morgan & Co., wrote to U.S. secretary of state Frank Kellogg to inform him that, following a recent visit to Rome, Morgan was prepared to provide the Italian government a banking credit of $50 million. Italy also soon won favorable terms for the repayment of its wartime debts to the United States, an issue that had festered since the war's end. And in November 1925, the House of Morgan came through with yet another loan, this time for $100 million. Lamont emerged as an enthusiastic backer of Mussolini, playing a crucial role in bankrolling the early Fascist state. At the start of 1926, Lamont lectured the Council on Foreign Relations on the success of fascism in restoring Italy's economy and winning the loyalty of its people. The press could not get enough of Il Duce. On July 12, *Time* put a photo on its cover of Mussolini stroking a lion cub. "I am like the animals," he said. "I can feel the future as it approaches. Some instinct guides and warns me. My blood speaks!"[31]

What was it Americans found so alluring about Italian fascism? Anne McCormick, Ida Tarbell, Richard Washburn Child, Thomas Lamont, and countless others imagined that Mussolini had found answers to the crises of the age: Bolshevism and class conflict, labor strikes, unemployment, parliamentary stalemate, fractious politics—Mussolini's fascism somehow swept these aside and replaced them with harmony and order, they told themselves. "He is the perfect dictator," McCormick sighed in 1926, "cool before bombs, passionate when passion will move, masterful when there is need of mastery." Interviewing him at 8 p.m. after a long, hot workday, McCormick found Mussolini "fresh and animated," his voice "low, throaty, musical"; "he talks of Rome like a poet." The "whole country is keyed up by his energy." Liberalism looked stagnant and passive by comparison to the active, muscular fascists. Even liberals said this: Herbert Croly of the venerable *New Republic*, in an editorial called "An Apology for Fascism," asserted that "whatever the dangers of Fascism, it has at any rate substituted movement for stagnation, purposive behavior for drifting, and vision of a great future for collective pettiness and discouragement." Yes, there might be dangers in promoting intense and violent nationalism. "But it may be better for the Italian people to venture upon a costly and tragic experiment which arouses their passionate cooperation than to remain satisfied with the cheap corruption and stagnation of their former parliamentary politics."[32]

Vision, passion, movement: Here is what Mussolini promised, and who could blame Italians for rallying to the handsome strongman? Americans developed a kind of romantic attraction to what they saw as a young, unruly people suddenly called to their nation's flag and submitting to the discipline of their leader, a bold chief who, though he might have murdered a few Socialists along the way, had forged a new kind of unity and order. No wonder, then, that Americans looked on with fascination as another fascist experiment took hold just a few hundred miles to the north, led by a former German army private who the American press quickly dubbed "the Bavarian Mussolini."

CHAPTER 3

LAND OF FISTS

"He is inconsequent and voluble, insecure—the very prototype of the Little Man."

—DOROTHY THOMPSON

I

"The situation in Bavaria is giving us all some concern," wrote U.S. ambassador Alanson B. Houghton in a report from Berlin to Secretary of State Charles Evans Hughes in late November 1922. Armed antidemocratic groups, Houghton said, had joined forces in Bavaria, and "a young Austrian named Hitler" had emerged as the leading figure due to his "dominating and attractive personality." Houghton labeled Hitler a "monarchist" and went on to say that the "Fascisti" movement was "spreading throughout Germany."[1]

It was natural that American observers, when they first started to pay attention to the militant nationalist movement around Munich, reached for comparisons with Mussolini. Like the Fascist Party, this German group attracted mainly war veterans, wore uniforms, hated Communists, and rallied around a single charismatic leader. The *New York Times* described the new National Socialist party in May 1922 as "modeled on the lines of the Italian Fascisti." The *Chicago Tribune* considered the German movement a mélange of Italian fascism and "the American Ku Klux Klan," and with similar aims: "to clean Germany" of Jews, Communists, "usury, speculation, and other manifestations of Jewish spirit." Cyril Brown of the *Times* penned his first portrait of "the Bavarian Mussolini" just one month after the fascists had come to power in Rome; he described Hitler's "rare oratorical gift of spellbinding whole audiences," and noted that this radical movement was "reactionary, nationalistic, and anti-Semitic." This feature differed from Mussolini's ideology, yet "reliable, well-informed sources" assured Brown that "Hitler's anti-Semitism was not so genuine or violent as it sounded." Brown asserted that the Nazi leader only used antisemitism as "bait to catch masses of followers and keep them aroused."[2]

Karl H. von Wiegand, the German-born correspondent for the Hearst-syndicated Universal News Service, did not mention antisemitism at all in his first profile of the Nazi leader, stressing Hitler's anti-Communism instead. Hitler, wrote von Wiegand in an admiring tone, had "eyes that spurt fire" and "finely chiseled features, with a complexion so remarkably delicate that many a woman would be proud to possess it." Yet he was also a man of "dynamic energy," "a man of the people, a private soldier during the war . . . a magnetic speaker, having also exceptional organizing genius." In a tone set by the press coverage of Mussolini and Italian Fascism, von Wiegand uncritically reported Hitler's plan to save Germany from "internal" foes.[3]

Feeling the need for more firsthand information, Ambassador Houghton ordered the assistant military attaché in the embassy, Captain Truman Smith, to go to Munich and prepare a report on the far-right movement in Bavaria. Smith, a Yale-educated infantry officer from an old Connecticut political family, had won a Silver Star in the Great War while serving as a battalion commander. (He later became a close wartime aide to General George C. Marshall.) In November 1922, he spent a remarkable week in Munich interviewing Bavarian politicians and journalists in hopes of understanding the political scene there. He became the first American official to meet with Adolf Hitler.

Munich, once known for beer halls and gaiety, had not recovered from the shattering impact of the Great War. It looked shabby and worn, beset by skyrocketing prices and shortages of every kind. "In the markets of Munich," according to von Wiegand, "shivering groups of half-starved women stand about and pick up the ends of carrot and turnip tops." Upon arriving there on November 15, Smith went straight to the American consulate to meet with Robert Murphy, a young diplomat working overtime to prepare visas and travel papers for Germans who wished to immigrate to America—and there were many. Murphy (who would go on to a long and influential diplomatic career) told Smith that "the National Socialists are increasing their strength rapidly," and that Hitler was brilliantly "exploiting all latent discontent." But Murphy downplayed the prospect of Hitler emerging as a national figure capable of uniting the nationalist right.[4]

As Smith moved through his rounds in Munich, he found that many officials in the Bavarian government had a certain admiration for Hitler's aims, which were described mainly as combating Marxism. The Bavarian government let the Nazis do what they wanted, he learned. Captain Smith was astonished to witness a demonstration of Nazi Party members, "1,200 of the toughest roughnecks I have ever seen in my life," goose-stepping down Munich's wide Corneliusstrasse. Hitler greeted the marchers and made a speech that cursed the Jews. "There was frantic cheering. I never saw such a sight," Smith would write in his official report.

More was to come, for the following day Smith found himself listening to a long disquisition from General Erich Ludendorff on the grave threat to Germany posed by Marxism. Second only to Field Marshal Paul von Hindenburg in influence and prestige, Ludendorff had served as quartermaster of the German General Staff during the Great War and exercised near-dictatorial control over Germany in the last two years of the war. Following the defeat in 1918, Ludendorff stoked the flames of the "stab in the back" legend, alleging that Jews and Socialists had betrayed Germany, triggering domestic revolution and chaos that undermined the war effort. Someone must be responsible for Germany's defeat and humiliation, and it certainly was not the army, Ludendorff insisted. To Smith, Ludendorff openly hailed the emergence of fascism as "the beginning of a reactionary awakening in Europe." He pleaded with the American visitor to urge the U.S. government to accept that only a strong, nationalist Germany could fend off the mortal danger of Communism.

And then at last, Smith met the man himself on November 20 at 4 p.m., in a small dingy office on Munich's Georgenstrasse. Hitler, with his "short cropped black hair and stubby moustache" gave the appearance of a "middle-class shopkeeper." But his eyes, "gleaming with fanaticism, intense and unceasing," bored into Smith. And his voice, "derisive, rasping, often angry," made an arresting impression on the American. "A marvelous demagogue," he wrote of the Nazi leader when he returned to his hotel that evening. "I have rarely listened to such a logical and fanatical man. His power over the mob must be immense." Hitler presented himself as determined to defeat Marxism in Germany; the issue of antisemitism and his desire for revenge after the defeat of 1918 did not arise. Hitler instead stressed his fight against the Communists; the only way to defeat them was through a dictatorship. Like Ludendorff, Hitler stressed that "if America does not help German nationalism, Bolshevism will conquer Germany." Hitler had often been described in newspapers as leader of the "monarchist" forces, but to Captain Smith, Hitler dismissed the appellation with contempt. "Monarchy is an absurdity," he declared, and had no desire to resurrect the tarnished royals who had failed to win the last war. He wanted dictatorship and he meant to impose it on Berlin.

Smith left the interview unnerved. Germany was an angry, desperate country and Hitler had the capacity to exploit this unrest. Like other American analysts, Smith did not really grasp the ideological content of the emerging Nazi movement. If Hitler was just a Bavarian Mussolini, he could be expected to rely on nationalism and fear of the left, and perhaps the use of belligerent street bullies, to build his political movement in the service of order, discipline, and anti-Communism. But Smith did get one thing right: Hitler possessed sufficient talent and fanaticism to shake the fragile foundations of German democracy. At a time when Germans were enduring widespread hunger, poverty, and ideological conflict, "the magnetism and oratorical ability of the National Socialist leader," Smith concluded, would insure "a rapid and consistent development of the German 'Fascisti.'"[5]

II

Born in Braunau am Inn, Austria, on April 20, 1889—a date that millions of Germans would later fanatically celebrate—Adolf Hitler was the spoiled, indolent son of a doting mother, Klara, who had once toiled as a charwoman, and an abusive, distant father, Alois Schicklgruber, a minor customs official in the Austrian civil service who was himself born out of wedlock. (In adulthood, to wipe away the stain of illegitimacy, Schicklgruber got a court to recognize his stepfather, Johann Georg Hiedler, as his biological father; soon after, he began to spell his new last name as Hitler.) The young Adolf had a nasty, cross temperament. He was friendless and did poorly in school; he affected an artistic air and dabbled with paints and music. After his father died suddenly in 1903, Hitler began to plan his escape from his dreary small-town life. He dreamed of studying painting at the Vienna Academy of Fine Arts, but his middling talents could not propel him into that elite institution. His mother's death in 1907 left him an orphan but also released him from any family expectations. He could roam where he wished.[6]

From 1908 to 1913, he whiled away his late teens and early twenties in polyglot, multiethnic Vienna, living off a small savings from his family and earning a little money by selling amateur paintings of famous Viennese buildings. Lazy, verbose, full of scorn toward the "mongrel races" that crowded the streets of his adopted home city, Hitler loafed in dingy cafés, where he pored over antisemitic newspapers and nourished his grievances. He lived among the city's transient day laborers in a men's hostel. His only passion was music, and he saved his coins to buy cheap standing-room-only tickets to lavish performances at Vienna's magnificent opera houses.

As with Mussolini, the outbreak of war in August 1914 altered Hitler's course. Having moved to Munich a year earlier, he joined the German (rather than the Austro-Hungarian) army—the 16th Bavarian Reserve Infantry Regiment—and within weeks found himself at the front in Belgium. The war gave this unremarkable failure of a man a sense of purpose and belonging. During four years in the trenches in the Great War, he served as a dispatch runner, carrying messages between command posts. Though rewarded twice with an Iron Cross for bravery, he never advanced beyond the rank of corporal. His fellow soldiers found him peculiar: He did not drink, smoke, express a desire for women, or receive packages from home. He seems to have made only one close friend: a white terrier named Fuchsl.

In the aftermath of Germany's defeat in the war, Hitler was adrift. His parents were dead, his youthful hopes of becoming a painter long since dashed. The army was the only institution in which he had found a home. Hitler returned to his barracks in Munich, and the army put him to work as an informant, eavesdropping on meetings of fringe political groups and demobilized veterans. Like Hitler, the veterans were angry and sullen. They had fought bravely and at great cost—2 million dead, over 4 million more disfigured and traumatized—and returned home to a shattered, defeated nation in the grip of political turmoil.[7]

Kaiser Wilhelm II, confronted with military defeat as well as a growing insurrection from the radicalized working class, abdicated on November 9, 1918, and fled the country. Two days later, a delegation of Germans, meeting with Allied officials in a railway car in northern France, signed an armistice that brought the fighting to a close and required the Germans to evacuate occupied French and Belgian territory and to withdraw completely from all German soil on the western bank of the Rhine River. A makeshift provisional government of Social Democrats and centrists took the reins of power under Friedrich Ebert, the Socialist leader. But Ebert was no radical. The extreme leftists in Germany thought him a mere bourgeois politician, a product of the capitalist system they aimed to topple. The Spartacus League, named for the leader of a Roman slave rebellion, took inspiration from the Russian Bolsheviks; they believed the time was ripe for a Soviet-style revolution. Launching an uprising under the red flag of Communism, the Spartacists staged massive protests and strikes in January 1919.

Facing a violent and determined revolutionary movement, Ebert mobilized irregular militia units, the Freikorps, made up of recently demobilized German army troops and officers, to crush the uprising. For two weeks, gunfire filled Berlin's streets as the Spartacists were hunted down. Their leaders, Karl Liebknecht and Rosa Luxemburg, were arrested on January 15 and then murdered in cold blood. Yet the Communists' revolutionary ardor did not fade. Another outburst of strikes seized the country in March, and left-wing insurgents took control of official buildings in Berlin. The defense minister,

Gustav Noske, declared a state of emergency and sent the Freikorps into action. A bloodbath followed, with as many as two thousand people gunned down in Berlin. The Communists were suppressed, but the specter of a red revolution haunted Germany for many years and induced a deep anti-Communist paranoia among Germany's politicians and military leaders.[8]

Ebert, who had turned back the tide of the "Red" revolution, seemed to have mastered the moment, and a hastily convened national assembly now elected him president of the Reich. Meeting in the Thuringian city of Weimar to avoid the street fighting in Berlin, this assembly turned to the task of writing a new constitution, which became the law of the land on August 11, 1919. The war had swept away the monarchy and the German Empire; in its place, the new Weimar Republic offered not Bolshevism or monarchy, but a liberal capitalist democracy based on the rule of law. The constitution gave adult men and women the right to vote; it offered religious protection for all; and gave rights to privacy, speech, assembly, and equality before the law. Amid the ashes of the old imperial order—ashes now mixed with the blood of the revolutionary Spartacists—a fragile democracy sprouted tentative roots.[9]

Yet Weimar was saddled with a heavy burden: In June 1919, the new German government was compelled to accept the harsh terms of the Versailles Treaty, the much-criticized peace settlement that lopped off 13 percent of Germany's territory (and 10 percent of its population), demanded enormous reparations to be paid to the victors, and limited the German military to a tiny fraction of its former size. The Allies insisted that the kaiser should be put on trial as a war criminal and, perhaps most notorious, the Versailles Treaty specified that Germany bore the responsibility for having started the war. The Allied governments made it plain: If Germany refused to sign, they would restart the war, march to Berlin, and occupy the country.

Many German leaders, shocked at the severity of the peace terms they faced, blamed Woodrow Wilson for approving this "diktat" (imposed or forced) peace; they had looked to Wilson as the man who had championed a "peace without victory" and who would broker a conciliatory settlement based on the principles of the Fourteen Points. Rather than accept their own responsibility for the war and its costs, many in Germany blamed others—Wilson, the French, the British, the Socialist government, and of course the Jews—for what they saw as a deceitful and unjust peace process, forced on the Germans at the point of a bayonet. And for many demobilized soldiers, the families who had lost loved ones, and the citizens who remained in thrall to the nationalism and chauvinism of the dethroned kaiser, this bitter peace, with its odor of failure and shame, could never be tolerated.[10]

Hitler was one of these unmoored, resentful veterans. And in the taverns of Munich, he found comradeship with men of like temper. The Bavaria to which Hitler returned after the war was in a state of complete chaos and turmoil. Long an independent kingdom, Bavaria chafed under the rule of Prussian Berlin and still nursed separatist ambitions. In early November 1918, as the kaiser's rule was disintegrating, left-wing radicals, led by a socialist (and Jewish) journalist named Kurt Eisner, took power in Munich, and declared a People's State of Bavaria. This political experiment was a fiasco. Amid mass unemployment, shortages of food and fuel, and the complete collapse of municipal authority, Bavaria drifted into violent anarchy. Eisner was murdered by a right-wing nationalist on February 21, 1919, opening the way for two months of chaotic rule by a far-left Communist junta. The central government in Berlin, itself embattled by forces of the far left, at last sent in the Freikorps units to take control of "Red Munich." The repression of May 1919 left hundreds of dead in the streets. The army took command of the city and installed a pliant reactionary government.[11]

Hitler witnessed all this upheaval from the relative safety of his Munich army barracks, and he drew lifelong lessons about the existential threat of Marxism—what he later termed a "doctrine of destruction," a "plague," "a stream of poison." He saw the potential power of the working class united under a banner of revolution and it terrified him. He also placed great emphasis on the Jewish background of the leftists who had tried to launch both the revolution in Berlin and in Munich. When he was assigned by his regiment to penetrate groups of disaffected veterans and report on their activities, Hitler did more than watch. He leaped at the chance to enter their ranks. In September 1919, he joined a small group of disillusioned nationalists and right-wing antisemites, who styled themselves the German Workers' Party. With the approval of his army superiors, Hitler took a leading role in this party, helping to frame its infamous "Twenty-Five Points" program of February 1920.[12]

Adolf Hitler in 1921.
Keystone / Hulton Archive / Getty Images

This party manifesto, issued to a rambunctious meeting in the cavernous hall of Munich's Hofbräuhaus, gave voice to the grievances of many disaffected former soldiers caught up in the backwash of war. It called for a purifying of the German racial community, or *Volk*; the annulment of the Versailles Treaty; the banning of Jews from German public life; a halt of immigration into Germany, especially by Jews fleeing the upheaval of war and persecution in Russia and Poland; and economic measures designed to reward the working and middle classes with pensions, land reform, and profit sharing from big business. Making its antisemitic character perfectly clear, the party demanded that the news media be purged of all "Jewish influence," and that art and literature be cleansed of "Jewish-materialistic spirit." Above all, a strong government of "unquestioned authority" must replace the cacophony of democracy.

The Twenty-Five Points manifesto was no less than a declaration of war on the nascent Weimar Republic. Hitler, who immediately emerged as the group's most electrifying speaker and rabble-rouser, insisted the party amend its name to the National Socialist German Workers' Party (*Nationalsozialistische Deutsche Arbeiterpartei*, or NSDAP), the word "socialist" acting as a lure to working-class voters. In July 1921, at the age of thirty-two, Hitler became the party's chairman and adopted the title of leader: *der Führer*.

III

As Americans contemplated the wreckage of Germany in the wake of its devastating defeat in the Great War, they had every reason to worry. Hitler's emergence in Munich was just one of many indications that postwar Germany would face a very difficult future. Three themes stood out to American observers: the desperate economic crisis the country faced; its deep political and ideological divisions; and the intense hatred of Jews that coursed through public discourse, part of the search for someone to blame for Germany's misfortunes.

The economic crisis could be seen everywhere. Shortages of coal and raw materials brought the German economy to a near halt, and unemployment spiked dangerously. Germany had suffered badly from four years of a naval blockade that halted imports of food and fertilizer. Though the war had ended, the blockade continued into 1919 until the German government accepted the peace treaty. The spring of that year was an especially acute period of malnutrition and aching hunger for millions. Factories that once churned out war matériel had been shuttered. Returning soldiers could not find work. George Renwick, a travel writer returning to Germany in the spring of 1919 after an absence of four and a half years, described Berlin as "a phantom city," its cafés dark, the streets in a state of "underworld gloom." By the Brandenburg Gate, disfigured soldiers hawked pathetic wares. The once-gleaming shops along Unter den Linden were shuttered and dark. By summer, a few Berliners who had made money during the war in war-related industries were filling the nightclubs and dance halls, but in the less affluent streets, gaunt men still in their field-gray uniforms stood sullenly, selling matches and trinkets. Tea, sugar, butter, and meat were all in desperately short supply. Germany, Renwick sadly concluded after a five-month visit, is "a nation broken not just physically but mentally."[13]

American military intelligence officers, part of a small occupation force left in the demilitarized Rhineland after the war, believed that such conditions would spawn further left-wing upheaval. One officer, after crossing Germany in March 1919 by convoy train, reported that in Bavaria he saw "thousands of dejected loafers wandering aimlessly about the streets . . . soldiers in unbuttoned uniforms, dirty and unshaven," selling newspapers and postcards. "The people are under-nourished and in poor mental, moral and physical condition." Bands of demobilized soldiers had resorted to looting and robbery. Only "food and work will check Bolshevism and save the situation for the more moderate influences." One gloomy assessment insisted that food relief must come immediately: "Six weeks from now it will be too late; Germany will be Bolshevistic." These dire assessments were leaked to the American press: "Feed Germany or Reds Rule," the *Chicago Tribune* declared, featuring a story that drew on these confidential U.S. military reports. The message reached Washington. In April, the United States shipped tons of grain and meat into Germany to stave off famine. But the much-hated blockade remained in place until July.[14]

Though emphasizing the threat of left-wing violence, U.S. observers did report on the sharp rise of antisemitism in postwar Germany, stoked by the far right. Propaganda spread across Berlin asserting that Jews were responsible for the Communist revolutionary activity that had so destabilized the country. This notorious conspiracy theory, the "Judeo-Bolshevik" myth, aimed to demonize Communist political radicalism by associating it with Jews—a community of people that millions of Germans considered alien, un-German, and potentially threatening. At a time when thousands of Polish and Russian Jews were fleeing into Germany due to the persecutions and political instability in Eastern Europe, flyers and handbills circulating in Berlin gave vivid testimony to the antisemitic atmosphere. One poster in Berlin called on demobilized soldiers to "wake up" to the Jewish attempt to seize power and destroy Germany from within. "Wake up, Comrades! You know the bloodsuckers!" The flyers asked rhetorically about German Jews, "Who stayed home?" during the war. Who avoided service, shirked, went to cafés, wrote critical essays in newspapers? The Jews. Such scurrilous handbills alleged that Jews were behind the Spartacist uprising (pointing out that Luxembourg was Jewish), and these left-wing radicals were part of a Jewish conspiracy against the German nation that aimed to "arouse the masses of the working classes and excite them everywhere to civil war." Now was the time to get rid of the Jews, this agitprop declared. "Our rallying call must be 'Germany for the Germans.'"[15]

American journalists, too, reported on sharp outbursts of brutal antisemitism that spiked across postwar Germany. Just weeks after the war ended, the *New York Times* described "a Jew-baiting campaign in Berlin . . . inciting the populace against the alleged Jewish dominance in government circles and the Socialist parties." During the counterrevolution in Munich in the spring of 1919, the American papers reported that many Germans felt the bloody repression of the Bavarian leftists was fully justified as a measure against "foreign" Jewish influence. In early May, the papers carried reports of placards pasted on the walls of Berlin calling for a massacre of Jews in retaliation for the murder of "200 children at Easter"—a foul canard that conjured up the blood libel allegation. A *Chicago Tribune* journalist in Berlin noticed that "anti-Semitic agitation" had been stirred by nationalists who declared that "the Jewish element is behind all the bolshevist trouble."[16]

This ominous threat hung over Berlin throughout the first postwar summer. "Jew-baiting has been revived among certain reactionary elements," reported the *New York Times* in August. "It is believed by well-informed persons that pogroms are being prepared." Affluent Jews living along Berlin's commercial boulevard called the Kurfürstendamm were told to expect "savage riots." "New clubs and secret associations" had formed for the purpose of "liberating Germany from Jewry." These attacks caused American Jewish leaders much anguish: Rabbi Stephen S. Wise in a speech in Manhattan's Rodeph Sholom synagogue sharply denounced the "cruel and barbarous" antisemitism that was "made in Germany" and exported "throughout the world."[17]

Beset by these political upheavals, Germans went to the polls in June 1920 to elect deputies to the Reichstag. The results of the voting showed the vast rift splitting Germany apart. The centrist Socialists lost seats but remained the largest party. A more radical offshoot of the Socialists won sixty-one seats and became the second-largest party. But most worrisome, the elections demonstrated the rising strength of the antidemocratic far right, as the German National People's Party (DNVP), a precursor of the Nazi Party, tripled its seats in parliament. The DNVP rallied many antisemitic, anti-Bolshevik, nationalist, and reactionary supporters to its banner, and called for the abolition of the Republic and the restoration of the monarchy. In its search for an explanation of Germany's miseries, the DNVP routinely deployed the stab-in-the-back myth that put the blame for Germany's defeat on Jewish leftists, who undermined the war effort. The party leaders gave spittle-flecked speeches about the Jewish "conspiracy" to use Bolshevism to destroy Christianity and Western civilization. These accusations joined the long-standing antisemitic tropes of Jewish corruption, swindling, and hoarding. Such ideas found support across Germany, and after the 1920 elections, the DNVP became the third-largest group in the parliament.

With the nationalist, antisemitic right now gaining momentum, violence against Jews continued—and was noted in the American press. In early 1921, the *Chicago Tribune* reported that "hundreds of university and upper-school students, armed with clubs and stones, raided the Jewish section [of Berlin] and then invaded the Kurfürstendamm," home to many Jewish jewelry and high-end clothing stores. "Hundreds of Jews were attacked and many were beaten." Jews from Eastern Europe, fleeing pogroms in Poland and the upheaval of the Russian Civil War, were particularly sought out and terrorized. Nationalist politicians routinely denounced Jewish immigrants as a foreign danger to Germany and goaded their supporters into violence. In March 1922, antisemitic rioters attacked the synagogue on Berlin's Fasanenstrasse in the ritzy Charlottenburg neighborhood. American papers recounted that when the police arrived to break up the violence, the crowds shouted, "Death to the Jews!"[18]

IV

In this toxic environment of economic chaos, extremist political division, and antisemitic scapegoating, the small Bavarian Nazi Party began to grow rapidly. As Truman Smith had noted, Hitler's oratorical performances mesmerized Bavarian audiences with their theatrical anger and fanaticism. Like other political parties of the era, the Nazis adopted a signature symbol—the swastika, an ancient religious ideogram that, in Hinduism, had betokened good luck. Set in a white circle on a red field, that hooked cross, or *Hakenkreuz*, would soon be affixed to armbands, helmets, banners, and flags carried by the movement's members. Followers began to greet Hitler with an outstretched stiff-armed salute, and a shouted greeting: "Heil!"

Though still a minor figure on the national scene, Hitler attracted ever more support from across the ethno-nationalist right, including some wealthy elites who liked his anti-Marxism, such as Fritz Thyssen, the scion of a mining and steel-manufacturing fortune. Thyssen would later write an apologetic memoir about his early support for the Nazis called *I Paid Hitler*. Ernst Hanfstaengl, a Harvard-educated, half-American publisher of high-end art books, also rallied to Hitler's side as an informal press secretary; a well-connected Bavarian and fluent English speaker, Hanfstaengl used his oily charm and excellent piano-playing skills to beguile foreign journalists and reassure them about Hitler's pure motives.[19]

It wasn't only wealthy German industrialists who liked Hitler; one important American tycoon seemed especially intrigued by Nazism. Tipped off by a notice in the *Berliner Tageblatt*, a *New York Times* reporter visited Hitler's cramped office in Munich in December 1922 to track down "a rumor . . . that Henry Ford, the American automobile manufacturer, is financing Adolf Hitler's nationalist and anti-Semitic movement in Munich." He found ready corroboration. The wall next to Hitler's desk "is decorated with a large picture of Ford. In the antechamber there is a large table covered with books, nearly all of which are a translation of a book written and published by Henry Ford." The book in question was *The International Jew*, a digest of articles from Ford's notorious newspaper, the *Dearborn Independent*, which had been publishing grotesque anti-Jewish lies and calumnies since 1920. *Chicago Tribune* reporter Raymond Fendrick called on Hitler in Munich in March 1923 to dig deeper into the story that Ford had bankrolled the Nazis. Hitler denied any direct ties but spoke warmly of the American car manufacturer. "We look on Heinrich Ford as the leader of the growing *Fascisti* movement in America," Hitler said. "We admire particularly his anti-Jewish policy which is the Bavarian *Fascisti* platform. We have just had his anti-Jewish articles translated and published. The book is being circulated to millions throughout Germany." Hitler's loyal party workers, Fendrick reported, were distributing Ford's filth around Bavaria "by the carload."[20]

In January 1923, France inadvertently did the Nazi movement a great service. In retaliation against Germany for its failure to pay the war reparations required by the Treaty of Versailles, French and Belgian armed forces rolled into the Ruhr valley, home to many of western Germany's largest coal-mining and steel-producing industries. If Germany refused to abide by the treaty, the French would simply seize control of the country's mines and forges. Outraged by the invasion, German workers downed tools rather than work for the hated French. The economy lurched to a halt. The German government, which had already been resorting to inflation of the currency to ease the burden of reparations payments, now pushed the printing presses into high gear, spitting out piles of paper currency that soon grew worthless. Within months, unemployment spiked, savings evaporated, and hunger began to stalk the land.[21]

Just two weeks after the French invasion of the Ruhr, Hitler organized the first Nazi Party rally—a march of six thousand storm troopers on a parade ground in Munich. His violent speeches, given at various meetings of the assembled faithful across the city during January 27 and 28, focused not on France but on the internal enemy: the "November criminals," who had accepted the armistice in 1918, as well as the Jews, the Bolsheviks, the union organizers, the moneylenders who had betrayed Germany during the war and who remained in power in Berlin. At each of a dozen beer hall meetings, hundreds of delirious supporters greeted Hitler with shouts and cries, confirming his personal sway over the young movement. In an interview with Hearst newsman von Wiegand, Hitler said that German people, facing such unendurable humiliation, might "choose gigantic ruins as their death monument and like Samson pull down on all what may remain of the structure of civilization." The French had triggered a wave of nationalist hatred and "a terrible reckoning" lay ahead.[22]

In the spring and summer of 1923, Hitler kept up a manic pace of public appearances, filling large halls with ever-more-numerous gatherings, keeping himself at the center of the swirling plots and conspiracies in Munich. American papers now regularly reported on his "blood-curdling speeches" that denounced "Sovietism and Jewish domination." The *New York Times* reprinted a report from the Jewish Telegraphic Agency recounting a resolution of the Nazi Party in March "that all Jews in Germany should be interned," and if they did not report for incarceration voluntarily, "they should be shot." By midsummer, with runaway inflation having wiped out savings and depleted pocketbooks, the *Wall Street Journal* described Germany as on the brink of anarchy, facing a civil war between socialism and the nationalist right. "Germany today is a land of fists," the paper declared. The right-wing groups wanted to settle scores with "foreigners and Jews," and had behind them both "old men with bitter memories" and "young men of ardent, romantic aspirations." They all shared the common aim of "cleansing" Germany of "Jews, democrats, internationalists, and all hangers-on of the loathed republican heresy."[23]

In September 1923, Hitler appeared alongside General Ludendorff at a massive rally of veterans' groups and nationalist associations in Nuremberg;

one hundred thousand former soldiers crammed into the city, forming a sea of uniforms, medals, gold braid, and slashing sabers. The *Chicago Tribune* reporter George Seldes described countless "Fascisti banners" flashing in the autumn sunshine. Penetrating through the colorful pageantry, a leading American Jewish newspaper noted with genuine fear that Hitler, were he to take power in Germany, would "inaugurate a forced exodus of Jews from Germany that would make the exodus of the Jews from Egypt appear as child's play in comparison."[24]

They had every reason to worry. A canny demagogue, Hitler sensed that the German people had reached a breaking point—they were hungry and impoverished by the total collapse of the currency (by November, it took 4.2 *billion* marks to buy a single U.S. dollar). They also felt the daily humiliation of the French invasion of the Ruhr and the requisitioning of German timber, coal, and goods while people went hungry. Incessant invective by the nationalist far-right against Weimar, the Socialists, and the Jews fueled a boiling cauldron that spilled over in early November when food riots in the capital city quickly evolved into a violent pogrom. On the evening of November 5, angry mobs, decrying a sudden spike in the price of bread, flooded into Berlin's Jewish quarter and blamed residents—especially newly arrived Eastern European immigrants—for speculation and hoarding. In grotesque scenes over two days, Jews were publicly stripped and robbed, their belongings plundered, their shop windows smashed. The Associated Press reported that thugs had seized Galician Jews and clipped off their beards. "Kill them!" shouted the mob. "Kill the Jewish stock exchange dealers!" Men and women both were beaten with "fists, clubs and whips." And it was not just Berlin that saw such scenes: In Nuremberg, four Jews were killed. Antisemitism marched in lockstep with the fascist assault on democracy.[25]

By the fall of 1923, with his party having grown to fifty thousand members, his restless young thugs straining for action against the hated Berlin government, and the country facing a total economic collapse, Hitler decided to risk everything. Inspired by Mussolini's extraordinary success in Rome, Hitler hatched a plot to seize power in Berlin through a coup d'état. First, relying on the prestige and authority of General Ludendorff to rally far-right militants to the cause, Hitler would topple the state government of Bavaria, then mobilize Bavarian troops to march on Berlin and install himself as Germany's new leader. The Bavarian government was led by a triumvirate of hard-right monarchists who hated the Weimar regime; in fact, the state commissioner of Bavaria, Gustav Ritter von Kahr, a right-wing separatist, had been engaged in conspiratorial discussions with nationalist groups for months about combining forces against Berlin. Hitler, by acting first, hoped his coup in Munich might precipitate a rallying of the Bavarian leaders to him, and the Nazi banner. He believed columns of dedicated Nazis would sweep away the rotten Weimar edifice like a house of cards.[26]

He set his plot in motion on the night of November 8, 1923—when the leaders of the Bavarian state government were gathered at Munich's large and popular beer hall, the Bürgerbräukeller, for an address by state commissioner von Kahr. Hitler's plan was to seize the government leaders at the beer hall and compel them to join the conspiracy; Hitler and Ludendorff would then lead a march on Berlin. It began well enough: Hitler (in formal dinner dress) strode boldly into the middle of the large hall during von Kahr's speech, climbed up on a chair, and fired a pistol into the ceiling, announcing that the Bavarian government had been deposed. Hermann Göring, a highly decorated flying ace and one of Hitler's top lieutenants, imperiously rushed into the hall at the head of a column of gun-laden Brownshirts, who filled the aisles. Hitler announced his plan to lead a Bavarian army to seize power in Berlin; and then at gunpoint he offered von Kahr and his close associates positions in a new government headed by himself if they would now agree to rally to his leadership. General Ludendorff soon arrived, resplendent in his imperial army uniform, and assured the ministers that the coup had his approval. Under duress, von Kahr and his men sullenly submitted to Hitler's demands.[27]

But in a matter of hours, the coup unraveled. The Bavarian police were alerted to the coup attempt and rushed to secure the main government offices in Munich. The officials who had been detained at gunpoint were released on their word of honor—and they immediately repudiated their pledge to support Hitler. The government in Berlin denounced the "crazy mutiny" and labeled Hitler both a "foreigner" and a traitor. Army troops took up positions across Berlin, awaiting an onslaught of Bavarian putschists that never materialized.[28]

The band of plotters, their momentum ebbing, remained in the beer hall all night, morosely drinking until the morning of November 9, unsure what to do. In a last roll of the dice, they hit upon the idea of staging a march toward the War Ministry building in central Munich, hoping to trigger off a popular uprising. At midday, a formation of about two thousand armed Nazis set off from the beer hall in a noisy march toward the center of the city. But as they approached the Odeonsplatz, a large square in central Munich, they ran into a line of entrenched police. The column marched on, with Ludendorff and Hitler near the front. Shots rang out, and after a furious exchange of fire, sixteen Nazi troops fell dead, with dozens wounded. Hitler's column of Brownshirts scattered in disarray.

In the melee, Hitler was wrenched to the ground, his shoulder dislocated. He was bundled into a car and smuggled out of the city. Göring suffered a serious gunshot wound to his leg; Ludendorff walked, unscathed, into the ranks of the police, where he surrendered himself. A dejected Hitler, hiding out at the country home of his acolyte, Hanfstaengl, contemplated suicide. But he did not take his own life. Instead, after hastily scribbling down a few commands for how the Nazi movement was to be run in his absence, he gave himself up to the police, who carted him off to the fortresslike prison at Landsberg am Lech. A newly built facility with copper-domed turrets and thick stone walls, it looked more like the ancestral home of a minor German aristocrat than a jail. The warden obsequiously ushered Hitler into cell number 7, a large suite of rooms. The date was November 11, 1923—five years to the day since the armistice that marked Germany's defeat in the Great War. The beer hall coup, now jauntily dismissed in the foreign press as "a comic opera monarchist revolt," had been a miserable failure.[29]

"Hitler is confined in the fortress of Landsberg about 30 miles west of Munich," the *New York Times* told its readers. "Landsberg is by no means an unpleasant place of confinement," with ample rooms, books, good food, regular guests, and a garden for walking. Over the course of his yearlong confinement in Landsberg, Hitler busied himself with dictating a long, bloated screed titled *Mein Kampf* (My Struggle) to members of his entourage, who wrote down every poisonous syllable. On December 19, 1924, he was released from prison on parole. The event caused barely a ripple. In fact, the *New York Times* published a small article under the headline "Hitler Tamed by Prison." "Once the demi-god of the reactionary extremists," Hitler now looked "sadder and wiser" and was "no longer to be feared. It is believed he will retire to private life and return to Austria, the country of his birth."[30]

V

Was the Hitler chapter over? Had Nazism expended all its energies in a single failed coup attempt? For a brief moment in 1924, it seemed as if the toxin of far-right violence might dissipate. While Hitler was loafing morosely in his Landsberg Prison suite, the great powers, with the significant help of the United States, took a creative step forward to stabilize postwar Europe—and keep extremist politicians like Hitler at bay. They agreed to an international financial arrangement called the Dawes Plan, named for Charles G. Dawes, a Midwestern Republican banker and former director of the Bureau of the Budget. In early 1923, President Harding asked Dawes to work with British, French, and German officials to find a way to bring order and equilibrium to the European economy. Dawes discovered a fortunate partner in the sturdy, intelligent center-right German foreign minister Gustav Stresemann and the two men set to work.[31]

At the heart of the matter lay the problem of reparations, the huge sums stipulated by the terms of the Treaty of Versailles that Germany must pay Britain and France. The Germans claimed they could not pay, especially in light of France's costly and chaotic occupation of the Ruhr industrial areas, which severely hampered German productivity. But if Germany did not pay its reparations in a regular and timely fashion, then France and Britain in turn could not pay off the war loans they had taken out in the United States. And as long as those loans remained unpaid, U.S. bankers were loath to send more money down the rabbit hole to assist postwar Europe. The result was a stalemate in the world economy that could have severe political repercussions by opening the way to extremist parties on both the left and the right. Stresemann understood that the key to breaking the deadlock was to accept the reparations obligations and get French troops out of the Ruhr. Then, perhaps, the Americans could be persuaded to allow private capital to flow into Germany and spur an economic recovery. The Republican leadership in Washington aligned itself with those objectives.[32]

Dawes and his team knew that U.S. banks were willing to float a large loan for German reconstruction, provided the loan would be backed by some kind of collateral. The Germans put up their railroads and other national property for mortgage and agreed to reconfigure their monetary system and impose tax reforms in return for a pause in reparations payments for a brief period, to be followed by an escalating scale of payments as Germany's economy grew. Although the nationalists in Germany opposed yet another treaty that in their eyes placed Germany at the mercy of foreign powers (Ludendorff predictably howled that the Dawes Plan was the "devilish handiwork of the Jewish spirit"), Stresemann appeased them by saying that a new reparations plan backed by American loans offered the only path to ensure French evacuation of German soil, and that the new arrangement would result in lower overall reparations payments.[33]

In a high-stakes and often tense series of negotiations in London in August 1924, during which Thomas Lamont of J. P. Morgan worked the corridors, assuring Europeans of the willingness of banks to provide the necessary loans, U.S. and European officials set down the details of a major agreement that served as a kind of bookend to the woeful Versailles peace negotiations. The historian Patricia Clavin argued that "the Dawes Plan marked the re-entry of the United States into European affairs" after America had rejected the League of Nations. The host of the London meeting, British prime minister Ramsay MacDonald, called the Dawes Plan "the first peace treaty, because at last we have turned our backs on the terrible years of war and war mentality." The Germans had not been forced to sign under the threat of war, as with the Versailles Treaty. Rather, they were welcomed as equal participants in negotiating a just settlement.[34]

And it paid off. U.S. banks now provided large loans to Germany and found investors eager to buy into the promise of a German "take-off." Immense sums of capital flowed into Germany after 1924, more than offsetting the German reparations payments the government could now fulfill. Far from hunkering down in glorious isolation, the United States government mobilized private banks to lubricate the German economy, thus underwriting German and European stabilization. Within a year, the German economy lurched back into life. Success followed success: In October 1925, at the Swiss resort town of Locarno, diplomats from Germany, Britain, France, and Belgium signed a pact that committed these states to accept their mutual borders as inviolable; they also agreed to a peaceful settlement of any disputes. In this spirit of reconciliation, Germany joined the League of Nations in 1926, once again a welcome partner in the European great-power family. Stresemann and French prime minister Aristide Briand shared the Nobel Peace Prize in 1926. At last, it seemed that the Great War had come to a close.[35]

It certainly looked that way to Lilian and Edgar Mowrer, who arrived in Berlin in 1924, after eight years in Rome, to take over the office of the *Chicago Daily News*. Their timing was impeccable: Germany had entered on a brief but dazzling golden age. Edgar recalled that Berlin became "the center of social and cultural effervescence such as has rarely ever been equaled." Innovations in film and theater, music and art, philosophy and architecture, and especially science blossomed alongside a notoriously uninhibited nightlife and cabaret scene. "For the first time in their entire existence," Lilian wrote, "Germans were really popular." Paris and London seemed tame by comparison, and Americans and English visitors flocked to Berlin to catch a taste of the excesses. It wasn't just culture that blossomed; the economy, underpinned by the Dawes Plan, shifted into high gear. Foreign bankers, especially Americans, poured their money into major infrastructure projects in roads and railways, public buildings and stadiums, parks and housing, cinemas and theaters, and the total overhaul of Germany's aging industrial plant that had been worn out by the war. In an essay for *Harper's* magazine marking the tenth year since the 1918 armistice, Edgar hailed the "stubborn good sense of the people" and the "sturdy, commercial middle-class independence" that had kept the Weimar Republic alive, despite its difficult birth. Various "hotheads," meaning Communists and Nazis, still lurked around the edges of the political scene, Mowrer said, but the economic acceleration had blunted their appeal. "No such example of economic rebound has ever been chronicled," he noted, and he felt sure "that the German Republic will stand."[36]

The Mowrers reveled in the gaiety of Berlin with little sense of the fragility of the moment. As Lilian remembered it, "Germany offered so many thrilling experiences that it was difficult to realize that, under the peaceful surface of the Republic, forces were already at work which threatened it with destruction." As Lilian and Edgar would soon see, the Weimar Republic had been constructed on shifting, unstable foundations. The proportional representation system of Germany's parliament encouraged a proliferation of small political parties and made stable governments difficult to form. A mere sixty thousand votes won a seat in the Reichstag, in a country of 65 million people. Over forty parties competed in the 1928 elections and fifteen of them won at least two seats in parliament. To form a government, a chancellor needed five or six parties in a coalition, and as Edgar put it, "keeping them together is like collecting live guinea pigs on an unfenced lawn." The largest party of the era, the Social Democratic Party, won 30 percent of the vote in 1928, but still needed help from the conservative Catholic Center Party as well as the smaller center-right parties to govern. Two political parties, the far-right German National People's Party and the Communist Party (KPD), won 15 percent and 10 percent, respectively, in national elections in 1928, and both of them were utterly hostile to parliamentary democracy and wanted Weimar overthrown. Meanwhile, outside of the Reichstag, powerful opponents of the system had begun to collude. Germany's large industrial combines hated being forced by the government to pay for the social gains the labor movement had won, like shorter workweeks and higher wages. And the army, too, chafed under the humiliating restrictions imposed by the Versailles Treaty and was working secretly to train the core of a future German military force.[37]

Although the Nazi Party remained small and on the fringes of politics in the late 1920s, its core leadership was hard at work staging a comeback. Hitler left prison in late 1924 on parole, which meant that any trouble with the law could send him back to Landsberg Prison. The Nazi Party would have to operate legally and give up further beer hall coup attempts. Hitler relied on the talents of Gregor Strasser, a former soldier and Freikorps fighter of a middle-class, educated background, who possessed genuine administrative talent. Strasser had joined the Nazis in Munich before the putsch, and while Hitler was incarcerated, Strasser kept working to build the party organization, opening new regional offices and enrolling new members. At the same time, a small, pockmarked, and slightly crippled young academic named Joseph Goebbels took command of the party's work in Berlin. A philologist who had earned a PhD in Romantic literature, Goebbels was a gifted, theatrical propagandist and orator, emerging by 1926 as one of the most effective Nazi public speakers. The party held a "refounding" rally in Weimar July 1926. In the Reichstag elections of May 1928, the Nazis won 800,000 votes and took 12 seats. This was a pitiful result compared to the 9 million votes and 153 seats of the Social Democrats. Even the Communists swamped the Nazis, winning over 3 million votes and 54 seats. Yet the Nazi Party held its ground, and by the end of 1929, counted about 150,000 members. A large rally in Nuremberg in August 1929 pulled in 100,000 enthusiastic participants; street clashes with Communists left two dead and inflamed the Nazi rank and file.[38]

As long as the post-Dawes economic growth spurt continued, Hitler's appeal remained limited. But Germany's luck began to run out in the last two years of the decade. As the stock market in America soared in 1928, investors who had sent dollars into Germany redirected their money into the high-octane New York markets; the head-spinning returns were too good to miss. But the drying up of loans slowed the German boom. At the same time, the overproduction of food during the war had glutted the market, and prices of farm goods plummeted all across the Western industrial world, sending many farmers into bankruptcy. Nazis were quick to seize on this crisis in agriculture to build strength in rural farming communities, where they promised to raise tariffs and keep foreign goods out of Germany. Meanwhile, unemployment started to tick up, reaching 8 percent in 1928. With the October 1929 stock market crash in America, U.S. banks now called in the many short-term loans they had made to Germany. The sugar high of plentiful foreign money broke, and the economy ground to a halt. By the end of 1930, 22 percent of the workforce was out of a job, and voters began to look for extreme solutions.[39]

Now the weaknesses of Germany's political system began to tell. In March 1930, Germany's Socialist-led coalition government fell, and President Paul von Hindenburg asked the leader of the Center Party, Heinrich Brüning, to take over. But this conservative economics professor and former army officer could not hope to cobble together a coalition that would support the harsh measures he wanted to impose to stop Germany's free fall, like cutting unemployment benefits and increasing taxes. So he appealed to Hindenburg to let him rule through the emergency decree powers vested in the president—the infamous Article 48 of the Weimar Constitution. Hindenburg gave Brüning the authority to enact deflationary measures, sharply reducing government expenditure, despite opposition from the Reichstag. Brüning dissolved the parliament and set elections for September 14, hoping for the best. Instead, he got the worst.

The election results shocked the world because while the Social Democrats won a quarter of the votes, the Nazi Party won 18.3 percent and 107 seats in the Reichstag, becoming the second largest party. To add insult to injury, the Communists came in third with 13 percent of the vote. Including the votes of the extreme nationalist DNVP, almost 40 percent of the German people had voted for parties that wanted to overturn the Republic, end democracy, and form a dictatorship—either of the extreme left or extreme right. The Nazis received a burst of support from white-collar workers, shopkeepers, anxious farmers, as well as merchants and business owners, all joined together by their frustration at the failed efforts of the government to improve the economy. The results, however, only made matters worse, as foreign investors panicked, leading to a run on German banks. The economic crisis continued its downward spiral.[40]

In retrospect it is fairly easy to identify the reasons for the success of the Nazis in 1930. Hitler and his propaganda chief, Goebbels, preyed on the people's anxieties and built the party around a series of powerful mobilizing passions: hatred of the great powers for the humiliation of Versailles and the burden of reparations; anger toward the international economic system, including the gold standard, which imposed a tight money policy and made Germans feel subjected to foreign pressure; the collapse not only of family farms but the traditions and customs associated with rural life; scorn for democracy, which produced only a stalemate in the Reichstag; shock at the loose morals and vulgar tastes of Weimar's urban culture; horror at the power of the Communist Party, which took its political orders from a foreign country and which was deeply hostile to German nationalism; and through it all, fury at the Jews, whether impoverished new immigrants from the East or wealthy industrialists, bankers, intellectuals, or skilled professionals who allegedly operated the levers of power. Despite the small number of Jews in Germany, Nazi propaganda inflated them into a monstrous, crypto-Communist menace, in league with international finance, that sought the destruction of the German people.[41]

The Nazis proposed simple solutions to deal with these threats: destroy the Versailles system and break the grip of the Allied powers over Germany;

create a new autarkic empire by reuniting all lost territory and acquiring new lands in Poland and Ukraine to make Germany self-sufficient and invulnerable to blockade; restore the armed forces to glory; eliminate the embarrassing misrule of the democratic Reichstag; provide work and bread for the suffering ordinary people; close down the "lying" news media (*Lügenpresse*); and cleanse the nation of the toxic Jewish virus that threatened German racial purity. Above all, the Nazis promised order, strength, and economic security in a new unified empire. Packaged in the muscular imagery of disciplined young men marching shoulder to shoulder beneath swastika flags and banners, this was a message filled with hate and fear, but also with a yearning to restore German might.[42]

VI

Just as the Weimar Republic began its tailspin toward fascist dictatorship, Dorothy Thompson returned to Berlin. She was already one of the best and most well-informed journalists covering Central Europe; and she was on the cusp of a career that would make her a household name in America, becoming the decade's most important analyst of world affairs and the global crisis of democracy. The daughter of a Methodist minister from upstate New York, Thompson was educated at Syracuse University. After working in the suffrage movement, she decided to set off for Europe in 1920 in search of a career. She made her way to Vienna, where her meager income went a long way and she started selling short articles to American newspapers and magazines, whose readers took great interest in postwar European life. She proved enormously resourceful, and a brilliant portraitist of personalities and policy. She was soon offered steady work on the staff of the Philadelphia *Public Ledger*, a distinguished newspaper that was looking to add some pizzazz to its pages.

In 1925, the *Ledger* promoted her to run its Berlin bureau, giving her a pass to the city's dazzling cultural and political scene. She rented a large house on Händelallee, a curved lane just on the edge of Berlin's vast green Tiergarten park. She invited the Mowrers to live on the first floor, while she nested in a large, sun-filled top floor that looked out onto a profusion of leafy trees. But after three years in Berlin, including a long stay in Moscow to report on the Soviet economic experiment of the mid-1920s, she left the *Ledger* and her career to marry Sinclair Lewis, who she had met one evening at a party in her own house. Lewis was then one of America's leading novelists, the author of *Main Street*, *Babbitt*, *Arrowsmith* (which won a Pulitzer Prize that Lewis declined), and *Elmer Gantry*, piercing satirical novels about American mores. The couple settled in a large rambling farmhouse on three hundred acres in Barnard, Vermont, and invited a parade of intellectual guests for long stays amid the farm's orchards, gardens, and rolling green hills. In 1930, Dorothy gave birth to a son, Michael.[43]

But her gift for reporting and her intense wanderlust propelled her back to Europe. When Lewis, to the astonishment of the literary world, won the Nobel Prize for Literature in the fall of 1930, Thompson—then referred to in newspapers as Mrs. Sinclair Lewis, though she never changed her last name—joined her husband on a trip to Stockholm in December, where he received his award. (Lewis did not decline this one.) She then went directly to Berlin, took rooms at the Adlon Hotel, the favorite stopping place for foreign journalists, and began intensive research for a series on Germany for the *Saturday Evening Post*, the largest-circulation magazine in America. Thompson's style—vivid, argumentative, opinionated, extremely well-informed, and deeply hostile to the emerging Nazi movement—suited the essay format of the *Post* well, and her articles in the spring of 1931 surveyed the German scene with brilliance and insight.

Dorothy Thompson: an assured, incisive anti-fascist voice.
Bettmann / Getty Images

She opened her first essay with a description of Joseph Goebbels, "the wizened, club-footed and frenetic" Nazi propaganda chief. Goebbels gave a speech in the Berlin Sportpalast, normally used for indoor bicycle races and now bedecked with Nazi banners and slogans blazing "Germany Awaken!" in Gothic script. The hall was full of "shock troops" outfitted in brown uniforms, "neat and grim, their steps precise and military"; choruses of "Heil!" erupted from fifteen thousand throats. She described Nazism to her readers as "a peculiar mixture of Nordic myth, antisemitism, militaristic tradition, desperado nationalism and moronized socialism." She listened intently to a two-hour speech from Goebbels, trying to grasp why 6 million voters had recently supported the Nazi Party, yearning for Hitler to take power. Germany, the snarling Goebbels announced, had been enslaved by the Versailles Treaty, kept in poverty and shame by the great powers, shackled by foreign control of the economy and by outrageous reparations demands.

What baffled Thompson, she confessed, was that Germany possessed the world's finest infrastructure, roads, subways, ocean liners, airplanes, hospitals, universities, public parks and pools, museums and theaters, yet all anyone could talk about was its poverty and desperation. She acknowledged that Germany had 5 million unemployed workers to subsidize, and bankruptcies of farms and businesses were cascading. But Germany remained a wealthy and productive nation with a large trade surplus whose industrial output rivaled that of Britain and the United States. The real problem, she saw, was less economic than political: The far left and far right were never reconciled to the Republic and its parliamentary democracy, while the Social Democrats promised so many lavish benefits to their constituents that the country was going bankrupt paying unemployment and health insurance. The state imposed massive taxes to fund these handouts, along with all its cultural and infrastructure spending. (A good Republican, she bristled at this state largesse.) But the budget crisis, combined with unemployment, gave Hitler a wedge issue and he used it brilliantly, blaming foreigners for Germany's troubles when they were mostly self-inflicted.[44]

Thompson returned to the United States briefly in the middle of 1931, but could not stay away from Germany and the compelling, tragic story it revealed: a democracy filled with intelligent, innovative, creative, and industrious people that could not find a way to survive, searching instead for radical solutions offered by various demagogues and extremists. Back in Germany in November, she was shocked at how much worse the scene looked. "Unless things change radically," she wrote to Lewis, "there will be war in Europe within the decade—before the 1930s are out." Yet in diagnosing Germany's ills, she did not place all the blame on Hitler and the Nazis. In her reporting, she stressed the economic headwinds and structural weaknesses of the country's institutions. In her next major article for the *Post*, she again argued that the social welfare state was Germany's real handicap, as the country was driving itself into bankruptcy by generous handouts combined with an overregulated economy. And worse, the use of emergency decrees by Brüning meant that, functionally, Germany had ceased being a democracy. The danger for Europe lay in the argument, made by Nazis as well as industrialists and farmers, that only high tariff walls could save the German economy, keeping out foreign goods and propping up domestic production. The movement toward European integration that had characterized the 1920s was grinding to a protectionist halt.[45]

Perhaps her focus on Germany's economic and administrative difficulties led her to underestimate Hitler. Or perhaps it was her profound admiration for the sophistication of German culture that made her refuse to believe that a dreary little Austrian foot soldier could succeed as a politician in Germany. In December 1931, she finally secured an interview with the Nazi leader himself. It was held at Hitler's preferred Berlin residence, the enormous and luxurious Kaiserhof Hotel. The article she produced—memorably titled "I Saw Hitler!"—appeared in *Cosmopolitan* in March 1932, and was then published by Farrar & Rinehart as a small book with many accompanying photographs. Thompson began by reminding readers of Hitler's shabby beginnings, his failed coup and prison time, and the rise of the party as the economic crisis deepened. By 1930, with the party's electoral breakthrough, "it was impossible to laugh off Hitler" and his Brownshirts, those "gymnasium-trained bruisers" who beat up Communists on the streets in rolling, prolonged waves of violence. She readied herself to meet the future dictator of Germany: "I was nervous."

But within "fifty seconds" of meeting Hitler, she wrote, she became certain that the man was a fraud. A talented fraud, perhaps, but little more than a mediocre huckster. "He is formless, almost faceless; a man whose countenance is a caricature; a man whose framework seems cartilaginous, without bones. He is inconsequent and voluble, insecure—the very prototype of the Little Man." Compared to rock-hewn Hindenburg or the austere Brüning, Hitler was gray, weak, with eyes that had "the peculiar shine which often distinguishes geniuses, alcoholics, and hysterics."

The interview was difficult, she wrote, because Hitler gave a roaring speech as if he were standing at the rostrum of the Sportpalast; he evaded direct questions. But he did make clear his plan to abolish parliament and establish a dictatorship. Taking the measure of this ludicrous figure, Thompson felt sure that his extreme views combined with his vulgar, manic temperament would lead the conservative forces around Hindenburg to keep Hitler at bay as his movement lost steam. His ideas were "weak," his cry of "Down with the Jew!" one of the oldest scams in Europe, unoriginal and repulsive. But he was "the most golden-tongued of demagogues" who appealed to the emotions, not reason, and millions of "little people, weighted with inferiority," would vote for him and feel exalted as they did so. In Hitler, Thompson saw the desire of the lower middle class for revenge, pure and simple, rather than any rational political program. Thompson's essay captured so many of the baffling features about Hitler's rise: his lack of stature, his grievances, his irrationality, his whiny complaints, his racism, above all his mediocrity. Thompson was not alone in failing to see why anyone would look to this grubby opportunist as a savior.[46]

It wasn't only Thompson who misjudged Hitler. A few months after her article appeared, three of the most experienced correspondents in Europe met with Hitler for a long interview at Hitler's chalet in Berchtesgaden, in the Bavarian Alps: Louis Lochner of the Associated Press, Karl von Wiegand of the Hearst syndicate, and Hans V. Kaltenborn, a German American radio broadcaster who had known Hitler's press secretary, Ernst Hanfstaengl, at Harvard. When these men arrived at Hitler's summer cottage in Berchtesgaden, the political context had changed dramatically since the Thompson interview. In March 1932, Hitler challenged President von Hindenburg in the presidential election. The elder statesman, now eighty-four years old and increasingly feeble, found it intolerable that the Austrian upstart would dare suggest himself as a suitable successor to Germany's renowned president and former field marshal. But Hitler and two other candidates did well enough to deny Hindenburg a first-round majority; he would have to endure a runoff. On April 10, in the second round, Hindenburg won easily with 53 percent of the votes. But Hitler won 13.4 million votes; 36 percent of the electorate wanted this man in power. (The Communist leader Ernst Thälmann won 10 percent.) It was a sign of things to come. Hitler was now seen as the leading statesman of the right, the man to rescue Germany from its travails. Three months later, in the July 1932 Reichstag elections, Hitler's party won 230 seats and 37 percent of the vote, becoming the largest party in the parliament. Though he did not have an absolute majority, a sense of inevitability now hung about Hitler: It seemed clear that he would determine Germany's future, one way or another. When Kaltenborn, von Wiegand, and Lochner met with Hitler on August 17, 1932, they knew he stood on the cusp of power.

Kaltenborn tried to deny Hitler the chance to begin one of his usual monologues by throwing out a question even before they had been seated: Why did the Nazis discriminate against Jews? Hitler, with sulfurous contempt, threw American immigration policy back at Kaltenborn. "You exclude any would-be immigrants you do not care to admit," he said. "We demand the same right." Jews, Hitler said, were "anti-German." As the interview progressed, Kaltenborn, like Thompson, concluded that Hitler had "no capacity for logical, consecutive thought." But when Lochner asked why Hitler felt he should be allowed to form a government despite not having a majority, Hitler answered that Nazi voters were "the bravest, the most energetic, and in every way the best German material in Germany." The voters wanted fascism because democracy was "not native to us" and had failed. The people had expressed themselves, said Hitler. "I don't have to march on Berlin, as they say I propose to do. I am already there." Kaltenborn concluded that Hitler was provincial, narrow, doctrinaire, an introvert who could speak to huge crowds, but shied away from normal conversation. As he later admitted, "We underestimated the fanatical drive and magnetic power of the man. . . . I could not see how a man of his type, a plebian Austrian of limited mentality, could ever gain the allegiance of a majority of Germans."[47]

It just didn't make sense that this proud, cultured, class-conscious country, with a long history of skilled statesmen, would fall for this loud street gangster and his inflammatory rhetoric. H. R. Knickerbocker, a legendary reporter who had covered every European capital since the 1920s, recalled that when he first saw Hitler make a speech, in Munich in 1923, "I broke out laughing." Even as Hitler kept gaining strength, Knickerbocker wrote, it seemed unreal. "This fatty-hipped, slope-shouldered, lonely figure, standing so inflexibly, his arm outstretched so tautly, his eyes staring over the heads of his subjects, is incredible. 'No,' you say to yourself, 'this can't be true.'" Lilian Mowrer sensed it, though. Hearing Hitler give an election speech in 1932, she thought he was "talking nonsense," but looking at the glowing faces of the audience with their eyes aflame in adoration, she heard them murmuring, "*Richtig! Richtig!*" (Right! Right!) at every falsehood and accusation. The crowds "pitied themselves, wept with him, were refreshed," and went away certain that Hitler would fulfill their fondest dreams.[48]

If journalists expressed exasperation and bewilderment at Hitler's appeal, the diplomats in the U.S. embassy tended to see Hitler as an opportunist who would make whatever compromises he needed to get into power. Ambassador Frederic Sackett, a former Republican senator from Kentucky who made good in the mining business, went to Berlin in February 1930 as President Hoover's envoy, and he and his staff reported dutifully on the parliamentary bickering, the street brawls, the profound hatred between left and right, and the sheer ungovernability of Germany. Hitler was, in their reports, foam on a turbulent sea, a symptom of these larger structural problems. The diplomats tended to see Hitler and the Nazis as a second-tier threat to the German Republic when compared with the militant left. They socialized with the Nazi leaders, spoke with them in regular interviews, and found them compelling, in a way.

John Wiley, the counselor of embassy on Sackett's staff, spoke of Joseph Goebbels as "more intelligent than any other Nazi I have met. He obviously has first-rate ability and much personal magnetism." In a report to the State Department in January 1932, Wiley summarized a recent talk with the Berlin

Nazi chief. Goebbels tried to explain that Nazism had similar goals to Italian Fascism, such as unifying the state and putting a halt to ceaseless party strife. Wiley reported that Goebbels assured him, with respect to the Nazi Jewish policy, that "the Nazi idea is not to harm a hair of any Jewish head, but to treat them as foreigners; to tax them, but not to subject them to military service; to deport eastward as many Polish and Russian Jews as possible." Wiley seemed pleased at this and concluded, "The Nazis have become . . . more and more moderate."[49]

Embassy officials also assumed that Hitler's wealthy industrialist supporters would contain his more radical impulses; they wanted stability, order, and a powerful nation, not chaos or war. If Hitler could not discipline his most radical members, the Americans believed, the conservatives, nationalists, and military officers around President Hindenburg would shun him and look for an alternative strongman to hold the reins of power. Many American analysts made the same mistake, assuming Hitler to be merely a tool of the conservatives, rather than the other way around. Yet Hitler's strength became apparent with the enormous victory in the election of July 1932. In a normal parliamentary system, the largest party would try to cobble together a coalition with other parties. But the Socialists and Communists, the second and third largest parties respectively, were bitter enemies of Hitler and each other. The stalemate therefore continued, since none of the major parties could build a governing coalition.[50]

The Nazi success in July shocked Dorothy Thompson, and in the summer and fall of 1932, she abandoned her earlier sarcastic tone of the "I Saw Hitler" essay. Now she sensed a catastrophe coming, though even she could not see into the future. As the army and the conservatives rallied around Hindenburg to keep both the Nazis and the Communists from seizing power, she wrote that "reaction is settling over Germany." Democracy "is finished," she observed, because the people of Germany wanted order and security far more than they wanted a Republic, with its street violence and uncertainty. "*Wir müssen Ordnung haben*" (we must have order) was the only thing the German people seemed to agree on, and she guessed that President Hindenburg, if he lived long enough, would use the army to forestall a Nazi government while imposing order in the streets.

It seemed as if Thompson was right about Hindenburg. On August 13, the president told Hitler in a private meeting that he would not appoint him chancellor. Hindenburg would not yield power to this street thug he waspishly called a "Bohemian corporal." And since Hitler refused to join a cabinet in any other role but as chancellor, the Reichstag could not produce a functioning coalition. Another round of elections would have to be held, in November. No one could tell what might happen. Thompson, even as late as September 1932, did not really think Hitler would take power. "What will develop within Germany in the next ten years is therefore not certain," was her rather feeble effort to make sense of it all. Thompson reported lucidly on what Hitler *said* he would do should he become chancellor; but in her heart, she simply could not imagine such a radical, horrifying outcome.[51]

VII

Everyone underestimated Hitler. Or perhaps more precisely, they underestimated the foolishness and stupidity of the conservatives, who believed they could use Hitler for their own purposes. Although he had demonstrated his electoral strength in the presidential elections and in the July Reichstag election, Hitler still remained out of power. The November Reichstag elections did not change much, for the Nazis had a slight decline in their vote total, winning only 33 percent compared with 37 percent in July. The Nazis, it seemed, had hit a ceiling of about a third of the popular vote—a large slice, but not decisive. Hitler therefore could only gain power in a coalition, forged with the help of conservative, nationalist political elites. And in January 1933, they finally offered him what he had long demanded.

The middleman who engineered what he considered a brilliant scheme to break the political logjam was Franz von Papen, a tall, graying aristocrat and former army officer whom Hindenburg had appointed chancellor in June 1932, hoping he could forge a right-wing nationalist government. He failed. Hindenburg then asked another military man, General Kurt von Schleicher, to form a government; he, too, floundered. Von Papen now made his historic blunder: He persuaded Hindenburg that Hitler—the little corporal, the foaming radical, the shrieking populist—should be named chancellor at the head of a new government in a coalition with the smaller German National People's Party and the Catholic Center Party, which held fifty-one and seventy seats, respectively, in the Reichstag; together with the Nazis they could form a right-wing bloc. Von Papen sold this plan to Hindenburg by insisting that the real power in such a coalition would remain with the conservative insiders, especially von Papen himself, who proposed to serve as deputy chancellor. In von Papen's scheme, Hitler would serve as the pack mule of the nationalist right, carrying its policies through the Reichstag.

Hindenburg had long mistrusted Hitler for his distasteful style, his use of violent storm troops in the streets, his long history of hostility to the constitution—and his low birth. Yet von Papen assured the president that Hitler could be contained in a cabinet of non-Nazi ministers. To appease Hindenburg further, von Papen stressed that there would be continuity between this new cabinet and the previous ones, as various technocrats and conservatives would agree to serve under Hitler. Von Papen deftly persuaded Hindenburg that Hitler was the key to forging a "front" of nationalist conservatives against the left. Yes, Hitler would hold the title of chancellor, reflecting the strength of the Nazi Party in the Reichstag. But he would be outnumbered in the cabinet, for von Papen had contrived to limit the Nazi members to three: Hitler himself; Wilhelm Frick as interior minister; and Hitler's wingman, Hermann Göring, as minister without portfolio. For good measure, Hindenburg could place his own man, General Werner von Blomberg, in the post of defense minister. At long last, against his better judgment, Hindenburg gave in. The clever von Papen felt he had accomplished a masterstroke. Hitler would place the fervor of the Nazi Brownshirts into the service of the traditional right. Von Papen memorably chuckled about manipulating Hitler: "We've hired him."[52]

In the bitterly cold mid-morning of Monday, January 30, 1933, a group of sullen, darkly dressed politicians converged on the Reich Chancellery in Berlin, which Hindenburg was using as a residence while the nearby presidential palace underwent extensive renovations. Five of the men arrived on foot, through the back garden, having walked along the private path between the chancellery and the Interior Ministry next door. Their heavy leather shoes crunched in the evenly raked gravel as they passed under bare trees. Others arrived separately, in black cars that glided down the broad Wilhelmstrasse in Berlin's government district. By quarter to eleven, the men had gathered in the ground-floor office of bull-necked, gash-faced Otto von Meissner, the president's private secretary. At 11:30 a.m., the men trudged upstairs to Hindenburg's chambers, where the president administered the oath of office to the cabinet of Chancellor Adolf Hitler.

The face of a tyrant.
Hulton Archive / Getty Images

That evening, Hitler's faithful followers celebrated. The flames from thousands of orange and red torches stabbed into the cold Berlin night sky as joyful Brownshirts staged a giant procession through the capital. The French ambassador André François-Ponçet, with a dreadful sense of foreboding, took in the scene from the nearby French embassy. "The torches they brandished formed a river of fire," he wrote later, "sweeping with a sovereign rush over the very heart of the city. From these brown-shirted, booted men, as they marched by in perfect discipline and alignment, their well-pitched voices bawling warlike songs, there rose an enthusiasm and dynamism that were extraordinary." Hour after hour they came, surging up from Berlin's large park, the Tiergarten, their faces lighted by the flames, through the Brandenburg Gate, and down Wilhelmstrasse, past the chancellery, where they hailed two men standing in adjacent windows: President Hindenburg, his cane in hand, stone-faced, a symbol now of the past; and a beaming, ebullient Chancellor Adolf Hitler, his arm raised in salute, the man who would make Germany's future.[53]

CHAPTER 4

THE NEW DEAL IN A FASCIST AGE

"I tell you, lady, the day Roosevelt is elected will be a national holiday."

—NEW YORK TAXI DRIVER

I

March 4, 1929, dawned gray and cold, with rain expected. Some 150,000 well-wishers had poured into Washington, D.C., in the preceding days to attend the inauguration of Herbert Hoover as the nation's thirty-first president. Rooming houses and hotels had long been filled, and balls and galas dazzled the city for days. Carpenters had erected a huge wooden structure across the east portico of the Capitol, and it was festooned with radio and telegraph wires so Hoover's words could fly westward toward Chicago, Dallas, and to his adopted home state of California, thence across the Pacific to the American territory of the Philippines, to Tokyo, Leningrad, Berlin, Paris, and London: a globe-circling message of American confidence.

A calm, unperturbed Hoover ate breakfast alone in his S Street home and then waited out the morning in his library, his family milling nervously about. At 10 a.m. he donned his morning coat and silk top hat and, with Mrs. Hoover, rode by car to the White House, where an unusually sunny Calvin Coolidge greeted them in the Blue Room. Following a rather awkward period of idle conversation between two men known for their taciturn demeanor, the president and president-elect traveled together in an open car toward the Capitol behind a splendid cavalry escort, Hoover mute and stone-faced as the motorcade passed the cheering throngs lining the way. A few raindrops, fat and wet, began to fall.

At the Capitol, cabinet members, justices of the Supreme Court, diplomats and envoys, admirals and generals, politicians and close friends of the president-elect all crammed the platform to watch Chief Justice William Howard Taft, a former president now garbed in a flowing black robe and soft skullcap, administer the oath of office. Hoover kissed his own Bible, which he had opened to Proverbs 29:18—"Where there is no vision, the people perish: but he that keepeth the law, happy is he." As he approached the rostrum and began to speak, "the heavens emptied," according to one report, soaking every observer to the skin. Cold rain spattered onto Hoover's papers as he read his thirty-minute address, a joyless message that stressed law and order, the enforcement of prohibition, and limited government interference in the economic life of the nation.

Yet this virtuous Quaker also reveled in America's material abundance. "We have reached a higher degree of comfort and security than ever existed before in the history of the world," said Hoover. In a bold statement of American exceptionalism, he declared, "We are steadily building a new race—a new civilization great in its own attainments." The future beckoned. "Ours is a land rich in resources; stimulating in its glorious beauty; filled with millions of happy homes; blessed with comfort and opportunity. In no nation are the institutions of progress more advanced. In no nation are the fruits of accomplishment more secure. In no nation is the government more worthy of respect. No country is more loved by its people." Few could begrudge Hoover his bold peroration: "I have no fears for the future of our country. It is bright with hope." Hoover left the stage, shook hands with the departing Calvin Coolidge, and headed back to the White House for a grand buffet lunch.[1]

Despite the damp start to his presidency, Hoover had reasons for optimism. The accelerating growth of the U.S. economy in the decade of the 1920s, spurred by remarkable innovation in the automotive, radio, electronics, steel, and construction industries, augured an era of continuing expansion. Industrial production had soared 70 percent since 1921 and business earnings were rising. An ethos of consumerism took hold in America, and families began to borrow money to purchase durable goods—buying on credit or the installment plan. Large shopping concerns like Sears and J. C. Penney began to bring mass-produced goods to the middle class. Using assembly lines and routinization of labor, Ford Motor plants by the middle of the decade churned out an average of one motorcar every ten seconds. Unemployment stayed close to the statistical vanishing point of 4 percent, while America's high tariff walls kept out cheap foreign goods and assured domestic manufacturers of high prices. Low taxes and tight, balanced federal budgets kept the government small, lean, and wedded to the philosophy of laissez-faire. No wonder the *New York Times* could predict that Hoover would preside over "an era of unprecedented prosperity."[2]

American growth also helped bring stability to the world economy, which had been so disrupted by the war. During that terrible ordeal, private banks and the U.S. government had acquired enormous reserves of gold and foreign exchange, the result of serving as a marketplace for the European belligerents who desperately bought American textiles, food, and industrial products. These same banks had also loaned billions of dollars to France and Britain, putting Europe at the mercy of American financiers. By the time the dust had settled in late 1918, America had become the world's largest creditor and controlled 40 percent of the world's gold supply. This gave Washington, and especially private banks, enormous leverage over the indebted European nations. And Republican administrations, wedded to ideas of fiscal orthodoxy, used that leverage in the 1920s to reestablish what they considered to be the bedrock of global economic stability: the gold standard.

This mechanism linked currencies to one another by valuing them in terms of gold, facilitating trade and making the prices of goods on the world market predictable. In theory, the value of each national currency reflected the value of the gold held by central banks. Nations on the gold standard could not suddenly print money (or suddenly make money easy to borrow by lowering interest rates) if there was not enough gold in the national vaults to cover the new currency. In the late nineteenth and early twentieth century, the adoption of the gold standard by most of the world's leading economies had helped to keep inflation low, keep interest rates high, impose tight budget-balancing upon national governments—all while making global trade easier. The result was an era of financial stability and robust international trade.

The First World War disrupted this stabilization mechanism, because suddenly governments at war had needed huge sums of money to fund their war efforts. They raised taxes, launched bond drives to encourage patriotic citizens to lend money to their governments, and, of course, borrowed from the United States. To ensure that all this additional money they were pushing into their economies to pay for the war did not trigger inflation or lead to sudden loss of gold reserves, European nations fixed prices and imposed various controls over the exchange of gold, effectively abandoning the gold standard—another casualty of the Great War.

As soon as the war ended, European governments began to roll back some of these wartime controls in the hope of a quick return to business as usual. But with so much money in circulation, and so many persistent shortages of goods in the aftermath of the war, European economies experienced a terrific spike in inflation. To make matters worse, the continuing disagreements about the payment of war reparations by Germany, and payment of war debts owed by France and Britain to the United States, inhibited the international cooperation so essential to the functioning of the gold standard. National economies were set adrift into a kind of anarchy, and the German hyperinflation of 1923 following the French invasion of the Ruhr provided a shocking illustration of the consequences.

With the Dawes Plan of 1924, the scene brightened. Germany's economy sprang back to life, the country began grudgingly to pay war reparations to Britain and France, and inflation came under control. The magic sword of the gold standard seemed to have slain the dragon of inflation at last. In April 1925, Britain returned to the gold standard, setting the value of the pound at the prewar rate of $4.86. Italy followed suit in 1927 and France in 1928; by then over thirty-five nations had pegged the value of their currencies to gold. In this manner, the priorities of orthodox conservatives in Washington bound Europeans together with what one historian has called "golden fetters." Though in fact the gold standard restricted the freedom of states to meet the needs of their people for higher wages and lower borrowing costs, at the time, this return to monetary orthodoxy seemed certain to halt inflation, impose balanced budgets, and encourage world trade.[3]

Hoover opened his presidential campaign trumpeting these indices of progress: "We in America today," he said on August 11, 1928, in Palo Alto, "are nearer to the final triumph over poverty than ever before in the history of any land.... We shall soon with the help of God be in sight of the day when poverty will be banished from this Nation." In late October, in New York City, he confidently declared that "by adherence to the principles of decentralized self-government, ordered liberty, equal opportunity, and freedom to the individual, our American experiment in human welfare has yielded a degree of well-being unparalleled in all the world." Small government, tight money, and individual gumption were the keys to success. The public agreed and sent Hoover to the White House with a mandate to keep the good times rolling. He took office at a moment of hope and confidence. The terrible upheaval and senseless slaughter of the Great War began to recede in the public mind and a future of abundance and stability beckoned.[4]

II

There were a few clouds on the horizon, however. The prices of agricultural goods had been falling across the decade of the 1920s, the result of wartime overproduction, immense harvests, and the decline of European demand after the war. American farm foreclosures had been increasing for years, and by Hoover's inauguration, one in five family farms had gone bankrupt. As one of his first presidential acts, Hoover called a special session of Congress to address the crisis; he wanted, and got, a national Farm Board that could assist farmers in selling their products and supporting higher prices. Meanwhile, steel production began to slow in mid-1929, while housing construction had been slowing for a few years.

And the red-hot stock market also caused Hoover some concern. The New York Stock Exchange had been in a frothy and volatile state throughout 1928, with sharp spikes and dizzying drops. With Hoover's election in November, and the promise of more pro-business Republican policies ahead, buyers swarmed into the market. During the year of 1928, the *New York Times* average of industrial stocks was up 75 percent. And the rise carried over into 1929: On March 1, just days before Hoover's inauguration, the stock exchange traded a record number of shares in what the *Chicago Tribune* called "a session of speculative frenzy." Reporters styled the behavior of investors as "a pre-inauguration orgy" of "buying hysteria." Such speculation in the stock market had become extremely easy because banks and stockbrokers were happy to lend money to allow buyers to purchase stock on margin. Buyers put down a fraction of the price, typically 10 percent, and borrowed the rest. Inevitably, borrowed money poured into equity markets, and stock prices soared. Since the market had been zooming upward and the fundamentals of the economy looked so strong, it seemed to buyers to be a foolproof system to get rich quickly.[5]

President Hoover, a conservative who disliked frenzies of any kind (and who wisely sold much of his own stock in the spring of 1929), expressed anxiety about the stock bubble to his cabinet officers soon after taking office. Something should be done. But what? The orthodox principles of his administration dictated that government should not interfere with the invisible hand of the marketplace. No one expressed this view more firmly than the secretary of the treasury, Andrew Mellon, the fabulously wealthy Pittsburgh banker who since his appointment in 1921 had concerned himself chiefly with tax cuts and balanced budgets. When asked by Hoover to consider measures to help cool off the stock market, Mellon said there were none. The only remedy: allow the bubble to burst and sort the winners from the losers in the aftermath. The market continued its wild fluctuations, surging one week only to fall back to earth in another. On September 3, the stock market hit what would be its peak before losing steam and beginning a gradual decline.[6]

In October, with signs that the economy was cooling, the market began to drop further, feeding the impression that the height of the market had been reached and a correction loomed. On Thursday, October 24, 1929, there came a sudden, stomach-churning drop: The market lost 10 percent of its value, and a classic panic took hold. The more stocks were sold, the more their prices fell, and anxious sellers rushed to get out before their portfolios completely collapsed. Furthermore, since so many holders of equities had bought stocks on margin—meaning they borrowed most of the money they needed to buy stocks in the first place—they felt added pressure to recoup some portion of their investment once the market began to nose-dive.

To restore confidence in the market, several wealthy bankers, Thomas Lamont of the House of Morgan among them, publicly announced their intention to pool their funds and buy stocks at the lower prices; by Friday, the markets stabilized. But when trading opened on Monday, October 28, the sell-off continued as spooked investors concluded that the end of the boom had come. The stock market average fell 13 percent in a day (still the second-worst day on Wall Street after October 19, 1987). The following day, on what became known as Black Tuesday, the plunge continued, dropping another 12 percent. In those two days of trading, the stock market lost almost a quarter of its value. Between September and November 1929, the market declined by half; by July 1932, stocks were down almost 90 percent from their high mark three years earlier. Huge paper fortunes vanished. The White House issued reassuring messages, declaring the fundamentals of the economy to be sound, and emphasizing the small numbers of Americans who actually had any money in the stock market. Inside the White House, the treasury secretary gloomily advised Hoover to do nothing—a "purge" of speculation and greed would do the country good, he breezily asserted.[7]

The stock market drop acted like a stone thrown down a rocky hillside, triggering an avalanche. The market decline did not by itself cause the depression that followed, but it exacerbated preexisting structural weaknesses and created a climate of fear and anxiety about the future growth of the U.S. economy. With so much institutional wealth having been wiped out in the sharp correction of late October, investment of all kinds began to slow, with the inevitable ripple effect of job losses. Americans quite suddenly curtailed their purchases of expensive and durable goods, sharply slowing aggregate demand, forcing manufacturers to slow production and lay off workers. The impact on the already struggling farmers was devastating, leading to foreclosures and abandonment of countless small family farms across the country. The downward spiral had begun. President Hoover convened titans of industry at the White House to urge on them a voluntary cooperative scheme of sustaining high wages and avoiding any rapid layoffs of workers. But exhortations of this kind could not by themselves halt the gradual slowdown of America's economy. The only question was whether the inevitable recession would be short or prolonged.[8]

The answer emerged fairly soon. Although the federal government did not yet keep regular and accurate labor statistics, scholars believe that the unemployment rate jumped from under 4 percent in 1929 to 8.7 percent in 1930, and then further upward to the shocking figures of the early thirties: 16 percent in 1931, 24 percent in 1932, and 25 percent in 1933. And the unemployment rate would stay in the high teens until 1940. As industry contracted, the nation's GDP fell by 8 percent in 1930, another 6 percent in 1931, and a staggering 13 percent in 1932. Workers in the machine, auto, and durable-goods industries were hit especially hard as those sectors imploded for lack of demand. The decade of the 1930s, both in America and in most industrial nations, became the years of the breadline, the soup kitchen, the sagging shoulders of the despairing job seeker trudging the streets in search of work and food. Memories of the inconceivably prosperous carefree 1920s vanished like a shimmering mirage on a scorched plain. The Great Depression struck at America's sense of confidence, self-reliance, and optimism; it traumatized a generation of people who soon grasped that the world could never return to life before the Crash of 1929.[9]

Herbert Hoover, once lauded as the "great engineer," a man of supreme administrative competence, managerial skill, and a theorist of "American individualism," found himself facing a problem he could not solve. The columnist Walter Lippmann, then the editor of the *New York World* newspaper, wrote a devastating portrait of the president as a man who in theory had all the intelligence and skill needed to master the crisis, yet proved in fact to be hesitant, indecisive, bewildered, and unwilling to enter the political fray in search of a solution. Hoover was "tender-minded, thin-skinned," Lippmann wrote, quite the opposite of the "natural politicians like Roosevelt and Al Smith." Unlike running a business, governing required skill in "the political art," which Hoover lacked. Lippmann, a brilliant Harvard graduate, co-founder of the *New Republic*, and a Wilsonian internationalist, had emerged in the 1920s as a leading thinker of progressivism. In November 1930, Lippmann told Felix Frankfurter he was "genuinely concerned about Hoover in a human way." His temperament was not suited for public office, and "ambition and anxiety gnaw at him constantly. He has no resiliency." Lippmann thought Hoover seemed on the brink of a breakdown.[10]

In truth, Hoover had few tools at his disposal to fix the crisis. The federal government's share of total spending in the late 1920s was tiny compared to later decades, and even had Hoover been inclined to initiate a large federal spending program, it would not by itself have had much effect. Instead, Hoover sought to restore confidence in the economy by stressing the basic soundness of the American system. At a December 1929 conference of business leaders convened by the U.S. Chamber of Commerce, he laid out a strategy of urging greater private investment in industrial expansion as well as state and municipal spending on jobs and public works programs. Amid cheers and applause from the gathered businessmen, Hoover admitted that the stock panic had led to some job losses, but that the moment of fear had passed, the economy was robust, and with a little concerted effort by industry, the worrisome employment picture should improve.[11]

Sticking to his guns into the new year, Hoover announced in February 1930 that "this is not the time for a general expansion in public expenditures." The government must balance its budget, since any shortfall would have to be met by tax increases upon an already hard-up population. By the start of May, Hoover was telling another meeting of the Chamber of Commerce that the country had "passed the worst of the great economic storm" and that "America is finding herself on the road to secure social satisfaction." In June, Hoover would say to White House visitors that "the depression is over."[12]

Although there had been a few signs of life in the economy in mid-1930—industrial production had picked up since late 1929, while railroads and some utilities were expanding their operations—Hoover evidently refused to accept other alarming data. New home construction had collapsed; steel production slumped; and prices of key agricultural products, already at record lows before the stock market crash, plunged still further, endangering the livelihoods of American farmers even as they crammed city-bound railroad cars with record harvests. And Hoover made matters considerably worse in June 1930 by signing into law an ill-conceived tariff bill, the Smoot-Hawley Tariff Act. Hoover had campaigned on increasing tariffs on agricultural products to keep out foreign competition and help the beleaguered American farmer. But as the draft law worked its way through Congress, tariffs on thousands of products were added onto the list in hopes of providing protection to every sector of the economy. Notwithstanding the counsel of economists, journalists, some of his own advisers, industrialist Henry Ford, J. P. Morgan chief Thomas Lamont, many foreign leaders, and his own private reservations, Hoover signed the bill, knowing that it was popular with his party rank and file.[13]

Predictably, many nations retaliated by raising tariffs against American goods, thus slowing global trade just at the very moment that American producers were desperately searching for markets where they could off-load their wares. No less significant, the tariffs shut off U.S. markets to Europeans who needed to sell their goods inside the United States to earn dollars with which to buy more American goods or to pay off loans to American banks.

Narrowly conceived to protect American producers, Smoot-Hawley in fact jammed a wrench into the fragile gears of the global economy. American imports in the next four years dropped by two-thirds, but the tariff law cut both ways: American exports dropped by 60 percent during Hoover's presidency. Hoover's promise of abundance and eternal prosperity, made so confidently in March 1929, now mocked him. Capitalism, that miraculous engine of prosperity, had stalled, and Hoover simply had no ideas about how to restart it.[14]

III

From the moment Franklin Roosevelt narrowly won election to the governorship of New York in 1928, the press speculated about his future. "It is too early to select the new leader of the Democratic Party or to predict nominations for a date so remote as 1932," the *New York Times* editorial page stated a few days after his victory. "Yet by a most extraordinary combination of qualities, political fortunes, and diversified associations, Governor-elect Roosevelt is within reach of the elements of party leadership." Upon arriving in Warm Springs for a postelection rest, Roosevelt found "the Southland hailing him as the heir apparent to the leadership of the Democratic Party," while people arrayed along the train tracks as he rolled into Georgia waved enthusiastically at "the 1932 standard bearer." Celebrants at a barbecue guffawed at references to his Warm Springs cottage as "the summer White House after 1932." He cheerfully mugged for the reporters in his buoyant hot swimming pool, play-

FDR shows off his vigor in the pool
at Warm Springs, Georgia.
FDR Library

ing a vigorous game of water football. "Roosevelt Proves Physical Fitness," the headlines helpfully stated.[15]

Unlike Warm Springs, Albany on the first of January 1929 was cold and slushy when Roosevelt was sworn in as governor for a two-year term. He faced a Republican-controlled legislature that planned to block any ambitious plans the new governor might have. And he certainly sounded a note of progressive ambition in his inaugural address. Not only did he praise the departing Al Smith as a bold and liberal governor, but he also struck a philosophical note that jumps out at any student of FDR's view of government and its wider purpose. "Our civilization cannot endure," he said, "unless we as individuals realize our personal responsibility to and dependence on the rest of the world." In a passage strikingly at odds with the mythical image of America as a nation of brawny individualists, FDR stressed community: "It is literally true that the 'self-supporting' man or woman has become as extinct as the man of the stone age. Without the help of thousands of others, any one of use would die, naked and starved." He painted a picture of countless laborers in mines, forges, fields, and factories spinning the web of prosperity and comfort that Americans then enjoyed. This was a concept of the economy as an interdependent system of labor and consumption, in which the role of the government was to protect the health, the rights, and the wages of working people who needed advocates in a capitalist society. Speaking at the peak of the roaring gold rush of the 1920s, FDR signaled his belief that an active, interventionist government must help to build and then equitably distribute prosperity. His clear message: Individualism was "extinct." In modern society, citizens rise or fall together.[16]

The legislative proposals FDR made in Albany, though rarely approved by the legislature, foreshadowed the New Deal. On issues such as a minimum wage, the regulation of utilities to provide cheap electricity to consumers, old-age pensions, unemployment support, jobs programs, investment in public infrastructure, and conservation of public lands, Roosevelt took the side of the workers and farmers against the owners. "The first duty of a State," as he put it in January 1930, "is to promote the welfare of the citizens." That included protecting them from "disease, from ignorance, from physical injury, and from old-age want." This concept had roots in the progressive era of Wilson, of course, but in many ways, it was more radical and far-reaching than the reforms proposed under the New Freedom. His aim was not simply to regulate free-market capitalism but to make it more democratic by bolstering the relative power of workers and farmers in a capitalist system. Rather than refereeing conflicts between owners and workers, FDR's state would pick sides. In this manner, he believed, the federal government would fend off revolution, limit the power of oligarchs, and renew the confidence of working people in democracy itself.[17]

As the economy worsened in 1930, FDR sharpened his critique of Hoover and the inaction of the federal government. He felt that Hoover remained beholden to a small clique of superrich businessmen and bankers; Hoover's administration was "government by oligarchy masquerading as democracy." Violence among the unemployed was rising. On March 6 and 7, 1930, the Communist Party of the United States organized mass protests across the country; in New York City's Union Square forty thousand people marched and clashed with police. Similar protests popped up in some thirty U.S. cities. In Washington, police deployed tear gas to disperse angry protests at the White House. To fend off revolution, Roosevelt argued that government must act boldly. As he put it in May 1930, "it is time for the country to become fairly radical for at least one generation. History shows that where this occurs occasionally, nations are saved from revolutions." Democracy needed to prove that it could deliver security; without that, "there will be a gain throughout the country of communistic thought."[18]

In a way, he was lucky to face determined opposition in Albany to his proposals; Republican inaction became one of FDR's favorite topics. He began his fireside chats while governor, using the intimate medium of radio to tell the voters personally that the Republicans were halting progress. He wanted cheap electricity for consumers; the Republicans refused to allow it. He wanted to help farmers get better prices for their crops and dairy produce; the Republicans objected. He wanted reforestation and conservation of eroded soil; the Republicans stood in the way. He wanted better local schools, improved roads, shorter working hours for women and children, and above all, the regulation of private companies making money on publicly financed utilities like water, gas, electricity, telephones, and transportation. He made some progress in reforming the Public Service Commission to oversee utilities, but the legislature blocked serious reform, giving FDR another campaign issue.[19]

It was at times a frustrating first term, but the public understood that Roosevelt had made their welfare his primary aim. In November 1930, FDR was returned to the governor's office for a second two-year term by a record-breaking margin of three-quarters of a million votes, an astonishing improvement on his narrow first-term victory. Most impressive, he nearly swept the rock-solid Republican upstate counties. The platform of progressive, active government looked like a winner, especially as the economic slowdown of 1930 showed signs of worsening. With strength like that in New York, Roosevelt instantly confirmed his place as the leading candidate to take on the now-struggling Herbert Hoover in 1932.

These were the crucial years when Roosevelt put together the rather small group, one could say an official family, of men and women who would help him win the presidency and launch the New Deal. He already relied for daily scheduling and paper flow on the talents of Marguerite "Missy" LeHand and Grace Tully, who managed every waking hour of his time and would accompany him to the White House. Missy gradually came to occupy the role of chief of staff; and she served, too, as a kind of surrogate wife, offering the devotion and complete subservience that Roosevelt expected and desired. To pair with Louis Howe, the loyal factotum of twenty years, FDR brought onto the team James A. Farley, a Catholic from Rockland County who managed the state Democratic Party and who rebuilt a defunct upstate organization into a serious vote-getting operation. Tall, bald, red-faced, unfailingly polite, and privately ambitious to become president himself, Farley worked fiendishly to get Roosevelt into the White House, believing he could cling tightly to the governor's coattails. Howe and Farley set up their operation in New York City, and from late 1930 on were devoted solely to preparing FDR's bid for the Democratic presidential nomination.[20]

Three other figures who became central to FDR's presidency joined him first in New York. Frances Perkins, educated at Mount Holyoke College, worked at Hull House and other settlement houses in Chicago under the tutelage of the influential social activist Jane Addams. She then moved to New York and joined the women's suffrage movement while earning a degree in economics at Columbia. Living in Greenwich Village, she witnessed the horrific Triangle Shirtwaist Factory fire in March 1911, in which 146 garment workers, nearly all women and girls, were consumed in the flames. Perkins threw herself into the cause of workers' rights and industrial safety and was placed by Al Smith on the New York Industrial Commission in 1919. FDR appointed her to lead the commission in 1929 and eventually would bring her to Washington as secretary of labor, making her the first female cabinet officer.[21]

Henry Morgenthau Jr., son of a prominent real estate developer and diplomat, was a neighbor and friend of Roosevelt's in Dutchess County and a fellow gentleman farmer. Not an intellectual—he never received either a high school or college degree—he dabbled in farming, managed his family's considerable fortune, and published a farmer's almanac called *American Agriculturist*. Roosevelt brought him into state government to oversee agricultural policy and later appointed him secretary of the treasury. He became a stalwart ally of liberal programs during the New Deal as well as a faithful diarist: His personal papers would yield enormous insights into the daily operations of the Roosevelt presidency. Morgenthau had "a dog-like devotion" to Roosevelt that proved invaluable in the many bureaucratic struggles ahead.[22]

Harry Hopkins was perhaps the most significant member of the inner circle who joined FDR in New York. Raised in Iowa, educated at Grinnell College, he, too, went into the settlement house movement in New York and worked his way into the network of social welfare programs in the city. A slight, tough, sharp-elbowed man who endured painful stomach ailments, Hopkins spent a decade in New York's philanthropic and charitable community, directing funds to the needy. He served as head of the New York Tuberculosis Association in 1924 until taking a job as the number two man at the Temporary Emergency Relief Administration, established by FDR in 1931. The following year, Hopkins became its director and demonstrated enormous administrative talent in standing up work relief programs for the unemployed. His success in New York set him on a path to become the most influential official of the Roosevelt presidency, other than Roosevelt himself.[23]

IV

The day after Roosevelt's landslide reelection in November 1930, James Farley released a statement to the press. "I do not see how Mr. Roosevelt can escape becoming the next presidential candidate of his party, even if no one should raise a finger to bring this about." Of course, Farley and Howe would work tirelessly during the subsequent eighteen months toward that end; but Roosevelt also got help from America's accelerating economic meltdown. Soon after the election, a banking crisis rippled across the country that belied Hoover's rosy statements about an imminent recovery.[24]

In the 1930s, some eight thousand U.S. banks belonged to the Federal Reserve System, giving them some access to liquidity in case of a sudden panic by depositors. But sixteen thousand banks, mostly small local institutions, did not; they were simply on their own if their cash reserves ran low. When Caldwell & Co., a large Southern financial services company based in Nashville, lost heavily in the stock market crash, it began to pull cash out of banks it controlled, leading to the closing of some banks in Tennessee and Kentucky. Within days, a domino effect occurred, and hundreds of small independent banks suspended operations to avoid having their own vaults drained by frightened depositors. Over six hundred banks failed in just the last two months of 1930. Deposits were lost, businesses closed, the economy contracted further, and the unemployment numbers grew. Similar waves of bank failures rolled through the economy in 1931 and 1932, with shocking results: Between 1930 and 1933, over nine thousand banks would go under, taking $7 billion worth of deposits with them. The entire banking system seemed headed for collapse, adding to America's sense of despair and anxiety.[25]

Nor were such bank failures limited to the United States. As the U.S. economy slowed, as prices of commodities plunged, as tariffs went up, as unemployment grew, banks everywhere came under pressure because their outstanding loans could never be made good. Any bank that was overextended might find itself in trouble, and it was the weakest ones that went first. In May 1931, Austria's Creditanstalt, once the most important bank in the Austro-Hungarian Empire, collapsed. The contagion quickly spread to Germany, where large banks faced massive withdrawals by anxious clients, who often took out their money in the form of gold. A run on German banks, and a loss of gold reserves, gained momentum that summer, and Germany's central Reichsbank had to appeal to Britain, France, and the United States for help.

Germany's bank crisis in turn made it impossible for the country to pay its reparations, and Hoover, pressured by his own diplomats to help shore up the Brüning government lest the crisis further help the Nazis or Communists at the polls, agreed to a one-year moratorium on the payment of reparations and war debts. It was a constructive proposal and went into effect in July 1931; but it only stanched the bleeding for a short while. Britain, which had made large loans to continental banks to help prop them up, was now hit with a panic of its own as nervous holders of sterling, worried about the Bank of England's overexposure, began to cash in their pounds for gold. A major run on Britain's gold supply ensued. The only way to halt this was to abandon the gold standard, which Britain did in September. With the gold standard disrupted, each nation faced the Depression more or less on its own, with little international coordination. The overall picture was grim indeed: unemployment, economic contraction, austerity, deflation, and fear swirling together to fuel a worldwide tempest.[26]

As the global banking system seized up, the economic crisis in New York State devolved into a major human catastrophe. New York City initially could bear the brunt of the Depression better than smaller cities in the Midwest or West because of its size, wealth, strong municipal and state government, and because of its well-funded churches and charitable institutions. But by the winter of 1930–31, terrible signs of human misery appeared across metropolitan New York: men selling pencils and apples on the street corners, tin-and-cardboard shacks sprouting along the mucky shoreline of the Hudson and

East Rivers, destitute and homeless families camping in filth in Central Park, scrawny children arriving at their public schools without adequate clothing, faint from malnourishment. The unemployment crisis, which had first taken hold among the seasonal laborers and the industrial working class, now reached into the white-collar sector, hitting the clerks, bookkeepers, bank tellers, and secretaries, whose labor was no longer needed. Tenants who couldn't pay the rent found themselves on the streets. A New York City lyricist named Yip Harburg wrote a song called "Brother, Can You Spare a Dime?" that was recorded by the great crooner of the day, Bing Crosby; the Great Depression now had a mournful anthem. If even shimmering, glittering New York City, for so long a symbol of America's wealth, power, and industrial might, could be thrown into hunger and despair, no place in America was safe.

All of this could have been used as material for a demagogic campaign of hatred, anger, and fearmongering of the kind Hitler had orchestrated between 1930 and 1933. Hitler attributed the suffering of Germans to a devious conspiracy hatched by Jews, Bolsheviks, and international bankers to destroy the German *Volk*. His solution to the crisis called for putting an end to democracy with its divisive political parties, expelling the Jews, and conquering new territory to create an autarkic German empire in Europe, thus securing the economic and racial supremacy of the German people. This kind of warped fever dream was repugnant and alien to Roosevelt. For him, the Depression

Christmas, 1931: hungry men waiting to get a hot meal in New York City's Municipal Lodging House on East Twenty-Fifth Street.
Rolls Press / Popperfoto via Getty Images

proved that unrestrained capitalism needed drastic reform. The solution to the economic crisis lay in better, wiser, more creative democratic government, led by civic-minded public officials, working to enhance human security.

He responded to suffering in New York in imaginative ways that would serve his presidential ambitions. In a sharp contrast with the inaction of the federal government, Roosevelt on August 28 made "an extraordinary and startling proposal," as Rosenman described it: the creation of a Temporary Emergency Relief Administration (TERA), with a budget of $20 million, to employ New Yorkers on short-term public works projects—improving parks and forests, roadways, schools, public buildings, and the like. The program reflected Roosevelt's still-Victorian sensibility that a mere handout would ruin character, whereas work promoted order and self-respect. But in the speech to the legislature proposing this new agency, FDR elaborated on his theory of government. As he put it, "the duty of the state toward the citizens is the duty of the servant to its master." In the midst of a catastrophic economic breakdown, the state "owes the definite obligation to prevent the starvation or the dire want of any of its fellow men and women who try to maintain themselves but cannot." The state must serve the people "as a matter of social duty," he said. Here Roosevelt expressed as clearly as he ever did a political creed. And it stood in contrast not just to Hoover's conservative nostrums but also to the fascist concept in which individuals are bound together into a single mass, compelled to subsume their individuality in a unitary and all-powerful one-party state under the guidance of a singular dictator. Roosevelt, here in August 1931, began what would become a decade-long rhetorical effort to mark out the fundamental opposition between democratic capitalism and totalitarian conceptions of power.[27]

TERA became, in the words of historian Mason Williams, "easily Roosevelt's greatest achievement as governor of New York." It pushed millions of dollars into local relief, set thousands of New Yorkers to work on public improvement projects, and kept families afloat with a small paycheck. By the fall of 1932, after a year of operation, the agency had vastly expanded its work and was providing aid to 370,000 families, in total 1.4 million people. In what Harry Hopkins, who had become its administrator, called "one of the greatest social experiments ever undertaken," TERA spent $25 million in its first year. But it needed more, as much as $10 million a *month* to sustain millions of New Yorkers. Roosevelt and Hopkins got a $30 million bond issue placed on the ballot for voters in November 1932; it passed by an overwhelming majority. TERA was popular, effective, and a showcase of what the federal government might do under the right leadership.[28]

V

And yet, there was no coronation of Franklin Roosevelt by the Democratic Party elders. Roosevelt remained for them an unknown quantity. Yes, he had shown remarkable strength in New York, and his position among Southern Democrats was strong. But some found his jaunty bearing condescending, others thought him shifty and unprincipled, still others feared he was a lightweight and just not up to the heavy responsibilities of the presidency. His unwillingness to crack down on corruption and influence peddling in the New York City Democratic Party tarnished him in the eyes of some critics. And he was seen as presumptuously elbowing his way into the leadership ahead of the still-revered Al Smith. Hoover was vulnerable, some of the party insiders said; why not give Al another shot at the presidency in 1932?

The case made against Roosevelt was based upon personal judgments more than real policy differences. Walter Lippmann, for example, found something lacking in Roosevelt's character. Writing in November 1931 to Newton Baker, an Ohioan who had served with distinction as Wilson's secretary of war, Lippmann poured out his worries: "I was an enthusiastic Roosevelt man up to the week of his first inauguration as Governor," he wrote. But having watched him closely for two years, Lippmann concluded FDR "just doesn't happen to have a very good mind. . . . He never really comes to grips with a problem which has any large dimensions." In making policy decisions, Roosevelt cared only about "political advantage." That was a curious complaint to make about a politician, but Lippmann captured something that others felt, too: FDR was too quick to sacrifice principles to get ahead.

And he was inexperienced. "I am convinced," Lippmann continued, "that he has never thought much, or understood much, about the great subjects which must concern the next president, about such matters as the tariff, foreign policy, taxation, currency and banking. He is best on certain questions of social welfare, old age pensions, and that kind of remedial legislation, but on the real problems of statesmanship, my impression, from many long talks in the last few years, is that he is a kind of amiable boy scout." Lippmann, who clearly hoped Baker himself would let his name go forward as a candidate for the nomination, summed up: "I consider it extremely important that he shouldn't be the Democratic candidate for president."[29]

Lippmann did not limit these observations to his private correspondence. On January 8, 1932, in his new regular column for the *New York Herald Tribune*, he published a remarkably condescending assessment of Roosevelt's qualities. In Lippmann's view, Roosevelt was inconsistent, too eager to please, forever changing his views, always "carrying water on both shoulders." FDR dealt in "two-faced platitudes"; he was a man "without a firm grasp of public affairs and without very strong convictions." To the progressives and populists in the West, he spoke of smashing the oligarchy; to the oligarchs in Wall Street, he gave "private assurances" that they need have no fear of him. As governor, he had been cautious and taken no risks. He was not "a crusader" nor an "enemy of entrenched privilege." Lippmann ended with a droll, dismissive comment, as if he were flicking away the ash at the end of his cigarette: "He is a pleasant man who, without any important qualifications for the office, would very much like to be president."[30]

Walter Lippmann, an early Roosevelt skeptic.
Library of Congress

This immortal gaffe shows more than Lippmann's poor judgment in gauging political talent. It reveals the headwinds FDR faced in winning the nomination of his party. On January 23, Roosevelt took the plunge, allowing his name to be placed on the primary ballot in North Dakota. Two weeks later, Al Smith, backed by the wealthy party chairman John Raskob, announced that if the party beckoned him to run again, he would accept the call. "Smith Declares War," stated the *Washington Post* editorial page. Both New Yorkers were formidable candidates; neither could assume he would accumulate the required two-thirds of the delegates at the Democratic National Convention, to be held in June in Chicago. The ugly specter of a divided party forced to choose a compromise candidate—as in 1924—now loomed on the horizon. Governor Albert Ritchie of Maryland, a Southern conservative, began to assess his chances; Speaker of the House "Cactus Jack" Garner looked like a plausible alternative; Baker, the Midwest progressive, stood impassively in the wings. "A desperate battle," said the *Post*, had begun.[31]

The Lippmann critique stung Roosevelt and it may have had something to do with his effort to get more brainpower into his campaign. In March, Sam Rosenman gathered a small group of academics to meet and consult with Roosevelt in Albany, where they discussed a wide range of domestic policy issues in agriculture, banking, railroads, trade, tariffs, utilities, and job programs. Three Columbia University professors—Raymond Moley, professor of government; Adolph A. Berle Jr., professor of law; and Rexford G. Tugwell, professor of economics—formed the core of what FDR called his "privy council" and what the press soon called "the brain trust." FDR needed the help badly. As Tugwell remembered it, Roosevelt's "lack of knowledge was total." He possessed little more than "a general attitude of liberal progressivism."

But unlike Lippmann, these men immediately perceived Roosevelt's underlying intelligence and confidence. He had "a phenomenal capacity for growth," Tugwell recalled. "Meeting him was somewhat like coming into contact with destiny itself. It was a tremendous, an unnerving experience." As they briefed Roosevelt, they saw his extraordinary power to grasp the essentials of complex problems. "Facts stuck to his mind like flies to old-fashioned flypaper," Tugwell saw. "He had an exceptionally agile mind." Moley noted his inexhaustible energy: "The stories about his illness and its effect upon him are the bunk," he wrote his sister. "Nobody in public life since TR has been so robust, so buoyantly and blatantly healthy as this fellow." FDR was warm, alive, quick-witted, fun to be around. "I had faith in him," Moley said. This brain trust of obscure academics, with their briefcases bulging with technical papers and their talk so full of abstractions, found themselves in the presence of a man who could draw from them their best work and translate it into the language of practical policy. Tugwell confessed "the Albany of that spring can only be described as given over to euphoria."[32]

They had their own theories and pet projects and did not often agree with one another; indeed, they often did not agree with Roosevelt. Perhaps because it emerged from open-ended bull sessions with the professors, the early New Deal never lost a certain patchwork, unsystematic character. As one caustic historian wrote in 1948, "the New Deal will never be understood by anyone who looks for a single thread of policy, a far-reaching, far-seeing plan. It was a series of improvisations, many adopted very suddenly, many contradictory. Such unity as it had was in political strategy, not economics." Unlike the continental fascists, Roosevelt abjured fixed ideological systems. He knew generally the direction he wanted to go, but he kept his options open and secured his lines of retreat.[33]

The brain trusters first saw the results of their work in one of FDR's most memorable stump speeches. Such public addresses were designed to lay out what Tugwell called a "grand strategy" that Roosevelt intended to follow as president. On April 7, in a radio address from Albany, Roosevelt spoke about the grave crisis in farming—a sector of the economy that then employed 20 percent of the workforce. Using a text prepared by Moley, he identified three knotty economic problems that needed fixing. The farmers of the country could not earn a living by selling their crops because prices had fallen too low; farmers could not send their goods abroad because the world's tariffs were too high; and the farmer was in danger of defaulting on his mortgage and losing his farm. These issues formed a nexus and needed to be dealt with as part of an overall plan devised by government, banking, and farmers. It was time, Roosevelt said, for the leaders of the country to "put their faith once more in the forgotten man at the bottom of the economic pyramid." The speech was instantly taken out of context by Al Smith who accused Roosevelt of inciting class warfare. But Smith missed the point: What FDR wanted was an economic program that connected the farm crisis, the banking and foreclosure crisis, the tariff and trade crisis, and the social and human crisis that America faced. Roosevelt did not set class against class; he asked only that government serve *all* the classes, and not just the one at the top.[34]

In an era of socialist and fascist experimentation with the reordering of society, Roosevelt had to be careful not to open himself up to the charge of going "red." Yet at Oglethorpe University in Atlanta on May 22, he sounded like a prophet of collectivism. American capitalism, he said, was characterized by haphazardness and waste, the scramble to make money today while forgetting about building security for tomorrow. The current crisis, he believed, "could have been prevented by greater foresight and by a larger measure of social planning." America was enormously rich. Why then were millions jobless and hungry? "Raw materials stand unused, factories stand idle, railroad traffic continues to dwindle, merchants sell less and less, while millions of able-bodied men and women, in dire need, are clamoring for the opportunity to work. This is the awful paradox with which we are confronted, a stinging rebuke that challenges our power to operate the economic machine which we have created." The solution lay in an active government ironing out the inequities inherent in capitalism, and in "controlling by adequate planning the creation and distribution of those products which our vast economic machine is capable of yielding." This was radical stuff: The American system could not endure "unless we can bring about a wiser, more equitable distribution of the national income." Exactly how he proposed to share out America's wealth, he did not say. But no one could hear this speech and think that Roosevelt was just "an amiable boy scout." These were words designed to set the country ablaze.

Tugwell wrote later that of all his speeches, the Oglethorpe address most accurately captured Roosevelt's true convictions. For the rest of the campaign, he tended to shy away from such talk of a "more equitable distribution of the national income." Even so, he had sent up a signal that the choice before his party lay between Al Smith, buttressed by the wealthy conservative Raskob, and the promise of new ideas, even a new order. "The country needs and, unless I mistake its temper, the country demands bold, persistent experimentation," Roosevelt said at Oglethorpe. "It is common sense to take a method and try it: If it fails, admit it frankly and try another. But above all, try something." A simple bromide, perhaps: but memorable.[35]

FDR on the eve of victory.
FDR Library

At the Democratic Party's convention in Chicago in June, the two factions of the party bitterly clashed in what became a sad, even tragic finale for Al Smith. He had no chance to win the nomination for himself. Coming into the Chicago gathering, he had amassed only 200 delegates to Roosevelt's 667. Yet a candidate needed 770, or two-thirds of the delegates, to clinch the nomination. In an atmosphere of intense rivalry and bitterness going back years, in the heat of a Chicago summer, the delegates and campaign strategists endured sleepless nights, exhausting days, poor food, perspiration and noise, and all the tumult of a political convention without a script. Three rounds of balloting went forward. Roosevelt was well ahead, but the Smith forces held firm and no winner emerged. The delegates grew restless. Should they rally to a compromise candidate? No—Jim Farley, worn red with fatigue and worry, fearful that his long-sought prize might slip away, brokered a deal. Jack Garner of Nevada would come onto the ticket as Roosevelt's running mate and bring with him into the Roosevelt camp the crucial states of Texas and California. On the fourth ballot, conducted on July 1, the delegates, with the scent of victory now breaking through the odor of stalemate, rallied to Roosevelt. With excitement mounting in the hall, 945 delegates stood up for FDR; an embittered 190 stayed with Smith until the end, resigned to defeat and oblivion.[36]

VI

In the spring of 1932, while engaged in his own presidential campaign, Adolf Hitler did something designed to amaze the public: He traveled by airplane across Germany, making it possible for him to be seen and heard at mass meetings in several cities and towns every day. With a flair for the dramatic, and his desire to connect himself to symbols of modernity, Hitler created immense publicity for what he termed his "Flights over Germany." His propagandists issued a newsreel and a booklet of photographs of the flight; later, in 1935, the filmmaker Leni Riefenstahl, in her epic pro-Nazi film *Triumph of the Will*, returned to the theme of Hitler in flight, descending godlike from the clouds. It was a powerful motif, for in this era, aviation signaled strength, modernity, and daring.

It is therefore striking, and revealing, that the day after his nomination, Franklin Roosevelt set out for Chicago and the convention by airplane—a chartered American Airways Ford Tri-Motor passenger craft with seating for eleven and two pilots. He became the first presidential candidate to fly, and the first to attend a nominating convention in person. It was a way of dispelling the whispers that he might not have the physical vigor to handle the duties of the presidency. The plane had been sitting on a grass field in Albany for a few days, awaiting the moment. At 8:30 a.m. on July 2, Roosevelt, Eleanor, their two sons, Elliott and John, Missy LeHand, Grace Tully, Sam Rosenman, and two state troopers took off, heading to Buffalo, then on to Cleveland, refueling along the way. The aircraft, boxy and heavy, had a top speed of only 130 miles an hour and met headwinds and rain squalls along the route; the plane did not reach Chicago until 4:30 p.m. Ten thousand people greeted the family at the Chicago airport with a hearty roar. A motorcade of sixty cars whisked the party off to the teeming Chicago Stadium, through streets choked with gleeful supporters. FDR knew how to make an entrance.[37]

There was no time to lose. Roosevelt was late, and the weary, punch-drunk crowd of twenty thousand people in the vast arena had become fractious. The candidate, red carnation in the lapel of a blue suit, a cane in one hand and the arm of his tall son James in the other, walked slowly into the arena to a tumultuous howl of cheering. Democratic dignitaries rose as he made his way carefully to the speaker's podium, where he stood for many minutes, absorbing the clamorous scene of happy Democrats going berserk. Gripping the stand for balance, he began in a deep, confident voice by giving the traditional thanks to the party leaders for their work and their support. But he moved quickly to the great economic crisis at hand, which would be his most effective weapon against Hoover. He revisited the "forgotten man," and indicted the Republicans for wanting to help only "a favored few" while hoping that "some of their prosperity will leak through" to the farmer and laborer. This method he rejected in favor of "liberal thought" and "planned action." It was a substantive, policy-heavy speech, demonstrating how much he had learned from his seminars with the brain trust.

But there was also a puritanical tone, a paternal scolding for the collective failures of a people. "Let us be frank," he told the crowd, "many amongst us have made obeisance to Mammon," and been seduced by "the profits of speculation, the easy road without toil." Those "false prophets" must now be abandoned. Instead, new leaders must blaze a path "back to the places of security and of safety in our American life." Work and security: The people demanded and deserved those basic rights. His final words that night in Chicago, echoing Christian themes of suffering, redemption, and renewal, promised a new beginning:

> I pledge you, I pledge myself, to a new deal for the American people. Let us all here assembled constitute ourselves prophets of a new order of competence and of courage. This is more than a political campaign; it is a call to arms. Give me your help, not to win votes alone, but to win in this crusade to restore America to its own people.[38]

Historians have often noted that Roosevelt's 1932 campaign for president lacked meaningful policy details and stuck to the high ground of generality. But that critique can be overstated. FDR's campaign was animated by a clear and expansive vision of the role of the federal government in the lives of the American people. In over forty campaign speeches, Roosevelt hammered home the thesis that capitalism had been warped by the abuses and greed of economic elites or "oligarchs." To fix this imbalance, he demanded banking reforms to curb the abuses of Wall Street, sought the regulation of agriculture to raise crop prices, and envisioned powerful new agencies to administer—even control—sectors of the economy. He planned to provide jobs and paychecks to the unemployed, he sought a broad national program of environmental conservation, and he called for investment in major new hydroelectric power projects to benefit rural communities. Of course, there would be much added later, but these ideas all found their way eventually into legislation.[39]

Roosevelt sought nothing less than a new economic order in America, one that served the needs of all the citizens, that was disciplined by the guidance of a democratic state and was legitimized by the people at the ballot box. In fact, Roosevelt believed that capitalism could *only* survive by becoming more democratic—by delivering prosperity, job security, and social harmony to the nation. He outlined this vision simply and memorably in a speech on "social justice" in Detroit in October. Two philosophies of government were locked in a great struggle, he said. One was the idea that if the rich could only get richer, their wealth would "trickle down to the rest of us." The other theory proposed that if average American families were secure and prosperous, "their prosperity will rise upward." He belonged to the second school of thought. The primary purposes of government, he believed, included caring for the poor and eradicating poverty, providing pensions to the old, ensuring adequate health care to the community, and offering the most basic "protection of humanity." These goals were not only just and humane; they made good economic sense, as they would encourage greater productivity in the long run. This connection between social justice and democratic capitalism ran through his campaign and formed the foundation of the New Deal. Any attentive listener in 1932 would have instantly perceived how sharply FDR had broken from the shibboleths of the Harding-Coolidge-Hoover years. As the historian Eric Rauchway has persuasively argued, "the New Deal was on the ballot in 1932."[40]

Certainly, Herbert Hoover had no doubts about that. Already struggling from the self-inflicted wound of sending the army to clear out a large encampment of World War I veterans who had come to Washington during the summer to demand the payment of their wartime bonus, he was baffled about how to counter FDR's ambitious ideas. Unable to run on his own disastrous record, he fell back on tried-and-true Red Scare tactics. At the end of his campaign, he made a desperate attempt to cast the New Deal as dangerous, foreign, and a menace to "the American system of life." At a huge rally at Madison Square Garden, Hoover called FDR's proposals "a radical departure" from 150 years of American history. They would bring "regimentation of men," the suppression of free speech, and the government control of the economy. The New Deal would stifle innovation, Hoover said, vastly expand government bureaucracy, bankrupt the Treasury, spur corruption, destroy the savings of workers by inflation, and "cripple mental and spiritual liberty and progress." Roosevelt's plans would "crack the timbers of our Constitution" and result in dictatorship. Hoover threw every imaginable insult and epithet he could find in Roosevelt's direction. It didn't work.[41]

It seems possible, maybe even probable, that the thousands upon thousands of people who mobbed the streets and parks and railway tracks during

Roosevelt's whistle-stop tours across the country that autumn, and the 23 million Americans who voted for him, did not know the details of FDR's farm program, or his views on tariffs, or conservation, or hydroelectric power. Of course, he laid them out in a series of policy-rich speeches during the campaign, taking up one big issue at a time and unfolding the basic principles of the New Deal. In Topeka, Kansas, it was agriculture; in Portland, Oregon, it was electric power; in Albany, he examined the unemployment problem; in Pittsburgh, he promised a balanced budget (a sop to the economic conservatives in his party who had not yet heard of Mr. Keynes and his 1930 study of deficit spending). In San Francisco, he positioned himself as the inheritor of Jefferson's legacy in the modern world, determined to free the country from the control of "a group of financial Titans" and to guide the government in "distributing wealth and products more equitably." He aligned himself with "enlightened administration" in the service of democracy and equality in America.[42]

Whether or not voters understood his nuanced addresses, they certainly knew that Roosevelt promised a change from Hoover. They knew he would help "the forgotten man." And they knew he carried himself with the unmistakable air of a winner. By Election Day, voters identified FDR with criticism of Wall Street, with the regulation of farming and utilities, and with big public works projects to provide jobs. They heard his indictment of capitalism in America as inherently unfair and in need of serious reform. This was not the New Deal in toto, but campaigns do not turn on policy details. They are for declaring values, and for assuring the voters that they could consign the fate of the nation to a safe, trustworthy pair of hands. "For a sick country," noted Anne O'Hare McCormick on election eve, "the Democratic candidate has the ideal bedside manner, recognizing the symptoms with due gravity but convinced, himself, and convincing the patient, that there is a cure." The inevitable cabdriver, always a source of wisdom for journalists, put it this way to McCormick: "I tell you, lady, the day Roosevelt is elected will be a national holiday. . . . If we get rid of Old Gloom and put in a feller that can laugh and act human, the depression will be half over."[43]

The isolated, brooding Hoover, bitter and sulking, watched Roosevelt sweep to a massive landslide victory on November 8, winning 57 percent of the vote. He won forty-two states to Hoover's six and amassed an Electoral College margin of 472–59. The Democrats in the House of Representatives won ninety-seven seats and would enjoy a 313–117 advantage in the next Congress; in the Senate, Democrats won twelve seats and would hold an unassailable majority of 59–36. It was an electoral tidal wave. The people had spoken, decisively.[44]

VII

A year before the election, as the economic pain of the Great Depression really started to bite, Walter Lippmann wrote of his fear that the American people were "hankering for supermen." He caught a whiff of this desire at the American Legion national convention in Detroit that year, where war veterans approved a resolution stating that the economic crisis could not be met "promptly and efficiently by existing political methods." Lippmann took this to mean that they wanted the president to assume war powers and "dictate national action." Lippmann decried this appeal to a strongman. He thought it was a fantasy to imagine "a conclave of great executives meeting at Washington to formulate a constructive plan to re-create prosperity." This yearning for some all-knowing leader to act with a firm hand must be suppressed, Lippmann wrote. American democracy had the capacity to solve its problems. Politics could still work, he believed.[45]

But in the wake of FDR's huge victory, Lippmann made a startling pivot. Now he, too, hankered for a superman. During the very long interval between the presidential election and the inauguration on March 4, 1933 (a four-month period that would be shortened by the Twentieth Amendment), the economy went into a rapid tailspin with bank failures cascading across the country and breadlines lengthening. An anxious Lippmann called for "the leadership and discipline of a strong national executive." FDR's warm, optimistic personality was welcome, but to master the crisis, Lippmann insisted, "there must be a birch rod in the closet. There must be steel under the velvet." Lippmann wanted the president to "compel" the bureaucracy, "impose" his will on the government, and "mobilize" the people. Two days after Hitler took power in Berlin on January 30, Lippmann lunched with Roosevelt in Warm Springs. "The situation is critical, Franklin," Lippmann said to his old acquaintance. "You may have no alternative but to assume dictatorial powers." In his next column, Lippmann told his readers "this is an emergency" and the president must do "extraordinary things quickly." He considered Congress "impotent except to delay and obstruct." Congress must be "disciplined," a word that had become Lippmann's favorite. The president must have "for a period of, say, a year, the widest and fullest powers possible," while Congress should essentially dissolve itself for a while. "This is strong medicine. It is meant to be."[46]

Did America need a dictator? The question hung on the lips of many worried political elites during that winter of 1932–33. Woodrow Wilson's unctuous counselor Colonel Edward M. House published his own musings on the question, claiming that if things did not improve, Americans would be prepared for a "limited" dictatorship. "There is to be found considerable sentiment favorable to a Mussolini-style dictatorship in conservative circles in America," House confessed. After all, Italy seemed to have pulled itself together under Il Duce's firm hand. In light of the snowballing economic crisis, perhaps it was time for America to suspend democracy for a while.[47]

At the end of December, John Garner, now the vice president–elect and still Speaker of the House, let it be known that he was devising legislation to give Roosevelt "a dictatorship with strings tied to it." Congress would give the new president unlimited authority to slash the federal budget and dissolve federal agencies. FDR would become "dictator of government finance." Democratic leaders in both houses, emboldened by the enormous majorities they now enjoyed, briefly rallied around the idea, seeing it perhaps as way to deflect unpopular budget cuts onto the incoming chief executive. The press announced on February 10 a plan "to confer dictatorial powers . . . equal in many respects to those now held in Italy by Mussolini." Henry T. Rainey, who would take over the duties of Speaker upon Garner's elevation to vice president, said that Roosevelt needed "autocratic power" in these terrible times. "Drastic remedies are necessary."[48]

The so-called "Garner dictatorship plan" soon aroused a good deal of indignant spluttering from the rank and file in Congress, and the *New York Times* editorial page doubted that the legislators had the courage to agree to such a "suicide pact." But *Barron's*, a weekly financial paper, acknowledged that the country was "longing to see the superman emerge." In fact, "a genial and lighthearted dictator might be a relief from the pompous futility" of Congress. "A mild species of dictatorship will help us over the roughest spots in the road ahead," said *Barron's*, which also praised Italy's progress under Mussolini. Lippmann, too, kept up the drumbeat: "In their hearts, the American people know that their hope of relief depends on suspending the power of Congress. . . . 'Dictatorial powers,' if that is the name for them, are essential." He backed off a little a week later, trying to draw a distinction between dictatorship and "a concentration of authority during an emergency." No matter: It was a time for action. Even Al Smith, who late in the campaign had mended fences with Roosevelt, supported extreme measures. He put the case with typical flair: "We are in a state of war. The only thing to do now is to lay aside statutes and do what a Democracy must do when it fights. During the World War, we wrapped the Constitution of the United States in a piece of paper, put it on the shelf and left it there until the war was over." Once again, the moment called for extreme measures.[49]

These remarks, borne of fear and frustration in the face of an unprecedented economic meltdown, reveal both the euphoria many Democrats felt at Roosevelt's enormous victory and the feeling that democracy's built-in inefficiencies and compromises could never meet the scale and scope of the crisis. In the first weeks of 1933, the entire banking system faced collapse. A panic that started in February engulfed thirty-eight states by Inauguration Day as bank doors across the country slammed shut. Washington seemed powerless; perhaps only an iron hand could bring results. This context explains the stress Roosevelt placed on decisive action in his inaugural address. Rejecting fear as irrational—"the only thing we have to fear is fear itself"—he promised "a leadership of frankness and vigor," insisted America had all the tools needed to correct the economic crisis, and laid blame on "the rulers of the exchange of mankind's goods" and "unscrupulous money-changers" for the nation's problems. He would chase these money changers "from their high seats in the temple of our civilization" and begin work immediately to repair the damage. Borrowing from the "dictator" talk of the previous weeks, he said that if the national emergency should endure, or if Congress should fail to follow his lead, he would assume "broad Executive power to wage a war against the emergency," as if the nation had been invaded by foreign armies. The war theme ran through the speech: He demanded unity and discipline as in a "time of armed strife" and called for a "loyal army willing to sacrifice" in the service of saving American democracy. The war against calamity was on, and Roosevelt would lead the charge.[50]

"Roosevelt Inaugurated, Promises War-Time Action," blazed the *Herald Tribune* headline the next day. And indeed, he moved like a commander in chief. On his first night in office, Roosevelt and his treasury secretary, William Woodin, drafted emergency banking legislation to close the banks until they could be assessed and strengthened, and he halted transactions in gold. He also called Congress into a special session. His first fireside chat as president, on March 12, explained his actions and buoyed confidence. Banks soon reopened and the panicky withdrawals stopped. Now began that remarkable run of legislation—the 100 Days of the congressional session between March 9 and June 16, 1933—when the president and Congress passed fifteen major bills that laid the foundations of a new era in American economic and political history.[51]

Though it seemed to come in spasms, scattershot, the legislation FDR signed in those fourteen weeks fell into three general baskets. First there were the banking and economy measures: the Emergency Banking Relief Act, the Economy Act, the Securities Act, and the Glass-Steagall Banking Act, followed a year later by the Securities Exchange Act of 1934. Historians have noted that these laws hardly expelled the money changers from the temple. Rather, they bailed out banks, cut federal spending, and regulated the activities of Wall Street to restore confidence in the marketplace. In a second basket came the relief efforts and jobs programs: the Civilian Conservation Corps (CCC), which promised to put half a million unemployed young men to work in forests and parks; the Federal Emergency Relief Act, which would get cash into the hands of unemployed Americans; and the Public Works Administration, which would send billions of dollars into major infrastructure projects across the country. The Home Owners' Loan Act and the Farm Credit Act offered good terms to refinance mortgages and borrow money to keep people out of bankruptcy.[52]

Yet the third basket, dealing with the restructuring of key sectors of the economy, contained the big, far-reaching programs that FDR and the brain trust had discussed most intensively. These included the Agricultural Adjustment Act, which sought the reduction of crop acreage in order to limit production and lift prices of farm goods; the Tennessee Valley Authority Act, which created a federally owned electric utility corporation to spearhead development and provide electric power in a wide area including Tennessee, Alabama, Mississippi, Kentucky, Georgia, North Carolina, and Virginia; and the National Industrial Recovery Act, which aimed to restart industry by allowing major corporations to work together to set prices and wages, conduct sector-wide planning, and guarantee workers the right of collective bargaining. This was the New Deal's most ambitious law and eventually its most visible failure. But in three months, Roosevelt had certainly followed through on his promise to take daring measures in the hopes not of overturning capitalism but of making it work for average Americans. Only in this manner, he felt, could America follow the path of reform and avoid the road to revolution.[53]

To his critics, and even to some of his friends, Roosevelt suddenly looked like a dictator, sweeping all before him. He had a pliant Congress that barely paused to read most of these bills and passed some simply by shouting approval. To build up a cult of personality, he spoke directly to the nation in the new medium of radio. And he projected decisive leadership, showing the same enviable certainty as the European strongmen. In an ironic twist, a German newspaper on March 5 opined that "America is ripe for a dictator, and it is possible for Roosevelt to become this dictator" by pushing his legislative program through. *New York Times* journalist Arthur Krock, who would become a constant thorn in Roosevelt's side, thought Congress had effectively made Roosevelt a "Constitutional dictator . . . in possession of more arbitrary authority than any American statesman has had since the Constitution was framed." FDR had already been empowered to run the banks; now Agriculture Secretary Henry Wallace said the president would seek "dictatorial powers" to fix the prices of wheat, corn, cotton, hogs, cattle, sheep, rice, tobacco, and dairy, while curtailing production. In late March, there was talk of "the appointment of a dictator with full power to control the railroads." The *Chicago Tribune*, hostile to FDR, claimed America "was drifting into a dictatorship like that of Mussolini and Hitler." By early May, some Republicans openly referred to FDR as "the Dictator" who would not relinquish his powers once the period of emergency had passed.[54]

The leitmotif of a dictatorial Roosevelt shaped public discourse in 1933. In a glowing profile of the new president, Anne O'Hare McCormick depicted FDR as a man of destiny, imposing his will on a stricken, inert nation. "Energy is the note he strikes," she wrote. His office was filled with "a sense of movement. Everybody seems receptive, primed to go. 'Let's try it,' says the president and there is a groundswell as if the nation waited for the word." Roosevelt seemed naturally at ease in command, she noted, breaking precedents in the name of forward movement. "Nothing wears him out. Even his temper is practically shock-proof." His radio talks gave an air of "friendly intimacy" and established "a personal relation between the president and the people." He issued orders like an "autocrat," and wrote the bills that a dumbstruck Congress swiftly approved. He had "caught the imagination of the world, awakened its hope." McCormick drew parallels to another strongman, reporting that the atmosphere in Washington, D.C., had become "strangely reminiscent of Rome in the first weeks after the march of the Blackshirts." But FDR, she said, had not used force to attain power. He had won a mandate to impose "a permissive dictatorship" and get on with the job of fixing America.[55]

In April, the Washington press corps held its annual Gridiron Club dinner, a tradition in which the president is subjected to off-the-record jibes by journalists. A jaunty after-dinner revue featured a skit with five dictators—Mussolini, Hitler, Stalin, Mustafa Kemal Atatürk of Turkey, and Marshal Józef Piłsudski of Poland—welcoming FDR to the dictator's club. Gilbert and Sullivan songs were repurposed to roast Roosevelt for his dictatorial temper, while woeful bankers behind bars sang self-pitying lamentations. Henry Wallace and Rex Tugwell, the new farm "dictators," were turned into Soviet commissars with the names Wallaceowski and Tugwellovitch. A crowd of notables including Vice President Garner, Chief Justice Charles Evans Hughes, cabinet officials, and foreign ambassadors roared with laughter. This ribald take on dictatorship carried on through the year, and by January 1934, FDR himself made fun of it, hosting a birthday party at the White House in which he dressed as Caesar, complete with a crown of laurel, attended by a train of toga-robed "vestal virgins."[56]

But the idea of an American dictator did not always prompt chuckles. In April, a film called *Gabriel over the White House*, bankrolled by the media tycoon William Randolph Hearst, opened in theaters across the country. It was a weird political fantasy in which a cynical careerist politician, Judd Hammond, who has been elected president, suffers a head injury in a car crash and receives a visit from the Archangel Gabriel. Emerging from his coma, the president is a man transformed. He sheds all interest in party politics, dissolves Congress, declares martial law, and sets out to heal the suffering nation with forceful, sensible orders that restore life to the economy. He succeeds—and then drops dead, a martyr and hero. As entertainment, it was weak stuff, but as a plea for a superman, or fascist dictator, it hit home just as these issues were being debated feverishly across the country. Roosevelt knew about the film, had seen an early cut, and told Hearst rather coolly that he found it "tremendously interesting." Its call for swift, decisive action did not go unnoticed.[57]

FDR celebrated his birthday in January 1934 dressed as Caesar, mocking the "dictator" criticism.
FDR Library

VIII

The "dictator" charge was easy enough to rebut. Roosevelt, after all, had not turned the police and army into his personal bodyguard; had not banned all opposing political parties, or jailed his enemies, or silenced the press. Even Congress would soon begin to exercise its normal function as a check on executive authority. There was, however, another criticism frequently directed at the New Deal that particularly annoyed Roosevelt: the charge that it bore a strong resemblance to fascism.

An Italian fascist newspaper described New Deal policies as the same "that have been practiced under Fascism now for a long time in Italy," and others made the similar claims. When the CCC proposal went before Congress, William Green of the American Federation of Labor opposed it as "smacking of fascism, Hitlerism, and in some respects of Sovietism." The idea of sending hundreds of thousands of men to army training camps and then into the forests to work for a dollar a day seemed exploitative and echoed the "regimentation" of the fascists, Green contended. Roger Baldwin of the American Civil Liberties Union described the emerging New Deal as "economic fascism," because it had effectively merged business and government into joint custodians of the economy. Norman Thomas, the leader of the Socialist Party, agreed and argued that the New Deal substituted "State capitalism" for the old laissez-faire version. Roosevelt, by pushing the federal government so boldly into the economic life of the nation, had proposed "the economics of fascism without its politics." And under the rule of any demagogue, Thomas concluded, such state capitalism could be joined with nationalism and racism to create a distinctive brand of American fascism.[58]

The strongest piece of evidence for fascist influence in the New Deal came from the National Recovery Administration, the office created by the National Industrial Recovery Act. The agency aimed to boost industrial activity by developing a set of fair practices or codes in every industry, whereby employers would agree to pay decent wages, allow workers to unionize, limit working hours, and ban child labor and sweatshops. In return, industry would be exempted from antitrust laws and allowed to collude in fixing prices so that employers could be guaranteed a decent income without the fear of being undercut by unscrupulous manufacturers. Through this regulatory device, the NRA aimed to reshape capitalism through the cooperation of business, the government, and labor. When signing the law, Roosevelt predicted it would become "the most important and far-reaching legislation ever enacted by the American Congress." The NRA promised to end "piratical methods and practices" of the unregulated marketplace, which led to low wages, union-busting, and cutthroat competition.[59]

To run the NRA, Roosevelt appointed Hugh S. Johnson, a flamboyant, hard-driving, cantankerous (and alcoholic) army officer who had been educated at West Point and received a BA and law degree at the University of California, Berkeley. Though he did not see combat during World War I, Johnson—who reached the rank of brigadier general at the age of thirty-five—worked closely with the War Industries Board, headed by Bernard Baruch, the businessman and financier who had strongly backed Roosevelt's presidential campaign. With Baruch's support, Johnson elbowed his way into the brain trust and soon found himself running one of the biggest and most ambitious experiments of the New Deal. He spent his first months in the job working tirelessly to secure the voluntary commitment of all the major industries to abide by industry-wide codes that set prices and wages.[60]

In doing so, it was perhaps natural that Johnson would take an interest in fascist economic planning then underway in Italy. After all, Mussolini's state had compelled labor unions and industry to submit to government supervision for the setting of prices, wages, and hours; and Italians hailed their model as one other industrial economies should follow. Johnson's counterpart in Italy, Giuseppe Bottai, the minister of corporations, wrote an essay in *Foreign Affairs* talking up the ways in which the NRA reflected fascist practices, and one of the key brain trusters, Rex Tugwell, traveled to Italy and concluded that the country was "doing many of the things which seem to me necessary." Italy had become a "disciplined" nation as a result of Mussolini's leadership, he thought, and had "made enormous progress." Roosevelt's newly appointed ambassador to Italy, Breckinridge Long, sent home many admiring memos about Mussolini and fascism. Rather like Anne McCormick, Long saw Italy under fascism as "the most fascinating experience imaginable," and its merging of business, labor, and the state into a cooperative system was "the most interesting political experiment" since 1776. Long told Roosevelt about the enormous strides Italy had made in restoring economic growth and employment, reclaiming swampland for cultivation, rolling out miles of new roads, all done in a spirit of national unity under the watchful eye of impressive young men "in their black shirts." Taxes were high and the rich were feeling the pinch, but "the trains are punctual, well-equipped, and fast," and the nation was full of dynamism. Roosevelt delighted in Mussolini's success and told Long he was "deeply impressed by what he has accomplished."[61]

The NRA also launched a vigorous campaign of publicity and education that clearly borrowed from propaganda techniques visible in Rome and Berlin. Because participation in the NRA's code system was voluntary, Hugh Johnson believed he needed to stigmatize noncompliance and embarrass those employers who did not sign up to the new rules. Johnson also chose a symbol for the NRA—a Blue Eagle bearing electric bolts and a gearwheel in its talons—which soon became a talisman of patriotic conduct. Blue Eagle buttons, cards, posters, and flags, with the slogan "We Do Our Part" emblazoned on them, were sent by the millions across the country for public display to encourage support and enthusiasm for this nationwide program.

In the summer of 1933, Johnson threw himself into an exhausting campaign of public appearances, radio programs, and speeches lauding the NRA and calling on citizens to "Buy now!" at shops that displayed the Blue Eagle in their windows. Johnson mocked the "witch doctors of the let-things-alone school of thought" and urged mass participation in this effort to restart the nation's economy. The Blue Eagle, the *Los Angeles Times* said, would become "one of the most powerful weapons of enforcement ever wielded by the federal government." One and a half million canvassers were enrolled in NRA armies to knock on doors and get consumers to sign a pledge card stating they would only buy from NRA stores. Parades with banners, brass bands, fireworks, and speeches popped up in major cities throughout the summer. At the end of August, Johnson offered the wildly optimistic boast that 2 million people "had been removed from the ranks of the unemployed" by NRA policies. On the eve of a mass rally in New York City, he spoke to ten thousand people in Madison Square Garden and hailed the early success of the program. Eighty-five percent of the nation's employers had signed up to industry codes, which he styled "charters of freedom" for American business. The NRA had begun to pull America up from the "inky blackness" of the Depression. The "sneers and sarcasm" directed at the Blue Eagle, he said, came from the very same men who had led the country into disaster in 1929. The program had put

The Blue Eagle and slogan of the National Recovery Administration.
Library of Congress

"heart and hope into a whole people." The next day, 2 million New Yorkers turned out for one of the city's largest marches: a miles-long stream of citizens running up Fifth Avenue, hailing the great program of national recovery.[62]

Was any of this fascist? Certainly, the NRA featured flags and eagles, exhortations to unity and sacrifice, and new designs for state intervention in the economy. But fascism this was not. Max Ascoli, an Italian philosophy professor who had fled fascism in 1931 for America, wrote a barbed essay in *The Atlantic* in November 1933 that put it well: Those who believed the New Deal had put America on the road to fascism "do not know what Fascism is." He reminded readers that the NRA's style of economic planning was not fascism: It was an effort to soften the harshness of capitalism by relying on voluntary codes of conduct in the marketplace. By contrast, fascism was a violent movement with roots deep in the blood-soaked soil of war. It was led by lower-class veterans and angry young men who hated what the war had done to them and to their nation. They appealed to emotion, not reason; they sought power in order to punish their enemies, not to improve the lives of their supporters. They desired to use the state to wipe out opposing political parties, crush dissent, close down centers of independent thought, and completely bind the economy to their plans of war and imperialism. They aimed to supplant individual liberty with a rigid social hierarchy in which all individuals became unthinking servants of the state and its leader. Ascoli saw Roosevelt as the antithesis of the fascism he had known in Italy: "We now see in America a leader who has never played the role of hero or savior, and whose greatest ambition appears to be to look like a common human being." Under his leadership, Americans were grappling with a grave economic and social crisis. They had not solved their problems, but they were fighting toward a solution. And that great national effort, Ascoli suggested, could best be described with "the good old word 'democracy.'"[63]

Roosevelt, too, leaned into the argument. Marking the end of his first year in office in the spring of 1934 with various speeches, he laid down the narrative that would define his presidency. The country had teetered on the brink of anarchy in March 1933. The people cried out for leadership, and Roosevelt offered them not dictatorship but democracy. "I am always a little amused and perhaps at times a little saddened," he said in a public address in March 1934, by the charge that America under the New Deal is "committed to Communism and collectivism or that we have adopted Fascism and a dictatorship." He rejected that accusation. The National Recovery Administration "follows the American method rather than any of the experiments being tried in other nations." The NRA embodied the ethos of the New Deal. The way to fix capitalism, Roosevelt believed, was not through dictatorship or revolution but by making it more democratic, more equitable, more just. To those who wailed about the tyranny of the state, he asked simply, "Are you better off than you were last year?" followed by "Have you lost any of your rights or liberty or constitutional freedom of action and choice?" No, he insisted. Recovery was moving forward with due respect for the American democratic system.[64]

In the end, the NRA did little to restart the American economy, and in 1935, the Supreme Court struck down much of the law, finding that it usurped the role of Congress in regulating commerce. But that disappointment lay in the future. By the end of his first year in office, Roosevelt felt confident about what he called, in his inaugural address, "essential democracy" in America. The New Deal showed that democracy could meet and manage the global crisis of capitalism without resorting to the rubber truncheon or the jackboot. But what Roosevelt perhaps did not yet grasp was that the principal threat to American democracy would not come from within, but from overseas. In Europe and Asia, democracy was dying, and the shadows of totalitarian rule had grown wider and darker with every passing hour. Roosevelt's greatest test still lay ahead.

CHAPTER 5

IGNORING HITLER

"Our wisest policy would be to maintain a passive attitude."

—CORDELL HULL

I

In January 1933, as Franklin Roosevelt prepared to take office, the president-elect had a brief exchange about Adolf Hitler with Rex Tugwell, the razor-sharp, left-leaning member of the brain trust. As Tugwell recalled this conversation, FDR said he viewed the rise of Hitler as "a portent of evil for the United States," and that Hitler's "black sorcery appealed to the worst in men; it supported their hates and ridiculed their tolerances." A clash between Germany and America seemed inevitable because Nazism "could not exist permanently in the same world with a system whose reliance on reason and justice was fundamental." Tugwell, writing about this conversation in 1952, was looking back at the start of FDR's presidency through the thick black fog of World War II. He attached great importance to Roosevelt's words in that pre-inauguration period. "What he was intending to say," Tugwell wrote, "was that he would have no fear of a military trial of strength." Roosevelt also expressed his concern about a more pressing threat: the "latent Nazism in America." Tugwell in retrospect thought that the struggle with "Hitlerites in our own electorate" eventually wore Roosevelt down, compelling him to make "successive retreats" from the firm policy he would have preferred to follow. Public opinion did not support "the necessary hard policy" Roosevelt wanted, and so there was "nothing to do after a certain point but build up strength and wait for the show-down."[1]

This interpretation, that at the start of his presidency FDR anticipated an armed confrontation with fascism but was obstructed in awakening the nation by the combined forces of the neutrality bloc, the peace movement, and pro-fascist American "Hitlerites," is an influential one among New Dealers and historians alike. But it is a curious argument, since many of the authors who believe Roosevelt was intimidated and rendered helpless by isolationists also see him as a creative, bold, imaginative leader, a gifted communicator, a man quite willing to take risks to move his far-reaching domestic policy forward. Did this confident commander in chief, so easy in the saddle when he was fighting on the field of domestic politics, suddenly lose his nerve when facing fascism? Not exactly. However much FDR hated fascism and Nazism, he was determined to avoid a confrontation with them. Tugwell's memories do not match the evidence. In his first year in office, and for some time after that, FDR *chose* to ignore the threat of Nazism, even while leading public figures and some of his own officials urged him, pleaded with him, to speak out. Yet Roosevelt would not be moved.[2]

Why did he stay silent about the Nazi menace? It was never a question of not knowing. In 1933, Roosevelt and his staff learned a great deal about how the Nazis were reordering German society in their first weeks in power. Diplomats and foreign correspondents of all the major newspapers covered the shocking descent of Germany from a troubled but functioning democracy into a brutal dictatorship. Yet FDR viewed events in Germany in the first year of Hitler's rule through the lens of America's domestic crisis. Overwhelmed by America's own problems, he had no appetite for confronting the horrors of Nazi brutality. When he took notice of German developments at all, he sought to ease U.S.-German frictions and proposed negotiated solutions to ongoing disagreements about trade and disarmament. He tried to look past the hatred and violence of Hitler's first year in power, hoping that after a period of upheaval, German politics would settle down. As he waited, many witnesses to the Nazi seizure of power sent to the president a steady supply of news showing that Hitler's madness had only just begun.

II

It all happened so fast. In his first cabinet meeting just hours after being sworn in by President Hindenburg, Hitler showed that he would not be constrained by norms or laws. He spoke casually about banning the Communist Party altogether, thereby opening the way for the Nazis in the Reichstag to form a majority government. Since disenfranchising 6 million Communist voters would probably trigger a general strike and political chaos, he proposed instead new elections, obviously hoping to secure an outright Nazi majority. On February 1, Hitler gave a radio address warning that the "Communist method of madness is trying as a last resort to poison and disrupt the *Volk.*" Invoking the legacy of Hindenburg as their former commander in the Great War, Hitler declared that the president had "appealed to us men of the nationalist parties and associations to fight under him again as once we did at the front, but now loyally united for the salvation of the Reich at home. . . . Germany must not and will not sink into Communist anarchy." It was a call to arms against the left.[3]

To ensure a favorable outcome in the election, now set for March 5, Hitler promulgated a new "Decree for the Protection of the German People," allowing the government to ban political meetings, suppress newspapers as well as labor strikes, and to impose severe penalties for impugning members of the government. At a stormy rally in the Berlin Sportpalast on February 10, Hitler—wearing the brown uniform of the storm troopers—screeched about the "14 years" of treachery and horror inflicted by the Weimar Republic on the German people. In place of the "misery" of millions of unemployed and hungry Germans, Hitler offered work, food, and glory: a recovery of Germany's place in the world, a return to grandeur, and a final reckoning with the November criminals. The political parties and the class warfare they promoted would be swept away; in their place, Hitler promised racial and spiritual unity. The *New York Times* headline got it right: "Hitler Proclaims War on Democracy."[4]

The election campaign opened with bloody street violence between the Brownshirts—the Sturmabteilung, or SA—and Communist militias. In Prussia, Germany's largest state, Hitler's brutal acolyte Hermann Göring had taken control of the Interior Ministry, giving him direct control of the Prussian police force—a powerful army in street battles with the leftists. U.S. ambassador Frederic Sackett, a Hoover appointee who would soon resign his post, sent detailed reports to Washington of Nazi intimidation, censorship, mass jailings, beatings, and murder. Such "acts of terrorism" were intended to suppress left-wing votes and create an atmosphere of crisis and chaos.[5]

And chaos there was, especially on the night of February 27, when the Reichstag erupted in flames. Controversy still hangs over the act of arson that left the parliament building a burned-out hulk—was it done deliberately by the Nazis, or did the Dutch Communist who was immediately arrested on the spot actually set the blaze? Whoever the arsonist, the Reichstag fire perfectly suited the Nazis. As Ambassador Sackett reported back to Washington, the fire gave the Nazis "the pretext they needed for further repressive measures against political opponents." Hitler lost not a moment. The fire, he asserted, was the first act in a general Communist uprising that must immediately be suppressed.

The next day, Hitler presented to President Hindenburg an emergency decree "for the protection of the people and state," suspending civil liberties and extending press censorship; Hindenburg duly signed it. Göring began arresting Communists by the thousands along with prominent journalists, authors, intellectuals, lawyers, and Social Democrats. The Brownshirts were deputized as auxiliary police, and they brutalized anyone suspected of leftist tendencies. Meanwhile, as the election campaign continued, huge Nazi banners and placards occupied every public square, mass parades of armed storm troopers thumped through the streets, torchlight processions bathed the night in flickering amber, and voices of Nazi spokesmen blared from the radios. To the increasingly horrified Sackett, it seemed that "now there is only one large party in Germany."[6]

On March 5, 1933, in the last plausibly democratic election that the German people would know for the next twelve years, 89 percent of registered voters, the highest yet in German history, cast ballots. Forty-four percent of them willingly voted for Hitler's Nazi Party. Eighteen percent supported the Social Democrats, and even the much maligned and persecuted Communists won 12 percent of the vote. Hitler had won a thumping victory, though only a plurality of the vote. Once again, he would have to rely on his coalition partner, Alfred Hugenberg's German National People's Party, whose 52 seats, when combined with the 288 Nazi deputies, gave Hitler a governing majority in the Reichstag. The *Chicago Tribune* did not mince words: "Germany," it stated, "is now well on the way to Fascist dictatorship."[7]

The talented newsman for the *Chicago Daily News*, John Gunther, saw it all in person. "The Hitler people, especially Göring," he confided to a friend, "are running simply wild, and I don't think anything will get them out for years. It is a shocking catastrophe for Germany, I do think, and for the world. Those bloody people are likely to cause a war, deliberately, and then we are all dished." Dorothy Thompson, who had come up from her post in Vienna to cover the Nazi elections, had been shattered by what she saw in Germany that spring. "There is a wholesale terror and pogrom going on the like of which I have not seen in my years as a journalist," she wrote privately. "These SA men have gone perfectly mad . . . they don't like anyone who is a pacifist, an internationalist, a Jew, a socialist, a Catholic, or a radical." The Brownshirts, she asserted, would take their victims to special blocs of flats, "beat them with steel rods, knock their teeth out with revolver butts, break their arms . . . urinate on them, make them kneel and kiss the Hakenkreuz flag . . . it is all too horribly degrading for words." The German newspapers were cowed into silence, but she feared the British and American papers were too restrained in their coverage as well. "I feel myself starting to hate Germany. And already the world is rotten with hatred."[8]

By the end of March, fifteen thousand people had been swept into the prisons, a number that soared to one hundred thousand by October. On March 22, the first truck convoys of political prisoners arrived at an abandoned munitions factory about ten miles northwest of Munich, near a town called Dachau, marking the opening phase of a campaign to liquidate enemies of the Nazi state. Ambassador Sackett, taking his leave of Germany, could not grasp why the German people had willingly chosen this fate for themselves. Hitler, "with avowed dictatorial aspirations, has managed to obtain power by means of the secret ballot. . . . Democracy in Germany has received a blow from which it may never recover," he mournfully concluded. "The much heralded Third Reich has become a reality."[9]

III

Throughout these months of upheaval, the State Department learned in great detail about Nazi methods from George Messersmith, the head of the U.S. consulate in Berlin. A schoolteacher by training, Messersmith came from a Presbyterian and Pennsylvania German background, and had joined the consular service in 1914. He'd worked in Canada, Curaçao, Belgium, and Argentina before taking up the post of consul general in Berlin in 1930 at a time of mounting political and economic crisis. Standing about five feet, six inches tall, sporting steel-rimmed glasses and thinning dark hair, the fussy, plump, fifty-year-old Messersmith was hardly an imposing figure. But his looks were deceiving. He was immensely intelligent, indefatigable, constantly active, and oversaw thirty consular offices across Germany. His role was to protect the commercial and personal interests of Americans in Germany, a job that became increasingly difficult as American travelers, journalists, and businesspeople—many of

George S. Messersmith saw the danger of Nazism from his post as consul in Berlin.
United States Holocaust Memorial Museum

them Jewish—fell afoul of SA thugs, who routinely harassed and beat them on the streets.

Throughout 1933, Messersmith lodged firm protests with the German authorities, demanding a halt to abuse of Americans and seeking the release of those who had been wrongfully detained. To the German government, he insisted that such treatment of U.S. citizens would become a scandal in America and harm the reputation of the new German government. To his superiors in Washington, Messersmith wrote long, detailed cables that tried to alert the State Department to the depraved character of the Nazi government. His grim assessments were rarely welcomed. After a week of chaotic anti-Jewish outbursts, Hitler on the evening of March 10 ordered the storm troopers to cease their helter-skelter attacks on foreigners, worried lest their violence against Americans bring about untimely friction with the United States. According to Messersmith, Hitler's command "had a decisive effect," and attacks on Americans stopped. However, Messersmith very quickly concluded that the Nazi regime had no intention of abandoning its plans for a purging of Jews from the nation. "Anti-Jewish sentiment," he wrote to the State Department, "has in no sense abated." Jewish judges and lawyers, doctors and scientists, figures from the arts, music, and film, university professors: The Nazis aimed "to eliminate them from all positions of importance."[10]

The culmination of this period of anti-Communist and antisemitic agitation came on March 23, when Hitler, again wearing the uniform of the Brownshirts, presented to the Reichstag an Enabling Act designed to give the chancellor nearly unlimited power to govern the nation. With the Communist deputies languishing in prison, and the conservative nationalist parties cowed by intimidation, only the Social Democratic members opposed the measure. The Enabling Act passed by a vote of 444–94, giving Hitler full powers to make and enforce laws for a period of four years. Ambassador Sackett, in his last telegram from Berlin, stated that the Nazi leader could now "reconstruct the entire system of government." Hitler had achieved a legislative coup d'état. Though Hindenburg remained president and reserved the right to dismiss the chancellor if he chose, the legislature surrendered any role in governing the nation. The Reichstag, having made itself irrelevant, adjourned, and Germany passed into a complete dictatorship.[11]

The United States government made no public statements about these developments in Germany. American Jewish leaders and newspapers, however, mobilized to express their horror and shock at Hitler's dismantling of German democracy and the Nazi treatment of Jews. Rumors flew about "the most staggering massacre the world has ever known" being drawn up in Berlin. On the Jewish holiday of Purim, which fell on March 11 to 12, rabbis in many U.S. cities gave sermons likening Hitler to Haman, the evil figure in the Purim fable who desired to exterminate the Jews in Persia. Albert Einstein, who had only just fled to the United States from Germany three months earlier, appealed for the "moral intervention of the world" against Nazism. A conference of Jewish organizations expressed its "profound indignation and loathing which the recent anti-Jewish excesses in Germany under the Hitler regime have aroused" and began to plan protest meetings. Along with large city dailies, smaller Jewish papers like the *American Israelite* of Cincinnati, the *Jewish Advocate* of Boston, and the *Jewish Exponent* of Philadelphia published detailed analyses of the new Nazi regime.[12]

As the press ran increasingly hair-raising stories about atrocities in Germany—reports of Jews thrown into prison cells, beaten until unconscious, of fathers bludgeoned in the presence of their wives and children, of public flogging of Jewish businessmen as well as mock executions and death threats—Jewish leaders demanded action from Washington. Denouncing Nazi outrages as "medieval barbarism," the American Jewish Committee, an advocacy organization in New York led by some of the most prominent lawyers, bankers, philanthropists, and political leaders in the city, asked the State Department to lodge a protest with the German government. By contrast, the American Jewish Congress, founded a decade after the more elitist Committee and spurred on by its outspoken leader, Rabbi Stephen Wise, called for a bolder strategy: public denunciation of Nazi antisemitism. One of the most renowned Reform rabbis in America, and an unsparing critic of the Nazi movement, Wise planned a rally at Madison Square Garden to bring attention to Nazi brutality. "The time for caution and prudence is past," he said. "We must speak up like men. . . . What is happening in Germany today may happen in any land on earth unless it is challenged and rebuked." Catholic and Protestant church leaders spoke out to express solidarity with Rabbi Wise.[13]

Rabbi Stephen Wise, a tireless advocate for Europe's Jews.
Library of Congress

Pressured by Wise and other Jewish leaders, Secretary of State Hull on

March 22 promised that the American embassy in Berlin would investigate the allegations of Nazi brutality. Hull privately believed that noisy protest rallies by American Jews would only inflame the Nazis further and hoped that an expression of concern from him might tamp down Jewish criticism of the Nazi government. With Ambassador Sackett on his way home, it fell to George A. Gordon, the forty-eight-year-old acting chief of the embassy, to provide Hull with an assessment of Nazi actions. Gordon was an experienced diplomat, like FDR a graduate of Harvard and Columbia Law School. He had served as an officer in the Great War and a staff member of the American delegation at the Paris Peace Conference. He married the wealthy socialite Alice Vandergrift Garrett in 1930 and established his family in great luxury in Berlin. He spoke with an affected accent, never went out without his silk hat, gloves, and walking stick, and sported an elaborately waxed mustache. Yet for all that, in 1933 Gordon proved a discerning judge of the Nazis.[14]

Gordon told Hull that while the worst of the brutal public attacks by Nazi Brownshirts on Jews seemed to have diminished on Hitler's orders, "another phase of anti-Semitic action, however, is now manifest. Jews in administrative, executive, and even judicial positions in the Reich Government are being expelled from their positions in large numbers." As Gordon put it, "a far-reaching revolution has actually taken place" in Germany. Nonetheless, Gordon, like Hull, worried that any loud protests in America would be dismissed by the Nazis as mere "atrocity propaganda" and would strengthen the hands of the more vociferous antisemites in Hitler's entourage.[15]

With the Madison Square Garden protest set for the evening of March 27 and talk of a boycott of all German-made products starting to gain momentum, Hull released a public telegram to Rabbi Wise, declaring that upon examination of the facts, the U.S. embassy in Berlin had found that "physical mistreatment of Jews" had ceased in Germany. There had been abuses in early March, Hull acknowledged, but Hitler had "issued an order calling upon his followers to maintain law and order," and as a result "a stabilization appears to have been reached in the field of personal mistreatment." He continued: "I feel hopeful in view of the reported attitude of high German officials and the evidences of amelioration already indicated, that the situation . . . will soon revert to normal." Hull hoped his message would halt Jewish protests at home and encourage Hitler to maintain control over his street thugs. Hull concerned himself more with soothing German feelings than speaking out against Nazis. A woeful chapter in American diplomacy had begun.[16]

Hull's statement failed to reassure Rabbi Wise, who moved ahead with plans for the mass meeting. On the evening of March 27, twenty-three thousand people packed into Madison Square Garden. At least thirty thousand more filled the streets outside, listening to a live broadcast of the rally. It was a remarkable moment: That night, Americans wanted to make their own foreign policy and place the nation on record as opposing Nazi barbarity. Not only Jewish leaders came to the rostrum in the great hall. Former governor Al Smith, U.S. senator Robert Wagner of New York, American Federation of Labor president William Green, and prominent Christian clergy all stood united in condemnation of Nazi antisemitism. In a fiery speech that brought the crowd to its feet, Al Smith insisted that Nazism should be given "the same treatment we gave the Ku Klux Klan." Religious intolerance, whoever the target, is all the same, he said with a wry quip: "It doesn't make any difference to me if it is a brown shirt or a night shirt." For Smith, the Klan and the Nazis were branches of the same poisoned tree.[17]

A more somber Rabbi Wise in his remarks returned to a theme he had repeated in his sermons since Hitler became chancellor, namely, that Jews would not be the only victims of Nazism. All Germany would suffer in the end and "go down to moral defeat and spiritual disaster." Before the immense crowd at the Garden, Wise took aim at the argument that the American people had no right to interfere in German affairs. He insisted that anti-Jewish policy of Nazi Germany was no mere internal matter, for "the conscience of humanity has made a world problem of the present situation of the Jews." Senator Wagner, an immigrant born in Prussia and a stalwart ally of Roosevelt and the New Deal, insisted that he did not come to the meeting to denounce Germany, but "to awaken her" to the disastrous course the Nazi government had taken. All who cared about civilization and progress, said Wagner, looked with "horror and dismay" at Nazi attacks on Jews.[18]

Sure enough, the Nazi regime viewed the New York protest as an intolerable provocation. Hours before the meeting in the Garden, Joseph Goebbels announced that Jewish "lies" would be met by new measures, namely, a boycott of Jewish businesses in Germany. From Berlin, George Messersmith reported to the State Department that "the mass meeting" in New York triggered "almost hysteria" in the Nazi government about "propaganda against Germany abroad." Messersmith included a clipping from the Nazi Party newspaper, *Der Angriff* (The Attack), which called Jewish accusations of brutality "fairy-tales" and "criminal propaganda." The announcement of a boycott of Jewish stores, Messersmith noted, only heightened the sense of "terror in which the Jews in Germany live."[19]

And no wonder: When the official boycott order came down from party headquarters, it drew from the filthy lexicon of Nazi Judeophobia, asserting that Hitler's "liberation" of Germany had "filled the international Jew with hatred and fury"; the Jewish plan for making Germany into a "Soviet-Jewish colony" had been stymied; and so Jews had flooded the press with atrocity tales. Against this "criminal agitation," the German government would respond with a total boycott of Jewish commerce. The order was posted on giant signboards around Berlin and ended with these words: "Show the Jews they cannot degrade us and throw dirt upon German honor without being punished!" Even the normally reticent editorial board of the *New York Times* described this language as reminiscent of the Dark Ages and declared that "the modern world cannot sit by in silence while [Jews] are singled out for exceptional punishment." The *Chicago Tribune* summed it up at the end of March: "Hitler Nazis Declare War on World Jewry."[20]

IV

The White House remained silent. Roosevelt's foreign policy aimed chiefly to avoid conflict with other states while trying to find a path to restart the global economy that had completely broken down. He planned to send a delegation to the World Economic Conference, set for June in London. Other than that, he left the State Department to run foreign affairs. Roosevelt's appointment of Cordell Hull as the secretary of state put a political ally with limited experience in world affairs at the helm of the State Department. A veteran of the Spanish-American War, a local judge and state politician in Tennessee, Hull served in the House of Representatives for twenty-two years, where he developed a reputation as a Wilsonian progressive, favoring low tariffs, a federal income tax, and the League of Nations. He won election to the Senate in 1930 and played a large role in crafting the Democratic platform on which FDR ran in 1932.

Cordell Hull, though an internationalist, spent most of his energy protecting his turf at the State Department.
Library of Congress

FDR admired Hull and respected his political clout. But they were not friends. Courtly, at times vain and defensive, Hull avoided socializing and lived quietly at the Carlton Hotel, a few blocks from the White House. He allowed himself only a weekly game of croquet as a diversion from work. He did not go to Hyde Park or on sailing excursions on the presidential yacht, nor did FDR visit the State Department. Hull resented any interference from other cabinet officers in his domain, occasionally with tragic consequences. For example, in his memoirs he chided Treasury Secretary Henry Morgenthau Jr. for urging action on Jewish matters. "Emotionally upset by Hitler's rise and his persecution of the Jews," Hull wrote of Morgenthau, "he often sought to induce the president . . . to act contrary to our better judgement." Some ambassadors, aware that Hull liked to keep the White House at arm's length, developed the habit of writing letters directly to the president, leaving Hull out of the loop. FDR needed Hull, a leading Southern Democrat, in his cabinet, but he would forge his own foreign policy. One of Hull's assistants noted in his diary: "To such a degree our foreign affairs centralize on the president that no one here really knows what is going on." It would become FDR's pattern for the next twelve years.[21]

Hull's small, tightly knit senior staff comprised conservative officials who jealously guarded their privilege in the insular world of the State Department. William Phillips, Hull's undersecretary, came from an elite Boston lineage and had studied at Harvard just a few years before Roosevelt. Independently wealthy and a close friend of the president's, he'd already held many senior appointments and served as ambassador to Belgium and Canada. Jay Pierrepont Moffat, another product of Groton and Harvard, served as chief of the Western European division, and his copious diaries show that he shared in the persistent antisemitism so common in this social milieu. Assistant Secretary Wilbur J. Carr possessed deep knowledge of the department's legal and personnel machinery and had helped design the quota system of the Immigration Act of 1924—a law that gave American consuls in foreign countries great power to issue, or deny, immigration visas for entry into the United States. His reluctance to allow European Jews into the country would have doleful effects throughout the 1930s. R. Walton Moore, another assistant secretary whose pedigree went back to the Founders, had been active in Virginia politics for decades and had developed a close friendship with Cordell Hull when both men served in the U.S. House of Representatives; he was committed like all Southern Democrats to the ideology of Jim Crow and white supremacy. This coterie of elitists was bound together by courtly professionalism, a sense of their own importance, a generally understood dislike of immigrants,

African Americans, and Jews, and a belief that the province of foreign affairs was best left to the experts. Amateurs from the press, the philanthropic and business worlds, were made to feel unwelcome.[22]

It is tragic but hardly surprising, then, to find that in response to the early antisemitic outrages in Germany, Secretary Hull, rather than condemn the planned Nazi boycott of Jewish businesses, chose a course of appeasement. As Phillips explained to Hamilton Fish Armstrong, the editor of the influential monthly *Foreign Affairs*, the State Department wanted "to reduce the volume of Jewish complaints and actions here, so that the Nazis may have no alibi." That is, Hull wanted to silence American Jews so Hitler's regime would in turn halt anti-Jewish measures. Hull directed George Gordon to sound out the German foreign minister, Konstantin von Neurath, about a deal that can only be described as immoral and degrading. Hull offered to make a public statement casting doubt on reports of anti-Jewish violence; he would also call for an end to U.S. protest rallies against Nazi Germany. The Germans, in turn, would cancel the April 1 boycott of Jewish stores. "You should make it clear," Hull stressed to Gordon, "that it is not the purpose of this Government to interfere in any way in matters which are essentially the domestic concern of Germany." The next day, Phillips told Gordon on a static-filled transatlantic phone call that Hull was prepared to say publicly "that many of the accounts of acts of terror and atrocities which have reached this country have been exaggerated, and I fear that the continued dissemination of exaggerated reports may prejudice the friendly feelings between the peoples of the two countries." Gordon hurried off to ask von Neurath if such a statement would help halt the boycott, but learned it was too late: The orders had been given and there could be no backtracking now.[23]

In the end, the Nazi government found that a boycott of Jewish stores was in fact hard to implement—for example, what if a "Jewish" business employed non-Jewish workers? Should it be closed, despite the ensuing economic hardship? Hitler, concerned about the economic damage of a long-term boycott, decided to limit it to one day, serving as a warning of further reprisals. Yet even while it lasted, the April 1 boycott revealed the ugliness of the new Nazi state and the ready compliance of the German public with Nazi antisemitism. Brown-shirted youths daubed Jewish shopwindows with the word "Jude" in white or yellow paint. They also affixed a black sign with a yellow circle in the middle, "the mark of disease and quarantine the world over," according to one reporter. Trucks of SS men cruised through the streets of Berlin, rushing reinforcements to every quarter. Placards enjoined the public: "Germans: Defend Yourselves! Do Not Buy from the Jews!" In Berlin, commerce slowed, and many storefronts remained shuttered. A few flags of the defunct Weimar Republic were burned amid general cheering, and throngs of grinning Nazis sang and caroused into the night in an atmosphere of vengeful celebration.[24]

The day after the anti-Jewish boycott, George Gordon, who had expected much worse, reported to Washington that the events of April 1 had "passed off extremely peacefully," giving the "moderates" around Hitler a victory. Perhaps such forces of moderation, Gordon naively hoped, would now guide the Nazi regime. He got it wrong. There were no moderates in Hitler's inner circle. In fact, the boycott was just the start of a three-month period of ruthless action by Hitler to seize control of the machinery of the German state, permanently suppress his political opponents, and expunge Jews from the life of the new Reich. On the last day of March, Hitler announced that all the German state governments, the *Länder*, would henceforth be merged with the Nazi Party's own administration through a process of "coordination," or *Gleichschaltung*. New Reich governors, all loyal Nazis, would be appointed as masters of the once independent states. On April 7, the regime issued a "Law for the Restoration of the Professional Civil Service," excluding Jews and other political opponents of the Nazis from all civil service positions including the legal profession, teaching, and the bureaucracy. Two weeks later came a law reducing the number of Jewish students in public schools. On May 2, Hitler ordered the arrest of most of Germany's labor leaders and dissolved the once-powerful trade unions.[25]

Accompanying this seizure of the institutions, the Nazis staged one of the more shocking public demonstrations of their nihilist ideology. On May 10, zealous pro-Nazi university students in Berlin, aided by detachments of Brownshirts, gathered thousands of "un-German" books into a giant pile on the Opernplatz, right in front of the library of Humboldt University. As evening came, they set the books alight. Propaganda Minister Joseph Goebbels presided, howling about the decadence of Jews and Communists as some forty thousand onlookers shouted and danced before the pyre. In his diary, Goebbels raved about his performance as the "trashy and obscene books" blazed into the night: "I am in top form. Huge crowd." But to outsiders, the effect was indelible. "The burning of books affected me more deeply than anything else," recalled Lilian Mowrer, who watched the flames devour pages written by so-called decadent authors. "It was like burning something alive."[26]

To complete the Nazi seizure of power, the remaining nationalist political parties, once Hitler's allies, dissolved themselves, and on July 14, the government banned all but the Nazi Party. On that same day, the government passed the "Law for the Prevention of Offspring with Hereditary Diseases," mandating the forced sterilization of certain individuals with physical and mental disabilities. "Germany can be lifted to a higher cultural level only by race purity," said Goebbels. Any hereditary deformity must be wiped out of the body politic, and the nation purified. The first step on the road to euthanasia and genocide had been taken.[27]

The sharpest American observers now saw the character of the Nazi regime quite clearly. Hamilton Fish Armstrong arrived in Berlin in late April and immediately noted its dour, anxious atmosphere. "There is no use pretending that this is a temporary regime, or that the country is badly divided. The Nazis are Germany," he ruefully noted in his diary. The political opposition had been crushed, and the army had capitulated. Armstrong, working through the oily Ernst Hanfstaengl, got an interview with Hitler and found him "mystical and obscurantist," always ready to launch into a high-pitched monologue and annoyed by any interruption. He expressed his usual obsessions: hatred of Versailles, the Poles, the arrogance of the great powers toward Germany. Armstrong asked about the Jewish boycott and got no reply. He came away thinking the Führer seemed fanatical, angry, histrionic, awkward, naive—and very dangerous. After his return to America, Armstrong gave a radio interview in which he said the old order and old leaders of Germany were gone, "swept away" along with journalists, professors, judges, and labor leaders. "All has been swallowed up in the roaring Nazi cataract," he said.[28]

George Messersmith, as consul, interacted with German police and lesser authorities on a regular basis and reported to the State Department on the shocking swiftness of the Nazi repression, especially the opening of concentration camps across Germany for housing the regime's opponents. He also informed Washington of the continuing brutalization of Jews throughout Germany and the increasing numbers of suicides among Jewish professionals who had been forced out of their jobs by new Nazi laws. Though he held out hope that the Nazi regime might evolve in a more orderly and moderate direction, Messersmith noted that the revolution had taken on a momentum of its own that even Hitler could not, had he wished, entirely contain. Nazi leaders—who he characterized as "psychopathic cases"—had done everything to encourage a warlike, "Spartan" spirit among the people. "I wish it were really possible to make our people at home understand," he wrote despairingly to William Phillips.[29]

Dorothy Thompson tried to do just that. In mid-May, she returned from several weeks in Germany to give public lectures in America. Hitler was far more dangerous than she initially thought, she told her audiences. The Germans were experiencing "a mass movement," a revolution against the norms of the past; Hitler was a brilliant demagogue, she said, who had triggered a nationwide "psychosis." George Gordon, too, could see by midsummer that his hopes for a moderation of the regime had been misplaced. As he reported to Washington, the principle of "totality" had been imposed on Germany: civic society, political activity, intellectual and educational pursuits, and the administration of every facet of German life would now be controlled solely by the Nazi Party. The American chargé wrote dolefully that "all potential sources of resistance to the Nazi regime . . . have now been either absorbed by the Nazis or largely, if not totally, crushed."[30]

It had been a breathtaking assault on German democracy: the suppression of civil liberties, the elimination of the once mighty Communist and Social Democratic parties, the absorption by the Nazi Party of the once independent states, the brutal targeting and segregation of Jews, the dissolution of the labor movement, and the final stroke, the ban on rival political parties—all constituted the complete seizure of power by Hitler's movement. A struggle with the fractious and ever-more-restive SA and its leader Ernst Röhm lay ahead, but Hitler would sweep aside that obstacle with customary brutality and bloodshed. And the army had yet to be fused completely to the Hitler cult. That would come soon enough, for by the middle of 1933, Hitler stood supreme as Germany's dictator. The complete destruction of Weimar democracy had taken less than six months.

V

President Roosevelt had a lifelong interest in Germany. He had spent time there as a child, spoke and read German, and had already played a significant role in one great war against the former German Reich. He had read at least portions of *Mein Kampf* in German and followed the rise of Hitler and the collapse of German democracy closely. The American press featured stories about the persecution of Jews and the consolidation of Hitler's cult almost every day during these early months of 1933. The State Department sent cables from U.S. officials in Berlin to the president regularly. And Roosevelt also learned about conditions inside Germany from important friends and advisers who carried to him the alarming news of Hitler's seizure of power.

One of these, James G. McDonald, came to visit the president on the first of May and spent a long evening and night at the White House. McDonald, a tall, angular man with a thick shock of fair hair, was educated at the University of Indiana and Harvard and raised in a Catholic family with German roots; he spoke German well. He took a job as a university lecturer on history and international affairs just as America entered World War I and became a fervent advocate of American membership in the League of Nations. In 1919, he was named the director of a public advocacy organization called the Foreign Policy Association (FPA), which promoted education on world affairs. Traveling extensively overseas during the 1920s, McDonald developed close ties to many liberal statesmen, bankers, journalists, and diplomats. He also developed a national reputation by giving short weekly radio broadcasts on international politics for NBC. Eleanor Roosevelt became involved with the board of FPA, and through her, McDonald met and consulted with FDR during the 1932 campaign.[31]

In late March, appalled by the press reports coming from Berlin, McDonald boarded the *Europa*, a German ship and one of the fastest transatlantic passenger liners afloat, and sailed from New York to Bremerhaven. He arrived by train in Berlin just as the anti-Jewish boycott got underway. His first meeting, with George Gordon at the embassy, brought him up to date on the Nazi violence against Communists and Jews, as well as the suppression of political parties and newspapers. He met with Hitler's press agent Hanfstaengl over steins of beer at Horcher's, the Berlin restaurant that catered to the Nazi elite; Hitler's press secretary spoke "almost poetically" about the regime and its ambitions to destroy the Jews. Old friends, political contacts, and journalists confirmed reports of tens of thousands of people languishing in prisons, tormented by Brownshirt sadists. Observing the boycott firsthand, McDonald saw "the jeering, the hatred of the crowds" toward Jews and the "medieval signs of Jewish ostracism" the Nazis had brought back to life in modern Berlin. Whenever he met with Nazi officials, they spoke obsessively and zealously about the racial threat to German purity presented by mongrel races. Germany, they said, was "fighting the battle for the world, the battle of the white race."[32]

McDonald met with Hitler on April 8 in an interview arranged by Hanfstaengl. To McDonald's inquiry about Nazi policy toward the Jews, Hitler shot back: "The United States has shut out such people. We did not do so. Therefore, we cannot be blamed if we now take measures against them." A day earlier, Hitler had delivered a speech to an assembly of German doctors making just this argument: America had long used racial difference to organize its society, and "through its immigration law America has inhibited the unwelcome influx" of undesirable people, he asserted. Americans had no right to complain now. McDonald later told close friends that Hitler promised to show the world "how to get rid of the Jews."[33]

After a three-week stay, a despairing McDonald sailed for home. He soon received a telegram from Eleanor Roosevelt, asking him to visit and stay overnight at the White House. "President most anxious to hear your impressions," she wrote. Hoping this visit might be a preliminary step to naming him ambassador to Germany, McDonald leaped at the chance. Arriving on Monday afternoon, May 1, he found himself in a scrum of Brazilian and Argentinian diplomats who had been invited for a formal dinner. As various distinguished guests began to arrive, including the secretary of state and leading congressional figures, FDR pulled McDonald aside and said theatrically, "after dinner you and I will talk about Germany." McDonald retorted, "Mr. President, what I have to say is not a bed-time story."

Once the guests had gone, McDonald sat with Roosevelt from 10 p.m. until midnight, huddled in the second-floor oval room that the president used for his private office. McDonald delivered a briefing about the state of affairs in Germany and the nature of the Nazi regime; FDR peppered him with questions. It became clear to McDonald that the president had "a real grasp of the situation," and had "a program to deal with it." FDR said he planned to meet soon with a representative of the Nazi government, the director of the German central bank, Hjalmar Schacht. Through him, he would convey his personal anxiety about Germany's treatment of Jews. He also had an idea for a public statement to the governments of the world calling for disarmament and economic cooperation, policies McDonald strongly supported. McDonald came away from this long conversation with "an extremely favorable" impression of the president. But the next day, when he stopped in at the State Department, he got a chilly reception. Undersecretary William Phillips, "though knowing most of the facts, did not really sense the urgency of the situation" in Germany. When McDonald asked to see Secretary Hull, he was waved off. McDonald got the message that his personal diplomacy was unwelcome.[34]

There was no way to avoid the subject, however. On May 10, as the grotesque scenes of book burning made headlines in the United States, New York responded with a gigantic anti-Nazi protest march, spearheaded by the indefatigable Rabbi Wise and the American Jewish Congress. Some one hundred thousand people carrying banners and signs walked through the streets, past City Hall, ending at a mass rally in Battery Park. Once again, Jews, Protestants, Catholics, students, uniformed war veterans, rabbis in long black robes, labor officials, and politicians walked shoulder to shoulder and denounced Nazi antisemitism. The marshal of the parade, World War I general and New York politician John F. O'Ryan, called Nazi brutality against Jews "a challenge to civilization" and a "challenge to Christianity and its basic teaching." Amid the field of protesters, a moment of dark humor: The men of the Undertakers Union carried a sign declaring "We Want Hitler."[35]

The story of Nazi persecution in 1933 stayed in the public eye through the activism of Jewish organizations and the prominence of the people willing to support them. On June 14, FDR's successor as governor of New York, Herbert Lehman, headlined a fundraising dinner at the Commodore Hotel in New York City with the aim of raising $1 million for the American Jewish Joint Distribution Committee, a leading Jewish aid group that had been founded at the start of World War I. Philanthropist Harry F. Guggenheim offered his support, as did Felix M. Warburg, the German-born financier and senior partner of the banking firm Kuhn, Loeb & Co. A prominent New York Republican, F. Trubee Davison, who like FDR had been educated at Groton, told the well-heeled diners that Christians like himself "who believe in the brotherhood of man must not remain silent" in the face of Nazi persecution of six hundred thousand German Jews. James McDonald also spoke, invoking the Christian obligation to help the suffering.[36]

And the American press continued to comment extensively on Nazi antisemitism and brutality. That spring, Dorothy Thompson wrote two brilliant essays on the Nazi seizure of power and the persecution of Jews for the *Saturday Evening Post*, making perfectly clear that Nazi Germany was now a brutal police state. She then spoke at the annual convention of B'rith Sholom in Atlantic City in mid-June. To over one thousand delegates of the venerable Jewish fraternal organization, she courageously confessed her error in underestimating Hitler. She had once believed that since Nazism was illogical, contradictory, and certain to harm Germany, the German people would never embrace it. But they had done so, and now the Jews faced torment, expulsion, or worse. The world was outraged and she believed action against the Nazis would follow. Major newspapers, weeklies like *Time* and *Newsweek*, and intellectual magazines like *The Nation* and the *New Republic* gave anti-Jewish measures extensive attention and did not hide the plain fact that the Nazis intended to hound the Jews out of Germany or destroy them. *Time* ran a story on Nazi Germany virtually every week in the first half of 1933, often lightly mocking Hitler as the "pudgy little vegetarian with the Charlie Chaplin mustache," but also taking his ideology seriously. *Time* reported on anti-Jewish brutality, new race laws, the April boycott, and the firing of Jewish university professors. In July the magazine put Joseph Goebbels on its cover, accompanied by a caption that summarized the propagandist's simple message: "THE JEWS ARE TO BLAME!" There can be no doubt: The American public was well-informed about Nazi racial ideology.[37]

Yet no word of criticism came from President Roosevelt. Rabbi Stephen Wise's son, James Waterman Wise, who had just published a short and alarming book called *Swastika: The Nazi Terror* about what he termed a Nazi war on the Jews, expressed stupefaction in a public address on June 25: "It is difficult for Americans—Jews and Gentiles alike—to understand the silence of President Roosevelt in the face of one of the great human disasters of our time." The genteel tone American officials maintained toward Nazi Germany enraged the young Wise: "In a crisis such as exists in Germany today, diplomatic discretion must yield to moral indignation."[38]

Why did FDR not address Nazi persecution of Jews in 1933? Some scholars have suggested that a kind of casual, implicit antisemitism explains the president's silence. Undeniably, both Franklin and Eleanor Roosevelt shared the cultural biases against Jews that were common in their families and class, and FDR frequently made remarks that revealed what one biographer has called his "jocular anti-Semitism." Roosevelt took at face value the crude stereotype of Jews as pushy upstarts, money-obsessed, and vulgar. Yet in his political and personal life, he welcomed Jews as loyal partners and counselors, like speechwriter Sam Rosenman, Dutchess County neighbor and future treasury secretary Henry Morgenthau Jr., Harvard Law professor and future Supreme Court Justice Felix Frankfurter, and brain-trust prodigy Benjamin V. Cohen. Antisemitism, then, would seem an inadequate explanation of Roosevelt's silence in the spring of 1933.[39]

Besides, even Jewish leaders were divided about whether to raise their voices. Many of the prominent Jews that FDR knew from New York or from the political world counseled a policy of quiet diplomacy that would allow Hitler to ease up on Jewish persecution without appearing to lose face. Judge Irving Lehman, the brother of Governor Lehman and an active member of the American Jewish Committee, opposed talk of anti-German boycotts and noisy public rallies; they would only stir up further reprisals against Jews in Germany, he believed. Cyrus Adler, the leader of the Committee, concurred. He opposed the May 10 rally in New York in response to Nazi book burning because it would "inflame already highly wrought feelings." And he denounced a proposed boycott of German goods in America, fearing it "will cause the persecution of Jews in Germany to become even more severe." With crosscutting opinions even within the Jewish community, it was no wonder Roosevelt himself thought he could evade any firm action on the matter.[40]

VI

FDR shared the concerns of Jewish leaders, but his reticence about condemning Germany grew from another source. In the spring of 1933, Roosevelt made a calculated gamble—a naive one, as it turned out—that the German problem could be resolved as part of a general European agreement on economic stabilization and disarmament. Rather than alienate Hitler through condemnation, FDR wanted to preside over a diplomatic breakthrough that would bring the dictator states back into the family of nations. There were two prongs to this strategy: to win a deal on reducing arms; and then to construct an agreement at a conference in London to stabilize international monetary policy that would restore international trade. In the end, neither attempt worked and FDR's first foray into foreign affairs flopped.

The failure of the World Economic Conference in London was predictable. The idea for convening dozens of national delegations in London to agree on lowering tariffs and returning everyone to the gold standard had been in circulation for two years, though Herbert Hoover, facing a difficult election in 1932, dragged his feet. With FDR in office, hopes were rekindled that Washington might pursue a fix to the Depression through international economic cooperation. FDR encouraged this hope in his fireside chat of May 11. But did Roosevelt really want to lower tariffs, allow cheaper imports into America, and lock the dollar into a fixed value? All the policies of the 100 Days required just the opposite approach to succeed. FDR wanted to raise agricultural prices, not lower them; he wanted the dollar to float, allowing for more favorable terms of trade. Nor did Roosevelt pull back the Smoot-Hawley tariffs in his first months. Furthermore, all the major European economies had erected high tariff walls.

When the conference opened in London on June 12, the participating countries were far apart and the American delegation itself was riven by factions, uncertain of the president's desired position. The conference had been underway for three weeks when Roosevelt made a public statement on July 3 casting doubt on the entire undertaking and effectively withdrawing U.S. participation. In making this peevish public declaration, Roosevelt made himself appear in European eyes as an unhelpful nationalist and a poorly informed, inexperienced executive who did not really grasp the need for a global economic cooperation of the great powers. As an effort to encourage international comity through negotiation, the conference was a dramatic failure and seemed to vindicate the argument of the dictator states that national recovery required autarky and economic nationalism.[41]

The disarmament program, by contrast, held a much more important place in the political culture of the 1920s and '30s. If there was any "lesson" to be learned from the horrible tragedy of World War I, it seemed the simplest one of all: Piling up armaments was not just a waste of money but would certainly result in war. In a Depression-racked world, surely all leaders could find a way to halt such madness. This position found widespread support in virtually every democracy of the era. Since February 1932, diplomats had been engaged in fitful and slow-moving talks in Geneva on the reduction of arms, and FDR embraced the opportunity of striking a deal there, burnishing his reputation as a man of peace. As his envoy to the talks in Geneva, Roosevelt relied on Norman Davis, the son of a whiskey distiller and an old Tennessee friend of Cordell Hull, as his special envoy for disarmament. Davis, who in the Wilson administration had held various advisory roles on financial matters, sped across the Atlantic to London and Paris to discuss a European disarmament treaty. He then proposed to the State Department on April 4 that he go to Berlin to meet Hitler to gauge his interest in a disarmament pact. But the timing was awkward. The anti-Jewish boycott had just happened three days earlier. Sending a high-ranking official to Berlin would create, as William Phillips wrote to the president, "the presumption that he was going to discuss the Jewish question," a mission that would embarrass the Nazi government. The department was determined to avoid the impression that it was bending to pressure from American Jews to intercede on behalf of Jewish victims.[42]

But Roosevelt, eager to engage Hitler through diplomacy despite the recent antisemitic outrages, personally directed the State Department to approve Davis's trip to Berlin. "I think it is important enough for Davis to go to Berlin at once," he wrote to Hull, emphasizing that the chance for a breakthrough on disarmament would "outweigh the Jewish problem." Hull reluctantly approved Davis's meeting with Hitler but instructed the envoy to tell the press he would not discuss "the attitude of the German Government toward the Jews." This order to avoid any criticism of the Nazi outrages toward Jews was sent to Davis just days after the scandalous boycott, an act of terror the world had condemned. The Jewish question, FDR and Hull decided, must not derail any chance of a diplomatic breakthrough.[43]

On April 8, Davis met with the German chancellor to discuss an agreement on European disarmament. Hitler treated Davis to one of his evasive, maudlin performances. "Germany believed in disarmament," he said, "but that did not mean solely the disarmament of Germany." The other European states must also disarm. "Germany," Hitler insisted, "had no intention of leaving herself as defenseless as she now is with France and her Allies having a crushing superiority over her." Hitler, using a favorite tactic to generate sympathy for Germany, asked Davis to imagine, for example, if after the U.S. Civil War, Southerners "had been forced to sign an agreement that held them in subjection for an indefinite period of years." Who could tolerate such injustice?

This historical analogy provoked Davis, a Southerner. He launched into a lecture filled with untruths that revealed his own blinkered ideology of race. He told Hitler of the shameful treatment of the South by the federal government after the Civil War, saying it was far worse than anything France had inflicted on Germany. Davis, drawing on the Lost Cause mythology that so saturated the South at this time, conjured up the most shocking of all the outrages: "The North," he sputtered, "even went so far as to put in ex-negro slaves as judges." Davis, repeating the worst fictions of the Southern lament about Reconstruction, all but mocked Germany's postwar suffering when compared to the alleged horrors of Yankee rule in the South. It was a remarkable moment: An American presidential envoy diminished Hitler's self-righteous German claims of ill-treatment by pointing to what he considered a far greater injustice white Americans had once faced: Black men in power. If the American South could endure that horror and yet return to the Union as loyal citizens, Davis implied, Germany could overcome a few years of postwar punishment.

Davis's interjection clearly knocked the Nazi leader off balance. He sought refuge in the old complaints, that France was militarily far stronger than Germany, had been "trying to force Germany forever to live under treaty conditions which no self-respecting nation could tolerate," and must take the first step toward disarmament. Davis, in another awkward blunder, conceded that the Versailles Treaty had been "too harsh," and that a revision of the treaty might be obtained "quietly," through diplomacy. Hitler made it plain that he saw Germany as surrounded by hostile neighbors, and while he did not want war, Germany must be able to defend itself in case of an attack. In fact, Davis's mission was stillborn, since the French would never disarm while Hitler talked about rejecting the Versailles Treaty and about the resurrection of German power in Europe. Only if Britain and the United States would pledge to defend France in case of an attack by Germany would the French even think of disarmament; and the U.S. Congress would never give such a blanket protection. Davis persevered, but by mid-May, there had been no movement toward any agreement and Germany seemed inclined to withdraw from the talks and renounce the Versailles Treaty—an act that could have triggered war.[44]

Matters grew still more gloomy during the visit to Washington of Hjalmar Schacht, the president of the Reichsbank and Hitler's emissary. Schacht was a former banker with close ties to the industrialists that bankrolled the Nazi Party in the early 1930s. He came to discuss preparations for the World Economic Conference scheduled for June in London, and FDR went out of his way to curry favor with him. On May 6, Roosevelt welcomed him to lunch at the White House, where the marine band struck up "*Deutschland, über alles*," and FDR toasted the health of President Hindenburg. In a short private meeting, Roosevelt raised the question of the Nazi treatment of German Jews. Schacht wrote back to Berlin that FDR did not seem to speak from any "particular sympathy for the Jews but from the old Anglo-Saxon sense of chivalry toward the weak. But he did not elaborate," Schacht reported, "and said this hurdle would be cleared even if its importance should not be underestimated." FDR swiftly dropped the subject and pressed Schacht to help bring about a disarmament plan in which Germany's interests would be served through the reduction of arms by France and Poland over a number of years. Schacht, a temperamental and vain man who knew that Hitler was going to begin a secret rearmament program, grew increasingly impatient during his weeklong visit and felt that the Americans had been condescending toward Germany during his visit. Upon taking his leave, he seethed at Undersecretary Phillips that "if the world proceeded to hold Germany down there would be a smash." The prospects for a disarmament deal seemed dim indeed.[45]

Hoping to forestall a total breakdown, Roosevelt on May 16 made a public appeal to all fifty-four governments participating in the disarmament discussions at Geneva to abolish "the weapons of offensive warfare," and to sign a nonaggression pact between all nations. He even suggested, going a good deal further than Congress would allow, that the United States would participate in a worldwide conference to ensure peace and punish any belligerent nation. Though it earned kudos from the press, FDR's proposal in retrospect has the feel of a bid for attention by a new president hoping to notch an early success. Yet the next day, Hitler, evidently wishing to avoid the blame for breaking up the disarmament talks, embraced the president's proposals. In a speech to the Reichstag, he claimed Germany wanted peace and would agree to disarmament and a nonaggression pact, just so long as the Reich was treated equally, and the signatories all reduced their war matériel simultaneously. Delighted by this unexpected act of Nazi statesmanship, Roosevelt felt he had accomplished something of a coup. "I think I have averted a war," he gleefully exclaimed to Henry Morgenthau. The disarmament talks were back on. It seemed as if FDR's policy of engaging with the Nazis and avoiding criticism of their barbarism had paid off.[46]

To be sure, some American officials saw through Hitler's unpersuasive declaration. George Gordon in Berlin composed a long, skeptical memo to Hull arguing that conflict and struggle were far too important a part of Nazi ideology to be abandoned. "The glorification of war by Hitler's own party, as reflected in speeches of its leaders, the Nazi songs and literature, the militaristic propaganda over the Government-owned radio, the so-called patriotic films which are now so much in vogue in Germany" all gave the lie to Hitler's appeals for peace. Whatever Hitler might say about his desire for peace in Europe, argued Gordon, "the real Hitler—the advocate of the doctrine of force, as laid down in his book *My Struggle*," would soon reemerge. Roosevelt and Hull brushed these caveats aside and planned to take Hitler at his word. And that meant overlooking the most sinister aspect of Hitler's new regime.[47]

VII

On the morning of June 8, 1933, the telephone rang in the office of Professor William E. Dodd, a modestly renowned historian at the University of Chicago. The president was calling to ask if Dodd would accept an appointment as U.S. ambassador to Germany. Dumbfounded, Dodd begged for time to speak to his wife and to the president of the university. Roosevelt gave him two hours to consider and, having done so, Dodd took the job.

Sending William Dodd as ambassador to Berlin just at the beginning of the Hitler dictatorship was a curious decision. FDR had tried to fill the post by offering it to various well-known figures, including James Cox, the 1920 Democratic nominee for president; Newton Baker, Wilson's secretary of war; and Columbia University president Nicholas Murray Butler. All refused. But why Dodd? He was a diffident, awkward, at times caustic man, the son of an impecunious North Carolina farmer; in his school days, he had shown a flair for learning and made his way to Virginia Tech to study history. At the suggestion of a teacher, he decided to pursue a doctoral degree in Germany, home to some of the world's most respected universities. In 1897, young Dodd set out for the University of Leipzig—and there, over three years, wrote a dissertation, in German, on Thomas Jefferson's political career in the 1790s. He returned to Virginia to teach at Randolph-Macon College, where he became the subject of some controversy for arguing that slavery lay at the heart of the U.S. Civil War, a view that set him at odds with elite Virginians. Exhausted by constant criticism, Dodd moved to the University of Chicago in 1908 and established himself as a leader in the field of Southern history.

In his scholarship, Dodd developed his ideas about Jefferson, whom he saw as the embodiment of the democratic ideal—a farmer who mistrusted elites and venerated the wisdom of the common man of the soil. When Woodrow Wilson emerged onto the national stage, Dodd became his ardent supporter and eventually his biographer, seeing in him the second coming of the Sage of Monticello. Dodd became close to Wilson personally, edited his papers for publication, and in these years became known in Democratic political circles. He cultivated Wilson's adviser Colonel Edward House, and befriended Josephus Daniels, the North Carolina newspaper publisher and Wilson's secretary of the navy. Dodd occasionally crossed paths with Daniels's lieutenant, the ambitious assistant secretary of the navy, Franklin D. Roosevelt, with whom he remained in touch during Roosevelt's rise to prominence. He had written to Governor Roosevelt frequently, offering advice on party politics in Virginia. His appointment as ambassador in 1933, then, could be explained by Dodd's knowledge of Germany, his record as a liberal internationalist and Wilsonian, and his Democratic Party connections. But an experienced diplomat he was not.[48]

Ambassador William E. Dodd never found his footing in Berlin.
Dodd Papers, Library of Congress

A week after answering Roosevelt's fateful phone call, Dodd visited the president for a personal chat at the White House. As waiters served them a simple lunch, Roosevelt reviewed various problems of U.S.-German relations. He then introduced "the Jewish problem," Dodd later wrote in his diary. FDR said the Germans were treating Jews "shamefully," but went on to say that "this is also not a governmental affair." Dodd should rely on "unofficial and personal influence" to urge the Nazis to moderate their antisemitic policies. Beyond that, the president said, "we can do nothing." Dodd made a pilgrimage a few days later to the Massachusetts home of the gray eminence,

Colonel Edward House, and got rather similar advice. "You should try to ameliorate Jewish sufferings," said Wilson's former adviser. But Dodd need not protest too much because, said House, "the Jews should not be allowed to dominate economic or intellectual life in Berlin as they have done for a long time." House pithily expressed the patronizing antisemitism of the American elite.[49]

Dodd had a far more bracing meeting at the Century Club in New York with some of the leaders of the American Jewish community. During a ninety-minute conversation, Felix Warburg, Judge Irving Lehman, and Rabbi Wise gave Dodd a somber and serious warning. "The Germans are killing Jews all the time, they are being persecuted to the point where suicide is common . . . and all Jewish property is being confiscated," Dodd recalled them saying. Dodd replied that he could not intervene officially, but would "exert all possible personal influence against unjust treatment" of Jews. As it happened, Dodd would see Rabbi Wise again soon, for on July 5 the Dodd family set off to Europe on the luxury liner SS *Washington*, on which Wise was also a passenger. This gave Wise an opportunity to restate his hope that Dodd would intervene on behalf of suffering Jews. And Dodd spent a portion of his ocean crossing immersed in a new and controversial book by Edgar A. Mowrer, the journalist who had covered Mussolini's rise and then moved to Berlin in the mid-1920s. Mowrer's book, titled *Germany Puts the Clock Back*, had appeared in late 1932, just before Hitler became chancellor, and it was a bitter denunciation of the Nazi Party and the conservative nationalist politicians who were gutting German democracy. By the time he arrived in Berlin, Dodd had received an unvarnished picture of the new Nazi order.[50]

And yet Dodd's first months in Berlin are remarkable for their absence of urgency. His diary records few discussions about Jewish affairs; instead, it gives evidence of Dodd's quirks and insecurities. He found the embassy staff, particularly the chargé George Gordon, too formal and too wedded to diplomatic protocol; he bemoaned the expensive habits of the diplomatic corps and insisted that, unlike many wealthy ambassadors, he would not exceed the limits of his modest salary. He drank and ate little and insisted that American embassy social affairs be restrained and spartan. He found the evening dinners he was obliged to attend dull, and he frequently left social functions early in an affront to his hosts. His staff rather quickly took a dislike to him, no doubt because he disliked them, especially the independently wealthy junior officers at the embassy who entertained in grand style. Journalists and scholars frequently came to tell him about Nazi abuses of various kinds, but Dodd viewed most of these reports with suspicion.[51]

Just a week after arriving in Berlin, Dodd wrote to Rabbi Wise that the Hitler regime was inclined to listen to American private protests, and that he saw "an improvement" in their treatment of Jews. Dodd still believed "private conversations" and unofficial appeals yielded better results than public rebuke. He also wrote to the president, stating his opinion that the Hitler government would likely take "a more moderate course." Yet just a few days after Dodd sent these missives, eighty thousand storm troopers held a mass meeting at Tempelhof airfield, where a pro-Nazi Christian pastor, Friedrich Tausch, delivered a sermon that declared "Jews and their confederates have robbed, trampled, and vilified the German soul. The German nation was near death when God almighty sent Hitler. . . . Let us thank God that he gave us such a leader." Dodd's style of quiet diplomacy could never hope to contend with this kind of fanaticism.[52]

In some ways, Roosevelt had placed Dodd in an impossible position. His orders were to establish cordial ties to the German government, focus on issues such as trade and economic relations, and generally stay out of German domestic politics. Moreover, Dodd and his family—he arrived with his wife and two grown children, Martha and Bill—liked Germans, enjoyed the dazzling dynamism of Berlin and the beauty of the countryside, and tended to discount the antisemitic propaganda they heard from government officials. Martha Dodd, twenty-five years old and a vivacious, indiscreet socialite who rapidly developed amorous relations with dozens of journalists, diplomats, and even high-ranking Nazi officials, wrote candidly in her frothy 1939 memoir that she was deeply impressed by the Nazi revolution. "I thought there was a rebirth in Germany as exciting as anything I had ever witnessed," and she believed the press exaggerated the brutality of the Nazi government.[53]

Martha would eventually change her tune, but in 1933 these illusions were common enough, even among seasoned journalists who knew Germany as well as any foreigner could. The major American newspapers and news services had all sent reporters to Berlin to cover the bewildering and menacing story of Hitler's rise. They formed a close-knit circle, professional rivals but personal friends, working and even living side by side and sharing drinks and dinner long into the evenings. Their favorite hangout was the Taverne, an Italian restaurant on Kurfürstenstrasse that allowed them to keep a table permanently reserved for their nightly gatherings. Their personal views on Nazism varied considerably. Some were deeply hostile, like Mower of the *Chicago Daily News*. Sigrid Schultz of the *Chicago Tribune* preferred a less judgmental style in her reporting, mindful of the archconservative politics of her paper's publisher, Colonel Robert McCormick. Karl von Wiegand of the

Hearst syndicate was close to members of the old monarchy and viewed Hitler quite benevolently. Otto Tolischus, Guido Enderis, and Frederick Birchall of the *New York Times* soft-pedaled Nazi violence in their reporting, though Birchall won a Pulitzer Prize in 1934.[54]

Anne O'Hare McCormick, who had a roving commission for the *Times*, interviewed Hitler in July 1933. In much the same tone of her Mussolini articles a decade earlier, McCormick wrote of Hitler that "his eyes are almost the color of the blue larkspur in a vase behind him, curiously childlike and candid." Not only that; Hitler "has the sensitive hand of the artist." Leaving aside the antisemitism and vulgarity of Nazism, she styled Hitler as a man of undoubted political gifts whose main aim was to create "jobs for all Germans." Of course he engaged in "cleansing," McCormick wrote, but the economic crisis demanded such measures. Besides, this man did not seem menacing to McCormick. He "seems a rather shy and simple man, younger than one expects. . . . His sun-browned face is full and is the mobile face of an orator." Hitler expressed admiration for Roosevelt, who he said "marches straight ahead toward his objective over Congress, over lobbies, over stubborn bureaucracies." Hitler, too, was "cutting red tape," McCormick wrote. When asked about Jews, Hitler stiffened briefly, then said he would be happy if those nations that criticized German policies toward Jews "would open their doors to them." Besides, he said, Germany's fight was not directed chiefly at Jews but at the Communists. McCormick dropped the subject, returning to Hitler's "disarming smile." At the conclusion of the interview, the chancellor kissed McCormick's hand "in the best German manner, turned and marched from the room with a light military step."[55]

Such soft-soap reporting would carry on for months and indeed for years, despite the antisemitic and anti-communist terror and the destruction of parliamentary democracy. In early 1936, the *New Yorker* columnist Janet Flanner put out a long three-part profile of Hitler that dwelled on his clothing, his sleeping habits, his sweet tooth (he liked Linzertorte), his humble vegetarian diet, his utter ordinariness; and though his ideas were unappealing, Flanner reassured her readers that Hitler's violent opinions "have definitely mellowed." These journalists understood that the Nazi government watched the foreign news carefully and too much negative reporting could lead to their expulsion from Germany. As one of the leading figures of the group, the Associated Press bureau chief Louis Lochner put it, "our orders from our bosses were to tell no untruth, but to report only as much of the truth, without distorting the picture, as would enable us to remain at our posts." Reporters chose to trim their stories rather than lose the favor of the regime.[56]

Edgar Mowrer, on the other hand, never pulled his punches. Martha Dodd described him as "slender, stoop-shouldered, with a dark, gaunt, early-Christian-martyr face," and animated by a profound hostility toward Fascism. He and his talented wife, Lilian, had been in Germany since 1924, and from his perch as the Berlin bureau chief for his newspaper, Mowrer had done a superb job of relaying to American readers the dark political scene in Germany. His powerfully argued book *Germany Puts the Clock Back* took stock of the German political crisis of 1932, laying blame on everyone from the far left to the far right. Mowrer saw Hitler as just one of several crude opportunists on the make, a jackal waiting to pounce on the mortally wounded Weimar Republic. Dangerous and capable, Hitler remained for Mowrer "an unconvincing figure . . . with dark hair and Charlie Chaplin dab on the upper lip . . . the epitome of reaction masquerading in revolutionary bonnet." His ideology was "a bird's nest of odds and ends" rather than anything coherent. Finishing his book in November 1932, Mowrer guessed that the forces of the reactionary right around Hindenburg, the army, and the plutocrats would block Hitler's bid for the chancellorship.[57]

He got it wrong, of course, and in March 1933, as Hitler clamped down on the press, Mowrer found himself a target of the Nazi regime. A government functionary called him in to berate him for his coverage of German affairs and told him that the Führer had not liked his book. "That's alright," Mowrer shot back. "I feel the same way about *Mein Kampf.*" Joseph Goebbels wanted him out of the country, but as Mowrer had just been elected president of the Foreign Press Association in Germany, and in May won a Pulitzer Prize for his journalism, a direct expulsion might seem too provocative. Instead, the Nazi government had him followed, bullied his friends and sources, and began to spread the word that Mowrer was a "secret" Jew. Mowrer could take it, but by August, the publisher of his newspaper, Frank Knox, learned that the regime would not vouch for Mowrer's safety. Knox decided he should be transferred.[58]

Mowrer felt the principle of an independent press was at stake and appealed to Ambassador Dodd for help in backing his request to remain in Berlin. Dodd, however, thought Mowrer had become a problem—he was, Dodd recorded privately, "as vehement in his way as the Nazis." The German Foreign Office put pressure on Dodd to get Mowrer out of the country. "In view of the intensity of feeling" against the journalist, Dodd wrote in his diary, "I agreed to advise Mowrer to go by September 1." Martha Dodd later claimed that Mowrer "never quite forgave my father for this advice," and indeed Mowrer would later call Dodd a "purblind professor," hopelessly out of his depth in Nazi Berlin.[59]

When Mowrer boarded the train that would carry him out of Germany to Paris, his fellow journalists stood on the platform and gave him a hearty send-off. A sneering Nazi official, there to verify that he actually departed, asked, "And when are you coming back to Germany, Herr Mowrer?" The journalist replied with a snarl, "When I can come back with about two million of my countrymen." He would fulfill that prophecy twelve years later when he returned, along with an army of occupation, to an utterly ruined Berlin and a transformed world.[60]

VIII

Just as Mowrer left Berlin, the Nazi Party opened its annual rally at Nuremberg—the first since Hitler's seizure of power. It bore the name "Congress of Victory," a celebration of Hitler's triumph over democracy and the Weimar Republic. The Nazis chose Nuremberg because it was a convenient city with a large fairground they could use for the immense gathering of hundreds of thousands of Brownshirts. But the city presented another advantage: It lay within the district of Franconia, and its district leader, or gauleiter, was Julius Streicher, one of the most depraved and fanatical Nazis. A war veteran, Streicher had been a Nazi since 1921 and had participated in the failed coup attempt of 1923. He went on to publish the rabidly antisemitic tabloid *Der Stürmer*, a paper with an avid readership among Nazi rank and file, and he had been the chief organizer of the April 1933 anti-Jewish boycott. Streicher set out to make Nuremberg an example of a pure Nazi city, which meant regular atrocities against Jews there. On July 20, 1933, Streicher ordered the roundup of some three hundred Jewish merchants, bankers, and professionals and had them marched through the streets toward a military barracks, where they were stripped and beaten with iron rods. They were then set to do manual labor while being jeered and kicked by Brownshirt guards.[61]

In mid-August, as workmen began to transform Nuremberg for the upcoming rally, a nineteen-year-old girl named Betti Suess was seized by local Brownshirts on the grounds that she had a Jewish boyfriend. Her long black hair was cut from her head, and a gang of Nazis then placed a placard around her neck: "I have offered myself to a Jew," it read. They paraded her through the streets of the town, stopping at every bar and cabaret to compel the wretched girl to stand on the stage to be mocked and threatened by the vicious crowds. As it happened, Ambassador Dodd's children, Martha and Bill, witnessed the scene. Having set out for some sightseeing with Quentin Reynolds, a journalist then working for the Hearst chain, the group stayed overnight in Nuremberg and stumbled across a noisy mob abusing the girl in the street. Martha recalled that the girl's "tragic and tortured face" had the pale green color of "diluted absinthe." Afraid of being noticed, the Americans skulked away into a nearby bar and drowned their sorrows in champagne.[62]

This kind of spontaneous brutality set the stage for the minutely planned Nuremberg rally of August 30 to September 3. Though Ambassador Dodd, after some waffling, had decided to decline the official invitation to the rally, some one thousand journalists from around the world covered the mass gathering. Nuremberg city officials had made an immense effort to erect vast tent cities for the Brownshirts, Nazi youth, and spectators who came to take part. From every windowsill in the ancient city hung a vivid red, white, and black Nazi swastika flag. Hitler's arrival on the afternoon of August 30 triggered an immense crush of people who wanted to catch a glimpse of the Führer cruising past in his car, on his way to the city hall. There he was greeted by the mayor and a chorus of children singing music from Wagner's *Die Meistersinger von Nürnberg*, Hitler's favorite opera, renowned for its intense nationalism and, some believed, its coded antisemitism. At 8 p.m., all the bells in the city rang in unison for half an hour, tolling the start of the *Reichsparteitag*.[63]

Frederick Birchall of the *New York Times*, who spent a week in Nuremberg to cover the rally, thought the townspeople regarded Hitler "as a prophet and almost as a god." In his various utterances throughout the festival, Hitler returned to his usual themes: the danger of debasement of German blood and culture by foreign and Jewish influence, the suffering of Germany be-

Hitler taking the salute at the 1933 Nuremberg rally.
Photo by Robert Sennecke / UllsteinBild via Getty Images

fore 1933, and the heroic awakening of the nation that had occurred under his leadership. But the real impact of the rally, which would be repeated and expanded in subsequent years until 1939, lay in its monumental scale and its elevation of a new national origin story that culminated in the birth of the Third Reich. From disarray and suffering, the Nazi Party had rescued and revived Germany; its new principles were discipline, organization, unity, and total veneration of the Führer. Even the tattered and bloodstained Nazi flag, the *Blutfahne*—the very standard carried by the 1923 putschists in Munich—made an appearance, held aloft as new Nazi banners were consecrated by brushing past this holy relic.[64]

On September 3, after one hundred thousand brown-clad storm troops bearing fifteen thousand Nazi flags marched past the reviewing stand, Hitler gave his final address to the vast congress. He praised himself for destroying a weak and corrupt German democracy; and expanded on a racial theory of history in which the natural rivalry of races would open the way to Aryan domination and conquest of weak and submissive peoples. No one could possibly miss the centrality of war, conquest, and genocide in these words.

Certainly, Birchall noticed it, and after the fourth day, he wrote a summation for his newspaper in which he confessed his inability to capture the power and shocking weirdness of the entire "stagey and unreal" event. The "endless undulating rhythm of brown caps, gray blanket rolls, and knapsacks" as the immense wave of storm troopers marched through the town made it clear to him that Germany was on the march again and National Socialism "is here to remain for a very long time." Hitler served as the idol at the center of the new faith, venerated and worshipped by his followers. There would be no moderation, no middle way, no return to political norms, Birchall concluded. And above all, the Jews would be relentlessly targeted. "Aryanism is now the keystone of Nazi policy," he wrote. "Its corollary is persecution even to extermination—the word is the Nazis' own—of the non-Aryans." Germany under the Nazis had become a nation enthralled, reinvigorated, ready to turn on its Jewish citizens and destroy them, and ready to redraw the boundaries of Europe to place Germany in a position of mastery.[65]

On October 14, 1933, Adolf Hitler took a gamble—not the first of his life. He announced that Germany would withdraw from the ongoing disarmament talks in Geneva, as well as from the League of Nations. The move carried some risk. Germany seemed to be repudiating the entire postwar system of diplomacy, and implicitly announcing its own program of rearmament—a violation of the Versailles Treaty. The great powers might respond with sanctions, or even launch another invasion as in 1923. But by now, Hitler had taken the measure of his European adversaries and expected they would do nothing. "They don't dream of making war!" he scoffed. "A pretty crew they are. They'll never act. They'll just protest. And they will always be too late."[66]

In a long speech to the nation carried by radio on the evening of October 14, Hitler rehearsed the old grievances, insisting that Germany had accepted Wilson's Fourteen Points, had accepted the reparations demands, had disarmed after the war, and swallowed all the humiliations of the Treaty of Versailles. Yet in return, the victor nations refused to treat Germany with respect. And even now, with the rise of National Socialism to power, the rest of the world "has been persecuting us for months with a flood of lies and slander," by which he meant, of course, what the Nazis called Jewish "atrocity propaganda." The German people wanted only equality of rights, Hitler declared; if the League of Nations and the disarmament negotiators continued to treat the Reich as if it was on probation, then Germany would go its own way. And to show that Hitler spoke for all Germans, he announced a plebiscite, to be held on November 12, to allow Germans to show their support for his decision. It was masterpiece of Hitlerian double-talk: Even as he privately assured the German army of a major arms buildup and the conquest of new lands in the East, he presented Germany to the world as a weak nation only concerned with recovering its honor from the vindictive tyranny of France and Britain.[67]

American official reactions to these bold maneuvers reflected the confusion that prevailed at this moment toward the Nazi government. In Berlin, Ambassador Dodd went to see Hitler for his first personal meeting with the chancellor. He climbed the broad stairs of the palace, where the famous Iron Chancellor Otto von Bismarck had once lived, and noted Nazi soldiers standing guard, arms outstretched in salute, throughout the building. Hitler, in a simple suit, greeted him, alongside Foreign Minister von Neurath. "Hitler ranted about the Treaty of Versailles," Dodd recorded later, and spoke of the terrible injustices Germany had been forced to endure after the war. Hitler showed "belligerence and self-confidence" during this meeting, yet Dodd in a report to Washington insisted that Hitler did not want war. Dodd believed that Hitler had abandoned the League for domestic political reasons, seeking to shore up his support among the more extremist rank and file at a time when the Nazi revolution seemed to have lost some of its radical character. Once having solidified his regime, Dodd thought, Hitler might come back to the negotiating table. "The total effect of the interview," Dodd wrote Hull afterward, "was more favorable from the point of view of the maintenance of world peace than I had expected." Despite all the evidence accumulating before him, Dodd still thought Hitler might agree to international treaties limiting German military power.[68]

Similarly, Norman Davis breezily told the president that "I am not hopeless at all." The German government did not want war, he believed; negotiations could still yield fruit. To that end, Davis and Roosevelt, talking on a transatlantic telephone line, agreed that the United States must not appear to be pressuring Germany or unduly chastising it for the breakup of the disarmament conference, lest such criticism make it impossible for Hitler to come back to the bargaining table. Davis insisted that the withdrawal from the League was "primarily an internal political move." The U.S. should continue to work with the chancellor because "Hitler is the best one of the lot" in the German government, and he "certainly wants to make peace with France." Davis and the president wished to avoid any appearance of joining Britain and France in ganging up on Germany. Cordell Hull endorsed this view. The government should avoid criticism of Germany and wait until Hitler had dealt with his internal problems. "Our wisest policy," said Hull characteristically, "would be to maintain a passive attitude."[69]

To a later generation reading these flaccid and evasive memorandums, the lack of alarm in official circles about the Nazi regime appears intolerable and incomprehensible. Of course, the effects of the Great Depression dominated the first year of Roosevelt's presidency and FDR concentrated primarily on legislation keyed to domestic economic recovery. And certainly, the State Department believed a strategy that kept Germany inside the family of nations, where deals might be struck, served world peace better than a complete break. Yet even so, in 1933 some Americans who had spent time in Berlin and in the presence of Nazi officials could see through the curtain of lies. Edgar Mowrer, Dorothy Thompson, Hamilton Fish Armstrong, George Gordon, and James McDonald, all had tried to sound the alarm about the menace of Nazism. Rabbi Stephen Wise had mobilized thousands of American Jews in an effort to awaken the world to the existential danger the Nazis posed.

And no one had documented Nazi policy in more damning detail than George Messersmith from his post in the American consulate. By the fall of 1933, he concluded that antisemitism was no passing phase, but a core principle of the Nazi government. Hitler was obsessed with the specter of a looming Jewish threat. Inside Nazi circles, Messersmith wrote, it was widely believed that President Roosevelt "had practically nothing but Jewish advisers." Jews were enduring so much brutality in Germany not because of their religion, Messersmith correctly noted, but because Hitler insisted that they posed a threat to Aryan "race and blood." In this biological conception of the Jewish threat, extreme measures must be taken to expunge the Jews not merely from the professions but from the body of the German nation. Recalling the Nuremberg rally of early September, Messersmith said that Hitler and Goebbels, "at the most important meeting the Party has ever held," delivered "their principal speeches on racial questions." Messersmith, though under the restraints of diplomatic usage when writing official cables, had clearly come to believe that Hitler aimed at the very least to wage a racial war on Germany's Jews.[70]

John Gunther of the *Chicago Daily News* saw Messersmith at work in Berlin and described him as "one of the most absolutely just, stern, and righteous men I've ever met." This temperament showed in his reporting about the Nazi assault on the Jews. In contrast to the blinkered views of Davis and Hull, and the temporizing of Dodd, Messersmith saw that there was no moderate or rational Hitler waiting in the wings; Hitler had been "deified," and his position was "stronger than ever." The regime had shown "a complete absence of humanitarian principles," Messersmith wrote, and its leaders issued "extraordinary fairy tales" to stoke fear and paranoia among the public. Any utterances from Hitler about peace must be discounted, Messersmith believed. "They are getting ready for war just as rapidly as it is possible for them to do so." Germany, he reported, had become a "madhouse" led by "pathological cases" who lied constantly and without shame. The withdrawal from the League, he guessed, was designed to gin up nationalism and hatred of the other European powers—a prelude to war.[71]

The plebiscite of November 12 posed a simple question: Did the voters approve of withdrawing from the League of Nations and the disarmament talks? The campaign that preceded the vote featured the usual Nazi methods. The press and radio were flooded with propaganda about German victimization and ill-treatment since the end of the Great War. Hitler placed the question as one of Germany's very right to exist. "I will not have this nation treated as a shoeshine boy," he howled on the stump. The creaky, decrepit President Hindenburg urged German voters to support the government's policy of "peace, honor, and equality." On Election Day, Nazi Party members and SA men walked through the streets, knocking on doors, checking lists of names, pushing voters to the polls. When the results were tallied, Hitler had won an overwhelming victory: 95 percent of the voters—some 40 million people—had given him a "yes" vote. A despairing Messersmith urged the State Department not to be fooled: The German people were "completely cowed" by Nazi intimidation. It had been a massive spectacle designed to give Hitler "blanket approval" for any action he might now wish to take.[72]

Yet there could be no doubt, for all the chicanery and pressure from the regime, that the German public approved of Hitler. He had come to power in January 1933 by a shabby backroom political deal when his party had the support of no more than a third of the voters. By the end of 1933, Hitler had transformed Germany, fused its administration with the Nazi Party itself, crushed the opposition parties, labor unions, and free press, imposed a dictatorship on the Reich, and begun a planned assault on Jews who he styled as the chief enemy of the German race. Far from seeking an escape from what Messersmith had called this "madhouse," the German people in November pledged Hitler their devotion and loyalty, as if he had truly saved them from the humiliations and torments of parliamentary democracy. American observers saw that living conditions in Germany were not improving under the Nazis. Louis Fischer, a seasoned journalist who was then based in Moscow, spent a week in Germany in April 1934 and saw that "wages are going down, the standard of living is going down, industry is deteriorating, the quality of goods grows worse . . . fear of informers is widespread." Still, thought Fischer, "the regime sits firmly and cannot yet be unseated from within." Hitler's revolution was secure. And his success in transforming Germany soon led him to encourage Nazis in his own homeland, Austria, to join the greater Reich Hitler was building.[73]

IX

Like many European states of this era, Austria had struggled to build a functioning liberal democracy in the chaotic aftermath of the Great War. The Austro-Hungarian Empire, a polyglot, multiethnic federation ruled loosely from Vienna and Budapest, disintegrated in the last days of the war, and at the postwar peace conference, the Allied powers divided the carcass up among the small successor states of central and southeastern Europe. A sliver of its former self, with a population of just six and a half million (97 percent Catholic) citizens, Austria sat squeezed between Germany, Czechoslovakia, Hungary, Yugoslavia, and its large southern neighbor, Italy. Insignificant in itself, Austria served as a sort of keystone in the arch of Central Europe: As long as it remained in place and independent, it helped hold the European system in place. But since Germany and Italy sought to exert control over the small mountainous republic, Austria became the first place where the great powers tested the durability of the post–World War I order.

Vienna attracted American and British foreign reporters like moths to a bright if unsteady flame. John Gunther, whose *Daily News* beat covered Central Europe and who would soon become an international sensation with his 1936 book, *Inside Europe*, moved to Vienna in June 1930. His neighbors and friends there included Dorothy Thompson, then writing for various newspapers and popular magazines; G. E. R. Gedye, the British leftist who reported for the *New York Times* until his sympathies with the anti-fascists became too pronounced for that paper; Marcel Fodor, the rotund, twinkling Hungarian-born correspondent for the *Manchester Guardian* and close friend and mentor of both Thompson and Gunther; William Shirer, until the *Chicago Tribune* owner Colonel Robert McCormick fired him in October 1932; and countless other visitors who wanted to get as close as possible to the story of fascism in Germany and Italy. The new Austrian Republic dazzled foreign visitors who lounged in Vienna's cafés, skied in the snowcapped mountains, and gushed about the bold experiments undertaken by the Socialist city council in public housing, free schools, elegant parks, and health care.

But under the placid exterior, Austria was being torn to shreds by the conflicting political ideologies of the day. The left and the right clashed openly and violently, much in the way German parties had done during the Weimar Republic. Adding to this unstable political mixture, Austria also had a Nazi Party, which had emerged in the early 1920s, just as Hitler was giving life to the German Nazi Party. Small and fractious, the Austrian Nazi Party had little impact on politics until Hitler's movement had its dramatic success in the 1930 elections. From then on, Austrian and German Nazis colluded on a common platform: Anschluss, or annexation of Austria by Germany. Hitler had long dreamed of merging his homeland into a greater German Reich, gathering all the German *Volk* under one flag and one leader: himself. Linking the two countries would also knock yet another pillar out from the hated postwar peace treaties that had expressly forbidden the union of the two countries. As soon as he took power in 1933, Hitler began to pressure the Austrian government, using a combination of economic blackmail, saber-rattling, and a subversive terrorist campaign of bombings and violence carried out by his Austrian Nazi proxies to humiliate the government and compel it to merge with Germany.[74]

Chancellor Engelbert Dollfuss refused to submit to German demands. Though a man of the right, a Catholic nationalist, and no friend to democracy, Dollfuss did not want to surrender Austria's sovereignty to Hitler and his fifth column of Nazis. Diminutive at four foot eleven, Dollfuss was tough, crafty, and willing to take quite drastic steps to prepare his country to fend off Nazi subversion. In the spring of 1933, he merged his political party with other conservative nationalists into a single Fatherland Front; he circumscribed the powers of the parliament; and in mid-1933, he banned the Austrian Nazi Party in response to the increasing violence it had deployed to destabilize the government. Dollfuss struck a deal with the right-wing militia, the Heimwehr, to join forces against their shared enemies: the Socialist left as well as the Nazis. John Gunther wrote of Dollfuss: "I admire the courage and tenacity of the little man; I deplore his reactionary parochialism." But perhaps that was the only way to keep the Nazis out of Austria.[75]

When in early February 1934, Austrian police claimed to have uncovered explosives and weapons hidden at various Socialist strongholds in Vienna and across the country, the leftists rose in resistance, firing on police. Alleging a plot to overthrow the government, Dollfuss gave the Heimwehr the green light to destroy the Socialist Party and its armed militia. A spectacularly violent weeklong settling of scores now opened as Heimwehr troops and police forces stormed through socialist neighborhoods, apartment blocs, and working-class quarters. Several hundred people were killed, while the leaders of the Socialist Party, along with thousands of rank-and-file socialists, were imprisoned.[76]

American journalists now rained down criticism on Dollfuss. William Shirer had lived in Vienna in the 1920s and married an Austrian woman; he had many close friends among the socialist political class, people whose politics he shared. He looked on aghast at the destruction Dollfuss had wrought. "There goes democracy in Austria," Shirer wrote in his diary, "one more state gone." Other reporters emphasized the foaming antisemitic fascism of the Heimwehr forces that had crushed the Socialists, and told of artillery firing into residential apartments, killing civilians indiscriminately. Gunther, who witnessed the ugly violence, wrote that to speak of a Socialist insurrection was "absurd." He saw "an army of 19,000, equipped with machine-guns," wipe out "a cold and ragged handful of hungry workers." Gunther insisted that "the events of February were a fascist coup d'état." Hamilton Fish Armstrong wrote directly to President Roosevelt to say, "I am afraid that Dollfuss has killed Austria," and urged FDR to speak out against this rapid consolidation of fascism in Europe.[77]

American officials in Vienna, though, took a different view. In reports back to Washington, they described the bloody events of February as a "Socialist revolt" that had been met by the Austrian government's "unusually vigorous and efficient suppression." Criticizing the media coverage of the violence, the chargé of the U.S. embassy, A. W. Kliefoth, asserted that Socialist armed resistance "necessitated artillery action and veritable assault methods. . . . The public and foreign press correspondents [are] unable to understand that the struggle was a real warfare between two armies and not merely the effort of police forces to put down an unarmed mob." Furthermore, by acting so decisively against the left, Dollfuss had boosted his prestige and could now turn against the other looming threat, the Nazi terrorists trying to destroy his government. He was "the only person in the country that has a possibility of holding back [the] Nazi wave," the embassy claimed. Far from alienating other nations with his bloody tactics, Dollfuss had emerged as a plucky figure of defiance.[78]

But his actions destroyed Austria's democracy. On May 1, 1934, he unveiled a new constitution that turned Austria into a one-party corporate state loosely modeled on Fascist Italy, putting an end to Austria's brief experiment of democratic government. Dollfuss was not a classic Fascist. He had no mass party, he wore no uniform, he did not strut in jackboots. Dollfuss aimed chiefly to impose a reactionary, colorless Catholic dictatorship that could, he wagered, effectively unify the country to fend off both the far left and the Nazis.

In Washington, Roosevelt carefully watched the Austrian crisis. One report that crossed his desk called the Austrian problem "the most dangerous question today in Europe" because Hitler's ambitions there could easily trigger a wider war. If Hitler succeeded in swallowing Austria, that would give the Führer "control of the entire Danube basin," and make the states of Czechoslovakia, Hungary, and Yugoslavia easy pickings for this new "Reich of Napoleonic grandeur," the memo argued. Roosevelt dejectedly wrote to an adviser that he hoped "the German sanity of the old type that existed in the Bismarck days when I was a boy at school in Germany will come to the front again." He wanted to avoid "the very real danger" of Hitler gaining control in Vienna.[79]

That meant lending support to Dollfuss, whose hands were now stained by the bloody attack on the Socialists and who had imposed a one-party dictatorship. In 1934, Roosevelt appointed George Messersmith, the tireless consul in Berlin, as ambassador to Austria. FDR was impressed by Messersmith's frank reports from Berlin and took real pleasure in seeing him made ambassador. Messersmith, with his good German-language skills and his long experience in dueling with the Nazi government in Berlin, was in some ways the perfect man for the delicate job. In his first meeting with Dollfuss in Vienna in mid-May 1934, Messersmith listened to the chancellor's lament that Hitler remained determined to launch a coup inside Austria. Dollfuss spoke with clarity and candor about his country's predicament. As a deeply religious nationalist who was determined to protect Austria's sovereignty, he was willing to use any available tool to strengthen his country against internal and external subversion. Messersmith warmed to this sinuous, clever politician. Although Dollfuss had smothered democracy in Austria, Messersmith considered him "a good man" of "outstanding" personal qualities who had done something extremely rare: He had fought off the far left and also defied Hitler. Messersmith and Roosevelt hoped Austria would emerge as an effective roadblock to Hitler's ambitions. They would soon be disappointed.[80]

X

At the start of 1934, Ambassador William Dodd had been in Berlin about six months, long enough to tire of the exhausting social duties of a diplomat in a European capital. Most evenings involved donning formal dress to attend elaborate dinners, occasions that Professor Dodd, with his insistence on frugality and his lack of personal wealth, felt unable to reciprocate. Scholarly and withdrawn, Dodd preferred a quiet night at home among his academic journals and books. He considered receptions "tiresome," he wrote in his diary, and bemoaned the expense of hosting such pointless charades.[81]

Averse to rubbing elbows in Berlin high society, Dodd often failed to pick up the political gossip these evenings could generate; he sometimes missed the subtle signals of who was in favor in the Nazi regime, who was feuding with whom, and where the strange, unstable government was heading. He saw Hitler rarely, in settings like a New Year's Day reception at the presidential palace, where he chatted briefly with the aging Hindenburg and the nervous, awkward Führer. But Dodd was uneasy at these official functions. After one particularly excessive reception for seven hundred guests at the Hotel Kaiserhof given by the German foreign minister that featured immense quantities of food and drink, Dodd angrily scribbled in his diary about the "useless" evening where guests merely gossiped and ogled "women's exposed backs or breasts." Dodd went home early that night, "drank a glass of milk and ate a stewed peach" before retiring to bed.[82]

Even the introverted Dodd, however, perceived the growing fissures within the Nazi regime. As early as November 1933, he described to FDR the curious trio of men at the top of the government, all with their own roles and their own sources of strength. There was Hitler, of course, the "romantic-minded" but bellicose leader whose guiding philosophy Dodd summed up briskly: "A people survives by fighting and dies through peaceful policies." Then there was the reptilian, darkly theatrical Dr. Joseph Goebbels, a "past master" at bloodcurdling oratory whose talents lay in "stirring animosities and hatred." Propaganda Minister Goebbels fired up the ideological rank and file, the true believers, the antisemites, and maniacs who served as Hitler's foot soldiers. Dodd felt Goebbels was "much more belligerent than Hitler." And the third leg of the stool was Hermann Göring, the former aviator, "intensely war-like," who appealed to the aristocrats, the Prussian army officers, as well as the conservative barons of industry. Though superficial, Dodd's analysis hit on an essential truth: Hitler's regime in its early stages remained a coalition of factions, an unstable and unpredictable mixture of rivalries and jealousies.[83]

In trying to normalize U.S. relations with the Nazi government, Dodd placed his hopes on the strata of what he considered rational officials with whom the Americans might forge an understanding. The German economy remained stagnant; well over 20 percent of the workforce was unemployed in 1934. Many basic foods were beyond the reach of ordinary Germans. The country needed foreign trade, especially imports of raw materials like cotton, copper, and oil, but had little foreign exchange with which to buy these products on the world market. Dodd observed signs of discontent with the government everywhere and felt sure that these economic woes would compel the Nazis to see reason. He believed he could work with von Neurath at the Foreign Office; the chief of the Reichsbank, Hjalmar Schacht; and Kurt Schmitt, a former insurance executive who had entered the cabinet in June 1933 as head of the Economics Ministry. Possibly, Dodd hoped, these figures could educate Hitler in the realities of international relations, in particular the dire need of Germany to forge agreements with other nations to maintain the flow of imports and exports that the economy desperately needed. Dodd told Roosevelt that a "conciliatory" attitude toward Germany would empower these technocrats and help lead Hitler in a more moderate, statesmanlike direction.[84]

But Hitler would not cooperate. On March 7, 1934, Dodd held one of his rare meetings with the chancellor, and the Führer was in a foul mood. At that very moment, twenty thousand Americans were jammed into Madison Square Garden in New York, participating in a "trial" of the Hitler government for "crimes against civilization." The mock trial, organized by Rabbi Wise and the American Jewish Congress to denounce continuing Nazi persecution of Jews, incensed the German government. Hitler had instructed his Foreign Office to lodge the strongest possible protests in Washington and demand that the Roosevelt administration intervene to halt the event. Secretary of State Hull, who privately opposed such inflammatory events, sadly explained to the German ambassador that the government could not forbid citizens from exercising their rights of free speech. The trial went forward, duly finding Nazism guilty as charged.

Dodd explained to Hitler that the mock trial had been staged without the participation of the U.S. government, but Hitler "broke in frequently with such expressions as 'Damn the Jews!'" He said it was the Jews alone who were creating a rift between America and Germany, and he insisted that "if such agitation continued in the outside world, he would make an end of all Jews in Germany." Dodd expected that protests in America, and the boycott against German goods that had harmed German exports, would bring Hitler to his senses. Instead, Hitler reacted violently to the insolence of Jews denouncing him as a menace to Western civilization when, as he thundered to Dodd, he alone had "saved Germany from Communism."[85]

Dodd returned to the United States for two months in the spring to give a few lectures, confer with officials at the State Department, and attend to affairs on his beloved farm in Loudoun County, Virginia. He desperately desired a break from his stressful work at the embassy. But news from Berlin followed him to Virginia. In early April, George Messersmith, just on his way to take up his new post in Vienna, wrote to him of the "increasingly serious situation" in Germany. Goebbels and Göring were feuding, Messersmith wrote, while the leader of the Brownshirt militia, Ernst Röhm, was fighting openly with General Werner von Fritsch, chief of the Army High Command. Röhm had made a proposal to amalgamate his storm troops into the army, which Röhm himself would then lead. The radicals, Messersmith asserted, were pushing Hitler to take bolder, faster steps to wipe out Jews, consolidate power, and undertake a "second revolution" against internal and external enemies. Messersmith painted a portrait of a government split between the radicals who wanted the Nazi regime to intensify its policies, and those who wanted to consolidate power and muzzle the extremists.

Goebbels seemed to favor the extremists, calling for more radical action against Jews. On May 12, he delivered a wildly antisemitic speech in the Berlin Sportpalast in which he blamed the Jews for Germany's economic malaise and called Jews "the syphilis of all European peoples." In his newspaper, *Der Angriff*, Goebbels urged a reckoning with "world Jewry" for the harm it was inflicting upon Germany. If Germany had been harmed by a Jewish boycott, Goebbels declared, then Jews will be the first to suffer the consequences. Sigrid Schultz in early June reported that Goebbels wanted to see mass demonstrations against "world Jewry" and was using *Der Angriff* to stir the pot of race hatred. Was this an effort to pressure Hitler to act more audaciously? To Hamilton Fish Armstrong, it seemed that Goebbels and the ideologues like

Röhm, Himmler, Streicher, and Rosenberg wanted a violent clash now, while Göring, von Papen, Schacht, von Neurath, and the functionaries wanted order, discipline, and economic stabilization. Was there a serious internal divide threatening to break the regime apart?[86]

When he got back to Berlin in late May after his leave in America, Dodd found a city on edge, rife with speculation, rumor, and anxiety. Over lunch in a quiet, discreet restaurant in the government quarter, Hans-Heinrich Dieckhoff, a senior foreign ministry official, confided to Dodd that "Hitler would be overthrown soon" because he had neither solved the country's economic problems nor carried out the extreme antisemitic cleansing of Germany that his radical followers had expected. Other officials like von Neurath and Schmitt confided their fears to Dodd. They, too, worried about the "calamitous" state of Germany's finances and about the restive radical faction of Nazis that could push Germany to war. Messersmith also felt the same sense of panic and instability. In a series of dispatches that William Phillips sent on to President Roosevelt, Messersmith argued that the constant shortages of food, imported goods, and raw materials had left business elites grumbling, and ready for a change of course. The Hitler government, he felt, "cannot continue for more than five or six months at the most."

When Vice-Chancellor Franz von Papen gave a speech at the University of Marburg on June 17 decrying the random violence and radicalism of the Brownshirts and calling for a return to order and lawful rule, many observers took it as the starting pistol for a counterrevolution by the traditional right and army, perhaps with the support of President von Hindenburg. But who would dare take such a step? Dodd thought perhaps Göring would make a bid for power, in alliance with the nationalist and conservative military leaders of the army, or Reichswehr. Unless, perhaps, Hitler struck first? Dodd recorded in his diary that "the Berlin atmosphere [is] more tense than at any time since I have been in Germany." His daughter, Martha, felt it, too. One of her lovers, Rudolf Diels, was the head of the secret state police, or Gestapo, and he had been extremely jumpy during the month of June. Martha recalled that "the atmosphere had become tense and electric. Everyone felt there was something in the air but didn't know what it was."[87]

By late June, Dodd started to get concrete reports, which he sent to Washington, that the army and the SS—the Schutzstaffel, or "protection squadron," the fanatically loyal police guard led by Reichsführer-SS Heinrich Himmler—wanted a final reckoning with Ernst Röhm. His Brownshirt militia, the Sturmabteilung, was created to engage in street warfare with the Communists in the early days of the Nazi movement, and it had grown rapidly—too rapidly in fact. By 1934 it had 3 million young zealots enrolled in its ranks. Fueled by a fanatically antisemitic, anti-capitalist, anti-Bolshevik ideology, the SA threatened to become a state within the state, independent of Hitler's control. Röhm, a short, pudgy beast with a face badly scarred by war wounds, had been a Freikorps leader and a gleeful participant in Hitler's 1923 beer hall putsch. In addition to his reputation as a fiercely loyal Nazi, Röhm was notorious for his vulgar sexual exploits among men and boys handpicked for his tastes. The Führer had primly ignored Röhm's deviance out of loyalty to his old friend.[88]

But he was becoming an embarrassment. The angry, mostly lower-class storm troops wanted to bash heads and noisily demanded more violence—against Jews, the churches, the Communists, the big industrialists, the wealthy landowners, elites of every kind. Known for their drunken sprees, for beating up passersby, for humiliating local police officers, the SA acted with impunity. Röhm's challenge to the authority of the army proved to be the last straw. When von Papen publicly rebuked the SA and the disorder they had brought to Germany, Hitler understood this as a direct challenge from conservative circles, from President Hindenburg, and from the army that the Führer must act to bring order and discipline to the country—or suffer the consequences. Hindenburg, now gravely ill, reinforced this message to Hitler directly on June 21 at his Prussian estate: Bring the Brownshirts under control, or he would impose martial law and let the army rule.

Reluctantly, Hitler chose to move against his oldest and most fervent supporters. Himmler now went into high gear, manufacturing evidence that Röhm and the SA were planning a coup d'état. Hitler met with army leaders to gain their support for a direct strike against the SA and Röhm in particular. On June 30, in the early-morning hours, the axe fell. Röhm and his key lieutenants were enjoying a vacation at a hotel in Bad Wiessee, a lakeside resort town in southern Bavaria. Hitler himself led an expedition of guards to the hotel, where the debauched SA leaders were sleeping off a night of carousing. Hitler confronted Röhm, ordered his arrest on grounds of treason, and had the lot of them sent off to the Stadelheim prison in Munich. Röhm was shot to death in his cell the next day (having refused to shoot himself) and the others swiftly met a similar fate. Hitler then raced to Berlin, where Hermann Göring had been rounding up other political enemies and rivals in a vast settling of scores. Anyone who had crossed Hitler at any time was suddenly vulnerable, and within twenty-four hours, nearly a hundred leading figures of the political world were dead, shot down in cold blood on Hitler's orders, accused of participation in a vast conspiracy against the Reich.

It was as if something had snapped, as if some tether, frayed and worn, connecting the world to law and order and decency, had finally given way. Of course, there had been plenty of arbitrary violence and murder during Hitler's rise to power; the concentration camps were already brimming with political enemies. But June 30, 1934—the "night of the long knives," as it was called ever after—marked a complete rupture with the figment of legality that Hitler had half-heartedly upheld since January 1933. Now, the Führer eagerly took credit for the wave of assassinations, bragging in the Reichstag on July 13 that "I gave the order to shoot," acting as the sole judge and executioner. Ambassador Dodd, profoundly shocked by the bloodletting and by the disappearance of the old Germany he had known of courtly aristocrats, fine universities, and genteel manners, considered resigning his post. "The situation here is the heaviest nervous strain imaginable," he wrote to Walton Moore at the State Department. Many people he knew and respected had been murdered, including the former chancellor General Kurt von Schleicher and his wife, who were ruthlessly gunned down in their own home by an SS squad. "Hitler-Goering-Goebbels are half-crazy," Dodd lamented. He decided he would never again meet with Hitler. "He is such a horror to me," he told the British ambassador Sir Eric Phipps. "I cannot endure his presence."[89]

XI

The bad news kept coming, landing like repeated blows on an already painful bruise. Just three weeks after the slaughter in Germany, a shocking twist to the Austrian drama shook Europe to its core: On July 25, some 150 Austrian Nazis, disguised in army uniforms, stormed the Vienna offices of Chancellor Dollfuss during a cabinet meeting in what turned out to be a botched coup attempt. Two men rushed up the central stairs of the chancellery, clearly looking for the chancellor, and found him in his study, where they fired two shots at him, one striking his armpit and the other his neck. He fell to the floor, his life slowly ebbing. The radio station, briefly seized by the Nazi insurgents, announced that Dollfuss had resigned and his place would be taken by a minister sympathetic to the Nazi cause. Almost immediately, the coup went awry. Most of the cabinet had managed to escape before being rounded up, and they announced their determination to carry on as the legitimate government. Kurt Schuschnigg, the minister of justice, was immediately appointed acting chancellor and defied the plotters. Austrian police surrounded the building, and within five hours the Nazi plot fizzled. A few days of violence flared up across the country as police forces clashed with Nazi foot soldiers, but the ringleaders were arrested, tried, and either jailed or hanged.

John Gunther saw the carnage up close. Just about to head out for an afternoon swim, he got a call from a tipster that a coup was underway. He raced to the chancellery, but at first nothing seemed out of the ordinary; the place was locked and an armed guard stood at the large oak doors. He did not yet know the plotters had locked themselves in. Soon enough, as armed police surrounded the building and sent in a series of ultimatums, he grasped the larger picture. The standoff came to an end with promises to the plotters that they could have free passage to the German border. But once the word came that Dollfuss had been murdered, the deal was off: The plotters were instead arrested and hauled off to prison. Gunther rushed into the building and got a look at the corpse of the fallen chancellor: "The body was completely shriveled like a raisin and was clammy and blue. The face was uncovered and wore an expression of extremest agony. . . . There was a terrible wound in the throat." And on the floor beneath the sofa where the dying man had been laid, "a lake of blood."

Despite the murder of Dollfuss, the Nazi coup attempt failed because the intended head of the new government got cold feet and disavowed the coup, and also because in Rome, word of the putsch launched Mussolini into action. He had warned Hitler to leave Austria alone; the little state, in its Fascist guise, had become something of an Italian satellite and Mussolini had ambitions to exert influence across southern and southeastern Europe. He rushed troops to the Austrian border in a show of force, an action that certainly deterred Hitler, especially once the Führer saw that the coup attempt had come apart. The Austrian Legion, forty thousand strong, made up of pro-Nazi Austrians who had been armed and sheltered inside Germany, did not march on Vienna. Gunther believed that the failure of the coup, and the death of Dollfuss, might reinforce peace in Europe. It united Austrians against the Nazis; it left in place a Dollfuss cabinet albeit without its martyred leader; and it brought Mussolini into the role of guarantor of the status quo. "The death of Dollfuss is a heavy price to pay for temporary security," Gunther reckoned. "But he died to keep anarchy out of central Europe." Hopeful words.[90]

If the thwarting of a Nazi coup in Vienna briefly raised hopes, news from Berlin dashed cold water on them. On August 2, 1934, at about 9 a.m., President von Hindenburg finally died after a long illness. Within the hour, in a carefully prepared move, Hitler merged the offices of Reich president and chancellor, making himself head of state, head of government, and commander in chief of the armed forces. In a stroke, he consolidated in his own person all the executive power of the regime. On the same day, the entire armed forces were ordered to swear an oath of "unconditional obedience" to the person of Adolf Hitler. What a month it had been! The Führer, with the army now fully behind him, had eradicated the threat of the powerful Sturmabteilung; four weeks later, he defanged the aristocratic and conservative faction in German politics, subsuming the powers of the presidency and by extension, the powers of the old monarchy for which the president had been a weak substitute. By the end of this tragic European summer of 1934, Adolf Hitler stood as the uncontested, all-powerful leader of a totalitarian dictatorship.

Certainly, Ambassador Dodd drew the gloomiest possible conclusions. In a sad letter to Secretary of State Hull, he said that Hitler no longer had any rivals to worry about, and the world would now face "an even more terroristic regime than we have endured" since Hitler's arrival in power. He was even darker in a personal letter to his friend, Daniel Roper, the secretary of commerce. Dodd had taken at face value the many statements by Nazi officials that they would moderate their course eventually and work toward peace. Instead, Hitler's regime had intensified its attacks on Jews, imprisoned countless enemies, murdered hundreds of rivals on June 30, and engineered a coup attempt in Vienna. Germany had descended into "medievalism." And to President Roosevelt, Dodd sent the alarming assessment that Germany was preparing for war and had more soldiers trained and armed than in 1914, when the last cataclysmic war began. "War, not peace, is the objective," he now believed.

To this, FDR replied that he, too, saw trouble ahead. "Your situation cannot exactly be called a rosy one," he wrote to Dodd in a weak attempt at gaiety. "It confirms my fear that the drift in Germany, and perhaps in other countries in Europe, is definitely downward and that something must break within the next six months or a year." But he continued, in an epistolary shrug, "I too am downhearted, but I watch for any ray of hope or opening to give me an opportunity to lend a helping hand. There is nothing in sight at present." So far, Nazism remained an internal matter for Germany, and since Austria had been saved, there had been no essential rupture of the European order. A fragile peace had held, and Roosevelt would accept that.[91]

But something *had* changed after June 30, and a vivid example of how the new dictatorship would treat unflattering news stories came soon enough. In early August, Dorothy Thompson arrived back in Germany, having set out from Vienna to report on the aftermath of the "night of the long knives." Driving across the border into Germany, she recalled, she was struck by the innumerable flags hanging from every window she passed, a banner of bright red with a white circle pierced by a black, menacing swastika. Upon her arrival, a friend told her the place had changed: "These people are crazy. They think Hitler is God." Her usual haunt, the Adlon Hotel, seemed unchanged, however. There was the familiar bartender making dry martinis; there was the doorman, quick with a warm welcome and addressing her by name; here came the manager, offering to install her in her usual room. "The French doors were open into the garden," she recalled, "and the fountain was sparkling, and the little lawn was smooth as the finest broadloom. . . . All the courtesy, all the cleanliness, all the exquisite order which is Germany."[92]

Three weeks after her arrival, however, a young man in a trench coat of the sort Hitler often wore appeared at her door with a formal letter asking her to leave the country. He was from the Gestapo. They gave her twenty-four hours to depart, and if she defied this request, she would be deported by force. The reason, allegedly, was her pointed, mocking remarks in the 1932 essay "I Saw Hitler." She obeyed, politely taking her leave. But the expulsion brought enormous attention to Thompson herself, turning her into something of a heroine, a woman so feisty and fearless that the Nazis simply could not abide her presence. Every major U.S. paper, and many European ones as well, splashed the news of her expulsion on their front pages. "Nearly the entire corps of American and British correspondents went to the railway station to see her off," Frederick Birchall reported. And as she boarded the train for Paris, she delivered a parting shot. Germans could do what they liked inside their country, she asserted, but Nazism was "a world outlook which is frankly directed against the liberal and democratic conceptions under which a great part of the world still lives." If the Germans attack such principles, they must expect "a robust and energetic opposition." For the rest of her career, Thompson would unceasingly fight against Nazism.[93]

As soon as she got to Paris, she rushed out her own account of the expulsion, saying that her real crime was "blasphemy": She had treated Hitler not as a god but an "ordinary man." She also predicted a "campaign of terrorism against foreign correspondents," and described Germany as "the most comfortable and most hygienic prison in the world." She depicted Germany as a place where law was improvised, changing every day on the whim of the dictator. "Force and the arbitrary and unchallengeable decisions of a small oligarchy" now ruled: "What was legal today may be established as illegal tomorrow." As for silencing journalists, it would never work: Others "will rise to shout the forbidden truths." Thompson sailed for home in mid-September, finding upon her arrival in New York that she had become a celebrity. She used her platform to denounce the Nazis. "Germany has gone to war already," she told one audience in October, "and the rest of the world does not believe it."[94]

In truth, Ambassador Dodd believed it, and from mid-1934 on, that is exactly what he tried to impress upon President Roosevelt, Cordell Hull, Walton Moore, and anyone else who would listen. The murders of June 30 left the people "terrorized," he wrote to Hull. There seemed "no alternative to Hitler now." By the end of August, he felt "the general tendency is toward war on a grand scale." Across Germany, there is "feverish arming and drilling of 1.5 million men." Whatever the Nazi leaders might say in public, "a vast war is the one objective." The only way to counter this trend was a policy of engagement with the world: "to abandon our so-called isolation," join the League of Nations, and work with Britain, France, and Russia to check Germany and Japan. Dodd counseled a total reversal of American foreign policy to counter the threat of fascism.[95]

Though presumptuous, Dodd's message was prophetic. "Hitler is here to stay," he wrote to Moore in October. "Rome, Berlin, Warsaw, and Moscow are all centers of arbitrary and ruthless social and political control." Germany was arming to the teeth, for "war is the German purpose," he declared, underlining his words for emphasis. In November, he recounted a trip he made with his son to Wittenberg, Leipzig, Nuremberg, Stuttgart, and Erfurt. "In almost every city or town, there was marching, either of the *Hitler Jungend* or of SS and SA men in uniform." Whereas a year ago, the factories were idle, now "every smokestack showed great activity . . . there is great preparation for war." Young lads marched by his hotel in Hechingen singing a once-forbidden war song, *"Siegreich wollen wir Frankreich schlagen"* (Victoriously We Will Conquer France). Moore passed this letter on to the president, with a covering note drawing attention to Dodd's "rather dark picture of what is going on in Germany."[96]

Roosevelt saw Dodd's correspondence. He read of Thompson's travails, he bemoaned the sad fate of Dollfuss in Austria, and he looked on anxiously as Fascists tried to forge mass parties in France and Britain. After this awful year, he grasped the nature of the threat Hitler posed, as he revealed in a somewhat indiscreet "off the record" press conference in September. After a lunch with the French foreign minister Pierre-Étienne Flandin, he told journalists gathered in his tiny study at Hyde Park that German rearmament was moving ahead so rapidly that they were going to exhaust their domestic resources quite quickly. Even "synthetic rubber and gasoline" would not meet their needs. To find more raw materials, "leaders over there . . . will start to march on something, to walk across the border." The French were convinced, he went on, that Germany was hiding a giant rearmament program, churning out artillery and airplanes at a staggering clip, training schoolchildren to use gas masks, and building bomb shelters. "If I were a Frenchman, I would be scared too," the president chuckled.[97]

This offhand remark suggests that Roosevelt now perceived the innately expansionist character of the Nazi regime. And while he remained unwilling to confront Germany directly, he could at least start to build ties to Germany's enemies as a hedge against the future.

CHAPTER 6

ROMANCING THE REDS

"Nothing is impossible in the Soviet Union."

—LOUIS FISCHER

I

It was winter, December 20, 1933, and William C. Bullitt stood on the threshold of history. The new American ambassador would that night be the guest of honor of the leaders of the Soviet Union, dining in splendor at the Kremlin apartment of the small, dapper Kliment Voroshilov, the people's commissar for military and naval affairs. To his Soviet hosts, the arrival of Bullitt meant that the United States had finally ended fifteen years of frosty disdain for the revolutionary Bolshevik regime and agreed officially to recognize the government. It was the start, they all hoped, of a new relationship between the United States and the USSR, two nations bound together, if not by shared values, then at least by the threat of common enemies.

Bullitt had only arrived in Moscow nine days earlier and had been much caressed by Soviet officials. They knew Bullitt's story well: As a mere twenty-eight-year-old, then a member of the American delegation to the Paris Peace Conference following World War I, he had been sent by President Wilson on a secret mission to Moscow in March 1919. The British, French, and American governments despised the Bolsheviks, who had toppled the Romanov dynasty, murdered Czar Nicholas II and his family, taken Russia out of the war, and surrendered huge swaths of territory to the Germans. Still worse, this bloodthirsty regime openly sought to export class warfare across Europe. To punish the revolutionaries, the Western allies blockaded Russia and sent soldiers to Arkhangelsk and Vladivostok in a menacing gesture. A larger conflict beckoned.

But intervening in Russia remained a half-hearted effort of war-weary leaders who were trying to impose order on Europe, not inflame the continent further. Wilson sent Bullitt to sound out the Bolshevik leader, V. I. Lenin, on whether he would be willing to negotiate an end to hostilities on terms acceptable to the Western powers. Reaching Moscow after an arduous journey through Sweden and Finland, Bullitt found Lenin eager for a respite in light of the brutal civil war and famine then ravaging Russia. Bullitt and Lenin drafted a deal for what would amount to a pause in hostilities; Bullitt enthusiastically rushed back to Paris, expecting Wilson's gratitude. Instead, he got the cold shoulder. Word of his mission had leaked. The conservative press in London and Paris denounced any parley with the murderous and treacherous Bolsheviks. The British and French governments, deeply hostile to the revolutionaries, were unmoved by the truce Bullitt had secured. Wilson, now focused on securing European support for his League of Nations, disavowed the mission and the deal slipped away, to Bullitt's lifelong disappointment.

His first assignment to Russia had failed. Yet here he was in 1933 with a rare second chance to broker a new era in Russian-American friendship. He presented his credentials to the nominal head of state, President Mikhail Kalinin, on December 13, and received not only a warm welcome but fulsome praise for Franklin Roosevelt and the New Deal. Kalinin conveyed to Bullitt his belief that President Roosevelt "really cared about the welfare of the laboring men and the farmers" and he applauded the president's scorn for America's oligarchs. On December 15, the people's commissar for foreign affairs, Maxim Litvinov, gave the ambassador a formal welcome dinner. This chubby Lithuanian Jew wore a wire pince-nez and black tie that made him look more like an English country doctor than a revolutionary; Litvinov had in fact spent many years in Britain, had an English wife, and spoke English well. Bullitt, a Yale-educated, cocksure egotist with a bald head and feline eyes, gleefully reported to FDR that Litvinov's banquet featured "food and wines of a quality that no one in

Ambitious, brilliant, and devious, William C. Bullitt became FDR's indispensable envoy to Russia and France.
Library of Congress

America would dare to serve nowadays, and many toasts were drunk to you and to me and to the United States." It seemed a promising beginning.

But in a week filled with waist-expanding luncheons and dinners, the Voroshilov gala stood out, as Bullitt explained in a long and detailed letter to FDR. Bullitt had clearly taken to the handsome, compact Voroshilov, who was "one of the most charming persons I have ever met," a man who kept himself in enviable physical condition and radiated good humor and liveliness. In fact, Bullitt in his first days in Moscow got rather carried away, declaring that all the Soviet leaders "are really intelligent, sophisticated, vigorous human beings." He was falling for them, and no wonder. At Voroshilov's apartment, a military honor guard welcomed Bullitt to this conclave of party and government heavyweights. "This is the whole gang that really runs things," Litvinov whispered to Bullitt as they surveyed the room, "the inside directorate."

And there among them was the top man, the *vozhd*, the leader, Joseph Stalin. Bullitt reported to FDR that he was at first taken aback: Rather than a hulking man of steel, Stalin appeared rather short, "dressed in a common soldier's uniform with boots, black trousers and a gray-green coat without any decorations of any kind." His eyes were "curious, giving the impression of a dark brown filmed with dark blue. They are small, intensely shrewd, and continuously smiling." His thick mustache obscured his mouth, but when he laughed, Bullitt wrote, "his lips curl in a curiously canine manner." The pockmarked and swarthy Georgian cupped a curved pipe that he never put down even at dinner. Bullitt had trouble getting a read on Stalin, who looked like "a wiry Gypsy with roots and emotions beyond my experience."

The evening began with a sequence of appetizers "of every conceivable kind of caviar and crab and other Russian delicacies." Stalin, now warming to the task of welcoming the American envoy, proposed a toast to President Roosevelt, and all the guests rose from their places to knock back a tumbler of vodka. More toasts followed, perhaps as many as fifty, each requiring Bullitt to drain his glass. After some time, "the table got into the mood of a college fraternity banquet," Bullitt recalled. A breathy Litvinov, seated at Bullitt's right, leaned in to say that the ambassador had been accepted as one of the "inner gang," and the table talked loudly about geopolitics. Stalin asked Bullitt if the United States could send steel railroad tracks to help the Soviets prepare their defenses against Germany and Japan, those worrisome enemies that had begun to growl at Russia's doorstep. After consuming this tremendous feast, the party staggered into an adjoining room and gathered around a piano for a riotous chorus of folk songs, with Stalin, wreathed in smiles, presiding.

At last, Bullitt and Stalin sat together privately for some time. Stalin was feeling "extremely gay, as we all were," and the *vozhd* now gushed about Roosevelt, America, and the new friendship between their countries, which, he hoped, "would cooperate with the greatest intimacy." When Bullitt, sensing an opportunity, asked Stalin to approve his request for a fourteen-acre parcel of land in a park overlooking the Moskva River on which to build a new embassy, Stalin replied simply, "you shall have it." Bullitt extended his hand to shake on it, but Stalin took his smooth bald head in his hands "and gave me a large kiss! I swallowed my astonishment and, when he turned up his face for a return kiss, I delivered it." The new era had begun.[1]

Why did FDR decide to open relations with the Soviet Union in 1933, just at the moment when the Soviet experiment was entering its darkest period? Roosevelt received significant public criticism for reaching out to the "godless" Communists, and most of the senior State Department staff opposed the overture to the Russians. Stalin was a supremely powerful autocrat, and Americans had been instructed for two decades that Communism was inherently evil and a danger to their values. Yet FDR went ahead, nonetheless. Part of the explanation lies in misinformation: Like many Americans, Roosevelt was led to believe by sympathetic journalists that the Soviet Union was a dynamic, progressive force in the world, entering an exciting period of economic growth after the upheavals of the revolution and civil war. Its officials seemed hungry to make contact with the outside world, and the Soviet commitment to science, engineering, mass production, and state planning might hold interesting lessons for Western capitalist states. FDR's new agriculture secretary, Henry Wallace, wanted to know about the great collectivization programs just getting underway. Russia already showed promise as a valuable trading partner.

Yet in addition to these economic considerations, there lay a less explicit motive, perhaps stowed away in the back of Roosevelt's mind: The Soviet Union in the fateful year of 1933 was the chief bulwark against Nazism, and was also locked in a frosty standoff with Japan over the fate of northeastern China. "Two great nations like America and Russia," FDR said to Cordell Hull, "should be on speaking terms." A relationship with the mysterious denizens of the Kremlin might be useful one day.[2]

II

Roosevelt in recognizing the USSR engineered a major reversal of American foreign policy. From its earliest days, Bolshevism terrified Americans. The term referred to the Bolshevik faction of the Russian Social Democratic

Labor Party, a group led by Lenin that had seized control of the Russian government in November 1917. In the fraught years immediately following the Bolshevik seizure of power, Americans of every stripe—politicians and jurists, bankers and industrialists, newspaper editors and essayists, soldiers and spiritual leaders—denounced Bolshevism in lurid terms. To them, the term was synonymous with anarchy, regicide, atrocity, atheism, and the oppression of human liberty. In the words of a well-known essayist of the era, Agnes Repplier, Bolsheviks were "men who rob treasuries, repudiate debts and murder opponents"; they "spit at religion and despoil marriage." The last American ambassador to Russia, David R. Francis (a former governor of Missouri), who witnessed the chaotic days of the revolution, described Bolshevism as a "monstrosity" and a "world-wide danger." Lenin, he asserted, "was a German agent from the beginning," doing the work of the kaiser by knocking Russia out of the war. According to Francis, the Bolshevik leaders were "inhuman brutes" who had imposed "a tyranny worse than absolute monarchy."[3]

Certainly a few American observers of the revolution, like the irrepressible ideologue John Reed and the muckraking journalist Lincoln Steffens (who had accompanied Bullitt on his abortive 1919 trip to Russia), wrote with breathless enthusiasm of the triumph of the Bolsheviks over czarist tyranny. Reed, an eager young Socialist who wrote for *The Masses* magazine, traveled to Russia during World War I and covered the revolution not only as a journalist but as an active participant, serving briefly as a translator in the revolutionary government. His 1919 account, *Ten Days that Shook the World*, painted a heroic portrait of the revolution and its leaders. Steffens, equally taken by the ideals of the Bolsheviks, uttered a memorable epigram after his Russian adventure: "I have seen the future, and it works." Progressive intellectuals echoed this kind of enthusiasm in the pages of Herbert Croly's *New Republic* and Oswald Garrison Villard's *The Nation*.[4]

Yet Bolshevism prompted more fear than admiration in America because it looked as if this foreign ideology might well take root at home. These were years of ferment: During the Great War, an openly revolutionary labor union, the Industrial Workers of the World (IWW), grew to 150,000 members, and its call for radical workplace democracy caught on across the country. In the fall of 1919, hundreds of thousands of Americans—steelworkers, coal miners, and even the Boston Police Department—went on strike in search of better working conditions and higher pay. The leader of the Socialist Party of America, Eugene V. Debs, had been arrested in 1918 for speaking out against the war; while sitting in a federal penitentiary, he won nearly a million votes in the 1920 presidential election.

Adding to the palpable sense of dread, anarchists launched a campaign of letter bombs, slipping explosives into unmarked packages destined for the homes of leading politicians and officials, including Woodrow Wilson's attorney general, A. Mitchell Palmer. On June 2, 1919, an anarchist named Carlo Valdinoci delivered a lethal package to Palmer's front door on R Street in Washington, D.C., but inadvertently blew himself up. Some of his remains landed in the front garden of Palmer's neighbor, the assistant secretary of the navy, Franklin D. Roosevelt. The next morning Roosevelt's young son James gleefully brought a pink chunk of collarbone to the breakfast table. The threat posed by radicalism was real enough, even to those far from Moscow and St. Petersburg.[5]

Using the powers granted to it by the Espionage Act of 1917 and the Sedition Act of 1918—wartime measures passed to suppress dissent and left-wing agitation—the Justice Department arrested, jailed, and deported thousands of suspected Communists and anarchists, with little regard for the rules of due process. Although these "Palmer raids" of 1920 were criticized as unlawful, public opinion welcomed the harsh measures. Many shared the sentiments of the commander of American forces in Europe during the war, General John J. "Blackjack" Pershing: "America for Americans, until there is not a single half-breed, draft-dodging, IWW or bomb-throwing Bolshevik left in this country."[6]

American attitudes toward Russia evolved in the years after the revolution, moving from undisguised hostility to grudging acceptance and even, in some circles, genuine admiration. This shift followed a tactical retreat initiated by Lenin in early 1921 when he launched his New Economic Policy (NEP). Facing the total collapse of the Russian economy after seven years of uninterrupted war and social dislocation, Lenin announced that the wholesale nationalization of the economy would be scaled back somewhat to allow for small businesses, traders, shopkeepers, and farmers to produce and sell goods in a free market. Releasing the economy from smothering state control, Lenin's NEP spurred a significant increase in industrial and agricultural output, and by 1928 Russia had just about returned to its 1914 level of activity. Along with monetary reforms like the creation of an autonomous central bank, a new currency, and a new tax system, Russia slowly stabilized.

American business saw opportunities in the Union of Soviet Socialist Republics, as it was named in 1922. Entrepreneurs like Armand Hammer and the investment banker Averell Harriman worked out mining deals in the resource-rich country. The Soviet government gave out contracts to Sinclair Oil and Standard Oil in hopes of restoring oil production and earning valuable foreign exchange. In 1928, General Electric signed a six-year contract for sales of up to $26 million of technology to help Russia build a power grid. The Ford Motor Company had been selling cars in Russia since 1909; in 1929, Ford signed a deal to build a new plant in Nizhny Novgorod, along the Volga River, in exchange for Soviet purchases of millions of dollars of Ford parts. And American exporters found a large and needy market in Russia, sending cotton, tractors, railway locomotives, heavy industrial machinery as well as engineers and experts to the USSR. By 1930, U.S.-Soviet trade reached an annual value of $100 million, twice that of 1914.

Yet still the U.S. government refused to offer diplomatic recognition of the government, pointing to the explicit Soviet intention "to bring about the overthrow of the existing political, economic and social order throughout the world." Private American companies were undeterred, and the State Department counted two thousand American engineers and technical workers from forty-four companies at work in the Soviet Union at the end of 1930. U.S. politicians started making inspection trips and returned full of enthusiasm. "I never saw such optimism," Senator Alben Barkley of Kentucky said of what he had seen in Russia. Others agreed: There was money to be made in Russia at a time when Americans were out of work. "We're just a bunch of suckers if we do not recognize them," argued Senator Burton K. Wheeler of Montana.[7]

These encouraging indexes of growing commercial ties between the U.S. and USSR, which appeared regularly in the newspapers, told only one side of the story. In fact, Americans had little knowledge or understanding of what was transpiring inside the Kremlin. There, a power struggle had been unfolding since in 1924, when Lenin, the beloved helmsman of the revolution, died of a brain hemorrhage. Joseph Stalin, from his powerful position as general secretary of the Communist Party, proved the cleverest schemer, gradually outmaneuvering his chief rival and ideological antagonist Leon Trotsky, and then pushing aside his onetime allies and friends Grigory Zinoviev and Lev Kamenev. Deftly using a combination of ideological arguments, tactical alliances, as well as outright treachery, Stalin by 1928 had solidified his position as the unquestioned leader of the party and the state.

He then decided upon a drastic change in course, breaking away from the slow and cautious NEP in favor of a dramatically accelerated program of industrialization. Stalin argued in the Politburo that it was taking too long to build Soviet socialism. The economy was stagnating, the harvests were inadequate, and the capitalist nations might see Soviet weakness as an invitation to mount a counteroffensive. Only by transforming the Soviet Union into a powerhouse of heavy industry, capable of producing not just steel and tractors, but tanks and artillery, could the leadership ensure the survival and success of the Bolshevik experiment. By building "socialism in one country," and postponing the bid for world revolution, the Soviets could construct a glittering example of socialist progress while also arming themselves for future struggles against the inevitable capitalist reaction.

In October 1928, the USSR launched a Five-Year Plan that set out wildly ambitious—indeed, fantastical—objectives for the acceleration of industrial production. This plan received enormous attention from the Western press and buttressed the argument of those who found the Soviet political experiment admirable. A young Texan named Hubert R. Knickerbocker, who had worked for William Randolph Hearst's International News Service before emerging as the Berlin and Moscow correspondent for the *New York Evening Post*, wrote a detailed series of articles on the Five-Year Plan that started out with the portentous statement "The Soviet Union is a land at war." This war for industrialization, Knickerbocker reported, "holds Russia in a feverish grip." The workers toiled under martial law and Knickerbocker described them as "ill-fed, ill-clothed, ill-housed, and partly terrorized." Knickerbocker was one of the few Westerners who honestly reported the terror apparatus deployed by the state to extract labor from a cowed, brutalized workforce. The Soviets sought nothing less than to overtake and defeat the capitalist nations at their own game. Knickerbocker's series won the 1931 Pulitzer Prize and formed the basis of a widely acclaimed study of Soviet economics that appeared in 1931.[8]

The colossal plan to expand Soviet heavy industry required money: more precisely, foreign currency with which to purchase machinery and technology from abroad, which the Russians as yet could not produce themselves. How could the Bolsheviks secure enough hard currency to buy the basic tools needed for this giant leap forward? Exports of grain could solve the problem, but the 1928 harvest had been disappointing, and the peasants had begun to resist selling their grain to the state at low fixed prices. Furthermore, world markets were awash in wheat, and prices had markedly slumped to historic lows. To earn enough foreign exchange by exporting wheat to pay for the import of industrial products, the Soviet Union would have to sell a great deal of grain.

To wring increased grain production from the land now became the prerequisite for fulfilling the Five-Year Plan, and Stalin moved ruthlessly to impose upon the country's 120 million peasants a revolution in their modes of production. In the immense grain-producing regions of Ukraine, the North Caucasus, the Volga basin, and Kazakhstan, Stalin envisioned the peasants being force-marched from their small plots, which they had plowed for generations by hand or with oxen and horses, into vast collective farms, where tools, tractors, livestock, and seed would be pooled and shared, triggering what he believed would be a surge in agricultural output. At last, the peasants—people the Bolshevik elites tended to scorn as backward, illiterate, conservative, hidebound peons—would be lashed to the great engine of Soviet socialism.

In the phrase of historian Robert Tucker, the Five-Year Plan signaled the start of Stalin's "revolution from above"—a total reconfiguration of economic and agricultural life in the Soviet Union, designed both to hasten industrialization but also to transform the state into an instrument of his own will. If Lenin's revolution had energized the masses and shaken off the czarist yoke, Stalin's would forge a new socialist great power under his iron rule. Stalin understood that this transformation would meet with opposition. Indeed, he relished the prospect of full-scale war on the petite bourgeoisie, the little capitalists of the NEP, and especially the fat country squires (*kulaks*) who he had been told presided over the Soviet grain supply. In words that served as a death sentence for millions, Stalin thundered in December 1929 that the state had "developed an offensive along the whole front against the capitalist elements in the countryside." His goal, he said, was nothing less than "eliminating the *kulaks* as a class." Quite clearly, Stalin intended to conduct a mass terror campaign on the peasants.

And he did. Landowning peasants who objected to collectivization were deported to labor camps, their livestock seized, and their acres turned over to local collectives. And not just the *kulaks*, or better-off farmers, suffered. Poor peasants who expressed the slightest resistance to collectivization and the seizure of their crops and animals could be arrested or shot; tens of thousands were executed at the start of the collectivization period. The result of this "war," quite predictably, was widespread disruption of agricultural production. But when yields fell and harvests dwindled, Stalin merely blamed "wreckers" and recalcitrant peasants, and insisted on even harsher measures to seize grain he imagined they were hoarding. He sent his most powerful lieutenants into the rural areas to oversee the ransacking of grain stores, the expropriation of property, and the deportation of millions of uncooperative and bewildered peasants to the gulag. They left unspeakable horror in their wake.

With grain requisitioned to feed the urban industrial workers or for export, food shortages soon mounted into a full-scale famine. Over the course of the Five-Year Plan (1928–32), 2 million peasants were deported to labor camps, and hundreds of thousands more died during forced population transfers. Stalin, determined to break Ukrainian nationalism while also seizing the grain supply, waged a vast murderous war in Ukraine that intentionally starved at least 4 million people to death there. Another 2 million people in North Caucasus and Kazakhstan died of hunger. At the very moment that Stalin kissed Ambassador Bullitt's bald head in late 1933, the emaciated corpses of millions of peasants were still lying unburied across the most fertile grain-producing regions of the Soviet state.[9]

III

As Roosevelt considered opening ties to the USSR, though, the human costs of the Five-Year Plan were hidden from public view by a counternarrative of Soviet progress. Russia's industrial and agrarian transformation received extensive press coverage in U.S. newspapers, and Western journalists competed for access to what they invariably called Russia's second revolution. Although their work was scrutinized by the Soviet press office, and the conditions of life in Moscow were often hard—even those with dollars to spend faced shortages of food, poor housing conditions, and constant government surveillance—reporters thrilled at the chance to write about the vast socialist experiment. Some of these observers brought with them a deep ideological sympathy toward the Soviet project, while others simply wanted a good story. Because of the absence of any U.S. government presence in the USSR, the handful of American journalists who were allowed to work in Moscow became the sole conduit of news to a public eager to learn about Russia's industrial awakening.

No one worked the story more successfully than Walter Duranty, the *New York Times*'s man in Moscow. An Englishman of middle-class background who had made good by getting scholarships to Harrow and Cambridge, Duranty had drifted to France just before World War I. Because of his language ability, he got work doing odd jobs at the *Times*'s office in Paris; late in the war, he finally got the chance to do his own reporting from the front. His powerful style, vivid description, and storytelling ability made his writing stand out, and the *Times* assigned him to cover the Paris Peace Conference and the postwar political upheaval in Germany.

A short, balding, talkative cynic, Duranty was brilliant, ambitious, and unscrupulous. From the Baltic states, before Western journalists could enter Russia, he wrote about the Bolshevik revolution in distinctly unflattering tones, describing it as "a compound of force, terror, and espionage, utterly ruthless in conception and execution." But in hopes of gaining an entry visa to Russia, he started to change his tune, penning a handsome tribute to Lenin and the NEP in 1921. The ploy worked, and Soviet authorities granted him a coveted pass to the great Russian drama. For the next twelve years, Duranty filed a steady stream of reporting on Soviet politics and became the principal source of information about Russia to the Western world—and a valued ally of the Kremlin.[10]

Duranty settled into the good life of a foreign correspondent, hiring a cook and manservant, renting a large apartment and lavishly entertaining fellow journalists and friends. He became the most well-connected foreigner in Moscow. In 1924, he lost part of his left leg in a freak train derailment in France, but the limp he acquired only added to his quirky renown; the Soviet government soon furnished him with a car with which to move around the capital. Duranty played a clever game in his journalism. Knowing of his newspaper's distinctly hostile outlook—the *Times* ran numerous skeptical editorials about the Soviet Union in this period—Duranty regularly reported on problems and disappointments that beset the government: lags in production, food shortages, the dirt of the capital, the internecine power struggles in the Kremlin, and so on. At the same time, in order to curry favor with his Soviet hosts, who had made his life in Moscow so comfortable, he always insisted such difficulties paled against the brilliant future the Communists were building. In fact, Duranty often included the statistics and storylines provided to him by his government handlers to demonstrate Russia's unstoppable progress. He was no ideologue, just a self-centered and influential opportunist.

To his large American readership, Duranty pitched the Five-Year Plan as the greatest news story of modern time. In the summer of 1929, he described the opening of new factories in Moscow, Leningrad, and Nizhny Novgorod and the joy among workers due to higher wages, "new schools, houses, clubs, sports organizations, and movie theaters." Yes, he acknowledged, there was a food shortage, but that would soon be solved by the collective farms, which "have made a good start and seem to be efficiently managed." He uncritically passed on Soviet reports of their own prodigious industrial growth, noting an unlikely 24 percent increase from October 1928 to August 1929 alone. He praised Stalin for "gathering the reins of power firmly" in his hands: "Under the lash of his will," the Five-Year Plan "will be accomplished." Duranty likened Stalin both to the French revolutionary Danton, known for his belief in audacity, and to Jesus Christ, who had said that faith "can move mountains." With coverage like this, it is little wonder he became the Politburo's favorite foreign reporter.[11]

Duranty wrote in the heroic register the Soviets themselves often used in describing their staggering achievements. Hailing Stalin's "genius," he praised the "vigorous drive of socialism in the villages" as the "outstanding feature of the economic year just ended." The Five-Year Plan had "captured the popular imagination," Duranty claimed; "no country in the world ever made so swift a forward jump as Russia plans this year." As for the food shortages that hit every major city during the war on the peasantry, Duranty argued that "birth pangs are ever painful" and the road to this new utopia would be hard. There would of course be "setbacks and difficulties," but "the socialization movement in agriculture is making tremendous headway." Collectivization was "the greatest revolution in world history," he wrote, predicting that "if the Kremlin keeps its nerve," it could win the war against the recalcitrant peasants. He praised the unsentimental attitude of the Soviet leaders: "If it is war, class war or civil war or any other war—it is no good weeping over innocent victims."[12]

Reporting on Stalin's speech to the 16th Congress of the Communist Party in June 1930, Duranty noted that "the Red lord of the Kremlin made full use of the contrast between the growing unemployment and falling production in capitalistic states and the upward drive of the Soviet Union." Duranty again passed along Stalin's own statement that "the grain problem has already been solved" and that "the assault on capitalist elements in the country" had proceeded mercilessly. By the fall of 1930, as chaos, murder, and deportations in the countryside had started the rural areas on the path to full-scale famine, Duranty asserted that "the food situation looks much brighter, and the success of the Kremlin's agrarian policy" had boosted the Kremlin's confidence. All of this was untrue, of course. Famine stalked the countryside, and collectivization impeded agricultural growth for decades. Not until the 1950s did the USSR output reach the level of 1917.[13]

At the end of November 1930, Duranty scored an interview with Stalin himself. He turned the meeting into three lengthy articles about this "outstanding world figure," and no historical or literary reference was beyond Duranty's reach as he likened the "man of steel" to Napoleon, Agamemnon, Clemenceau, and Dr. Frankenstein. As Stalin expounded on the inevitable implosion of capitalism, Duranty found that "he showed no sign of doubt, weakness or uncertainty." Stalin was a man of discipline, a leader who had "tamed his hot Georgian blood" in the harsh school of war, revolution, and Bolshevism. "He is veritably like steel, not rigid like iron, but resilient and able to bend." Stalin was "the reticent lord of all the Russians," a "legend of hardness and icy decision" with a "genius for political organization." And so on. At the end of the year, he summed up Stalin's "gamble" on collectivization as "the greatest victory won by the Communist cause."[14]

Even when he was reporting obviously horrific news, such as the deportations of hundreds of thousands of *kulaks* to concentration camps in the north or in Siberia, Duranty asserted such actions were necessary "to remove subversive individuals from their familiar milieu." He adopted the government line that landowning peasants were the source of the trouble in the countryside. Besides, he went on, "the concentration camp forms a sort of 'commune' where everyone lives comparatively free, not imprisoned but compelled to work for the good of the community. They are housed and fed *gratis*." In his eleven-part series published in June 1931 on the Five-Year Plan, Duranty outdid himself in his praise for Stalin's success in making "eager, conscious workers out of a nation that was a lump of sodden, driven slaves." In the spring of 1932, Duranty received the Pulitzer Prize for these articles (a decision that Columbia University, which awards the prizes, would regret for decades). There can be no doubt: Duranty had snowed his readers. He helped hide the horrors of Stalinism and popularized a cynical defense of mass murder, namely, that rapid progress toward modernity justified some unpleasantness along the way.[15]

One of the great liars in an age of deceit, Walter Duranty whitewashed Soviet atrocities.
John Rooney, Associated Press Images

Duranty was by no means alone in lauding the Soviet experiment and covering up its horrors. As the crisis of global capitalism took hold in the early thirties, as breadlines in American cities stretched down city blocks, as men sleeping under cardboard and newspapers became a common sight, and as joblessness turned into despair, some American journalists, sympathetic to the socialist critique of capitalism, sent back glowing reports to their newspapers, encouraging Americans to see Russia as the front line in a war against poverty and unemployment and injustice.

Louis Fischer of *The Nation*, for example, was an eager publicist for Stalinism. He grew up in Philadelphia, the son of Orthodox Ukrainian Jews who had fled the pogroms of the late nineteenth century; his father worked as a day laborer and fish peddler. Louis was a star student in Philadelphia's Southern High School, and his youthful Zionist idealism led him to join the British Army's Jewish Legion in 1917. In 1922, he traveled to Moscow where, after seeing Lenin speak, he became an ardent believer in the promise of Communism. During the 1920s, Fischer wrote occasionally for the U.S. press on Russian affairs and started a regular stint at *The Nation* in 1930 as the Five-Year Plan gained momentum. Fischer's articles told of the "powerful, all-enveloping, newly released wave or wall of energy and enthusiasm" in Russia under the Plan. Its goal was nothing less than "the complete destruction of capitalism in the Soviet Union." This conflict had "tapped gushers of popular will," he went on. "Everything moves here. Life, the air, people are dynamic. . . . Nothing is impossible in the Soviet Union."[16]

As for collectivization, Fischer could only sing its praises in lyrical prose. From Rostov-on-Don in August 1930, he wrote of vast open prairies filled with sunflowers and wheat, gleaming new concrete buildings on the collective farms, the immense acreage under cultivation, the sophisticated farming techniques the Soviets deployed, and "results far beyond the wildest expectations" of Soviet planners. Would there be disruptions and hardships? Perhaps. But in the end, "the nation will be grateful to the Soviet regime for its persistence and courage in carrying out a difficult program despite the terrific costs." The Kremlin could not have produced better copy.[17]

Among the ranks of Western apologists, few became such fiery and unrepentant followers of Stalinism as Anna Louise Strong. The daughter of a Nebraskan minister, Strong attended college at Bryn Mawr and earned a PhD in philosophy in her early twenties. Like so many elite, well-educated women of that era, she went into humanitarian work in the inner cities and became a noted child welfare advocate. An outspoken pacifist during the Great War, she traveled to Poland and Russia in 1921 to assist war victims, and soon became radicalized by Communism, just as Louis Fischer had been.

Strong started writing dispatches from Europe for left-wing newspapers in America and eventually founded the *Moscow News*, an English-language newspaper in the Soviet capital that fully supported government policies. In late 1930, after traveling widely across the country, she filed a series of feature stories for the *New York Times* on the "fateful drama" of Russia's economic transformation. Each piece was filled with portentous phrases about the "great struggle" underway to tear Russia free of the grip of its backward ways. In the *Washington Post*, she also hailed Stalin's increasingly dictatorial leadership, expressed admiration for the "unity" of the Communist Party, and wrote admiringly of the policy of "eliminating the kulaks as a class." In December, she insisted: "I know of no one starving in Moscow, or elsewhere in the Soviet Union for that matter." If there were shortages of food, it was because "the Soviet system has been chiefly concerned with making power plants and tractors and steel mills." The Bolsheviks, she said, had begun to "remake the whole face of the land." Some disruptions along the way were "inevitable."

Strong echoed this tone in her 1931 book, *The Soviets Conquer Wheat*, a shameless hymn of praise to "the revolution in farming" in the USSR. The "veritable war" in the countryside had been concluded, she asserted, "with stupendous success." The regime had pushed "one hundred million of the world's most backward peasants almost overnight into ultra-modern farming, more modern than is known in America." The harvest of 1930, which she declared to be surpassingly abundant, was "the most important harvest that has ever occurred since prehistoric man." The fierce resistance of the peasants against collectivization proved no match for the heroic Bolshevik leaders, men who "were used to riding the whirlwind." In some places, her text was copied directly from the speeches of the June 1930 Party Congress.[18]

Why did they do it? Louis Fischer, in a moving confession written after World War II, admitted that he had been swept up by the ideals of the Bolshevik Revolution. "It envisaged the world-wide abolition of war, poverty, and suffering," he wistfully recalled. The Russia he encountered in the 1920s "throbbed with dynamic energy," propelled by young, forward-thinking people eager to build a new future. The Harding-Coolidge years in America seemed repulsive by comparison. "I preferred fresh, sweeping winds to stagnant air," he wrote. Even as the true character of the revolution emerged, with its censorship, arrests and executions, show trials, and the famine, Fischer remained steadfast, certain that these sacrifices would be made good in the end. "I did not want to forswear a cause in which I had made such a large spiritual investment." By 1934, as the regime began more ferocious persecution of its internal enemies, Fischer grew increasingly wary of "this new search for heretics," as he put it in a letter to his editor, Freda Kirchwey. He anticipated the dark years ahead. But his celebration of the great Soviet experiment had already done much damage, falsely portraying Stalin's rule as a glorious chapter of Soviet history.[19]

For the duration of the Five-Year Plan, U.S. journalists like Duranty, Fischer, and Strong helped the Soviet Union cover up monstrous aspects of the regime. They self-censored their reporting to remain in good favor with the government rather than risk expulsion and lose their prestigious positions in Moscow. This deliberate whitewashing had a significant impact on the direction of U.S.-Soviet relations in 1933.

IV

When FDR made it known in mid-1932 that he would be inclined as president to establish diplomatic relations with the Soviet Union, one of the first people he consulted on the matter was none other than Walter Duranty. Home for a speaking tour in the glow of his Pulitzer Prize, Duranty received an invitation to meet with Governor Roosevelt in Albany. The two spent several hours in conversation on July 25, 1932, and FDR told reporters afterward in his usual jaunty style that "I turned the tables; I asked all the questions this time. It was fascinating!" No record was kept of the discussion, but Duranty later claimed the governor wanted to know about the state of Russian finances. Did they have the gold reserves to allow them to be reliable partners in international trade? he asked. Duranty, eager for ties between the two countries to improve, offered assurances. And the *Times* issued an article about the meeting that pointed to FDR's interest in "a policy of experimentation, socially and politically." The Soviet Union's centralized planning "has been one of the factors that account for his interest in the work there," the paper stated.[20]

FDR carefully avoided committing himself during the election. Although industrial leaders urged recognition and the extension of credits to the USSR to purchase American goods, opposition to the Bolsheviks remained strong among patriotic societies, church leaders, immigrant groups, and the American Federation of Labor, which feared a flood of cheap imports into the country that might undercut prices of domestic goods. The *Washington Post* editorialized that "the American people are unalterably opposed to recognition of the Soviet" because of its revolutionary propaganda and "Bolshevist intrigue." Reverend Edmund Walsh, the founder of Georgetown University's School of Foreign Service, spoke for many religious leaders in opposing any opening to Moscow. The noisy anti-communist Republican congressman Hamilton Fish (who represented Hyde Park) denounced FDR's "pussyfooting and ducking" on the issue and declared his steadfast opposition to any dealings with the avowedly revolutionary Bolsheviks.[21]

After the election, while FDR went to Warm Springs to recover from the strain of the campaign, Walter Duranty reported that the Soviet leaders had high hopes for a change of policy from the Hoover administration. "Roosevelt appears in an almost roseate light in Russia" for his openness to new ideas of governance, the newsman wrote. In the newly Democratic Senate, two dozen senators went on record favoring prompt recognition of the Soviets in the hopes of expanded commercial ties. Senator William Borah, the progressive Republican from Idaho who had so strenuously opposed America's membership in the League of Nations, now championed recognition as a way to reconcile old ideological foes. Some 800 college professors from 268 institutions also endorsed recognition in an open letter spearheaded by theologian Reinhold Niebuhr. Recognition of Russia, his group asserted, would help the cause of peace by deterring the warlike expansion of the Japanese Empire in Asia. Luminaries such as Jane Addams and Amelia Earhart joined the American Women's Committee for Recognition of Soviet Russia, urging recognition "in the interest of peace and trade." The momentum in favor of renewing ties to Moscow was gaining, it seemed.[22]

But in March 1933, an unwelcome series of news stories pushed the terrible famine back into public view. Though the scale and scope of the famine had been carefully hidden from outsiders by the Soviet government and compliant Western journalists, a few brave souls took enormous risks to get the story out. Malcolm Muggeridge, a young English journalist with communist sympathies, arrived in Moscow in 1932 to write a few pieces for the *Manchester Guardian*. Soon disillusioned by what he saw, Muggeridge set off in the spring of 1933, without official approval, on a trip into Ukraine and North Caucasus to investigate rumors of famine.

He smuggled his reports out through the diplomatic pouch of the British embassy, and they gave searing testimony of what he called "an active war" on the peasantry. He saw "soldiers everywhere . . . and the civilian population was obviously starving." Not undernourished, he insisted: dying of starvation. In the Kuban district of the North Caucasus, there had been no bread for three months. A dismal marketplace sold strange foods he described as unfit to be fed to animals. "We have nothing," he heard again and again. "They have taken everything away." Muggeridge made it clear: "The famine is an organized one." The towns were hopeless and barren, the people bereft and ill, "the fields choked with weeds, the cattle dead." Whole villages had been exiled. A piece of bread he examined was made of weeds and straw. Death hung over every town. Returning to Moscow, he concluded that the USSR had become "a slave state."[23]

Just days later, a Welsh journalist named Gareth Jones arrived in Berlin with an equally shocking story. Jones, a Russian-speaker and aide to former prime minister David Lloyd George, had just emerged from three weeks in Ukraine. Walking through some twenty villages, he saw the same signs of famine and military occupation that Muggeridge did. There was no food; no seed for sowing; and the peasants were too weak to work the land. He predicted millions would soon die from hunger. And he, too, pointed the finger at the government: "The policy of collectivization" was responsible. Over the course of the next few months, Jones published twenty-one articles in several leading British papers about his shocking findings, and his reporting made news in U.S. papers as well.[24]

True to form, Walter Duranty leapt at the opportunity to debunk this news. In an article that carried an infamous headline—"Russians Hungry, but Not Starving"—Duranty belittled the reports of famine as "a big scare story." He allowed that the Soviet government's effort to transform backward peasants who relied on techniques "from the days of Abraham and Isaac" into "1933 collective grain farmers" had perhaps been mismanaged. But once again, he applied his handy epigram—"you can't make an omelette without breaking eggs"—and asserted that the Bolsheviks were determined to modernize Russia whatever the cost. There was a food shortage, Duranty agreed, but "there is no actual starvation." In early May, he reported that the prospects for the 1933 fall harvest looked excellent and that there was no evidence of famine anywhere.[25]

Alarming news kept trickling out of the USSR, however. On August 19, 1933, Cardinal Theodor Innitzer, the archbishop of Vienna, made a striking public appeal to the International Red Cross in unambiguous language:

> Famine conditions there [the USSR] are accompanied by such cruel phenomena of mass starvation as infanticide and cannibalism. In the interest of the eternal laws of humanity and charity, the undersigned raises his voice and appeals to all those organizations and centers in the world which work in serving humanity and justice in order that they can undertake, before it is too late, a general plan of rescue on a basis above nationality and above religious affiliation for those who are threatened with starvation in Russia.

The cardinal said his information came from "hundreds of touching letters from the famine-stricken North Caucasus. . . . Eyewitnesses about whose competence there can be no doubt have described shocking details of the crisis." The very same day, the Soviet Foreign Ministry issued an adamant denial, calling the charges "pure fabrication."[26]

Duranty once again rose to the defense of the regime. "Any report of a famine in Russia is today an exaggeration or malignant propaganda," he insisted. A food shortage might have increased mortality from "diseases due to lowered resistance," but he saw no famine. Duranty, though, had not traveled to the stricken regions to verify the reports, and merely gave voice to Soviet official denials. People who did pass through Ukraine offered eyewitness testimony of mass death, cannibalism, and armed occupation of the grain-producing regions. Duranty's prestige proved adequate to wave off such reports as mere fiction.[27]

Franklin Roosevelt, planning to bury the hatchet with Russia and renew diplomatic ties, read both the stories about the famine and Duranty's adamant denials. But the press was not the only source of information about the dire Ukrainian situation. Under the Hoover administration, the State Department had been receiving worrisome reports from U.S. officials in Warsaw, Vienna, Berlin, Helsinki, Brussels, Paris, and from the specially trained Russia watchers stationed in Riga, Latvia. They noted the turmoil of collectivization, the plummeting agricultural production, increased refugee flows, and the mounting evidence of famine. This material had been gathered before FDR took office, but even after his inauguration in March 1933, the president received appeals and letters from Ukrainian immigrants calling for intervention to assist the starving peasants. These were usually turned over to the State Department without comment. According to a leading scholar of the subject, "the State Department and the White House had access to plentiful and timely intelligence concerning the famine of 1932–33 in the Ukraine and made a conscious political decision not only to do nothing about it, but never to acknowledge it publicly." Roosevelt had settled on a policy of improving ties to Moscow, and that meant stifling any concerns about the government-orchestrated famine.[28]

Why did FDR ignore the horrific man-made catastrophe in the Soviet countryside? Partly because he and Secretary Hull believed in the principle of noninterference in the internal affairs of other states. This principle formed the bedrock of Roosevelt's "good neighbor" policy, a policy Hull strongly endorsed. It was meant to reflect American tolerance for other forms of government and to deny any aggressive intent from the United States toward other nations—a departure from the repeated armed interventions in Latin America, the Pacific, and the Caribbean by the United States from 1898 through 1919. The famine had resulted from Soviet collectivization policy; it was Russia's problem. FDR and Hull could not have demanded a halt to collectivization without making a mockery of their pledge to keep out of other nations' domestic affairs. And indeed, the Americans were demanding a promise from the Soviets that they stay out of America's internal politics and stop sending their Communist propaganda into the United States. By insisting on a mutual policy of noninterference, Roosevelt made the famine disappear as a matter of discussion.[29]

FDR may also have shared in the weary condescension toward undeveloped peoples that was so common in this era. After all, famine had gripped Soviet Russia in 1920 to 1921, the result chiefly of drought and the dislocations of war. The American Relief Administration, founded in 1919 to assist postwar Europe, had appropriated $20 million to assist hungry populations in the USSR, though as many as 5 million people may have died from hunger despite outside help. In the late 1920s, famine also gripped China, again the result of drought and war; 6 million people may have died between 1928 and 1930. Reports of famine, then, were not uncommon, and perhaps some shock fatigue had set in among Western observers. Advocates of opening diplomatic relations with Russia could argue that more trade with Russia, which would assist its industrial development, might mitigate future crop failures. The reassurances of Walter Duranty that famine stories had been exaggerated, combined with reports that the harvest in the fall of 1933 was at long last a plentiful one, allowed American officials to turn a blind eye to the entire affair.

V

In the fall of 1933, therefore, Roosevelt pressed ahead with his plan for the diplomatic recognition of the Soviet Union. He tasked a small committee of State Department officials with the job of preparing the ground. This group included Assistant Secretary of State Walton Moore, a lawyer and former Virginia congressman who FDR had appointed to the State Department; as well as Robert Kelley, the chief of the Division of Eastern European Affairs, a staunchly anti-communist Russian expert who had trained young diplomats like George Kennan and Charles "Chip" Bohlen—two future ambassadors to the USSR. It also included William Bullitt, who had not known Roosevelt for long, but who in 1932 had joined the Roosevelt campaign and then offered his services—and knowledge of Russia—to the new president. FDR, warming to the talented, aristocratic loyalist, appointed Bullitt as assistant to the secretary of state in June 1933, with a roving commission to make himself useful to the president.[30]

The senior officials at State, especially Kelley, Moore, and their boss, Secretary of State Hull, looked askance at the Bolshevik regime and quietly opposed diplomatic recognition. Knowing Roosevelt favored it, these men sought to drag out the preliminary negotiations with the Soviets by introducing a long list of conditions that the United States should insist upon before recognizing the Moscow government. These included repayment of nearly $300 million in loans made to Russia before the Bolsheviks took power, restitution of American property and assets confiscated by the Bolsheviks, assurances that Americans in Russia could freely practice their religion and would not be subject to improper arrest or detention in the USSR, and above all, a cessation of revolutionary propaganda aimed at the United States. Moore counseled the president to "take the time necessary" to hammer out specific agreements on all these matters before offering diplomatic recognition. Bullitt, however, counseled speed and daring. On October 10, using Bullitt as a back channel, Roosevelt delivered a private message to the Soviet government inquiring about its willingness to begin discussions. After the Soviets agreed to talk, FDR issued a public invitation to the Russians to send a representative to Washington "to explore with me personally all the questions outstanding between our two countries." Reports reached FDR that on balance, most editorial pages of the nation's newspapers favored recognition of the USSR, easing any concerns of serious political repercussions.[31]

When Foreign Minister Litvinov arrived in Washington on November 7, however, he initially played hard to get and rejected many of the conditions the State Department demanded be settled before diplomatic relations could be established. Walton Moore huffed that Litvinov wanted "unconditional recognition." But after a week of hard bargaining, in which Bullitt played a crucial role as negotiator, Litvinov and the president announced a breakthrough. On some of the softer issues like freedom of religion, and respect for American business practices in Russia, the two agreed to some innocuous and reassuring language that Roosevelt could use to assuage domestic critics. Litvinov made a significant concession by declaring that the Soviet government would "refrain from interfering in any manner in the internal affairs of the United States," and halt "any agitation or propaganda" on behalf of revolutionary organizations—a promise they never intended to keep. On the much tougher problem of debt repayments, they announced a "gentleman's agreement" to continue negotiations on the problem as soon as a new ambassador was appointed—precisely the concession Moore and Kelley had cautioned against. FDR did not want the haggling over old debts to block his important diplomatic success. On November 16, an exchange of notes made the recognition formal. FDR sidestepped his fussy diplomats and cut a deal.[32]

At the time, his advisers privately worried he'd given away the store, offering recognition in exchange for nothing but platitudes. Roosevelt, however, reckoned that good ties to Moscow would be far more valuable in the long run than the modest political cost he had to pay now. "I believe sincerely," he said a day after reaching the agreement with Litvinov, "that the most impelling motive that has lain behind the conversations which were successfully concluded yesterday between Russia and the United States was the desire of both countries for peace and for the strengthening of the peaceful purpose of the civilized world."[33]

Certainly, recognizing Russia meant an accommodation with Bolshevism, which many Americans still saw as an abomination and a genuine threat to capitalism and religious liberty. But in 1933, a worldwide depression hung over every industrial nation. The Japanese conquest of northeast China opened Manchuria's raw materials, labor, and railways to the exploitation of an autarkic and menacing Japanese Empire, which seemed poised to strike next at Siberia or Mongolia. And the European scene looked bleak. Just days after FDR issued his invitation to Litvinov to come to Washington, Hitler announced Germany's withdrawal from ongoing disarmament talks in Geneva as well as from the League of Nations. During Litvinov's stay in Washington, Hitler's November 12 plebiscite overwhelmingly affirmed the desire of millions of Germans to break up the international order. Everyone could feel the dreadful undertow of war.

Roosevelt hoped that by courting the Soviets he might build a bulwark against the drift to war. That is how Felix Frankfurter, one of Roosevelt's closest informal advisers, saw it. A law professor at Harvard, a mentor to many New Deal lawyers, and a future Supreme Court justice, Frankfurter wrote to Roosevelt that the recognition of the Soviet Union "may, in view of the new constellation of the Great Powers, be of really momentous significance to the world's peace. There surely can be little doubt that Germany and Japan are moving on converging lines, full of ominous significance." Frankfurter derided critics of Roosevelt's Russia policy as "myopic" and insisted that the new relationship with the USSR would be "a most important chapter in the pursuit of world peace."[34]

Frankfurter grasped the president's thinking. FDR sensed that a time might come when the Soviet Union and the United States, divided though they were by ideology, would find themselves on the same side in a global struggle against the expansionist, imperialist powers. Time would prove him right, though his pursuit of friendship with Stalin came at a far greater cost than he could ever have imagined.

VI

Bullitt, who had steered the negotiations competently, was named the first U.S. ambassador to the Soviet Union, and he departed for Europe on the liner *President Harding* almost immediately. "You are a very great human being and a great president," Bullitt wrote FDR during the crossing. It was the first of many intimate expressions of loyalty. Bullitt's first stay in Moscow was brief, just long enough to enjoy the many banquets in his honor, including the one in December that ended with Stalin's kiss. He met with leading figures of the government, and once again stressed in his messages home that Soviet fear of a Japanese, and possibly a joint Polish and German, attack made the new American ambassador a popular man indeed. "It is difficult to exaggerate the cordiality with which I was received," an ebullient Bullitt wrote to the president. Stalin himself told Bullitt that "at any moment, day or night, if you wish to see me, you only have to ask."[35]

Bullitt returned to Washington after just a few weeks to pull together a staff for the embassy and put his own affairs in order. In the meantime, he left the thirty-year-old George Kennan in charge in Moscow. A fluent Russian speaker who would go on to an influential career as a Cold War hawk, Kennan lived in the winter of 1933–34 in the National Hotel with his wife and one employee—an intrepid young American named Charlie Thayer, whom Kennan called his "man Friday." Although Kennan found Russia "a filthy, sordid country, full of vermin, mud, stench, and disease," he recalled the start of his service in Moscow as "a wonderful and exciting time," since Russians were still allowed to interact with foreigners. Kennan attended the "uproariously informal parties" that Walter Duranty and other journalists threw each weekend and enjoyed getting to know the Russian people. "Russia, Russia," he reflected later, "unwashed, backward, appealing Russia, so ashamed of your own backwardness . . . so sensitive and so suspicious in the face of the wicked, civilized west." He saw the leaders of the regime as "strong-nerved, lean, ruthlessly competent," and he admired their strength while hating their political ideology. But it was a time flush with possibility. Kennan lived in a drafty, cramped hotel room; his wife prepared his meals there on a camp stove. It was a spartan existence and the ascetic Kennan loved it.[36]

Bullitt had more refined tastes and grander ideas. He returned to Moscow in March 1934, but as he wrote in a letter to his fellow ambassador Breckinridge Long, then in Italy, "the only furniture which had arrived from America was six clocks and a small picture of George Washington." The embassy team, which grew to about forty people, had to camp out in various hotels until their official chancery, a seven-story apartment block at 13 Mokhovaya Street in central Moscow, had been completed. The ambassador was offered Spaso House for his residence, a large neoclassical mansion built by a textile magnate just before the war. It was completely empty of furnishings, and Bullitt could do little entertaining for some months after his arrival. No matter, chirped Bullitt: "For the moment at least the United States is extremely popular in the Soviet Union."[37]

The moment ended abruptly. At the end of March, Bullitt wrote to Walton Moore in the State Department that the atmosphere had changed and the "underlying emotion toward all capitalist nations is one of hostility." The Soviets had become difficult as the threat of a Japanese attack had diminished. And Bullitt was shocked to discover that the Soviets believed Roosevelt, in working out the recognition deal with Litvinov in Washington, had agreed to provide the USSR loans for economic development. When Litvinov pressed Bullitt for the loans that he thought FDR had promised, Bullitt had to tell him that there had been a grave misunderstanding. The American government did not plan to loan the Russians anything. Credits to buy U.S. goods might be arranged—but only after the USSR agreed to settle the debts from loans the U.S. had granted during the war.

Litvinov, stunned, felt the Americans had been duplicitous. Suddenly, Bullitt's request for a large, prominent parcel of land on which to build an embassy got hung up in red tape and did not come through. Ongoing negotiations about repaying wartime debts stalled. Bullitt found it hard to reach Litvinov and even harder to get him to agree to anything at all. Life had suddenly become "extremely unpleasant" in Moscow, he told Moore, as he had no furniture in his house and he missed Washington and the thrill of seeing the president every day. In April, he wrote to Roosevelt that "the honeymoon atmosphere had evaporated," as the Russians made life difficult with a thousand small indignities and delays.

Bullitt tried to improve ties to the host government with gestures like teaching Red Army cavalry units how to play polo and baseball. But he noted that with the Japanese having turned their attention away from Siberia and toward China, the Soviet government had "stiffened" toward the Americans. In September, Bullitt wrote to FDR that the Russians were feeling "cocky" and seemed unwilling to cultivate the Americans as they had done at the start of the year. In his memos to the president, Bullitt sounded homesick and frustrated. He left Moscow on October 10 for a long journey home via Japan and China during which he fell ill with a viral infection; he would not return to his post until April 13, 1935.[38]

During his absence, a political earthquake struck the Soviet Union. On December 1, 1934, Sergei Kirov, the head of the Leningrad Communist Party organization, was assassinated in the corridor outside his office. The assassin, Leonid Nikolaev, was apprehended immediately, tortured, and forced to confess to being a part of a conspiracy led by Stalin's old rival Grigory Zinoviev. He was then dispatched to the executioner. Kirov was enormously popular within the party and a charismatic and talented orator. He had been an intimate friend of Stalin's, but possibly Kirov had become too popular. Almost immediately, rumors flew that Kirov had been the victim of a Kremlin plot orchestrated by Stalin, who had grown suspicious of the handsome, magnetic Kirov and saw him as an emerging threat to his grip on power.

Though incontrovertible evidence of Stalin's complicity has long eluded scholars, most believe Stalin was involved in Kirov's murder. He certainly used the event for his own ends—an uncanny echo of the Reichstag fire in Berlin. On the very day of the assassination, Stalin signed two new laws authorizing the secret police to arrest anyone suspected of plotting acts of terrorism, and to imprison them and even execute them with no recourse to the courts. A dragnet swiftly snapped up thousands in Leningrad and Moscow on charges of conspiracy. The great purges that Stalin would use to wipe out rivals, real and imagined, had begun. An atmosphere of gloom and suspicion descended across the country. Eventually, hundreds of thousands would die as Stalin tightened his grip on the levers of power. And the brief period of warm U.S.-Soviet relations plunged into a deep chill.[39]

Ambassador Bullitt, long absent from Moscow, had little feel for the sinister turn of events that had occurred while he was gone. In fact, he had wired ahead to his staff that he wanted to throw a large and dazzling party in late April 1935 to mark the advent of spring, and perhaps to make up for his five-month sojourn away from the capital. The planning was given over to the youthful Charlie Thayer, who, with the wives of some of the senior staff, settled upon a design theme for the ball: They would turn Spaso House into a collective farm and decorate it with all the color and life they imagined rural life to entail. Tulip bulbs were shipped in from Helsinki, live birch trees were uprooted and replanted in vast pots, half a dozen mountain goats and a few bear cubs were borrowed from the zoo, fishing nets were hung from the ceiling and filled with zebra finches to herald the coming of spring. Accordion players and dancers, attired as cheerful peasants, gamboled gaily throughout the ballroom, while lights of green and gold turned the interior into a phantasmagoric scene. The drinking and dancing carried on all night, the finches escaped their nets and careened around the house, a bear cub got into the champagne and became copiously sick, and five hundred amazed guests passed through this dazzling display that ended with breakfast amid the debris.[40]

Bullitt crowed to FDR about his ball, calling it "astonishingly successful... the best party in Moscow since the revolution." In retrospect, however, the party seems an act of appalling bad taste, collective farms being the site of untold horrors associated with the recent famine. And Bullitt's fete clashed with the atmosphere in Moscow, which had become funereal and tense with ever-widening accusations of conspiracy taking hold. Indeed, some prominent guests present that evening would not survive the purges. Bullitt may have held this ostentatious debauch precisely as an act of defiance against a regime he now loathed. "The terror, always present, has risen to such a pitch that the least of the Muscovites, as well as the greatest, is in fear," he told the president. "The arrest and exiling of innocent human beings in all quarters of the Soviet Union continues apace." Quite clearly, there would be no return to the optimistic days of early 1933.[41]

His charm offensive having failed, Bullitt grew miserable in Moscow, unable to work effectively with the Soviet leadership, far from the action in Washington, and bitterly disappointed that the new era in U.S.-Soviet relations had come to naught. His reports from Moscow turned caustic, notably during the summer of 1935, when the Third International Congress of the Communist Party opened in Moscow. Although the Soviet Union had settled on a strategy of building a "popular front" against fascism and Nazism, thus welcoming tactical alliances with non-communist parties across Europe, the Soviets had also invited representatives of the American Communist Party to Moscow for the Congress. This Bullitt took as a violation of the pledge made by Litvinov that the USSR would stay out of internal U.S. politics. He thought the president should publicly tell the American people that the Soviet Union was attempting to subvert American democracy and he should restrict visas of Russians coming into the United States. Roosevelt rejected this and instead asked the State Department to issue a written protest note to the Kremlin. That done, he chose to let the matter drop. As the dust settled, FDR wrote to Bullitt simply, "I know you have been having a bad time in many ways," and urged him to get more rest.[42]

After a little more than two years at his post, Bullitt sent a long memo to the secretary of state (drafted by George Kennan) that amounted to an epitaph for his term as ambassador in Moscow. By this point, he planned to leave Moscow and had hopes of being appointed ambassador to Paris—which indeed he was in August 1936. He remained completely loyal to Roosevelt despite their now entirely divergent views on Russia. Compiling his thoughts into a formidable anti-Soviet screed, Bullitt declared that the United States could never rely upon the Soviet Union as an ally or friend. The Soviets, he believed, had every intention of pursuing world revolution and the destruction of all forms of liberal democracy. Communism held its fanatical adherents in its grip with a messianic appeal that Bullitt likened to Islam. Stalin he described as "the most absolute dictator in the world." On the international scene, the USSR would toggle whichever way best suited its interests. The Communist parties of the world, he wrote, "believe in mass murder," and were perfectly prepared to "kill millions of Americans" on the road to world domination.

Soviet foreign policy, Bullitt concluded, now sought chiefly to inflame Franco-German animosity in hopes of setting the two old enemies at each other once again in a fight to the death between Nazism and capitalism. Once ruined by another great war, the states of the old order would crumble away, and the Communists could swoop in and build a new Soviet Europe in the rubble. Moscow also desired a U.S.-Japanese war because the Soviets believed it would end in Japan's defeat, opening an opportunity to spread Communism into China. American diplomacy, Bullitt insisted, could do nothing to tame or befriend the zealous Bolsheviks. Roosevelt should encourage Franco-German reconciliation and close ranks against the Soviet threat. This view meant working with the Nazi government against the Soviets, something that Bullitt accepted as the only way to avoid a red tide spreading across Europe.[43]

Bullitt's lieutenants in the Moscow embassy shared these strident views. Having lived in the eerie, frightening, and ever-more-controlled society of the Soviet Union, and watched the earthy, humane Russian people crushed by Stalin's vast machinery of repression, they, too, developed an intense hatred of Communism and its brutal practitioners. George Kennan, mentored by the ebullient ambassador, praised Bullitt in his memoirs and claimed his only weakness was impatience and perhaps overoptimism. "We took pride in him and never had occasion to be ashamed of him," Kennan recalled of Bullitt. Kennan "whole-heartedly" supported his hard line and wrote bitterly about Roosevelt's softness toward the Russians. In fact, Kennan even wondered if FDR's effort to cultivate the Stalin regime was the result of "pro-Soviet influence somewhere in the higher reaches of government"—a provocative claim that he never substantiated.[44]

If FDR's Russia experts were so united in their fierce animosity toward Stalin's government, why then did the president continue with his efforts to court, and indeed appease, the Soviets? Had he been duped? Was he a fool? A crypto-communist? None of these claims, all made at the time and after, bear scrutiny. FDR's position on the USSR emerged from a tactical, and hard-headed, calculation. As U.S.-Soviet relations became increasingly strained, FDR accepted that the Soviet regime was malevolent, and he was perhaps chastened about developing friendly relations with the Kremlin. But there was a larger strategic picture to consider. In 1933, Hitler had withdrawn Germany from the League of Nations; in 1934 the Nazi leader liquidated his few remaining domestic rivals in a bloody purge; in 1935, he set out to rearm the German military and air force. Germany could only be preparing for war. In Asia, the scene had also darkened. Japan's invasion of Manchuria in 1931, and the establishment there of the puppet state of Manchukuo the following year, had placed northern China under the Japanese thumb. Japan's withdrawal from the League in March 1933 signaled the alignment of authoritarian, expansionist nations that wanted to redraw the world map in their favor.

In such a dangerous world, the United States needed partners—not friends, exactly, but nations that shared an interest in halting the spread of fascism. Roosevelt knew all too well that Congress and the public had no desire to become entangled in Europe's affairs; all the more important, then, to find states willing to oppose Nazism. FDR accepted the emerging political typology of his era: that Communism, however odious, was above all anti-fascist. Left-wing political parties across the Western world had started to sound the alarm about the fascist threat coming from the right, and FDR's New Deal ideology emerged in that context. To him, and to millions of others, fascism, often in league with big business and cynical monied elites, sought to destroy democracy. His own political movement at home, the New Deal, aimed to strengthen democracy, lessen inequality, encourage political participation of the working classes whose toil had built America, and to bring them along with him in an effort to revitalize American values as he understood them. In this reading, democracy and fascism could hardly coexist.

FDR did not of course align himself with communism or socialism, but his anti-fascist instincts made for uncomfortable bedfellows. Perhaps his anxiety about the growing fascist menace hindered him from grasping the expansionist ambitions, murderous character, and immense cynicism of the Soviet Union and its leader. But Roosevelt's critics like Bullitt and Kennan, and the right-wing plutocrats that had started to organize at home in opposition to the New Deal, seemed ready to make the same mistake about Hitler: to overlook the Führer's malevolence in the hopes of forging an anti-communist bloc that would hem in Communism while tolerating fascism. Forced to choose between equally tyrannical regimes, FDR believed that a tactical alliance with Stalin, animated by the goal of containing Nazism and Japanese militarism, would serve American world interests. The grand alliance that he shaped during the Second World War would bear out his gambler's instincts. Bullitt and Kennan never reconciled themselves to FDR's complacent view of the Soviets, and they would not cease to undermine the policy of cooperation with a government they considered monstrous and dangerous. Their day in the spotlight would come, but not until Roosevelt had left the stage.[45]

CHAPTER 7

ETHIOPIA AND THE NEUTRALITY TRAP

"I am a little puzzled as to just where the conquest of Ethiopia leads the pacifists."

—W. E. B. DU BOIS

I

Dorothy Detzer stood up, spread out the pages of her text, with its marginal notes hastily penciled in at the last minute, and began her remarks to the assembled two thousand delegates of the International Congress of Women, then meeting in Chicago in July 1933. She spoke sharply. Despite the past decade's efforts to build a durable peace, she said, war, dictatorship, and persecution were spreading across the world, from Latin America to Manchuria, from India to Africa, from Russia to Italy and Germany. Endless meetings of earnest statesmen in the marble halls of the League of Nations at Geneva had proved fruitless. With a certain bitterness in her voice, Detzer, the executive secretary of the U.S. branch of the Women's International League for Peace and Freedom (WIL), likened the Geneva organization to a missionary who wished to bring Christianity to the "savages." After years of toil, countless Bibles distributed, and innumerable prayer meetings, the missionary returned home to his church to report that he had made progress. Yes, the savages still ate one another, "but now they did it with knives and forks." Similarly, she asserted, the League of Nations had provided silverware and lace tablecloths to the nations of the world so they could gorge on the bodies of the innocent in an atmosphere of genteel elegance.[1]

Detzer had been active in humanitarian work since leaving high school in Fort Wayne, Indiana, working at Hull House in Chicago and traveling to Russia in the early 1920s with the American Friends Service Committee during the postwar famine that ravaged the Volga basin. After losing her brother to a wartime gas attack, and then encountering the mass suffering the war had unleashed in Europe, Detzer devoted her life to anti-war activism.

Slender and prim, she was invariably called "the attractive young lobbyist" by reporters, though by the time of her Chicago speech, she was thirty-nine years old and had accumulated two decades of hard experience in the field. And she saw that since its founding in 1920, the League had been unable to broker a meaningful agreement on world disarmament.

Article 8 of the League of Nations Covenant had committed its members "to the reduction of national armaments to the lowest point consistent with national safety," but with the exception of a 1922 naval arms limitation treaty hammered out between the U.S., Britain, France, Italy, and Japan, the members of the League had accomplished little. And they had failed miserably to do anything about Japan's seizure of Manchuria in 1931, flunking their first big test. The United States and the USSR had not joined the organization, Japan left it in March 1933, and with Hitler now in power, declaring his intention to reorder the map of Europe and destroy the Versailles system, the collective security idea of 1920 lay in tatters; it seemed plausible to imagine Europe and Asia slipping once again into global war. To avoid that horrific fate, Detzer argued, citizens must demand that their governments dismantle their arsenals of weapons and settle their differences at the conference table rather than on the battlefield.[2]

Utopian as it may sound, the cause of disarmament was not a peripheral or fringe idea. Religious and labor organizations, veterans' groups, college teachers and students, and hundreds of national and international peace societies had been calling for an end to war since the guns went silent in Europe on November 11, 1918. The Great War, they believed, proved that when nations built vast naval and land forces, they created irreversible momentum toward war. The principal lesson seemed obvious: To avoid future wars, abolish the weapons used to fight them.

And in fact, President Roosevelt had embraced this very logic in one of his first foreign policy gestures. On May 16, 1933, he launched an appeal to fifty-one heads of state that proposed the elimination of offensive weapons combined with a global nonaggression pact. In a message to the U.S. Congress, he linked the cost of armaments to large budget deficits and national insolvency. In his mind, eliminating "weapons of aggression" was not only fiscally prudent but consistent with the pursuit of human rights and social justice at home. The peace movement, stunned and delighted by FDR's bold statements, showered him with praise and hoped his appeal would jump-start the campaign for world disarmament.[3]

That cause enrolled some of the most well-known activists of the era, in particular the savvy, battle-tested leaders of the women's suffrage movement.

Fresh from their stunning victory in securing the right to vote in 1920, leading suffragists took aim at the problem of war and how to stop it. In 1924, Carrie Chapman Catt, leader of the National American Woman Suffrage Association and founder of the League of Women Voters, turned her attention to anti-war work, creating an umbrella organization of peace groups called the Committee on the Cause and Cure of War. Its members wrote letters to Congress, held public meetings, and gathered petitions to urge progress upon legislators. Jane Addams, perhaps the leading female activist of her time, had been a leader in the anti-war movement for decades. The founder of Hull House and an originator of the field of social work, she founded the Women's Peace Party in 1915. Once demonized for her anti-war statements on the eve of America's entrance into the Great War, she now looked like a prophet for opposing a conflict that much of the world had come to see as a mistake. She started the WIL in 1919 to champion the anti-war cause and won the 1931 Nobel Peace Prize for her efforts.[4]

With figures as distinguished as Catt and Addams among America's peace campaigners, the movement possessed genuine political clout. Along with the WIL, the National Council for Prevention of War, headquartered in Washington, supported neutrality legislation, an anti-war referendum, and total disarmament. They joined with the Fellowship of Reconciliation, the National Peace Conference, and the Emergency Peace Campaign to form a powerful, transnational network that captured the attention of the public and political leaders in Europe and America. They demanded drastic cuts in arms spending, limits on navies and air forces, and the abolition of submarines, poison gas, and chemical weapons. "Disputes Will Continue Between Nations," read one handbill from the National Council; "Do You Want Them Settled by Reason or by Poison Gas?" One delegate to the International Congress in Chicago gave her speech an arrestingly simple title: "Civilization or War?"[5]

Under enormous popular pressure for action, the League of Nations promised to convene a World Disarmament Conference in Geneva, starting in February 1932. The WIL made the most of this opportunity. In a theatrical publicity stunt, Detzer arranged for a transcontinental caravan to drive from Los Angeles to Washington, stopping in over one hundred cities along the way to collect signatures on an enormous scroll that would be presented to President Hoover as a sign of the immense national support for disarmament. Other organizations had accumulated similar bundles of signatures and converged on Washington in January 1932, on the eve of the Geneva meeting, in a "pageant of petitions." The *Ladies' Home Journal* joined the cause, urging its readers to send letters and telegrams in favor of a plan for disarmament that included the automatic economic boycott of any nation that started a war. Millions did so, including college presidents, governors and elected officials, religious leaders, industrialists, and hundreds of civic organizations. In the spring, when the Geneva Conference got underway, marches and anti-war protests popped up in major cities. Students, pastors, labor leaders, and concerned citizens locked arms and shouted, "No More War!" and "Disarm Now!" By one count, 12 million Americans—a tenth of the U.S. population—had joined at least one of sixty major anti-war organizations by the start of the 1930s.[6]

The Geneva talks on disarmament, however, proved an immense disappointment. Germany, forever complaining of its weakness and vulnerability, demanded equality in armaments with France, while the French insisted on maintaining arms strong enough to compel Germany to fulfill its obligations under the Versailles Treaty. Britain welcomed a reduction of land armaments, but its navy remained crucial for projecting imperial power in Asia, where Japan's rapid shipbuilding program threatened to challenge Britain's preeminence. Japan's army had grown exponentially as it gobbled up Manchuria, while Fascist Italy was pouring money into naval and military expansion to serve its own renewed imperial ambitions. After a frustrating year of inaction at Geneva, Carrie Chapman Catt issued a public letter with the headline: "Lost! One international disarmament conference!" With barbed sarcasm, she inquired, "What has become of it? No one seems to know."[7]

In light of the League's failures, American anti-war activists called for action by Congress to mandate an arms embargo on nations that went to war in violation of the 1928 Kellogg-Briand Pact. The idea seemed simple enough: Stop selling weapons to combatants, and they would soon be incapable of waging war. But the embargo idea was tricky and would mark a decisive break with America's traditional idea of neutrality. For over a century before 1917, the United States had insisted that other warring nations respect its rights as a neutral, which meant the right to send its commercial ships across the open sea in wartime to engage in commerce with anyone. During the first three years of World War I, this position had been good for business, allowing weapons, textiles, food, raw materials, and loans to flow out to the combatants in the European conflict. Some Americans got very rich on war. But when Germany began to attack American shipping on the grounds that war matériel and commercial loans from America were sustaining the British and French war effort, the United States had no choice, President Wilson concluded, but to enter the war against Germany.

Jurists, scholars, activists, and public figures drew the conclusion from this experience that trade with warring states had embroiled America in Europe's conflict. To stay out of future wars, they argued, America should cut off trade completely with all nations at war. In addition to keeping America out of harm's way, the measure might also help the cause of peace by shutting down the supply of arms, food, raw materials, and loans to warring nations. With the Japanese invasion of Manchuria in 1931, Congress debated measures to halt the arms trade with Japan. An arms embargo won the support of the peace movement, and some internationalists thought an embargo, if wielded by the president, could become a useful tool in America's diplomatic arsenal. In August 1932, President Hoover's secretary of state, Henry Stimson, drew up draft legislation that would allow the president to act against aggressor nations by embargoing arms shipments. But Hoover's departure from office brought a halt to the initiative.[8]

At the start of 1933, Senator William Borah (R-ID), the outgoing chairman of the Senate Foreign Relations Committee, picked up the torch. Borah, who had been one of the most strident opponents of American membership in the League of Nations, had a long history of supporting disarmament and had helped stand up the talks that resulted in the Naval Armament Limitation Treaty of 1922. He did not believe in "collective" security, that is, a binding commitment to police the world that might compromise U.S. independence. But he did believe that disarmament, as well as a ban on arms sales to nations at war, would encourage peace. Detzer and the WIL made common cause with Borah. On May 21, 1933, when Detzer's group held a rally in Farragut Square in Washington, Borah, now in the minority party in the Senate, was there. The group marched on the White House with a petition bearing one hundred thousand signatures, demanding drastic cuts in armaments. Borah delivered remarks making the case that disarmament was "the keystone to the arch of international amity." He declared it would be impossible to "stabilize currencies, adjust tariffs, open up markets, and to bring trade and commerce back to normal conditions while nations are piling up armaments . . . pauperizing their people to pay the expense." On the same day, the WIL called for a Senate investigation of the weapons industry and its role in pushing America into war in 1917.[9]

The pressure for action had already reached a fever pitch upon FDR's arrival in office, and the new president readily agreed to support the emerging embargo legislation. FDR and Cordell Hull, both old Wilsonians who approved of international cooperation, believed that an arms embargo law that gave the president the authority to block sales of weapons to select nations would allow the United States to deter and punish aggressor nations; it would also open the door to cooperation with European governments, should they also deploy an embargo. In April 1933, the House of Representatives passed legislation that would give this power to the president. But in the Senate, a combination of opponents emerged to slow the bill's progress. Senators from states with a big munitions industry balked. Those opposed to collective security—the same bloc that stymied Wilson's plans to join the League of Nations—got a whiff of FDR's internationalist intentions and came out against the bill. And a vocal minority argued that a *selective* embargo imposed by the decision of the president on an aggressor nation was tantamount to an act of war. They believed if Roosevelt imposed an arms embargo on Japan in light of its invasion of Manchuria, Japan could well view this as an act of war and respond with hostilities. America would immediately be dragged into war, defeating the entire purpose.

In May 1933, Senator Hiram Johnson, a progressive Republican from California who was also a staunch anti–League of Nations man, proposed a clever refinement to the embargo bill: It would have to apply impartially to *all* nations involved in a war. The president could not pick favorites. This measure, Johnson believed, would demonstrate America's genuine neutrality, while keeping the country out of war. FDR and Hull saw immediately that the Johnson amendment, by removing the element of executive decision-making from the embargo bill, weakened the power of the president to conduct foreign policy. They decided to withdraw their support. Wrapped up in the complexities of the legislative proposals of his first hundred days in office, FDR did not wish to fight over foreign policy. The embargo proposal would have to wait.[10]

II

The cries for disarmament did not abate, however. The anti-war movement drew much support from a growing academic and popular consensus that the Great War, and in particular America's involvement in it, had been either a dreadful mistake, or the result of deliberate deception by unscrupulous propagandists, arms manufacturers, bankers, and militarists. The Great War, this argument ran, had been sold to the American people as a crusade to rid the world of Prussian militarism. But what had been the result? The death of 20 million people; enormous and now unpayable national debts; the birth of Bolshevism; an unfair "peace" settlement that had driven the Germans toward Nazism; and an artificial boom economy that went bust in 1929, triggering a worldwide depression. If the war to "make the world safe for democracy" had led to such ruin, who could possibly argue for more of it? Only the arms dealers, who had accumulated enormous wealth during the war while ordinary soldiers were fed into the slaughterhouse. Detzer believed the arms trade should be treated like opium trafficking in an earlier era: The "munitions racket" must be stopped by coordinated international action. In December, she again called for a Senate inquiry into the arms manufacturers to determine their role in starting and prolonging the recent war. If they could be exposed and then restrained by Congress, peace just might have a chance.[11]

Detzer had accumulated a decade of experience as a lobbyist on Capitol Hill and she knew a good deal about parliamentary procedures. To win Senate approval for a munitions investigation, she needed a sponsor to put a resolution on the Senate floor and win its approval. She asked various senators of both parties for help; they all declined, pleading the press of other business. A few whispered that taking on the arms industry would be "political suicide." But Detzer persisted until, just after Christmas 1933, she found a willing partner: Gerald Nye of North Dakota, a forty-one-year-old Western progressive Republican with an independent streak. Nye grew up in Wisconsin and went into his father's line of work as a newspaper editor. In 1916, he moved to North Dakota and bought a small newspaper, which he used to advocate the interests of farmers against big business. Though a Republican, he had supported Wilson's progressive domestic policies. But the collapse of farm prices after World War I fueled his antipathy to bankers, industrialists, railroads, and middlemen who, he believed, conspired to gouge the hard-pressed farmer. Like many farm-state progressives, Nye also developed a suspicion of arms manufacturers who had made profits out of imperialism, naval expansion, and war—wars paid for in the lives of conscripted soldiers from the heartland. He ran unsuccessfully for Congress in 1924, but caught the eye of the progressive governor, who appointed him to a U.S. Senate seat when the incumbent died suddenly in 1925. Nye won the seat in his own right in the 1926 election and set out on a twenty-year career in Washington.[12]

Senator Gerald Nye, a stubborn isolationist and effective critic of the arms merchants.
Library of Congress

Nye knew some of his colleagues from the West shared his beliefs. Progressive Republicans such as Borah of Idaho, Johnson of California, and George Norris of Nebraska were part of the "irreconcilables," the group that successfully blocked American membership in the League of Nations. Another progressive, Robert "Young Bob" La Follette Jr. of Wisconsin, joined this isolationist caucus when he entered the Senate in 1925. Along with some Democrats like Burton K. Wheeler of Montana and Bennett Champ Clark of Missouri, they all opposed collective security and any cooperation with the League, which they saw as likely to drag America into European troubles. As progressive populists (and largely supportive of FDR's New Deal), they could be counted on to rail against big banks and big industry. Borah, in fact, had recently called arms manufacturers "international criminals" who seemed intent on fomenting war with Japan. But even with these allies, Nye knew he had to pick his moment to introduce a resolution asking the Foreign Relations Committee to take up a munitions investigation. He bided his time until early February when, noting the absence of a few obstreperous senators from the floor, Nye casually put his proposal to a vote; it was passed with a minimum of fuss and sent to the Foreign Relations Committee for discussion.[13]

There still remained some maneuvering to determine the shape of the investigation and its precise purpose. As Nye worked the corridors, a storm of helpful publicity broke. In March 1934, *Fortune* magazine published a profile of the world's biggest arms manufacturers like Krupp (Germany), Bethlehem Steel (U.S.), Vickers (Britain), Schneider-Creusot (France), and Škoda (Czechoslovakia), showing how these conglomerates operated, often across national borders, and how much money these companies made during the war. "Every time a burst shell fragment finds its way into the brain, the heart, or the intestines of a man in the front line," said the essay, the arms producers got richer. These corporations were so big and so wired into legal, political, and banking networks that their power exceeded that of their own governments. They would sell arms to any buyer, friend or foe, who could pay for them. These companies, *Fortune* claimed, had a simple method: "Keep Europe in a constant state of nerves. Publish periodical war scares. Impress governmental officials with the vital necessity of maintaining armaments against the 'aggressions' of neighbor states. Bribe as necessary. In every practical way create suspicion that security is threatened." In a nutshell: "When there are wars, prolong them. When there is peace, disturb it."[14]

A month after the *Fortune* piece appeared, a new book with an unforgettable title hit the bookstores and became an instant bestseller: *Merchants of Death: A Study of the International Armament Industry*, by muckraking journalists Helmuth Engelbrecht and Frank Hanighen. The book added more substance to the story told in *Fortune*'s piece, and it lent an air of conspiracy and subterfuge that rocked the nation and spurred Congress to act. On April 12, after committee chairmen had passed around Nye's proposed investigation like a hot potato, the Senate approved the creation of a select committee to examine the "munitions trust." Seven senators were assigned to the committee, and Gerald Nye would serve as its chairman. The tall, humorless, energetic senator with dark, slicked hair leaned into his new role as a champion of truth against the secretive machinations of a sordid industry. "The time is coming," he told the press, "when there will be a realization of what monkeys the munitions makers can make of the otherwise intelligent people of America."[15]

Given the headaches this investigation would later create for his administration, it seems odd that FDR did not use the immense Democratic majority in the Senate to strangle the inquiry before it began. In fact, Roosevelt endorsed it. Why? Clearly, the enormous media storm around the "merchants of death" created momentum for the investigation. And the president needed the support of the progressives in Congress for New Deal legislation. In mid-May, he gave the inquiry his public support, adopting Nye's rhetoric: "The grave menace to the peace of the world," FDR said, "is due in no small measure to the uncontrolled activities of the manufacturers and merchants of engines of destruction." FDR here was also aiming to appease the peace movement and its effective lobbyists like Dorothy Detzer and Carrie Chapman Catt. The anti-war ideal had even taken root in the White House: FDR knew that Eleanor Roosevelt had agreed in June 1934 to contribute an essay to a book to be edited by Catt titled *Why Wars Must Cease*. Eleanor's essay argued that war had become "obsolete"—a view the president shared.[16]

Furthermore, Roosevelt had long experience with arms dealers from his time at the Navy Department, and he knew perfectly well that this industry often tried to bilk the government by demanding top dollar for deliveries of munitions; more supervision and regulation of the arms business would be a good thing and consistent with Roosevelt's New Deal ethos. And there was no doubt in the back of his mind that a Senate investigation of the arms industry would shine a bright light into the cloaked and secretive world of some of FDR's political enemies, especially the du Pont family, whose large company included gunpowder and arms-manufacturing plants in half the states of the Union. The du Ponts were sharp critics of the New Deal and were at that very moment drawing up plans to launch a public outreach organization—

the American Liberty League—to combat New Deal policies. FDR met with Nye's committee in early June and breezily spoke about "clipping the wings of the arms manufacturers"; he promised full cooperation of the White House in securing documents to aid the investigation.[17]

And as the committee began its work, it seemed he had made the right decision. The Senate munitions inquiry was catnip to the media and became a daily story in the nation's newspapers. In July, Nye promised that his staff of eighty sharp-eyed investigators were poring over secret company records and would soon produce "startling facts." The committee subpoenaed one hundred officials from the arms industry to testify, and reporters clamored for revelations of "international intrigue, activities of secret agents . . . high finance, and extraordinary profits." When the hearings opened on September 4, they did not disappoint. Nye's team revealed the giant sums that had been creamed off government contracts by the arms makers. Unscrupulous middlemen took bribes to guide war contracts into the hands of select industries, and arms dealers operated free from government supervision. The committee also found the perfect villain to hold up to public scrutiny: the Anglo-Greek arms merchant Sir Basil Zaharoff, a fabulously wealthy businessman who had served for decades as a discreet intermediary between European firms and numerous governments—work that earned him hefty commissions. The hearings turned Zaharoff into "Europe's High Priest of War" and "master arms salesman" who typified the "extraordinarily sordid" world of the merchants of death.[18]

Nye also put the heat on the du Pont family, calling brothers Irenée, Lammot, and Pierre, along with cousin Felix du Pont, to answer questions before the committee. These men held the reins of an enormous munitions business, and Nye tried to pin them down on their wartime windfall. At one moment, Irenée, "his face flushed, eyes sparkling," tried to rebut the insinuation that he had placed profit before country. Du Pont's munitions had helped win the war and kept America from turning into a German "colony," he declared. Nye countered by pointing out how lucrative the trade had been for the family: From $6 million in profits in the four years before the war, the company had raked in $58 million between 1914 and 1918. "The world is going to see," Nye roared, "the need for curbing these merchants of death and their business." At the close of the first round of hearings in late September, Senator Nye called for a 98 percent tax to be levied on all incomes over $10,000 during wartime. "Do that," he declared, "and then observe the number of jingoists diminish."[19]

In this same tone of inquisition, Nye's committee carried on hearings through all of 1935, tarnishing the arms industry and alleging connivance of government officials in taking the country to war to protect the interests of big industry and banks. Nye and his committee even threw mud at the legacy of Woodrow Wilson, who they increasingly saw as a tool of big business in taking the country to war. These aspersions stirred the anger of many Democratic senators who still revered the departed president, and they mobilized to cut off the Nye committee's funding in early 1936. The peace movement, though, saw Nye as a hero. Dorothy Detzer believed that the "record of intrigues and bribery; of collusion and excessive profits; of war scares artificially fostered and conferences deliberately wrecked" showed the public that war had become nothing less than a gigantic criminal enterprise. She believed that "no Senate committee ever rendered to the American people a more intelligent or important service."[20]

A bold claim, and not without controversy. For Nye's committee also did much damage. Scattershot, hyperbolic, self-righteous, Nye persuaded the public that the arms industry was an "unadulterated, unblushing racket" that traded death for dollars. The idea of building up the armed forces for its deterrent power seemed ludicrous to Nye and to a generation of Americans. Had not war come in 1914 precisely because of the gigantic arms race that had preceded it? Nye formed part of that thread in American public life that saw conspiracy and deception as the chief characteristic of government. Collusion between industry and political elites got America into war in 1917, Nye believed. Henceforth, the public should stand watch against the trickery and deceit of public officials and business leaders. Nye also urged the public to reject pleas from embattled Europeans for aid in containing fascism; America had no place in those ancient quarrels. Stay home, stay out, keep clear. These were Nye's watchwords. Never again, he vowed, would the country be conned into a war for profit, and the public heartily agreed.[21]

III

While Americans spoke of hammering their swords and spears into plowshares and pruning hooks, the European dictators were preparing for war. Mussolini always believed that Fascism meant empire—his creed of violence, virility, and militarism demanded conquest. From the early 1920s, Italy had been waging an immensely destructive war in its own colony of Libya, where an anti-Italian resistance movement had emerged. Italian forces used tanks, aircraft, concentration camps, and mustard gas against Senussi tribesmen, eventually subduing them in 1932. Flush with victory, Mussolini now took aim at Ethiopia.[22]

This independent kingdom, one of the last remaining outposts of African autonomous rule, had delivered a humiliating defeat to Italian troops at the Battle of Adwa in 1896 when Italy had attempted to grab Ethiopia during the European "scramble for Africa." Called Abyssinia by Europeans, Ethiopia had successfully fended off colonial marauders since then. Geography helped: The capital, Addis Ababa, lay smack in the center of this vast country that was three times the size of California and larger than France and Germany combined. But it was surrounded, and cut off from any access to the sea, by the Anglo-Egyptian Sudan; British East Africa; the British, French, and Italian colonies in Somaliland; and Italy's valuable possession of Eritrea, a narrow strip of coast on the strategically important Red Sea. Ruled by a young Christian monarch, Haile Selassie, who had been crowned in 1930, Ethiopia joined the League of Nations as a sovereign state. But it lived an uneasy existence, dependent on the European great powers for access to the sea and to world trade; its railway system, too, was built and owned by foreign powers. Ethiopia looked like a tempting prize for Mussolini, who thought Britain and France too timid, and preoccupied with European matters, to halt a daring Italian campaign to seize Ethiopia. At the start of 1934, Mussolini ordered his generals to draw up a plan of invasion that would eventually consolidate Fascist control of the entire Horn of Africa.[23]

All he needed was a pretext, and in December of that year, a skirmish between Italian and Ethiopian soldiers at an oasis along the ill-defined Ethiopia-Somalia border in the wastes of the Ogaden desert provided it. A few hundred Italian and Somali troops, wandering across the border, confronted Ethiopian guards who, after some days of icy confrontation, began to shoot at one another. A few dozen soldiers on both sides were killed. Il Duce demanded an apology and the payment of a huge indemnity; Emperor Haile Selassie refused and took the case to the League of Nations for arbitration. Unfortunately, the League, dominated by France and Britain, was not a disinterested party. France desired above all to remain on close terms with Mussolini, encouraging his continued resistance to Hitler and his staunch defense of independent Austria. The French government could ill afford a break with Mussolini over colonial issues.

In early January 1935, Pierre Laval, the French foreign minister (who would end his days in front of a firing squad for his wartime collaboration with Nazi Germany), secretly offered Mussolini a deal. In return for Mussolini's continued veto of a German move to swallow Austria, France would turn a blind eye to Italy's conquest of Ethiopia and try to keep the League from interfering. Pocketing this promise, Mussolini sought a similar green light from Britain. But the British government proved less amenable, fearing the massive blow to the reputation of the League of Nations if it simply allowed Italy to swallow a sovereign member state. The British called for diplomacy and reconciliation; Mussolini dragged his feet. And while negotiations began between Italy and Ethiopia in the spring of 1935, he accelerated the transport of a vast quantity of arms, supplies, and soldiers to Italy's colonies of Eritrea and Italian Somaliland. There could be little doubt of Il Duce's intentions.[24]

Could the United States do anything to halt the drift to war? As much as President Roosevelt deplored Italy's saber-rattling, he simply did not have any tools to deploy on the international stage. In fact, at just this moment of increasing international tension, the Senate delivered a cruel blow to FDR's internationalist hopes by rejecting U.S. membership in the World Court (officially the Permanent Court of International Justice). The Court was created by the League of Nations in 1920, but it presented no threat of an entangling alliance, and it had no binding powers. It simply provided a tribunal for the arbitration of disputes between states. FDR thought that joining this organization would serve as an American pledge to uphold law and advance the cause of peace. But even this gesture of international cooperation proved too much for the same bloc in the Senate that had halted U.S. membership in the League. William Borah, Hiram Johnson, and Homer T. Bone of Washington, among others, spoke out against joining the Court in rash, exaggerated terms. Europe, with its defaulting debtors, its manipulative munitions barons, its tolerance for colonialism, its corrupt political system—all of it should be kept at arm's length, they declared. On January 29, 1935, the proposal to join the Court won the support of fifty-two senators, but fell seven votes short of the two-thirds majority required for a treaty. This, in a Senate with sixty-nine Democrats. It was a shocking rebuke, made worse by Roosevelt's poor management of the debate and the vote. A downcast president wrote to Ambassador Dodd in Berlin that the country would "go through a period of non-cooperation in everything, I fear, for the next year or two."[25]

Nursing wounds from that defeat, FDR got more bad news from Ambassador Breckinridge Long in Rome. A wealthy Kentucky lawyer and scion of a powerful family who had donated heavily to FDR's campaign, Long had been rewarded with this important foreign post. Like many elite Americans, Long admired Mussolini enormously and even had many nice things to say about Fascism as a solution to modern problems. But in February 1935, he informed the president that Italy was on the warpath. "Italian steel mills and factories are busily engaged in the manufacture of all kinds of guns and ammunition—even large cannon," he wrote. Italian men were being mustered for service in Ethiopia and "enormous supplies of barbed wire, trucks, and all that sort of thing continue to be sent." Long calculated that Mussolini had mobilized an army of four hundred thousand men for Ethiopia and was preparing for a general European war as well, which Long predicted would break out within two years. "I see no escape," he concluded, "from a real cataclysm." Roosevelt, normally so buoyant, replied, "I fear I must agree with you about the general situation. . . . These are without doubt the most hair-trigger times the world has gone through in your lifetime and mine. I do not even exclude June and July 1914."[26]

The press certainly fed the fire with daily reports on the Ethiopian crisis. Headlines in February 1935 boldly announced that "Duce Mobilizes"; "Mussolini Hurls Threat of War"; "Italy's Troops Gather"; "War Nearing as Ethiopia Defies Italy." A report from Rome described "scenes reminiscent of world war days" at the central train station, as young men with "sprays of Italian wildflowers in their helmets" packed off to Italy's southern ports. Frederick Birchall of the *New York Times* wrote in a resigned tone that Ethiopia's fate was sealed: "It is only a question of time" before the Ethiopians were "put under the rule of white races further advanced in civilization and better equipped with the tools of war than they are." Italy's brazen move against Ethiopia threatened not just to destabilize Africa but to deliver a death blow to the League of Nations, a body evidently incapable or unwilling to stop the Fascist powers and their march to war.[27]

On top of this worrisome news from Rome came another provocation, this time from Nazi Germany. At 5 p.m. on March 16, 1935, in the Propaganda Ministry in Berlin, Joseph Goebbels, in a voice shaking with emotion, read out to over one hundred breathless foreign correspondents a shocking statement. Because of the failure of the Geneva Disarmament Conference, and because of the refusal of other nations to disarm themselves, Germany would form an army of thirty-six divisions, and expand its navy and air force. Germany would also reestablish mandatory conscription of young men into the armed forces. The Germans had already been rearming secretly; now Hitler dared the world to do anything about it. William Shirer, busily scribbling notes as Goebbels spoke, understood immediately that "Hitler had of his own accord wiped out the military sections of the Versailles Treaty." The German people, Shirer knew, would be thrilled by this demand for equality and respect from the other great powers. But "it is a terrible blow to the Allies," he noted, because Hitler had called the bluff of the entire postwar system. Shirer went to bed late that night, "sick at this Nazi triumph."[28]

Other close observers noted the immediate change in Germany. Sigrid Schultz of the *Chicago Tribune* reported that "all Germany rejoiced" at the news of Hitler's proclamation. This "bold stroke came as a thunderbolt," and the reaction was "deliriously enthusiastic," she wrote. The people, long instructed to see Germany as a victim of the terrible peace treaty, felt that "the fetters of shame had been broken," according to Schultz. Not since the outbreak of war in August 1914 had Germans shown so much "unity of spirit" as they did after Hitler's proclamation. Ambassador Dodd, already inclined toward gloomy assessments, wrote to Walton Moore that following the rearmament announcement, "Hitler is stronger today than he has ever been." More pointedly, Dodd wrote that the popularity of neutrality in America provided Hitler a golden opportunity to fulfill his expansionist ambitions. Dodd imagined Hitler's reasoning this way: "With the United States and Great Britain aloof and divided, why should not the Third Reich dominate Europe and Japan the Far East?"[29]

In Washington, Hitler's announcement "put furrows in the brows of American statesmen," as the *Washington Post* put it. But it did nothing to stiffen their spines. President Roosevelt, after the World Court defeat, had concluded "most Americans would prefer a policy of isolation," according to the *Post*. In his press conference on March 20, Roosevelt said that he would not comment on the news from Berlin except to "maintain the general principles of the good neighbor and hope that that American principle will be extended to Europe." This was pretty weak stuff. But even Germany's European neighbors did not do much more than talk. In mid-April, British, French, and Italian ministers met at Stresa, on the glimmering shores of Italy's Lake Maggiore, to confer and denounce Germany's unilateral rearmament move. Talk like this, without any action, only confirmed in Hitler's mind the weakness of his rivals. Roosevelt, in a private letter to the elder statesman Colonel Edward House, mused about the prospect of the European states placing a blockade around Germany, a measure U.S. ships would then respect. But House in reply pointed out a blockade would surely trigger a general war in Europe: "Of course," House wrote, "you know how overwhelmingly the sentiment in this country would be against our participation in another European conflict."[30]

Yes, Roosevelt knew; and he had occasion to be reminded on April 12, 1935, when over one hundred thousand American college students staged a walkout from their classrooms in a "protest against war and fascism." Organized by the League for Industrial Democracy (a section of the Socialist Party of America) along with half a dozen church and student organizations, the daylong "strike" spread across the country. The ringleader, twenty-six-year-old Joseph P. Lash, told the press that "our strike is a dress rehearsal for what we intend to do the day your Congress declares war. We say send Congress to Shanghai. Send the warmakers there. We're not going." (Lash would later become a close friend of Eleanor Roosevelt's and a sympathetic chronicler of the New Deal.) At Columbia University, three thousand students massed together in the gymnasium and hoisted placards with slogans like "Build Schools, Not Battleships." The pacifist cofounder of the American Civil Liberties Union, Roger N. Baldwin, shouted, "We refuse to bear arms for our country in time of war," eliciting wild cheers from the crowd. Reports poured into the press of similar protests at universities and colleges across the country; the same event a year later drew half a million students.[31]

These students had reason to fear a new war as the Ethiopian crisis dominated newspaper headlines in the spring of 1935. Anne O'Hare McCormick, who rushed to Italy to take the temperature of the people, found them "readied for war. . . . It is common talk in the streets and cafés that operations will begin in October at the end of the rainy season." In London, British officials expressed bafflement at Mussolini's determination to start a war; they were immensely frustrated that Il Duce forced them to choose between defending Ethiopia's sovereignty or watching Italy quit the League, rush into Germany's arms, and seize Ethiopia anyway. In mid-May, Mussolini ordered another two hundred thousand men to report to their barracks for mobilization. He also made a clever offer to the French and British to partition Ethiopia among them. But this was mainly to show up the hypocrisy of the European colonial powers: Why should they block Italy from possessing a few colonies, given their own voracious appetite for conquest?

Anne McCormick grasped the essential point: "Mussolini is seizing the opportunity to inaugurate the second phase of his program," she wrote. "Collecting an empire is a riskier business than reforming a nation. But the die is cast. Sooner or later, the Fascist state was bound to strike out for a Roman empire." The Italian strongman confirmed this analysis with a thundering speech to his farcical Fascist parliament in late May: "Let everyone keep well in mind," he said, "that when there is a question of the security of our territories and the lives of our soldiers, we are ready to assume all, even the supreme, responsibilities."[32]

IV

War was coming, in Africa certainly and perhaps in Europe, too. How would FDR and Congress respond? In this atmosphere of crisis and anxiety—with Italy sharpening its bayonets to slice up Ethiopia; with Germany laying out plans to create an army of half a million men; with the League of Nations cowering; with a vocal minority of U.S. senators opposed even to the mildest form of international cooperation such as membership in the World Court; with an ongoing congressional probe into the nefarious world of the arms trade and its "merchants of death"; with American pacifists effectively mobilizing across the country—with all this swirling around the president, Roosevelt took the most significant foreign policy decision of his presidency so far: He signed the Neutrality Act of 1935.[33]

By 1935, "neutrality" had become a word of talismanic power in America. Everyone favored it, everyone invoked it, everyone associated it with virtue, wisdom, reason, and restraint. The Italians could rush into Africa, guns blazing; the Nazis could unveil jackbooted phalanxes. Let them. America would not fall for the false patriotism of war ever again. But talk of this kind was easy enough; crafting legislation to inscribe neutrality into law proved more complex. It was made more difficult by the crowded legislative calendar. FDR and Congress had been exceptionally busy in the first half of 1935. In early April, FDR signed the Emergency Relief Appropriation Act, transforming the relief program set up in the early months of 1933 into a job-creation program through the Works Progress Administration. In May, the Supreme Court ruled a major component of the National Industrial Recovery Act unconstitutional, gutting one of the signature pieces of New Deal legislation. Far from deterring FDR, the court's ruling seemed to energize him. He pushed through the Wagner Act in July, setting up the National Labor Relations Board and guaranteeing the right to unionize. On August 14, he signed the Social Security Act, creating a safety net for the elderly and unemployed. A few days later, he signed the Banking Act that tweaked the working of the Federal Reserve and Federal Deposit Insurance Corporation, which had been created by his earlier legislation. On August 26, he signed the Public Utility Holding Company Act, which allowed for the regulation of electric utilities. And at the end of August, he signed the Revenue Act, which featured a "wealth tax"—a heavy tax on incomes over $1 million. Each of these bills had required intensive debate and negotiation. Taken together, these laws formed what historians have termed a "second New Deal," and indicate how successful FDR had been in 1935 in working with progressive leaders in Congress to reshape American society. But it also meant there was precious little room to contemplate world affairs. And by the end of August, everyone in Congress and the White House was tired and ready to go home.[34]

Yet Mussolini's saber-rattling over Ethiopia, combined with the strident calls from the Nye Committee for action to "take the profits out of war," pushed both Congress and the State Department to draft legislation to address the thorny problem of neutrality in wartime, and in particular the question of arms sales to nations at war. Nye's committee had helped drive home the lesson of the Great War: The surest means to keep the United States from getting drawn into future hostilities overseas was to ban arms sales to all nations waging war. While this action might not bring about peace, an embargo would at least ensure that American ships, travelers, and weapons were not sent into a war zone.

FDR accepted the logic of the argument. On March 19, only a few days after Hitler's shocking rearmament announcement, the president met with the members of the Senate munitions inquiry. In his usual breezy fashion, he urged Nye's committee to press on, and to design legislation both to tax arms manufacturers during wartime and to limit U.S. arms sales to combatants. In what to the assembled senators would have been a remarkable statement, FDR said "he had come around entirely to the ideas of Mr. Bryan." This referred to William Jennings Bryan, the secretary of state under President Wilson who had resigned in June 1915 after Wilson had strongly protested the German sinking of the *Lusitania*—a British passenger ship whose destruction killed 128 Americans. Bryan saw that Wilson was poised to take the country to war to protect the freedom of the seas, and the right of neutral American ships to conduct commerce in wartime. But strict neutrality in the war, Bryan believed, required the U.S. to halt its commerce with the belligerents rather than go to war to protect it. For FDR to align himself with Bryan over Wilson in the context of new neutrality legislation marked a massive shift in U.S. policy. No wonder that Senator Nye left the meeting feeling "extremely pleased" by the discussion.[35]

Secretary Hull, by contrast, was aghast at FDR's apparent nonchalance. He feared that Congress was leaning toward neutrality legislation of the kind Hiram Johnson had put forward in 1933: an embargo law that compelled the president to block arms sales to *all* nations at war, regardless of circumstances. The heart of the matter, as Hull saw it, was presidential authority. Neutrality legislation that forced the president to impose an embargo on all combatants in a conflict would weaken his ability to exert any influence in a time of crisis. Cases might emerge, Hull believed, when the president would want to punish an aggressor with an arms embargo while allowing sales of weapons to an aggrieved party. The president might also wish to coordinate an embargo action with other nations. The proposed legislation offered no room for maneuver and would not serve American interests, Hull insisted.[36]

But Congress would not be deterred. In late March 1935, Senator Nye, referring to Hitler's ominous announcement about rearming Germany, gave a robust statement in favor of keeping America out of another war "at all costs." To a crowd in Lexington, Kentucky, he said the president agreed with him on the need "to guarantee our neutrality in the event of European hostilities." Nye had it slightly wrong. The president and Hull only wanted a neutrality bill that kept the power to impose an embargo on select nations in the president's hands. During the summer, Hull and the State Department fought to ensure that whatever the final shape of the neutrality legislation, at least the principle of presidential discretion was protected. But they got nowhere. Senator Key Pittman, the Democratic chairman of the Foreign Relations Committee, told the White House that "the fool Munitions Committee" had stirred up so much fury against arms dealers that Congress would never accept an embargo law that relied on the decision of the president for enforcement. They wanted ironclad assurance that once a war broke out, the president could not lean to one side, as Woodrow Wilson had done between 1914 and 1917.[37]

With Nye and members of his committee threatening to hold a filibuster until they got a vote on neutrality legislation—thus holding up major domestic priorities as well as blocking the adjournment of Congress at the end of August—FDR gave in. He would rather accept a bad neutrality law than spend another month or more fighting with Congress and watching his domestic agenda go down the drain. He also had word from Rome on August 19 that Mussolini had told the American chargé, who had carried a personal appeal for peace from FDR to Il Duce, that "it was now too late to avoid an armed conflict"; the Italian people "unanimously supported" the government. With war imminent, FDR accepted the need for a neutrality law.

On August 21, after conferring with the White House, Pittman pushed Senate Joint Resolution 173 through the Foreign Relations Committee and presented it to the Senate. It allowed the president to determine if a foreign war had commenced; but once he did so, "it shall thereafter be unlawful to export arms, ammunition, or implements of war from any place in the United States, or possessions of the United States, to any port of such belligerent states, or to any neutral port for transshipment to, or for the use of, a belligerent country." There was no room here for the president to choose which nations would be cut off from U.S. arms and munitions sales. The Senate, now running out of steam and desperate for a recess, passed the bill almost without discussion, so keen were the senators to go on record as having kept America out of any foreign wars.[38]

Accepting the inevitable, Roosevelt now asked only that the House of Representatives amend the resolution by placing a six-month limit on the new law, asking that Congress reconsider it at the end of February 1936. That way, should Italy go to war in Ethiopia, at least Mussolini would be unable to buy American arms for his colonial venture. Congress and the president could reassess the picture in six months. The House accepted the compromise on August 23, passed the bill, and sent the amended bill back to the Senate, where it was approved the next day. Congress overwhelmingly supported a mandatory arms embargo against all nations at war, whether friend or foe, victim or aggressor. Should war break out anywhere in the world, the United States would call back its ships, isolate itself from the conflict, and let the chips fall where they may.[39]

The entire affair left Secretary Hull and his advisers deeply depressed and thoroughly bewildered at how easily FDR had given in to congressional pressure. Shortly after the resolution passed but before FDR had signed it, Walton Moore, the assistant secretary of state who had done so much of the negotiating with the Senate, wrote a memo to the president explaining his serious concerns. "The president," he insisted, "should be vested with discretion to apply the embargo not necessarily to all but to any of the belligerents he might designate." Why was this flexibility so important to Moore? Because he could conceive of circumstances in which America might wish to aid a victim of aggression. "The unwisdom of the mandatory embargo provision," he stressed, "is illustrated by assuming that a war may occur between two nations, one of which is really fighting our battle and entitled to our assistance." For example, what if the United States, wishing to protect its interests in the Philippines, should wish to send arms to China to halt Japanese aggression in Asia? Such a policy would now be illegal. Moore concluded, "this is certainly not a time, when the future is so unpredictable, to tie our hands in advance."[40]

FDR also received sharply worded criticism from Secretary Hull, who considered the Neutrality Act both an "invasion of the constitutional and traditional power of the Executive to conduct the foreign relations of the United States," as well as a foolish restraint upon America's ability to exercise its influence in the world arena. In November, Hull gave a radio address in which he told his listeners that they could not "complacently sit back with the feeling that we are secure from all danger." In fact, Hull went on, sounding like an old Wilsonian, "our own interest and our duty as a great power forbid that we shall sit idly by and watch the development of hostilities with a feeling of self-sufficiency and complacency." Hull's call for engagement with the world rather than retreat would go unheeded for the rest of the decade.[41]

FDR signed the Neutrality Act on August 31, 1935, and issued a statement that showed that he understood the criticisms of Hull and Moore. While declaring the goals of the act "wholly good," he noted that "the inflexible provisions might drag us into a war instead of keeping us out." He did not elaborate, but this statement echoed the fears of his advisers. They saw that neutrality as conceived by Congress meant unilateral U.S. withdrawal from world affairs and resignation in the face of aggression. Under pressure from a united Congress and a powerful anti-war movement, preoccupied with his domestic agenda, and determined to avoid some accidental involvement in Italy's colonial conflict in Africa, FDR made a tactical error of enormous magnitude. For the next five years, his hands remained tied as aggressors around the world set out on the pitiless march to war.[42]

V

With the passage of the Neutrality Act, politicians on Capitol Hill felt relief and satisfaction. They showed the voters with this law that they had learned the hard lesson of the last European conflict and would not be hoodwinked or bamboozled into another war. Yet not all their constituents refused to confront the march of fascism. Just as Roosevelt and Congress were joining hands in a pledge to stay out of foreign conflicts, Black Americans were taking up the cause of Ethiopia with fury and urgency. For them, Italy's war on Ethiopia became a catalyzing moment in an ongoing struggle for racial justice, and in the summer and fall of 1935, Black journalists, educators, and pastors mobilized for action. They made a case that Italy's threat to Ethiopia represented a front in the wider global struggle of white imperialism against non-white people, and that it also mapped onto their own daily lives in America where white supremacists routinely subjected Black Americans to violence and humiliation. And many Black critics pointed out, Ethiopia was not just a Black problem: If the Italians were allowed to succeed in Ethiopia, they argued, fascists everywhere would be emboldened, and Europe and America would soon be the target of fascist aggression. Ethiopia became a test case for the fragile new order the great powers had erected after 1918. If they failed to uphold it, chaos beckoned. In the words of columnist Roi Ottley, a chronicler of daily life in Harlem for the *New York Amsterdam News*, "the Ethiopian-Italian conflict is filled with dynamite."[43]

Ethiopia had long occupied a privileged and sacred place in the cultural vocabulary of Black Americans. It represented the marvel of an independent Black empire ruled by a Christian monarch, and a people that had defied invasion and white colonization. There was also a powerful spiritual echo in the very word. The Ethiopian prophecy of Psalm 68:31 had been on the lips of abolitionists throughout the nineteenth century: "Princes shall come forth out of Egypt; Ethiopia shall soon stretch forth her hands unto God," a passage that connected the enslaved of Egypt, and their emancipation, with eventual freedom for enslaved African Americans. And that verse had remained a spiritual call for the ongoing Black freedom struggle in the Jim Crow era. Ethiopia meant African agency, autonomy, and liberation. News that Europe's strutting Italian dictator wished to despoil this place, subdue it, and enslave it angered and united African Americans as no other cause had yet done in the twentieth century.[44]

It was no coincidence that the first planning session for public demonstrations against Italy was held at the Abyssinian Baptist Church in Harlem, a church founded in the early nineteenth century by Ethiopian sailors in New York who had been barred from segregated white churches. Its pastor, Adam Clayton Powell Sr., called together the Provisional Committee for the Defense of Ethiopia to plan for action, and on March 9, 1935, "3,000 indignant Harlemites of all political shades" gathered to form an action plan amid shouts of "Africa for the Africans!" There was no talk of neutrality here: Ethiopia needed money, arms, and munitions, they agreed, and they set in motion plans for a huge demonstration to raise the nation's awareness of the crisis. "The time is at an end when the white race can continue to ride on the backs of the darker races," said Arthur Reid of the Provisional Committee to wide agreement. Adam Clayton Powell Jr., the minister's son and a rising political star in Harlem, noted that Italy's threat to Ethiopia formed part of a rising tide of fascism, "the fingers of which are daily digging into the vitals of our people," he boomed from the pulpit. The *Baltimore Afro-American* editorial page painted a lurid picture of the consequences of Italian victory. "If Italy wins this war, there will follow murder, pillage, rape, and enslavement of the Ethiopian people for the next two hundred years.... For dear old Rome, Italy, the Pope, and Protestant Christianity, Ethiopians will be raped, worked to death, robbed, cheated, beaten, mutilated" into extinction. "Back into Italy will flow a hoard of yellow gold, oil, minerals and wool—wealth wrung from Ethiopian sacrifice."[45]

Harlem's sudden engagement with Ethiopia drew condescending commentary from the *New York Times*, which suggested only an "aggressive minority" of the city's Black residents cared about the cause; despite their raucous protest meetings, they were "doing precious little about it." Instead, clever propagandists had seized upon the issue "to hammer home the lesson of the white man's perfidy and chicanery." Black street-corner demagogues turned the fate of Ethiopia into a "racialist" call to arms against white people everywhere, the paper claimed. To be sure, some Black writers wondered at the passion for a cause so distant from the present crisis of African Americans. Roi Ottley wrote in his column that "the United States has its Mussolinis in the public utilities, captains of industry, and princes of finance" who strictly policed the color line at home. "If war is to be declared, cast the first stone in their direction," he urged. And Roosevelt himself might have agreed with that sentiment. In late July, at two consecutive press conferences, he responded to repeated questions about Ethiopia by saying his policy would be to emphasize "the good neighbor," and to make every effort "to keep us from getting involved in specific cases that do not concern us." The most he would do was issue a public statement on August 2 calling for "an amicable solution" to the "differences" between Italy and Ethiopia.[46]

This call for calm fell on deaf ears, for the very next day, a large protest march gathered in New York City. On a hot, sticky Saturday afternoon, about twenty-five thousand people, including anti-Fascist Italian Americans walking side by side with African Americans, wound their way through Little Italy and lower Manhattan. Led by Reverend William Lloyd Imes, pastor of St. James Presbyterian Church in Harlem, the parade demonstrated the role church leaders were taking in the Ethiopia movement in alliance with left-wing groups like the American League Against War and Fascism, founded by the U.S. Communist Party and led by Dr. Harry F. Ward, a Methodist minister and socialist. Marching bands of Black musicians walked alongside members of the Brotherhood of Sleeping Car Porters, war veterans, mothers pushing baby carriages, and students. According to the *Afro-American*, students from Columbia and Hunter College joined "trade unionists galore, anti-militarists, anti-Fascists, and anti-Hitlerites." As the march flowed through the city streets, "a multitude of banners, floats, and placards made up the colorful singing, clapping, shouting pageant." Signs with slogans dotted the crowd: "Hands Off Ethiopia!" "Fight War and Fascism!" "Down with Mussolini!"[47]

The Ethiopian cause spurred interracial solidarity of leftists. At a rally at Madison Square Garden on September 25, organized by the Committee for Ethiopian Independence, a crowd of seven thousand people, "about one-fourth of whom were Negroes," according to the *New York Times*, raised their voices in protest. They heard speeches from the minister Harry Ward (who had co-founded the ACLU in 1920), the director of the NAACP Walter White, John Haynes Holmes of the New York Community Church, Rabbi Stephen Wise of the Free Synagogue, and the educator and leading Black intellectual W. E. B. Du Bois. A large effigy of Mussolini wielding a bloody knife appeared on the stage, only to be ripped to shreds while the audience booed and hissed. In its place, a new papier-mâché figure appeared depicting, as the *New York Times* described it, "a Negro and a white man standing side by side as friends."[48]

Beyond Harlem, the world spoke out against Mussolini. In London, the International African Friends of Ethiopia, founded by the Trinidad historian and journalist C. L. R. James, held its first meeting at the end of July 1935 and arranged a protest in Trafalgar Square, calling on Britain and the League to stop Mussolini's planned invasion. Frederick Birchall, writing from Geneva, noted that the protest movement had become global, and that unless Italy was stopped, "the entire white race will stand arraigned before black opinion." The backroom appeasement of Mussolini by the European powers had not gone unnoticed, Birchall claimed. Once the Africans realized that the Western powers were planning to impose an arms embargo on both Italy and Ethiopia that could only benefit the well-prepared Italian forces, they will see it as one more piece of evidence for "the eternal subjugation of the colored races [which] is considered necessary for the well-being of the whites." Dan Burley of the *Chicago Defender*, a leading Black newspaper with a national reach, agreed. "The time will soon come when race advocates of the American conception will be knocked down and trodden underfoot... when something else in its stead, a creation awesome and inspiring, will take form and grow from the morass of blood, broken bones and bodies of the warrior dead." Conflict in Ethiopia, in these accounts, marked the start of a global racial showdown.[49]

W. E. B. Du Bois linked fascism to European imperialism and U.S. segregation.
Library of Congress

Perhaps no one articulated the global connections of the Ethiopian crisis as powerfully as did Du Bois, the renowned sociologist and historian of Atlanta University. A cofounder of the NAACP in 1909, he was a Pan-Africanist, an anti-colonialist, a socialist, and author of (among many other works) the immensely influential study *Black Reconstruction*, which appeared in June 1935, just as the Ethiopia crisis reached the boiling point. In that book, Du Bois completely overturned the long-held idea that Reconstruction after the American Civil War was a failure that could be blamed on Black knavery and Yankee carpetbagging. Rather, Du Bois showed that newly freed Black people had seized upon the opportunity that emancipation had given them to reinvent the South, experimenting with new forms of economic and social relations, only to have massive white resistance, violence, and terrorism undo their efforts. He emphasized Black agency and consciousness, writing African Americans back into the story from which they had been erased.

In a similar way, Du Bois wanted to place Ethiopia at the center of world politics of the 1930s. In speeches, newspaper columns, and an important article in *Foreign Affairs*, he connected Ethiopia to a global conflict of race, a conflict engineered by white imperialists in search of African wealth, labor, and commodities, against which all people of African descent must fight. The new language of human rights, international law, and collective security that could be heard in Geneva at the League of Nations was not on offer to Black people, he believed. Just as African Americans were still subjugated by Jim Crow in a nation that prided itself on the principles of democracy and liberty, so, too, would white nations tolerate the Italian conquest of Ethiopia in the name of intra-European amity and harmony. For Du Bois, the color line was the most important boundary of geopolitics.[50]

The concept of race, though, was malleable enough so that it could be used to oppress European Jews with the same kind of merciless intensity that had been meted out to people of color around the world. In July, as the U.S. Congress mulled over how best to tie the president's hands in foreign affairs, Ambassador Dodd reported to the State Department about a gruesome spike in antisemitic violence in Germany. This "particularly ugly phase" of Nazi antisemitism, Dodd wrote, focused on the threat to German purity from "what is portrayed as Jewish 'miscegenation' with Aryans"—namely, sexual contact. Not only were marriages between Jews and non-Jews being blocked, but groups of Brownshirts regularly mobbed the homes of women alleged to have had contact with Jews. On July 15, 1935, in Berlin, some two hundred Brownshirts had invaded the fashionable Kurfürstendamm district, savagely beating people who they believed were Jewish. Some of the thugs carried placards that read "The Jew is the cause of all our troubles," and on shopwindows they pasted notices reading "I am a Jew, Aryans enter my establishment at their own risk." The American Jewish Congress rushed out a statement asking why the U.S. government, "which indicates a deep and sincere interest in the maintenance of peace as between Italy and Abyssinia," had not lodged a formal protest with the Nazi regime. But the White House and State Department remained silent.[51]

Just two weeks before Italy's armies marched into Ethiopia, the Nazi government on September 15 announced two laws inscribing their conception of "race" into German law: the Reich Citizenship Law and the Law for the Protection of German Blood and German Honor, both unveiled at the Nazi Party rally in Nuremberg that month. Premised on the idea that the "Aryan" German race was threatened from within by miscegenation and pollution from Jews, the Nuremberg laws now limited citizenship only to those of "German blood." Since German blood looked exactly like the blood of any other human, the term had no scientific value. The Germans used it as a legal fiction to deny Jews access to the rights and privileges of citizenship. The Nazis also banned intermarriage and sexual contact between Germans and Jews. In the words of the Nazi Reich commissar for public health, Gerhardt Wagner, "the fight for our national future . . . calls for a perfect man—a strong man. That struggle cannot be fought with men who go about begging for mercy or whine and crawl."[52]

Seen in global context, these Nazi laws echoed the widespread (and entirely false) consensus in Western nations that human beings were inherently, biologically different from one another, and that these differences could be codified as "racial." This theory had a pedigree that predated the Nazis. After all, the idea of immutable racial difference fueled the eugenics movement, so popular in America and essential in nourishing the European fascist mindset. It had long served as justification for racial segregation, Jim Crow, and sterilization laws in America. And it underpinned the colonization and subjugation of Africa and Asia, long practiced by France and Britain, and now mimicked by Mussolini. The roots of Nazi race laws lay deep in the soil of Western race ideology.

In fact, some Nazis delighted in pointing out the parallels between antisemitic race laws in Germany and Jim Crow in the American South. On the eve of the unveiling of the new Nuremberg statutes, the propagandist Julius Streicher, publisher of the filthy Nazi rag *Der Stürmer*, mocked Americans for criticizing Germany's Jewish policy while practicing "lynch justice" and "Negro executions" at home. Streicher was not the only one to make the connection. Some observers familiar with racial segregation in the United States readily connected Nazi anti-Jewish policy with the brutality of Jim Crow. "Jews are being subjected to discriminations similar to those practiced against colored people in the Southern states of the United States," noted the *Baltimore Afro-American* with undeniable candor. From this perspective, the Nazi assault on Germany's Jews formed part of an ongoing global race war against Jews, Black Americans, Ethiopians, and colonized peoples in Asia and Africa.

Black and Jewish Americans, in protesting Mussolini's Ethiopian conquest and Hitler's brutality, pulled together the lines of an argument that when plotted out on a map crisscrossed the globe. From London to Cape Town; from Rome to Addis Ababa; from Berlin to Nuremberg; from Paris to Algiers; from Washington, D.C., to Warm Springs, Georgia, Western governments—both democratic and dictatorial—embraced the principle of racial hierarchy, revealing the kinship ties between an older order of empire and segregation and the new fascist racial order that the European despots aspired to build. To those who had experienced the humiliation of colonial subjugation in the European empires, or who had witnessed the flames consuming the writhing body of a lynch victim in Georgia or Mississippi, the racial obsessions of the German Nazis and Italian Fascists looked very familiar.[53]

VI

President Roosevelt spent most of that eventful September 1935 at Hyde Park, glad to escape the heat and humidity of Washington after a hard summer during which he and Congress had hammered out so many legislative achievements. Speaking in an impromptu address at the Women's Democratic Club of Hyde Park, he called it "probably one of the most important sessions that the Congress of the United States has ever had." His excuse for a long stay in his Hudson Valley home was the renovation of the White House electrical wiring, making the mansion "uninhabitable," he said. He returned to Washington on September 23, and three days later set out on a cross-country train passage to San Diego in the company of Eleanor Roosevelt; Interior Secretary Harold Ickes; the press team of Marvin H. McIntyre and Stephen T. Early; his personal secretary, Missy LeHand; his doctor, Ross T. McIntire; and his close pal and helpmate Colonel Edwin M. "Pa" Watson. The trip had numerous purposes, the first being the inauguration of the enormous Hoover Dam in the Black Canyon of the Colorado River. (Ickes, in a fit of partisan pique, had renamed it Boulder Dam, but Congress restored Hoover's name in 1947.) Started in 1931 by his predecessor, the dam nonetheless embodied FDR's ideals of using public funds to control floods and generate cheap hydroelectric power. His dedication speech at the massive new dam gave a powerful defense of the ways that major government spending projects improved lives, created jobs, and harnessed nature's power.[54]

On October 1, FDR motored through Los Angeles to a rapturous welcome and headed to the Memorial Coliseum, where he spoke to seventy-five thousand cheering spectators. In the four speeches he made on this western trip, FDR tried out his pitch for reelection in 1936, confidently summing up the progress his administration had made since the dark days of 1933. In San Diego, he contrasted his policies with the inaction of the Republicans. Facing an economic meltdown, his administration had chosen to use the tools of government to initiate radical change. He refused, he said, "to let nature take its course," await total collapse, and then "take the long gamble of rebuilding on the ruins." Instead, he reconfigured the banking and regulatory laws of the country, massively intervened in the agricultural sector, and found new ways of putting people back to work with a wage that allowed them to eat. "An American government cannot permit Americans to starve," he thundered, to heartfelt applause.[55]

If he had done much to revive the "spirit of America," he nonetheless recognized that foreign problems loomed over the world. Though privately, FDR had criticized those in "the school of thought which holds that we can and should withdraw wholly within ourselves and cut off all but the most perfunctory relationships with other nations," publicly he still stressed America's distance from Europe's turmoil. "It is not surprising," he said to the immense crowd in Los Angeles, "that many of our citizens feel a deep sense of apprehension" at the prospect of a new war, so soon after that last cataclysm ended. He assured them, however, that "the United States of America shall and must remain—as long ago the father of our country prayed that it might remain—unentangled and free." The government, he insisted, "will continue to preach the gospel of the good neighbor," encouraging peace, conciliation, and "the principles for which our flag has long been the lofty symbol." But America would not resort to force to impose those principles on others. It was a sentiment fully shared by his listeners, who cheered lustily at this repudiation of foreign intervention. With that, FDR and his party boarded the USS *Houston*, a nine-thousand-ton cruiser, for a vacation that began by observing naval maneuvers off the Cortes Bank west of San Diego, and then continued with a pleasant cruise along the coast of Baja California. The president planned on three weeks of fishing.[56]

On October 3, 1935, as the president's ship ran south through untroubled waters, two hundred thousand Italian soldiers, accompanied by convoys of lumbering tanks, trucks, and artillery pieces, crossed Ethiopia's borders. Italian bombers took aim at Adwa, close to the Eritrean border and the site of Italy's humiliation in 1896, indiscriminately hitting civilian targets in a showcase of fascist violence. *Time* magazine archly reported on the incongruity. While "the Italian troops advanced on Aduwa . . . Mr. Roosevelt, anchored near Cerros Island, listened to the World Series by radio. War-scared, the New York Stock Exchange had plummeted in the worst one-day break since

July 1934. In Magdalena Bay, the President went fishing." Three days into his excursion, on October 5, the president did what the neutrality law now required him to do. Over the *Houston*'s radio, he proclaimed: "A state of war unhappily exists between Ethiopia and the Kingdom of Italy," and he ordered an embargo to be placed on "the export of arms, ammunition or implements of war . . . to Ethiopia [and] to the Kingdom of Italy." As the sun dipped into the cobalt-blue Pacific, FDR veered west toward the uninhabited and spectacularly beautiful Cocos Island, 340 miles west of Costa Rica, mixing cocktails and swapping fishing stories with his guests.[57]

At dinner that night in the president's stateroom, the talk was all about war. Harold Ickes recalled that "the sympathies of everyone were with Ethiopia." The president's advisers quietly chatted about whether it was appro-

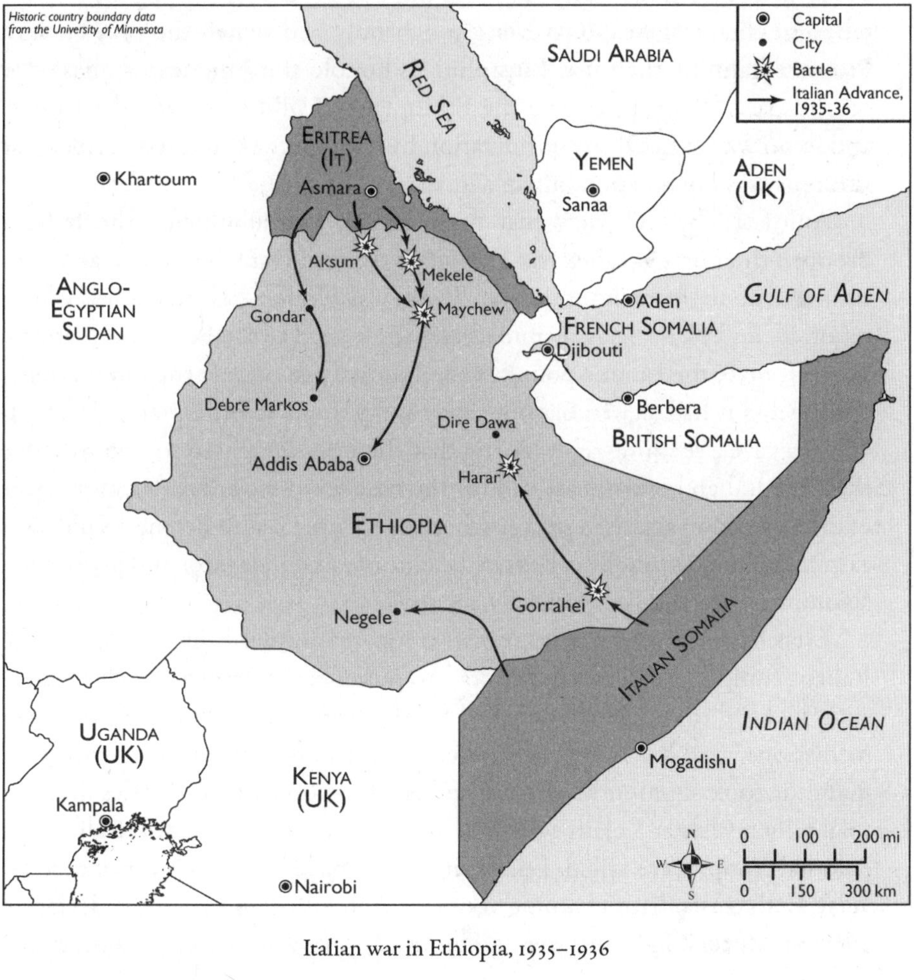

Italian war in Ethiopia, 1935–1936

priate for the fishing vacation to continue in light of the news. Ickes thought FDR should return to Washington, but the president ignored the suggestion. Instead, he enjoyed long days of leisurely fishing followed by evening drinks on deck and raucous games of poker and blackjack. The *Houston* threaded its way through the Panama Canal before finally arriving at Charleston, South Carolina, on October 23. In all, Roosevelt had been away from Washington for nearly two months.[58]

In that time, Italy's invasion of Ethiopia ground on. The Italians had built up an enormous force for the attack, using the Red Sea port of Massawa to stage huge quantities of food, ammunition, fuel, and weapons. The bulk of the invasion came from this Eritrean stronghold while a smaller force struck toward Addis Ababa from Italian Somaliland, crossing the Ogaden. With an immense advantage of weapons, and especially aircraft, the Italians seized the initiative from the start. They also did not shy from breaking the terrible taboo of chemical weapons, even though Italy had signed the 1925 Geneva Protocol banning their use. Mussolini, as he told the American ambassador on the eve of the war, viewed the Ethiopians as "illiterate, wild, barbarous, and in no way entitled to consideration by or respect of civilized nations, for Ethiopia was not a nation but an aggregation of slaves."

Animated by this view that their enemy was subhuman, the Italians dropped their first gas shells on Ethiopian troops in late December, and continued to do so throughout the war. The news of Italian gas attacks was widely reported, and Haile Selassie immediately protested to the League of Nations. In April 1936, the League politely called on Italy to respect the international agreements it had signed banning such weapons. The Ethiopian delegate in Geneva gave a seething reply, saying that the League refused to acknowledge that "the Italian government had for the past seven months carried on a war of extermination against a people whose only crime was to defend its political existence," and essentially called the League members cowards and hypocrites. (Not until 1996 did Italy officially acknowledge its use of gas in Ethiopia.)[59]

Eventually pinning the Ethiopian troops with their backs to capital, the Italians could use artillery and aircraft to pummel the defenders into submission. In April 1936, Mussolini called for the "total annihilation of Ethiopian formations," and his use of mustard gas gave a sinister overtone to this command. It took six months and a number of major set-piece battles, but the final tally reveals at a glance the horrific mismatch. About 9,000 Italian and colonial troops were killed. Ethiopian deaths have been a subject of controversy, with the Italians claiming about 70,000 killed and Ethiopia declaring 275,000 officers and men were killed in action. Ethiopia also claimed that

478,000 civilians had died as a result of the war, though these figures remain difficult to verify. By all accounts, the war took a shocking toll on Ethiopia. On May 5, the Italian commander Marshal Pietro Badoglio marched into Addis Ababa. In Rome, Mussolini gave a sneering victory speech in which he declared "Ethiopia is Italian. . . . Civilization triumphs over barbarism, justice triumphs over cruel barbarism." In Rome, Louis Fischer noted that flags adorned every building and "Mussolini's prestige was never higher." Meanwhile, Emperor Haile Selassie fled into exile; he would spend the next five years in England, a proud symbol of his defeated and wounded nation.[60]

Ethiopia was not the only casualty of this dreadful war. The League of Nations and the idea of collective security—of nations working together to police the international order—also sustained a mortal blow. Like the fictional murder on the Orient Express, there were many assailants. Italy drove in the knife first, but Britain and France soon followed. Britain's hypocrisy in the Ethiopian affair still has the power to shock. The coalition or "national" governments of Ramsay MacDonald and Stanley Baldwin both repeatedly stressed their commitment to the League and to collective security. During the general election of November 1935, when Baldwin was hoping to strengthen his hand by winning a larger Conservative majority, candidates of both parties gave stirring stump speeches denouncing Italy's invasion and calling for meaningful economic sanctions to be imposed by the League. In fact, on November 18, the League did impose a rather sophisticated set of financial sanctions on Italy, including an arms embargo, a freeze on loans and credits, some restrictions of exports of important goods, and most significant, a restriction on the import of Italian products, a move designed to make it impossible for Italy to earn the hard currency that it needed to purchase oil and raw materials on the world market. For a brief moment, it seemed that the League was at last living up to its promise: Over fifty nations cooperated in sustaining these financial sanctions on Italy. Had the war continued for a year or two, Italy's ability to buy vital supplies abroad—and Italy imported half its coal and all its oil—would have been crippled.[61]

But privately, Prime Minister Baldwin and his ministers feared the consequences of treating Italy too harshly. A naval blockade to halt Italy's oil imports, or the closing of the Suez Canal, might trigger war with Italy. Indeed, Mussolini had said as much. Such a European war, Baldwin's advisers told him, would propel Mussolini into the arms of Hitler in a powerful fascist combination in Europe; Austria would immediately be endangered, as would Poland, Czechoslovakia, southeastern Europe, and perhaps Russia. British ships in the Mediterranean would be harassed by the Italian navy, thus endangering British supply lines through the Suez Canal to India and Asia. A war with Italy, when added to worsening tensions with Japan in the Pacific, would immensely complicate Britain's imperial security. Despite the gradual progress the League had made in imposing sanctions, Britain wanted to avoid a worsening of the picture, and hoped to strike a deal with Mussolini to end the war. If that meant partitioning Ethiopia, it seemed to Baldwin's government a price worth paying.

Once Baldwin had won the general election, he gave his foreign minister, Samuel Hoare, leeway to explore a negotiated deal to end the war. Working with Pierre Laval, who had become French prime minister in June 1935, Hoare hammered out a proposal to offer Mussolini. About half of southern Ethiopia would be turned into a sort of mandate under Italian supervision, while smaller slices of the country in the east and north would be annexed outright by Italian Eritrea and Somaliland. It gave much of Ethiopia to Mussolini and spared him the trouble of having to fight for it. But before any deal could be reached, the Hoare-Laval plan was leaked to the French press on December 9, triggering an immense international outcry. To the British and French public, so proud of their governments for using the League to defend right over might, the plan looked like an unconscionable betrayal of the League. Hoare and Laval stood accused by the press, and many legislators in both countries, of stabbing the League in the back just as it was gaining real standing as the arbiter of world affairs. In Washington, the State Department was astounded and thought this proposal immoral. Baldwin pretended to know little about the deal, but backbench Conservatives screamed for a scalp, and Hoare was forced to resign a week after the plan leaked. At the end of January 1936, Laval, too, resigned.[62]

The Hoare-Laval plan showed that behind the scenes, Britain and France would gladly give up Ethiopia to appease Italy. With the public outcry having scotched the shameless backroom partition plan, however, the League's sanctions against Italy took on new importance. Could they work and perhaps punish Mussolini for his aggression without, at the same time, starting a wider European war? The economic sanctions needed time to work, and Mussolini by the start of 1936 knew this, too. His resort to chemical weapons in December was driven in part by his need to win the war quickly before the sanctions could bite.

But the League did have a powerful weapon in its arsenal that it had not yet used, and which might just have compelled Italy to back down: the threat of an oil embargo. To deprive Italy of oil would immediately slow and eventually halt the Italian war machine in its tracks. It was a very risky act to take because Mussolini had stated directly that he would see an oil embargo as an act of war. There was not much point in taking such a risk if the oil sanctions did not work, and the only way to assure its success was if the United States joined in the oil embargo.

At this time, U.S. companies produced 60 percent of the world's oil supply. So far, oil had not been placed on the list of embargoed exports by the U.S. because it did not match the criteria of "arms, ammunition, and implements of war" that the Neutrality Act enumerated. If the United States took the bold step of imposing an oil embargo on Italy, the League members might follow, and Italy would be choked into submission in a matter of weeks. At a crucial moment at the end of 1935, American actions, if combined with British and French resolve, might just have stopped Mussolini, rescued the League of Nations, and showed Germany and Japan that the world could act effectively against aggressors.[63]

But the Roosevelt administration failed to take this important step, and this is why the U.S. must be considered one of the assailants who inflicted a death blow upon the League of Nations. It is a devastating "what if" of history: What if FDR and Congress had come together in common cause to denounce Italy as an aggressor and international outcast that must be punished with stiff sanctions? What if FDR had the power to impose a discretionary embargo on Italy, using America's huge oil market as leverage? What if Hitler had seen a concerted and successful effort to use sanctions to halt aggression? It was not to be, of course. The Neutrality Act that FDR had so blithely signed in mid-1935 now blocked him from applying a selective embargo of specific goods only on one party to a conflict. When the League began to sound out the Americans about whether the United States might join in an oil embargo, all that Cordell Hull could do was stress that oil did not appear on the list of banned exports to the combatants in the Italo-Ethiopian War. The senators who designed the Neutrality Act knew that halting oil shipments to a nation at war would be provocative; it might also require a multinational blockade—precisely the kind of "collective security" confrontation that could lead to war. While the League wanted to impose penalties on Italy for its aggression, the U.S. Congress wanted to avoid taking any unneutral act against a single nation that might be interpreted as an act of war.

Frustrated by his inability to use U.S. economic power to curtail Italy's invasion, Roosevelt resorted to a "moral embargo," namely, urging American companies not to *increase* their sales of war matériel to Italy to meet the shortfall created when Europe closed off its markets. He issued a statement from the moral high ground: "I do not believe that the American people will wish for abnormally increased profits that temporarily might be secured by greatly extending our trade" in materials that would allow Italy to keep fighting. But he was wrong, for at the end of October, the State Department received figures showing that U.S. exports of copper, iron, and steel scrap to Italy had more than doubled between October 1934 and October 1935, while oil was flowing to Italy at three times the prewar rate. American companies had the goods and were glad to sell them, moral embargo or no. The British and French rightly concluded that the U.S. would not close off its oil supply to Italy. In that case, they chose not to take the risk of imposing their own oil embargo. American inaction opened an escape hatch for the League that it gladly used.[64]

Roosevelt in his January 3, 1936, State of the Union speech expressed his anxiety about the state of world affairs. He had told Henry Morgenthau two weeks earlier that he wanted to "say something about Nazism," and to link the Fascists in Italy to the various far-right groups forming in America. In fact, he toned down his remarks considerably. "The people of the Americas must take cognizance of growing ill will, of marked trends toward aggression, of increasing armaments, of shortening tempers—a situation which has in it many of the elements that lead to the tragedy of general war," he said, giving much more than usual attention to foreign affairs. He asserted that autocrats and dictators had "reverted to the old belief in the law of the sword, or to the fantastic conception that they, and they alone, are chosen to fulfill a mission and that all the others among the billion and a half of human beings in the world must and shall learn from and be subject to them."

In the face of this intensifying aggression, FDR stated his dual policy: "First, we decline to encourage the prosecution of war by permitting belligerents to obtain arms, ammunition or implements of war from the United States. Second, we seek to discourage the use by belligerent Nations of any and all American products calculated to facilitate the prosecution of a war in quantities over and above our normal exports of them in time of peace." But by the time he spoke these words, his policy had already failed. It had not slowed Italy's march, nor had it stopped American oil from going into Italian trucks and tanks. FDR's use of the language of peace and moral example may have pleased the ears of those Americans who wished never to wage war again. But it also brought joy to the very dictators he condemned. For he made it plain: America would take no overt act to stop aggression overseas.[65]

The tragic Ethiopian war had significant consequences for American foreign policy. At the end of February 1936, the Neutrality Act was set to expire. Congress had been discussing how to renew it, and if necessary, how to strengthen it. FDR had welcomed the Neutrality Act in 1935 because he, too, desired to avoid inadvertent entanglement in war. But the Ethiopian conflict showed how the act could hamstring the president. He could not adapt to circumstances and use America's huge economic power in the interest of peace. FDR hoped to get Congress to agree to revise the act in such a way as to keep the mandatory features of the arms embargo but allow the president discretion over exports of raw materials. Secretary Hull worked hard to try to alter the act to allow the president some discretion over exports of war-related commodities. He argued that the Neutrality Act kept the United States from sending arms to combatant states; why not add to that legislation the additional ability to impose export controls on strategic materials used in war-making?[66]

Congress refused. Too many senators feared that a policy of presidential discretion would give Roosevelt the leeway to align the United States with the collective security principles of the League and that, they felt sure, would draw America into war. Senator Nye and his allies drew attention to the conclusion of the Senate munitions investigation: Presidential discretion over trade with belligerents is just what got America entangled in the last war, they argued. During the month of January 1936, the White House wrangled with Congress, but the stalemate endured. Roosevelt feared the cost of a damaging and prolonged fight, and he gave in, agreeing to accept an even more stringent Neutrality Act that forbade loans to belligerents as well as arms sales. The 1936 Neutrality Act was set to last for fourteen months, at which point it could be revisited. Once again, Roosevelt chose not to expend his political capital to secure greater presidential power to conduct foreign policy. That proved a grave miscalculation, for it would become only more difficult, as war clouds darkened in Europe, to win concessions from Congress and free the president to act against the forces of fascism and Nazism.[67]

VII

The neutrality debates, combined with the remarkably flaccid administration response to the Italian invasion of Ethiopia, put the world on notice: For fear of getting ensnared in foreign crises, the United States would restrain itself from exerting any meaningful influence over world affairs. It was a remarkable act of unilateral withdrawal, fueled by a loud chorus of anti-militarists, anti-business populists, anti–League of Nations politicians, and those who still carried the bitter wounds of the last war. Roosevelt emerged from this ordeal a diminished leader. He failed, twice, to find a winning formula to defuse a congressional attack upon the powers of the presidency to conduct foreign relations. In the interest of his domestic priorities, and because he himself had adopted so much of the pacifist language of the day, he refused to defend the right of the chief executive to choose when and where to use the power that by law and tradition belonged to him.

American inaction sent a message. In Europe, the British and French governments now understood that they were on their own in facing the fascist threat. And Hitler felt confirmed in his assessment of the democracies: Confronted with a daring, decisive action like Mussolini's invasion of Ethiopia, they would huff and puff and, in the end, do nothing. Mussolini embodied the fascist creed, showing that boldness would win out over parliamentary dithering every time. A statesman with far less cunning and ambition than Adolf Hitler would have concluded that the Western powers had absolutely no desire to meet the challenge of fascism on the field of battle. On March 7, 1936, in another calculated gamble, Hitler ordered German troops into the demilitarized Rhineland. This vital buffer zone between Germany and France had been occupied by Allied troops at the end of the war, but those forces had been removed in 1930. By the terms of the treaty, the Rhineland was to remain free of any military fortifications or German soldiers. Hitler guessed, after watching the confusion of the democracies during the Ethiopian crisis, that Britain and France would do nothing in response. He was right.

The fascists were riding high. Anne O'Hare McCormick, who in the 1920s had been so dazzled by Mussolini and fascism, skillfully sketched a portrait in 1936 of the new Italy that had eagerly gone to war to expand the Italian empire. Fascism, she wrote, stirred a passion in Italians that "democracy seems to have lost the power to inspire." Nationalism, unity, pride, and a willingness to sacrifice for the nation: These were emotions the Fascists knew how to stir. By contrast, she wrote, "democracy cannot compete with these new systems unless it summons the young to pay an equal price for freedom." The Western democracies spoke of their devotion to peace. But what were they willing to give for it? McCormick now believed that it would take "sacrifices beyond any yet conceived" to beat back the forces of nationalism and build a lasting peace in Europe and the world. A Fascist war against democracy was coming, she believed, because war was the raison d'être of fascism. Would democracy defend itself?[68]

Writing in the grim aftermath of Italy's successful conquest, W. E. B. Du Bois, too, came to a tentative conclusion that fascism, along with its twin, white supremacy, would never yield unless met with an organized global campaign in favor of freedom. Ethiopia had been left to suffer a "Golgotha of murder, destruction, and cruelty." What was to be done? If people of African descent wanted to save Africa from further despoliation, they would have to join together, build a common commitment to their liberation across national boundaries, and organize themselves against global white supremacy. The lynching of Black people in America, the seizure of Haiti, the conquest of Ethiopia, "these are pieces of one cloth," and they required a common struggle against fascism and white supremacy.[69]

To that end, Du Bois was willing to ask the question that no one in the peace camp had the courage to pose. To fight against such oppression, was force necessary? "Ethiopia has thrown new light on pacifism," he argued in his *Pittsburgh Courier* column. He had once been a pacifist and opposed all wars. Now, he confessed, pacifism looked hollow. "There must be world policemen, just as we have city policemen; otherwise, a criminal like Mussolini is always free to stab a gentleman like Haile Selassie in the back and crow over it." In the intellectual climate of the left in the 1930s, Du Bois uttered an almost heretical opinion. The use of force had been condemned by the peace movement as barbaric and uncivilized behavior. But Du Bois countered: "I am a little puzzled as to just where the conquest of Ethiopia leads the pacifists." He imagined a bully on a city street attacking and strangling a "half-grown child." Was it civilized to stand and watch, and do nothing? "If a world war, or the threat of it, could have stopped Italian aggression in Ethiopia," he insisted, "it would in the long run have cost humanity less in the murder of human beings and the overthrow of human ideals." Du Bois, a socialist and pacifist, had come early to the conclusion that there are things worse than war, namely, the unmourned destruction and conquest of an entire people by Fascist tyranny.[70]

The leaders of the world's democracies, no less than their people, were not yet ready to consider this kind of talk. It remained only for Haile Selassie, now a king without a state, to deliver the epitaph of the whole grisly affair. On June 30, 1936, this slight man, grayed by the agonies of war, came to Geneva to address the League of Nations Assembly. He spoke in an accented French and a thin voice to the representatives of all the League's member states. He delivered a warning. "It is my duty to inform the Governments assembled in Geneva," he began, "of the deadly peril which threatens them, by describing to them the fate which has been suffered by Ethiopia." He spoke of the chemical weapons, the gas shells, and the sprayers attached to aircraft that released a fine lethal mist over Ethiopian troops, as well as nearby towns and villages, so that "soldiers, women, children, cattle, rivers, lakes and pastures were drenched continually with this deadly rain. In order to kill off systematically all living creatures, in order more surely to poison waters and pastures, the Italian command made its aircraft pass over and over again. That was its chief method of warfare."

Behind this unspeakable act lay a larger moral failure: the unwillingness of the world's most powerful nations to defend the rights of the weak. "In October 1935, the 52 nations who are listening to me today," he said, "gave me an assurance that the aggressor would not triumph, that the resources of the Covenant would be employed in order to ensure the reign of right and the failure of violence. . . . I had placed all my hopes in the execution of these undertakings. My confidence had been confirmed by the repeated declarations made in the Council to the effect that aggression must not be rewarded, and that force would end by being compelled to bow before right." Instead, behind closed doors, the great powers plotted Ethiopia's partition and destruction, awarding to the aggressor the spoils it desired. The League turned its back on a weak African state, unwilling to stand up for the rule of law and the dignity of a sovereign people. Selassie quietly concluded his speech with a simple and devastating envoi: "God and history will remember your judgment."[71]

CHAPTER 8

IT CAN'T HAPPEN HERE

"There are enough good people who believe in the flag and the Bible to seize and control the government of America!"

—GERALD L. K. SMITH

I

By the middle of the 1930s, fascism had established itself as the most dynamic and successful political ideology in Europe. Fascists built their movement on the claim that liberal democracy could neither solve the global economic crisis of the Depression nor beat back the menace of Communism that threatened to turn Europe into the devil's playground. Pointing to the experience of the Soviet Union since 1917, fascists conjured up the specter of bloody revolution and Stalinist tyranny as the fate that threatened civilization. In response, powerful industrialists, Catholic church leaders, senior military officers, press barons, and even some classical conservatives accommodated themselves to rising fascist parties, seeing fascism as a bulwark against the "reds." Fascist governments had taken power in Germany, Italy, Austria, Portugal, and Greece by the end of 1936, and fascist generals in Spain would soon seize power there, too. Fascist political parties were surging in Britain, France, the Low Countries, Scandinavia, and southeastern Europe; by the end of the decade, fascism would rule over much of the European continent. It undoubtedly looked like the wave of the future.

Did it ever stand a chance in America? In a country with 20 percent unemployment—down from 25 percent in 1933, but still shockingly high—a restive public might well be primed for a new kind of political order. The right leader, with the right message, just might be able to turn discontent into revolutionary action. In late 1935, Sinclair Lewis, the Nobel Prize–winning novelist and the husband of columnist Dorothy Thompson, published a short satirical novel titled *It Can't Happen Here*. Its general argument was that it very well could happen here. Fascism in America might not look like the black-shirted variety in Rome. But in an era of economic desperation and a loss of faith in democracy, a populist leader who could draw upon a familiar American vernacular of Christian zeal mixed with class resentment and xenophobia could quite possibly win wide support.[1]

As Franklin Roosevelt began to shape his 1936 reelection campaign, the threat of domestic fascism transformed American political discourse. Whereas in 1932, FDR positioned himself as the outsider who promised to turn the "moneychangers" out of the "temple of our civilization," in 1936 he had to defend a record of experimentation that featured both successes and failures. From both the right and the left, FDR heard bitter criticism of the New Deal and his efforts to reshape American capitalism. The business class argued that the New Deal was too radical, had intervened too much into the marketplace, and threatened to make the federal government into a tyrannical, overbearing dictatorship. Conservatives, including many in his own Democratic Party, accused the president of violating the Constitution, abusing his power, and going socialist. From the other side of the political spectrum, soapbox populists called the president a liar and a traitor for bailing out big banks, allying with industrial leaders, failing to address glaring economic inequality, and providing only undignified, stopgap, low-wage relief work for the unemployed. With mounting bitterness, some of his early supporters, who had expected much greater daring and radicalism, turned on him with intense ferocity, calling for a root-and-branch cleansing of the American elite and a final reckoning with the bankers and industrialists who kept their hands coiled around the neck of the American working man.

In designing a response to these attacks on him and his signature policies, Roosevelt had to do more than simply defend his record of achievement in his first term. He had to show that American democracy could still provide effective solutions to the grave crises of the moment. FDR urged the American people to reject would-be dictators and authoritarians who promised that only they, armed with suitable powers, could solve America's problems. Borrowing some of the class-warfare rhetoric of the populists, Roosevelt moved away from the "happy warrior" style he perfected in his first term—the air of pragmatism, buoyancy, and good cheer he projected as he muddled through the problems the country faced. Instead, he forged a new argument for his 1936 campaign: Democracy at home was under threat from unaccountable, powerful elites who threatened to sink the New Deal just as it was gaining momentum. Positioning himself as a champion of the voiceless and powerless against special interests and reactionaries, FDR began to connect the antidemocratic tendencies of his domestic critics to the rise of the dictators abroad. Europe offered a cautionary tale of how easily democracy could be surrendered to charlatans and vulgar hate-mongers. Democracy was under siege at home no less than abroad, and Americans were called to fight on its behalf. The kernel of an idea, too dreadful yet to be spoken aloud, took hold in his mind: that to secure democracy at home, Americans might have to face, and vanquish, fascism in the world.

II

As early as 1933, some public officials believed that the fascist threat to America would come directly from Europe, transported by sympathizers who wanted to build a simulacrum of the Nazi movement in America. "The Nazi Government has reached into this country," declared Congressman Samuel Dickstein of New York in a statement to the press on October 9, 1933. No less than three hundred Germans, "personally selected by the German Minister of Propaganda" and supplied with "millions of Marks," had entered the country with the purpose of flooding the United States with pro-Nazi propaganda. The ultimate objective of these agents: "overthrowing our government and installing in its place a dictatorship on the Nazi model." As chairman of the House Committee on Immigration, Dickstein took it upon himself to launch a preliminary investigation into the matter. On a nationwide radio broadcast that week, he asserted that "here in America, an insidious, well-planned and well-financed Hitler propaganda is rapidly taking root." The Nazis were already "drilling their Storm Troops on American soil," Dickstein alleged, and an investigation now was a "matter of self-defense."[2]

Dickstein had a reputation as a brash, pugnacious publicity hound. Born in a Jewish family in Vilnius, Lithuania, in 1885, he had been brought to the U.S. as a small boy and grew up in the tenements of the Lower East Side of Manhattan. Bright and ambitious, he made it through City College and New York Law School and went into politics, gradually rising through the Democratic Party machine in New York and landing a seat in Congress in 1922. When the Democrats won control of the House in 1930, Dickstein got a plum job as chairman of the Immigration Committee, from which he launched a personal campaign against fascism and its adherents in America. He painted an alarming picture of a vast Nazi conspiracy to undermine democracy, and he positioned himself as the fearless crusading congressman who could expose it.

In America, a nation with over 8 million inhabitants of German origin, hundreds of Germanic cultural organizations had proliferated for decades.

Mainly, they sponsored gatherings of immigrant families who liked to hoist frosted mugs of German beer, eat grilled sausage, and sing songs from the old country. But with the emergence of the Nazi Party in Germany in the early 1920s, a small number of naturalized German Americans as well as recent German immigrants identified themselves with the magnetic if still marginal figure of Adolf Hitler. A group called the National Socialist Teutonia Association was formed in Detroit in 1924 by two immigrant brothers, Peter and Fritz Gissibl, who shared the antisemitic and conspiracy-laden ideology of the young Nazi Party. Detroit had a large working-class German community, with plentiful jobs in the sprawling Ford auto plant—until the Depression hit, when many men found themselves out of work. Although the number of members in the pro-Nazi Teutonia group remained small, the seed of a larger organism had been planted, and cells of Teutonia were set up among German communities in Chicago, Milwaukee, St. Louis, New York, and Cincinnati.[3]

When the Nazis took power at the start of 1933, their eager U.S.-based imitators imagined that they could serve as the pioneers of a robust, ideologically coherent Nazi movement in America with direct support from Berlin. An ambitious member of the Detroit Teutonia group, German-born immigrant Heinz Spanknöbel, traveled to Germany in the spring and managed to secure the blessing of Hitler's deputy, Rudolf Hess, to build a new organization in America that coordinated its efforts with the Nazi high command. Hess and his minions believed that "Aryan blood" ran through the veins of these far-flung German brothers who congregated in significant numbers in the American Midwest and East Coast. Nazism, it seemed, already had a foothold in the New World. Hess gave Spanknöbel the green light, and in May 1933, Spanknöbel rolled up other German fraternal groups into the *Bund der Freunde des Neuen Deutschland*: the Association of the Friends of New Germany.

With the help of the German consul in New York, Spanknöbel set up an office in the heavily German Upper East Side neighborhood called Yorkville and declared himself the singular leader of the new Nazi movement in America. He issued viciously antisemitic pamphlets, urged his followers to daub synagogues with swastikas, and tried to intimidate local German-language newspapers into supporting Hitler. He also planned a large public "German Day" rally for October 26, where he planned to unveil the new nationwide Nazi movement amid a sea of Nazi banners and stiff-arm salutes. But given the intense opposition across New York to the Hitler regime at this very moment, and the successful anti-German boycott spearheaded by Jewish leaders, this proved an unpropitious time and place to launch an American Nazi movement. Congressman Dickstein caught wind of Spanknöbel's activities, and pressured New York City mayor John P. O'Brien to cancel the German Day rally out of fear that New Yorkers would meet it with violence. (A Nazi assembly in Chicago that day featured Nazi flags, Hitler salutes, and 350 Germans singing the "*Horst Wessel Lied*," the Nazi Party anthem.) Dickstein went even further: He used his influence to get a grand jury empaneled to charge Spanknöbel with illegally acting as an agent of a foreign government. Dickstein wanted him deported. The mayor banned the German Day meeting, stating that "there is no room here for the preaching, in these days of crisis, of any such un-American doctrine, whether it be anti-Semitism, Ku-Kluxism, or any related phase of bigotry." Spanknöbel, now fearing arrest, slipped down to the dockyards, boarded the German liner SS *Europa*, and sailed for home.[4]

All this was grist to Dickstein's mill, and he used the skulduggery of Spanknöbel to point to a larger pattern of Nazi infiltration in America. His preliminary hearings in mid-November were abruptly terminated when it became clear that without funds or congressional approval, a temporary inquiry would not be able to achieve much. That winter, Dickstein gave incendiary speeches alleging that German agents were at work in eighteen states across America, distributing thousands of pieces of vile propaganda. He spoke of "40,000 to 50,000 aliens" smuggled into the country who were trying to link their movement to other fascist-style groups like the "Silver Shirts" based in Asheville, North Carolina, led by an obscure antisemitic publisher and self-proclaimed oracle named William Dudley Pelley. Dickstein's public agitation about the domestic Nazi threat worked: In March 1934, he won passage of a resolution to create a Special Committee on Un-American Activities focused on the threat of Nazi propaganda in the United States. This committee would be led by John McCormack of Massachusetts with Dickstein as his cochair.[5]

Despite the growing federal interest in their activities, the Friends of New Germany did nothing to hide their allegiance to Nazism. In December 1933, German-American organizations in New York, appealing to the mayor to lift the ban on their annual German festival, won approval for a rally in Madison Square Garden. Despite promises that the event would be apolitical, the evening was punctuated with pro-Nazi propaganda. The German ambassador, Dr. Hans Luther, stood on the huge stage and raised his right arm in a Hitler salute; this was met with a universal shout from the twenty thousand people in the hall of "Heil Hitler" and the impromptu singing of "*Horst Wessel Lied*." Other speakers denounced the "Jewish boycott" of German goods. When these antics were criticized as evidence of a plan organized in Berlin to promote Nazism in America, Hitler's government denied any overt interference in American politics. It was a half-hearted denial, though, because the Deutsches Ausland-Institut, the central office for documenting the global German diaspora, issued a statement saying that it had a right to "give our brothers abroad the spiritual and moral equipment effectively to fight systematic propaganda and lies against the Reich." Nazis in America, then, had a spiritual duty to oppose Jewish "slander" against Germany.[6]

In addition to their rallies, the Friends of New Germany built a reputation in New York as a kind of Nazi mafia. Following Spanknöbel's flight from America, Fritz Gissibl, the cofounder of the group, took the helm and intensified its anti-Jewish activities in New York, organizing a counter-boycott of Jewish shops in Manhattan. Under the guise of the Deutsch-Amerikanischer Wirtschafts-Ausschuss (DAWA), or German-American Business Committee, the Friends created an extortion racket. They bullied storeowners in Yorkville and the greater New York area to pay a five-dollar fee for the right to hang a card in the shopwindow with the DAWA symbol: a black eagle that looked remarkably similar to the Blue Eagle of the NRA that many Americans had affixed to their lapels and storefronts. In return for this "privilege" of hanging the Nazi eagle in their windows, store owners promised to avoid any commerce with Jewish merchants in New York until they ceased their anti-German boycott. Failure to abide by the DAWA demands could lead to smashed windows or physical harm. About ninety German American organizations promoted the DAWA counter-boycott, and the Friends soon boasted that five hundred thousand German Americans (surely an exaggeration) were actively involved. The money raised by this crude scheme went into the coffers of the Friends for more newspapers, handbills, and posters denouncing Jewish perfidy.[7]

In May 1934, the simmering tension in New York came to a rolling boil. In just the same week when the McCormack-Dickstein committee began its hearings, the Friends of New Germany organized a "Day of Awakening of Germandom," yet another rally at Madison Square Garden at which speakers planned to denounce "the unconstitutional Jewish boycott." Seven hundred New York policemen and mounted officers formed a picket all around the hall on the evening of May 17 as over twenty thousand ticket holders pushed to get inside. Nazi swastika flags hung down the massive walls of the Garden, and a company of burly storm troopers, in full regalia, but wearing white shirts rather than brown, stood in the aisles. Among the speakers was George Sylvester Viereck, a notorious pro-German propagandist during the First World War who edited a magazine called *The Fatherland*. He was a regular traveler to Germany and had met with Hitler and his entourage numerous times. Other speakers denounced Samuel Untermyer, the prominent lawyer and leader of the Non-Sectarian Anti-Nazi League, which had organized the anti-German boycott. They railed against the "Jewish domination of America," as one speaker put it. As the Nazi rally-goers filed out of the Garden, about five hundred Communists met them in the street and hurled abuse at them; only a thin blue line of nervous patrolmen kept the confrontation from turning bloody. Meetings like this, with swastika flags, costumed thugs in militia-style uniforms, and oaths of loyalty to Hitler, could be seen in a dozen cities across the country in 1934 and into 1935. The Nazi movement in America, it seemed, could not easily be suppressed.[8]

But did such regular rallies reveal the existence of a plot directed from Berlin to undermine the American way of life? The McCormack-Dickstein committee, whose hearings ran all summer and into the fall of 1934, set out to make the case. But its conclusions did not quite live up to the hype. Despite deposing hundreds of witnesses and gathering thousands of pages of written material, the committee could show only that some German diplomatic staff in America had worked with the Friends of New Germany to purchase and distribute pro-Nazi propaganda—a violation of the rules of diplomatic behavior, but hardly a threat to the Republic. Certainly, witnesses made it plain that the Friends of New Germany shared the racial and ideological tenets of Nazism, and their frequent gatherings put the swastika on display in cities and suburbs around the country. And it was uncomfortable to learn that the Friends had set up a summer camp for German children near Princeton, New Jersey, called Camp Wille und Macht (Will and Power). Dickstein visited the campsite personally and reported, "we have found too much goose-stepping and no saluting of the American flag. . . . They have a four-inch American flag, but the Nazi swastika flags are four feet long." None of this quite rose to the level of threat to national security, but Dickstein did not relent. In wrapping up his committee in early 1935, he portrayed pro-Nazi gatherings in New York, Boston, Chicago, Philadelphia, Detroit, and Cincinnati in sinister terms: "There is going on in this country at this time an extensive campaign for Nazism" and against America's democratic values.[9]

Dickstein had tried his best to raise awareness in the United States about the potential threat of these Nazified Americans. But his investigation had perhaps greater impact in Berlin than in Washington. Hitler and especially the German Foreign Office began to grow wary of the antics of this band of ill-disciplined foot soldiers operating on American soil. At a time when Hitler's Germany was still trying to maintain stable relations with the Roosevelt administration, the congressional investigation of subversive Nazi activities threatened to turn American public opinion decisively against the German government. In October 1935, the Foreign Office, calling the group a "nuisance," forbade all German nationals in America from joining the Friends of New Germany, and ordered German citizens in the organization to resign. Jew-baiting, so common at Nazi rallies in Germany, had become a liability in America. Hitler wanted the group shut down. Hess duly delivered the news, and this first iteration of a Nazi movement on U.S. soil soon withered. But Hitler and his minions could not control the actions of *American* citizens of German origin, should they choose to carry on the work of the Friends of New Germany. And there were many German immigrants with American passports who yearned to carry the Nazi torch. The dream of a Nazi America did not die quite yet.[10]

III

At least through the middle part of the decade, these Nazi sympathizers did not pose a serious threat to America. More worrisome were homegrown threats coming from some of the most powerful men in America. Ironically, the most important revelation of the McCormack-Dickstein committee had nothing to do with Nazis. On November 21, 1934, a retired Marine Corps officer, Major General Smedley D. Butler, appeared before the committee to tell a remarkable tale. He claimed that he had been approached by an intermediary of powerful Wall Street banking interests to mobilize an armed force of U.S. veterans that would overthrow the Roosevelt administration and install a form of fascist dictatorship. The story seemed outlandish, but Butler swore under oath that a New York bond salesman named Gerald MacGuire had spoken with him on numerous occasions starting in July 1933, and showed him bank books with thousands of dollars of cash supplied by highly placed financiers for Butler's use in organizing a military march on the White House.

General Butler, who during a long career had compiled an infamous record of helping coup plotters and imperialists in the Caribbean and Central America, showed no interest in the scheme. He told the investigating committee that "he smelled a rat." But MacGuire persisted, and in August 1934, he came to see Butler again after making a long trip to Europe to examine how fascist organizations had been built in Germany, Italy, France, and Spain. MacGuire told Butler that the French Croix de Feu—a fascist militia composed of former soldiers—was exactly the model he had in mind for America. He imagined Butler leading an American corps of volunteers to throw FDR out of office or, perhaps, to act as a kind of praetorian guard with the power to make decisions while relegating the president to a mere figurehead. "We need a Fascist government in this country to save the nation from Communists," MacGuire allegedly said. And General Butler was the man to lead former soldiers in this cause. MacGuire was called before Dickstein's committee and admitted meeting Butler, discussing a leadership role for him in the American Legion, and reporting on right-wing politics in Europe. But in halting, contradictory testimony, he denied proposing a coup d'état.[11]

Inevitably, the press gave this tale of an alleged plot to overthrow the government, led by wealthy business interests, plenty of attention. "New York capitalists," reported the *Washington Post*, were planning a "Fascist march on Washington somewhat along lines of Mussolini's march on Rome." Dickstein, after hearing the closed testimony from Butler, told reporters that "some rather important personages have been proposing ideas that are distinctly un-American." But emphatic denials immediately came from the men named by Butler as taking up roles in this proposed junta, including General Hugh Johnson, the former NRA administrator; Thomas Lamont of J. P. Morgan; and General Douglas MacArthur, the U.S. Army chief of staff. Meanwhile, Dickstein and his committee prepared a compressed summary of Butler's testimony for release to the public. It looked to them as if Butler had been duped by a small group of unscrupulous plotters who made unverifiable claims about having the backing of New York banking interests. Butler, possibly imagining himself as a savior of the Republic, insisted that "there is a potential menace in these movements unless they are exposed," and he stuck with his story. But given the prominence of some of the figures alleged to be involved, and the shakiness of the testimony they heard, the Dickstein-McCormack committee preferred to drop the matter.[12]

It has long been a subject of speculation and debate among historians: Was there really a "business plot" to overthrow the government and install a kind of junta in Washington? It is possible that such a scheme might have been discussed among disgruntled bankers or old soldiers, but the story had too many holes to be plausible. In normal times, Butler's story might easily have been dismissed. Yet it resonated in 1934 because of the sharp resistance the New Deal had encountered from business elites. In a fireside chat on June 28, FDR acknowledged that his policies threatened monied interests, bankers, and wealthy industrialists. "In the working out of a great national program which seeks the primary good of the greater number," the president explained, "it is true that the toes of some people are being stepped on and are going to be stepped on. But these toes belong to the comparative few who seek to retain or to gain position or riches or both by some short cut which is harmful to the greater good." FDR thought he was simply leveling the playing field that for too long had tilted in the direction of the wealthy.[13]

His opponents called this class warfare and plotted to strike back. On August 23, just when the "business plot" was allegedly being hatched, some of the country's most powerful corporate titans and political insiders announced the formation of a pressure group to fight the radicalism of the New Deal and return the nation to what they claimed were its bedrock constitutional principles. The group was called the American Liberty League, and its founding gave credence to the idea that bankers and plutocrats were plotting to take back control of the government and purge it of every last vestige of the New Deal.[14]

FDR knew the men behind the Liberty League very well. Its director was Jouett Shouse, the former chairman of the Democratic National Committee who had opposed Roosevelt's nomination for president. Right behind Shouse was Al Smith, FDR's former mentor in New York, who since losing out to FDR for the nomination in 1932 had become a bitter enemy. Smith had turned sharply to the right and developed close ties with leading business and financial heavyweights, who now joined him in the League. With Smith stood the wily millionaire John J. Raskob, the former chairman of General Motors and corporate board member of the Du Pont industries; Alfred P. Sloan Jr., the president of General Motors; and the du Pont family, in particular Irenée du Pont, vice-chairman of Du Pont & Nemours, the very same man who Senator Gerald Nye had called a "merchant of death" for his profit-making in the arms business. John W. Davis, the deeply conservative Democrat who got thumped by Calvin Coolidge in the presidential contest of 1924, also joined the list of well-known but notably unsuccessful politicians who hoped that the League could succeed in doing what they had been unable to do: halt the New Deal.[15]

Naturally, Shouse told the press the new organization was nonpartisan and apolitical. The group sought only to "educate" the country about "the necessity of respect for the rights of persons and property." Property and its acquisition ran like a red thread through all their founding documents, giving away the real intention behind the League: to halt government encroachment, by way of taxation, regulation, pro-labor policies, and administrative power, over corporate control of America's economy. The enemy, according to Shouse, was "radicalism," and few doubted that the stop-Roosevelt group from 1932 wanted to stop Roosevelt again in 1936.[16]

Roosevelt did not bat an eye. He had bested the Smith-Raskob-Shouse team before, and he saw this confrontation with elite voices from the past as a political gift. In fact, FDR instantly grasped the political opportunity the

Liberty League gave him: Here was a group of rich reactionaries that he could use as a foil for his progressive policies. In a press conference on August 24, FDR skillfully parried the thrust of the League by saying that all Americans naturally subscribed to its stated goals of protecting individual and property rights; that was "axiomatic," he said. "Personally," he went on in a carefully prepared rebuke, "my own feeling is this: that when you come down to the definition of American principles you want to go the whole hog; you want to go all the way, instead of stopping short. An organization that only advocates two or three out of the Ten Commandments may be a perfectly good organization in the sense that you couldn't object to the two or three out of the Ten Commandments, but it would have certain shortcomings in having failed to advocate the other seven or eight Commandments."

Warming to this theme, he flayed the Liberty League for its hostility to the little man: "There are quite a number of other things that the average, and more than average, human gets out of government" besides the protection of property. "There is no mention made here," he gleefully pointed out, "about the concern of the community, in other words the Government, to try to make it possible for people who are willing to work, to find work to do. For people who want to keep themselves from starvation, keep a roof over their heads, lead decent lives, have proper educational standards: Those are the concerns of government." Furthermore, he continued, with a sharp stab at the bankers and corporate titans behind this new group, the Liberty League did not address "the protection of the life and the liberty of the individual against elements in the community that seek to enrich or advance themselves at the expense of their fellow citizens." He closed the matter by saying that when he read in the papers that the Liberty League had the fulsome support of Wall Street stockbrokers, "I lay in bed and laughed for ten minutes."[17]

He had reason to chortle. On November 6, 1934, Americans went to the polls for the first midterm election of FDR's presidency and delivered an unmistakable mandate in favor of Roosevelt and the New Deal. Bucking the historic trend of incumbent presidents losing support in Congress in the midterms, the Democratic Party gained nine seats in the House and nine in the Senate, giving them a supermajority in the upper chamber. The Republicans were pushed to the brink of extinction, holding on only in New England, the upper Midwest, and slivers of the West Coast. No wonder the Liberty League went into overdrive now, shrieking about the dangers of one-party rule and the snuffing out of democracy.[18]

Yet, there could be no doubt that the whiff of reaction hung in the air, and for the next two years, the Liberty League pumped out a stream of pamphlets with impassioned arguments against the New Deal. They itemized and repudiated Roosevelt's excessive spending and usurpation of the power of Congress, his expansion of the federal bureaucracy and the regulation of business. FDR sought "socialized government," said the League, and had placed America on the road to tyranny. "Wherever in the world today there is serious dabbling in Socialism," alleged one broadside, "those countries end up in dictatorship, either Fascist or Communist." Al Smith, former Democratic standard-bearer, told an audience of Liberty League faithful in Washington that it was not easy to criticize his own party, but the unconstitutional policies of the president compelled him to state the "facts," namely, that the New Deal was not just contrary to Democratic Party ideals but was profoundly un-American. Invoking the nation's founders, he claimed the Constitution had been written by "refugees and sons of refugees, by men with bitter memories of European oppression" who were willing to die for their personal liberty. The free nation they built now lay imperiled by the autocratic, power-hungry chief executive in the White House.[19]

IV

The fulminations of the Liberty League, along with rumors of a fascist-style coup to oust FDR, demonstrated the growing anxiety on the right that the New Deal would succeed in curtailing the privileges and power that economic elites long enjoyed in America. But did this conservative critique represent a real threat to Roosevelt? *The Nation* magazine thought not, making the astute observation that "the march on Washington will probably not be led by Smedley Butler or by any of the gentlemen publicly mentioned in connection with the fascist plot." Rather, if the New Deal failed to fix the economic and social crisis of the Depression, Americans would turn not to corporate boardrooms or cigar-chomping former pols for answers. They would lurch leftward, demanding more radical solutions increasingly on offer from grassroots populists like Senator Huey Long of Louisiana. And FDR did not laugh about the "Kingfish" from the bayou.[20]

With his receding chin and blubbery face, pug nose and curly mop of uncombed hair, his loud neckties and Delta twang, and especially his herky-jerky lecture style in which he thrust a fist straight into the air and then brought it down into the palm of his hand again and again, Huey Long seemed an unlikely herald of a new political order. Yet he emerged as the most charismatic, energetic, and disconcerting politician of the early 1930s—a match even for Franklin Roosevelt, who famously called Long "one of the two most dangerous men in the country." (The other was General Douglas MacArthur, who had so eagerly rousted out the striking veterans from their temporary camps in Washington in July 1932.) Born and raised in rural northern Louisiana in a moderately prosperous farming family, Long grew up with a chip permanently affixed to his shoulder. Impatient, argumentative, easily bored by school, but blessed with a quick wit and fierce debating skills, Long barely made it through a year in college before taking up work as a traveling salesman. His success at selling vacuum cleaners to housewives could not satisfy him for long. He aimed to make something of himself. He attended night classes at Tulane Law School and, after less than a year of study, passed the state bar exam. He set up shop as a country lawyer at the ripe age of twenty-one.[21]

But he was drawn to politics, armed with the gift of gab, and driven by a desire for status and recognition. His election in 1918 to the state Railroad Commission, a once-moribund board that in fact had considerable authority to regulate utilities across Louisiana, marked the start of his rapid ascent. Using his influence over this regulatory agency, Long developed a reputation as a fighter willing to go toe-to-toe with big industries like the Standard Oil Company, with its huge refinery plant along the Mississippi River at Baton Rouge, as well as the railroads, the natural gas companies, and the electric utilities. He demanded lower prices for the consumer and proposed higher taxes on the corporations to help fund infrastructure in the state. As his legal practice grew, making him a well-off squire, he tested the waters of statewide politics with a run for governor in 1924. He lost, but established his name and his reputation as the champion of the common man. In 1928, the same year FDR won election to the governor's mansion in Albany, Long sailed to victory in the Louisiana governor's race with 57 percent of the vote, running especially well in rural counties among the small farmers who expected great things from the fiery populist.[22]

Senator Huey Long of Louisiana, a progressive populist and a gifted demagogue.
Library of Congress

Limited by law to one term, Long worked fast to build a political machine that would endure even after he had left office. He pushed through development projects that could directly benefit his poor constituents, such as schools, hospitals, paved roads, and toll-free bridges. He also built monuments to himself, like the new state capitol building, a new governor's mansion, and a hugely expanded Louisiana State University. He doled out favors to his friends and relentlessly harassed his enemies, using patronage and graft to get his way. He handpicked judges and legislators who then cleared a path for his programs. In 1930, he ran for an open U.S. Senate seat and won, though he refused to resign as governor because the lieutenant governor who would replace him was a political enemy. Long used his control of the courts to unseat this rival and placed a subservient crony in the post. He then took his new seat in the Senate in early 1932, yet still controlled state politics through his compliant puppet governor. Though he held no office in the state legislature, Long would preside over its sessions anyway and force through the measures he wanted. Not without reason, the press referred to him as "the dictator of Louisiana."[23]

But in the U.S. Senate, Long quickly found that he had no levers to pull, no executive authority such as he enjoyed as governor. He was merely one voice in a chamber full of blowhards where power derived from seniority. Too impatient to climb the Senate pecking order, Long went rogue. As the country spiraled downward into a bleak economic depression, Long demanded action to help the little man and directed scathing attacks on both parties for their failure to respond to the plight of the hungry and poor. He attacked his own Democratic Party leadership for its ties to wealthy banks and big business; he filibustered against bills his colleagues favored; he broke the rules of decorum on the Senate floor by insulting his rivals and wearing clownish combinations of pink shirts, loud ties, and flamboyant suits. But in the process, he attracted national press attention, and he used his notoriety to advance his own pet project: the redistribution of America's wealth. In April 1932, he called for confiscatory taxes on the very rich and the sharing of that excess with the poor who could afford neither a home nor food for their families. His Democratic colleagues like Senator Pat Harrison of Mississippi, a member of the powerful Finance Committee, quickly denounced Long's ideas as un-American. "I think America ought to give a fellow the opportunity to make money," Harrison said, especially during a depression. But Long understood the tenor of the times. His words resonated in a hard-hit, anxious nation—so much so that Governor Roosevelt would borrow some of these ideas in his 1932 presidential campaign.[24]

Long strongly backed Roosevelt's bid for the White House, seeing in the New Yorker a man who had the courage to take on the "money-changers" and the elites in corporate boardrooms. He campaigned across the country for FDR, showing off his remarkable speaking skills and his talent for attracting publicity. But after Roosevelt took office, the relationship between the two men quickly soured. Long spoke out against many of the signature pieces of legislation during the 100 Days because he felt they focused too much on rescuing big banks rather than saving the little man. He denounced the Economy Act, which slashed government spending just when the country needed the federal spigot turned on. In particular, he opposed the National Industrial Recovery Act that allowed businesses to fix prices and wages, fearing collusion of the big industries against workers. He thought FDR had been snookered by the big bankers and squandered an enormous opportunity to impose enduring change on the American economy.[25]

In early 1934, Long took a step that marked his break with his own party and the president. In a national radio speech on February 23, 1934, he unveiled his "Share Our Wealth" plan. Long told his listeners that the New Deal had failed to take the bold steps the people wanted. "Had Mr. Roosevelt proceeded along the lines that he stated were necessary for the decentralization of wealth, he would have gone a long way already," Long said. But FDR pulled up short and protected the interests of the banking class. Therefore, Long laid out a plan for a national movement to build pressure upon the president. "We have in America today, my friends, a condition by which about 10 men dominate the means of activity in at least 85 percent [of the economy]. . . . They own the banks, they own the steel mills, they own the railroads, they own the bonds, they own the mortgages, they own the stores, and they have chained the country from one end to the other." Long outlined a federal program to tax the very wealthy to provide a basic guaranteed income of $5,000 to all households. He also called for a cap on working hours, the provision of old-age pensions, and free college education. The superrich in America could still keep plenty of their money, but not at the expense of the struggling farmer and unemployed working man.[26]

His radio address was an irresistible performance, larded with sentiment and pathos. "People today," he said, "are seeing their own children hungry, tired, half-naked, lifting their tear-dimmed eyes into the sad faces of their fathers and mothers, who cannot give them food and clothing they both need, and which is necessary to sustain them, and that goes on day after day, and night after night." America had the power to fix this calamity. Drawing on the Scriptures for support, Long called on the government to do the Christian thing and help the poor. "We have got to hit the root with the ax. Centralized power in the hands of a few, with centralized credit in the hands of a few, is the trouble." Long urged his listeners to form "Share Our Wealth" clubs in their community and keep the pressure up on their representatives. With the assistance of a devoted follower named Gerald L. K. Smith, a former evangelical minister from Wisconsin, Long oversaw the construction of a genuine national organization that mushroomed into twenty-seven thousand Share Our Wealth clubs with millions of members. By the start of 1935, Huey Long had built a political movement that made him a household name across the country.[27]

Though Long presented himself in public as a champion of the little fellow in his struggle against big government and big banks, he used his power in Louisiana in the style of an authoritarian bully. Throughout 1934 and 1935, he waged a bitter fight with the mayor of New Orleans, T. Semmes Walmsley, the patrician scion of an influential New Orleans family whose support came from the city's leading lawyers and business interests. Long wanted to run his own handpicked cronies in races for office in the U.S. Congress, the state supreme court, and the Public Service Commission. Walmsley's New Orleans machine controlled a significant bloc of votes that could foil Long's plans. (Given the lack of Republicans in the state, victory in the Democratic primary made winning the post in the general election a certainty.) Alleging corruption in New Orleans by the mayor, Long ordered the National Guard to occupy the city's voting registration office. Walmsley accused Long's men of purging the voting rolls of potential opposition voters. The month before the primary, Long jammed through the state legislature twenty-seven bills that gutted the power of elected officials across the state, replacing them with supervisory commissions whose members would all be appointed by Huey Long's rubber-stamp governor. The national press likened Long to "a dictator of an authoritarian state." But his bills rolled through the kangaroo legislature by a nearly two-thirds margin, so completely had Long cowed its members.[28]

On September 11, 1934, all of Long's candidates won, even in districts where the Walmsley forces expected to be strong. Emboldened by this triumph, Long went back to the state house to push through another forty-four laws to ensure that the Public Service Commission—which his men now dominated—would have complete authority over the state's utilities; other boards were to be appointed to govern all aspects of public life, including the public schools. The hog-tied legislature passed these bills in under two hours with Senator Long sitting in chair of the Speaker of the House. When opponents asked Long if they could at least read the bills, he laughed and told them they'd pass anyway. The national press gave Long's actions a great deal of attention, and even the British newspaper the *Manchester Guardian* seemed stunned by Long's assault on democracy. "Many Americans," that paper reported, "are even asking themselves whether he is not now in a position similar to that of Hitler about the time of the Munich putsch." No one now doubted Long's intention to run for the presidency.[29]

President Roosevelt believed Long was a danger not just to his own reelection but to the country. In typical style, he launched an indirect attack on the senator in ways that allowed the president plausible deniability. The Treasury Department suddenly found cause to investigate the tax returns of many of Long's closest supporters, finding significant irregularities. Federal funds for public works and jobs in Louisiana dried up. In March 1935, General Hugh Johnson, the former administrator of the NRA, launched a blistering personal attack on Long, calling him the "dictator of the Delta," "the Hitler of one of our sovereign states," a "mad mullah," a "dancing dervish." Johnson, speaking before a tuxedoed dinner audience at the Waldorf-Astoria in New York, admitted that the country still faced big problems, but denied that Huey Long had the solutions. His Share Our Wealth program was all "mumbo-jumbo," Johnson thundered, and his rule by fiat in Louisiana showed Long's true nature. "Huey is a dictator by force of arms and Adolf Hitler has nothing on him." A day later, the distinguished, courtly Senator Joe Robinson of Arkansas, a Democrat and former governor of his state, called Long an "egotistical, arrogant and ignorant" man whose ideas for wealth distribution were simply "the ravings of a madman." The establishment was striking back.[30]

To FDR's great concern, however, attacks like these did little to dent Long's national popularity. He told Ambassador William Dodd, who was in Washington on leave, that "Long plans to be a candidate of the Hitler type for the presidency in 1936." Long planned to split the Democratic Party, allowing "a reactionary Republican" to win. This, FDR went on, would so inflame the country that by 1940, the people would clamor for a savior. "Long thinks he would be made dictator," FDR said. He had reason to worry. A secret poll taken by the Democratic National Committee in April 1935 showed that in the 1936 presidential race, Huey Long could win anywhere from 10 to 15 percent of the vote in a three-way contest against FDR and the Republican candidate. While FDR still had a commanding lead in popularity over both Long and the as-yet-unnamed Republican, Long might win enough votes to deny Roosevelt a majority in the Electoral College. Jim Farley, the campaign manager, considered Long "a source of annoyance rather than a threat in 1936," but the poll made it clear that Long could complicate FDR's reelection.[31]

It was certainly not coincidental that in mid-June 1935, Roosevelt announced a reform of the nation's tax laws, using language that carried a faint echo of the bayou. "Our revenue laws," FDR wrote to Congress, "have operated in many ways to the unfair advantage of the few, and they have done little to prevent an unjust concentration of wealth and economic power." He went on to argue that great fortunes were never the result of one person's toil or industry but the product of the work of the community. The community ought therefore to share in this wealth. Massive fortunes handed down from one generation to another perpetuated economic inequality and should be taxed. Incomes over $1 million should likewise be taxed heavily, and on an upward scale so that the superrich paid taxes at the highest rates. "Social unrest and a deepening sense of unfairness are dangers to our national life which we must minimize by rigorous methods," he said, in words that many construed as a nod to Huey Long's demagoguery. The government must step in and lessen the most glaring examples of inequality in the nation. The press treated the president's "soak-the-rich" tax message, which became the Revenue Act of 1935, as a direct riposte to the Kingfish. It was, said one paper, a "master stroke of politics and cuts much ground from under the feet of Senator Huey Long." Senator Long would be "smothered" by the new proposal, said another report. One reporter heard "a note of bitterness and disappointment" when Long responded to FDR's proposals. He knew that the president "really had taken the wind out of his sails." Roosevelt followed this with the Social Security Act, designed chiefly by Frances Perkins and signed by FDR on August 14, 1935—a signature piece of legislation that showed that while Huey Long could talk about a new economic order for America, FDR was actually building it.[32]

By the fall of 1935, the battle lines were drawn for a bruising political fight between the popular sitting president and a clever, unpredictable, gifted rival. Long's appeal to millions of voters rested on his uncanny skill in diagnosing America's problems as the result of the criminal greed of a privileged few, and in offering solutions that had a beguiling simplicity about them. As he geared up for a presidential run, Long published a book in September 1935 called *My First Days in the White House*. Rather than offer a boring summary of his policy ideas, Long's book imagined a near future in which he had already been elected president. Sweeping into Washington, President Long appointed a coalition cabinet made up of figures like Herbert Hoover (secretary of commerce), General Smedley Butler (secretary of war), Al Smith (director of the budget), and Senator William Borah (secretary of state). Even FDR would find a place in this cabinet, though demoted to secretary of the navy. One by one, Long imagined, he would call these men into his office and order them to undertake gigantic public works projects costing billions. The government would also take over the banking system, provide medical care for all, jobs for all, guaranteed income for all, grant pardons to petty criminals, and fund college for America's young people. The immense cost of this transformative undertaking would easily be paid for by heavy taxation of the richest few. In this weird fever dream, the titans of industry looked upon Long's bold actions with such alarm that they caved in immediately. In Long's fantasy, John D. Rockefeller offered to surrender his entire fortune to be distributed to the people. "The barons of Wall Street," Long wrote, "were content at last to accept democracy in America."[33]

Of course, this futuristic scenario never materialized. On September 8, 1935—just about the time his book appeared—Long was shot in the belly by an aggrieved young man whose family had been the target of one of Long's political vendettas. Long lay in a hospital bed in agony for two days before sepsis set in and he died. He would never get a chance to rule America, either as the benevolent Father Christmas of his own kaleidoscopic daydream or the power-hungry tyrant his enemies knew him to be. The single greatest political threat Franklin Roosevelt faced during his first term vanished. Yet Long's importance lies less in his political challenge to FDR—who, after all, could expect strong nationwide support in the 1936 election—than in the way it legitimized antidemocratic political action. Democracy, even when facing the emergency of the Great Depression, seemed slow, cumbersome, inefficient, prone to compromise and half measures. Long showed in Louisiana that a singular leader could cut through the red tape and get results, even if success meant riding roughshod over democratic procedure.

Though some commentators drew a parallel between Mussolini and the Louisiana senator, Huey Long was not a fascist. He lacked many of the conventional signifiers: no glorification of militarism, no ethno-nationalism, no rallies of jackbooted storm troops, no ideology steeped in racism and antisemitism, no flag or emblem, no "shirts" of black or brown. Nor did he have the tacit support of conservative elites, the military, or landowners, as Hitler and Mussolini did. Instead, Long used class antagonism to fuel his rise to fame. He preyed upon the anxieties of the impoverished and destitute who felt, with some reason, that the Wall Street fat cats were stealing bread from the mouths of their children. In this sense, he drew from a long tradition of agrarian populists in the American South who had built movements of the have-nots against the haves. To be sure, he had many of the personal attributes of the strongman: the lust for power, the scorn for compromise, the immense self-regard, the eagerness to construct a cult of personality, the inability to tolerate even the slightest criticism (he had the editor of the LSU student newspaper dismissed for publishing a critical editorial). But Huey Long did not need fascism; his own brand of populist class warfare and demagoguery was successful enough without aping Hitler. At a time of grave economic dysfunction in America, Long built a powerful base in Louisiana that just might have been enough to propel him into the White House. It was merely a twist of fate that Senator Long never got the chance to fulfill his ambitions.[34]

V

Long's death did not mark the end of anti–New Deal demagogy. In fact, it opened up the field to new competitors. Gerald L. K. Smith, Long's zealous right-hand man who had venerated the slain Kingfish, acted swiftly to claim the leadership of the Share Our Wealth movement. A tall, vigorous son of rural Wisconsin, Smith moved to Louisiana in 1929 to take a post as minister in an evangelical church in Shreveport. After hearing Long's thundering denunciation of the wealthy, Smith left his position in the church in 1933 to work for the senator full-time. A charismatic apostle of Long's radical message, Smith enjoyed immediate success across rural Louisiana, inveighing against bankers, gold hoarders, trusts, corrupt monopolists, Communists, and bureaucrats.[35]

At Long's funeral on September 12, 1935, Smith told a crowd of a hundred thousand mourners that he would carry on the movement, which, he said, "shall never rest as long as lean human frames stand naked, as long as homeless wretches haunt this land of plenty." To F. Raymond Daniell, the *New York Times* reporter who had covered Huey Long's rise, Smith looked like a cheap imitation of the real thing. He borrowed the same physical gestures, wore an old suit once owned by the deceased senator, and let his forelock fall in his face while giving thundering speeches against the misrule of the banking class. "Mr. Smith stands for the old-time religion and old-time Americanism with Fascist trimmings," noted Daniell. But for all his gifts as a sermonizer, Smith had no access to the levers of power, and he quickly found himself sidelined in Louisiana by factions vying for the leftover pieces of Long's empire.[36]

Smith went looking for new allies who could help him stay in the limelight, and he found one in Dr. Francis Townsend, an elderly and frail-looking California physician who had been making national headlines in promoting a scheme to kick-start the economy and help vulnerable elderly people. Townsend's scheme sounded simple. If the government would pay Americans over sixty years of age a monthly stipend of $200 (funded by a small national sales tax) and require them to spend that money within the month, this would supply them with basic needs and help stimulate national economic activity. In a depression-racked nation that did not yet have a Social Security program, Townsend's plan, called the Old-Age Revolving Pension (OARP) plan, caught fire. Thousands of clubs sprang up across the country to lobby elected officials in favor of the plan. It echoed Long's Share Our Wealth program and was, in economic terms, just as impractical: Its cost would far outstrip any revenue it generated. But Smith sought out Townsend and proposed they make common cause, linking the earnest if naive doctor with the fire-breathing, tub-thumping antics of an evangelical preacher. Together, they hoped to forge their supporters into a powerful bloc in the run up to the 1936 elections.

To have any hope of success, however, Smith and Townsend needed to win over to their side the most well-known, influential figure of the anti–New Deal wave in America: Father Charles E. Coughlin, the Catholic "radio priest" who had started his rise to national fame in 1930. Born in Ontario of Irish American parents—his father was a laborer who had moved back and forth across the boundary with Canada looking for work around the Great Lakes—he was raised in a devout Catholic family and ordained as a priest in Toronto in 1916. He moved to Detroit in 1923 and the archdiocese there soon assigned him to a small church called the Shrine of the Little Flower (devoted to the recently canonized St. Thérèse of Lisieux) in the heavily Protestant town of Royal Oak. In 1926, aged thirty-five, Coughlin (pronounced kawg-lin) oversaw the construction of a modest new church for his humble flock. The day after it opened, the local KKK chapter set a cross alight on its front lawn—a fearful gesture of anti-Catholic bigotry that only spurred the fighting cleric to greater action.[37]

In a few short years, Coughlin went from being a small-time church leader in a bland suburb on the fringes of industrial America to become a nationally known figure, venerated by millions. How did it happen? It began through the medium of radio. In an effort to spread the message of his sermons to a wider audience, he proposed to a local radio station that he be allowed to broadcast live from his pulpit. He would pay the cost of the transmission. After his first radio sermon in October 1926, Coughlin received an enthusiastic response, which grew over the next few months. Not only did the number of worshippers in his church increase, but letters of thanks, along with small contributions, began to arrive in the mail. If his wire-rimmed spectacles and carefully combed brown hair made him look like a modest clergyman, his thick neck, fleshy face, and broad shoulders, hinting at his collegiate career as a football player, suggested latent power. Above all, though, it was the voice. His rich baritone carried a hint of an Irish brogue that he exaggerated for effect. Coughlin could modulate his tone from a quiet, pastoral message of assurance to the loud, booming command of an Old Testament prophet. He came across as a confiding, assuring, omniscient presence. In the memorable phrase of the novelist Wallace Stegner, Coughlin possessed "a voice made for promises."[38]

Initially, Coughlin drew on the Scriptures for his lessons and showed no particular interest in politics. But once the Depression hit Detroit's motor industries, leading to huge layoffs, breadlines, hunger, and increasing desperation among the working class, Coughlin began to address the economic and social crisis directly. He offered sinister explanations for its cause—the greed of international bankers and "unelected and selfish financiers"—and mesmerized his listeners with his distinct combination of sincerity, authority, and moral certainty. He stoked fears that economic distress provided "a breeding place" for communism, "the worst form of paganism that ever appeared on the face of the Earth." He denounced the gold standard as a tool of the bankers to impose austerity on hard-pressed laborers. He called for the monetization of silver in order to push more currency into circulation, and he wanted the government to take control of the banking system, in order to pry it out of the hands of plutocrats like "the Morgans, the Kuhn-Loebs, the Rothschilds, the Warburgs." (His repeated emphasis upon Jews in the banking world would become even more pointed toward the end of the decade.) In language that spoke directly to the gnawing anxiety of many jobless Americans, Coughlin painted a picture of heartless kingpins of finance rolling in ill-gotten gains while the weak, the poor, the hungry, the masses, struggled for survival. His message resonated across the Midwest and Northeast, where it could be heard spilling out of countless windows every Sunday afternoon. He received an average of eighty thousand letters a week. By 1932, over thirty radio stations carried his program to 30 or 40 million regular listeners.[39]

Father Charles Coughlin.
Library of Congress

Unlike fascist leaders in Europe, Coughlin did not call for a revolution against democracy; he claimed that he wanted its radical revival, in the manner of William Jennings Bryan, the "great commoner" who had run for president three times on a platform of anti-corruption, trust busting, abandoning the gold standard, and bringing greater democracy to the people. Coughlin in 1932 became an enthusiastic supporter of Roosevelt's, hoping he would shatter the orthodox shibboleths of Republican monetary policy. After FDR won, Coughlin showered him with praise. "The new deal is here," he bellowed to his flock in March 1933, led by "new men, enlightened men, who will transform America." Following the passage of the Emergency Banking Act in March 1933, which gave the Federal Reserve Bank the power to issue additional currency and take control of troubled banks, Coughlin declared that "Roosevelt shall be immortalized for having broken the bonds of financial slavery." The president welcomed these expressions of loyalty but always remained politely cool and distant from Coughlin.[40]

Over the next two years, however, Coughlin soured on FDR. The president kept him at arm's length and would not adopt his legislative proposals. The boldness he expected from the new president yielded to political compromises. The Depression endured, wages stayed stagnant, unemployment persisted. Coughlin's enormous weekly mailbag told him of the ongoing suffering of the public. Perhaps in response to these frustrations, Coughlin announced in November 1934 the creation of a new pressure group called the National Union for Social Justice (NUSJ), which would lobby elected officials to act on Coughlin's demands. He quickly demonstrated its clout: In January 1935, as the Senate considered passage of the treaty that would bring the United States into the World Court, Coughlin gave a fiery sermon against it, asserting that the Court would turn over American sovereignty to international bankers. As a result of Coughlin's last-minute opposition, telegrams flooded Capitol Hill echoing the priest's arguments. The Senate narrowly rejected the measure, to FDR's profound dismay.[41]

Coughlin discovered that stoking fear and pointing an accusing finger got him bigger audiences than rooting for the president. His sermons became more sharply political and polemical. He aimed his barbs in every direction, at bankers, labor leaders, bureaucrats, Communists and Socialists of every variety, the New Deal, capitalism, the American Liberty League, and FDR himself. In April 1935, he announced that his NUSJ had swelled to 8.5 million members. He planned to mobilize these voters to "drive out of public life the men who practice the philosophy of plutocracy," he told fifteen thousand followers at the Olympia Stadium in Detroit. He was vague when it came to stating what he was for, but he never stinted in declaring what he opposed: "racial Hitlerism," "industrial fascism," "plutocratic individualism," "immoral capitalism," as well as "the dictatorship of a President." The next month, speaking to an even larger and noisier crowd at Madison Square Garden in New York, he condemned such figures as Baruch and Warburg and Morgan—his familiar roll call of sinister bankers. He demanded "protection for the small industrialist, production at a profit for the farmer, a just and living wage for every American," but it was his feverish condemnation of Wall Street and the banks that brought enormous, thundering waves of applause. Shouts of "Coughlin for President" could be heard rippling across the sea of hopeful faces.[42]

In early September, Coughlin got a call from Joseph P. Kennedy, at that time chairman of the Securities and Exchange Commission, and a prominent and well-connected Catholic. "The Boss wants to talk to you," Kennedy told the cleric. In person. Kennedy directed Coughlin to take the train to Albany, where he would meet him and drive him to Hyde Park. As it happened, the visit occurred on September 11, the morning after Huey Long died. Coughlin had heard newspaper boys at the train station shouting the news, and he conveyed it to Roosevelt upon arriving in the early morning at the Hyde Park mansion. "He blanched white," Coughlin recalled. "It was a shock to him." FDR then sat Coughlin down over breakfast at the kitchen table and demanded an explanation for the priest's rants against the New Deal. Coughlin replied that he wanted the president to act more boldly to address the economic crisis; Roosevelt insisted that he was doing more than any Republican would do, and that if Coughlin kept up his attacks, he would open the way to a GOP win in 1936.[43]

Coughlin was not moved, and if anything grew firmer in his resolve to break publicly with the president. In late November 1935, the moment came. Coughlin went on the air to confess his error in supporting FDR in the 1932 election. The New Deal had been a sham, he said, providing only "slave wage" relief work to millions, while deceiving the farmers and labor. To these accusations of deceit at home, Coughlin added deception abroad, alleging that FDR secretly made a pact with the League of Nations to support sanctions against Italy in the Ethiopian conflict. "Move by move," thundered the priest, "the checkers are being played which will force us into the corner of an inevitable war. . . . The jobless American youth will be herded to the slaughterhouse abroad" by a deceptive and untruthful president. As one newspaper put it, Coughlin "ran up his battle flags" with these words.[44]

Battle flags there were, but did Coughlin have the troops? He claimed that millions supported him, and millions more listened to his broadcasts.

It was time to find out if they would follow him into combat against a popular, and immensely clever, president. Coughlin had often denied wanting to start a third party. He had no experience in electoral politics, nor did he know how to build a get-out-the-vote operation. He needed foot soldiers to do that kind of work. Two stood ready to assist: Gerald L. K. Smith and Francis Townsend, the pair of hucksters whose fix-the-Depression schemes had garnered nationwide attention. Each of them believed he could mobilize millions of downtrodden and penniless Americans into a mighty movement to unseat the fat cats and redistribute America's wealth. But it would be a very peculiar set of bedfellows, the effete, moralizing Coughlin under the covers with a septuagenarian doctor and a second-rate Huey Long impersonator.

Gerald Smith by mid-1936 had taken his rabble-rousing to new heights, asserting that he and Townsend "would get rid of Roosevelt and capture the U.S. government." Smith adopted a crazed kind of rhetoric that might have been too vulgar even for Coughlin. In a spittle-flecked speech on June 6 in New York, Smith promised to rid America of "Rosey-velt and his gang of Frankfurter pinks and his Fascist lash of terror and his stupendous plot to communize America." This was impolite language. But on June 19, Coughlin made an astonishing announcement. His National Union for Social Justice would join forces with Smith and Townsend in a Union Party, and they would back a hitherto-unknown North Dakota congressman named William Lemke for president. Townsend claimed that the combined forces of these men would control 20 million votes in the 1936 election. A skeptical media termed this curious coalition "the lunatic fringe."[45]

There was a good deal of lunacy on display in midsummer of 1936, as the Townsend organization staged a convention in Cleveland, Ohio, to allow members of nationwide Townsend clubs to give their blessing to the new anti–New Deal party. On July 15, about eleven thousand people gathered in the city's Public Auditorium. According to one observer, they were "ample, motherly women and old men who have spent their years in hard work," people who slept in cheap motels or in their cars during the convention, eating humble boxed lunches brought from home. They wanted to hear Dr. Townsend explain why the balding no-name teetotaler from North Dakota, William Lemke, was the man to back in the presidential election against Roosevelt. What they got instead was a high-octane performance from Gerald Smith. Coatless, drenched in sweat, and clutching a Bible, Smith electrified the audience with his foaming denunciations of Wall Street and his howling anti-communism. He got them clapping, standing on their chairs, howling, hissing, booing, and cheering in the aisles. It was an old-time revival meeting that only lacked a parishioner speaking in tongues. "There are enough good people who believe in the flag and the Bible," he shouted, "to seize and control the government of America!" The crowd simply exploded as Smith reached his climactic utterance, telling his audience that America faced a clear choice: "It is the red flag or the Stars and Stripes! It is Lenin or Lincoln! Stalin or Jefferson!" And of course, the demonic Roosevelt or the holy Union Party.[46]

Father Coughlin, who thought of himself as the star attraction and who was visibly annoyed by Smith's success at lathering up the crowd, now came to the podium to give his blessing to the new political party. He began by trying to restore some dignity to the proceedings, but as he warmed up, his speech turned into a bitter denunciation of "the great betrayer and liar, Franklin D. Roosevelt—he who promised to drive the money changers from the temple and succeeded in driving the farmers from their homesteads and the citizens from their homes in the cities." This personal attack was a departure for Coughlin, who always said he hated FDR's policies, but not the man himself. But now he laid it on thick, knowing he had to match Smith's intensity. He took aim at all his usual targets, from the bankers to the gold hoarders to the communists to the rigged media. In the stuffy, sweltering auditorium, Coughlin halted in mid-speech to remove his black jacket and his tight clerical collar, as if stripping down for a fight. Then he returned to his attack: "I ask you to purge the man who claims to be a Democrat from the Democratic Party, and I mean Franklin Double-Crossing Roosevelt." Bedlam in the hall.[47]

Overheated: Coughlin harangues the faithful in Cleveland.
Library of Congress

VI

Did Huey Long, Charles Coughlin, Gerald L. K. Smith, and Francis Townsend constitute a fascist threat to America? Looking back through the lens of the Second World War and all its horrors, no one could find in these amateur demagogues and self-appointed saviors anything like the genocidal ambitions of Hitler or the imperial chauvinism of Mussolini. But to many Americans at the time, the populist, anti-elite, increasingly antisemitic Christian nationalism of the "lunatic fringe" sounded familiar, like a fascist anthem transposed to an American key. Despite the absence of an organized fascist party or militia, Coughlin's angry, conspiratorial message gripped millions of Americans. James Waterman Wise, the son of the heroic Rabbi Stephen Wise, who had worked so hard to raise the alarm about Nazism in Germany, neatly captured the danger of the American homegrown variety. If fascism comes to America, he said in February 1936, it would not be wearing the uniform of a storm trooper or bearing an insignia on its sleeve. It would be "wrapped up in the American flag and heralded as a plea for liberty and preservation of the Constitution."[48]

Those themes ran through Coughlin's innumerable sermons and speeches: The modern world, he believed, had perverted the simple enduring principles of American self-government. In Coughlin's view of America, the individual farmer and shopkeeper felt powerless in the face of huge concentrations of wealth. He had lost his home or farm to unnamed bankers, while distant, all-powerful chiefs of industry refused to give him a job or a decent wage. He felt betrayed by political parties that had cynically made promises they never would keep. He had lost his dignity standing in breadlines. His family and town no longer seemed to protect him from the harsh winds of capitalism. He had fought, or sacrificed his sons, in foreign wars started on behalf of bankers and arms dealers. In return he got nothing.

But Long and Coughlin did share something with the continental fascists. They proposed to use *more* government to solve these problems. They called for the government to seize banks and nationalize the banking system; to tax the rich and redistribute their huge fortunes; to issue new currency; to lower interest rates; to forgive the debts of farmers; to halt all flows of loans and gold out of the country; to remove the profit motive from the economy and assure high prices for farm goods; to develop huge work programs that paid good wages out of government coffers. These measures, taken by a government of true patriots like themselves, would restore a lost world, turn back the red tide of Communism, revive America's faith in God, and fulfill the vision of the Founders of an orderly Christian society. Here lay the germ of fascism: a belief that a corporate state, freed from the compromises and half measures of democracy, could impose a unitary system upon its citizens, and build an enduring social structure in which everyone knew his place and gave his loyalty to the visionary leaders who had brought order out of chaos.

Many of the sharpest political minds in the country saw the link between the European fascist movements and their American imitators. As early as January 1935, the radio commentator and journalist Raymond Gram Swing, in a multipart series in *The Nation*, argued that Coughlin's state-centered, corporatist solutions to America's problems bore a "technical similarity to those of Hitler." Like the harangues of the German Führer, Coughlin's speeches "are vague and emotional," tapping into "the underlying prejudices of listeners." While Swing considered Huey Long merely a goggle-eyed, power-hungry strongman, he sensed in Coughlin something more sinister. "More nearly than any demagogue in America, he has the formula for a Fascist party," Swing concluded. Dorothy Thompson, too, saw the likeness. The Union Party, she wrote in the summer of 1936, "is a nearer approach to a national Fascist tendency than any which America has yet developed." Thompson noted that the demagogues appealed to the same audiences as Hitler had done before taking power: the "dispossessed and humiliated of the middle classes, bankrupt farmers, cracker-box radicals," as well as conservative elites who secretly hoped the populists would bring down Roosevelt. Add to this mixture the demagogues' habit of "Scripture-quoting" and their Klan-like hostility to foreigners, Thompson concluded, and you had a recipe for American fascism.[49]

American Jews, too, felt the cold chill of hate in the words of Coughlin and Smith. As the Union Party coalesced in the summer of 1936, Smith infused it with antisemitism, tapping into the usual tropes. Linking FDR to Communism and Jews, he told one audience that the New Deal was a "cake baked in Moscow by Ezekiel and Cohen," that is, the agricultural economist Mordecai Ezekiel and the lawyer and brain truster Benjamin V. Cohen. Coughlin, too, started to drift into the overt antisemitism so typical of fascists. His ringing denunciations of Jewish investment bankers like Bernard Baruch, the Rothschild family, and the Lazard Frères investment firm became so heated and nasty that Jewish leaders called him out for his "scurrilous demagogy." At the end of August, Coughlin declared that Jewish bankers were heartless loan sharks because they adhered to the principle of "eye for an eye, tooth for a tooth," rather than the Christian ethic of brotherly love. This weird Jew-baiting brought forth a flood of criticism from national newspapers, but his followers did not mind. They agreed with the cunning cleric that "Jews are too sensitive and too jittery in view of what has happened in Germany." They should not be so "thin-skinned," Coughlin said.[50]

Amid widespread criticism of Coughlin's increasingly toxic public statements, the *Washington Post* editorial page in mid-August delivered one of the most pointed and brutal assessments of the radio priest. Calling the Lemke campaign a lot of "hooey," the paper likened the Union Party rallies to a recent public lynching in Kentucky, when thousands of people had jostled for a good view of the hanging. Like European fascists, the *Post* continued, Smith and Coughlin were manipulating their supporters, inflaming their passions, lavishing them with promises they could never keep, and insisting on the need to restore "American" values against foreign and un-American enemies. Should a Lemke, Smith, or Coughlin ever take actual power, they would have to resort to dictatorship "to suppress the outcries of their disillusioned supporters" who would demand to know why the promised Utopia had not arrived. Coughlin was "America's No. 1 potential Fascist leader" who had mastered "the Hitler technique." Preying on the misplaced hopes of a desperate public, Coughlin made American democracy look deceitful and corrupt. There was no doubt: Given his skills, the paper concluded, he "could easily bring it down in ruins."[51]

VII

Since the death of Huey Long, Franklin Roosevelt did not worry much about the electoral threat of the Coughlinites. But the evidence is clear that he took seriously the assaults launched by the populist Union Party and the reactionary Liberty League on the integrity of America's democracy. In his 1936 reelection campaign, he devoted many speeches to two intertwined themes: that the New Deal, in recalibrating the national economy to make it fairer, would revive American democracy; and that in rescuing democracy, his administration would light a beacon of hope to embattled people around the world. During 1936, in no small measure as a response to America's own would-be dictators and demagogues, Roosevelt found the words he would later use to confront fascism in the world.

He set the tone in his January 3, 1936, State of the Union address to Congress. In an unprecedented act, FDR insisted not only on delivering his message in person (his predecessors Herbert Hoover and Calvin Coolidge preferred to send written reports), but doing so at 9 p.m. so that it could be carried by radio across the nation after most people had returned home from work. Not since Woodrow Wilson came to ask for a vote to declare war in 1917 had a president spoken to Congress at night. The Republicans cried foul, believing that Roosevelt would make a partisan campaign speech, and so he did.[52]

Speaking before a bank of microphones to a rowdy joint session of Congress, the president began with an uncharacteristic discussion of world affairs. The "twin spirits of autocracy and aggression" had been unleashed upon many nations by dictators against the will of the majority, he said. Though not naming them, FDR clearly had Italy and Japan in mind when he spoke of aggressor nations reverting to "the law of the sword." America in response would continue to emphasize the "good neighbor" policy of nonintervention, encourage economic growth through bilateral trade deals, and ban sales of arms to nations at war. But after this survey of a darkening world scene, Roosevelt made a startling move: He explicitly connected the rise of dictators in Europe and Asia to the forces of reaction in the United States.

"Peace is jeopardized by the few, not the many," he declared, and that is why democracies must "prevent the continuance or the rise of autocratic institutions that beget slavery at home and aggression abroad." Sharpening this barbed message, he now argued that the threat of autocracy in the United States came not from storm troops or would-be dictators, but from "financial and industrial groups" who had in the past dominated government. "In the United States, as in the world at large, popular opinion is at war with a power-seeking minority," he said. In this view, the New Deal was just one battlefront in a global contest between the people and the tyrants that sought to rule them. In America, he went on, the New Deal had broken the grip of those wealthy and illiberal powerbrokers who opposed economic justice for the people. These "discredited special interests," he warned, wanted to climb back up into positions of power from which the New Deal had expelled them.

Clearly directing his wrath at the potentates of the Liberty League, FDR accused them of engaging in "vast propaganda to spread fear and discord among the people." These corporate board members and acquisitive robber barons, he said, would "gang up on the people's liberties," undo the progress of the previous four years, and misuse for their own ends the "new instruments of public power" that the New Deal had built. In language that might have come from a Union Party rally, he accused these "political puppets of economic autocracy" of seeking "power for themselves [and] enslavement for the public." It was an astonishing, violently polemical speech, denouncing the big-money conservatives for their hypocrisy, greed, and worse—their assault on American democracy. And by connecting the threat of autocracy at home to the rise of dictatorships abroad, he likened the Liberty Leaguers to strutting militarists in Berlin, Rome, Tokyo, and elsewhere who ruled their people with iron fists. Everyone had expected FDR to fire the first shot of the 1936 campaign in this speech, but as Arthur Krock noted, "few expected it to be of such a high caliber."[53]

Although publicly Roosevelt would keep his campaign focused on the successes of the New Deal and the danger of returning to the dark days of Coolidge and Hoover, privately he did worry about the worsening world picture. He told Ambassador Dodd in Berlin that he felt "extreme disquiet in regard to European and Asiatic affairs," and hoped his speech would resonate in Germany. To his disarmament negotiator, Norman Davis, he confessed that "I still worry about world affairs more than domestic problems, which includes the election." To Ambassador Jesse Straus in Paris, he wrote he "could not help feeling that the whole European panorama is fundamentally blacker than at any time in your lifetime or mine." Toward the end of February, he confided to Breckinridge Long in Rome that "we all watch the daily news from Europe with, I think, the feeling each day that the next will bring a major explosion." And these comments preceded the two disasters of the spring and summer of 1936: the German invasion and remilitarization of the Rhineland in early March, and the outbreak of civil war in Spain in July, which FDR called "a terrible catastrophe" in a message to Ambassador Claude Bowers in Madrid. Clearly, the onrush of fascism weighed on him.[54]

Still, Roosevelt planned to run on his domestic record and to keep foreign affairs mostly out of the picture. Talking about war overseas only raised the possibility of American involvement, something he and the public were determined to avoid, and FDR had his hands full running against an opposition that had started to gain some momentum. Sam Rosenman, the lead speechwriter from 1932 who FDR brought back for the 1936 campaign, recalled that "in the spring, the prospects for reelection did not seem quite that bright." The Republicans had been encouraged by the decisions of the conservative Supreme Court that had invalidated some significant aspects of the New Deal—notably the National Industrial Recovery Act and portions of the Agricultural Adjustment Act. The GOP found an attractive moderate governor from Kansas, Alf Landon, to carry its standard. FDR repeatedly expressed his exasperation that by his reckoning 85 percent of newspaper publishers opposed him. And the Democrats were starting to fissure along regional lines as some conservative Southerners began to chafe at FDR's progressive policies. The acerbic columnist for the *Baltimore Evening Sun*, H. L. Mencken, wrote that with the Supreme Court defeats, FDR had "lost his halo," and noted that the president's "chances in November continue to worry his partisans."[55]

Roosevelt chose to advance rather than retreat. Upon accepting the Democratic Party nomination for president in Philadelphia on June 27, he gave a "militant, bare-fisted statement" in defense of his record. FDR spoke outdoors on a wet night at Franklin Field, the University of Pennsylvania's huge football stadium. His arrival, wrote Arthur Krock, "was greeted by a real demonstration, as distinguished from the artificial efforts of conventions. One hundred thousand people rose and roared unmistakable acclaim as Mr. Roosevelt entered the platform on the arm of his eldest son and clasped the hand of Vice President Garner while 'The Star-Spangled Banner' was sung." Here, for the first time, Roosevelt labeled his opponents "economic royalists," a term that Rosenman said "expressed vividly the president's feeling about the concentration of economic power" in the hands of a few.

Ironically, it was the kind of epithet Father Coughlin had thrown at Roosevelt himself, accusing him of making peace with the bankers and big shots. Now, tacking sharply leftward, FDR repackaged the insult for his own purposes. These royalists, FDR said, "carved new dynasties" out of the industrial revolution and had subverted the political freedoms American patriots had wrested from English royalists in the eighteenth century. The "privileged princes," FDR went on, created "a new despotism . . . to regiment the people." Working hours, wages, and prices were set by an "industrial dictatorship" that had built an "economic tyranny." His administration, he believed, had given heart to those who wanted to fight this tyranny, who wished to raise "the flag and the constitution . . . against a dictatorship by mob rule and the over-privileged alike." Those who would take up this fight, he said in one of his most memorable lines (suggested by domestic policy adviser Tommy Corcoran), "have a rendezvous with destiny."

The president closed by returning once again to the connection between the fight against elites at home and the fight for democracy abroad. Europeans had "yielded their democracy" to militant fascists. What could or should America do about those now suffering under such oppression? Reverting again to warlike imagery, he said, "I believe in my heart that only our success can stir their ancient hope. They begin to know that here in America we are waging a great and successful war. It is not alone a war against want and destitution and economic demoralization. It is more than that; it is a war for the survival of democracy. We are fighting to save a great and precious form of government for ourselves and for the world." These words became the thesis of the rest of his presidency. Americans must fight to save democracy not only for themselves but for the world; the fight against royalists, princes, oligarchs, and fascists became, in FDR's words, a global struggle for democracy everywhere. As the hall erupted in applause, Roosevelt concluded with a ringing declaration of battle: "I accept the commission you have tendered me. I join with you." His last phrase was drowned out by the delirious crowd: "I am enlisted for the duration of the war."[56]

VIII

A war for democracy at home, then, a war that could inspire others around the world to keep faith in their own struggle against the tyrants. Did these words signal a new, firm policy of confrontation with fascism? Alas, not yet. When Spain lurched into a violent civil war in midsummer, the United States followed Britain and France in a hurried declaration of noninterference in the conflict. Fearful that war in Spain could draw in the rest of Europe, Roosevelt ordered his acting secretary of state, William Phillips, to release an unequivocal statement to the press on August 11. Noting that the neutrality acts only applied to war between two or more nations, Phillips stressed nevertheless that the United States had committed itself to staying out of "internal affairs" of other countries, and it "would scrupulously refrain from any interference whatsoever in the unfortunate Spanish situation." The State Department urged, but could not order, American businesses to refrain from selling any supplies that could assist either side in the conflict.[57]

This policy statement provided the backdrop to Roosevelt's major speech at the historic camp meeting site in Chautauqua, New York, on August 14. The address, drafted by William Bullitt, who had left his Moscow post to assist in the campaign, was aimed at reassuring the country that America would stay out of war while also pointing up the inexperience of FDR's opponent, Governor Landon, in dealing with the tricky issues of foreign policy. "I am more concerned and less cheerful about international world conditions than about our immediate domestic priorities," Roosevelt told the vast crowd of twenty-five thousand people. The world of 1936, he said, "faces wars between conflicting economic and political fanaticisms in which are intertwined race hatreds." Worse, some American business leaders in pursuit of "fool's gold" were poised to start selling goods to nations at war, placing profits over peace. War profiteers, he suggested, were always willing to plunge the country into war to make a fast buck.

Americans, however, should not worry so long as Roosevelt sat in the White House. For "I have seen war," he said portentously. "I have seen blood running from the wounded. I have seen men coughing out their gassed lungs. I have seen the dead in the mud. I have seen cities destroyed. . . . I have seen the agony of mothers and wives. I hate war." This statement elicited the loudest and longest applause from the crowd. Not only did he hate war, FDR continued, but he "passed unnumbered hours thinking and planning how war may be kept from the nation." That was the thrust of the speech: Voters could trust FDR to keep America out of war, whether in Spain, Ethiopia, Europe, or

Asia. In a passage that signaled his determination to remain unentangled by foreign conflicts, he said, "we seek to isolate ourselves completely from war." This speech expressed an unambiguous position: FDR would not bring the country into a foreign war, as his Democratic predecessor Woodrow Wilson had done.[58]

No war overseas; that was his firm commitment. But there were threats at home to consider, from the Friends of New Germany to the Coughlinites to the Communists. The government should keep an eye on them, Roosevelt believed. On August 24, he called J. Edgar Hoover, the director of the Federal Bureau of Investigation, to the White House for a remarkable conference. FDR told Hoover that he was concerned about "Communist activities in this country, as well as Fascist activities." The president wanted Hoover to draw up "a broad picture" of such movements in the United States, but Hoover replied that there did not exist any "governmental organization which is getting any so-called 'general intelligence information' upon this subject." When prompted by FDR, Hoover offered a solution. While the FBI had no appropriation for general domestic intelligence gathering, "under our present authority," the FBI could undertake an investigation of foreign subversives in the United States if asked to do so by the State Department. Roosevelt, wanting to avoid creating a paper trail, told Hoover to return the following day, when he would have Cordell Hull on hand to make this request to Hoover orally. The three men duly met, and Hoover got his marching orders: to start spying on certain un-American activities at the personal behest of the president. A long chapter of domestic surveillance of political activities in America had begun.[59]

FDR, for the time being, was too preoccupied with winning reelection to spend time on peripheral extremists. In September and October, he followed a grueling campaign schedule, belying any thought of overconfidence. His train rolled through the Midwest, to the Dakotas and Wyoming, Colorado, Missouri, Illinois, and North Carolina. He assessed the condition of the drought-racked Western states and examined construction projects of the Works Progress Administration. In early September, he delivered a fireside chat on the drought in nine states. As in his Chautauqua speech, Roosevelt positioned himself as a witness to tragedy: "I shall never forget the fields of wheat so blasted by heat that they cannot be harvested. I shall never forget field after field of corn stunted, earless and stripped of leaves, for what the sun left, the grasshoppers took. I saw brown pastures which would not keep a cow on fifty acres." He assured the country that "the indomitable American farmers" would battle through this temporary calamity with help from federal and state governments—all part of his administration's effort to deliver "economic freedom for the average man."[60]

At the end of September, Roosevelt took on the accusation made by the powerful newspaper publisher William Randolph Hearst, and echoed by his opponents in the Liberty League as well as in the thundering speeches of Father Coughlin, that somehow the New Deal was un-American, too radical, and in fact a "Communist" program. Hearst alleged that FDR had, since the moment he took office, "adopted the platform of the Karl Marx socialists in almost every word and letter," and then had granted diplomatic recognition "of the bloody dictatorship of Stalin in Moscow." The idea of the Groton- and Harvard-educated squire of Hyde Park as a Communist seems laughable, but his enemies would not give up this theme: The New Deal was bringing left-wing doctrines into America and subverting the Constitution.[61]

Roosevelt cleverly found a way to fend off this pike thrust. In Syracuse, at the New York Democratic State Convention, he explicitly repudiated the support "of any advocate of communism or of any other alien 'ism' which would by fair means or foul change our American Democracy." But he went on to say that his policies were designed to address the economic crisis that made communism attractive to desperate people in the first place. This became an opportunity to recount the myriad ways the New Deal had improved the lives of the most vulnerable, the hungry and homeless and jobless, thus helping restore faith in democracy while restarting the nation's economy. In the face of destitution, unemployment, bank failures, and farm foreclosures, FDR used government to "wage war" against inequality, injustice, unfairness. In doing so, Roosevelt said, Americans "proved that democracy can work." A packed and partisan crowd gathered at the Syracuse Armory erupted in applause. "It was a fighting speech and it went over big," Harold Ickes noted. While conservatives like H. L. Mencken bitterly attacked FDR's "concept of government as a milch cow with 125 million teats," one for each American, the president had a simple rebuttal: The country was immeasurably better off in 1936 than it had been in 1932. Only the monied "royalists" wanted to return to the past.[62]

The final few days of the campaign seemed like a victory lap as Roosevelt grew ever more certain of the outcome. On October 28, he made a triumphal return to New York City, where enormous crowds crammed the streets to catch a glimpse of him. He passed through Manhattan and enjoyed a ticker-tape parade in lower Broadway; he drove through Brooklyn and Staten Island; he was ferried to Bedloe's Island (now called Liberty Island), where he gave a speech marking the fiftieth anniversary of the unveiling of the Statue of Liberty. The horns of hundreds of vessels, as well as the batteries at Fort Jay on nearby Governors Island, erupted in salute to the commander in chief. During this day, his motorcade logged thirty miles, according to one witness, "without passing a block whose sidewalks were not jammed with enthusiastic crowds."[63]

His last major campaign address came on Halloween eve at Madison Square Garden, where twenty thousand people crushed into the hall as one hundred thousand more shivered in the chill outside. Here, Roosevelt offered a belligerent, stirring address, once again conjuring up the sinister, faceless forces of the robber barons and selfish capitalists who had directed so much hatred at him. "I welcome their hatred," he crowed to an audience carried away in euphoria. "The familiar golden voice of the President," wrote one observer, "investing the paper words with warmth and color, worked on the crowd with such authority that the entire audience seemed to sway expectantly under his featherweight touches until he slammed home a body blow," and their voices exploded in delight. Blasting twelve years of Republican misrule, he declared that in his first term, "the forces of selfishness and of lust for power met their match." After his next four years, he expected the people would say of his presidency that "these forces met their master."[64]

For a man who had regularly been accused of seeking to set up a one-party dictatorship in Washington, this was a belligerent phrase. And truthfully, this tone had permeated the entire campaign: a bare-knuckled attack on the bastions of privilege and power by a president determined to overcome their defenses and storm the gates. Mencken spoke for many conservatives when he called FDR's campaign "socialistic folderol" and labeled the New Deal nothing more than "a political racket" that bought voters with federal largess. But if the president resorted to purple campaign oratory, it was in the service of a vision of progress to which his entire political career had been dedicated. As the always astute Dorothy Thompson (a Republican) noted in her *Herald Tribune* column, Roosevelt was popular because he "was actively doing something," whereas Landon and the conservatives gave an air of "timidity, of apprehension," and even fear. At a moment when democracy around the world was under siege, FDR insisted that Americans could meet the crisis of the moment without resort to the rubber truncheon and the goose step.[65]

On November 4, Roosevelt won 61 percent of the popular vote, and crushed Governor Landon in the Electoral College by a vote of 523–8. Only Maine and Vermont went for the Republican. The Union Party went down to stinging defeat, winning a mere 892,000 votes. The Lemke-Coughlin-Townsend-Smith experiment simply crumpled, done in by internal jealousies and outmaneuvered by a crafty president who stole much thunder from the "lunatic fringe." Franklin Roosevelt adopted a populist theme, that a corrupt elite sought to deny prosperity and security to the American people. In the campaign, he never shied away from using the term "war" to describe his struggle against "economic dictatorship." Effectively combining the roles of warrior and teacher, he educated the public about the stakes of this fight and the role that active government could play in making America a more equal, more just, and more democratic society. The country gave him an extraordinary mandate to carry on.

Yet it remains puzzling, even vexing, to find that again and again, Roosevelt shied away from a sustained discussion of the looming *world* crisis, and the threat that fascism, imperialism, autarky, and war posed to American democracy. FDR understood these threats. In some of his most important speeches during 1936, he connected demagogues at home with dictators overseas. But he did not insist that Americans face that problem until they had regained their domestic security. In his first term, he remained fundamentally a nationalist and a noninterventionist, aware of the looming global dangers but choosing to concentrate his fire on what he liked to call America's own tyrants and autocrats. During his second term, however, events in the world from Spain to Austria, from China to Czechoslovakia, would force him to choose. Would he remain content in trying to solve America's domestic problems or was he willing to take the fight for democracy into the world?

CHAPTER 9

SPANISH EARTH

"This war is a conspiracy of the Fascist powers to destroy democracy in Europe."

—CLAUDE BOWERS

I

On the same day in August 1936 that Franklin Roosevelt spoke of his hatred of war before thousands of eager, upturned faces at the outdoor gathering at Chautauqua, New York, Spanish rebel soldiers, part of a nationwide military uprising against the leftist government in Madrid, fought their way into the town of Badajoz, an old walled city of forty thousand residents on the Portuguese border. As aircraft dropped incendiary bombs, troops from the Spanish Foreign Legion, accompanied by Moroccan soldiers from Spain's colonial outpost across the sea, battered Badajoz with artillery. They then swept into the town, dynamited buildings, shot civilians in the streets, and disarmed the city's defenders. On orders from the commander of the fascist insurgents, Lieutenant Colonel Juan Yagüe, the surrendering militia forces were hauled to the city's bullfighting arena, where machine guns awaited on fixed tripods. The executions began that night and carried on into the early morning. By the end of it, fascist soldiers had murdered about four thousand people, including unarmed civilians. The blood ran thick and dark in the streets of the sacked town.[1]

"We seek to isolate ourselves completely from war," Roosevelt said on that warm evening of August 14 in western New York, reassuring the public of his determination to remain unentangled in Europe's crises. But in Spain, that date is known for this ghastly act of wanton murder that opened three years of mass killing and atrocities. Badajoz shocked world opinion in a way that the Italian gassing of thousands of Ethiopians had not. The Spanish war was a European war, on European soil, and fueled by recognizably European ideologies: Fascism, Catholicism, and the power of traditional landed gentry mobilized against the revolutionary ideas of Socialism, Communism, anticlericalism, and working-class solidarity. From the first days of this bitter internecine conflict in Spain, everyone understood it not as a colonial war of the kind Europeans had exported to Africa or Asia for centuries, but as a terrible prophecy of Europe's own future.

The war started a month earlier, on July 17, when a group of right-wing generals put into action a long-nourished plan to seize control of the colonial army in Spanish Morocco and trigger a rising of the armed forces in Spain. Relying on German aircraft helpfully supplied by Hitler to ferry their insurgent troops across the strait of Gibraltar, rebel officers seized Cádiz and then Seville, establishing a beachhead in the south of the country. Army units in the north quickly rallied to the rebels. By September, the rebel forces held about half the country in the shape of a fat letter *C*, stretching from the northern city of Zaragoza, toward the Atlantic coast, and down to Salamanca and Seville to Gibraltar.

The Spanish government, facing the betrayal of the army, hastily improvised ragtag militias, made up of civilians and soldiers who remained loyal. Variously called Republicans or Loyalists, these troops held firm in the capital of Madrid and controlled the Mediterranean coast from the French border to Barcelona and Valencia on down to Málaga. The rebels called themselves Nationalists, and they included conservative Catholic army officers, Fascist militia, monarchists, and an assemblage of militant anti-Communists. Speaking to *Chicago Tribune* reporter Jay Allen, who barged his way into rebel headquarters a few days after the war began, one leader discounted the term "fascist," suggesting that "what Spaniards mean by fascist is a government that keeps order. That is what they want—that, and to destroy the Marxists." A week later, Allen got a major scoop, interviewing one of the leading generals behind the coup, the diminutive, pudgy, forty-three-year-old Francisco Franco. "I will save Spain from the Communists," he coolly told Allen. "And I will pacify it."[2]

Spain had been in upheaval for decades before the civil war began, fractured along lines of class, religion, ideology, and national identity. The military, in conjunction with King Alfonso XIII, had ruled in an uneasy dictatorship until 1931, when rising frustration and unrest led to the declaration of Spain's Second Republic and the abdication of the king. For a moment, reformers and leftists had a golden opportunity to push Spain forward into the world of modern, progressive democracy, and they took it—instituting a liberal constitution, curtailing the power of the Catholic Church and the military, allowing home rule for Catalonia and giving autonomy to the Basques,

Spanish Civil War, 1936–1939

granting votes to women, and beginning an ambitious program of land reform. Inevitably in such a traditional society, these policies were met with a powerful reaction from the army, the Catholic Church, the landed elites, and large farming interests, as well as many middling people of a conservative bent who disliked such rapid change. Across five uneasy years, the nation's already-existing fault lines pulled further apart. When a coalition of left-wing and centrist parties grouped under the Popular Front banner won elections to parliament in February 1936, the right-wing parties and military stirred fears of an imminent Bolshevik takeover and laid down their plans for a coup.[3]

Among European elites, the outbreak of civil war in Spain provoked only dread. They felt that nothing good could come of a victory in Spain of either a fascist junta, which would embolden Mussolini and Hitler, or of a victorious left-wing government, whose success would hearten Communist parties across Europe. The British ambassador in Washington, Sir Ronald Lindsay, reflected the typical view of the matter when he casually declared, while knocking balls around a golf course in Washington with former secretary of state Henry Stimson, that it did not make "any long-standing difference which side won out. The result would be a dictatorship in any event." With atypical speed, the British and French moved to limit any collateral damage. In London, Prime Minister Stanley Baldwin, having failed to halt Mussolini's conquest of Ethiopia and then done nothing when Hitler sent German troops into the Rhineland, saw war in Spain as a regional brushfire that should be contained lest it draw in other European states. Britain's government had committed itself to a policy of cultivating better relations with Germany and Italy, hoping that by offering Hitler and Mussolini concessions on certain territorial disputes, the dictators would agree to support a stable, anti-communist order in Europe. Keeping the dictators "inside the tent" mattered far more in Whitehall than sending aid to the decidedly left-wing, revolutionary Popular Front in Madrid.[4]

So, when French prime minister Léon Blum, himself a Socialist and leader of a Popular Front coalition that included Communists, briefly considered selling weapons to the Spanish government, the British pounced, making it plain that if France should find itself embroiled in war with the fascist powers as a result of its interference in Spain, Britain would remain entirely aloof. Blum quickly trimmed his sails and instead of assisting the Spanish Republic, proposed an alternative: an international agreement of nonintervention, binding the states of Europe to halt any arms sales to either side in the civil war. The theory was that at least in this way, the war would not spread or be likely to drag outside powers into it. Twenty-seven nations signed up, including Britain and France as well as Nazi Germany, Fascist Italy, and the Soviet Union. They pledged to join a Non-Intervention Committee that would supervise Europe's hands-off policy. Even figures later known for staunch antifascism supported this nonintervention scheme. Winston Churchill, then a backbench Conservative MP, argued strenuously in favor of "the strictest neutrality" in the conflict, seeing the Spanish government as too friendly with Moscow to deserve Britain's military support. What mattered now was to wall off the Spanish war from the rest of Europe.[5]

With European democracies choosing neutrality toward the conflict, it was easy for Franklin Roosevelt to do the same, especially in the midst of a reelection campaign. The State Department informed the U.S. embassy and consulates in Spain on August 7 that the government "will of course scrupulously refrain from any interference whatsoever in the unfortunate Spanish situation," as if American neutrality was a given. FDR then released that statement to the press, as a way to make plain his conformity with the Neutrality Act. His anti-war speech at Chautauqua followed a few days later, in which he made his case to the neutralists and pacificists that he could be relied upon to keep America out of any foreign conflict. Both his statement on Spain and his Chautauqua speech won praise from across the progressive anti-war left. Roosevelt's quick insistence on American neutrality in the Spanish Civil War, a conflict in which a democratically elected government was under attack by rebellious army officers with close ties to Fascist Italy and Nazi Germany, aligned with the views of many Americans at the start of the conflict.[6]

While FDR did not share the widespread belief that the "Red" government in Madrid was as bad as, or worse than, the rebel forces under Franco, the Hearst newspapers were pushing exactly that line. With a combined circulation nearing 20 million readers, the Hearst press openly backed Franco's "insurgents" as a "bar to the Red Menace," as one article put it. Franco's promise that he would suppress the "savage hordes of Marxists" met with warm support in the *San Francisco Examiner*, the flagship Hearst paper. In the early months of the war, both sides committed heinous acts of brutality, from killing civilians and raping women to shooting prisoners, burning churches, and murdering priests. But only the government forces attracted the ire of Hearst's editorial writers. "Nuns Shot Down," blared the headlines in early August. "Communist Jungle Law," screeched another banner. "The Spanish Reds are taking their cue from Moscow," claimed an editorial in the *Examiner*. The Spanish Popular Front, this paper insisted, stood for nothing more than "assassinations, confiscation, pillage, rapine, and hatred." Government forces were always called "reds" and "radicals," and when two Communist ministers were brought into the cabinet in September, the *Examiner* accused "Spain's radical regime" of setting up "a Soviet state." From the two dozen papers of the Hearst empire, readers learned that the Spanish Republic was a bloodthirsty Bolshevik tyranny, while Franco's patriotic, nationalist uprising could fairly be admired for coming to the rescue of Christian civilization.[7]

In stressing American neutrality, FDR also had in mind the attitudes of Catholic voters, who formed an important component of his New Deal coalition. He knew that America's Catholic leaders considered the Civil War not a struggle between fascism and democracy, but a fight to the death between Christianity and godless Communism. When reports came back from the front lines that Spanish leftists were attacking churches and murdering priests—a ghastly and all too common occurrence in the first few months of the war—Catholics erupted in protest. "Five Bishops Slain in Spain," blazed a headline in the *Chicago Tribune*, which gave particular attention to leftist atrocities. The bishops had been shot or, in the case of Eustaquio Nieto Martín, the bishop of Sigüenza, allegedly burned alive. Eyewitnesses told reporters of seeing priests clubbed with rifle butts and churches looted. In one particularly morbid case, militia soldiers had dug up the bones of Carmelite nuns and displayed them in public in order to mock Catholic promises of an afterlife.[8]

Lurid stories of attacks on Catholic priests and holy sites filled the American press, accompanied by accounts of Pope Pius XI falling ill from worry over Spain's conflict. Yet the Holy Father roused himself from his sickbed in mid-September to denounce communism as a "Satanic" ideology, "a program of hate, subversion, and destruction" that aimed to overturn "every form of institution, human and divine." Following this lead, American Catholics mobilized support for Franco and his Nationalist forces, raised funds for the "victims of Communism in Spain," published pamphlets, magazines, and editorials about the war, and hosted large public meetings to denounce the "red" Spanish government. Decrying the alleged left-wing sympathy of the mainstream press, the editor of the Catholic review *Commonweal* asserted that U.S. journalists had become "unconscious propagandists" for the Spanish government cause. Father Coughlin poured out his anguish about the horrific Judeo-Bolshevik conspiracy to destroy Catholicism in Spain. And President Roosevelt could hardly ignore the sentiments of Cardinal Patrick Joseph Hayes, the archbishop of New York, who had spoken at the 1924 Democratic National Convention and supported Democrats in congressional elections since then. He became a staunch supporter of the rebels, and in 1938, he admitted that he prayed for Franco's victory in the conflict.[9]

II

If the Hearst papers and the Catholic hierarchy conjured up a picture of barbarous leftist militias on the rampage, Roosevelt's ambassador to Spain offered a strikingly different assessment. Claude G. Bowers, born and raised in Indiana, was a self-taught writer, journalist, and biographer who had emerged as a sort of in-house court historian of the Democratic Party. An ardent Jeffersonian and champion of the little man and yeoman farmer, Bowers had written numerous books on Jefferson, Jackson, and the struggle of the Democratic Party against the entrenched privilege of elites. His bestselling 1929 book on post–Civil War Reconstruction, called *The Tragic Era*, was a book

FDR particularly admired. It depicted the Republican program to cleanse the South of secessionism and pro-slavery ideology as unjust and cruel. Like many in FDR's circle of foreign affairs specialists, such as William Dodd, Norman Davis, Breckinridge Long, and Josephus Daniels, Bowers possessed a political outlook quite typical of 1930s Democrats: sentimental sympathy for the Confederacy; hostility to big-city banking interests and corporate elites; belief in the enduring importance of racial segregation; and progressive views on the role of government in protecting white farmers and shopkeepers from the harsh winds of capitalism. After Bowers played a helpful role in ghostwriting speeches during Roosevelt's first presidential campaign, he was offered his choice of foreign ambassadorships and selected Spain (though he did not know the language).[10]

In light of his career as a popularizer of Democratic Party ideals, it is not surprising to find that Bowers viewed the Spanish Civil War through the lens of America's history. Bowers saw the Spanish peasants and downtrodden workers as luckless and forgotten men who embodied the virtues that came from working the land. Drawing from Jacksonian ideology, he considered Spanish landlords, aristocrats, bankers, business leaders, and Catholic prelates as malevolent, persecuting the honest toiler and wage earner in Spain just as they had done in America. His sympathies for the Spanish Republic and its cause had nothing at all to do with the left-wing politics of the Popular Front. Rather, he Americanized the Spanish struggle and portrayed it in letters to FDR as one that pitted scheming elites and heartless monied interests against the honest sons of the soil.

From the start of the Spanish crisis, Bowers urged FDR to ignore the Hearst press, whose papers carried nothing but what he called "persistent and outrageous propaganda." Instead, he offered a simple framework to understand the conflict. He told FDR that the Spanish Republic's president (and former prime minister) Manuel Azaña was a man cast in the Roosevelt mold. A progressive reformer, but not a doctrinaire leftist, Azaña had led the Popular Front government in introducing land reform, boosting working-class wages, and breaking the hold of the Catholic Church over Spain's public schools. "His purpose," Bowers told FDR, "was to change Spain from a 16th century state into a modern European state, and to end feudalism." Linking Azaña's policies to the New Deal, Bowers assured FDR of the Spanish leader's political centrism: "in his government, there is not even a socialist. All ministers are stout republicans."

In contrast, Bowers depicted the fascist rebels under Franco as radical extremists: They wanted to impose military dictatorship, suspend civil liberties, abolish parliament, restore the Church to its position of influence, and repeal all land reform measures. Putting the conflict in terms that might resonate with Roosevelt, Bowers wrote: "Of course my sympathy is with the government. The rebels are of the same element as those opposing your administration." Connecting Franco and his fascist foot soldiers to the tycoons of the Liberty League, Bowers transformed the Spanish Civil War into a battlefront in the global contest between democracy and oligarchy. Roosevelt responded guardedly to Bowers, agreeing with him that "the Hearst papers and most of the conservative editors are playing up all kinds of atrocities on the part of what they call the Communist government in Madrid—nothing about atrocities on the part of the rebels." Yet FDR also insisted that precisely because the war was an internal Spanish affair, the United States must follow a policy of "complete neutrality." If Europe was on the brink of a wider war, as Bowers believed, FDR wanted to remain as far from it as possible.[11]

While Bowers loyally followed FDR's chosen policy of neutrality, he told the president frankly that the Germans and Italians had broken their pledge to the Non-Intervention Committee to stay out of the war. In mid-September, he noted "abundant evidence that Italy is sending matériel all the time," while the Germans had sent bombers and aircrews as well as arms and ammunition. Both fascist powers were engaged in "an international conspiracy to destroy the democracy of Spain under the pretext of saving it from Communism." Italian soldiers lounged in cafés in Nationalist-held territory "with true fascist arrogance," making no secret of their presence. "Only a moron fails to see that the purpose [of the dictators] is to make Spain a base for the international fascist fight on democracy," Bowers wrote FDR. "Make no mistake," he insisted, "this is not a fascist war on communism, it is a fascist war on democracy in Europe." In his personal messages to the president, Bowers began to lay the groundwork for an argument he would actively push later: Supporting the Spanish government against the fascist rebels, and beating back the fascist challenge now, might forestall a wider war for control of the European continent.[12]

Roosevelt refused to be drawn into the European morass. He held firm to the view that neutrality and disarmament provided the surest means to limit the spread of war. He believed, like so many scholars, politicians, and peace activists in the 1930s, that the outbreak of the world war in 1914 could be laid at the feet of unscrupulous arms dealers, jingoistic press barons, vulgar nationalists, militarist generals and admirals who built up huge navies and standing armies, and secret alliances that committed nations to inflexible and aggressive war plans. He thought he could dodge all of these tricky political traps, and he believed that banning arms sales to combatant nations was an important additional step in containing the contagion of war.

He also mulled over the idea of an American-led conference of the great powers in the hopes of securing a global peace settlement and halting the drift to war that the Spanish crisis had accelerated. FDR launched a trial balloon on this topic in August 1936 during a personal conversation with *New York Times* columnist Arthur Krock, who duly printed up a story about a possible meeting with Stalin, Hitler, Mussolini, and the Japanese leadership to sort out their various demands. To Joseph E. Davies, the man he had just asked to serve as ambassador to the Soviet Union, Roosevelt said he "sympathized with Germany's need for access to raw materials," and thought Europe could be stabilized by "providing living room for the German people." It was a hopelessly naive idea, one that raised quizzical eyebrows in his own State Department. But FDR asked Ambassador Dodd in Berlin to gauge the appetite of German leaders for a negotiated settlement to meet their demands for a favorable European order. Dodd reported back that the Nazis had no interest in an American initiative. After all, he wrote, "the dictators mean to dominate Europe" and so far were achieving their aim without war. Since the European democracies had let the fascists roll on unimpeded, the dictators had no reason to respond to an American-led peace initiative. But the idea did not disappear.[13]

With his huge electoral victory in November 1936, Roosevelt could have tried to change his Spanish policy and seek some means to aid the loyalist government in its war with the fascists. He did nothing of the kind, hoping instead to play the role of peacemaker. This idea aligned with advice he received from his new ambassador to France, William Bullitt, who urged FDR to avoid a pan-European meeting with the world's revisionist powers in favor of a narrower policy of appeasement toward Nazi Germany. Bullitt argued that Roosevelt, who European leaders now considered a "miracle man" after his huge reelection victory, should try to bring about a Franco-German reconciliation. Germany wanted economic dominion of southeastern Europe; why not urge the French and British to offer this in return for "limitation of armaments and a general revival of a feeling of European unity"? Bullitt, whose profound anticommunism had been whetted to a fine gleam during his miserable ambassadorship in the Soviet Union, personally believed that the greatest menace to Western democracy came from Moscow, not Berlin. He hoped to encourage FDR to engineer some kind of agreement that might consolidate the Western powers—democratic and fascist—against the Soviet Union.[14]

The announcement in late October that Nazi Germany and Fascist Italy had forged a new "Rome-Berlin Axis" seemed to lend support to Bullitt's scheme. Hitler had given Mussolini formal recognition of Italy's conquest of Ethiopia, in exchange for Italy's support of German economic interests in the Balkans. Bullitt believed that the fascist powers need not be at odds with America or the European democracies, who after all had empires of their own. The main thing, Bullitt believed, was to build an anti-communist bulwark in Europe. Bullitt pushed this idea for months, arguing that "the only chance of preserving peace in Europe lies in the possibility that the French and Germans may reach some basis of understanding." If war broke out, "the only winners will be Stalin and Company." In order to play the mediating role that Bullitt imagined for him, however, Roosevelt would have to remain scrupulously neutral on the Spanish war—and not allow that unfortunate conflict to spoil the possibility of a general détente between the fascist states and the west.[15]

Faced with a choice between the fierce anti-fascism of Bowers and the equally determined anti-communism of Bullitt, FDR ignored both. In the days following his reelection, he continued to burnish his reputation as a world envoy for peace. On the morning on November 18, he boarded the USS *Indianapolis* in Charleston, South Carolina, for a monthlong trip to South America. He rested, sunbathed, fished, and engaged in the usual hijinks during the ceremony for those mariners who, including himself, crossed the equator for the first time. In Buenos Aires, he was met by a staggering public demonstration of affection and esteem, with huge crowds lining the streets shouting, "*Viva la democracia*" as his entourage motored along. He crowed about this later: "Those people down there were for me," he said, "for the simple reason that they believe I have made democracy function and keep abreast of the times, and that as a system of government it is, therefore, to be preferred to Fascism or Communism."[16]

In a speech on the first of December to gathered heads of state from the Americas, he held up the example of neighborly relations in the Western Hemisphere as an example to the world while warning of the darkening storm clouds in Europe and Asia. "We see continents rent asunder by old hatreds and new fanaticism," he said. "We hear the demand that injustice and inequality be corrected by resorting to the sword and not by resorting to reason." Economic walls of protectionism had been built higher, and vast new armaments were being deployed to defend them. Such trends only reinforced his "horror of war and all that war means." Yet still, FDR gave no concrete plan to reverse the drift to war except to rededicate himself to the "hard and consistent effort" of peacemaking: shoring up democracy, expanding rights of free expression and liberty, and meeting the economic and security needs of the people. Educating the world in the arts of peace, he suggested, would be the gift of the Americas "to our brethren overseas."[17]

When he returned to Washington, Roosevelt made a gesture—a regrettable one in retrospect—of his commitment to peace by calling for an embargo on arms sales to Spain. Because the Neutrality Act did not address the matter of civil wars, American businesses could technically still sell arms and related war matérial to the Spanish government. To head off any opportunistic arms merchants, Roosevelt sought new legislation—and Congress answered his call on January 8, 1937, with an arms embargo, barring U.S. companies from selling weapons to Spain. That this ban would harm chiefly the Republican government rather than the Nationalist rebels, who were already receiving aid from Italy and Germany, caused no concern in the Capitol. Senator Key Pittman, chairman of the Senate Foreign Relations Committee, stated that the embargo showed that America was "not taking either side." *The Nation* magazine, though, disagreed. By cutting off access of the besieged Republic to arms, the United States was in fact taking sides—"the side of the Spanish militarists, Hitler, and Mussolini against the government chosen by the Spanish people." The president who had so recently hailed the blessings of democracy in Buenos Aires now seemed to be "actively supporting fascism." The debate over Spain would only get uglier.[18]

III

To many American writers, journalists, and intellectuals, FDR's bloodless response to the crisis in Spain seemed almost unforgivable. How could he not see the obvious stakes of the war? It certainly was not for lack of information. Starting in the summer of 1936, a few American journalists published searing descriptions of the war and its extraordinary brutality in newspapers the president regularly read.

Jay Allen, who had been working for the *Chicago Tribune* in Europe since 1926, wrote about the early days of the war with skill and a deep familiarity with Spain. He had lived there for long stretches during the early thirties, developing close ties with mostly left-wing politicians and writers. Just a few days after the coup of July 1936, Allen landed an interview with its leader, General Franco, and memorably portrayed him in unflattering terms: Franco was a "midget" with "tiny feet and hands" and a "nascent paunch." Yet there was no doubting his deadly purpose. "Spain cannot be allowed to go communist," Franco told him, and the general suggested that Britain, France, and Italy would support his cause against the "red propaganda" from Moscow.

Allen might have belittled the man, but he did not doubt Franco's fanatical belief in his cause, or his determination to crush the left in Spain.[19]

In the first days of the revolt, Allen wrote encouragingly about the rapid mobilization by the Spanish government of armed militias, which he initially believed had been effective in pinning down what he called the "monarchist-Fascist" forces in Andalusia, Spain's southernmost province. Since most of the army had joined the rebellion, the government had to arm workers, students, teenagers, and anyone else who could wield a rifle. In Málaga, the first large town on the road toward Madrid, militia troops blew up bridges, dug trenches, and prepared to meet the mutineers. Yet the rebel generals relied upon "Moorish troops"—seasoned Moroccan conscripts in Spain's colonial army—who according to Allen unleashed pitiless horror upon militia forces and civilians. In order to emphasize the sinister and alien quality of the fascist cause, Allen conjured up the image in his reports of Nazi aircraft transporting "tribesmen in turbans and the homespun chilaba, sharpshooters, guerilla warriors," flown in the from the "savage, bloodstained hills" of colonial Morocco to fight on behalf of the fascist coup.[20]

In August, Allen reported on the role that Fascist Italy, Nazi Germany, and Portugal were playing in arming the rebel forces. Though the Italians and Germans denied it, Allen provided detailed evidence that their planes, artillery, and soldiers had been crucial to Franco's initial success and that Franco was busily seeking further supplies from his fellow fascists. "Thanks to the Italian and German-piloted planes," Allen wrote on August 4, "the rebels were able to transport 1,000 men today directly" from Spanish Morocco to the outskirts of Cádiz, "and they expect to get 2,000 across tomorrow." Allen also broke the story that a trainload of war supplies brought to Portugal by German boats had crossed into Spain toward rebel-held Salamanca. This was only the start of what became a flood of military aid from the fascist states. Italy provided the Nationalists with 660 aircraft, 150 tanks, almost a thousand artillery pieces, as well as 70,000 soldiers. With Nazi Germany sending squadrons of newly built aircraft, pilots, and ground crews in the so-called Condor Legion, Franco enjoyed an early advantage over the struggling government defenders.[21]

It was Allen's reporting from Badajoz, however, that established his name as a leading witness of fascist barbarism. Allen was not the first reporter to see the ruins of the town that was seized and burned by Franco's insurgents on August 14. But he was the first American, and after getting to the hideous scene nine days after the fall of the town, he wrote a long a personal story of the kind that would become characteristic of the civil war. "This is the most painful story it has ever been my lot to handle," he began. "I write it at 4 o'clock in the morning, sick at heart." He went to the bullring, where thousands had been murdered. He saw the bullet-riddled walls with dried blood caked on them. "It was a hot night," Allen wrote of his trip to the gruesome site. "There was a smell. I can't describe it and won't describe it." Through the ruined town, ashen-faced women stumbled in search of lost sons and husbands. He tersely summarized the story: "Thousands of republican, socialist, and communist militiamen and militiawomen were butchered after the fall of Badajoz for the crime of defending their republic against the onslaught of the generals and the landowners," he wrote. It became clear that Franco's army intended the massacre at Badajoz as a warning: Any city that did not surrender, the rebel armies stated, "will be taken in the same fashion as Badajoz." And their next target was the capital city, Madrid.[22]

But Jay Allen would not be covering that story for the *Tribune*. For reasons that he and his friends suspected had to do with his obvious sympathies for the Republican cause, and perhaps because of noisy complaints from Catholic leaders in Chicago, Allen was let go in October by the newspaper's imperious publisher, the right-wing anti–New Deal isolationist Colonel Robert McCormick. The paper had already established an editorial line that was strongly critical of the "communist" government in Spain, and McCormick did not like Allen's melodramatic and left-leaning articles. However, Allen's place as a sympathetic chronicler of the agonies of Spanish democracy would soon be taken by many others.[23]

Louis Fischer was one of them. Fischer—the very same journalist who settled in Moscow in the 1920s and then worked so hard in the 1930s to whitewash Stalin's murderous tyranny—had become disaffected with life in Moscow once the 1936 show trials began that led to the deaths of many of the leading figures of the Russian revolution. "Communist morality and idealism," Fischer recalled later, "were disintegrating." Anyone caught expressing dissenting ideas "received a 2 a.m. visit from the secret police" and was shipped off to Siberia. His hope for a democratic Russia that could counter the aggressive fascist bloc lay in tatters. "I sensed the oncoming night and knew that I no longer wished to live in the Soviet Union," he confessed. But he had not soured on Communism as an ideal yet, and in Spain, he thought he found a true example of men and women fighting against fascism on behalf of a genuinely democratic, just society. "I was glad there was a Spain to work in and work for," he thought. "Spain was salvation."[24]

He was not alone: Millions of idealists in Europe and America who had grown wary of the hardening Soviet experiment saw in Spain something both frightening and inspiring. Fischer got it right when he wrote that "the Republic's struggle against Fascism in Spain was probably the zenith of political idealism in the first half of the twentieth century." Across the United States in the fall of 1936, organizations to support Spanish democracy mushroomed, and they usually looked a good deal like the Popular Front itself. Protestant pastors, labor organizers, Communist and socialist activists, writers, professors, and artists set aside narrow doctrinal differences to awaken the American public to the stakes of the war. Their leftist affiliations would make them easy targets of the pro-Franco propagandists for they were indeed part of a global Communist effort to raise the alarm about fascism. Yet in 1936 and 1937, many American supporters of Spanish democracy wore accusations from the Francoists as a badge of honor. These groups, like the American Friends of Spanish Democracy, the American League for Peace and Democracy, the American Committee for Spanish Freedom, and the League of American Writers, saw fascism as a sinister, aggressive ideology that aimed to destroy democracy and set up totalitarian rule across Europe. They wanted above all to demonstrate the global character of Spain's crisis: The struggle for survival of the Spanish government looked to them like a front in a widening world conflict.[25]

Louis Fischer captured this worldview in his writing. He arrived in Madrid in September 1936 and set himself up in the Hotel Florida for an extended stay. With a contract from *The Nation* for his essays, he traveled to the front lines, interviewed leading government figures, inspected airfields, labor halls, barracks, even night clubs and cafés. What he found alarmed him: indiscipline, lack of urgency, a flagging offensive spirit, food shortages, a serious shortfall in weapons, artillery, aircraft, and ammunition, and constant ideological bickering between communists, socialists, and anarchists that made decision-making impossible. The press failed to tell the public just how bad the war was going, and the political leadership seemed powerless to impose order. Everywhere, militia men in blue overalls lounged in cafés, uncertain of the war's purpose. For a man who had seen the Russian revolution and followed the birth of the Soviet state, the absence of discipline among the leadership shocked him. "There is no political work, there are no mass meetings," he wrote in his diary. "It is an informal war." He went to see Ambassador Bowers and found him "accessible and friendly," but without a staff or the authority to do anything. He "sits at his typewriter sucking an unlit cigar and hammers out his own dispatches with two aching fingertips," Fischer ruefully noted. This dismal impression formed the basis of Fischer's long piece in *The Nation* in late October, "On Madrid's Front Line," in which he stated plainly that "what the Spanish government needs at this moment is a well-trained army." The government, he believed, could win the war with five thousand disciplined fighters; it did not have even that many.[26]

In early November, in the most acute phase of the civil war so far, Franco's rebels took aim at Madrid. They expected to take the capital in a matter of days, assuming that the disorganized government had failed to prepare adequate defenses. The rebels began with indiscriminate air attacks on the city, using German and Italian aircraft. "A bomb killed five women standing in a milk queue," Fischer wrote, one of whom was holding a baby in her arms as she died. Fischer believed that Franco wanted to terrorize the population into surrender. He venomously attacked the great powers for their indifference: "These air raids can have no military object," he said. "That Italian and German pilots should attack noncombatant Spaniards with bombs and machine-guns without provoking a protest so violent as to force democracies to intervene to protect Spain's progressive republic is a pretty fair gauge of the world's moral caliber these days."[27]

One bright spot appeared, however: starting in early November, foreign volunteers began to arrive to help the beleaguered republic. French, Belgian, Italian, German, Polish, British, Canadian, and American young people, mostly connected to Communist parties in their homelands, trickled into Madrid and took up places in the line. Enthusiastic, amateur, poorly armed, these fighters in the International Brigades nonetheless showed immense courage and plugged crucial gaps in the defenses of Madrid, sustaining high causalities while helping to stave off the Nationalist attack in November and December. "Nothing is more important," Fischer told *Nation* editor Freda Kirchwey, than the impact of these foreign fighters. Combined with deliveries of Soviet aircraft, which Stalin had belatedly agreed to sell in exchange for virtually all of Spain's gold reserves, the Brigades helped deliver a major win for the republic. Madrid would not fall to Franco for another two and a half years. Fischer exulted at the sudden jolt of effort by the Republican side. Madrid, "shaken out of its lethargy, went fearlessly to work at the task of defending itself. In innumerable streets, sandbag barricades have been erected and houses converted into fortresses," he wrote. Foreign Socialists and Communists had rallied to Spain's side, showing "unprecedented valor" and lifting the morale of the Spanish forces. So thrilled was he at the sight of the Brigades that Fischer signed up with them and for two months served as their quartermaster, a role in which he used his connections to marshal weapons, food, and transport for the few thousand foreign troops who had come to fight.[28]

Fischer's essays countered the Hearst-designed narrative of Red hordes on the loose in Spain with a powerful story of a heroic, democratic people's army facing terrible odds against a well-armed fascist military machine. He also gave voice to the anger building among leftists the world over: Why did Europe and America do nothing? After recounting another gruesome bombing raid that left countless Spaniards dead or homeless, Fischer asked "where is the humanitarian heart of the millions who go to church and pray to God, or of the millions who call themselves idealists yet go about their business signing letters, having manicures, seeing cinemas, while a city of culture and beauty is being ground to dust?" The war in Spain, he argued, pitted "two vast world forces" against one another. The fascists were more daring, more ruthless, more ready to kill civilians. The democracies, by contrast, were "no match for fascist arrogance," and in such places as Abyssinia and the Rhineland they had shown that they would not fight to uphold their own ideals. If Spain should fall, it would not be long, Fischer believed, before Hitler and Mussolini took aim at the rest of the continent.[29]

By no means did all reporters adopt the style and sympathies of Allen and Fischer. The lead reporter for the *New York Times* in Spain, William P. Carney, produced a steady flow of critical articles about the Spanish government. Having observed some of the early atrocities of the militias toward priests and churches, he repeatedly emphasized the "red terror" the Popular Front had imposed in Spain. Likening the Spanish government to Soviet-style tyranny, he referred to Francisco Largo Caballero, the government's prime minister during the first year of the war, as "the Spanish Lenin." He published chilling details of mass executions and arrests in Madrid by agents of the Popular Front, and he gave extensive attention to repressive police and censorship measures the government imposed.[30]

In early December, Carney filed an incendiary story from Paris that claimed to be the first "uncensored" reporting from Spain. "All semblance of democratic forms and usages of government has disappeared in Spain," it began. Madrid was cloaked in fear and secrecy, he alleged, and foreign journalists were harassed and frequently arrested. Huge portraits of Stalin bedecked the streets and squares of Madrid. He asserted that the Soviet Union was not only aiding the Madrid government with arms but was "running the show in Spain" through the agency of the Soviet ambassador, Marcel Rosenberg. (In fact, Rosenberg was already under suspicion in Moscow and was recalled, and later executed, on Stalin's orders.) He described the mass of the citizens as apolitical, tired, and hungry, while the militia soldiers were well-fed. Above all, he expressed his horror at the "anti-religious campaign" led by atheistic Marxists against the traditional faithful Catholics of the country. "All churches that were not burned have been converted into fortresses," he claimed. Even the simple expression "*adiós*" had been banned because it derived from the saying *a Dios seas*, or "may you be commended to God." In its place: a raised fist and the word "*Salud!*" Carney also floated the idea that the atrocities of Badajoz had been invented by the communists, and he would go on to describe areas seized by the rebel forces as "liberated" towns where grateful Spaniards breathed freely and enjoyed a "perpetual holiday atmosphere."[31]

Fortunately, Carney was not the only *Times* man in Spain. Herbert L. Matthews arrived in Madrid in December 1936, fresh from covering the appalling war in Abyssinia. Tall, lanky, impeccably dressed, a true professional, Matthews stayed in Madrid to report on the republican side, while Carney packed off to Franco's headquarters to continue his flattering portrayals of the fascist cause. Matthews's reporting was careful, factual, empathetic, and above all gutsy: He refused taking anybody's word for events that he could verify himself, and he spent countless days among republican soldiers in trenches and dugouts at the front lines. Matthews would later write of his own method: "I held back no facts and wrote only what I saw or believed to be true. . . . To ask that a correspondent have no feelings or ideas or even prejudices and bias of his own is asking the impossible. We, too, are human." In his humanity, he fell hard, as did so many foreign observers, for the antifascist cause. He believed that the war pitted democracy against fascism and believed that the righteous courage of the republicans could win out in the end. "For the first time since the Fascist movement started," he wrote, "men are willing to die to crush it. Is that not significant?"[32]

IV

Roosevelt kept Spain at arm's length in 1937, preoccupied by a major domestic crisis he himself had triggered: the infamous "court packing" episode. In his second inaugural address on January 20, he declared that the New Deal was not a "patch-work job with second-hand materials." Rather, he aimed to build a new political and economic order on the foundations of the old. The suffering, poverty, and unemployment of 1933 had been ameliorated, but not ended. "One third of a nation," he admitted, remained "ill-housed, ill-clad, ill-nourished." The New Deal had put out the fire of the Depression; now it must rebuild the very structure of American life.

But the president needed the right tools. And so, to meet the ongoing crisis, FDR demanded that the federal courts get in line with the needs of the hour. The New Deal, Roosevelt felt, had been endorsed by the people in two presidential elections and Congress had passed far-reaching legislation to enact it. Yet again and again, the people's will had been thwarted by the Supreme Court, which had ruled that eight of FDR's signature programs, designed to jump-start the economy and deliver meaningful relief to farmers and workers in America, were unconstitutional. To bend the court to his will, on February 5 he sent to Congress a proposal for the reform of the federal judiciary that, as the hostile *Chicago Tribune* put it, "exploded like a bombshell."[33]

The plan was simple enough. Roosevelt proposed that for every federal judge over the age of seventy who had served at least ten years on the bench, another justice would be appointed by the president. FDR tried to justify this idea on the grounds that the federal docket had become too crowded with cases and that the older justices needed the help of a younger generation of jurists. But that argument fooled no one, for the measure would immediately allow Roosevelt to appoint six new justices to the Supreme Court, one for each seventy-year-old with more than a decade of service. The court would then have fifteen members, six new ones joining two reliable liberals already there to assure the president of eight favorable votes—a locked-in majority. In short, FDR wanted to pack the court.

His scheme met a furious backlash, as conservatives (including many Democrats) likened Roosevelt to the power-crazed tyrants in Europe. Progressive Republican Senators Hiram Johnson and William Borah, who had supported much of the New Deal, now abandoned the president. The Catholic weekly *America*, which had supported aspects of FDR's policies, called the measure "the most dangerous attack in all our history upon the government established by the Constitution." If Roosevelt wanted a fight over the court, he certainly got one.[34]

After a few weeks of this kind of invective, FDR struck back. In the first fireside chat of his second term, he laid the blame for America's troubles at the feet of the Supreme Court. On a national radio broadcast, he said, "We must take action to save the Constitution from the Court and the Court from itself. . . . I want—as all Americans want—an independent judiciary as proposed by the framers of the Constitution. That means a Supreme Court that will enforce the Constitution as written—that will refuse to amend the Constitution by the arbitrary exercise of judicial power." It was a clever argument: "We cannot yield our constitutional destiny," he summed up, "to the personal judgment of a few men who, being fearful of the future, would deny us the necessary means of dealing with the present. This plan of mine is no attack on the Court; it seeks to restore the Court to its rightful and historic place in our system of Constitutional Government." The court, not the president, was out of step with the Constitution.[35]

Going to the country over the radio had so often worked for Roosevelt in the past, but this time, his magic touch deserted him. Republicans maintained total hostility, while his own party split over the issue. Many conservative Southern Democrats fiercely attacked the plan as the act of a dictator. At the end of May, polls showed 54 percent of the public opposed the court-packing scheme, despite the president's huge personal popularity.[36]

With a vacancy now open on the court, FDR did have a chance to bring a liberal supporter onto the bench and slightly improve his chances of getting New Deal laws sustained. On August 12, the president nominated Alabama senator Hugo L. Black to fill the seat; the Senate confirmed him five days later and he took the oath of office the following day. Black came from a farming family in the rural South and had started out his career as a lowly country lawyer. He served in the artillery during World War I, and in the 1920s he went into politics. Like many Southern Democrats with political aspirations, Black joined a number of civic and fraternal organizations, the better to make useful connections. One of those groups was the Birmingham chapter of the Ku Klux Klan.

This chapter (or "klavern"), called the Robert E. Lee Klan No. 1, did not operate in the shadows. In 1921, it held a public initiation ceremony for hundreds of new recruits at the Alabama State Fairgrounds, forming a giant cross in the middle of the racetrack. To be sure, the Klan of the 1920s did not operate as a vigilante group in the way its notorious nineteenth-century predecessor did, but it did normalize anti-Catholic and antisemitic bigotry, decried immigration of non-white people, and rigorously supported the practices of Jim Crow segregation. On September 12, the *Pittsburgh Post-Gazette* reporter Ray Sprigle published a major exposé (and later won a Pulitzer Prize for it) showing that Black joined the Klan in 1923. Though he resigned in 1925 just before running for the Senate, the newspaper alleged that he had been welcomed back into the organization in 1926 as a lifetime member.[37]

Did FDR know of Black's ties to the Klan? Harold Ickes did, and noted in his diary a month before the news broke that Black certainly had the support of the Klan in Alabama during his Senate campaign. But the news story left Roosevelt dumbfounded. The story was "very bad for the president," Ickes wrote. FDR himself had stood against the Klan and its loathsome hatreds his whole career. Yet here the newspapers now reported that Black swore an oath of allegiance to the Klan and had given his "sacred unfailing bond" to support white supremacy. Justice Black, faced with the evidence, admitted that he had joined, but insisted he'd had nothing to do with the Klan since 1925. While some in the Democratic Party of the 1930s would have welcomed Black's ties to the Klan, for FDR the affair became yet another crisis that made it hard to think about problems beyond American shores. It also made FDR especially eager to mend fences with his Catholic supporters, and that meant turning a blind eye to Franco's war in Spain.[38]

V

By the spring of 1937, the U.S. government could no longer feign ignorance over the role of Fascist Italy and Nazi Germany in the Spanish war. Ambassador Bowers, in a seething letter to the president, confirmed that "the Italian army [in Spain] numbers fully 70,000 men, they fight in regular Italian army uniform, respond to the orders of Italian officers, and use guns, planes, and tanks." The Republican government, though hobbled by lack of supplies as well as its own internal divisions, was showing coherence and strength, he wrote. They fought for that most basic of aims: to preserve their national independence from foreign armies. Stressing again the high stakes of the conflict, Bowers told FDR that "this war is a conspiracy of the Fascist powers to destroy democracy in Europe." His cries fell on deaf ears.[39]

The drumbeat from Spain grew louder. Louis Fischer took to the road, traveling across the United States in the spring and summer of 1937 on a lecture tour to raise awareness about the civil war. In *The Nation*, he wrote a scathing essay denouncing America's neutrality policy as selfish and dangerous. In his view, FDR's stay-out policy "increases the likelihood of foreign war" and "plays directly into Hitler's hands." He pointed out that the United States was not in fact neutral, because the Neutrality Acts allowed business as usual for exports of products like oil—which Mussolini happily purchased even as he "sprayed the Ethiopians with poison gas." At the same time, the embargo on arms sales meant the legitimate, democratic government of Spain could not buy arms from America to defend itself from the fascist insurgents and their German and Italian allies.

The United States, Fischer said, must bear the blame for the "daily bombing and wounding and killing of thousands of women and children in Madrid and elsewhere." The civil war was a death struggle between democracy and fascism; and if Spain fell to the fascists now, "the turn of the larger states will come later." In a furious coda to his essay, Fischer said he assumed that Roosevelt and Hull were "anti-fascist in their convictions," but their neutrality policy "has made America effectively pro-fascist." America still had a chance to delay and perhaps halt the outbreak of a wider war by selling arms to the

Spanish. But if Spain should succumb for lack of arms, the larger war Fischer feared would be a certainty.[40]

The Spanish Republican cause picked up influential new supporters in the spring of 1937. Ernest Hemingway, a star of American literature whose books had already secured him international fame, arrived in Madrid in March with a commission from the North American Newspaper Alliance to cover the war. Hemingway knew Spain well, had traveled and lived there, and his 1926 novel, *The Sun Also Rises*, was set partly in Pamplona. In 1932, he published *Death in the Afternoon*, a nonfiction study of bullfighting. "Spain is a bad war," he wrote a friend just before setting off, "and nobody is right." But Hemingway was not neutral. His sympathies lay, he said, "with the exploited working people against the absentee landlords." His thirty-odd color pieces for the news service featured his spare, detached style and covered not just the battles but their aftermath, with deft portraits of the soldiers, the civilians, the wounded, and the dead. Without making his stories overtly political, he expressed unmistakable admiration for the struggle of the ordinary people against the generals, the landowners, the Church, and the foreign fascists.[41]

Hemingway took up the cause of the Spanish Republic.
John Springer Collection / Corbis via Getty Images

Hemingway took rooms in the frequently shelled and half-ruined Hotel Florida on the Plaza del Callao in central Madrid, which had become a caravanserai for the many writers and journalists passing through the city. He arrived in the company of Joris Ivens, a Dutch Communist filmmaker, and together the two men set out to the front to capture the essence of the Spanish struggle in a film they planned to call *The Spanish Earth*. Well-connected and treated like a special guest of the government, Hemingway did not lack the luxuries that had long since disappeared from the Madrid markets: coffee, liquor, tobacco, sugar, tinned goods, and gasoline for a government-supplied car with which to tour the front lines. He traveled, wrote, drank, and caroused along with a rotating cast including the French author and pilot Antoine de Saint-Exupéry; the British Communist Claud Cockburn, who wrote for the *Daily Worker*; Sefton Delmer of the *Daily Express*; George Steer of the London *Times*; and Geoffrey Cox of the London *News Chronicle*. Vincent "Jimmy" Sheean, the peripatetic writer who had won acclaim for his 1935 book, *Personal History*, joined Hemingway, with whom he had been friends since they overlapped in Paris in the 1920s.[42]

In this atmosphere saturated with male self-regard and ambition, Martha Gellhorn stood out as one of the few female journalists and, as soon became obvious to all, one of the most talented. Raised in St. Louis by well-to do, progressive parents, Gellhorn had dropped out of Bryn Mawr, hoping to make a career in journalism. Like many bright young Americans who wanted to escape the suffocating social conventions of the era, she shipped herself off to Paris in 1930 and spent four years there writing advertising copy and working as a clerk at the United Press office. She returned to America in 1934 and was introduced by a mutual friend to Harry Hopkins, the director of the Federal Emergency Relief Administration. Hopkins needed people to travel to the most destitute parts of the country and describe what they found, adding eyewitness accounts to the sterile statistical tables he received about America's economic crisis. Gellhorn jumped at the chance to do something like real journalism. With a few dollars a week as salary, she made first for the Carolinas, then moved north to the idle mill towns of New England. Both in the South and the North, she found unspeakable poverty, destitution, inequality, disease, and utter despair among the unemployed. Working for Hopkins, she developed the sharp reporting and writing skills, as well as the political consciousness, that would come to define her contribution to journalism over the next half century.[43]

Gellhorn had a knack for attracting powerful patrons, and one of her close friends and mentors was none other than Eleanor Roosevelt. Gellhorn's mother, Edna, a feminist and a founder of the League of Women Voters, had known Mrs. Roosevelt for many years, and Martha, while under Hopkins's tutelage, soon sought out the First Lady. Eleanor admired young Martha's courage in digging into the dirty underside of America's failing economy. Eleanor even invited Martha to stay at the White House while she was drafting a book of semi-fictional stories about the crushing poverty she had seen during her travels. *The Trouble I've Seen* came out in September 1936 and Eleanor helped publicize it, thus securing Gellhorn's status as an up-and-coming talent in American letters.

Trailing glory from the success of her book, Martha set out for Spain with a vague promise from *Collier's* magazine to consider any pieces she might write on the war. Gellhorn became an active partisan in the cause of Spanish democracy, and she kept Mrs. Roosevelt informed about the war and its importance. To be sure, Gellhorn's decision to go to Spain in the spring of 1937 was influenced by more than professional ambition. She had met Ernest Hemingway while on Christmas vacation at Key West the previous year, and though Ernest was married, he took an instant shine to the vivacious, smart, spirited Gellhorn. Meeting again in the shabby but thrilling setting of the Hotel Florida in Madrid, the two soon became lovers (and would marry in 1940). The Spanish war, then, attracted some of the most talented writers of the era, and they all seemed to know that their work in covering the death throes of the Spanish Republic would be the most important and meaningful job of their lives. As Herbert Matthews put it, they shared the conviction of the Republican fighters and the International Brigade volunteers that "this world will not be worth living in if Fascism triumphs."[44]

American novelist and war correspondent Martha Gellhorn.
FPG / Archive Photos / Getty Images

VI

It wasn't only American journalists who raised awareness of the stakes of the war. The Fascists played a large role, too, by committing war crimes on a shocking scale. In the spring of 1937, Franco's Nationalist forces took aim at the Basque country, the small pocket of territory that runs along the northeastern coast of Spain from the French border to its main city of Bilbao, a significant port and industrial center. A fiercely independent ethnic group, the Basques had sought and received self-governing status from the Popular Front government in October 1936, making them a natural ally of the Republic and a foe of the Fascists. As part of his assault into the Basque heartland, Franco deployed the planes and pilots so generously provided by Hitler and

Mussolini to carry out bombing raids on small towns and cities on the route to Bilbao. On March 31, German and Italian bombers struck Durango, a village of about 10,000 people. The town center, along with two churches, was set ablaze; a dozen nuns were among the 250 civilians killed. As many as a thousand refugees fled Durango to the neighboring city of Guernica.

Guernica had been a significant site of Basque identity for six hundred years; here, under an old spreading oak tree, the city fathers would gather to discuss politics and so established a long tradition of self-government. Over the centuries, Spanish monarchs came to Guernica to reaffirm their respect for Basque autonomy, and the parliament of the province of Biscay sat there. These historical details meant little to the villagers and farmers who came to Guernica on April 26 for the usual Monday market day. The town itself possessed no military importance, but it lay on the road to Bilbao, and the Basques had set up a blocking position nearby. At 4:40 p.m., the first wave of German and Italian bombers appeared in the sky above the town and began dropping five-hundred-pound bombs as well as small incendiary explosives designed to set the town on fire. Fighter aircraft then dove from the clouds to strafe people fleeing the blaze. After about three hours, the entire town was engulfed in flames.[45]

Early press reports drew a horrific picture of the atrocity. "Hundreds of men, women, and children were literally roasted alive and torn to pieces by machine gun bullets today in a savage rebel air attack," said one report from the Reuters news service that appeared in papers across the United States. George Steer of the London *Times* happened to be in the Basque country when the attack took place; he set out for Guernica as soon as he could, arriving within hours of the bombing. In a long eyewitness report titled "The Tragedy of Guernica," Steer laid out in impeccable detail the raid and its consequences. He identified the fascist aircraft used in the strikes. The town had become "a horrible sight, flaming from end to end. . . . Houses were falling until the streets became long heaps of red impenetrable debris." He saw where civilians had been trapped in underground air-raid shelters; he saw people searching in vain for family members beneath the rubble; he saw the roads choked with bewildered refugees trudging behind horse-drawn carts en route to Bilbao. In a phrase that would frequently be repeated, he wrote, "The raid on Guernica is unparalleled in modern history."[46]

The bombing caused a sensation, gaining immense coverage in the international press. At least three hundred people were killed, though initial estimates placed the death toll between eight hundred and one thousand. "Wholesale arson and mass murder," the *New York Times* called it. The *Wash-*

ington Post insisted that the world now knew what kind of regime Franco would build in Spain: a totalitarian one, imposed "with a savagery and mercilessness without parallel.... It is not war which the Spanish rebels are now waging: it is mass murder of helpless and innocent civilians." Another *Post* editorial called Guernica "an inhuman holocaust of savagery." In the House of Commons, the foreign secretary, Anthony Eden, had to answer pointed questions about the British government's response to this "deliberate effort to use air power as an instrument of massacre and terrorism." Eden fell back on the most notorious of evasions, deploring the bombing of civilian populations "wherever it may occur and whoever may be responsible." After all, Eden insisted, "bombardments have been inflicted on both sides."[47]

But this equivocation did not silence the outrage. When the German government denied having bombed Durango or Guernica, blaming the destruction on the Spanish government forces, George Steer angrily called out the use by the fascists of "false news" and propaganda, and said that German planes were still active in the Basque territory, now bombing Bilbao. An unimpeachable witness, the dean of the cathedral at Valladolid, gave his own testimony of the burning of Guernica: "Fire enveloped the whole city," he said. "Screams of lamentation were heard everywhere and the people filled with terror." And more was to come. The Nationalist general commanding the attack, Emilio Mola, threatened to turn the entire Basque territory "into a cemetery" unless Bilbao surrendered. The Basques fought a bitter defensive struggle, but could not match the weapons and the field experience of the Nationalists. After a weeklong battle in mid-June, Bilbao fell to Franco's armies.[48]

What impact did these tragic events have upon President Roosevelt? In a doleful twist of fate, FDR set out on a two-week fishing trip on the day after the fascists destroyed Guernica. "Will Spend Next Two Weeks in the Gulf of Mexico to Catch Up on Sleep," as one headline put it. On April 27, his entourage left the White House and boarded a train for New Orleans, where he was greeted by a huge and cheering throng; the streets were bedecked in American, Confederate, and French flags. On April 29, he inspected the new Bonnet Carré Spillway, a large flood-control project, then lunched at the famous Antoine's restaurant, and boarded a ship to carry him down the Mississippi and out to meet the waiting USS *Potomac*, the yacht the press called "the floating White House." He was hoping to fish for tarpon as he cruised the warm waters of the Gulf of Mexico.[49]

As soon as he came on board, he was presented with a newly passed piece of legislation: the 1937 Neutrality Act, which Congress and the State

Department had been shaping all spring in anticipation of the expiration of the 1936 act. The 1937 version of the law carried the same mandatory prohibitions against arms sales and loans to any nation at war and banned travel on ships belonging to belligerent nations. It contained a new feature that allowed the president some discretion: If he felt that the sale of even *non-military* goods—such as oil, textiles, raw materials—to nations at war might risk American embroilment in their affairs, he could require that such sales be paid for in cash (to avoid another experience of accumulated war debts) and transported from American shores to the purchasing nation on their own vessels. Yet because this feature of the new law was not mandatory, it meant that until the president said otherwise, American markets for all goods except weapons were open for business, even to nations at war. Indeed, even if the president invoked this provision of the act, any nation with ready cash and a big merchant marine would have no trouble buying goods from the United States. For all the hand-wringing and pious speeches about neutrality in the 1930s, Congress proved unwilling to halt *all* trade with belligerent nations because there simply was too much money to be made in selling American goods to them. Thus, the law banned arms sales to the Spanish government, but permitted the sale of oil, steel, cotton, copper, and scrap-iron sales to Italy, Germany, and Japan. Sitting in his tiny stateroom aboard the *Potomac*, FDR signed the act on May 1, 1937, even as the embers of Guernica were still hot to the touch.[50]

VII

Though the president and most of Congress appeared unmoved by the horrors of the war in Spain, Americans after Guernica began to express concern over their government's inaction. Four left-wing Democrats in the House called for the president to impose the Neutrality Act upon Italy and Germany, halting them from purchasing war matériel in the United States. The congressmen condemned the "unprecedented barbarism" of the Guernica bombing and the "merciless undeclared war against a people whose main offense in Fascist eyes is loyalty to democratic institutions." Yet since the Germans and Italians denied that they were involved in the war, and the State Department did not want to make any provocative move against them, FDR chose to avoid triggering the Neutrality Act provisions—vivid testimony to its toothless, hypocritical character.[51]

On May 10, a public letter of protest against "the monstrous crime of Guernica" appeared in the press. It was launched by the New York Methodist bishop and chairman of the North American Committee to Aid Spanish Democracy, Francis J. McConnell, and carried the signatures of seventy-six leading public figures in religion, education, and politics. "This ruthless aerial warfare upon women and children stands outside the pale of morality and of civilization," the letter stated. Senator William Borah, a pacifist and neutralist but possessed of a sharp conscience, described the attack as "the most revolting instance of mass massacre of modern times." He took aim at the "ruthless creed" of fascism, which "is grounded in force" and which in Spain "presented to the world its masterpiece." Guernica "was not war, but butchery.... It is a repudiation of civilization." One well-seasoned correspondent who had covered Germany during the Great War despaired that Americans seemed not to realize what they were witnessing. Hitler, he argued, descended from a long line of militarists who embraced the doctrine of total war—and aimed not just to destroy enemy armies but eliminate entire peoples. Once Germany set out on the war path, Guernica would be repeated a thousand times over.[52]

The outcry grew. On June 4, the League of American Writers gathered 3,500 people for a mass meeting at Carnegie Hall to denounce the Nationalists as an arm of a global fascist conspiracy in Europe. One of the organizers, the poet Archibald MacLeish, managed to get his close friend Ernest Hemingway to speak there in return for a screening of *The Spanish Earth*, his now-completed film about the war. Hemingway, just back from the front, gave a brief but powerful address, foreshadowing ideas that would become common enough in the early 1940s. Drawing on his recent experience, he laid out in his distinctive prose why the war in Spain mattered so much:

> When men fight for the freedom of their country against a foreign invasion, and when these men are your friends—some new friends and some of long standing—and you know how they were attacked and how they fought, at first almost unarmed, you learn, watching them live and fight and die, that there are worse things than war. Cowardice is worse, treachery is worse, and simple selfishness is worse.

The fascists, Hemingway said, were undertaking an operation of "murder on a large scale," and they planned to kill not just soldiers but civilians as well. He said that he would not describe what the fascists were doing to civilians in Spain because "if I described it, it would only make you vomit. It might make you hate. But we do not want hate. We want a reasoned understanding of the criminality of fascism and how it should be opposed." How indeed? He offered a simple reply: "There is only one way to quell a bully, and that is to thrash him." Hemingway claimed that the Spanish loyalists and the International Brigades would give Franco a thrashing, but they needed help. The fascist war was no longer just distant thunder that Americans could ignore. It was a destructive tempest spreading over the world.[53]

Call it the Guernica effect. It could be seen across the newspapers and magazines in mid-1937. Hemingway framed a new argument that hitherto had been drowned out in the flood of American pacifism since the end of the Great War: Cowardice is worse than war. To allow fascists to murder a free people and do nothing would forever give the lie to any claim of moral superiority by the world's democracies. Drawing the same conclusions from the Spanish war, Dorothy Thompson lashed out at the pacifists and neutralists, calling the Guernica attack "the ruthless, cold-blooded, vicious extermination of one of the rare peoples of the Earth, the Basques." She condemned America's indifference: "To sit by and not to protest with all the breath in one's body rules one out of Christian society." It was a fierce indictment of America's fence-sitting and shoulder-shrugging toward foreign disasters.[54]

Thompson did not stop there. In a razor-sharp editorial in the *Ladies' Home Journal*, she took aim at pacifism more generally. "All my life I have been a pacifist," she began, but "today I seriously question whether our ways of seeking peace are not playing directly into the hands of those who love war." In the age of fascist dictatorships, with war fever encouraged by state-controlled mass media, the Russians, Germans, Italians, and Japanese were raising a generation of young people who desired only to die for their country in wars against some ideological enemy of the state. And America had so far given only one answer: We don't care. "Break treaties," Thompson wrote sarcastically, "invade other nations, bomb cities, blockade ports, starve women and children, and we will take our ships off the seas and fold our hands. You can count on our doing nothing." But Americans, she went on, had forgotten that "in a world where anarchy rules, no one is safe." Echoing Hemingway's remarks about moral courage, Thompson wrote with steely directness: "I know there are things for which I am prepared to die," namely, political freedom and the right to live, love and work without the constraint of a "dictator's code." She did not want war, but "if the fight comes unsolicited, I am not willing to die meekly, to surrender without an effort." Words like these could not be found in the national press before Guernica.[55]

Thompson's article resonated. Eleanor Roosevelt herself, in her immensely popular syndicated daily column called "My Day," mused about Thompson's piece. "I wonder how many of you have read Dorothy Thompson's 'The Dilemma of a Pacifist' in this month's issue of the *Ladies Home Journal*?" she asked in her usual conversational tone. "She has reached much the same conclusion as I have, namely, that an attitude of letting the rest of the world stew in their own juice, is rather a dangerous one." The First Lady in one sentence had called into question America's neutrality policy, a policy her husband had shaped. "Perhaps in our own interest we may have to take the initiative and have sufficient interest in other people's affairs to really want to help them remain at peace. . . . If war comes into your own country, then even a pacifist, it seems to me, must stand up and fight for their beliefs." Millions of readers of "My Day" would have wondered if the Roosevelt administration was about to alter course after five years of fence-sitting.[56]

In fact, there *was* something brewing in the White House. Not yet a change of course, but at least a quiver on the tiller. Martha Gellhorn may have had something to do with it. Returning to the United States from Spain for the writers' conference, she visited Mrs. Roosevelt in the White House on May 27. Eleanor wrote about this visit in "My Day," telling her readers that Martha had come back from Spain with "one deep conviction: 'the Spanish people are a glorious people, something is happening in Spain which may mean much to the rest of the world.'" Martha and Eleanor conspired to arrange a viewing of *The Spanish Earth* for the president. In a letter of June 1, the First Lady offered possible dates for Gellhorn, Hemingway, and their Dutch filmmaker friend, Joris Ivens, to visit and show the film. She encouraged Martha's work: "You are right to try to make people realize that what is happening in Spain might happen anywhere." Martha's letters to the First Lady showed how the raw emotions of her experience in Spain followed her to America. "The future of Europe is our future, no matter how much we want to be apart," she wrote in a long, sorrowful letter, full of rage toward Hitler and Mussolini—"dangerous criminals," she called them—as well as toward the governments that turned a blind eye to the destruction of Spain. Still, she took solace in Eleanor's support, ending a letter with: "Please know how very much and how very admiringly I love you." The two agreed on a date for a viewing of Ernest's "very, very beautiful film" at the White House.[57]

Eleanor Roosevelt: the most admired and influential woman in America.
Library of Congress

On July 8, 1937, Gellhorn, Hemingway, Ivens, Harry Hopkins, the president, and the First Lady sat together for an amiable dinner followed by a screening of a dark, brooding art film, written and narrated by Hemingway, that purported to tell the story of the Spanish Civil War and its chief victims, the poor but proud farmers and ordinary people who took the brunt of Franco's pitiless war. Hemingway wrote later that it was "damned nice of the Roosevelts to have us there," but his description of the scene, in his curious telegraphic style, has gone down as one of the more uncharitable descriptions of the Roosevelt White House ever written:

> Mrs. Roosevelt is enormously tall, very charming, and almost stone deaf. . . . The President is very Harvard charming and sexless and womanly, seems like a great Woman Secretary of Labor, say, he is completely paralyzed from the waist down and there was much skillful maneuvering of him into the chair and from room to room. The White House, when we were there, was very hot, no air conditioning except in the President's study, and the food was the worst I've ever eaten. (This between us. A guest cannot criticize.) We had a rainwater soup followed by a rubber squab, a nice wilted salad and a cake some admirer had sent in. An enthusiastic but unskilled admirer.

What really mattered, of course, was that both Roosevelts "were very moved by the Spanish Earth picture," but thought it too oblique. "Put more propaganda in it," said FDR to Hemingway and Ivens, in so many words.[58]

To Martha, who had been "very nervous lest anything go wrong with the film," the evening was a great success. About the film, the Roosevelts told them "to make it stronger . . . by underlining the causes of the conflict." In fact, Mrs. Roosevelt made this point in her "My Day" column on July 19, describing the film to her readers, and offering Hemingway and Ivens some advice: "I think they presuppose too much knowledge of old-world conditions," in particular the thorny historical problem of land ownership and the vulnerability of the peasantry to exploitation. "The pity of it all, however, kept running through my mind. When will we learn to talk things out and not go at each other's throats like wild beasts?"[59]

The film itself was critically acclaimed, with the *New York Times* calling it the most successful appeal for Spanish democracy yet produced. In its realism, its close-ups of individual farmers, or the dark faces of civilians huddled in basement bomb shelters, or the grim, tired tramp of marching Republican militia soldiers, the film showed clearly that the Spanish people were not fighting for "Muscovite Marxism" but for the right to work and own land long neglected by absentee landlords. When it opened in Los Angeles, leading celebrities came out in droves; crowds were turned away at a few of the early showings. Money from the film was spent on purchasing ambulances for the Spanish government forces.[60]

Still, the fortunes of the Spanish Republic dimmed as the war ground on, and attitudes in Washington did not change much. Roosevelt did not want to get embroiled in European affairs, as he casually reminded reporters in a press conference in mid-July. To a question of whether he would take the initiative in convening a world economic conference, he said that "about once a day" he got a call asking him to play a role in helping Europe solve its problems. Europe was "up against a stone wall," he said, and "it is a perfectly logical thing for them to look around for somebody to come forward with a hat and a rabbit in it; and they think I got a hat with a rabbit in it." Chuckling in a somewhat tetchy manner, he said: "Well, I haven't got a hat, and I haven't got a rabbit in it." Laughter erupted, but the message was plain: America wasn't going to make any heroic measures in European affairs.[61]

As ever, American elites just did not want to hear lectures about the threat posed by fascism. William Shirer, who had spent three years in Berlin watching Hitler consolidate power, began a new job in Vienna in the fall of 1937. He looked back on his time in Berlin with regret. As he wrote in his diary, he tried to alert the world to "Nazi fanaticism, sadism, persecution," to no avail. The Nazis were preparing for a world war, he believed, but when he spoke of such things to visiting American officials, "they laughed." Shirer found that Americans could not grasp the "dynamics of this movement, the hidden springs that are driving the Germans on, the ruthlessness of the long-term ideas of Hitler . . . the Nazi goal is domination!" He could not get the words of the well-known Nazi marching song out of his ears:

Today Germany belongs to us,
Tomorrow the whole world.[62]

One man who did understand was Claude Bowers, who kept up his steady flow of letters to the president, begging him not to ignore the catastrophe gaining momentum in Spain. On the one-year anniversary of the start of the Spanish war, Bowers sent a sharply worded nine-page memo to the president that essentially indicted FDR's hands-off policy in Spain. "The civil war ceased to be a civil war many months ago when great numbers of the Italian and German armies were brought into Spain," he cabled Roosevelt. "No doubt in my mind that non-intervention has prolonged the war" by starving the Spanish government of the means to protect itself. Cynicism drove this policy, Bowers said: Spain's democracy had been sacrificed to buy peace in Europe. But, he prophesied, the dictators would renege on the deal, for "at every surrender, beginning long ago with China, followed by Abyssinia and then Spain, the fascist powers, with vanity inflamed, will turn without delay to some other country—such as Czechoslovakia."[63]

Jay Allen, who after being fired by the *Chicago Tribune* had found work editing a glossy high-brow (and short-lived) magazine titled *Ken*, wrote of Bowers that he had done "a magnificent job of informing his government of the truth," and his reports to Washington "constitute a definitive history of the war." But Bowers could not claim to have altered the mind of the only man that mattered in making U.S. foreign policy. To his latest letter, FDR responded with extraordinary indifference. "It is good to get your letter," he wrote. "It is tremendously interesting." But, he continued, "I have missed having you at home and having the services of your pen in a period when we have needed a great deal more in the way of publicity than we have been able to secure." The fight to change the Supreme Court had occupied so much of his time, he complained, and the "fat-cat newspapers" damned the administration at every turn. He did not have to say it directly, but the message to Bowers was clear enough: For now, Spanish democracy would have to make do without America.[64]

CHAPTER 10

JAPAN STRIKES

"China is really fighting our battle for freedom and peace in the Orient today."

—HENRY STIMSON

I

Can a photograph start a world war? Surely not by itself. But one snapshot taken hurriedly in China in 1937 did have a significant impact on the course of world events and helped place the United States on a direct collision course with the Empire of Japan. On August 28, Japanese aircraft bombed the Shanghai South Railway Station, where thousands of anxious civilians were trying to board trains to flee the city. A news photographer named Wang Haisheng, who worked as a stringer for the Hearst newspapers under the name H. S. Wong, rushed to the station to find a scene of unspeakable horror. Bodies lay mangled, bits of flesh and limbs were scattered across the ruins of the station, and Wong's shoes were soon soaked in blood. Later reports suggested two hundred people had been killed in the bombing. Using both a small newsreel camera and his Leica, Wong gathered pictures of the gruesome slaughter. One of his photos showed a baby, sitting amid the wreckage in apparently burned clothes, smeared with blood and ash, screaming into the void. No other life form is visible: The crying child is cocooned in twisted metal, rubble, bent train tracks, and dust.

Other photographs Wong took showed a crumpled, lifeless body nearby—perhaps the child's mother. Wong also saw the baby being carried off to an aid station on a stretcher. Within two weeks, Wong's film footage and photographs reached the United States, and soon appeared in newsreels in thousands of movie houses across the nation. William Hearst's news empire published the photo of the screaming child in all of its papers, and Hearst shared the image with other newspapers at home and overseas. On Octo-

Shanghai South Railway Station, August 28, 1937.
H. S. Wong

ber 4, the hugely popular and influential weekly magazine *Life*, published by Henry Luce, carried the searing photo, for which Wong later won an award. According to the accompanying caption, the picture had by that date been seen by 136 million people around the world in newsprint and movie form. Whatever the exact numbers, there can be no doubt: That bloodied, terrified child became the face of Japan's war in China.[1]

The chain of events leading to that murderous bombing of the Shanghai train station extended back across many years of Japanese expansion into northeast Asia. After the Japanese victory in the 1905 Russo-Japanese War, Japan took control of a web of railways that connected the interior of Manchuria, a strategic and contested borderland province of China, to coastal cities and ports. Along with Japan's annexation of Korea in 1910 and its possession of Taiwan, the control of Manchuria transformed Japan into the dominant power of East Asia. Japan deployed soldiers in Manchuria to guard its network of rail lines and open the region's mines, timber, and natural resources to Japanese exploitation. When the world war broke out in 1914, Japan seized the German-controlled port of Qingdao in Shandong Province and then compelled a weakened Chinese government to recognize Japan's "Twenty-One Demands," drastically extending Japanese economic and political rights in Manchuria and north China.

As the influence of military officers and right-wing national organizations took hold in Japanese politics, the Japanese occupation forces in Manchuria envisioned a bold strike to seize all of Manchuria and entrench Japan's control of the region. In 1931, they manufactured a crisis by alleging Chinese sabotage of the South Manchurian railway; there followed the swift annexation by Japan of all of Manchuria. The League of Nations condemned Japan's brazen act, but beyond issuing this public statement, the great powers chose to do nothing. The Hoover administration declared that it would not recognize political changes made by force—the so-called "non-recognition doctrine" designed by then–secretary of state Henry Stimson. This policy allowed the United States to register disapproval without taking any punitive steps. The seizure of Manchuria went forward unimpeded.[2]

Japan's grip on Manchuria created friction on the Chinese-Manchurian border, which was exacerbated by the presence of Japanese military units posted along the Beijing-Tianjin railway. On July 7, 1937, while Japanese forces were staging a military exercise near the Marco Polo Bridge a few miles west of Beijing, Chinese and Japanese forces exchanged fire. Who fired first is an issue that remains clouded in controversy, but it was clear that by 1937, both Japan and the Chinese government were spoiling for a fight. The Japanese viewed their control of northern China as a benevolent civilizing mission similar to European colonization. From the Japanese perspective, China was a lawless, backward region of bandits and warlords that should be harnessed to a new order in Asia. The weak civilian control of the military in Japan allowed the voices of the government's most bellicose advisers to push through a plan for the conquest and control of China as the first step of a greater imperial project: an eventual confrontation with Communist Russia in the north combined with the conquest of Southeast Asia and its valuable supplies of oil, rice, and tropical products. The skirmish at the Marco Polo Bridge in July provided a convenient pretext to initiate this program, and within days, Japanese forces in China marched on the historic capital of Beijing and the nearby port city of Tianjin. They both fell to the Japanese at the end of July.

In its penetration and conquest of Manchuria, Japan benefited from China's internal political weakness; in the years since the 1911 revolution and the fall of the Qing dynasty, China had passed through years of civil war and chaos. But by 1937, China was no longer an anarchic, collapsing nation. It had a central government that ruled, albeit unsteadily, over the vast and fractious coun-

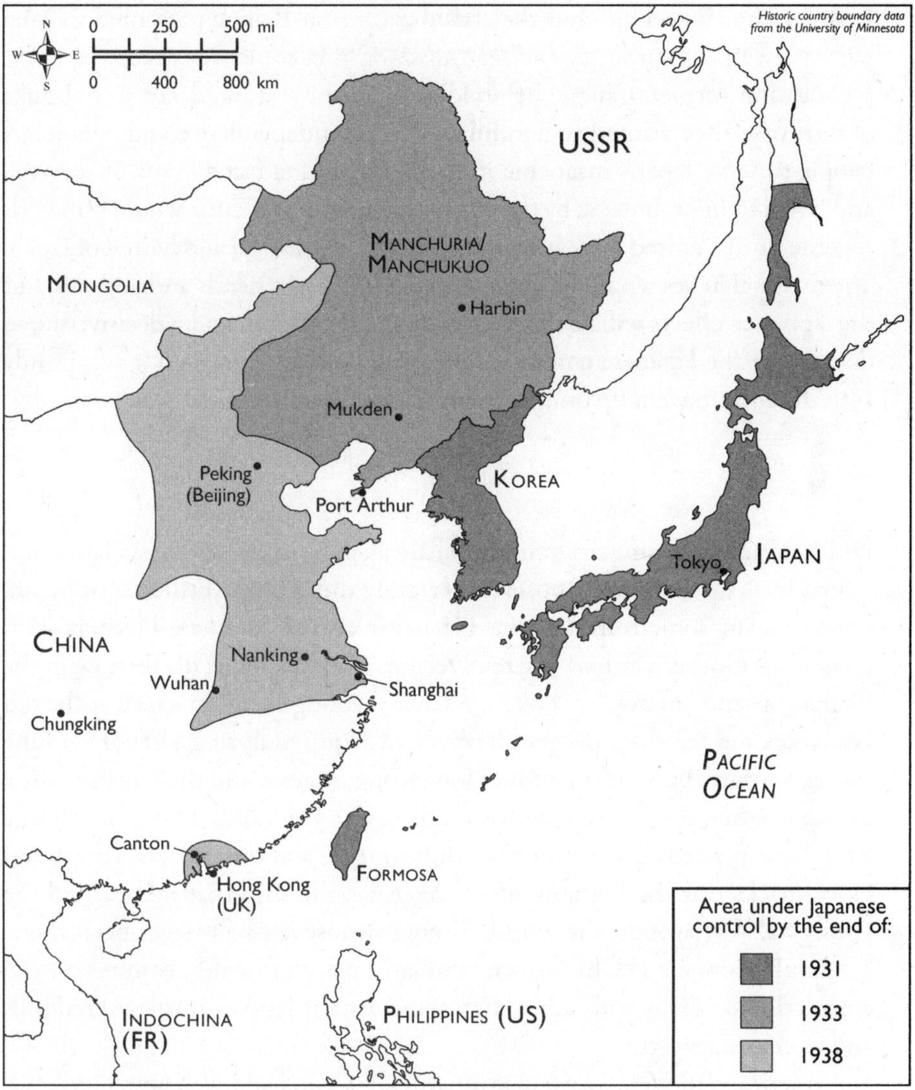

Japanese expansion in China, 1931–1938

try. Through the Kuomintang, or Nationalist Party of China, a military officer named Chiang Kai-shek had either defeated or coopted regional warlords and established his claim to leadership of the Republic of China. Though he faced a major challenge from the growing Chinese Communist Party, Chiang Kai-shek had consolidated his hold on most of the country and ruled from his capital in Nanjing (then called Nanking). Chiang had sought to avoid war with Japan throughout the early 1930s, knowing that China could not match

Japan's military strength, but the armed clash near Beijing presented Chiang with a test of his authority and legitimacy. China could not accept Japanese provocation forever, Chiang believed. The Japanese wanted not just chunks of territory; they wanted to annihilate China's independence and compel its people to serve Japan's insatiable imperialism. China faced a war of survival, and it had to fight. Indeed, by fighting, Chiang hoped, China would pull itself together into a united force bound together by patriotism and hatred of Japan. The material losses would be great, Chiang told his generals and advisers, but the "spiritual effects will last forever." Chiang chose war, and a decisive showdown with the Japanese empire. Though no one quite grasped it yet, in July 1937 the curtain went up on the first act of the Second World War.[3]

II

Did Americans care much about the outbreak of hostilities between Japan and China in 1937? Franklin Roosevelt certainly did. Unlike Ethiopia or Spain, China meant something to him. He never ceased to regale listeners with tales of his mother's father, Warren Delano, who had made his fortune in the China tea (and later opium) trade. As a boy, young Franklin gazed at the old keepsakes and treasures his grandfather had acquired during a life of working the trade routes between Canton, Hong Kong, Macau, and the United States. FDR's mother, Sara, when she was only seven years old, made the passage from New York to China with her family in 1862, and one of FDR's cherished knickknacks was the logbook of the *Surprise*, the ship that had carried the family halfway around the world. Though Roosevelt had never been there, his family's lore made China seem familiar, a place of wealth, commerce, and connection to the world rather than some distant land of mist-covered hills and uncharted rivers.[4]

Americans too felt a certain sympathy for China and welcomed its emergence from centuries of feudalism and civil war. Although anti-Chinese racism *inside* the United States was rampant and extreme, and had led to the 1882 Chinese Exclusion Act, barring virtually all Chinese immigration to America (it was not repealed until 1943), some Americans saw glittering opportunities in this vast Asian kingdom. A generation of American missionaries had been active in China; hospitals and schools with American doctors and educators sprang up; American investments flowed into the construction of China's infrastructure; and American merchants considered China a huge untapped market for American goods. European powers, too, had been pressing claims in China since the middle of the nineteenth century, using gunboats and war to carve out "concessions"—zones in port cities where foreigners could live, own property, run churches, and build trading posts, free from interference of Chinese authorities. Foreign concessions had their own police forces and military contingents. Tianjin, Shanghai, Nanjing, Canton, Kowloon in Hong Kong, along with many other cities, featured thriving foreign communities.[5]

America would not be left out. In 1898, the United States annexed Hawaii and took control of the Philippines from Spain (and proceeded to wage a brutal colonial-style war of conquest there that did not fully end until 1913). The following year, the U.S. called for an "open door" agreement among the great powers to preserve access to China's markets, thus avoiding a colonial carve-up of the kind then going on in Africa. During the anti-foreign Boxer Rebellion in 1900, an international alliance sent troops into China to protect foreign citizens and keep the open door from slamming shut. The political disarray in China allowed the great powers to secure preferential rights to build railways, dig mines, establish banks, construct settlements for their citizens, and garrison soldiers to protect them. To impose some order on this economic rivalry in China, the nations with the greatest economic interests there—including both the United States and Japan—signed the Nine-Power Treaty in 1922, affirming China's sovereignty while making the Open Door a formal international agreement. To enhance its presence in the region, the U.S. Navy created a Pacific Fleet in 1907 and soon began building fortifications in Hawaii. The Navy in 1924 adopted "War Plan Orange"—a Mahanian scheme to use naval power to defend American territorial possessions in the Pacific from the most likely enemy, Japan. By the 1920s, the United States controlled a Pacific archipelago of maritime outposts that reached from the Aleutian Islands in the north to Hawaii, Midway, Wake, Samoa, and Guam in the central Pacific, all the way to the Philippines, a mere seven hundred miles from the coast of China.[6]

Americans were introduced to China in these years by able popularizers like Pearl Buck, whose huge bestseller of 1931, *The Good Earth*, created a sympathetic portrait of a peasant family, its earthy values and mores, and the human drama of daily life in rural China. As historian Gordon Chang notes, the Chinese of Buck's book were superstitious, poor, simple-minded, but possessed of a certain human warmth that made them appealing and accessible. The daughter of Presbyterian missionaries, Buck spent most of her first forty years in China; her book "more than any other single contemporary work, shaped an American image of China," in the words of historian Michael Hunt. Another American, Edgar Snow, reported from China throughout the 1930s for the *Saturday Evening Post* and other U.S. periodicals, and published a wildly successful book in 1937 called *Red Star over China.* This volume myopically portrayed the Chinese Communist leader Mao Zedong as a nationalist, a "Lincolnesque" figure, a wise and well-read man, and a sincere anti-fascist who was joining in the struggle against the Japanese occupiers; his movement, Snow claimed, attracted disciplined, idealistic youths who wanted land reform, reduced taxes on peasants, and women's rights. Admirable and decent, these young revolutionaries seemed to Snow much like Americans.[7]

Not only writers and evangelicals went to China: It became an important location for the training and education of some of the most influential future officers of the U.S. Army. General George Marshall, for example, the man FDR would tap in 1939 to serve as army chief of staff, spent three years in China from 1924 to 1927 in command of the 15th Infantry Regiment, stationed in Tianjin. Marshall and his wife enjoyed their time in China and Marshall studied Mandarin intensively, becoming reasonably proficient. In China, Marshall worked alongside Joseph Stilwell, a China hand who was fluent in Chinese and who Marshall later assigned to organize and train the Chinese military during the war against Japan. Claire Chennault, a retired military pilot, arrived in China in June 1937 to begin a long stint as Chiang Kai-shek's adviser on the Chinese air force; he would later pioneer the use of American volunteer pilots to fly for the Nationalist forces against Japan.

Another American with early connections to China was Henry Luce, who, by 1937, had become a media mogul and owned some of America's most important newsmagazines including *Time*, *Life*, and *Fortune*. Luce was born in 1898 in Shandong to missionary parents and lived his first fifteen years there. He became a warm admirer of Chiang Kai-shek and an advocate of American aid to China in its struggle against Japan. To Luce, Chiang Kai-shek was a charismatic figure who could unify China, fend off powerful regional warlords as well as the growing Chinese Communists, and keep China aligned with the West. Luce helped popularize Chiang's wife, the Wellesley-educated Soong Mei-ling, who had been raised in a rich and politically powerful Methodist family from Shanghai, and who persuaded Chiang to convert to Christianity. With Luce's help, Chiang and his wife became media darlings in America, and the two of them often graced the pages of Luce's magazines. By the mid-1930s, then, China had been transformed in American eyes from a dangerous, chaotic arena of warlords and violence into an appealing and promising ally against an ever-more-ambitious Japan.[8]

Not everyone accepted this narrative. To some leading African American intellectuals and editorialists, white America had the story backward: Japan was the nation that, through discipline, unity, and ambition, had demonstrated the capacity of non-white people to govern themselves and perhaps expel European colonizers from Asia. No American did more to make this case for Japan's civilizing mission than W. E. B. Du Bois, who traveled extensively in Europe and Asia in 1936, writing columns for the *Pittsburgh Courier*. Du Bois was considered in the Black community "a statesman, historian, creative writer, editor, scholar," a leader who had spent years "raising voice and pen" against racial oppression. Having passed through Brussels, Paris, Berlin, Munich, and Moscow, he set out in mid-November 1936 on the Trans-Siberian Railroad bound for Manchukuo, as the Japanese called their colony in Manchuria. As a guest of the Japanese government, who knew of his outspoken criticism of European colonialism, Du Bois received special attention from his hosts in Harbin and Changchun. He was captivated by the Japanese and their achievements in China. "I brush aside as immaterial," he wrote, "the question whether Manchukuo is an independent state or a colony of Japan." More important, he argued, was the absence of racism, the visible orderliness, the provision of public services, utilities, health care, libraries, education, and housing, and the dynamic and industrious people. Japanese rule in Manchukuo, he said, was "nothing less than marvelous."[9]

In fact, he considered the Chinese at fault for resisting Japanese leadership. Visiting Shanghai, he found it "the epitome" of European racial colonialism, a large city controlled by a small avaricious European population. In his eyes, the Europeans had imposed an Asian version of Jim Crow there. He saw a small white boy order three Chinese adults off the sidewalk. "They meekly obeyed; it looked quite like Mississippi." Du Bois lectured Chinese business and government officials about their aping of Western manners and their foolish hopes that Europeans would ever treat them as equals. Demonstrating astonishing ignorance of Japan's own racism toward other Asian peoples, Du Bois wondered why the Chinese did not join with Japan to create a dynamic Asian community of their own. "With China and Japan in rivalry, war, and hatred," he told them, "Europe still continues to rule the world for its own ends." Ending his trip with a visit to Tokyo and Kyoto, Du Bois declared himself "overwhelmed" by Japanese courtesy, modernity, and racial tolerance. Japan gave the world a shining example of "a country of colored people run by colored people for colored people." This thesis that Japan held the key to a new order in Asia, one that would break the choke hold of Western imperialism and showcase self-rule by non-white people, found its way into many editorials in the American Black press.[10]

Such pro-Japanese views would not be found inside the State Department, where a foreign service officer named Stanley K. Hornbeck emerged as the leading Asia specialist. Hornbeck had spent his late twenties teaching in China and immersed himself in its history. He earned a PhD in political science from the University of Wisconsin, where he studied tariffs and trade relations, and published his first book in 1916 on politics in Asia. He was attracted, like many Americans, to the entrepreneurial spirit of the Chinese and the potential of a modern, Western-oriented China. After service in World War I as an intelligence officer, he played a role as a special adviser on the Far East in the American delegation to the Paris Peace Conference. He later joined the State Department and soon rose to become the chief of the Division of Far Eastern Affairs, where he advocated a get-tough policy toward Japan. He believed the United States and Japan were on a collision course in Asia. The Japanese, Hornbeck asserted, did not have any regard for law or treaties, and only "speak and understand the language of force," he wrote in a memorandum in 1934. America must meet the Japanese on similar terms by building a powerful navy so that "the Japanese will not dare to take the risk of resort to force against us." Hornbeck took the view that China, though inefficient and messy, had a sparkling future because its people were industrious, democratic, and genial; whereas the Japanese were imperialists, militarists, and obsessed with martial traditions. Although initially out of step with the cautious Hull and his team, Hornbeck's advice to treat Japan firmly would ultimately prevail.[11]

Despite the best efforts of these active China lobbyists, however, the American government did little in reply to Japan's new assault in July 1937. Hull issued a characteristically aloof public statement on July 16 about respect for international treaties and the importance of conciliation and restraint in world affairs. When the British inquired through diplomatic channels if the Americans would welcome "a combined Anglo-American *démarche*," that is, a protest, against Japanese actions, Hull immediately squelched the idea. He told the British ambassador in Washington that the United States preferred to act "on parallel but independent lines." This meant that Hull wanted to be able to say publicly that America was not joining in any kind of cooperative venture with Britain, even though he decried Japanese aggression. America, it seemed, wanted to stand with, but a good distance from, the British in confronting Japan.[12]

Roosevelt took a slightly different view from Hull. The accelerating Japanese offensive after July 1937, which clearly aimed at the total subjugation of all of China, struck him as a breathtaking violation of international law and a direct threat to American security. Japan must not be allowed to close off this vast area to the rest of the world while harnessing its unlimited natural resources to its war machine. That summer, "the president grew increasingly restive," according to his adviser and friend Sumner Welles. He wanted to sound out the European powers about a coordinated effort to isolate Japan. He anticipated that because of their vast colonial possessions in Asia, from French Indochina to the Dutch East Indies and British-held Hong Kong, Singapore, Malaya, Burma, and India, the Europeans shared an interest with America in containing Japan's advances. Thinking of Britain's large navy, FDR imagined a joint Anglo-American force hemming in Japan's imperial ambitions. According to Welles, who FDR had elevated to undersecretary of state in May 1937 despite Welles's frosty rivalry with Cordell Hull, the president pored over large maps of the Pacific Ocean in his study, and from these he developed an idea for a trade embargo on Japan enforced by the U.S. and British navies. So dependent were the Japanese on imports of American goods, especially petroleum, cotton, wool, and scrap iron, FDR reasoned, that Japan would immediately grasp the threat of an embargo and reverse course in China.

Did not the president fear such a blockade would lead to war? Welles asked. No, FDR replied. The Japanese were overextended in China already and could not risk opening another front against the powerful British and Americans. FDR calculated that the new British prime minister, Neville Chamberlain, would prove a leader with more "guts" than his predecessor, the discreet and restrained Stanley Baldwin. So, at the end of July, FDR personally invited Chamberlain to visit Washington for discussions of their common problems, a meeting that would instantly have conveyed to the world that the democracies were moving to join forces.[13]

Neville Chamberlain—six feet, two inches tall, high-necked, his angular face bisected by a thick boot-brush mustache with eyebrows to match—did not fit the usual mold of British prime ministers. Unlike his predecessor, the wily Baldwin, who was educated at Harrow and Trinity College, Cambridge, and who had proven his political skills over a lifetime of backroom deals and careful conciliation, Chamberlain came to politics late after a career as an accountant and businessman. He began public life by working in municipal government in his home city of Birmingham, where he showed a talent for urban planning; in 1915, he became Lord Mayor. He was neither religious nor intellectual, only briefly attending a technical college. He grew up in the shadow of his charismatic father, Joseph Chamberlain, a wealthy manufacturer who also had a glittering and controversial career as the arch-imperialist secretary of state for colonies. Joseph's oldest son, Austen, spent forty-five years in politics and notched a distinguished term as foreign secretary in the 1920s. Neville, by contrast, only decided to go into national politics after the Great War, and in 1918, at the age of forty-nine, he was elected a member of Parliament from a Birmingham constituency.[14]

His experience in local government, his head for numbers, and his tireless work ethic opened the way to rapid advancement. For much of the 1920s, Chamberlain was an especially successful minister of health, and in 1931, became chancellor of the Exchequer, where he imposed high tariffs on foreign imports, cut spending especially on armaments, reduced the giant national debt that had accrued during the war, and seemed to have put British finances on steady ground by 1935. When he became prime minister in May 1937 at the age of sixty-eight, Chamberlain could be described as forceful, seasoned, egotistical, censorious, and thin-skinned. Neville Chamberlain rose to the height of British politics through hard work and mastery of the bureaucratic machinery rather than social connections or likeability or because of any fixed political ideology. Indeed, he had few friends, confiding chiefly in his sisters, to whom he wrote extensive, indiscreet, and revealing letters.

British prime minister Neville Chamberlain: confident, smug, and inflexible.
Popperfoto via Getty Images

Though he had no experience in external affairs, he made it clear to his foreign secretary, Anthony Eden, that he would largely run foreign policy himself; Eden, far more favorable to a firm foreign policy against the dictators, immediately clashed with the new prime minister. Surveying the international scene upon taking office, Chamberlain rightly perceived that Britain faced an array of global obligations without the resources to meet them all. Appeasement—that is, a process of negotiation through which European great powers could meet the demands of the restive fascist nations while avoiding war—seemed to Chamberlain, as well as the cabinet, the press, and much of the British public as wise, normal, and indeed magnanimous and honorable. Britain had lost nearly nine hundred thousand soldiers in the Great War—6 percent of the adult male population. Offering conciliation to the dictators while limiting arms spending was for this generation of British statesmen the ethical, righteous thing to do. And peace, even at the price of territorial revisions in Europe, would postpone any reckoning with Britain's overstretched imperial commitments, Chamberlain believed.[15]

These calculations framed Chamberlain's reaction to Roosevelt's invitation to meet in Washington to discuss some sort of coordinated action against Japan. The new prime minister felt that a meeting with the president would arouse the suspicions of Germany and Italy about an Anglo-American alliance, undermining his efforts to propitiate the dictators. Furthermore, he suspected a Washington trip would remain only symbolic, doing enough to aggravate relations with Japan, but too little to halt Japanese expansion. Chamberlain was not alone in rejecting any Anglo-American initiative. Cordell Hull also believed that a formal protest coordinated by Washington and London would be perceived as tantamount to an alliance against Japan, thus worsening rather than easing the crisis. Even when Japanese officials in early September publicly announced their intention to deliver a "decisive blow" to China—a prospect that directly threatened the interests of all the other great powers in the Pacific—Hull continued to insist that the United States would not work jointly with other nations to lodge a protest, for fear of precipitating the country into a war that the American people would not support. At the end of September, Neville Chamberlain declined the president's invitation to visit. Privately, he snidely remarked that "the Americans have a long way to go yet before they become helpful partners in world affairs."[16]

III

The absence of any Anglo-American response to Japan's aggression looked especially feeble in light of the ghastly news that began to pour out of China in August, and which American newspapers reported in depth to a worried nation. After seizing Beijing in late July, Japanese forces chose to attack Shanghai, planning to seize this important port city and use it to stage an assault on the Nationalist capital in Nanjing, located some 180 miles up the Yangtze River.

Shanghai, a city of three and a half million people, was also home to many thousands of foreign missionaries, tradespeople, doctors, and teachers, drawn from across Europe, America, and Japan. Four thousand Americans, along with a thousand marines, lived there, dwelling in the enclaves designated many decades before as exclusive zones for Westerners. Rising from the banks of the Huangpu River—and a short distance upstream from the mighty Yangtze—Shanghai was a showcase of Westernization, precisely what had antagonized Du Bois. The art deco Cathay Hotel, ten stories high with indoor plumbing, stood next door to the Palace Hotel, a redbrick structure that featured the city's first elevator. Cafés and restaurants, shopping centers, banks, headquarters of shipping lines, all clustered together along a handsome riverfront district called the Bund, where foreign and Western elites strolled, viewed the boats at their moorings, or hailed a rickshaw for swift transport around town. "People of all walks of life, all nationalities, all creeds, pass through Shanghai," said the manager of the Palace. "Nowhere, not even in London or Paris, is there such a distinctly international hotel patronage." Perhaps with this foreign presence in mind, Chiang Kai-shek chose to throw a great deal of effort into defending the city from the Japanese attack: should the Japanese harm foreign interests in Shanghai, the outside world might awaken sooner to the implications of Japan's war on China.[17]

The Battle of Shanghai turned this cosmopolitan city into a charnel house. When the Japanese cruiser *Izumo* menacingly appeared in the river just off the Bund, along with other ships and gunboats preparing the way for the landing of infantry, the small Chinese air force tried to sink it at its mooring. On August 14, inexperienced Chinese pilots made a dreadful mistake, dropping bombs intended for the *Izumo* on the packed streets of central Shanghai—striking the Palace and Cathay hotels directly as well as the markets that were full of Saturday afternoon shoppers. In a flash, hundreds of people were blown to pieces, glass windows along the Bund were shattered, and burning cars became ovens that incinerated their trapped passengers. In the lobby of the Palace, a young Princeton professor named Robert Reischauer had a portion of his heel sliced off by falling sheet glass. Dazed and bleeding, he got his friends to rush him to a hospital where he died from loss of blood, making him the first American death of the Second World War. (His brother Edwin would later become a renowned Asia expert and the U.S. ambassador to Japan in the 1960s.) As many as a thousand people were killed in this one terrible accident.[18]

Two days later, the Japanese began a methodical shelling of the city, using naval gunfire and aircraft. The State Department swung into action, attempting to coordinate the departure of Americans from the city, but the intense exchange of fire between Japanese and Chinese forces threatened them at every turn. Cordell Hull announced that a contingent of 1,200 U.S. Marines would be sent from San Diego to assist in protecting the American community, joining the USS *Augusta*, the flagship of the American Asiatic Fleet, which had arrived off Shanghai a few days earlier to lead the evacuation. Meanwhile, the Japanese poured shells into the city relentlessly, taking no heed of civilian causalities. Panic-stricken residents, fleeing burning homes, trudged through the streets, hauling pathetic bundles of belongings. Explosions rang through the densely settled city, and on August 20, an explosion—probably caused by a Chinese antiaircraft round—landed on the deck of the *Augusta*, killing Seaman First Class Freddie Falgout of Raceland, Louisiana. He was later immortalized as the first American military death of World War II. (The *Augusta*, too, found a place in history as the vessel that carried FDR in August 1941 to meet Winston Churchill at Placentia Bay, Newfoundland, where the two leaders signed the Atlantic Charter.)[19]

As Japanese soldiers swarmed into the city and Chinese defenders fought for every street, billows of black acrid smoke cloaked Shanghai, the result of incendiary bombs dropped by the invaders. City landmarks, like the large shops Sincere and Co. and Wing On's department store, took direct hits at a time when people in search of dwindling food supplies had crowded into them. One eyewitness reported that "headless bodies, arms, and legs were scattered in macabre patterns all through the area." Fires burned fiercely in northern and central Shanghai, which included large portions of the foreign settlements. No one was safe: The British ambassador to China, Sir Hughe Knatchbull-Hugessen, was strafed in his car by a Japanese plane and severely wounded.[20]

On August 28, Japanese bombers destroyed Nantao, the old walled district of historic Shanghai, its narrow roads turned into graveyards for thousands of refugees that had sought shelter there. As this neighborhood went up in flames, bombs rained down on the nearby South Railway Station, where huge crowds of anxious Chinese had gathered in hopes of catching a train away from the fighting. At least two hundred people were killed there. "About 1,000 Chinese, many of them homeless and half-starved, were jammed in the station," wrote one journalist. After the bombing, "the railway yards were littered for several hundred yards with arms, legs, and heads." When one American reporter toured this district two days later, "the sickly stench of rotting human flesh" hung in the air. Chinese soldiers also suffered enormous casualties, and those that surrendered to the Japanese were often murdered. The bodies of Chinese POWs, hands tied behind their backs, were found by the score in the rivers and canals. Inevitably, a cholera epidemic hit the city on September 1, the result of the putrefaction in the summer heat of so many corpses.[21]

The battle for the city ground on through September, October, and into November as both sides threw in more and more troops. Japan eventually sent 300,000 soldiers into Shanghai to face 750,000 Chinese defenders, making it the largest urban battle until Stalingrad in late 1942. If the Chinese had more men under arms, the Japanese had the advantage of greater firepower and training, which began to tell as the fight for the city dragged on. Under sweltering heat, in narrow alleyways and across endless creeks and canal networks strewn with barbed wire, mines, and machine-gun nests, the armies fought to the death for every inch of Shanghai. The city was ground into rubble and ash by repeated mass bombardments from Japanese bombers and artillery. The Chinese lost 250,000 soldiers there and the flower of the Nationalist Army officer corps.[22]

Chiang Kai-shek appeared willing to pay this extremely high price in order to dramatize the stakes in China to Western governments. He wanted to show the world the brutality deployed by the Empire of Japan in its march of conquest, and Shanghai gave vivid witness of that. His charismatic wife, Soong Mei-ling, helped to spread the word in the West with targeted radio addresses, bemoaning China's isolation. "China is fighting," she said in mid-September, "not only for her sovereign rights and existence but also for the sanctity of treaties, while foreign nations watch their rights and interests being destroyed. . . . No other nation seems to care." As Roosevelt and his advisers discussed whether to invoke the Neutrality Act of 1937, Soong Mei-ling asserted that China would fight on with "swords, sticks, and stones" if necessary. But America's policy of preventing China from defending itself, she said in an echo of the argument made by Spanish Republicans, would bring tragedy not just for China, "but also for the world."[23]

The press coverage of the conflict did a great deal to fix in American minds the idea that Japan was a uniquely ruthless, fanatical empire—entirely different from the "civilized" empires in Europe. The historian John Dower has shown how certain words, phrases, and images that took hold in American rhetoric during World War II—depicting Japanese as rodents, monkeys, lice, and other undesirable non-human creatures—prepared the public for the "extermination" of hundreds of thousands of Japanese civilians through aerial bombardment during the war. This process of treating the Japanese as "uncivilized" and even inhuman intensified in 1937, and the keyword of the moment was "barbarism." The *Washington Post* felt that Japan's bombing of Shanghai "bids fair to make the name of Japan a synonym for brutality and barbarism and makes a mockery of the pretensions of the island empire to the status of a civilized state." The "barbarous action" and "savagery" in Shanghai "was a sheer act of terrorization" and the *Post* even hinted that Japan would reap what it had sown: "For a nation whose own cities are peculiarly vulnerable to air attack, Japan is clearly acting in a suicidal manner," and would not be able to invoke the norms of international law for the protection of its own "crowded noncombatant areas." The *New York Times* also condemned Japan's "unprecedented barbarism" and its "unbridled terrorism" in Shanghai and other cities.[24]

In early October, pulpits across the country rang with indignation as clerics condemned Japan for demonstrating "a barbarism and a savagery which people find it hard to believe, wreaking a merciless slaughter" on civilian refugees. "Heathens are always cruel and ruthless," thundered Reverend John H. McComb of the Broadway Presbyterian Church in New York City. The British *Manchester Guardian* labeled the Japanese "the new barbarians" for bombing undefended cities; the British government formally expressed its "horror" at Japanese methods while the *Daily Express* and the *Evening Telegraph* called for boycotts of Japan. The British labor movement in late September, condemning "the barbarous and systematic massacre by Japanese aircraft and submarines of the defenseless Chinese civilian population," also urged a boycott. On October 7, the American Federation of Labor followed suit.[25]

Americans could agree that Japan's war in China was "barbarous," but they asked: What does it matter to us? In the fall of 1937, Roosevelt came under pressure from some in Congress, the press, and anti-war organizations to invoke the Neutrality Act and cut off all sales of weapons and war-related matériel to the combatants. "That the U.S. should go to war because Japan has attacked China," complained the *Chicago Tribune* editorial page, "would seem one of the most unreasonable things imaginable." The paper later demanded that Roosevelt withdraw "every soldier and warship away from the troubled zone. . . . We have no interests in China which are worth a war." Roosevelt sought to assure his critics of his own desire to steer clear of the conflict in Asia, yet he did not want to hamper China's ability to defend itself using some American-made armaments. In a characteristic maneuver, on September 14 he banned government-owned merchant ships from transporting arms to China or Japan, but also said that he would not yet invoke the Neutrality Act, since the two warring nations themselves had not declared war against each other. His action meant that thirteen vessels of the U.S. Merchant Marine that regularly carried goods to China would now be forbidden from carrying arms, aircraft, or war matériel. But privately owned merchant ships could continue to do so, albeit at their own risk. The Chinese felt betrayed.

Soong Mei-ling expressed her shock: "Our very life is being strangled from us," she asserted, yet "we find America operating to prevent our securing the means to defend ourselves and therefore aiding our enemy to fulfill her threat to beat us to our knees." The Chinese, she bitterly noted, had been "struck in the face by the great republic whom we had been taught to look up to with respect."[26]

IV

Yet beneath his equivocation, Roosevelt was searching for some kind of action that might signal a new degree of engagement with the global crisis. Harold Ickes, a close Roosevelt adviser, a leading liberal, and the most outspoken anti-fascist in the cabinet, told Roosevelt privately that American inaction only reinforced the argument of the dictators that democracy had failed. He referred to the huge Nazi rally going on at that very moment in Nuremberg, where Hitler and his minions denounced democracy as weak and withered, offering instead a Rome-Berlin fascist alliance for "safeguarding Europe from chaotic madness." Ickes insisted that Cordell Hull's State Department had become far too timid in generating a suitable response to these outrageous statements. FDR agreed and said, "he would have to take the ball in international relationships from Hull." As a first step, he imagined writing an open letter to the world's nations calling for the isolation of the international "bandits," namely Germany, Italy, and Japan, and an imposition of a blockade around them to deny them raw materials. While nothing could be done to save Spain or China, he said, this idea might serve as "new policy for the future." Ickes urged him to act: FDR possessed, the secretary said, "the only voice in the whole world that could speak out for the democratic principle." Ickes said that the rogue states of the world presented a case of a "contagious disease" and that "neighbors had a right to quarantine themselves" to limit the spread. FDR replied: "That is a good line; I will write it down."[27]

With the images of the September Nuremberg rally and the pictures of slaughter in Shanghai fresh in his mind, Roosevelt departed Washington on September 22 for a two-week train trip to the Pacific Northwest, chiefly to visit three major Public Works Administration projects that the New Deal could rightly claim as major success stories: the Fort Peck Dam on the Missouri River in Montana, and two dams nearing completion: the Bonneville Dam on the Columbia River near Portland, Oregon, and the Grand Coulee Dam, also on the Columbia, about eighty miles west of Spokane. These were enormous engineering feats, designed to control floods, provide irrigation, and generate huge amounts of hydroelectric power. In scale and daring, they exemplified the New Deal imagination. For Roosevelt, this was an "epic pilgrimage," as one journalist on board the presidential train put it, for FDR had envisioned the great potential of the nation's waterways since his earliest days as a state legislator in Albany. The Grand Coulee Dam was simply "the biggest thing on Earth," and the three dams together "constitute the most far-reaching construction program ever undertaken by the Federal Government." Even in the fall of 1937, when the economy had stumbled into a recession and when Roosevelt had lost considerable prestige in the bruising battle over the Supreme Court, these stupendous projects showed the latent power of the United States and embodied a belief in the future—a future of abundance, strength, and limitless possibility.[28]

Yet the world crisis would not be ignored. While en route to Seattle, FDR learned that Mussolini had arrived in Berlin for a state visit. Millions of Germans lined the streets of the capital to greet the Italian strongman and cheer this alignment of Europe's antidemocratic forces. Il Duce spoke, in German, of the ideological solidarity of the Rome-Berlin axis. Nazism and Fascism formed together "a revolutionary movement" with a common enemy, Bolshevism; the Axis powers were destined to emerge victorious from that struggle. "The Europe of tomorrow will be Fascist," he roared. Mussolini's preening in Berlin made it plain: The fascist states had forged an ideological alliance. Their vision of the future—a world of militarist empires, discipline, the domination of the weak by the strong, racial purification, all imposed by powerful dictators—would consign the feeble democracies to oblivion.[29]

Roosevelt, a self-described pacifist, did not wish to threaten these tyrants with war. He remained convinced that war would jeopardize the very economic and social progress he celebrated on his long western tour. But he also felt that the world he wished to see emerge from the global crisis of the decade—a world of law, commerce, intellectual achievement, and human freedom—would never succeed as long as aggressive fascism and militarism grew unchecked. Could America galvanize the world's nations to resist the march of the dictators? Roosevelt and Cordell Hull decided that some kind of public statement should be made when FDR arrived at Chicago on his return journey from the Northwest. Chicago, a hotbed of pro-neutrality sentiment and home to the anti-Roosevelt *Chicago Tribune* newspaper, also gave Roosevelt an opportunity to celebrate another New Deal achievement: the opening of a bridge over the Chicago River, built by the PWA. State Department officials sent in pages of possible text, and FDR's speechwriting team adopted much of their high-minded language; but Roosevelt added to the speech a memorable phrase from the conversation he had with Ickes in the previous month.

As it happened, October 5 was a propitious day to decry the horrors of war: The infamous photo taken by H. S. Wong in Shanghai of the dazed and terrified baby appeared in *Life* the day before. Standing on a platform next to the new Outer Drive Bridge, Roosevelt cleverly set up a comparison between the prosperous America he had just seen on his western train journey and the obscenities of war around the world. He painted a picture of the busy farms and factories he had passed, the huge federal projects he inspected, the undoubted progress America had made to recover from the global Depression. But overseas, a "reign of terror and international lawlessness" gripped the world. Careful to avoid naming names, he declared that "the very foundations of civilization are threatened." Civilians, women, and children were being slaughtered by indiscriminate bombing. Ships were being attacked by submarines, nations were taking sides in civil wars, and "greed for power and supremacy" were driving nations to ever more violent action. Americans must take note of this global crisis, he insisted. Should these wars merge into a world conflict, "let no one imagine that America will escape . . . through mere isolation or neutrality." The world had become interdependent: A war against civilization would touch all people, everywhere.

This diagnosis reappeared more frequently in Roosevelt's speeches in the coming years: American security, liberty, and democracy, he argued, could not thrive in a world of dictatorships and war. But what could America do about it now? Here came FDR's prescription: "When an epidemic of physical disease starts to spread, the community approves and joins together in a quarantine of the patients in order to protect the health of the community." If war, as he put it, was a "contagion," then it followed that it must be isolated and cut off from the rest of the world. Roosevelt avoided specifics. Did he mean to impose a blockade, or economic sanctions, against the bandit nations? He did not say. Did he mean that America would risk war in order to stop the dictators? No: "America hates war. America hopes for peace. Therefore, America actively engages in the search for peace."[30]

Some historians have asserted that the speech received overwhelmingly negative reviews, compelling Roosevelt to disavow it in the coming days and weeks. And indeed, figures like Senator Gerald Nye, the publisher William Randolph Hearst, and the editorial pages of the *Chicago Tribune*, *Wall Street Journal*, and the *New York Herald Tribune* did denounce the message as warlike and provocative. In the *San Francisco Examiner*, Hearst wrote that Roosevelt's quarantine meant war; FDR was misleading the country about the consequences of his proposal. Governor Alf Landon, still smarting from the beating he had received at the polls in 1936, said Roosevelt was about to make a "tragic" mistake that would put American lives at risk. And the peace movement also spoke out, claiming Roosevelt "points the American people down the road to world war."[31]

Yet far more revealing is the often-overlooked enthusiasm generated by the "quarantine" message. Harold Ickes, who could take some credit for the quarantine metaphor, called the speech "the most important one on the international situation that he [Roosevelt] has ever made." Ickes asserted that the president's words "created a sensation around the world" and "stiffened the backbones of Great Britain and France." In Britain, the *Manchester Guardian* noted that although the precise measures Roosevelt envisioned remained murky, there seemed "no doubt that the United States is prepared to approve and to aid any League efforts to apply economic sanctions against Japan." In Moscow, Ambassador Joseph Davies noted that the speech caused "a sensation" where it was understood as a chastising of both Nazi Germany and Imperial Japan, and a new engagement of the United States with collective security. From Spain, Claude Bowers sent glowing Spanish Republican newspaper editorials, and he himself called the Chicago speech "the first courageous, honest facing of ugly facts by any responsible statesman of the world . . . a splendid summons to the Democracies of the world to stop their pitiful policy of retreating before the gestures of the bullies." In Washington, the Chinese ambassador exulted; in Tokyo, the Japanese foreign ministry issued a cold rebuttal.[32]

Dorothy Thompson, speaking to her millions of listeners on her regular radio program, called Roosevelt's address "the most momentous and courageous speech of his career," and asserted that "it foreshadows a break with the policy of international isolation that has dominated our foreign relations since 1918." At last, she felt, FDR had told the American people the brutal truth: War in Asia and Europe menaced their own security. The country "cannot preserve its present political and economic system, nor hope for prosperity, in the face of catastrophic shocks from world conflicts," she wrote. The United States is "deeply, intimately, irrevocably a part of the world," she went on, and she hailed Roosevelt's assertion that isolation could never protect America from the consequences of global war and economic disruption.[33]

Still more significant, editorials in many American newspapers welcomed the speech, applauding the president's tone of outrage at the aggressors in Europe and Asia. *Life* magazine asserted that FDR "turned the course of history" in his "landmark" address. Papers in Philadelphia, Cincinnati, St. Louis, New

Orleans, San Francisco, and Portland, Oregon, all chimed in with robust support for the president's firmness. The *New York Daily News*, no friend of the president's, praised the speech, as did Frank Knox's paper, the *Chicago Daily News*. *Time* magazine asserted that Roosevelt had "correctly gauged public psychology." The *New York Times* thought FDR had "thrown the door wide open for collaboration" with other countries in containing Japan's aggression. The speech was "the strongest statement yet made by any government" about Japan's brutal war. The *Los Angeles Times*, a longtime critic of the New Deal, spoke of "a vigorous new foreign policy" and noted that the speech "stirred the imagination and wonder of diplomatic circles." The *Washington Post* editorial page vigorously applauded this "strong plea for effective international cooperation." The new policy "permits the American people again to take pride in their country as one which is at last willing to take a stand on principle." The *Post* welcomed the end of the "flabby, vicious, humiliating doctrine" behind America's neutrality acts, and envisioned an end to the "organized vandalism" of Germany, Italy, and Japan. The next day, the League of Nations stirred itself from its slumber and announced that it would host a meeting of the Nine-Power Treaty signatories in Brussels to discuss a peaceful end to the Japan-China conflict.[34]

Ironically, the press and public response to his speech might have been a bit too enthusiastic. For the next day, in an off-the-record press conference with weary and bedraggled reporters in Hyde Park following an overnight train ride east, Roosevelt tried to lower expectations about any change in U.S. policy. He specifically called out "old man Hearst" for his editorial, calling it "the silliest thing ever written . . . perfectly terrible—awful." He insisted that he did not have in mind economic sanctions, which he viewed as "coercive," and emphasized that whatever action the U.S. might take to pressure Japan did not in any way hamper or undermine American neutrality. He refused to go in detail with the reporters, but he clearly imagined "peace-loving nations" agreeing in some way to restrain their trade with Japan, thus compelling a change in behavior from the import-dependent Japanese government. The press had misread his speech, he implied, and were "unable to visualize the thing at all." He suggested "there were a lot of methods in the world that have never been tried yet," and admonished one of the reporters, Ernest Lindley: "Put your thinking cap on, Ernest."

This colloquy with an obviously frustrated press corps reveals that Roosevelt's quarantine address was never meant to lead to any belligerent measures at all. FDR imagined it as a collective act to isolate Japan, one that might contain and deter the onward march of Japanese conquest. "I am fighting," he wrote to an old friend from the World War I days, "against a psychology of long standing—a psychology which comes very close to saying 'peace at any price.'" He said he thought quarantine was a "practical and peaceful" way to censure lawless nations without provoking war. Yet even so, the sudden surge of support for Roosevelt's message reveals that important sections of the American public had begun to make the turn away from passive neutrality and were prepared to act in the face of ongoing savagery in the world. It was up to Roosevelt to cultivate that shift in American attitudes.[35]

V

Roosevelt saw the meeting in Brussels, set for November, as an opportunity to test the appetite of other leading states for some version of his quarantine idea. This willingness to confer with other states marked a change from America's normal wariness toward any international initiatives. FDR turned to his peripatetic special envoy Norman Davis to represent the United States at the conference. Davis, the well-connected, well-traveled, wealthy Southern Democrat with close ties to Cordell Hull (they were both from Tennessee) was not a member of Hull's staff at the State Department. He shared FDR's belief that a vigorous demonstration of American power and prestige, combined with subtle threats of economic quarantine, might deter Japan and open the way to a resolution in China. If it worked, the Western powers could stamp out the fire that threatened to engulf all of Asia.

On October 19 at Hyde Park, Roosevelt and Davis met and talked through various strategies for the upcoming conference. Davis expressed some concern about the unduly restrained official American attitude and said there were two schools of thought in the State Department: one that believed that if Japan conquered China, it would proceed to seize British and Dutch colonies in Asia and "also the Philippines, and that war with Japan would become inevitable." The other view argued that Japan would exhaust itself fighting an endless war in China, thus diminishing the future Japanese threat to America. Roosevelt said "he agreed with the first school of thought." War and anarchy in Asia, he said, "would inevitably endanger our own security and stability." Thus, Davis had as his mission to help bring about a ceasefire in the Sino-Japan conflict. And if such a ceasefire proved unobtainable? Roosevelt said that in such a case, "public opinion of the world and of the United States by that time would most probably demand that something be done." And here, in the privacy of his Hyde Park study, he told Davis what he meant: that neutral countries could concert together, "ostracize Japan, break off relations," and possibly halt commercial exchange—in short, an embargo. Yet

Roosevelt did not want to overcommit the United States and find the other powers too cautious. "We must avoid getting out front alone."[36]

Predictably, the conference at Brussels, which went on for three weeks, failed to create any consensus on how to halt the Japanese invasion of China. The Japanese refused to attend the meeting and rejected Western offers of mediation. The French and British wanted the Americans to stand up to the Japanese, but wanted to steer clear themselves of any conflict in Asia. Davis had anticipated this and wanted to rally the powers at Brussels to discuss some sort of united action against Japan. But the State Department insisted that the United States must not take the lead and to find itself "holding the bag," as Roosevelt put it. Stanley Hornbeck was one of Davis's assistants at the meeting and rued the contradiction in U.S. policy: "We do not want to take leadership in the conference," he wrote, yet "we wish that the conference accomplish something constructive." Hornbeck envisaged coercive measures—embargoes, boycotts, blockades—against Japan. He argued that the Japanese did not care about "a concert of adverse opinion;" they had contempt for Western verbal protests. "If we mean business, and if we intend to be realistic," he went on, "we must consider earnestly whether we are willing to do anything beyond and further than express opinions."[37]

A frustrated Davis appealed to Hull and to Roosevelt. The conference was getting nowhere, and the Japanese were simply ignoring the appeals to come to the peace table. He thought it was time to develop "united pressure on Japan" through curtailing trade, commerce, and shipping. He went further than that. He suggested that Roosevelt seek "a repeal or a suspension of the existing neutrality legislation at least insofar as concerns the Sino-Japanese conflict. This would startle and worry Japan, encourage the Chinese and have a dynamic effect upon world opinion." Hull rejected all this, desiring to take no firm steps against Japan. America must "keep the door open for possible mediation in the Far Eastern conflict," and that meant remaining neutral and passive. Davis drafted a red-hot memo to Hull: "Unless we are willing to share in possible measures of some sort . . . the majority of the powers would lose heart and sit back and do nothing." He went on, saying if "we confine ourselves to preaching," the Japanese would conclude "that they can, with no danger or interference, continue on their present course." Davis toned down this letter slightly in its final form; but his anger came through. Clearly, Roosevelt had abandoned Davis and dropped the robust talk of the Hyde Park meeting. FDR stood back and let Hull throw cold water on any talk of collective action against Japan. It was arguably a low point for American diplomacy in the interwar period.[38]

The meeting at Brussels deeply depressed the hawks who wanted a firm policy toward Japan. Henry Stimson's reaction to Roosevelt's meandering diplomacy is emblematic of internationalist opinion. A man with a towering reputation as a former secretary of war and state, Stimson knew the China problem well; in the spring of 1937 he published a book about his own efforts to deal with Japan's 1931 annexation of Manchuria. Stimson emerged as one of the leading voices of confrontation with fascism, urging the Roosevelt administration to assert American power in the world as a force for stability. Indeed, the very day after FDR's quarantine speech—and quite by coincidence—a long letter by Stimson about China appeared in the *New York Times*. Stimson painted a picture of a happy, peace-loving, and democratic China assailed by a barbarous, militarist Japan, and he called for an American embargo on sales of war-related materials to Japan. Stimson hailed FDR's Chicago speech but grew downhearted when he saw the administration fail to follow up.[39]

On Sunday, November 7, Stimson invited the brilliant economist and State Department official Herbert Feis to "Highhold," his country home on Long Island. Feis gave Stimson "a very gloomy picture" of the atmosphere in the State Department. He reported that Hull was exhausted by the constant pressure of world events, stubbornly insisting that statements of high moral principle would eventually win over the rest of the world. According to Feis, Stanley Hornbeck told Hull to his face that he had become "a preacher only" as if he was some kind of religious figure. He told Hull he "must consider action as well as preaching." Feis also told Stimson that Norman Davis in Brussels had become discouraged and depressed. Only Sumner Welles and Walton Moore in the State Department wanted to take serious measures to deter and contain Japan; Pierrepont Moffat, who went to Brussels with Davis, was "defeatist and isolationist," said Feis. When he sighed that a wary public was inhibiting Roosevelt, Stimson insisted that "the American people take their leadership from just one person—the President." Stimson claimed he had seen many cases when firm leadership from a president "could reverse a previous apparently insuperable attitude of the people."[40]

In hopes of prompting such presidential initiative, Stimson wrote to Roosevelt personally. Drawing on his own experience, he called the war in China "one of the very the gravest crises that have confronted us in my lifetime." (Stimson was then seventy years old.) He stated that "China is really fighting our battle for freedom and peace in the Orient today." Their people and government were "largely influenced by American education and traditions," while Japan is "feudal" and "wholly guided by military purposes." The war there was a struggle for the future of Asia, and China was at a huge disadvantage in arms and supplies. The U.S. must "alleviate the disparity under which China is fighting." A Japanese victory would have enormously bad consequences for U.S. security. If America imposed an arms embargo on China under the terms of the Neutrality Act, such a policy would have "permanent and damaging effects upon China's faith in us and our civilization." A failure to help China and to contain Japan would cause "incalculable harm." He closed with a powerful appeal for action: "the world crisis of freedom . . . is trembling in the balance on the fields of China today."[41]

This was a remarkable message from an unimpeachable source. Yet still Roosevelt refrained from any significant act against Japan. What happened? Why did Roosevelt go from his ringing oration at Chicago about halting the contagion of war to letting Cordell Hull squash even the hint of American cooperation in a "quarantine" against Japan? It is always difficult to know exactly how Roosevelt weighed his options, but surely the fear of becoming "the tail to the British kite"—a phrase Hearst had thrown at him—made him wary of starting down a path to confrontation with Japan and finding the British lagging far behind. There was also the Hull factor: Hull was a political force in his own right, a leading Southern Democrat, and a respected advocate of negotiation rather than confrontation. Roosevelt could not overrule Hull on such a serious matter without alienating members of his own party in Congress, many of whom were Southerners.

Roosevelt also wanted to avoid being drawn into the war in Asia; he saw the gathering crisis in Europe as far more menacing to America's national interests than Japanese imperialism. That meant relying on words rather than warlike action to contain Japan. He still believed, he wrote to Lord Robert Cecil, a leading British internationalist, in "the eventual effectiveness of preaching and preaching again." He saw himself as a Cassandra rather than an Achilles: "we cannot stop the spread of fascism unless world opinion realizes its ultimate dangers." And as for the appeal by Stimson, Roosevelt had the State Department draft a reply that said the Europeans were trying to push America to take "energetic measures," but Congress and the public opposed any such risk-taking. FDR would not be hectored into any provocation of the Japanese.[42]

VI

Roosevelt may also have been influenced by his ambassador to Japan, Joseph C. Grew, one of the most distinguished members of the diplomatic corps and an advocate of restraint in U.S.-Japan relations. From a wealthy Boston family,

Grew was two years ahead of FDR at Groton and Harvard. He had already had a successful career as ambassador to Turkey, Switzerland, and Denmark before going to Tokyo in 1932. He was popular among his Japanese counterparts, and he understood the importance of polite, behind-the-scenes diplomacy instead of public declarations. He told the State Department that the Japanese government was divided between civilians and the militarists who had plunged Japan into the latest China assault, and he urged Washington to avoid strident condemnation lest it serve to inflame the situation. He admired Hull's cautious, steady appeals to the principle of international law and feared Roosevelt's "quarantine" address was an empty threat that would only encourage Japanese defiance. In his diary, he noted that the "moral thunderbolts" of the great powers against Japan were worthless and tended to undermine the less aggressive faction in Japan's government. Grew believed his style of quiet diplomacy stood a better chance of winning Japanese cooperation than a policy of naming and shaming. And Grew soon showed that he could deliver results.[43]

When the Battle of Shanghai neared its grim final days, the Japanese army decided to press on to Chiang Kai-shek's capital, Nanjing, about 180 miles west, up the winding Yangtze River. Seizing Nanjing, they thought, could end the war. In a rapid campaign, the Japanese reached Nanjing's fortified walls on December 9 and commenced a massive final assault on the besieged city. Chiang and his officers abandoned the capital on December 12 and the Japanese breached its walls late that night. Amid the raging battle, the few remaining foreigners fled, heading for naval vessels waiting in the river to evacuate them.

One of these ships was the USS *Panay*, a river gunboat that formed part of an American naval patrol on the Yangtze. The *Panay* had been ferrying Americans away from Nanjing for some weeks. On December 11, the last Americans there, including four officers of the U.S. embassy, boarded the ship. Operating in a dangerous war zone, the ship's crew had painted fourteen-by-eighteen-foot American flags on the deck and on an overhead canvas awning; it was also flying a large flag from its stern. At 1:30 p.m. on December 12, a Sunday, a dozen Japanese aircraft appeared in the sky above the *Panay*. Three planes dropped bombs on the ship, and then the fighters dove down to strafe the vessel, pouring bullets into the hull and deck. Three other ships, tankers of the Standard Oil Company traveling in a convoy with the *Panay* and full of civilians, were also hit and set ablaze. The *Panay* was badly damaged, its captain seriously wounded, and the ship rapidly began to sink.

Among the ship's passengers were Universal Newsreel cameraman Norman Alley and Fox Movietone News cameraman Eric Mayell, who had been filming the torment of Nanjing under Japanese shelling. They took film footage of the sudden air attack that clearly showed how close the Japanese planes came to the ship; the pilots could easily see the American flags. As the *Panay* sank, the Japanese aircraft returned to strafe lifeboats filled with wounded passengers. Three Americans were killed; survivors, of whom nearly fifty were wounded, waded through thick mud to a nearby village and were eventually rescued by British and American vessels.[44]

Such an act of aggression could easily have triggered a war between Japan and the United States. Ambassador Grew made sure it didn't. As he wrote in his diary, it was "a black day indeed" when the Japanese foreign minister, Koki Hirota, came unexpectedly to the U.S. embassy and personally reported the news of the attack on the *Panay*. Grew recalled that Hirota expressed "profound apologies and regrets" and "seemed as genuinely moved as any Japanese is capable of registering emotion." He confessed to Grew, "I can't tell you how badly we feel about this." The State Department, now fully informed of the events on the Yangtze, passed along a protest and demands for a full explanation, and conveyed to the Japanese government that the president was "deeply shocked." Grew feared that this incident could lead to a rupture of relations and even war. He wrote sadly in his diary of the "two Japans"—the Japan he admired that had nourished a long friendship with America, and the Japan of martial ferocity whose army was "running amok and perpetuating atrocities." When additional details came to Grew four days after the attack that the Japanese pilots had deliberately fired on the lifeboats, he feared the worst.

Yet the Japanese government moved quickly to accept blame, apologize, and offer to pay an indemnity for all damages. More surprising, on Christmas Day, the United States accepted the apology and assurances that such an incident would never be repeated. Eventually, Japan paid a $2.2 million settlement. Grew called it "an eminently happy day" and was heartened that the two countries "refused to be stampeded into potential war." He even described the *Panay* incident in his diary as "a blessing in disguise," since it showed how easy it would be for the two countries to slip into a war that neither of them desired. Instead of war, Grew's swift intervention helped arrange a dignified apology and settlement of the issue. Grew felt vindicated that his patient work over five years to build trust with his Japanese counterparts had paid off. "Table-thumping is absolutely useless here," he wrote.[45]

Roosevelt seemed to agree. For a few hours after hearing of the *Panay* attack, he considered taking serious measures and asked Treasury Secretary Morgenthau to develop a plan for seizing Japanese assets in America and other forms of economic retaliation. Within days, though, he dropped the matter and accepted the Japanese apology. He did not want America to be ensnared by the Sino-Japanese War; he knew the public did not want it; he knew the U.S. Navy was not ready to send major forces to the region anyway while maintaining a presence in the Atlantic; and so he deliberately lowered the temperature and moderated his rhetoric. The *Panay* attack would not lead to a break in relations.[46]

This restraint of the American government in response to the deadly *Panay* attack is remarkable, especially when coupled with the horrific behavior of Japanese troops upon entering Nanjing. On December 16, American papers started to carry shocking reports of the mass executions of Chinese prisoners of war and of civilians by Japanese troops, combined with looting, burning, and a vast campaign of sexual assault. "'Four days of hell' would be the most fitting way to describe the siege, capture, and rape" of the capital, wrote Archibald T. Steele, the first Western news reporter to get word back to the United States about the fate of the city. Steele said the last thing he saw before fleeing the city was "300 Chinese being methodically executed" in front of a pile of corpses. The Japanese upon entering Nanjing did not restore order but instead "chose the course of systematic extermination. It was like killing sheep."[47]

F. Tillman Durdin of the *New York Times*, who slipped out of the city with Steele, reported witnessing "wholesale atrocities and vandalism" by the Japanese. Mass murder, incessant rape, looting, and mayhem turned Nanjing into "a city of horror." Durdin saw "civilian dead on every street," and captured Chinese soldiers slain on the spot. The fall of Nanjing was a disaster for China, Durdin wrote, "one of the most tragic military debacles in the history of modern warfare." And he did not see the worst of the killing that carried on for weeks afterward. We now know that as many as two hundred thousand people would be killed in Nanjing over two months; that sexual violence of unspeakable brutality accompanied this organized slaughter; and that the assault on the city would be etched into history's darkest pages.[48]

Yet it did not trigger any major change in policy from the United States government. Even combined with the *Panay* assault and the deliberate machine-gunning of American sailors and civilians in their pathetic, blood-spattered lifeboats, Nanjing did not become a rallying cry for American leaders. Indeed, what is remarkable is the silence of the Roosevelt administration, despite dozens of credible eyewitness reports that came out of China in the early days and weeks of 1938 about the scale of the Japanese savagery there. In fact, according to Harold Ickes, FDR said at a cabinet meeting in late January that he was receiving "reports of Japanese atrocities in China" that were "so terrible in their details that he could not read them" in the presence of a woman, meaning Secretary of Labor Frances Perkins. Henry Luce received regular reports from sources in Nanjing that detailed the horrible atrocities there. One doctor wrote in early February of the "large number of women from 16 to 30 . . . who are ridden with venereal disease from frequent raping. All of them have gonorrhea, most have syphilis, and a large proportion have chancroid as well." These details were kept secret so as to avoid reprisals against the Western doctors and missionaries still in the city, but the broad outlines of the story were well-known: *Life* magazine depicted the sack of Nanjing in its pages on January 10, 1938, with photos displaying dismembered corpses; *Time* added written details. And in the newspapers, periodic reports offered chilling hints at what had transpired there.[49]

Nor did the violations of American property or interests cease after Nanjing fell. In late January, John M. Allison, the chargé left behind to staff the deserted U.S. embassy, was slapped across the face by a Japanese soldier when Allison tried to enter a barracks in search of information about the rape of a woman with ties to Ginling College, an American school for women established by missionaries in the city. This "Jap Slap," as the *Chicago Tribune* labeled it, triggered yet another round of protests and half-hearted Japanese apologies, and again the Americans closed the matter. Yet the public by early 1938 had enough information to draw its own conclusions. The newsreel filmed by the unlucky reporters on the *Panay* went out to theaters in January and millions of Americans now saw for themselves the ruthless, pitiless assault of the Japanese fighter planes as they bore down on the hapless vessel. Detailed reporting in various papers about the horrors of Nanjing left no doubt that the Japanese had launched a campaign of mass terror and destruction on an unprecedented scale, designed to break Chinese resistance, sow fear, and compel China's surrender to the new Japanese Empire.[50]

Even the African American community, which under Du Bois's tutelage had welcomed the prospect of a strong, anti-European Japan that could guide Asia toward modernization, grew wary of Japanese ambitions. The Afro-Caribbean writer and Communist Cyril Briggs, who had been an important figure in the Harlem Renaissance, acidly rebuked the "dupes" who had fallen for the propaganda that depicted Japan as the "the hope of the darker races." In fact, he wrote in the *Philadelphia Tribune*, Japan showed its true colors in joining with Nazi Germany and Fascist Italy—the conqueror of Ethiopia—in the Anti-Comintern Pact of November 1937. This argument was echoed by Ben Davis Jr., a Harvard-trained lawyer who had become a Communist in the mid-1930s, and who edited the *Negro Liberator* and the *Daily Worker*. Fascism was a global threat and must be opposed by a global anti-fascist movement, he stated to an audience in Norfolk, Virginia; "Japan is not our friend."[51]

And it wasn't just Communists who made this case. Another rising voice in Black politics, the Harlem-based Baptist minister Adam Clayton Powell Jr., castigated Black indifference toward China's suffering. Neutrality in the face of fascist brutality and imperialism was immoral and contrary to the best interests of African Americans, he asserted. "We must aid China, Loyalist Spain, the Jew in Germany," and push for a federal anti-lynching bill—these issues were all connected. "This world of ours is too interdependent and interrelated for any one part to feel it can stand aloof from the problems of the whole." Race prejudice, he said, was "a world-wide, organized menace," and when it succeeds in Germany, Spain, or China, it endangers "us so-called free Negroes right here in Harlem." Here lay the outlines of an African American commitment to fighting fascism in the name of improving American democracy.[52]

Roosevelt, however, remained quiet on all this. Had he disowned his bold if vague proposal launched in Chicago three months earlier for a quarantine of lawlessness and the contagion of war? Not exactly. He was in no sense indifferent or unaware of the potential threat Japan posed, especially when united in a three-way alliance with Germany and Italy. Together, these three militarist imperiums could hem in American power by dominating Europe and Asia. A few days after the attack, he spoke to the cabinet about using British and American naval vessels to blockade Japan; according to Ickes, FDR said "Japan could be brought to her knees within a year." Roosevelt—as Stimson had noted—tended to overestimate the hold of neutralist and pacifist opinion on the American public, and he kept private all such talk of using the navy to contain Japan. But behind closed doors, he took an important step in that direction.[53]

The story is well-known to historians, though it was kept very secret at the time. Just four days after the sinking of the *Panay*, while still in a rage over this outrageous attack, Roosevelt asked the British ambassador, Sir Ronald Lindsay, to come to the White House. It was late in the evening of December 16, and Roosevelt was in an expansive mood. In response to a British inquiry that arrived on December 13 about a possible joint Anglo-American naval response to the Panay attack, Roosevelt told Lindsay that Britain and the United States should commence informal naval staff talks with an idea to establishing a direct line of communication between the American and British navies in case it became necessary—after the "next grave outrage"—to set up a quarantine or blockade of Japan. The two great powers would establish a picket along a vast expanse of the Pacific Ocean, from the Aleutian Islands to Hawaii, then over to the Philippines and to Hong Kong. By setting out a curtain of cruisers and smaller craft, the Anglo-Americans could cut the Japanese off from their access to any seaborne trade, which would immediately starve them of vital imports, especially oil.[54]

Roosevelt argued (much to Lindsay's astonishment) that such an act of blockade would not lead to war: it was merely a way of using methods short of war to deter Japan from further aggression. He wanted to send a naval officer to London immediately to get plans for such naval cooperation sketched out. Lindsay in his private communication to London said he thought the scheme itself unlikely to come into effect, but he seized on this new American enthusiasm for deploying its naval power alongside the Royal Navy to intimidate the Japanese. Though Chamberlain in London sniffed at the idea and considered it naïve, Eden argued that London must welcome this sign of American cooperation in Asia, and he won the day. Chamberlain reluctantly agreed. Within days of the White House meeting, Captain Royal E. Ingersoll of the United States Navy embarked on a liner and reached London on New Year's Eve for two weeks of talks with senior British naval officers. The discussions were serious, detailed, and professional—undoubtedly those present felt they were taking the first step toward a coordinated naval response to Japanese aggression.[55]

What does the Ingersoll mission tell us about Roosevelt's foreign policy in 1937? Some historians have seen this mission as evidence that Roosevelt was preparing for war; according to David Kaiser, FDR "already anticipated a resumption of the Anglo-American alliance to meet aggression in the Far East and, conceivably, in Europe." Others, like Robert Dallek, argued that Roosevelt saw any potential naval demonstration as a means "to prevent rather than risk a war." Roosevelt also, according to Dallek, "backed away from a boycott or a blockade" and stood down from taking any financial steps like seizing Japanese assets. The staff talks, Dallek believed, were merely "technical discussions" and after the Japanese apologized for the *Panay* attack, "Roosevelt closed the case." Clearly, Roosevelt's impulses in late 1937 have baffled scholars: Did he want a robust Anglo-American naval demonstration to deter Japan, or did he care chiefly about Europe and hoped to avoid any further incident in the Pacific? It is perhaps understandable that scholars have been unsure how to characterize Roosevelt's Far Eastern policy, for FDR himself seems to have yawed back and forth between talk of peace conferences and proposals for a naval blockade, only to turn the other cheek again and again as Japan kept striking. It seems fair to conclude that he was feeling his way, hedging his bets, preparing for a future he could not see, anticipating trouble but hoping, like a skilled river navigator, to fend off the rocks ahead with a long barge pole.[56]

Since Roosevelt did not explain to the public the substance of his foreign policy, it fell to media analysts to do it for him. And the reviews were critical. "We still remain without a foreign policy," Dorothy Thompson wrote after the *Panay* incident had been settled, "because we remain without a clear public opinion. Our interests, material and cultural, are scattered around a dangerous and disturbed world, in which wars may conceivably occur anywhere and at any time. What rights we will insist on maintaining in such a world are entirely unclear. And this is the most dangerous possible condition of affairs. For it encourages adventures against us, in the expectation that they will meet no opposition." Thompson felt that it was wise to avoid a clash over the *Panay*. But she wondered if this meant America would make a habit of backing down. "Nobody, not even we ourselves, knows what we stand for," she ruefully concluded. By failing to define America's fixed, unalterable interests in the world, the Roosevelt administration was "contributing as much as any nation in the world today to the danger of a general conflagration." It was time, she said, for America to let the world know what it stood for, and what it would fight for.[57]

CHAPTER 11

1938: BLOOD AND SOIL

"Fascism constitutes the greatest threat in the world today."

—HAROLD ICKES

I

"The world is in turmoil," sighed Mrs. Carrie Chapman Catt. "Nothing like it has been known for two centuries." When the thirteenth annual meeting of the National Committee for the Cause and Cure of War convened in January 1938 at the elegant Washington Hotel, a stone's throw from the White House, no one could miss the sense of gloom in the air. A thousand delegates came together in panels, lectures, and roundtables as the frightful news from Spain and China poured in. In a notable shift, members of the group began to discuss the merits of sanctions and boycotts to punish aggression. Recognizing that such steps could further inflame an already combustible world, the conference nonetheless rejected inaction and isolation. It was time to "serve notice on the world," one delegate insisted, "that the moral character and the conscience of this country were still alive."

The anxious, earnest convention-goers had become impatient. They called for greater U.S. cooperation with other democracies and the much-maligned League of Nations. They argued about how the Neutrality Act was impeding aid to victims of attacks, like Republican Spain and China. And in its final conference report, the National Committee stated that the United States must be "prepared to enter into progressive economic sanctions which involved economic measures and even the use of military force" against nations engaged in aggressive war. The pacifist tide, it seemed, was ebbing; Americans had begun to stir.[1]

The guest of honor at the meeting, Eleanor Roosevelt, gave further evidence of a shift in tone among American public figures on the problem of war and peace. She spoke to the group at a gala dinner on January 19, and summarized the argument of her new book, *This Troubled World*, that had appeared in the shops only two weeks earlier. Leadership in favor of peace, she said, "does not come from isolation." Rather, the United States must engage, guide, and push the world toward "what we think the principle of world behavior should be." While she abhorred war, she said, "we must pay a price for international peace, and we may have to pay a good deal of a price to uphold the principles of honesty and justice to which we hope to draw all nations." These words departed from the usual State Department script, which insisted on keeping America at arm's length from international institutions and foreign conflicts.[2]

In her book, she went even further. Mrs. Roosevelt called for new machinery to impose economic boycotts on aggressors, and she even imagined an international police force that could interpose itself between warring countries. Disarmament and isolation, so beloved of the early peace movement, she argued, would do nothing on behalf of world peace, nor make America more secure. Given the interdependence of human affairs, wars in Asia and Europe would eventually hit home. With no place to hide, Americans should instead step forward and lead the world in a new direction. The historian Blanche Wiesen Cook, in her biography of Eleanor, has shown that the First Lady tried to push FDR to lead the democracies toward some kind of collective action against fascism. Personally touched by the sufferings of Spanish Republicans and by the Chinese victims of the Japanese, Eleanor used the promotional book tour for *This Troubled World* as an opportunity to embrace collective security, reject isolationism, support naval rearmament, call for the lifting of the Spanish arms embargo, and urge trade sanctions on aggressor states. Far out in front of her husband on these matters, Cook concluded, Eleanor "sought to create a groundswell of public opinion to move her husband's policy along."[3]

In the preceding year, FDR had been unmoved by the plight of the Spanish government. And he had chosen to step back from the brink of war in China after the *Panay* incident. But during 1938, in characteristic zigzag fashion, he moved away from the neutralism that had characterized his foreign policy. There were signs of a new resolve to engage with world problems, as his effort to assist Jewish refugees shows. Pressure from Eleanor played a role, but in this tumultuous year, the First Lady's quiet activism joined a chorus of powerful voices in the press and the cabinet, in foreign governments and religious communities, and among the armed forces and foreign policy experts. From many quarters of American life came calls for Roosevelt to prepare the country to face the fascist challenge. In 1938, this advocacy began to tell, as Nazi Germany set out on a course—one that FDR now recognized as irreversible—toward the conquest and domination of Europe. That grim prospect the president could no longer ignore.

II

Roosevelt was always an imaginative thinker when it came to domestic policy, but in foreign affairs his occasionally quirky ideas did not always land. On January 10, 1938, while Captain Ingersoll was still in London for his highly secret naval talks, Roosevelt put one such proposal into circulation: What if the leading nations of the world came together to strike a grand bargain? In exchange for a serious program of disarmament, the largest economies of the world—the United States working in cooperation with the empires of Britain, France, Belgium, and the Netherlands—would draw up a scheme for the equitable distribution of raw materials to all industrial nations. Might this not give the dictatorships—so eager for access to oil, grain, coal, and iron ore—an incentive to pursue their industrialization without war? The idea was not Roosevelt's alone: Since 1936, Undersecretary of State Sumner Welles had been honing this scheme, arguing that dictatorships resorted to wars of conquest because they lacked sufficient raw materials to generate economic prosperity. If the United States could take the lead in reducing world tariffs and opening world markets, the fascists might not feel the need to conquer: They could simply participate in international commerce. Of course, a new international trade arrangement like this would require the active support of the globe-straddling and highly protectionist British Empire, and Roosevelt tasked Welles to get a message to Prime Minister Neville Chamberlain, outlining his plan. The following day, Welles handed a memo to the British ambassador in Washington, Sir Ronald Lindsay, who enthusiastically accepted it as a sign of America's growing determination to play a creative role in world affairs.[4]

A frosty reply, however, came back from London. The prime minister thanked the president for his "courageous" proposal, but Roosevelt was too late. Chamberlain had already devised his own plan for a grand bargain with the dictators that would open the way to a final settlement of European troubles. Chamberlain wrote that the first step in his plan had been set in motion: Britain was going to offer Mussolini the de jure recognition of the conquest of Ethiopia, something that Il Duce desperately desired as a sign of respect toward his own imperial ambitions. Chamberlain was also going to turn a blind eye to Mussolini's military intervention in Spain. These gifts would bring about "reconciliation with Italy," Chamberlain believed, thus picking off Italy from the Rome-Berlin axis while soothing the troubled waters of the Mediterranean. Following this achievement, Chamberlain continued, he would turn to Hitler, and ask him "in what measure German aspirations might be satisfied." Chamberlain expected Germany to offer a list of demands that might include colonies in Africa and some revision of the borders of Eastern Europe. Chamberlain clearly expected to strike a deal on these matters. Certain that his plan for the appeasement of the dictators would yield fruit, the prime minister asked Roosevelt to suppress any talk of an American-led peace initiative, which risked "cutting across our efforts here."[5]

Chamberlain's swift rejection of the Roosevelt plan, against the judgment of Eden and the British ambassador in Washington, marked another of his rebuffs of an American offer to work together in facing the world crisis. And Chamberlain's plan to recognize Italy's possession of Ethiopia left the president and his advisers in considerable shock. Replying to Chamberlain's message, FDR agreed to withdraw his own idea for a global bargain over raw materials, but he sharply questioned Chamberlain's judgment in recognizing Mussolini's conquest. At a time when world opinion was united in condemning Japan for invading China, the British offer to legitimize Italy's outrageous assault on Abyssinia would make a mockery of the doctrine of "non-recognition." Worse, it would have "a serious effect upon public opinion in this country," because Americans would ask, if Britain was cutting deals with dictators to buy peace in Europe, why should America not do the same with Japan? Roosevelt urged the British to think through the global consequences of recognizing Italian imperial spoils: If the United States should follow suit and turn a blind eye to Japan's aggression in China, what would stop the Japanese from pressing on to British possessions like Hong Kong, Singapore, Burma, even India? Cordell Hull made the same point to Ambassador Lindsay: Rewarding Italy for its pitiless war in Ethiopia would be a godsend to the "desperado nations" and only encourage their aggression elsewhere.[6]

It was no use: By the start of 1938, Chamberlain had made his decision. Britain, he knew, could not face a coalition of Japan, Germany, and Italy all at once. Chamberlain had to find a way to break apart this emerging phalanx of fascism. Appeasement offered a chance. That meant accommodating the dictators, finding common ground, pressuring lesser states to give up some territory in the interest of world peace, and avoiding a war that no one wanted and for which Britain was unprepared. With enough good will and creativity,

Chamberlain believed, Germany and Italy could be satisfied without resort to conflict. The fascist leaders might be vulgar, strutting upstarts, but if they won a few of their demands, they could help impose order on the continent and keep the Communists at bay. A peaceful settlement in Europe would in turn free up resources to defend the British Empire in Asia.[7]

This policy had a certain logic to it if one believed that Hitler and Mussolini would negotiate in good faith. Foreign Secretary Anthony Eden, however, did not. He sharply disputed Chamberlain's decision to recognize Italy's conquest of Ethiopia, feeling that it rewarded aggression and would make Hitler even more eager to press on with his revisionist demands. After months of backroom bickering, much of which was leaked to the press, Eden resigned over the issue in late February. A handsome, popular public figure, Eden was a man of integrity who had earnestly counseled Chamberlain to cultivate the Americans and rebuff the fascists. Chamberlain seemed determined to do the opposite. Dorothy Thompson erupted in outrage, styling Eden as "the last knight of Europe," a young veteran of the Great War who "believes that freedom will die in this world for countless years unless it is willing to take a risk." Eden's ouster shocked the State Department, too: Jay Pierrepont Moffat, chief of the Western European desk, wrote in his diary that it showed that Chamberlain's decision "to play ball with Hitler and Mussolini has reached a concrete stage." With Eden gone, Moffat continued, "the smaller states [in Europe] will feel that the chief democracy has ceased fighting, and that the juggernaut of totalitarianism can proceed forward unchecked." The American public, Moffat feared, might see Europe's resignation before the Nazi onslaught and demand that the country "withdraw into our own hemisphere."[8]

Eden's departure was unpopular in Britain, too: A Gallup poll showed that the British public opposed Chamberlain's policy of dealing with the dictators by 56 percent to 25 percent, and over 60 percent of respondents supported Eden in his clash with the prime minister. Winston Churchill, the hawkish, anti-appeasement Conservative MP who, because of his long history of party-switching and belligerent policy beliefs was widely distrusted by most of his fellow Conservatives, lofted an acid remark from the backbenches of the House of Commons. "This has been a good week for dictators," he seethed. "Mussolini has won again." Chamberlain ignored this. He replaced Eden with Edward Wood, the Earl of Halifax, a cadaverous, laconic, High-Church Anglican who had been a reliable adviser to the prime minister and who had made a trip to Berlin in November 1937 to sound out the Germans on an improvement of relations. The Chamberlain-Halifax team would shape British foreign policy for the next two years, with disastrous results.[9]

Like Eden, some American diplomats doubted the assumptions behind Chamberlain's policy. Hitler wanted to control all of Europe, they believed, and appeasement would only make his path to continental domination easier. George Messersmith, the former U.S. minister in Vienna who had been promoted in July 1937 to take Sumner Welles's place as assistant secretary of state, completely rejected the logic of appeasement. Adopting the same interpretation that Ambassador Dodd voiced in Berlin before he retired the previous December, Messersmith argued that "Germany is proceeding on a fixed course" that had not altered since 1933. Hitler wanted "mastery in Europe." He had already begun a vast rearmament program and seized the Rhineland, violating the Versailles peace treaty. His next target was certainly Austria, then Czechoslovakia, the Balkans, and perhaps Poland. Hitler could not be bought off with small concessions like colonies in Africa or a minor redrawing of borders in Europe: "No concession has yet satisfied Germany and none will satisfy her," Messersmith argued. British faith in negotiations with Hitler was "utterly futile and fatal." Other U.S. diplomats on the scene agreed. The Nazis "undoubtedly envisage the ultimate incorporation of Austria into the Reich," wrote Prentiss Gilbert, the number two man at the embassy in Berlin. And the chargé d'affaires at the American Legation in Vienna, John C. Wiley, noted that the Austrian Nazis were working hard to create a narrative of persecution that would give Hitler a pretext to invade the country.[10]

Hitler soon made prophets of these men. Though they did not know it, in November 1937, in a secret conference with his military chiefs, Hitler had outlined his plan to seize Austria and Czechoslovakia in order to use their wealth and raw materials to accelerate Germany's military rearmament. In February 1938, he set out to test, yet again, the resolve of the Western powers to sustain the much-maligned Versailles Treaty, which had explicitly ruled out the unification of Austria and Germany. Hitler believed he could get around that problem by destabilizing Austria from within, using Austria's own Nazis to do his bidding. On February 12, he summoned the Austrian chancellor, Kurt von Schuschnigg, to Berchtesgaden, the Bavarian town where the Führer had built his sprawling mountain chalet. Schuschnigg was an autocratic Christian nationalist in the mold of the martyred Engelbert Dollfuss. As the leader of the Austro-fascist Fatherland Party, he was no democrat, but nor was he a Nazi. Like Dollfuss, Schuschnigg opposed Nazism and any German domination of Austria. Hitler, with three top generals from the Wehrmacht by his side, subjected the Austrian leader to a few hours of bloodcurdling screams and threats, and then ordered Schuschnigg to revoke the ban on the Nazi Party in Austria that Dollfuss had put in place, release some three thousand

Nazis from prison (where they were doing time for attempting the violent overthrow of the government), and appoint several Austrian Nazi leaders to his cabinet—or else suffer the consequences of Hitler's wrath.[11]

Shattered by his encounter with Hitler, Schuschnigg told John Wiley the trip to Berchtesgaden had been "the most horrible day of his life." The Führer was "undoubtedly a madman with a mission" and would stop at nothing "to annex Austria." Schuschnigg felt he had no choice but to give in to Hitler's demands and bring some Nazis into his government. The atmosphere upon his return to Vienna was funereal. The country had suffered a "crushing defeat," as *New York Times* correspondent G. E. R. Gedye put it, and the people were "awaiting only the triumphant entry of the victors." The man Hitler picked to run Austria's Interior Ministry and internal police force was Arthur Seyss-Inquart, a soulless lawyer and functionary who had served in the Austro-Hungarian Army in World War I, and only recently joined the Austrian Nazis. (He would later become the brutal overseer of occupied Holland.) Now he could use his office to sideline Schuschnigg and complete the Nazi takeover of the state. "Write it down," Dorothy Thompson wrote in her column. "On Saturday, February 12, 1938, military bolshevism, paganism, and despotism started on the march across all of Europe east of the Rhine." William Shirer, the CBS radio correspondent now stationed in Vienna, noted in his diary what a terrible blow this had been to the country's sovereignty. "I dropped by the Legation this evening," Shirer wrote on February 16. "John Wiley was pacing the floor. 'It's the end of Austria,' he said."[12]

On Sunday, February 20, Hitler made a victory speech in Berlin. At the Kroll Opera House, where the German Reichstag still met, the Führer stood before a giant backdrop of red silk and a thirty-two-foot golden eagle bearing a swastika in its talons. For three tedious hours, Hitler brayed to his audience of compliant, uniformed Nazis about all he had done to rescue Germany from its defeat and despair after the last war. This was nothing new; what made reporters stand up and take note, however, was Hitler's discussion of the "10 million Germans" in Europe that did not live under the rule of the German Reich, and who had been persecuted unfairly by other nations. Shirer, listening to the radio broadcast, observed that Hitler meant "the seven million in Austria and the three million Sudeten Germans in Czechoslovakia." Hitler insisted that those Germans had a "right to racial self-determination," and he could not tolerate his "racial comrades" being deprived of their rights. "Germany will know how to defend the rights of Germans living on the other side of the border," he shrieked. Nobody could miss the veiled threat of war in Hitler's words.[13]

III

Certainly, Dorothy Thompson didn't miss it. By the spring of 1938, she had been writing her column for the *New York Herald Tribune* for two years and had become, as *Time* magazine put it, the most influential woman in America after Eleanor Roosevelt. Her sharp, even strident opinion pieces appeared in 200 newspapers with a total of 7.5 million readers; she was also giving weekly broadcasts on NBC radio to some 5.5 million listeners; and she wrote a column for the popular monthly *Ladies' Home Journal*. These outlets paid her handsomely and her accountant reckoned her annual income in 1938 at about $100,000—a sum that would have the purchasing power of over $2 million today. She was by this time estranged from her husband, Sinclair Lewis, whose alcoholism had transformed the former Nobel Laureate into a violent, jealous crank. Though her personal correspondence reveals how much Lewis had wounded her, Thompson kept that part of her life private. In public, she appeared, in the words of the anonymous profile writer of *Time*, as "a plump, pretty woman of 45, bursting with health, energy and sex appeal." Another portrait styled her as "the kind of woman who hates dictators . . . a woman of depth, charm, and brains."[14]

Her column, "On the Record," toggled between foreign affairs and domestic politics. It consistently reflected her hatred of fascism and any other form of government that seemed overbearing, centralized, and undemocratic. To her, Roosevelt's New Deal looked at times like it was drifting toward fascism, as it gave too much power, she thought, to the federal bureaucracy and unaccountable technocrats. She called herself a conservative because she wished to preserve older forms of civilization and society, especially the tolerant, aristocratic culture of Europe that she knew so well. She also called herself a liberal, by which she meant a champion of the greatest amount of human freedom consistent with an organized society. She feared that Americans, too wrapped up in their own troubles, did not grasp the nature of the threat posed to them by fascism and Nazism. Too many people, she believed, tolerated fascism because it was anti-communist. She rejected that dialectic. Communism and fascism were equally hateful, tyrannical systems that aimed to destroy democracy and liberalism everywhere. She characterized the great crisis of the world as a struggle not between variants of authoritarianism but between, as she put it, "freedom and slavery." And Americans needed to choose a side in that contest.[15]

The agonies of Austria in early 1938 struck her especially hard. Vienna had been her home for many years in the 1920s when she was emerging as a young reporter. She had countless friends there, and relished its cosmopolitan, sophisticated character. The city, she said on her radio program, wove together the strands of a great Central European civilization: "Latin culture, Slavic melancholy, Bohemian energy, Jewish talent, and German craftsmanship and organization." That Austria should be squeezed by Nazis from within, backed by Hitler from without, enraged her, and she was determined to awaken Americans to the stakes of the Austrian crisis. A few days after Schuschnigg capitulated to Hitler's demand at Berchtesgaden to appoint Nazis to his cabinet, Thompson wrote in her column that Germany had just undone the outcome of the Great War. The new German empire would dominate Central Europe after all, she believed. With Austria swallowed up, "Czechoslovakia is now surrounded, and the wheat fields of Hungary and oil fields of Romania are now open." Hitler would not stop with Austria, she felt certain. He had launched "a new crusade under a pagan totem, worshipping blood and soil, preaching the holiness of the sword, glorifying conquest." It was time, she insisted, for the democratic world "to capitulate or to take a stand."[16]

She claimed in a column in early March that some public figures in America were ready to take up the fight—people "who opposed the passage of the Neutrality Acts" and wanted the United States "actively to collaborate for the maintenance of international law in the world." Among this group was Harold Ickes, the secretary of the interior, who often gave voice to the fiery, provocative words the president felt he could not say. In December, for example, Ickes had given a memorable, and incendiary, address to the American Civil Liberties Union in New York—a speech that FDR read ahead of time—titled "Nations in Nightshirts." He stated that the same racist, antidemocratic madness that fueled the Ku Klux Klan had engulfed nations abroad. "The Kleagles and the Klokards," said Ickes, using the Klan's terminology for its members, "now ride bombers, tanks, battleships and submarines," laying waste to undefended cities. A worldwide struggle between totalitarianism and democracy was underway, he said, as "ventriloquists for dictators sneer at and condemn the democratic ideal." Fascism, far from being quarantined, had shown that "it is capable of leaping wide oceans." Wake up, Ickes begged his listeners. The fascists were coming for American democracy.[17]

Ickes returned to this theme in a radio broadcast at the invitation of the British Broadcasting Corporation, directed to the British people. This was one of a series of talks the BBC had arranged for Americans to speak to Britain, and Ickes used the opportunity to launch a pointed attack on appeasement. Speaking just two days after Hitler's shrieking February 20 address to the Reichstag, Ickes stated quite simply that "fascism constitutes the greatest threat in the world today." It was a threat to European democracies, of course, but it also threatened the United States because the fascists would use war and conquest to build a powerful, closed economic system, suffocating world trade and global prosperity. A world of rival empires and war would deepen the global economic crisis, halt domestic reform in its tracks, and gradually undermine democracy, Ickes asserted. There could be no compromise with such an expansionist, belligerent ideology; a world divided, half fascist and half democratic, could not endure.[18]

Significant coming from a member of the cabinet, the speech also gives ample evidence of Roosevelt's own frame of mind. Ickes had dutifully shown the speech to the State Department before delivering it, and there the draft had been torn to shreds, neutered and stripped of any provocative language. Ickes fought back and asked the president for help. FDR, examining the draft, restored virtually all the excised text of the speech. Ickes therefore reflected the president's views when he implied on the BBC that Britain's policy of appeasement, by rewarding the aggression of fascist states, would turn the democracies into accomplices of their own destruction. FDR's critical attitude toward British policy also emerged in a frosty and direct conversation between Sumner Welles and the British ambassador in early March. Welles told Sir Ronald Lindsay that the president "had made it emphatically clear that this government did not intend to participate in any way in the questions of European political appeasement." As Roosevelt himself put it about the appeasement gamble, "some people are, I think, taking very long chances." Roosevelt was not going to risk losing his shirt by backing appeasement; the Brits were on their own.[19]

Prickly, progressive, and pugnacious, Harold Ickes urged FDR to adopt a bolder stand against fascism.
Library of Congress

Roosevelt's poker-playing instincts about the risk of appeasement were soon vindicated in a few shocking days in March, when Hitler made his most daring geopolitical move yet. Ever since Chancellor Schuschnigg's humiliation at Berchtesgaden, the Austrian Nazis had been busy stirring up loud mobs in the streets to call for union with Germany. In reply, Social Democrats as well as Schuschnigg's right-wing Fatherland Front joined together and staged protests in favor of independence. The country found itself on the brink of civil war, with angry cries of "Heil Hitler!" clashing in the streets with shouts of "Heil Schuschnigg!" Amid this turmoil, Schuschnigg gambled. He decided to call for a plebiscite to prove to the world that Austrians did not want to be annexed by Germany. In fact, the country was deeply divided over the question and the plebiscite was a courageous though highly risky decision. On March 9, he announced that a nationwide vote would be held just four days hence on a single question: Shall Austria remain an independent Christian nation? This act of defiance infuriated the Austrian Nazis as well as Hitler, who had planned to bring Austria to heel by a soft coup, using the Nazi minion Seyss-Inquart to exert control. Now Hitler was faced with a direct challenge that could foil his plans—an intolerable affront.[20]

The Führer responded violently. On March 11, he gave Schuschnigg an ultimatum: cancel the plebiscite immediately and resign or face a full-scale invasion by German armed forces. Schuschnigg, his confidence collapsing, chose to give in rather than fight, hoping to avoid unnecessary bloodshed. He resigned. But Hitler had in fact already ordered the invasion. To provide cover for this aggression, Seyss-Inquart, replacing Schuschnigg as chancellor, sent out an "invitation" to Germany to send troops into Austria and restore order. On the morning of March 12, sixty-five thousand German soldiers poured into the country. "The worst has happened!" wrote William Shirer in his diary. "Schuschnigg is out. The Nazis are in. The Reichswehr is invading. . . . Austria is finished. Beautiful, tragic, civilized Austria! Gone. Done to death in the brief moment of an afternoon." Shirer went to get an update from the American Legation. "John Wiley was standing before his desk, clutching his invariable long cigarette-holder, a queer smile on his face—the smile of someone who has just been defeated and knows it. 'It's all over,' he said quietly." That night, amid thousands of fluttering swastika banners, a massive torch-light parade snaked through Vienna, the orange flames illuminating the flushed faces of gleeful, singing Austrians.[21]

Hitler still had another coup de théâtre in the works—a triumphal tour of his new conquest. He crossed into Austria near his birthplace, Braunau am Inn, and proceeded on to Linz, the city in which he spent his miserable youth, and where now he received a rapturous welcome. On March 15, he spoke to a massive crowd at Vienna's Heldenplatz, the enormous open space in front of the palace that housed the Austrian government. "A revolutionary transformation has taken place within the German racial community," Hitler bawled into the microphones to hundreds of thousands of roaring Austrians. "I proclaim forthwith," he bellowed, that Austria—"the most thoroughly German outpost of the German people—shall from henceforth be the newest bulwark of the German nation." He called the Anschluss (meaning joining together) "the greatest achievement of my life," the final entry of "my native land into the German Reich."[22]

Even the closest observers did not expect so much enthusiasm among Austrians for Hitler. Watching the pro-Nazi rallies in Vienna that week, Shirer wondered at the sudden rush of fanaticism. "The faces! I had seen these before at Nuremberg—the fanatical eyes, the gaping mouths, the hysteria. And now they were shouting like Holy Rollers: '*Sieg Heil! Sieg Heil! Sieg Heil! Heil Hitler! Heil Hitler! Heil Hitler! Hang Schuschnigg! Hang Schuschnigg! Hang Schuschnigg! Ein Volk, ein Reich, ein Führer!*'" Walking through the city on March 12, Shirer was dumbfounded: "Vienna was scarcely recognizable this morning. Swastika flags flying from nearly every house. Where did they get them so fast?" The Austrians were rushing into Hitler's stiff-armed embrace.[23]

Not all Austrians, of course. Hitler's invasion opened up a period of terror for two hundred thousand Austrian Jews, now subjects of a dictator who desired their destruction. The blows fell immediately: To prepare for Hitler's arrival in Vienna, gangs of Nazi thugs pulled Jewish men and women from their homes and set them to scrubbing pro-Schuschnigg graffiti from the city's streets and walls, as passersby jeered them with shouts of "*Juda verrecke!*"—perish the Jews. With unseemly speed, Austrians turned on their Jewish compatriots, smashing store windows, plundering homes, gaily carting away their stolen loot. Hundreds, perhaps thousands of Jewish doctors, professors, bankers, journalists, and religious leaders were immediately arrested. John Wiley, his office now besieged by Jews seeking entry visas to the United States, could scarcely believe the cruelty he saw, to say nothing of the rapacious looting: "even the knives, forks, and spoons are being confiscated in Jewish homes," he reported to Washington. In the coming few weeks, the Germans imposed an extremely harsh regime of segregation, dispossession, and forced migration upon Jews in Austria. Using legal decrees that had evolved over five years in Germany, they transformed Austria at a single stroke into a horror for now-stateless Jews.[24]

"The news from Europe is the blackest since 1914," Dorothy Thompson told her radio audience. "All Austria is in the hands of the Nazis." The fact of the invasion did not shock her as much as the feckless, unworthy response of the democracies. "Today," she wrote a few days after the Anschluss, "the defenders of liberal culture, with enormous wealth and power at their disposal, are totally paralyzed," even as "lists are drawn up for thousands to be sent to concentration camps, as Jews are beaten in the streets." The British leaders she found especially disgusting, for they had watched this coming for five years, done nothing, and continued to believe that "they could come to some nice dignified peaceful terms with the military despotisms." But there was no appeasing Nazi Germany, she believed. Only two paths lay ahead: "war, or the surrender of all democracies." Americans should understand what was at stake now: "we have something very precious to lose, which is the right to breathe the air of freedom. Hundreds of thousands of people have lost that right in Austria tonight."[25]

IV

Both the invasion of Austria by Hitler's forces and the wave of brutality and hate that broke upon the country's Jewish population profoundly disturbed Franklin Roosevelt. Not only had Hitler violated the rights of a sovereign state and defied the terms of the Versailles Treaty again, but he clearly would not stop with Austria. Roosevelt told Henry Morgenthau in a private conversation on March 16, just a day after Hitler took his victory lap through Vienna, that he thought "Germany will take Czechoslovakia in its stride. I have said so three months ago, and I also said at cabinet a week ago that it is perfectly clear that Hitler has made a deal with Mussolini by which Hitler gets a complete free hand in Central Europe and Mussolini in the Mediterranean." He understood the alignment of forces in Europe perfectly well. And although he did not announce a dramatic change of course in American foreign policy as a result, the evidence suggests that from the spring of 1938, he began to reconsider America's overall strategy toward the dictators and toward the crisis of fascism in Europe.[26]

An important sign of this shift came on March 17, when Secretary of State Cordell Hull gave a long, carefully worded speech at the National Press Club that sounded a new note of firmness. This speech had been deliberately crafted in the administration in response to the combined Asian and European crises. Although he did not outline any decisive break with the temporizing of the past, Hull wanted to make one thing plain: The regional conflicts in China,

Spain, and Central Europe did impact America's national interests in the world, and the country would defend those interests. Speaking at the National Press Club to a room full of reporters, Hull began with his favorite and slightly threadbare sermon: that world peace depended upon the rule of law and respect for treaty obligations. But the reporters in the hall caught a shift of tone in Hull's remarks. Whereas Hull had always publicly stressed the wisdom of America's neutrality and distance from world quarrels, he now spoke of the need "to cooperate by peaceful means in the defense of law and order."

In advocating a middle course between "extremes either of internationalism or isolation," Hull explicitly ruled out "the use of American armed forces for 'policing the world.'" After all, Americans overwhelmingly viewed U.S. participation in the last world war as a mistake. Still, Hull urged the prompt passage of the significant naval rearmament bill then working its way through Congress, and he did not rule out embargoes, sanctions, boycotts, and economic coercion—the kinds of things FDR had in mind when he spoke of imposing a "quarantine" of aggressive states. Hull also pointedly stressed that America possessed "legitimate national interests abroad" and if the country should "abandon them at the first sight of danger," then aggressors would roll on unimpeded while America became "a self-constituted hermit state." Isolation meant to Hull the collapse of free trade, a spike in the cost of goods, a scarcity of materials, unemployment, economic distress, and the necessary "regimentation in every phase of life." Isolation, he implied, led to dictatorship. "We cannot withdraw from the world itself. Isolation is not a means to security; it is a fruitful source of insecurity." To run from trouble in the world, Hull asserted, just invited anarchy. This argument—that an isolated America was a weak, vulnerable America—would become Roosevelt's common refrain in the coming years.[27]

As Japan laid waste to China's capital city, as Franco's air force bombed civilians in Barcelona, and as Hitler's thugs brutalized Jews in the streets of Vienna, Hull's speech received much attention from the national press. Dorothy Thompson in particular believed the speech marked a turning point. "It repudiates the doctrine of isolationism which lies behind America's neutrality legislation," she asserted in her column the day after the secretary spoke. More than that, she inferred that Hull and the president now agreed that fascism and democracy could not co-exist in the world. Fascism bred war and autarky, two forces that impeded democratic capitalism. Up to now, the "faltering weakness" of the democracies had only invited further aggression from the fascists. Hull's speech boldly set out a new direction, she thought. The administration had made a decision to defend "free governments, free institutions, and freedom of the seas," to give "moral and material support" to peaceful nations under attack, and to align itself with the safety and security of Britain and France.[28]

No doubt Thompson read too much into Hull's remarks. But the vigorous response of the neutrality bloc suggests that they too saw the administration adopting a new, and they thought dangerous, course. William Randolph Hearst issued a reply to Hull on the front page of his newspapers, completely contradicting the secretary of state. The publisher claimed that "magnificent isolation" had made America "the most powerful, the most prosperous, the most intellectually influential nation in the world," and that in fact it was the New Deal that had imposed regimentation and dictatorship at home. Hearst claimed the only people who welcomed Hull's change of policy lived in Moscow: The Communists know "the speech means war, and war on behalf of Soviet Russia." Hamilton Fish, FDR's own congressman from Dutchess County, announced his "whole-hearted" agreement with Hearst, alleging that FDR and Hull were trying to get American into war in Europe and Asia.[29]

And Republican senator William Borah, the former chairman of the Senate Foreign Relations Committee and an irreconcilable opponent of any involvement in European affairs, declared that the secretary of state had been seduced by "the dreamers, the sentimentalists" who wanted to spend American lives in the pursuit of abstract ideals. "Our supreme and imperative task is here at home," he said, not fighting the wars of other nations. "We went into the world war to make the world safe for democracy and we made it a breeding camp for dictators." Fighting overseas did nothing to advance democracy and merely hampered prosperity at home. These were powerful and popular arguments, ones that Hull and Roosevelt could not ignore.[30]

Yet even in this context of a struggle with isolationist sentiment, Roosevelt wanted to find a way to demonstrate America's capacity for cooperation on the world stage. Could a bold effort of humanitarian assistance serve that purpose? The day after Hull's speech, Roosevelt raised the issue in the cabinet: What could the United States do for Austrian refugees? Harold Ickes recalled that "the president thought we ought to make it as easy as possible for political refugees to come into this country." Henry Morgenthau noted for his diary that Roosevelt spoke about the "many fine Germans" who had come to America after the political upheavals of 1848; "why couldn't we offer them again a place of refuge," Roosevelt wondered. But as he surely knew, the legal obstacles were too great. Secretary of Labor Frances Perkins reminded the president that since 1924, American law had severely limited immigration, allocating on the basis of national origin only a small number of entry visas.

Even when FDR by executive order combined the annual quota for Germany and Austria, he could offer visas only to 27,370 immigrants from these two countries. It was hopeless to imagine Congress agreeing to an increase of immigration quotas, especially on behalf of European Jews, and at no point did Roosevelt ask Congress to do so. Immigration during the Depression was unpopular and in the cabinet meeting, Vice President Garner told FDR that if it could, Congress would gladly halt *all* immigration. There was no chance of further opening America's gates now.[31]

The only answer to the refugee crisis would have to be a cooperative, international one, which suited the tone of Roosevelt's increasingly active foreign policy. On March 22, after discussion with Sumner Welles and Henry Morgenthau, he tasked the State Department with setting up an intergovernmental conference to help refugees in Europe. In describing these refugees, FDR insisted on using the term "political" rather than "religious" or "racial" so as to avoid the impression that this was a rescue plan primarily for Jews. In a press conference, he insisted that the term political refugees included "a very large number" of Christians, but the initiative was clearly prompted by his own revulsion at the vicious Nazi treatment of Jews in Vienna. Invitations went out on March 25 to European and Latin American nations to join in the effort.[32]

The American initiative received a gratifying reply and before long, thirty-two nations had agreed to send delegates to a meeting at Évian-les-Bains, a pleasant French resort town on the shores of Lake Geneva. Predictably, the prospect of a world rescue program for Jews in distress kicked up some ugly reactions that made plain the challenges ahead. Hitler, with his usual talent for hitting a nerve, sneered at the American proposal, saying he was only too happy to "put these criminals at the disposal of other countries." The Nazi tabloid *Der Angriff* was even more vulgar, asserting that Jews who were taken in by Roosevelt would introduce into America's "blood circulation" the poison of Moscow Bolshevism and create "many grave domestic disturbances until the healthy strength of the Anglo-Saxon people has been destroyed." The refugee proposal also stirred up fearmongering at home. Martin Dies, Democratic member of Congress from Texas, wrote to Hull that 15 million unemployed people in America constituted the country's first priority, while more immigrants would take jobs away from citizens or become a burden on the taxpayer. Dies proposed sending Jewish refugees to Paraguay, where "millions of acres are available to colonists."[33]

FDR's scheme for assistance to Jewish refugees also had to contend with the nasty climate of racism in America. While vivid photographs of Jewish persecution in Vienna were appearing in American dailies, the United States

Senate was putting on a display of racist demagoguery that sounded precisely like language Joseph Goebbels might have used. From January 5 to February 22, 1938, the Senate was brought to a halt by a filibuster staged by a vigorous group of Southern Democrats. Their purpose: to oppose a vote on a bill that would make lynching a federal crime. The Wagner–Van Nuys bill would empower the federal government to intervene in any case where local authorities did not attempt to halt, or failed to punish, extra-judicial murder. Congress had considered anti-lynching laws in the past, and they invariably met the staunch opposition of Southerners who claimed that such an intrusion by the federal government violated the right of states to police themselves. But in the early months of 1938, the anti-lynching debate acquired new meaning. As the world heard Hitler's raucous celebration of the racial triumph of Aryan Germans over what he called mongrel Jews in Austria, and as President Roosevelt launched a long-shot effort to assist in the rescue of persecuted Jews, Southern senators were vigorously defending the doctrine of white supremacy in America.

Their language requires some attention, because it meshed so neatly with the sorts of calumnies that Nazis regularly used to generate fear of Jews. Senator Allen J. Ellender, a former floor leader for Huey Long in the Louisiana legislature, spoke for twenty-seven hours against the anti-lynching bill. He believed that protecting Black men from "Judge Lynch" would simply encourage them to commit crimes, particularly the raping of white women, which in turn would lead to the mongrelization of "white civilization." His colleague, Theodore Bilbo of Mississippi, elaborated on this thesis in lurid terms. The bill, by removing the threat of lynching, would immediately endanger "the wives, mothers, daughters, and sweethearts of Dixie." Lynching, though unpalatable, provided a necessary tool to sustain white supremacy, to halt race mixing, and to keep order in the South. Taking away the hallowed tradition of lynching would "open the floodgates of hell," and the authors of the bill would be stained "with the blood of the raped and outraged daughters of Dixie." If Congress wanted to halt the use of lynching, a far better solution would be to deport all 12 million Black people in America to Africa. "We removed the Indians," said Senator Bilbo. "Why can we not move the Negro in the same way?" Transporting millions of Black citizens to Africa, thought Bilbo, offered the most "satisfactory solution of this great national question." After listening to twenty-nine days of this disgusting torrent of hate, a weary Senate voted 58–22 to set aside the bill.[34]

These statements formed part of the context in which Roosevelt had to navigate the Jewish refugee crisis. Racism and white supremacy remained the bedrock of the Southern Democratic Party—Roosevelt's own. These legislators formed an important bloc of votes in Congress that FDR needed to pass his many priorities. Civil rights for Black Americans were not among those priorities. That is why the president remained silent during the filibuster against the Wagner–Van Nuys bill, despite urgent, vigorous lobbying from Walter White, the head of the NAACP. White had developed close ties to Eleanor Roosevelt and pressed the White House to take up the anti-lynching cause. With FDR now intervening on behalf of European Jews, White renewed his efforts. "We applaud your courage," White wrote to the president, in denouncing the "repression of the Jewish population in Europe. This gives us hope that you will speak out as unequivocally for the protection of your own citizens against mob violence in this country." But Roosevelt would not antagonize the Southern Democrats. Not until the bill had been safely shelved by Congress did he express even mild support during a press conference for some federal anti-lynching measure. Too little, too late—by design.[35]

On Jewish matters, though, he gingerly moved forward. In mid-April, he conferred with an informal network of advisers on Jewish affairs, including James McDonald and Rabbi Wise. Wise had praised Roosevelt's conference proposal as a "great gesture of good will" and told him, "you will never know what it means to millions of the homeless." His friend, the Harvard professor Felix Frankfurter, wrote in similar terms, thanking Roosevelt for "the hope that your actions and your words must be bringing to literally hundreds of thousands of victims of brute unreason." At this meeting, FDR spoke of America's "historic opportunity" to show its sympathy with victims of Nazism (though, as one participant noted, he remained anxious not to use the word "Jewish"). The group suggested that any direct call for a revision to immigration laws would trigger a storm of protest, so the president would have to proceed through executive action.[36]

Roosevelt also reached out to a powerful figure of the American establishment, Henry Stimson, and asked him to serve as chairman of the American delegation to the Évian conference. By calling on Stimson, a Republican of great integrity and experience, FDR signaled his serious commitment to making the conference a success. Stimson immediately began sounding out friends and colleagues about the project, and soon grew wary. He saw that FDR had announced the conference before doing any of the preliminary legwork. The most important factor had yet to be nailed down: Would the German government let Jewish refugees leave? If so, would they be allowed to take with them their capital—the very funds Roosevelt had breezily said would be used to pay for this large-scale exodus? Knowing that if the Germans refused, or proved difficult, the effort would fail, Stimson regretfully declined the president's invitation. Eventually, Roosevelt secured the commitment of Myron Taylor, the former head of U.S. Steel and a pragmatic, civic-minded Republican businessman, to take the job. As Nazis continued to harass and deport Jews from Austria, Taylor set to work preparing for the Évian meeting, now scheduled to convene in July.[37]

V

Did the Évian conference signal a new departure for Roosevelt, and a more active international role for America? The record is at best ambiguous. In the first half of 1938, as U.S. policy toward the Spanish Civil War painfully shows, FDR remained suspended between the passive neutralism of his first term and the robust interventionism that many in his inner circle now yearned for. A sudden and brief improvement in the military fortunes of the Spanish Republic gave Roosevelt an opening to rally the American public to the cause of the beleaguered Loyalists. Yet he refused to act, failing to seize an opportunity to revive the prospects of Spanish democracy.

In January, in the middle of a desperately cold winter in the high altitudes of wind-swept Aragon, Spanish government troops took the town of Teruel from the rebels, showing the world that they could still go on the offensive successfully against Franco's forces. This battlefield victory briefly raised hopes that the Republic, despite a huge disadvantage in matériel and arms, might still be able to save the country from fascism. Spanish officials quickly reached out to American diplomats to insist that they were capable of victory—provided only that they could purchase American military supplies. Meanwhile, American enthusiasts of the Loyalist cause redoubled their efforts. Louis Fischer, back in Barcelona on behalf of *The Nation*, praised the high morale and fighting qualities of the Republican soldiers and dismissed any talk of defeat. The victory at Teruel showed that the fascists had met their match in Spain and if only they had a few hundred more planes they could win the war. "The Spanish people are paying heavily for the privilege of fighting the world's battle against fascism," he wrote, but they did so "with mounting vigor and enthusiasm."[38]

Not everyone shared this optimistic outlook. Virginia Cowles, a twenty-eight-year-old freelance reporter, spent five months in Spain and reported at length in the *New York Times* on the struggles of daily life under the Republic: The people faced desperate food shortages, no gasoline, state appropriation of private property, limited electricity, and constant bombing, with Madrid,

Valencia, and Barcelona under nightly air and artillery attack. Bracingly, she assessed the chances of success of the government's army—made up of peasants and laborers who scarcely knew how to load a rifle—as slight. The Republic's soldiers were "untrained, unequipped, and badly led." Franco knew that time was on his side: He could rely on inexhaustible supplies of weapons from Hitler and Mussolini; in a war of attrition, the Spanish Republic could not win.[39]

Teruel proved Cowles right. Spurred by the loss of prestige the Republican victory had inflicted, Franco mounted a huge counteroffensive to retake the town, no matter the cost. After two months of bitter fighting in blizzard conditions, the rebels surrounded shattered Teruel, capturing thousands of Republican soldiers and their precious equipment. With the Republican troops exhausted, the fascist army could now drive east to the Mediterranean and divide the Republican territory in two, leaving Barcelona isolated and cut off. In Washington, Spanish officials pleaded unsuccessfully with the State Department to find a way to circumvent the January 1937 embargo on arms to Spain. But there was little appetite in the administration for a change of policy.[40]

Washington's inaction left Ambassador Claude Bowers in a rage. He bitterly informed Roosevelt that the Germans and Italians had hugely increased their supplies to Franco, with devastating results. "The fascist powers," he wrote, "have converted Spain into a laboratory for the testing of the efficiency of their improved methods of destruction," including the use of five-hundred-pound bombs dropped into the center of Barcelona on a market day to maximize casualties among women and children. Bowers wrote that the nonintervention agreement designed by the British and French at the outset of the war, combined with America's arms embargo against Spain, was "responsible for the lives of hundreds of thousands" of Spanish civilians. He told FDR that "the Fascist International" was waging and winning a war, not on communism, but on democracy. The president, stung by this indictment of his own policy, ordered Hull to see to it that Bowers's letter "should not be handed around in the Department." Bowers remained a voice crying in the wilderness.[41]

Roosevelt could not keep the public quiet, however. Everyone seemed angry about Spain. African Americans had long seen the war in Spain as part of a global struggle between the forces of reaction and the forces of progress, between oligarchy and the working classes, between the racial imperialism of the fascists and the multiracial solidarity of the Spanish people. The labor leader, A. Philip Randolph, speaking to the annual meeting of the National

Negro Congress, said the "non-intervention sham" of the United States, Britain, and France was responsible for the "massacre" of Spanish civilians. He called for an end to the arms embargo which unfairly punished the Republican government. "If the dikes of democracy break" in Spain, he said, "a world flood of fascism may not be far behind." Addressing this gathering, Dr. Harry Ward, the Methodist minister (and Marxist) who had been active in protesting Italy's invasion of Ethiopia, also stressed the global nature of the threat: "It is not simply a war in Ethiopia, a war in Spain, and a war in China. It is a general war," and the outcome "will be decided by collective action of the democratic people of the world."[42]

Others also placed Spain in a global context. The poet and writer Langston Hughes, one of the brightest stars of the Harlem Renaissance, spent six months in Republican Spain in late 1937 through the spring of 1938. What struck him most was the racial dimension of the war. In Madrid and Valencia and Barcelona, he met fighters from Cuba, Haiti, Puerto Rico, the West Indies, and Africa, as well as many Black Americans who had found a great cause in the anti-fascist struggle. Late at night in besieged Madrid, Hughes saw men and women, drawn from across the world, dancing quietly under the stars to American jazz music. "In Spain," he marveled, "there is no color line." The war in Spain seemed to him a struggle for racial liberation as much as an ideological conflict; a victory for fascism in Spain would mean a victory for global segregation and imperialism.[43]

Spain galvanized the American left. Under the influence of the popular front model, labor groups, socialists, communists, religious groups, and Black civil rights organizations rallied together and staged public meetings such as the National Congress of the American League Against War and Fascism in Pittsburgh in late November 1937. Its members sought to connect the Spanish war to a global fascist assault on democracy. "Spain's heroic resistance to Fascist invasion, China's last-ditch stand against Japanese aggression, Germany's colonial threats, the withdrawal of Italy from the League of Nations, the Tokyo-Rome-Berlin pact of aggression," these events joined with "the current drive of reactionary forces against democratic and labor rights in the United States" to form a global fascist onslaught. Harry Ward, who chaired this huge meeting, spoke of a "Fascist International" on the march against democracy, and praised FDR's "quarantine" speech a month earlier. He demanded an end to the arms embargo on Spain which only helped Franco, and greater activism to mobilize Americans to pressure the government to act. Reinhold Niebuhr, Joseph P. Lash, James Waterman Wise, and the Spanish ambassador to the United States, Fernando de los Ríos, all urged action against fascism in the world.[44]

Alongside such left-wing voices, the political establishment in the United States was growing restless about the failure to assist the Spanish government. In mid-February, as the Battle of Teruel was nearing its bloody conclusion, former secretary of state Henry Stimson and former ambassador William Dodd signed a petition organized by the American Friends of Spanish Democracy to lift the arms embargo on Spain. The petition asserted that American policy, by starving Spain of the means to defend itself, had prolonged a bitter, costly war and endangered democratic institutions. Using a legal argument that Roosevelt would eventually adopt, the signatories argued that the embargo conflicted with America's historical neutrality, by which any nation might buy arms in the U.S. market. According to international law, a government was entitled to defend itself, and in singling out the Spanish government in its embargo, the United States had effectively taken the fascist side in the war. The letter was signed by leading educators, clergy, and various advocates of international diplomacy. A week later, the National Lawyers Guild also called for an end to the Spanish embargo, and in mid-March, three hundred attorneys and law professors followed suit with a public statement. At the same time, Raymond Leslie Buell, president of the distinguished Foreign Policy Association, began a series of public letters to Secretary of State Hull, calling the embargo unjust and urging the government not to let Spain become "a second Austria." Hull rebuffed these pleas.[45]

As the rebels pressed their advantage in the wake of Teruel, Mussolini ordered a series of air strikes on Barcelona in an attempt to break the morale of the "reds." From March 16 to 18, an uninterrupted stream of bombers flew from airfields in Mallorca with a shield of fighter aircraft to protect them. In what has been called the first carpet bombing in history, the Italians pummeled the defenseless city, with devastating results: over one thousand civilians killed and twice that number wounded. It was front-page news in America: "Air Raiders Kill 1,000 in Barcelona," blazed the *New York Times*; "Hail of Bombs Spreads Death in Barcelona," announced the *Chicago Tribune*; "Half a Million Flee Barcelona," the *Los Angeles Times* reported. The Spanish ambassador held a press conference in Washington, asking why Spain was denied arms to defend itself from fascist aggression. The State Department issued a terse statement from Hull that the administration sought no change to the U.S. embargo law.[46]

This defiant use of indiscriminate bombing triggered a significant spike in public debate in the United States. Rallies and petitions mushroomed as Americans called for an end to the arms embargo. A rally at Union Square headed by Joseph Lash of the American Student Union clamored for aid to

Spain. On Capitol Hill, delegations from civic, student, and labor groups worked the corridors, pressing senators to act. On April 5, Rabbi Stephen Wise spoke to ten thousand people in Madison Square Garden at a rally calling for revision of the Neutrality Act to allow Spain to buy arms. Wise took aim at American leaders like Herbert Hoover who brushed off the Spanish war as a conflict of "old world ideologies" of no concern to Americans; but to Wise, the war in Spain was a life and death struggle between fascism and democracy with global implications. Protestant clergy joined Rabbi Wise, with the Episcopal Diocese of Albany sponsoring the rally alongside the Methodist Episcopal Church. On the same day, 1,500 Spanish Americans converged on the State Department and the Capitol, hoisting placards and singing songs, pressing the case for lifting the embargo.[47]

To leading writers and intellectuals, the destruction of Spanish democracy epitomized the tragedy of the era: Fascism was getting away with murder everywhere, in Germany, Austria, Italy, Spain, Ethiopia, and Latin America, while the Western democracies did nothing. Just as the Anschluss took place, the League of American Writers invited its members to state their views on the civil war; 418 letters from leading literary figures came in, denouncing Franco and fascism in the strongest terms. Louis Fischer's reports from the front now struck a desperate tone after the "heartbreaking" loss of Teruel and the "repeated barbarous bombings of Barcelona." He wrote with acidic contempt of the ludicrous nonintervention policy, which had done nothing to stop Nazi and Fascist war supplies pouring in to Spain. Though full of admiration for the heroic effort of loyalist soldiers, Fischer now wrote gloomily of the end: "it is nobler to die fighting than before a firing squad, and the Spaniard cares a great deal about nobility and about style."[48]

Ernest Hemingway also had been at Teruel and reported on the fighting there. In an April essay for the literary magazine *Ken*, he poured out his anger over what he had seen: "The fascist nations act, while the democratic nations talk, vacillate, connive, and betray." Taking aim at U.S. policy, he wrote that "if the democratic nations allow Spain to be overrun by the fascists through their refusal to allow the legal Spanish government to buy and import arms to combat a military insurrection and fascist invasion, they will deserve whatever fate brings them." Like many critics of U.S. policy, he believed that if the democracies did not stop fascism in Spain, they would soon find themselves fighting it all around the world.[49]

If Hemingway's articles were aimed at the literary set, Claude Bowers kept his fire trained on Roosevelt. "My heart bleeds for this fine and lovely people," he wrote to the president, just a few days before Franco's forces reached the coast at Vinaròs, cutting off Catalonia and Barcelona from Republican territory. Bowers expressed a seething hatred of Neville Chamberlain, who in an effort to cultivate a good relationship with Mussolini had just offered to recognize Italian control of Ethiopia at the very moment that the Italian air force pounded Barcelona and Valencia. Chamberlain's conduct, said Bowers, was "the most dishonorable and treacherous, antidemocratic and deceptive in the history of England." Perhaps realizing that his time in Spain was coming to a close, Bowers told FDR that the people fighting fascism in Spain were "the only people in the world in these days of fascist triumph and bullying who have the spirit and the guts to stand up and fight and die for liberty and democracy. Just now they are literally fighting for democracy against the entire world."[50]

Eleanor Roosevelt received similar messages from Martha Gellhorn who, after a grueling U.S. lecture tour in January to raise awareness about the stakes of the war, returned to Spain in the spring to report for *Collier's* magazine. She was in Barcelona just as Franco's troops reached the sea and started massing a hundred miles south of the city. The news was "terrible, too terrible," she wrote the First Lady. "It makes me helpless and crazy with anger to watch the next Great War hurtling towards us. . . . The whole world is accepting destruction from the author of *Mein Kampf*, a man who cannot think straight for half a page." Martha sent detailed descriptions to the White House of German planes bombing the city, the food shortages, the lack of weapons, the courage of the Spaniards. "I am again impressed by the unshakably democratic quality of Loyalist Spain," Gellhorn wrote to Eleanor. "I never saw better men in my life in any country . . . and hope to God that America at least will not go on letting this country down."

Eleanor replied sympathetically, expressing her frustration at the unneutral Neutrality Act and wondering at the selfishness of the isolationists who thought only of their "own skins." Gellhorn's anguish deeply impressed Eleanor, who shared these reports with the president. But she admitted that even "our own State Department has people who are not very anxious to do much for the Loyalists." In fact, she later revealed that Roosevelt himself wanted to aid the Spanish government but felt he could not get Congress to go along. He remonstrated with Eleanor, saying that the League of Nations had asked the U.S. and other nations to stay out; but as she put it tartly, he "was simply trying to salve his own conscience."[51]

Another man with a bad conscience was Senator Gerald Nye, the chief architect of the neutrality legislation that had tied the government's hands since 1935. With public pressure rising, Nye on May 2 introduced a resolution in the Senate calling for a repeal of the Spanish arms embargo. Nye stated that he was not taking sides in the conflict but wanted "to right an injustice growing out of the embargo program," namely, that U.S. policy was not in fact neutral but "partial to one side." Coming from the man who had done so much to demonize arms manufacturers as "merchants of death," this was a remarkable volte-face. Walter Lippmann put out a column expressing sympathy for the senator's reversal. The whole country wanted both to avoid getting entangled in war, and to help valiant Spain beat back the fascists. Lippmann called the embargo "unsound, unworkable, and unjust," and urged its repeal. It certainly looked as if, with just a gentle shove by the administration, the embargo could be lifted. After briefly reviewing the issue, however, Hull and Roosevelt chose not to take the golden opportunity Nye had presented. Hull announced that they would stand by the policy of "strict non-interference" in Spanish affairs. With that, the Senate Foreign Relations Committee tabled Nye's resolution. The embargo would stay, and in fact it was never lifted until the end of the war in 1939.[52]

Why did FDR refuse to act? His secretary of state wanted to keep the embargo in place, arguing that a change of course now would be seen as intervention in the war. Roosevelt could not undermine Hull directly, since he carried too much political weight in Congress. The British also opposed lifting the embargo, and Prime Minister Chamberlain felt his policy of appeasement was starting to show some results; for America to sell arms to Spain now would wreck Chamberlain's initiatives. Roosevelt's most important ambassadors, William Bullitt and Joseph Kennedy, opposed lifting the embargo because they too wanted to improve relations with the Axis. FDR was pushing a major naval rearmament bill through Congress that required cooperation on the Hill. A divisive debate on Spain might derail that program. And there was the Catholic issue. When Harold Ickes confronted Roosevelt in the Oval Office about the embargo—"a black page in American history," Ickes called it—Roosevelt said he had discussed the matter with allies in Congress. "He said frankly that to raise the embargo would mean the loss of every Catholic vote next fall and the Democratic members of Congress were jittery about it and didn't want it done." The result of these pressures led Roosevelt to halt discussion of lifting the embargo.[53]

It is also possible that Roosevelt, by avoiding a public fight over the embargo, was diverting attention from a secret scheme to subvert it. There is some evidence to suggest that Roosevelt had initiated a covert plan to get U.S. planes shipped to Spain through France in defiance of the embargo. In June, none other than Eleanor Roosevelt's younger brother, G. Hall Roosevelt, turned up in Paris with a remarkable story. Hall, an electrical engineer and former pilot in the American Army Air Service in World War I, told Ambassador Bullitt in Paris he was acting with FDR's secret approval to help get 150 aircraft shipped to France and then across the border into Spain. Bullitt, quite shocked by this news and opposed to any U.S. intervention on behalf of the left-wing Spanish government, sent a long cable to the president denouncing Hall's plan and implying that if it got out to the public, a very damaging scandal would transpire. Bullitt did not need to spell it out, but the cat had clearly got out of the bag and Bullitt was warning FDR to disavow the whole plan. Whether Roosevelt personally intervened with Hall is unknown, but the two did speak by telephone in late July, and at that point, the plan fizzled out. It is a tantalizing possibility: that FDR's private frustration with the embargo led him to use his brother-in-law in a secret and probably illegal plan to get warplanes to the Spanish government. Though nothing came of it, the plan points to a president who was having some second thoughts about his own foreign policy.[54]

VI

At least some part of the reason for Roosevelt's hesitation in starting a fight over the Spanish embargo relates to what he saw as a more pressing, urgent priority: rearmament. On May 17, FDR signed into law the Naval Act of 1938, which outlined a ten-year building program, at a cost of $1.1 billion (worth about $22 billion today), for the expansion by 20 percent of the U.S. Navy, including three new battleships and two new aircraft carriers. The passage of the bill proved to be unusually swift, despite the immense cost, showing that by the spring of 1938, a new consensus was starting to take hold: The era of disarmament that the United States had championed after the Great War had come to an end.

Roosevelt made his position clear in a message to Congress on January 28. In his statement, the president pointed to the calamitous world situation in Asia and Europe and declared frankly that long-standing efforts to strike a permanent arms reduction deal "have failed up to the present time." Instead, the world powers were increasing their armaments "at an unprecedented and alarming rate." A quarter of the world's population was embroiled in "devastating conflict," and new bombing technologies turned undefended cities into battlefields. "Tension throughout the world is high," he said ominously. In this context, Roosevelt went on, America's military capabilities were "inadequate for the purposes of national security." At a time when other nations were discarding treaties and violating international law, the United States must prepare for a difficult and uncertain period ahead. That meant a major expansion of America's defense capabilities.[55]

The president's chief ally in Congress on naval matters was Representative Carl Vinson of Georgia, chairman of the Naval Affairs Committee in the House of Representatives. Vinson was one of those powerful Southern Democrats that FDR relied upon to carry his policies through Congress: he was an ardent segregationist as well as a supporter of the New Deal, especially major federal spending on military and naval infrastructure. Vinson authored the 1934 Vinson-Trammel Act, which laid out a roadmap for naval expansion within the limits of the 1930 London Naval Conference that had committed Britain, Japan, and the United States to a cooperative framework for naval construction. But as of 1938, the U.S. had not come close to meeting even those modest treaty limits. With Japan having abrogated the various naval limitation agreements by 1936, Roosevelt believed the United States must counter Japan's growing naval strength in the Pacific. Vinson worked up the legislation, putting into place a dramatic program of naval construction that proved of vital significance for waging the war after 1941.[56]

Since the end of the world war, the navy had shrunk badly; by 1933, it had only 132 surface warships afloat (not including auxiliary craft and submarines), half of them out of date. The Vinson bill proposed adding 46 warships, 26 auxiliary craft, and 950 airplanes, and the expansion of navy yards for construction. And the legislation specified that the U.S. Navy must be big enough to protect the Atlantic and Pacific coasts, as well as "the Panama Canal, Alaska, Hawaii, and our insular possessions," including the Philippines, Guam, Wake and Midway Islands. To project American power into the Atlantic and far across the Pacific, the U.S. Navy needed more and better ships. Despite some opposition, most legislators agreed. On May 3, the Senate passed the bill by a vote of 56–28, and after a conference with the House, Congress reached final agreement on the massive building program. With a minimum of press coverage, Roosevelt signed the bill into law, opening a new era of American naval power. By the time of the Pearl Harbor attack in 1941, the navy could count 225 surface warships—a 70 percent increase since FDR's inauguration. Whatever Roosevelt's earlier commitments to neutrality, disarmament, and peace, the president in 1938 began to prepare the nation for war.[57]

Throughout the debate over the bill, the administration gained valuable support from Walter Lippmann, whose nationally syndicated column carried weight in progressive political circles. Lippmann in 1938 applauded the new direction of Roosevelt's foreign policy. He understood that Roosevelt and Hull had a certain "conception of the world," one he shared, which Lippmann described this way: "If respect for the lawful processes is not upheld in the outer world, then anarchy will inevitably invade us at home and engulf the whole world." Their opponents clung to the idea "that the United States can remain an island of law and liberty no matter what happens elsewhere." Rejecting isolation, Lippmann saw the rearmament bill as "an act of world-wide significance," because it committed the navy to defend American interests well beyond the nation's shores. And he applauded its scope. In an earlier time, perhaps, the U.S. could retrench and rely upon negotiations to manage the world. But by 1938, the world had changed. "Japan has freed herself of all limitations under the treaties" and was embarked on "unlimited naval construction." If Japan achieved its imperial ambitions in Asia and the Pacific, it would rule over "one-half the population of the globe." Germany too had extravagant aspirations not just in Europe, but in Africa and Latin America. And Germany, he noted, "is a military ally of Japan." After FDR signed the Naval Act, Lippmann rejoiced: The naval program would "reverse the tragic and disastrous error of the democratic nations" when they had embraced "grandiose ideals of collective security accompanied by the gradual dissolution of their military power." Weakness only earned the contempt of the dictators, Lippmann concluded. The best way to keep the peace was to prepare for war.[58]

That view started to emerge more fully in public statements from writers as well as policy officials. Dorothy Thompson, in a public debate with Senator Gerald Nye, insisted that America should use its power in the world to impose the rule of law and contain the dictators. Thompson, in her usual pithy fashion, put it this way: "The world is always run on somebody's terms. I prefer that it should be run on the terms of the democracies." The distinguished educator and president of Columbia University, Nicholas Murray Butler, agreed. Like so many elite Americans, Butler had been an apologist for Mussolini in the early days of fascism, but by the 1930s, he was worried. In his commencement address in June 1938, Butler declared that the democracies had abdicated their role in world affairs. "There is a point at which the rule of force may be needed in order that democracy can survive," he argued. "If democracy is to continue in any form, it must assert the power which belongs to it." And most significant, Secretary Hull delivered another condemnation of isolationism in a public address to the state bar association of Tennessee. Repeating the themes of his March address, he called the theory that isolation would bring peace "a bitter illusion." The world faced a choice between anarchy and the rule of law; should America "withdraw from the world," the chaos stirred up by the dictators would engulf everyone.[59]

Even the normally frigid editorial page of the *New York Times* expressed sudden warmth on the topic. "American opinion today is openly and overwhelmingly on the side of China" and "aligned against the seizure of Austria," stated the editorial board. "We are inevitably the natural allies of the democracies of Europe," including plucky Czechoslovakia, Hitler's next target. "We shall be fully prepared, if war on a large scale envelops Europe, to choose the side of the democracies," insisted the *Times*. This position went considerably beyond the calls for world engagement that Hull had been preaching, but it was a view Nicholas Murray Butler saw taking hold across the country. "American public opinion is turning away from isolation under the pressure of world events," he wrote at the end of June. "Isolationist sentiment," which had given shape to the Neutrality Act, had lost its appeal. The misguided neutrality legislation only aided aggressors and left the victims defenseless, and Butler hoped to see it repealed. Clearly, establishment figures in the press, the universities, the navy, and in the government—revolted by the bestiality of Japan's war in China, frustrated by FDR's inaction on Spain, and shocked by the brutality of Nazi aggression in Austria—wanted America to pick a side, and get into the fight.[60]

VII

Roosevelt seemed unwilling to commit himself. On Spain, he chose to do nothing; meanwhile, he put into place a naval expansion program that hinted at a more robust presence in the world, perhaps including the naval "quarantine" of the dictatorships. Certainly, his overriding goal had not changed: keeping America out of a major war. He remained convinced that war was unpopular, a tragic waste, would wreck all the progress of the New Deal, and destroy American democracy. He judged American moves on the world stage by their effectiveness in diminishing the risks of war. Indeed, this may have been his chief motive in convening the Évian conference on refugees. As Sumner Welles put it to a group of newspaper editors when trying to gain support for the conference, the United States aimed "to make it possible for these populations in certain Central European countries to find a refuge to which they can go." Welles continued, "if this proves successful . . . one of the causes for European war in the future will be, if not completely avoided, greatly alleviated." The idea of rearranging the ethnic map of Europe was not new: Population transfers and mass migrations had occurred in the aftermath of the Great War, and the Treaty of Versailles itself had brusquely drawn the national borders of the new Europe with an eye to ethnic homogeneity. In the interests of avoiding war, why not do more of the same?[61]

As reports continued to stream out of Vienna about Nazi sadism—"an unbroken orgy of Jew-baiting such as Europe has not known since the darkest days of the Middle Ages," as the London *Times* put it—the Évian conference opened on July 6 at the Hôtel Royal, situated by the blue-green waters of Lake Geneva. The diplomats conferred on a plan, as Myron Taylor described it at the outset, of "population dispersal in order to relieve the pressure at certain explosive points." Moving clumps of Jews around the globe—perhaps to Paraguay? Madagascar? Congo? Kenya?—seemed to these men an entirely plausible way to ease tensions in international relations, and they discussed these matters in an atmosphere of genteel concern. The hotel offered sumptuous accommodations and kept the delegates well-fed with multi-course dinners of fresh cantaloupe, velvety borscht, Dover sole, roast lamb, fresh berries and ice cream, all washed down with bottles of Chateau Latour 1920. Dabbing their lips after dinner and lighting their cigars, they got down to business. Taylor said the Americans would take twenty-seven thousand Jewish refugees from Germany and Austria. How many Jews would the other nations accept? As it turned out, infamously, the answer was none.[62]

From the opening moment of the conference, the ambassadors explained why they could not help. Lord Winterton, the British delegate, threw cold water on Taylor's hopes. "The United Kingdom is not a country of immigration," Winterton said in his first words to the conference. It is "fully populated" and still faced an unemployment problem. Winterton also discouraged any talk of Jewish refugees going to Palestine: "local political conditions," he said, referring to the ongoing Arab Revolt against both British rule and Jewish political aspirations in Palestine, "hinder or prevent any considerable immigration." Perhaps a small number of refugees might be offered settlement in East Africa; that was as far as he could go. The Australian delegate said that his country could not give special treatment to any particular class of refugees, and in any case Australia preferred British immigrants, not foreign ones. "As we have no real racial problem, we are not desirous of importing one by encouraging any scheme of large-scale foreign migration," he said frankly. Canada followed suit: "Unfortunately," said its delegate, "serious unemployment and economic uncertainty . . . still limits severely Canadian power to absorb any considerable number of immigrants."[63]

The reporter Jimmy Sheean, coming to the Hôtel Royal straight from observing the atrocities against Jews in Vienna, found these speeches full of "stupid, sanctimonious, heartless pomposity," and knew that nothing would be accomplished. The delegates were "glossing over a living horror with dead and empty words." Sheean noted that most of the conferees spent long evenings in the hotel casino playing roulette and baccarat (as did Sheean himself), quietly complaining that the champagne was not sufficiently chilled.[64]

The Évian meeting lasted ten days. It set up a permanent organization in London to open channels with the German government and work toward the organized departure of Jews from the Reich. That London committee was run by an American, a progressive lawyer and friend of FDR's from Groton and Harvard named George Rublee. With this done, Évian sputtered to a close. It was a worthy but limited exercise. If the Jewish refugee crisis had stayed fixed, with only six hundred thousand or so Jews to assist, and if war had not come in 1939, perhaps that London committee would have notched some successes. After all, the United States by law could take twenty-seven thousand Germans and Austrians each year, and if just nine other nations had taken the same number, a quarter of a million people could have been sheltered, with more in subsequent years. The American Jewish Congress appreciated the limited but meaningful help the U.S. government offered, only wishing that others would follow suit. But the Jewish crisis did not remain fixed. It was expanding, and not just because of Nazi persecution. In the spring of 1938, Italy joined Germany in the war on the Jews.[65]

VIII

In early May, Mussolini had welcomed Adolf Hitler to Italy for an excessively opulent, weeklong state visit. Il Duce spared no expense, driving the Nazi leader through miles of flag-bedecked streets past cheering multitudes and goose-stepping Blackshirts. He put on a vast naval review at Naples, and in Rome he arranged night-time spectacles, fireworks, searchlights, and artillery salutes. The visit signaled the close embrace of the Axis partners and showed that Mussolini harbored no ill will over the Anschluss. More than that, the visit kicked off a new intensification of Mussolini's drive to make Italy into a racial empire in the Mediterranean and Africa, along the lines of Hitler's own in Central Europe. Italy had a small Jewish community that was highly assimilated into Italian public life. Jews had been active in the professions, the universities, the military, business and trade for centuries. Indeed, Mussolini's mistress, Margherita Sarfatti, was born into a wealthy Jewish family in Venice. But as Mussolini pushed Italy closer into Hitler's orbit, he found it expedient to adopt some of the racial theories so eagerly promulgated by the Nazis.[66]

On July 14, at precisely the same moment that the worthy diplomats were wrapping up in Évian, a racial "Manifesto" appeared in the government-controlled Italian press. Ambassador William Phillips—the former under-secretary who Roosevelt had sent to Rome in August 1936—summarized the central points of the document for the State Department: Different human races exist; race is a biological fact; Italy is an Aryan civilization and different from Asian and African peoples; and finally, "Jews do not belong to the Italian race." The newspapers, Phillips said, all rushed out editorials in line with this new directive, asserting that "the racial principle has always been a basic doctrine of the Fascist regime and demonstrating that the strength of a nation is lost when its racial purity is weakened through the introduction of other racial strains."[67]

By themselves, these statements would not have caused trouble in America of the 1930s. Such sentiments might have been expressed in a seminar room at Harvard, on the floor of the U.S. Senate, or indeed in the State Department itself. Ambassador Phillips, a casually antisemitic Boston Brahmin, was the sort of man who went to the trouble of recording his frustration in his extensive diary when a beach vacation to Atlantic City was ruined by Jews: "The place is infested with Jews," he noted mournfully. "In fact, the whole beach scene on Saturday afternoon and Sunday was an extraordinary sight—very little sand to be seen, the whole beach covered by slightly clothed Jews and Jewesses." But in the context of the ghastly persecution in Vienna, and the president's close interest in the Évian meeting, Phillips wanted to know if this Italian racial manifesto portended a significant change.

The ambassador went to see the Italian foreign minister, Galeazzo Ciano (who happened to be Mussolini's son-in-law). Ciano confirmed that the move was part of a larger effort, as Phillips summarized it, "to preserve the purity of the Italian civilian throughout the Empire. The movement originated from the necessity of keeping the Italian and black races apart in Ethiopia in order to prevent miscegenation . . . [and] . . . the Jewish race which had always regarded itself as a separate race also came into the picture." Ciano insisted there would be no "persecution," just segregation. Although Phillips did not report it to the State Department, Ciano said more than that. In his diary, Phillips wrote that Ciano "likened the situation somewhat to the attitude of our southern states with regard to the negroes and to the segregation of the blacks from the white race." The Jews would not be physically harmed, Ciano insisted, but "they would not be permitted hereafter to have political or social influence in Italian life." Phillips cautioned Ciano to avoid explicit persecution, because in America, the ambassador asserted, the "Jewish influence in the American press was strong," and any harsh measures like those being imposed in Vienna would alienate Americans from Italy. Phillips seemed reassured that Italy planned mere segregation of Italy's Jews, with which he could sympathize, rather than giving them the full-on Nazi treatment.[68]

But within a month, Phillips realized that the Manifesto was just the start of a broader campaign. On September 1, in what Phillips called a "drastic anti-Jewish move," the government issued a decree that ordered the expulsion of foreign Jews from Italy. The next day, Jews were banned from the teaching profession. A few weeks later, marriages between Jews and non-Jews were banned, and Jews were prohibited from employment in the civil service, the military, journalism, banking, and insurance sectors. It all came as "a complete shock" to Phillips. He had received assurances from Ciano that "segregation" would not lead to "persecution," and Phillips had taken the foreign minister at his word. Now he was less sure, writing directly to the president that "I think we may include this anti-Jewish campaign in Italy's foreign relations." Mussolini pretended to remain an independent actor in world affairs, "yet everything he does has the appearance of being done under pressure from Berlin."[69]

Phillips may have been loath to admit it, but his hopes of weaning Italy away from the Axis had been dashed. Mussolini made his choice to follow Hitler's racial imperialism—the determination to reconstruct the European continent on racial lines, with so-called Aryans in a dominating position and the rest treated like helots or simply discarded and annihilated. As the great Italian novelist Ignazio Silone put it at the time, "Italian racism will be useful in scaffolding the national pride, now suffering from an inferiority complex aggravated by the increasingly intimate relationship with the blonde Germans." A shared racial-imperial project now bound Hitler and Mussolini together in an iron grasp. Acquiescing in Hitler's invasion of Austria as well as his radical racial policies, Mussolini could have no objection to Hitler's next gamble: the dismemberment of Czechoslovakia.[70]

CHAPTER 12

THE MEANING OF MUNICH

"A black pall is being spread bit by bit across the face of civilized Europe."

—HAMILTON FISH ARMSTRONG

I

In the summer of 1938, as Europe staggered from one crisis to another and Japan sliced ever deeper into China's heartland, Franklin Roosevelt's chief concerns lay not overseas but at home: with the stubborn unemployment numbers of the recession of 1937–38; with the forthcoming midterm elections, scheduled for November 8; and above all, with the progress of the New Deal, which he continued to believe gave an example to the world of how democracy could meet the challenges of modernity without resort to totalitarian rule. He spoke about these themes constantly that summer, as the Nazi threat grew more menacing. Democracy in America was working, he insisted. America was resilient and gaining strength. Liberal, progressive government offered solutions to a struggling people in need of help. In this grand narrative, Roosevelt provided a striking contrast to the stricken, defeatist European leaders whose only answer to fascism so far had been to retreat from it. While they mournfully clasped their hands and predicted catastrophe, Roosevelt projected confidence. And his voice carried no hint of accommodation to the dictators.

To be sure, he had an advantage: The United States was located far from the borders of Nazi Germany, well beyond any direct military threat. But if Roosevelt did not yet fear German bombers filling the skies above Washington, he did fear the persistent appeal of fascism as an ideology, and the evident weakness of the democracies. Should they fail to deliver, the dictators stood ready with alternative forms of rule. So when he spoke of the accomplishments of the New Deal in the middle of 1938, he was making not merely a partisan claim about his political achievements, but an ideological one as well. Consider the title of the fireside chat he gave on June 24, broadcast from the White House: "Advance, Not Retreat!" This speech is usually referred to as the start of an effort by FDR to "purge" the Democratic Party of a few difficult congressmen who had too often stood in the way of the New Deal. The president decided that he would make speeches to help his preferred liberal candidates in the Democratic primaries that summer. But this address evoked broader themes. He summarized the remarkable victories of the New Deal over the previous year, including new laws on conservation, farm aid, crop insurance, a federal minimum wage, a new civil aviation authority, and a new public housing authority. The WPA and the PWA, the CCC, the rural electrification program, the navy—all had received more funds for more construction projects.[1]

This was not a time for slowing down, he said. "After 1936, I was told . . . that I should coast along, enjoy an easy Presidency for four years." He heard that "people were getting weary of reform through political effort." He was met, he said, with a "concerted campaign of defeatism." He rejected this. "The American people do have confidence in themselves, have confidence in their ability, with the aid of government, to solve their own problems." This was the liberal credo: "new conditions throughout the world call for new remedies," as he put it. And these new remedies must be applied "through democratic processes instead of fascism or communism." Democracy, not authoritarianism, would empower people to battle through to victory over the troubles of the moment.[2]

On July 7, he set out by train on a remarkable four-thousand-mile cross-country whistle-stop tour to take his case to the people. In Ohio, Kentucky, Arkansas, Oklahoma, Texas, Colorado, Nevada, and California, his speeches returned again and again to the theme that liberal government had carved a pathway forward for America, out of the Depression and into a new era. And Americans had pulled together to share the burden. "We have been trying," he said in Pueblo, Colorado, "to make this nation conscious of the fact that it is a nation. If we succeed in that, it means we can make democracy work, and that is our big objective. We don't want and we are not going to copy other forms of government. Ours is good enough for us."[3]

After reviewing the U.S. Fleet in San Francisco Bay, the president and his party headed east, into the mountains, for a visit to Yosemite National Park, one of the wonders of the North American continent. He cruised through the park in an open-top car along the Merced River, past the majestic bare granite slope of Sentinel Dome, reflecting on the horseback tour his famous cousin Theodore had made here in 1903 in the company of the naturalist John Muir. Onward his car slowly progressed through the towering Sequoias in Mariposa Grove, past the thundering crash of Yosemite Falls, to the commanding heights of Glacier Point and its view across the endless vista of the High Sierra. Nothing could offer a greater contrast to the dismal and, as he thought, decadent European capitals than this extraordinary open vastness. It was two years almost to the day from his dedication speech at the Shenandoah National Park in Virginia. Then, he had spoken of what the parks meant to the toilers and city dwellers of the United States, as they set out for a brief summer vacation to renew and refresh themselves:

> Those people will put up at roadside camps or pitch their tents under the stars, with an open fire to cook by, with the smell of the woods, and the wind in the trees. They will forget the rush and the strain of all the other long weeks of the year, and for a short time at least, the days will be good for their bodies and good for their souls. Once more they will lay hold of the perspective that comes to men and women who every morning and every night can lift up their eyes to Mother Nature.

A nation with such inexhaustible resources, with an endlessly innovative and inventive people, aided by a responsive, generous government: What could it not accomplish?[4]

A day later, in the company of his official "family"—the ever-present Missy LeHand, Edwin "Pa" Watson, his physician Ross T. McIntire, press secretary Stephen Early, friend and business partner Basil O'Connor, and a naturalist from the Smithsonian Institution, Dr. Waldo Schmitt—the president boarded the USS *Houston* for a three-week cruise along the coast of Mexico and out to the Galápagos Islands. The expedition was chiefly a fishing trip (and poker-playing junket), but FDR invited the scientific staff of the museum to collect marine and botanical specimens on the voyage. Amid much of the usual shipboard hijinks, cocktailing, and backslapping that FDR enjoyed, the team collected specimens of plants, mollusks, sponges, and other invertebrates, and even named a newly discovered shrimplike crustacean for the president—*Siriella roosevelti*.[5]

Following his long return journey—through the Panama Canal to Pensacola, Florida, stopping briefly at Warm Springs, and then back to Washington—he gave a radio address on August 15 to mark the third anniversary of one of the New Deal's signature achievements: The Social Security Act, which by offering a basic minimum of support to millions of Americans in the years after they stopped working, had enhanced "the security and well-being of this great democracy." In a phrase that foreshadowed his famous Four Freedoms declaration of January 1941, he stated that "there is still today a frontier that remains unconquered—an America un-reclaimed. This is the great, nationwide frontier of insecurity, of human want and fear. This is the frontier, the America, we have set ourselves to reclaim." That work lay ahead.[6]

In these speeches, Roosevelt adopted the tone of a nationalist and an American exceptionalist. While democracy was embattled elsewhere, in the United States it was strong and proving its worth. And why should he not have felt this way? By the middle of 1938, the New Deal had already left its mark on the landscape of America. That breathtaking engineering marvel, the Boulder Dam (later renamed Hoover), started generating electricity in 1935. The Triborough Bridge between Manhattan, Queens, and Brooklyn opened in 1936. The New Deal would build about 800 airports, including the one in New York named to honor Mayor Fiorello La Guardia, which opened in 1939, in time for the New York World's Fair. The San Francisco–Oakland Bay Bridge was built in just three years and opened in 1936; its neighbor, the Golden Gate Bridge, finished in 1937, was at that time the longest and tallest suspension bridge in the world. As war loomed in Europe in the fall of 1938, the PWA had funded 34,000 construction projects across America, from airports to bridges, dams, schools, post offices, libraries, and hospitals. The WPA had overseen the construction of 650,000 miles of roads. The CCC had planted 3 billion trees. Surely, Roosevelt had every right to feel confident about the prospects and strength of American democracy.

Like fascist states, the New Deal's CCC deployed images of young, brawny men at work to animate its slogan "We Can Take It!"
WJ Mead / PhotoQuest / Getty Images

Only one speech in this summer of public addresses mentioned the European crisis directly. On August 18,

Roosevelt arrived in Kingston, Ontario, to dedicate the Thousand Islands Bridge across the St. Lawrence River, connecting New York to Canadian soil. He also received an honorary degree from Queens University. Here he discussed U.S.-Canadian friendship, contrasting it to the roiling hatreds in the Old World. "Civilization," which in his mind meant peace, tolerance, order, and reason, was in danger around the world. Rumors of war swirled around them, he said, and "we in the Americas are no longer a faraway continent, to which the eddies of controversies beyond the seas could bring no interest or no harm." The very strength of the American republics meant that fascists looked enviously upon them and plotted their downfall. In the face of such threats, Canada and the United States stood together, part of a community dedicated to democracy and liberty—"a strong citadel wherein civilization can flourish unimpeded." To what one witness described as a "suddenly electrified" audience, Roosevelt stated: "The Dominion of Canada is part of the sisterhood of the British Empire. I give you my assurance that the people of the United States will not stand idly by if domination of Canadian soil is threatened by any other empire." A thunderous wave of applause broke out even before Roosevelt had finished that passage and rolled over the stadium for several minutes. The Monroe Doctrine had just been shifted a few thousand miles northward.[7]

Roosevelt's sense of confident purpose, of forward momentum, his certainty that America's greatest problems could be met and solved through expedient and strong leadership—here lies the key to understanding how FDR approached European affairs in 1938, as Hitler set out to expand the Nazi empire beyond the borders of the Reich. In the course of 1938 he became ever more convinced that there lay ahead a great reckoning with the forces of fascism, racial imperialism, autarky, and dictatorship. But in facing those threats, he began from a position of confidence and strength that would have been completely foreign to the beleaguered European leaders.

A clear expression of FDR's worldview at this moment can be found in a letter to his old Harvard classmate William Phillips, now the ambassador in Rome. FDR had left Hyde Park on September 6 to head to the Mayo Clinic in Rochester, Minnesota, where his son James faced a delicate operation on a gastric ulcer. On the fourteenth, after an anxious week at James's bedside, the president boarded his train for Washington, eager to get back to the White House as the picture in Europe grew ominous. Phillips, in a recent missive, had commented on both the ignorance among Italian leaders about America and the likelihood of a fascist war breaking out soon. While his train rattled along the southbound tracks, Roosevelt dictated a response to Phillips that began with his estimate that Europe was headed for "an inevitable conflict within the next five years." He then told a little story about geopolitics that opens a window into a mind that is so often closed to historians:

> The complete ignorance of American conditions and fundamental strength on the part of highly placed Italians reminds me of Johnny's conversation with an Italian, I think it was the Minister of Finance, in Venice a year ago. [FDR's son John had made a tour of Italy and met Mussolini July 1937.] The Minister suggested to Johnny that I should pay a visit to Mussolini. Johnny very properly suggested that Mussolini might well pay a visit to the president. The Minister could not comprehend the suggestion, and Johnny told him with complete politeness that the United States had three times the population and ten times the resources of Italy, and that the whole of Italy would fit very comfortably into the state of Texas.

The letter gives just a hint of the pride Roosevelt took in America's immense power and in its freedom of movement. And he went on: "You are right in saying that we are an emotional people over here in the sense that we do not easily lose our heads, but *if we get the idea that the future of our form of government is threatened by a coalition of European dictators, we might have to wade in with everything we have to give.*" Unlike in 1914, Americans would not be neutral in thought or action if war broke out in Europe again. "Ninety percent of our people are definitely anti-German and anti-Italian in sentiment," the president wrote, and Americans would feel that a fascist war of aggression in Europe directly affected their own security. In closing, he reassured Phillips that he had no thought "of sending troops to Europe." No matter: There were other ways to help the European democracies, and to that subject his mind had already turned.[8]

A sense of power; an abiding hatred of fascism; a devotion to democracy as it struggled forward from the darkest days of the Great Depression; a feel for the public revulsion toward the dictators; no small amount of scorn for the truckling of Chamberlain and the appeasers; and a desire to keep American boots off the soil of the European continent. These were the principles and ideas that animated Roosevelt as he returned to Washington in mid-September. From the fall of 1938 onward, they provided Roosevelt with a kind of compass as he steered into the storm ahead, where Hitler was setting out on his greatest gamble yet.

II

The seizure of Austria in March 1938 had followed a well-conceived plan: Hitler used Nazi proxies to create a political crisis inside Austria and then insisted that only total absorption by Germany could resolve the matter. He turned to the same playbook to provoke what he expected to be a short, decisive war against Czechoslovakia that would allow the Nazi Reich to swallow it whole. Formed in 1918 at the Paris Peace Conference as part of the breakup of the Austro-Hungarian Empire, Czechoslovakia had a large German-speaking population, most of which was massed in the western and northern part of the country in a horseshoe-shaped mountainous territory called the Sudetenland. Although these 3.5 million ethnically German people had never been ruled by the German Empire and had for almost a millennium been part of Bohemia, Hitler decided to treat them as a lost German tribe that lived under the brutal oppression of a tyrannical Czech government. In fact, the Sudeten Germans had significant regional autonomy within the Czech state, but German nationalists in the region insisted on total separation. Hitler deftly encouraged this tension, hoping to use the alleged persecution of the Sudeten Germans as a casus belli against Czechoslovakia.

Just two weeks after the Anschluss, which had left Czechoslovakia surrounded by hostile powers including Germany, Poland, and Hungary, Hitler ordered the leader of the Sudeten German Party, Konrad Henlein, to manufacture a crisis by demanding from the Prague government the virtual independence of the Sudetenland. Henlein, a gymnastics instructor and veteran of the Austro-Hungarian Army, had been involved in right-wing nationalist politics since the end of the world war, and gloried in this sudden attention from the German Führer. On April 24, Henlein threw down the gauntlet at a meeting of his political party in Karlsbad that had all the trappings of a Nazi rally, including shouts of "Sieg Heil!" that erupted upon Henlein's arrival. In a violent, warlike speech, he made eight demands of the Czech government, including full equality and autonomy of the Sudeten Germans, reparations for all the oppression and damages allegedly done to the German minority since 1918, expulsion of Czech officials in the administration of Sudeten territory, and full freedom for the German minority to proclaim the pan-German ideology of the Nazi Reich. Although not yet an explicit demand for secession, in practical terms it was a declaration of war on the Czech state. Of course, these demands had been approved by Hitler, who expected Prague to refuse them, after which he would launch a war and break the Czech state to pieces. In the meantime, he ordered his military chiefs to prepare "Case Green"—the operational plan for the invasion.[9]

Everyone expected Hitler's strike on Czechoslovakia, yet no one knew if it would trigger a wider continental war. In 1925, France had signed a mutual defense pact with the Czechs; ten years later, the Soviet Union followed suit, both nations pledging to defend Czechoslovakia against attack. Czechoslovakia formed an important brick in the wall that the French and Soviets had built to contain German power. But would these countries really go to war to defend the territorial integrity of a new, multiethnic nation whose borders were arbitrarily drawn only a few years earlier? From the French point of view, a war against Germany without the backing of Britain would be suicide: French leaders convinced themselves they could not successfully fight Germany alone. So the decision about how, or whether, to contain Hitler's ruthless designs on Czechoslovakia lay in London: What would England do to defend the Czechs?

As early as mid-March, Prime Minister Chamberlain had made his position clear to his cabinet colleagues: He would not go to war to defend the Czechs if the Czechs themselves did not pursue every possible path to peace. In any case, Britain could not do much militarily to assist the far-off Czech state; and a war with Germany would bring a devastating aerial bombing attack that Britain's meager defenses could not repel. War over Czechoslovakia was out of the question, especially if there was some compromise that could be struck to avert it. At the end of April, Chamberlain met with his French counterpart in London and won Édouard Daladier's agreement to pressure the Czech government to meet the demands of the Sudeten Germans. Giving away control of the Sudetenland to the local German minority under pressure from Hitler was no small matter. Since the Sudetenland abutted Germany, the Czechs had spent many years building up significant defensive positions in the region, planning to use the mountainous terrain to their advantage against a possible German attack. The Sudetenland was Czechoslovakia's Maginot Line. But now, the British and French were proposing that the Czech government surrender control of this very territory to Hitler's proxies, thus leaving the remaining part of the country completely undefended.[10]

Yet Chamberlain felt fully justified in pursuing the appeasement of Germany in this manner. On April 16, British and Italian representatives signed the long-sought deal giving Italy the recognition of its empire in Ethiopia in return for the withdrawal of a token force of Italian troops from Spain. Chamberlain saw the Anglo-Italian agreement as evidence that appeasement was working, and he felt sure that a peaceful agreement over the Sudetenland could just as easily be arranged. Appeasement meant finding negotiated solutions to outstanding grievances, and if the Czechs had to pay the bill for a wider European peace settlement, so be it. Dorothy Thompson totally rejected Chamberlain's thesis. "The failure to comprehend the dictatorial mind is the greatest weakness of democracy," she wrote. The democracies assumed that negotiation and flexibility could satisfy dictators and lead to peace, when in fact the dictators saw such expressions as a sign of weakness and an invitation to ask for more. "The effect of all this," Thompson bitterly concluded, "is not only to fill the Fascist powers with arrogance but, what is much worse, to fill the democracies with a sense of defeatism." Having done nothing about the Anschluss, the democratic camp signaled to Hitler that he could carry on and grab whatever he wanted in Central Europe.[11]

That was exactly Chamberlain's problem: Hitler did not want peace at all. He wanted a swift, localized war with the Czechs that would allow him to seize control of the entire country while demonstrating his strength and daring as a dictator. His agitation about the Sudeten Germans was merely a pretext for a full-scale invasion. On May 28, Hitler ordered his generals to be ready for a military strike against Czechoslovakia by October 1; two days later, he signed a directive declaring his "unalterable decision to smash Czechoslovakia by military action in the near future." The British government's appeasement policy, therefore, complicated matters for Hitler by offering to resolve the dispute, and carve up Czechoslovakia, without war. Determined to extinguish any spark of disagreement that might set off a greater conflagration, as had happened in 1914, the British intensified their pressure campaign on Prague to accede to the demands of the Sudeten Germans for virtual autonomy and even outright secession from Czechoslovakia. Convincing himself that Hitler would be satisfied with a resolution of the Sudeten issue, Neville Chamberlain threw himself into the pursuit of peace. He felt he was on the side of the angels.[12]

Unfortunately for Chamberlain, the Czech government, led by President Edvard Beneš, did not want to slice itself up into pieces at the behest of Adolf Hitler. While the government participated in negotiations with Henlein and the Sudeten Germans over their demands for greater autonomy, Beneš refused to consider the complete transfer of the territory to Germany, knowing that it would spell the destruction of the country. Facing a stalemate between Henlein and the Czech government, Chamberlain sent a British mission to close to the deal, led by the sixty-eight-year-old Lord Walter Runciman, a stodgy fixture of British governments going back to 1908 (he defeated Winston Churchill in the 1899 Oldham by-election, the first time Churchill ever stood for Parliament). Runciman's task was to make Beneš and the Czechs understand that if they did not give in, they would be abandoned by the West. William Shirer, the CBS radio journalists, watched Runciman and his entourage arrive in Prague in early August with a huge train of luggage and take rooms "at the town's swankiest hotel, the Alcron, where they have almost a whole floor." He characterized the visiting British dignitary as "a taciturn thin-lipped little man with a bald head so round that it looks like a misshapen egg. . . . Runciman's whole mission smells." In fact, it smelled of failure; Henlein was under orders from Hitler to agree to nothing, since a stalemate is just what Hitler wanted as he fueled the crisis. He ordered Henlein to have his men launch armed attacks on Czech police barracks and border guards in the Sudetenland, hoping to provoke some violent response that could serve as evidence of Czech barbarism toward the German minority. Runciman continued with his pantomime, meeting various officials and going nowhere in reaching a resolution. British military intelligence reported to the cabinet that Hitler's war plans were moving forward rapidly. Barring some dramatic breakthrough, war in late September seemed inevitable.[13]

On September 12, Hitler turned up the temperature even higher when he addressed the 10th Nazi Party Congress at Nuremberg, the theme of which was the celebration of "greater Germany" after the successful annexation of Austria. The rally had been under way since September 5, and Hitler's closing address formed the high point of the mass gathering. Even before Hitler spoke, observers noted that the talk about Czechoslovakia had shifted from seeking autonomy for the German-speaking minority to its complete absorption into the Reich. Amid flyovers of new German bomber aircraft, endless marches of goose-stepping soldiers, half-naked men doing calisthenics, and some two hundred thousand people shouting their loyalty, Hitler took the podium before the party faithful. He laid it on thick, speaking of "tortures and oppression" that the Sudeten Germans had endured, a "defenseless people" subjected to "slow extinction" and treated like "animals" by "an alien state" created by Versailles. Germany, he howled, would no longer accept "further oppression and persecution of these 3.5 million Germans!" No one, hearing what Shirer called "the poison in his voice," could have doubted Hitler's eagerness to resolve the Sudeten question by force of arms. (Among the many listeners was President Roosevelt, who tuned in on the radio from Jimmy's bedside in Rochester.)[14]

Digesting Hitler's performance at Nuremberg, Neville Chamberlain concluded that he must take the initiative in searching for a peace deal, lest a Czech-German war embroil all of Europe. He wrote to Hitler on

Hitler at the center of the vast Congress of the Nazi Party, September 12, 1938.
Roger Viollet via Getty Images

Hitler reviews the rank and file at Nuremberg with Reichsführer-SS Heinrich Himmler.
United States Holocaust Memorial Museum

September 14, asking if he could come visit him to discuss a negotiated settlement. Hitler accepted, which Chamberlain took as a sign that the Führer might be coaxed away from the warpath. A burst of supportive headlines in the British press boosted Chamberlain's confidence. The next day, September 15, the prime minister motored to the small Heston Airport west of London and boarded a silver Lockheed 10 Electra—an American-made twin-engine aircraft, similar to the one Amelia Earhart had attempted to fly around the world. Chamberlain flew to Munich, where upon landing he reviewed a smartly turned-out honor guard. In fact, it was composed of SS-Totenkopf (death's head) guards—the troops assigned to police concentration camps. He then boarded a special train for a three-hour journey to Berchtesgaden, to meet Hitler at the Berghof, his retreat in the Bavarian Alps.[15]

Hitler greeted Chamberlain on the steps of his chalet; Chamberlain later described Hitler as "the commonest little dog he had ever seen." But it was Chamberlain who was doing the begging. In so many words, he asked Hitler what he wanted; Hitler launched into a speech about the alleged slaughter of Germans in the Sudetenland by Czech police and border guards. "From his youth," he insisted, he had dreamed of uniting all Germans into one Reich. He wanted "racial unity," and to eliminate the "danger" that Czechoslovakia posed to Germany's security. "I am determined to settle it." Chamberlain said that while he would have to discuss the matter with the British cabinet, he himself "had nothing to say against the separation of the Sudeten Germans from the rest of Czechoslovakia," provided it could be done through some face-saving procedure. (In a letter to his sister Ida, he put it more coarsely: He "didn't care two hoots whether the Sudetens were in the Reich or out of it.") He then asked Hitler to "keep his people quiet" while he went back to London, spoke to his colleagues, and got the French in line. Chamberlain returned to England the next day and told the cabinet that Hitler's objectives were "strictly limited," and Hitler could be trusted to keep his word. The policy of appeasement, Chamberlain hoped, would soon lead to an amicable adjustment of the map of Europe and preserve peace for another generation.[16]

III

How did Roosevelt view these developments? Historians have debated the question for years: Did FDR favor appeasement, or at least some negotiation to pacify Europe? Or had he already made up his mind about the inevitable confrontation between fascism and democracy? Perhaps he simply wanted to steer clear of the whole mess? As is so often the case with Roosevelt, the evidence is patchy and open to interpretation. Although he said little publicly during the high-stakes face-off over Czechoslovakia, Roosevelt sifted information from a variety of sources: from his ambassadors in the American embassies, as well as from Hull and Welles in Washington; from his inner circle of trusted cabinet officials like Morgenthau and Ickes and Hopkins; and above all, from the press, which commented in depth on the Hitler-Chamberlain duel and its import. These sources often contradicted one another, unable to agree on the appropriate American response to the European situation. To guide him, FDR fell back on a few foundational ideas—his confidence in American power; his determination to defend democracy at home and bolster it overseas; his desire to keep the United States out of a *combat* role in any European conflict; and his sensitivity to the volatile American public debate about the fascist threat. These fixed points provided FDR with a kind of road map as he picked his way through the thicket of bad faith and deceit that produced the fateful Munich agreement of September 30, 1938. The evidence suggests that FDR did not want to be associated with British appeasement policy, which he expected would fail. But he saw its value as a means to buy time, so that the democratic states could prepare for the war he saw as all but inevitable.[17]

His key envoys to Europe generally supported Chamberlain's appeasement of Nazi Germany. They counseled Roosevelt to embrace the role of arbiter or peacemaker. This idea came mainly from the ambassador in France, William Bullitt. Since he began his tour at the embassy in Paris in October 1936, Bullitt had been pushing the idea of an American-brokered reconciliation between France and Germany. Profoundly anti-Communist, full of hate toward Stalin, who he considered an "Asiatic" despot with ambitions to seize all of Europe, Bullitt feared a European war would end with the hammer and sickle flying above every capital on the continent. Far better, he thought, to seek an anti-Soviet entente between Nazi Germany and France and perhaps Italy as well. The scheme revealed Bullitt's faulty reading of Nazism—Hitler, too, had ambitions to rule Europe—but he relentlessly pressed the idea on Roosevelt, writing of the "real chance" FDR had of bringing France and Germany together. He admitted that such a reconciliation would come at the expense of German domination of Eastern Europe, but he predicted that Germany would swallow Austria and Czechoslovakia anyway; conceding the Nazis a sphere of influence could open the way to a broader settlement.[18]

To strengthen his preferred policy of appeasement, Bullitt regularly sent Roosevelt messages about the dire state of the French air force, comparing it unfavorably with the German Luftwaffe. Bullitt used wildly inflated numbers on German aircraft production—the Nazis were building three hundred to five hundred planes a month, he said (he was wrong)—and depicted the French as totally incapable of matching the Germans. Although the French were planning to buy one hundred of the new American Curtiss P-36 Hawk fighter aircraft, these would not match German power in the air, Bullitt believed. He used this alleged air gap to beef up his argument for appeasement. He painted an apocalyptic picture of a war as "an unspeakable tragedy" for France, "the slaughter of the entire younger generation" of French youth, "the complete destruction of Western Europe, and Bolshevism from one end of the continent to the other." He predicted that "Paris would be destroyed by air raids" that would make Guernica "seem infantile by comparison." This tone of alarm and defeatism permeated all his memos in 1938, the better to drive Roosevelt toward accepting appeasement and German domination of central and eastern Europe. From the spring through the late summer, Bullitt advised FDR to step into the leadership vacuum in Europe and host a four-power conference—with Germany, Italy, France, and Britain—at which Czechoslovakia would be partitioned and a wider peace achieved through the recognition of German demands. In short, Bullitt wanted Roosevelt to play the role to which Neville Chamberlain aspired: architect of appeasement, blessed peacemaker, defender of Western civilization from the Red menace.[19]

Another source of pressure and advice came from the self-centered, publicity-seeking, ambitious ambassador to Great Britain, Joseph P. Kennedy. FDR appointed Kennedy to the Court of St. James partly as a return for Kennedy's financial support for his two presidential campaigns, and partly to get a dangerous political rival out of Washington. These were poor criteria to select an ambassador, however, and Kennedy soon disappointed the president. A self-made millionaire who considered himself an expert on financial matters, Kennedy believed that the key to world peace lay in American economic growth that would pull along the ailing European economies. War, by contrast, would gravely threaten Europe's economic health and open the path to totalitarian domination of the continent. Like Bullitt, Kennedy placed great stress on the need for some kind of general settlement with Germany and Italy. Arriving in London just as Hitler seized Austria, he quickly found favor among the British elite that supported Chamberlain's policy of appeasement. Kennedy liked Chamberlain, who he described as a "strong, decisive man," and believed that Germany would naturally secure a predominant position in eastern Europe. There was no point in fighting a senseless war to oppose this evolution of German power. "If Chamberlain is successful," Kennedy wrote to FDR, "he will be a hero."[20]

Kennedy underwrote Chamberlain's appeasement policy by emphasizing to his British hosts the distance of the United States from European concerns.

Just a day after Secretary Hull delivered the March 17 address denouncing isolationism, Kennedy gave his maiden speech as ambassador to a gathering of royals and cabinet ministers at a dinner hosted by the Pilgrim Society, a group dedicated to Anglo-American friendship. Kennedy stated frankly that if war broke out in Europe, America would stay out. "The average American has little interest in the details of foreign affairs," he said, and the U.S. government would not get involved in overseas quarrels. "Nothing constructive can be built on false hopes and fears," he firmly stated to his British audience; no one should expect America to help Europe out of its troubles. Americans "oppose any entangling alliance," and will be guided only by the national interest. "Economic appeasement" and a restoration of trade, he stressed, were the key to international peace. Secretary of State Hull had seen a draft of this speech and asked Kennedy to tone it down, striking out the sentence, "The United States . . . has no plans to seek or offer assistance in the event of war." But Kennedy reinforced the impression that the United States remained firmly disengaged from Europe in its foreign policy and he viewed Chamberlain's policy as sensible. Writing to columnist Arthur Krock, Kennedy said that "Germany will get whatever it wants in Czechoslovakia." Why not meet German demands at the conference table rather than on the battlefield?[21]

Along with Bullitt and Kennedy, the new ambassador in Berlin, Hugh Wilson, also pressed the case for appeasement. A career diplomat who had done a long stint in Switzerland and then served briefly as an assistant secretary of state in Washington, Wilson replaced the rather sad figure of William Dodd. Professor Dodd, because of his fierce anti-Nazi opinions as well as his talent for alienating everyone from leading Nazis to members of his own staff, was pushed out of his post in December 1937. He was the victim of a vigorous campaign for his ouster by William Bullitt, who felt Dodd inhibited any chance of mending fences with the Nazis. Roosevelt seemed to like Dodd's perceptive missives, which laid bare the bestial nature of the Third Reich with an honesty few of his envoys emulated. But Dodd was indeed a caustic, embittered man and had become a source of genuine irritation to the Germans. FDR was persuaded by Bullitt and Sumner Welles to replace him with Wilson, who arrived in Berlin on the eve of the Anschluss.[22]

Wilson took the view that the United States should avoid controversy, remain aloof from the passions of the Europeans, avoid criticizing Germany publicly, and generally pour oil on troubled waters. Arriving in Berlin, Wilson expressed admiration for all Hitler had achieved, especially his economic recovery program. He was charmed by the stimulating Joseph Goebbels, and he told FDR that Hitler was an "artist" and an intuitive leader of rare qualities. He described Hermann Göring to the president as a man of "iron will, ruthless determination, brutal frankness, and underneath it a certain likeableness." He reported to Washington that the Anschluss was an enormous success for Hitler, that the Führer enjoyed the absolute loyalty of the people, and that Germany had become "indubitably the most powerful nation on the continent." Wilson generally considered that Jews in America—who he alleged controlled much of the U.S. press—had made U.S.-German relations difficult by stirring up hatred of the Nazi government. And he believed that public haranguing of the Nazis in the U.S. press distracted from the basic fact that Americans were overwhelmingly opposed "to support any policy of military aid to any country of Europe." On the eve of the Czech crisis of September, Wilson counseled the head of the German Foreign Ministry, Ernst von Weizsäcker, to show just a little patience, because Hitler could gain virtually everything he wanted through negotiation rather than war—precisely the argument Neville Chamberlain had made to Hitler.[23]

In promoting appeasement, Bullitt, Kennedy, and Wilson were heavily influenced by what they had learned about the German air force from the aviator Charles Lindbergh. As a mere twenty-five-year-old, Lindbergh in 1927 became the first person to fly across the Atlantic, from New York to Paris. This feat earned him a place in the pantheon of American heroes. He was promoted to the rank of colonel in the Air Corps Reserve, awarded the Medal of Honor, and acclaimed by millions. Following the fatal kidnapping of his son, Charles Jr., and the subsequent trial of the accused kidnapper that generated immense and distressing publicity, Lindbergh and his wife, Anne, moved to England in 1936, and then to a small, isolated island off the coast of Brittany, France. He remained deeply interested in aviation, however, and in May 1936, the U.S. military attaché in Berlin—Truman Smith, the very same man who in 1924 had reported to Washington about the then-unknown right-wing nationalist Adolf Hitler—asked Lindbergh if he would like to tour German aircraft plants and inspect some of the new planes the Germans were building. Smith, guessing that the Germans would welcome having such

Aviator Charles Lindbergh at the peak of his fame in 1927.
Library of Congress

a world-famous figure observe their sophisticated aviation program, got the Germans to extend an invitation.[24]

In late July, just on the eve of the Berlin Olympics, Lindbergh flew to Berlin and went on an extensive tour of German aircraft plants. He received a lavish welcome from the Nazi government, including a meeting with the Luftwaffe chief Hermann Göring. "I cannot help liking the Germans," Lindbergh would write later in his diary. "They are like our own people." He saw the new Heinkel medium bomber He-111 at the Heinkel factories at Rostock. At the Junker factory in Dessau, he inspected the new medium bomber Ju-86, as well as the new "Stuka" dive bomber Ju-87. He was deeply impressed and concluded that Germany could produce more and better planes than any country in the world. In October 1937, Lindbergh returned for a second trip, and was able to inspect the new Luftwaffe fighter, the Messerschmitt 109, at the Rechlin testing facility sixty miles northwest of Berlin. After this visit, he and Smith co-wrote a report for U.S. Army Intelligence in which they concluded that "Germany is once more a world power in the air." By contrast, when he toured British aircraft factories in the spring of 1938, he expressed contempt for the lack of progress and innovation he found. "God! How they will have to pay for it in the next war," he noted in his diary.[25]

Lindbergh's assessments reached Roosevelt as early as February 1938, sent by Joe Kennedy to the president even before Kennedy had taken up his role as ambassador. According to Lindbergh, the German aircraft industry was "without parallel." The Germans were now "the strongest air power in Europe," and their factories were capable of churning out hundreds of planes a month, he believed. On May 5, 1938, Lindbergh met both Joe Kennedy and William Bullitt at Cliveden, the grand Buckinghamshire estate of Lady Nancy Astor, where Lindbergh and his wife were often guests, and they discussed aviation and the general European scene. Soon after, Kennedy reported to Hull that Germany could defeat its enemies in thirty days and was "building an air force designed to demolish London completely in one fell swoop." In June, Bullitt and Lindbergh again discussed the state of the French air force, with Lindbergh concluding that France could not "even put up a show in case of war." He had been told by Bullitt that Communists had thoroughly infiltrated the French air corps. In early September, Bullitt arranged for Lindbergh to meet with the French minister responsible for the air force, Guy la Chambre, who confessed that France could only build forty-five planes a month against Germany's pace of five hundred to eight hundred a month. Any French-German war now would be "suicide" for France, Lindbergh believed.[26]

IV

Appeasement reflected the British sense of vulnerability to German military power, and it also grew from a genuine desire to avoid the terrible slaughter of war. Yet Roosevelt remained uneasy about it. Possibly he leaned more toward the views of another envoy overseas, John Cudahy, ambassador to Ireland, a headstrong former soldier and real-estate developer who Roosevelt had patronized with a diplomatic appointment to Poland in 1933. There he honed his dislike of both Russia and Nazi Germany; after taking up his new post in Ireland, he grew hostile to the British as well. After the Anschluss, Cudahy told Roosevelt that "Chamberlain's is the most weak, vacillating, humiliating policy England has ever presented. It is a drifting, not a policy at all." The long-standing British aim of promoting a balance of power in Europe had been discarded when Britain let Germany gobble up Austria without even a mild protest. "Now there is no balance on the continent. . . . There is no leadership to oppose the dictators." Chamberlain's policy was not only immoral but fundamentally bad geopolitics, Cudahy argued. And no one penned more sulfurous missives to Roosevelt than Claude Bowers, still lobbying hard and in vain for aid to the Spanish Republicans. He called Chamberlain's foreign policy "the most dishonorable and treacherous, antidemocratic and deceptive in the history of England for a century."[27]

These criticisms resonated with FDR. He believed that Germany could not be appeased; its ambitions were unlimited, he felt, as indeed were those of Japan. These were aggressive powers whose appetites would only grow with every meal they made of the smaller, weaker powers. Furthermore, Roosevelt disliked appeasement in part because he disliked Neville Chamberlain and thought him dishonorable, or "slippery," as he put it to Henry Morgenthau and Cordell Hull at the start of September. "You could not trust him [Chamberlain] under any circumstances"—a remarkably dismissive verdict. FDR felt that "Chamberlain was interested in peace at any price if he could get away with it and save his face," and he would ask for American support for his policy, so that if appeasement failed, Britain alone would not have to bear the blame. Sensing a trap, Roosevelt refused to give Chamberlain any encouragement.[28]

But there was another angle. Roosevelt's sixth sense for the domestic politics of foreign policy made him sensitive throughout the crisis to the air of shame that hung over Chamberlain's initial approach to Hitler on September 14. Coming just two days after Hitler's poisonous address at the Nuremberg rally, the humble request of the British prime minister, leader of the world's greatest empire, for an audience with a gutter gangster like Hitler shocked American public opinion. "Chamberlain Visit Stuns Reich," as one headline put it. "Nazi chests swelled with pride," a reporter in Berlin wrote of the prime minister's request to meet the Führer. "Nazis celebrated tonight what they regarded as a big victory," noted Sigrid Schultz in Berlin. Chamberlain's overture to Hitler appeared to the *New York Times* editorial page as a "breathtaking" and "unconventional" gesture. Only time would tell whether it was "a supreme stroke of imaginative statesmanship or a spectacular admission of desperation." Either way, Chamberlain's offer to broker a peace deal transformed Hitler from law-breaking outcast into "the arbiter, or co-arbiter, of Europe," signaling Britain's fear of Nazi Germany as a great power.[29]

Privately, Harold Ickes expressed a sentiment surely shared by Roosevelt: "the once proud lion seems now to have its tail thrust firmly between its legs," he wrote in his diary, as the British prime minister stooped to beg for an audience with "the ex-corporal, ex-house painter." Chamberlain had brought "humiliation" to Britain, as Ickes saw it. Even the editorial page of the *Chicago Tribune*, which applauded Chamberlain's visit, acknowledged that the prime minister had to surrender his "dignity and prestige" to travel to Hitler's doorstep. Not surprisingly, Roosevelt made no public statement of support for Chamberlain's visit to Berchtesgaden.[30]

Press coverage of Chamberlain's September 15 trip—and Roosevelt would have paid very careful attention to such reporting—was unflattering to all involved. A narrative took hold, depicting the courageous Czechs, abandoned by their friends, trying to survive the onslaught of a vicious Nazi bully. According to news reports from Prague, the Czechs, worn and exhausted from months of facing down the threats of Henlein and his Sudeten secessionists, were shattered by the blow Chamberlain had delivered: "There was no concealing the conviction," as one reporter in Prague put it, "that the British premier had gone to Berchtesgaden to sell out Czechoslovakia." Meanwhile, Hitler was described as "flattered" by the prime minister's visit, while Chamberlain granted Hitler recognition as an equal—the very thing "Germany has wanted more than anything else." However laudable his desire for peace, Chamberlain appeared willing to join with Hitler in slicing up a small, sovereign nation to achieve it.[31]

On September 16, Roosevelt convened the cabinet. The president did not yet know exactly what Chamberlain had proposed to Hitler at Berchtesgaden; Chamberlain was back in London working with a French delegation to hammer out an offer to take back to the Nazi leader. As Ickes recorded it, Roosevelt repeated his view that "Chamberlain is for peace at any price."

If war comes, Czechoslovakia will be "left by these supposed allies to paddle its own canoe." The president expected that Poland and Hungary would join in the feast and grab contested portions of the prostrate country. With Czechoslovakia dismembered, "England and France . . . will wash the blood from their Judas Iscariot hands," he told the cabinet. Accepting that Czechoslovakia's fate was sealed, Roosevelt's thoughts ran to the question of how Germany could be beaten in a larger war. He guessed that a combination of a naval blockade and aerial bombing, which would shatter German morale, could bring the Germans to their knees. He also seemed confident that Britain and France, if they fought, would be able to purchase all the matériel they needed in America, where they held significant gold supplies and assets. In a long struggle, he asserted, the democracies, sustained by American economic might, could outlast the dictatorships.[32]

Chamberlain, however, was moving in precisely the opposite direction. On September 19, the world learned the details of what he and Édouard Daladier had concocted in their London meetings. It was a shocking surrender to Hitler's demands, surpassing even the dreams of Konrad Henlein and his Sudeten Germans. The French and British governments proposed that Czechoslovakia transfer to Germany all districts where Germans made up more than 50 percent of the population; an international body of some kind would redraw the boundaries and possibly oversee the movement of affected populations (i.e., the forcible expulsion of non-German Czechs from the areas to be turned over); and in return for this sacrifice, the British and French governments would offer an "international guarantee of the new boundaries of the Czechoslovak State against unprovoked aggression." As payment for this bounty, Hitler would give exactly nothing, except his word to refrain from invading what remained of Czechoslovakia.[33]

Officials in Prague reacted with "incredulity," while in Berlin, Germans reveled in "another victory for Reichsführer Hitler," in fact, "the greatest diplomatic victory of his career." The U.S. national press saw the Anglo-French proposal as "a completely humiliating defeat;" "the beginning of the end of the British Empire;" "a betrayal;" "the great surrender;" and in any case unlikely to stop Germany's further expansion. Dorothy Thompson, who had been writing about the crisis in an increasingly anxious tone, said that Britain and France "had decided to throw the last democratic republic east of the Rhine into the jaws of the Nazis." And as she rightly pointed out, by giving in to German demands that German-speaking Czechs should be grouped into the Reich, the democracies "have aligned themselves on the side of the racial theories of Hitler." Law and national sovereignty were meaningless now; only race mattered.[34]

On this same day, as FDR read the shocking headlines and mused over what appeared to be a complete Western surrender in the face of Hitler's demands, he held an extraordinary conversation with the British ambassador, Sir Ronald Lindsay. A career diplomat with wide service abroad and in Whitehall, Lindsay had been ambassador in Washington since 1930 and was the dean of the diplomatic corps. He knew Roosevelt well, and just as important, he understood American public opinion and the constraints it placed on FDR's freedom of action. Still, it was remarkable for Roosevelt to call Lindsay on the phone and ask to see him immediately for what turned into a "long conversation" under conditions of "absolute secrecy." Roosevelt told Lindsay he would not even tell the State Department about the talk. Lindsay sent a report back to London at 2:30 a.m. the following morning summarizing the astonishing conversation.

The president began by stating his belief that the Anglo-French proposal—which the morning newspapers had thoroughly covered—asked for the Czechs to make "a terrible remorseless sacrifice" and would "provoke a highly unfavorable reaction in America." He went on to say that while he himself would forbear from any criticism, and while he sincerely hoped Chamberlain's policy would work to avoid war, he expected that war was imminent. In fact, he anticipated that the Czechs would refuse the proposal, fight to defend their country, "and be overrun in three weeks." Even if the Czechs gave in and accepted the cannibalizing of their state, Germany would not stop there: "other demands would follow," Roosevelt said. One way or another, FDR believed that the European democracies would be at war with Germany and Italy "sooner or later, but as he thought, sooner." That amounted to a fairly direct repudiation of appeasement.

Roosevelt now came to the point—as he put it, "the very secret part of his communication" whose contents must not be shared with anyone. He believed that when war came, England, France, and Russia, even if they joined together, could not defeat Germany through a ground offensive into the Reich. The only way to win was through a combination of naval blockade and bombing. And here, the United States could help. A war by blockade that relied mainly on sea power to contain Germany and Italy—Lindsay thought FDR had in mind the "quarantine" idea from the Chicago speech—would find popular support in the United States, Roosevelt said. It could be conducted on "humanitarian" grounds and did not involve sending U.S. troops to Europe. Under the Neutrality Act, the president could forbid U.S. vessels from sailing into a war zone, which effectively gave him the power to halt commerce with the enemy. While under the law, the U.S. could not sell munitions directly to combatants, FDR felt "free to export parts of munitions to Canada to be set up there." Better yet, if the Western powers did not declare war on Germany at all—"let them be called defensive measures or anything plausible but avoid actual declaration of war"—the president need not invoke the Neutrality Act at all. Roosevelt pointed out that so far, he had been able to skirt the issue in the undeclared China-Japan conflict. In such circumstances, Lindsay reported, Roosevelt believed that "prohibition of export of arms need not be applied to us." There was a loophole in the American law Roosevelt hoped the British would exploit.

This remarkable discussion with the British ambassador reveals FDR's strategic thinking at this moment. War, he plainly believed, was coming; he wanted to help Britain and France fight it; and there were ways of doing so, provided America's constraints were taken into account. Roosevelt may have been trying to buck up the British leaders and put a bit of backbone into them; but more likely, he wanted the British to know how America would respond to an all but inevitable war with Nazi Germany, whatever the outcome of the Czech crisis. When war came, Roosevelt wanted the British to know that America would help. He was, Lindsay wrote in his report, "quite alive to the possibility . . . that the United States might again find themselves involved in a European war," and it was even conceivable that "an American army might be sent overseas." That was a wildly risky message to share with the ambassador and explains why FDR stated at the outset of the discussion that if his ideas leaked to the press, "he would almost certainly be impeached."[35]

Roosevelt was wrong in one piece of his analysis: the Czech government, after an agonizing series of meetings, decided to accept the Anglo-French proposal rather than fight the Germans alone. President Beneš, seeing his great-power allies betray him, consulted with his military chiefs and got the bad news. They told him that with no allies, fighting alone, the country could hold out for three weeks at most against the Germans. Beneš gave in and accepted the terms of the proposal rather than force his country to endure certain destruction. Upon hearing this news, people in Prague stopped in their tracks, unable to believe it. One reporter saw men and women in tears, "tears of rage because they had been deserted by their allies and tears of humiliation because they had surrendered without firing a shot." A huge, silent crowd soon formed, pouring across the Charles Bridge toward the Prague Castle where the government was still meeting. The people stood mutely, defiantly, until Beneš briefly addressed them, urging calm. The Information Ministry issued a sharper statement, saying that the government had accepted the terms imposed on them to avoid bloodshed. "We make no reproaches to those who have deserted us. History will condemn them." It concluded sadly, "all is not lost and somehow we will keep our country." The mass of assembled people, said one observer, made "an unforgettable spectacle of a nation stricken down in peacetime, moved with great sorrow and vast anger." It was a humiliating surrender, and it would leave the rest of Czechoslovakia terribly vulnerable to a later German attack, though at least for now, a bloodletting had been avoided.[36]

Chamberlain, it seemed, had won the day; appeasement had delivered, and the Czechs would pay the price for a European peace. It would be strong medicine, but it would cure the war fever, Chamberlain thought. On September 22, certain that his great gamble had paid off, Chamberlain cheerfully headed back to Germany to work out the details of the agreement, flying this time to Cologne to meet Hitler at Bad Godesberg, a small town along the Rhine. Hitler often used the luxury hotel there called the Rheinhotel Dreesen; in June 1934, he plotted the murderous events of the "night of the long knives" here, so it was an appropriate setting to consider the carve-up of the Czech state.

But now Chamberlain learned what it really meant to rely on the word of a sociopathic dictator. For no sooner did Chamberlain arrive at Bad Godesberg than he discovered that Hitler rejected the deal. "No, I am very sorry, but it won't work anymore," he casually said to a stunned Chamberlain. The assaults on Germans in the Sudetenland were intensifying, he insisted, and a solution could no longer be delayed. He wanted immediate action. Instead of accepting the gradual transfer of majority-German portions of the Sudetenland to Germany, Hitler now demanded the complete transfer of the entire region to Germany within six days; following this transfer, a plebiscite would be held within two months (under the watchful eye of German authorities, naturally) to demonstrate the desire of the population there to join the Reich. The entire Sudeten area must be handed over intact, with no destruction or removal of military, economic, or agricultural infrastructure. He also insisted that territorial demands by Poland and Hungary for their slices of the Czech state would also have to be met. And if the Czechs did not agree to this new ultimatum by October 1, German armed forces would seize the region by force (and very likely keep going all the way to Prague).[37]

It was a shocking act of bad faith. Hitler clearly sought a rupture in the talks that he could blame on the Czechs, allowing him to unleash his military attack. Chamberlain, dumbstruck, suddenly saw his triumphant achievement, his brilliant gamble, snatched from his hands. He said to Hitler in a revealing moment of desperation that he "had got exactly what the Führer wanted and without the expenditure of a drop of German blood. In doing so, he had been obliged to take his political life into his hands." His legacy as a peacemaker, the vindication of his policy of appeasement, lay it tatters. Hitler seemed determined to have his war, and where that might lead, no one could tell.[38]

The Czechs, showing considerable sangfroid, rejected this new set of demands. In part, they calculated that the French and British would have to stand with them now that Hitler had brushed aside a reasonable settlement. The Czech army mobilized and a million well-trained and determined troops went into the line, ready for a German assault. The French government at last found its footing and announced it would not accept Hitler's diktat. Chamberlain skulked backed to London to meet with his gloomy and angry cabinet colleagues who now felt the sting of shame at being treated so shabbily by Hitler. At least half a dozen members of the government threatened to resign if Chamberlain tried to accommodate Hitler's new round of demands. One of those, the First Lord of the Admiralty Duff Cooper, wrote in his diary that "Hitler has cast a spell over Neville." Even Foreign Secretary Lord Halifax, whose moribund conscience suddenly showed signs of life, now argued that Britain had gone far enough. It was time to call Hitler's bluff and reject his latest demonstration of deceit. The Foreign Office released a robust statement that if Germany should attack Czechoslovakia, France would be bound to respond, and Britain would "certainly stand by France." The Admiralty put the Royal Navy on alert while workers in London began distributing gas masks, digging trenches, and filling sandbags. War loomed, just days away.[39]

V

Roosevelt's hunch that war would come sooner rather than later seemed fully vindicated. And when it came, he expected the results would be horrifying. On the evening of September 22, the day Chamberlain went to Godesberg, FDR received a fresh report from Ambassador Kennedy about the unpreparedness of the British for the coming air war. Kennedy, who had been seeing a good deal of Charles Lindbergh, had again asked the aviator to set down on paper his assessment of the situation. Kennedy sent this to Hull and asked him to pass it on to Roosevelt. Lindbergh described the German air fleet as "stronger than that of any other country in the world," and greater than all the European countries combined. Germany could produce twenty thousand aircraft a year, he guessed, and the Nazis "now have the means of destroying London, Paris, and Prague." The French air force was "pitiful," and the British little better. "For the first time in history, a nation has the power either to save or to ruin the great cities of Europe. . . . England and France are far too weak to protect themselves." Ambassador Kennedy seems to have leaked this memo to the press, for the next day the newspapers amplified the story: "Germany Is Reported to Have 10,000 Planes Ready for War," announced a breaking story in the *New York Times*. Although we now know that Lindbergh's figures were wrong and massively overstated—Germany had about 1,670 first-line aircraft available for use at the time of the Munich crisis—who could contradict the world's best-known aviation expert? The Germans evidently were so pleased by Lindbergh's assessment of their strength that the following month, Hermann Goering bestowed the Service Cross of the German Eagle on the American aviator—an award Lindbergh, tone-deaf to the growing outrage toward Germany, accepted with pleasure.[40]

When Roosevelt met with the cabinet the next day, September 23, he reviewed the European situation, only vaguely aware that the conversation between Chamberlain and Hitler at Godesberg had gone so badly. FDR made clear his "desire to avoid any embroilment in European quarrels," but as Ickes noted in his diary, the president wanted "to be ready for whatever may happen." The State Department prepared a memo for this meeting that suggested the Czechs would probably fight rather than submit to Germany even if the French and British abandoned them. Anticipating the possibility of a large-scale war on the continent, FDR's remarks show his confidence in the collective strength of the democracies. Britain and France could "bottle up" the Axis powers with a sea blockade while waging "a defensive war," the president told the cabinet. The problem remained "the overwhelming preponderance of Germany and Italy in the air." But the British had plenty of financial assets on deposit in America and had begun "a large program in Canada for buying and assembling munitions of war." This was the scheme he had floated to Ambassador Lindsay, that "even if we had to enforce our neutrality laws, there would be a large outlet by such methods for munitions to flow toward England and France by way of Canada." Roosevelt clearly intended to take measures short of war to help the democracies.[41]

The scene darkened on the twenty-fourth as telegrams arrived with details of the extreme new demands made by Hitler at Godesberg. Compromise seemed ever more out of reach. With his mind focused on how he would justify to the public the kind of aid program he had in mind, Roosevelt fastened on to an idea proposed by Ambassador Bullitt: "I am certain," Bullitt wrote that day, "that in the long run all Americans will feel that some effort by our government is essential even though the effort may prove to be a failure." Bullitt reiterated his favorite idea, convening a major conference of heads of state at a neutral site like The Hague "to discuss ways and means to preserve European peace." Roosevelt had waved off a gesture like this previously; now he thought it might have some merit. The following day, he and a team from the State Department drafted an appeal to Hitler, Chamberlain, Daladier, and Czech president Edvard Beneš, asking them to consider the "unspeakable horror" of war and to return to the negotiating table in search of a peaceful settlement. The message contained no offer of American arbitration, as Bullitt had wanted, and merely exhorted the parties to keep talking. It seems plausible that the message had a domestic audience, for if war came now, at least the president could say he did everything to halt it.[42]

While Roosevelt worked on this message in the White House, a prominent group of public figures held a major rally of twenty thousand people at New York's Madison Square Garden on the evening of September 25 in support of Czechoslovakia. It featured a who's who of the anti-fascist cause in America, including journalists Dorothy Thompson, John Gunther, Heywood Broun, and Jay Allen—people who had been raising their voices for years against the threat of Nazism. They were joined by church leaders, peace activists, and representatives of the Czech American community, and they all spoke earnestly in defense of plucky Czechoslovakia. But one figure captured the hearts of all in attendance: the German novelist Thomas Mann, recipient of the 1929 Nobel Prize in Literature, who had fled Germany in 1933 for Switzerland and become an outspoken critic of Nazism. "Hitler must fall," Mann said to an immense uproar of support from the crowd. And he sounded a note of fierce defiance that caught the spirit of the meeting. "I always loved peace and detested war. I detest it even today. But I feel that it would be a shame and an infamy if Europe and the world would accept without resistance this misdeed against a gentle little country which wishes to save civilization and freedom and which would be dismembered and delivered to slavery." Appeasing Hitler by destroying the Czech state was "a fatal mistake" and he was heartened that finally the great powers seemed ready to defy Hitler. No one would want to live in a "distorted and dishonored world" that allowed Hitler to act with impunity against peaceful, sovereign states.[43]

Mann's sentiments were echoed by other public figures in these anxious days: It was time to resist Hitler's fanaticism. Raymond Leslie Buell, the president of the Foreign Policy Association—a venerable internationalist organization that had been founded to advocate for American membership in the League of Nations—published an opinion piece on September 16 that laid out a plan to stop Hitler. "There is only one means of escaping from this dismal future" of Nazi domination, he wrote. "This is for the liberal powers to increase their military and economic forces until they have a clear superiority over the totalitarian dictatorships." Once unified and well-armed, making clear that the dictators could never prevail, then the democratic states could offer to address legitimate grievances at the negotiating table. This could work only if the United States participated. "The surest way to keep from being pulled into war," Buell concluded in words that would eventually take root in Roosevelt's mind, "is for us to use our vast power in averting the outbreak of conflict." Peace came through strength, Buell argued, not through neutrality and disarmament.[44]

Buell was not alone in laying the groundwork for a shift in American foreign policy. In a scathing editorial titled "Speaking of Betrayals," the *Washington Post* editorial page indicted America for two decades of diplomatic isolation which were to blame for Britain's policy of appeasement. The Neutrality Acts "told Hitler that when he gets ready to invade Czechoslovakia, we will draw no distinctions whatsoever between Germany and her victim." Americans made it plain to the world that "there is no cause, short of invasion of our own territory, for which we are willing to make a positive stand." Since the 1920s, this editorial continued, U.S. diplomacy had compiled a record "without parallel for pusillanimity, moral cowardice, and stupidity," making America "a country at which Hitler can—and does—contemptuously thumb his nose." This piece triggered a torrent of supportive articles to the *Post*'s offices, with writers calling for America to back the Czechs and defy Hitler. "Readers Favor a Strong Foreign Policy," declared the headline. There was a shift of tone in the air.[45]

In this atmosphere of mounting anger at Nazi Germany and intensifying scorn for appeasement, Hitler threw more fuel on the fire by delivering a strident, bellicose broadcast on Monday, September 26, at the Berlin Sportpalast before thousands of deranged and delirious Nazis that attempted to shift the blame for war onto the Czech president, Edvard Beneš. Germany had made a proposal for rightful and just transfer of Germans now in captivity in Czechoslovakia to the Reich, Hitler insisted; it was for Beneš to decide if the Sudetenland would go to Germany by war or by negotiation. As Germany's "first soldier," however, Hitler bellowed that he would never yield in protecting Germans—wherever they might live. He seemed entirely to have settled upon war on the first of October, and it would be the fault of the Czechs for not allowing Germans the right of self-determination. To Harold Ickes and the cabinet, "war seemed to be inevitable, with every tick of the clock bringing it closer."[46]

Hitler's framing of the crisis needed an immediate contradiction, and on Tuesday, September 27, Neville Chamberlain gave a radio address that sought to specify where the blame lay. Quite exhausted by this time, and fairly certain that his efforts had failed, he mused in a quiet voice that he found it "horrible, fantastic, incredible that we should be digging trenches and trying on gas masks here because of a quarrel in a faraway country between people of whom we know nothing." More peculiar, he said, was that the quarrel had already been settled in principle and now was just a matter of timing. Surely there lay some great misunderstanding beneath Hitler's refusal to accept the plan as it had been offered to him at Godesberg. But in any case, Chamberlain concluded, "I can see nothing further I can usefully do in the way of mediation." These were the words of a defeated man.[47]

Chamberlain's address aired in America at 2 p.m. on Tuesday the twenty-seventh and precipitated two actions by President Roosevelt. Almost immediately, he sent off a private telegram to Mussolini, urging him to intercede with Hitler to resume negotiations and avoid war. Mussolini in fact had been the target of appeals by the British government, too, for it was known that although he promised to stand by Hitler, he did want to risk a general war in Europe. FDR's cable went to the embassy in Rome, arriving well after business hours. Curiously, Ambassador William Phillips had chosen this grave moment to travel with his wife and daughter to Florence for a few days to stay at the magnificent villa of the steel tycoon and presidential envoy Myron Taylor. FDR's cable for Il Duce therefore sat all night in the embassy telegraph room, undelivered. Not until the next afternoon did Phillips arrive back in Rome and rush the message over to Mussolini's office.[48]

While Phillips luxuriated in Florence, Roosevelt, on the afternoon of the twenty-seventh, called a special cabinet meeting to discuss whether he ought now to intervene in the Czech crisis with some personal gesture of mediation. He had already sent one message to Hitler urging the Europeans to keep negotiating; this had prompted a long, boring screed from the Führer rehearsing the evils of Versailles. Should FDR try again? According to Harold Ickes, "no one, even the president, believed that another message would have any effect. It was clear that what he had in mind was the importance of clarifying the issue so that if war started, there could be no doubt in the mind of anyone as to who was responsible for starting it." That was Roosevelt's view, too. At ten o'clock that evening, Roosevelt sent another plea to Hitler, echoing Chamberlain's radio address: "Agreement in principle has already been reached" between Germany and Czechoslovakia; their differences were mainly over timing of the transfer of Sudeten territory. Surely, with a settlement so close, negotiations should continue, FDR suggested. Americans "demand that the voice of their government be raised again and yet again to avert and to avoid war." This appeal, arriving in Berlin in the early hours of September 28, was an empty gesture designed mainly for American consumption. Hitler did not bother to answer it.[49]

Nor did FDR's message to Mussolini matter. By the time Ambassador Phillips arrived at Mussolini's office on the afternoon of the twenty-eighth, the picture had changed completely. Il Duce told the ambassador that at the urging of the British government, he had already reached out to Berlin and urged Hitler to convene a four-power meeting to reach a negotiated settlement to the Czech crisis, and Hitler had accepted. "There was to be a meeting in Munich tomorrow," Mussolini told the crestfallen Phillips, who now must have realized that he had failed the president in waiting almost twenty-four hours to deliver his message. For a time, Roosevelt did not know about the delay and boasted that his crucial intervention had led the dictators to step back from the brink. But Phillips had dropped the ball (and covered up his fumble in his memoirs).[50]

It may have been just as well that Roosevelt could claim no responsibility for the events of the subsequent days. What unfolded contained a lifetime of pathos and drama, ending in tragedy. Neville Chamberlain, the tired and strained leader, trudged into the House of Commons on the afternoon of September 28 to report on his failed peace efforts. While concluding his remarks, he received a hastily written notice of Hitler's invitation to Munich to continue negotiations and avoid war. Sharing this welcome news, Chamberlain broke out into a hugely relieved smile and the House erupted in thundering, full-throated cheers. The reversal was complete, and Chamberlain once again became the hero of the hour.[51]

Why did Hitler change his mind, and agree to return to the negotiating table? Many pressures converged on him. The sudden firmness from the great powers, pointing to a big war rather than Hitler's preferred swift strike at Czechoslovakia; the doubts long expressed by his military commanders about the difficulties of fighting their way through the Czech defenses, as well as the vulnerability of western Germany to a simultaneous French attack; the dilapidated German navy having to face a British blockade; the strong opposition of his Italian ally to a war that could easily embroil the continent; and the realization that Britain was offering to serve up the valuable Sudetenland prize for free, without a risk of any kind, allowing Hitler to snap up a much weakened Czech state at a later time: All this finally tipped the balance.[52]

Upon receiving an eyewitness account of the day's events in Parliament from Joe Kennedy, FDR cabled immediately to Chamberlain a two-word congratulatory message: "Good man." This curious message suggests FDR's relief that war might be delayed, even avoided. Perhaps, too, it signaled his grudging respect for the "slippery" prime minister who genuinely had given all of himself for his cause. On the early afternoon of September 29, at the hideously ugly Nazi headquarters building in Munich, Chamberlain, Daladier, Mussolini, and Hitler convened. In a strained atmosphere, with only Mussolini (who relished his role as middleman) enjoying the proceedings, they finalized the agreement that would slice off the Sudetenland and hand it over to Germany. The Czechs were not invited to attend, the assumption being that if for some reason they refused to accept the dismemberment of their state, they would be destroyed by the Germans and no one would lift a finger in their defense. Indeed, Chamberlain asked Hitler that, if the Czechs should be "mad enough to refuse" the terms of the Munich deal and resist a German invasion, could the Führer at least promise not to carpet bomb Prague, killing women and children? Hitler assured the prime minister that he would "always try to spare the civilian population," and chillingly said, "he hated the thought of little babies being killed by gas bombs." Chamberlain "thanked Herr Hitler" for his promise.[53]

In the early hours of September 30, the Munich agreement was signed, and war averted. The deal won a bit more time—ten days—for the Czechs to evacuate the Sudetenland, and it kept alive a role for an international commission to set the precise future boundaries of the mauled rump of the Czech state. At the last moment, Chamberlain won from Hitler an additional promissory note: a piece of paper stating that Britain and Germany agreed never to go to war with each other—a sop to Chamberlain so that he would not return to England empty-handed. This was the paper he waved aloft when clambering down from his airplane at Heston airfield on the afternoon of September 30, declaring he had secured "peace for our time." The name "Munich" would go down in history as a moment of craven surrender and shameful weakness. For now, however, most Europeans welcomed the news with relief and joy. Neville Chamberlain returned home to the hero's welcome for which he desperately yearned.[54]

VI

Franklin Roosevelt did not have much impact on Munich, but Munich had an enormous impact on him, and on American statecraft. For five and a half years, FDR had promoted disarmament and neutrality, even after he had lost confidence in these measures to arrest the drift toward global war. Munich was the moment when FDR pivoted away from those policies. He recognized the need for a sharp change of course. The weakness of the democracies had invited and enabled Hitler's assault on the political order in Europe. As William Bullitt put it in a message to the president, "The moral is: if you have enough airplanes, you don't have to go to Berchtesgaden." The larger strategic meaning of this bon mot was obvious now to Roosevelt: In a contest between democracy and fascism, strength must match strength. War seemed likely now, and soon; the democracies were unready for it; and only prompt American aid could help stem the fascist tide. While Neville Chamberlain spoke of peace for our time after Munich, Roosevelt prepared for war.[55]

He was not alone in drawing such dire conclusions from the events of September. In Britain, amid the cheering for Chamberlain's achievement at Munich, a small but determined chorus of dissenters raised their voices against it. Duff Cooper, First Lord of the Admiralty, chose this moment to resign, and in the House of Commons called the British conciliation of Hitler "treachery and perfidy." Clement Attlee, the leader of the opposition Labour Party, stated that the Czechs had been "shamefully betrayed." And Anthony Eden, so recently Chamberlain's Foreign Secretary, said that Britain had done "a grave injustice to a small, friendly nation" which did not even have a say in its own destruction.[56]

Yet nobody struck so deeply at the Munich accord as Winston Churchill. Speaking on the third day of the Commons debate on Munich, the former minister, long out of step with the Conservative leadership, grumbled that "we have sustained a total and unmitigated defeat. . . . Silent, mournful, abandoned, broken, Czechoslovakia recedes into the darkness. She has suffered in every respect by her association with the Western democracies." That maimed country, he predicted, would not last long as an independent state but would soon be completely "engulfed" by Nazi Germany. "I fear we shall find that we have deeply compromised, and perhaps fatally endangered, the safety and even the independence of Great Britain and France. . . . We are in the presence of a disaster of the first magnitude." Churchill ended with a dark prophecy:

> Do not suppose that this is the end. This is only the beginning of the reckoning. This is only the first sip, the first foretaste of a bitter cup which will be proffered to us year by year unless by a supreme recovery of moral health and martial vigor, we arise again and take our stand for freedom as in the olden time.

Churchill's coruscating words received widespread coverage in the American press. The *New York Daily News*, calling Churchill the "cherub-faced veteran of many of Britain's stormiest political battles," reported his final assessment that only by building "the mightiest air fleet in the world" could Britain halt Hitler. Such reports were surely noted by Roosevelt.[57]

American journalists echoed this line of criticism. Dorothy Thompson called Munich "an international fascist coup d'état," a bloodless takeover with Hitler winning the spoils of war merely by threats and bullying. If it was peace, she wrote, it was built on lawlessness, dictatorship, and betrayal, and could not last. Anne O'Hare McCormick, seasoned witness of Europe's travails, saw that Czechoslovakia "has been offered up as a whole burnt-offering on the altar of peace," even though the peace itself looked like "German domination." And perhaps no editorial so scathingly captured the essence of the Munich deal than the one in the major Black newspaper, the *New York Amsterdam News*. "Four gangsters met last week to divide the property of an innocent victim," it began, referring to Chamberlain, Hitler, Mussolini, and Daladier. Their carving up of Czechoslovakia was "nothing new," just another chapter of iniquity following the destruction of Ethiopia, Spain, and Austria. "War cannot be far behind as long as these four greedy, selfish men plot, plan and divvy up the face of the Earth. For thieves are bound to fall out."[58]

Winston Churchill: a prophetic voice in 1938.
Library of Congress

Unexpectedly, even Ambassador Bullitt, who had so strongly supported appeasement and advised Roosevelt to sponsor a peace conference, now began to change his tune. At lunch in Paris a few days after the Munich meeting, a morose Prime Minister Daladier told Bullitt that Munich would be just the start of Hitler's demands, and that France must use the time they had bought to prepare to meet the German military threat. With greater air power, France could at least resist Hitler on equal terms. Munich was "an immense diplomatic defeat" for France and England, Daladier said sadly. Only with a rapid recovery of military strength could Europe avoid another "fatal situation." Two days later, Bullitt boarded the *Normandie* and sailed for home, intending to speak to the president in private about the strategic predicament the democracies now faced.[59]

The change in atmosphere in the White House was palpable. "High officials in the administration," the *Washington Post* reported just two days after the Munich meeting, "believe that the president will push ahead vigorously not only with his national defense program but with preparations for cushioning the economic shock of a war when it comes." The story was correct in its inference. As Harold Ickes noted in his diary at the end of September, the cabinet expressed full support for FDR's decision that if war came, "this country ought to do everything that it could to help the democratic countries." Ickes thought Roosevelt had emerged as the leader of the "democratic countries of the world," insofar as Chamberlain's weakness at Munich had tarnished England's prestige. A week later, after assessing the negative reaction to Munich in the country, Ickes called Munich "a totally disgraceful thing," and felt certain that Roosevelt would quickly dissociate himself from it. It was a bad deal, bought at far too high a price.[60]

By the time Bullitt arrived in Washington on October 13, Roosevelt seemed ready to act. He stayed up late that evening, as Bullitt related to him in detail the weaknesses of the French military that lay behind the deal at Munich. At the start of his press conference the next day at 10:45 a.m., Roosevelt told journalists of his late-night conference with Bullitt and announced that "new developments in national defense require a complete restudy" of the military budget that he would soon send to Congress. The events of the last month, he said, had forced an acceleration of his own plans. He suggested that one area that needed swift attention was standardization and "mass production" of aircraft, and this is where his attention remained in the coming days. He had secretly ordered Harry Hopkins to take a tour of American aircraft plants on the West Coast and assess its potential for rapid expansion. On October 16, the president left town for Hyde Park, but not for rest: He convened there some of the crucial players of his administration to sketch out a plan to mass produce military aircraft for purchase by the European democracies.[61]

The gathering at Hyde Park had a conspiratorial feel to it. Under strict secrecy, Treasury Secretary Henry Morgenthau Jr., William Bullitt, and chief of the Works Progress Administration, Harry Hopkins, gathered to talk about how to build and transfer airplanes to France and Britain, despite the restraints of the Neutrality Act. They were joined by two Europeans. One was an old friend from World War I days, the Scot Arthur Murray (later Lord Elibank), who though no longer in government was very well-connected in London. The other, to round out the Agatha Christie–like scene, was a Frenchman, Jean Monnet, a discreet technocrat who would go on to an almost legendary career during and after the war as the architect of French economic policy. Monnet had been sent by Daladier to determine if he could establish a corporation in Canada that could construct aircraft, using American raw materials, for shipment back to France, and Roosevelt heartily supported the scheme. The discussions were remarkable for revealing the clarity and ambition of Roosevelt's idea. As Murray later recalled it, Roosevelt felt it was "a certainty that Germany definitely intended to launch another war upon civilization," and he wanted to help the democracies defeat the dictators.[62]

Over the course of a few days of discussion, FDR's vision became clear. He wanted to build fifteen thousand airplanes a year in a public-private partnership with government and industry. He wanted eight plants set up around the country, mainly near large cities. And he wanted a thousand antiaircraft guns built as well. Hopkins, always ready to get to work, told FDR he could get the WPA to start "leveling ground and building these plants," which would put one hundred thousand men to work. Morgenthau was shocked at the scale and the possible cost. Roosevelt swept these objections aside, as he often did when thinking about ambitious projects. And to Murray, Roosevelt entrusted a message for Chamberlain: In the event of war, "he said he wished the prime minister to feel that he had . . . the industrial resources of the American nation behind him." In particular, FDR wanted Chamberlain to know that America would redress the imbalance in air power by building as many as twenty thousand to thirty thousand airplanes, which when added to European production, would "give the necessary overwhelming superiority over Germany and Italy." FDR was on a mission to arm the democracies and do it despite the restrictions of the Neutrality Act. Even if his ideas at first seemed overly ambitious and even impossible to achieve, these conversations in Hyde Park make plain that America was now in the game.[63]

Publicly, FDR made clear his plans to rearm in a speech to the *New York Herald Tribune* Forum, an annual gathering of thousands of writers and influential people. "Ordinary rules of national prudence and common sense require that we be prepared," and that meant building enough arms and aircraft to defend "our way of life." The United States would not pursue disarmament "while neighbor nations arm to the teeth." The *New York Times* welcomed this message and hoped it would mean a much greater expansion of American air power; for Munich made clear that the nation "which carries the most guns in the sky speaks with the greatest authority in the contemporary world." Roosevelt would have agreed; as he told Herbert Pell, his ambassador in Portugal, "the dictator threat from Europe is a good deal closer to the United States and the American Continent than it was before."[64]

Perhaps Roosevelt embraced his role as commander in chief because his leverage with Congress had fallen to an all-time low. The results of the November 8 midterm election came as a hard blow and seemed to signal the end of the road for the New Deal. The Republicans picked up eighty-one seats in the House, eight seats in the Senate, and twelve governorships. The country as a whole still admired the president, and Congress remained firmly in Democratic hands. But the recession had hurt Roosevelt—unemployment reached 19 percent in 1938—and he was bedeviled by the conservative faction in his own party that had turned against the New Deal and its support for labor unions, government spending, and aid to the poor and to minorities. The Southern Democrats were ready to pare back sharply the progress FDR had made since 1933. With conservative Democrats joining Republicans against the New Deal, FDR faced the prospect of a lame-duck presidency.[65]

Yet the sphere of military preparedness, where he could act with executive authority, offered a means to build upon his legislative legacy. He returned to Washington from Hyde Park, where he had spent Election Day, late on November 10, and the following day attended a memorial service at Arlington National Cemetery to mark Armistice Day. On the following afternoon, he brought Morgenthau, Hopkins, and the assistant secretary of war, Louis Johnson, into his office and asked them for a progress report on the aircraft program. Morgenthau haggled and argued with the president about the cost of the program and the need for increased taxes and the dangers of a large deficit. He thought Roosevelt "was rushing the whole thing terribly." For his part, FDR wanted action, and he told the men to return for a larger meeting in two days' time with the chief of staff of the army.[66]

A little after 2 p.m. on November 14, Roosevelt met at the White House with Morgenthau, Hopkins, Johnson, as well as Army Chief of Staff Malin Craig, Deputy Chief of Staff George C. Marshall, and General H. H. "Hap"

Arnold, the chief of the Air Corps. FDR took command and spoke at some length about the weakness of the U.S. armed forces in the air, and why this weakness must be remedied. He knew that Craig and Marshall were not enthusiasts of a large air force except as it might provide support for ground forces. Roosevelt clearly had something entirely different in mind. "The recrudescence of German power at Munich," he said, "had completely reoriented our own international relations." In light of new technologies, the Americas were suddenly vulnerable to air attack, while the Europeans were at Hitler's mercy. As a result, the United States needed "immediately a huge air force so that we do not have to send a huge army to follow that air force." In his thinking, air power would both deter Hitler from further conquest and arm the democracies adequately to meet Hitler in battle. At this point, of course, American troops in Europe were "politically out of the question." But aircraft could fill the gap.

He made it clear to the military men around the table that he wanted the new powerful air capability for two purposes: to defend the Western Hemisphere "from the North Pole to the South Pole, including all of North America and South America," and also to deter German aggression in Europe. A large fleet of planes would provide him and the Europeans with the ability to resist Hitler's bullying. He recounted his own recent missives to Hitler, and said, "when I write to foreign countries, I must have something to back up my words. Had we this summer 5,000 planes and the capacity immediately to produce 10,000 per year, even though I might have to ask Congress to sell or lend them to the countries in Europe, Hitler would not have dared to take the stand he did." There lay a clue as to Roosevelt's strategic purpose: He wanted planes not only for hemispheric defense but to send them to the Europeans so they could deter Hitler from starting a war. This strategy, to have any chance of success, would require an immense commitment. The United States could barely make one thousand fighter aircraft per year in 1938. The president now said he wanted a public-private partnership to build a fleet of ten thousand combat aircraft immediately, while constructing a nationwide factory capacity to build, if needed, as many as twenty thousand planes a year. He knew the program would stir controversy but said he planned to get it going through executive action "before Congress had a chance to act on it" and slow things down. He concluded the meeting by saying that he wanted a detailed plan drawn up immediately "to carry the thing through."

At this meeting, just six weeks after the Munich agreement that was supposed to deliver peace in Europe, FDR laid out a breathtaking proposal for the expansion of American global power. The president wanted an air force not just to defend the homeland but to project American power overseas and to deter Nazi aggression. In the meantime, he knew he would have to educate the public about the Nazi threat and the steps needed to halt it. "I must begin to lay the matter before the country," he said. It would be a difficult task of persuasion. But tragic, indeed shocking, events in Germany gave Roosevelt an opportunity to awaken the country—an opportunity that, at last, he did not fail to take.[67]

CHAPTER 13

1939: RUMORS OF WAR

"To stand aside before such injustice is the worst defeat there is."

—MARTHA GELLHORN

I

Attentive readers of the major American newspapers, inundated with alarming news from Central Europe during the upheavals of 1938, could be excused for overlooking reports in late October about the sudden arrest and deportation from Germany of some seventeen thousand Polish Jews who lived and worked in the Reich. Amid the vile persecution already meted out to Jews in Germany and Austria, the news that Hitler's SS had started roundups of another group of unfortunate victims slipped below the top fold of the morning papers. But it did receive attention. "Germans Oust Polish Jews," the *Chicago Tribune* announced; "Germany Deports Jews to Poland," added the *New York Times*; "Ousted Jews Left Penniless," was the *Los Angeles Times* headline.[1]

The origin of this latest atrocity lay in the bitter aftermath of the Anschluss, when the Nazi takeover of Austria meant that two hundred thousand Jews there, in a desperate panic, began to flee the clutches of their new overlords. The notoriously antisemitic Polish government, aware that many Jews in Austria and Germany had Polish citizenship, feared the sudden return of these unwanted Jewish citizens. The Polish parliament therefore passed a law that allowed the government to revoke citizenship from Poles who had been living abroad for more than five years—a clever way of abandoning expatriate Polish Jews to their fate. The German government immediately perceived that Poland was trying to unburden itself of some of its Jewish population. Given that there were still thousands of Jews with Polish citizenship in Germany, the Nazis leaped into action to ensure that these foreign Jews did not become Germany's problem. In two furious days at the end of October, the German security services rounded up thousands of Polish Jews in Germany, shoved them onto trains, and rushed them to the Polish border, denying them permission to carry personal belongings or money. Arriving hungry and terrified at the border, they were forced at gunpoint to march across open fields into Poland, where they were promptly arrested and penned up in barracks or train sheds. At the small border town of Zbaszyn, the refugees were herded into an unused flour mill and imprisoned.[2]

Among these unfortunate expellees were the parents of a seventeen-year-old boy named Herschel Grynszpan, who had fled Germany in 1936 for Paris, where he lived with an uncle. Herschel received a hastily scribbled postcard from his father, a tailor from Hanover now detained on the Polish border, that described their predicament and the suffering they had endured. Enraged by the persecution of his parents, Herschel bought a gun with the intention of striking back at the Germans. At 9:30 a.m. on November 7, he went to the German embassy in Paris, then on the Rue de Lille. He told the doorman that he had an urgent communication for the ambassador, but he was instead shown into the room of a lower official, Third Secretary Ernst vom Rath. Upon entering the room, he raised his revolver and shot at vom Rath five times, hitting him in the shoulder and abdomen. Mortally wounded, vom Rath was rushed to the hospital; he died two days later. Herschel defiantly told the French police that he wanted to exact revenge for the mistreatment of his family. Within hours, hundreds of thousands of Jews would come to regret Herschel's brazen act.

The shooting of vom Rath came at a moment of acute crisis for Jews in Germany. Since the spring of 1938, while Hitler was initiating the dangerous brinkmanship that would win him Austria and the Sudetenland, the Nazi government had been perpetrating another of its periodic Aryanization drives, making Jewish life intolerable in the Reich. During this year, the government banned Jews from medicine and the law, required them to adopt Israel or Sara as their first names, and generally encouraged vandalism and looting of Jewish shops, homes, cemeteries, and synagogues. In June, Hitler ordered the destruction of Munich's main synagogue; in August, the Nazi authorities in Nuremberg followed suit. While Hitler remained wrapped up in his high-stakes diplomatic gamble, his propaganda minister, Joseph Goebbels, urged a faster pace of cleansing. In Berlin, where Goebbels was the gauleiter (district leader), Jews were now banned from parks and trains and compelled to carry identity cards. Goebbels wished to accelerate the departure of Jews from the Reich through these discriminatory measures, and the murder of vom Rath gave him a golden opportunity to do so.

On November 9, as Nazi leaders convened in Munich to celebrate the anniversary of Hitler's failed 1923 Beer Hall Putsch, Goebbels reported to the Führer the news that vom Rath had died from his wounds. Hitler directed Goebbels to give the order for a nationwide pogrom. "Pull back the police," he said. "The Jews should for once get to feel the anger of the people." A wave of violence now crashed upon German Jews, as mobs of thugs, joined by SA Brownshirts, took to the streets in a mass campaign of incendiarism. Miscreants in the distinctive leather boots of storm troopers arrived by truck and even by taxi to synagogues in every major city; they carefully and often laboriously set fire to about three hundred holy sites. They ransacked and destroyed Jewish shops, apartments, and homes, tossed sacred scrolls into the flames, and arrested about thirty thousand Jewish men who were hauled off to the now-brimming concentration camps at Dachau, Buchenwald, and Sachsenhausen. At least ninety-one Jews were murdered; the number may have been significantly higher.

Late on November 10, following twenty-four hours of unrestrained violence, Goebbels issued a public statement, saying the attacks sprang from the "justified and understandable anger of the German people" and should now cease. Only a people already steeped in years of fanatical anti-Jewish propaganda could have responded so swiftly to the direction from their leaders to carry out this immense assault and, with equal obedience, to end it. Far from spontaneous, the violence that would come to be called "Kristallnacht" (referring to broken shopwindows) came down the chain of command from Hitler. Kristallnacht was no unrehearsed outburst but the first step toward a carefully planned genocidal war on the Jews.[3]

II

In the following days, Americans responded with an uproar of outrage, as if they now accepted what countless witnesses had been reporting since 1933: that the Nazis planned to destroy the Jews of Germany and in any additional lands they might incorporate into the Reich. The press gave the attack extensive, detailed news coverage, despite the effort of the Nazi government to suppress foreign reporting of the pogrom. This "unprecedented show of violence," as one paper called it, pulled back the curtain to reveal once and for all the true nature of the Nazi regime. The *Los Angeles Times* gave their story a lurid headline: "Nazi Mobs Riot in Wild Orgy." A story by Sigrid Schultz in the *Chicago Tribune* carried this banner: "Homes Burned; Stores Looted; Terror Reigns." Otto Tolischus of the *New York Times* termed the violence "unparalleled in Germany since the Thirty Years War."[4]

Kristallnacht spawned, as the *New York Times* editorial page put it, "scenes which no man can look upon without shame for the degradation of his species." Anne O'Hare McCormick, the doyenne of the foreign correspondents in Europe, noted that of all Germany's postwar complaints about its humiliation by the unfair Versailles Treaty, nothing had harmed Germany more than the decision of its own government to send "organized gangs recruited from the ruling party" into the streets, to destroy "the homes, the shops and the altars of a helpless minority of German citizens." Sigrid Schultz reported on harrowing scenes: "hundreds of Jewish women stood today before police headquarters in Berlin, weeping and begging for word of their fathers, husbands, brothers, or sons who have been arrested in the great Nazi anti-Semitic campaign." Dorothy Thompson as usual saw the larger picture: "The crisis is not a Jewish crisis. It is a human crisis."[5]

Across the United States, editorial pages burned; protests called for boycotts and the breaking of diplomatic ties with Germany and an embargo on trade with the Reich. The Non-Sectarian Anti-Nazi League, the National Conference of Christians and Jews, the Federal Council of Churches of Christ, and the bishops of the Methodist Church all issued impassioned statements. The Episcopal bishop of New York, Reverend William Manning, called German barbarism "an open defiance of God." Former president Herbert Hoover, Governor Alf Landon, Harold Ickes, labor leader William Green, the B'nai B'rith, and the American Jewish Congress, all condemned the Nazi pogrom with righteous anger. Thompson used her column not only to decry Nazi brutality but to launch an appeal for money to hire "the best lawyer in France" to defend the imprisoned teenager who had killed vom Rath. She feared a French kangaroo court would send Grynszpan to the guillotine to appease the Nazis before the boy had a chance to explain how the persecution of his parents had driven him to his desperate act. Telegrams and letters poured in with money and support.[6]

In reply to these furious comments from America, Dr. Goebbels mocked the assertion that Kristallnacht had been organized by top German officials, sneering that if he had led the pogrom, it would have been far more effective, murderous, and "radical." The Nazi regime then imposed a fine of 1 billion marks—about $400 million—upon the Jewish community of Germany as a penalty for the killing of vom Rath and announced that all insurance payments for damages to Jewish property must be forfeited to the state. German authorities crowed about their decisive and brutal strike on the Jews. In the chilling words of the *Berliner Tageblatt*, "we are now approaching a final solution of the Jewish question in Germany." Defiant in the face of world criticism, the paper promised that Germany "will continue our course with equanimity." There would be no slackening in the Nazi war on the Jews.[7]

America's official reaction lagged a few days. FDR had been preoccupied with the disappointing midterm election results of November 8 and was traveling to Washington by train from Hyde Park on November 10. The *New York Times* front page of that day had a large-type headline declaring "Coalition in Congress to Halt New Deal Urged as the Republicans Appraise Victory; Gain 80 in House, 8 in Senate, 11 Governors." It looked like a major setback for the president and his policies, and the news from Germany could not compete with this blow to the New Deal. On that same day, the anti-Jewish violence was given only a single column and a muted headline: "Berlin Raids Reply to Death of Envoy." Still, details were reaching Roosevelt. Ambassador Hugh Wilson sent a short cable describing "systematic breaking of Jewish-owned shop windows throughout the Reich and the burning of the principal synagogues in Berlin." Wilson also noted that while the Nazi news office asserted the riots were spontaneous, it was inconceivable that such attacks could have happened without government approval. On the same day, FDR received a cable from Dr. Stephen S. Wise reporting horrific scenes in Germany and "scores murdered." In a short press conference the next morning, however, Roosevelt had no statement to make about the assaults on Jews, and when pressed by journalists, he referred them to the State Department.[8]

Three days later, he shifted his tone. Having digested the immense national outcry about the Nazi pogrom, Roosevelt decided to recall Wilson as an act of protest. The press reported that it seemed "improbable" that Wilson would return to Berlin and indeed, he never did. On November 15, Roosevelt came to his press conference with a prepared statement. "The news of the past few days from Germany has deeply shocked public opinion in the United States. . . . I myself could scarcely believe that such things could occur in a twentieth century civilization." And there the statement ended. The next day's papers characterized this rebuke as "vigorous," "sharp" and "icily phrased." But his words were brief and cautious, especially given the monstrous nature of the Kristallnacht attacks. Journalists at the press conference asked FDR what measures he might take to aid Jews in peril. He replied "the time is not ripe" for specifics. Would the president "recommend a relaxation of our immigration restrictions so that the Jewish refugees could be received in this country," one reporter asked. "That," said the president tersely, "is not in contemplation." Roosevelt seemed eager to change the subject and spoke volubly about the meeting of his military chiefs he had held the previous day. He talked about the impact of air power on America's security and his plans "to place the defense of the United States . . . on a safer basis." It was a curious, elliptical performance: a restrained condemnation of Nazi atrocities, followed by a bold discussion of America's need for significant rearmament.[9]

In truth, Roosevelt had no means available to halt the pitiless behavior of the Nazis. He did use his authority to extend the short-term travel visas of about twelve thousand German and Austrian Jews already in the country. "It would be a cruel and inhuman thing to compel them to leave here" and send them back to "concentration camps," he told reporters. At the suggestion of Labor Secretary Frances Perkins, whose department oversaw immigration, their visas were extended six months. He also allowed a surrogate, Harold Ickes, to deliver a red-hot speech to the Cleveland Zionist Society in which the interior secretary likened the Nazi leaders to "voodoo high priests" and said that the only comparison to the current German regime was "that period of history when man was unlettered, benighted and bestial." The German embassy protested, but Sumner Welles, in the frostiest possible manner, replied that Ickes's outburst of indignation "certainly represented the feeling of the overwhelming majority of the people of the United States." Yet Roosevelt himself did not wish to dwell publicly on Nazi atrocities or begin an unwinnable fight over raising immigration quotas. His prestige had slumped in the wake of the November 1938 midterm elections, and his own party was riven by factional disputes. Instead, he accelerated what he called his program of education: persuading Congress and the public to see Nazism not simply as a German crisis but as a looming threat to American security.[10]

Starting just before Christmas, and working with two of his most able advisers, Thomas Corcoran and Benjamin Cohen, Roosevelt began drafting his State of the Union speech, which he would deliver on January 4 at the opening of the 76th Congress. Corcoran by the end of 1938 had earned a reputation as a legendary strategist in the administration. A student of Felix Frankfurter at Harvard Law and later a clerk for Justice Oliver Wendell Holmes, "Tommy the Cork" served as special counsel of the Reconstruction Finance Corporation, where he helped design some of the most important pieces of New Deal legislation. He shared a Washington apartment with Cohen, who he called his brother, also a Frankfurter protegee and key New Deal brain truster. The two men were so inseparable that they acquired a nickname: the "gold dust twins," a tagline taken from a popular advertising campaign for washing detergent. Corcoran came from a devoutly Catholic family; Cohen was a Jew who had once done legal work for the American Zionist movement. Together with FDR and chief speechwriter Sam Rosenman, they penned one of the most intelligent and prescient statements of national purpose that Roosevelt would ever deliver. Echoing themes first raised in the Quarantine speech in

October 1937, it marked the revival of Roosevelt's intermittent campaign to awaken America to the dangers posed by fascism.[11]

Roosevelt delivered the speech before a packed House of Representatives, wearing a light gray cutaway morning suit; Eleanor and his mother sat in the gallery, among throngs of listeners. Even with Republican gains in the recent election, Democrats outnumbered Republicans in the chamber, and a few rebel yells went up among the cheers as the president was assisted to the dais. With his text fixed into a black notebook in front of him, Roosevelt spoke in a deliberate and somber voice. It was not a campaign address, or a partisan speech: It was a message of warning. Despite the recent Munich accord, he said, peace in Europe "was not assured." The world still faced undeclared wars, an unprecedented arms race, and threats of aggression from dictators and tyrants; the images of Kristallnacht were still fresh in the minds of his listeners. Rejecting the comfortable nostrums of the pacifists and neutralists, he asserted that these "storms from abroad directly challenge three institutions indispensable to Americans," namely freedom of religion, democracy, and respect for international law, which he called "international good faith."

These three principles formed the foundation of the American experiment, and the country must decide what it was willing to give to secure them. "There comes a time in the affairs of men," he said solemnly, "when they must prepare to defend, not their homes alone, but the tenets of faith and humanity on which their churches, their governments and their very civilization are founded." To save freedom of religion, to save democracy, to save the rule of law in world affairs, "is all the same fight. To save one, we must make up our minds to save all." Roosevelt had reached the moment in his presidency when he dared to connect the security of American institutions and the well-being of the nation with the defense of democracy and freedom abroad. After all, Americans could no longer think of the wide oceans as protective barriers: "the world has grown so small, and the weapons of attack so swift, that no nation can be safe" from a determined aggressor. Here lay the theme he would return to many times in the coming months: Isolation offered no security to American democracy.

Of course, he veered away from calling for an armed confrontation with fascism. Instead, he emphasized "methods short of war" to express America's opposition to Nazism. He gently suggested that the Neutrality Act might be revised—in practice, it had operated "unevenly and unfairly," cutting off arms sales to victims of aggression like loyalist Spain and China while allowing regular commerce to continue with aggressors like Germany, Italy, and Japan. Most important, he called for rearmament: "we must have armed forces and defenses strong enough to ward off sudden attack," including a significant investment in installations and infrastructure to support rapid deployment of military power if necessary.

But in a brilliant rhetorical move, FDR exhorted his listeners to think of preparedness not just in terms of military defense. To meet the ideological challenge of dictatorship, Americans had "to make democracy work." Since 1932, using the tools of a redesigned and expanded government, Americans had shown the world that democracy could meet and master the crisis of the Depression. Look at all we have achieved, Roosevelt urged: food and shelter and work for a stricken people; better stewardship of natural resources; sound labor rules and labor rights; a secure banking system; investment in education, agriculture, medical care, security and dignity for the elderly. This was the best of America, "and all this has been done without any dictator's power to command . . . without concentration camps, without a scratch on freedom of speech, freedom of the press, or the rest of the Bill of Rights." Democracy, he said with a flourish, allowed Americans to solve these vast problems without transforming the people into obedient drones or "pawns molded and enslaved by a machine." America's greatest power, he argued, was its example, and the way to secure freedom and liberty in the world lay in restoring and strengthening American democracy.

Perhaps inspired by the 1939 short film *Lincoln in the White House*, which he watched just a few days earlier, FDR ended his address with a famous passage from Lincoln's 1862 annual message to Congress. In the face of the fascist threat and the horrors of war, FDR said, this generation of Americans would "nobly save or meanly lose the last best hope of earth." FDR once again drew a portrait of America as an exceptional nation, uniquely blessed but also fired by a restless quest for freedom and justice that placed it on a collision course with the dictatorships.

Was this his new battle cry? Was he ready at last to cast aside irresolution and unequivocally join the struggle against the fascist threat? Perhaps he had made up his *own* mind. But in the eight months before war broke out in Europe, Roosevelt found it immensely difficult to bring the people and their congressional representatives around to his way of thinking. Americans now knew enough about fascism to hate it and recoil from its brutality. But a natural antipathy to bloodletting, a sense of comfort born of distance and geopolitical good fortune, as well as some well-timed conspiratorial jingoism and hate speech from a variety of demagogues, all combined to befog the American mind. And Roosevelt, despite his gifts as a leader, could not easily dispel the thick mist.[12]

III

A week after his speech in the Capitol, Roosevelt sent a budget request to Congress for $552 million in new appropriations for air, land, and naval forces. This emergency request came on top of $1.3 billion regular budget estimates for defense through 1940. $330 million of the additional funds were tagged for building three thousand new combat aircraft—fewer than he originally wanted but a robust start for America's puny and underfunded aircraft industry. "Military aviation is increasing today at an unprecedented and alarming rate," Roosevelt said in a written statement to Congress, and the United States had to adapt to new strategic realities. There was no reason for "hysteria," but he called these additional measures "imperative" to prepare for a possible attack on American soil. On January 17, the Senate Committee on Military Affairs opened hearings on the president's request, with most Democrats lined up in support. Robert Taft, Republican of Ohio, a staunch isolationist and stern foe of the New Deal who had just begun his first term in the Senate, archly said of FDR's budget request that "the logical conclusion is another war with American troops again sent across the ocean." Other than some dour remarks like these, few legislators wanted to stand in the way of swift passage of the defense bill.[13]

But Taft's remark took on greater meaning when, in the midst of the hearings, Congress learned that Roosevelt had engineered a secret plan to sell hundreds of the planes he proposed to build to the European democracies so that they could meet the threat of Hitler's Luftwaffe. And the way this news broke only heightened congressional suspicions: On January 23, a prototype of the Douglas DB-7 light bomber, a newly designed aircraft that the army wanted to add to its fleet, crashed near the Los Angeles Municipal Airport with a French air force official on board. The American pilot was killed, the Frenchman badly injured, and ten people on the ground were wounded. The Associated Press ran a story that hinted at skulduggery: The Douglas company "first gave an incorrect identity and then refused explanation as to why Paul Chemidlin, 33, of the French air ministry," was a passenger on the "secretly designed bomber." The defense hearings on Capitol Hill, which had started in a collegial atmosphere, now flared up with senatorial indignation.[14]

The story of the scheme to get American planes into the hands of the French air force—Britain's air industry was in better shape than France's and did not rely on U.S. aircraft—presents a classic example of Roosevelt's sinuous method of policymaking and the trouble it often created. The president knew from Ambassador Bullitt that France could not possibly defend itself from

German air attack. Why not build planes in America for sale to France, Roosevelt thought? He proposed as much to Jean Monnet when they met at Hyde Park in October. But the army, which oversaw the nascent Army Air Corps, opposed the idea. The army liked neither FDR's overemphasis on air power nor his plan to share scarce planes and their secret designs with Europeans before American needs were fully met. Feeling this resistance, FDR simply went around the army and ordered Secretary of the Treasury Henry Morgenthau to work with a French purchasing team to allow them to place orders for the planes they needed; if U.S. factories were not yet ready to produce enough planes, this purchase order would act as a spur to get them going.[15]

By the time the Senate started hearings on the defense request in mid-January, Roosevelt had already approved an agreement for the French to buy 555 American-built planes—a combination of bombers, fighters, transport, and training craft—at a cost of $60 million. The army fought it all the way, but Morgenthau and FDR pushed it through. They were also responsible for allowing the French Air Ministry officials to test the U.S. planes before purchasing them; the fiery crash at the Douglas factory in Los Angeles blew the scheme wide open. In fact, it was perfectly legal—the Neutrality Act only forbade the sale of military equipment to nations at war—but the French sale confirmed suspicions among his congressional critics that Roosevelt was trying to subvert the principle of U.S. neutrality. In arming France, they believed, FDR could be taking the first steps toward sending Americans back to Europe to fight. And he pushed the sale despite objections from his own defense officials.[16]

The Senate Military Committee immediately summoned General H. H. "Hap" Arnold, the commander of the Air Corps. Democratic senator Bennett Clark, a vociferous foe of Roosevelt's, demanded: "Do you know what this Frenchman was doing in that plane?" When Arnold replied, "He was out there under the direction of the Treasury Department with a view of looking into possible purchase of the airplanes," the fat dropped into the fire. Did the War Department approve the agreement to sell planes to France? Did the planes carry secret technology? Was it wise to send planes to France when America's own cupboard was bare? Why should the Treasury have been involved in selling advanced planes to France? Senator Clark started to thunder about a special investigation to get to the bottom of it. Senator Ernest Lundeen, an unscrupulous opportunist from Minnesota (whose ties to the American Nazi movement were just coming under investigation by the FBI), said that sending advanced planes to France would lead the U.S. into war: "Have we already picked our enemies and our friends in the next conflict?" Gerald Nye took up his now well-worn cry, calling for a complete ban on all exports of munitions of war, even in peacetime. General Arnold insisted that only the plane's bombsight was of a secret design, and it had been removed before the French got a look at the aircraft. As for why the Treasury was involved at all, Arnold suggested that Secretary Morgenthau should be asked about the matter.[17]

Two days later, at 10:30 a.m. on January 27, President Roosevelt held a press conference, carefully timed to begin at the precise moment that Morgenthau arrived on Capitol Hill to speak to the Military Affairs Committee. The press whiffed the scent of scandal, and asked Roosevelt if he had taken "any steps to assist or facilitate France in buying planes in this country?" The president, untruthfully, replied: "As you put the question, no." He pretended that he and the cabinet wanted to get the idle aviation industry going for purposes both of jobs and the future readiness of national defense. The French expressed an interest in buying planes, and the president told them "there was no reason why they should not place orders for planes." In fact, FDR had been pressing the army to allow the French access to new models of aircraft and had smoothed the way for the foreign air force officials to get access to the aircraft they wanted. When asked why Treasury was involved at all, FDR said that department was "interested in building up the trade of the United States."

That answer was an artful dodge. Treasury was involved because Roosevelt used Morgenthau to get around the army. Morgenthau admitted as much when he testified at a closed hearing that same morning. He first stated that his role was merely "to play host to this mission" and treat France as a "friendly country." After some prodding about why Treasury was involved, Morgenthau said simply, "The president asked us to do it." Privately, after the hearings, Morgenthau and Roosevelt debriefed, and the secretary said, "You gave me a mission to perform, namely, to get the French these planes, and I have done it." Had it been left to the War Department, it would have taken years or never happened at all. "That is right," FDR admitted. But he did not like the Senate nosing into his handling of defense matters. When the committee asked him for documents relating to the French plane deal, he refused to comply, citing executive privilege.[18]

The press made a considerable fuss over the episode, reporting on "a serious conflict between the President and officer heads" of the armed services. The *Chicago Tribune* laid it on thick, asserting that FDR had ordered the army to share the "military and technical secrets" with the French. Worse, the *Tribune* reported, FDR may have "entered into a secret military alliance with France." That, at least, was the accusation made by Senator Nye to the press. The closed hearings, with all the top military officials being called to the Capitol, only spurred the interest of reporters; headlines spoke of Roosevelt's "Secret War Pact."[19]

To quench the flames of this controversy, Roosevelt, in a remarkable gesture, invited the entire committee to the White House for a private talk at which he could place the sale of aircraft to France in a wider strategic context. Seventeen men in great coats and fedoras arrived at the White House on Tuesday, January 31, just after noon, to meet the chief executive in a session all agreed would be absolutely confidential. It was a gloomy atmosphere. The evening before, Hitler gave an aggressive and wildly antisemitic speech to the Reichstag to mark his sixth year in power. He served notice, as the newspapers summarized it, that Germany had not yet seized enough territory and would now move to acquire a colonial empire abroad; in tandem with Italy and Japan, Germany would redraw the imperial boundaries of the world. The only people who would oppose Germany's rightful claims were the Jewish bankers and press lords, but they must be warned. To the ecstatic cheers of the Nazi faithful arrayed before him, Hitler howled that "if the international Jewish financiers in and outside Europe should succeed in plunging the nations once more into a world war, then the result will not be the Bolshevization of the earth, and thus the victory of Jewry, but the annihilation of the Jewish race in Europe." As the senators filed into the White House, this speech weighed on Roosevelt, less for its horrific prophecy toward the Jews than for Hitler's naked declaration of Germany's global ambitions.[20]

Once the legislators had taken their seats, FDR began a long, at times mesmerizing, soliloquy about American security in a troubled world. (Uncharacteristically, FDR ordered a note-taker to prepare a verbatim transcript.) He began with an unusually bold statement of his strategic thinking: "I am very much exercised over the future of the world . . . and I do not belong to a school of thought that says we can draw a line of defense around this country and live completely and solely to ourselves." While he said he did not wish to frighten the public, he wanted them alerted to the "potential danger" ahead. Ever since the 1936 Anti-Comintern Pact between Germany and Japan (joined soon after by Italy), the world faced an offensive and defensive alliance of these three aggressive powers. FDR laid his cards on the table: "We must try to prevent the domination of the world."

To do that, America needed a global strategy. "What is the first line of defense in the United States?" he asked. In the Pacific, the navy relied on a string of islands—the Philippines, Guam, Midway, and Hawaii—to hem in the Japanese. In the Atlantic, U.S. security depended on various European nations whose independence was now threatened. He rattled off their names, moving from eastern and southern Europe to France and Britain. These nations needed American support—aircraft especially—to fend off Hitler. The German leader was a paranoid, bellicose, irrational "nut," said Roosevelt, but he was also the dictator of a powerful state that posed a direct threat to Western Europe. Should France and England fall, all the "small nations would drop into the basket" next, including the republics of South America. He went through a list of them: Argentina, Brazil, Venezuela, Colombia, and the small central American states—all would be Hitler's for the taking.

"Do not say it is chimerical," he went on. "Do not say it is a pipedream." Look how much Hitler had accomplished in a mere six years. Who would bet against him now, especially knowing the weakness of the democracies? A war against democracy looked imminent in Europe; America must make its productive capacity available to those states defending themselves from Nazi aggression. If the U.S. could build ten thousand planes a year, and sell them to France and Britain, it would restore the balance to Europe and keep America out of a future war. He finished with great firmness: "I will do everything I can to maintain the independence of these other nations by sending them all they can pay for, on the barrelhead . . . Now that is the foreign policy of the United States." The senators broke into applause.[21]

This was the real Roosevelt, and one of the great puzzles, even tragedies, about the Roosevelt presidency is that he rarely spoke like this in public, at least before 1939. He kept his counsel, carefully pushing through his rearmament program. But he failed to orchestrate a sustained national lobbying effort to bring the country with him. Worse, he backtracked when directly challenged. Almost immediately, someone leaked the details of the meeting with the senators to the *Chicago Tribune* and its politics reporter Chesly Manly. "The President," wrote Manly, "went so far as to say that our present first line of defense is in France. . . . He gave them a lecture on present world conditions, pointing to the menace of Nazi Germany's territorial aspirations in a manner that was calculated to be terrifying." Senators who spoke to Manly said that "all pretense of American neutrality in foreign wars has been abandoned; that steps already have been taken which would lead us inevitably into Europe's next war." Roosevelt "took the position that France and England must be saved at all costs and that this country stands ready to give them all possible assistance." According to Manly's sources, FDR had expressed little concern about the restrictions of the Neutrality Act. As for how many planes America might build for the democracies, the president was quoted as saying, "The sky's the limit." The next day, after this report made the rounds, neutralists in Congress loosed off angry volleys at Roosevelt. Republican Hiram Johnson, a vehement critic of any U.S. involvement with Europe going back to the fight against the League of Nations, was scandalized by FDR's secret commitments to Europe. "Good God, gentlemen," he said to reporters, "do you not think the American people have the right to know if they are going down the road to war?"[22]

Stung by the leak, Roosevelt tried to discredit the report when he spoke to the press two days after the *Tribune* story broke. He blamed "agitators" in Congress, as well as antagonistic newspaper owners, for spreading a story that was "pure bunk—b-u-n-k." These people were trying to stir up fear among the public to score partisan points, he said. He called the assertion that he placed the American security frontier on the Rhine "a deliberate lie," and said America's foreign policy remained fixed: no entangling alliances, the promotion of world trade, the search for disarmament, and the independence of nations. The reporters wondered at the discrepancy between his account and the leaked information they possessed. They asked if a "stenographic record" had been made of the conference. Roosevelt again dodged, saying, "I do not know." He did have a record, of course, and it clearly showed him describing Britain and France as America's "first line of defense" in Europe. Two weeks later, reporters continued to badger him about the matter, and Roosevelt chalked the whole thing up to "unscrupulous" people like Senators Nye and Clark, who would gladly twist his words for political purposes. The French had "an absolute right to purchase planes in this country," Roosevelt said, and with that, he headed off to Key West, Florida, to board the waiting USS *Houston*, his favorite vacation vessel, for a two-week cruise in the Caribbean.[23]

The discovery of the French plane mission, which FDR had inexplicably tried to keep secret, set back the internationalist cause. It prompted allegations of hidden alliances, secret arms sales, and defiance of Congress. It also caused despair in anti-fascist intellectual circles. In a critical editorial, *The Nation*, now under the ownership of a worldly progressive named Freda Kirchwey, wondered at FDR's "wavering." Did he favor arming the democracies? Did he believe the United States must help bolster European security? If so, why not say it publicly? Instead, when confronted, FDR "decided to dilute to the point of vagueness his realistic prescription" that he gave the senators behind closed doors. In a decisive judgment, Kirchwey predicted that FDR's "shillyshallying will inevitably play into the hands of the isolationists." His penchant for secrecy and evasion would make breaking the shackles of the Neutrality Act infinitely more difficult.[24]

IV

Developments on the home front, however, gave Roosevelt at least one tool he might use to pick the lock of neutrality. Just two days after the president and his entourage slipped away on the *Houston*, heading southeast toward Puerto Rico for ten days of fishing, sun, and conferences with leading naval officers, an astonishing political rally took place back in icy, brooding New York City that spurred national anxiety about the threat to America from an "enemy within"—and FDR certainly was not above exploiting such fears for his own purposes.

The scene was Madison Square Garden, home to so many political rallies of this era. But this February 20 demonstration shocked the country. Over twenty thousand American Nazi sympathizers crammed into the large hall, bedecked with immense swastika banners and American flags, to celebrate George Washington's birthday—a ruse designed to link Americanism with Nazism. Slogans like "Wake Up, America! Smash Jewish Communism!" and "Stop Jewish Domination of Christian America!" blazed out from placards. Hundreds of young, grim-faced men dressed in military-style uniforms stood guard; an array of German American speakers rose to denounce Jewish Bolshevism, speaking beneath a giant portrait of Washington himself. These American Nazis provided vivid, indelible imagery of a dystopian future in which Hitler's minions had taken power and brought their race war into the

Timed to coincide with George Washington's birthday, the Nazi-themed rally at Madison Square Garden outraged most New Yorkers.
Records of the German American Bund, National Archives and Records Administration

heart of America's most diverse city. They also gave FDR an opportunity to discredit his political opponents by linking his foreign policy critics to the racism and bigotry of a secretive "fifth column" that was ready to do Hitler's work inside the United States.[25]

The rally was the brainchild of Fritz Kuhn, the leader of the *Amerikadeutscher Volksbund*: the German-American Bund. Kuhn built this organization out of the ashes of the Friends of New Germany, which had collapsed in 1936 when the Nazi government officially disowned it. A German-born veteran of the First World War (he won an Iron Cross and briefly served in the right-wing Stahlhelm militia in the postwar years), Kuhn immigrated to Mexico in 1923 and eventually moved north to Detroit in search of work. He joined the Friends organization there and rose to become its Midwestern district leader. By 1934, he had acquired naturalized American citizenship (though he never lost his strong German accent when speaking English). As he set out to build his new Nazi movement, he emphasized its American roots, inspired but not directed by the German government. America, he stressed, must remain a white, Christian, Aryan country and guard against pollution from Jews, African Americans, and Communists; he proposed Nazi methods to rescue America from these perils.

Though the German government remained wary about this would-be American Führer, Kuhn did manage to meet Hitler in person once—a brief encounter on the eve of the 1936 Olympic Games in Berlin, providing Kuhn a priceless photograph of himself with Hitler that he used to establish his bona fides among his followers. The Bund, like the Friends before it, set up chapters across the country, held rallies and marches, ran summer camps (Camp Hindenburg in Wisconsin, Camp Nordland in New Jersey, Camp Siegfried on Long Island) for German American children, and sought to normalize the appearance of the swastika flag fluttering in the heartland of America.[26]

By the time of the rally in New York, Kuhn was well-known to federal authorities for organizing such provocative public demonstrations. A military-style parade at the Bund-owned camp in Yaphank, Long Island, in August 1937 attracted twenty-five thousand people for a day of "swastika waving, heiling, and Hitler praising," according to one report, and smaller marches popped up frequently in New York and Chicago. In January 1938, Attorney General Homer Cummings cleared the Bund of any illegal activity. Though repulsive, the Bund did not seem particularly dangerous. The Nazi government explicitly banned German residents in the United States from joining it, and nationwide, Bund membership never passed twenty thousand.[27]

A German Day rally at Camp Siegfried in Yaphank, New York, in August 1937, replete with swastikas.
Joseph Rossteuscher / Archive Photos / Getty Images

Yet the "brown panic" was only just getting started. In February 1938, the New York police arrested Guenther Rumrich, a U.S. citizen of German ancestry who had volunteered to carry out espionage for German intelligence. Rumrich and the dozen or so associates he worked with were amateurs—they got work at defense plants and shipyards and tried to purloin blueprints of navy vessels as well as blank passports. Tipped off by British intelligence that a group of Germans was passing information to Berlin, the FBI arrested and interrogated Rumrich. By late April 1938, the authorities had amassed a fat dossier on some two dozen Germans active in intelligence gathering in the United States. In June, the FBI issued eighteen indictments against these German agents, though by then most of the accused had fled the country, leaving just four suspects in custody. Inspired by the FBI's success in prosecuting foreign agents, Congress formed the House Un-American Activities Committee (HUAC) in May 1938—it built on the work of the Dickstein committee—with the broad remit of unveiling "subversion" in America.[28]

Under the chairmanship of a conservative, publicity-hungry, anti–New Deal Democrat from Texas, Martin Dies, HUAC would spend most of its time investigating alleged Communist penetration of New Deal agencies and labor unions. But in its first hearings, in August 1938, the Dies committee summoned the Chicago reporter John Metcalfe to hear his arresting allegations. Metcalfe claimed that the Bund planned espionage and sabotage on behalf of Germany while encouraging "national socialism for the United

States." He also asserted that the German ambassador in Washington, Dr. Hans-Heinrich Dieckhoff, was orchestrating this secret Nazi cell (a charge the ambassador swiftly denied). Metcalfe showed that Fritz Kuhn was an ugly antisemite and a fanatical anti-communist, but he did not have decisive proof that the Bund took its orders from Berlin. At the start of 1939, HUAC asked the FBI to investigate allegations of Nazi sympathizers working "in the Navy yards and airplane factories of this country," as well as the activities of the Silver Shirts, William Dudley Pelley's fascist militia. Fear of Nazi spies conducting espionage and sabotage gripped the public.[29]

The Bund's Madison Square Garden rally of February 20, 1939, therefore landed at a moment of peak anxiety about covert Nazi agents at work in America. The event garnered significant press coverage, and some New Yorkers planned to demonstrate against it. Dorothy Thompson, fearless as ever, went to the rally and used her press credentials to gain entry to the great hall. She loudly heckled the speakers, cackling theatrically at their ludicrous statements. As American Nazis on the platform praised Hitler and Mussolini and denounced "President Rosenfeld," she noisily harrumphed and repeatedly shouted at the dais: "Bunk! Nonsense! *Mein Kampf*, word for word!" After some minutes of this, a throng of Kuhn's thugs hustled her out of the hall. As Kuhn began to harangue "Jewish financiers" and Jewish Bolshevists

Dorothy Thompson silenced by pro-Nazi members of the Bund in Madison Square Garden.
Thompson Papers, Syracuse University

for tricking America into the last war, a young man named Isadore Greenbaum rushed the stage to strike at Kuhn; he was caught and beaten by Kuhn's Nazi bodyguard. With these disruptions cleared away, the speeches carried on, indicting the international Jew for the world's troubles and invoking "Americanism" as the solution to the Jewish onslaught. Kuhn's storm troops raised stiff-armed salutes to the giant image of George Washington affixed to the stage alongside Nazi banners and slogans. When the meeting ended, city policemen had to clear the streets around the auditorium where an estimated fifty thousand angry New Yorkers had gathered in protest.[30]

The next day, laughing no more, Thompson wrote in her column that the Bund's antisemitism and Hitler worship directly threatened American democracy, and she called on Americans to stand up against the ideological onslaught sponsored by Berlin. Noting that her husband, Sinclair Lewis, had prophesied this exact scenario in his 1935 novel, *It Can't Happen Here*, she said that the Bund dressed up its hate and bigotry in the name of "Americanism," but wanted to use Nazi methods to rid the country of anyone who was not a "white Gentile." Thompson saw the Bund as part of a larger challenge thrown at America not just by minor would-be Führers like Kuhn but by Hitler: Would Americans defend their political system, or acquiesce in the collapse of democracy? She connected the domestic Nazi sympathizers with the world threat to democracy and took aim at those who cowered behind a failed neutrality policy: "No great nation," she wrote, "ever maintained itself in the long run by making the desire to avoid war the prime foundation of its international policy." If Americans would be worthy of their democracy, they must rise to defend it—even if that meant war.[31]

V

The surreptitious activities of German spies, combined with the Bund's mimicry of the Nazi Party, served Roosevelt's interests as he set out to win revision of the Neutrality Act by stoking fears of a "fifth column" in the United States. In the spring of 1939, the administration set up an inter-departmental committee of the Justice, State, and Labor Departments to devise legislative measures that would allow the government, as Sumner Welles put it privately, "to protect ourselves against these un-American activities of aliens who enjoy our hospitality" but remained loyal to a foreign government. FDR wanted to tighten laws on political activity by aliens; to change naturalization laws to allow courts to cancel naturalized citizenship of people, like Kuhn, who had acquired U.S. citizenship but effectively worked for Nazi

Germany; and to suppress organizations like the Bund in which members wore military uniforms.[32]

The Foreign Agents Registration Act, signed into law on September 6, 1938, had already forced foreign lobbyists and agents to register with the Justice Department. In September 1939, Roosevelt designated the FBI as the organization that would "take charge of investigative work in matters relating to espionage, sabotage, and violations of neutrality regulations," and he ordered all law enforcement agencies to turn over to the FBI any relevant information they possessed, creating a network of informers across the country. In the same month, FBI director J. Edgar Hoover began to compile the Custodial Detention Index, a list of German, Italian, and Communist-linked people in the United States who might be arrested in time of war on the grounds of disloyalty. These measures found further expansion in the Smith Act, or Alien Registration Act of June 1940, which required all aliens over age fourteen to register at their local post office and submit to fingerprinting.[33]

The paranoia about a "fifth column" only intensified, and Roosevelt played it to his advantage by winning more appropriations for the FBI and Hoover's G-men. As for the Bund, it proved easy enough to defang. Within days of the February rally, New York's mayor, Fiorello La Guardia, in tandem with District Attorney Thomas Dewey, launched an investigation of the Bund's finances. After seizing documents and combing through the books, they indicted Kuhn for larceny and fraud, accusing him of embezzling thousands of dollars from his own organization. At the end of 1939, Kuhn was convicted and sentenced to five years in Sing Sing prison. His successors blamed this persecution on "the warmongering international Jew" and tried to raise money for his defense, but the Bund never recovered. It was a precipitous fall.[34]

Still, there was one political challenge from the "lunatic fringe" that Roosevelt could not so easily rebuff as he accelerated his policy of confrontation with fascism. It came from his old nemesis, the sanctimonious and increasingly menacing priest of the Shrine of the Little Flower, Father Charles E. Coughlin. The Detroit radio impresario had been relatively quiet since his humiliation at the polls in November 1936, when his National Union of Social Justice spectacularly failed to halt FDR's reelection. With his church superiors growing uneasy about his foray into politics, he piped down for most of 1937. But he reemerged at the start of 1938, blasting his usual targets: Roosevelt, internationalism, big banks, Communists, and—most notably—Jews. He relaunched his drab black-and-white newspaper, *Social Justice*, as a glossy color magazine; it immediately gained 350,000 paid subscribers and the presses could not keep up with demand.[35]

In the pages of his new rag, Coughlin struck out at FDR's rearmament plans and his alleged secret pact to defend the British Empire in a repeat of "the folly of 1917–18." He threw at the New Deal every epithet that came to hand, calling it Communist, Fascist, a dictatorship, and a capitalist conspiracy against hardworking Americans. In his weekly editorials, Coughlin impugned James Warburg (an early brain trust adviser) and Jacob Schiff (Warburg's father-in-law, an influential banker and Jewish community leader, dead since 1920), to conjure up the specter of omnipotent Jewish financiers. While claiming to support democracy, Coughlin published puff pieces about dictators. In March, the cover of *Social Justice* featured a handsome portrait of General Francisco Franco petting his dog, followed by a glowing report on the "corporative state" Franco planned to construct in Spain after crushing the Communists. Under Franco, Spain would become a utopia, an ordered hierarchical society with no political parties, unswervingly loyal to the Catholic Church. Another issue hailed the dictatorship of Antonio Salazar of Portugal for bringing "justice" and "ending class conflict" in that now-happy Iberian land. A smiling country girl in traditional costume beamed out from the article, which blamed left-wing journalists for inaccurately labeling the Portuguese dictator a fascist. And the magazine effusively praised Mussolini as "the first efficient statesman to check the onrush of Red Communism: his Blackshirts saved Italy for Christian civilization."[36]

In early April 1938, Coughlin flexed his political muscles and ordered his followers to flood the Capitol with telegrams in opposition to FDR's government reorganization plan—an effort to improve the bureaucracy of the executive branch that Coughlin inevitably described as FDR's scheme for a personal dictatorship. Instantly tens of thousands of outraged messages lit up the wires, intimidating Congress and slowing the progress of FDR's proposal. In May, *Social Justice* featured a drawing of Labor Secretary Frances Perkins on the cover in a ghoulish shade of dark blue, with an accusation that her embrace of foreign, and likely Communist, immigrants endangered the dream of "America for the Americans." A commemorative Memorial Day issue at the end of May 1938 pasted an unflattering picture of Henry Morgenthau (the Jewish secretary of the treasury) onto a drawing of a military cemetery, implying that Jews would once again get American boys into a foreign war.[37]

Starting that summer, Coughlin plunged deeper into the addled underworld of antisemitic conspiracy theories. The July 18 issue of his magazine began to serialize the *Protocols of the Elders of Zion*, that disgusting antisemitic forgery already popularized by Henry Ford, which was drawn up at the turn of the century by Russian secret agents. The *Protocols* purported to be the blueprint for Jewish world domination. Coughlin, in a signed article, wove all the threads together, arguing that the plot of a global Jewish conspiracy outlined in the *Protocols* was coming true in the Jewish-dominated Soviet Union and the Jewish-dominated New Deal of Franklin Roosevelt. Like a con man in a rapid-fire game of three-card monte, Coughlin dealt out Theodor Herzl, Walther Rathenau, Karl Marx, New Deal wage increases, agricultural subsidies, and Communist labor unions, claiming they were all part of a conspiracy to destroy Christian America. And since Coughlin had long established that Communism was a Jewish idea, that Jews had financed the Russian Revolution, and that FDR's White House was full of Jews, it stood to reason that the New Deal was a Judeo-Bolshevik wolf in sheep's clothing. If it was exhausting to make sense of any of this, Coughlin simply asked his readers to trust him: He would decode it all for them.[38]

Kristallnacht accelerated Coughlin's descent into the gutter. The sight of America's newspapers denouncing Nazi persecution of Jews—instead of what he insisted was the far greater horror of Communist persecution of Christians—triggered a volcanic outburst from the radio priest. On November 20, just ten days after the atrocities in Germany, Coughlin read out to his millions of weekly listeners a sermon called "Persecution—Jewish and Christian." He asked, why are Jews being persecuted in Germany? The answer, naturally, was that Jews gave birth to Communism, and Nazism was merely, in his phrase, "a defense mechanism" against this terrible ideology. Communism was "anti-God, anti-Christ, anti-patriotism, and anti-property," and because Jews had unleashed this toxic poison on the world, they naturally had become the targets of abuse. Coughlin instructed his listeners to recall that in Germany, the Jews had been especially malevolent, bringing defeat in the world war, the hated Treaty of Versailles, the "red" revolution of 1918, and the economic crisis. Coughlin's sequence of evils might have come directly from *Mein Kampf*—it was standard Nazi storytelling. And in the Soviet Union, Coughlin claimed, the Jewish- Communist regime killed off 20 million Christians—an atrocity that, because of the Jewish domination of the media, had been suppressed. Instead, Jewish suffering got all the limelight.[39]

Even for Coughlin, this was a breathtakingly false and noxious broadcast. Within days, three radio stations, including New York's WMCA, announced they would break Coughlin's contract and bar him from future radio appearances. Newspapers ran extended denunciations and factual contradictions of Coughlin's outlandish claims. The Boston-based paper *The Jewish Advocate* called him a "genuine Fascist." Blasted as an antisemite, Coughlin doubled down a week later, repeating his claims that Jews (Kuhn, Loeb and Company, headed by Jacob Schiff, was his favorite fictional Judeo-Bolshevik banking conglomerate) had financed the Russian revolution. On December 4 came his third antisemitic sermon in a row, reiterating his claims of Jewish control of banks, newspapers, and radio. "I shall continue my crusade," he shouted to his millions of listeners.[40]

Now even the church hierarchy started to get worried. The Catholic weekly *Commonweal* stated that "the habit of specious selection in loading blame on the Jews recalls vividly the propaganda of the Nazis." The archbishop of Chicago, Cardinal George Mundelein, a friend of Roosevelt's, stated firmly that Coughlin "is not authorized to speak for the Catholic church nor does he represent the doctrine or sentiments of the church." Lay Catholic leaders took to rostrums across the country to denounce Coughlin. And then the picture darkened still further. On December 17, *The Nation* published a revelatory article by an anti-fascist Episcopal (and later Catholic) priest from New Jersey named William C. Kernan that showed not only that Coughlin's sources for his "facts" about Jews were phony, but that some of Coughlin's very language had been cribbed from a Nazi outlet called *World Service*, published in Hamburg. Journalists began to search through previous issues of *Social Justice* for more damning echoes of Nazism and quickly found them. The *New York Daily Post* reported that a Coughlin article of December 5 was plagiarized from a 1935 speech by Joseph Goebbels; the tabloid printed full paragraphs from each article side by side to demonstrate the near-identical language. "Nazi Sources of Coughlin's Talk Now Proven," said a headline in the *Jewish Advocate*. There could be no doubt now: Coughlin was singing from Nazi sheet music.[41]

Coughlin's antisemitic tirades resonated: At political meetings in favor of Franco or in support of the neutrality acts, rally-goers could be counted on to send up hearty cheers at the mention of Coughlin's name. Millions saw him as a truth-teller and visionary, a figure silenced by radio censors who foretold a dictatorial Roosevelt taking America into a Jewish-inspired war—a war that could only abet the ultimate victory of Communism. Coughlin in his sermons used "internationalism" as a synonym for a Jewish cabal of financial and media barons who wanted to send arms to Britain and France; the day before the February 1939 Bund rally in New York, Coughlin told his huge flock of listeners that the "system of international finance which has crucified the world to the cross of the Depression was evolved by Jews both for their own defense as well as holding the peoples of the world under control." He made plain the direct threat posed by this world Jewish conspiracy: "If this policy of internationalism continues, war will eventuate, capitalism will cease, and communism under some form will follow." With words like this filling millions of living rooms across the country, it was certainly not a surprise that at the Bund rally, every mention of the Detroit priest drew approving roars from the crowd.[42]

In late 1938 and early 1939, Coughlin accomplished what no other public figure of this era could achieve: He pulled together many once-disparate threads of the conspiratorial right—anti-New Deal sentiment, antisemitism, anti-communism, anti-militarism, fear of all-powerful so-called international bankers (a code word for Jews), Catholic support of General Franco in the Spanish Civil War, as well as advocacy of U.S. neutrality and disengagement. He injected the fevered anger and delirium of the conspiracy theorist into the national discussion about world affairs. In doing so, he unified those opposed to Roosevelt's rearmament plans. But he also gave FDR a political gift, allowing Roosevelt to paint all his foreign policy critics with Coughlin's toxic brand of varnish.

VI

March 1939 blew in full of dismal portents. In that pitiless spring, European fascists delivered the coup de grâce to two bloodied, broken, once-democratic nations: Czechoslovakia and Spain. On the fifteenth, Hitler sent the Wehrmacht into Bohemia and Moravia (the western portion of Czechoslovakia), completing the absorption of the country whose dismemberment began at Munich. Since losing the Sudetenland, and its ability to defend itself, Czechoslovakia had become a vassal of the Third Reich. President Edvard Beneš resigned a few days after Munich, replaced by an elderly and inexperienced lawyer, Emil Hacha, who placed his country's fate in Hitler's hands. Hitler now encouraged the Slovaks to seek independence, which they did, and bullied Hacha into signing away the rest of the country. Hitler followed his troops into the dismembered country, spent the night in Prague at Hradčany Castle, home of Bohemian kings since the ninth century, and the next morning issued a declaration that Bohemia and Moravia were now German protectorates. At a stroke, Germany snapped up the huge Škoda Works industrial complex that would now supply tanks and trucks to the Wehrmacht. Also in Hitler's hands were the iron and steel industries, the gold reserves, the raw materials and the skilled factory workers of this newly acquired land. The outcome that every honest observer prophesied at the time of Munich came to pass. Dorothy Thompson ran a column titled "Cassandra Speaking" that quoted liberally from her many previous articles predicting the destruction of the Czech state. Her bitter message: I told you so.[43]

In Prague, the Nazi coup was bloodless. In Spain, however, murder and retribution accompanied General Francisco Franco's armies into Madrid on March 28. The city had been besieged for two and a half years, and its fall—two months after Franco seized Barcelona—marked an end to the civil war. It did not bring an end to the killing, however. As refugee columns of Republican fighters and fearful civilians snaked northward toward the French border, the roundups began. Franco's triumphant forces arrested, tortured, and executed anyone who had fought for the Republic. Some were shot by firing squad, others dispatched by the medieval strangulation method called the garrote. The cleansing of the anti-fascist forces carried on for months, indeed for years.[44]

For those American supporters of Spanish democracy, these days triggered intense despair. William Shirer, the CBS radio correspondent who had covered Europe for years, wrote in his diary a brief comment: "Madrid surrendered yesterday, the end of Republican Spain today. There are no words to express what I feel tonight." Martha Gellhorn, who had spent so much time reporting on the Spanish war, poured out her grief in a few remarkable letters to her mentor and friend Eleanor Roosevelt. The defeat "is like having a death in the family, only worse," she wrote. "I cannot endure to think about it." The democracies had failed Spain in every way, and she could not forgive or forget. "In our time, there has been no spectacle as tragic," she said, feeling that something essential had died in Spain: "There will be millions like me who will never know what to believe again. . . . It is impossible to tell people to believe in democracy when those who control democracies will not believe in it themselves." War would be better than selling out, she wrote. "To stand aside before such injustice is the worst defeat there is."[45]

Franklin Roosevelt, it seems, had come to feel the same way. In a remarkable scene, in fact a truly tragic moment, he welcomed Ambassador Claude Bowers to the White House for lunch on March 11. Bowers had been ordered home for "consultation" by the State Department, a preliminary step toward replacing this outspoken anti-Franco envoy with a more pliant ambassador who would be less objectionable to Franco's new fascist government. Over three years, Bowers wrote powerful, emotional cables to Washington, begging for military aid for the Spanish government. It never came. Like many other witnesses, Bowers believed the war was "the only fight being made for democracy any place in Europe," but the Spanish Republic fought the fascists alone, "deserted by those who should have been its friends." Returning to Washington in March, he found State Department officials cool toward him; Secretary Hull met him but "seemed disinclined to discuss the Spanish situation," perhaps out of shame. Roosevelt showed at least a brief flash of frank honesty. As Bowers came into the president's office, FDR, looking "more serious and grave than I had ever seen him," blurted out his confession: "We have made a mistake; you have been right all along." Still, just two weeks after this admission, the United States offered diplomatic recognition to Franco's government, a pathetic coda to three years of unconscionable neglect of the war in this battered land.[46]

The twin disasters in Prague and Madrid gave Roosevelt an opportunity to move ahead with revising the Neutrality Act. His State Department officials had been quietly preparing for this since the late fall of 1938, working out proposals for the repeal of the act or its substitution with a law that gave the president discretion to lift an arms embargo on a nation that had been attacked (a measure that might have saved Spain). FDR himself said privately that he wanted the law entirely repealed, though there was little appetite for so bold a move in Congress. That spring, public opinion moved notably in support of selling arms to Britain and France, and the gap widened in the summer. Yet no one could deny the un-neutral impact of the act in practice, and if war broke out in Europe now, U.S. law would cut Britain and France off from purchases of arms vital to their survival. To avert this fate, the administration, working through the chairman of the Senate Foreign Relations Committee, Senator Key Pittman, proposed what it considered a compromise bill, the cleverly titled "Peace Act of 1939," that would eliminate the arms embargo from the Neutrality Act and allow arms sales to combatants, provided they paid in cash and transported the goods on their own ships (the so-called "cash-and-carry" proposal).[47]

Pittman mobilized powerful allies to speak in favor of a revised law, beginning with former secretary of state Henry Stimson. His views were well-known: A month earlier, Stimson penned a long letter to the *New York Times* stating that "fascism is a radical attempt to reverse entirely the long evolution out of which our democracies of Europe and America have grown." The fascist dictators, he wrote, formed "the most serious attack on our underlying principles" that the democracies had ever faced and that "the safety of our civilization" was now in jeopardy. Addressing the Senate committee in the packed Caucus Room on April 6, Stimson hammered home his argument. "I believe our present Caucasian civilization is threatened by the greatest danger with which it has been confronted in four centuries," he said, appealing to ideals of Western solidarity against barbaric fascism. He mocked isolation as "shopworn," and blamed American policy for the defeat of the Spanish Republic. To critics who argued that arms sales would irritate the Axis powers, making them more likely to declare war, the former artillery officer bristled:

"The very fact that we are a democracy irritates the Axis." Americans were not a "timid" people with some "inferiority complex," he declared. They must not kowtow to dictators but assist their fellow democracies in this dark hour.[48]

Pittman also called Dorothy Thompson to testify, who echoed Stimson. "The way to keep peace is not by inactivity, and not by declaring to the world the total disinterestedness of the greatest economic power of the world," she said. The president needed freedom of action to respond to aggression when it threatened America's interests. And the survival of Britain and France, she believed, was in America's interest. Others supported this line. Mrs. Louise Leonard Wright spoke for a large group of women's organizations that supported collective security in the face of fascist threats. On behalf of the League of Women Voters, the American Association of University Women, the General Federation of Women's Clubs, the National Council of Jewish Women, and the National Committee on the Cause and Cure of War, she stated that "the Neutrality Act thwarts the desire of the American people for peace and security." Adopting an argument Roosevelt was also making at this time, she said that America's "traditional neutrality," which insisted on freedom of the seas and allowed commerce with any nation even in wartime, would protect U.S. commercial interests while also giving democracies a chance to arm themselves adequately against aggression. In the long run, that policy would deter the dictators and keep the dogs of war on a tight leash.[49]

And those dogs appeared particularly restive. A week after his entry into Prague, Hitler demanded from Lithuania the return of the Memel territory, a coastal slice of East Prussia that had been ceded to the newly independent Baltic nation at the Paris Peace Conference. Abandoned by the British and French, the Lithuanians gave in—another win for the Führer. In late March, Hitler demanded that Poland return the port city of Danzig over to the Reich, another assault on the 1919 peace settlement that had placed this German city under international control. Unlike the Lithuanians, however, Poland refused and insisted they'd fight for Danzig. As tensions rose, the British government, infuriated by Hitler's invasion of Prague, pledged to defend Poland from German attack—a significant reversal of years of unrequited appeasement of the Nazis. The French government supported this gesture and joined in the security guarantee to Poland. The Anglo-French move was designed to deter Germany, though it was unknown if pledges by the democracies, so often broken before, would impress Hitler. Enraged by this sudden resolve from the Western powers, Hitler secretly ordered the preparation of an assault on Poland to subdue, and destroy, this obstreperous, defiant nation. Europe wobbled on the edge of the abyss.[50]

This would have been an obvious moment for Roosevelt to enter the congressional debate about revising the neutrality law, but he equivocated. On April 11, back in Washington, he refused to be drawn into a discussion about Europe with reporters at his press conference, though he did strongly emphasize his agreement with a *Washington Post* editorial that had appeared that morning. "I almost fell out of bed when I read it," he said. The newspaper asserted that Americans did not sufficiently grasp the "tremendous implications of the impending catastrophe for every citizen of this country." A Nazi war in Europe would represent an attack on Western civilization as a whole and "immediately affect us vitally." The only way to avoid such a disaster, the *Post* continued, was a prompt "show of preponderant force." To the fascists, "force is a real deterrent." The editorial ascribed to Roosevelt a desire to halt war by joining forces with Britain and France "to avert a shattering disaster." That the president would urge the White House press corps to read this "very good, very clear and very honest" editorial shows both the direction of his thoughts and his desire to appear aligned with public opinion.[51]

As if warming to the theme, three days later he gave a muscular address at the anniversary of the Pan American Union. Directing his message to the dictators, he insisted that the United States did have an interest in the fate of Europe, "an interest wider than that of the mere defense of our sea-ringed continent." As new technologies made the world ever more interdependent, the well-being of the United States was "necessarily involved" with Europe's, "whether we like it or not." If the dictators flung their people "into the tragic vortex of unending militarism punctuated by periodic wars," the United States would not sit idly by forever. "We, too, have a stake in world affairs," he said.[52]

Yet Roosevelt could maddeningly shift his tone, and did so that very evening, April 14, when he cabled letters to Hitler and Mussolini that were reminiscent of the fruitless missives he sent during the Munich crisis. His letter asked the dictators to commit themselves to a ten-year nonaggression pact toward thirty-one nations in Europe and the Near East named in the letter. If they would make such a pledge, America would help convene a great world conference on disarmament and trade to resolve their various territorial demands. "We are doing what we can to save humanity against war," FDR explained to the press the next morning. Although the president spoke about this overture with some enthusiasm, it was thin gruel indeed, the same warmed-over porridge he had been serving up since his first term. It was a return to the discredited appeasement strategy and suggested that Roosevelt was willing to look past the assaults on Ethiopia, Spain, Austria,

Czechoslovakia, and Italy's recent invasion of Albania in hopes of halting further aggression. Perhaps these billets-doux were designed mainly for domestic consumption—to prove his commitment to peace even as he was asking for a revision of the Neutrality Act. But the gesture elicited only contempt from Hitler and Mussolini and won him no sympathy from the peace bloc at home.[53]

Where FDR vacillated, the internationalist lobbying organizations forged ahead. In mid-March, Clark M. Eichelberger, the longtime director of the League of Nations Association, an ardent Wilsonian and advocate of collective security, announced the creation of the American Union for Concerted Peace Efforts, essentially a coordinating office for the dozens of proliferating groups that wished to see a revision or repeal of the neutrality laws. Eichelberger assembled one hundred leading scholars, lawyers, and journalists in early April at the Shoreham Hotel in Washington to create the impression of a groundswell in favor of overturning the Neutrality Act. Eichelberger's group organized a "Peace and Security Week" of radio broadcasts, mass meetings, and speeches by legislators and activists, underwritten by funding from the Carnegie Endowment for International Peace. The speakers made the case that the United States could not be neutral in the face of fascism, and that by engaging its strength now on the side of democracy, a calamitous world war could be avoided.[54]

These were influential and determined people, but their efforts, lacking significant public support from Roosevelt, had little impact. Roosevelt deferred to Congress to make the first move in altering the neutrality law, but the administration's allies handled the issue badly, allowing the debate to drag on for weeks, then months. Roosevelt, a lame duck president in what everyone assumed was his last year in office, had accumulated enough enemies in both parties to ensure that numerous legislators stood ready to deny him any victory. His chief foreign policy critics like Senators William Borah, Gerald Nye, and Hiram Johnson, along with Congressman Hamilton Fish, knew their arguments cold and repeated them with fervor: that American arms sent to Europe would soon be followed by American armies.[55]

The issue came to a head in a typically hot and stifling July in Washington. Roosevelt told the press he wanted the arms embargo repealed in order to deter the dictators and keep the peace; he insisted Congress stay in session as long as it took to get it done. But Senator Pittman, the administration's unfortunate field general, was mortally ill and relied heavily on alcohol to keep himself going. He procrastinated while the opposition mobilized. Senators Johnson, Nye, Clark, Borah, and others joined a caucus of at least thirty-four legislators who publicly opposed any modification of the Neutrality Act—and that number of votes would be enough to halt passage of any revision. In fact, it never got to the floor for a vote. On July 11, the Senate Foreign Relations Committee took up the matter. Though Democrats enjoyed a majority on this committee, anti-war and pro-neutrality sentiment crossed party lines, as did a general dislike of FDR and the New Deal. Two Democratic senators on the committee, Walter George and Guy Gillette, had been targets of Roosevelt's ill-conceived "purge" in the primaries of the spring 1938; they had been reelected anyway and now planned to exact their pound of flesh. In the meeting, Senator Clark made a motion to postpone discussion of neutrality legislation for the rest of the year. While eleven senators voted against the postponement, twelve voted for it. Five Democrats and two independents joined five Republicans to kick the can down the road until the next Congress, which would reconvene in January 1940. On an acute issue of foreign policy, the Senate punted—an egregious failure of responsibility.[56]

Privately, Roosevelt fairly screamed about what he considered obstreperous and provincial legislators in Congress and told Henry Morgenthau that they ought to erect swastika-draped statues to them in Berlin. Publicly, he was more restrained and simply asked Congress to continue discussion of neutrality revision before adjourning. Even Mrs. Roosevelt got in on the lobbying, calling for Congress to amend the neutrality law "to give it some backbone."[57]

On the evening of July 18, FDR gathered senior legislators from both parties at the White House and personally appealed to them to push through a new neutrality law that allowed the sale, on a cash-and-carry basis, of American munitions. But the old tricks, the cajolery, flattery, appeals to conscience, came to naught. Senator Borah waved off the president's request, casting doubt on doom-laden State Department reports about an imminent outbreak of war in Europe. He knew better from his own sources, he said, leaving Cordell Hull apoplectic and red-faced. The gathered leaders were unmoved by Roosevelt's request. Vice President Garner, who had just launched his own presidential campaign to succeed FDR in 1940, acidly remarked to the chief: "You haven't got the votes, and that's all there is to it."[58]

For that, FDR must bear much of the blame. He tried to break out of the neutrality trap but no longer had the political levers he needed to move his priorities along. After this disappointing defeat, he headed north to the cooler weather of Hyde Park; in mid-August, as war came ever closer in Europe, he embarked on the USS *Tuscaloosa*, a heavy cruiser that carried him from New York to his beloved retreat, Campobello Island, and then two weeks of fishing off Newfoundland. The bold language he used in his State of the Union message in January had evaporated. Dorothy Thompson wrote bitterly of the president's apparent defeatism. "We can hardly be said to have a foreign policy at all," she said, with Congress and the president unable to free themselves from the outdated, parochial notions of embargoes and neutrality—as if that could protect them from the global aspirations of fascism. American leaders seemed oblivious that Germany, Japan, and Italy planned to divide the world and set up new empires ruled by a "master race." Like it or not, "we are already entangled in this" sinister plot, she insisted, which if successful would totally smother U.S. independence in the world. The failure of Congress to revise the neutrality law "has strengthened the courage of the Axis powers" while the president fell back on vague platitudes.[59]

No less baffled than Thompson, later historians have struggled to explain Roosevelt's unwillingness to make the revision of the neutrality law a signature public fight that summer. Some put his caution in the debate down to a realistic assessment of the forces arrayed against him, as well as his fear that a prolonged public struggle would only embolden the dictators by revealing the depth of anti-war sentiment in America. But others sense that FDR had lost his touch. James M. Burns, in his 1956 biography, put the question plainly: "In the greatest international situation the nation had ever faced, where was the leadership of the man whose very name since 1933 had become the symbol of candor and courage?" In reply, Burns argued that FDR had become captive to the political forces around him, no longer their master. He had always preferred mediating rather than striking out boldly and calling his followers to step in line behind him. A skillful manipulator, FDR "lacked that burning and almost fanatic conviction that great leadership demands." A harsh verdict, and one others have rendered. Robert Divine in his influential 1962 study of neutrality concluded that Roosevelt should have fought harder, only if to show that he gave his all to the task of redirecting American foreign policy. And given FDR's abilities in political battles, "he might have won." Instead, Roosevelt allowed himself to be carried downstream by events, adrift on a current he could not control, and unable to anticipate what lurked around the bend in the river.[60]

VII

Drift; uncertainty; crepuscular gloom pierced occasionally by a flash of ambition, like heat lightning on a torpid summer night. This was Roosevelt's presidency in midsummer 1939. And in his temporizing, FDR perfectly embodied many of the crosscutting attitudes in American life in those uncertain months. In foreign affairs as well as domestic matters, the nation, like the president, toggled between engagement with the world and isolation; between progress and retreat; between moral purpose and inertia; between the risks of change and the lure of inaction. In this environment of equivocation, small gestures took on enormous significance. On Easter Sunday, April 9, on the steps of the Lincoln Memorial in the nation's segregated capital city, the renowned African American contralto Marian Anderson gave a short concert to a rapt audience of no less than seventy-five thousand people, with millions more tuned in by radio. As all those who witnessed it knew, this was no ordinary musical performance.

Anderson had earned a world reputation for her voice and her interpretations of spirituals, familiar American ballads, as well as the classical European repertoire. In Washington, D.C., a city with a large Black population that was banned from most restaurants, cafés, theaters, opera houses, hotels, and trains, Howard University wished to host Anderson for a concert at the historic Constitution Hall. The organization that owned the hall, the Daughters of the American Revolution, refused to give permission. The space by rule could not be used by Black performers. A powerful champion of racial equality now

The crowd on the National Mall listening to Marian Anderson sing, April 9, 1939.
National Archives and Record Administration

stepped in. First Lady Eleanor Roosevelt publicly announced her resignation from the DAR, writing to its leadership that "you had the opportunity to lead in an enlightened way and it seems to me that your organization has failed." Anderson told the *Baltimore Afro-American* that she was not surprised by the First Lady's action because "she really comprehends the true meaning of democracy." But the singer went on: "I am shocked beyond words to be barred from the capital of my own country after having appeared almost in every other capital in the world." Prodded into action by Walter White of the NAACP, Interior Secretary Harold Ickes, whose department supervised the National Mall, proposed to stage the concert at the feet of the Great Emancipator himself. Ickes received the president's explicit approval, and the concert became a world sensation, and a promise of what American might yet become.[61]

In front of an enormous crowd of African American and white residents of the city, surrounded on the dais by two hundred public officials, Anderson stood calmly and bravely, looking out toward the Washington Monument. She closed her eyes, drew in her breath, and confidently sang the indelible first line of the popular hymn, "America": "my country, 'tis of thee." Then she slightly altered the following words: "sweet land of liberty, *to thee we sing*," making the song an appeal rather than an homage. With her frail frame enveloped in a large fur coat on that chilly spring afternoon, Anderson embodied the hope, however fleeting, of racial equality in America, just at a moment when Hitler's racial imperialism had placed so many millions of vulnerable people in terrible jeopardy. One reporter said her voice "drowned out the rumblings of war machines, quieted the clouds of hatred and strife and brought sublimity and peace to many hearts."[62]

Just three weeks later, another message of hope and optimism went up from New York City, where the 1939 World's Fair opened on the former site of a vast ash dump in Flushing Meadow, Queens. Organized around a central theme—"the World of Tomorrow"—the fair put on display hundreds of head-spinning exhibits, inventions, futuristic machines, and cultural programs from sixty-two nations. It drew immense crowds: Over 45 million people would come to walk the miles of paths, attend musical shows, watch newfangled electrical devices, climb aboard heart-stopping rides, and gaze at the monumental pair of structures, the Trylon and Perisphere, that greeted visitors at the gates. (Sadly, the pavilion built by Czechoslovakia remained in limbo, its flag at half-mast since the German invasion had extinguished the nation's existence.) President Roosevelt opened the fair on April 30, becoming the first president to have his words broadcast on the new technology of television. He spoke of peace and good will, avoiding any direct mention of the world crisis. And Marian Anderson appeared there as well, singing in the fair's Hall of Music on May 28 to a full house of 2,375 people. She dazzled listeners with "her stage deportment and regal carriage," and held the crowd "spellbound" with the very last song of her second encore—her signature performance of Schubert's "Ave Maria."[63]

Nothing could compete for sheer scale and spectacle with the World's Fair—except the June visit to the United States of King George VI and Queen Elizabeth of Great Britain, which FDR had been planning for a year. No reigning British monarch had ever come to America, and in a time of international tension, Roosevelt hoped this demonstration of Anglo-American solidarity could soften the suspicions that many citizens held about the British Empire. On June 8, Roosevelt hosted the royals at a state dinner for seventy-eight guests at the White House. The president, who had planned every detail of the visit down to the bedclothes the monarchs required, gave a fulsome toast of thanks for "the bonds of friendship that link our two peoples." The guests dined on a distinctly American menu, including cornbread, Maryland terrapin, capon with cranberry sauce, beets, sweet potatoes, and maple walnut ice cream; the tables were festooned with orchids and lit by six immense gold candelabras. The queen stunned everyone with her tiara and necklace of innumerable diamonds, making her look, as one breathless reporter put it, "like something from a fairy tale." For a White House notorious for its bad food and miserly kitchen, this was a royal welcome indeed.[64]

It was capped by an evening of American music, featuring the booming, joyful voice of Kate Smith, a chorus of African American singers from North Carolina performing spirituals, and—once again—the great Marian Anderson, who filled the mansion with her exquisite voice singing "My Soul's Been Anchored in the Lord." For Black Americans, this moment, when a king and a president sat transfixed by the singing of the brilliant contralto, possessed transcendent meaning. The *Afro-American* editorial page said it was "impossible to overestimate the significance" of her presence that evening, and asked readers to "take out a mental measuring rod and stretch it over the distance colored people have traveled in the seventy-five years since they were chattel slaves and human animals." By privileging Black voices that night, the White House concert "slaps die-hard American color prejudice in the face." The event had global significance, and "Hitler and Mussolini, with their fanatic racial purity programs, will get word about it." Fight on, the paper urged its embattled Black readers. "We are winning."[65]

In these volatile spring months of 1939, many Americans saw themselves already engaged in a struggle—a moral and political struggle against Jim

Crow, Coughlinism, the sneering chauvinism of the Bund, the racism of the DAR. And in that fight, they were making headway. Yet the contradictions and hypocrisies of American life have a way of reasserting themselves, tempering hopes for radical change. For example, on May 27, the day before Marian Anderson wowed the crowds at the World's Fair, a transatlantic liner called the *St. Louis* docked in Havana, Cuba. It had left Hamburg, Germany, two weeks earlier, with over nine hundred Jewish passengers on board, all fleeing Nazi persecution. Arriving in Havana, the refugees discovered that Cuba would not admit them, having changed its immigration rules and canceled their landing permits. Cordell Hull and Henry Morgenthau interceded and urged the Cuban government to reconsider, but to no avail; the ship departed Havana with no certain destination. Lawyers from the American Jewish Joint Distribution Committee, a humanitarian organization in New York, tried desperately to persuade U.S. officials to admit these people; as they waited, their ship bobbed uneasily in the blue-green waters off Miami, within sight of Florida's white-sand beaches.

But without visas, these unhappy exiles had no hope of gaining entry to the United States. On June 8, as FDR and his beaming royal guests, King George and Queen Elizabeth, took their seats at the White House state dinner, the *St. Louis*, which the *New York Times* called the "saddest ship afloat today," departed for Europe, its passengers awash in bitter tears. Thanks to the work of the New York committee, they were disembarked not in Germany but in Britain, France, the Netherlands, and Belgium. A temporary reprieve, of course: 254 of these passengers would soon be murdered by the Nazis during their intensifying genocidal war on the Jews. That American gates remained closed to most Jewish refugees should hardly have come as a surprise. A poll soon after Kristallnacht showed that 72 percent of the public did not want to give safe harbor to more Jews from Germany. A congressional bill to allow the entry of twenty thousand German Jewish children, proposed in February 1939, was so unpopular it never even made it to the floor of Congress for a vote.[66]

Antisemitism coursed through the bloodstream of American public life in 1939. In universities, clubhouses, and the homes of the elite, it remained genteel; elsewhere it flared up into the ugliest kind of race-baiting. Throughout the spring, as war drew ever closer, Father Coughlin released an unceasing flood of invective against the movement to repeal the Neutrality Act. FDR and his minions, Coughlin insisted, aimed to "further the cause of tyranny and aggression under the name of liberty and democracy." The federal government, the priest alleged, planned to use war as an excuse to control the press, conscript labor, and direct all business activity, thus assuring a Roosevelt dictatorship. He called for a stronger neutrality law to punish any propagandist speaking in favor of war. Coughlin even saw the visit of the British royals as part of a conspiracy to circumvent neutrality laws and forge an Anglo-American alliance. War, he insisted, "would spell the destruction of Americanism, the cancellation of our Constitution, the abolition of liberty of conscience and freedom of speech." Those who spoke of confronting foreign dangers were doing the work of a power-crazed president hungry for war.[67]

Coughlin's sermonizing spurred the creation of white Christian nationalist organizations with names like American Patriots, American Federation Against Communism, American Nationalist Party, Christian Mobilizers, and, most significant, the Christian Front. These groups sold copies of Coughlin's *Social Justice*, held provocative rallies, sought out street fights, and beat up Jews on the streets of New York. *The Nation* ran a detailed investigation written by the investigative reporter James Wechsler, who reported that the Christian Front held as many as thirty public rallies a week in the New York area, each attracting crowds of about two thousand supporters. They often gathered near Jewish-owned storefronts, shouting anti-Semitic slogans ("Kill the Jews!" or "This is a Christian Country!") and engaging in brawls. The New York City police, "overwhelmingly Catholic" according to Wechsler, looked the other way. Though the *New York Times* pulled its punches, reporting that the Front's "patriotic rallies" had an "anti-Semitic tinge," Wechsler was far more direct in his reporting. "There is no longer any ambiguity about the link between anti-Semitic violence and Coughlin propaganda," Wechsler concluded. Under Coughlin's intoxicating influence, New York had become, in Wechsler's view, "a laboratory for carefully developed fascist experimentation" that could soon metastasize across the nation.[68]

Coughlin initially denied playing any role in stirring up these mobs. But in an August sermon, he seemed to embrace the need for such direct action. Inveighing against Communist-inflected Popular Front coalitions that had become so active across the democratic nations, he called for action: "If the enemies of our Americanism and Christianity have been successful in building up a following of millions of propagandized supporters, is it not right and just for us to organize a counterforce? Call this counterforce the Christian Front or any other name you please. But organize yourselves!" He himself would not stoop to lead the movement in the streets but he promised "to preach encouragement" and to "unveil the betrayers." And his preaching worked. In an incisive report in September published by *Look* magazine, journalist William A. Mueller concluded that Coughlin had far exceeded the

German-American Bund in rallying Americans to the antisemitic cause. He had "dignified" Jew-hatred and sent thousands of recruits into the ranks of fascist gangs. The Detroit radio priest "has done more to unify anti-Semites in nine months than the Bund has in six years."[69]

Coughlin's hate speech did not go unchallenged. Many of his most vociferous critics were religious leaders whose remarks could be read in every newspaper following each of Coughlin's nasty radio sermons. These churchmen explicitly linked the radio cleric to Nazi ideology. The Friends of Democracy, for example, set up in 1937, was led by Reverend Leon M. Birkhead of the All Souls Unitarian Church in Kansas City. Birkhead pulled no punches in linking Coughlin to Hitler and Nazism and set out to raise money for a campaign of counterpropaganda. In March, Monsignor John A. Ryan of Catholic University launched what became a long-running campaign against Coughlin, denouncing him for his cruel attacks on Jews. The influential Catholic magazine *Commonweal* followed suit. Reverend Walton E. Cole of the First Unitarian Church of Toldeo spent almost two years lambasting the Detroit priest, using Coughlin's favorite medium—radio. "Of all the propagandists now operating in the United States," Cole claimed, "none is more skilled, more vocal, and more destructive of established American ideals of tolerance and goodwill than the verbal magician, Father Charles E. Coughlin." Father William Kernan of Bayonne, who had uncovered the Nazi origins of Coughlin's sermons, gave a series of radio addresses that charged Coughlin with trying to bring fascism to America—"fascism that sets race against race and makes men pawns of the totalitarian state."[70]

Joining Catholics and Jews in a common front, Father Kernan spoke at a Chicago dinner in honor of Rabbi Stephen S. Wise's sixty-fifth birthday; his address was titled "An Answer to Father Coughlin" and took down every one of Coughlin's repulsive antisemitic claims. The moral stature of Coughlin's critics, and the connection they made between the radio cleric's bigotry and the global threat of fascism, carried real weight. This community of courageous, outspoken public figures repudiated not just Coughlin's theories of Jewish malevolence, but also his jeremiad against any engagement with the outside world.[71]

Yet alone, they could not shift American public opinion; the country resisted efforts to mobilize it toward a single purpose. The columnist Walter Lippmann caught something of this reluctance in an essay in *Life* magazine called "The American Destiny." The people, he wrote, were disillusioned by promises of their leaders, fearful of the great challenges ahead, persuaded by demagogues that they should "withdraw, retreat, fence in, batten down, plow under . . . and risk nothing." Lippmann believed the public was entrapped in "a mood of withdrawal, denial, defeat." But this attitude stood in stark contrast to the geopolitical realities of the moment, when America had become, through its power and size, the "political center of the Occident." A great world role, Lippmann believed, was "the American destiny," one the country could not refuse. Americans must "allow themselves to become conscious of their greatness, conscious not only of their incomparable inheritance but of the splendor of their destiny."[72]

Roosevelt had tried since his January State of the Union address to connect America's innovative achievements in economic recovery and social reform to a global campaign of anti-fascism. But since he remained unwilling to consider meeting fascism with force, with arms, his sermons to the country remained only hortatory exercises. It would require a decisive event to make the threat seem real to the American public. As FDR set out on the ocean on August 12 for a few weeks of sun and rest, Adolf Hitler provided the crisis that at last would awaken the world.

CHAPTER 14

THE AWAKENING

"A new page starts today in the history of the world."

—DOROTHY THOMPSON

I

August 1939 in Washington. The temperature above ninety degrees every day. The president literally at sea, fishing off the coast of Newfoundland. Secretary of State Cordell Hull away on a three-week holiday. James Dunn, the special adviser on European affairs, gone for a month. Undersecretary Sumner Welles, unsmiling, always flawless in a double-breasted suit even in the heat, presiding over a motionless bureaucracy. "Everything is still very quiet," noted assistant secretary Pierrepont Moffat in his diary, though he carefully read the cables clattering in from embassies across Europe and knew an explosion was imminent.

Hitler's demands to Poland to surrender Danzig had grown increasingly shrill; if the Poles did not cede the city and the strip of land around it (the "corridor") that gave Poland access to the Baltic Sea, Germany would take it by force. Yet the Poles, armed with a British and French military guarantee, stood firm; they also believed, as the Polish ambassador told Moffat, that German armed might was vastly overrated, that Hitler was unpopular in Germany, that the public opposed war, and that an attack on Poland, leading to a large war in Europe, would be "suicidal" for Germany. No chance for a climbdown, then, either from Hitler or the Polish government. Going into a silent State Department every morning, Moffat had the feeling "of sitting in a house where somebody is dying upstairs. There is relatively little to do and yet the suspense continues unabated."[1]

The situation had a tragicomic quality to it: Whereas the Western democracies had rolled over for Hitler and meekly allowed him to swallow Austria and Czechoslovakia, they now decided to stand rock-solid in defense of . . .

Danzig? If they were willing to surrender the Sudetenland, a territory that had never been part of Germany, why precipitate a world war to halt Hitler from taking back a Prussian port city, long a part of the German empire, that had been gerrymandered in 1919 by the Paris peace treaties, placed under the joint control of Poland and the League of Nations, and whose large German population had repeatedly voted for the local Nazi Party in free elections? It seemed absurd to ask English and French boys to die so that Poland could keep the German city of Danzig.

Neville Chamberlain hoped to avoid that outcome. His aim in giving the Poles a security guarantee on March 31, 1939, was to deter Hitler from attacking Poland in the first place. But he had given that pledge in a flash of anger over Hitler's entry into Prague and before checking with the one state that could actually have helped him make deterrence work: the Soviet Union. A British-French-Soviet front might just keep Hitler penned in, but Chamberlain instinctively recoiled from the prospect of allying with the untrustworthy Communists. "I regard Russia," he wrote to his sister Ida, "as a very unreliable friend with very little capacity for active resistance." He confessed to being "deeply suspicious" of the Russians, who were only out for themselves and would gladly see Germany fight anybody but themselves. And he seemed to

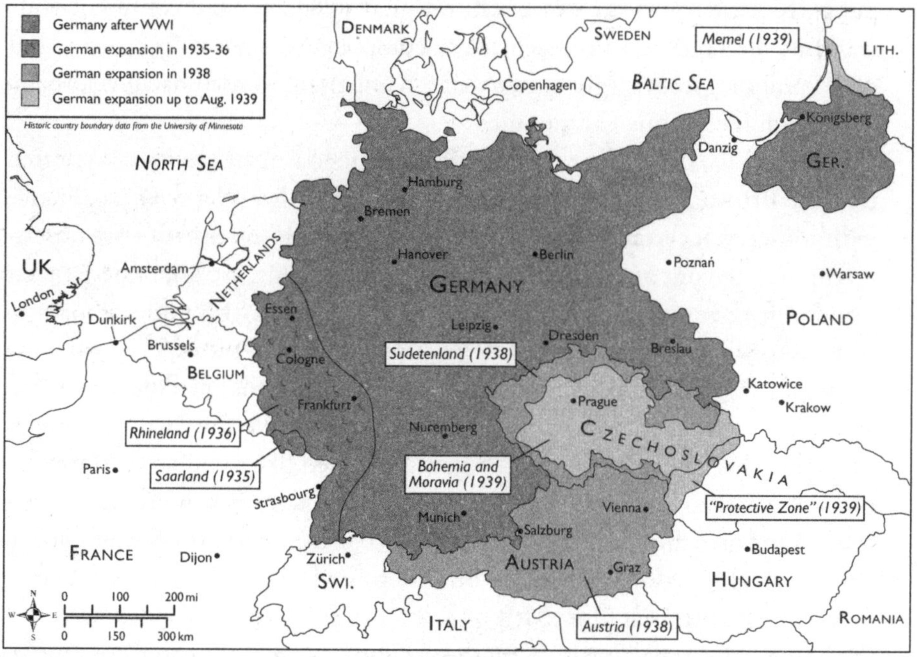

German expansion, 1935–1939

think that Britain's guarantee by itself could keep the Führer from making any "new challenge." Nonetheless, the British cabinet and military chiefs insisted that bringing in the Soviets was the best way to fence in the Führer. So Chamberlain reluctantly approved an approach to the Russians in the late spring that soon revealed Stalin's asking price for cooperation with the democracies: Stalin wanted to send troops into Poland before the Germans attacked—something the wary Poles, who had waged a fierce war against the Russians in 1920, steadfastly rejected. The stalemate in these Anglo-Soviet talks endured and by the end of July, Chamberlain had grown "sick and quite disgusted with the Russians," as Ambassador Joe Kennedy reported to Washington.[2]

Losing a Soviet alliance, however, did not bother Chamberlain unduly because he had not yet lost faith in appeasement, remarking privately that "if Hitler were asking for Danzig in a normal way it might be possible to arrange things." He only objected to Hitler asking for the city at the point of a gun. With a little pressure on the Poles, perhaps Chamberlain could broker a deal with Hitler and avoid a war. Chamberlain told Kennedy that Hitler was "highly intelligent" and surely could grasp that his chances of getting Danzig back would be better at the negotiating table than on the battlefield. So Chamberlain, while feeling out the Soviets about an anti-Hitler alliance, persisted in the appeasement strategy: urging the Poles to enter into direct talks with Hitler in search of a solution that would avoid a continent-wide war. But the Poles had no incentive to compromise, since they could count on the military security guarantee that Chamberlain himself had given them. The standoff continued all summer.[3]

Meanwhile, the Russians, observing Chamberlain's maneuvers, suspected that the British prime minister preferred a deal with Hitler over an alliance with Moscow. It certainly looked to the Russians as if the British were unserious in their pursuit of security cooperation. In early August, Chamberlain left London for a fishing vacation in Scotland, while the British military mission to Russia, when it finally got underway, embarked on a leaky, slow-moving merchant ship that took over a week to reach Leningrad. Even then, the British military advisers had not been empowered to make any final agreement. To Stalin, this lack of zeal from the British seemed like a deliberate slight, an obvious effort to buy time for Chamberlain to make a deal with Hitler over Poland and give the Nazi leader a free hand to make war on the Soviet Union. Perhaps, Stalin reasoned, it might be wise to strike his own deal with Hitler before the British beat him to it.[4]

In fact, Hitler had been laying the groundwork for a possible opening to Moscow. Hitler wanted a war with Poland—it would bring him the military glory he desired and fulfill his ambitions of a greater German Reich. In April, he ordered his military chiefs to draw up an operational war plan. But he wanted to keep it a short, local conflict, avoiding a wider conflagration. The Anglo-French guarantee to Poland, and the prospect of an Anglo-French-Russian encirclement of Germany, presented a major obstacle to Hitler's ambitions. However, if he could neutralize the Soviets, taking them out of the emerging anti-German coalition, he might induce the Western democracies to abandon their pledges to Poland, as they had abandoned the Czechs. Then Hitler could crush the Poles with no fear of a wider war. In the spring, he began his courtship of Stalin with trade talks, offering to purchase great quantities of Soviet raw materials, from cotton, grain, and timber to petroleum products and iron ore—a glittering sales opportunity for the cash-strapped Soviet Union. In return, the Soviets would get credits to purchase German industrial machinery. As these discussions gained momentum, Hitler pushed his foreign minister, Joachim von Ribbentrop, to go further, and sound out the Russians about a far-reaching pact to rearrange the map of Eastern Europe.[5]

Neville Chamberlain, still preoccupied by an unsuccessful search for Scottish salmon, remained oblivious to these developments. Yet the new American ambassador in Moscow, Laurence A. Steinhardt, quickly grasped the picture. In August, Steinhardt took over from the hopelessly unqualified Joseph Davies, whose brief term as ambassador had been forever stained by his credulous reporting to Washington about the Soviet purge trials of 1937. Steinhardt was a Columbia-trained lawyer from a well-connected New York Jewish family, a decorated World War I veteran, and a fervent New Dealer who was rewarded for his work in the 1932 campaign with an ambassadorship to Sweden and then Peru. Perceptive and experienced, Steinhardt within days of his arrival picked up what was afoot: The Nazis and Bolsheviks, despite ferocious ideological hatred and years of the bitterest conflict, were moving rapidly toward a reconciliation.[6]

Steinhardt had a confidential source who reported to him that the German ambassador in Moscow, Friedrich-Werner Graf von der Schulenburg, had seen Soviet foreign minister Vyacheslav Molotov late on August 15 and passed along a message directly from Hitler. Clearly prodded into action by the presence of the Anglo-French military mission in Moscow and hoping to outbid the democracies for Stalin's favor, Hitler sent word that the German government had "no aggressive intentions whatsoever against the Soviet Union" and that the Germans would gladly send a high-ranking official immediately to Moscow to resolve "any territorial questions in Eastern Europe."

Molotov responded cagily to this opening by laying out the steep price of winning Soviet cooperation. The Germans would have to agree to a nonaggression pact with the USSR, put an end to Germany's pursuit of an anti-Soviet alliance with Japan, and agree to recognize Soviet interests in the Baltic states. Steinhardt, reporting these extraordinary developments to the State Department, could not be certain the talks would result in an overt alliance, but the "steady progress" of Nazi-Soviet contacts certainly looked ominous.[7]

Progress toward a pact was moving even faster than Steinhardt knew. Hitler promptly accepted the terms the Soviets laid down, and on August 19, Stalin agreed to welcome a visit from Ribbentrop to consummate a deal. The world learned of these shocking developments on August 21, when the German press office announced that the German and Soviet governments had agreed to a nonaggression pact with one another and that Ribbentrop would reach Moscow by air on August 23 to sign the papers. Hitler, not waiting for Ribbentrop to arrive in Moscow, called his military chiefs together on August 22 and boasted of his clever maneuver. After much self-congratulation, Hitler told his generals to plan for the "complete destruction of Poland," after which would follow the plunder of Poland's valuable raw materials such as "grain, cattle, coal, lead and zinc." He would create some pretext for starting the war—"never mind whether it be plausible or not," he said. "In starting and making a war, what matters is not the Right but Victory." He stressed that he wanted at last "to test the military" because so far, he had gained his Greater Germany through "bluff." The conditions were now perfect for a swift strike. He had contempt for the British and French—"no personalities, no masters, no men of action," he said—and assumed that, having lost the Soviet Union as an ally, they would break their pledge and find some excuse not to come to Poland's aid. "Our enemies are little worms," Hitler sneered about Chamberlain and Daladier. "I saw them in Munich." He told his generals to adopt "a brutal attitude" in conquering Poland. "Have no pity."[8]

In Washington, Pierrepont Moffat described the news of the pact as a "bombshell" and wrote in his diary that "Germany has pulled off one of the greatest diplomatic coups for many years." He suspected that the agreement would involve giving the Soviets a sphere of influence over Estonia, Latvia, and even a large portion of eastern Poland. His instincts were right, as Ambassador Steinhardt confirmed. Ribbentrop arrived in Moscow on the afternoon of August 23; within about twelve hours, he and Molotov worked out the details of the pact, with Stalin actively participating. Steinhardt learned that when the agreement was signed in the very early hours of August 24, Stalin "drank a toast to Hitler and to the 'revival of the traditional German-

Russian friendship'"—an astonishing moment of world-class cynicism, given the deep ideological hostility between these two totalitarian systems. The pact included a secret protocol giving the Soviets a free hand in Estonia, Latvia, Finland, eastern Poland, and a slice of Romania called Bessarabia. On August 24, at 9 a.m. Moscow time, the nonaggression pact (without its secret annex) was made public. With this agreement in his pocket, Hitler could now strike at Poland with no fear of a Soviet response.[9]

In light of these developments, Sumner Welles reached President Roosevelt, who was still cruising off the Canadian Maritimes, and suggested that the president cut short his vacation and return to Washington. Roosevelt did so, and even before reaching New Jersey, where he disembarked from the *Tuscaloosa*, he penned an earnest appeal to the king of Italy, urging him to call for a world peace conference "in which the United States would gladly take part." He also sent a message to Hitler asking him to negotiate with Poland to resolve their differences peacefully. In retrospect, these letters—they had become a rather embarrassing habit—seem jejune and out of step with the realities of the moment. Moffat felt there was not "one chance in a thousand" that such messages would impact events. Still, they might make it easier for Roosevelt to pin the blame for war unambiguously on Germany, which could be of use in future discussions with Congress over American neutrality laws. FDR arrived at Union Station at 1:30 p.m. on August 24 and rushed into meetings with Hull and Welles at the White House, poring over the latest cables from Europe. The next day, he tried to play down the growing alarm, saying to journalists at his press conference, "You all know just as much about the situation as I do"—a not entirely candid statement.[10]

For the next week, the world held its breath in anxious anticipation, unable to get much news from London or Berlin. Would war come? Would Britain and France defend Poland, or offer Hitler a new Munich agreement, winning a peace by sacrificing Poland? To Hitler's surprise, Chamberlain, despite what he called "Russian treachery," did not abandon the Poles and instead announced on August 24 in the House of Commons his country's unalterable determination to honor its obligation to defend Poland. This sign of firmness briefly flummoxed Hitler, and on the next day he sent word to his generals to halt the invasion that had been set for the twenty-sixth. Hitler wanted a little more time to try to peel Britain away from its Polish commitment, perhaps by offering a compromise solution that the British might accept but that the Poles would reject, making the outbreak of war appear to be the fault of the uncompromising Poles. He also summoned the British ambassador, Sir Nevile Henderson, and offered a deal: Give Germany a free hand in Poland, and in return Germany would agree to an Anglo-German pact as wide-ranging as the one he had just concluded with Stalin—a sort of global partition between the German and British empires. Chamberlain brushed this off as the product of Hitler's fevered imagination. In any case, the proposal was wholly insincere: On August 26 Hitler renewed the order to his army to prepare for war, setting September 1 as the start date of the invasion of Poland. Hitler would have his war, whatever Britain and France decided to do. On August 31, Hitler confirmed the order to attack Poland the following day. He issued fictitious and totally unpersuasive atrocity stories of Polish attacks on Germans in Danzig as the justification for war.[11]

Just before daybreak on the first of September, one and a half million German troops launched themselves into Poland. William Bullitt in Paris, having heard the news from his colleague Anthony Biddle, U.S. ambassador to Poland, called the White House at 3 a.m. to awaken the president with the news. The Second World War had begun.[12]

II

In America, the news broke at 5 a.m. on Friday with a radio broadcast of Hitler's address to a hastily assembled Reichstag. "We have all been suffering under the tortures that the Versailles Treaty has been inflicting on us," Hitler howled, and then went on to argue, with astounding mendacity, that he had always wanted a peaceful settlement of the Danzig issue. His proposals had been rejected by the stubborn Poles and their bellicose British masters, and meanwhile the Poles had been abusing and murdering Germans in the "German city" of Danzig. And he made a chilling threat: "The Poles have shot regular soldiers upon our territory," he falsely asserted, "and from now on bomb will be met by bomb. He who fights with poison will be met by poison. He who departs from the rules of humane warfare can expect the same from us." As usual, this was a projection onto others of the horrors he intended to inflict: Just a few weeks after this outrageous speech, he approved a euthanasia program for the gassing of certain groups of incapacitated or infirm human beings in the Reich who did not fit his idea of Aryan perfection. Martial music then resumed on the German radio broadcast, and Berlin was ordered to prepare for air raids.[13]

Roosevelt, who had returned to his slumbers after Bullitt's 3 a.m. call, spent the morning as usual in bed, cloaked in his blue cape, breakfasting amid the morning papers. The stiff and formal Sumner Welles came to the executive bedside for consultation. Once dressed, Roosevelt met with Hull and worked the phones to his ambassadors overseas. The word came through unambiguously: The British and French would certainly fight this time. Their parliaments still had to convene to ratify the decision for war, but there was little doubt of the outcome. FDR immediately thought of the need to repeal the arms embargo and hoped the outbreak of war would give him the leverage he needed with Congress; he would wait a few days to let the news from Europe sink in and then call a special session to consider revision of the Neutrality Act. But when the cabinet convened that afternoon, Roosevelt insisted over and over to his subordinates: "we aren't going into this war." There is no reason to doubt his sincerity. Sympathetic as he was to the democracies, Roosevelt had absolutely no intention of going to war with Nazi Germany now or in the near future. The United States had no alliances to honor; its territory faced no direct threat; it had made no ultimatums.[14]

This tone of caution, of distance from the looming crisis, carried through in his fireside chat to the country on the evening of September 3. He avoided direct accusations against Germany and insisted that America would stay neutral. He hinted at the likely impact of war by telling his listeners that Americans could not "shrug our shoulders" and ignore the war in Europe. "Every battle that is fought *does* affect the American future." But he hastened to stress that no American armies would be sent to Europe, and that America remained committed to the "spirit of the New Testament—a great teaching which opposes itself to the use of force." He knew the public loathed Hitler and admitted that while official policy must remain neutral, "I cannot ask that every American remain neutral in thought as well. Even a neutral has a right to take account of facts. Even a neutral cannot be asked to close his mind or close his conscience." He concluded with an assurance: "I hope the United States will keep out of this war. I believe that it will." It was an elliptical talk, suppressing any warlike words, pointing no fingers, and stressing neutrality.[15]

If Roosevelt met the outbreak of war with caution, other voices were not so restrained. On September 1 at 8 p.m., on a nationwide NBC radio program, Dorothy Thompson reflected on Hitler's Reichstag address that morning. She found his tone "of defiance, of self-pity, of self-congratulation" all too familiar. For a decade she had been ringing the alarm about the threat of Nazism, about its false grievances, its use of hate and conspiracy, its rhetoric of racial struggle. Now, with the opening of the war, Hitler and his "Praetorian Guard of finks, thugs, informers, terrorists, and professional liars" aimed to subdue all of Europe. This war was not about Danzig, or even Poland, she insisted. It was about freedom, liberty, and the survival of civilization, and for that the British, French, and Poles would fight.

Thompson wanted her listeners to understand that the outbreak of war was not an accident, or the result of some misplayed diplomatic game. No: Nazism from its first days promised war, mass murder, and imperial conquest. Her mind went back to January 1933, when Hitler first took power in Berlin. She had watched the torchlight parades, the ghoulish specter of Nazis seizing control of the liberal Germany she knew and loved. She told her listeners of the premonition she had then:

> Men with a type of face I had never seen in Germany—maybe they'd been there all the time, but I had never noticed them—seemed to come out of the ground, clad in brown. They were marching four abreast, through the quiet, orderly, tree-lined streets. And they were crying in that fierce and yet monotonous tone which seems to have become the characteristic expression of the Nazi Revolution: "Juda Verrecke! Juda Verrecke!" over and over again. Perish the Jews! Perish the Jews! Later it was "Perish the Czechs! And Perish the Poles!"

Now, those same thugs were marching on Warsaw. She knew they would not stop there. A storm of merciless conquest and persecution had broken on the world.[16]

Like Thompson, many American newspapers placed the blame for war squarely on Hitler. In retrospect, this may seem obvious, but it needed saying. For twenty years, intellectuals and governments had been arguing over who was responsible for the Great War of 1914, and the lack of consensus on the matter lent support to the pacifist view that unscrupulous militarists and "merchants of death" had pushed the world into an unnecessary war. In the case of Poland, however, the matter was plain: "This is a war of wanton aggression, deliberately launched by a single dictator," said the editorial page of the *Washington Post*. "The verdict of history must lay responsibility at the door of a single individual," wrote the *Los Angeles Times* editors. The *New York Times* published a long list of Hitler's warlike and deceitful actions since 1933, proving the case for his culpability in bringing war. "No future scholar," opined military correspondent Harold Callender, "will need much time to determine the immediate and more remote causes of the European war." Hitler had long planned to reduce Poland to a "vassal state" and conquer all of Europe, he wrote. Assessing national opinion, *Newsweek* reported that thirty-two out of fifty nationwide newspaper editors wanted to see the arms embargo lifted immediately.[17]

Voices in the African American press went even further. William Jones in the *Baltimore Afro-American* asserted that Hitler's racism was not limited to

Jews; the Führer would wage war on Black people too, seeing them as a threat to the Aryan race. It was time to rid the world of such fanatics, he believed. The editors of that paper agreed that Americans must help "crush Hitler." The world would never know peace "so long as crazy men like Hitler are allowed to dictate the policy of any nation." The *New York Amsterdam News* reported that Harlemites felt "nothing but hate and plenty of it for Adolf Hitler," and that many men declared themselves ready to fight now. Charles P. Howard in the *Atlanta Daily World* said that Black Americans wanted "to go to the aid of England and France with money, supplies, and men." Said Howard, "we favor the complete destruction of Hitler and all that he stands for." There was no equivocation toward fascism in the Black community.[18]

Most surprisingly, the usually frosty *New York Times* demonstrated real heat in an editorial titled "The Sword Unsheathed":

> We know where the responsibility lies for this reckless act that has plunged Europe into war. We know in our hearts. . . . that the democracies of Europe are the outposts of our own kind of civilization, of the democratic system, of the progress we have achieved through the methods of self-government. . . . Hitler has said that this is victory or death for him. It is also victory or death for decent standards of international conduct and the democratic way of life.

This editorial set out the dramatic stakes of the war: The German attack on Poland was just the first chapter in a global clash between two irreconcilable ideas of civilization. Who could be neutral on that question? Key public voices, then, had no problem labeling Nazism as a threat to America and to democracy everywhere; it would be some months yet before Roosevelt dared to speak so boldly.[19]

In Britain, a nation that had been deeply polarized by the agonizing arguments over appeasement, a remarkable atmosphere of unity now reigned. Neville Chamberlain, his appeasement policy discredited and disgraced, steeled himself for war. On September 1, he issued an ultimatum to Germany to withdraw its forces from Poland. He ordered the full mobilization of the army and fleet, began the evacuation of hundreds of thousands of children from London and other cities, and announced the creation of a five-man war cabinet, including Winston Churchill, his perennial goad and critic, as First Lord of the Admiralty. On September 2, in the House of Commons, the deputy Labour Party leader, Arthur Greenwood, pledged full support for war, and said the country would fight "to overthrow and destroy that system of government which has trampled on freedom, crucified men and women, and has brought the world back to the jackboot of militarism." Here was a call not simply to defend Poland but to eradicate Nazism. John Gunther, prowling the London pubs to take the temperature of the average Briton, reported that the country was "calm and confident." No panic, no complaints, just an overall sense of what Gunther described as "fed-upness." We cannot go on like this, he heard everywhere. Hitler must be stopped. A proverbial taxi-driver told *New York Times* correspondent Frederick Birchall that there was no use talking to Hitler anymore: "'Let's get on with it now and settle 'im.'"[20]

Chamberlain went on the radio just before noon on September 3 to inform the country that the Germans had rejected his ultimatum to withdraw from Poland; "consequently, this country is at war with Germany." He sounded tired and worn, as if his heart was not in it. "You can imagine what a bitter blow it is to me that all my long struggle to win peace has failed," he said pitifully. But others were not so gloomy. Churchill, sitting in the Commons at noon that day, felt "a serenity of mind. . . . The glory of Old England, peace-loving and ill-prepared as she was, but instant and fearless at the call of honor, thrilled my being." And he rose to speak in a voice that would become familiar to Britain and the world in the coming years:

> The Prime Minister said it was a sad day, and that is indeed true, but at the present time there is another note which may be present, and that is a feeling of thankfulness that, if these great trials were to come upon our Island, there is a generation of Britons here now ready to prove itself not unworthy of the days of yore and not unworthy of those great men, the fathers of our land, who laid the foundations of our laws and shaped the greatness of our country.
>
> This is not a question of fighting for Danzig or fighting for Poland. We are fighting to save the whole world from the pestilence of Nazi tyranny and in defense of all that is most sacred to man.

Reflecting on this declaration of war, Dorothy Thompson told radio listeners late that night: "A new page starts today in the history of the world."[21]

And there came from Paris equally firm language, a sharp break from the years of dithering and submission to Hitler's bullying. Prime Minister Édouard Daladier in many ways had a harder challenge than Chamberlain. France was deeply divided. The Communists in France, taking orders from Hitler's new ally, Stalin, opposed any war. And the far-right fascist movements like the antisemitic *Parti Populaire Français* favored an outright alliance with

Nazi Germany. Even within the center-right French government, as Bullitt reported to Washington, the foreign minister, Georges Bonnet, still pressed for negotiation and appeasement over war. Nonetheless, in uncompromising terms, Daladier told the French parliament on September 3 that the German invasion of Poland marked "a new phase in the march of the Hitler dictatorship toward its goal—domination of Europe and of the world." The time for appeasement had passed; Hitler's appetite had only grown with each conquest. France had given its word to defend Poland; further concessions now would leave France's prestige in ruins, the nation at Hitler's mercy, insecure, fearful, "a miserable people doomed to defeat and servitude." The parliament accepted Daladier's argument. It was time to fight for freedom and honor, whatever the cost; a new spirit of resolution had taken hold.[22]

III

While parliaments in London and Paris deliberated, the Nazi war machine swept into Poland. With 60 divisions, 2,750 tanks, 3,600 aircraft, and a vast array of mobile artillery pieces, the Germans overwhelmed the courageous but poorly equipped Polish defenders. From staging grounds in Pomerania and East Prussia, the Wehrmacht formed a giant pincer movement to cut off the Polish corridor and Danzig; a naval assault on the port of Gdynia sealed the fate of this contested pocket, securing for Hitler his chief war aim in forty-eight hours. But Hitler wanted more than the Polish corridor, as he had made clear to his commanders on August 22. He wanted to destroy and dismantle the entire Polish state and annex its most valuable territory. The largest German battle groups struck in the south, pushing into Silesia and the heavy industrial and mining areas of Poland, toward Gleiwitz, Cracow, Czestochowa, Lodz, and aiming at Warsaw itself. The Luftwaffe established air superiority early and used it to sow terror in cities and strike at retreating Polish columns. By September 8, only a week from the start of the invasion, the Germans had surrounded Warsaw; a three-week battle for the capital began that killed tens of thousands of civilians and ended with the fall of the city at the end of the month.[23]

In a flash, Poland fell. The invaders coined a new term in modern warfare that would soon become well-known: *Blitzkrieg*, or lightning war. Otto Tolischus, the *New York Times* correspondent embedded with German forces in Poland, used a more modest metaphor: "The Germans are today crushing Poland like a soft-boiled egg. After having broken through the shell of Polish border defenses, the Germans found inside . . . little more than a soft yolk."

As a coda to the tragic story, the Soviet government announced on September 17 that, due to "internal instability" in Poland and the disintegration of the Polish state and government, Red Army forces would cross into eastern Poland and seize the spoils promised in the Molotov-Ribbentrop Pact. This move, though anticipated, came as a staggering blow nonetheless: Adolf Berle, an assistant secretary in the State Department and occasional Roosevelt speechwriter, described this Soviet-German carve-up as a return to the age of Genghis Khan. Like the fierce Mongol warrior whose empire stretched across all of Eurasia, Hitler and the Soviets now controlled all the world between Manchuria and the Rhine. "For the time being, Europe is gone," he noted mournfully in his diary.[24]

As the Germans and Russians squeezed the life out of Poland, events in Washington picked up momentum. Roosevelt began to mobilize his political network to launch a bid to revise the Neutrality Act. He told the press on August 29 that he believed the law had emboldened Hitler by taking American power off the European chessboard. Writing to a fellow Democrat, he said that the isolationists should "now realize the gravity of the mistake they made"—forgetting perhaps that he himself supported the act when it emerged in 1935. The September 3 sinking of a British passenger liner the *Athenia* by a German submarine, leading to the deaths of 117 people including 28 U.S. citizens, fueled growing anti-German sentiment. By law, the president was required to declare America's application of the Neutrality Act, and he did so on September 5; but he followed this three days later with a declaration of "national emergency" to allow himself some freedom to speed up rearmament, and it delivered a significant message of America's growing disquiet over European affairs. FDR learned on September 7 from his press aid Stephen Early that a careful count of senators suggested that sixty of them would support "cash-and-carry," that is, an end to the embargo and the return to arms sales to any nation provided they paid in cash and carried the arms away in their own vessels. The next day, at his press conference, a journalist asked about reports of "a rising sentiment in the country for the repeal of the embargo." FDR did not comment on that and insisted the country would "remain on a peace basis." Still, three days later, he felt confident enough to write to Neville Chamberlain to say that "I hope and believe that we shall repeal the embargo within the next month."[25]

Public opinion seemed to be moving favorably as well. Dr. George Gallup, the leading national pollster, published his findings showing the American people "overwhelmingly" on the side of Poland. They believed Germany's claims to Danzig were unjustified, and that Hitler was solely to blame for war. Three polls in September showed that well over 60 percent of the public believed that the United States should "sell airplanes and other war supplies to England and France." When the question was phrased as "do you think England and France should be allowed to buy war supplies here if they pay cash and take them away in their own ships," 79 percent of the respondents answered yes. A September 19 poll found that 62 percent of the public favored revision of the Neutrality Act. For a nation whose public discourse had been so saturated by calls for neutrality and isolation, these numbers show a remarkable degree of support for FDR's "methods short of war" to aid the democracies. Gaining confidence from these trends, Roosevelt on September 13 summoned Congress to meet in a special session to consider repealing the arms embargo and amending the Neutrality Act.[26]

And then gales of opposition began to blow. In a carefully prepared barrage, a few formidable public figures immediately denounced any talk of neutrality revision. Sen. William Borah of Idaho was the first to cry out. While still on vacation in Maine, he summarized the cautionary tale of the First World War in language anyone could grasp: "In the world war, we got rid of the kaiser, but got Hitler instead. In the meantime, we spent forty billions and our boys are dead, maimed, and insane." Why repeat that experience? he asked. Borah hastened back to Washington to deliver a nationwide radio broadcast against any change to America's neutrality law. Speaking for what he termed the "peace bloc," he said that selling arms to one side in the conflict would be an unneutral act and "inevitably bring us into the war." Borah tried to simplify the issue: Repeal of the arms embargo, he said, was tantamount to American intervention. An old lion of the pacifist and neutrality movement, Borah appealed to the age-old dream of a peaceful, prosperous America, free from the quarrels of any other nation or people. He imagined America hunkered down in inward-looking serenity, able to ignore the harsh winds of war. Such a complete isolation from world affairs would, he prophesied, "not only shelter our homes from mass murder, our people from poverty and premature graves, but also will go far toward guaranteeing anew the blessing of free institutions."[27]

Borah had allies both in Congress and out. In addition to senators such as Gerald Nye of North Dakota, Hiram Johnson of California, Robert La Follette of Wisconsin, Bennett Clark of Missouri, and Arthur Vandenberg of Michigan, Borah told the press that a "vigilante" campaign was underway to derail the president's hopes for neutrality revision. Borah dropped the names of Henry Ford and Herbert Hoover, Pierre du Pont and historian Charles A. Beard, as supporters. He could also count on the caustic radio cleric, Father Charles Coughlin. On September 17, in his weekly sermon, Coughlin argued that cash-and-carry would get America into war within a year, and he called for a march on Washington to protest any change in the neutrality law. Coughlin actually spoke of forming an "army of peace" under the leadership of former soldiers in the American Legion and the Veterans of Foreign Wars—remarks that some likened to a call for insurrection. And just a day after Borah gave his radio address, a new member of the "peace bloc" emerged into public view: Colonel Charles Lindbergh.[28]

By the start of 1939, Lindbergh's reputation had lost some of its former glow. The fact that he accepted a decoration from the hands of Hermann Göring was widely noted; and it was said that his alarming reports on the Nazi air force had encouraged Neville Chamberlain to accept the dismemberment of Czechoslovakia at Munich in 1938. Lindbergh did privately admire certain aspects of Nazi Germany and Hitler, as he regularly noted in his diary: "Much as I disapprove of many of the things Germany has done," he wrote, "I believe she has pursued the only consistent policy in Europe in recent years." He liked Nazi Germany's strength and discipline and thought that Hitler "has established a new tempo—a tempo possibly more in keeping with this modern age." Still, as war in Europe neared, he decided to leave his secluded seaside home in France and return to America in order to serve the country. The commander of the Army Air Corps, General Hap Arnold, promptly invited him to conduct a summer-long survey of the American military aircraft industry, its planes, designs, airfields, and general readiness for war, a task Lindbergh gladly accepted. Yet even as he welcomed the expansion of American air power, he fiercely opposed any American involvement in a European war. In his diary, he expressed his fears that the country was being pushed by British and Jewish propaganda to get involved in fighting Hitler. He feared in particular "Jewish influence in our press, radio, and motion pictures."[29]

Lindbergh decided to put his fame to use, scheduling a radio address for September 15 to make an appeal to the public to stay out of the conflict. He wrote in his diary: "I do not intend to stand by and see this country pushed into war if it is not absolutely essential to the future welfare of the nation." For Lindbergh, a war would weaken America and "leave affairs chaotic—and always the best men lost." He had grown deeply suspicious of Roosevelt, who he felt "would sacrifice this country in war if it were to his own personal interests." That low opinion of Roosevelt only hardened when, on the day of his radio address, he learned that the White House was "very much worried by my intention of speaking over the radio and opposing actively this country's entry into a European war." He was told a "secretaryship of air" would be created in the cabinet if he would halt his speech. Rejecting this emolument, he went ahead with the address at 9:45 pm, broadcasting from a room at the Carlton Hotel in Washington.[30]

It was a curiously tone-deaf speech. Nobody in mid-September was calling for America to enter the European conflict—certainly not Roosevelt. Yet that was Lindbergh's chief message to America: Resist "foreign"—meaning Jewish and British—propaganda and stay out of war. The reasoning he gave revealed his sympathy for Nazism. Lindbergh dismissed claims that Hitler posed some kind of existential threat to Western civilization, as so many had claimed. Hitler was "no Genghis Khan." The war in Europe was not a clash of civilizations; there was no threat to the West from "some Asiatic intruder" that would require "the banding together to defend the White race against foreign invasion." The war in Europe was just another round in an "age-old quarrel" arising from "errors" of the last war. It was certainly not America's business to settle. If America entered the war, the cost would be "a million men, possibly several million—the best of our youth." And democracy itself would not survive the regimentation that modern warfare demands: "If we enter fighting for democracy abroad, we may end by losing it at home."

Charles Lindbergh begins his career as a critic of Roosevelt and apologist for Nazi Germany.
Library of Congress

Lindbergh's speech went further than calling for isolation from Europe. He insisted on unmasking the forces within that would manipulate the country with false propaganda. Amplifying Father Coughlin's persistent claims of Jewish domination of the media, Lindbergh called on Americans to reject "insidious" propaganda that would lure them into war. "We must learn to look behind every article we read and every speech we hear" to determine the "personal interests and nationality" of the writer; we must uncover "who owns and influences the newspaper, the news picture, and the radio station." As he made clear in his diaries, he had Jews in mind. America must avoid Europe's new "Dark Age," take shelter behind its oceanic buffers, and protect the "gift" of Western civilization.[31]

Lindbergh's entrance into the debate about American policy toward Nazism made it all too clear where the famous aviator stood. And if listeners did not quite grasp the gist of it, Dorothy Thompson jumped in to clarify things. Deeply offended by his assertion that Nazism was not a threat to Western values, that Europe was not worth saving, and that Jews were conducting a propaganda campaign to trick America into war, she wrote a ferocious column five days later that took up his challenge to examine the "personal interests" of the Colonel himself. He was known to hate America, she said, and had fled the country for seclusion in Europe. He once contemplated giving up his U.S. citizenship. He won the affection of Reichsmarschall Göring and accepted the second highest military decoration of the Nazi government. He closely associated with Dr. Alexis Carrel, a French eugenicist who wished to rebuild and repair modern mankind through ideas of selective breeding. He, along with Ambassador Kennedy, urged the British on in their policy of appeasement. In the horrific days after the Kristallnacht pogroms, Lindbergh actually considered moving to Berlin. His "inclination towards fascism is well known to his friends," Thompson concluded. It was a brutal but accurate assessment, one that discredited the Colonel and cleverly positioned Lindbergh and his cause as sympathetic to Nazism. Evidently, Dorothy Thompson also knew how to make propaganda.[32]

The Roosevelt administration did not have to rely only on Thompson to rebut Borah and Lindbergh. Henry Stimson, Republican stalwart, urged the repeal of the "foolish and dangerous embargo" and advocated a return to "traditional" neutrality—a term FDR would also stress—which allowed the sale of arms to warring nations. Halting such sales to the victims of an attack, Stimson said, only favored an aggressor who had stored up a large arsenal in advance. In two public statements that fall, the former secretary of state argued that if America closed its harbors and arsenals to the British and

French, Hitler would win the war, leaving America itself far more vulnerable to attack. Walter Lippmann in his newspaper column dismissed Borah's argument as a "false dilemma" between war or peace; in fact, no such decision was on the table. The issue was simply how best to assist the Western democracies while staying out of the war. As the *New York Times* put it, to lift the arms embargo was to promote the traditional American interest in free markets, with the added benefit of enabling those nations "which are now resisting unprovoked aggression and defending our own democratic way of life, to obtain in our markets the instruments of self-defense." The sheet music had been set, and now dozens of public figures began to sing this refrain.[33]

More important than these spokesmen, Roosevelt himself entered the fray. On September 20, he met with a small number of congressional leaders from both parties to preview his tactics in the coming debate. The next day, he addressed Congress, assembled in a special session, and made his appeal for neutrality revision. He insisted that everyone in the country, including himself, belonged to the "peace bloc." However, the 1935 Neutrality Act had been shown to encourage war, not thwart it. It allowed aggressors to start a war, knowing the outcome would be the withdrawal of all American power from all sides in the conflict. He did not have to mention Ethiopia, Spain or China, as his audience knew the ways the law had harmed those countries. In a rare admission of error, he said: "I regret that the Congress passed that act. I regret equally that I signed that act." In its place, he proposed the cash-and-carry formula to allow the democracies a fighting chance against the German aggressors, accompanied by a ban on U.S. ships and U.S. travelers from transiting a designated war zone. That prohibition would limit the chance that a sinking of merchant or passenger vessels would become a tripwire for American entry into the war. He also accepted the continuing prohibition on loans to combatants. FDR's proposal was hardly interventionist: After all, the Europeans who bought American war matériel would still have to accept all the risk of transporting it; and Americans would be required to keep their ships out of harm's way.[34]

Although he insisted that his primary aim was to keep America out of war, he also implicitly rebuked the belief that the war would not touch the homeland. The war in Europe cast "a shadow over the world," he said. The shadow would not pass swiftly, and "darker periods may lie ahead. The disaster is not of our making . . . yet we find ourselves affected to the core." As "heirs of European culture," he concluded, America's "destiny" was not isolation but something nobler: "to assume the task of helping to maintain in the Western world a citadel wherein that civilization may be kept alive." Here at last, Roosevelt moved toward embracing the argument, already current in public discourse, that a clash of civilization between democracy and fascism had broken upon the world, and America could no longer absent itself from that fight.[35]

IV

In the coming weeks, many familiar voices rose to support the president. One in particular may have been especially helpful. Eleanor Roosevelt, whose newspaper column, "My Day," was read by millions every morning, rejected Borah's argument on moral grounds, where she had the greatest authority. She had long been the most prominent advocate of racial justice in the administration and had become a beacon for liberals among the New Dealers. In 1939 she began to address the global crisis more frequently.

"I read recently a statement made by a United States Senator on neutrality," she wrote in mid-September of Senator Borah's recent speech. "Why must we approach these questions solely from the point of view of what will save our skins and our pockets? In the end, if the skins of the rest of the world are removed and the pockets of the rest of the world are empty, we will grow thin and lean." America could play a constructive role, she believed; neutrality did not require passivity. While she abhorred the violence of war, she argued that "if certain ideas triumph, then what our forefathers founded in this nation in the way of ideas and ideals would receive a very serious blow." America must consider its obligations to the world. "What we need to think about today is how we can be useful as well as neutral. We must keep alive the ideals which now make life worth living for us. Hundreds of thousands of men, women and children are dying. Are we going to think only of our skins and our own pockets?" And she closed her short essay by asserting that American neutrality must not encourage indifference to suffering: "We have a right to stay at peace, if by doing so we render a greater service to a war-torn world." That service, she suggested, meant offering refuge to the endangered, and promoting the value of democracy in a world of tyrants. The inward-looking isolation of Borah she firmly rejected.[36]

These statements from both Roosevelts triggered a significant surge in calls to aid Britain and France. Associate Justice of the Supreme Court Felix Frankfurter, Reverend William T. Manning (Episcopal bishop of New York), and even Roosevelt's great antagonist Al Smith, all joined the call for action. Bishop Manning had championed American entry into World War I and risen to aid Stephen Wise in 1933 in condemning Nazi attacks on German Jews. He declared to his flock that "we all want peace, but right is more important." With Soviet Russia now on Hitler's side, he said, the issue before the world was a simple one: whether "totalitarianism with its barbarous and inhuman despotism, its anti-God philosophy, and its declared war on Christianity, is now to dominate the world." The *Chicago Defender* published a smoldering editorial that offered Black America's view on the matter: "Neutrality is a fine word rolled from the lips of reactionary congressmen whose speeches too often camouflage a sympathy for the Nazi dictatorship." America's neutrality law had "helped to slaughter Republican Spain." The chief opponents of revoking the act, claimed the *Defender*, were on friendly terms with Father Coughlin's Christian Front, the German-American Bund, "and other organizations that would bring the blessings of castor oil and the concentration camp to America." Dorothy Thompson was not the only writer who could land a blow for the anti-fascist cause.[37]

To be sure, the headwinds continued to howl. Borah accused the British and French of sitting on their hands rather than attacking Germany while the Wehrmacht was busy in Poland. "There is something phony about this war," he said, coining a phrase. Maybe the democracies were merely awaiting rescue by the Americans, Borah implied. Adolf Berle noted in his diary that FDR's congressional address produced "a considerable convulsion of feeling in the country. Propaganda began to pour in on the Congress, chiefly in the form of letters and telegrams." Much of this was the work of the clever radio priest from Detroit. Berle was worried because "our side has no demagogue like Coughlin" to make the case for repeal. And FDR expressly declined to play that role. Far from taking the case to the country, Roosevelt decided he should stay quiet. "I am almost literally walking on eggs," he wrote to his friend Lord Tweedsmuir, the governor-general of Canada, "and having delivered my message to the Congress, and having good prospects of the bill going through, I am at the moment saying nothing, seeing nothing, and hearing nothing."[38]

Roosevelt's best ally in pressing his case for neutrality revision was Hitler himself. During September and October, the American press reported in excruciating detail on the pitiless destruction of Poland. *Life*, one of America's most popular magazines with a circulation of two million per week, went into overdrive, filling every issue with colorful maps, extensive photo essays of war damage, and historical summaries of the European crisis. The September 18 cover with the title "Britain Goes to War" showed a ghoulish British soldier wearing a gas mask and pushing cartridges into an antiaircraft gun. Renderings of the sinking of the *Athenia* accompanied analysis of the ground war in the East. In a tone set by the publisher Henry Luce, one article on the history of American neutrality emphasized the volatility of American opinion. Americans wanted to stay out of war, but no one should underestimate "the final hatred of Adolf Hitler and Hitlerism which Americans have felt since the morning of September 1."[39]

Meanwhile, the daily newspapers and wire services pushed out a stream of terrible stories from the front. The *New York Times* on September 13 reported that the Germans were preparing "a solution of the Jewish problem" through the "removal" of all 3 million Polish Jews. Exactly what this meant, no one yet surmised. After the fall of Warsaw, the *Los Angeles Times* likened the German attack on the Polish capital as something out of the age of Attila the Hun. "If a country can be killed," the paper editorialized, "then surely Poland is dead." Reporters who saw the battered city spoke of hundreds of fires burning out of control and countless corpses among the debris. "Warsaw has been blown off the map," said one correspondent. On October 5, Hitler arrived in the shattered, captive city to review his victorious troops during a two-hour military parade. He preened and strutted through the charred ruins.[40]

The following day, back in Berlin, Hitler offered a victor's peace. Germany, he said, had fulfilled its historic task of destroying the Versailles system. With its Soviet ally, Germany would now reorder the borders—and resettle the people—of central and eastern Europe. In essence, the war in the East was over. "Why should there be any war in the West?" Hitler asked his adoring Nazi deputies of the Reichstag. Poland was gone and "would never rise again." It would be absurd, he said, "to destroy millions of human lives" to resurrect the failed prewar system in Europe. A triumphant Hitler presented a fait accompli to the world and dared any country to wage war against the new German Reich. Leaders in London, Paris, and Washington summarily rejected this cynical overture. And besides, Hitler's idea of peace included more horror for Poland, to which Americans could hardly remain indifferent. At the start of November, headlines instead carried frightful forebodings: "1,500,000 Jews in Poland Face Death By Hunger," reported the *Chicago Tribune*.[41]

As stories of Poland's martyrdom filled the U.S. media, a dedicated corps of lobbyists in New York, spurred by the president's address to Congress, went into action to get the arms embargo repealed. Clark Eichelberger, the tireless leader of the League of Nations Association and the Union for Concerted Peace Efforts, brought together an elite team of seasoned veterans of the internationalist cause to form the Non-Partisan Committee for Peace through the Revision of the Neutrality Law. Eichelberger prevailed upon the elderly Kansas editor, William Allen White, to take the role of chairman. A Pulitzer

Prize–winning progressive Republican whose wise essays and editorial balance had earned him the moniker "the Sage of Emporia," White had been an eager supporter of Teddy Roosevelt, a faithful advocate of U.S. membership in the League of Nations, and, despite his party allegiance, a supporter of the New Deal as well. He joined the anti-war movement of the 1920s, but as the fascists took power and began their rampages, he grew hostile to appeasement and recognized that a conflict with the dictators was coming. "We cannot forever be turning the other cheek," he wrote in March 1938. He was also an outspoken opponent of racial and religious bigotry from the Klan and the Bund. He was an ideal person to make the president's case.[42]

Within days, Eichelberger and White won the support of dozens, and soon hundreds, of the most influential public figures in the country. Many had been active in earlier causes, but this time, their work aligned exactly with Roosevelt's publicly declared policies. The Non-Partisan Committee for Peace was a powerhouse public advocacy group that included newspaper editors and publishers, university and college presidents, bishops, clerics and rabbis, journalists, lawyers, and businesspeople. Carrie Chapman Catt, late of the peace movement, joined, as did Henry Sloane Coffin (president of Union Theological Seminary), Rabbi Stephen Wise, banker Marshall Field III, John Gunther, Freda Kirchwey, Dorothy Thompson, James Shotwell, Monsignor John A. Ryan, playwright Robert Sherwood, and hundreds of other members of the anti-fascist intelligentsia. Even Hollywood figures like Tallulah Bankhead and Edward G. Robinson signed on. A vigorous publicity campaign on letterhead that listed the committee's influential membership soon yielded sponsorship of lunches and dinners, money to build a staff, telegrams to Congress, and public rallies. The committee could make the case in words Roosevelt remained reluctant to use: Its purpose was to urge repeal of the arms embargo in order to help "the democracies who are resisting the spread of dictatorship."[43]

White put his folksy wordsmithing skills to use in a nationwide radio address on October 15, called "The Hour Is Striking." Insisting that he wished above all to keep America out of war, White repeated the now well-rehearsed argument that the Neutrality Act unfairly blocked Britain and France from buying the means to defend themselves against the terrible threat of Nazi aggression. And that should matter to Americans because the British and French were democracies that shared America's devotion to "freedom of worship, the freedom of speech and of the press, the trial by jury and the writ of habeas corpus." He called the war in Europe "a clash of ideologies" and asserted that European soldiers "are carrying our banner, fighting the American battle." While Americans need not risk "our flesh and blood," the country had a moral obligation to assist Britain and France in "defending our own homes, making our own liberties secure." White, with an essayist's talent, positioned the repeal of the arms embargo as an act of self-defense as well as an act of solidarity with the defenders of global democracy.[44]

Against such arguments, the neutrality bloc struggled to mount a successful riposte. Senator Borah, seventy-four years old, was losing steam. Gravely ill, he would die in January 1940. Charles Coughlin, though still able to conjure bag loads of telegrams through his radio sermons, had been tainted by his association with the Christian Front, the Bund, and other openly antisemitic groups. He was coming under sustained public fire from church organizations that openly denounced him for encouraging racist groups like the Crusaders for America, the American Patriots, and the Christian Mobilizers. Herbert Hoover, a constant critic of the president's, wrote various articles warning that war would lead to dictatorship in America, but these lines had grown rather stale. That left Charles Lindbergh as the most prominent public figure to champion isolation from the European war. Lindbergh regularly talked with Hoover, Borah, and Henry Ford about how to combat "the hysteria sweeping the United States" that threatened to push the country into war to rescue Britain and France. Yet Lindbergh was no political pugilist. He had no skill in the art of policy debate. On October 13, he gave another radio speech that actually began by supporting a robust, well-supplied U.S. military establishment to provide for hemispheric defense. "From Alaska to Labrador, from the Hawaiian Islands to Bermuda, from Canada to South America, we must allow no invading army to set foot," he said, sounding much like Roosevelt. "These are the outposts of the United States. They form the essential outline of our geographical defense. We must be ready to wage war with all the resources of our nation if they are ever seriously threatened." Furthermore, he did not object to the sale of what he called "defensive arms" to any European state, and he supported the administration's proposal for restrictions on the travel of American ships into the European war zone.[45]

But Lindbergh did not stop there. Both in his radio talk and in an article he drafted in September that appeared in *Reader's Digest*, Lindbergh expanded on his own sinister theory of world politics. Stressing his favorite theme—the survival of the white race—he said that for Americans to join an internecine war among white Europeans would be a terrible mistake, for "our bond with Europe is a bond of race and not of political ideology. . . . It is the European race we must preserve; political progress will follow." Racial solidarity should draw Europeans together, not drive them apart: "If the white race is ever seriously threatened, it may then be time for us to take our part in its protection, to fight side by side with the English, French, and Germans, but not with one against the other for our mutual destruction." The white race, he believed, existed uneasily in "a pressing sea of Yellow, Black, and Brown." The war in Europe might well "destroy the treasures of the white race . . . [and] lead to the end of our civilization."

Far from fighting the Nazis, Lindbergh insisted, Americans should join their racial brothers and "build our White ramparts again." It was time to stand with Britain, France, and Germany and build "a Western Wall of race and arms." White people must not "commit racial suicide" by fighting one another, when a war against the "Mongol and Persian and Moor" loomed. Coming at the very moment when Nazis were grinding Warsaw into dust and plotting the destruction of Poland's Jews, Lindbergh's timing was, to say the least, poor. In fact, his utterances were so weird, tortured, and disconnected from reality that only his world celebrity as an aviator kept him from being tossed onto the ash heap with cranks like William Dudley Pelley and Fritz Kuhn. And politically, Lindbergh did his cause few favors. He made it easy for Roosevelt to link his critics to the racial imperialism of the Nazis. William Shirer in Berlin noted that all Lindbergh's public remarks received adulatory coverage in the Nazi press.[46]

In the end, Roosevelt won the battle over the arms embargo rather easily. On October 27, the Senate passed what would become the Neutrality Act of 1939—a revised measure shorn of the controversial ban on arms sales—by a wide margin of 63–30, matching the predictions of FDR's legislative advisers two months earlier. The House of Representatives followed suit by a wider margin than the president had expected: 243–181, a buffer of 62 votes. Roosevelt signed the act into law on November 4 at the White House with Cordell Hull, Vice President Garner, and congressional leaders arrayed behind him. It represented "an outstanding victory," as Harold Ickes put it. Historian Wayne Cole has noted that "it was the first of an uninterrupted succession of Roosevelt administration triumphs over isolationists" who, from this moment on, "were never able to defeat any presidential short-of-war proposal actually put up to a vote in Congress. The initiative and advantage had shifted to the president." There remained debates ahead about *how* to aid Europe, but the era of non-involvement and isolation was all over but the shouting.[47]

Four factors explain FDR's remarkable success in November 1939. First, Hitler's bestial slaughter of the Poles, so vivid in the minds of all Americans, helped the cause of repeal. No nation, the public agreed, should be denied the ability to defend itself from the Nazi *Blitzkrieg*, and the cash-and-carry plan proved to have wide support across the country. Second, the administration framed the bill so that it would extend certain aspects of the old neutrality laws—keeping American ships and travelers away from the war zone and continuing the ban on loans to combatants. In that sense, the new act was, as historian Robert Divine wrote, "a perfect expression of the contradictory mood of the American people" who favored the cause of the European democracies but did not want to fight themselves. Third, Roosevelt's own description of the bill as a peace measure, while convoluted and possibly insincere, gave many wavering Congresspeople some political cover to join his cause. FDR in a public statement said that the accusation that he planned to send Americans to fight in Europe was "one of the worst fakes in recent history . . . the deliberate setting up of an imaginary bogeyman." Rather, his plan would do exactly the opposite, he declared. By helping Britain and France to fight with American-made arms, the new law could be explained to the public as a way of keeping American boys out of European trenches.[48]

Yet the most important element in winning the revision of the neutrality law lay in the ability of the internationalist camp to capture the public arena from the neutralists and pacifists whose once-fiery arguments had gone cold. Since the end of the Wilson presidency in 1921, the ideas of pacifism, neutrality, antimilitarism, and isolation had dominated public discourse about America's role in the world. They had been bolstered by xenophobia, antisemitism, and some outright admiration of fascism. The mantra had been clear and unshakeable: American entry into the Great War had been a terrible mistake, caused by unscrupulous bankers and arms merchants; the war failed to make the world safe at all. Never again should America fight the wars of other nations, no matter the cause. The New Deal had accelerated this inward-looking tendency, focusing on reviving and repairing a broken nation. Yet gradually, Americans lost faith in this introverted perspective, as did Roosevelt himself. The tragic assault on Ethiopia, the bloody strife in Spain and China, the Anschluss in Austria, the sickening sellout to Hitler at Munich, then the swallowing of Prague, and finally the murderous destruction of Poland—all these events gave the internationalists the evidence they needed to shape a new argument about America's world responsibilities. When FDR proved too cautious and maddeningly tongue-tied, these advocates of America's engagement with the world elevated the sense of danger to democracy posed by aggressive fascism. They worked to awaken the American public to its responsibility for the survival of liberty both at home and abroad.

In doing so, they appealed to an American tradition that was as old and venerable as George Washington's admonition against "permanent alliances," namely, the idea of an American "empire of liberty." Articulated by the man FDR looked to as the spiritual founder of the Democratic Party, Thomas Jefferson, as early as 1780, this vision of continental expansion had an elastic quality. For Jefferson, who in 1803 doubled the size of the United States through the Louisiana Purchase, an act taken without congressional approval, an empire of liberty implied the conquest and civilizing of the American continent, including of course the subjection and removal of Native peoples. An empire of liberty, in Jefferson's mind, could offer the world an example of a great nation that embodied liberty as well as dominion over land, peoples, and oceans. A paradoxical idea, the empire of liberty reflected perfectly the experience of a slaveholding Republic devoted to freedom for the white men who designed it. That idea flowed through the bloodstream of American nation-builders from the period of continental conquest and expansion through the acquisition of territories in the Pacific and Caribbean, up to Woodrow Wilson's globe-encircling vision of a "world made safe for democracy." Far from being an anomaly or accident, the Wilsonian worldview grew from a long American tradition of expansion—commercial, territorial, and ideological. That tradition had its ebbs and flows, peaking between 1898 and 1917, subsiding in the 1920s.

Franklin Roosevelt had been educated in that school of globalism, full of admiration for the symbols of empire—a big navy, territorial acquisition (he fabricated a story about writing the constitution of Haiti while serving in the Navy Department), and merchant ships plying the trade routes from America's coasts to every corner of the world. For Roosevelt's generation, it was natural to see America as exceptional: blessed by Providence in its wealth, its freedom from Old World decadence, and its founding ideals of self-government. Such an America had a "destiny," a word Roosevelt used frequently, to enter the world and transform it. Roosevelt never tired of speaking of America as a role model and example to the world.

In 1939, as war loomed, he and his internationalist brain trust rediscovered Wilson's vocabulary, which had been mothballed after the bitter fight over the League of Nations. Looking upon a European continent once again ravaged by the flames of war, Roosevelt told Congress in September that the United States must "maintain in the Western world a citadel wherein that civilization may be kept alive." America, Roosevelt suggested, was like the Ark of the Covenant, holding within it the precious tablets on which were written the principles of democracy. The forces of fascism and war threatened these principles. As a matter of self-defense, America had to assist the Europeans to fight fascism and Nazism, to uphold the ideals of law, justice, and what he called Western civilization. Many people had helped Roosevelt shape this argument and this cause. He was now awake to the task and embraced it as his own.

V

On the last day of November 1939, what Senator Borah sneeringly called "the phony war" erupted into a very real conflict in Finland, as the Soviet Union began an invasion of its small neighbor. Since the nonaggression treaty with Nazi Germany, the Soviets had occupied the eastern half of Poland and forced Estonia, Latvia, and Lithuania to accept Russian military bases in those countries, ostensibly for the forward defense of Leningrad. Stalin then turned to Finland and demanded the ceding of a significant slice of territory along the Finnish-Soviet border, in particular the Karelian Isthmus, a land bridge connecting the two nations. The Finns refused; and the Soviet government mobilized its armed forces in an attempt to annex Finland outright or at least place a pliant Finnish Communist government in charge in Helsinki. About nine Red Army divisions struck at the heavily defended isthmus and ran headlong into Finnish guns as well as swamps and thick forests. For a moment, the Russian advance was halted, though Soviet aircraft bombed and strafed Helsinki and a dozen other cities as Soviet divisions poured across the long border running from Lake Ladoga to the Arctic Sea, a distance of over eight hundred miles. Foreign Minister Molotov ludicrously blamed the conflict entirely on "abominable provocations by Finnish militarists" aided by "foreign imperialism."[49]

Americans responded with extraordinary outrage to what became known as the Winter War, a three-month-long fight for survival by Finland against the Russian behemoth. While the Nazi destruction of Poland provoked sympathy and criticism, something about the fate of Finland hit a peculiar American nerve. As commentators noted at the time, Americans were aroused by the David vs. Goliath nature of the war and felt affection for democratic Finland—the only nation in Europe to pay its World War I debts without complaint. More important in stirring Americans into fury, however, was a simple fact: the attackers were Communists. For years, the Soviets and their fellow travelers had positioned themselves as the leading anti-fascists in a global struggle against imperialism and militarism. They claimed to speak for the workers and the downtrodden as they fought the capitalists, fascists, and plutocrats of the world. But since the Molotov-Ribbentrop Pact and Stalin's collaboration with Hitler, this self-righteous language had been revealed as cynical nonsense. Many U.S. observers felt that Soviet behavior in Poland and Finland showed the Communists to be no different from the Nazis. "Identical evils," the *Washington Post* called them. "Different labels for the same poison."[50]

As early reports of Soviet bombing of Finnish cities came in, Roosevelt expressed his "profound shock" and issued a sharp rebuke of Russia's "wanton disregard for law"; Herbert Hoover, glad to join the Red bashing, likened the "Communist attack on peaceful Finland" to "the butchery of Genghis Khan." This reaction marked a shift. After all, Nazi Germany's attacks on its neighbors in 1938 and 1939 had generated precious little American action, while the Spanish Republican government had been unable to buy even a single cartridge in America during its long civil war. Now U.S. newspapers called for military aid to the plucky Finns immediately. Like "a predatory animal which has once tasted blood," Russia would keep stalking more prey unless it was punished harshly, as one paper put it. Talk of neutrality and nonintervention evaporated. Walter Lippmann believed giving arms to Finland was essential to halt the Soviets in their bid to bring Sweden, Norway, the North Sea, and the Atlantic under Red influence. With genuine pathos, Lippmann insisted that the defense of the "free, honest, innocent northern peoples" of Scandinavia was "in the interest of mankind."[51]

The country took a good deal of delight at Finland's effective resistance, with Anne O'Hare McCormick writing that "Finland fights alone, but on the side of the angels." That tone carried through the reporting about the "tough and hardy race putting up a stiff fight against overwhelming odds." In a radio broadcast to America, the Finnish premier Risto Ryti emphasized that Finland's struggle against Soviet imperialism was one front in a war for the defense of "western culture." The *New York Times* editorial page agreed, stating that "Finland, standing alone, is reawakening the conscience of the world. . . . Liberty is at stake in Europe." The *Washington Post* added a call for immediate aid to Finland: The spread of Communism across Europe was not an issue to be met with "neutrality legislation." The U.S. government must aid those "manning the outposts of democracy in Finland." The Soviet attack on Finland, more than Nazi slaughter in Poland, completely changed American perceptions of the stakes of the European war.[52]

Contempt for Russia now saturated public commentary. Newspapers scorned the "immorality, sickening hypocrisy, and the complete ruthlessness of Stalin," and even slighted the backwardness of the Soviet Union. "Going from Russia into Finland, the traveler leaves a dirty, primitive country, ruled by a fanatical terrorization, to enter a spotless and highly civilized democracy," said one report. Finns show "immeasurable superiority" over Russians. *Newsweek* snickered that the Russians, whose armies could not overcome the resistance of the stalwart Finnish citizen-soldiers, resorted to spewing out elaborate insults instead, describing the Finns as maniacal, malicious hangmen, beasts of prey, clowns, buffoons, lackeys, marionettes, snakes, mad dogs, and bandits. In contrast, *Life* magazine, always a good barometer of American interventionist opinion, called the Finns "the best winter soldiers in the world" and cast doubt on the capabilities of the "Red Steamroller." A morbid photo essay by photographer Carl Mydans showed numerous pictures of dead Soviet soldiers, frozen into the Finnish ice in grotesque shapes, with jocular captions such as "Wolf Food" and "Red Dead."[53]

Some newspapers went so far as to depict Stalin as more dangerous than Hitler. This had been the theme of Lindbergh's talks, and the *Chicago Tribune* picked it up. The publisher of that paper, Colonel Robert McCormick, styled the Soviets as "Asiatic barbarians" who threatened all of Europe. Britain and France must seek a rapid peace with the Germans, McCormick urged, so they could face the Red barbarian together. Dorothy Thompson did not favor one over the other, arguing that the Nazis and the Soviets, along with the Japanese and Italians, were all international gangsters using force to attack the world order. The question that Soviet and Nazi aggression posed, she wrote, was "whether the United States can survive as a free people . . . in a world of illimitable terror." Americans lived in a "hideously dangerous world in which there are going to be no free rides to freedom and security." If the United States wanted a peaceful, law-abiding world system, it would have to build it and defend it.[54]

The war carried on until March, when the Finns, massively outnumbered by half a million Red Army troops, began to falter and sued for an armistice. They "fought like white demons," *Life* wrote, "to the last frayed nerve of resistance," but could not hold out against Russia's reinforced divisions. The international outcry had not led to any significant military aid for Finland, though the British and French had started to plan a joint naval expedition to bring some relief to the struggling defenders. In a peace treaty signed at Moscow on March 12, 1940, the Soviets got their slice of Finnish territory. It had cost perhaps one hundred thousand Soviet soldiers their lives; far more were wounded or frostbitten. Hitler duly took note of Soviet military ineffectiveness and began to think of the Red Army as a paper tiger—a factor in his later decision to attack the Soviet Union in 1941.[55]

If the American outcry did not rescue Finland, the war nonetheless profoundly shaped the public discussion of America's world role. Former pacifist and neutralist critics now joined forces with internationalist groups to decry

Soviet intervention and mobilize aid. Herbert Hoover took up the leadership of a new Finnish Relief Fund, and at a mass meeting at Madison Square Garden he firmly denounced "the primitive savagery unloosed upon the world." New York Mayor Fiorella LaGuardia, sharing the podium with the former president, pointedly said, "when 3.5 million people are attacked by a nation of 160 million, you can't invoke the laws of neutrality . . . only the laws of decency and humanity may be invoked." Senator Robert F. Wagner of New York said that "although our geographic borders have not been invaded, the common frontier of civilized mankind has been violated." He asked the teeming crowd: "Shall we abandon this brave outpost of civilization?" At the same rally, Dorothy Thompson, always going to the heart of the matter, called it the duty of America to mobilize aid "not only for the sake of Finland but for the sake of our own souls." By mid-February 1940, Hoover's campaign had raised over a million dollars for the Finns.[56]

It wasn't just sentimental humanitarians who called for purposeful action from Washington to meet the growing world crisis. Business leaders also began to see FDR's methods-short-of-war policies as beneficial to their bottom lines. In January 1940, *Fortune* magazine (published by Henry Luce) released the results of a round table discussion with leading business executives, virtually all of whom opposed FDR and the New Deal. They wanted the United States to stay out of any combat role in Europe. But they believed that a German victory would "severely injure the welfare of the American people." The triumph of "totalitarian" governments in the war, they feared, would compel America to build its own garrison state and weaken democracy at home. Americans would live "under the fear of attack from without and subversive propaganda from within." To avoid this nightmare scenario, these Republican stalwarts supported a robust assertion of America's trading rights in the world—meaning defiance toward any warring nation that sought to inhibit U.S. ships from reaching any port in the world. That was a far more daring policy than the one codified in the revised neutrality law, which banned American ships from the European war zone. America should also reject Japan's "new order" in Asia, said these executives, give loans to China, send ships to ply trade routes around the world, and beef up national military preparations. Roosevelt could hardly have asked for a better statement of his own policy preferences.[57]

Popular culture in 1940 also began to reflect the growing feeling in the country that the world's dictators threatened the American experiment itself. Robert Sherwood, a tall, gaunt, Harvard-educated playwright and Great War veteran, emerged in the late 1930s as one of the most influential voices in favor of confrontation with the totalitarian menace. Despairing over American inaction during the Winter War and ashamed of the sneering indifference by many toward the fascist threat, Sherwood set out in January 1940 to dramatize the Finnish tragedy in a new play called *There Shall Be No Night*. He was already renowned in the theater, having won a Pulitzer Prize for his 1936 play, *Idiot's Delight*, a lighthearted satire of nationalism and militarism. His 1938 play, *Abe Lincoln in Illinois*, marked a shift to more explicitly political work, which emerged from his admiration of Roosevelt and his anxiety over the march of fascism in Europe. In that play, Sherwood presented Lincoln as a man of peace who faced a terrible decision: to fight for democracy and union or to succumb to the pressures of appeasement and indifference to evil. After much soul-searching, Sherwood's Lincoln decides to rouse the nation in a great fight to defend the idea of self-government and freedom. Hailed as an instant classic when it opened in October 1938, the play toured the country in hundreds of performances, pulled in huge audiences, and won Sherwood his second Pulitzer. A film version appeared in February 1940, as the flames of war spread across Europe.[58]

Robert Sherwood: playwright, speechwriter, and astute Roosevelt chronicler.
Library of Congress

Slapped together in an intensive six-week burst of furious work, *There Shall Be No Night* opened in New York in late April 1940. It told the story of a Finnish doctor, a specialist in the causes of insanity, caught in the horror of the Soviet invasion. Initially a pacifist, the doctor evolves into a combatant in the war, finally deciding that until the evil of aggressive tyranny is defeated, "there can be no peace—no freedom from fear—no hope of progress for mankind." The doctor and his son eventually face the invaders and die for the cause of liberty, leaving audiences to conclude that though they have given their lives, they have also redeemed the human race with their struggle. According to *Life* magazine, New York audiences were in tears throughout every performance.[59]

The play was a smash hit, generating wide acclaim, filling theaters, and prompting anti-war picketing, too. Brooks Atkinson in a *New York Times* review wrote that the play, in speaking the truth about the terrible troubles of Finland, illuminated the "spiritual agony that torments enlightened men today." Justice Felix Frankfurter told Sherwood that the play, using the emotional register available to the artist, had broken through the indifference and fatigue of public opinion toward Nazi and Communist atrocities. The play gave the cause of freedom "a vivid concreteness" that Frankfurter felt certain would help spur action in defense of "the painfully gained achievements of civilization." Eleanor Roosevelt too wrote to Sherwood, describing herself as deeply moved: "I hope I will have the courage to meet whatever may come to me as splendidly as do your characters." The play would earn Sherwood his third Pulitzer. It was no accident that Sherwood in October joined FDR's internationalist brain trust, helping to frame the moral argument for intervention against the fascist threat.[60]

An even greater popular success, Charlie Chaplin's film *The Great Dictator* appeared in October 1940. It brilliantly satirized Hitler's manic speeches, his narcissism, and the fawning loyalty of the Nazi toadies of the Third Reich. In the remarkable concluding scene, Chaplin, playing a Jewish barber who is impersonating Hitler, climbs a platform to speak to the nation. Abandoning his role-playing, he begs his hearers to embrace tolerance and to abandon plans for conquest and empire. Improbable, acidly witty, and sentimental at the same time, *The Great Dictator* subjected Nazism to derision and belly laughs, popping the inflated balloon of Hitler's ego.[61]

But if *The Great Dictator* prompted snorts and guffaws, another storied film of this moment poignantly captured America's particular dilemma in the face of the European war. In mid-1940, a young writer named Murray Burnett traveled to Vienna, where he was trying to help his wife's Jewish relatives escape the Nazi persecution unleashed there after the Anschluss. Burnett learned that Jews with enough money could possibly make their way on an underground railroad of sorts from Vienna to Marseilles, then to French Morocco, and from there to Lisbon and the United States. He decided to see for himself, and traveled into southern France toward Nice, where he stopped at a nightclub on a bluff above the Mediterranean.

There, in the smoky gloom of the café, a Black American jazz pianist played sentimental songs, army officers knocked down cocktails, and people of a dozen nationalities met and conversed nervously about their plans to get away from the rising Nazi threat. Inspired by the scene, Burnett returned home to write a play with a co-writer named Joan Alison. It featured a cynical expatriate bar owner named Rick, whose saloon in Morocco attracted black marketers, spies, police officers, and refugees desperate to get to America. Rick had a past—he fought for the Republicans in the Spanish Civil War and tried to help the Ethiopians beat back the Italian Fascists. Now, desperate travelers came to him, pleading for help, money, and false papers. But Rick had grown weary and wary; he just wanted to make a quiet living and avoid politics.

Burnett and Alison sold the rights to the play, titled *Everybody Comes to Rick's*, to Warner Bros.; in late 1941, the story was renamed and went into movie production as *Casablanca*—the greatest anti-fascist film to emerge from World War II. Rick's dilemma—whether to keep his head down or to help fugitives evade the Nazis at the risk of his own safety—was America's, too, and just to make the connection to contemporary affairs perfectly clear, the writers had Rick grapple with this thorny problem in a place called "white house." In a heart-warming final scene, Rick overcomes his hesitations, helps a resistance hero escape the Gestapo, and joins the war.[62]

CHAPTER 15

STOP HITLER NOW!

"There is no such thing as isolation."

—ELEANOR ROOSEVELT

I

At the start of 1940, Franklin Roosevelt, like Rick in his Casablanca saloon, was taking ever more daring steps toward the European war. Repealing the arms embargo had been an enormous achievement. Victory in that debate marked a decisive shift in U.S. politics: The pacifist and neutrality camp would never meaningfully shape defense policy ever again. Certainly, isolation as a rhetorical tool, wielded against Roosevelt and the internationalists, continued through 1941, but it had been put on the defensive and would never recover its former chokehold over U.S. foreign policy. Noisy critics prophesied that FDR would take America into war and transform the nation into a militarized dictatorship. But these now familiar attacks no longer had the power they did before Hitler's invasion of Poland. The decision to help Britain and France meet the Nazi threat had been made. The problem shifted now to implementation: how to get meaningful amounts of military equipment across the Atlantic within the constraints of the cash-and-carry formula, and how to do it quickly.

The French in particular were desperate for American aircraft, artillery, machine guns, ammunition, aluminum, and countless other supplies they needed to prepare for the expected German onslaught in the spring of 1940. Prime Minister Édouard Daladier told Ambassador Bullitt he wanted to order ten thousand planes from the United States—a fantastic number and about twice America's annual production capacity at the time. Roosevelt replied to Bullitt that he was "ready to handle the whole matter over here," though he cautioned that any large orders would run into trouble if they slowed down America's own rearmament program. Hoping to avoid piecemeal orders for arms, he urged the French and British governments to work together and send two men "who will sleep in the same bed and lay all their cards on the table to prevent crossing wires." He wanted the French prime minister to know that he would "give every facility to the export of all types of American products."[1]

But the bureaucratic wheels did not turn as swiftly as Roosevelt wished. The War Department, led by Harry Woodring, opposed his efforts. A former governor of Kansas who joined the administration in 1933 as assistant secretary and moved up to the top job in 1936, Woodring was a classic Midwestern isolationist. His parochialism did not matter during FDR's early years in office, when army budgets were pitifully small. But now Woodring became a problem, telling the French that sales of aircraft and other matériel to foreign governments would have to wait until the U.S. government's orders with private manufacturers had been filled. Woodring's staff even denied the sale to France of a large supply of field shoes sitting in a warehouse in New York. Roosevelt responded to this army foot-dragging in the same way he had helped France in late 1938: by ordering Treasury Secretary Henry Morgenthau to work around the War Department. At a cabinet meeting on December 8, at which Woodring was present, Roosevelt made clear his desire that in the event of European requests running up against army orders for aircraft and other supplies, "we would let England and France have the first call." He reiterated this view in mid-January at a meeting with military chiefs and Morgenthau. Roosevelt was "very much in favor of assisting the foreign powers to every reasonable extent," noted a minute-taker.[2]

The president grew anxious about the lack of urgency he perceived in the country to get arms to Europe. "The world situation seems to me to be getting rather progressively worse," he wrote to William Allen White. Hitler and Stalin had subdued Poland and Finland and settled their affairs in the East. The Germans were starting a major buildup of offensive forces along the front facing France and the Low Countries. "Your civilization and mine is indeed in peril," he wrote. He worried that "public opinion over here is patting itself on the back every morning and thanking God for the Atlantic Ocean (and the Pacific Ocean). We greatly underestimate the serious implications to our own future." And while he hoped the United States would stay out of war, "things move with such terrific speed these days, that it really is essential to us. . . to warn the American people" of the global consequences of a German-Soviet victory. In a letter to *Chicago Daily News* publisher Frank Knox, who he was considering for a cabinet post, Roosevelt reiterated this anxiety "that the country as a whole does not yet have any deep sense of world crisis." He said he wanted to awaken, though not frighten, the public.[3]

He certainly did not mind frightening the public a little, as he did in his annual message to Congress on January 3, 1940. Once again, Sam Rosenman, Ben Cohen, and Tom Corcoran worked on this speech with the president. He painted a dark picture of world affairs. "Whether we like it or not, the daily lives of American citizens will, of necessity, feel the shock of events on other continents," he said. "The work, the security, the prosperity, the happiness, the life of all the boys and girls in the United States" would be shaped by the war. Those who denied this—"those who wishfully insist, in innocence or ignorance or both, that the United States of America as a self-contained unit can live happily and prosperously, its future secure, inside a high wall of isolation"—were wrong, dangerously so. He asked his listeners to imagine a world dominated by force, war, and tyranny; a world in which children were "compelled to worship a god imposed by a military ruler or were forbidden to worship God at all"; a world in which news and information was controlled by a dictatorial state; a world closed to trade and the free movement of peoples. That world, he suggested, was being built in Europe and Asia, and misguided politicians must open their eyes to that hard truth. "I hope," he said with a grim chuckle, "that we shall have fewer American ostriches in our midst. It is not good for the ultimate health of ostriches to bury their heads in the sand." With the ambassadors of Poland and Finland watching grimly from the gallery, he called for an increase in the defense budget and more taxes to pay for it.[4]

In this same speech to Congress, Roosevelt also reminded the public about the internal threats to American democracy. "Some in our midst have sought to instill a feeling of fear and defeatism in the minds of the American people about this problem," he ominously said. In Europe, he pointed out, "doctrines that set group against group, faith against faith, race against race, class against class, fanning the fires of hatred in men too despondent, too desperate to think for themselves, were used as rabble-rousing slogans on which dictators could ride to power. And once in power they could saddle their tyrannies on whole nations and on their weaker neighbors. This," he declared, "is the danger to which we in America must begin to be more alert." In America there circulated many "apologists for foreign aggressors, and equally those selfish and partisan groups at home who wrap themselves in a false mantle of Americanism to promote their own economic, financial or political advantage." Such tricks, he said, must be exposed and defeated.

And just two weeks later, J. Edgar Hoover's FBI launched a raid on the Christian Front, arresting eighteen members and seizing rifles, ammunition, and explosives. Many of those arrested had been in the military or the New York National Guard. Hoover charged that the men had plans to terrorize Jews and to blow up the offices of Jewish and leftist newspapers in the New York area. As *The Nation* put it, the plot of the Christian Front "contains all those recognizable elements of antidemocratic and anti-Semitic terror which were the preludes of European fascism." Another investigation described the Christian Front as "a domestic storm-troop mob running amuck, spewing racial hatred, fomenting violence. . . . Crowds have been exhorted to liquidate the Jews in America." Such reports of extremist cells plotting domestic attacks while also urging America to "keep out of war" served FDR's broader purposes: linking critics of his foreign policy to the subversive actions of an "un-American" fifth column.[5]

Although he told a British friend, Arthur Murray (later Lord Elibank), that public opinion was "in good shape in spite of the extreme isolationists," Roosevelt still had to fight ostriches in his own administration to get the ball rolling. In late February, newspapers reported that an Anglo-French Planning Commission was en route to the United States to place a huge order for American planes. General Hap Arnold, commander of the Air Corps, and Secretary Woodring still tried to block the sale of aircraft in light of America's own rearmament needs. Henry Morgenthau complained that "the whole War Department have fought us to a standstill on this thing," and he pleaded with the president to intervene. Roosevelt always preferred using intermediaries to fight these kinds of battles but occasionally he put his thumb on the scale. If General Arnold would not carry out the president's policies, he told Morgenthau, "maybe we will have to move him out of town." On March 13, he delivered that message to Arnold in person at the White House, specifying the destination he had in mind for recalcitrant officers: Guam.[6]

Roosevelt also told the press at length that the sale of aircraft had already spurred economic growth and accelerated the expansion of a crucial sector of the economy. He was right: According to a survey done by *Fortune* in March, the aircraft industry was booming. In 1937, it sold $86 million worth of planes, engines, and parts. As of January 1940, it "had on its books more than $600 million in unfilled orders," 60 percent of which were foreign contracts. Companies like Curtiss-Wright, Douglas, Lockheed, North American Aviation, and Bell Aircraft had plans for rapid expansion to meet the demand. All the swank hotels in Washington were swarming with foreign purchasing agents trying to snap up American goods. U.S. exports surged: By January 1940, they were up 70 percent over the previous year, and everyone was buying, not just the British and French: Italy, Japan, Canada, and the Soviet Union all increased purchases not only of aircraft and engines but trucks, cotton, copper, iron, and steel.

The huge backlog of aviation orders made the War Department uneasy, but Roosevelt had confidence that the capitalist system, fueled by massive government spending, would rise to the challenge. United Aircraft, for example, had increased its workforce from 3,000 to 12,000 in a matter of months. At the end of March, Roosevelt pushed through a new policy to "liberalize" foreign sales and told his still-unwilling subordinates to follow it. This opened the way for the Anglo-French mission to place a new order for 4,600 fighter and bomber aircraft as well as 13,000 aircraft engines. Well before the German Blitzkrieg struck into the Low Countries and France, FDR was already stocking the vast arsenal of weapons and matériel that would soon be put to use around the world. "When the president wants to," Morgenthau happily chirped, "he can take two hours to get a thing straightened out."[7]

II

Above all these efforts to help rearm Europe hung the biggest political question of the year: Would Roosevelt run for a third term? Journalists twitted him by likening him to the Sphinx—that inscrutable creature who never told its secrets. But it was not a subject of mirth to Roosevelt; the matter had enormous significance. If he revealed publicly a decision to retire after completing his second term, he would become a lame duck and immediately lose his political leverage to push through his methods-short-of-war plans. On the other hand, if he announced his intention to break the third-term taboo and run again, his policies would be met by ferocious partisan opposition, no matter how wise or necessary they might be. He chose, characteristically, to say nothing. Even to his friends, his plans remained obscure—intimates like Ickes and Rosenman had no idea of his thinking, though in the spring of 1940 they expected he would not run. If he mentioned the subject at all, he insisted he was exhausted and could not take the punishment of another term in office. His Hyde Park presidential library and separate little house, Top Cottage, were nearing completion. There was a memoir to write, trees to plant, cocktails to mix, stories to tell.[8]

And his health was failing, though he kept that fact from the public and even from his family. One detailed examination of the admittedly sketchy medical evidence speculates that FDR, who battled melanoma, hypertension, dental trouble, chronic lung irritation from smoking two packs of Camels a day, heart disease as well as anemia requiring occasional blood transfusions, might also have been battling prostate cancer. Enduring these illnesses, FDR was bedridden for most of the spring, and even less inclined to seek a third term. To those who saw him in March and April, he looked worn, thin, and unwell. He would not run for reelection, he told a few friends, unless the situation in Europe got very much worse.[9]

But how could he foresee the future? The war might flare up dramatically, or it might devolve into a stalemate, or a negotiated settlement. Hitler had achieved everything he wanted, hadn't he? In any case, the massed armies glaring at one another across miles of fortifications on the French-German border had not budged. It was not unreasonable in the quiet stillness of February 1940 to imagine that Europe might settle down into a grim but stable cold war between the democracies and the dictators. Roosevelt wanted to know which way the wind was blowing: toward a negotiated peace or total war? He had ambassadors to report to him, but men like Joe Kennedy and Bill Bullitt were so personally ambitious, and so strident in their (quite differing) views that they might not be telling the president the full story. In fact, the Hearst newspapers, anticipating a Roosevelt third-term bid, prophesied that the public might welcome a Roosevelt "dictatorship" in place of democracy unless a strong alternative to FDR were available; Hearst began booming Joe Kennedy as a "good American" who opposed any involvement in Europe's war and who would be a strong candidate for president. For Roosevelt, Kennedy was both a political rival and a defeatist, and not a reliable source on the state of European affairs.[10]

On February 9, at his weekly press conference, Roosevelt read a statement to the journalists crowded around his desk. He announced that he had asked Sumner Welles, undersecretary of state and a trusted personal friend, to visit leaders in Germany, Italy, France, and Britain "solely for the purpose of advising the president and the secretary of state as to present conditions in Europe." When a reporter asked him why he could not rely on his diplomats for information, he replied that "it might be a good thing to get somebody to see all of the conditions in all of the countries so that one mind would be able to cover the situation instead of having four separate minds reporting on separate things."[11]

The Welles trip immediately stirred up criticism from every possible quarter. Secretary Hull bitterly resented this poaching on his own prerogatives and in any case neither liked nor trusted Welles. Ambassadors Bullitt and Kennedy, both sensitive egotists, were furious at being sidelined. The British and French governments feared that FDR might be returning to the now-discredited policy of appeasement, raising hopes that a peace deal could be struck with Hitler. Chamberlain made it known through his ambassador in Washington that no peace was possible with Germany as long as Hitler held that country in its tight grip, and for America now to undercut his position risked a serious "embarrassment." And indeed, the American press did interpret the Welles mission as a "peace offensive," confirming Chamberlain's worst fears.[12]

Historians have long puzzled over the purpose of the Welles trip. Some argue that Roosevelt wanted to burnish his reputation as a peacemaker and cultivate support among anti-war voters. Others believe that by sending an envoy to European capitals, he wanted to buy a little more time for the French and British to rearm. Still others believe he wanted to keep Mussolini, who had not joined Hitler in the attack on Poland in September, from entering the war, and perhaps even coax Il Duce into leading a peace conference that the United States, as a fellow neutral, could join. These are plausible theories but remain speculative, for FDR and Welles never explained exactly what they wished to come out of the trip. Given the upcoming Democratic primaries and the looming decision about a third term, Welles's impressions could at the very least help Roosevelt make up his mind about running again by answering the big question facing the world: Did Germany's successful conquest of Poland mark the end of war in Europe, or only the beginning?[13]

Welles and FDR made a curious pair: Though both men shared the pedigree of Groton, Harvard, and elite New England society, Welles was an excessively formal, tight-lipped, repressed man whose career would end in disgrace in 1943 after his bisexuality was used against him. (His crime: propositioning Pullman train porters for sex.) Yet Welles had the sort of eye for detail that Roosevelt relied on to take the measure of people he could not meet in person. Welles did as the president asked, making a six-week tour in February and March to Europe, meeting Hitler, Mussolini, Daladier, Chamberlain, and many other leading officials. The long report he wrote and submitted upon his return in late March gave Roosevelt vivid impressions of the world leaders—and little hope for peace.[14]

Welles visited Mussolini first and returned at the end of his tour to see him a second time—clues to the importance he and Roosevelt placed upon winning Mussolini to the cause of peace. But Il Duce was no longer the lithe, energetic, and independent-minded figure of the fascist myth. His face obscured by "rolls of fat," Mussolini seemed "ponderous and static," moving with heavy, "elephantine" effort, according to Welles. He appeared oppressed, leaden, and under immense strain. And while Welles perceived the petty jealousies and rivalry between Hitler and Mussolini, he also astutely picked up the enormous bitterness in Italy toward Britain, whose naval power blocked Il Duce's imperial ambitions in the Mediterranean and loomed as a constant source of irritation and humiliation for Italy. Though he tried to cajole and inspire Mussolini toward taking steps that might open peace negotiations, Welles learned from the rueful Foreign Minister Galeazzo Ciano that the Germans were determined to take the offensive soon and would impose a German diktat upon conquered Europe. No peace talks could possibly appeal to the Nazi leadership which, after all, had already swallowed Austria, smashed Czechoslovakia, and wiped Poland off the map.

In Berlin, Welles sat and listened to an extended harangue from Hitler on the unendurable humiliations Germany had suffered since the end of the last war, and the legitimacy of Germany's attacks of the monstrous Versailles peace settlement. Göring and Ribbentrop piled on, blaming the British for the war and insisting that they would now pay for their aggression against Germany. Welles took a certain pleasure in sketching a portrait for the president of the corpulent Göring, whose fat fingers were bedecked with giant gemstones and whose face appeared heavily rouged. Welles described Göring's vast, soulless country retreat, stuffed with trophies and gifts from

Sumner Welles and George Kennan in Berlin,
still hoping for a reconciliation with Nazi Germany.
Bettmann / Getty Images

obsequious admirers, as the ugliest building he had ever seen. If Göring possessed a certain barracks-room charisma, Ribbentrop was completely repellent, a craven, deranged dog obedient only to his master's every command. "I have rarely seen a man I disliked more," Welles wrote of the foreign minister. He left Berlin deeply discouraged, feeling that "all decisions had already been made." These men relished the thrill of waging war and winning it.

Perhaps more surprising to Welles than the Nazi leadership's fanaticism was the warlike resolution he encountered in London. Expecting a dejected, anxious, appeasement-addled governing class, Welles instead found British leaders united in their determination to fight and win the war. Prime Minister Neville Chamberlain, with his dark hair, piercing eyes, low voice, and determined air of "physical strength," deeply impressed Welles. Meeting his American guest at the green baize table in the cabinet room at 10 Downing Street, Chamberlain immediately ruled out a negotiated peace with Hitler. He bitterly recounted that he had made "every possible concession" to Hitler and been deceived and lied to in return. He spoke with the fervor of a convert: Hitler wanted only German domination, not peace, and England would fight "to preserve the institutions of liberty and democracy which were threatened with extinction." Over the course of many dinners and meetings, Welles heard the same message from virtually every cabinet official and political leader, including Clement Attlee of the opposition Labour Party. There could be no peace with Nazism; the Germans must be taught a lesson they had not learned after World War I; and Britain would fight it out. Welles returned to Washington clearly frustrated—he had hoped he might bring home to the president the outlines of a peace deal. Instead, he had to admit that only a "miracle" could bring peace to Europe now.[15]

Instead of peace, Hitler offered a wider war. On April 9, ten days after Welles arrived home, the Führer launched the first stage of the long-anticipated invasion of Western Europe with a brilliant and daring assault on two neutral nations, Denmark and Norway. He had started planning this assault in January, fearing that the war in Finland would precipitate an Allied invasion of Norway that could help tighten the blockade of Germany and interrupt the flow of Swedish iron ore that Germany relied on for steel production. In April, the British were indeed gathering forces for a limited invasion of the Norwegian coast; Hitler rushed ahead and beat them to it. Coordinating air, naval, and ground forces, the Germans landed small mobile teams at Oslo, Kristiansand, Bergen, Trondheim, and Narvik, and took control of airfields at Oslo and Stavanger—an astonishing coup of combined arms. Simultaneously, the Danish government, taken completely by surprise and without any means to defend itself, surrendered immediately with barely a shot being fired.

The British, caught completely off guard, mounted a response to try to oust the Germans from Norway, but it was too late; and unlike the Germans, the British armed services were simply not prepared. Naval landings were slow and poorly organized. Troops lacked equipment, arriving in hip-deep Norwegian snow with unsuitable clothing. And though the Royal Navy battered German ships, British vessels took a heavy pounding from the Luftwaffe. The effort to counter the German attack ended in total humiliation. Gerhard Weinberg, the preeminent scholar of the Second World War, has accused the British Army of "gross incompetence."[16]

In America, Roosevelt blurted out in a press conference on April 9 that the German attack came with a silver lining: It was "a grand thing," and even "a damned good thing" for Americans to see the proximity of war "and not take everything for granted." Ten days later, he expanded on this sentiment to nearly 300 newspaper editors gathered at the White House. "Last year," he scolded them, "you thought that I was—oh, let us say—an alarmist about the situation of the world." The rapid intensification of the war proved, he said, that "I was right, and most of you—the majority of you—were wrong." The German advance into Scandinavia, he believed, would prompt the American people "to take their heads out of the sand," and consider the prospects of a Nazi victory in Europe. He mocked a senator who on April 9 (presumably unaware of what was happening that day) praised Scandinavia's neutrality as a model for the United States to follow. "At that particular time," FDR archly pointed out, "Copenhagen was in the hands of the Germans and so was Oslo." Neutrality was no defense against fascist aggression, and he believed that the rich, soft target of "North, Central and South America" would be among Hitler's next targets.[17]

In London, another silver lining: The Norway campaign precipitated the fall of Chamberlain's government. The prime minister, for all his brave talk to Sumner Welles in March, appeared out of his depth as a war leader and at the end of April, the leader of the Liberal party Sir Archibald Sinclair attacked him for his "defeatist" attitude. When on May 3 Chamberlain ordered the withdrawal of all British forces from the southern half of Norway, critics in the Commons ferociously attacked the government's handling of the war. Labour's Herbert Morrison, then running the London County Council, called for Chamberlain's resignation. David Lloyd George, the seventy-seven-year-old Welshman and Liberal who had led the country in the Great War, roused himself from the opposition benches to call the government "faulty, feeble, and foolish," and demanded a change of leadership. On May 7, in a demonstration of democratic self-government unimaginable in Berlin, Rome, Tokyo, or Moscow, a parliamentary debate opened on the conduct of the war. There, Chamberlain, looking tired and discouraged, defended his war leadership in the face of jeers and shouts so frequent that at one point he sat down and let his head fall into his hands. When he continued, he admitted that the failure of the Norway campaign had been a profound shock, but he appealed for unity to continue the fight.

Labour leader Clement Attlee, a small, balding former army major, drove in the knife. "This is a reverse," he said. "We have got to face the facts." He blamed Chamberlain for lack of preparation and foresight, for poor decision-making, and for irresolution. Expressing the frustration so many felt toward three years of Chamberlain's smug and yet disastrous appeasement policy, Attlee said "the government are blind and deaf if they do not realize there is widespread anxiety among the people of this country." Chamberlain lacked "energy, drive, and capacity," and it was time for a change of leadership. "In the life-or-death struggle of this country, we cannot have our destinies in the hands of failures or people who need a rest," he said, looking at the exhausted (and in fact mortally ill) Chamberlain. Winston Churchill, the First Lord of the Admiralty who in fact bore much of the blame for the poor showing in Norway, rose to defend the heroism of the navy in its gallant fight against the Kriegsmarine, but he was unable to stem the tide. On May 8, Morrison called for a vote of confidence and Chamberlain testily agreed, saying, "At least we shall see who is with us and who is against us."

The verdict was damning. The Conservative Party enjoyed a massive majority in the Commons, and Chamberlain could normally count on about 420 members to back his government. But this time, he was in for a shock. The tally on the vote of confidence was 281–200—a sign that support for the prime minister had collapsed. 134 MPs abstained, and some 40 Conservatives voted against their leader. When the results were announced, cries of "Go!" and "Resign!" cascaded through the House. Chamberlain, stricken, knew his time had come and sought the advice of his ministers on a replacement. The foreign secretary, Lord Halifax, was the heir apparent. He was a senior figure closely identified with Chamberlain, and he had wide support in the Conservative Party. Yet Halifax, a rather withdrawn, ecclesiastical type, quiet and spectral, knew he was not the man for the moment. Perhaps unwilling to face the awful task that awaited the next prime minister, he took himself out of the running, using as an excuse that it would be too difficult to serve as prime minister while also being a member of the House of Lords. His withdrawal opened the way for the person who desperately wanted the job, who had been closely guiding the war effort so far, and who had wide experience in naval and military affairs. On May 10, King George VI accepted the resignation of Chamberlain and rather reluctantly asked Winston Churchill to form a government.

Britain showed the world that even in wartime, democratic self-government could work uninterrupted, as the Commons peacefully deposed a prime minister and replaced him with one of his harshest critics. Age sixty-five, with wide experience in government but a spotty record of party loyalty and a considerable number of mistakes and fiascos to his name, Winston Churchill nonetheless possessed exactly the skills Britain needed at this moment. His ability to frame moral issues in simple language, his drive and work ethic, his daring and courage, his familiarity with military strategy, his single-minded focus on victory, all would stand him in good stead now. He later claimed that as he took over from Chamberlain, he felt "a profound sense of relief. At last, I had the authority to give directions over the whole scene. I felt as if I were walking with Destiny."

Perhaps. But his country stood on the threshold of the most perilous and desperate moment in its history. For at dawn on May 10, the same day that Churchill took office, Hitler's armies smashed across the borders of Belgium, the Netherlands, and Luxembourg, and knifed through the hilly Ardennes Forest, a tactical surprise that allowed the Germans to skirt France's heavily defended Maginot Line. This was the start of a massive assault that within a few days threatened to envelop the Allied forces and open the way to Paris. Suddenly, a hideous nightmare loomed: Hitler could soon enjoy total mastery of the European continent and take aim at Britain next. Never had democracy been more imperiled.[18]

III

War has a way of accelerating history. In times of dire crisis, great shifts in the tide of world events can occur in an instant, with breathtaking speed and enduring consequences. In the thirty-one days between May 10 and June 10, 1940, Franklin Roosevelt and Winston Churchill, moving on parallel but not yet coordinated paths, took a series of decisions that laid the foundation of the Anglo-American alliance which, in the long run, would wage and win a global war for democracy. Facing unimaginably bad news and the collapse of world order, Roosevelt and Churchill recast what had been a European conflict about the last war into a struggle over the future of human rights and liberty everywhere in the world. Rarely is the historian given a moment in time when the factor of individual courage, vision, and decisive action can change the trajectory of human society for centuries. This is one of them.[19]

Roosevelt and Churchill did not act alone, however. They stepped forward in the company of a coalition of anxious prophets, men and women who had spoken out about the fascist threat when it was unpopular to do so and whose judgments had now been brutally vindicated by Hitler's aggression. Historians therefore must give attention both to the role of political leaders as well as the ideas they drew upon to mobilize their citizens. In this, Roosevelt and Churchill were fortunate. For nearly two decades, various observers and analysts in the press had been alerting the Western world to the nature of the fascist threat. They were often maligned for doing so, mockingly called Cassandras by people who perhaps forgot that the mythological Cassandra could accurately foresee the future; the curse she bore was that no one would ever believe her prophecies. Now, in May 1940, few could doubt that the visionaries had been right all along. (As Dorothy Thompson put it, "By being consistently pessimistic, I have been oftener right than I would wish.") The words that cascaded from Roosevelt and Churchill in the summer of 1940, the epigrammatic rallying cries that shaped a generation, did not originate solely in the capacious minds of the president and prime minister. They had been in the making since 1922, when fascism first trod the colonnaded streets of Milan and Rome, leaving its sinister reek in the air.[20]

The news of the German invasion came to the president from Ambassador John Cudahy in Belgium late in the evening of May 9. Brussels itself was under attack and German bombs had shattered the embassy's windows. Roosevelt and his press secretary Steven Early monitored news reports coming from Europe until nearly 3 a.m. before turning in for the night. At ten thirty the next morning, May 10, he met with a hastily assembled group of advisers: Secretary of State Cordell Hull, Attorney General Robert H. Jackson, Treasury Secretary Henry Morgenthau Jr., Sumner Welles, army chief of staff General George C. Marshall, and the chief of naval operations, Admiral Harold R. Stark. He directed the men to prepare summaries of American military readiness and lay out precisely what deficiencies must now be corrected to close the gap with the German military behemoth. After meeting individually with the ambassadors from the Netherlands, Denmark, and Belgium, Roosevelt convened the cabinet at 2:00 p.m.

At that moment he had little detailed information on how fast the Germans were progressing. It seemed for a few hours as if the Dutch and Belgians would offer firm resistance. The French and British forces were marching north as planned into central Belgium toward the river Dyle, to meet and stem the German onslaught. Roosevelt said he thought Mussolini would soon join the war and snatch a few scraps from Hitler's table. Commerce Secretary Harry Hopkins alerted the cabinet to the shocking shortfall of American supplies of rubber and tin—essential for aircraft production. And then the news came into the cabinet room of Chamberlain's resignation. Given the damage he had sustained in the Norway debate, this news did not come as a surprise. Roosevelt expected Churchill to succeed Chamberlain and described him as "the best man that England had."[21]

Roosevelt was scheduled to speak that night at Constitution Hall to the Eighth Pan-American Scientific Congress, a periodic gathering of scientists from North and South America that had started in 1908. He kept the appointment but altered his remarks to meet the gravity of the moment. He began by saying to the scientists that he came to them "with a heavy heart." Speaking slowly and firmly, in a voice that kept the delegates riveted, he noted that while scientists gathered in Washington in the spirit of peaceful inquiry, a pall of war had been thrown over the world. The basic belief that "men and women have an inherent right to hew out the patterns of their own individual lives, just so long as they as individuals do not harm their fellow beings," was in jeopardy. "We call this ideal by many terms which are synonymous—we call it individual liberty, we call it civil liberty and, I think, best of all, we call it democracy."

The dictators on the march that night wanted to destroy democracy, and they would not halt at the English Channel. They "seek to dominate hundreds of millions of human beings in vast continental areas—and, if they are successful in that aim they will, we know down in our hearts, enlarge their wild dream to encompass every human being and every mile of the earth's surface." In a remarkable passage that presaged so many of his future speeches, he asked his audience if the Americas could be secure once the rest of the world passed under the rule of totalitarian governments. "Can we continue our peaceful construction if all the other Continents embrace by preference or by compulsion a wholly different principle of life? No, I think not." This proposition—that American democracy could not endure in a world beset by war and tyranny—would become the great theme of his wartime leadership. In a ringing peroration, he nailed his colors to the mast: "I am a pacifist. . . . But I believe that by overwhelming majorities in all the Americas you and I, in the long run, if it be necessary, will act together to protect and defend by every means at our command our science, our culture, our American freedom and our civilization." His words had been carried across the country by radio, and within hours, telegrams began to arrive in the White House, 90 percent of which praised his speech. There could be no doubt that, as May 10 came to a close, Roosevelt was preparing for war, and public opinion had begun to rally behind him.[22]

Roosevelt now moved swiftly along the channels he had already cut when getting planes to France in 1939: He turned to Morgenthau and General Marshall and ordered them to work together to identify the immediate needs of the armed forces and to put together lists of materials that could immediately be sold and shipped to Britain and France under the cash-and-carry law. Morgenthau had to bypass the secretary of war to do it, an example of the chaos FDR had allowed to persist in his administration even this late in the day. On May 11, Morgenthau and Marshall spent a long time together hammering out the outlines of a vast mobilization effort for the army, which was in a pathetic state and needed everything from guns and ammunition to shovels and clothing. On top of this, the Air Corps had only 1,900 combat planes, most of them under-powered and under-gunned. More factories would have to be set up and the whole program would cost unprecedented sums. "It makes me dizzy," Marshall confessed to Morgenthau. And Marshall was not a man known for light-headedness.[23]

In Britain, the events on the continent propelled Churchill into action. While he was still assembling the members of his new government, he gave his first address as prime minister to the House of Commons on May 13. In a kind of transatlantic echo of FDR's remarks, Churchill spoke of the terrible struggle now opening. "We have before us an ordeal of the most grievous kind," he told the House in a low growl, "many, many long months of struggle and of suffering." He offered only "blood, toil, tears, and sweat." But he committed himself and the country to one objective—"victory at all costs, victory in spite of all terror, victory, however long and hard the road may be." This was a new tone, and not entirely welcomed in the House. Churchill was still seen by many of the old guard Tories as an ambitious and unscrupulous cad who had undercut Chamberlain and who had a weakness for theatrical language. But this opening address marked the arrival in high office of more than a gifted orator. Like Roosevelt, Churchill saw the war as an existential conflict between the values of English democracy and "a monstrous tyranny, never surpassed in the dark, lamentable catalogue of human crime."[24]

Heartening words. But they alone could not dispel the gloom coming from Prime Minister Paul Reynaud in Paris. Reynaud had replaced Daladier in a typical though ill-timed cabinet reshuffle in March, after Daladier was saddled with the failure of the Allied forces to aid Finland. A conservative,

Reynaud had a long record of opposing appeasement, demanding rearmament, and favoring close military ties with Britain. Like Churchill, he was seen by his own party as a warmonger. However determined he may have been to lead France in war, he was quickly overwhelmed by the swift collapse of his country's military position. On May 14, he told William Bullitt that France was "at one of the most terrible moments in human history." The Germans had broken through the French lines in the north, crossed the Meuse River, and cut through tank obstacles as if they were made of straw. The German armored attacks, supported by aircraft, speared through the thick and hilly Ardennes woods and overwhelmed French positions. Paris now stood nearly defenseless. Reynaud begged Bullitt to ask the president for more fighter aircraft, without which the war would be lost. Said Reynaud desperately, Europe faced "enslavement" by "a barbarism which would crush twenty centuries of Christian civilization." He had every reason to fear such an outcome for at that very moment, about 80 Heinkel He 111 bombers of the Luftwaffe were unloading their deadly payloads in the center of the Dutch city of Rotterdam, turning the historic town into an inferno and killing 1,150 people in an instant. The terrible prophecies that modern war would bring a rain of death from the sky were coming true.[25]

The next morning, May 15, Churchill was awoken by a telephone call from a now despondent Reynaud who shouted into the receiver, "We have been defeated." When Churchill did not immediately reply, he said again, "We are beaten; we have lost the battle." The Germans had broken through the front at Sedan. "They are pouring through in great numbers." Just a few hours later, news came that the Dutch armed forces had surrendered to the Germans. As the Allied forces collapsed, Churchill desperately cabled Roosevelt a long list of arms he hoped the U.S. could supply, including aircraft, "forty or fifty of your old destroyers" to help deal with the Nazi submarine menace, antiaircraft guns and ammunition, as well as steel. Churchill understood Roosevelt's legal constraints but put the issue simply: If America did not act, "you may have a completely subjugated, Nazified Europe established with astonishing swiftness." In no way did Churchill exaggerate the threat. When he flew to Paris the next day to buck up Reynaud, he found the French generals in a state of "utter dejection." He also observed that the staff of the French Foreign Ministry, where the two prime ministers met, were industriously burning their archives; the courtyard was filled, Churchill noted, with "curling wreaths of smoke from the bonfires of the State documents of the French Republic."[26]

In Washington, Roosevelt hoped he could help meet the immediate needs of the democracies but remained anxious about the political problem.

Rearmament required congressional support, which Roosevelt still doubted. Marshall and Morgenthau had drawn up a staggeringly expensive list of needs and argued for it to Roosevelt on May 13. The president worried that Congress would resist such a big program. Marshall, however, made a direct and powerful case for rearmament and then told the president, "if you don't do something . . . and do it right away, I don't know what is going to happen to this country." Roosevelt relented. Although he had to tell Churchill on May 16 that he could not send him the destroyers he asked for—that would require congressional action—he went that same day in person to Capitol Hill to dramatize the stakes of the moment. In an address as significant as any he made in the first hundred days of his presidency, Roosevelt painted a chilling picture of the threat the world now faced. "These are ominous days—days whose swift and shocking developments force every neutral nation to look to its defenses in the light of new factors," he began. "The brutal force of modern offensive war has been loosed in all its horror. New powers of destruction, incredibly swift and deadly, have been developed; and those who wield them are ruthless and daring."[27]

The United States was vulnerable as never before to attack, he claimed. Wide oceans no longer shielded American coastal cities from bombers, parachute troops, and lightning attacks. "We have had the lesson before us over and over again—nations that were not ready and were unable to get ready found themselves overrun by the enemy." The vital element of defense was air power, he asserted, and while the country had begun to speed up production, it must go faster still. "I should like to see this nation geared up to the ability to turn out at least 50,000 planes a year," he said to audible gasps. (The nation had produced 2,100 military aircraft in all of 1939 and most of those were for training purposes.) Furthermore, the army needed "motor transport and artillery, tanks, antiaircraft guns and full ammunition supplies. It had been planned to spread these requirements over the next two or three years. We should fill them at once." There was no dithering now: "I ask for an immediate appropriation of $896 million. And may I say that I hope there will be speed in giving the appropriation."

Understanding the political dimension of this enormous program, he placed his request for money into a broader context. American democracy faced a historic test, he believed. "There are some who say that democracy cannot cope with the new techniques of Government developed in recent years by some countries—by a few countries which deny the freedoms that we maintain are essential to our democratic way of life. That I reject." A democratic and capitalist United States could outperform the totalitarian states in the business of war production, he insisted. Yes, meeting the crisis required "a toughness of moral and physical fiber." But the country had come through a decade of struggle and would once again meet this new task with courage. In words that got the assembled legislators up off their feet and thumping their hands together in a roar, he concluded:

> We stand ready not only to spend millions for defense but to give our service and even our lives for the maintenance of our American liberties. . . . These are the characteristics of a free people, a people devoted to the institutions they themselves have built, a people willing to defend a way of life that is precious to them all, a people who put their faith in God.

Americans did not want war. But with these words, Roosevelt made it plain that if war came to the United States, the people would understand it as a great moral contest between democratic government and the jackbooted phalanxes of fascism. After listening to the speech, Justice Felix Frankfurter told Roosevelt that he felt an almost spiritual sense of gratitude, and he wondered at "the mysterious good fortune" that he was president at this time of crisis: "You are the embodiment of hope and of faith of all the peoples of the earth."[28]

It was an indication of the power of Roosevelt's message that Charles Lindbergh rose immediately to attempt to deflate it. In a nationwide radio speech on May 19, Lindbergh rejected Roosevelt's appeal for rearmament. America was not vulnerable to bombing or air attack, he said, and the country had no business building planes for use in Europe. "Our danger in America is an internal danger," the aviator said, suggesting that Roosevelt, along with unnamed Jewish media tycoons and foreign interests, wanted to drag the country into war. America need not have any concern over events in Europe, Lindbergh argued. It did not matter who won the war, for the United States could make peace with either side and coexist perfectly well in a fascist-dominated world. He called on Americans to "stop this hysterical chatter of calamity and invasion that has been running rife these last few days." At a moment when a hundred thousand young Frenchmen were being gunned down by the Wehrmacht, when Rotterdam was still burning, and when democracy hung by a thread, Lindbergh's xenophobic, sneering criticism prompted genuine fury from Roosevelt. Speaking to Henry Morgenthau about this speech, he said, "If I should die tomorrow, I want you to know this. I am absolutely convinced Lindbergh is a Nazi." The next day, in a letter to Henry Stimson, Roosevelt identified Lindbergh with "fifth column" activities and said his speech "could not have been better if it had been written by Goebbels himself." In FDR's mind, Lindbergh was now the face of America's pro-Nazi movement.[29]

The news from the European battlefields grew worse every hour. Bullitt passed on Reynaud's assessment that the Germans were driving to the English Channel to cut off the best of the British and French armies then engaged to the north in Belgium. Reynaud thought "the war might end in an absolute defeat of France and England" quite soon, and should that occur, the United States would be Hitler's next target. Churchill also cabled a desperate message to Roosevelt the same day: "We are determined to persevere to the very end . . . we must expect in any case to be attacked here on the Dutch model before very long," a reference to the German use of parachute landings in Holland as well as indiscriminate bombing of Rotterdam. The next day, Sunday, May 19, Churchill gave his first radio broadcast as prime minister. It was a courageous speech, acknowledging the serious situation on the battlefield yet speaking of ultimate victory. "Arm yourselves, and be ye men of valor," he beseeched his British listeners, using lines from the First Book of Maccabees: "Be in readiness for the conflict; for it is better for us to perish in battle than to look upon the outrage of our nation and our altar."[30]

The next day, more dreadful news: The first German forces reached the English Channel at Abbéville. Churchill put into action the plan for a general retreat of the British Expeditionary Force toward the Belgian coast, converging on the seaside town of Dunkirk, where just possibly some of the men might be rescued by the Royal Navy. The forces of the Western European alliance were falling to pieces like papier-mâché in a heavy downpour. In another fretful message to Roosevelt, Churchill again expressed his interest in acquiring U.S. destroyers and added a request for the "largest possible number of Curtiss P-40 fighters" to beat off the Luftwaffe. He also restated his personal determination "to fight on to the end in this Island" but hinted that if Roosevelt "left this country to its fate," some future British government might have to ask the Germans for "a parley amid the ruins" and accept whatever harsh terms the Nazis would mete out. Even the indomitable Churchill now seemed prepared for the worst.[31]

IV

Roosevelt could not send ships and aircraft to Britain immediately: The Americans had too few of them. Yet there was a good deal of surplus small arms and ammunition that he thought could fill the urgent needs of the British forces. He urged Morgenthau and Marshall to work on that problem while setting into motion a new administrative machinery to oversee national mobilization and rearmament. He established the National Defense Advisory Commission and Office of Emergency Management to supervise production of weapons and economic mobilization; meanwhile, he ordered an assessment of available stocks of arms and ammunition that could be declared "surplus" and therefore legally sold to another country. This was easy enough, since most of the material had been produced for use in World War I.[32]

Roosevelt acted with the confidence of a man who has been vindicated by events. "I was a sort of—who was the fellow? John the Baptist—'voice crying in the wilderness' all last summer," he said in a press conference on May 23. "I was perfectly sure there would be a war," but he had been called an alarmist. Now, with Hitler's armies on the march, he felt it was his right to lay down a new course for the country. On Sunday evening, May 26, the same day that the British began to evacuate thousands upon thousands of their soldiers from the now-encircled pocket at Dunkirk, Roosevelt spoke to the country in a fireside chat to explain his defense program. The atmosphere was tense and anxious. Sam Rosenman, who had drafted the speech with Harry Hopkins, recalled the scene in the White House: "There was no levity. There was no small talk. . . . It was a dejected dinner group" that assembled before the radio broadcast. As Harold Ickes put it in his diary, "there is no doubt in my mind that this country is in the most critical situation since we won our independence."[33]

Millions of Americans, tuning in on a restful Sunday evening, heard FDR's familiar voice tell of the terrible events in Europe. "Tonight," Roosevelt began, "over the once peaceful roads of Belgium and France millions are now moving, running from their homes to escape bombs and shells and fire and machine gunning, without shelter, and almost wholly without food." These "almost incredible" scenes were the result of a horrifying attack on peaceful countries by the Nazi war machine—a threat that many in America had discounted. "There are some among us who were persuaded by minority groups that we could maintain our physical safety by retiring within our continental boundaries," he said. To these doubters, "the past two weeks have meant the shattering of many illusions. They have lost the illusion that we are remote and isolated and, therefore, secure against the dangers from which no other land is free." He explained the work already accomplished in rearming, but made it clear the country needed a full-scale national effort. "It is our purpose not only to speed up production but to increase the total facilities of the nation in such a way that they can be further enlarged to meet emergencies of the future." And in a sign of the growing linkage he saw between American security the safety of the world, he placed this rearmament effort in global terms: "We defend and we build a way of life, not for America alone, but for all mankind."

In another sign of things to come, he called for Americans to be on guard against "the Trojan Horse, the fifth column that betrays a nation," internal subversives who sow discord and use "false slogans and emotional appeals." In fact, just five days earlier Roosevelt had authorized the Justice Department to use "listening devices" to gather information on "persons suspected of subversive activities against the Government of the United States." He did not reveal this publicly because the Supreme Court had ruled that information gathered by wiretapping was inadmissible in court. To FDR, wiretapping provided a vital tool in gathering intelligence for national defense, even if such evidence could not be used to win a conviction. "It is too late to do anything about it after sabotage, assassinations and fifth column activities are completed," he told Attorney General Robert Jackson in his secret May 21 directive ordering him to allow wiretapping. To the public, in his fireside chat, he made clear his purpose: "New forces are being unleashed, deliberately planned propaganda to divide and weaken us in the face of danger." Some of this language had been prompted by a recent report from Ambassador Bullitt that Communists in Belgium and France were sabotaging their military forces from within. He also knew about the Nazi infiltration into America, which J. Edgar Hoover had been monitoring. From now on, the swift mobilization of the country went forward accompanied by an ever-more intrusive government surveillance of suspected aliens, foreign agents, and their accomplices.[34]

Reports from Europe did nothing to dispel the gloom. On May 28, the Belgian king announced the surrender of his armed forces, clearing a path for the Germans to complete their drive to the coast. Reynaud in a fury told Bullitt that France had been "stabbed in the back" by the king's precipitous decision. Now the whole British force on the continent, along with the excellent French First Army, were caught in a rapidly closing German trap. Reynaud, his nerves shattered, again told Bullitt that the war would end soon in total defeat and that "Hitler would move almost immediately against the United States." He begged for American intervention, and also said he expected another "stab in the back" from Mussolini who would not scruple to attack France in her most vulnerable hour. Reynaud presented a sad contrast to Churchill, who on that same day told the House of Commons that despite "hard and heavy tidings" from the battlefield, Britain would not fail "to defend the world cause to which we have vowed ourselves."[35]

In fact, Britain's commitment to the cause was not quite as ironclad as Churchill suggested. At this moment, out of public view, Churchill faced a rearguard action from his own Foreign Secretary Lord Halifax who, over the preceding few days, had been urging Churchill to open a line to Mussolini to see if Il Duce might act as a go-between to Hitler on the subject of peace negotiations. Churchill strenuously opposed this, but Halifax kept pressing the issue. What could be wrong, he asked, with at least sounding out Mussolini about terms to end the war? Churchill replied that the Germans would make outrageous demands, such as the surrender of the fleet, perhaps some colonies and naval bases, and that the British government would have to refuse any such deal; but the mere act of inquiring about peace would deflate morale in the country and certainly alienate the Americans, who were watching closely to gauge British determination in the war. Halifax would not yield.

Only when Churchill took the issue to the full cabinet of some thirty ministers on the evening of May 28 did he win the point. To that body, he made plain that he had no interest in negotiations now, and that "whatever happens at Dunkirk, we shall fight on." His colleagues, upon hearing this, immediately rushed up to him, shook his hand, patted him on the back, and exhibited numerous un-English signs of emotion. The Halifax proposal fell away into embarrassed silence. The historian John Lukacs, in a penetrating study of this moment, believes it was a turning point in the war. Had Halifax been prime minister instead of Churchill, history might have turned out very differently. Instead, on this day, May 28, Churchill won a final victory over the appeasers and gained the support of the cabinet to carry on the war. There would be no more talk of peace with Hitler.[36]

In Washington, Roosevelt was tireless. "I am hitting on all cylinders, about 17 hours a day," he wrote to his daughter Anna. On May 31, he presented another enormous request for $1.3 billion for the army and navy, just two weeks after asking for $1.2 billion for the same general purpose. The funds would not help in the immediate crisis but would put into motion the building of a new American military establishment. As those requests churned their way through Congress, General Marshall on June 3 approved the sale to Britain and France of a large shipment of surplus weapons and ammunition. At that very moment, an armada of British naval and commercial vessels were scooping up the sodden, defeated remnants of the British army off the beach at Dunkirk. In a daring and much-celebrated operation, 338,000 British and French soldiers were rescued by June 4, though they left behind virtually all of their weapons and equipment.[37]

Though Dunkirk was a serious defeat, it also contained within it the material of legend, which Churchill seized upon for an address to the Commons. After explaining the heroic British and French resistance that kept the beaches open long enough for 215,000 British and 123,000 French soldiers to withdraw, and after excoriating the Belgian King for surrendering his armies without any warning to his allies, he praised the Royal Air Force and Navy for their exceptional efforts. The successful operation at Dunkirk was "a miracle of deliverance, achieved by valor, by perseverance, by perfect discipline, by faultless service, by resource, by skill, by unconquerable fidelity." He acknowledged that "wars are not won by evacuations," yet the keynote of his message was that Britain would fight on, and not seek peace terms. Churchill spoke of the possibility of a German invasion, but insisted that the British people "shall prove ourselves once again able to defend our Island home, to ride out the storm of war, and to outlive the menace of tyranny, if necessary for years, if necessary, alone." He ended with an indelible flourish designed especially for the still-tentative American people and government:

> We shall defend our Island, whatever the cost may be, we shall fight on the beaches, we shall fight on the landing grounds, we shall fight in the fields and in the streets, we shall fight in the hills; we shall never surrender, and even if, which I do not for a moment believe, this Island or a large part of it were subjugated and starving, then our Empire beyond the seas, armed and guarded by the British Fleet, would carry on the struggle, until, in God's good time, the New World, with all its power and might, steps forth to the rescue and the liberation of the old.[38]

The New World, at precisely that moment, was doing its best to help. Hoping surplus U.S. matériel could make good some of the losses at Dunkirk, General Marshall ordered the loading of 70,000 tons of surplus arms, then stored in armories along the East Coast, onto freight cars for transfer to the loading docks at Raritan, New Jersey. After the paperwork was signed and these weapons duly purchased, the first British transport ship, *Eastern Prince*, set sail for Britain on June 13, loaded with 12,000 rifles, 15,000 machine guns, 48 75-millimeter field guns, and 37 million rounds of ammunition. This was scarcely enough to outfit a single division for a few days of fighting. But it was a start.

By the end of June, a dozen ships had sailed. Fifteen more crossed the Atlantic in July. In these shipments, the United States sent to Britain half a million Lee-Enfield rifles, 130 million rounds of ammunition, 900 75-millimeter guns and a million shells, along with 25,000 Browning automatic rifles, the legendary Great War infantry weapon. They also threw in 20,000 revolvers. Shipments intended for France were diverted after the French asked the

Germans for an armistice on June 17. These old weapons, made for the last war, might be useful to a home guard in defense of the British Isles but they mainly served a symbolic purpose. "In terms of the supplies needed in modern war," the official British history stated, "the amounts involved in the surplus arms transaction were small; but from a strategical and political point of view they were of the greatest importance." Churchill himself later called these shipments "a supreme act of faith and leadership" in support of a nation that "many deemed already beaten." This Anglo-American collaboration contained within it the seeds of a future alliance, and even though the American cupboards were now bare, they could be resupplied. More important, Roosevelt had taken the first steps to commit the United States to supply Britain in its hour of peril.[39]

At his press conference on June 7, Roosevelt made clear that he envisioned more such military aid getting into British hands. He also let it slip that other far-reaching measures were in train. A journalist asked him if he had seen the *New York Times* editorial that morning calling for a program of universal compulsory military training—in effect, a draft. Such an idea a month earlier would have been thought wildly excessive and unneutral. Instead, FDR said simply, "I only read the first paragraph, and I liked it." The paper argued that "the logic of events" made such a measure necessary, and more than that, "we must face in all frankness the worst that can possibly happen," namely the defeat of France, Britain, and the domination of Europe by a Nazi dictator who could turn the British and French fleets against the United States. Germany, combining with Japan, would throttle America's trade, its security, and its democracy. Congressional timidity should be countered, said the *Times*, by the strong desire of the America public to defend "the only way of life they believe to be worth living." The United States was not yet at war, but the rhetorical foundations of a global struggle to defend democracy were being laid.[40]

Roosevelt expressed his new policy vividly in his speech at the University of Virginia commencement ceremony in Charlottesville on June 10. To that huge audience of expectant parents, youthful university graduates, and assembled faculty, he dropped the mask of equivocation once and for all. The shocking events of the previous few weeks, he began, had raised the fundamental question of the "future of the country" and of democracy at home and in the world. The students had heard the principles of individual liberty, free elections, tolerance, and peace mocked by nations that embraced the philosophy of force. Now suddenly the American public faced the immediate threat of war and dictatorship. Some people still clung to the "obvious delusion" that the United States could ride out the coming tempest as "a lone island in a world dominated by the philosophy of force." That he rejected. An isolated America meant "a people without freedom, a people lodged in prison, handcuffed, hungry, and fed through the bars from day to day by the contemptuous, unpitying masters of other continents." It was time, he said to face "certain truths," namely, that "military and naval victory for the gods of force and hate would endanger the institutions of democracy in the Western world, and that equally, therefore, the whole of our sympathies lies with those nations that are giving their life blood in combat against these forces." The audience burst into applause and shouts at this.[41]

And while much of the rest of the speech addressed the decision of Mussolini to enter the war by invading southeastern France—the "stab in the back" Reynaud had predicted—the president ended by stating clearly his new policy: "we will extend to the opponents of force the material resources of this nation; and, at the same time, we will harness and speed up the use of those resources in order that we ourselves in the Americas may have equipment and training equal to the task of any emergency and every defense." There would be no hesitation or restraint in this cause, for "once more the future of the nation and of the American people is at stake." With these remarks, a decade of neutrality, of repeated invocations of great ocean barriers and the blessings of isolation, gave way to a new vision: the mobilization of American industrial power in a world war for democracy.

Speechwriter Sam Rosenman called this address "the beginning of the policy of all-out aid to the democracies. It was still a 'measure short of war.' It was a logical extension of the quarantine speech and the policy of collective security. The isolationists still wailed; but the preponderance of American public opinion was rallying in back of the president." Henry Luce, the publisher of *Time*, *Life*, and *Fortune* magazines, wrote to FDR that "it was the most important human utterance since Lincoln's at Gettysburg," and the incoming telegrams to the White House overwhelmingly expressed similar views. Felix Frankfurter wired FDR his "wholehearted gratitude" for the address which "effectively summoned our people to our duty." *Time* magazine called it "a fighting speech, more powerful and more determined than any he had delivered since the war began." And even more than that, "the U.S. had taken sides. Ended was the myth of U.S. neutrality."[42]

While Roosevelt made his way back to Washington after speaking to his son's graduating class, the legislative wheels that would appropriate money for rearmament were already whirring. Congress—for so long anesthetized by the appeal of pacifism and neutralism—had been kicked into action by the collapse of France, by Mussolini's entrance into the war, and by the desperate threat of Hitler's forces to Britain. Legislators had already passed bills amounting to \$3.3 billion in appropriations by the time of the Charlottesville speech; two days later, the House passed a \$1.7 billion additional request for army and navy funds—a sum that matched the entire defense budget of the previous year—after only six hours of discussion, and by a vote of 401–1, the lone holdout being Vito Marcantonio, a socialist from East Harlem, New York. In the Senate, a few noisy critics like Burton Wheeler of Montana and Ernest Lundeen of Minnesota wailed that British propaganda, backed by bankers from J. P. Morgan, were pushing America toward war. But their appeals drifted harmlessly upward with the hot air of the Washington summer. Nothing could stop rearmament now.[43]

On June 18, a week after Roosevelt spoke at the University of Virginia, the House sent to the Senate—by a unanimous vote and after only two hours of discussion—a bill for the construction of a two-ocean navy that would cost \$4 billion over six years. The Vinson-Walsh Two-Ocean Navy Act envisioned two hundred new warships, including aircraft carriers, battleships, destroyers, and submarines. The bill was then passed on July 10 by the Senate without debate and without even taking a recorded vote. Roosevelt signed the measure on July 19. As C. P. Trussell of the *New York Times* noted, this act fueled "the largest single naval expansion program ever undertaken by any nation in world history." The Vinson-Walsh Act pumped new blood through the veins of the American shipbuilding industry, funding contracts at dry docks and shipyards from Bath, Maine, to Los Angeles, from New York, Boston, and Camden, New Jersey, to Newport News in Virginia and Puget Sound in Washington. By early September, the armed forces had placed orders with the aircraft industry for thirteen thousand planes. On September 9, Roosevelt, in his small office at the Hyde Park family home, signed a defense bill that totaled \$5.2 billion, the largest peacetime appropriation measure in American history. Within hours of the signing, the navy placed orders for \$3.8 billion in new construction.[44]

In late September, the press reported that \$7 billion of contracts had been sent out to private industry for the construction of aircraft, tanks, guns, and ships, as well as the infrastructure for expanding the size of the army. According to one tally—the press struggled to add up the dazzling flood of new spending—the 76th Congress, by the time it adjourned in late September, had approved \$12 billion (about \$265 billion today) in defense-related appropriations for fiscal year 1940–41. To put this into perspective, the previous year's defense budget had barely hit \$1.5 billion. In just a few frenetic months, the United States multiplied its defense budget *by a factor of eight.* These appropriations, often passed by voice vote without debate, show that while a few politicians and public figures still urged a policy of neutrality, disarmament, and disengagement from the global crisis, a new reality had overtaken the nation. Whatever appeal isolation once held as an actual strategy for the defense of the United States, its time had passed. Under Roosevelt's consistent pressure, Congress acted with rare unanimity, approving enormous and unprecedented expenditures with scarcely a word of dissent. Now, in the summer of 1940, American forges, mills, mines, factories, and dockyards sprang to life, infused with federal money and the urgency of war.[45]

V

It is natural that biographers of Roosevelt depict this remarkable eruption of defense spending as the personal achievement of the president. No one emphasized that point more than Robert Sherwood, whose admiring postwar biography insisted that Roosevelt alone must be credited with getting aid to Britain and starting the great rearmament effort: "the decision was entirely on his own. There was no time in his presidential career when he met with so much opposition" from his advisers. Sherwood called it "appropriate" that Roosevelt should have outlined his new policy of aid to the democracies in Charlottesville "in the presence of the genius of Thomas Jefferson, who had boldly without congressional authority set the young United States on the way to continental dominance" by acquiring the immense Louisiana Purchase. The empire of liberty had been Jefferson's legacy, Sherwood implied, and FDR would follow the Sage of Monticello in pushing America to accept "nothing less than the leadership of the world." In Sherwood's eyes, FDR had done it all by himself.[46]

Yet it does a disservice to the historical record to depict FDR as acting alone. After all, for many years before 1940, he had *failed* to act while others beseeched him to respond to the rise of fascism. Now that he moved the country onto a new path, he benefited from the labors of many advocates for American action in the world, public figures who had long been urging him to adopt a more vigorous policy. Operating in overlapping spheres of public action—in a fashion quite typical of the New Deal itself—these columnists, lobbyists, military officers, university presidents, religious leaders, business executives, publishers, and some former federal officials served as an extended brain trust for Roosevelt, making the moral case for aiding the democracies and advising on how to stand up the gigantic rearmament program the president wanted. Over the summer of 1940, these public allies helped grease the wheels of government as America moved to take on an ever more ambitious global role. Even more valuable, they helped Roosevelt—in a presidential election year—find a way to ensure that ongoing partisan differences about the New Deal would not block or hamper the emergence of a new coalition dedicated to the cause of saving democracy from the undeniable, and imminent, threat of fascism.[47]

Some interventionists never ceased pushing for action during the spring and summer. In April 1940, Dorothy Thompson boarded the SS *Manhattan* for Europe, arriving just in time for the German invasion of Scandinavia. Her trip was cut short by the subsequent attack on the Low Countries and France; by May 19, she was on a return ship to New York, her mind full of images of the collapse of the Western world she knew so intimately. She poured out a flood of furious columns that made the case for an immediate American mobilization in defense of democracy and civilization itself. She wrote from Paris to indict the Western democracies for "complacency, overconfidence and unwillingness to face the facts." They had enjoyed a position of dominant strength in the early 1930s and frittered it away. She argued that Hitler's battlefield success showed that such passive ideas as "defensive" warfare, which the French had banked on, were illusory. Neutrality itself was "a myth" that had not saved Scandinavia, Belgium, or the Netherlands.

Dorothy Thompson shaped the call for intervention.
J. A. Hampton / Topical Press Agency / Getty Images

She called for immediate aid to Britain and even proposed that the allies go on the offense to attack Germany: "The dark beast of the Nazi world must not be allowed to crouch upon its exhausted victims and feed upon them" while preparing to strike again. "It must be attacked," she insisted. To meet the crisis immediately, she suggested the two political parties in the U.S. call off their looming nominating conventions and place FDR and Republican hopeful Wendell Willkie on a joint bipartisan ticket. Only Roosevelt, she wrote (enraging Helen and Ogden Reid, the staunch Republican owners of the *Herald Tribune*), could lead the country in the coming conflict against fascism. In a private letter to the president, she went even further: She asked FDR to set up a "Committee of Public Safety to legally suppress the leaders of subversive movements aimed against our freedoms," namely Bundists and Communists who both opposed rearmament and aid to Britain.[48]

In these same weeks, Thompson's fellow *Herald Tribune* columnist Walter Lippmann issued equally powerful calls for mobilization and action. Normally, Lippmann wrote in a more abstract style than Thompson, philosophical and with less heat. He had been quite late to the interventionist cause, favoring neutrality for most of the 1930s. But the crisis of May and June brought new fire to his pen. Washington was facing, he said, "decisions which are as momentous as any in our history," and he feared that the country and Congress remained insufficiently alert. He blamed political leaders for not speaking "the hard truth" to the public or preparing them for the work and sacrifice that lay ahead. Writing in *Life* on June 3, he declared "the hour of our destiny has come." Using a term FDR had already placed into current use, he said the United States must become a "citadel so strong in its defenses that by our own example the world can eventually be redeemed and pacified and made whole again." Lippmann inveighed against the propaganda of the isolationists. He called them "misguided zealots" who believed that quotations from Washington's Farewell Address would suffice to defend America. In the gravest crisis since the founding of the United States, Americans must decide "how much of our great inheritance we are able and willing to defend." To secure democracy from fascism's global threat, he argued, the country needed to be led toward "a wholly new mood of duty, sacrifice, and honor." A total rearmament program, along with rationing, allocation of labor and raw materials, even the surrender of some civil liberties—these discomforts would now have to be endured. "The price will be heavy," he said. "Let us pay it like men."[49]

Contemplating the source of America's failure to wake up to the fascist threat, Lippmann had some choice words for the generation of Americans who, after the last war, had sworn off conflict forever. They styled themselves as realists, "hard-core, buncombe-proof, un-bamboozleable, antiseptic to flag waving, deaf to the bugles." But Lippmann believed they had been "duped by a falsification of American history . . . miseducated by a swarm of innocent but ignorant historians, by reckless demagogues" who spawned the myth that Woodrow Wilson, British propagandists, American bankers, arms manufacturers, and jingoist press lords had tricked the American people into war in 1917. Such stories were fanciful and false, he said. America had gone to war to protect the national interest against the German submarine threat to the Atlantic Ocean. That threat now loomed again, as the German Reich stood poised to thrust its tentacles into the Western Hemisphere.[50]

This theme, that a disillusioned "lost generation" of intellectuals had ill-served the country by promoting cynicism toward national defense, became something of a leitmotif of the summer of 1940. On June 10, the same day of FDR's Charlottesville address, the Librarian of Congress, Archibald MacLeish, published in the *New Republic* a direct accusation against a handful of popular writers who, he felt, had encouraged distrust of patriotism, national duty, and sacrifice. MacLeish, a Harvard Law graduate by way of Hotchkiss and Yale, had abandoned his promising law career for a penurious life of letters in Paris in the 1920s, and became an intimate friend of Ernest Hemingway, F. Scott Fitzgerald, John Dos Passos, and others of the expatriate set who shaped interwar literature. In the 1930s, MacLeish worked as an editor for Henry Luce's *Fortune* magazine and grew increasingly interventionist in his outlook. His law teacher Felix Frankfurter had helped him win the librarian job in 1939, and from this prestigious position of public service, MacLeish acted a bit like Roosevelt's minister of culture, weighing in on all manner of political subjects. In his June essay, MacLeish expressed his anxiety that "the moral and spiritual unpreparedness of the country is worse than its unpreparedness in arms." He feared that "a free people cannot fight fascism unless it believes with even greater conviction that freedom is good, and that slavery is evil." But such convictions, he went on, had been mocked by postwar writers who exhibited only distrust of slogans and flag-waving.

MacLeish pointed an accusing finger at Hemingway, who had written in *A Farewell to Arms* that "I was always embarrassed by the words sacred, glorious, and sacrifice. . . . I had seen nothing sacred, and the things that were glorious had no glory, and the sacrifices were like the stockyards at Chicago." To MacLeish, the bestselling books of the lost generation "have done more to disarm democracy in the face of fascism than any other single influence." Given that both Hemingway and Dos Passos had served as ambulance drivers in the First World War and had gone to Spain in the 1930s to encourage Americans to support the Spanish Republican cause, this charge seemed un-generous, and it kicked off a significant literary spat. But MacLeish diagnosed a critical problem that the internationalist camp faced: After the bitter experience of World War I, too many Americans closed their ears to any moral appeal or clarion call for sacrifice and struggle, even on behalf of democracy. In a personal appeal to FDR on June 14, he asked the president to make rearmament into "a great affirmative forward effort . . . requiring discipline, requiring sacrifice, requiring much suffering and pain, but an effort which, if it succeeds, will create upon the continent the realization of our possibilities as a people." In short, mobilization for war, and even war itself, could make America into a more virtuous republic.[51]

If Thompson, Lippmann, and MacLeish adopted a tone of pugnacious moral certainty akin to the Four-Minute Men of the First World War—those trained speechifiers who whipped up patriotic sentiment in theaters and concert halls before the curtain went up—Eleanor Roosevelt used a lighter touch. In her "My Day" columns, she had perfected a kind of pragmatic empathy that could reach readers inured to robust appeals for intervention in European affairs. In the early summer, she frequently invoked the Christian ideal of kindness and ministry to make the case for aid to war-torn Europe. "Oppression and misery anywhere," she wrote on the day the Nazis invaded Western Europe, "menaces the spirit of democracy all over the world and therefore is a concern of ours." Here she gave voice to a theme FDR had tentatively begun to incorporate into his own public messages: that if democracy is threatened abroad, Americans must act. "There is no such thing as isolation," Mrs. Roosevelt wrote. "We cannot cut ourselves off from the conditions which prevail in other nations. What they suffer, we must feel one way or the other." This did not strike the same militarist note as Dorothy Thompson, but the First Lady frequently quoted the columnist when their views coincided. She praised Thompson for writing about both the moral and material unpreparedness of the country. "I think she is entirely right that the two go together. . . . We in the democracies . . . have almost forgotten that a bandit may turn up who does not understand our language nor hold to any of our beliefs."[52]

And she used her platform to push for more than just rearmament. She insisted on protecting the advances of the New Deal, ensuring that the government redouble its commitment to social and economic progress as it prepared for war. Defending democracy meant proving that it works, she argued, and that meant renewing the national commitment to social progress alongside rearmament. "If democracy is to survive, it must be because it meets the needs of its people," she wrote in mid-May as the Nazis menaced Paris. The challenge the nation faced was to "make democracy something for which every citizen will feel he will willingly die." Toward the end of June, she particularly praised a column of Thompson's that demanded social progress alongside war preparation and said, "even though we rearm . . . we must have more housing, better health services and jobs that ensure a decent livelihood to every family." Her insistence on fighting for a better, fairer, more secure society would find its way into many of the speeches and pronouncements the president would make in the coming weeks and months, culminating in the "Four Freedoms" address of January 1941. With unparalleled prestige and popularity in America in these anxious days, the First Lady could say with no hint of equivocation that in a world of cruel tyrants and aggressive war, the United States must stand "as a beacon of light to all people who believe in freedom and the triumph of the theory of government which is based on spiritual values."[53]

In this tumultuous summer, interventionist voices from across the political spectrum dominated public debate about the war and its danger to America. Henry Luce, a Republican and no friend of the New Deal, stridently declared on the ABC radio network on June 1 that the fascists threatened everything Americans valued, including a high standard of living, free enterprise, labor unions, arts and letters, the right to vote, the trial by jury, and freedom of religion. It was time, he said, "to strip off our false cloak of neutrality and announce to the world—to the brown men and the black men and the yellow men and to all the white men of the world—that we stand now . . . for democracy." And that meant getting arms to Britain and rearming America. Luce's *Time* magazine, summing up the new atmosphere in a mid-June essay, claimed that the hesitation and timidity of the recent past was gone. Now "it was a matter of citizens ringing doorbells, handing out petitions, joining committees that urged aid." *Time* saw the country pulling together. General John J. Pershing, commander of American forces during World War I, told the country that it now faced "a war for civilization" and must prepare to fight. A few days before the president's Charlottesville speech, thirty educators, writers, lawyers, and executives signed a petition calling the Nazi regime "our mortal foe" and urged the United States to declare war on Germany. Even Charles Lindbergh's mother-in-law, Mrs. Elizabeth Morrow, called for aid to the allies. An author and acting president of Smith College, she proclaimed that "there are some things worse than war," unknowingly borrowing a line coined by Ernest Hemingway in Spain. "There are some things supreme and noble that are worth fighting for."[54]

The German Spring offensive also propelled William Allen White back into action. The Kansas editor, ably assisted by Clark Eichelberger, announced on May 19 the creation of a new lobbying organization in favor of getting arms to Britain immediately: the Committee to Defend America by Aiding the Allies. Among its earliest members were Henry Stimson, former secretary of war; Governor Herbert Lehman of New York; Frank Knox, publisher; and Columbia University president Nicholas Murray

Butler. Within days, other prominent internationalists, many of them veterans of the embargo-repeal effort, joined the new organization. The list of signatories included the cream of America's elite, drawn from business and industry, the universities, Congress, the legal profession, banking, religious institutions, the arts, and the press. Robert Sherwood signed on with a public statement that denounced "the false prophets of isolationism." To beat back "the swelling forces of evil," Sherwood continued, the United States must confront, not duck, the threat of fascist aggression. The country must drop the "cardboard mask of neutrality" and "go to the Allies' aid with all the power that we can command." By the end of the summer, over six hundred chapters of CDAAA had been set up, and though the conceit of the organization was that aid to Britain would keep Americans out of combat, few could deny that words like Sherwood's prepared the ground for the country's direct entry into the war.[55]

Sherwood was also responsible for a full-page newspaper ad that ran on June 10, paid for by CDAAA. The ad featured a simple slogan in large block letters: "Stop Hitler Now!" Beneath it appeared a message exhorting readers to urge their congressional representatives to support immediate aid to Britain. "If Hitler wins," it said, "the United States will find itself alone in a barbaric world, a world ruled by Nazis, with 'spheres of influence' assigned to their totalitarian allies." Hitler, Mussolini, Stalin, the Japanese militarists—all agreed on one thing, said the ad: "Democracy must be wiped from the face of the Earth!" In such a dystopian world, America would have to become a militarized garrison state, always on alert, in a state of never-ending war. "We shall exist only under martial law—or the law of the jungle." The ad urged "patriotic Americans" to "tell your president—your senators—your congressmen—that you want them to help the allies to stop Hitler now!"[56]

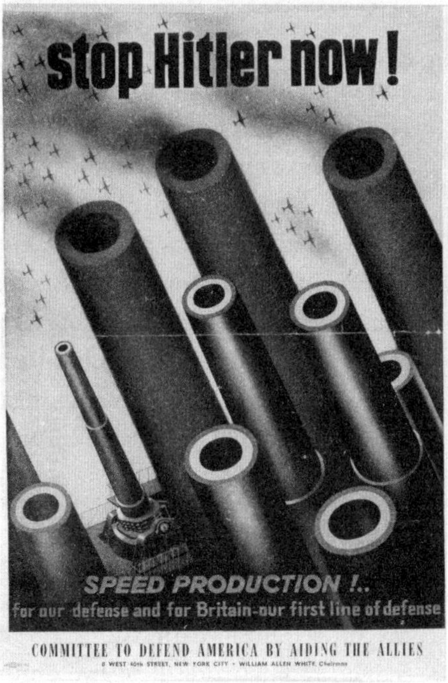

Robert Sherwood's slogan became a rallying cry.
Library of Congress

Sherwood certainly deployed a strident tone, but Roosevelt approved: During a press conference in the Oval

Office the next day, reporters spotted a copy of the ad laid out on the president's desk and invited him to comment on it. Basking in the success of his Charlottesville speech, he called the ad "a great piece of work, extremely educational for the people of this country. . . . It is a mighty good thing that Bill White and his committee are getting things like this out for the education of this country." The *Chicago Tribune*, which had criticized FDR's rearmament policy, put out a churlish article that Sherwood's ad was mocked in Berlin and indeed Hitler's armies entered Paris on June 14, showing just how hard it was to stop him. But Sherwood's full-page ad, reprinted in news stories across the country, resonated. In fact, "Stop Hitler Now!" became a slogan the government used in bond drives all the way through the Second World War.[57]

Revealing its ambitions to mobilize public opinion across the country, the CDAAA commissioned Dr. Ralph Bunche, a thirty-five-year-old professor of political science at Howard University, to write an addendum to Sherwood's broadside called "Stop Hitler Now—The Negro Must Help." Bunche argued that the triumph of Nazism would force African Americans into a "permanent status of sub-marginal existence" more ruthless than "the paternalism of the southern slave system." Should Hitler win the war, "the Aryan Cult of Racial Supremacy will dominate the world" and African Americans would be used as "slaves of the master race—the Nordic Nazis." Of course, American democracy was imperfect, Bunche wrote. But between a flawed democracy and "a totalitarian system bent upon the enslavement of the weak," Black Americans had only one choice. The *Baltimore Afro-American* agreed: "our welfare is intimately tied up with the welfare of America," said an editorial, "and the colored man cannot save himself by sticking his head ostrich-like in the sand and saying, 'it ain't none of my business.'" Charles P. Howard, writing in the *Atlanta Daily World*, showed no fear of fighting for democracy. Hitler meant to send Black Americans back to the worst days of slavery, he said. "If our descendants shall be free, it looks like we must die. If that is a necessity, let it come. There are those who died that we might be free. Why shouldn't we die, that those whom we love should be free?" Sherwood could not have made the case more powerfully.[58]

VI

As these public expressions of support for the "Stop Hitler" movement gained momentum, Roosevelt announced on June 20 his decision to bring Henry Stimson and Frank Knox into the cabinet as secretaries of war and the navy, respectively. Both were prominent Republicans—Knox, the publisher of the *Chicago Daily News*, had been Alf Landon's running mate in 1936, and Stimson had been Herbert Hoover's secretary of state (and before that, William Howard Taft's secretary of war). Both men were former artillery officers and outspoken interventionists. In fact, just two days earlier, Stimson gave a stirring address at the Yale University commencement in which he said the United States "faces the greatest crisis in its history," that all neutrality laws should be repealed, that planes and munitions of every kind should be sped across the ocean to Britain immediately, that the country should institute a draft, open its doors to refugees, and "combat the defeatist arguments" being made by a few holdouts in Congress and the press who failed to see the urgency of the Nazi threat. Stimson came very close to advocating war against Germany now, and he was far out in front of FDR's public views. Roosevelt was under no illusion about Stimson's position when he called him the next day to offer him the cabinet post.[59]

In making these appointments, FDR placed the rearmament program in the hands of two experienced leaders who shared his outlook on the growing threat to America's national security. He also strengthened the position of General George Marshall by ensuring that the army chief of staff would be paired with a powerful secretary of war who, unlike Harry Woodring, was impatient to rebuild the armed forces. The Republican leadership, then gathering in Philadelphia for its presidential nominating convention, immediately expelled Stimson and Knox from the party, while some of FDR's Democratic critics like Burton K. Wheeler and Bennett Champ Clark took to the floor of the Senate in a fury to denounce Roosevelt for plotting to get America into war. But a Gallup poll showed that 71 percent of Americans approved the appointments. Both Stimson and Knox were confirmed in the Senate by wide margins, another defeat for the dwindling number of Senate isolationists.[60]

General Marshall viewed these appointments with delight. He knew Stimson would be a powerful ally in mobilizing the nation. As he put it in a speech to the annual meeting of the Veterans of Foreign Wars in Akron, Ohio, the American people "want the nation to be prepared. They want a large army, fully equipped with the latest vehicles and weapons; and they want this transformation to be accomplished immediately. . . . The time for endless debate and other differences of opinion is past. We must get down to hard pan and carry out our preparations without vacillations or confusion." If there was one topic Marshall feared might divide the country, however, it was conscription. With an immense amount of money now flowing into shipbuilding, aircraft production, and arms manufacturing, Marshall knew he would need manpower to fill out the armed services. The army had dwindled to a pitiful figure of 270,000 active-duty soldiers; by contrast, Hitler had mobilized 1.5 million men just for the invasion of Poland and sent about 3 million into France and the Low Countries. Marshall felt that voluntary enlistment could never produce enough soldiers; the country needed a selective service program. But he felt the proposal must come from civilians or from Congress. Fortunately, a savvy band of veterans of the World War I preparedness movement, anticipating the urgent need for men in uniform, issued a call for the immediate adoption of universal compulsory military training—in effect, an unprecedented peacetime draft.[61]

In May, the Military Training Camps Association, with about fifty thousand members in chapters across the country, passed a resolution at a board meeting in New York stating that the war in Europe "endangers the safety and free institutions of the United States," and called for an immediate program of training and recruitment. The principal leader behind the effort was Grenville Clark, a Great War veteran and well-connected New York lawyer (Henry Stimson had been one of his law partners). He was also a longtime friend of Roosevelt's going back to Harvard. Clark denounced "the defeatist and ignorant" belief that it was too late to help the European democracies. He called for rapid aid to Britain as well as the mobilization of at least 3 million soldiers for all the branches of the military.[62]

Roosevelt, sensing that a peacetime conscription bill could stir up a hornet's nest on Capitol Hill, remained wary, though privately he gave Clark conditional approval to move ahead. In the typical New Deal fashion of relying on citizens to play leading government advisory roles, Clark drafted a selective service bill that would register men between the ages of eighteen and forty-five (later reduced to ages twenty-one to thirty-five) for training and service. He then found allies in Congress to help get it passed. On June 20, the same day FDR brought Stimson and Knox into the cabinet, Senator Edward R. Burke, a Nebraska Democrat, introduced the necessary legislation; it was cosponsored in the House by a conservative Republican, Representative James Wadsworth of New York. A few increasingly frustrated senators like Gerald Nye tried to paint the selective service plan as the work of a cabal of Anglophile bankers and militarists who wanted to get America into war. Senator George Norris, a progressive independent from Nebraska and a longtime antimilitarist, howled that conscription would lead to war and dictatorship in America. Yet these kinds of vitriolic attacks had lost their bite and Grenville Clark's organization had the more powerful argument: "the [Burke-Wadsworth] bill," it stated, "takes cognizance of the Nazi-

Fascist-Communist threat to individual freedom everywhere and authorizes the mobilization and training of the nation's manpower for the preservation of peace and the American way of life." That message could not easily be rebutted.[63]

Polls showed the public supported the conscription bill by significant majorities; so did Congress, the press, the CDAAA, governors, executives in business and industry, General Pershing, even William Randolph Hearst (though he preferred a Swiss model of universal citizen training with no standing army). Surprisingly, given the pacifism then popular on college campuses, university presidents beat the drum for conscription. Nicholas Murray Butler of Columbia was a fervent internationalist; in January 1940, he spoke of the war in Europe as a clash of civilizations and described the storm clouds in Europe as "the darkest and most threatening since the fall of the Roman empire." He urged the U.S. government to provide "world leadership" in the struggle against totalitarianism and threatened to fire any Columbia faculty member who opposed mobilization efforts.[64]

The most active university leader was James Bryant Conant of Harvard, who eagerly joined the CDAAA and gave regular public pronouncements about the threat of fascism. He asserted that Hitler clearly aimed "to dominate the world" and that America must rapidly prepare to stop him, even at the risk of war. A "complete totalitarian triumph" looked possible, Conant said, placing American freedom in grave danger. The day after FDR spoke in Charlottesville, Conant called for immediate passage of a compulsory military training law. Acknowledging the popularity of pacifism on some campuses, he alleged that students "were suffering from overexposure to one particular ideal—a noble one but not always sufficient—the ideal of peace." Now, he said, Americans had woken up to the imminent threat of war. In early July, Conant testified in the Senate in favor of the Burke-Wadsworth bill, insisting that "our entire way of life" was under attack and that the immediate mobilization of fighting men "takes precedence over all other considerations." Others followed Conant's lead: As of early July, twenty-three presidents of colleges and universities had publicly backed the plan for selective service. On college campuses everywhere, the Military Training Camps appeared at commencement ceremonies that spring, staging officially sanctioned rallies in favor of conscription. In late August, despite the outcry of a few "irreconcilables," the Selective Service Act of 1940 passed the Senate easily, by a vote of 58–31; it cleared the House by a vote of 263–149. FDR signed the measure into law on September 16.[65]

There can be little doubt that the shocks of 1940—from Hitler's extraordinary success in Scandinavia to the swift collapse of Belgium, the Netherlands, and France and the start of an air war on Britain—transformed America's perception of the war in Europe. As Hitler drew up plans for a cross-Channel invasion, it seemed entirely plausible that Nazism would soon rule all the Old World from the Russian border to the Irish Sea. By the middle of 1940, a growing majority of the American people came to accept, however unwillingly, some responsibility for halting the further spread of fascism. Few sought formal entry into the war, nor did Roosevelt. But there were other measures the public now agreed must be taken. The day after the Charlottesville speech, polls showed 80 percent of the public approved of selling weapons to Britain and France, and 73 percent wanted "to do everything possible to help England and France, except go to war," which was FDR's position exactly. This number went up to 76 percent in September. And Americans were prepared to accept greater risks as the summer turned to fall. By November, 60 percent of the public favored aiding Britain "even at the risk of war" with Germany.[66]

The ground was shifting. The appeal of pacifism, neutrality, and isolation—for so long articles of faith to much of the country—had waned. Walter Lippmann penned an alarming essay in *Life* on "The Economic Consequences of a German Victory" that envisioned a global economy controlled by "totalitarian" empires (the use of this word peaked in late 1940). If Britain should

FDR signs the Burke-Wadsworth conscription law.
FDR Library

fall, Americans would face a world controlled by "a totalitarian monopoly" in Europe and Asia. Americans, alone and cut off, would become "isolated and impoverished and demoralized." Robert Sherwood, in a *Reader's Digest* essay titled "Rush All Possible Aid to Britain," argued that Americans could no longer "hide behind the tattered rags of our neutrality." For Sherwood, the purveyors of antimilitarism, neutrality, and isolation stood accused of willful ignorance, and worse, of beguiling the public with a fraudulent argument that only aided the dictators. Roosevelt of course could not use such language, but he shared Sherwood's view. And these interventionists were no longer alone. In these shocking, horror-filled months of 1940, as German armies rolled like an unstoppable tide across Europe, Roosevelt and his many public allies and supporters succeeded in winning the country over to the position that Nazi domination in Europe, aligned with Italian Fascism, Soviet Communism, and Japanese imperialism, directly threatened America, its values, and its form of government. And that Americans, at long last, must act.[67]

VII

No one knows exactly when Roosevelt made up his mind to run for a third term. Sam Rosenman thought he decided sometime between the invasion of Norway on April 9 and the evacuation at Dunkirk on June 4. Henry Morgenthau thought he made up his mind sometime during the month of June. Harold Ickes, who had been urging a third term on FDR for months, wrote in his diary at the end of June that "I have no doubt now that the President will run, for he must realize that failure to do so will mean the loss of all that he has done during the last seven years." And not just the fate of the New Deal hung in the balance: In the early summer, the Republicans vying for their party's nomination included two staunch isolationists—Senators Robert Taft of Ohio and Arthur Vanderburg of Michigan. A third hopeful, New York District Attorney Thomas Dewey, shifted his position with the prevailing breeze, and said he favored strict U.S. neutrality. Contemplating these uninspiring, conventional men, the Republican delegates to the national convention did something quite unexpected. They nominated for president not a familiar insider, but a charismatic business executive, political neophyte, and lifelong Democrat named Wendell Willkie.[68]

A lawyer from a small town in Indiana, Willkie had been a supporter of Woodrow Wilson and the League of Nations. He served as a delegate to the Democratic convention in 1924, where he supported Al Smith in his unsuccessful campaign against the Klan. His legal career led him into the utility business and in 1929 he took a position as the legal counsel for Commonwealth and Southern, an electric utility holding company, rising to become its president in 1933. Although an early supporter of FDR's, he soon tangled with the New Deal's effort to produce and transmit cheap electricity through the Tennessee Valley Authority. Fighting the overreach of the TVA, he became a noted spokesman for the idea that government intrusion in the free market was un-American and bad for business. This argument placed Willkie and Roosevelt on a collision course and made Willkie a possible contender for the Republican nomination. With the country increasingly resolved to aid Britain in its life-and-death struggle with Hitler, the internationalist wing of the GOP thought Willkie's foreign policy views would neutralize the issue and allow the 1940 contest to become a referendum on the New Deal alone, about which the public remained divided. A worldly professional with Midwestern values and a bluff, hearty charm, Willkie sported wrinkled suits and floppy, unkempt hair that gave him a look of a windswept everyman. He was an appealing figure to whom many of the Republican delegates were drawn. On June 27, he snatched the nomination away from Dewey at the last minute and rolled out of Philadelphia with momentum and an admiring press corps along for the ride.[69]

Wendell Willkie: charismatic, honest, rough-hewn, but a poor campaigner in the end.
Library of Congress

Roosevelt instantly understood the political threat Willkie posed, seeing him as an advocate of the "corporate state," that is, the theory, popularized by Mussolini, that business elites and a political strongman should join forces, creating a system that could exploit workers, crush unions, extract wealth from the people and fill the pockets of executives while promising to provide security and order. In fact, according to Harold Ickes, FDR thought Willkie wanted to impose a more friendly, less aggressive version of fascism. (He was not alone: Freda Kirchwey wrote in *The Nation* that Willkie spoke for Wall Street appeasers who had no qualms about doing business with the dictators.)

Roosevelt feared that Willkie would empower the economic royalists he had been fighting for over a decade and usher in an era of corporate rule. With this diagnosis of his opponent in mind, Roosevelt resolved to break the third term taboo. He would fight Willkie on the ground he liked best: the safeguarding of democracy.[70]

He hinted at this strategy in a remarkable and quite lengthy monologue delivered on July 5 to his traveling press entourage in Hyde Park. The previous day, he had opened his just-completed presidential library and in a small ceremony, handed over the keys to R. D. W. Connor, the archivist of the United States—a testament to FDR's belief that the activities of the president should be subject to public scrutiny. In his press conference, he interrupted the first questioner and took the floor, speaking for some time without interruption about the state of the world and America's place in it. His remarks signaled the start of his campaign and prefigured many themes that would soon become familiar.

"Today the world is facing a very definite upheaval," he began, "because certain new systems of Government have arisen to such an extent that they already control and are seeking to enlarge their control over a very large portion of the world's population." This new form of government, he said,

> is called by various names; probably the easiest name, as a symbol, is the corporate state. The corporate state—we think of Italy, but it applies equally to Germany and Russia—is extremely efficient. It has abolished two of the three safeguards of democracy, the Legislature and the Courts. It puts the supreme power into a group, in some cases a very small group, in some cases very large, which exercises administrative functions, and there are no legislative functions and there are no court functions. It is efficient. And I am sorry to say there are a large number of Americans—not proportionate to the population but still a large number of Americans—who are willing to consider, because of its efficiency, the corporate state.

This was a swipe at Willkie, of course, and a way of linking him to fascism: In the name of efficiency, Roosevelt implied, the oligarchs and corporations supporting Willkie would snuff out the inefficient but consensual processes of American democracy.

And what were the chief elements of this democratic tradition? He enumerated them, in what was a rough draft of his later "Four Freedoms" speech. They included the freedom of speech and religion. They also included the freedom from fear—"so that people won't be afraid of being bombed from the air or attacked, one way or the other, by some other nation"—and freedom from want—that is, human security through "the removal of certain barriers between nations, cultural in the first place and commercial in the second place." These were America's core values, he believed. As he wrapped up his impromptu remarks on this warm July day in rural New York, he made plain that he saw Willkie as a threat to those values, a threat as serious as Hitler himself:

> And so the question really comes down to whether we are going to continue to seek those freedoms or whether we are going to give up, at the behest of . . . those nations which have removed those four freedoms in the interest of a greater efficiency of Government—a temporary efficiency, I might say.[71]

As the Democratic National Convention opened in the enormous indoor Chicago Stadium on July 15, Roosevelt had still not publicly stated his decision to run, feeling that he could not be seen to *want* the nomination but would accept it only by acclamation and because of the world emergency. This sort of vanity and even narcissism infuriated most of his advisers, but they swallowed their frustration, disciplined the delegates, and swept aside the somewhat pathetic competition of Jim Farley, the party chairman, and Vice President John Nance Garner, a bilious and alcoholic conservative who Roosevelt had come to loathe. Roosevelt was nominated on the first ballot, and after a tense couple of days, he compelled the party to accept Henry Wallace, the peculiar but reliably liberal secretary of agriculture, as his running mate.

Only then, as July 18 stretched into the early dawn hours of the nineteenth, did Roosevelt address the convention and the country by radio from the White House to explain what he saw as the stakes of the election. He was prepared for this moment. Some days earlier, he had asked two of his most devoted advisers, Felix Frankfurter and Archibald MacLeish, to send him the strongest argument they could make for why he should run for an unprecedented third term. Using their words, as well as some polished phrases of Sam Rosenman, Tom Corcoran, and Ben Cohen, Roosevelt placed the issue in terms of duty and service in a time of national emergency:

> Like most men of my age, I had made plans for myself, plans for a private life of my own choice and for my own satisfaction, a life of

> that kind to begin in January 1941. These plans, like so many other plans, had been made in a world which now seems as distant as another planet. Today all private plans, all private lives, have been in a sense repealed by an overriding public danger. In the face of that public danger all those who can be of service to the Republic have no choice but to offer themselves for service in those capacities for which they may be fitted.

As thousands of Democratic conventioneers sat quietly in the stifling hall, exhausted, sweaty, fanning themselves, the familiar voice filled the cavernous space. Eleanor sat motionless on the stage; a blue-white spotlight shone on a flag-draped portrait of the president hanging from a balcony. FDR's voice cascaded down from the loudspeakers, enveloping the party faithful. The president explained the "public danger" that lay ahead. Hitler wanted to destroy "the form of Government, the kind of society that we in the United States have chosen and established for ourselves." Something much bigger and greater than just a clash of nations now threatened Europe. "It is not an ordinary war. It is a revolution imposed by force of arms, which threatens all men everywhere. It is a revolution which proposes not to set men free but to reduce them to slavery—to reduce them to slavery in the interest of a dictatorship which has already shown the nature and the extent of the advantage which it hopes to obtain." If that was true, then Americans had no choice but to meet, and somehow defeat, this assault on democratic government. He could not set down the cares of his office at such a time.

And in a remarkable conclusion, he returned to a theme that he had voiced before, and which Frankfurter in his memo had underscored: that a war for democracy must be waged in the name of what he called "human security . . . to better the condition of life of the many millions of our fellow citizens." The struggle against Nazism and totalitarian rule was, for FDR, a fight for "human decency" on behalf of "the common people." It was a clash between "the continuance of civilization as we know it versus the ultimate destruction of all that we have held dear—religion against godlessness; the ideal of justice against the practice of force; moral decency versus the firing squad; courage to speak out, and to act, versus the false lullaby of appeasement. . . . The American people must decide whether these things are worth making sacrifices of money, of energy, and of self." Roosevelt, for his part, had made up his mind, and the roar of approval from the delegates suggested they would follow him into battle.[72]

VIII

One person who took heart from Roosevelt's robust statements in favor of stopping Hitler was Winston Churchill. He wrote to FDR after the Charlottesville speech to praise "the grand scope of your declaration" and to thank him for his "strong encouragement in a dark but not unhopeful time." He followed this with a request for ships—in particular, the small, nimble destroyers that could fend off Axis submarines and provide protection to shipping in the English Channel and the western approaches of the British Isles. "The next six months are vital" because the Germans, now with the immeasurable advantage of access to the French Atlantic ports, could tighten the noose around Britain and halt the shipping on which Britain's survival depended. Sending about fifty old American destroyers that were not needed by the U.S. Navy would help "bridge the gap," Churchill said, until Britain's own crash program of shipbuilding could yield fruit. Churchill told Roosevelt that Hitler was staging an enormous force for an invasion of Britain, and the matter of getting American destroyers into the battle was now "a matter of life and death."[73]

Initially, Roosevelt refused. He feared that Congress would never approve the transfer of the ships to Britain, and in any case, he did not want such a fight on his hands as he was just starting on his reelection bid. But the stakes of the issue rose rapidly after July 10, when the German Luftwaffe began regular air attacks across the Channel. A week later—just as the Democratic convention reached its climax—German bombing intensified, hitting British shipping, ports, coastal airfields, and aircraft manufacturing plants. The ensuing Battle of Britain, featuring waves of German fighters and bombers engaging with swarms of British Hurricane and Spitfire planes above the southeastern British countryside, prompted Churchill to renew his request. On July 31, with Hitler's divisions massing in coastal ports in preparation for an invasion and the outcome of the war in the balance, Churchill sent FDR a point-blank demand for ships: "It has now become most urgent for you to let us have the destroyers. . . . Mr. President, with great respect I must tell you that in the long history of the world, this is a thing to do now."[74]

With the nomination safely behind him, with Willkie largely leaving foreign policy out of his campaign, and with the resilience of Britain now on display in beating back the German onslaught, Roosevelt changed his mind. He seized upon an idea initially proposed by the British ambassador in Washington, Philip Kerr (Lord Lothian), that an informal exchange might be arranged: The United States would give the ships to Britain and in return, Britain would offer the U.S. government a long-term lease on naval bases in the Caribbean. In this way, both sides could shore up their defenses against the German naval threat, and Roosevelt could sell the deal as a national security measure. This plan, which Lothian circulated to various cabinet officers like Frank Knox, Harold Ickes, Henry Morgenthau, and Henry Stimson, became the principal subject of debate on August 2, at what Ickes called one of the most important cabinet meetings of the Roosevelt presidency. (It was so important that FDR prepared a record of it, something he rarely did.) When Knox pressed the matter at that meeting, Roosevelt was much more sympathetic. He still thought it would need congressional approval, but figured that if Willkie would lend support to the plan, it might get through Congress. FDR put in a call to William Allen White, asking him if he would intercede with the GOP candidate and win his support. Roosevelt also wanted assurances from Churchill that under no circumstances would the Royal Navy be allowed to fall into German hands, should the worst happen, and Hitler succeed in his invasion of Britain.[75]

White did more than send out feelers to Willkie; he redoubled his own Committee's efforts to create a groundswell of support for the destroyers deal. The interventionist cause did not lack for talent and star power. The CDAAA deployed the country's greatest living soldier, Gen. John "Blackjack" Pershing, to plead for aid to Britain, and others were summoned as well. Robert Sherwood, Ambassador William Bullitt (back from Nazi-occupied France), Florida Senator Claude Pepper, Ralph Ingersoll—editor of the new high-brow New York newspaper called *PM*—Governor Herbert Lehman of New York, all spoke of the horror of a German victory in Europe. The strangest bedfellows were brought together by the cause, with left-wing Freda Kirchwey of *The Nation* proclaiming that "we must lend all possible strength to the struggle against totalitarianism" just as General Douglas MacArthur, a man of Napoleonic ego and right-wing political tastes, thundered that a failure to help Britain immediately would be "the greatest strategical mistake in all history." The actress Helen Hayes, a Catholic and a Republican, gave public readings of Shakespeare's "sceptered isle" speech from *Richard II*, trying to drum up sympathy for "this England;" and religious leaders like Rabbi Stephen Wise, Monsignor John A. Ryan, and Henry Sloane Coffin and Reinhold Niebuhr, both from the Union Theological Seminary, all signed on to public appeals. Pamphlets titled "Hitler's American Ambitions" and "Destroyers Today or Destruction Tomorrow!"

flooded mailboxes across the country. White himself delivered a nationwide radio address in late August asserting that America was in "mortal danger," with Hitler planning to impose a "slave economy on the world" that would crush "our free enterprise, our free commerce, our free institutions." The war in Europe was not limited by geography: "this is a world struggle for freedom," he said.[76]

In Washington, the cabinet hawks also pushed Roosevelt; on August 13, in a meeting with Stimson, Knox, and Sumner Welles, Stimson strongly argued that as commander in chief, the president had the authority to consummate the deal without Congress: It fell under his traditional powers to direct foreign and defense affairs. Stimson was strengthened by a long letter published on August 11 in the *New York Times*, written by Dean Acheson, one of Felix Frankfurter's protégés and a former undersecretary of the Treasury. Acheson laid out an ironclad case that the destroyers-for-bases deal was well within the prerogative of the executive and did not need congressional approval. This brief emerged from conversations among a group of well-connected former government officials and lawyers who had been meeting privately for over a month to brainstorm about how to get aid to Britain quickly.[77]

Self-anointed as the Century Group for its regular meetings at New York's exclusive club, the Century Association, this circle of men epitomized how influence and power worked in the Roosevelt years. The group included about thirty experienced public figures, a cross-section of what sociologist C. Wright Mills would later term "the power elite"—people who had schooled together, socialized together, worked in government, law, finance, or publishing, and who shared many beliefs about America's world role. Among them could be found publisher Henry Luce, journalist Joseph Alsop, cotton broker William L. Clayton, lawyer and war hero Colonel William J. Donovan, Roosevelt's former director of the budget Lewis Douglas, banker James P. Warburg, lawyer Dean Acheson, diplomat (and later spymaster) Allen Dulles, Harvard president James B. Conant, and the group's informal coordinator, Francis P. Miller, a Virginia legislator who was active at the Council on Foreign Relations. They carried real weight in Washington and gave Roosevelt access to timely but unofficial advice. Indeed, a small delegation of the Century Group met with Roosevelt on August 1 at the White House to urge him to push ahead with the destroyers-for-bases exchange. When word came through that Willkie would not openly criticize the proposed plan (he later changed his mind), Roosevelt decided to move ahead with it. There followed two weeks of exchanges with Churchill and the British authorities over the deal's exact terms, and on September 2, the United

States offered fifty destroyers in return for ninety-nine-year leases on naval and air bases located on Newfoundland, the Bahamas, Jamaica, Bermuda, Saint Lucia, Trinidad, Antigua, and British Guiana.[78]

What mattered far more than the actual ships—only a few of them, leaky and rust-covered, arrived in time to be useful in 1940 in any case—was that the United States had taken a significant step in joining forces with Britain in the war. Roosevelt's antagonists understood this. William Randolph Hearst in his "In the News" column stated that "it is obvious that the United States is preparing not merely for defense but for war." Hearst still urged a negotiated settlement with Hitler to "preserve our religion and our civilization," since he saw Russia as the war's only victor. But these counsels of appeasement had long since been rejected by Roosevelt and indeed Willkie too. And the insiders took heart from the destroyers deal; Henry Stimson, who had been impatient for action since joining the cabinet, saw it as "enormously encouraging," one that might later be judged as "the turning point in the tide of the war." Churchill gleefully considered the destroyers-for-bases

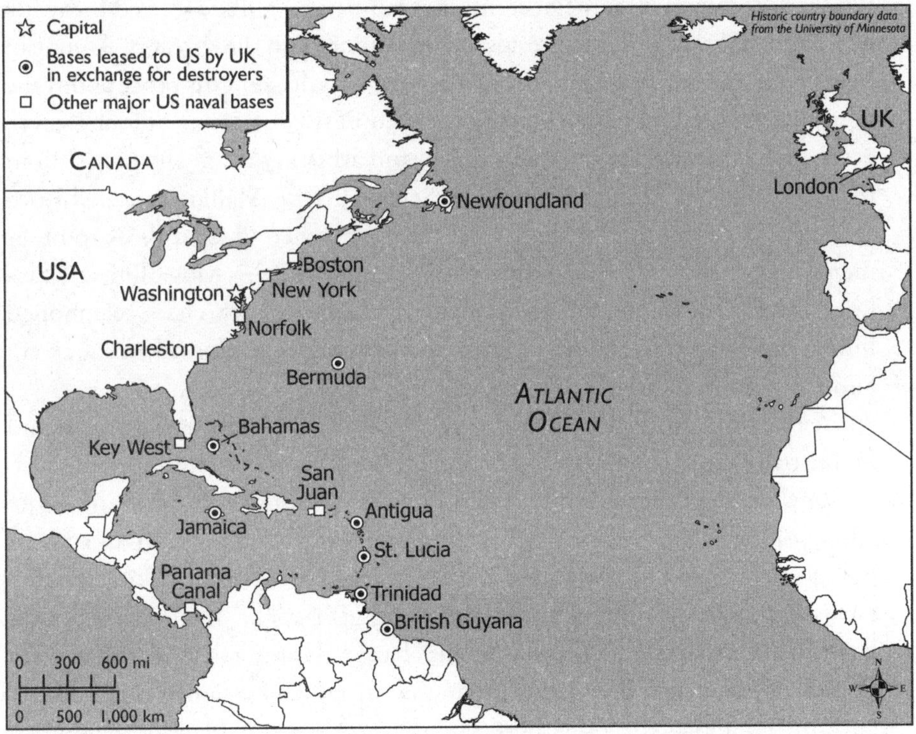

Destroyers-for-bases deal, 1940

trade "a decidedly unneutral act," placing the United States on a course that in due time would bring America into the war. *Fortune* magazine, reflecting Henry Luce's exuberant interventionism, saw America on the verge of "a great awakening," recovering "our old aggressive spirit," perhaps even "reacquiring a sense of manifest destiny." That was rather lofty language; but undoubtedly, these fifty aging warships had become a symbol of America's turn away from neutrality and toward something that looked a good deal like war.[79]

IX

The election of 1940 did not begin as a referendum on Roosevelt's foreign policy. Since Willkie agreed with FDR on sending military aid to Britain, he took aim instead at what he called the "state socialism" of the New Deal and its lackluster record in creating jobs and restarting the economy. Willkie offered himself as a more competent manager whose knowledge of business and dedication to free enterprise would turn things around. But he struggled to gain traction. There was talk of a Willkie slump by early September. Searching for a way to inject some heat into his campaign, Willkie started throwing the "dictator" charge at the president and conjured up the threat of American boys being sent into combat. Though he had initially kept his peace about the destroyers-for-bases deal, Willkie now called FDR's bypassing of Congress to get ships to Britain "the most dictatorial and arbitrary act of any president in the history of the United States." On September 14, Willkie attacked Roosevelt for violating the third-term tradition and then likened FDR to other men who saw themselves as indispensable, namely, Hitler, Mussolini, and Stalin. For good measure, he called Roosevelt an appeaser who had "telephoned Hitler and Mussolini and urged them to sell Czechoslovakia down the river." Suddenly, politics did not stop at the water's edge.[80]

Yet it was a confusing message: As Willkie told it, FDR was weak and ineffective, but also an all-powerful dictator; he was a warmonger but also an appeaser; he imposed state control of the economy yet could not create enough jobs or get the arms program going quickly enough. In an address billed as a foreign policy speech, Willkie accused FDR of provoking the dictators by "talking loudly and carrying a swagger stick." Just a few minutes later, Willkie renewed the appeasement charge, claiming that FDR was "very proud" of Munich. "The campaign doesn't make sense," sighed one reporter covering Willkie. The polls bore out that assessment. In mid-September,

Fortune published a survey showing Willkie trailing Roosevelt by eighteen percentage points. His train was stoned by passersby in labor heavy districts; eggs and tomatoes occasionally arced through the air in Willkie's direction. On September 20, George Gallup came out with a poll predicting an FDR victory of "landslide proportions," with thirty-eight states going to the president and only ten to Willkie. (That forecast turned out to be precisely accurate.) As Mayor Fiorello La Guardia of New York put it, the voters seemed to prefer "Roosevelt with his known faults than Willkie with his unknown virtues."[81]

By contrast, the nation's daily newspapers were overwhelmingly for Willkie. One analysis concluded that 66 percent of the press favored the Republican, and *Time* magazine reported that of 120 dailies in the 41 largest cities, a staggering 78 percent were for Willkie. In New York, FDR won the support of the *New York Daily News*, which had the largest circulation in the country; but the *New York Times* and the *New York Herald Tribune* endorsed Willkie. On October 9, Dorothy Thompson—a Republican who opposed most New Deal measures and who had voted for Landon in 1936—came out for Roosevelt. It was a gutsy decision, one that would eventually cost her the job she loved. But she made a simple, powerful case. Roosevelt had experience; he had courage; and he had enormous prestige in the world. Above all, there was greatness about him. "The president can be a very great man in times of emergency," she wrote, citing his brilliant leadership in 1933 as well as in the crisis of June 1940, when he pulled together a bipartisan cabinet, brought businessmen into the defense program, and took a huge political risk in pushing for conscription. Thompson knew her man: Seasoned, worldly, and statesmanlike, FDR, she believed, was made for this moment.[82]

And the moment was filled with looming dread: As the U.S. presidential campaign kicked off, the German Luftwaffe began the relentless bombing of London and other British cities that would soon be called "the Blitz." Though the Germans had been hitting England since mid-July, Hitler's failure in the air battles that summer led him to order indiscriminate nighttime attacks on London, in hopes of damaging British dockyards, shipping, airfields, and industry before launching his planned invasion. From September 7 on, Britain endured fifty-seven straight nights of bombing, and the death toll mounted with horrific regularity. Each night took a new harvest: women and children, mothers and fathers, workers and shopkeepers, grandmothers and teachers, smashed into bits amid the rubble of thousands of buildings. "The glow of fire spread over sections of London tonight," wrote

Drew Middleton for the Associated Press after that first night of the Blitz. Walking through ruined areas, he noted that the roar of the fires was so great that it drowned out everything else. In the Elephant and Castle district south of the Thames River, Middleton saw people frantically searching for bodies, "a look of horror and incredible bitterness on their faces." He saw a man return late from work to find his house a smoking pile of rubble. "He flung himself into the ruins of what had been his home and started calling 'Mary! Mary!'"[83]

Amid the fires and destruction caused by the Blitz, the CBS journalist Edward R. Murrow pioneered a new kind of radio reporting, broadcasting live to America from a jury-rigged underground studio in London. Murrow's voice, laconic, low, smooth, but with a tinge of darkness to it, captivated his listeners with word-pictures of the bombing that the Luftwaffe nightly inflicted on London. The theme of his broadcasts rarely varied: "I've seen some horrible sights in this city during these days and nights, but not once have I heard man, woman, or child suggest that Britain should throw in her hand. These people are angry." Murrow not only described what he saw; he captured the sounds, too, broadcasting into American living rooms the noise of the bombers and their explosions, the sound of the sirens wailing and the icy crunch of feet walking through broken glass. Observing thousands of red-eyed, weary Londoners emerge from underground shelters one morning, to open up businesses and shops amid the shocking wreckage of the city, Murrow could only marvel at their resilience: "these people are stubborn. Often, they are insular, but their determination must be recorded."[84]

And this was just the beginning. All through September, all through October, night after agonizing night, London and other industrial cities were struck by high explosive and incendiary bombs designed to start fires and burn people to death. No district was safe. The East End, the working-class area with the most industrial sites, was regularly bombed, but on September 17, James Reston reported in the *New York Times* that the tony West End, including Piccadilly, Regent Street, Berkeley Square, and swank Savile Row, had been pulverized. Top-hatted nabobs were forced, along with everyone else, into the subway system in search of shelter. In the midst of this horror came another act of unspeakable barbarism: On September 17, a British passenger ship called *The City of Benares*, carrying 406 civilians en route to Canada, was torpedoed by a German submarine; 258 people were killed. Of 123 children on board, 98 perished in the black, gale-swept North Atlantic. Every day, American newspapers were filled with reports of British suffering and stoicism. Occasionally, photographers staged a scene to make a point. On October 9, after a huge daytime raid on London and nearby airfields that was as bad as any yet, photographer Fred Morley dressed up his assistant as a milkman and had him walk resolutely through the ruins of London while carrying a load of bottles. The photograph Morley took suggested to the American public that the milk would be delivered, and London could take whatever the Germans might throw at them. "Keep Calm and Carry On" was the apt government-designed slogan.[85]

The news from Asia joined the horrific images from London to create a sense of a world under siege. On September 22, the Japanese, profiting from France's surrender to Germany, sent forces into northern Indochina to ensure continued access to the tropical products, and labor, of this French colony; and to close off supply routes into China. The United States responded immediately with another tightening of the economic screws. In early July, Roosevelt had signed the Export Control Act, giving him the power to limit the sale overseas of certain strategic materials. On July 26, he restricted the sale of aviation fuel, lubricants, and some iron and steel scrap, all crucial for Japanese aircraft production. Now, just days after the Japanese moved into Indochina, he curtailed the shipment to Japan of all grades of iron and steel scrap as an act of retaliation. He also announced a new $100 million credit for China. Exports of oil to Japan had not yet been cut off, but the threat was now clearly posed. It did not deter the Japanese government, however, for on September 27, it signed the Tripartite Pact with the Germans and Italians. The revisionist "Axis" powers were formally allied now: a dynamic, well-armed, aggressive bloc that aimed to reorder the world.[86]

FDR's demonstration of firmness toward Japan in imposing a scrap iron and steel embargo bucked up the interventionists. At a CDAAA rally at the World's Fair ground on October 6, Gov. Lehman, Robert Sherwood, and Clark Eichelberger all praised the move. The public approved, too, with Gallup showing almost unanimous support for the anti-Japan embargo, as well as a pronounced shift in support for the aid-to-Britain policy. The interventionists felt they were winning the argument, and Japanese aggression had helped their cause.[87]

X

Back in the presidential race, the polls tightened slightly in late October, as they usually do. FDR still held a commanding lead, but a few states seemed to be softening. The *Chicago Tribune*, intensely hostile to Roosevelt, claimed that Willkie now had a chance of carrying New York, Pennsylvania, Ohio, and Illinois, thus propelling him into the White House. This was wishful thinking (and Willkie won none of those states), but it spurred Roosevelt into a flurry of activity. So far, he had spent the campaign visiting defense plants, navy yards, and factories, pointing up his steady leadership as commander in chief. Not leaving anything to chance, he now decided to come out of his corner and throw some punches. In five speeches, compressed into just two weeks before Election Day on November 5, Roosevelt made his pitch to the country for four more years as president.[88]

In these final days, FDR got some valuable help. Robert Sherwood joined the speechwriting team, having been brought in by Harry Hopkins. Sam Rosenman later recalled that of all the people he worked with over seventeen years in the Roosevelt camp, Sherwood was the man he liked best. The playwright had an elegant way with language, and his passion blazed through his cool appearance: "If anything," Rosenman said, "he had to be restrained rather than encouraged." Sherwood experienced the thrill of hearing the president give voice to his own words on October 12, when FDR gave a Columbus Day speech at Dayton, using a text Sherwood helped write. He sat with a carbon copy of the speech on his lap by the radio, listening as Roosevelt emphatically stated America's policy of aiding the forces fighting for freedom: "No combination of dictator countries of Europe and Asia will halt us in the path we see ahead for ourselves and for our democracy. . . . Our course is clear. Our decision is made. We will continue to pile up our defense and our armaments. We will continue to help those who resist aggression, and who now hold the aggressors far from our shores." In words surely written by Sherwood, Roosevelt said: "The men and women of Britain have shown how free people defend what they know to be right. Their heroic defense will be recorded for all time. It will be perpetual proof that democracy, when put to the test, can show the stuff of which it is made."[89]

Roosevelt's final speeches were designed chiefly to rebut many of the falsehoods and exaggerations the Republican candidate had uttered. In Philadelphia and New York, Roosevelt hit the Republicans mercilessly for their hypocrisy and inconsistencies, pointing out that those who criticized him now for going too slowly on rearmament had earlier voted against the repeal of the arms embargo and charged Roosevelt with alarmism and war hysteria. At Madison Square Garden, he got cheers when he spoke of the "timidity, weakness, and shortsightedness" of the Republican party's attitude to national defense. He assured his audiences that he viewed rearmament as America's best path to staying out of war, and in Boston on October 30, he laid out in detail the massive program of military expansion he had led, cherishing the opportunity to point out that many Republicans in Congress voted against it. "What kind of political shenanigans are these?" he asked, in a calculated jibe. "Can we trust those people with national defense?"

The Boston speech is perhaps best known for the remark FDR made in reply to Willkie's assertion that he was a reckless warmonger. "I have said this before," he said, "but I shall say it again and again and again. Your boys are not going to be sent into any foreign wars. They are going into training to form a force so strong that, by its very existence, it will keep the threat of war far away from our shores." But more significant than this well-known bit of campaign oratory was FDR's announcement of a new commitment to help Britain. Two days earlier, FDR had received an anxious message from Churchill about the desperate state of Britain's air and naval defenses. He wrote of the "extreme urgency of accelerating delivery" of aircraft. "The world cause," Churchill wrote, "is in your hands." FDR replied in that Boston speech, telling the public that he would meet Britain's request for twelve thousand more American aircraft, bringing total British orders to twenty-six thousand planes, along with purchases of artillery, tanks, and ammunition. On this night in Boston, Roosevelt pledged to keep "your boys" away from European battlefields but simultaneously promised that American factories would be harnessed to the war effort.[90]

After a stop in Brooklyn, Roosevelt and his team headed to Cleveland in vote-rich Ohio to give the last major speech two days before Election Day. It would serve as a summation of his campaign, a summation of his eight years in office, across all the highs and lows of the New Deal. Rosenman and Sherwood, exhausted and running out of ideas, crammed themselves into a rattling train compartment (Sherwood, at six foot six, could barely fold himself into the seats), and worked through the night. They were fortunate in having some ideas on paper from Archibald MacLeish, Dean Acheson, and Dorothy Thompson, who wired in some themes and phrases she hoped Roosevelt would use. Rosenman later recalled of the Cleveland speech that "a great deal of it was based on the draft Dorothy Thompson had submitted." This moment marked the convergence of the two most powerful anti-fascist voices in the United States at this time. Thompson had been among the first Americans to raise the alarm about the fascist threat, and after almost a decade of tireless work, she would hear the president of the United States read words she had written, words that carried her unmistakable tone of urgency, determination, and confidence.[91]

It was a speech that knitted together their shared concern that democracy at home was at risk from fascists abroad, that America could not be secure while dictators trampled down the rights of all the other free nations in the world. To Rosenman, it was the best speech Roosevelt ever delivered, laying out "a blueprint for the America of the future as he would wish it." In a raucous hall of twenty-five thousand people, with one hundred thousand more outside listening on a public address system, Roosevelt stated his theme: "This generation of Americans is living in a tremendous moment of history. The surge of events abroad has made some few doubters among us ask: 'Is this the end of a story that has been told? Is the book of democracy now to be closed and placed away upon the dusty shelves of time?'" His audience answered with shouts of "No!"

He asked his listeners to look at "the old world of Europe. It is an ugly world, poisoned by hatred, greed and fear." In contrast, he offered a vision of a future America secure in a peace guaranteed by its growing military strength, but also an America of economic justice, of tolerance, of conservation of natural resources, of prosperity for the "common man." Connecting the New Deal to the great task of defending democracy abroad, he said, "the true measure of our strength lies deeply imbedded in the social and economic justice of the system in which we live. For you can build ships and tanks and guns galore; but they will not be enough. You must place behind them an invincible faith in the institutions which they have been built to defend." As he launched into a vigorous defense of the New Deal, he connected America's material strength with the confidence of its people in the habit of self-government, a faith that acted as a beacon to the world. "It is the destiny of this American generation," he said, "to point the road to the future for all the world to see. It is our prayer that all lovers of freedom may join us—the anguished common people of this earth for whom we seek to light the path."[92]

This speech drew on the language of American exceptionalism, an old tradition dating to the Puritans that asserted America's providential, God-given responsibility for the peace of the world. Roosevelt believed that if the American people joined together to defend democracy wherever it might be endangered, then the United States would become "a light of the world and a comfort to all people. And the forces of evil shall not prevail against it." Echoing Thompson's Methodism and Roosevelt's Episcopalian tutelage under Reverend Endicott Peabody, this closing election appeal did much more than ask voters for their support. It sent a message to the world: that a renewed and awakened nation, proud of its democratic faith, its progress toward greater economic equality and fairness, ever-more confident in its moral and material strength, was ready to rally the free world—an expression soon to come into regular use—for the coming battle with the dictators.

And with that, the Roosevelt campaign train rattled away into the night toward Hyde Park, where FDR would await the verdict of the voters.

CHAPTER 16

EVERYWHERE IN THE WORLD

"The United States will never survive as a happy and fertile oasis of liberty surrounded by a cruel desert of dictatorship."

—FRANKLIN D. ROOSEVELT

I

"It was a narrow escape," Roosevelt wrote to Sam Rosenman on November 13, eight days after the election. "I wonder whether people will ever realize that."

By narrow escape, he could not have meant the result of the vote: FDR defeated Willkie by ten percentage points and won thirty-eight of forty-eight states. He even won his own reliably Republican hometown of Hyde Park, 376–302, a first for him. To be sure, this was not quite the landslide of 1932 or 1936, but given the unprecedented step Roosevelt took in seeking a third term and given an unemployment rate that stood stubbornly at about 14 percent, Roosevelt's victory was historic. What he had in mind was not the outcome of the election but the very fact that so many Americans still did not seem to grasp the dangers that lay ahead for "our type of civilization." Too many Republicans, he wrote, "thought in terms of appeasement of Hitler," and the temper of those elites, he felt, had become intolerant, shrill, even dangerously undemocratic. "Those newspapers of the nation which most loudly cried dictatorship against me," he confided to Rosenman, "would have been the first to justify the beginnings of dictatorship by somebody else."[1]

In truth, it had been a tough election, one FDR did not enjoy. The New Deal had come under withering fire from conservatives who claimed it was socialist and un-American. Roosevelt ably defended his record of progress since 1933 but the chief reason for seeking a third term lay overseas. FDR asked an unsettled, anxious people to commit themselves to a policy of active support for Britain (and less explicitly for China) in their wars against Germany and Japan. He persuaded the public that helping Britain now would keep America out of war, and although they may have had doubts about that argument, voters decisively endorsed his leadership. But the resistance of some Americans to his policy of aiding Britain in its fight for "our type of civilization" worried Roosevelt and undoubtedly influenced his policy throughout 1941.[2]

During that year, Roosevelt moved along two planes of action that might seem to be in tension with one another. He remained determined to keep the country out of war if possible. To that end, he deployed American economic and industrial power to sustain Britain in its life-or-death struggle with Nazi Germany. He held to this policy even though it frustrated nearly all of his senior military advisers, including Secretary of War Henry Stimson, Army Chief of Staff George Marshall, Secretary of the Navy Frank Knox, and the Chief of Naval Operations Harold "Betty" Stark. They were much more hawkish than Roosevelt and consistently pressed the president to prepare for what they saw as an inevitable war with Germany and possibly Japan. In fact, they believed that American entry into the war was the only way to defeat Hitler. Roosevelt allowed these men to write their memos and do their table exercises but avoided giving official approval to their war plans. It is ironic that soon after World War II, some strident critics would claim that FDR secretly connived to get America into the war. At least through August 1941, the evidence shows that Roosevelt wanted to stay out of the war and had to restrain his military advisers who advocated getting into the fight as soon as possible.[3]

At the same time, though, Roosevelt worked hard to establish the rhetorical foundations of a new and ambitious world role for the United States. Leaving aside the precise question of whether the United States would enter the war as a belligerent, he made it clear to the public that in a broad sense, America was already fighting for the survival of democracy. The battle front was on the factory floors, in the forges and blast furnaces and assembly lines of the American heartland, and on the Atlantic shipping lanes to Britain. In 1941, Roosevelt sought to blur the line between active belligerency and material aid to America's embattled friends. He believed and ardently hoped that the United States could decisively impact the war's outcome without sending men into battle. Events would prove this hope illusory. But what mattered was that in the year before Pearl Harbor, Roosevelt established a moral and ethical framework to legitimate America's fight against fascism and tyranny. In doing so, he deployed a vocabulary of internationalism honed by some of the most active anti-fascists of the era. Because of their collective intellectual effort, reaching back across the many tragedies of the 1930s, when war came,

Americans knew what they were fighting for, and what they were fighting against.

II

In the wake of the election, FDR returned to the White House from Hyde Park to face a serious, even desperate, global strategic picture. The Asian scene had grown ominous. In August, Japan publicly declared its breathtaking ambition to build a "Greater East Asia Co-Prosperity Sphere," a Japan-centered, autarkic colonial system designed for intensive resource extraction and the military domination of a vast swath of Asian peoples. The following month, the Japanese leadership threw in its lot with the Nazis by signing the Tripartite Pact; they then sent troops into the northern part of French Indochina. Japan now looked covetously at the oil-rich Dutch East Indies, and the rubber and tin resources of British Malaya. The Japanese also planned to spear into British-held Burma and cut off the Burma Road—the sinuous seven-hundred-mile-long dirt track that allowed supplies to flow into southwest China in support of Chiang Kai-shek's Nationalist forces. Every success by Hitler in Europe increased the likelihood of Japan snapping up British, French, and Dutch possessions in Asia.

Fortunately, Hitler's assault on Britain had been blunted in the summer of 1940 by Royal Air Force fighter pilots who, with unmatched skill and courage, denied Göring's Luftwaffe control of the skies over southern England—the crucial prerequisite of a German cross-Channel invasion. In mid-September, unbeknownst to the British, Hitler postponed the invasion. But he redoubled the saturation bombing of London and other industrial cities, hoping to strangle the British war economy and terrorize the population. An even greater menace to Britain that fall came from the shocking German success in finding, and sinking, enormous numbers of merchant ships that carried food, supplies, and weapons from North American factories and ports, across the black, windswept Atlantic, into besieged Britain. That lifeline was frayed and vulnerable as never before. Without drastic action, it might snap completely.

Roosevelt in early October 1940 received a detailed report on Britain's circumstances from two Army officers of the War Plans Division who had returned from a monthlong investigation in London. They observed that British morale was high, and the country was united behind Churchill, but there were serious troubles ahead. British factories were vulnerable to German bombing, and aircraft production would be hampered should the Blitz continue. Furthermore, Britain's "financial outlook is dubious, if not distinctly bad," they wrote. Britain had a dwindling supply of dollars and gold with which to buy American supplies. And even if they could pay for these supplies, transporting them across the Atlantic had become perilous. Without enough destroyers or aircraft to provide a shield to Britain's merchant ships, the losses "will be crippling." These officers believed that Britain simply could not hold on much longer alone. They called for a drastic increase in U.S. aircraft and artillery production to help Britain and hinted at the larger problem of what might happen should Britain run out of money to pay for all these supplies.[4]

Winston Churchill sent much the same message. In his telegrams to Roosevelt, Churchill always tried to accentuate the fine fighting spirit of the British people while relaying his country's desperate circumstances. In late October, he wrote to FDR that German submarine and air attacks on "our only remaining lifeline, the northwest approach," were taking a serious toll. "We feel, however, confident of our ability, if we are given the necessary supplies, to carry on the war to a successful conclusion." But he did not hide Britain's dependence: "We depend upon American deliveries. . . . The world cause is in your hands." Roosevelt responded to this appeal in his October 30 campaign address in Boston, when he told the public that America would meet Britain's latest request for twelve thousand more aircraft. Two days after the election, Churchill sent Roosevelt a warm and moving message, confessing his enormous relief at Roosevelt's victory. A "somber phase" of the war loomed ahead, but he drew comfort from American "confidence and goodwill" toward Britain. Stressing Anglo-American solidarity, he wrote in a typical flourish: "Things are now afoot which will be remembered as long as the English language is spoken in any quarter of the globe."[5]

With the election behind him, Roosevelt felt more comfortable in promising to meet Britain's needs. In a press conference, he breezily said that as a "rule of thumb," America would share all its war production with Britain on a fifty-fifty basis. "In other words," he told the journalists around his desk, "we take half; they take half." Privately, though, he admitted this arrangement could not endure because of Britain's exhausted finances. He told the cabinet that same day that "the time would surely come when Great Britain would need loans and credits," and according to Harold Ickes, Roosevelt said "he thought we could lease ships, or any other property that was loanable, returnable, and insurable." Ickes thought this a "very good suggestion." The germ of an idea began to grow.[6]

Yet Roosevelt's impromptu, slapdash approach to the war, strong on inspiration and weak on organization, simply was not addressing the larger strategic problem America and Britain faced. That opinion came through clearly in mid-November when the chief of naval operations, Admiral Harold Stark, drafted and circulated a probing memorandum that asked fundamental questions about America's role in the war. In a twenty-four-page paper, Stark told his superior, Navy Secretary Frank Knox, that in his view, the British were far too optimistic about their chances against Germany. He was not at all confident that the British could endure for more than six more months, and "should Britain lose the war, the military consequences to the United States would be serious." By itself, Stark argued, Britain could not defeat Germany. It simply lacked the manpower and the industrial capacity. It could possibly defend itself, but its hold on the Eastern Mediterranean, the Suez Canal, and even Gibraltar, was extremely vulnerable to German and Italian attack; should these crucial outposts be lost, Britain's Asian empire would probably collapse, and Japan could then swoop down upon its resource-rich colonies.

Stark's memo was a bracing, crystal clear assessment of America's strategic dilemma. The defense of Britain required massive American aid; getting that aid across submarine-infested waters in turn required winning the Battle of the Atlantic; and that could only be done through a major offensive by Britain and the United States, fighting as allies in the Atlantic against Germany. A war with Germany, however, would eventually demand major naval and ground forces to be sent to Europe and North Africa, a vast undertaking that required the United States to avoid war with Japan for now. Stark, with dispassionate strategic logic, made the case that "methods short of war" would not succeed in achieving America's objectives. The United States, he believed, must prepare for a global war against the Axis powers, concentrated on Germany. On November 12, a revised version of Stark's paper, with the blessing of Knox, Stimson, and Marshall, went to the White House.[7]

At the same moment, public voices who supported the aid-to-Britain effort were growing louder and more insistent. William Allen White, still leading the Committee to Defend America by Aiding the Allies, denounced any talk of a negotiated peace deal with Hitler to stop the war—an idea Charles Lindbergh kept pushing. Such a path would allow Hitler to keep all his conquests and consign many democratic peoples to oblivion in a Nazi-dominated continent. "If you consider that this is a war not of Empires but ideas, appeasement is treason to democracy," he wrote. James Bryant Conant, a leading member of the CDAAA and the president of Harvard, turned up the heat in a WABC radio talk. "Our free way of life," he said, "can be secured only by a defeat of the Axis powers." He felt Americans had not fully grasped "the true nature of our peril," and demanded even greater mobilization on behalf of Britain. Dr. Robert A. Millikan, the head of Cal Tech, joined Conant, saying that "in the struggles of mankind to escape from the law of the jungle, the democratic, peace-loving people must unite to defend themselves from international bandits."[8]

And banditry there was. On the night of November 14, a series of Luftwaffe attacks on the city of Coventry destroyed some 4,300 homes and set off a firestorm that engulfed the fifteenth-century cathedral there. Americans did not need much prompting to loathe Nazism any more intensely, but this kind of bombing seemed well outside the laws of war. Ten days later, the CDAAA issued a new policy paper calling for greater industrial mobilization on the home front, the transfer of U.S. merchant vessels to Britain to keep supplies flowing, the embargo of all oil sales to Japan, and the repeal of the remaining clauses of the Neutrality Act so Britain could finance these supplies through loans or credits. The war had become "a moral issue of world import to civilization itself. The fate of human freedom, freedom of thought, of religion, of individual initiative, is dependent upon victory of Britain and her allies." In a rousing closing passage, the CDAAA stated that "it is time for democracy to be militant against the Axis theory that life can only be organized if it is regimented by dictatorship." Behind all this there hung the obvious implication: If America would save democracy, it must fight for it.[9]

Did Stark's memo, or these well-intentioned appeals, impress Roosevelt? If so, he revealed little about his thinking. He did not give Stark's paper formal approval, and when questioned on November 22 by the press about his plans for increasing aid to Britain, he refused to give out any more details. "We are just talking glittering generalities that don't mean one damned thing," he said rather peevishly. He was doing everything he could. "If you will show me a way of turning out airplanes faster than we are doing it now, that is a different thing. You cannot pass a bill and issue an order and get the plane the next day." He was certainly right about that. In fact, U.S. aircraft production was still meager. At the start of 1941, the U.S. Army Air Corps possessed a mere 733 tactical aircraft for use in combat. The rest were trainers or transports. For all of FDR's robust declarations about sending Britain 12,000 planes, the United States could barely deliver to the British 400 per month. By comparison, the Luftwaffe had deployed about 2,500 fighter planes in the Battle of Britain alone. No wonder Roosevelt was feeling irritable. Perhaps the campaign had taken a toll on him. Harold Ickes thought so. "The tragic thing is," noted Ickes in his diary, "that the President, as tired as he is, is isolating himself more and more." Only Missy LeHand and Harry Hopkins, who had been living in the White House since May 1940, could get regular access to him. "Altogether," complained Ickes, "it is not either a happy or too helpful situation, considering that the world is in such desperate straits for real leadership." As if demonstrating his intention to postpone any major decision on further aid to the allies, Roosevelt headed out of Washington by train on December 2, en route to Miami, where he would board the USS *Tuscaloosa* for a two-week vacation in the Caribbean.[10]

While Roosevelt sunbathed, fished, and enjoyed time away from the strains of Washington, his lieutenants worked feverishly to find mechanisms that would keep supplies flowing to Britain. Stimson met with a weary Cordell Hull, who in a meeting at the State Department on December 3 bemoaned the immense damage inflicted by constant German bombing combined with the terrible harvest of merchant ships taken by the German submarines. Stimson asked what could be done and both men agreed: send them more airplanes and defend the British merchant ships by escorting them across the Atlantic with American naval vessels in convoys. That would be tantamount to entering the war, a step only Knox and Stimson now favored. But as Stimson put it in his diary, the country was "still asleep" and badly needed awakening.[11]

Later the same day, Henry Morgenthau Jr., who by default had become the point person on the British aid program, gathered Stimson, Knox, Marshall, Sumner Welles, and other Treasury officials together and unburdened himself. "I can't take this alone," he said. The president had told Morgenthau to find a way to build additional industrial capacity "to manufacture for the English what they needed." But where would he get the money? The British didn't have it. His figures, which he shared with the others, showed a drastic shortfall of British assets. They did not have enough money to pay for current orders, much less additional purchases. "You can see why I sent out the distress signal," Morgenthau said, sighing. Turning to his colleagues, he asked, "are we going to let them place some more orders or not," even if the British were broke? Knox interjected briskly: "Got to. No choice about it." The U.S. was going to build what the British needed and find some way to get the supplies to them swiftly.[12]

And there was no time to lose, as Winston Churchill made perfectly clear to Roosevelt in a letter that reached the president on December 9 while he bobbed in the balmy waters of the Caribbean. In a carefully scripted appeal that had gone through many drafts, Churchill again stressed the desperate crisis triggered by German attacks on Atlantic shipping. By shutting off Britain's sources of supply, Germany could win the war. Here, Churchill said, "the crunch of the whole war will be found." Taking extraordinary liberties, the prime minister proposed that America suspend the Neutrality Act and give or lend American merchant ships to Britain; he also suggested the U.S. Navy be used to escort merchant ships, a task he called "constructive non-belligerency." He also envisioned getting more U.S. destroyers into British hands.

These actions, Churchill believed, would help keep the shipping losses to "manageable proportions." Yet Britain also needed to bulk up its air force, and Churchill asked that more American aircraft be sent to Britain at a rate of two thousand per month—five times what the U.S. was then supplying. Above all this hung the problem of finance: "the moment approaches," he wrote, "when we shall no longer be able to pay cash for shipping and other supplies." Somehow, the Americans must find a way to help Britain get the material all the same, no matter the method. "We shall prove ourselves ready to suffer and sacrifice to the utmost for the Cause," he concluded, but America would have to do its part for "the achievement of our common purpose." It was a plain appeal: Without a great deal more American war supplies, at a greater pace and scale, Britain would lose the war, and America would have to face Hitler alone.[13]

III

The story of Roosevelt's remarkable initiatives in the few weeks after his return to Washington from his Caribbean vacation on December 16 has often been told, but it still bears analysis as a perfect example of his policy-making method: a long period of apparent drift, indecision, and improvisation followed by decisive, far-reaching action. Robert Sherwood, one of his closest observers, believed that Roosevelt "had put in his time on this cruise evolving the pattern of a masterpiece, and once he could see it clearly in his own mind's eye, he made it quickly and very simply clear to all." The masterpiece was a legislative device designed to get huge quantities of U.S. military aid to allied nations, and to hammer home the last nail in the coffin of the Neutrality Acts.[14]

During his December 17 press conference, a suntanned, rested, and energetic Roosevelt alerted the assembled journalists that he was working on a plan to loan war matériel to Britain without worrying about the "silly, foolish, old dollar sign." He deployed what became a famous analogy: A homeowner who loans his neighbor a garden hose to put out a fire—so that the blaze will not spread to his own house—does not concern himself with the cost of his garden hose. He knows he'll get it back after the fire has been doused. Britain's house was on fire; why could not America simply lend or lease the hose—or a few billion dollars' worth of armaments—and settle up after the fire was out? The gist of this phrasing was suggested by Harold Ickes in a personal letter back in August, but Roosevelt transposed this idea into his own style, and produced a simple, memorable image of a neighborly garden hose that instantly took hold in the public mind.[15]

The message came as a relief to the key officials handling the supply effort. Stimson, Marshall, Knox, and Stark had just met the day before to review what Stimson called America's "grand strategy," and found his colleagues in full agreement that "this emergency could hardly be passed over without this country being drawn into the war eventually." Stimson arranged a meeting with the president for December 18 and went in with Knox to the Oval Office. He feared that Roosevelt would delay things in his usual manner, telling fishing tales and wasting time. In his diary, Stimson penned a memorable remark about the president: "his mind does not follow easily a consecutive chain of thought, but he is full of stories and incidents and hops about in his discussions from suggestion to suggestion and it is very much like chasing a vagrant beam of sunshine around a vacant room." But after some preliminary rambling, FDR said he had in mind a new organization to speed up the production of weapons, and he returned to his idea of leasing munitions to Britain. Stimson was "very much encouraged" by these signs of action. When at the cabinet meeting the following day, Stimson urged Roosevelt "to forcibly stop German submarines by our intervention," FDR resisted this. He did not want to enter the war yet and preferred to send arms to Britain. The next day, he announced the creation of the Office of Production Management, a four-man executive team including Stimson, Knox, labor leader Sidney Hillman, and William S. Knudsen, the Danish American president of General Motors who had already been advising on war production.[16]

Now it was time to lay the idea before the country. Four days after Christmas, Roosevelt spoke to the nation in a fireside chat and made the case for his Lend-Lease proposal. For all the informality of these talks, with FDR seated in front of a large chimneypiece in the ground-floor Diplomatic Reception Room in the White House, they were the result of many days of hard work by the speechwriting team, in this case Sam Rosenman, Harry Hopkins, and Robert Sherwood. According to Sherwood, FDR enjoyed the opportunity this speech gave him to "lash out against the apostles of appeasement." It was a pitch-perfect appeal to the country for supporting an even greater military production effort. Hull, Stimson, Morgenthau, Knox, and their wives assembled in the room to watch Roosevelt deliver what he called a talk on "national security." His tone was serious, and his pace deliberate.

"Never before since Jamestown and Plymouth Rock has our American civilization been in such danger as now," he began. "The Nazi masters of Germany have made it clear that they intend not only to dominate all life and thought in their own country, but also to enslave the whole of Europe, and then to use the resources of Europe to dominate the rest of the world." There could be no talk of peace with a regime that sought to destroy American democracy. Nor could Americans blithely ignore the war, he said, for "if Great Britain goes down, the Axis powers will control the continents of Europe, Asia, Africa, Australasia. . . . It is no exaggeration to say that all of us, in all the Americas, would be living at the point of a gun." He mocked the timidity of those who wanted to steer clear of wars in Europe and Asia. "We well know that we cannot escape danger, or the fear of danger, by crawling into bed and pulling the covers over our heads." Peace with Nazism and fascism was unthinkable, for "the history of recent years proves that the shootings and the chains and the concentration camps are not simply the transient tools but the very altars of modern dictatorships."

Having diagnosed the problem, he then offered a solution. "The people of Europe who are defending themselves do not ask us to do their fighting. They ask us for the implements of war, the planes, the tanks, the guns, the freighters which will enable them to fight for their liberty and for our security. Emphatically we must get these weapons to them." The nationwide effort would be massive and unprecedented. "I want to make it clear that it is the purpose of the nation to build now with all possible speed every machine, every arsenal, every factory that we need to manufacture our defense material. We have the men—the skill—the wealth—and above all, the will." And his peroration gave an indelible name to his policy: "We must be the great arsenal of democracy. For us this is an emergency as serious as war itself."[17]

The press reaction was immediate and favorable. As the *New York Times* saw it, Roosevelt "summoned the American people for their mightiest effort yet." The speech was considered his most important since March 1933, when he gave his first fireside chat in the worst days of the Depression. The *Washington Post* welcomed his clear assertion that the defeat of Nazi Germany was an American national interest, while the *New York Herald Tribune*, a frequent New Deal critic, praised the address as "superb in its directness, its realism, its courage and its purpose." The *Louisville Courier-Journal*, a longtime ally of the president's, expressed relief: "We have prayed the president would be thus courageous, and give us the leadership we have so sorely needed." The nation's editors unreservedly rallied to Roosevelt's call. With this kind of public support behind him, he could anticipate a swift passage of a Lend-Lease bill through Congress.[18]

Roosevelt's message went out across the networks at 9:30 p.m. Shortly afterward, the German Luftwaffe sent 136 bombers over London, each with a payload of incendiary bombs. With the purpose of showing Roosevelt that his words were powerless against Germany's air bombardment, the bombers hit the central business district, the City of London, setting over a thousand blazing fires that engulfed offices and buildings, threatening St. Paul's cathedral, and gutting the Guildhall, London's fifteenth-century administrative building. Firemen struggled against the superhot magnesium-fueled flames as their water supply ran low. The damage according to one reporter "outdid anything experienced by London since the intense German raids started last September." Two days later, on New Year's Eve, Edward R. Murrow went on the air from his underground studio in London. The people of that city were suffering, besieged by terror bombing, trapped amid smoking ruins. Murrow asked his American listeners to reflect on their good fortune on that last day of the year. "You will have no dawn raid as we shall probably have if the weather is right. You may walk this night in the light. Your families are not scattered by the winds of war." But looking ahead into 1941, Murrow told his audience that like it or not, they held Britain's fate in their hands. "The decisions you take will overshadow all else during this year."[19]

Roosevelt made just this point to Congress in his annual State of the Union message on January 6, just a week after London had been set ablaze. "Every realist knows that the democratic way of life is at this moment being directly assailed in every part of the world," he declared. "The future and the safety of our country and of our democracy are overwhelmingly involved in events far beyond our borders." He rejected appeasement of the dictators and recommitted himself to arming those resisting aggression. And he linked America's domestic progress and the security of its democracy with the war against fascism abroad. He envisioned America waging a two-front war, one against the Nazis and the other against entrenched privilege, oligarchy, and economic inequality. The people fighting Hitler in Europe wanted the same things as the people fighting economic royalists in America: equality of opportunity, the security of well-paid work, and the protection of civil liberties. In simple, unadorned but powerful phrasing, Roosevelt sketched an image of a world worth fighting for, a world "founded upon for essential freedoms":

> The first is freedom of speech and expression—everywhere in the world.
>
> The second is freedom of every person to worship God in his own way—everywhere in the world.

> The third is freedom from want—which, translated into world terms, means economic understandings which will secure to every nation a healthy peacetime life for its inhabitants—everywhere in the world.
>
> The fourth is freedom from fear—which, translated into world terms, means a world-wide reduction of armaments to such a point and in such a thorough fashion that no nation will be in a position to commit an act of physical aggression against any neighbor—anywhere in the world.[20]

In time, these Four Freedoms came to epitomize the American war effort. Roosevelt wanted not only to beat back fascism but to clear the ground so that a revived democracy could take root and flourish, in America and across the globe. In a sense, this speech marked the end of a long road that Roosevelt had traveled since 1933, when his outlook was limited by the Great Depression, and his policy concerns strictly focused on domestic recovery. With these words, Roosevelt took the country across the threshold of a new age, in which the United States would identify itself as the guarantor of democracy in the world.

IV

Not everyone rallied to his call. The introduction of the Lend-Lease bill, cleverly numbered H.R. 1776, to Congress on January 10, 1941, prompted a furious reaction from across the anti-war, pro-neutrality, and isolationist spectrum, and well it might. For Lend-Lease did envision granting Roosevelt a great deal of authority to send American war material overseas. The bill proposed that "the President may, from time to time, when he deems it in the interest of national defense, authorize the Secretary of War, the Secretary of the Navy, or the head of any other department or agency of the Government . . . to sell, transfer title to, exchange, lease, lend, or otherwise dispose of, to any such government any defense article," a defense article being defined capaciously to include weapons, aircraft, ships, artillery as well as machinery and agricultural and industrial materials. Congress would still have to appropriate funds for the immense quantity of arms Roosevelt envisioned, and the law would expire in June 1943, when it could be renewed. Yet to those who feared wider American involvement in the war, the Lend-Lease bill did indeed look as if it would give Roosevelt a blank check to send virtually anything to Britain or to any other nation he designated. Giving FDR so much authority, his critics believed, would assure further entanglement in the war.[21]

If ever the America First Committee (AFC) had an opportunity to strike a blow at Roosevelt's foreign policy, it was now, as Congress began public hearings on the Lend-Lease bill. AFC was founded in September 1940 by some plucky and well-connected Yale Law School students who feared their generation of young men might be fed into the slaughterhouse of war as their fathers' generation had been. R. Douglas Stuart Jr., son of the wealthy manufacturer of Quaker Oats, a Chicago-based food conglomerate, got the organization started; the bright *Yale Daily News* editor (and future Yale president) Kingman Brewster Jr. joined Stuart and helped mobilize the Yale campus. Stuart's contacts in the strongly isolationist Chicago area gave him access to corporate and publishing tycoons who soon helped to bankroll the fledgling group. The Hearst newspaper chain immediately expressed its support for the organization and spread the news of its founding across the country.

AFC scored its first big win by enrolling as its titular leader General Robert E. Wood, a decorated Great War soldier and the board chairman of Chicago-based Sears, Roebuck and Company. With Wood lending his name to the enterprise, AFC began to attract support from across the country. In its first statements, the group stressed that it favored a strong hemispheric national defense but opposed aid to Britain because it would draw needed supplies away from American arsenals. Contradicting Roosevelt's chief argument, the group also argued that participation in the European war would not rescue but fatally undermine American democracy. Indeed, many of the Committee's leading members thought that Roosevelt aspired to use the wartime emergency to seize dictatorial powers.[22]

The administration sent its heavyweights to the Hill to plead for Lend-Lease. Secretaries Hull, Morgenthau, Stimson, and Knox, joined by the production administrator William Knudsen, all testified before the House Committee on Foreign Affairs, and coordinated their testimony carefully in advance. They faced hostile questions from Representative Hamilton Fish, the New York congressman and perennial Roosevelt scourge. Stimson stressed in his first words to the committee that "the effective defense of this country in the pending emergency depends in large part upon our giving effective help to Great Britain." That policy was overwhelmingly supported by the public, he said, and the bill would implement it with speed and efficiency. In reply to various outlandish statements from Fish that Lend-Lease would allow Roosevelt to "give away our Navy," Stimson expressed veiled contempt. Asked if the Lend-Lease law adopted "the totalitarian method of placing all power in the hands of one man," Stimson said simply that in wartime, "it is necessary to concentrate our means of self-defense and make them more effective." Over two days of testimony, the opponents of the bill could not rattle the secretary of war, an old and experienced hand at such performances. The critics of the bill drew from "the well-worn grab bag of isolationism," Stimson later wrote.[23]

Those hostile to the Lend-Lease plan were not all of the same mind. Some, such as two former FDR appointees who had soured on the president, Ambassador Joseph Kennedy and General Hugh Johnson, testified in favor of sending aid to Britain; they simply feared that the bill gave too much power to the president alone. But these figures were not the main attraction. On January 23, the star of the opposition appeared: Colonel Charles Lindbergh. Not yet a member of the AFC, he nonetheless was the leading spokesman for a policy of keeping out of Britain's war with Hitler. Outside the newly built House office building (later named for former Speaker Nicholas Longworth), lines of people hoping for a chance to enter the large hearing room formed well before 10 a.m. Once seated, the packed crowd of five hundred people repeatedly interrupted the proceedings with applause and hurrahs for the aviator and his message.

Henry Stimson, Republican interventionist and secretary of war.
Library of Congress

But the message itself was defeatist and craven. Britain could not beat Germany, Lindbergh said, even with American help. In any case, the outcome of that war was of no consequence to America. He believed the U.S. Navy could protect the country from a German invasion, though he wanted to see a much larger Air Force and the construction of a belt of air bases from Canada to the Galapagos Islands to the Amazon basin. Showing that he certainly favored intervention when it came to Latin America, he called the acquisition of such foreign bases "vital to our national defense." Did he think it would be in the best interest of the United States to see Hitler defeated? "No," said he. A "negotiated peace" would be best. "I prefer to see neither side win." He went on: "I believe this is not our war," and that getting into it would be "disastrous" for the country. Invited to say a few critical words about Hitler, he declined, replying "we should maintain as far as possible a position of complete neutrality." He spoke like a man who had received a decoration from the Nazi government, which of course he had. In fact, a German official called the testimony "courageous" and declared "hats off!" to Lindbergh.[24]

The colonel's tolerance for Nazi control of the European continent did his cause no favors. Two days later, Dorothy Thompson came before the committee and with her usual verve, demolished Lindbergh's position. She insisted that "the Germans intend to encircle this country and drive it to a purely defensive position and eliminate it as a world power." A German victory over Britain would give the fascists and Nazis control of much of world trade, and America would become a satellite in a Nazi empire, governed by some pro-Hitler satrap. Lindbergh's negotiated peace, she pointed out, was not on offer. Hitler was winning the war and would go on winning unless America stopped him. "If we do not greatly increase aid to Britain, there will be a dictated peace wholly on German terms." Dazzling the panel with her verbal dexterity (and cheered on by applause from observers), she painted a dark picture of what passivity and appeasement would bring. "I was in France this spring. France was not defeated. France collapsed." The country fell to pieces because of its indecision: "France had never really made up her mind whether wholeheartedly to resist Hitler or to make a deal with him." If America were to remain divided and hamstrung, and allow Britain to fall to the Nazi invaders, "we will have dealt a very serious blow to democracy right here on this soil. I doubt whether we would survive it as a democracy." When she concluded, warm applause rippled across the room and the Chairman of the committee, Sol Bloom of New York, had to reprimand the visitors, though he confessed, "I have felt like applauding myself."[25]

The House, unmoved by Lindbergh's apologetics for Hitler, swiftly passed the Lend-Lease bill on February 8 by 260 votes to 165. The momentum appeared to be with the president. But the hearings in the Senate, and the weeks of prolonged, fractious, and windy debate that followed in that chamber, arrested the progress of the bill, to the despair of Stimson and other officials. Again, Hull, Stimson, Morgenthau, and Knox came to spell out the immediate need for the Lend-Lease aid to Britain. James Conant of Harvard and theologian Reinhold Niebuhr also gave powerful support for the bill; in over a month of hearings, Niebuhr was the only person to mention the Nazi "intention of annihilating the Jewish race."[26]

The Republicans called in various outspoken isolationists. *Chicago Tribune* publisher Robert R. McCormick, whose paper referred to Lend-Lease as the "war dictatorship bill," said it was "fantastic to suggest that we are in any danger of attack." He then told the senators that "I pray to God that hysteria, propaganda, and ambition will not become strong enough to immolate our present generation of young men." One of those young men was twenty-one-year-old Kingman Brewster, chairman of the Yale chapter of the AFC. Appearing before the senators with considerable poise, he said that his generation would not hesitate to serve their country in wartime if needed, but much preferred to avoid "a devastating transoceanic war." (In fact, Brewster volunteered for the navy in 1942 and served throughout the war as a navy aviator.) Sympathetic as he was with Britain's plight, he said he "put the peace of this hemisphere even above the victory of Great Britain."[27]

Less genteel was General Wood, the chairman of the America First Committee, who blasted the bill. Commissioned in 1900, Wood served in the Philippines, the Panama Canal Zone, and in the Great War, where he rose to the rank of brigadier general. He pulled no punches. "This bill," he began, "is not a defense measure or a lend-lease bill; it is really a war bill, transferring the war-making powers of Congress to the president." Using talking points outlined by AFC, Wood called the bill "a blank check on the American taxpayer's money for the defense of Britain." Lend-Lease, he argued, would certainly lead to war, perhaps within ninety days. And if war came, the public "will believe that we have been tricked into the war" and that "their leaders in Congress have betrayed them." Another leader of the AFC, Hanford MacNider, echoed Wood. An Iowa manufacturer and decorated Great War soldier, MacNider was a former national commander of the American Legion. He called the struggle of the British a gallant one, but he "was unwilling to commit my sons or any American's sons to the policing of the rest of the world, or the maintenance of the British Empire, much as I hope that it may survive." Similar words would be uttered across the country in the coming months.[28]

And of course, Charles Lindbergh did not miss a chance for more public adulation. The same standing-room-only crowd welcomed him to the Senate; the same society hostesses cancelled lunch plans to attend the hearings. But this was not a lighthearted affair. Lindbergh grew defensive, even dark. Britain would not win the war, he insisted; American aid would only prolong the conflict but not save England. Germany was now "the natural air power in Europe" and would soon crush Britain with air bombardment. Lend-Lease aid would just compound a failed policy of helping Britain by wasting valuable American matériel. Worse, the bill would, he implied, make FDR a dictator and create "conditions in our country as bad or worse than those we now desire to overthrow in Nazi Germany." Lindbergh had hit a new low. He ended by asserting that the real threat to America came not from abroad. "It lies here at home in our own midst." It was just the start of the flier's rapid descent.[29]

The debate in the Senate that followed these hearings became acrimonious at once, and no one seemed to enjoy it more than Senator Burton K. Wheeler. A progressive, pro-labor, anti-corruption Democrat from Montana, he had been in the Senate since 1923 and strongly backed the New Deal. But the court-packing controversy, and Roosevelt's increasing involvement in European affairs, pushed him into the opposition. By the time of the Lend-Lease debate, Wheeler had become a caustic, conspiratorial critic of the president. He described the Lend-Lease bill on January 12 as a "New Deal Triple-A foreign policy." Like the Agricultural Adjustment Administration, which emphasized destroying crops and livestock to reduce overall output, Lend-Lease, according to Wheeler, would "plow under every fourth American boy." Roosevelt at a press conference called this statement "dastardly" and "unpatriotic" and the "rottenest thing that has been said in public life in my generation." Not long after, Roosevelt—making an uncharacteristic personal attack—implied that Wheeler was soft on Nazism, and believed the Nazi victory in Europe was "inevitable." Wheeler barked backed immediately, accusing the president of making a "scurrilous attack" on him because he opposed the president's foreign policy. A few days later, Wheeler, brandishing a sheaf of leaked documents, tried to embarrass the administration by claiming that Roosevelt had stripped the American army of all its aircraft and shipped them to Britain. Though Henry Stimson was hustled out to tell reporters that those were obsolete, older models of planes, the press described the personalization of the Lend-Lease debate as "one of the bitterest feuds in the capital's history."[30]

The critics of Lend-Lease smelled blood. As the debate in the Senate began, they poured concentrated fire on the administration. Champ Clark of Missouri said the bill would lead to "war abroad and dictatorship at home." Hiram Johnson of California saw the bill as a "pure grant of power to the President to do as he pleases with any foreign nation for any purpose and on any terms as he sees fit." Robert La Follette, a Progressive from Wisconsin, claimed that Lend-Lease would reduce Congress to a rubber-stamp "Hitler-Reichstag." On February 20, Gerald Nye and Wheeler attended an America First rally at the Mecca Auditorium in New York City, where Wheeler indulged in characteristic bombast before 3,500 people, including some members of Father Coughlin's Christian Front. "American mothers," he said, "see their sons taken to camps to be trained in the refinements of mass murder. . . . And then they hear the War Department announce contracts to purchase identification tags and make inquiries for coffins. . . . Is it any wonder these mothers have stormed the halls of Congress?" he howled.[31]

In fact, the "mothers" who popped up in Washington to protest Lend-Lease were mobilized by a professional agitator and notorious red-baiter named Elizabeth Dilling of Chicago, who in 1934 wrote *The Red Network—A Who's Who and Handbook of Radicalism for Patriots*, a self-published catalog of slurs and accusations about Communists in America. Dilling elaborated on this in her 1936 screed, *Roosevelt's Red Record and Its Background*, in which she denounced the "Jew Deal" and its Communist authors. In 1941, Dilling formed the Mothers' Crusade to Defeat Bill 1776 and bundled a few dozen ladies off to Washington, where on February 19 they threw themselves onto the steps of the Capitol and shouted their opposition to Lend-Lease. Dilling followed this publicity stunt by bringing an effigy of Dorothy Thompson to the White House and hanging it on the fence; police seized the grotesque figure, to which was pinned an insulting message about the warmongers Eleanor Roosevelt, Dorothy Thompson, and (for the anti-Semitic effect) Congressman Sol Bloom. A few days later, Dilling was arrested for attempting to occupy the office of Senator Carter Glass of Virginia, an outspoken supporter of aid to Britain.[32]

Dilling and Wheeler made predictable allies, for Wheeler often resorted to familiar antisemitic codewords: The pressure for intervention in the war, he said at the Mecca Auditorium, was coming from "international bankers," while "real Americans" opposed involvement. Wheeler asserted that Lend-Lease was being pushed by a "financial oligarchy" made up of "Morgans, Warburgs, and Kuhn-Loebs"—the favorite targets of Father Charles Coughlin. The "New York capitalists," which his audience understood to mean Jews, were trying to get America into the war to save their "cartels and monopolies." By 1941, the phrase "international bankers" was a well-established synonym for Jews, and no one could feign ignorance of the sinister undertones this anti-Jewish trope carried. Yet Wheeler persisted, unable to see how this kind of bigotry tarnished his campaign. In fact, when Wheeler and Nye spoke in New York, the audience included members of the American Destiny Party, an explicitly Nazi-style gang led by Joe McWilliams, a New York–based follower of Coughlin and the Christian Mobilizers. His men shouted antisemitic slurs throughout the rally. Wheeler disavowed these ruffians but a few weeks later he was back on the radio alleging that Jewish banking families like "the Sassoons of the Orient and the Rothschilds and Warburgs of Europe" were agitating for war so America could save their overseas investments. It was weird stuff, very like the twisted conspiracies that Coughlin had spun so effectively. But the act had worn thin, as the debate over Lend-Lease soon showed.[33]

V

Perhaps the most striking feature of these attacks on Lend-Lease, on Roosevelt, and on internationalism in general, is that they didn't work. Voices in Congress and in the public made a case even more compelling and urgent in favor of aid to the allies than the AFC made in opposition. Senators such as Claude Pepper of Florida, Josiah Bailey of North Carolina, Majority Leader Alben Barkley of Kentucky, and Warren Austin of Vermont (a Republican), all stood up for aid to Britain. Pepper declared that peace in the world could only be secure once "Hitler was crushed into an earth that absorbs and assimilates him until he is remembered only as a nightmare." Austin, accepting the risk of war, thundered that "a world enslaved is worse than war!" While the president and his advisers tried to keep a low profile and ride out the storm—a *New York Times* reporter counted at least fifty-two senators in favor of Lend-Lease in late February—many anti-fascist voices did not stay silent.[34]

Politicians grew bolder in urging a confrontation with fascism because, in part, they had been given plenty of ammunition by public figures who defined the opponents of Lend-Lease as isolationists, appeasers, and genuine national security threats. Harold Ickes never missed a chance to strike at Lindbergh, who he called a "native fascist," doing the work of the dictators on the inside. Lindbergh was "a busy appeaser who would voluntarily surrender his sword even before it is demanded," Ickes said. The *Des Moines Register* editors called Lindbergh's defeatism "BUNK" in capital letters and said the airman did not grasp that in wartime, "determination and ideals can count as much as bullets and bombs." Because America stood for democracy, it possessed a universal appeal that could overcome even Hitler's Wehrmacht. To Herbert Agar, the editor of the *Louisville Courier-Journal*, people like Senators Robert Taft of Ohio and Wheeler of Montana wanted to appease the dictators because they feared that a war against fascism would lead to national unity and progressive social and economic change at home, the very thing they sought to arrest. That is why they objected to joining the fight against "the murderers of freedom."[35]

Dorothy Thompson kept up her withering assaults on Lindbergh. On February 17, she teased out the implications of Lindbergh's recent testimony, where he had spoken of "hemispheric defense" as if it was a passive, peaceful retreat from the dangers of war. Thompson argued on the contrary that Lindbergh was an imperialist. He wanted a new form of American empire and autarky, "which is a copy of Hitler's continental imperialism." Lindbergh, she said, hoped for a great world carve-up, with Hitler getting Europe, Japan taking Asia, and America grabbing Canada, South America, the Caribbean, and much of the Pacific. This would serve as "lebensraum"—Thompson used the Nazi term for "living space"—so desired by the American Fascist movement, with which she identified Lindbergh. In the aviator's mind, she said, "we are to be the Master Folk of the Western Hemisphere and conclude a binding alliance treaty with the Nazis." Lindbergh and his isolationist allies were "attempting to delay and sabotage aid to Britain" so that Hitler could force the British to the negotiating table where he would impose this global partition.

Thompson also alleged that Lindbergh and his partners were plotting to build a new Republican party, purged of Willkie and the internationalists, led by Lindbergh himself, and backed by a few powerful newspaper chains "to smear, calumniate, and blackmail opponents into silence." American fascism, she claimed, would bring "war on neighbors, war on liberals, war on racial minorities, militarism, and the concept of America as a gigantic land power with a permanent huge standing Army . . . all masked as 'progressivism' and 'peace.'" Once again, Thompson showed an uncanny ability to expose the dark underside of Lindbergh's world view.[36]

If Ickes, Agar, and Thompson went for the jugular, Henry Luce tried to inspire American elites—the sort of people who read his magazines like *Fortune* and *Life*—to assume world leadership. On February 17, as the Lend-Lease fight raged on, he published a long essay titled "The American Century," a meditation on the "gloomy or apathetic" state of public life in the United States. Frightened to act in the present and fearful of the future, Americans, Luce claimed, were "filled with foreboding," beset by "moral and intellectual confusion." Americans were fooling themselves about the war, imagining that they could avoid it somehow. In fact, the United States was already in the war, and Luce saw it as a good war, "a war to defend and even to promote, encourage and incite so-called democratic principles throughout the world." Why be fearful of using "big words like Democracy and Freedom and Justice?" he asked. In truth, the United States had become "the most powerful and vital nation in the world," yet so far, Americans had failed to play their part, failed to "accept wholeheartedly our duty . . . to exert upon the world the full impact of our influence."

Though clumsily written and meandering in its style, Luce's essay had the benefit of good timing. Just as the vote in the Senate on Lend-Lease neared,

Luce struck out hard at "the moral and practical bankruptcy of any and all forms of isolationism." He bemoaned the hold of "this virus of isolationist sterility" on much of the Republican Party and hoped both political parties would rally to a common goal of using American strength to make a just world order. Roosevelt, who had temporized for so long, now offered the country a great chance, Luce believed. "With his leadership, we can make isolationism as dead an issue as slavery, and we can make a truly *American* internationalism something as natural to us in our time as the airplane or the radio." With a flourish, he concluded, "the world of the 20th Century, if it is to come to life in any nobility of health and vigor, must be to a significant degree an American Century."[37]

Luce was certainly not the only Republican to support Lend-Lease. In his testimony before the Senate in mid-January, Wendell Willkie also broke ranks and threw his support to FDR's program. He then met with Roosevelt at the White House on January 19, and two days later he flew to Britain to meet with Prime Minister Churchill and other government officials. He carried a famous note from FDR to Churchill. It said simply, "Wendell Willkie will give you this—He is truly helping to keep politics out over here," followed by the passage from Longfellow's epic poem, "The Building of the Ship":

Sail on, Oh Ship of State!
Sail on, Oh Union, strong and great!
Humanity with all its fears
With all the hope of future years
Is hanging breathless on thy fate!

It was just the sort of sentimental gesture that Roosevelt enjoyed making, and which Churchill found especially moving. That Willkie was the intermediary between the two leaders shows that a new cross-party consensus about an Anglo-American partnership had formed. Willkie's visit to Britain was an enormous success, and when he inspected the bomb damage in devastated Coventry, hundreds of local people flooded the streets and heartily cheered him.[38]

But Willkie did more than act as a messenger. Upon returning to New York, he gave the keynote address on Lincoln Day at the National Republican Club. Though many Republicans were angry at Willkie for his support of Lend-Lease, he got a warm welcome from 2,200 bejeweled and tuxedoed diners in the ballroom of the Waldorf-Astoria Hotel. Speaking without notes in the hearty style of the campaign trail, Willkie urged his party to leave behind the bitterness of the 1940 election and rally to the defense of freedom. Sounding much like

Luce and Thompson, and Roosevelt, too, Willkie asked his audience to reflect that a short distance away across the Atlantic, "bombs are dropping, destroying cities lived in by free men, free men like us, and some men rise and say, 'that's no problem of ours, let us preserve ourselves alone.'" The Republican Party had become, he said, the party of negation and opposition, and that attitude led them down the road to defeat. Now it was time to stand up, "to say here are free men like ourselves, struggling to preserve themselves; here is a war that will determine the course of American history . . . [and] offers the opportunity to America for world leadership." It was time for the Republican Party to join the fight for democracy. Though Willkie had burned his bridges with the old-time Republican leaders, that night the ballroom erupted in cheers and shouts of "We Want Willkie!" and the next day, his suite at the Commodore Hotel was flooded with supportive telegrams. He could not cure his party of its hatred toward the New Deal, but he did make it possible for Republicans to embrace the cause of defending Britain and perhaps democracy itself.[39]

With some prominent Republicans joining the bulk of the Democratic Party, with able cabinet officers explaining why the United States must protect Britain's lifeline to North America, and with writers and essayists elevating the Lend-Lease debate to a higher plane of ideals and morals, the momentum behind the bill became unstoppable. On March 8, the Lend-Lease bill finally came up for a vote in the Senate and passed easily, sixty votes in favor and only thirty-one against. Ten Republican senators voted yes; thirteen Democrats opposed the measure. The administration accepted an amendment that specified the bill did not authorize the U.S. Navy to convoy merchant ships, and that made it palatable to the final few fence-sitters. After a speedy and lopsided House vote on the slightly altered bill (it passed that chamber by 317–71), Roosevelt signed the Lend-Lease law at 3:51 p.m. on March 11. Roosevelt's patience had paid off, and he secured overwhelming support for the measure from Congress. Within hours, millions of dollars of war matériel started moving toward Britain; and the president announced he would seek $7 billion from Congress to fund the vast manufacturing effort the new law envisioned. The era of neutrality, mortally wounded by Hitler's aggression, was now dead and buried; FDR had delivered the coup de grâce. The arsenal of democracy fully opened its doors, and over the next four years, no less than $50 billion worth of supplies (valued at about $1.1 trillion today) would flow out to embattled allies across the globe.[40]

A few days later, Roosevelt took a victory lap at the cheerful, boisterous annual White House Correspondents Dinner, among journalists he knew well and genuinely liked. The occasion allowed him once again to define fascism in contrast to democracy. The new dictators, he said, "openly seek the destruction of all elective systems of government on every continent—including our own. . . . Yes, these men and their hypnotized followers call this a new order. It is not new, and it is not order." The American people showed that democracy, though slow and deliberative, could still work. The Lend-Lease debate had been a tough fight, "argued in every newspaper, on every wavelength, over every cracker barrel in all the land; and it was finally settled and decided by the American people themselves."

Once and for all, Roosevelt claimed, the debate was over: There would be no half measures or accommodation with fascists. "This decision is the end of any attempts at appeasement in our land; the end of urging us to get along with dictators; the end of compromise with tyranny and the forces of oppression." He used war imagery throughout the speech, placing the United States right in the middle of the conflict, not on the sidelines, and asked his listeners to make unstinted sacrifice "for our defense against the most ruthless brutality in all history; for the ultimate victory of a way of life now so violently menaced." FDR's great gift as a political communicator was his ability to link his policy decisions to a larger sense of moral purpose and democratic action. He understood Lend-Lease as more than a production program. It marked the joining together of America's vast industrial power with the ideals of the Four Freedoms. Roosevelt proposed a world order founded not on terror and tyranny but upon democratic capitalism and political liberalism. With the passage of Lend-Lease, Henry Luce's "American Century," with all its promise and its danger, had begun.[41]

VI

The fight over Lend-Lease did not come without costs. The venerable director of the CDAAA, William Allen White, felt that the organization he had led since the spring of 1940 had begun to lean strongly toward embracing war—a position he consistently rejected. After releasing a statement about his own determination to keep America out of war and insisting that the U.S. Navy should never be used to shield British merchant ships in convoys across the dangerous Atlantic, White found himself at odds with his board and resigned. The *Chicago Tribune* crowed that White had been pushed out by "warmongers," and in truth, the Lend-Lease program of unlimited aid to nations fighting Hitler and Japan did seem risky. White rightly assessed that some of the leaders in his group believed that war might be America's only choice for defeating Hitler.[42]

Another casualty of the argument over the war was Dorothy Thompson—or rather, her *Herald Tribune* column. At the end of 1940, Thompson learned that the publishers of the paper, Ogden and Helen Rogers Reid, were unhappy with her strong support for Roosevelt in the 1940 election and felt her unflagging attacks on Lindbergh, appeasement, and fascism had become tiresome to their readers. They suggested she vary her topics and occasionally discuss non-political, lighthearted subjects. Predictably, Thompson told Helen Reid that "I do not see how a political commentator can avoid the major political questions of the moment." She refused to be reined in, and in early January placed an ultimatum before her employers: either she could write what she pleased, or she would leave the paper when her contract expired in March. In the end, she told Reid that "I think we shall be happier divorced." She did not want to leave the *Herald Tribune* and give up the prestige and visibility of the column. But she would not be bound by the narrow world view of the paper's owners, and so she did not seek to extend her contract. In mid-March, she joined the Bell Syndicate instead, where she continued writing columns for national papers. She told Eleanor Roosevelt that "I do not suffer financially from the change," but the effort of the Reids to muzzle her revealed how some wealthy Republicans had grown censorious and resentful about expressions of support for Roosevelt and his policies.[43]

At the same time, the passage of Lend-Lease opened up a new frontier in the public campaign to fight fascism. On April 20, 1941, a new lobbying organization called the Fight for Freedom (FFF) announced itself. Made up of some former CDAAA members, Century Group supporters, and other influential figures in New York and Washington, Fight for Freedom sought direct U.S. entry into the war. In its first public statement, the group pledged to "do whatever is necessary to insure a Hitler defeat." It was led by the Right Reverend Henry W. Hobson—an Episcopalian bishop of southern Ohio. Hobson was born in Denver, attended Yale, and enlisted in the Great War, where he won a Distinguished Service Cross for heroism in France (before he was ordained). The honorary chairman of FFF was the elderly Senator Carter Glass of Virginia, a man born before the Civil War who had served as Treasury Secretary in the Wilson administration. He was, like so many Southern Democrats of the early 1940s, a strict segregationist, a critic of the New Deal, and an active interventionist.[44]

The group featured quite a few activists already known for their support of a muscular confrontation with Hitler, such as Herbert Agar and Ulric Bell of the *Louisville Courier-Journal*, Grenville Clark, Colonel William Donovan, Allen Dulles, banker James Warburg, the decorated soldier General John

F. O'Ryan of New York, and Freda Kirchwey of *The Nation*. University leaders James Bryant Conant and Frank P. Graham both joined in early May. The premise of the group was that America was already in the war, and it was foolish to withhold leadership and military power from the task at hand: destroying aggressive fascism. "Do You Want Hitler to Win?" blared their full-page ad in many newspapers. "If not, now is the time to act!" Action meant using U.S. naval power to protect convoys, arrest fifth columnists, and deploy "the power and majesty of the United States" to beat Hitler. With the FFF prepared to take on the America First Committee, the national debate about aid to Britain devolved into a bitter argument: whether America should get into the fight against Nazism or keep clear of the European morass altogether.[45]

The America First Committee, though bloodied by its defeat in the Lend-Lease campaign, did not back down. Senators Wheeler and Nye joined forces with Lindbergh, who became an AFC member in April, and they went on a coordinated nationwide tour, often appearing together, blasting Roosevelt's "warmongering." In Denver, Wheeler denounced the British "propaganda machine" that had successfully drummed up support for Lend-Lease. (Wheeler was right: The British were running a propaganda operation, placing favor-

Senator Burton K. Wheeler and Charles Lindbergh at an America First rally hailing the U.S. flag with the "Bellamy salute"—a gesture with fascist overtones.
Wheeler Papers, Montana State Archives

able editorials and news coverage in many news outlets.) He alleged that Hollywood had taken up the interventionist cause and threatened the film industry with an investigation. In Salt Lake City, Wheeler's rally "took on a revival meeting intensity," as the senator attacked the administration. "Hitler and Hitlerism can never dominate the world so long as America remains a strong democracy," Wheeler argued, but if the country entered the war, it "would cease to be a democracy."[46]

The AFC's real star, though, was the heroic young flier who had become a political sensation. When Lindbergh rolled into New York City for a speech on April 23 at the Manhattan Center, the six-thousand-seat auditorium on West Thirty-Fourth Street, the city was ready with two hundred uniformed police outside to contain the throngs of people trying to get in. Hawkers of Father Coughlin's rag, *Social Justice*, worked the crowds and elderly mothers waved miniature flags and shouted, "Phooey on England!" A hundred or so brave protesters with anti-Lindbergh signs were set upon by thugs and beaten, some senseless. Inside the theater, Lindbergh told the audience that America was not prepared to wage war in Europe. The only way to save Britain now was to seek a negotiated peace with Hitler. The British were avoiding the facts and trying to hook the U.S. into the war. The interventionists were raising Britain's hopes cruelly, delaying the moment of reckoning, costing lives, when in the end the British would be forced to accept a settlement, or worse, accept defeat. Countless boys had already died needlessly. Rather than mount a hopeless operation to aid Britain, America's only choice now was to withdraw behind a well-defended hemispheric curtain, ride out the storm, and develop its own "civilization."[47]

Roosevelt responded to this speech with a passing but barbed remark in his press conference two days later. He said that some people, out of one corner of their mouths, claimed to oppose dictatorship; but then from the other corner they said, "it's going to beat democracy . . . might as well accept it." FDR, showing his talent at political name-calling, continued: "Now I don't call that good Americanism. . . . I don't want to lie down and say, 'dictatorship is inevitable.'" Going a little further, he described the pro-peace spokesmen as "Vallandighams," referring to Clement Vallandigham, the Ohio Democrat who, during the Civil War, called for a negotiated peace and a recognition of Southern demands. Vallandigham incurred the wrath of President Lincoln and was labeled a "Copperhead"—a slithery, dangerous snake in the grass who, like a Fifth Columnist, might betray the country. "Vallandigham, as you know, was an appeaser," Roosevelt told the reporters. Was the president thinking about Mr. Lindbergh, the journalists asked? "Yes," came the emphatic reply.[48]

In the overheated rhetorical atmosphere of the moment, this slight against Lindbergh was depicted by the AFC and sympathetic newspapers as a full-frontal attack by the president against Lindbergh's loyalty and his right to free speech. Lindbergh himself resigned his commission in the Army Air Corps Reserve and issued a public letter, saying that since the president impugned his loyalty, character, and motives, "I can see no honorable alternative to tendering my resignation." Senator Wheeler said that "for anyone to attack Colonel Charles A. Lindbergh as a Copperhead is shocking and appalling to every right-thinking American." But of course, Lindbergh did call for a negotiated peace, and seemed willing to accept a Hitler-dominated Europe.[49]

Throughout that spring, Lindbergh kept at it, rejecting any support for the British Empire and asserting that a war for democracy abroad would destroy democracy at home. With more power centralized in Roosevelt's hands, America would be transformed into a dictatorship "as bad or worse" than Hitler's Germany. "Does anyone think," he asked rhetorically to a huge crowd in Madison Square Garden in May, "that freedom can exist even in America if we are forced into such a war?" In Philadelphia on May 29, he went so far as to say that Roosevelt, not Hitler, had dreams of world conquest. Repeated ovations and shouts of "We Want Lindbergh!" rose up into the rafters of the great city arenas at these rallies. In mid-June, on a nationwide radio broadcast, he said the administration and its supporters were sending aid to Britain in hopes of being dragged into war. They had "baited the trap of war." But America would be destroyed in a prolonged conflict against the Nazi war machine; at best, America would find itself stuck in a quagmire of war for "for the next generation," and democracy would be snuffed out. An iconic AFC poster showed the Statue of Liberty blown to pieces by an artillery shell, accompanied by the slogan: "War's First Casualty."[50]

Lindbergh's charges that Roosevelt wanted to get America into the war seemed laughable to Henry Stimson, who despaired that FDR was doing *too little* to put the country on a war footing. Though he favored aid to Britain, he believed the United States "cannot permanently be in a position of toolmakers for other nations which fight." Young American lads, he was sure, "will not be satisfied unless they are offering the own bodies to the flames." Stimson worried that Roosevelt after the Lend-Lease success had been coasting, waiting for developments rather than maintaining his momentum and exercising strong leadership. FDR often showed "flashes of genius," Stimson confided to his diary, but was a dreadful administrator. Stimson told the president that convoys of merchant ships, no matter how provocative, would be necessary to sustain Britain, and Navy Secretary Frank Knox agreed. FDR knew the strategic necessity, but he declined to take the convoy fight to Congress. Stimson bemoaned FDR's unwillingness to bend Congress and the public to his way of thinking. "I feel very keenly that something must be done in the way of leadership here in the center at Washington, and I am beginning to feel very troubled about the lack of it," he noted in his diary. In early May, Stimson went on the radio with an unambiguous call for active naval support of the British—an act that would very likely lead to war.[51]

The theme of a president adrift, or at least suspended between thought and action, came out sharply in a mid-April column by Walter Lippmann. Prompted perhaps by Lindbergh's campaign as well as the mounting disasters in the Battle of the Atlantic, Lippmann said simply that Roosevelt was failing as a leader. The people "are not getting leadership from the president," but being treated like "inquisitive children." Lippmann claimed that the American public, once told the facts of the global situation, would gladly authorize more money for defense, agree to the conscription of young men into the armed forces, and pay more taxes. But Roosevelt, "by his cleverness and his maneuvers and his devices and his casual comment on great issues," appeared condescending and insincere. FDR was "separating himself from the American people, denying to them the guidance which is their right and depriving himself of the support of the people's convictions." Lippmann delivered a bruising conclusion: "That is not the way to make democracy work and prove itself in the greatest test to which it has ever been subjected. To fail to inform the people, waiting for them to lead him, is not democracy but demagogy. To act as if the people had to be manipulated is to deny the very virtues on which rests the hope of democracy." Here was Stimson's lament too: Why did Roosevelt hesitate, when the public could easily be persuaded to fall in behind him?[52]

Harold Ickes, always prickly and impatient, had grown downright churlish about Roosevelt's apparent passivity. He wrote in his diary that he felt Roosevelt's foreign policy had been far too soft "since Ethiopia" and that the U.S. had not acted speedily in getting arms to Britain. Ickes joined Roosevelt on a fishing cruise in early April, where they debated whether the country ought to enter the war, and Roosevelt implied that he would have to wait for a German "incident" before committing the country to fight. Ickes also felt deeply concerned about the attacks of the AFC on Roosevelt and wondered why so little had been done about it. Ickes shared his worries with Archibald MacLeish, who also favored prompt intervention. "In every direction I find a growing discontent with the President's leadership," Ickes wrote. "People are beginning to say, 'I am tired of words. I want action.'" Ickes even began to doubt if he should have supported FDR's bid for a third term. Some of this may have reflected the usual friction and rivalries with other cabinet members. But Ickes claimed to have found this sentiment in many senior members of the administration. In late May, at a cabinet meeting with these headstrong advisers pressing for action, Roosevelt said simply, "I am not willing to fire the first shot." He would wait until the Germans "create an incident." This picture of a passive Roosevelt was quite different from the one the America First Committee portrayed.[53]

Roosevelt's caution that spring is all the more surprising in light of the evolution of public opinion toward the European war. In mid-March, Hadley Cantril at the Princeton Public Opinion Research Project sent to the White House polling data that showed well over 60 percent of the public felt it was more important for the U.S. to help Britain win the war than for the U.S. to stay out of the war. At the end of April, the Gallup poll showed that 68 percent of the public agreed that America should enter the war "if it appeared certain that there was no other way to defeat Germany and Italy." Only 24 percent favored staying out. And as for Lindbergh, his giant crowds masked the fact that his speeches did not persuade the rest of the country. Of those who knew about Lindbergh's views, 63 percent disagreed with them; a mere 24 percent agreed. A *Fortune* survey, also in late April, showed a consensus around key elements of the interventionist argument: that Hitler did indeed intend to dominate the United States (70 percent), that a Hitler victory over Britain would have a "very serious" effect on the United States (72 percent), that the U.S. should send half or most of the war matériel it produced to Britain (57 percent), and that the isolationist committees leaned more toward outright propaganda than the interventionist groups did. In mid-May, polls also showed support (54 percent to 39 percent) for using the U.S. Navy to convoy war materials to Britain. Despite the pizzazz of Lindbergh's appearances, America First was losing ground, as the public began to accept the prospect of intervening in the war.[54]

On May 27, in a much-anticipated speech, Roosevelt spoke to the nation by radio. His text had been written largely by Sherwood and Rosenman. Sumner Welles had also carefully reviewed it. It attempted to do a number of things: to appease the warhawks in his cabinet with a clear expression of American principles; to counter the worrying news of British military reversals in Greece and North Africa; and to lay the ground for a bolder, more assertive naval policy in the Atlantic that ran the risk of an open clash with Germany. On an oppressively hot night in Washington, the president spoke from the large East Room of the White House, seated at a desk in front of a crowd of Latin American diplomats whose gathering for the annual meeting of the Pan American Union offered an occasion for a speech. The Nazis, Roosevelt said, were waging "a world war for world domination. . . . Unless the advance of Hitlerism is forcibly checked now, the Western Hemisphere will be within range of the Nazi weapons of destruction." No peace was possible with such a monstrous regime, and in words that sounded much like Dorothy Thompson's columns, Roosevelt ventured that in any so-called peace deal with Hitler, "Germany would literally parcel out the world—hoisting the swastika itself over vast territories and populations," including eventually North and South America. Free labor, free trade, freedom of speech and religion, all would be crushed under the jackboot.

"Yes," he said darkly, "even our right of worship would be threatened. The Nazi world does not recognize any God except Hitler." Only the valiant defense by Britain and China, he said, had halted the complete victory of the tyrants. In language that resonated far more than Lindbergh's inward looking, shoulder-shrugging approach to the world crisis, he came to the powerful peroration:

> Today the whole world is divided between human slavery and human freedom—between pagan brutality and the Christian ideal.
>
> We choose human freedom—which is the Christian ideal.
>
> No one of us can waver for a moment in his courage or his faith.
>
> We will not accept a Hitler-dominated world.

FDR closed this address with "a proclamation that an unlimited national emergency exists and requires the strengthening of our defense to the extreme limit of our national power and authority."[55]

Rhetorically it was, as usual, a stirring and inspirational speech, and it announced an extension of U.S. naval patrols—not convoys—further into the Atlantic. Beyond that, though, had Roosevelt really made up his mind? Stimson and his wife listened to the radio broadcast outside in his garden under the trees, where the evening air gave a bit of relief from the early spring heat wave. Stimson, who had sent in suggestions for the speech and had read an early draft that he much liked, was crestfallen: "Lo and behold, the speech had been softened," he wrote in his diary. It lacked specifics and pulled up short of the boldness Stimson wanted. For two days, he remained in a funk, "exhausted by the letdown occasioned by the president's speech." Harold Ickes, always eager for action, felt "the president has not aroused the country; has not really sounded the bell." The British were fighting heroically but losing their hold on the Mediterranean; an invasion of southern England looked imminent; the U.S. production effort was behind schedule; and shiploads of arms and food were being sunk at an ever-greater rate. "And we are still talking," noted Ickes sourly.[56]

VII

Roosevelt was, of course, a gifted talker. By the spring of 1941, he had framed the national rearmament and production effort as America's contribution to the global war against fascism. "We choose human freedom," he said, and he committed the United States to help sustain democracy "everywhere in the world." *Fortune* magazine endorsed this world view by calling Nazism "a counterrevolution against freedom" that America must oppose, with war if necessary. In a soaring editorial, the magazine declared that "we must be willing to fight for freedom and the world must know that we are willing." Otherwise, democracy was doomed. Isolationism would lead to fascism, *Fortune* asserted, for America, "ringed around by a world hostile to our way of life," would become an armed redoubt, a tyrannical warfare state. In July, Walter Lippmann bolstered this argument, calling isolationism "America's greatest mistake," perpetrated by a minority in Congress, leaving the nation vulnerable, weak, and unprepared to defend the democratic world from the insatiable fascist empires.[57]

But for some citizens, such words about preserving American freedom rang hollow. At the start of 1941, A. Philip Randolph, the labor leader and civil rights activist, expressed outrage that Black workers had been shut out of the expanding war industries. "Negroes are not getting anywhere with National Defense," he wrote in January. "The whole National Defense setup reeks and stinks with race prejudice, hatred, and discrimination." As Congress channeled billions of dollars into defense manufacturing, Randolph fumed that Jim Crow segregation kept Black workers out. The arsenal of democracy, it seemed, offered no place to African Americans.[58]

A veteran of the labor movement, A. Philip Randolph had led the Brotherhood of Sleeping Car Porters since 1925. A charismatic figure who had toiled in backbreaking manual labor in his native Florida, Randolph moved to New York City on the eve of World War I. He became active in union organizing and edited a radical magazine called *The Messenger*. Randolph believed that public pressure on government officials could work if African Americans organized and pulled together. In 1940, he pleaded with White House officials to end segregation in the military. He was politely rebuffed. He now settled on more confrontational tactics. Starting in January, he assembled a national organization devoted to staging a protest march on Washington. The demands were simple, "namely, jobs in National Defense and placement as soldiers and officers of all ranks we are qualified for in the armed forces." But these achievements would not come easily: "We must fight for it, and fight for it with gloves off."[59]

In his public messages about the march, Randolph repeatedly stressed that Black Americans were loyal citizens and wanted to shoulder their share of the national burden. During the Lend-Lease debate, he spoke out in favor of aid to Britain at a time when Communist organizations like the National Negro Congress opposed it. As Randolph put it at the height of the debate, Britain was "fighting for the cause of democracy, the only hope and salvation of minority groups." He knew that Britain had governed a racist and oppressive empire. But the Nazis, he wrote, were far worse than the British, and their racial ideology showed "utter contempt and disdain for the Negro people." He argued that "no group would suffer more from the dreadful darkness and tragic terrorism of a totalitarian world—Nazi, Fascist, or Communist—than the Negro people." Randolph had the support of educator and activist Mary McLeod Bethune, who asserted on a CBS radio program that "the Negro people have always demonstrated their allegiance to the American Republic. . . . This is our country. We have helped to build it. . . . We now stand ready to defend it." Randolph also rejected participation by Communists so that detractors could not depict the movement as subversive or "red." The march organizers "consider Communists a definite menace, pestilence, and nuisance," and disavowed their support. The March on Washington Committee wrote in its public appeal for support that the march formed part of the global struggle against "Fascism, Nazism, Communism, and all forms of dictatorship."[60]

By positioning himself as a supporter of Roosevelt's program, Randolph hoped to increase his leverage when he demanded federal action on desegregation. The march on Washington would go forward under a powerful banner, Randolph said: "We Loyal Negro-American Citizens Demand the Right to Work and Fight for Our Country." Randolph here anticipated what became the "Double-V" campaign: victory over fascism abroad, and victory over Jim Crow at home. In mid-May, the *New Journal and Guide* reported that the excitement around the march had pushed the expected number of participants to over fifty thousand people; by June, that number had grown to one hundred thousand. Church leaders like Adam Clayton Powell Jr. of New York City actively promoted participation in the march by their parishioners. Randolph in a public letter said, "We hope that this march will serve to shake up white Americans and official Washington to an appreciation of the rights of Negro America." Walter White, the executive secretary of the NAACP, endorsed the march. "If we demonstrate to the United States Government and the people of America that we mean business, it will help towards the attainment of a real democracy in the United States while we are fighting for it abroad."[61]

Roosevelt now faced a serious problem. Washington, D.C., in 1941 was in every respect a Southern town. All its public facilities—trains, rest rooms, hotels, restaurants, movie theaters, and streetcars—were segregated. If one hundred thousand determined Black Americans marched down the main boulevards toward the Lincoln Memorial, there was every possibility that they would be met by violence, some of it inflicted by Washington's own police force. Roosevelt could easily imagine scenes of bitter racial violence on the streets of America's capital city. All his recent efforts to position the United States as the champion of democracy and human freedom might be dashed in a single afternoon. FDR pressed the First Lady to intercede and stop the march.

Because of her work with civil rights leaders, Eleanor Roosevelt knew Randolph and Walter White well. In fact, Randolph sent her a copy of the "Call to Negro America" laying out the purpose of the march and asking her to promote it her "My Day" column. Instead, she threw cold water on the march. She replied to Randolph on June 10 with a strongly worded plea. "I have talked over your letter with the President, and I feel very strongly that your group is making a very grave mistake at the present time to allow this march to take place." She predicted "it may engender so much bitterness that it will create in Congress even more solid opposition from certain groups than we have had in the past." She went on to call the march "unfortunate" and "unwise." Three days later, Eleanor met with Randolph and White in New York, with Mayor Fiorello La Guardia acting as the host. The mayor had just been named director of a new Office of Civilian Defense to prepare the home front for the possibility of war. He too pressured Randolph to cancel the march.[62]

Randolph and White refused to budge. "Negroes have awakened to a definite sense of their mass power," they said, and demanded a meeting with the president to make their case for an executive order banning racial discrimination in the defense industry. On June 18, he and Walter White, accompanied by members of the organizing committee, met with Roosevelt, La Guardia, Stimson, Knox, and the head of the Office of Production Management, William Knudsen. Roosevelt made it clear that the march would be perceived as an effort "to coerce the government" and he wanted it halted. Randolph replied that "a wave of resentment, bitterness, disillusionment and desperation was sweeping the Negroes throughout the country because of discrimination in national defense," and only an executive order "that had teeth" would break Jim Crow in the war industries.

The discussion continued in the cabinet room after Roosevelt left the group. Frank Knox, the navy secretary, asked Randolph if he would go so far as to compel Black and white sailors "to live together on ships," and Randolph said firmly, "yes." Knox said that in a time of national emergency, "experiments of this kind cannot be carried on." Randolph made it clear that even if he could not win the desegregation of the military, he demanded that the federal government deny contracts to any defense plant that engaged in systematic discrimination. Knudsen rejected the need for an executive order and said more could be done through "persuasion and education than by force." Randolph said simply that such methods had been tried in the past and failed. Intervening with the decisive argument, Layle Lane, the vice president of the American Federation of Teachers and a Black New York City labor activist, laid out the stakes of the issue. "If the government really wants to assume the leadership in fighting for the preservation of democratic institutions and traditions," she said, "it would have to recognize that it could not ignore the rights of the Negroes." Progress in the world must start with progress at home.[63]

Aware that the march would be a serious embarrassment, and possibly also aware that Randolph had given him an opportunity to advance civil rights through executive action rather than through a hostile Congress, Roosevelt yielded. He asked Joseph L. Rauh Jr., a Felix Frankfurter protégée and member of the Cohen-Corcoran legal team that had been so important in the early years of the New Deal, to draft an executive order that would meet Randolph's demands and get the mass protest canceled. It required tough negotiating, but on June 25, just six days before the scheduled march, they reached a deal. Roosevelt issued Executive Order 8802, which mandated that all defense production industries that contracted with the federal government must pledge "not to discriminate against any worker because of race, creed, color, or national origin." And a new supervisory body, the Fair Employment Practices Committee (FEPC), would see to it that these rules were followed.

It was a breakthrough for civil rights in America, made possible by Randolph's skills as an organizer. Randolph saw the opportunity created by Roosevelt's year-long campaign to awaken the country to its moral duty as the defender of democracy. He used the leverage of mobilized Black citizens to make the case that, before America could rescue democracy in the world, it must advance democracy at home. Of course, the road ahead remained steep and rocky, and the FEPC by no means met the high expectations Randolph had for it. But those struggles remained in the future. The March on Washington organizers in June 1941 could take satisfaction that, with just the right kind of pressure at just the right moment, they had wrung from the president a pledge to use his authority to begin, however tentatively, the rollback of racial segregation in America.[64]

VIII

In the early days of June 1941, in small leafy towns and pavement-ringed cities, hundreds of thousands of young people donned black gowns and wobbly mortarboards, and headed toward the central green, quad, or gymnasium of their universities to receive their hard-won academic degrees. In normal times, graduation brings joy and celebration, and commencement speakers deliver words of encouragement, wisdom, and inspiration. This particular year, though, with the world in flames and the future clouded with the smoke of war, the graduates heard appeals for action that were directed not to them but to President Roosevelt.

At the Stevens Institute of Technology in Hoboken, New Jersey, 17 men in the class of 115 received commissions in the Naval Reserve, and listened to an address from Rear Admiral Harry E. Yarnell, the former commander of the Asiatic Fleet and veteran of the 1937 *Panay* incident. "We are at war," Yarnell told the graduates, and he called for the unrestricted use of naval and sea power to defend Britain and China from their attackers. Wendell Willkie, who received an honorary degree that day, vigorously applauded Yarnell's words from the seats. At Cornell, where 39 young men received navy commissions and 117 joined the Army Reserve, the university president, Dr. Edmund Ezra Day, said the United States must send aid to Britain "with whatever means are necessary." Using a word much on the lips of editorialists in those days, he said that "destiny has a way of overcoming indecision." Hinting at Roosevelt's fence-sitting, he said, "right now, America is facing destiny. The immediate need is for decision and action. We have no option but to take a stand."[65]

At New York University, the dean of the faculty told 4,571 graduates that the world faced a menace "far greater than the Black Death," which killed 50 million people. The university chancellor, Harry Woodburn Chase, described the ongoing war as "a struggle for the human spirit," and urged his listeners to sacrifice themselves gladly and willingly for such ideas as "freedom and justice and opportunity and respect for the individual." The university gave an honorary degree that day to Anne O'Hare McCormick, thanking her for serving as "a guide and interpreter, fearless and resourceful, in the savage thickets of politics both foreign and domestic."[66]

Close advisers of the president could be found on many platforms that month; they took the liberty of urging prompt intervention in the war. Attorney General Robert H. Jackson told the graduates of the Albany Law School that the defeat of Britain by Nazi Germany would leave the United States trapped "like a bug in a bottle." Associate Justice of the Supreme Court Felix Frankfurter, addressing Radcliffe graduates, rejected the pacifist thesis that "war never settles anything." Not only did the U.S. Civil War "settle slavery," he said, but democracy in wartime Britain was more vigorous and progressive than ever. And at West Point, Secretary of War Henry Stimson set aside any words of congratulation and spoke honestly about the great tasks that awaited the 424 future Army officers arrayed before him.[67]

"Our nation," Stimson began, "is confronted by the most dangerous threat which has ever faced its political and economic independence." The ideals of justice and law had been overthrown; freedom of speech and religion had been "trampled under by ruthless barbarity and the organized slavery of fellow men." Those who spoke of negotiation and appeasement were dangerously wrong. Perhaps thinking of Roosevelt's description of Lindbergh as a war-shy Copperhead, Stimson now invoked Lincoln's solemn words from 1858. A house divided against itself cannot stand, Lincoln said; a nation divided over slavery could not long endure. To Stimson, the world now faced the same kind of dilemma. "The world today is divided between two camps and the issue between the camps is irreconcilable. It cannot be appeased. It cannot be placated. Humanity cannot permanently make terms with injustice, with wrong, and with cruelty. . . . There is no possibility for this country, with its principles and its methods of life, to live safely in a world dominated by the methods and practices of the Axis powers." Like Lincoln, Stimson knew the issue could only be settled by war. And these very men would bear the burden: Forty of them, so handsomely bedecked that day in their dress gray uniforms, would die in combat in the coming conflagration.[68]

Some of these scenes might have come from the pages of the great anti-war novelists of the interwar generation, from authors like Erich Maria Remarque who, in his bestselling 1928 book, *All Quiet on the Western Front*, mocked the crusading spirit of the German schoolteachers who had inculcated millions of young men with a passion for war and a mortal dread of cowardice. But during the decade of the 1930s, some of the caustic anti-war attitudes of Remarque's generation had dissipated. In America, at least, some young people were prepared to join the fight against fascism.

At Dartmouth College, for example, a member of the class of 1941 published an open letter to President Roosevelt in the college newspaper, and it became something of a national sensation. Prompted by the defeat and occupation of Greece by German forces that April, Charles Guy Bolté of New York began his letter with a strikingly powerful sentence: "Now we have waited long enough." With the characteristic impatience of a twenty-one-year-old college grad, he demanded action from Roosevelt. "All over the world men are waiting for you. In Greece, in Yugoslavia, in Norway, in France, in Belgium, in Holland, in Poland, you are the only hope of men who fought and lost. In England, you are the only hope of men who are still fighting. It must be that in Germany itself there are men who think of you as the only hope." Bolté repeated his refrain, "now we have waited long enough," and continued:

> We have seen the United States move slowly toward war, through conscription, industrial defense mobilization and the Lend-Lease act; we have known that it moved too slowly.
>
> We have not produced enough guns, tanks, airplanes, bombs.
>
> We have not supplied the ships to carry what we have produced across the seas.
>
> We have not supplied the men to fight the battle other men have been fighting for us.
>
> Now we ask you to order complete industrial mobilization of this country on wartime lines. We ask you to set in motion the executive and legislative machinery which will stop the farce of producing automobiles, washing machines, gaudy fashions, and aluminum salad bowls while the peaceful world which is enhanced by these products is being blasted to pieces.
>
> Now we ask you to authorize the sending of supplies across the seas in American ships, convoyed by the American navy.
>
> Now we ask you to send American pilots, mechanics, sailors and soldiers to fight wherever they are needed.
>
> In the dark catalogue of our public events no other answer can be given.[69]

The letter was widely reprinted and even read into the *Congressional Record*. To his credit, Bolté did not wait for America to join the war. That spring, he went right from the sylvan comfort of Dartmouth's New Hampshire campus to besieged Britain, where he enlisted in the British Army and was eventually commissioned as a second lieutenant in the King's Royal Rifle Corps. In October 1942, he fought in the Second Battle of El Alamein, one of the most significant British victories of the war. Bolté, badly wounded by a shell, lost his right leg. He returned home and went on to become an organizer of the American Veterans Committee, a progressive group that championed the cause of racial integration in the U.S. military. If the Four Freedoms were ever going to be realized, it would be because impatient young people like Chuck Bolté stepped forward to say, "Now we have waited long enough."

IX

"This morning the news broke of the attack of Germany on Russia," wrote Henry Stimson in his diary on June 22, 1941. After meeting with George Marshall and other colleagues in the War Department, he put together a short letter to the president. With Germany bogged down in Russia for at least one month and possibly three, the United States must seize the initiative. (Like most analysts, Stimson dismissed Soviet military capabilities and assumed Hitler would beat the Russians rapidly.) Stimson believed the president should send troops to Iceland to secure the shipping lanes in the north Atlantic, rush more aid to Britain, and act "with the utmost vigor" to establish control over the Western Hemisphere. "Germany's action seems like an almost providential occurrence," Stimson wrote. His counterpart at the Navy Department, Frank Knox, sent Roosevelt a brief note of his own: The German invasion of the Soviet Union "provides us with an opportunity to strike and strike effectively at Germany."[70]

Like all great human dramas, wars have turning points, and historians use these moments to bring structure to what at the time seemed like a fluid, uninterrupted stream of events. The invasion of Poland in 1939, the fall of France in June 1940, followed by Dunkirk and the Battle of Britain in the summer of 1940, the seesawing conflict between the British, Italians, and Germans for control of North Africa—as world-shattering as these milestones looked to contemporaries, they cannot match in historical significance Operation Barbarossa. It was an invasion of unprecedented scale—the Germans threw 3.5 million soldiers in 138 divisions into this fight, accompanied by Allied forces from Romania, Hungary, Italy, Slovakia, and Finland, along a front that ran nearly 1,200 miles from Latvia down to the Black Sea. And it was also a colossal strategic error, expending the bulk of the German armed forces in an unnecessary war in the East while giving Britain a reprieve from the terrible blows it was then receiving. Barbarossa also granted the United States a most valuable commodity—time—with which to speed up its production and delivery of weapons to its allies. Roosevelt immediately perceived the opportunity Barbarossa offered to the anti-Hitler powers: If it developed into a long struggle, "it will mean the liberation of Europe from Nazi domination."[71]

For the United States, the outbreak of the German-Soviet war acted like a giant railway turntable—one of those old-fashioned disks that could rotate a locomotive from one track to another in an instant, completely changing a train's course and destination. If at the start of June 1941, American grand strategy had been stuck, with Roosevelt awaiting an "incident" in the Atlantic and mulling over just how to deploy his still modest naval resources to protect aid shipments to Britain, by the end of July the global strategic picture had completely changed. And Roosevelt, rather than waiting upon events, at last directed them. The rearmament plans he had pushed through Congress, the mobilization of the naval and air forces, the rolling back of portions of the Neutrality Act, the implementation of the Selective Service law, the Lend-Lease program—these policy achievements positioned Roosevelt to act, now that the context had changed. After Barbarossa, the fog of uncertainty lifted, and a clear picture emerged. Although formal declarations of war would not come until December, the United States in July 1941 effectively joined the war against Nazi Germany.

Immediately upon hearing the news of Hitler's misguided invasion, Roosevelt casually told reporters at a press conference that "of course we are going to give all the aid we possibly can to Russia." In fact, the decision to aid Russia was controversial. During the debate on Lend-Lease, some opponents had tried to slip a prohibition on aid to the Soviet Union into the bill. FDR, with great foresight, had thwarted that end-run, and now freely promised swift support for Russia's fight. Sumner Welles told the Soviet ambassador two days later that "any request which the Soviet government might make of the United States for material assistance would be given immediate attention." Ambassador Laurence Steinhardt conveyed a similar message to Foreign Minister Vyacheslav Molotov on June 29, and by June 30, the State Department had set up the bureaucratic machinery to handle Soviet aid requests. Given that the Soviet Union had for two years been an ally of Nazi Germany, a source of immensely valuable raw materials for the German war machine, and a partner in the partition of Poland, the decision to let bygones be bygones for the purpose of fighting a common enemy reveals Roosevelt's strategic judgment as well as a characteristic cold-bloodedness. In a larger sense, this moment was a triumph for FDR, who had a hunch back in 1933 that the United States might one day find a useful ally in the Soviet Union. That day had come.[72]

By contrast, Charles Lindbergh rushed to the microphones to denounce any talk of helping Russia. He told an AFC rally in San Francisco on July 1 that "I would a hundred times rather see my country ally herself with England, or even with Germany, with all her faults, than the cruelty, the godlessness, and the barbarism that exists in Soviet Russia." This talk of preferring Nazi Germany "with all her faults" to an alliance with the Soviet Union gave Lindbergh's critics an opening, and Harold Ickes seized it. On July 14—at a Bastille Day ceremony hosted by French exiles in New York—Ickes took a brickbat to Lindbergh. In front of two thousand cheering people, he delivered "one of the most bitter attacks ever made on Lindbergh by any member of the Roosevelt administration," according to the *New York Times*. "Lindbergh now denounces communism because it defends itself against the aggression of Hitler," Ickes said.

> But I have never heard this Knight of the German Eagle denounce Hitler or Nazism or Mussolini or Fascism. I have never heard him raise his voice for any of the raped countries of Europe. . . . I have never heard him express a word of pity for the Poles or the Jews who have been slaughtered by the hundreds of thousands by Hitler's savages. I have never heard Lindbergh say a word of encouragement to the English for the fight they are so bravely making for Lindbergh's right to live his life in his own way. . . . As a matter of fact, I have never heard Lindbergh say a word for democracy itself.

On the same day that Ickes spoke, the Committee to Defend America hosted a rally of seventy-six thousand people at Manhattan Beach in Brooklyn at which the actress and political activist Tallulah Bankhead theatrically buried the head of a large stuffed ostrich in a large pile of sand. The ostrich had a placard around its neck labeled simply "Lindbergh."[73]

With his lieutenants effectively swatting down the ever-more egregious and increasingly antisemitic Lindbergh, Roosevelt could focus on the massive problem of supplying both Britain and Russia with war matériel. Barbarossa, by diverting Hitler's attention away from the Atlantic for a moment, allowed Roosevelt to take the significant step of sending a detachment of marines to neutral Iceland, a nation the British had occupied in 1940. There, the British had improved dock facilities and built airfields for planes involved in anti-submarine operations. On July 8, in a coordinated handoff, U.S. forces landed to replace the British troops. American aircraft soon arrived to continue the air patrols in the north Atlantic. *Time* magazine had no doubt about the significance of the Iceland operation. "This week," the magazine reported, "Franklin Roosevelt moved the U.S. squarely into the Battle of the Atlantic." From Reykjavik, "New York was 3,900 miles away, but Norway's Nazi-occupied Bergen was only 1,800 miles, Scotland's port of Glasgow only 1,600 miles, and Berlin a mere 2,800 miles as the bomber flies. The Western Hemisphere had stretched once more. The President had taken another great step." Roosevelt told Congress of his actions in unambiguous terms. "As Commander in Chief I have . . . issued orders to the Navy that all necessary steps be taken to ensure the safety of communications in the approaches between Iceland and the United States, as well as on the seas between the United States and all other strategic outposts." The last phrase vaguely extended America's area of operations all the way to the British Isles.[74]

Roosevelt did not have to expend any additional political capital to implement these decisions. The work of framing the argument had been done in the preceding year, in a patient effort of persuasion about the stakes of the war for the United States. When he delivered a brief radio address on July 4, 1941, speaking from his newly opened presidential library in Hyde Park, he adopted a serious, firm tone appropriate for a nation at war. With the exiled Crown Princess Martha of Norway and her children seated nearby (the Roosevelts had offered her refuge in the White House in 1940), Roosevelt said that freedom was in jeopardy around the world, and if the forces of democracy failed now, the American experiment of self-government would quickly be crushed by a "juggernaut of force." Fighting fascism abroad was the only way to sustain democracy at home. In one of his most memorable lines, he summarized a worldview that would shape the rest of the century: "I tell the American people solemnly that the United States will never survive as a happy and fertile oasis of liberty surrounded by a cruel desert of dictatorship." He asked Americans on that Independence Day to pledge themselves not only to their flag, and to prepare to give "our work, our will and, if it be necessary, our very lives" to the defense of freedom. These words struck home. In New York City's Times Square, auto traffic came to a complete stop for the seven minutes that Roosevelt spoke. Americans hung on every word.[75]

No doubt they paid such careful attention because the war no longer seemed far away. Conscription had been under way for almost a year. Since the previous September, a million young men had donned fatigues, endured hard physical training, learned how to use weapons, dig trenches, and follow orders. But the 1940 Selective Service Act had required only one year of service for young recruits, and it was nearing expiration. In mid-July, Army Chief of Staff George Marshall pleaded with the Senate to extend the law; otherwise "our present trained forces will largely melt away." He had "no doubt whatever about the gravity" of the emergency the country faced. Letting the newly trained soldiers slip back into civilian life on the eve of a global crisis would be "a fundamental and tragic error." On July 21, Roosevelt sent a special message to Congress stating that the interests of the United States were "definitely imperiled," and calling for speedy action. In early August, the Senate passed legislation allowing the president to extend the terms of enlisted men, National Guardsmen, and reserve officers by eighteen months. The vote was 45–30, a comfortable if not overwhelming margin. The legislation faced stiff headwinds in the House, however, where many Democrats felt uneasy about extending the term of service. It cleared the hurdle on August 12, but only by one vote.[76]

As Congress wrangled with extending the draft, Roosevelt grasped yet another nettle he had been avoiding. The German invasion of the Soviet Union directly altered the strategic balance in Asia, for now Japan, which had been anxious about a Soviet threat to its control of northeast Asia, had to make a decision about its long-term strategy. The Japanese began to mass troops in Manchuria and Korea for an assault on Vladivostok and the Soviet far east. But the resilience of the Red Army, and the absence of any Soviet troop withdrawals from its easternmost territory, made the Japanese government hesitate about going on the offensive against the Russians. As they dithered, American actions tipped the scale against a Japanese invasion of the Soviet Union. In late July, the Japanese government demanded the acquiescence of the Vichy French government to the extension of Japanese forces into southern Indochina; the French agreed under duress. As the Japanese prepared to land forces there at the end of July, Roosevelt chose to punish the Japanese by freezing their assets in America, making the purchase of U.S. products, especially oil and aviation fuel, all but impossible. He followed this on August 1 with a total embargo of oil and gasoline exports to Japan, a catastrophic loss for the Japanese, who bought 80 percent of their oil in the United States. The Japanese high command now abandoned plans for a northward military strike against Russia and took aim instead at Southeast Asia, where they could make good the lost American supplies of oil. Roosevelt had hoped to deter Japan by blocking their ability to buy oil in America, but as the historian Akira Iriye has written, Japanese military planners now believed a "fatal clash" with America lay ahead, and that the United States and Japan had reached "the point of no return."[77]

Amid the rising tide of war, Roosevelt now put into place the foundations of the great alliance that would wage and win the Second World War. On July 13, Roosevelt's personal envoy and Lend-Lease administrator Harry Hopkins departed for Britain to meet with Prime Minister Winston Churchill. Hopkins, who had occupied a bedroom in the White House since May 1940, had become Roosevelt's closest adviser on national security matters, and a crucial go-between with Churchill, who he had met in London in January. Hopkins served FDR as a sounding board and consigliere, a person who could brighten White House evenings with good talk, amusing stories, and friendship—something FDR needed after his faithful companion of 20 years, Missy LeHand, suffered a debilitating stroke in June 1941. She never recovered.

Hopkins too was fragile: In 1939, much of his cancerous stomach was removed and he was chronically undernourished and fatigued. He was fueled mainly by cigarettes and a profound loyalty to Roosevelt. He traveled to London in July to review Anglo-American relations with Churchill and his senior military staff. And Hopkins also laid the ground for a personal meeting between Churchill and Roosevelt—an event that would fix in the public mind the close bond between the United States and Britain. FDR did not trust anyone in the State Department, nor in the U.S. embassy in London, to carry out such a task, and in fact he kept the planning of the Churchill meeting secret from Cordell Hull and just about everyone else in Washington.

After ten days of close consultations with the British service chiefs on the war and the supply problem, Hopkins wired the president on Friday, July 25, suggesting that he continue his mission by going to Moscow to meet Stalin. Hopkins thought that Roosevelt, by sending his personal envoy to the Kremlin, would show Stalin "in an unmistakable way that we mean business on a long-term supply job." It was an inspired suggestion—evidence of why Hopkins was so valuable as a lieutenant—and Roosevelt immediately approved the trip. Hopkins spent the weekend at the prime minister's country home, Chequers, in an atmosphere much like the Roosevelt White House—aides, servants, and important dignitaries all jostled together, messages flying to and fro, and intimate, highly secret conversations mingling with country-house gossip. None other than Dorothy Thompson appeared for Sunday lunch, full of opinions and provocations, her spirit of defiance crackling in the air as it had done for the entire decade.

On Sunday evening, July 27, Hopkins delivered a speech for the BBC from Chequers that gave a morale-boosting (and inflated) version of the robust American aid program. "Even now as I speak," he said dramatically, "sleek grey destroyers flying the American flag are plunging their bows into the waves of the North Atlantic," on a mission to protect shipping lanes to Britain. He spoke of the immense rate of American aircraft production and the vast armada of ships carrying supplies to the embattled allies. "No enemy action can stop the ceaseless tide of ships coming here daily," he said in words that would be put to the test in the coming years during the prolonged Battle of the Atlantic. "Your fight is a fight for freedom in the world," he said to his British audience, "and will not fail." In effect, Hopkins declared that a wartime alliance now prevailed, a bond of "friendship, sympathy and admiration" between Britain and the United States. And with that, Hopkins boarded a night train to Scotland, where a U.S.-made PBY Catalina awaited to take him on a flight over Norway, Sweden, and Finland to Archangel, on what Robert Sherwood called "one of the most extraordinarily important and valuable missions of the whole war."[78]

Following a long low-altitude flight in an unpressurized, freezing cold aircraft equipped with only a canvas cot for occasional naps, Hopkins and his small party made it to Archangel, just south of the Arctic Circle. A "monumental" feast awaited him, he recalled, and he was plied with caviar, bread, vodka, and immense tables of delicacies much like those that greeted William Bullitt in the Kremlin in December 1933. But it was Stalin Hopkins came to see, and he rushed onward to Moscow the next day. He was met by Ambassador Steinhardt and another large welcoming committee; at 6:30 p.m. the next day, July 30, he arrived at the Kremlin to meet Stalin.[79]

Hopkins later described Stalin as "an austere, rugged, determined figure in boots that shone like mirrors, stout baggy trousers, and snug-fitting blouse. He wore no ornament, military or civilian." He was built like a football player, low to the ground; "his hands are huge, as hard as his mind." He spoke tersely, directly. "He never wastes a syllable." Like Bullitt before him, Hopkins was transfixed by his manner, imperious and earthy at the same time. Hopkins came prepared with a personal statement from President Roosevelt, which emphasized America's admiration for Russia's valiant struggle and his determination to see that Russia received as much military aid as possible. Hopkins stated that "the President considered Hitler the enemy of mankind and that he therefore wished to aid the Soviet Union in its fight against Germany."

In reply, Stalin delivered (apparently with a straight face) a little homily on the importance of "minimum moral standards" in world affairs and said the Germans had violated even those. The two men then quickly got down to business, with Stalin telling Hopkins of his need for antiaircraft guns, machine guns, rifles, gasoline, aluminum, and bomber aircraft. At a longer conference the next day, Stalin emphasized his confidence in his country's resilience. Hitler had underestimated Russia's strength and now his panzer divisions were discovering that "moving mechanized forces through Russia was very different than moving them over the boulevards of Belgium and France." Stalin anticipated that by October, the Germans would face heavy rain and then freezing cold and be forced to go on the defensive. Brave words, considering that even as Stalin and Hopkins met in the Kremlin, German armored divisions were within 150 miles of Moscow.

At the close of this meeting, Stalin drew Hopkins in, rather in the way he had courted Bullitt seven and a half years earlier. He told Hopkins that "Hitler's greatest weakness was found in the vast number of oppressed people who hated Hitler and the immoral ways of his government. He believed these people and countless other millions in nations still unconquered could receive the kind of encouragement and moral strength they needed to resist Hitler from only one source, and that was the United States. He stated that the world influence of the President and the Government of the United States was enormous." Stalin expressed confidence in his ability to stem the German attack, but to defeat Hitler, he needed America's help. With America in the war, Hitler's fate would be sealed. "He repeatedly said," Hopkins wrote, "that the President and the United States had more influence with the common people of the world today than any other force." Hopkins related these sentiments to Roosevelt, who was always susceptible to such flattery, even when it came from a ruthless tyrant. For now, what mattered was that a grand alliance had come into being, and its linchpin, the central component holding the whole architecture together, was Roosevelt himself.[80]

X

No one understood Roosevelt's centrality more than Winston Churchill. As he prepared for a secret summit with his American counterpart, Churchill spoke in reverent tones of the president. Harry Hopkins later chuckled that "You'd have thought Winston was being carried up into the heavens to meet God!" But American support in the war against Hitler was the lifeline that had kept Britain afloat, and Churchill naturally wanted to transform the Anglo-American relationship into a fighting alliance. On August 4, Churchill slipped out of London on a train for Thurso, on the northern tip of Scotland, and then embarked on a destroyer that bore him across to Scapa Flow and the waiting battleship HMS *Prince of Wales*. His destination was Placentia Bay, off the coast of Newfoundland, where he would meet Roosevelt at a shipboard rendezvous. Along for the ride was Harry Hopkins, who had returned from his Moscow mission thoroughly exhausted. After a long rest in his cabin, Hopkins revived and spent the Atlantic crossing writing up his notes on the Moscow trip and playing backgammon with a doggedly competitive Churchill.[81]

In Washington, Roosevelt engaged in some good-natured subterfuge to keep the Atlantic conference a secret from the press—and presumably from German submarines, too. On August 3, he left the White House by train for a widely publicized fishing trip off Cape Cod. He boarded the presidential

FDR and Churchill on HMS *Prince of Wales*, observed by Admiral Ernest J. King and Admiral Harold Stark of the U.S. Navy.
Imperial War Museum, UK

yacht *Potomac* at New London, Connecticut, and stood out into Long Island Sound, where he was whisked onto the fast cruiser USS *Augusta*. The *Potomac*, still flying the presidential flag, carried on through Cape Cod Canal; three figures impersonating Roosevelt, Stephen Early, and General "Pa" Watson could be seen by the curious public casually chatting on deck. Meanwhile the *Augusta* sped northeast toward the naval station at Argentia, a base that came into American hands as part of the destroyers-for-bases deal. On August 9, as Churchill steamed into the bay aboard the *Prince of Wales* and passed the *Augusta*, the president stood at attention. The national anthems, *God Save the King* and *Star-Spangled Banner*, rippled out across the green water. Churchill hastened on board the *Augusta* to greet a waiting Roosevelt. "At last, we've gotten together," said FDR as he shook Churchill's hand. And with that clasp, an alliance was born.[82]

Three days of conversations followed. Churchill hoped to win a firm commitment from Roosevelt for a joint Anglo-American statement to Japan that any further advance in Southeast Asia—Churchill justly feared for Singapore, Hong Kong, Burma, even India—would be met by war. Roosevelt demurred but agreed to send a unilateral statement of warning in tones only

Beneath the guns, FDR and Churchill set a course for war.
FDR Library

slightly less belligerent than Churchill wished. The service chiefs met and confirmed generally the policy they were already following of concentrating their efforts against Germany while remaining on the defensive in the Pacific. And two diplomats, Sumner Welles of the State Department and Sir Alexander Cadogan of the Foreign Office, honed and polished a proposed statement that the president and prime minister would issue at the close of the meeting.[83]

With their exquisitely sensitive feel for politics and public gestures, the two leaders arranged for a Christian church service on Sunday, August 10, that gathered hundreds of men in uniform arrayed on the deck of the *Prince of Wales* beneath its imposing fourteen-inch guns. There they sang hymns known to both Roosevelt and Churchill since childhood, hymns that drew on a common heritage of shared values, ideals, and faith: "Onward Christian Soldiers," "O God Our Help in Ages Past," and the naval hymn "Eternal Father, Strong to Save." Nothing could more clearly demonstrate the affinity between Roosevelt and Churchill, and between the United States and Britain.

Everyone understood, and deeply felt, the significance of the Argentia meeting. Churchill explained to the British people upon his return that the meeting of the two leaders "symbolizes, in a form and manner which everyone can understand in every land and in every clime, the deep underlying unities which stir and, at decisive moments, rule the English-speaking peoples throughout the world. Would it be presumptuous for me to say that it symbolizes something even more majestic, namely, the marshalling of the good forces of the world against the evil forces which are now so formidable and triumphant, and which have cast their cruel spell over the whole of Europe and a large part of Asia?"[84]

Roosevelt was not quite so florid in speaking of the meeting. Keenly aware that talk of secret understandings had long been a charge leveled at the statesmen from the era of the First World War, he strove to characterize the Atlantic conference as a general discussion related to Lend-Lease arrangements. As for the joint statement that came from the meeting, FDR called it a "declaration of principles . . . which is worthwhile for our type of civilization to seek." Yet it was of course much more than that.[85]

The Atlantic Charter, issued to the press on August 14, 1941, was both a statement of war aims and a vision of a future world that offered a sharp contrast with the New Order the fascists were building. Against the one-party state, the jackboot and the concentration camp, Roosevelt and Churchill set down eight principles for a future based on international law, free trade, and basic human rights. The two nations stipulated that they would seek no territorial conquests for themselves and would encourage the principles of national sovereignty and democratic self-government. They would work toward open and equitable trade arrangements, freedom of the seas, and promote social and economic security for all. And "after the final destruction of Nazi tyranny," they would dedicate their nations to maintain a peaceful world order, starting with the total disarmament of any states that "threaten aggression outside of their frontiers." The Atlantic Charter reflected many compromises. Neither the United States nor Britain, after all, practiced free trade in 1941, while the language about "the right of all peoples to choose the form of government under which they will live" might fatally undermine the foundations of the British empire.[86]

Such talk of a future world might have seemed incompatible too with the terrible crisis of the moment. In August 1941, Hitler and his fascist allies still held Europe by the throat and were closing in on Moscow; German submarines knifed silently through the cold Atlantic, sending countless merchant ships and their lifesaving cargoes to the bottom; Japanese forces, already occupying Korea, Manchuria, and much of coastal China, were set to pounce on Indochina, Thailand, Burma, the Dutch East Indies, and the Philippines. In 1941, the democracies could muster against these vast imperial conglomerations only promises of a better world.

But the Second World War was at its heart a war of ideas, and Roosevelt understood this intuitively. His great challenge had been to explain to a skeptical, war-weary nation why America must help defeat fascism, and what the people had a right to expect in return for their sacrifice. In the preceding few months, in his own fashion, he had erected four pillars that would provide the supporting architecture for the new world he wanted to build. The United States, through Lend-Lease, would serve as the arsenal of democracy, lashing its great industrial power to the cause of anti-fascism. The Four Freedoms gave hope to occupied peoples around the world that their long night would not last forever, and that help was on the way. Roosevelt's recent step, belated and tentative, to bring racial equality to the American workplace foretold of a civil rights revolution that the war would accelerate. And the Atlantic Charter beckoned anti-fascist nations and peoples to join together in a common struggle for freedom and human dignity.

None of these foundations could have been envisioned in 1933, or even in 1938. Roosevelt, feeling the constant and determined prodding and encouragement of many Americans in the press, government, and in his own intimate circle of advisers and friends, chose to reconfigure America's role in the world. By August 1941, he had committed the United States to a great struggle against fascist tyranny, one he knew would demand unstinting effort and perhaps bitter loss. The precise contours and timing of America's war still lay in the future, but here, along the gentle mist-shrouded hills of the coast of Newfoundland, Roosevelt set a course that would carry the country toward the sound of the guns.

ACKNOWLEDGMENTS

In early 2020, as I set out on what would become a long journey into the history of American anti-fascism and democratic politics, the world lurched into the global COVID pandemic, forcing many institutions, including schools, universities, and libraries, to close. These closures presented scholars with great professional and personal difficulties. At a time when America's own democratic political structures were coming unglued, the pandemic reminded us of our vulnerability as well as our need for fellowship and human connection in times of crisis. Over the past five years, work on this book brought me into contact with countless other historians, journalists, students, and public audiences who have all been supportive and generous. Despite the shadow that hangs over our world, these friends and colleagues brought light in a dark time.

My first tentative steps into the topic took place in a weeklong seminar with the University of Virginia Library staff, who made many suggestions about archival sources I otherwise would not have found. They also introduced me to digitized sources and collections that became essential during the pandemic closures. My sincere thanks to Judith Thomas, Keith Weimer, Molly Schwartzberg, Bryan Kasik, and Christine Slaughter.

I owe a special thanks to my colleagues and friends at the National World War II Museum in New Orleans. The Museum is national treasure. At a time when history is losing its appeal on college campuses, the Museum draws millions of enthusiastic visitors to conferences, workshops, lectures, and of course to its peerless exhibits. To my fellow Presidential Counselors at the Museum, as well as its President and CEO Emeritus Nick Mueller, President and CEO Stephen Watson, historian Rob Citino, Vice President and Chief Operating Officer James B. Williams, Vice President of Education and Access Pete Crean, Executive Director of the Jenny Craig Institute for the Study of War and Democracy Michael S. Bell, and Director of Conferences and Symposia Jeremy Collins, my sincere thanks for all you have done to support my work over the years. And to Sarah Kirksey, Senior Director of

Educational Travel, thank you for your joyful spirit and friendship over the years.

Much of the archival work for this book took place in the Franklin D. Roosevelt Library in Hyde Park, New York, and in the manuscript collections of the Library of Congress in Washington, D.C. I am extremely grateful for the professionalism of the staff at these institutions. My thanks also to Harold Holzer for a memorable tour of FDR's New York townhouse at 47–49 East Sixty-Fifth Street. At the University of Virginia, many colleagues helped me with conversations, suggestions, and inspiration. A warm thanks to Brian Balogh, Melvyn P. Leffler, Philip Zelikow, Sarah Milov, Kyrill Kunakhovich, Grace Hale, Claudrena Harold, and to the recent chair of the History Department Tom Klubock. Ian Iverson gathered some valuable material on the interventionists held at UVA's Small Special Collections Library. For their professionalism and unfailing support, I thank Karly Kovalcik, Latricia Washington, and Carol Anne Brown. I am fortunate indeed to share a workplace with such fine, generous people. I also benefited from the insightful comments of Nicole Hemmer of Vanderbilt University, who read many draft pages. Brooke Blower, a leading scholar of the transnational history of the interwar years, helped me shape and improve the introduction. Three outstanding scholars and close friends gave the manuscript a thorough "scrub" in May 2025, offering excellent advice at a crucial stage of the writing process. With characteristic generosity, Beth Bailey, David Farber, and Andrew Preston took time away from their own commitments to share their wisdom and experience. I am forever grateful.

I was enormously fortunate to find myself at two superb research institutions as I worked on this book. In the academic year 2023–24, the Rothermere American Institute at Oxford University, skillfully led by Adam I. P. Smith, offered me access to a fabulous library and an opportunity to present my work and hone my arguments. And in the fall of 2025, I completed the book at the extraordinary American Academy in Berlin, where I found a cohort of brilliant fellows with whom I spent four months in deep and sustained conversation. The Academy is superbly run by President Daniel Benjamin, Christian U. Diehl, and Ana Ramic. I am deeply grateful to them and the superb and attentive Academy staff for helping me push the book across the finish line.

My agent for the past twenty-five years, Susan Rabiner, has been an invaluable counselor and advocate. At Simon & Schuster, Bob Bender helped me shape the book's central idea, and Jonathan Jao has brought it to life. I'm lucky to work with such experienced and supportive editors. Jennie Miller expertly guided the manuscript through production. My thanks to Gabriel Moss for his speedy work on the maps.

To Liz Varon, my most careful reader, most helpful critic, funniest friend, and lead guitarist: all my love. And to my brilliant and delightful sisters, Lucy and Effie: Like many of the courageous women in this book, you have never been afraid to speak up and speak out. This one's for you.

NOTES

ABBREVIATIONS

APP:	American Presidency Project, online resource at UC-Santa Barbara
BAA:	*Baltimore Afro-American*
CD:	*Chicago Defender*
CT:	*Chicago Tribune*
DBFP:	Documents on British Foreign Policy
DHFDRP:	*Documentary History of the Franklin D. Roosevelt Presidency*
FDR&FA:	Franklin D. Roosevelt and Foreign Affairs documentary collection
FDRL:	Franklin D. Roosevelt Library
FRUS:	*Foreign Relations of the United States*
LAT:	*Los Angeles Times*
LOC:	Library of Congress
MG:	*Manchester Guardian* (UK)
NARA:	National Archives and Records Administration
NMAH:	National Museum of American History
NYAN:	*New York Amsterdam News*
NYHT:	*New York Herald Tribune*
NYT:	*New York Times*
OF:	Official File, FDRL
PC:	*Pittsburgh Courier*
PP&A:	*Public Papers and Addresses of Franklin Delano Roosevelt*
PSF:	President's Secretary's File, FDRL
SEP:	*Saturday Evening Post*
SFE:	*San Francisco Examiner*
WP:	*Washington Post*

Prologue: No Lone Island

1. Papers of the President of the University of Virginia, Office Administrative Files, Accession #RG-2/1/2.491, IV, Special Collections, box 6, University of Virginia Library. "Once More U.S. Future Is at Stake, Roosevelt Tells U. of Va. Graduating Class," *WP*, June 11, 1940; "Our Help Pledged," *NYT*, June 11, 1940. Details on the scene in "Sidelights on Roosevelt's Talk," *WP*, June 11, 1940.
2. Robert Sherwood, speech at Naval War College, April 28, 1954, Sherwood Papers, box 63, Houghton Library, Harvard University.
3. The view of Roosevelt as an internationalist who was shackled by isolationist opinion is most insistently made by Robert Dallek. Part 1 of his book is puzzlingly titled *The Internationalist as Nationalist* and part 2 is called *The Internationalist as Isolationist*, suggesting FDR up to 1938 was engaged merely in a tactical retreat from a firm foundation of active anti-fascism. FDR, Dallek writes, was compelled "to align himself with the current nationalistic mood," but his silence on the threat of fascism "belied his true feelings." *Franklin D. Roosevelt and American Foreign Policy, 1932–1945* (Oxford, 1995), 20. Alonzo Hamby sees FDR as being forced to acquiesce in the isolationist sentiments of the country; "he had little choice." He knew terrible times were coming, but "the need to keep it private was urgent." *Man of Destiny: FDR and the Making of the American Century* (Basic, 2015), 286–87. For James MacGregor Burns, FDR "seemed to float almost help-

lessly on the flood tide of isolationism"; he was privately an internationalist, but in public "he often talked, in short, like an isolationist." *Roosevelt: The Lion and the Fox* (Harcourt, Brace, 1956), 262. Eric Rauchway argues that FDR saw Hitler's rise "with the greatest alarm" and as a "significant threat from the start." *Winter War: Hoover, Roosevelt, and the First Clash over the New Deal* (Basic Books, 2018), 185–87. William E. Kinsella Jr. writes that FDR "had always been eager to halt the fascist advance. . . . He anticipated the coming storm." Roosevelt "searched in vain for a response to the fascist challenge. He was constrained by isolationist sentiment, neutrality restrictions, and the appeasement solutions offered by other nations." *Leadership in Isolation: FDR and the Origins of the Second World War* (Schenkman, 1978), 209, 210, 214. Wayne Cole believes that FDR sacrificed any activism in world affairs to advance his domestic priorities. *Roosevelt and the Isolationists, 1932–1945* (University of Nebraska Press, 1983), 7–10. A much less-forgiving view is Arnold A. Offner, *American Appeasement: United States Foreign Policy and Germany, 1933–1938* (Harvard University Press, 1969). Frederic W. Marks III pulled no punches, either, saying of FDR that "the keynote of his approach to Hitler beginning in 1933 was appeasement." *Historical Journal* 28, no. 4 (1985): 969–82. Marks contends that even once FDR began to denounce fascism and autocracy, he still pursued appeasement. Donald Cameron Watt was equally pungent. See his "Chamberlain and Roosevelt: Two Appeasers," *International Journal* 28, no. 2 (1973), 185–204, and his *How War Came: The Immediate Origins of the Second World War, 1938–1939* (Pantheon, 1989), 255–70. Watt calls FDR's diplomacy in mid-1939 the work of "an inept and ignorant fool," 264.

4. In addition to Dallek, *Franklin D. Roosevelt and American Foreign Policy*, the most thorough survey of U.S. foreign policy in this period is Cole, *Roosevelt and the Isolationists*. Many works on FDR's world policies start around 1937 or 1938, as if Roosevelt's early restraint was irrelevant. See for example William L. Langer and S. Everett Gleason, *The Challenge to Isolation, 1937–1940* (Harper & Brothers, 1952) and Donald F. Drummond, *The Passing of American Neutrality, 1937–1941* (University of Michigan Press, 1955). A thoughtful book that tries to understand the sources of the shift in American foreign policy from isolationism to global activism is John Thompson, *A Sense of Power: The Roots of America's Global Role* (Cornell University Press, 2015). For an attempt to narrate this shift through the device of FDR's relationship with his ambassadors, see David McKean, *Watching Darkness Fall: FDR, His Ambassadors, and the Rise of Adolf Hitler* (St. Martin's Press, 2021).

5. Fascism is an umbrella term beneath which several variants of radical ethno-nationalism, including Nazism, can be grouped. This book relies on the broad definition as articulated by historian Robert Paxton: Fascism is "a form of political behavior marked by obsessive preoccupation with community decline, humiliation, or victimhood and by compensatory cults of unity, energy, and purity, in which a mass-based party of committed nationalist militants, working in uneasy but effective collaboration with traditional elites, abandons democratic liberties and pursues with redemptive violence and without ethical or legal restraints goals of internal cleansing and external expansion." Fascists took power in Germany and Italy, and Francisco Franco's regime in Spain was perceived as fascist by those who fought against it. There were fascist parties in many European states that never took power, but looked to Mussolini and Hitler as role models. There were fascist sympathizers in the United States in the 1920s and 1930s who expressed their particular ideas in an American vernacular and shared in the glorification of white Christians; they, too, directed violence and hatred toward Jews, Communists, and non-white people. Paxton suggests that scholars should consider the "mobilizing passions" of fascists rather than search for some fixed, fully articulated political ideology. Robert Paxton, *The Anatomy of Fascism* (Alfred A. Knopf, 2004), 41, 218–20. For three essential scholarly essays on the question of American fascism, see Joseph Fronczak, "The Fascist Game: Transnational Political Transmission and the Genesis of the U.S. Modern Right," *Journal of American History* 105, no. 3 (2018): 563–88; Olivier Burtin, "Fascism Has an American History, Too," *Reviews in American History* 49 (2021): 494–520; and Richard Steigmann-Gall, "Star-Spangled Fascism: American Interwar Political Extremism in Comparative Perspective," *Social History* 42, no. 1 (2017): 94–119. There is also now an excellent collection of essays on the topic: Gavriel David Rosenfeld et al., eds., *Fascism in America: Past and Present* (Cambridge University Press, 2023). On the political use and abuse of the term, see Bruce Kuklick, *Fascism Comes to America: A Century of Obsession in Politics and Culture* (University of Chicago Press, 2022). Scholars of fascism in America are indebted to the classic text by Leo P. Ribuffo, *The Old Christian Right: The Protestant Right from the Great Depression to the Cold War* (Temple University Press, 1983).

6. On FDR's description of Willkie as a fascist, see Harold Ickes, The *Secret Diary of Harold Ickes*, vol. 3 (Simon & Schuster, 1954), 221, 268, 290. For the campaign, see comments by Democratic Party national chairman Edward J. Flynn, reported in "Rule by Wall St. Held Willkie Aim," *NYT*, Sept. 6, 1940, and comments by Gov. Herbert Lehman in "Willkie Train Stoned in Michigan; He Scores Lehman, Gives Job Plan," *NYT*, Oct. 2, 1940. Dorothy Thompson wrote that "the Axis desires the defeat of Roosevelt" in a column titled "The Axis and the Campaign," *WP*, Oct. 14, 1940. Roosevelt connected foreign threats with domestic fascists explicitly in his "Address at Dedication of Great Smoky Mountains National Park," Sept. 2, 1940, Master Speech File, box 52, FDRL.
7. An important exception is Johnstone, *Against Immediate Evil: American Internationalism and the Four Freedoms on the Eve of World War II* (Cornell University Press, 2014). And there is work on the internationalization of society, such as Glenda Sluga, *Internationalism in the Age of Nationalism* (University of Pennsylvania Press, 2013). An excellent survey of the field is Erez Manela, "International Society as a Historical Subject," *Diplomatic History* 44, no. 2 (2020): 184–209.
8. Of late, the terms "isolationism" and "isolationist" have been discredited by some historians, who see them as propagandistic epithets designed by Roosevelt and his supporters to tarnish the legitimate cause of anti-war activism. These historians prefer the term "anti-interventionist" to describe critics of Roosevelt's world policy. The leading historian of "anti-interventionism" is Justus D. Doenecke, author of *In Danger Undaunted : The Anti-Interventionist Movement of 1940–1941 as Revealed in the Papers of the America First Committee* (Hoover Institution Press, 1990) and *Storm on the Horizon: The Challenge to American Intervention, 1939–1941* (Rowman & Littlefield, 2004). I take a different view from Doenecke, since some significant critics of Roosevelt's foreign policy were not "anti-interventionist" at all. Take, for example, Charles Lindbergh. He was pro-fascist and a champion of hemispheric defense, that is, he favored building a cone of naval and airpower that would completely dominate the Western Hemisphere from the North to the South Poles, including the Pacific Ocean as far as Hawaii. "From Alaska to Labrador, from the Hawaiian Islands to Bermuda, from Canada to South America," as he put it in October 1939, U.S. power must dominate. He believed in building U.S. air bases across the Western Hemisphere and in creating a closed-off American economic lebensraum in this portion of the globe. He could hardly therefore be called an anti-interventionist or a pacifist. Nor was he neutral about fascism. He accepted German domination of Europe. He did not want to go to war against Nazi Germany because he believed Hitler was defending an embattled white Western civilization from destruction by Communism, Jews, and non-white people from Asia and Africa. He repeatedly urged U.S. reconciliation with Hitler. To label him as "anti-interventionist" or "neutral" serves to normalize a man who placed himself at the center of an imagined racial conflict that spanned the globe. The same could be said about Father Charles Coughlin, who was not so much an "anti-interventionist" as a theorist, apologist, and active defender of fascist antisemitism *in the world*. Can his proselytizing on behalf of Francisco Franco, for example, be called "anti-interventionist"? Should his cheerleading for the Salazar dictatorship in Portugal be considered "anti-interventionist"? When he cribbed words from the speeches of Joseph Goebbels, was he demonstrating "neutrality" in the great global struggle of the 1930s? Certainly not. At the same time, there were many in the anti-war movement who favored international action and collective security, and might be called interventionists: Carrie Chapman Catt, for example, was a leader of the peace bloc in America who believed in the League of Nations, believed in the use of boycotts and sanctions against aggressors, and eventually accepted the need for the United States to rearm in order to deter the fascists. Finally, if advocates of the term "anti-interventionist" define it narrowly to mean only opposition to sending combat troops to Europe, then FDR was anti-interventionist until late 1941. Clearly, the term "anti-interventionist" obscures and confuses more than it clarifies. Thus, following Charles Kupchan, I use the term "isolationism" to describe a body of thought that (1) sought to block American military and diplomatic cooperation with other states, (2) insisted on American freedom to act unilaterally without regard to the interests of any other state, and (3) rejected any policy of confrontation with foreign dictators and authoritarian militarists. Defined in this specific way, "isolationism" fits the attitudes of many people in 1930s America (including Lindbergh, Father Coughlin, and Senate pacifists and neutralists like William Borah or Hiram Johnson), though as we shall see, its appeal *diminished* as the decade wore on, despite the active lobbying campaign of the America First Committee. This use of the term comports with the work of Wayne Cole. See *Roosevelt and the Isolationists*, 6–7. The historian Brooke Blower has argued

in an important essay that American political culture of the 1930s is probably too complex to be adequately named by any single term. Though she proposes "neutrality" as the term that most capaciously covers anti-war thought in America, she writes persuasively that "binaries" such as isolationism and interventionism "cannot encompass the confounding issues Americans faced during these years." See "From Isolationism to Neutrality: A New Framework for Understanding American Political Culture, 1919–1941," *Diplomatic History* 38, no. 2 (2014): 345–76, quotation from p. 353. A recent effort to place isolationism at the heart of the American diplomatic tradition is by Charles Kupchan, *Isolationism: A History of America's Efforts to Shield Itself from the World* (Oxford University Press, 2020).

9. One of the most insightful books on the FDR-ER relationship is Doris Kearns Goodwin, *No Ordinary Time: Franklin and Eleanor Roosevelt—The Home Front in World War II* (Simon & Schuster, 1994), which carefully draws on the extensive documentary record at the FDR Library at Hyde Park. Two other works on Eleanor Roosevelt are essential: the three-volume life by Blanche Wiesen Cook, *Eleanor Roosevelt* (Penguin, 1992–2016), and David Michaelis, *Eleanor* (Simon & Schuster, 2020). For discussion of FDR's "official family" and how it functioned, see Frank Costigliola, "Broken Circle: The Isolation of Franklin D. Roosevelt in World War II," *Diplomatic History* 32, no. 5 (2008): 677–718. The sources relating to the members of this inside circle are extensive. On Morgenthau, the essential source is John Morton Blum, *From the Morgenthau Diaries*, 3 vols. (Houghton Mifflin, 1959–1967), which is not a diary at all but a narrative history that quotes heavily from the diaries. Morgenthau's voluminous diaries have been digitized by the FDR Library. Harold Ickes kept and then published an extraordinarily detailed diary that almost serves as an official record of the inner workings of the administration: Ickes, *Secret Diary*, 3 vols. On Hopkins, the dual biography by Robert Sherwood is excellent: *Roosevelt and Hopkins: An Intimate History* (Harper and Brothers, 1950), and can be supplemented by David L. Roll, *The Hopkins Touch: Harry Hopkins and the Forging of the Alliance to Defeat Hitler* (Oxford University Press, 2013). Stimson's autobiography was curiously written in the third person (with help from MacGeorge Bundy): *On Active Service in Peace and War* (Harper & Brothers, 1948). Stimson's extensive diary has been digitized by the Yale University archives. For insight about Frankfurter, an essential source is Max Freedman, ed., *Roosevelt and Frankfurter: Their Correspondence, 1928–1945* (Little, Brown, 1967), which shows Frankfurter growing bolder in encouraging FDR's anti-fascism. For insight into two key New Dealers, Ben Cohen and Thomas Corcoran, see Joseph P. Lash, *Dealers and Dreamers: A New Look at the New Deal* (Doubleday, 1988). Samuel Rosenman wrote an insightful memoir: *Working with Roosevelt* (Harper & Brothers, 1952). Though Frances Perkins did not shape foreign policy in a significant way, her memoir of the White House years is invaluable: *The Roosevelt I Knew* (Viking, 1946). Harriet Hyman Alonso wrote a useful biography of four-time Pulitzer Prize winner and key speechwriter for FDR: *Robert E. Sherwood: The Playwright in Peace and War* (University of Massachusetts Press, 2007). The life of Archibald MacLeish reveals the growing boldness of internationalist opinion and the departure from interwar pacifism. See Scott Donaldson, *Archibald MacLeish: An American Life* (Houghton Mifflin, 1992).

10. Hull's memoirs are ponderous and self-serving. *The Memoirs of Cordell Hull*, 2 vols. (Macmillan, 1948). Sumner Welles produced two laudatory studies of FDR: *Seven Decisions That Shaped History* (Harper & Brothers, 1950), and *The Time for Decision* (Harper & Brothers, 1944). Invaluable insight on Welles is related in Irwin F. Gellman, *Secret Affairs: Franklin Roosevelt, Cordell Hull, and Sumner Welles* (Johns Hopkins University Press, 1995). Bullitt, who began with such early promise only to end in obscurity and failure, is best followed in the extensive letters he wrote to FDR: Orville H. Bullitt, ed., *For the President: Correspondence between Franklin D. Roosevelt and William C. Bullitt* (Houghton Mifflin, 1972). Like all the Kennedys, Joseph P. Kennedy has attracted much attention. His letters are revealing (and damning): Amanda Smith, ed., *Hostage to Fortune: The Letters of Joseph P. Kennedy* (Viking, 2001). His life is best handled by David Nasaw, *The Patriarch: The Remarkable Life and Turbulent Times of Joseph P. Kennedy* (Penguin, 2012). The sad tale of William Dodd became well-known after the somewhat unfair book by Erik Larson, *In the Garden of Beasts: Love, Terror, and an American Family in Hitler's Berlin* (Crown, 2011). Larson treats Dodd as a fool, but Larson's book ends much too soon, and readers can see Dodd evolve into a stern critic of the Nazis in his diary: *Ambassador Dodd's Diary, 1933–1938* (Harcourt, Brace, 1941). On Claude G. Bowers, see *My Life: The Memoirs of Claude Bowers* (Simon & Schuster, 1962). George Marshall's life and thought were painstakingly studied by Forrest C. Pogue in his five-volume life: *George C. Marshall* (Viking Press, 1963–1968). Marshall's papers are available

in six volumes edited by Larry I. Bland and Sharon Ritenour Stevens, *The Papers of George Catlett Marshall* (Johns Hopkins University Press, 1981–1996).

11. Grace Tully, *FDR: My Boss* (Charles Scribner's Sons, 1949), 76–77, 293. Scholarship on how FDR used the press to serve his policy goals includes Steven Casey, *Cautious Crusade: Franklin D. Roosevelt, American Public Opinion, and the War against Nazi Germany* (Oxford University Press, 2001); Michael G. Carew, *The Power to Persuade: FDR, the Newsmagazines, and Going to War, 1939–1941* (University Press of America, 2005); Richard W. Steele, *Free Speech in the Good War* (St. Martin's Press, 1999), and his *Propaganda in an Open Society: The Roosevelt Administration and the Media, 1933–1941* (Greenwood Press, 1985). On the role of the British in influencing U.S. public opinion, see Nicholas J. Cull, *Selling War: The British Propaganda Campaign Against American "Neutrality" in World War II* (Oxford University Press, 1995). For a fresh and important investigation of the major publishers who favored isolationism (and were often fascist apologists), see Kathryn S. Olmsted, *The Newspaper Axis: Six Barons Who Enabled Hitler* (Yale University Press, 2022). On Hearst's admiration of Hitler, see his 1934 interview, reprinted in the *Jewish Daily Bulletin* of Philadelphia, "W.R. Hearst Has Kind Words for Hitler—but None for Jews," Sept. 26, 1934.
12. Two excellent works that recover the world of these correspondents are Deborah Cohen, *Last Call at the Hotel Imperial: The Reporters Who Took on a World at War* (Penguin, 2023), and Nancy F. Cott, *Fighting Words: The Bold American Journalists Who Brought the World Home Between the Wars* (Basic, 2020). Andrew Nagorski offers a vivid treatment of the German scene as American correspondents encountered it in the 1930s: *Hitlerland: American Eyewitnesses to the Nazi Rise to Power* (Simon & Schuster, 2012).
13. The excellent and lively biography by Peter Kurth, *American Cassandra: The Life of Dorothy Thompson* (Little, Brown, 1990), remains authoritative, but Thompson's life and impact badly need more attention from scholars. John Gunther, "A Blue-Eyed Tornado," *New York Herald Tribune Magazine*, Jan. 13, 1935; Ronald Steel, *Walter Lippmann and the American Century* (Little, Brown, 1980), 360.
14. Dorothy Thompson, *I Saw Hitler* (Farrar & Rinehart, 1932), vi. Mowrer wrote his own account of his years overseas: *Triumph and Turmoil: A Personal History of Our Time* (Weybright & Talley, 1968). Martha Gellhorn has attracted many biographers, but the best place to encounter this luminous writer is in her letters: Janet Somerville, ed., *Yours, for Probably Always: Martha Gellhorn's Letters of Love & War, 1930–1949* (Firefly Books, 2019), and Caroline Moorehead, ed., *Selected Letters of Martha Gellhorn* (Henry Holt, 2006). Sigrid Schultz did not write a memoir, but she showed where her heart was in *Germany Will Try It Again* (Reynal & Hitchcock, 1944). On the *Chicago Tribune* publisher, see Richard Norton Smith, *The Colonel: The Life and Legend of Robert R. McCormick, 1880–1955* (Houghton Mifflin, 1997).
15. Daniel Victor, "She Was the Times's First Female Pulitzer Winner," *NYT*, Apr. 17, 2018.
16. On the shortcomings of the *New York Times*, see Deborah E. Lipstadt, *Beyond Belief: The American Press and the Coming of the Holocaust, 1933–1945* (Free Press, 1986). On key editors, see Sara Alpern, *Freda Kirchwey: A Woman of the Nation* (Harvard University Press, 1987); Alan Brinkley, *The Publisher: Henry Luce and His American Century* (Alfred A. Knopf, 2010); and Hamilton Fish Armstrong, *Peace and Counterpeace: From Wilson to Hitler: Memoirs of Hamilton Fish Armstrong* (Harper & Row, 1971). Murrow has received much attention, but readers can start with his own words: Edward R. Murrow, *In Search of Light: The Broadcasts of Edward R. Murrow, 1938–1961* (Alfred A. Knopf, 1967). Shirer wrote extensively about Europe's crisis years. Especially insightful is William L. Shirer, *Berlin Diary: The Journal of a Foreign Correspondent, 1934–1941* (Little, Brown, 1941). His magnum opus, based on captured German documents, is *The Rise and Fall of the Third Reich: A History of Nazi Germany* (Simon & Schuster, 1960).
17. These groups have received good treatments in Johnstone, *Against Immediate Evil*, and Mark Lincoln Chadwin, *The Hawks of World War II* (University of North Carolina Press, 1968). The public lobbying groups receive attention in Lynn Olson, *Those Angry Days: Roosevelt, Lindbergh, and America's Fight over World War II, 1939–1941* (Random House, 2013).
18. Standard and well-crafted biographies include the multivolume studies of Frank Friedel, *Franklin D. Roosevelt*, 4 vols. (Little, Brown, 1952), and Kenneth S. Davis, *FDR*, 4 vols. (Putnam, 1972–2000), neither of which is especially strong on foreign policy. Jean Edward Smith, *FDR* (Random House, 2007), combines thoroughness with lively narrative, but is surprisingly weak on world affairs. Robert Dallek's one-volume account, *Franklin D. Roosevelt: A Political Life* (Penguin, 2017),

gives limited attention to public debates on world politics, sticking closely to FDR and his advisers. H. W. Brands, *Traitor to His Class: The Privileged Life and Radical Presidency of Franklin D. Roosevelt* (Doubleday, 2008), though lively, draws mainly on previously published biographies. The somewhat dated but compelling works of James MacGregor Burns, unlike so many later biographies, do not hesitate to criticize: *Roosevelt: The Lion and the Fox* (Harcourt Brace, 1956), and *Roosevelt: The Soldier of Freedom* (Harcourt Brace Jovanovich, 1970). The biographical studies that are probably the most enduring and insightful on FDR's emergence and the early thinking behind the New Deal are Arthur M. Schlesinger Jr., *The Age of Roosevelt*, 3 vols. (Houghton Mifflin, 1957–1960); and Rexford G. Tugwell, *The Democratic Roosevelt* (Penguin Books, 1957), a true gem of a book.

19. Dallek's *Roosevelt and American Foreign Policy* is a heroic effort to touch on every foreign policy issue over a twelve-year presidency, but far too much domestic politics and public debate goes missing. The best one-volume work remains Cole, *Roosevelt and the Isolationists*. Langer and Gleason, *The Challenge to Isolation*, is insightful but one-dimensional, failing to address the domestic dimension of foreign policy. Good short works that illuminate the last two years before the U.S. entered the war are valuable: Waldo Heinrichs, *Threshold of War: Franklin D. Roosevelt and American Entry into World War II* (Oxford University Press, 1988); David Reynolds, *From Munich to Pearl Harbor: Roosevelt's America and the Origins of the Second World War* (Ivan Dee, 2001); Robert A. Divine, *The Reluctant Belligerent: American Entry into World War II* (John Wiley & Sons, 1965); and Susan Dunn, *A Blueprint for War: FDR and the Hundred Days That Mobilized America* (Yale University Press, 2018).
20. Olson, *Those Angry Days*; Susan Dunn, *1940: FDR, Willkie, Lindbergh, Hitler—the Election amid the Storm* (Yale University Press, 2013); H. W. Brands, *America First: Roosevelt vs. Lindbergh in the Shadow of War* (Doubleday, 2024); Paul M. Sparrow, *Awakening the Spirit of America: FDR's War of Words with Charles Lindbergh—and the Battle to Save Democracy* (Simon & Schuster, 2024).
21. An excellent exploration of how Americans were deeply entwined in Europe and the world in the interwar years is Brooke Blower, *Americans in a World at War: Intimate Histories from the Crash of Pan Am's Yankee Clipper* (Oxford University Press, 2023).
22. An effort to assess Roosevelt's changing views of Europe from his early years in the Wilson administration onward is John L. Harper, *American Visions of Europe: Franklin D. Roosevelt, George F. Kennan, and Dean C. Acheson* (Cambridge University Press, 1994), 7–131. An engaging and perceptive study by a journalist who watched him in action over many years is John Gunther, *Roosevelt in Retrospect: A Profile in History* (Harper & Brothers, 1950).
23. For the term, see Warren F. Kimball, *The Juggler: Franklin Roosevelt as Wartime Statesman* (Princeton University Press, 1994), 7: "You know I am a juggler," FDR said to Henry Morgenthau. "I never let my right hand know what my left hand does."
24. Ira Katznelson has written an extraordinarily rich and insightful study of the many moral compromises that lie at the heart of the New Deal. See *Fear Itself: The New Deal and the Origins of Our Time* (Liveright, 2013). A pathbreaking work connecting war and diplomacy to the goal of "security" both at home and abroad is Andrew Preston, *Total Defense: The New Deal and the Invention of National Security* (Harvard University Press, 2025).
25. At least one scholar believes FDR deliberately and deceptively pursued a permanent global military ascendancy from 1940 on: Stephen Wertheim, *Tomorrow the World: The Birth of U.S. Global Supremacy* (Harvard University Press, 2022).
26. FDR's immensely important role in shaping the modern FBI is outlined in detail in Beverly Gage, *G-Man: J. Edgar Hoover and the Making of the American Century* (Viking, 2022).

Chapter 1: The Most Magnetic Personality

1. "F. D. Roosevelt Has Infant Paralysis," *New York Herald*, Sept. 16, 1921. Another paper reported that "Mr. Roosevelt has regained control of his legs," *New York Tribune*, Sept. 16, 1921. "F. D. Roosevelt Ill of Poliomyelitis," *NYT*, Sept. 16, 1921. The same AP story ran in *CT* and *WP*, Sept. 16, 1921. Also "269 Poliomyelitis Cases Here in a Year," *NYT*, Sept. 18, 1921. For broader context, see Naomi Rogers, *Dirt and Disease: Polio Before FDR* (Rutgers University Press, 1996).
2. On FDR's illness and efforts to strengthen himself, see Geoffrey C. Ward, *A First-Class Temperament: The Emergence of Franklin Roosevelt, 1905–1928* (Random House, 1989), 600–648; Smith, *FDR*, 187–212; Ross T. McIntire, *White House Physician* (Putnam, 1946), 30–44; Frank Freidel,

Franklin D. Roosevelt: A Rendezvous with Destiny (Little, Bown, 1990), 41–52; Brands, *Traitor*, 142–97; and Hugh Gallagher, *FDR's Splendid Deception* (Dodd, Mead, 1985), 19–27. For a personal account by his son, see James Roosevelt, "My Father, F.D.R.," *SEP*, Oct. 24, 1959.

3. "Smith, Confident, Says He Is Unable to See Dark Horse," *WP*, June 21, 1924.
4. Reminiscences of Frances Perkins, Columbia Oral History Project, Columbia University; N. O. Messenger, "Smith Accorded Wild Acclaim Following Nominating Speech," and "Franklin D. Roosevelt, Crippled, Hailed as He Nominates Smith," both in the *Evening Star* (Washington, D.C.), June 26, 1924. The friend who recalled "the long hour" was Marion Dickerman, a suffragist, teacher, and Eleanor Roosevelt's close companion, in Kenneth Davis, *Invincible Summer: An Intimate Portrait of the Roosevelts Based on the Recollections of Marion Dickerman* (Atheneum, 1974), 30–31.
5. Reminiscences of Frances Perkins, Columbia Oral History Project, Columbia University; "Party Turning to Roosevelt as Sole Hope," *NYHT*, July 1, 1924.
6. Frank Freidel, *Franklin D. Roosevelt, Vol. 2: The Ordeal* (Little, Brown, 1954), 180; Kenneth Davis, *FDR: The Beckoning of Destiny, 1882–1928* (G. P. Putnam's Sons, 1972), 757. The scene in Madison Square Garden, as well as the preceding period, is beautifully rendered in Ward, *First-Class Temperament*, 690–99. See also James Roosevelt and Sidney Shalett, *Affectionately, FDR* (Harcourt, Brace, 1959), 204–6; and Reminiscences of Frances Perkins, Columbia Oral History Project, Columbia University.
7. In addition to the excellent treatments of FDR's early years by Ward, Smith, Brands, and Freidel, the older biography by Burns, *Roosevelt: The Lion and the Fox*, is especially shrewd on FDR's political career up to 1928, esp. 3–104. For details of family life, see the admiring tribute by Joseph Alsop, *FDR, 1882–1945: A Centenary Remembrance* (Viking, 1982). The FDR quotation is in Perkins, *The Roosevelt I Knew*, 316.
8. On James and his political leanings, see Davis, *FDR: Beckoning*, 46–48, 62–63, 93–101.
9. Alfred B. Rollins Jr., *Roosevelt and Howe* (Alfred A. Knopf, 1962).
10. For the evolution of the Democratic Party in the decades before FDR's rise, see Douglas B. Craig, *After Wilson: The Struggle for the Democratic Party, 1920–1934* (University of North Carolina Press, 1992); and Jules Witcover, *Party of the People: A History of the Democrats* (Random House, 2003). One careful observer felt that TR's legacy was often a burden for FDR, who feared he could never live up to his successful cousin. Tugwell, *The Democratic Roosevelt*, 46.
11. Alan Taylor, *American Revolutions: A Continental History, 1750–1804* (Norton, 2016), 408–11.
12. Merrill D. Peterson, "Bowers, Roosevelt, and the 'New Jefferson,'" *Virginia Quarterly Review* 34, no. 4 (1958): 530–43; and Thomas T. McAvoy, "Roosevelt: A Modern Jefferson," *Review of Politics* 7, no. 3 (1945): 270–79. FDR expressed his thoughts about running for president as early as 1907: Arthur M. Schlesinger Jr., *The Age of Roosevelt: The Crisis of the Old Order, 1919–1933* (Houghton Mifflin,1957), 330.
13. J. Simon Rofe, "'Under the Influence of Mahan': Theodore and Franklin Roosevelt and their Understanding of American National Interest," *Diplomacy and Statecraft* 19, no. 4 (2008): 732–45; Edward J. Marolda, ed., *FDR and the U.S. Navy* (St. Martin's Press, 1998).
14. Lee A. Craig, *Josephus Daniels: His Life and Times* (University of North Carolina Press, 2013).
15. For FDR's experience in the Navy Department, see Stanley Weintraub, *Young Mr. Roosevelt: FDR's Introduction to War, Politics, and Life* (Da Capo Press, 2013), 74–172. These years have been carefully examined in Davis, *FDR: Beckoning*. FDR's essay: "On Your Own Heads," *Scribner's*, 61, no. 4 (1917): 413–16.
16. For the text of Wilson's April 2, 1917, address, see Mario R. DiNunzio, *Woodrow Wilson: Essential Writings and Speeches of the Scholar-President* (New York University Press, 2006), 397–403.
17. For these intellectual links between Wilson and FDR, see Schlesinger, *Crisis of the Old Order*, 27–36.
18. The tragedy of Wilson's last two years as president and his struggle for the League is carefully discussed in John Milton Cooper, *Breaking the Heart of the World: Woodrow Wilson and the Fight for the League of Nations* (Cambridge University Press, 2001), and Cooper's *Woodrow Wilson: A Biography* (Alfred A. Knopf, 2009).
19. An excellent recent overview is Linda Gordon, *The Second Coming of the KKK: The Ku Klux Klan of the 1920s and the American Political Tradition* (Liveright, 2017), especially 163–79; and David H. Bennett, *The Party of Fear: The American Far Right from Nativism to the Militia Movement* (Vintage, 1995), 208–37. On the Johnson-Reed Act and the racist dimensions of U.S.

immigration policy, see Mae Ngai, *Impossible Subjects: Illegal Aliens and the Making of Modern America* (Princeton University Press, 2005), 16–55.

20. Floyd J. Calvin, "Ghostly Specter of the Invisible Empire Hovers over Democratic Convention," *PC*, June 28, 1924.
21. "Anti-Klan Plank Beaten by One Vote," *Evening Star*, June 29, 1924; N. O. Messenger, "War of Factions over Klan Issue Imperils Election," *Evening Star*, June 29, 1924. On the Klan's influence at the convention, see Robert K. Murray, *The 103rd Ballot: Democrats and the Disaster in Madison Square Garden* (Harper & Row, 1976), 108–64. Nationally syndicated columnist Mark Sullivan blamed the anti-Klan faction for making the Klan into a greater threat than it was: "Klan Issue Grew Out from Grave after Obsequies," *Atlanta Constitution*, June 29, 1924. "Anti-Klan Plankers Lose," *Fiery Cross*, July 4, 1924. On rallies, "Klan Rally Vents Anti-Smith Feeling, *NYT*, July 5, 1924; "Binghamton Sees Only 1,540 of Klan," *NYT*, July 5, 1924; "10,000 in Klan Parade at Little Rock," *NYT*, July 5, 1924. NAACP statement in *Cleveland Gazette*, July 12, 1924. "An Irrepressible Conflict," *NYT*, June 30, 1924.
22. Thomas G. Dyer, *Theodore Roosevelt and the Idea of Race* (Louisiana State University Press, 1980), 159–60.
23. Edwin Black, *War Against the Weak: Eugenics and America's Campaign to Create a Master Race* (Dialog Press, 2012), 99, 113–21.
24. "Infant Paralysis Starts a Cleanup," *NYT*, July 1, 1916.
25. Gallagher, *FDR's Splendid Deception*, 172. In addition, Ward, *A First-Class Temperament*, 702–9, 715–30; James Tobin, *The Man He Became: How FDR Defied Polio to Win the Presidency* (Simon & Schuster, 2013); Steven Lomazov and Eric Fettermann, *FDR's Deadly Secret* (Public Affairs, 2009).
26. Tobin, *The Man He Became*, 203.
27. Cleburne Gregory, "Franklin D. Roosevelt Will Swim to Health," *Atlanta Journal*, Oct. 26, 1924; Tobin, *The Man He Became*, 208, 219.
28. Theo Lippman Jr., *The Squire of Warm Springs: FDR in Georgia, 1924–1945* (Simon & Schuster, 1977), 91. Geoffrey Ward states that FDR at Warm Springs "was not inclined to intrude upon Southern folkways," and that in any case his own views on race were "maddeningly elusive." Beyond recounting a few racist jokes that FDR enjoyed retelling, Ward rarely discusses the subject. *First-Class Temperament*, 766.
29. Campbell Gibson and Kay Jung, "Historical Census Statistics on Population Totals by Race, 1790–1990," Population Division, Working Paper No. 56, U.S. Census Bureau, Sept. 2002, https://www.census.gov/content/dam/Census/library/working-papers/2002/demo/POP-twps0056.pdf.
30. Stewart Tolnay and E. Beck, "Lynching," *New Georgia Encyclopedia*, Jan. 26, 2007, https://www.georgiaencyclopedia.org/articles/history-archaeology/lynching/.
31. Edward Hatfield, "Segregation," *New Georgia Encyclopedia*, June 1, 2007, https://www.georgiaencyclopedia.org/articles/history-archaeology/segregation/. The data on lynching was well-known at the time of FDR's arrival in Warm Springs. In 1929, one of the leading figures in the NAACP, Walter White, published his own study based on years of carefully accumulated data: *Rope and Faggot: A Biography of Judge Lynch* (Alfred A. Knopf, 1929). On the decline in lynching, "Year Ending Shows Marked Decline in Number of Lynchings," *New Journal and Guide*, Jan. 3, 1925. On James Irwin, see "Georgians Soak Man in Gas, Burn Him Alive," *BAA*, Feb. 8, 1930; and Arthur F. Raper, *The Tragedy of Lynching* (University of North Carolina and the Southern Commission on the Study of Lynching, 1933), 6–7.
32. Turnley Walker, *Roosevelt and the Warm Springs Story* (A. A. Wyn, 1953), 23–24. On race and public health at Warm Springs, see Naomi Rogers, "Race and the Politics of Polio: Warm Springs, Tuskegee, and the March of Dimes," *American Journal of Public Health* 97, no. 5 (2007): 784–95. Two authors argue that Jim Crow has largely been erased from the record at the FDR museum at Warm Springs: John A. Lynch and Mary E. Stuckey, "'This Was His Georgia': Polio, Poverty and Public Memory at FDR's Little White House," *Howard Journal of Communications* 28, no. 4 (2017): 390–404. For further details on population and race relations in Warms Springs in the 1930s, see the application to the National Register of Historic Places made by the Eleanor Roosevelt School in Warm Springs, available at https://npgallery.nps.gov/GetAsset/80a75451-01b9-40f4-b3d7-f6dbc467387d.
33. Ward, *First-Class Temperament*, 755; "Offers Spa to Push Fight on Paralysis," *NYT*, Aug. 13, 1927; "FDR Quits Several Posts," *NYT*, Feb. 23, 1928.

34. Freidel, *The Ordeal*, 216–19, 233; "Smith Nominated for Fourth Term," *WP*, Sept. 29, 1926; "Text of Roosevelt's Democratic Keynote Speech," *NYT*, Sept. 28, 1926.
35. "Text of Keynote Speech by Claude G. Bowers," *NYT*, June 27, 1928; "Farm State Parade Started by Bowers," *NYT*, June 27, 1928.
36. "Roosevelt Named New York Governor," *NYT*, June 28, 1928; Freidel, *The Ordeal*, 231, 241–44. On FDR's view that a Democrat would most likely fail to win the presidency in 1928, Davis, *FDR: Beckoning*, 813.
37. David Farber, *Everybody Ought to Be Rich: The Life and Times of John J. Raskob, Capitalist* (Oxford University Press, 2013), 220–55.
38. *Congressional Record* (Jan. 28, 1928), 1st Session, 70th Congress, vol. 69, pt. 2, 1654–55, 1658, cited in "Warning Against the 'Roman Catholic Party': Catholicism and the 1928 Election," History Matters, http://historymatters.gmu.edu/d/5073/; James O'Donnell Bennett, "Al Smith Denounces Intolerance," *CT*, Sept. 21, 1928.
39. For the details of FDR's nomination, see Ernest K. Lindley, *Franklin D. Roosevelt: A Career in Progressive Democracy* (Blue Ribbon Books, 1931), 11–23. Lindley, a journalist, was present in Rochester as Smith and other New York Democratic leaders beseeched FDR to run for governor. For further details, see Davis, *FDR: Beckoning*, 843–53; Ward, *First-Class Temperament*, 788–94; Freidel, *The Ordeal*, 248–56. Eleanor Roosevelt gave her own account in *This I Remember* (Harper & Brothers, 1949), 44–47. She records that Raskob gave the Foundation over $100,000 between 1928 and 1931.
40. *Public Papers and Addresses of Franklin D. Roosevelt [PP&A], vol.1, The Genesis of the New Deal, 1928–1932* (Random House, 1938), Oct. 16, 1928, 13; and Oct. 22, 1928, 38.
41. Samuel I. Rosenman, *Working with Roosevelt* (Harper & Brothers, 1952), 14–16.
42. *PP&A*, vol. 1: Oct. 29, 1928, 59; Oct. 26, 1928, 53.
43. Rosenman, *Working with Roosevelt*, 22–24; Perkins, *The Roosevelt I Knew*, 44–45.
44. Herbert Hoover, *American Individualism* (Doubleday, Page, 1922), 13.
45. Hoover, *American Individualism*, 24; FDR speech of Nov. 1, 1928, *PP&A*, vol. 1, 67–72.
46. Gene Smiley and Richard H. Keehn, "Federal Personal Income Tax Policy in the 1920s," *Journal of Economic History* 55, no. 2 (1995), 285–303; and Gene Smiley, "The U.S. Economy in the 1920s," Economic History Association, June 29, 2004, http://eh.net/encyclopedia/the-u-s-economy-in-the-1920s/.
47. Text of Hoover's August 11 speech in Palo Alto accepting the Republican nomination for president, *CT*, Aug. 12, 1928.

Chapter 2: Falling for Fascism

1. Ida Tarbell's long series on Mussolini appeared in *McCall's* in four parts: November, December, January, and February, 1926–27. For her own account of her trip, see Ida Tarbell, *All in a Day's Work: An Autobiography* (Macmillan, 1939), 378–83. On the details of Tarbell's contract with *McCall's* and the sum she was paid, see Kathleen Brady, *Ida Tarbell: Portrait of a Muckraker* (University of Pittsburgh Press, 1989), 238–39.
2. The most thorough account of American perceptions of fascist Italy is John P. Diggins, *Mussolini and Fascism: The View from America* (Princeton University Press, 1972), which can be supplemented by Katy Hull, *The Machine Has a Soul: American Sympathy with Fascism* (Princeton University Press, 2021). For American perceptions of dictatorship generally, see Benjamin L. Alpers, *Dictators, Democracy, and American Public Culture: Envisioning the Totalitarian Enemy, 1920s–1950s* (University of North Carolina Press, 2003), esp. 15–58. A lively brief account of Mussolini's life and personality by an author who fought in Italy in the Second World War is Christopher Hibbert, *Mussolini: The Rise and Fall of Il Duce* (Little, Brown, 1962). Denis Mack Smith, *Mussolini* (Alfred A. Knopf, 1982), deftly synthesizes much literature. A more up-to-date account with an eye to social history is R. J. B. Bosworth, *Mussolini's Italy: Life under the Fascist Dictatorship, 1915–1945* (Penguin, 2005). A less accessible but thorough treatment of the politics of the era is Adrian Lyttelton, *The Seizure of Power: Fascism in Italy, 1919–1929* (Weidenfeld & Nicolson, 1973).
3. Anne O'Hare McCormick, "New Italy of the Italians," *NYT*, Dec. 19, 1920.
4. Wilson remarks on Fiume in *NYT*, Apr. 30, 1919; on Paris Peace Conference, "Italy Quits Peace Table!" *CT*, Apr. 24, 1919; and "Italians Decide to Quit," *NYT*, Apr. 24, 1919.

5. Italian response to Wilson, "Romans Cheer Envoys' Stand," *NYT*, Apr. 25, 1919; and "The American Dictator," *Observer*, Apr. 27, 1919. On stoning incident, *CT*, May 15, 1919; "Fiume to Be Free Under the League," *NYT*, May 30, 1919.
6. Michael Ledeen, *D'Annunzio: The First Duce* (Routledge, 2002); Dominique Kirchner Reill, *The Fiume Crisis: Life in the Wake of the Habsburg Empire* (Harvard University Press, 2020).
7. For a detailed analysis of strikes, see Paolo Spriano, *The Occupation of the Factories: Italy 1920*, translated and introduced by Gwyn A. Williams (Pluto Press, 1975).
8. Mussolini's early life and the founding of fascism: Ivone Kirkpatrick, *Mussolini: Study of a Demagogue* (Odhams, 1964), 1–88; Richard J. B. Bosworth, *Mussolini* (Bloomsbury, 2003), 47–128.
9. Lilian Mowrer, *Journalist's Wife* (Grosset & Dunlap, 1937), 76–79, 91–92.
10. "Nationalists War on Reds in Italy," *NYT*, Jan. 28, 1921; "Italy Recovering in Spite of Mobs," *NYT*, Feb. 20, 1921.
11. "Many Fatalities in Series of Riots in Florence," *NYT*, Mar. 1, 1921; "11 Dead, 500 Held in Florence Riots," *WP*, Mar. 2, 1921; "Civil War in Italian Cities," *NYT*, Mar. 2, 1921;"Fascisti Continue War on Socialists," *NYT*, Apr. 18, 1921; "14 Killed, 100 Hurt, as Reds Fight Fascisti," *CT*, Apr.19, 1921.
12. Anne O'Hare McCormick, "The Revolt of Youth," *NYT*, June 5, 1921.
13. "Fascisti Expanding as Election Nears," *NYT*, May 8, 1921; Edgar Mowrer, *Triumph and Turmoil*, 138.
14. "Rioting in Rome as Strike Goes On," *NYT*, Nov. 11, 1921; "Strike in Rome Ended," *NYT*, Nov. 12, 1921; Edgar Mowrer, "Rome Experiences Fascisti Menace," *Birmingham News*, Nov. 21, 1921. For an excellent summary of the early party building, Emilio Gentile, "The Problem of the Party in Italian Fascism," *Journal of Contemporary History* 19, no. 2 (1984): 251–74.
15. T. R. Ybarra, "Italy's Frankenstein and His Monster," *NYT*, Jan. 29, 1922.
16. Edgar Mowrer, "Law Enforcement Needed in Italy," *Charlotte News*, May 31, 1922; Mowrer, *Triumph and Turmoil*, 139; "Leader of Fascisti Threatens Revolt," *NYT*, July 21, 1922; "Scores Are Slain, Thousands Wounded, in Italy's Civil War," *NYT*, Aug. 6, 1922.
17. Anne O'Hare McCormick, "Politics à l'Italienne," *NYT*, Sept. 10, 1922.
18. V. De Santo, "Fascisti Shall Rule Italy, Says Chief Mussolini," *CT*, Oct. 7, 1922; "Fascisti Prepare to Control Italy," *NYT*, Oct. 7, 1922; Editorial, "Plans of the Fascisti," *NYT*, Oct. 20, 1922.
19. "The Fascist Congress at Naples," *NYT*, Oct. 25, 1922; "Fascisti Chief Warns Cabinet," *CT*, Oct. 26, 1922.
20. Lilian Mowrer, *Journalist's Wife*, 165–68; "King Bows to Fascisti Power," *NYT*, Oct. 30, 1922.
21. Luigi Barella, "Italy Pledged by Fascisti to Peace Policy," *CT*, Oct. 31, 1922; "Mussolini Forms Cabinet for Italy," *NYT*, Oct. 31, 1922.
22. *Baltimore Sun*, Nov. 1, 1922; *New York Tribune*, Nov. 1, 1922; Arthur Brisbane, "Today," *SFE*, Nov. 1, 1922.
23. "The Future of Italian Nationalism," *CT*, Nov. 4, 1922; J. W. T. Mason, *Duluth New Tribune*, Nov. 12, 1922; Walter Littlefield, "How the Italian Middle Class Rose," *NYT*, Nov. 5, 1922. See also Otis Swift and V. De Santo, "Fascisti Light Way for Europe Middle Classes," *CT*, Nov. 9, 1922.
24. "Mussolini Wars on Party He Ruled," *WP*, Nov. 5, 1922; Alice Rohe, "Mussolini, Hope of Youth, Italy's Man of Tomorrow," *NYT*, Nov. 5, 1922.
25. Editorial, "Mussolini," *CT*, Nov. 18, 1922.
26. Edgar Mowrer, "The Rule of the Fascisti," *Forum*, Mar. 1923; Lilian Mowrer, *Journalist's Wife*, 174–78.
27. Anne O'Hare McCormick, "Swashbuckling Mussolini," *NYT*, July 22, 1923; *Time*, Aug. 6, 1923.
28. "Calls Mussolini Latin Roosevelt," *NYT*, Oct. 7, 1923; Samuel Crowther, "Mussolini: New Napoleon or Demagogue," *McClure's*, Jan. 1924; "In Mussoliniland," *Time*, Feb. 11, 1924.
29. Richard Washburn Child, *A Diplomat Looks at Europe*, 154–220. Also note Childs's belief in Mussolini's historic greatness: "It may be shrewdly forecast that no man will exhibit dimensions of permanent greatness equal to those of Mussolini," in "Foreword," Benito Mussolini, *My Autobiography* (Charles Scribner's Sons, 1928), i–xix.
30. On Matteotti and the significance of the assassination, Denis Mack Smith, *Mussolini* (Alfred A. Knopf, 1982), 52–68; "Foe of the Fascisti Disappears in Rome," *NYT*, June 13, 1924; "Socialist Deputy Seized by Fascisti," *NYT*, June 14, 1924; Howard Sachar, *The Assassination of Europe, 1918–1942: A Political History* (University of Toronto Press, 2014), 49–65.
31. Thomas W. Lamont of J. P. Morgan & Co. to the Secretary of State Frank Kellogg, May 26, 1925, and Kellogg to Lamont, May 29, 1925, *FRUS 1925*, vol. 2, 358–59; Diggins, *Mussolini and Fascism*, 152–53. For Lamont at CFR, *Time*, Feb. 1, 1926.

32. Anne O'Hare McCormick, "*Il Duce* Pictures the New State," *NYT*, Oct. 24, 1926; "An Apology for Fascism," *New Republic*, Jan. 12, 1927.

Chapter 3: Land of Fists

1. Houghton letter to Hughes, Nov. 21, 1922, in Jeffrey J. Matthews, *Alanson B. Houghton, Ambassador of the New Era* (SR Books, 2004), 69.
2. "Fascisti Have Bavarian Imitators," *NYT*, May 29, 1922; "Bavaria Near Revolt," *CT*, Nov. 12, 1922; Cyril Brown, "New Popular Idol Rises in Bavaria," *NYT*, Nov. 21, 1922; see also the pieces on Hitler, *NYT*, Nov. 28, Dec. 14 and 16, 1922.
3. Karl H. von Wiegand, "Fascisti in Germany Defy Berlin," *SFE*, Nov. 13, 1923.
4. Karl H. von Wiegand, "Fascisti Vow to Overthrow Berlin," *Washington Herald*, Nov. 21, 1922. On his early discounting of Hitler, see Robert Murphy, *Diplomat Among Warriors* (Doubleday, 1964), 20–23.
5. Robert Hessen, ed., *Berlin Alert: The Memoirs and Reports of Truman Smith* (Stanford University Press, 1984), 48, 50, 56–59, 61–65, 73. Smith's reports also appear in National Archives and Record Service, Record Group 165, Military Intelligence Division Files: Germany, published on microfilm as *US Military Intelligence Reports: Germany, 1919–1941*, ed. Dale Reynolds (University Publications of America, 1983), reports dated Nov. 25, Nov. 28, and Dec. 4, 1922, microfilm, reel 1.
6. The outstanding biography is Ian Kershaw, *Hitler: 1889–1936: Hubris* (Norton, 1998), which is the first of a two-volume treatment. For comparison, see one of the earliest studies of Hitler: Konrad Heiden, *The Führer*, trans. Ralph Manheim (Carroll and Graf, 1944). In the vast literature on Hitler's rise, one excellent comprehensive synthesis is Thomas Childers, *The Third Reich: A History of Nazi Germany* (Simon & Schuster, 2019), which can be supplemented by Klaus P. Fischer, *Nazi Germany: A New History* (Continuum, 1995). A superb overview of the rise of Nazism is Richard J. Evans, *The Coming of the Third Reich* (Penguin, 2004), which was followed by two additional volumes taking the story through 1945.
7. Kershaw, *Hitler: Hubris*, 73–128.
8. "Dead Fill the Streets," *CT*, Jan. 12, 1919; "Troops Keep Order in Berlin Strike," *NYT*, Mar. 6, 1919.
9. Evans, *Coming of the Third Reich*, 69–76; Fischer, *Nazi Germany*, 41–73.
10. Klaus Schwabe, *Woodrow Wilson, Revolutionary Germany, and Peacemaking, 1918–1919: Missionary Diplomacy and the Realities of Power* (University of North Carolina Press, 1985), 3–8.
11. A lively account is David King, *The Trial of Adolf Hitler: The Beer Hall Putsch and the Rise of Nazi Germany* (Norton, 2017).
12. Adolf Hitler, *Mein Kampf*, trans. Ralph Manheim (Houghton Mifflin, 1943), 154; "Program of the German Workers' Party," Feb. 24, 1920, at https://ghdi.ghi-dc.org/sub_document.cfm?document_id=3910.
13. George Renwick, "Berlin Changed to City of Gloom," *NYT*, Mar. 19, 1919; and "Luxury and Famine Present in Berlin," *NYT*, Aug. 21, 1919.
14. Military Intelligence Division reports of Feb. 25, Mar. 3, Mar. 4, Mar. 11, Mar. 15, Mar. 20, 1919, in *US Military Intelligence Reports*, reel 3. Parke Brown, "Feed Germany or Reds Rule," *CT*, Mar. 10, 1919. A recent analysis of the impact of the blockade on children's health can be found in M. E. Cox, "Hunger Games, or, How the Allied Blockade in the First World War Deprived German Children of Nutrition, and Allied Food Aid Subsequently Saved Them," *Economic History Review* 68, no. 2 (2015): 600–31. On the U.S. aid in early 1919, see Charles E. Strickland, "American Aid to Germany, 1919 to 1921," *Wisconsin Magazine of History* 45, no. 4 (1962): 256–70. For a careful study of postwar Germany's demobilization, economy, and society, see Richard Bessel, *Germany after the First World War* (Oxford University Press, 1993).
15. "Anti-Semitism in Germany," Mar. 11, 1919, *US Military Intelligence Reports*, reel 3. For an excellent discussion of the origin of the belief that Communism was a Jewish conspiracy, see Paul Hanebrink, *A Specter Haunting Europe: The Myth of Judeo-Bolshevism* (Harvard University Press, 2018), 1–45.
16. "Junker Intrigue Rife in Germany," *NYT*, Dec. 3, 1918; "Report Commune Rules in Munich," *NYT*, Apr. 12, 1919; see also George Renwick, "Munich's Red Rule is a Grim Farce," *NYT*, Apr. 14, 1919; "Attack on Berlin Jews," *NYT*, May 9, 1919; Parke Brown, "Jews in Berlin Fear Pogroms," *CT*, July 7, 1919.
17. "Fear Incitement of German Pogroms," *NYT*, Aug. 17, 1919; "Berlin Reactionaries Plan War on Jews," *NYT*, Aug. 31, 1919; "Dr. Wise Blames Germans," *NYT*, Feb. 24, 1920.

18. "Students Beat Jews in First Berlin Pogrom," *CT*, Feb. 28, 1921; George Seldes, "Monarchists of Berlin Attack American, Jews," *CT*, Mar. 14, 1922; "Anti-Semitism in Germany," *American Israelite*, Mar. 23, 1922.
19. His remarkable, breezy memoir is a crucial source about Munich in these years. Ernst Hanfstaengl, *Hitler: The Memoir of a Nazi Insider Who Turned Against the Führer* (Arcade, 1994), originally published as *Unheard Witness* in 1957. For excellent portraits of Hitler's closest associates, see Richard J. Evans, *Hitler's People: The Faces of the Third Reich* (Penguin, 2024).
20. "Berlin Hears Ford is Backing Hitler," *NYT*, Dec. 20, 1922. See also Karl H. von Wiegand, "Ford Accused of Financing Berlin Fascisti," *SFE*, Dec. 19, 1922, and "Says Ford Aids Royalists," *NYT*, Feb. 8, 1923; Raymond Fendrick, "Heinrich Ford Idol of Bavaria Fascisti Chief," *CT*, Mar. 8, 1923. For the details of this story, see Victoria Saker Woeste, *Henry Ford's War on Jews and the Legal Battle Against Hate Speech* (Stanford University Press, 2012).
21. "Strike in Ruhr; Defy French: Miners, Rail and Wire Men Stop Labor," *CT*, Jan. 22, 1923. For the decision to invade the Ruhr, see Zara Steiner, *The Lights that Failed: European International History, 1919–1933* (Oxford University Press, 2005), 182–237.
22. "Bavaria Gives in to Hitler's Threats," *NYT*, Jan. 28, 1923; Larry Rue, "Rhineland Coup Set for Feb. 1, Germany Hears," *CT*, Jan. 29, 1923; Karl H. von Wiegand, "Fascist Chief Sees Peril in Ruhr," *SFE*, Feb. 15, 1923.
23. "War Talk Heard at Berlin Meeting; Monarchist Orator Attacks the Jews," *NYT*, Feb. 28, 1923; "Threaten German Jews: National Socialists Want to Intern All as 'Hostages' for the Ruhr," *NYT*, Mar. 17, 1923; "Germany Panicky and Pessimistic," *Wall Street Journal*, July 28, 1923.
24. George Seldes, "Thousands Hoch der Kaiser in Bavarian Mass," *CT*, Sept. 3, 1923; "Bavarian Fascisti Control City," *NYT*, Sept. 2, 1923; "Ludendorff Hails Prince as Ruler," *NYT*, Sept. 3, 1923; "Hitler Waiting to Succeed Stresemann," *American Israelite*, Oct. 4, 1923. See also Kershaw, *Hitler: Hubris*, 199–200. Film footage of the September march can be seen at "Der deutsche Tag in Nuernberg am 2 September 1923," United States Holocaust Memorial Museum, https://collections.ushmm.org/search/catalog/irn1003680.
25. "Berlin, in Hunger Blockade, Riots, Loots, Attacks Jews," *WP*, Nov. 6, 1923; "Bavarian Dictator Is Fast Losing Power," *WP*, Nov. 7, 1923; "Berlin Food Rioters Attack and Beat Jews," *NYT*, Nov. 6, 1923; "Berlin Rioting Resumed," *NYT*, Nov. 7, 1923; "Jews of Berlin Attacked by Mob," *Jewish Telegraphic Agency*, Nov. 6, 1923; Carl O. Groat, "Jews Mobbed in Berlin Riots," *Los Angeles Evening Express*, Nov. 5, 1923; John Clayton, "Storm Berlin Bourse; Raid Jews' Homes," *CT*, Nov. 6, 1923; Gustav M. Oehm, "Throngs Flee German City in Wild Panic," *Los Angeles Evening Express*, Nov. 6, 1923; "Anti-Jewish Riots in Various Parts of Germany," *American Israelite*, Nov. 15, 1923; "Kill Jews Is Cry Throughout Berlin," *American Israelite*, Nov. 22, 1923.
26. On rumors of a coup led by von Kahr, see "Berlin Sees Hostile Move," *NYT*, Sept. 27, 1923. Hitler's coup was a poorly kept secret: see "Arm for German Monarchy: Army of 30,000 Mass for Drive toward Berlin," *CT*, Nov. 1, 1923; "Monarchist Uprising Against Republic Planned for Wednesday, Berlin Hears," *NYT*, Nov. 5, 1923; "Bavarian Fascisti Impatient," *NYT*, Nov. 7, 1923.
27. "Ebert Summons People," *NYT*, Nov. 9, 1923; *CT*, Nov. 9, 1923; *SFE*, Nov. 9, 1923; "German Capital Prepares for Defense after Coup by Hitler," *NYT*, Nov. 10, 1923; Karl H. von Wiegand, "Rebes in Coup Seize Bavarian Rule," *SFE*, Nov. 9, 1923.
28. John Clayton, "Sharp Fighting Ends Royalist Coup in Munich," *CT*, Nov. 10, 1923; Cyril Brown, "Brief Battle Ends Revolt," *NYT*, Nov. 10, 1923.
29. "Latest Version of Putsch," *NYT*, Nov. 11, 1923; "Munich Mobs Defy von Kahr as Hitler Raises New Forces," *WP*, Nov. 11, 1923; "Hitler Seized Near Munich," *NYT*, Nov. 13, 1923. An eyewitness account appeared as "Munich's Riotous Saturday: Pandemonium and Panic; Hitler Troops' Final Ignominy," *MG*, Nov. 12, 1923; Karl H. von Wiegand, "Dictatorship Appeal Made by Germans," *SFE*, Nov. 11, 1923.
30. "Hitler a Prisoner in Landsberg Fort," *NYT*, Nov. 15, 1923; "Hitler Tamed by Prison," *NYT*, Dec. 21, 1924.
31. On the origins and diplomacy of the Dawes Plan, see Melvyn P. Leffler, *The Elusive Quest: America's Pursuit of European Stability and French Security, 1919–1933* (University of North Carolina Press, 1979), 82–122.
32. Manfred Jonas, *The United States and Germany: A Diplomatic History* (Cornell University Press, 1984), 173.

33. Jonas, *United States and Germany*, 175–81; Steiner, *The Lights That Failed*, 240; Ludendorff in "Assails Dawes Report," *CT*, July 7, 1924. For the details of the negotiations, see Stephen Schuker, *The End of French Predominance in Europe: The Financial Crisis of 1924 and the Adoption of the Dawes Plan* (University of North Carolina Press, 1976).
34. Steiner, *Lights That Failed*, 244; Patricia Clavin, *The Great Depression in Europe, 1929–1939* (Macmillan, 2000), 36–39; MacDonald in John Steele, "Europe Signs Dawes Pact," *CT*, Aug. 17, 1924.
35. On the inflow of dollars, see Natacha Postel-Vinay and Stéphanie Collet, "Hot Money Inflows and Bank Risk-taking: Germany from the 1920s to the Great Depression," *Economic History Review* 77, no. 2 (2024): 472–502. A self-congratulatory summary by the American overseeing the reparations program, S. Parker Gilbert, is in "What the Dawes Plan Has Accomplished," *Congressional Digest* 8, no. 8/9 (1929): 199–202.
36. Mowrer, *Triumph and Turmoil*, 194; Lilian Mowrer, *Journalist's Wife*, 236; Edgar Ansel Mowrer, "Germany After Ten Years," *Harper's*, Dec. 1928, 61–69.
37. Lilian Mowrer, *Journalist's Wife*, 230. For a careful explanation of the economic and political crises of this period, see Benjamin Carter Hett, *The Death of Democracy: Hitler's Rise to Power and the Downfall of the Weimar Republic* (St. Martin's Press, 2019), 35–93.
38. Evans, *Coming of the Third Reich*, 195–212; "2 Dead, 20 Hurt in Bavaria When Hitlerites Riot," *CT*, Aug. 5, 1929.
39. Clavin, *Great Depression*, 112, table 5.1.
40. Evans, *Coming of the Third Reich*, 247–65.
41. On the concept of mobilizing passions, see Robert O. Paxton, "The Five Stages of Fascism," *Journal of Modern History* 70, no. 1 (1998): 1–23.
42. Most of these ideas were foreshadowed in the 1920 "Program of the German Workers' Party."
43. Thompson's life has been the subject of one first-rate biography: Peter Kurth, *American Cassandra: The Life of Dorothy Thompson* (Little, Brown, 1990). There is an earlier account by Marion K. Sanders, *Dorothy Thompson: A Legend in Her Time* (Houghton Mifflin, 1973). Her friend and fellow journalist Vincent "Jimmy" Sheean wrote a gossipy study of the Lewis-Thompson marriage called *Dorothy and Red* (Houghton Mifflin, 1963). Her reporting in the 1930s has recently attracted more attention. See in particular Cott, *Fighting Words*, and Cohen, *Last Call at the Hotel Imperial*. Among the profiles written about her at the time, the most revealing is a two-part essay titled "The It Girl," by Margaret Case Harriman in the *New Yorker*, Apr. 20 and 27, 1940.
44. Dorothy Thompson, "Poverty de Luxe," *SEP*, May 2 and 9, 1931.
45. Kurth, *American Cassandra*, 160; Dorothy Thompson, "The State Dictates," *SEP*, Feb. 6, 1932; "The Gray Squirrel Complex," *SEP*, Feb. 20, 1932.
46. Dorothy Thompson, "I Saw Hitler!" *Cosmopolitan*, Mar. 1932, 32–33, 160–64.
47. Hans V. Kaltenborn, *Fifty Fabulous Years, 1900–1950* (Putnam, 1950), 185–6; Hans V. Kaltenborn, "An Interview with Hitler, August 17, 1932," *Wisconsin Magazine of History* 50, no. 4 (1967), 283–90.
48. H. R. Knickerbocker, *Is Tomorrow Hitler's?* (Reynal & Hitchcock, 1941), 3; Lilian Mowrer, *Journalist's Wife*, 264.
49. Bernard V. Burke, *Ambassador Frederic Sackett and the Collapse of the Weimar Republic, 1930–1933: The United States and Hitler's Rise to Power* (Cambridge University Press, 1994), 149–71; John Wiley, Counselor of Embassy, to Pierre de Boal, Chief of the Western Europe Division in the State Department, Feb. 17, 1932, *FRUS 1932*, vol. 2, 281–86.
50. Boal to Secretary of State, June 4, 1932, *FRUS 1932*, vol. 2, 295–96; Sackett to State, Aug. 1, 1932, *FRUS 1932*, vol. 2, 302–3.
51. Dorothy Thompson, "The Rise of the German Menace," *Redbook*, Sept. 1932, 30–31, 111–14. In another essay that month, she made perfectly clear the racial and dictatorial ambitions of the Nazis: "The Militant Disarmed," *SEP*, Sept. 17, 1932, 12–13, 88–93.
52. Henry Ashby Turner Jr., *Hitler's Thirty Days to Power: January 1933* (Addison-Wesley, 1996), 148. For other accounts of January 1933, see Kershaw, *Hitler: Hubris*, 413–27; Hett, *The Death of Democracy*, 170–83; Heiden, *The Führer*; and Timothy W. Ryback, *Takeover: Hitler's Final Rise to Power* (Alfred A. Knopf, 2024).
53. André François-Ponçet, *The Fateful Years: Memoirs of a French Ambassador in Berlin, 1931–1938*, trans. Jacques LeClercq (Gollancz, 1949), 48; Lilian Mowrer, *Journalist's Wife*, 280–81.

Chapter 4: The New Deal in a Fascist Age

1. These details emerge from contemporary accounts. "Capital Prepared to Greet Crowds," *NYT*, Mar. 1, 1929; "Crowds Wait New President," *CT*, Mar. 3, 1929; "Capitol Stage Set for 4-Year Drama," *WP*, Mar. 3, 1929; "Hoover Inauguration Broadcast to World in Greatest Hookup," *CT*, Mar. 5, 1929; "Hoover Enjoys Day; Busy From the Dawn," *NYT*, Mar. 5, 1929; "Hoover Is Grave, Coolidge Is Quiet, and Taft Jovial," *CT*, Mar. 5, 1929; "A New Hoover Is Heard," *NYT*, Mar. 5, 1929; "Air Parade Salutes a New Commander," *NYT*, Mar. 5, 1929; "Inaugural Address of Herbert Hoover," Yale Avalon Project, Mar. 4, 1929, https://avalon.law.yale.edu/20th_century/hoover.asp; John Kenneth Galbraith, *The Great Crash, 1929* (Houghton Mifflin, 1954), 6–8.
2. "Inauguration Seen as Business Omen," *NYT*, Mar. 3, 1929. On the growth of the economy, see Charles Kindleberger, *The World in Depression, 1929–1939* (University of California Press, 1986), 44–45; Maury Klein, *Rainbow's End: The Crash of 1929* (Oxford University Press, 2001), 27–41. On Hoover's intellectual world view, see Albert U. Romasco, *The Poverty of Abundance: Hoover, the Nation, the Depression* (Oxford University Press, 1965), 10–23.
3. Barry Eichengreen, *Golden Fetters: The Gold Standard and the Great Depression, 1919–1939* (Oxford University Press, 1992), 153–87; Adam Tooze, *The Deluge: The Great War, America and the Remaking of the Global Order, 1916–1931* (Penguin, 2014), 353–73; Clavin, *Great Depression*, 40–67.
4. "Address Accepting the Republican Presidential Nomination," Aug. 11, 1928, APP; "Campaign Address in New York City," Oct. 22, 1928, APP.
5. Tom Pettey, "Hoover Bull Market Sends Stocks Soaring," *CT*, Mar. 2, 1929; see also "Stocks Swept High as Inaugural Nears," *NYT*, Mar. 1, 1929. Gary Richardson et al., "Stock Market Crash of 1929," Federal Reserve History, Nov. 22, 2013, https://www.federalreservehistory.org/essays/stock-market-crash-of-1929.
6. Charles Rappleye, *Herbert Hoover in the White House* (Simon & Schuster, 2016), 75–86.
7. Rappleye, *Herbert Hoover*, 99–116; Klein, *Rainbow's End*, 207–39; Richardson et al., "Stock Market Crash of 1929."
8. Richard V. Oulahan, "Nation's Industrial Chiefs Confer with Hoover Today," and "Hoover to Set Up Business Council," *NYT*, Nov. 21 and 22, 1929.
9. Robert A. Margo, "Employment and Unemployment in the 1930s," *Journal of Economic Perspectives* 7, no. 2 (1993): 41–59.
10. Walter Lippmann, "The Peculiar Weakness of Mr. Hoover," *Harper's*, June 1930, 1–7; Lippmann to Felix Frankfurter, Nov. 8, 1930, in John Morton Blum, ed., *Public Philosopher: Selected Letters of Walter Lippmann* (Ticknor & Fields, 1985), 268.
11. "Executive Outlines Task: Country Has Regained Confidence Lost in Market Crash, He Says," *NYT*, Dec. 6, 1929; "Hoover Cites New Attitude," *WSJ*, Dec. 6, 1929.
12. "Hoover Against Expenditures Now," *WSJ*, Feb. 26, 1930; "Worst of Depression Over, Says Hoover," *NYT*, May 2, 1930; and Peri E. Arnold, "The 'Great Engineer' as Administrator: Herbert Hoover and Modern Bureaucracy," *Review of Politics* 42, no. 3 (July 1980): 329–48; and Romasco, *Poverty of Abundance*, 24–38.
13. Schlesinger, *Age of Roosevelt*, 163–64; David M. Kennedy, *Freedom from Fear: The American People in Depression and War, 1929–1945* (Oxford University Press, 1999), 49–50; Charles P. Kindleberger, *The World in Depression, 1929–1939* (University of California Press, 1986), 123–26.
14. Romasco, in *Poverty of Abundance*, shows that Hoover did try to launch various initiatives but was too wedded to outdated ideas. "The well of conservatism had been pumped dry," 232. Joan Hoff Wilson demonstrates Hoover's activism in trying to restart the economy, but concedes his intellectual limitations stymied progress. *Herbert Hoover: Forgotten Progressive* (Little, Brown, 1975), 122–67.
15. "The Emergence of Roosevelt," *NYT*, Nov. 13, 1928; "Roosevelt Hailed by South as Hope of Party in 1932," *NYT*, Nov. 11, 1928; "Roosevelt Hailed as 1932 President," *NYT*, Dec. 5, 1928.
16. "First Inaugural Address as Governor," Jan. 1, 1929, *PP&A, 1928–1932*, 75–80.
17. Rosenman, *Working with Roosevelt*, 31-2; "An Address Before the State Charities Aid Association," Jan. 17, 1930, *PP&A, 1928–1932*, 330–33.
18. "Address on States' Rights," Mar. 2, 1930, *PP&A, 1928–1932*, 569–75; on the protests: "Police Crush 2,000 Rioting Reds in Jam of 40,000," *NYHT*, Mar. 7, 1932; "Riots General over Nation on 'Red Thursday,'" *NYHT*, Mar. 7, 1930; "Many Hurt in Riots in Nation's Cities, *NYT*, Mar. 7, 1930; "fairly radical" in letter to John Kingbury, May 12, 1930, and "communistic" in letter to

William I. Sirovich, May 14, 1930, both in Elliott Roosevelt, ed., *FDR: His Personal Letters*, vol. 1 (Duell, Sloan and Pearce, 1950), 118–19.

19. For a detailed account of his time as governor, see Kenneth Davis, *FDR: The New York Years, 1928–1933* (Random House, 1979), and Bernard Bellush, *Franklin D. Roosevelt as Governor of New York* (Columbia University Press, 1955).
20. For a fresh perspective on his close associates, see Costigliola, "Broken Circle," 677–718.
21. Kirstin Downey, *The Woman Behind the New Deal: The Life and Legacy of Frances Perkins* (Anchor, 2009).
22. For a witty contemporary assessment, see Joseph Alsop and Robert Kintner, "Henny Penny: Farmer at the Treasury," *SEP*, Apr. 1, 1939.
23. Sherwood, *Roosevelt and Hopkins*. A short, lively portrait of the insiders is Joseph Alsop and Robert Kintner, *Men Around the President* (Doubleday, 1939).
24. Farley in Kenneth Davis, *FDR: The New York Years*, 198.
25. "Bank of U.S. Closes Doors," *NYT*, Dec. 12, 1930; Gary Richardson, "The Check Is in the Mail: Correspondent Clearing and the Collapse of the Banking System, 1930 to 1933," *Journal of Economic History* 67, no. 3 (2007): 643–71; and Gary Richardson, "Banking Crises and the Federal Reserve as a Lender of Last Resort during the Great Depression," *NBER Reporter* 3 (2013): 7–10; for comparative data, see Drew DeSilver, "Most U.S. Bank Failures Have Come in a Few Big Waves," Pew Research Center, Apr. 11, 2023, https://pewrsr.ch/43s9B07.
26. The precise causes of the Creditanstalt failure are still disputed, with some blaming French policy, others blaming Austria's own banking policy. See Flora Macher, "The Austrian Banking Crisis of 1931," Department of Economic History Working Paper no. 274, London School of Economics, Feb. 2008; Eichengreen, *Golden Fetters*, 262–69; Aurel Schubert, *The Credit-Anstalt Crisis of 1931* (Cambridge University Press, 1991). On the moratorium and subsequent British decision, see Kindleberger, *World in Depression*, 148–58; Clavin, *Great Depression*, 119–30; "Great Britain Suspends Gold Payments Today," *NYT*, Sept. 21, 1931.
27. This connection was made clear in Tugwell, *The Democratic Roosevelt*, 205. FDR's speech, Aug. 28, 1931, *PP&A, 192–1932*, 457–68. Rosenman wrote the speech under FDR's guidance. Rosenman, *Working with Roosevelt*, 50–52. Hoover's limitations, but also the legacy of some of his Depression-related policies, are considered in Ellis W. Hawley, *The Great War and the Search for a Modern Order* (St. Martin's Press, 1979), 172–200.
28. Mason B. Williams, *City of Ambition: FDR, La Guardia, and the Making of Modern New York* (Norton, 2013), 110; "$10,000,000 Monthly Asked for State Relief," *NYT*, Oct. 18, 1932; "Chairman Hopkins Explains Purpose of Relief Bond Issue," *NYT*, Nov. 4, 1932; "Beggary Avoided in State Relief, Report to Governor Stresses 'Revolutionary' Effort," *NYT*, Nov. 1, 1932; "Relief Issue Wins," *NYT*, Nov. 8, 1932; "Relief Bonds Approved, 4 to 1," *NYT*, Nov. 12, 1932.
29. Lipmann to Newton D. Baker, Nov. 24, 1931, in Blum, ed., *Letters of Walter Lippmann*, 280–81.
30. Walter Lippmann, "Governor Roosevelt's Candidacy," Jan. 8, 1932, reprinted in his book *Interpretations, 1931–1932* (Macmillan, 1932), 259–63.
31. "Replies to Leaders' Letter; He Accedes to Request to Let His Name Be Used There," *NYT*, Jan. 24, 1932; "Smith Declares War," *WP*, Feb. 8, 1932; Smith, *FDR*, 258–59. On Garner, see Arthur Krock, "Chief Cactus: The Frontier's Candidate," *NYT*, Mar. 13, 1932.
32. Tugwell, *Democratic Roosevelt*, 73, 212–17; the flypaper comment is in R. G. Tugwell, "The Preparation of a President," *Western Political Quarterly* 1, no. 1 (1948): 131–53. Raymond Moley, *After Seven Years* (Harper & Brothers, 1939), 9–10.
33. Richard Hofstadter, *The American Political Tradition and the Men Who Made It* (Random House, 1973), 431. Eric Rauchway agrees: "New Deal programs embodied no single approach to political management of the economy. They originated in no single book, speech, or person's thoughts." *The Great Depression and the New Deal: A Very Short Introduction* (Oxford University Press, 2008), 4.
34. "The Forgotten Man Speech," April 7, 1932, *PP&A, 1928 –1932*, 624–27.
35. "Address at Oglethorpe University," *PP&A, 1928–1932*, May 22, 1932, 639–47. This speech was written by the journalist Ernest Lindley for the campaign.
36. "Floor Resembles Stock Boom Scene," *NYT*, June 29, 1932; "He is Ready for Action," *NYT*, July 2, 1932; "Pick Roosevelt; Here Today," *CT*, July 2, 1932; "Roosevelt Vote Is 945," *NYT*, July 2, 1932. The story of getting Garner on the ticket is told in James A. Farley, *Jim Farley's Story: The Roosevelt Years* (McGraw-Hill, 1948), 19–27.

37. "Roosevelt Is Ready for Chicago Flight," *NYT*, June 30, 1932; Rosenman, *Working with Roosevelt*, 73–75; "Wild Acclaim Greets Him in Chicago," *WP*, July 3, 1932; "10,000 Greet Plane Bearing Roosevelt," *NYT*, July 3, 1932.
38. "Nominee Flies to Convention; Speaks; Asks for a 'New Deal,'" *CT*, July 3, 1932; "Text of Roosevelt's Address Accepting Nomination," *CT*, July 3, 1932; "Convention Throng Hails Roosevelt," *NYT*, July 3, 1932; "Governor Accepts the Nomination for the Presidency," *PP&A, 1928–1932*, July 2, 1932, 647–59.
39. William Leuchtenberg, *Franklin D. Roosevelt and the New Deal, 1932–1940* (Harper & Row, 1963), 33, 12. Another great student of the Roosevelt years argued that the New Deal was "awash in ideologies" and lacked "any single principle to bind its many diverse initiatives together." Not until 1937 did liberals begin to define precisely what they meant by the term "the New Deal." Alan Brinkley, "The New Deal and the Idea of the State," in Steve Fraser and Gary Gerstle, eds., *The Rise and Fall of the New Deal Order, 1930–1980* (Princeton University Press, 1989), 85–121.
40. Eric Rauchway, "The New Deal Was on the Ballot in 1932," *Modern American History* 2, no. 2 (2019): 201–13.
41. "President Hoover, New York City, Madison Square Garden, Oct. 31, 1932," in *Campaign Speeches of 1932* (Doubleday, Doran, 1933), 167–96; "Hoover Warns Foes Plan Complete Wreck of American System by Creed of Despair," *LAT*, Nov. 1, 1933; "Hoover Warns of Radicals," *CT*, Nov. 1, 1933. On the eviction of the Bonus Army and FDR's reaction, see Ted Morgan, *FDR: A Biography* (Simon & Schuster, 1985), 356–57.
42. Sept. 23, 1932, *PP&A, 1928 –1932*, 742–55.
43. Anne O'Hare McCormick, "Two Men at the Big Moment," *NYT*, Nov. 6, 1932.
44. For election results, Donald A. Ritchie, *Electing FDR: The New Deal Campaign of 1932* (University Press of Kansas, 2007), 157–60.
45. Walter Lippmann, "Hankering for Supermen," Sept. 25, 1931, in *Interpretations*, 30–33.
46. Walter Lippmann columns, "Today and Tomorrow," *LAT*, Jan. 17, Jan. 24, Feb. 10, 1933; Steel, *Lippmann and the American Century*, 300.
47. "Col. House Warns of Dictator Peril," *NYT*, Dec. 28, 1932. The *Nation* reported in mid-1932 that powerful banking interests were hoping for a dictator: "Wanted: A Mussolini," *Nation*, July 6, 1932.
48. "Dictator Proposed," *LAT*, Dec. 30, 1932; "Broader Power for Roosevelt," *WSJ*, Dec. 30, 1932; "Broad Powers for Roosevelt Being Mapped," *WP*, Dec. 31, 1932; "To Aid Roosevelt in Economy Power," *NYT*, Jan. 10, 1933; "Powers Equal to Duce Sought for Roosevelt," *LAT*, Feb. 10, 1933; "Two Year Plan Is Pushed," *NYT*, Feb. 10, 1933; "Leaders Differ on Garner Plan of Dictatorship," *CT*, Feb. 11, 1933; "Dictator Move Hit," *LAT*, Feb. 11, 1933.
49. "Will Congress Abdicate?," *NYT*, Feb. 11, 1933; "Semi-Dictator?," *Barron's*, Feb. 13 and 27, 1933; Walter Lippmann, "The Right Direction" and "Democracy and Dictatorship," *LAT*, Feb. 14 and 24, 1933; Smith quoted in "Smith Favors U.S. Dictator of Public Works," *NYHT*, Feb. 8, 1933, and in "A Blank Check for Roosevelt," *Newsweek*, Feb. 17, 1933. An editorial typical of the moment appeared in the Mar. 3, 1933, Georgia *Macon News*: "The feeling is strong that a measure of dictatorship is necessary. . . . In view of thousands of patriotic citizens, dictatorship must come by one means or the other." *The Nation* rejected Lippmann's argument emphatically: "Do We Need a Dictator?" *Nation*, Mar. 1, 1933.
50. "Inaugural Address," Mar. 4, 1933, *PP&A*, vol. 2, 11–16.
51. On the banking crisis and Roosevelt's first measures: Leuchtenberg, *FDR and the New Deal*, 18–45; "Roosevelt Inaugurated, Promises War-Time Action," *NYHT*, Mar. 5, 1933.
52. Ray Moley noted that the emergency bank acts were "thoroughly conservative policies." For the atmosphere of this grave hour, see Moley, *After Seven Years*, 138–61.
53. For a detailed timeline of New Deal legislation, see the Living New Deal at https://livingnewdeal.org/. The narrative of the 100 Days is brilliantly synthesized in Leuchtenberg, *FDR and the New Deal*, 41–62. Colorful details abound in Morgan, *FDR*, 367–412, and Jonathan Alter, *The Defining Moment: FDR's Hundred Days and the Triumph of Hope* (Simon & Schuster, 2006).
54. "Roosevelt Hailed by German Press," *NYT*, Mar. 5, 1933; "Europe Looks to Roosevelt as World Savior," *CT*, Mar. 5, 1933; Arthur Krock, "Roosevelt Gets Power of Dictator," *NYT*, Mar. 11, 1933; "Roosevelt Is Urged to Ask Wide Power as Farm Dictator," *NYT*, Mar. 12, 1933; Arthur Krock, "Roosevelt, as Crusader, Seeks Unequaled Power," *NYT*, Apr. 23, 1933; "Fear Congress Is Abdicating to a Dictator," *CT*, May 1, 1933; "Declares Roosevelt Failed in Remedies," *NYT*, May 8, 1933.

55. Anne O'Hare McCormick, "'Let's Try It!' Says Roosevelt," *NYT*, Mar. 26, 1933, and "Vast Tides That Stir the Capital," *NYT*, May 7, 1933.
56. "New Deal Sprung by Gridiron Club," *NYT*, Apr. 28, 1933. FDR himself addressed the dictator charge and rejected it: "Roosevelt Urges Cooperative Spirit as of Pioneer Days," *NYT*, Oct. 22, 1933; "Roosevelt Asks Cooperation; Sees No Need for Dictator," *CT*, Oct. 22, 1933.
57. FDR to Hearst, April 1, 1933, reproduced at "Dictatorship: The Road Not Taken," FDRL, http://www.fdrlibrary.marist.edu/archives/pdfs/dictatorship.pdf. The film was based on a book by the same name by Thomas Frederic Tweed. See Jeff Greenfield, "The Hollywood Hit Movie That Urged FDR to Become a Fascist," *Politico*, Mar. 25, 2018.
58. "America on the Road to Fascism Under Roosevelt, Italians Say," *CT*, May 13, 1933; "N. D. Baker Warns Against Dictator," *NYT*, May 20, 1933; "Job Bill 'Fascism' Alleged by Green," *NYT*, Mar. 25, 1933; "Roosevelt New Deal 'Fascism,' League Is Told," *CT*, June 18, 1933; "Is the New Deal Socialism? A Socialist Leader Answers," *NYT*, June 18, 1933. FDR rejected the association: see "No Dictatorship," *Time*, May 15, 1933. For further discussion of the "dictator" theme in American politics of the 1930s, see Alpers, *Dictators, Democracy*, 15–58; and Richard H. Pells, *Radical Visions and American Dreams: Culture and Social Thought in the Depression Years* (University of Illinois Press, 1973), 78–86.
59. "Statement on Signing the NIRA," *PP&A*, vol. 2, 246–7. For an early discussion of the issue, see Gilbert H. Montague, "Is NRA Fascistic?" *Annals of the American Academy of Political and Social Science* 180 (1935): 149–61.
60. The essential study is John Kennedy Ohl, *Hugh S. Johnson and the New Deal* (Northern Illinois University Press, 1985). Johnson wrote his own account: *The Blue Eagle from Egg to Earth* (Doubleday, 1935).
61. Giuseppe Bottai, "Corporate State and NRA," *Foreign Affairs*, July 1, 1935; Tugwell, *Diary*, 138; Long to FDR, June 27, 1933, Official File, FDRL, 447; Long to FDR, Aug. 14, 1933, Long Papers, box 100, LOC; FDR letter to Long, June 16, 1933, in Elliott Roosevelt, *F.D.R.: His Personal Letters*, vol. 1, 351–52.
62. "Johnson Issues 'Buy Now!' Appeal to Consumers," *LAT*, Aug. 11, 1933; "Drive on NRA Foes Started by Roosevelt," *WP*, Aug. 14, 1933; "NRA Lists Rules to Get Blue Eagle," *NYT*, Aug. 23, 1933; "Women Push Dor-to-Door NRA Canvas," *WP*, Aug. 26, 1933; "NRA Opens Drive to Line Up Nation," *NYT*, Aug. 29, 1933; "Giant Parade to End Gala NRA Program," *WP*, Aug. 29, 1933; "2 Million Jobs Are Attributed to NRA Code," *NYHT*, Aug. 30, 1933; "NRA Leader Hits Charges of Czardom," *WP*, Aug. 31, 1933; "Climax of Drive of NRA Is Set for Tomorrow," *NYHT*, Sept. 3, 1933; "Blue Eagle Drive Is Near Goal Here," *NYT*, Sept. 3, 1933; "Claims 85% of US Employers Enroll in NRA," *CT*, Sept. 13, 1933; "Heard by 10,000 Here," *NYT*, Sept. 13, 1933; "Fervor Sweeps Throngs," *NYT*, Sept. 14, 1933; "Johnson Pledges Credit," *NYT*, Sept. 14, 1933; "Parade Assembly a Vast Lake," *NYT*, Sept. 14, 1933; "Millions Join to Cheer NRA in New York," *WP*, Sept. 14, 1933.
63. Max Ascoli, "Fascism in the Making," *Atlantic*, Nov. 1933. For a similar judgment about the way FDR was using democratic methods to rejuvenate the economy, see Harold J. Laski, "The Roosevelt Experiment," *Atlantic*, Feb. 1934. A large scholarly literature has explored the fascism–New Deal links, sometimes stretching the case to prove intellectual kinship. See Maurizio Vaudagna, "The New Deal and Corporativism in Italy," *Radical History Review* (1977): 3–35; John A. Garraty, "The New Deal, National Socialism, and the Great Depression," *American Historical Review* 78, no. 4 (1973): 907–44; and more recently, Wolfgang Schivelbusch, *Three New Deals: Reflections on Roosevelt's America, Mussolini's Italy, and Hitler's Germany, 1933–1939* (Metropolitan Books, 2006). A deft analysis that keeps the New Deal just in the democratic camp is Katznelson, *Fear Itself*, 227–75. A careful study of the NRA and its alleged debts to fascism is James Q. Whitman, "Of Corporatism, Fascism, and the New Deal," *American Journal of Comparative Law* 39 (1991): 747–78.
64. Two speeches in the spring took up this topic: "Address to Representatives of Industry on NRA Codes," Mar. 5, 1934, *PP&A*, vol. 3, 123–31; and Fireside Chat, June 28, 1934, *PP&A*, vol. 3, 312–18. FDR rolled out a book to make this case: *On Our Way* (John Day, 1934), which was reviewed by Raymond Clapper, "New Deal, He Says, Is Neither Communism nor Fascism," *WP*, Apr. 15, 1934. The democracy vs. dictatorship dichotomy appeared in the midterm elections. See the James A. Farley speech at a dinner of the Democratic National Committee titled "Dictatorship—A Myth," in Roanoke, Virginia, on Oct. 19, 1934, Farley Papers, LOC.

Chapter 5: Ignoring Hitler

1. Michael Vincent Namorato, ed., *The Diary of Rexford G. Tugwell: The New Deal, 1932–1935* (Greenwood Press, 1992), 313–14.
2. Even the somewhat sympathetic account of Roosevelt's predicament by Richard Breitman and Allan J. Lichtman asserts nonetheless that in his first term, FDR was "a bystander to Nazi persecution." Though he showed initiative in pushing for the Évian conference in 1938, he really did not make any effort to help Jews until the establishment of the War Refugee Board in 1943. *FDR and the Jews* (Belknap Press, 2013), 2–4. A much more pointed critique by David Wyman argues that "anti-Semitism, nativistic nationalism, and the unemployment problem" led to the abandonment of the Jews by the Roosevelt administration. *Paper Walls: America and the Refugee Crisis, 1938–1941* (Pantheon Books, 1985), viii. Robert H. Abzug, ed., *America Views the Holocaust, 1933–1935* (Bedford/St. Martin's, 1995), shows that Roosevelt was aided by various apologists who tried to downplay Hitler's anti-Jewish measures. But many voices spoke up against the early Nazi moves, and the press made plain what was happening. For such evidence, see Daniel Greene and Edward Phillips, eds., *Americans and the Holocaust* (Rutgers University Press, 2022), 15–38.
3. Minutes of First Session of Cabinet of Adolf Hitler, Jan. 30, 1933, in Office of United States Chief of Counsel for Prosecution of Axis Criminality, *Nazi Conspiracy and Aggression* (Government Printing Office, 1946), 272–75; Sigrid Schultz, "Rule of Hitler Opened with Riots," *CT*, Feb. 1, 1933; "12 Shot in German Parade of Fascists," *WP*, Feb. 1, 1933; on the decree: Sackett to State Dept, Feb. 6, 1933, in *FRUS 1933*, vol. 2, 187–88; "Proclamation of the Reich Government to the German People (February 1, 1933)," in *Nazism 1919–1945*, vol. 1, *The Rise to Power 1919–1934* (University of Exeter Press, 1998), 131–34.
4. "Hitler Proclaims War on Democracy at Huge Nazi Rally," *NYT*, Feb. 11, 1933. Hitler's Feb. 10 speech in Max Domarus, ed., *Hitler: Speeches and Proclamations, 1932–1945*, vol. 1, 244–50.
5. Sackett to State Department, Feb. 16 and 27, 1933, *FRUS 1933*, vol. 2, 191, 199–200.
6. Sackett to State Department, March 3, 1933, *FRUS 1933*, vol. 2, 201–4. For a summary of the Reichstag fire controversy, see Benjamin Carter Hett, *Burning the Reichstag: An Investigation into the Third Reich's Enduring Mystery* (Oxford University Press, 2014). See also Kershaw, *Hitler: Hubris*, 457–59, and Childers, *Third Reich*, 240–47. "Decree of the Reich President for the Protection of the People and State," Feb. 28, 1933, https://ghdi.ghi-dc.org/sub_document.cfm?document_id=2325.
7. "Hitler Tightens Grip on German Rule at Polls," *CT*, Mar. 6, 1933.
8. John Gunther to William C. Bullitt, Mar. 7, 1933, Bullitt Papers, box 34, Yale University; Dorothy Thompson to Harriet Cohen, Mar. 18, 1933, in Harriet Cohen, *A Bundle of Time* (Faber, 1969), 175–76.
9. "Dachau," Holocaust Encyclopedia, https://encyclopedia.ushmm.org/content/en/article/dachau. On the rumors of torture and mass arrests, see "Nazi Terror Goes On," *MG*, Mar. 16, 1933; Peter Fritzsche, *Hitler's First Hundred Days: When Germans Embraced the Third Reich* (Basic, 2020), 156–64. Sackett to State Department, Mar. 9, 1933, *FRUS 1933*, vol. 2, 206–9. Sackett submitted his resignation on March 4; he left Germany on March 22, 1933.
10. Sigrid Schultz, "Hitler's Nazis Beat Yankees," *CT*, Mar. 8, 1933; Frederick T. Birchall, "3 More Americans Attacked in Berlin," *NYT*, Mar. 10, 1933; George Messersmith, U.S. consul in Berlin, to State Department, Mar. 14, 1933, cable #1184, in Messersmith Papers, box 1, University of Delaware; Sackett to State Department, Mar. 21, 1933, *FRUS 1933*, vol. 2, 210–13. For Messersmith's background and work in Berlin, see Jesse H. Stiller, *George S. Messersmith: Diplomat of Democracy* (University of North Carolina Press, 1987), 1–55; Max Domarus, ed., *Speeches and Proclamations, 1932–1945*, vol. 1 (Bolchazy-Carducci, 1990), 263–64; Sigrid Schultz, "Hitler Orders Nazi Troops to End Terrorism," *CT*, Mar. 11, 1933; Messersmith to State Department, Mar. 21, 1933, cable #1196, Messersmith Papers, box 1, University of Delaware.
11. Sackett to State Department, Mar. 24, 1933, *FRUS 1933*, vol. 2, 213–14; Sigrid Schultz, "Hitler Is Made Dictator," *CT*, Mar. 24, 1933.
12. "Apprehension Grows for Safety of German Jews," *American Israelite*, Mar. 2, 1933; "Hitler Denounced in Purim Sermons," "Dr. Einstein Urges Hitler Protests," "Plan Protest on Hitler," all in *NYT*, Mar. 13, 17, 19, 1933. The Haman parallel had been made before: "Adolf Hitler, a Modern Haman, Named Chancellor of the German Reich," *Jewish Advocate*, Jan. 31, 1933. The *American*

Israelite also published a fanatically antisemitic speech by Joseph Goebbels explaining why the Nazis sought to purge Germany of its Jews: "What Does Hitler's Triumph Really Mean?" *American Israelite*, Feb. 9, 1933.

13. "German Fugitives Tell of Atrocities at Hands of Nazis;" "Jews Here Demand Washington Action," "Protest on Hitler Growing in Nation," "Churches Protest on Anti-Semitism," "Attacks on Jews Scored in Pulpits," all in *NYT*, Mar. 20, 21, 23, 25, and 27, 1933. Many reports of anti-Jewish violence were compiled in a June 1933 report, *Jews in Nazi Germany: The Factual Record of Their Persecution by the National Socialists* (American Jewish Committee, 1933).
14. Martha Dodd, *Through Embassy Eyes* (Garden City, 1940), 20–1; "G.A. Gordon to Wed Mrs. Alice V. Garrett," *NYT*, July 5, 1930.
15. Gordon to State Department, Mar. 23, 1933, *FRUS 1933*, vol. 2, 328–30.
16. "Berlin Inquiry Ordered," *NYT*, Mar. 22, 1933; "Jews' Mistreating Abated, U.S. Is Told," *WP*, Mar. 27, 1933; "Nazis End Attacks on Jews in Reich, Our Embassy Finds," *NYT*, Mar. 27, 1933.
17. "55,000 Here Stage Protest on Hitler Attacks on Jews," "35,000 Jam Streets Outside the Garden," "Smith Calls for a World-Wide Fight on Religious Bigotry," "Leaders of Nation Send in Protests," all in *NYT*, Mar. 28, 1933. The American Jewish Congress sponsored simultaneous protest rallies in Chicago, Boston, Philadelphia, Baltimore, Cleveland, and seventy other cities. For simultaneous protests, "Crowds Protest Hitler Persecution," *CT*, Mar. 28, 1933.
18. For Wise's earlier remarks: "Score Nazi Religious View" and "Sorrows for Germany"; text of Wise speech: "'We Ask Only for the Right,' Says Wise," *NYT*, Feb. 27, Mar. 20 and 28, 1933.
19. Messersmith to State Department, #1210, Mar. 28, 1933; #1212, Mar. 31, 1933; #1214, Mar. 31, 1933, Messersmith Papers, box 1, University of Delaware. See also press coverage of boycott announcement: Sigrid Schultz, "Nazis Strike New Blow at German Jewry," *CT*, Mar. 28, 1933; Frederick T. Birchall, "Nazis Plan Order for New Boycott," *NYT*, Mar. 28, 1933; "More Jews to Go," *Wall Street Journal*, Mar. 28, 1933; "Jewish Retaliation Is Planned by Nazis," *WP*, Mar. 28, 1933; Sigrid Schultz, "Jews Face Drastic Boycott," *CT*, Mar. 29, 1933; Frederick T. Birchall, "Boycott on Jews Ordered by Nazis," *NYT*, Mar. 29, 1933; "Jewish Clamp Set Saturday by Nazi Chiefs," *WP*, Mar. 29, 1933; Sigrid Schultz, "Hitler Puts O.K. on Jewish Boycott," *CT*, Mar. 30, 1933.
20. "Nazis Lay Boycott to 'Lies' of Jews," *NYT*, Apr. 1, 1933; "The Larger Question," *NYT*, Mar. 30, 1933; "Hitler Nazis Declare War on World Jewry," *CT*, Mar. 31, 1933.
21. Hull's turf wars with the White House can be sampled in Hull, *Memoirs*, vol. 1, 202–8; and the Moffat diaries, Nancy Harvison Hooker, ed., *The Moffat Papers: Selections from the Diplomatic Papers of Jay Pierrepont Moffat, 1919–1943* (Harvard University Press, 1956), 93.
22. Katharine Crane, *Mr. Carr of State: Forty-Seven Years in the Department of State* (St. Martin's Press, 1960), 269–78; Alan M. Kraut, Richard Breitman, and Thomas W. Imhoof, "The State Department, the Labor Department, and German Jewish Immigration, 1930–1940," *Journal of American Ethnic History* 3, no. 2 (1984): 5–38. William Phillips wrote an opaque and dull memoir: *Ventures in Diplomacy* (Beacon Press, 1952). See also Paul Henry Reuter, "William Phillips and the Development of American Foreign Policy, 1933–1947" (University of Southern Mississippi, PhD dissertation, 1979). Moffat's attitudes can be seen in, for example, his diary entry of Apr. 3, 1934, *Moffat Papers*, 111.
23. Hull to Gordon, Mar. 30, 1933, *FRUS 1933*, vol. 2, 338; "Memorandum of Trans-Atlantic Telephone Conversation," Mar. 31, 1933, Gordon and Phillips, *FRUS 1933*, vol. 2, 342–43; Armstrong diary, Mar. 31, 1933, and text of interview, Aug. 23, 1933, in Hamilton Fish Armstrong Papers, box 99, Seeley Mudd Library, Princeton University.
24. Sigrid Schultz, "Hitler Cuts Jew Boycott to One Day," and "Hitler Orders Nazis to Halt Jewish Boycott," *CT*, Apr. 1 and 4, 1933; Frederick T. Birchall, "One Day Boycott in Reich Orderly," *NYT*, Apr. 2, 1933. Messersmith cabled detailed accounts of the boycott to the State Department: #1216, Apr. 3, 1933, Messersmith Papers, box 1, University of Delaware.
25. Gordon telephone call with Phillips, Apr. 2, 1933, *FRUS 1933*, vol. 2, 344–46; on the stages of the seizure of power, see Josef and Ruth Becker, eds., *Hitlers Machtergreifung 1933: Vom Machtantritt Hitlers 30. Januar 1933 bis zur Besiegelung des Einparteienstaates 14. Juli 1933* (DTV, 1983), 185–382; Childers, *Third Reich*, 229–64; Kershaw, *Hitler: Hubris*, 431–83. There was widespread chatter even among German nonpolitical officials in government that the Nazi Party might collapse or that Hitler could be sobered by the responsibilities of power. Hamilton Fish Armstrong, who visited Berlin in April 1933, gives some atmosphere of the moment: *Peace and Counterpeace,* 530–31; and "Hitler Sweeps Jews Out of Official Jobs," *NYHT*, Apr. 9, 1933.

26. *Die Tagebücher von Joseph Goebbels*, Teil I, Aufzeichnungen 1923–1941, Band 2/III, Oktober 1932–März 1934 (K. G. Saur, 2006), 184. Lilian Mowrer, *Journalist's Wife*, 291. For press comment: "Nazis Pile Books for Bonfires Today," *NYT*, May 10, 1933; and Walter Lippmann, "The Burning of Books," *LAT*, May 12, 1933. The American Jewish Congress compiled a list of authors whose books were burned: see Proquest, History Vault: American Jewish Congress Records, Series I: History, 1915–1974, Jews in Germany, 1933, box 1, folder 18, American Jewish Historical Society.
27. Guido Enderis, "Pure German Race Is Aim of New Law," *NYT*, Aug. 6, 1933. Extensive reporting on the sterilization law appeared in hundreds of American newspapers, as research of the U.S. Holocaust Memorial Museum shows: https://newspapers.ushmm.org/search/results?eventName=37.
28. Armstrong diary, Apr. 27, 1933, Armstrong Papers, box 99, Seeley Mudd Library, Princeton University. Armstrong interviewed Mussolini on May 16, and gave a radio address on August 23. Text of these also in box 99. He published his impressions of Germany in "Hitler's Reich: The First Phase," *Foreign Affairs* 11, no. 4 (1933): 589–608.
29. Messersmith to Hull, memo #1305, May 12, 1933; Messersmith to Hull, memo # 1369, June 17, 1933; Messersmith to Hull, #1370, June 19, 1933; Messersmith letter to Phillips, June 26, 1933; Messersmith Papers, box 2, University of Delaware.
30. "Hitler Power Seen in Middle Class; Dorothy Thompson, Back from Germany, Calls Him 'Apotheosis of the Little Man,'" *NYT*, May 12, 1933; Gordon to State Department, June 24 and 30, 1933, *FRUS 1933*, vol. 2, 236–39, 239–42.
31. Richard Breitman, Barbara McDonald Stewart, and Severin Hochberg, eds., *Advocate for the Doomed: The Diaries and Papers of James G. McDonald, 1932–35* (Indiana University Press, 2007), 3–5, 22.
32. *Advocate for the Doomed*, 27, 33, 35, 40.
33. *Advocate for the Doomed*, 48; "Hitler Challenges American Protests," *NYT*, Apr. 7, 1933.
34. *Advocate for the Doomed*, 59–64.
35. "100,000 March Here in 6-Hour Protest over Nazi Policies," *NYT*, May 11, 1933. In Cincinnati, civic and religious leaders also held a mass gathering to protest "the rebirth of medieval barbarism." "Hitlerism Fought on Local, National, and International Fronts," *American Israelite*, May 25, 1933.
36. "Drive to Aid Jews Opened by Lehman," *NYT*, June 15, 1933. McDonald called for American Jews to donate to Jewish relief in *Jewish Advocate*, June 27, 1933, and in July he began a speaking tour publicizing Nazi segregation policy. "Cruelty of Nazis to Jews Asserted," *NYT*, July 11, 1933.
37. Dorothy Thompson, "Back to Blood and Iron," and "Room to Breathe In," May 6 and June 24, 1933, both in *SEP*. "National Revolution," *Time*, Mar. 13, 1933; "Hitler is Criticized—Dorothy Thompson Is Speaker at B'rith Sholom Convention," *NYT*, June 19, 1933; text of her address: "What Dorothy Thompson Saw in Germany," *Jewish Exponent*, June 30, 1933. Goebbels story: "The Jews Are to Blame," *Time*, July 10, 1933. For a study of the American high-brow journals and their treatment of Germany in 1933, see Michael Zalampas, *Adolf Hitler and the Third Reich in American Magazines, 1923–1939* (Bowling Green State University Press, 1989), 28–42.
38. "Urges Anti-Nazi Stand," *NYT*, June 26, 1933.
39. Rafael Medoff, *The Jews Should Keep Quiet: Franklin D. Roosevelt, Rabbi Stephen S. Wise, and the Holocaust* (University of Nebraska Press, 2019), 32–33; Ward, First-Class, 251–55.
40. "Boycott Warning Sent from Berlin," *NYT*, Mar. 31, 1933; "Frown on Parades as Hitler Protest," *NYT*, Apr. 28, 1933; "Leader of Jews Warns on Boycott," *LAT*, Aug. 1, 1933.
41. Much valuable work has been done on the World Economic Conference. See Patricia Clavin, *The Failure of Economic Diplomacy: Britain, Germany, France and the United States, 1931–1936* (St. Martin's Press, 1996), and Barry Eichengreen, *Golden Fetters: The Gold Standard and the Great Depression, 1919–1939* (Oxford University Press, 1992), esp. 317–47. FDR's message that helped scuttle the conference is in FDR to Phillips, July 2, 1933, FDR&FA, vol. 1, 268–69. A doleful postmortem was written by the State Department economic adviser, Herbert Feis: *1933: Characters in Crisis* (Little, Brown, 1966). A characteristically lively narrative that highlights the divisions within the U.S. government is in Arthur M. Schlesinger Jr., *The Age of Roosevelt: The Coming of the New Deal, 1933–1935* (Houghton Mifflin, 1958), 179–232.
42. A detailed analysis of the disarmament discussions can be found in Offner, *American Appeasement*, 18–53. Phillips to Roosevelt and Hull to Davis, both Apr. 4, 1933, *FRUS 1933*, vol. 1, 80–82.

43. Memorandum by President Roosevelt, and message from Hull to Davis, both dated Apr. 4, 1933, *FRUS 1933*, vol. 1, 81.
44. Davis memo on his talk with Hitler, Apr. 8, 1933, *FRUS 1933*, vol.1, 85–89.
45. Schacht to Foreign Ministry, May 6, 1933, in *Documents on German Foreign Policy, 1918–1945*, Series C (1933–1937), vol. 1, 390–93. On Schacht's petulance, see *Moffat Papers*, 95–96.
46. This episode can be followed in Norman Davis to FDR, May 15, 1933, *FRUS 1933*, vol. 1, 140–42; and FDR's message of May 16, ibid., 143–45. FDR quoted by Freidel, *Rendezvous with Destiny*, 114. For Hitler's May 17 speech to the Reichstag, see *Documents on German Foreign Policy*, vol.1, 451–5.
47. Gordon to Hull, May 20, 1933, *FRUS 1933*, vol.1, 159–64. Hitler's speech certainly fooled Walter Lippmann, who took Hitler's speech at face value, hailed the statesmanship of the chancellor, and thought Hitler was "the authentic voice of a genuinely civilized people." Lippmann, "Hitler's Speech," *LAT*, May 19, 1933, in Abzug, *America Views the Holocaust*, 42–43.
48. John G. Deal, "William Edward Dodd (1869–1940)," *Dictionary of Virginia Biography*, Library of Virginia, http://www.lva.virginia.gov/public/dvb/bio.asp?b=Dodd_William_Edward; Robert Dallek, *Democrat and Diplomat: The Life of William E. Dodd* (Oxford University Press, 1968); Fred Arthur Bailey, "A Virginia Scholar in Chancellor Hitler's Court: The Tragic Ambassadorship of William Edward Dodd," *Virginia Magazine of History and Biography* 100, no. 3 (1992): 323–42. On October 30, 1947, Dodd's daughter Martha issued a statement to the press detailing Dodd's connection to FDR and the likely reasons for his appointment; journalists of the era, unaware of Dodd's biography, had started a rumor that Dodd had been an accidental appointment when FDR called the wrong Professor Dodd listed in the Chicago phone book. "Statement of Martha Dodd," Dodd Papers, box 60, Library of Congress. In his letter of March 9 to James M. Cox, FDR wrote, "I regard Berlin as of special importance at this time," but despite this plea, Cox refused the offer of ambassador: *FDR: His Personal Letters,* vol. 1, 337–38. For Dodd's advice to FDR during and after the 1932 campaign, see Dodd to FDR, July 30, Nov. 9, and Dec. 24, 1932, President's Personal File 1043, Dodd, William E., FDRL.
49. William E. Dodd Jr. and Martha Dodd, *Ambassador Dodd's Diary, 1933–1938* (Harcourt, Brace, 1941), 4–6, 9–10. The Dodd family experience in Berlin in 1933–34 received sustained examination in Larson, *Garden of Beasts*.
50. *Ambassador Dodd's Diary*, 11–12; Wise to Dodd, July 19, 1933, Dodd Papers, box 43, LOC.
51. For Dodd's anxieties about money and the cost of living in Berlin, see Dodd letter to Frederic Sackett, June 22, 1933, Dodd Papers, box 43, LOC. He wrote directly to FDR to complain of "cliques who jeopardize the service by favoring rich personal friends and kinfolk," and foreign service officers "imitating Louis XIV." Dodd to FDR, Dec. 23, 1933, PSF: Germany: Dodd, 1933–35, box 32, FDRL. He also complained to Hull about staff trying who undercut his efforts to economize at the embassy, letter of Apr. 17, 1934, Dodd Papers, box 44, LOC. For further details see Dallek, *Democrat and Diplomat*, 196–232.
52. Dodd to Wise, July 20 and Aug. 1, 1933, Dodd Papers, box 43, LOC; Dodd to FDR, July 30, 1933, Official File 523, W.E. Dodd, FDRL; Sigrid Schultz, "80,000 Storm Troops March in Berlin Review," *CT*, Aug. 7, 1933.
53. Martha Dodd, *Through Embassy Eyes*, 37.
54. Morrell Heald, *Transatlantic Vistas: American Journalists in Europe, 1900–1940* (Kent State University Press, 1988), 159–72. For social lives of the journalists, see Lilian Mowrer, *Journalist's Wife*, 286–7, and Martha Dodd, *Through Embassy Eyes*, 100. For further analysis of the restraints on reporters, see Lipstadt, *Beyond Belief*, 20–32. For details on the Taverne, see Norman Domeier, *American Journalists in Hitler's Germany* (Boydell & Brewer, 2025), 35–37.
55. Anne O'Hare McCormick, "Hitler Seeks Jobs for All Germans," *NYT*, July 10, 1933.
56. Louis Lochner, *Always the Unexpected: A Book of Reminiscences* (Macmillan, 1956), 252; Janet Flanner, "Führer," in 3 parts, *New Yorker*, Feb. 22, Feb. 29, and Mar. 7, 1936.
57. Martha Dodd, *Through Embassy Eyes*, 39; Mowrer, *Germany Puts the Clock Back*, 242, 287.
58. Mowrer, *Triumph and Turmoil,* 217, 219, 225. On the State Department's role in easing Mowrer out of Berlin, see *FRUS 1933*, vol. 2, 398–406.
59. *Ambassador Dodd's Diary*, 24, 26; Martha Dodd, *Through Embassy Eyes*, 39; Mowrer, *Triumph and Turmoil*, 224.
60. Mowrer, *Triumph and Turmoil*, 365–66.
61. "300 Jews Jailed in Nuremberg by Nazi Troops," *WP*, July 21, 1933; "Nuremberg Jews Brutally Treated," *NYT*, July 31, 1933; "Nuremberg Jews Ordeal," *MG*, Aug. 7, 1933.

62. Martha Dodd, *Through Embassy Eyes*, 28–29; Quentin Reynolds, "Woman's Place," *Collier's*, Nov. 25, 1933; "Nazis Use Penalty of Medieval Days," *NYT*, Aug. 19, 1933; "Women Paraded in Streets," *MG*, Aug. 23, 1933. The victim became "mentally deranged" as a result of the incident, according to later reports, and was sent to the Erlangen psychiatric clinic. "Nazi Victim Deranged," *NYT*, Sept. 4, 1933. Ambassador Dodd later confirmed that his children had been present during the attack, letter to Emil Ahlborn, Jan. 19, 1934, Dodd Papers, box 43, LOC.
63. Frederick Birchall, "Nazi Legions Mass at Greatest Rally," *NYT*, Aug. 31, 1933; Tom Service, "*Die Meistersinger*: 'It's Wagner's Most Heartwarming Opera,'" *The Guardian*, May 19, 2011.
64. Frederick Birchall, "Nazis Use Pressure for Big Party Rally," *NYT*, Aug. 29, 1933.
65. Frederick Birchall, "Lengthy Nazi Rule Indicated by Rally," *NYT*, Sept. 6, 1933.
66. Offner, *American Appeasement*, 50; Sigrid Schultz, "Hitler Evokes World Crisis," *CT*, Oct. 15, 1933.
67. Domarus, ed., *Hitler: Speeches and Proclamations*, vol. 1, 364–74. For analysis, see Ian Kershaw, *Hitler: Hubris*, 490–95; Evans, *Third Reich in Power*, 618–19; Shirer, *Rise and Fall*, 210–12.
68. *Ambassador Dodd's Diary*, 49–50; Dodd to Hull, Oct. 18, 1933, *FRUS 1933*, vol. 2, 397.
69. FDR and Hull phone call to Davis, Oct. 16, 1933, *FRUS 1933*, vol. 1, 273–76; Davis to FDR, Oct. 17, 1933, ibid., 278–79; Davis to Hull, Oct. 19, 1933, ibid., 289–91; Hull to Davis, Oct. 21, 1933, ibid., 296; Hull to Davis, Oct. 24, 1933, ibid., 298.
70. Messersmith to Hull, Sept. 21, 1933, and Messersmith to Phillips, Oct. 28, 1933, Messersmith Papers, box 3, University of Delaware.
71. John Gunther to William Bullitt, Nov. 26, 1933, Bullitt Papers, box 34, Yale University; Messersmith to Phillips, Sept. 29 and Oct. 19, 1933, Messersmith Papers, box 3, University of Delaware.
72. Frederick T. Birchall, "Nazis Cover Reich with Vote Pleas," *NYT*, Nov. 6, 1933; "Hitler Insists Voters Refute 'Beast' Brand," *WP*, Nov. 11, 1933; Frederick T. Birchall, "Hindenburg Urges 100% Hitler Vote," *NYT*, Nov. 12, 1933; Sigrid Schultz, "Nazi Votes Sweep Germany," *CT*, Nov. 13, 1933.
73. Louis Fischer to Freda Kirchwey, Apr. 18, 1934, Louis Fischer Papers, box 6, Seeley Mudd Library, Princeton University.
74. John Gunther, "Keeping Hitler Out of Austria," *Nation*, Feb. 14, 1938.
75. Gunther, "Keeping Hitler Out," and Gunther, "Dollfuss and the Future of Austria," *Foreign Affairs*, Jan. 1, 1934. For developments in Austria in 1933–34, see John W. Boyer, *Austria, 1867–1955* (Oxford University Press, 2022), 759–89.
76. For details on the February 1934 civil war, see Martin Kitchen, *The Coming of Austrian Fascism* (Routledge, 1980), 202–32. Kitchen concludes of Dollfuss: He "was determined to destroy Social Democracy. 'Anti-Marxism' was the guiding principle of his politics" (283). For an eyewitness account, see Louis Fischer to Freda Kirchwey, Mar.1, 1934, Louis Fischer Papers, box 6, Seeley Mudd Library, Princeton University.
77. G. E. R. Gedye, "Dollfuss Becomes a Legal Dictator, *NYT*, May 1, 1934; Shirer, *Berlin Diary*, 10; "Austria Uncovers a Socialist 'Plot,'" *NYT*, Feb. 9, 1934; David Darrah, "Austria in Civil War," *CT*, Feb. 13, 1934; Frederick T. Birchall, "Socialists Losing Fight," and "Socialist Fight Hopeless," *NYT*, Feb. 13 and 14, 1934; G. E. R. Gedye, "Dollfuss Ends 10-Year Rule of Socialists in Vienna," *NYT*, Feb. 18, 1934; John Gunther, "The Slaughter in Austria," *Nation*, Mar. 21, 1934, and "The Struggle for Power in Austria," *Nation*, May 16, 1934; Hamilton Fish Armstrong letter to FDR, Feb. 15, 1934; and in a memo dated Feb. 20, Armstrong noted that his letter did reach FDR. Armstrong Papers, box 99, Seeley Mudd Library, Princeton University; G. E. R. Gedye, "Austria Is Fascist, Says Starhemberg," *NYT*, Feb. 28, 1934. Johannes Steel, a German émigré journalist, thought Dollfuss had badly miscalculated and predicted that "Austria will soon go Nazi." "The Bloody Danube and Beyond," *Nation*, Mar. 7, 1934.
78. For the U.S. embassy view of the events as a Socialist revolt, see the cables by the chargé A. W. Kliefoth to State Department of Feb. 13, Feb. 15, Feb. 16, Feb. 17, Feb. 22, 1934, in *FRUS 1934*, vol. 2, 10–20.
79. Undated and unsigned "Memorandum on the Austrian Situation"; George Earle to FDR, Nov. 27, 1933, and FDR to Earle, Dec. 22, 1933, both in PSF, Box 23, Austria, 1933–1944, FDRL.
80. Messersmith to Under Secretary of State William Phillips, June 18, 1934, Messersmith Papers, box 4, file 24, University of Delaware. On FDR's high opinion of Messersmith, see memo of Hamilton Fish Armstrong, May 17, 1934, after having tea with Roosevelt. Armstrong Papers, box 99, Seeley Mudd Library, Princeton University.
81. Dodd, *Diary*, 54, 67–68, 71.

82. Dodd, *Diary*, 78.
83. Dodd to FDR, Nov. 27, 1933, PSF, box 32, Germany, Dodd, 1933–35, FDRL.
84. Dodd to FDR, Feb. 8, 1934, and undated memo titled "The Proposed German Commission," PSF, box 32, Germany, Dodd, 1933–35, FDRL.
85. Memos by Hull, Feb. 1, Feb. 19, Mar. 2, and John Hickerson, Mar. 1, 1934; Dodd to Hull, Mar. 6, and Hull to Dodd, Mar. 6, 1934; and memo by William Phillips, Mar. 7, 1934; and the protest made by the Foreign Office in Berlin to Dodd, Mar. 8, 1934, in *FRUS 1934*, vol. 2, 508–15; Dodd, *Diary*, 89–90. "Dr. Luther Protested Hitler Trial Here," *NYT*, Mar. 9, 1934; "Mock Trial in New York," *MG*, Mar. 9, 1934. For analysis of the trial, see Louis Anthes, "Publicly Deliberative Drama: The 1934 Mock Trial of Adolf Hitler for 'Crimes against Civilization,'" *American Journal of Legal History* 42, no. 4 (1998): 391–410; and *The Case of Civilization against Hitlerism: Presented under the Auspices of the American Jewish Congress at Madison Square Garden* (Robert Ballou, 1934).
86. Messersmith to Dodd, Apr. 3, 1934, Moore Papers, box 5, FDRL; "Goebbels Utters Threats to Jews," *NYT*, May 12, 1934; Otto Tolischus, "Nazi Press Pushes New War on Jews," *NYT*, May 13, 1934; Charles Farmer, "Hitler Jittery as German Faith in Him Slips," *CT*, May 17, 1934; Otto Tolischus, "Reich Exports Cut to New Low Level," *NYT*, May 18, 1934; Sigrid Schultz, "Hitlerists Open New Campaign to Crush Jews," *CT*, June 2, 1934; Hamilton Fish Armstrong, "Radicals, Reactionaries Joust for Rule of Germany's Future," *WP*, June 2, 1934. For the "syphilis" comment, see Dodd to FDR, Aug. 15, 1934, PPF 1043, FDRL.
87. Dodd, *Diary*, 101–5, 109–10, 114–15; Messersmith's memo summarized by William Phillips to FDR, June 5, 1934, PSF, box 31, Germany, 1933–38, FDRL; the von Papen speech in Louis L. Snyder, ed., *Hitler's Third Reich: A Documentary History* (Nelson-Hall, 1981), 173–77; Martha Dodd, *Through Embassy Eyes*, 134.
88. Dodd's reports were not entirely accurate, but he had gleaned the general outlines of the unfolding conflict. Dodd to Hull, June 20 and 26, 1934, *FRUS 1934*, vol. 2, 224–29.
89. Dodd, *Diary*, 123, 126; Dodd to Hull, July 14, 1934, Dodd Papers, box 44, LOC; Dodd to Moore, July 17, 1934, Moore Papers, box 5, FDRL. On the events of June 1934, Evans, *Third Reich*, 20–43; Kershaw, *Hitler: Hubris*, 499–526.
90. John Gunther, "Policy by Murder: The Story of the Dollfuss Killing," *Harper's*, Nov. 1, 1934. For an earlier and briefer summary, see Gunther, "After the Dollfuss Murder," *Nation*, Aug. 22, 1934. For further details of the role of Mussolini in thwarting a German invasion, see Messersmith letter to Hamilton Fish Armstrong, Oct. 2, 1934, Armstrong Papers, box 44, Seeley Mudd Library, Princeton University.
91. Dodd to Hull, July 14, 1934, Dodd Papers, box 44, LOC; Dodd to Roper, Aug. 14, 1934, OF 573, FDRL; Dodd to FDR, Aug. 15, 1934, and FDR to Dodd, Aug. 25, 1934, PPF 1043, FDRL.
92. Dorothy Thompson, "Good-by to Germany," *Harper's*, Dec. 1, 1934.
93. Frederick T. Birchall, "Dorothy Thompson Expelled by Reich For 'Slur' on Hitler," *NYT*, Aug. 26, 1934.
94. Dorothy Thompson, "Dorothy Thompson Tells of Nazi Ban," *NYT*, Aug. 27, 1934; "Expulsion Are Futile, say Ms. Thompson," *NYT*, Aug. 30, 1934; Dorothy Thompson, "Force Governs Germany," *Jewish Advocate*, Sept. 7, 1934; "Dorothy Thompson Expelled from Germany," *Jewish Exponent*, Aug. 31, 1934; Editorial, "Dorothy Thompson's Expulsion from Germany," *Jewish Exponent*, Aug. 31, 1934. Additional coverage appeared in the *CT* and *WP*, among other papers. Quote on Germany already at war, Kurth, *American Cassandra*, 204.
95. Dodd to Hull, Aug. 2 and Aug. 30, 1934, Dodd Papers, box 44, LOC.
96. Dodd to Moore, Oct. 5, 1934, Moore Papers, box 5, FDRL; Dodd to Moore, Nov. 5, 1934; Moore to FDR, Nov. 20, 1934, PSF, Germany, Dodd, 1933–35, box 32, FDRL.
97. "Press Conference," Sept. 7, 1934, *FDR & FA*, vol. 2, 207–10.

Chapter 6: Romancing the Reds

1. Bullitt's long personal letter to FDR detailing these events is dated Jan. 1, 1934, in William C. Bullitt Papers, box 71, Sterling Library, Yale University. For Bullitt's early days in Russia, see Will Brownell and Richard N. Billings, *So Close to Greatness: A Biography of William C. Bullitt* (Macmillan, 1987), 86–99; Beatrice Farnsworth, *William C. Bullitt and the Soviet Union* (Indiana University Press, 1967), 32–54; and Michael Cassella-Blackburn, *The Donkey, the Carrot, and the Club: William C. Bullitt and Soviet-American Relations, 1917–1948* (Praeger, 2004), 35–61.

2. *Memoirs of Cordell Hull*, vol. 1, 297. For the linkage between recognition of the USSR and the containment of Germany and Japan, see Blum, *Morgenthau Diaries: Years of Crisis, 1928–1938*, 54.
3. "Congress to Grasp Reins, Says Harding," *NYT*, May 19, 1919; and a roundup of opinion titled "Bolshevism—by Those Who Know It," *WP*, Feb. 8, 1920; David R. Francis, *Russia from the American Embassy* (Charles Scribner's Sons, 1921), vi, 226, 283, 333.
4. John Reed, *Ten Days That Shook the World* (Boni and Liveright, 1919). Lenin wrote the book's foreword. On Steffen's remark, see Peter Hartshorn, *I Have Seen the Future: A Life of Lincoln Steffens* (Penguin, 2012), 315, and 301–21 for the Bullitt mission.
5. On the bloody chunk of collarbone, Ward, *First-Class*, 456–7.
6. "Bolshevism—by Those Who Know It," *WP*, Feb. 8, 1920. For a fresh look at the Palmer raids, see Gage, *G-Man*, 61–74.
7. David Greenstein, "Assembling 'Fordizm': The Production of Automobiles, Americans, and Bolsheviks in Detroit and Early Soviet Russia," *Comparative Studies in Society and History* 56, no. 2 (April 2014): 259–89. For the nonrecognition statement, Frank Kellogg to Sen. William Butler, Feb. 23, 1928, *FRUS 1928*, vol. 3, 823–25. "44 American Firms Are Aiding Soviet," *NYT*, Nov. 30, 1930. The senators were quoted in "Russians Recruits," *Time*, Sept. 15, 1930.
8. H. R. Knickerbocker, "The First Five-Year Plan and Its Postulates," *New York Evening Post*, Nov. 17, 1930; "Five-Year Plan Forging Ahead in Reign of Terror," *New York Evening Post*, Dec. 15, 1930; his book was *The Soviet Five-Year Plan and Its Effect on World Trade* (Bodle Head, 1931).
9. The scholarship on forced collectivization and the famine is substantial. These numbers come from Stephane Courtois, et al., *The Black Book of Communism: Crimes, Terror, Repression* (Harvard University Press, 1999), 159, 167. For the origins and early phases of the plan, see Robert C. Tucker, *Stalin in Power: The Revolution from Above, 1928–41* (Norton, 1990), 44–118, and 139 for the "breaking" and "liquidation" of the kulaks; Robert Conquest, *Harvest of Sorrow: Soviet Collectivization and the Terror-Famine* (Oxford University Press, 1986), 87–116; Stephen Kotkin, *Stalin: Waiting for Hitler, 1929–1941* (Penguin Press, 2017), 9–83; and Anne Applebaum, *Red Famine: Stalin's War on Ukraine* (Random House, 2017), 96–164.
10. S. J. Taylor, *Stalin's Apologist* (Oxford University Press, 1990), 95–116.
11. Duranty, "Food Lack Menaces Soviet Prosperity," *NYT*, June 6, 1929; "Soviet Budget Rise Reveals Progress," *NYT*, Aug. 26, 1929.
12. Duranty, "Grievances Aired in Russian Press," *NYT*, Sept. 9, 1929; "Sees Soviet Ahead with 5-Year Plan," *NYT*, Oct. 3, 1929; "All Russia Lauds Five Years Plan," *NYT*, Oct. 6, 1929; "Soviet at a Crisis in Its Farm Plans," *NYT*, Oct. 14, 1929; "Soviet Farm Plan a Real Revolution," NYT, Nov. 3, 1929; "Bucharin Ousting Is Class War Sign," *NYT*, Nov. 19, 1929; "1929 Was Big Year for Soviet Russia," *NYT*, Jan. 1, 1930; "Soviet Drives Fast for Socialization," *NYT*, Feb. 16, 1930.
13. Duranty, "Stalin Triumphs at Red Convention," *NYT*, June 29, 1930; "Shock Period Set to Spur Red Output," *NYT*, Oct. 2, 1930. According to historian Robert Service, "mass collectivization meant that not until the mid-1950s did agriculture regain the level of output achieved in the last years of the Great War." Service 181.
14. Duranty, "Stalin Sees Capitalists Drifting Surely to War," Dec. 1, 1930; "Stalin Says Tyranny Made Him a Radical," Dec. 4, 1930; "Soviet Advanced by Farm Victory," Jan. 1, 1931; "Stalin: Man, Mouthpiece, Machine," Jan. 18, 1931, all in *NYT*.
15. "Millions are Held in Russian Camps," *NYT*, Feb. 3, 1931; "Red Rigor Likened to Puritans' Zeal," *NYT*, Feb. 15, 1931; "Red Russia of Today Ruled by Stalinism, Not by Communism," *NYT*, June 14, 1931.
16. Louis Fischer, "Russia's New Revolution," *Nation*, Mar. 19, 1930.
17. Louis Fischer, "Russia's New Revolution"; also "Why Stalin Won" and "Russia's Collective Farms," *Nation*, Aug. 13, 1930, and Oct. 8, 1930.
18. Anna Louise Strong, "All Russia Watches a Fateful Drama," *NYT*, Feb. 23, 1930; "Stalin's Strength Now Compared to that Lenin Showed," *WP*, Sept. 28, 1930; "Soviet Overcoming Shortage of Food by United Effort," *WP*, Dec. 7, 1930; *The Soviets Conquer Wheat: The Drama of Collective Farming* (Henry Holt, 1931), 3–6, and for passages taken from the recently held party congress, 272–88. Strong never tired of such exalted prose; she would write over thirty books in a similar vein, eventually settling down in China and becoming a devout Maoist.
19. Louis Fischer in Richard Crossman, ed., *The God That Failed* (Hamilton, 1950), 199–203, 215. Fischer to Freda Kirchwey, Jan. 1, 1934, Louis Fischer Papers, box 6, Seeley Mudd Library, Prince-

ton University. For further explanation of the way that the West collaborated in suppressing information about the famine, see Conquest, *Harvest of Sorrow*, 308–21.

20. "Roosevelt Confers on Russian Policy," *NYT*, July 26, 1932; Taylor, *Stalin's Apologist*, 184.
21. FDR's brain trust had discussed Soviet recognition in a May 1932 campaign memo, arguing that "the largest actual market" for the American surplus of wheat was Russia, and that Russia was "suffering likewise from an acute shortage of practically all products which the United States manufactures." Beatrice Bishop Berle, ed., *Navigating the Rapids, 1918–1971: From the Papers of Adolf A. Berle* (Harcourt Brace Jovanovich, 1973), 49. Russia "Politics in Soviet Trade," *WP*, July 27, 1932; "Women's Program Put Before Hoover," *NYT*, July 14, 1932; "Three Moves Begun to Aid Soviet Trade," *NYT*, Sept. 11, 1932; "Roosevelt Undecided on Soviet Recognition," *NYT*, Oct. 6, 1932; "Roosevelt's Stand on Soviet Sought," *WP*, Oct. 15, 1932; "Uninformed on Russia," editorial, *WP*, Oct. 8, 1932; "President Deciding on His Final Trips," *NYT*, Oct. 25, 1932.
22. Walter Duranty, "Russians Hopeful of a 'New Deal,'" *NYT*, Nov. 10, 1932; "Roosevelt Asked to Study Red Data," *NYT*, Nov. 23, 1932; John Boettinger, "Gov. Roosevelt Studies Russia at Dixie Home," *CT*, Nov. 26, 1932; "Democrats Expect Soviet Recognition," *NYT*, Dec. 4, 1932; "Senate Group Poll Indorses Soviet Accord," *WP*, Dec. 7, 1932; "Urges Soviet Recognition," *NYT*, Jan. 23, 1933; "Labor Protests New Recognition of Russia Move," *CT*, Jan. 30, 1933; "268 Colleges Join in Plea for Soviet," *NYT*, Jan. 30, 1933; "Soviet Recognition Urged by Women," *NYT*, Mar. 25, 1933.
23. "The Soviet and the Peasantry," three-part series, *MG*, Mar. 25, 27, and 28, 1933. Muggeridge expanded on his articles in "The Soviet's War on the Peasants," *Fortnightly Review*, May 1933, 558–64.
24. "Famine in Russia: Englishman's Story—What He Saw on a Walking Tour," *MG*, Mar. 30, 1933. For the publication history of Jones's pieces, see Ray Gamache, *Gareth Jones: Eyewitness to the Holodomor* (Ashley Drake, 2018), 122–47.
25. Walter Duranty, "Russians Hungry, but Not Starving," *NYT*, Mar. 31, 1933; Duranty, "Soviet Peasants Are More Hopeful," *NYT*, May 14, 1933.
26. "Cardinal Asks Aid in Russian Famine," *NYT*, Aug. 20, 1933.
27. "Famine Toll Heavy in Southern Russia," *NYT*, Aug. 24, 1933. For a report summarizing the testimony of an American couple in Ukraine, "Visitors Describe Famine in Ukraine," *NYT*, Aug. 29, 1933. Robert Conquest sees Duranty's impact as undermining otherwise credible reports emerging from the USSR about the scale of the famine. *Harvest of Sorrow*, 320–21.
28. James E. Mace, "The Politics of Famine: American Government and Press Response to the Ukrainian Famine, 1932–1933," *Holocaust and Genocide Studies* 3, no. 1 (1988): 75–94, quotation on 86. Also see the damning evidence of U.S. indifference in Commission on the Ukraine Famine, *Investigation of the Ukrainian Famine, 1932–1933: Report to Congress* (Government Printing Office, 1988), 151–84.
29. Hull, *Memoirs*, vol. 1, 167, 174, 300.
30. On connecting the origins of the Bullitt-FDR relationship and the natural affinity between the two, from 1932 on, see Louis Wehle's memoir, *Hidden Threads of History: From Wilson through Roosevelt* (Macmillan, 1953), 114–23. Bullitt's appointment letter of June 2, 1933, is in Bullitt Papers, box 111, Sterling Library, Yale University. On the extensive correspondence about Bullitt's 1932 trip to Europe on FDR's behalf, see Bullitt Papers, box 70 and 71, Sterling Library, Yale University.
31. Walton Moore, "Some Questions to be Studied," Sept. 27, 1933, in *DHFDRP*, vol. 27, 186–87; Moore memo, "What Soviet Russia Must Agree to in Order to Win American Recognition," Oct.1933, ibid., 195–97; Moore memo for Hull, Oct. 4, 1933, ibid., 296–99; FDR to Kalinin, Oct. 10, 1933, ibid., 312. Kelley had expressed his doubts in a paper dated July 27, 1933, *FRUS: The Soviet Union, 1933–39*, 6–11. And Hull counseled the president to secure ironclad guarantees before granting recognition. Hull to Roosevelt, Sept. 21, 1933, ibid., 12–13; and Hull, *Memoirs*, vol. 1, 299. The State Department supplied FDR with an analysis of newspaper editorial comment on recognition: William Phillips to FDR, Oct. 19, 1933, Official File 220, box 1, FDRL. On Bullitt's role as a back channel, see Bullitt to Hull, Oct. 11, 1933, Bullitt Papers, box 110, Sterling Library, Yale University. Bullitt had counseled Hull that the Russians wanted loans and a counterweight to Japanese threats, giving Washington "two powerful weapons" with which to negotiate with Moscow. Bullitt to Hull, Sept. 18, 1933, Bullitt Papers, box 110, Sterling Library, Yale University.
32. Moore, "Memorandum as to the Russian Conversations," Nov. 10, 1933, *DHFDRP*, vol. 27, 625–29; Moore to FDR, three memos dated Nov. 11, 1933, ibid., 632–33, 634–37, 638–39; FDR

to Litvinov, Nov. 16, ibid., 659; Memorandum by Roosevelt and Litvinov, Nov. 15, 1933, *FRUS: The Soviet Union*, 26–7; Litvinov to Roosevelt, Nov. 16, 1933, ibid., 28–29. The signed "gentleman's agreement," dated Nov. 15, 1933, is in Bullitt Papers, box 110, Sterling Library, Yale University.

33. "Address Delivered at Savannah, Georgia," Nov. 18, 1933, APP.
34. Frankfurter to FDR, Oct. 29, 1933, in Freedman, ed., *Roosevelt and Frankfurter*, 165–66.
35. Bullitt to FDR and Hull, Dec. 24, 1933, Bullitt Papers, box 70, Sterling Library, Yale University.
36. Frank Costigliola, ed., *The Kennan Diaries* (Norton, 2014), undated entry, 92; and "Memoirs Covering the Period 1933–1938," 1938, George Kennan Papers, box 240, Seeley Mudd Library, Princeton University.
37. Bullitt to Long, Mar. 16, 1934, Bullitt Papers, box 50, Sterling Library, Yale University.
38. Bullitt to Moore, Mar. 29, 1934, and May 4, 1934, Moore Papers, box 3, FDRL. Bullitt wrote extensively to Moore, both official and personal letters, and Moore duly showed the president the most important dispatches. Bullitt to Litvinov, Mar. 18, 1934, Bullitt Papers, box 50, Sterling Library, Yale University; Bullitt to Roosevelt, Apr. 13, 1934, in *For the President, Personal and Secret: Correspondence between Franklin D. Roosevelt and William C. Bullitt*, ed. Orville H. Bullitt (Houghton Mifflin, 1972), 82–84; Bullitt to Roosevelt, May 18, 1934; June 14, 1934; Sept. 8, 1934, Bullitt Papers, box 71, Sterling Library, Yale University. On the polo lessons, Bullitt to FDR, Aug. 5, 1934, in *For the President*, 92–94. For Bullitt's unsuccessful tour as ambassador, see Alexander Etkind, *Roads Not Taken: An Intellectual Biography of William C. Bullitt* (University of Pittsburgh Press, 2017); Brownell and Billings, *So Close to Greatness*, 139–86; Dennis J. Dunn, *Caught Between Roosevelt and Stalin: America's Ambassadors to Moscow* (University Press of Kentucky, 1998), 13–58.
39. Simon Sebag Montefiore, *Stalin: The Court of the Red Tsar* (Penguin, 2003), 126–66; Stephen Kotkin, *Stalin: Waiting for Hitler, 1929–1941* (Penguin, 2017), 188–220.
40. Charles W. Thayer, *Bears in the Caviar* (Russian Information Services, 2015 ed.), 168–76.
41. On the April 23 ball, Bullitt to FDR, May 1, 1935, Bullitt Papers, box 71, Sterling Library, Yale University. For Bullitt's reports on the arrests, Bullitt to FDR, Apr. 26, 1935, in *For the President*, 118–21.
42. Bullitt to FDR, July 15, 1935, in *For the President*, 130–31; Bullitt to Walton Moore, July 15, 1935, in *For the President*, 134–35; Bullitt to FDR, Aug. 3, 1935, in *For the President*, 135–36; Moore to FDR asking for approval of protest with FDR's approval penciled in, Aug. 23, 1935, Official File 220, box 1, FDRL; Moore to Bullitt, Sept. 3, 1935, Moore Papers, box 3, FDRL; and FDR to Bullitt, Sept. 26, 1935, in *For the President*, 139. See also Bullitt Papers, box 71, Sterling Library, Yale University; and Farnsworth, *William C. Bullitt*, 140–49.
43. Bullitt to Hull, Apr. 20, 1936, Bullitt Papers, box 135, Sterling Library, Yale University. A shortened version of this memo appears in *FRUS, The Soviet Union: 1933–39*, 291-96. An earlier statement along these lines is in Bullitt to Hull, July 19, 1935, "The Foreign Policy of the Soviet Union," Bullitt Papers, box 40, Sterling Library, Yale University.
44. Kennan, *Memoirs*, 84, 88.
45. On Bullitt's desire for the appeasement of Germany, see Farnsworth, *Bullitt and the Soviet Union*, 37–38, 160–63.

Chapter 7: Ethiopia and the Neutrality Trap

1. Dorothy Detzer, "Vested Interests in War," July 20, 1933, delivered at the International Congress of Women, Chicago, July 20, 1933, in Dorothy Detzer Papers, box 5, Swarthmore College Peace Collection. For a complete record of the conference, see International Congress of Women, *Our Common Cause, Civilization* (National Council of Women of the United States, 1933). "Women's Rally Lists Demands," *LAT*, July 21, 1933.
2. For some background on the movement, see Marcus Duffield, "Our Quarreling Pacifists," *Harper's*, Dec. 1, 1932. On her early life and work in Russia, see Dorothy Detzer, *Appointment on the Hill* (Henry Holt, 1948), 1–33.
3. "An Appeal to the Nations of the World for Peace by Disarmament," May 16, 1933, and message to Congress, May 16, 1933, in *PP&A*, vol. 2 (Random House, 1938), 185–93; "Back Roosevelt Policies," *NYT*, June 12, 1933.
4. Gertrude Bussey and Margaret Tims, *Pioneers for Peace: Women's International League for Peace and Freedom, 1915–1965* (Allen & Unwin, 1980), 17–22; Carrie A. Foster, *The Women and the*

Warriors: The U.S. Section of the Women's International League for Peace and Freedom, 1915–1946 (Syracuse University Press, 1995), 1–57.

5. Florence Brewer Boeckel, "Civilization or War?," in *Our Common Cause,* 688–94. For a discussion of how the pacifist movement differed from the collective security approach to containing war, see Charles Chatfield, ed., *Peace Movements in America* (Schocken Books, 1973).
6. "The Women's Program for Peace," *Ladies Home Journal,* March 1932, 24; "Program for Peace Wins World Favor," *NYT*, Feb. 12, 1932; "3,000 March Here in Anti-War Parade," *NYT*, May 22, 1932; on membership numbers, Duffield, "Our Quarreling Pacifists."
7. "Mrs. Catt Hunts 'Lost' Arms Parley," *NYT*, Jan. 19, 1933.
8. The history of these competing ideas of neutrality, trade, and embargoes are carefully explained in Robert A. Divine, *The Illusion of Neutrality* (University of Chicago Press, 1962), 1–80.
9. "Ask Hoover to Disarm World," *NYT*, Feb. 6, 1933; "Peace Groups Seek Arms Export Curb," Feb. 6, 1933; "Full Disarmament is Goal of Women," *NYT*, Apr. 17, 1933; "Women to Present Peace Pleas Today," *WP*, May 20, 1933; "Women Ask Roosevelt to Slash Army and Navy," *CT*, May 21, 1933; "Peace Plea Voiced at White House," *NYT*, May 21, 1933; "Borah Assails Peace Treaty," *LAT*, May 21, 1933; "Inquiry Demanded on Arms Concerns," *NYT*, May 22, 1933.
10. Divine, *Illusion*, 52–56.
11. Detzer, "Vested Interests"; "Women Adopt Program of World Action," *CT*, July 23, 1933; "Women Urge Peace in Series of Rallies," *NYT*, Aug. 28, 1933; "Women to Demand Munitions Inquiry," *NYT*, Dec. 13, 1933. On the debates about the lessons of World War I among scholars in the interwar years, see Justus Doenecke and John E. Wiltz, *From Isolation to War: 1931–1941* (John Wiley & Sons, 2015), 1–18; and Donald F. Drummond, *The Passing of American Neutrality, 1937–1941* (University of Michigan Press, 1955), 36–43.
12. Wayne Cole, "Gerald P. Nye and Agrarian Bases for the Rise and Fall of American Isolationism," in John N. Schacht, ed., *Three Faces of Midwestern Isolationism* (Center for the Study of the Recent History of the United States, 1981): 1–10.
13. Detzer, *Appointment*, 151–58; "Nye Demands Probe of All Deals in Arms," *WP*, Feb. 11, 1934; "Munitions Makers Assailed by Borah," *NYT*, Mar. 6, 1934.
14. "Arms and the Men," *Fortune*, Mar. 1934, 53–57, 113–26.
15. H. C. Engelbrecht and F. C. Hanighen, *Merchants of Death: A Study of the International Arms Industry* (Dodd, Mead, 1934); "Investigation of 'Munitions Trust' Voted; Senate Committee Gets Sweeping Power," *NYT*, Apr. 13, 1934; "Nye Assails Steps to Wage New Wars," *NYT*, May 1, 1934.
16. "A Message to the Senate on the Menace of Uncontrolled Manufacture of Arms and Munitions, May 18, 1934," *PP&A*, vol. 3, 239–42. For the contribution of the ER to the Catt volume, see Catt to ER, June 18, 1934; ER to Catt, June 29 and Sept. 3, 1934, in FDRL, Selected Digitized Correspondence of Eleanor Roosevelt, 1933–1945, Catt, Carrie Chapman, 1933–1943.
17. Matthew Ware Coulter, *The Senate Munitions Inquiry of the 1930s: Beyond the Merchants of Death* (Greenwood, 1997), 19–33; Cole, *Roosevelt and the Isolationists*, 149. For more on the du Ponts, see R. L. Dufuss, "Rulers of the Vast Empire of Du Pont," *NYT*, Sept. 30, 1934.
18. "Eighty Agents Push Inquiry on Munitions," *NYT*, July 26, 1934; "Munitions Heads Called in Arms Inquiry," *NYT*, Aug. 29, 1934; Franklyn Waltman Jr., "Senate Investigates Train Their Big Guns on Munitions Makers," *WP*, Sept. 2, 1934; Robert C. Albright, "Zaharoff and U.S. Firms in World Arms Trade," *WP*, Sept. 5, 1934; Osgood Nichols, "Mystery Man Leads World to War," *WP*, Sept. 9, 1934; Coulter, *Senate Munitions Inquiry*, 35–50.
19. "Nye Asks 98% Tax for War Incomes," *NYT*, Oct. 4, 1934.
20. Detzer, *Appointment*, 169, 171.
21. "Munitions Inquiry Intrigues Capital," *NYT*, Sept. 9, 1934; "The Munitions Scandal," *NYT* editorial, Sept. 9, 1934; Robert C. Albright, "Du Ponts Paid 458 Percent on War Profits," *WP*, Sept. 13, 1934; "Munitions Aid Cited," *LAT*, Sept. 14, 1934; "Munitions Inquiry to Bare War Deals," *NYT*, Sept. 16, 1934; "Nye Will Seek Confiscatory Wartime Tax," *WP*, Sept. 27, 1934.
22. Robert Mallet has done extensive work on Mussolini's imperial wars of conquest. For some of the debates among historians, see *Mussolini and the Origins of the Second World War, 1933–1940* (Palgrave Macmillan, 2003), 1–15; and for a careful analysis of the origins of the Ethiopia campaign, see his *Mussolini in Ethiopia, 1919–1935* (Cambridge University Press, 2015). For an account of the diplomatic history, see Stephen U. Chukumba, *The Big Powers Against Ethiopia* (University Press of America, 1979). An excellent study of U.S. policy is Brice Harris Jr., *The United States and the Ethiopian Crisis* (Stanford University Press, 1964).

23. Mallet, *Mussolini in Ethiopia*, 63–71, 100–106.
24. John Gooch, *Mussolini's War: Fascist Italy from Triumph to Collapse, 1935–1945* (Pegasus Books, 2020), 9–15; George W. Baer, "Sanctions and Security: The League of Nations and the Italian-Ethiopian War, 1935–1936," *International Organization* 27, no. 2 (1973): 165–79.
25. Robert D. Accinelli, "The Roosevelt Administration and the World Court Defeat, 1935," *The Historian* 40, no. 3 (1978): 463–78.
26. *FDR&FA,* vol. 2, Long to FDR, Feb. 3, 1935, 387–89; Feb. 8, 1935, 401–4; Long to FDR, Feb. 21, 1935, 426–29; FDR to Long, Mar. 9, 1935, 437–38. See also Long diary, entries for Mar. 20, Mar. 24, and Apr. 8, 1935, Breckinridge Long Papers, box 4, LOC. He estimated that Italy had 940,000 troops in total, ready for war.
27. "Duce Mobilizes," *WP*, Feb. 12, 1935; "Mussolini Hurls Threat of War," *LAT*, Feb. 11, 1935; David Darrah, "Italy's Troops Gather," *CT*, Feb. 12, 1935; "War Nearing as Ethiopia Defies Italy," *WP*, Feb. 13, 1935; "Prepare for War in Africa, Italy Told by Il Duce," *CT*, Feb. 17, 1935; Frederick T. Birchall, "Ethiopia Now Seems Headed for Doom," *NYT*, Feb. 17, 1935.
28. Shirer, *Berlin Diary*, 28–31; "Text of Hitler's Proclamation," *MG*, Mar. 18, 1935; "Hitler Orders Military Conscription in Germany," United Press, Mar. 16, 1935, https://www.upi.com/Archives/1935/03/16/Hitler-orders-military-conscription-in-Germany/5124911384073/.
29. Sigrid Schultz, "Germans Arm; Scrap Treaty," *CT*, Mar. 17, 1935; Dodd to Moore, Mar. 21, 1935, Dodd Papers, box 47, LOC. Dodd considered resigning over the Senate's rejection of the World Court, and also believed the U.S. should join the League of Nations in order to rescue Europe. See Dodd to Moore, Jan. 22 and Jan. 30, 1935, Moore Papers, box 5, FDRL. Dodd conveyed these same worries to a group at the home of Rex Tugwell on February 1, 1935. Withdrawing from the Court "means war," he said, because Hitler will now see America is "completely out of the European scene." Austria, he thought, would be Hitler's next target. Namorato, ed., *Diary of Rexford G. Tugwell*, 192–96.
30. "America Silent as Nazis Junk Separate Pact," *WP*, Mar. 17, 1935; Press Conference, Mar. 20, 1935, *FDR&FA*, vol. 2, 447–49; House to FDR, Apr. 20, 1935, *FDR&FA*, vol. 2, 488–89; Steiner, *Triumph*, 88–93; Long diary, entry for Apr. 15, 1935, Long Papers, box 4, LOC.
31. "Capital Schools Today to Join National Strike Against War," *WP*, Apr. 12, 1935; "Nation's Students 'Strike' for Peace," *NYT*, Apr. 13, 1935. Baldwin quoted in "War Strike," *Newsweek*, Apr. 20, 1935, 21. On the origins of the strike, "Plans a Student Strike," *NYT*, Apr. 1, 1935. For the origins and scope of the 1935 and 1936 walkouts, see Robert Cohen, *When the Old Left Was Young: Student Radicals and America's First Mass Student Movement, 1929–1941* (Oxford University Press, 1993), 73–97.
32. Anne O'Hare McCormick, "Italy Expects War in Africa in Fall," *NYT*, May 5, 1935; "Paris Asks London to Help Curb Italy in African Designs," *NYT*, May 11, 1935; "200,000 Italians Called to Colors," *NYT*, May 14, 1935; John Steele, "Italy Demands Ethiopian King Split Up Nation, *CT*, May 20, 1935; Anne O'Hare McCormick, "Italy's Hope Rises For Gain in Africa," *NYT*, May 20, 1935; Arnaldo Cortesi, "Mussolini Warns Italians May Fight," *NYT*, May 26, 1935.
33. The shaping of the act can be followed in Stuart L. Weiss, "American Foreign Policy and Presidential Power: The Neutrality Act of 1935," *Journal of Politics* 30, no. 3 (1968): 672–95; Divine, *Illusion*, 81–121; Cole, *Roosevelt and the Isolationists*, 141–86; Dallek, *FDR and American Foreign Policy*, 103–8.
34. On the major achievements of 1935, see William Leuchtenberg, *FDR and the New Deal*, 143–66. "No other session of Congress had ever adopted so much legislation of permanent importance," he writes (162).
35. "Memorandum by Mr. Joseph C. Green of the Division of Western European Affairs," Mar. 20, 1935, *FRUS 1935*, 1, 363–64.
36. Hull, *Memoirs*, vol. 1, 397–417. Henry Stimson, Hull's predecessor, agreed that the neutrality proposals would crimp presidential authority and contravene the Constitution. Henry Stimson, "The Illusion of Neutrality," *Forum and Century*, Nov. 1935. For the view inside the Department, see Herbert Feis to Henry Stimson, Aug. 15, 1935, Feis Papers, box 26, LOC.
37. "President to Avoid Any War, Says Nye," *NYT*, Mar. 31, 1935. For the back-and-forth between the State Department and Capitol Hill, see Phillips to Roosevelt, July 16, 1935, in *FDR&FA*, vol. 2, 558–60; Key Pittman to Stephen Early, Aug. 19, 1935, *FDR&FA*, vol. 2, 607–9.
38. Kirk to Hull, and cover note from Hull to FDR, Aug. 19, 1935, PSF, box 41, Italy, 1933–38, FDRL.
39. "Neutrality Act to Safeguard U.S. from War," *WP*, Sept. 1, 1935.
40. Walton Moore to FDR, Aug. 27, 1935, in *FDR&FA*, vol. 2, 624–28.

41. Hull to FDR, Aug. 29, 1935, in *FDR&FA,* vol. 2, 630–32; Hull, *Memoirs,* vol. 1, 417.
42. "Statement by Roosevelt on Approving Senate Joint Resolution 173," Aug. 31, 1935, *FDR&FA,* vol. 2, 632–33.
43. Roi Ottley, "Hectic Harlem," *NYAN,* Oct. 5, 1935.
44. Roy Kay, *The Ethiopian Prophecy in Black American Letters* (University Press of Florida, 2011). For the significance of the crisis to Black Americans, see Roi Ottley, *New World A-Coming* (Riverside Press, 1943), 111: "I know of no event in recent times that stirred the rank-and-file of Negroes more than the Italo-Ethiopian war." See also William R. Scott, "Black Nationalism and the Italo-Ethiopian Conflict, 1934–36," *Journal of Negro History* 63, no. 2 (1978), 118–34. Scott's excellent book is *The Sons of Sheba's Race: African-Americans and the Italo-Ethiopian War, 1935–1941* (Indiana University Press, 1993).
45. "Harlem Plans Mass Protest Against Italy," *NYAN,* Mar. 2, 1935; "3,000 Strike at Mussolini," *NYAN,* Mar. 9, 1935; "Why Ethiopia Must Win," *BAA,* Mar. 16, 1935; "Ethiopian Mass Meetings Urged All Over the U.S.," *BAA,* Mar. 16, 1935.
46. "Harlem Ponders Ethiopia's Fate," *NYT,* July 14, 1935; Roi Ottley, "Hectic Harlem," *NYAN,* July 20, 1935; FDR press conferences of July 24 and 26, 1935, FDRL; "Roosevelt Sets Hands-Off Policy in Ethiopian Crisis," *LAT,* July 27, 1935; "Roosevelt Voices His Hope for Peace," *NYT,* Aug. 2, 1935. Privately, FDR conveyed a brief message to Mussolini on August 19, not released to the press, "expressing his earnest hope that the controversy between Italy and Ethiopia will be resolved without resort to armed conflict. In this country it is felt both by the Government and by the people that failure to arrive at a peaceful settlement of the present dispute and a subsequent outbreak of hostilities would be a world calamity." The message had no effect except to elicit from Il Duce the statement that it was "too late" to avoid war. Hull to Kirk, and Kirk to Hull, Aug. 18 and 19, 1935, *FRUS 1935,* vol. 1, 739–42.
47. "Will March Today Protesting War in Ethiopia," *NYAN,* Aug. 3, 1935; "Italians to March in Anti-Mussolini Parade," *BAA,* Aug. 3, 1935; "Respectable Organizations Snub NY's Biggest Turn-out," *BAA,* Aug. 10, 1935.
48. "To Hit African War at Madison Square Garden," *NYAN,* Sept. 21, 1935; "7,000 Here Protest Ethiopian Invasion," *NYT,* Sept. 26, 1935; "10,000 Protest Mussolini's War in East Africa," *NYAN,* Sept. 28, 1935.
49. Frederick T. Birchall, "Race Issue Feared in African Dispute if It Is Not Resolved," *NYT,* Aug. 5, 1935; Dan Burley, "Sees Drastic Change in Social Order; Plight of Ethiopia Draws Blacks of World Together," *CD,* July 27, 1935.
50. W. E. B. Du Bois, "Inter-Racial Implications of the Ethiopian Crisis: A Negro View," *Foreign Affairs* 14, no. 1 (1935): 82–92. A thoughtful assessment of Du Bois and international politics is Zachariah Mampilly, "The Du Bois Doctrine: Race and the American Century," *Foreign Affairs,* Sept.–Oct. 2022.
51. Dodd to Secretary of State, July 17, 1935, *FRUS 1935,* vol. 2, 401–3; Moshe Gottlieb, "The Berlin Riots of 1935 and Their Repercussions in America," *American Jewish Historical Quarterly* 59, no. 3 (1970): 302–28.
52. Guido Enderis, "Perfect Man is Aim of Nazi Eugenists [*sic*]," *NYT,* Sept. 15, 1935; "Hope of Reich Jews Is Dimmed by Events," *NYT,* Sept. 22, 1935; "Hitler Shouts Warning to Jewry," *WP,* Sept. 16, 1935; Sigrid Schultz, "Hitler to Adopt Nazi Swastika as German Flag," *CT,* Sept. 14, 1935.
53. Sigrid Schultz, "Hitler Leader Assails U.S. 'Lynch Justice,'" *CT,* Aug. 16, 1935; "Reich Triumvirate Crushes Jews," *Jewish Exponent,* Sept. 20, 1935. On parallels between Nazi Jewish policy and Jim Crow, see Winfred B. Nathan, chair of the Education Department at Atlanta University, quoted in "Nazi Jew-Baiting Likened to U.S. Race Oppression," *BAA,* Sept. 14, 1935; "Scorching Note Scores Nazis, U.S. Jim Crow," *CD,* Dec. 14, 1935; Joel A. Rogers, "American Fascism Already Has Negroes in Grip," *PC,* Oct. 24, 1935; "Nazi Prejudice Against Jews Is Like Dixie's," *BAA,* Sept. 21, 1935. For an argument that links the Nazi Nuremberg laws directly to U.S. segregation codes, see James Q. Whitman, *Hitler's American Model: The United States and the Making of Nazi Race Law* (Princeton University Press, 2017).
54. Letter to Col. Edward M. House, Sept. 17, 1935, in *FDR: His Personal Letters,* vol. 1, 506–7. Speech text, Sept. 3, 1935, and calendar, http://www.fdrlibrary.marist.edu/daybyday/resource/september-1935/. "Roosevelt Draws Parable on Repair," *NYT,* Sept. 4, 1935. "President Starts Far West Journey; To Speak 4 Times," *NYT,* Sept. 27, 1935; "Text of President's Speech at Boulder Dam," *WP,* Oct. 1, 1935.

55. "75,000 on Coast Cheer Roosevelt Please to Liberals," *WP*, Oct. 2, 1935; "Roosevelt Urges Liberals to Fight on United Front," *NYT*, Oct. 2, 1935; "Roosevelt's Address at Los Angeles," *NYT*, Oct. 2, 1935; "Roosevelt's Address at San Diego Touching on Home and Foreign Problems," *NYT*, Oct. 3, 1935.
56. San Diego speech, Oct. 3, 1935.
57. "The Presidency: Fierce Foreign War," *Time*, Oct. 14, 1935; for details on the trip, *FDR Day by Day*. Will Barber, "Italy Hits with 4 Armies," *CT*, Oct. 4, 1935.
58. For a detailed account of the voyage, see Ickes, *Secret Diary*, vol. 1, 446–61.
59. Mussolini conversation with Breckinridge Long, Sept. 17, 1935, in Long diary, Long Papers, box 4, LOC. Lina Grip and John Hart, "The Use of Chemical Weapons in the 1935–36 Italo-Ethiopian War," SIPRI Arms Control and Non-Proliferation Program, Oct. 2009. "Take Ethiopia by June, Duce Orders Army; Troops to Open Drive with Poison Gas," *CT*, Feb. 16, 1936; "Two Kinds of Poison Gas Used by Italy in Air Raid," *NYT*, Mar. 17, 1936; "Italian Gas Raid Decried in Britain," *NYT*, Mar. 31, 1936. The League did convene meetings to discuss Italy's use of gas, but little came of it. "Italy and the Use of Poison Gas," *MG*, Apr. 6, 1936; "Committee to Make Poison Gas Protest," *WP*, Apr. 10, 1936; "League Council's Resolution," *MG*, Apr. 21, 1936.
60. Arnaldo Cortesi, "Mussolini Insists Foe Be Annihilated," *NYT*, Apr. 9, 1936. Mussolini's speech was sent by the embassy in Rome to the State Department: Gray to Hull, May 5, 1936, State Department Decimal File 865D01, in Gale Primary Sources digital database, "European Colonialism in the Early Twentieth Century: Italian Colonies in North Africa and Aggression in East Africa, 1930–1939." On casualties, Alberto Sbacchi, *Legacy of Bitterness: Ethiopia and Fascist Italy, 1935–1941* (Red Sea Press, 1997), 87–101. Louis Fischer to Freda Kirchwey, Apr. 21, 1936, Louis Fischer Papers, box 6, Seeley Mudd Library, Princeton University.
61. Nicholas Mulder, *The Economic Weapon: The Rise of Sanctions as a Tool of Modern War* (Yale University Press, 2022), 202–25; George W. Baer, "Sanctions and Security: The League of Nations and the Italo-Ethiopian War, 1935–1936," *International Organization* 27, no. 2 (1973): 165–79.
62. Steiner, *Triumph*, 112–36; R. A. C. Parker, "Great Britain, France, and the Ethiopian Crisis, 1935–1936," *English Historical Review* 89, no. 351 (1974), 293–332; Andrew Holt, "'No More Hoares to Paris': British Foreign Policymaking and the Abyssinian Crisis, 1935," *Review of International Studies* 37, no. 3 (2011): 1383–1401; James C. Robertson, "The Hoare-Laval Plan," *Journal of Contemporary History* 10, no. 3 (1975): 433–64. A detailed study of the diplomacy behind the crisis is Stephen U. Chukumba, *The Big Powers Against Ethiopia: Anglo-Franco-American Diplomatic Maneuvers During the Italo-Ethiopian Dispute, 1934–1936* (University Press of America, 1979). For opinion in State Department, see Hamilton Fish Armstrong, memo of Dec. 12, 1935, Armstrong Papers, box 99, Selley Mudd Library, Princeton University.
63. The administration possessed a detailed report on the impact of the League's economic sanctions, as well as the vulnerability of Italy to any embargo on oil, copper, cotton, scrap steel, and other raw materials. See George Haas to Secretary of the Treasury Henry Morgenthau, Dec. 6, 1935, "The effect of sanctions on Italy's African campaign," in FDRL, Morgenthau Diaries, book 13, 63–85.
64. Office of the Economic Adviser, Department of State, Nov. 7, 1935, tables on U.S. exports to Italy; and William Phillips to Hull, Nov. 14, 1935, on the likelihood that even with an appeal from the president, some 120 smaller oil companies would certainly not cease selling oil to Italy; both in PSF, box 41, Italy, 1933–38, FDRL.
65. "Monday Lunch, December 16, 1935," Morgenthau Diaries, book 14, 57, FDRL. State of the Union address, Jan. 3, 1936, Master Speech File, box 24, FDRL.
66. Ickes, *Secret Diary*, vol. 1, entry for Dec. 15, 1935, 483. On Hull's efforts, Hull, *Memoirs*, vol. 1, 460–67.
67. Divine, *Illusion of Neutrality*, 122–61.
68. Anne O'Hare McCormick, "The New Italy: Fact or Phrase?," *NYT*, May 17, 1936.
69. W. E. B. Du Bois, "Forum of Fact and Opinion," *PC*, Apr. 25, 1936, and May 2, 1936.
70. W. E. B. Du Bois, "Forum of Fact and Opinion," *PC*, June 6, 1936.
71. Haile Selassie speech, June 30, 1936, text at https://www.blackpast.org/global-african-history/1936-emperor-haile-selassie-ethiopia-appeal-league-nations/#:~:text=It%20is%20my%20duty%20to,Italian%20Government%20has%20made%20war. An original copy of his speech in French and Amharic is viewable at the Library of Congress: https://www.loc.gov/resource/gdcwdl.wdl_11602/?sp=21&st=image&r=-0.936,0,2.873,1.346,0. It is sometimes said that the

Emperor closed his speech with the words "Today it is us; tomorrow it will be you," but this phrase does not appear in his speech. Some reports say that he spoke these words under his breath as he left the podium. See his obituary in *Time* magazine, "The Lion Is Freed," Sept. 8, 1975, and Paul Hoffman, "The Lion at Sunset," *NYT*, Sept. 13, 1974.

Chapter 8: It Can't Happen Here

1. A recent survey of the scholarship on this topic can be found in Rosenfeld and Ward, eds., *Fascism in America*, 1–42. The classic study on the origins of the extremist politics of the era is Ribuffo, *The Old Christian Right*. For a lively and pointed contemporary account by the anonymous columnist "Unofficial Observer" (Jay Franklin Carter), is *American Messiahs* (Simon & Schuster, 1935). The writer and radio commentator Raymond Gram Swing penned an insightful essay on FDR's populist and elitist critics: *Forerunners of American Fascism* (Messner, 1935). See also Bradley Hart, *Hitler's American Friends: The Third Reich's Supporters in the United States* (Thomas Dunne, 2018). On the connections between Nazism and eugenics, see Stefan Kühl, *The Nazi Connection: Eugenics, American Racism, and German National Socialism* (Oxford University Press, 1994). For an exploration of how fascism was deployed as a term in modern American politics, see Kuklick, *Fascism Comes to America*.
2. "Nazi Actions Here Bring on an Inquiry," *NYT*, Oct. 10, 1933; "Many Offer to Aid Inquiry on Nazis," *NYT*, Oct. 11, 1933; "Washington Awaits Filing of Anti-Nazi Complaint to Start Immigration Inquiry," *WP*, Oct. 13, 1933; "Dickstein to Open Nazi Inquiry Soon," *NYT*, Oct. 18, 1933.
3. On the early years of the U.S.-based Nazi movement, see Sander A. Diamond, *The Nazi Movement in the United States, 1924–1941* (Cornell University Press, 1974), 85–103; and Susan Canedy, *America's Nazis: A Democratic Dilemma* (Markgraf, 1990), 49–70.
4. "O'Brien May Lift German Day Ban," *NYT*, Oct. 25, 1933; "Germans Hail Nazi Leader in Meeting Here," *CT*, Oct. 26, 1933; "Arrest is Ordered of Spanknöbel as German Agent," *NYT*, Oct. 28, 1933.
5. "Nazi Exposé Promised U.S.," *WP*, Nov. 13, 1933; "Nazi Inquiry Opens Behind Locked Doors," Nov. 14, 1933; "Investigation Ends Suddenly," *American Israelite*, Nov. 23, 1933; "Nazi Investigation by Dickstein Postponed," *Jewish Exponent*, Nov. 24, 1933; "Congressman Dickstein Flays Nazi Activities," *American Israelite*, Jan. 11, 1934; "Bares Nazi Propaganda," *NYT*, Jan. 21, 1934; "Cong. Dickstein Warns of Nazi Agents in U.S.," *CT*, Mar. 19, 1934; "House Asks Nazi Quiz," *LAT*, Mar. 21, 1934; "Wide Nazi Inquiry Is Voted by House," *NYT*, Mar. 21, 1933; "House Decides to Look into 'Brown Menace,'" *Newsweek*, Mar. 31, 1934. On the remarkable story of Dickstein and his later espionage for the USSR, see Peter Duffy, "The Congressman Who Spied for Russia," *Politico*, Oct. 6, 2014. Dickstein issued a preliminary report about his initial findings on Jan. 18, 1934: U.S. House of Representatives, Subcommittee of the House Committee on Immigration, *Nazi Propaganda Activities by Aliens in the United States* (Government Printing Office, 1934).
6. "German Day Set; Nazi Note Curbed," *NYT*, Dec. 2, 1933; "Germans in Rally Heavily Guarded," *NYT*, Dec. 7, 1933; "Dr. Luther Gets N.Y. Nazi Salute," *WP*, Dec. 7, 1933; Otto Tolischus, "Reich Propaganda Abroad Is Denied," *NYT*, Dec. 10, 1933.
7. "Nazis Here Spur Counter-Boycott," *NYT*, May 9, 1934; "Ninety German Groups Join DAWA Move," *Jewish Telegraphic Agency*, Mar. 30, 1934; "German Societies Defend the DAWA," *NYT*, May 10, 1934.
8. "U.S. Nazis Launch First Offensive Against the Jews of America," *Jewish Advocate*, May 15, 1934; "Nazi Friends Here to Be Heard Today," *NYT*, May 17, 1934; "American Nazis and Sympathizers Hold Open Demonstrations in New York and Boston," *Jewish Advocate*, May 18, 1934; "20,000 Nazi Friends at a Rally Here Denounce Boycott," *NYT*, May 18, 1934; "War on American Jews Opened by Nazis," *Jewish Advocate*, May 22, 1934.
9. "German Envoys Linked to Fund," *LAT*, June 6, 1934; "German Emissaries Linked Directly with Nazi Activities," *Jewish Advocate*, June 8, 1934; "Official Revelation of Hitlerism in U.S. Outrages Nation," *American Israelite*, June 14, 1934; "Nazi Leader Here Defends Drilling and Ban on Jews," *NYT*, July 10, 1934; "Nazis Open Camp in Jersey for Boys," *NYT*, Aug. 9, 1934; April C. Armstrong, "A Princeton-Area Nazi Boys Camp and Civil Liberties in New Jersey in the 1930s," Princeton University Archives blog, June 23, 2012; "Cong. Dickstein Reveals Amazing Information about Organized Nazi Propaganda," *Jewish Advocate*, Sept. 28, 1934; "Congress Inquiry Shows Fascist Danger Is Real," *American Israelite*, Feb. 21, 1935; "Dangerous Nazi Activities Traced," *Jewish Advocate*, Feb. 19, 1935. The hearings were published in multiple parts: House of

Representatives, 73rd Congress, *Investigation of Nazi Propaganda Activities and Investigation of Certain Other Propaganda Activities* (Government Printing Office, 1934–35).

10. "Nazis Are Angered by 'Friends' Here," *NYT*, Oct. 3, 1935; "Nazi Activity Here Limited by Hitler," *NYT*, Dec. 25, 1935.
11. "Public Statement of Special Committee on Un-American Activities," *U.S. House of Representatives*, 73rd Congress, Second Session, Nov. 24, 1934. Butler's testimony was published in "Public Hearings Before the Special Committee on Un-American Activities," *U.S. House of Representatives*, 73rd Congress, Second Session, Dec. 29, 1934. For a careful study of Smedley Butler's unsavory career as a soldier, see Jonathan M. Katz, *Gangsters of American Capitalism: Smedley Butler, the Marines, and the Making of Breaking of America's Empire* (Macmillan, 2023). Katz sheds little new light on the "business plot" and is unable to corroborate it (319–26).
12. "Butler Details 'Fascist Coup' in House Quiz," *WP*, Nov. 21, 1934; "Plot U.S. Coup: Gen. Butler," *CT*, Nov. 21, 1934; "Gen. Butler Bares 'Fascist Plot' to Seize Government by Force," *NYT*, Nov. 21, 1934; "Group in House Ends Inquiry of Fascist 'Putsch,'" *CT*, Nov. 25, 1934.
13. Fireside Chat, June 28, 1934, *PP&A*, vol. 3, 312–18.
14. "Leaders of 2 Parties Set to Sift New Deal," *WP*, Aug. 23, 1934; "Liberty League Program," *WP*, Aug. 23, 1934; "Unite in War on Radicalism," *CT*, Aug. 23, 1934; "League Is Formed to Scan New Deal, Protect 'Rights,'" *NYT*, Aug. 23, 1934.
15. "Fight to Rule New Deal Seen in Liberty League," *LAT*, Aug. 24, 1934; "See New League as New Deal Foe," *Wall Street Journal*, Aug. 24, 1934.
16. "End of NIRA Asked by Irenée Du Pont," *NYT*, Aug. 24, 1934; "Liberty League Nothing New, Says Du Pont," *WP*, Aug. 24, 1934; "Hope Roosevelt Will Drop NRA, Asserts Du Pont," *CT*, Aug. 24, 1934.
17. Press Conference, August 24, 1934, FDRL. "Liberty Body Frowned on by President," *WP*, Aug. 25, 1934; "Roosevelt Twits Liberty League as Lover of Property," *NYT*, Aug. 25, 1934; "President Sees Liberty League Hostile to Him," *CT*, Aug. 25, 1934. FDR's laughter was prompted by this article: "Finance Welcomes Liberty League," *NYT*, Aug. 24, 1934.
18. Jouett Shouse, "Progress vs Change," speech to the Bond Club of New York, Nov. 20, 1934; "Shouse Assails 'Regimentation' Under New Deal," *CT*, Nov. 21, 1934; "Shouse Defends Liberty League," *NYT*, Nov. 21, 1934.
19. For examples of the Liberty League's indictment against the New Deal, see Fitzgerald Hall, "The Imperilment of Democracy," July 18, 1935; Demarest Lloyd, "Fabian Socialism and the New Deal," July 9, 1935; Al Smith, "The Facts in the Case," Jan. 25, 1936; Jouett Shouse, "The New Deal vs. Democracy," June 20, 1936, all issued in pamphlet form by the League.
20. Editorial, *Nation*, Dec. 5, 1934.
21. The essential study of Long's career is T. Harry Williams, *Huey Long* (Alfred A. Knopf, 1969). For Long's early life, see Williams, *Huey Long*, 3–79. But Alan Brinkley places Long alongside Father Charles Coughlin in an excellent dual biography on the two most dangerous antidemocratic demagogues of the decade: *Voices of Protest: Huey Long, Father Coughlin, and the Great Depression* (Alfred A. Knopf, 1982). The comment on Long and Macarthur was reported twice in slightly different language by Rex Tugwell, first in *The Democratic Roosevelt*, 349, and later in *The Brains Trust* (Viking, 1968), 433–34.
22. Williams, *Huey Long*, 119–279.
23. "Louisiana Expects Troublous Times; His Nomination for the Senate Makes Gov. Long Virtually State's Dictator," *NYT*, Sept. 14, 1930; "Gov. Roosevelt Would Lose, He Avers," *WP*, Jan. 26, 1932; "Long Yet Kingfish in His Home State: Whips 4 Tax Bills Through Legislature as Minority Shouts 'Dictator!,'" *WP*, June 11, 1932.
24. "Fight in the Senate on 'Soak the Rich' Led by Harrison," *CT*, Apr. 5, 1932.
25. Williams, *Huey Long*, 572–640; Brinkley, *Voices of Protest*, 57–61.
26. Williams, *Huey Long*, 676–706; Brinkley, *Voices of Protest*, 61–81.
27. United States Congress, Senate, *Congressional Record*, 73d Cong., 2d sess., 3450–53. He published more details, larded with quotations of famous historical figures, in pamphlets like *Share Our Wealth: Every Man a King, Containing Authorities, Laws, Statistics and Published Comments of Leaders of All Times* (1935).
28. "Long Foes Ask U.S. to Halt Senator," *WP*, Aug. 1, 1934; "Long Jams 27 Bills Through the House," *NYT*, Aug. 7, 1934; "Long Made Dictator," *LAT*, Aug. 19, 1934; "Long Rushes Plans for Dictator Role," *NYT*, Aug. 19, 1934; "Louisiana Factions Press Mudslinging," *NYT*, Aug. 21, 1934; "Huey

Long Leads Troops Invading New Orleans," *LAT*, Sept. 1, 1934; "All State Troops Mobilized by Long," *NYT*, Sept. 7, 1934; Williams, *Huey Long*, 722–28.

29. "Louisiana Gives Long a Big Margin in Primary Vote," *NYT*, Sept. 12, 1934; "Kingfish Jams Dictator Plan Through House," *WP*, Nov. 16, 1934; "Huey Whips His 44 Bills in and out of Both Houses," *CT*, Nov. 15, 1934; "Dictator in Louisiana," *MG*, Nov. 20, 1934. Long did not give a direct answer about his plans to run for the White House, but in August 1935, sources told the *New York Times* that he would do everything to stop Roosevelt. "Huey Long to Seek Presidency in 1936," *NYT*, Aug. 14, 1935.
30. "Johnson Attacks Coughlin and Long," *NYT*, Mar. 5, 1935; "Text of Gen. Johnson's Denouncement of Father Coughlin and Huey Long," *NYT*, Mar. 5, 1935; "Long Denounced by Party Leader on Senate Floor," *NYT*, Mar. 6, 1935.
31. James A. Farley, *Jim Farley's Story: The Roosevelt Years* (McGraw-Hill, 1948), 51. FDR's comments of February 1935 about Long in Dodd, ed., *Ambassador Dodd's Diary*, 213–14.
32. "Message to Congress on Tax Revision," June 19, 1935, APP. On the matter of FDR responding to Long's program, see Edwin Amenta, Kathleen Dunleavy, and Mary Bernstein, "Stolen Thunder? Huey Long's 'Share Our Wealth,' Political Mediation, and the Second New Deal Author," *American Sociological Review* 59, no. 5 (1994): 678–702. Raymond Moley argued that "the threat [of a Long candidacy] definitely influenced Roosevelt's policies in 1935." Moley, *The First New Deal* (Harcourt, Brace, 1966), 373. The dean of FDR studies, William Leuchtenburg, sees little direct causality: "FDR and the Kingfish," *American Heritage* 36, no. 6 (1985), https://www.americanheritage.com/fdr-and-kingfish. Also see Robert E. Snyder, "Huey Long and the Presidential Election of 1936," *Louisiana History* 16, no. 2 (1975): 117–43. Raymond Clapper, "Roosevelt Message Stops Huey," *WP*, June 21, 1935; "Mr. Roosevelt's New Push," *MG*, June 21, 1935; "Tax Plan Befogs Congress," *CT*, June 23, 1935.
33. Huey Long, *My First Days in the White House* (Telegraph Press, 1935), 34–35, 69–71, 102–15; Williams, *Huey Long*, 845–47.
34. On the link between Long and Fascism, see Edward F. Haas, "Huey Long and the Dictators," *Louisiana History* 47, no. 2 (2006): 133–51; Raymond Swing in *Nation*, Jan. 23, 1935. Alan Brinkley, in a short appendix titled "The Question of Anti-Semitism and the Problem of Fascism," argues that fear of concentrated power and big government animated Long more than a desire to impose a new fascist order on America: *Voices of Protest*, 269–83. On the LSU fracas: "Long Is Accused of Cursing Editor," *NYT*, Dec. 5, 1934.
35. For an invaluable portrait of Smith, see Ribuffo, *Old Christian Right*, 128–77.
36. "Friends and Foes Battle for Scepter of Long's Empire," *LAT*, Sept. 11, 1935; "Carry On, Urges Parson at Huey Long's Funeral," *LAT*, Sept. 13, 1935; "Apostle of Long Stirs 10,000," *NYT*, Sept. 15, 1935; "Long Faction Split in Drive for Power," *NYT*, Sept. 18, 1935; "Preacher-Pupil Tries to Draw Long's Bow," *NYT*, Sept. 22, 1935; "Louisiana Sees Wane of the Dictatorship," *NYT*, Sept. 29, 1935.
37. On Coughlin's life see Sheldon Marcus, *Father Coughlin: The Tumultuous Life of the Priest of the Little Flower* (Little, Brown, 1973), and Donald Warren, *Radio Priest: Charles Coughlin, the Father of Hate Radio* (Free Press, 1996).
38. Wallace Stegner, "The Radio Priest and His Flock," in Isabel Leighton, ed., *The Aspirin Age, 1919–1941* (Bodley Head, 1950), 234.
39. "Christ or the Red Fog?" Sermon, Jan. 19, 1930; "The Red Serpent," Sermon, Jan. 26, 1930; "Prosperity!" Sermon, Jan. 11, 1931, in Charles E. Coughlin Collection, box 1, NMAH. On the numbers, see Brinkley, *Voices of Protest*, 101, 119. On Coughlin's antisemitism, see Lucilla Cremoni, "Antisemitism and Populism in the United States in the 1930s: The Case of Father Coughlin," *Patterns of Prejudice* 32, no. 1 (1998): 25–37.
40. "Banks and Gold," Sermon, Feb. 26, 1933; "The New Deal and the New Men," Mar. 12, 1933, in Coughlin Collection, box 1, NMAH.
41. Brinkley, *Voices of Protest*, 134–37.
42. "Coughlin Demands Cohorts Mobilize," *NYT*, Apr. 25, 1935; "Shuns Office, Fr. Coughlin Tells New York: Cheered Wildly, Priest Outlines Social Justice Program to Throng," *WP*, May 23, 1935; "23,000 Here Cheer Coughlin Attack on the President," *NYT*, May 23, 1935; "Text of Father Coughlin's Address Attacking Plutocrats and the Bonus Veto," *NYT*, May 23, 1935. See also Charles J. Tull, *Father Coughlin and the New Deal* (Syracuse University Press, 1965), 93–103.
43. On the Coughlin-FDR meeting, see Sheldon Marcus, *Father Coughlin: The Tumultuous Life of the Priest of the Little Flower* (Little, Brown, 1973), 98–100.

44. "Father Coughlin Airs Open Break with Roosevelt," *CT*, Nov. 18, 1935; "Coughlin and Roosevelt," *LAT*, Nov. 19, 1935; "Radio Priest Apologizes Belatedly for His Roosevelt Fervor," *Newsweek*, Nov. 23, 1935; "Coughlin Links U.S. to League in Secret Pact," *WP*, Nov. 25, 1935.
45. "Share-Wealth Leader Forms OARP Alliance," *WP*, May 31, 1936; "Townsend Obtains Aid," *LAT*, May 31, 1936; "Townsend, Aides Gird to Battle 'Dictatorship,'" *WP*, June 1, 1936; "Huey's Ghost Fights On, Says Successor," *LAT*, June 7, 1936; "United Front Announced," *NYT*, June 17, 1936; "Four Blocs Join Forces," *LAT*, June 17, 1936. The epithet "lunatic fringe" had been first launched by Gen. Hugh Johnson in his March 1935 speech, denouncing Long and Coughlin.
46. "Townsend Attacks on Roosevelt Rule Cheered by 11,000," *NYT*, July 16, 1936; Felix Bruner, "Townsendites Stage a Show That Makes Alice in Wonderland Tame," *WP*, July 19, 1936; Gerold Frank, "Huey Long the Second," *Nation*, July 25, 1936; Duncan Aikman, "Lemke's New Party," *NYT*, July 26, 1936.
47. "Text of Father Coughlin's Address to Townsendites," *NYT*, July 17, 1936. Coughlin was gently admonished by the Detroit archdiocese for calling FDR a liar and he later gave a half-hearted apology. "Coughlin is Chided by Detroit Bishop," *NYT*, July 19, 1936. A month later, Coughlin held a rally of his own National Union of Social Justice in Cleveland, and once again, a tedious speech from Townsend and rousing performance from Smith preceded Coughlin's own smears against FDR and the New Deal. A good survey of the Union Party story is David Harry Bennett, *Demagogues in the Depression: American Radicals and the Union Party, 1932–1936* (Rutgers University Press, 1969). "Lemke Endorsed by Coughlinites," *NYT*, Aug. 16, 1936; "Thousands Salute their Leader and Swear Fealty," *Newsweek*, Aug. 22, 1936.
48. James Waterman Wise, quoted in "Speakers Draw Dark Picture of Future," *Christian Century*, Feb. 5, 1936.
49. Raymond Gram Swing, "Father Coughlin: The Phase of Action," *Nation*, Jan. 2, 1935; Dorothy Thompson, "The Lunatic Fringe," *NYHT*, Paris ed., Aug. 5, 1936.
50. "Coughlin Denies Jew-Baiting," *Jewish Advocate*, May 3, 1936; "Uneasiness at Remarks by Coughlin," *Jewish Advocate*, July 31, 1936; "Strictly Confidential" column, *Jewish Advocate*, Aug. 4, 1936; "That Man Again," *Jewish Advocate*, Aug. 18, 1936; "Father Coughlin as He Seems to Us," *American Israelite*, Aug. 27, 1936; "Coughlin Denies Ant-Jewish Bias in His Speeches," *Jewish Advocate*, Aug. 28, 1936; George Sokolsky, "The Man of Hate," reprinted from *NYHT* in *Jewish Advocate*, Aug. 28, 1936. For further discussion, see James P. Shenton, "Fascism and Father Coughlin," *Wisconsin Magazine of History* 44, no. 1 (1960): 6–11.
51. "Watch Coughlin," *WP*, Aug. 18, 1936.
52. Turner Catledge, "Congress to Meet at Noon; Roosevelt's Speech Tonight Stirs Bitter Partisanship," *NYT*, Jan. 3, 1936.
53. Text of Jan. 3, 1936, speech in Master Speech File, box 24, FDRL. Franklyn Waltman Jr., "Foreign Affairs Stand Overshadows Domestic Issues," *WP*, Jan. 4, 1936; Arthur Krock, "Roosevelt Has Free Hand in Publicity Coup," *NYT*, Jan. 2, 1936.
54. Quotes from *FDR: His Personal Letters*, vol. 1, letter to Dodd, Jan. 6, 1936, 543; letter to Norman Davis, Jan. 14, 1936, 544–45; letter to Jesse Straus, Feb. 13, 1936, 555–56; letter to Breckinridge Long, Feb. 22, 1936, 560. FDR to Bowers, Sept. 16, 1936, in PSF, box 50, Spain 1933–1936, FDRL.
55. Rosenman, *Working with Roosevelt*, 98; Malcolm Moos, ed., *H.L. Mencken: On Politics* (Johns Hopkins University Press, 1956), 306, 310. For an example of FDR invoking trouble overseas only to insist that America would not get "tangled up" in foreign problems, see speech in Dallas, Texas, June 12, 1936, Master Speech File, box 25, FDRL.
56. Text of speech on June 27, 1936, in Master Speech File, box 25, FDRL. See also Freidel, *Franklin D. Roosevelt: Rendezvous with Destiny*, 203; Rosenman, *Working with Roosevelt*, 105–6; Arthur Krock, "Roosevelt to War on 'Economic Royalists'; Hailed by Throngs in Acceptance Ceremony," *NYT*, June 28, 1936.
57. Phillips to All Consulates in Spain, Aug. 7, 1936, *FRUS 1936*, vol. 2, 471.
58. Speech at Chautauqua, NY, Aug. 14, 1936, in Master Speech File, box 26, FDRL. "Peace Appeal by Roosevelt Warns World," *WP*, Aug. 15, 1936. On Bullitt's role in drafting the speech: *FDR&FA*, vol. 3, 377–84, and Rosenman, *Working with Roosevelt*, 108. For Phillips statement, "Neutrality Path Taken, Spanish Policy Outlined," *LAT*, Aug. 12, 1936; Charles Hurd, "Roosevelt Denounces War and Breakers of Pledges, Peace and Neutrality Promised in Speech at Chautauqua," *NYT*, Aug. 15, 1936. For Ickes and his advice to use Chautauqua to speak out on the war issue, see Ickes, *Secret Diary*, vol. 1, 655–63.

59. Official and Confidential Files of FBI director J. Edgar Hoover, 136/5, Federal Bureau of Investigation Library, available through Gale Primary Sources, Archives Unbound, Confidential memoranda prepared by Hoover, dated Aug. 24 and Aug. 25, 1936. See also Beverly Gage, *G-Man*, 204–7.
60. Fireside Chat, Sept. 6, 1936, reporting on drought conditions, Master Speech File, box 26, FDRL.
61. Hearst attack reported in "Hearst Raps White House Statement," *Omaha World-Herald*, Sept. 21, 1936. An example of the FDR-as-Communist language is in the editorial of the Hearst-owned *San Francisco Examiner*, "The Radical Brand on the New Deal," Sept. 6, 1936.
62. Speech at Syracuse, NY, to the Democratic State Convention, Sept. 29, 1936, Master Speech File, box 27, FDRL. Ickes comment in *Secret Diary*, vol. 1, 687. The theme of inequality as a threat to democracy came through strongly in his October 14 speech at Chicago. Master Speech File, box 28, FDRL. Mencken, Oct. 26, 1936, in *On Politics*, 329.
63. Russell Porter, "300,000 See the President," *NYT*, Oct. 29, 1936.
64. "Text of President Roosevelt's Address in Madison Square Garden," *NYT*, Nov. 1, 1936; Sidney Olson, "'Just Begun to Fight' Against His Enemies," *NYT*, Nov. 1, 1936.
65. Mencken, *On Politics*, Nov. 2, 1936, 336; Dorothy Thompson, "During the Campaign," *NYHT*, Paris ed., Sept. 25, 1936.

Chapter 9: Spanish Earth

1. On the details about Badajoz, see Paul Preston, *The Spanish Civil War: Reaction, Revolution, and Revenge* (William Collins, 2016 ed.), 120–23.
2. Jay Allen, "Civil War Rages in Spain," *CT*, July 20, 1936; and "Franco Orders: No Let-up in Drive on Madrid," *CT*, July 28, 1936.
3. On the Spanish Civil War generally, the most well-researched and balanced accounts in English include Hugh Thomas, *The Spanish Civil War* (Hamish Hamilton, 1977); Paul Preston's many works including an account of foreign journalists, *We Saw Spain Die: Foreign Correspondents in the Spanish Civil War* (Constable, 2009), and his study of ideology and atrocities, *The Spanish Holocaust* (Norton, 2012). The military details are laid out in Antony Beevor, *The Battle for Spain: The Spanish Civil War, 1936–1939* (Penguin, 2006). One of the best introductions to the ideas and politics of the war is by a German Communist writer who was there: Franz Borkenau, *The Spanish Cockpit* (Faber & Faber, 1937).
4. For the European context, see Enrique Moradiellos, "The Allies and the Spanish Civil War," in Sebastian Balfour and Paul Preston, eds., *Spain and the Great Powers* (Routledge, 1999), 96–126. Stimson Diary, Yale University Library, Mar. 27, 1937, vol. 28, Oct. 18, 1935–1938, 50.
5. Preston, *Spanish Civil War*, 141; Winston Churchill, "The Spanish Tragedy," *Evening Standard*, Aug. 10, 1936; and "Keep Out of Spain," *Evening Standard*, Aug. 21, 1936.
6. For example, see Oswald Garrison Villard, former editor and owner of the *Nation* magazine, to FDR, Aug. 18, 1936, *FDR&FA*, vol. 3, 389–90; and Dallek, *FDR and American Foreign Policy*, 127–29. The American experience is ably portrayed in Adam Hochschild, *Spain in Our Hearts: Americans in the Spanish Civil War, 1936–1939* (HarperCollins, 2017), and Cecil B. Eby, *Comrades and Commissars: The Lincoln Battalion in the Spanish Civil War* (Pennsylvania State University Press, 2007). Important U.S. diplomatic histories include Richard P. Traina, *American Diplomacy and the Spanish Civil War* (Indiana University Press, 1968); F. Jay Taylor, *The United States and the Spanish Civil War* (Bookman, 1956); and Dominic Tierney, *FDR and the Spanish Civil War* (Duke University Press, 2007).
7. "Insurgents Held Bar to Red Menace," *SFE*, Aug. 1, 1936; "Nuns Shot Down," *SFE*, Aug. 5, 1936; "Communist Jungle Law," *SFE*, Aug. 10, 1936; "Spain Soviet Near; New Red Regime Set Up," *SFE*, Sept. 5, 1936. These editorials and articles were reprinted across the Hearst news empire.
8. "Five Bishops Slain in Spain, Vatican Officials Report," *CT*, Aug. 23, 1936; "Chicago Woman Tells of Priest Murders in Spain," *CT*, Aug. 28, 1936.
9. "Pope Worn Down by Grief for Spain," *NYT*, Aug. 28, 1936; "Pope Summons World to Wipe Out Red Peril," *CT*, Sept. 15, 1936; "Pope Assails Foes of Church in Spain," *NYT*, Sept. 15, 1936; "Anti-Red Campaign Directed by Pope," *NYT*, Dec. 14, 1936; "Belloc Denounces Spanish Loyalists," *NYT*, Mar. 20, 1937; "15,000 at Rally Aid a Fund for Spain," *NYT*, May 20, 1937; "Bias Laid to Press in News from Spain," *NYT*, May 4, 1937; "Catholic Claims of Bias," *WP*, June 18, 1937. On the religious debates in America during the war, see F. Jay Taylor, *The United States and the Spanish Civil War*, 117–162; J. David Valaik, "Catholics, Neutrality, and the Spanish Embargo, 1937–1939,"

Journal of American History 54, no. 1 (1967): 73–85; Austin J. Clements, "'The Franco Way': The American Right and the Spanish Civil War, 1936–9," *Journal of Contemporary History* 57, no. 2 (2022): 341–64.

10. For a sympathetic portrait, see Oliver Knight, "Claude G. Bowers, Historian," *Indiana Magazine of History* 52, no. 3 (1956): 247–68. FDR expressed his admiration of *The Tragic Era* to Bowers in a letter of May 22, 1930: *FDR: His Personal Letters*, vol. 1, 122.
11. Bowers to FDR, Aug. 26, 1936, and FDR to Bowers, Sept. 16, 1936, PSF, box 50, Spain, FDRL.
12. Bowers to FDR, Sept. 9, 16, and 23, 1936, and Dec. 16, 1936, PSF, box 50, Spain, FDRL.
13. Stephen Early to FDR, Aug. 26, 1936, and Dodd to FDR, Aug. 31, 1936, *FDR&FA*, vol. 3, 405–8; Dodd to FDR, Sept. 21, 1936, in *FDR&FA*, vol. 3, 433–34; and Dodd to FDR, Oct. 19, 1936, in *FDR&FA*, vol. 3, 455–58, in reply to an August 5 letter from FDR to Dodd asking if Hitler could be drawn into arms control talks, *FDR: His Personal Letters*, vol. 1, 605–6; Arthur Krock, "Roosevelt, If Re-Elected, May Call Kings, Dictators, and Presidents to Great Power Peace Conference," *NYT*, Aug. 26, 1936. Joseph Davies was a successful trial lawyer and Democratic Party donor. His was married to the enormously wealthy Marjorie Merriweather Post, the daughter of cereal magnate C. W. Post. Among her many residences, she built and lived in Mar-a-Lago in Palm Beach, Florida. FDR's comment to him is in his diary, entry for Aug. 28, 1936, Joseph Davies Papers, box I:3, LOC.
14. Bullitt to FDR, Nov. 8, 1936, *FDR&FA*, vol. 3, 471–77.
15. Bullitt to FDR, Dec. 20, 1936, in *FDR&FA*, vol. 3, 550–53. On the Italian-German negotiations leading to the Axis, see Arnaldo Cortesi, "Italy and Germany Completing a Bloc," *NYT*, Oct. 25, 1936; "Germany and Italy: African Empire Recognized," *Observer*, Oct. 25, 1936; Sigrid Schultz, "Germany Formally Recognizes Italy's Conquest of Ethiopia," *CT*, Oct. 25, 1936; Guido Enderis, "Nazis Fell It Demonstrates Effectiveness of Hitler's Method," *NYT*, Nov. 1, 1936.
16. FDR to Dodd, Jan. 9, 1937, in *FDR: His Personal Letters*, vol. 1, 648–49.
17. Address to the Inter-American Conference for Maintenance of Peace in Buenos Aires, Dec. 1, 1936, in *FDR&FA*, vol. 3: 516–21 and Master Speech File, box 30, FDRL.
18. "Pro-Fascist Neutrality," *Nation*, Jan. 9, 1937, 33–34; "US Passes Embargo Bill," *WP*, Jan. 7, 1937.
19. "Civil War Rages in Spain," *CT*, July 20, 1936; "Franco Orders: No Let-Up in Drive on Madrid," *CT*, July 28, 1936.
20. "Spain Checks Rebels' Drive," *CT*, July 21, 1936; "Tell Atrocities of Rebel Moors in South Spain," *CT*, July 23, 1936; "Military Dictatorship Will Follow Rebel Success in Spain," *CT*, July 29, 1936.
21. "Keep Hands Off! Spain's Warning to Duce, Hitler," *CT*, Aug. 2, 1936; "Italian Flyers Join Rebels," *CT*, Aug. 4, 1936; "Italian-Nazi Aid for Rebels Stirs Europe!" *CT*, Aug. 5, 1936; "Riffians Invade Spain," *CT*, Aug. 6, 1936; "Portugal Helps Rebels Get Arms from Germany," *CT*, Aug. 24, 1936; "Ship German Guns to Rebels," *CT*, Aug. 24, 1936; "Spain's Revolt Leaders Find Help in Lisbon," *CT*, Aug. 29, 1936. For details on Italian aid to Franco, see Paul Preston, "Italy and Spain in Civil War and World War, 1936–1943," in Balfour and Preston, eds., *Spain and the Great Powers*, 151–84.
22. Jay Allen, "Slaughter of 4,000 at Badajoz, City of Horrors, Is Told by Tribune Man," *CT*, Aug. 30, 1936; on deliberately sowing terror, see "Mass Executions Spread Terror in Spain," *LAT*, Aug. 15, 1936, and "3 Shells Fall in Border Town," *WP*, Aug. 17, 1936. Other papers reported the testimony of a Portuguese newsman named Mário Neves of the *Diario Lisboa*, who arrived at Badajoz the day after it fell to the Nationalists. He spoke to a number of Western reporters by telephone, but could not publish what he had seen in Portugal because the dictatorship there supported Franco's rebellion. See the essay at https://www.newsmuseum.pt/en/imortais/mario-neves. For papers citing Neves, see "Badajoz Slaughter Reported," *WP*, Aug. 17, 1936; "Corpses Litter Badajoz," *NYT*, Aug. 17, 1936; "Dead Piled in Streets," *LAT*, Aug. 17, 1936; "Flyers Set City Afire," *CT*, Aug. 15, 1936; "Slaughter after Capture of Badajoz," *MG*, Aug. 17, 1936.
23. On Allen's story and his fate, see Paul Preston, *We Saw Spain Die*, 341–97.
24. Louis Fischer in Crossman, ed., *The God That Failed*, 210–18; and Louis Fischer, *Men and Politics* (Duell, Sloan and Pearce, 1941), 413, 442. For a portrait of Fischer, see Preston, *We Saw Spain Die*, 249–307.
25. For the atmosphere within these intellectual circles, see Franklin Folsom, *Days of Anger, Days of Hope: A Memoir of the League of American Writers, 1937–1942* (University Press of Colorado, 1994); Harvey Klehr, *The Heyday of American Communism: The Depression Decade* (Basic Books, 1984); and Robert A. Rosenstone, *Crusade of the Left: The Lincoln Battalion in the Spanish Civil*

War (Pegasus, 1969). For documents relating to the Soviet support—and eventual betrayal—of the Spanish Republicans, see Ronald Radosh, Mary Habeck, and Grigory Sevostianov, eds., *Spain Betrayed: The Soviet Union in the Spanish Civil War* (Yale University Press, 2001).

26. "Spanish Diary," Louis Fischer Papers, box 25, Seeley Mudd Library, Princeton University; Louis Fischer, "On Madrid's Front Line," *Nation*, Oct. 24, 1936.
27. Louis Fischer, "Madrid Keeps Its Nerve," *Nation*, Nov. 7, 1936.
28. Louis Fischer, "Madrid Fights Off Franco," *Nation*, Nov. 21, 1936. Fischer to Freda Kirchwey, Dec. 16, 1936, Fischer Papers, box 6, Seeley Mudd Library, Princeton University.
29. Louis Fischer, "Under Fire in Madrid," *Nation*, Dec. 12, 1936.
30. William P. Carney, "Madrid Executes More Insurgents," *NYT*, Aug. 26, 1936; and "Two Reds in New Madrid Cabinet, Headed by a Left-Wing Socialist," *NYT*, Sept. 5, 1936.
31. William P. Carney, "Madrid Situation Revealed; Uncensored Story of Siege," *NYT*, Dec. 7, 1936. The subtitle of this piece was "All Semblance of Democratic Forms of Government in Spain Disappears, 25,000 Put to Death by Radicals." On the joy in "liberated" areas, see his "Regime of Terror is Denied by Llano," *NYT*, Mar. 23, 1937.
32. Herbert L. Matthews, *The Yoke and the Arrows* (Brazillier, 1957), 35; and *Two Wars and More to Come* (Herrick & Evans, 1938), 185.
33. "Demands High Court of 15," *CT*, Feb. 6, 1937; "Roosevelt Seeks Way to Name Six Justices to Supreme Court," *Wall Street Journal*, Feb. 6, 1937.
34. On Hoover, "Hoover Sees Attempt to Change Constitution," *LAT*, Feb. 6, 1937, and "Hands Off Court, Hoover Says, Warning of Road to Suicide," *NYT*, Feb. 21, 1937. "Dodd Terms High Court Attack a Dictator's Move," *CT*, Feb. 7, 1937; Franklyn Waltman, "Politics and People," *WP*, Feb. 9, 1937; "Dictator Feared by Amos Pinchot," *NYT*, Feb. 15, 1937; "Catholic Weekly Assails Proposal," *NYT*, Feb. 17, 1937.
35. Fireside Chat, March 9, 1937, *PP&A 1937*, 122–33.
36. Examples of the heat FDR took can be seen in the press: "Calls Roosevelt Scheme Rape of Supreme Court," *CT*, Mar. 14, 1937; "Wrecks Argument for Packing Supreme Court," *CT*, Mar. 30, 1937; "Mr. Roosevelt as Dictator," *CT*, May 17, 1937; "Bill Now a Corpse, Sen. Burke Says," *WP*, May 19, 1937; "Two Polls Indicate Popularity Loss for Roosevelt," *WP*, May 24, 1937.
37. For a sympathetic view of Black's past, see Max Lerner, "Hugo Black: A Personal History," *Nation*, Oct. 9, 1937.
38. "Justice Black Is Recorded as Still a Member of Klan," *NYT*, Sept. 13, 1937. Ickes, *Secret Diary*, vol. 2, Aug. 15, 1937, 191, 215. Black gave a radio address about the issue on Oct. 1, 1937, called "I Did Join the Klan," published in *Vital Speeches of the Day*, Oct. 15, 1937.
39. Bowers to FDR, Mar. 31, 1937, PSF, box 50, Spain—1937, FDRL.
40. Louis Fischer, "Keeping America Out of War," *Nation*, Mar. 27, 1937.
41. Richard Freedman, "Hemingway Spanish Civil War Dispatches," *Texas Studies in Literature and Language* 1, no. 2 (1959): 171–80; David Sanders, "Ernest Hemingway's Spanish Civil War Experience," *American Quarterly* 12, no. 2 (1960): 133–43; Anton Nilsson, "Ernest Hemingway and the Politics of the Spanish Civil War," *Hemingway Review* 36, no. 1 (2016): 81–93. Hemingway remarks in Carlos Baker, ed., *Ernest Hemingway Selected Letters, 1917–1961* (Scribner, 2003), Feb. 5, 1937, and Feb 7, 1937, 456, 458.
42. On Hemingway's relations with these and other writers, see Preston, *We Saw Spain Die*, 72–108.
43. Martha Gellhorn has attracted much attention from scholars. See especially Caroline Moorehead, *Gellhorn: A Twentieth-Century Life* (Henry Holt, 2003); and a recent survey of the scene by Sarah Watling, *Tomorrow Perhaps the Future: Writers, Outsiders, and the Spanish Civil War* (Alfred A. Knopf, 2023). Gellhorn's letters are collected in Somerville, ed., *Yours, for Probably Always*; and Caroline Moorehead, ed., *Selected Letters of Martha Gellhorn* (Henry Holt, 2006).
44. For Gellhorn's many letters to Eleanor Roosevelt, see Somerville, ed., *Yours, for Probably Always*; Matthews, *Two Wars*, 207.
45. On the background and events at Guernica, see Beevor, *The Battle for Spain*, 230–33, and Thomas, *The Spanish Civil War*, 623–29.
46. The Reuters report can be seen for example in "800 Slain as Rebels Raid City," *Wilkes-Barre Times Leader*, Apr. 27, 1937. United Press followed with its own account, "800 Refugees Are Massacred as Insurgents Destroy Town," *WP*, Apr. 28, 1937; "Fascist Fliers Kill 800 in Raid," *Buffalo News*, Apr. 27, 1937; "Nazi Rebel Fliers Raze City, Kill 800," *New York Daily News*, Apr. 28, 1937; "Air Raids Kill 800 Civilians, Nazis Blamed," *Philadelphia Inquirer*, Apr. 28, 1937. George Steer,

"The Tragedy of Guernica," *Times* (London), Apr. 28, 1937. The articles appeared without a byline. About Steer, see Preston, "No Ordinary Purveyor of News," *History Today*, May 2007, 12–19; and Nicholas Rankin, *Telegram from Guernica: The Extraordinary Life of George Steer, War Correspondent* (Faber & Faber, 2003). Steer soon expanded his reports into a book about the Basques and the Guernica attack: G. L. Steer, *The Tree of Gernika: A Field Study of Modern War* (Hodder & Stoughton, 1938).

47. "Mass Murder in Guernica," *NYT*, Apr. 29, 1937; "Kultur for Spain," *WP*, Apr. 30, 1937. Eden's remarks in "The Bombing of Guernica," *MG*, Apr. 29, 1937.
48. G. L. Steer, "Basques Indignant on Guernica Raid," *NYT*, Apr. 30, 1937; "Destruction of Guernica: Priest's Account," *MG*, May 3, 1937.
49. "Roosevelt Goes Fishing Aboard U.S. Destroyer: President Welcomed Gaily by New Orleans After Day of Sight-Seeing," *WP*, Apr. 30, 1937. Further details at "FDR Day by Day," http://www.fdrlibrary.marist.edu/daybyday/.
50. The details of the 1937 Neutrality Act are laid out in Divine, *Illusion of Neutrality*, 162–99.
51. "U.S. Arms Ban on Reich, Italy Urged to Hull," *WP*, May 6, 1937.
52. "U.S. Leaders Voice Guernica Protest," *NYT*, May 10, 1937; "Borah Looses Scathing Attack on Fascist Rule," *WP*, May 7, 1937; S. Miles Bouton, "German Militarism," *WP*, June 8, 1937.
53. "Fight on Fascism Urged," *NYT*, June 5, 1937; Hemingway's talk was published as "Fascism Is a Lie," *New Masses*, June 22, 1937, 4.
54. "Babies, Bombs, and Battleships," *Time*, May 10, 1937.
55. Dorothy Thompson, "The Dilemma of a Pacifist," *Ladies Home Journal*, July 1937. A clipping is among her papers: Dorothy Thompson papers, box 80, Syracuse University.
56. Eleanor Roosevelt, "My Day," June 19, 1937, available online through the Eleanor Roosevelt Papers Project, George Washington University, https://erpapers.columbian.gwu.edu/my-day.
57. Eleanor Roosevelt, "My Day," May 28, 1937; ER to Gellhorn, June 1, 1937; Gellhorn to ER, July 3–4, 1937; and Gellhorn to ER, June 9, 1937, in Somerville, ed., *Yours, for Probably Always*, 167–68, 175–76, 168-69. Gellhorn had just written an excellent essay on Madrid: "Only the Shells Whine," *Collier's*, July 17, 1937.
58. Hemingway to Mrs. Paul Pfeiffer, his mother-in-law, Aug. 2, 1937, in Baker, ed., *Selected Letters*, 460.
59. Gellhorn to ER, July 8, 1937, Somerville, ed., *Yours, for Probably Always*, 177; "My Day," July 10, 1937.
60. John T. McManus, "Down to Earth in Spain," *NYT*, July 25, 1937; and McManus, "'The Spanish Earth' at the 55th St. Playhouse Is a Plea for Democracy," *NYT*, Aug. 21, 1937; Stacy Guill, "Now You Have Seen It: Ernest Hemingway, Joris Ivens, and the Spanish Earth," *Hemingway Review* 30, no. 1 (2010): 51–68.
61. Press conference transcript, July 13, 1937, FDRL.
62. Shirer, *Berlin Diary*, 83–87. The German words are: "*Denn heute gëhort uns Deutschland, Und morgen die ganze Welt.*"
63. Bowers to Hull, May 18, 1937, copied to FDR; and Bowers to FDR, July 21, 1937, PSF, box 50, FDRL. For scathing criticism of the neutrality policy, see Barnet Nover, "U.S. and Spain: The Latest Dilemma," *WP*, July 6, 1937.
64. FDR to Bowers, Aug. 1, 1937, PSF, box 50, FDRL; Jay Allen letter to Leo J. Callanan, American Consul in Malaga, Spain, Sept. 16, 1937, Hamilton Fish Armstrong Papers, box 1, Seeley Mudd Library, Princeton University.

Chapter 10: Japan Strikes

1. "The Camera Overseas: 136,000 Million People See This Picture of Shanghai's South Station," *Life*, Oct. 4, 1937. On Wong's prize, "Headliners Club Awards Its Prizes," *NYT*, July 11, 1938. Details of the scene at South Railway Station can be seen in "Foreign Protests Against Bombing," *North China Herald*, Sept. 1, 1937.
2. Akira Iriye, *The Origins of the Second World War in Asia and the Pacific* (Longman, 1987), 2–20. The League's summary of the issue is in Department of State, *Manchuria: Report of the Commission of Enquiry Appointed by the League of Nations* (Washington, D.C., 1932). Stimson's role is assessed in Armin Rappaport, *Henry L. Stimson and Japan, 1931–33* (University of Chicago Press, 1963); and his own account, Henry L. Stimson, *The Far Eastern Crisis* (Harper & Bros., 1936).
3. Rana Mitter, *Forgotten Ally: China's World War II, 1937–1945* (Houghton Mifflin, 2013), 95, and 56–97 generally for the origins of the war. A good fresh survey is available in S. C. M. Paine, *The*

Wars for Asia, 1911–1949 (Cambridge University Press, 2012), 49–122. The foundational and still crucial study of U.S. policy is Dorothy Borg, *The United States and the Far Eastern Crisis of 1933–1938* (Harvard University Press, 1964). This is now superseded by the excellent work of Richard Frank, *Tower of Skulls: A History of the Asia-Pacific War, July 1937–May 1942* (Norton, 2020).

4. R. J. C. Butow, "A Notable Passage to China: Myth and Memory in FDR's Family History," *Prologue Magazine* 31, no. 3 (1999), https://www.archives.gov/publications/prologue/1999/fall/roosevelt-family-history.
5. On the Chinese Exclusion Act, see Erika Lee, *America for Americans: A History of Xenophobia in the United States* (Basic, 2019), 75–111. On American activities in China, see Gordon H. Chang, *Fateful Ties: A History of America's Preoccupation with China* (Harvard University Press, 2015), 9–48, 90–129.
6. For a summary of some of the debates about the value of the China trade to American business, see Michael Hunt, "Americans in the China Market: Economic Opportunities and Economic Nationalism, 1890s–1931," *Business History Review* 51, no. 3 (1977): 277–307. For a discussion of the image-making, see T. Christopher Jespersen, *American Images of China: 1931–1949* (Stanford University Press, 1996). On war planning, see Louis Morton, "War Plan Orange: Evolution of a Strategy," *World Politics* 11, no. 2 (1959): 221–50.
7. Michael H. Hunt, "Pearl Buck—Popular Expert on China, 1931–1949," *Modern China* 3, no. 1 (1977): 33–64; Chang, *Fateful Ties*, 146–54. On Snow, see S. Bernard Thomas, *A Season of High Adventure: Edgar Snow in China* (University of California Press, 1996).
8. See Patricia Neils, *China Images in the Life and Times of Henry Luce* (Rowman & Littlefield, 1990); Alan Brinkley, *The Publisher: Henry Luce and His American Century* (Alfred A. Knopf, 2010), 3–25. Other examples of how the press described Madame Chiang Kai-shek are "The Man and the Woman Whom China Obeys," *NYT*, Nov. 7, 1937; and Pearl Buck's article, "The Sister 'Dictators' Behind the Chinese Dragon," about the Soong sisters, in *Hearst's International and Cosmopolitan*, Sept. 1937.
9. "Du Bois Gets Rousing Welcome as Harlem Hears Him Describe His Foreign Travels," *NYAN*, Jan. 30, 1937; "Forum of Fact and Opinion," *PC*, Feb. 13, 1937. David Levering Lewis, *W. E. B. Du Bois: The Fight for Equality and the American Century, 1919–1963* (Henry Holt, 2000), 388–421.
10. "Forum of Fact and Opinion," *PC*, Feb. 27 and Mar. 13, 1937. These essays were published after Du Bois returned to the United States. Further examples of this argument are in Kelly Miller, "Color and Character: The White Man's Burden," *New Journal and Guide*, Sept. 18, 1937; "We Don't Want War," *Philadelphia Tribune*, Oct. 14, 1937; Gordon Hancock, "Between the Lines: War with Japan," and "Between the Lines: Roosevelt in Reverse," both in *New Journal and Guide*, Oct. 9 and Oct. 30, 1937; George Pickens, "Race Issue Clear in Sino-Japanese War," *New Journal and Guide*, Dec. 4, 1937; and perhaps the most controversial editorial, "The Case for Japan," *BAA*, Jan. 15, 1938.
11. Hornbeck memo, May 24, 1934, in *FRUS 1934*, vol. 3, 189–93; and for another example of this line of argument, see Hornbeck memo, Jan. 3, 1935, *FRUS 1935*, vol. 3, 829–37.
12. Ambassador Joseph Grew to Hull, July 13, 1937, *FRUS 1937, The Far East*, vol. 3, 157; Stanley Hornbeck memorandum, July 14, 1937, *FRUS 1937, The Far East*, vol. 3, 161.
13. Sumner Welles, *Seven Decisions That Shaped History* (Harper & Brothers, 1950), 70–71. FDR letter to Chamberlain, July 28, 1937, *FRUS 1937*, vol. 1, 113.
14. The essential work is Robert Self, *Neville Chamberlain: A Biography* (Routledge, 2006).
15. For an insightful view of the long history of appeasement in British strategy, see Paul M. Kennedy, "The Tradition of Appeasement in British Foreign Policy, 1865–1939," *British Journal of International Studies* 2, no. 3 (1976): 195–215.
16. William R. Rock, *Chamberlain and Roosevelt: British Foreign Policy and the United States, 1937–1940* (Ohio State University Press, 1988), 28–31; David Reynolds, *The Creation of the Anglo-American Alliance, 1937–41* (University of North Carolina Press, 1982), 16–17; Andrew Kelly, "The Sino-Japanese War and the Anglo-American Response," *Australasian Journal of American Studies* 32, no. 2 (2013), 27–43; Borg, *United States and the Far Eastern Crisis*, 373–77; Hull, *Memoirs*, vol. 1, 538; Chamberlain to FDR, Sept. 28, 1937, PSF, Series 3, Diplomatic Correspondence, box 32, FDRL; Chamberlain to his sister Hilda, Aug. 29, 1937, in Robert Self, ed., *The Neville Chamberlain Diary Letters*, vol. 4 (Ashgate, 2005), 267.
17. Michelle Qiao, "Palace Hotel Reigned Over City's Most Famous Road," *Shanghai Daily*, May 27, 2017.

18. "Rain of Death on Shanghai," *CT*, Aug. 15, 1937; "Flyers! A Flash from the Sky and the Carnage," *CT*, Aug. 15, 1937; "3 Americans Among Slain; Big Hotels Shattered," *CT*, Aug. 15, 1937.
19. Colleen Carrigan, "Seaman First Class Freddie Falgout: First Military Casualty of World War II," *Sextant*, Sept. 3, 2021, published by the Naval History and Heritage Command. "5,000 Wounded; Battles Waged by Land, Air, and Sea," *WP*, Aug. 16, 1937; "Hull Gives Policy; 1,200 More Marines Will Be Sent to Reinforce Shanghai Guard," *NYT*, Aug. 18, 1937; "Night of Terror Reigns in Ruined City," *WP*, Aug. 18, 1937; "Smiling Chinese Defy Death as Bombs Tear Homes to Bits," *WP*, Aug. 19, 1937; "Shell Hits U.S. Warship; Sailor Killed," *CT*, Aug. 21, 1937; "Augusta Is Struck," *NYT*, Aug. 21, 1937.
20. "Japanese Air Bombs Spread Fire and Terror in Shanghai," *NYT*, Aug. 22, 1937; "Shell Kills 200 in Shanghai," *CT*, Aug. 23, 1937; "Wild Havoc Scene Told by Witnesses," *NYT*, Aug. 24, 1937; "Planes Bomb Auto; Ambassador is Struck," *NYT*, Aug. 27, 1937.
21. "Bombs Rain on Refugees Waiting Train to Safe Zone," *WP*, Aug. 29, 1937; "Japanese Bombs Kill 200 in Shanghai," *CT*, Aug. 29, 1937; "Only Civilians Hit," *NYT*, Aug. 29, 1937; "Hundreds Die as Japs Bomb Chinese Cities," *CT*, Aug. 30, 1937; "Shanghai Hit by Cholera as New Fighting Rages," *CT*, Sept. 1, 1937; "Unburied Bodies Add to Shanghai Horrors," *WP*, Sept. 1, 1937. An eyewitness described the scene in "Nantao Bombing," *North China Herald*, Sept. 1, 1937; and "50 Die in Early Morning Bombing," *North China Herald*, Sept. 8, 1937.
22. Frank, *Tower of Skulls*, 25–36.
23. Madame Chiang Kai-Shek, "No Other Nation Seems to Care," *MG*, Sept. 13, 1937; "Madame Chiang on U.S. Attitude," *Times of India*, Sept. 17, 1937; "'My Heart is Chilled': Nanking," *Time*, Oct. 11, 1937. See also "Chiang Condemns Neutrals' Policy," *NYT*, Sept. 25, 1937.
24. John Dower, *War Without Mercy: Race and Power in the Pacific War* (Norton, 1986); "Calling Japan to Account," *WP*, Aug. 30, 1937; "A City Faces Death," *NYT*, Sept. 22, 1937.
25. "Japan Bombing Scored in Pulpits," *NYT*, Oct. 4, 1937; "New Barbarians," *MG*, Sept. 24, 1937; "London in Protest," *NYT*, Sept. 25, 1937; "Britain Reasserts Protest at Tokyo," *NYT*, Sept. 28, 1937; "British Groups Hist 'Barbarism' in Chinese War," *WP*, Sept. 30, 1937; "Boycott of Japan Pressed by AFL," *NYT*, Oct. 8, 1937.
26. The editorials are "The USA in China: Too Few to Fight, Too Many to be Killed," *CT*, Aug. 21, 1937, and "Getting Out of China," *CT*, Aug. 31, 1937. Roosevelt's announcement in "U.S.-Owned Ships Forbidden to Take Arms to Far East; Private Lines are Warned," *NYT*, Sept. 15, 1937; Madame Chiang Kai-shek, "China Takes Her Stand," *Forum and Century*, Dec. 1937.
27. Ickes, *Secret Diary*, vol. 2, 209–14; 221–22. On the Nuremberg rally, "Hitler Hails Ties with Italy, Japan," *NYT*, Sept. 8, 1937; "Labor Has Its Day at Nazi Congress," *NYT*, Sept. 9, 1937. Norman Davis also suggested to FDR that "war is a contagion" in some draft memos he sent to FDR on Sept. 17, 1937, Norman Davis Papers, box 51, LOC.
28. "Two Dams in Series Near Completion," *WP*, Sept. 26, 1937; Richard L. Neuberger, "Roosevelt Goes to See," *NYT*, Sept. 26, 1937.
29. "Cheers of Million in Berlin Approve Tie with Mussolini," *NYT*, Sept. 28, 1937; "Texts of Speeches by Hitler and Mussolini," *NYT*, Sept. 29, 1937.
30. "Text of President's Speech at Link Bridge Dedication," *CT*, Oct. 6, 1937. For analysis on the origins of the speech, see Borg, *US and Far Eastern Crisis*, 380–86.
31. Langer and Gleason, *Challenge of Isolation*, 11, 19–24. "Japan Hurls Warning of War Danger," *SFE*, Oct. 6, 1937, with accompanying editorial likening Roosevelt to Wilson and the drift to war in 1917; "U.S. Brands Japan Aggressor," *SFE*, Oct. 7, 1937; "He Too Would Keep Us Out of War," *CT*, Oct. 6, 1937; "Whatever It's Called, It's War," *CT*, Oct. 8, 1937; "We Could Muddle Into War," *Wall Street Journal*, Oct. 7, 1937; "No Clarion Call for Us," *Wall Street Journal*, Oct. 9, 1937; "Critics of Mr. Roosevelt," *MG*, Oct. 20, 1937; "6 Peace Groups Hit Roosevelt 'Quarantine,'" *WP*, Oct. 7, 1937.
32. Ickes, *Secret Diary*, vol. 2, 222. "Interpretations of President Roosevelt's Speech," *MG*, Oct. 6, 1937; Davies comment, Journal, Oct. 5, 1937, Davies Papers, box I:6, LOC; "Roosevelt Hailed by Moscow Press," *NYT*, Oct. 9, 1937; Bowers to FDR, Oct. 11, 1937, PSF, box 50, Spain, 1937, FDRL. A careful study of the reception of the speech is Travis Beal Jacobs, "Roosevelt's 'Quarantine' Speech," *Historian* 24, no. 4 (1962): 483–502.
33. Dorothy Thompson, Pall Mall Broadcast, Oct. 8, 1937, transcript in Dorothy Thompson Papers, box 111, Syracuse University.
34. "On This Bridge, A U.S. President Turned the Course of History," *Life*, Oct. 18, 1937, 25–27; "Nation-Wide Press Comment on President Roosevelt's Address," *NYT*, Oct. 6, 1937; "The Pres-

ident Warms Up," and "Action Against Japan?" both in *LAT*, Oct. 6 and 7, 1937; "America Finds Her Voice," *WP*, Oct. 6, 1937; "President's Attack on Aggressor Nations Spurs League to Back China in War," *LAT*, Oct. 6, 1937.

35. Press Conference, Oct. 6, 1937, at Hyde Park, FDRL; Lord Elibank, "Franklin Roosevelt: Friend of Britain," *Contemporary Review* (1955): 362–68. See also Dorothy Borg, "Notes on Roosevelt's 'Quarantine' Speech, *Political Science Quarterly* 72, no. 3 (1957): 405–33. He used the same "peace at any price" phrase in a letter to Endicott Peabody, Oct. 16, 1937, in *FDR: Personal Letters*, vol. 1, 716–17.
36. Davis memorandum, Oct. 20, 1937, Davis Papers, box 4, LOC. For further analysis, see John McVickar Haight, "Roosevelt and the Aftermath of the Quarantine Speech," *Review of Politics* 24, no. 2 (1962): 233–59.
37. Two undated Hornbeck memos, presumably for Davis, Davis Papers, box 4, LOC. Sumner Welles made it plain to British ambassador Lindsay that the U.S. government wanted to concentrate on "the making of every effort to promote a pacific solution" to the crisis in China, and avoid discussion of economic or naval pressure. Memo by Welles, Nov. 13, 1937, in *FRUS 1937, The Far East,* vol. 4, 152–53.
38. Davis draft message of Nov. 14 to Hull in Davis Papers, box 4, LOC. The final version, dated Nov. 14, appeared in *FRUS 1937, The Far East,* vol. 4, 183–85.
39. "Text of Former Secretary Henry L. Stimson's Letter on the Crisis in the Far East," *NYT*, Oct. 7, 1937.
40. Stimson Diary, Yale University, vol. 28, 96–100, 109.
41. Stimson to FDR, Nov. 15, 1937, Feis Papers, box 26, LOC.
42. FDR to Viscount Cecil, Apr. 6, 1937, in *FDR: Personal Letters*, vol. 1, 671–72; FDR to Anthony Biddle, Nov. 10, 1937, ibid., 725–26; FDR to Hull about Stimson's letter, Nov. 22, 1937, ibid., 729
43. Joseph C. Grew, *Ten Years in Japan* (Simon & Schuster, 1944), 211–24. On the Grew-Hornbeck divergence and Roosevelt's position, see Abraham Ben-Zvi, *The Illusion of Deterrence: The Roosevelt Presidency and the Origins of the Pacific War* (Routledge, 1987), 31–87.
44. A detailed written report by the ship's captain, James J. Hughes, is in PSF, box 26, FDRL; "Shelling of Panay Related by Briton," *NYT*, Dec. 18, 1937; "Writer Tells of Machine Gunning by Japanese Planes," Dec. 18, 1937; "Roosevelt Active," *NYT*, Dec. 18, 1937.
45. Grew, *Ten Years in Japan*, 232–50; and his "blessing" remark, in Grew, *Turbulent Era: A Diplomatic Record of Forty Years, 1904–1945* (Houghton Mifflin, 1952), 1205; for the "deeply shocked" phrase, FDR to Hull, Dec. 13, 1937, in *DHFDRP*, vol. 29, 22. On the report of the strafing of the smaller boats, see Admiral William D. Leahy to FDR, Dec. 17, 1937, ibid., 101–2.
46. On the idea of Treasury action against Japan, see Blum, *Morgenthau Diaries, Years of Crisis, 1928–1938*, 485–92.
47. A. T. Steele, "Chinese Slain Without Mercy in 4 Days of Hell at Nanking," *Evening Star* (Washington, D.C.), Dec. 16, 1937. See also Arthur Menken, "Witness Tells Nanking Horror as Chinese Flee," *CT*, Dec. 17, 1937.
48. F. Tillman Durdin, "All Captives Slain," *NYT*, Dec. 18, 1937. There is a large literature on the Japanese atrocities in Nanking; a good recent synthesis is in Mitter, *China's World War II*, 124–44. For a careful collaborative assessment of the available evidence and its significance, see Bob Tadashi Wakabayashi, ed., *The Nanking Atrocity, 1937–1938: Complicating the Picture* (Berghahn Books, 2007).
49. Ickes, *Secret Diary*, vol. 2, 302; "Excerpts from the Letters of an American Doctor in China," Feb. 8, 1938, Henry Luce Papers, box 26, LOC; "The Camera Overseas: The Japanese Conqueror Brings a Week of Hell," *Life*, Jan. 10, 1938; articles in *Time*, Dec. 27, 1937, Jan. 3, 1938, Jan. 10, 1938, Feb. 14, 1938; "Nanking in Flames as Nipponese Take City," *LAT*, Jan. 1, 1938; "Hundreds Slain in Jap Bombing of Canton Area," *CT*, Jan. 2, 1938; "Plundering Japanese Rob Americans; Women and Children at Nanking Killed in Cold Blood," *LAT*, Jan. 9, 1938; "Americans Holdings Looted in Nanking since Its Conquest," *NYT*, Jan. 9, 1938; F. Tillman Durdin, "Japanese Atrocities Marked Fall of Nanking after Chinese Command Fled," *NYT*, Jan. 9, 1938; "Reign of Terror in Nanking," *MG*, Jan. 23, 1938; "Reign of Disorder Goes on in Nanking," *NYT*, Jan. 25, 1938; Hallet Abend, "Terrors in Nanking Told," *LAT*, Jan. 25, 1938; "Lawlessness in Nanking," *NYT*, Jan. 26, 1938; "Terrorism in Nanking," *MG*, Feb. 7, 1938. At the end of March, Stimson spoke with Hull at the State Department and Hull confirmed that he knew all about the atrocities, which he called "beyond description." Stimson Diary, vol. 28, Mar. 24, 1938, 122, and Apr. 12, 1938, 138.

50. "U.S. Envoy Tells of Jap Slap," *CT*, Jan. 29, 1938; "America Sends Sharp New Protest to Japan," *LAT*, Jan. 28, 1938; "U.S. Protests Anew to Japan," *NYT*, Jan. 28, 1938; "Diplomat Slapped by Tokyo Soldier," *NYT*, Jan. 28, 1938; "U.S. Protests Outrages to Japan," *WP*, Jan. 28, 1938; "Japanese Regret Slapping of U.S. Envoy," *WP*, Jan. 28, 1938; "Japan Makes Slap Apology," *LAT*, Jan. 31, 1938. The newsreel of the Panay incident was hastily put together. See "U.S. Panay Bombing as Shot by the Moving Picture Camera," *WP*, Dec. 30, 1937; "Panay Pictures: Rush!" *NYT*, Jan. 2, 1938.
51. Cyril Briggs, "Japan Proves Not to be the Hope of Darker Races," *Philadelphia Tribune*, Jan. 20, 1938; "Says Germany, Italy, Japan, Not Friends of American Negro," *PC*, Mar. 26, 1938.
52. Adam Clayton Powell Jr., "Soap Box," *NYAN*, Feb. 19, 1938.
53. Ickes, *Secret Diary*, vol. 2, 274–75.
54. British inquiry in Nelson T. Johnson to Hull, Dec. 13, 1937, *DHFDRP*, vol. 29, 26–27; and Sir R. Lindsay to Eden, Dec. 17, 1937, in Great Britain Foreign Office, *Documents on British Foreign Policy, 1919–1939*, 2nd series, vol. 21 (Her Majesty's Stationery Office, 1984), 589–92.
55. The British record of the talks is in *Documents on British Foreign Policy, 1919-1939*, 2nd series, vol. 21, 651–56. For more analysis, see Lawrence Pratt, "The Anglo-American Naval Conversations on the Far East of January 1938," *International Affairs* 47, no. 4 (1971): 745–63. On the missed opportunity for joint action, see Andrew Kelly, "The Sino-Japanese War and the Anglo-American Response," *Australian Journal of American Studies* 32, no. 2 (2013): 27–43. On the content and significance of the Ingersoll mission, see John McVicker Haight Jr., "Franklin D. Roosevelt and a Naval Quarantine of Japan," *Pacific Historical Review* 40, no. 2 (1971): 203–26.
56. David Kaiser, *No End Save Victory: How FDR Led the Nation into War* (Basic Books, 2014), 38; Dallek, *Franklin D. Roosevelt and American Foreign Policy*, 155. For a view of FDR as temporizing and unsure, and lacking a clear direction in foreign affairs, see Mark M. Lowenthal, "Roosevelt and the Coming of the War: The Search for United States Policy, 1937–42," *Journal of Contemporary History* 16, no. 3 (1981): 413–44.
57. Dorothy Thompson, "On the Record: Pany Tension Eased; Uncertainty Remains," *Buffalo News*, Dec. 29, 1937.

Chapter 11: 1938: Blood and Soil

1. "War Cause Parley Ends Conference," *WP*, Jan. 22, 1938; "Mrs. Catt, 79 Today, Saddened by Wars," *NYT*, Jan. 9, 1938. Further news coverage of the meeting is in "Sessions Open Tuesday on Cause, Cure of War," *WP*, Jan. 16, 1938; Anne Petersen, "Formula for World Peace Is Aim of 4-Day Rally in Washington," *NYT*, Jan. 16, 1938. The Communist-led American League for Peace and Democracy, which had been strongly pacifist, shifted its tone with the war in Spain and the Japanese attack on China. At the end of 1937, it adopted taking a more militant line in calling for embargoes, boycotts, even a blockade of Japan, and confrontation of aggressors. See the editorial in its monthly magazine, "Berlin-Rome-Tokyo," December 1937, *The Fight Against War and Fascism* 5, no. 2 (1937): 31.
2. "New League Urged by Mrs. Roosevelt," *NYT*, Jan. 2, 1938; "Mrs. Roosevelt's Views on Peace," *NYT*, Jan. 2, 1938; "Mrs. Roosevelt Decries Lack of Peace Plan," *WP*, Jan. 2, 1938; "Mrs. Roosevelt Sees a World in Danger," *WP*, Jan. 2, 1938; "U.S. Must End Isolation to Act for Peace, Mrs. Roosevelt Asserts at Conference on War," *WP*, Jan. 20, 1938.
3. Eleanor Roosevelt, *This Troubled World* (H. C. Kinsey, 1938). Blanche Wiesen Cook, *Eleanor Roosevelt, Vol. 2: The Defining Years, 1933–1938* (Penguin Books, 1999), 484–508, quote from 492.
4. Welles to Roosevelt, Jan. 10, 1938, *FRUS 1938*, vol. 1, 115-17. For the background and implications of the proposal, see Tim Bouverie, *Appeasement: Chamberlain, Hitler, Churchill, and the Road to War* (Tim Duggan, 2019), 152–53; Anthony Eden, *Facing the Dictators*, 622–27; Welles, *Seven Major Decisions*, 25–30; Welles, *The Time for Decision*, 66–68; and David Reynolds, *Creation of the Anglo-American Alliance*, 31–32. On Welles and "economic appeasement," see David F. Schmitz, *The Triumph of Internationalism: Franklin D. Roosevelt and a World in Crisis, 1933–1941* (Potomac Books, 2007), 42–50.
5. Welles to Roosevelt, Jan. 14, 1938, *FRUS 1938*, vol. 1, 117–20, containing Chamberlain's message.
6. Roosevelt letter, given by Welles to Lindsay, Jan. 17, 1938, *FRUS 1938*, vol. 1, 120–22; Hull memo of conversation with Lindsay, Jan. 17, 1938, *FRUS 1938*, vol. 1, 133–34.
7. For an excellent synthesis of the vast literature on the origins of appeasement, see Tim Bouverie, *Appeasement*, 131–36.

8. Ferdinand Kuhn, "Britain is Shocked: Foreign Secretary Quits over Issue of Seeking Deals with Dictators," *NYT*, Feb. 21, 1938; Dorothy Thompson, "The Last Knight of Europe," *Buffalo Evening News*, Feb. 23, 1938; Moffat, *Moffat Papers*, 190–91.
9. "The Gallup Poll: British Opinion Still Against Cabinet as Rome Conference Begins," *WP*, Mar. 11, 1938; "Laborites Lose as Turbulent Session Accords Him Right to Pursue Hitler-Mussolini Talks," *WP*, Feb. 23, 1938.
10. George Messersmith to Hull, Feb. 18, 1938, *FRUS 1938*, vol. 1, 17–24; Gilbert to Hull, Jan. 18, 1938, *FRUS 1938*, vol. 1, 384–85; Wiley to Hull, Feb. 4, 1938, *FRUS 1938*, vol. 1, 387–89. For Dodd's view, see his remarkable thirty-five-page-long memo, "A Survey of the German National Socialist Foreign Policy and Its Development," Nov. 28, 1936, in PSF, box 32, Diplomatic Correspondence, Dodd, William, 1936–38, FDRL.
11. For Hitler's plans, see the so-called Hossbach Memorandum , Nov. 10, 1937, "Minutes of a Conference in the Reich Chancellery, Berlin, November 5, 1937," at https://avalon.law.yale.edu/imt/hossbach.asp.
12. Otto Tolischus, "Reich Jubilant," *NYT*, Feb. 16, 1938; G. E. R. Gedye, "Amnesty Decreed," *NYT*, Feb. 16, 1938; Sigrid Schultz, "Czechs May Be Next for German Net, Berlin Hints," *CT*, Feb. 20, 1938; Dorothy Thompson, *NYHT*, Feb. 18, 1938; Shirer, *Berlin Diary*, 92.
13. "Herr Hitler's Speech of February 20," *Bulletin of International News* 15, no. 5 (1938): 23–27; Shirer, *Berlin Diary*, Feb. 20; Sigrid Schultz, "Hitler Demands Stir Europe, Nazis Seek Unity of All Germans," *CT*, Feb. 21, 1938.
14. "Cartwheel Girl," *Time*, June 12, 1939; "Dorothy Thompson—Lady Astor of the USA," *Radio News*, May 1938, 18. An earlier portrait, by her friend and colleague John Gunther, appeared as "A Blue-Eyed Tornado," *NYHT*, Sunday, Jan. 13, 1935; and see Don Wharton, "Dorothy Thompson," *Scribner's*, May 1937, which referred to her as "the first lady of American journalism." Clippings of these pieces are in Thompson Papers, box 73, Syracuse University. On her income, see John Moses to Thompson, Aug. 17, 1937, and Jan. 6, 1937, Thompson Papers, box 20, Syracuse University. On her split from Lewis, see in particular her heartbreaking letter to him of Apr. 29, 1937, Thompson Papers, box 48, Syracuse University.
15. Dorothy Thompson, "Freedom's Back Is Against the Wall," *Vital Speeches of the Day* 3, 18 (1937): 547–51. She delivered this speech at the commencement ceremonies at Russell Sage College, June 8, 1937. For a critical assessment of her opposition to the New Deal, see Margaret Marshall, "Dorothy Thompson," *Nation*, June 25, 1938, 721–24. Her self-description as a liberal is in "To Freedom!," *Ladies Home Journal*, Dec. 1937.
16. Dorothy Thompson, "Write It Down That a New Era Has Started," *Buffalo Evening News*, Feb. 18, 1938. This paper published her syndicated column. See also the transcripts of her radio broadcasts of Feb. 18 and Feb. 22, in Dorothy Thompson Papers, box 111, Syracuse University.
17. "Drive for Fascism Charged by Ickes," *NYT*, Dec. 9, 1937; "Ickes Calls Ku Klux Klan Menace to Entire World," *BAA*, Dec. 25, 1937. The full text was published as "Fascism's Trojan Horse," *Jewish Exponent*, Dec. 24, 1937. On FDR seeing the draft, Ickes, *Secret Diary*, vol. 2, 258. Herbert Feis was one of a core group in the State Department who wanted more action and fewer words: "It may, under some circumstances, be our national responsibility to employ force, to go to war, either for our own ultimate safety or to prevent the world from falling completely" under the control of tyrants. Feis to Felix Frankfurter, Feb. 11, 1938, Feis Papers, box 33, LOC.
18. Dorothy Thompson, "Opinion Shifting in Regard to Europe," *Buffalo Evening News*, Mar. 2, 1938; "Text of Ickes Broadcast," *NYT*, Feb. 23, 1938; "Economic Security Is Best Safeguard for Democracy," *WP*, Feb. 23, 1938; "Divided Views in Washington," *MG*, Feb. 23, 1938; "Ickes Address to Britain Condemned as Danger," *WP*, Feb. 25, 1938.
19. Ickes, *Secret Diary*, vol. 2, 321–24; Sumner Welles, Memorandum of Conversation, Mar. 8, 1938, *FDR&FA*, vol. 9, 68–77; FDR to John Cudahy, ambassador to Ireland, Mar. 9, 1938, *FDR&FA*, vol. 9, 87.
20. G. E. R. Gedye, "Schuschnigg Calls Independence Poll as He Defies Nazis," *NYT*, Mar. 10, 1938.
21. Sigrid Schultz, "Punish Austrian Leader! Hitler Instructs Nazis," *CT*, Mar. 11, 1938; Sigrid Schultz, "Berlin Jubilant as Vienna Falls to Hitler's Aids," *CT*, Mar. 12, 1938; G. E. R. Gedye, "Schuschnigg Goes," *NYT*, Mar. 12, 1938; "Nazi Crowds Rout Enemies in Vienna," *NYT*, Mar. 12, 1938; "65,000 Reich Troops Move into Austria," *NYT*, Mar. 13, 1938; "Under the Feet of German Troops the Map of Europe Changes," *NYT*, Mar. 13, 1938. Shirer on Wiley, *Berlin Diary*, 98; Kershaw, *Hitler: Nemesis*, 74–77.

22. "Hitler's Vienna Talk," *WP*, Mar. 16, 1938; Kershaw, *Hitler: Nemesis*, 78–82.
23. Shirer, *Berlin Diary*, 97, 103.
24. Wiley to Hull, Mar. 19, *FRUS 1938*, vol. 1, 457–60. Details in "Vienna Jews Beaten; Stores Plundered," *NYT*, Mar. 14, 1938; "Jews of Vienna Flee as Nazis Plunder Shops," *CT*, Mar. 15, 1938; "Jews Humiliated by Vienna Crowds," *NYT*, Mar. 16, 1938; "Austrian Jews Handed Brooms and Put to Work," *CT*, Mar. 20, 1938; "Terror Grips Vienna Jewry," *Jewish Exponent*, Mar. 25, 1938.
25. Dorothy Thompson, radio broadcast, Mar. 11, 1938, transcript in Dorothy Thompson Papers, box 111, Syracuse University; Dorothy Thompson, "Events in Europe Are Real Concern of U.S.," *Buffalo Evening News*, Mar. 16, 1938.
26. FDRL, Morgenthau Diary, book 115, Mar. 16, 1938, 27.
27. "Hull Outlines Foreign Policy Based on Peace," *CT*, Mar. 18, 1938; "Hull's Address Outlining Foreign Policy of the United States," *NYT*, Mar. 18, 1938; "Text of Secretary Hull's Admonition to Nation to Increase Its Armaments," *WP*, Mar. 18, 1938; Department of State, Our Foreign Policy: Address by the Honorable Cordell Hull, Washington, March 17, 1938 (Government Printing Office, 1938). For the significance of the speech inside the administration, see Messersmith to Wiley, Mar. 16, 1938, *FRUS 1938*, vol. 1, 451–53. Polls showed 70 percent thought it was a mistake to enter the world war. See George Gallup and Claude Robinson, "American Institute of Public Opinion—Surveys, 1935–1938," *Public Opinion Quarterly* 2, no. 3 (1938), 373–98.
28. Dorothy Thompson, "Now or Never Is the Time to Save the World," *Buffalo Evening News*, Mar. 18, 1938.
29. William Randolph Hearst, "Isolation or Participation in Foreign Complications? Which Is It Going to Be?" *SFE*, Mar. 20, 1938; "Peace Speech by Hull Assailed," *SFE*, Mar. 23, 1938.
30. "Borah Warns of War Peril in U.S. Foreign Policy," *CT*, Mar. 29, 1938.
31. Ickes, *Secret Diary*, vol. 2, 342–43, and for March 18 cabinet meeting, Morgenthau Diary, vol. 115, 38–81, FDRL. FDR discussed the issue in his press conference March 25—the United States had always been "a place for political refugees to come to." Press conference, Mar. 25, 1938, *FDR&FA*, vol. 9, 243–44.
32. Early planning documents put together by Sumner Welles can be seen in Morgenthau Diary, book 116, Mar. 22 and 23, 1938, 264–75, FDRL; Sumner Welles Papers, box 150, folder 1, FDRL; Hull to European Embassies, Mar. 23, 1938, *FRUS 1938*, vol. 1, 740–41; "30-Nation Bloc Sought to Help Emigration from Germany," *WP*, Mar. 25, 1938. Herbert Feis also played a role in trying to "awaken my colleagues to the plight particularly of the Jews in Austria." He pushed Hull to act, and he told Felix Frankfurter "the president seems definitely interested." Feis to Frankfurter, Mar. 22, 1938, and Feis to Hull, Mar. 22, 1938, Feis Papers, box 33, LOC. For the lobbying for action from leading Jewish organizations, see Maldwin Fertig of the American Jewish Congress to FDR, Mar. 25, 1938, *FDR&FA*, vol. 9, 242.
33. "Hitler Is Pleased to Get Rid of Foes," *NYT*, Mar. 27, 1938; "Texan Calls Hull's Refugee Plan New U.S. Tax Burden," *CT*, Mar. 27, 1938.
34. Ellender and Bilbo in *Congressional Record—Senate*, 1938, Jan. 20, 1938, 813–35; Jan. 21, 873–96. News coverage, especially in the Black press, was extensive. "Ellender Speaks 4 Days and Goes On," *NYT*, Jan. 19, 1938; "Sen. Bilbo Upholds Mississippi Traditions in Anti-Lynching Debate," *New Journal and Guide*, Jan. 29, 1938; "Bilbo Gets It Off His Chest," *PC*, Jan. 29, 1938; "'Deport All Negroes—Bilbo,'" *PC*, Jan. 29, 1938; "Anti-Lynching Vote," *NYT*, Feb. 22, 1938.
35. Walter White to Roosevelt, Jan. 22, 1938, asking FDR to intervene in the filibuster and push the bill through, in ProQuest, History Vault: Papers of the NAACP, Part 07: The Anti-Lynching Campaign, 1912–1955, Series B: Anti-Lynching Legislative and Publicity Files, 1916–1955. FDR press conference, Mar. 22, 1938, FDRL.
36. Wise to FDR, Mar. 28, 1938, in PPF 3292, Wise, Rabbi Stephen, FDRL. Felix Frankfurter to FDR, Mar. 26, 1938, in Freedman, ed., *Roosevelt and Frankfurter*, 449; Sumner Welles, preparatory memorandum for the meeting of April 13, dated Apr. 11, 1938, *FDR&FA*, vol. 9, 375–78; notes on the meeting of Apr. 13, 1938, in Richard Breitman et al., eds., *Refugees and Rescue: The Diaries and Papers of James G. McDonald, 1935–1945* (Indiana University Press, 2009), 127–29.
37. Stimson Diary, vol. 28, 1935–1938, 142–44, Yale University Library; FDR to Myron Taylor, April 26, 1938, in Myron Taylor Papers, Intergovernmental Committee on Political Refugees, 1938, Select Digitized Documents Related to the Holocaust and Refugees, FDRL.

38. The battle of Teruel is analyzed in Hugh Thomas, *Spanish Civil War*, 789–94; and Antony Beevor, *Battle for Spain*, 313–27. For Spanish arms requests, see Thurston to State, Jan. 5, 1938, *FRUS 1938*, vol. 2, 149–50. Louis Fischer, "The Loyalists Push Ahead," *Nation*, Jan. 1, 1938.
39. Virginia Cowles, "Behind the Fighting Fronts," *NYT*, Jan. 9, 1938; quotation from her excellent memoir, *Looking for Trouble* (Harper, 1941), 40.
40. Memo by Sumner Welles after conversation with Ambassador Fernando de los Ríos, Feb. 23, 1938, *FRUS 1938*, vol. 1, 161.
41. Bowers to FDR, Feb. 20, 1938; FDR note to Hull, Mar. 7, 1938, both in PSF, box 50, Spain, 1938, FDRL.
42. Proceedings of the Second Congress, Oct. 15–17, 1937, National Negro Congress, *African America, Communists, and the National Negro Congress*, Gale, Archives Unbound.
43. Langston Hughes, "Hughes Bombed in Spain; Tells of Terror of Fascist Raid," *BAA*, Oct. 23, 1937; Langston Hughes, "Langston Hughes Tells Poignant Tale of Spain: Men or Color Are Heroes on Madrid Front," *New Journal and Guide*, Oct. 30, 1937; "Langston Hughes, "Hughes Finds Moors Being Used as Pawns by Fascists in Spain," *BAA*, Oct. 30, 1937; Langston Hughes, "'Organ Grinder's Swing' Heard Above Gunfire in Spain," *BAA*, Nov. 6, 1937; Langston Hughes, "Soldiers from Many Lands United in Spanish Fight," *BAA*, Dec. 18, 1937. For more, see Isabel Soto, "'I Knew That Spain Once Belonged to the Moors': Langston Hughes, Race, and the Spanish Civil War," *Research in African Literatures* 45, no. 3 (2014): 130–46.
44. *Proceedings: People's Congress for Democracy and Peace*, Fourth National Congress, American League for Peace and Democracy, Nov. 26–28, 1937 (New York: Jan. 1938).
45. "U.S. Urged to End Embargo on Spain," *NYT*, Feb. 16, 1938; "Lawyers Denounce Aid to Gen. Franco," *NYT*, Feb. 23, 1938; "Lawyers Ask Help for Loyalist Spain," *NYT*, Mar. 13, 1938; "U.S. Not to Change Our Neutrality Policy," *NYT*, Mar. 23, 1938; "Buell Criticizes Our Stand on Spain," *NYT*, Mar. 27, 1938; Raymond Leslie Buell, "Faults in Our Neutrality Policy," *NYT*, Apr. 17, 1938.
46. "Hail of Bombs," *CT*, Mar. 17, 1938; "Air Raiders Kill 1,000 in Barcelona," *NYT*, Mar. 18, 1938; "Half a Million Flee," *LAT*, Mar. 19, 1938; "U.S. Embargo Is Scored by Spain," *NYT*, Mar. 18, 1938; "No Change on Spain," *NYT*, Mar. 19, 1938.
47. "Peace Aids Ask Boycott to Halt Wars," *WP*, Mar. 29, 1938; "Aid for Spain Demanded," *NYT*, Mar.29, 1938; "On Capitol Hill: Lifting of Arms Embargo Against Loyalist Spain Demanded," *WP*, Mar. 31, 1938; "Peace Rally Hears Attack on Clergy," *NYT*, Apr. 5, 1938; "Women Parade to Aid Spain," *LAT*, Apr. 5, 1938.
48. "Writers Take Sides," pamphlet published by the League of American Writers (New York: May 1938), with Hemingway's April 1 telegram; Louis Fischer, "What Can Save Spain?" *Nation*, Mar. 26, 1938; "Barcelona Holds Out," *Nation*, Apr. 2, 1938.
49. Ernest Hemingway, "Dying, Well or Badly," *Ken*, Apr. 21, 1938.
50. Bowers to FDR, Apr. 11, 1938, PSF, box 50, Spain 1938, FDRL.
51. Gellhorn to ER, Mar. 23 and Apr. 24, 1938, in Somerville, ed., *Yours for Probably Always*, 189–90, 191–92; ER to Gellhorn, Apr. 5 and June 29, 1938, 190–91, 214-15; Eleanor Roosevelt, *This I Remember*, 161-62.
52. On Nye, see Taylor, *United States and the Spanish Civil War*, 173; Walter Lippmann, "Senator Nye Grows Older," *LAT*, May 10, 1938.
53. "Hull Defends Embargo on Arms to Spain," *CT*, May 7, 1938; "Lifting of Ban on Arms for Spain Studied by Roosevelt," *WP*, May 9, 1938; "President Confers on Neutrality Act," *NYT*, May 10, 1938; "Move to Lift Spanish Arms Embargo Lost," *WP*, May 10, 1938; "U.S. Drops Plan to Repel Arms Embargo on Spain," *NYT*, May 14, 1938; "Text of Hull's Letter," *NYT*, May 14, 1938; "Senators Doom Hope of Selling Arms to Spain," *WP*, May 14, 1938; Ickes, *Secret Diary*, vol. 2, 390.
54. The case has been made by Dominic Tierney, "Franklin D. Roosevelt and Covert Aid to the Loyalists in the Spanish Civil War, 1936–39," *Journal of Contemporary History* 39, no. 3 (2004): 299–313. For Bullitt's June 21, 1938, message to FDR: *For the President*, 274–76.
55. "The President's Message," *NYT*, Jan. 29, 1938, and "Vinson Offers Bill," *NYT*, Jan. 29, 1938; FDR's own draft of the message is in Donald B. Schewe, ed., *FDR&FA*, vol. 8, Jan–Feb 1938, 168–73.
56. Jamie McGrath, "Peacetime Naval Rearmament, 1933–39," *Naval War College Review* 72, no. 2 (2019): 83–103; George V. Fagan, "FDR and Naval Limitation," *U.S. Naval Institute Proceedings* 81, no. 4 (1955), https://www.usni.org/magazines/proceedings/1955/april/fdr-and-naval-limitation.

57. "Naval Bill Drawn to Define Policies of 2-Coast Fleet," *NYT*, Feb. 12, 1938; "Navy Bill Passed in Senate, 56–28," *NYT*, May 4, 1938; "Senate Completes Naval Bill Action," *NYT*, May 14, 1938; "New Navy Bill Is Signed," *NYT*, May 18, 1938; Naval History and Heritage Command, "U.S. Ship Force Levels, 1886–present," at https://www.history.navy.mil/research/histories/ship-histories/us-ship-force-levels.html#1931.
58. Walter Lippmann columns in *Los Angeles Times*: "The Debate about American Rearmament," Jan. 25, 1938; "Some Plain Truths About American Foreign Policy," Feb. 4, 1938; "The Super-Super Navy," Apr. 25, 1938; "American Rearmament," June 11, 1938.
59. Dorothy Thompson, *Buffalo Evening News*, Mar. 25, 1938; Nicholas Murray Butler, "Democracy 1938," *NYT*, June 2, 1938; "Hull Calls on the Nation to Unite for 'World Based on Law,'" *NYT*, June 4, 1938. The text of the Nye-Thompson debate is in "What Does the European Situation Mean to Us?," *Bulletin of America's Town Meeting of the Air* 3, no. 21 (1938).
60. Editorial, "A Way of Life," *NYT*, June 15, 1938. The German government lodged a protest against this editorial. "Butler Sees Death of Neutrality Act," *NYT*, June 26, 1938.
61. Breitman and Lichtman, *FDR and the Jews*, 106; and see transcript of Welles's conference with the American Society of Newspaper Editors, Apr. 22, 1938, in Sumner Welles Papers, box 44, FDRL. FDR received praise from numerous friends in the Jewish community. See letters in OF 3186, Political Refugees, Jan.–May, 1938, FDRL. A summary of refugee policy in the U.S. government at this time is given in Richard Breitman and Alan M. Kraut, *American Refugee Policy and European Jewry, 1933–1945* (Indiana University Press, 1987), 52–70.
62. "Vienna Nazis Widen Drive on Jews; Every Family Reported Suffering," *NYT*, June 20, 1938, reprinting most of the London *Times* piece. Taylor's comment in "Confidential Memorandum Regarding Refugees, 1938–1947," July 30, 1947, in Myron C. Taylor Papers, Selected Digitized Documents Related to the Holocaust and Refugees, 1933–1945, FDRL. Menus in Myron Taylor Papers, Intergovernmental Committee on Political Refugees, 1938, FDRL. For a summary of the meeting and its failure, see S. Adler-Rudel, "The Évian Conference on the Refugee Question," *Yearbook of the Leo Baeck Institute*, vol. XIII (London, 1968): 235–73. On Madagascar as a possible destination for Jews, the economic adviser in the State Department, Herbert Feis, thought it could indeed support "a large white population" and he and Pierrepont Moffat asked William Bullitt to sound out the French government about the idea. Bullitt replied that he had been asking about Madagascar as a refuge for "more than a year," but discovered it was unappealing because of "the prevalence of syphilis among 100% of the population." Bullitt proposed Northern Rhodesia instead. Feis to Bullitt, May 18, 1938; Bullitt to Feis, June 1, 1938, Herbert Feis Papers, box 12, LOC.
63. Conference minutes and papers, Myron Taylor Papers, Évian Intergovernmental Committee Conference, July 1938, FDRL; "Agenda of the Committee," July 5, 1938, sent to participating governments; statements by delegates, July 7, 1938; all in Select Digitized Documents Related to the Holocaust and Refugees, FDRL.
64. Gerald Gross, "'Yes, But . . .'—Attitude Perils Progress at World Refugee Conference," *WP*, July 10, 1938; and Vincent Sheean, *Not Peace but a Sword* (Doubleday, 1939), 92–94. On Sheean losing all his money at the baccarat table, see Shirer, *Berlin Diary*, 120, as well as Dinah Sheean letter to Louis Fischer, July 10, 1938, from Évian, Louis Fischer Papers, box 11, Seeley Mudd Library, Princeton University. Henry Stimson in his diary noted that FDR adviser Bernard Baruch suggested the Congo as a suitable place for a new Jewish homeland. Stimson Diary, vol. 28, September 1938, 170, Yale University.
65. At the annual convention of the American Jewish Congress on Oct. 29–30, 1938, at the Biltmore Hotel in New York City, delegates recognized and applauded American efforts. See address of Dr. Nahum Goldmann at the meeting in American Jewish Historical Society, American Jewish Congress Records, Series VI: National Biennial Conventions, 1922–2005: box 835, 1938, National Convention.
66. Paul Baxa, "Capturing the Fascist Moment: Hitler's Visit to Italy in 1938 and the Radicalization of Fascist Italy," *Journal of Contemporary History* 42, no. 2 (2007): 227–42; Zara Steiner, *The Triumph of the Dark: European International History, 1933–1939* (Oxford University Press, 2011), 570–71.
67. Phillips to Hull, July 15 and 24, 1938, *FRUS 1938*, vol. 2, 583–84.
68. Phillips to Hull, July 29, 1938, *FRUS 1938*, vol. 2, 587–88; William Phillips diary, July 28, 1938, Phillips Papers, box 8, Houghton Library, Harvard University.

69. William Phillips diary, Sept. 1, 1938, Phillips Papers, box 9, Houghton Library, Harvard University; Phillips to Hull, Sept. 1 and 2, 1938, *FRUS 1938*, vol. 2, 588–89; Phillips to FDR, Sept. 1, 1938, in Schewe, ed., *FDR&FA*, vol. 8, 134–39.
70. Ignazio Silone, "Italian Antisemitism," *New Republic*, Nov. 22, 1938.

Chapter 12: The Meaning of Munich

1. On the "purge," see Frank Friedel, *Franklin D. Roosevelt: A Rendezvous with Destiny* (Little, Brown, 1990), 280–88.
2. Master Speech File, Fireside Chat #13—"Report to the Nation on National Affairs," (speech file 1138B), June 24, 1938, box 39, FDRL.
3. Master Speech File, Pueblo, Salida & Grand Junction, Colorado (speech file 1157), July 12, 1938, box 40, FDRL.
4. "Andrew Chosen Wage-Hour Chief; President Tours Yosemite Park," *NYT*, July 16, 1938; "Address at the Dedication of Shenandoah National Park," July 3, 1936, at APP.
5. Presidential Cruise of 1938, Smithsonian Libraries and Archives, https://www.si.edu/object/auth_exp_fbr_EACE0063.
6. Master Speech File, Radio Address on 3rd Anniversary of Social Security Act (speech file 1166), Aug. 15, 1938, box 41, FDRL.
7. Master Speech File, Kingston, Ontario, Canada - Address at Queens University (speech file 1168), Aug. 18, 1938, box 41, FDRL; "Aims at Dictators, 'We Won't Stand Idly By,' He Says in Extending Monroe Doctrine," *NYT*, Aug. 19, 1938.
8. FDR to William Phillips, William Phillips Diaries, box 9, Houghton Library, Harvard University. On John's visit to Italy: "Duce Meets a Roosevelt," *NYT*, July 13, 1937.
9. G. E. R. Gedye, "Czech Nazis Warn Prague to Accept German Demands," *NYT*, Apr. 25, 1938. Among the extensive writing on the Munich crisis, see especially Ian Kershaw, *Hitler: Nemesis*, 95–125; an excellent recent synthesis by Bouverie, *Appeasement*, esp. 192–296; and the enormous and detailed study by Telford Taylor, *Munich: The Price of Peace* (Random House, 1980).
10. Chamberlain's thinking is remarkably well outlined in his many letters to his sisters. See Robert Self, ed., *The Neville Chamberlain Diary Letters, Vol. 4: The Downing Street Years, 1934–1940* (Ashgate, 2005).
11. Dorothy Thompson column of May 20, 1938, in *Let the Record Speak* (Houghton Mifflin, 1939), 194–200.
12. Judgment of the International Military Tribunal at Nuremberg, "The Seizure of Czechoslovakia," at the Yale Avalon Project, https://avalon.law.yale.edu/subject_menus/judcont.asp.
13. Shirer, *Berlin Diary*, 120–21; on Runciman and the events of August, see David Faber, *Munich 1938: Appeasement and World War II* (Simon & Schuster, 2008), 200–29.
14. "Nazi Victory in Austria Stressed as Nuremberg Congress Opens," *NYT*, Sept. 6, 1938; "Reich Sees Climax," *NYT*, Sept. 12, 1938; "Hitler's Threat to Czechs," *NYT*, Sept. 13, 1938; "Hitler Says He'll Free Sudetens," *CT*, Sept. 13, 1938; "Partial Text of Historic Hitler Address at Nuremberg," *WP*, Sept. 13, 1938; Shirer, *Berlin Diary*, 126. On FDR listening to Hitler's speech, Robert Sherwood, *Roosevelt and Hopkins*, 77.
15. On the honor guard, Telford Taylor, *Munich*, 738.
16. "Commonest little dog": Bouverie, *Appeasement*, 250; "Notes by Mr. Chamberlain of his conversation with Herr Hitler at Berchtesgaden, Sept. 15, 1938, *DBFP*, 3rd series, vol. 2, 338–41; Chamberlain letter to sister Ida, Sept. 19, 1938, Self, ed., *Chamberlain Diary Letters*, vol. 4, 345–49.
17. Historians have had trouble pinning down FDR's thinking during the Munich crisis. Dallek sees him as "powerless," confined to making empty "gestures," and minimizes the impact of those events on FDR. *FDR and American Foreign Policy*, 166, 168. Arnold Offner argued that FDR largely shared the isolationist view and wanted to steer clear of the European tangle. His "chief concern was to encourage further negotiation without committing the United States," and the Munich agreement did not disappoint FDR. *American Appeasement*, 267–68. Robert Divine views FDR as having given appeasement his "official seal of approval," and hoped it would lead to further stability in Europe. Robert A. Divine, *The Reluctant Belligerent: American Entry into World War II* (John Wiley, 1965), 55. James MacGregor Burns argues that even if FDR personally anticipated the coming conflict with the fascists, in 1938 he remained "confined to a policy of pinpricks and righteous protest. No risks, no commitments, was the motto of the White House." *Roosevelt: Lion and the Fox*, 385. Barbara Rearden Farnham, in *Roosevelt and the Munich Crisis: A*

Study of Political Decision-Making (Princeton University Press, 1997), argues that Roosevelt was not constrained by isolationist public opinion, but was consciously following a course between isolation and intervention, searching for a way to aid the democracies without getting into war. Farham, *Roosevelt and Munich*, 8. Wayne Cole suggests that FDR knew Munich would encourage rather than restrain German ambitions, but among other factors was heavily influenced by Charles Lindbergh's reports of German air strength and so encouraged any effort to buy time. *Roosevelt and the Isolationists, 1932–1945* (University of Nebraska Press, 1983), 284–85, 288. William E. Kinsella Jr. gives perhaps the strongest defense of FDR's policies during Munich, believing that Roosevelt only urged acceptance of a deal because he knew Britain and France were woefully underprepared for war, and because it bought time to "to rally public opinion against Germany." *Leadership in Isolation: FDR and the Origins of the Second World War* (Schenkman, 1978), 124.

18. "Real chance": Bullitt to FDR, Jan. 10, 1938, in *For the President*, 249.
19. Quotations from Bullitt to FDR, May 20, 1938, *FDR&FA*, vol. 10, 144–50. For his further advice on handling Germany: Bullitt to FDR, Jan. 10, 1938, ibid., 63; Bullitt to FDR, Jan. 20, ibid., 120; Bullitt to FDR, May 12, 1938, in *For the President*, 257; FDR to Bullitt on planes, in *For the President*, 259–60; Bullitt to FDR, June 13, 1938, in *For the President*, 267–69; Bullitt to FDR, Aug. 17 and Aug. 31, 1938, in *For the President*, 279–83.
20. Joseph Kennedy diary entry, Mar. 4, 1938, in Amanda Smith, ed., *Hostage to Fortune: The Letters of Joseph P. Kennedy* (Viking, 2001), 239; Kennedy to FDR, March 11, 1938, ibid., 240–43.
21. "The text of the address delivered by Joseph P. Kennedy, the United States Ambassador to Great Britain, at the Pilgrims Dinner," *NYT*, Mar. 19, 1938; Hull to Kennedy, Mar. 14, 1938, in Smith, *Hostage to Fortune*, 243–44; Kennedy to Arthur Krock, Mar. 28, 1938, in Smith, *Hostage to Fortune*, 247–49; Kennedy to Hull, Aug. 30, 1938, in Smith, *Hostage to Fortune*, 269–70. See also Kennedy's comments to Henry Stimson about his admiration for Chamberlain, in Stimson Diary, July 27, 1938, vol. 28, 152, Yale University.
22. For Bullitt's views, see Bullitt to FDR, Nov. 23, 1937, in Orville Bullitt, ed., *For the President*, 232–38.
23. Wilson to FDR, Mar. 3, 12, 23, and May 2, 1938, PSF, box 32, Germany-Wilson, Hugh R., March-November 1938, FDRL; Wilson to Hull, Mar. 23, 1938, Aug. 6, 1938, and Sept. 1, 1938, *FRUS 1938*, vol. 1, 463–64, 542–43, 566–67.
24. A. Scott Berg, *Lindbergh* (Putnam's Sons, 1998), 355–56; Truman Smith, *Berlin Alert: The Memoirs and Reports of Truman Smith*, ed. Robert Hessen (Hoover Institution Press, 1984).
25. Charles A. Lindbergh, *The Wartime Journals of Charles A. Lindbergh* (Harcourt Brace Jovanovich, 1970), entries for Mar. 16, 1938, 5, and Apr. 2, 1938, 11. W. Karin Hall, "Truman Smith: United States Military Attaché: An Examination of His Career," (unpublished MA thesis, San Jose State University, 1992), 117.
26. PSF, box 58, Navy Department, January–February 1938, FDRL; *Wartime Journals*, entry for May 5, 1938, 26; entry for June 23, 1938, 35–36; entry for Sept. 9, 1938, 69–70; *FRUS 1938*, vol. 1, May 16, 1938, 55.
27. John Cudahy to FDR, Apr. 6, 1938, *FDR&FA*, vol. 9, 334.
28. FDRL, Morgenthau Diary, vol. 138, 34. Herbert Feis at this time wrote that Hull believed "the scope of the German program is indefinite; that there is no reasonable anticipation that it will find a feasible point of voluntary balance," and change its expansionist character. Feis to William Bullitt, Sept. 6, 1938, Feis Papers, box 12, LOC.
29. Guido Enderis, "Chamberlain Visit Stuns Reich," *NYT*, Sept. 15, 1938; Sigrid Schultz, "Germany Hails Premier's Visit as 'Big Victory,'" *CT*, Sept. 15, 1938; "Mr. Chamberlain Goes to Berchtesgaden," *NYT*, Sept. 15, 1938.
30. Ickes, *Secret Diary*, vol. 2, Sept. 15, 1938, 467; Moffat, *Moffat Papers*, Sept. 16, 1938, 205; "Chamberlain Talks to Hitler," *CT*, Sept. 16, 1938.
31. "Hitler Demands Sudetens; Chamberlain Goes Home Today," *CT*, Sept. 16, 1938; "Expect Wide Plan," *NYT*, Sept. 16, 1938. For the "heroic" Czechoslovakia view, see "Triumphant in Defeat," editorial, *WP*, Sept. 23, 1938.
32. Ickes, *Secret Diary*, vol. 2, Sept. 18, 1938, 467–72.
33. The proposal was conveyed to the Czechs in a cable from Halifax to the British ambassador in Prague, Sir Basil Newton, Sept. 19, 1938, *British Documents on Foreign Policy*, 3rd series, vol. 2, 404-5; and for details of the British-French plan, Taylor, *Munich*, 776–84.

34. "Czechs Astounded," *NYT*, Sept. 19, 1938; "Another Victory for Hitler Seen by Nazi Leaders," *CT*, Sept. 19, 1938; "Powers Draw Plan," *NYT*, Sept. 19, 1938; "American Editors Speak of Betrayal of the Czechs, but They Urge Isolation," *NYT*, Sept. 21, 1938; "Current Comment: Timid Democracies," *LAT*, Sept. 22, 1938; Dorothy Thompson, "On the Record: Obituary for Europe," *WP*, Sept. 21, 1938.
35. Sir R. Lindsay to Halifax, Sept. 20, 1938, *Documents on British Foreign Policy, 1919–1939*, 3rd series, vol. 7, 627–29.
36. Alex Small, "Stunned Czechs Broken-Hearted over Surrender," *CT*, Sept. 22, 1938; "Prague Gives Way; Public Is Furious," *NYT*, Sept. 22, 1938; for the three-week assessment: Taylor, *Munich*, 790.
37. The details of Hitler's demands were spelled out in what became known as the Godesberg Memorandum of Sept. 24, 1938, handed to Chamberlain. *Documents on British Foreign Policy, 1919–1939*, 3rd series, vol. 2, 495–96. Hitler's famous words rejecting Anglo-French plan were: "*Es tut mir leid, aber das geht nicht mehr.*" See Taylor, *Munich*, 806.
38. "Notes of a Conversation between Mr. Chamberlain and Herr Hitler at Godesberg," Sept. 22, 1938, *DBFP, 1919–1939*, 3rd series, vol. 2, 463–73.
39. John Julius Norwich, ed., *The Duff Cooper Diaries, 1915–1951* (Weidenfeld & Nicolson, 2022), entry of Sept. 24, 1938, 264–65. Bouverie, *Appeasement*, 263–70.
40. Kennedy to Hull, Sept. 22, in Smith, ed., *Hostage to Fortune*, 281–82; "Germany Is Reported to Have 10,000 Planes Ready for War," *NYT*, Sept. 23, 1938; "Nazi Air Force Worries Both London and Paris," *NYT*, Sept. 25, 1938; R. J. Overy, "German Air Strength 1933 to 1939: A Note," *Historical Journal* 27, no. 2 (1984): 465–71. On Lindbergh receiving the award on Oct. 18, 1938, see John T. Correll, "The Cloud over Lindbergh," *Air Force Magazine*, Aug. 2014, 76–82.
41. Ickes, *Secret Diary*, vol. 2, Sept. 24, 1938, 474; Moffat, *Moffat Papers*, Sept. 23, 1938, 209–10.
42. Bullitt to Hull, Sept. 24, 1938, *FRUS 1938*, vol. 1, 641–42; Roosevelt to Hitler, Sept. 26, 1938, *FRUS 1938*, vol. 1, 657–58; "Kellogg Pact Cited," *NYT*, Sept. 26, 1938. For the drafting, see Moffat, *Moffat Papers*, Sept. 24–25, 1938, 211–13.
43. "20,000 in Garden Cheer for Czechs," *NYT*, Sept. 26, 1938.
44. Raymond Leslie Buell, "What Price Isolation?" *WP*, Sept. 16, 1938.
45. "Speaking of Betrayals," *WP*, Sept. 24, 1938; and letters to the editor published as "'Speaking of Betrayals:' Readers Favor a Strong Foreign Policy," *WP*, Sept. 27, 1938. For further examples of an increasingly bellicose tone in the press, see Ernest Lindley, "Isolation Issue," *WP*, Sept. 26, 1938; Walter Lippmann, "Today and Tomorrow: The Burning of the Bridges," *WP*, Sept. 27, 1938; "The Answer to Hitler," *NYT*, Sept. 27, 1938; "On the Brink," *WP*, Sept. 27, 1938.
46. "Points in Hitler's Speech," *NYT*, Sept. 27, 1938. For criticism of this speech, see the editorial "Two Broadcasts," *NYT*, Sept. 28, 1938; Ickes, *Secret Diary*, vol. 2, 477.
47. Chamberlain broadcast in Taylor, *Munich*, 884–85.
48. FDR to Mussolini, 3:00 p.m., Sept. 27, 1938, *FRUS 1938*, vol. 1, 677.
49. Roosevelt to Hitler, Sept. 27, 1938, 10:18 p.m., *FRUS 1938*, vol. 1, 684–85. Even the authors of the second Roosevelt message knew it was "vague." Moffat, *Moffat Papers*, Sept. 27, 1938, 216.
50. Entry of Sept. 28, 1938, Phillips diary, Phillips Papers, box 9, Houghton Library, Harvard University. For the sanitized account, see Phillips, *Adventures in Diplomacy*, 220–22. Phillips later offered to resign over this incident: Phillips to Roosevelt, Oct. 1, 1938, *FDR&FA*, vol. 11, 267–70.
51. This scene is well-told by Bouverie, *Appeasement*, 275–76. "Commons Jubilant," *NYT*, Sept. 29, 1938; "Duce Sways Hitler," *NYT*, Sept. 29, 1938.
52. Kershaw, *Hitler: Nemesis*, 119.
53. Kennedy to FDR, Sept. 28, 1938, and FDR to Chamberlain, Sept. 28, 1938, *FRUS 1938*, vol. 1, 692–93 and 688; "Conversation between Prime Minister and Hitler," Sept. 30, 1938, *DBFP*, 3rd series, vol. 2, 635–40. Offner views the "good man" message as an endorsement of appeasement, *American Appeasement*, 269.
54. On the differences between the Godesberg demands and the final Munich agreement, Taylor, *Munich*, 900; for a detailed eyewitness account, "Note by Sir H. Wilson on the Munich Conference, Sept. 29–30, 1938," *DBFP*, 3rd series, vol. 2, 630–35; Kershaw, *Hitler: Nemesis*, 119–22; "Chamberlain Hero of Munich Crowds," *NYT*, Sept. 30, 1938; "'Peace with Honor,' Says Chamberlain," *NYT*, Oct. 1, 1938.
55. Bullitt to Roosevelt, Sept. 20, 1938, in Bullitt, ed., *For the President*, 288.
56. "Excerpts from Commons Speeches," *NYT*, Oct. 4, 1938; "'Democratic Idea Betrayed,'" *MG*, Oct. 3, 1938; "Debate on the Munich Agreement," *MG*, Oct. 5, 1938.

57. Churchill speech of Oct. 5, 1938, at https://www.nationalchurchillmuseum.org/disaster-of-the-first-magnitude.html. "Build Air Fleet to Check Hitler, Churchill Urges," *NY Daily News*, Oct. 6, 1938; "Munich Plan Is Denounced by Churchill," *Richmond Times-Dispatch*, Oct. 6, 1938 (an AP wire story); "Churchill in Speech Lashes at England," *Miami Herald*, Oct. 6, 1938 (a UP wire story); "Churchill See Prediction of Nazi Demands Come True," *Cincinnati Post*, Oct. 7, 1938 (a Scripps-Howard wire story).
58. "Dorothy Thompson, "Peace—and the Crisis Begins," *WP*, Oct. 1, 1938. See also her column titled "Toward a New Foreign Policy," which argued that America could "not exist on tolerable terms in a world" dominated by totalitarian powers: *WP*, Oct. 19, 1938; Anne O'Hare McCormick, "Thoughts as the Germans March into Czechoslovakia," *NYT*, Oct. 1, 1938; "Four Gangsters Met," *NYAN*, Oct. 8, 1938.
59. Bullitt to Hull, Oct. 3, 1938, *FRUS 1938*, vol. 1, 711–12.
60. Ernest Lindley column, *WP*, Oct. 2, 1938; Ickes, *Secret Diary*, vol. 2, 480–83.
61. Press conference #491, Oct. 14, 1938, FDRL. On Bullitt's visit to the White House: *For the President*, 302; and Mark Skinner Watson, *The United States Army in World War II: The War Department, Chief of Staff: Prewar Plans and Preparations* (Center of Military History, 1991), 131. On the Hopkins tour of aircraft factories: Sherwood, *Roosevelt and Hopkins*, 78.
62. Arthur Murray published an article recalling the Hyde Park meetings. Lord Elibank, "Franklin Roosevelt: Friend of Britain," *Contemporary Review* (1955): 362–68.
63. Transcript of conversation, Oct. 20, 1938, Morgenthau Diaries, vol. 146, 279–94, FDRL; and memorandum of Hyde Park discussions, Morgenthau Diaries, vol. 147, 185–90, FDRL; Elibank, "Franklin Roosevelt," 365, 366.
64. "Text of Roosevelt's Talk to Forum," *NYT*, Oct. 27, 1938; "U.S. Forced to Rearm, Roosevelt Tells World," *WP*, Oct. 27, 1938; "American Foreign Policy," *NYT* editorial, Oct. 28, 1938; Letter to Herbert C. Pell, Nov. 12, 1938, in *FDR: His Personal Letters*, vol. 2, 826.
65. Leuchtenberg, *Franklin D. Roosevelt and the New Deal*, 271–72.
66. FDRL, Morgenthau Presidential Diary, vol. 1, 52–55.
67. "Meeting at the White House," notes by Oliphant, Nov. 14, 1938, in Morgenthau Diary, vol. 150, 337–42, FDRL. A memorandum of the meeting was also prepared by General H. H. Arnold: "Memorandum for the Chief of Staff," Nov. 15, 1938, box 118, PPF 1P—Special Conferences, FDRL. General Marshall contradicted the president at this meeting; he thought building a large air force would harm the army's rearmament program. Larry I. Bland, ed., *The Papers of George Catlett Marshall*, vol. 1 (Johns Hopkins University Press, 1981), 650–55. This meeting received extended treatment in Watson, *Chief of Staff: Prewar Plans*, 136–41; and Farnham, *Roosevelt and the Munich Crisis*, 182–88.

Chapter 13: 1939: Rumors of War

1. Sigrid Schultz, "Germans Oust Polish Jews," *CT*, Oct. 29, 1938; "Germany Deports Jews to Poland," *NYT*, Oct. 29, 1938; "Ousted Jews Left Penniless," *LAT*, Oct. 31, 1938. A full account is in Otto Tolischus, "Reich Begins Deportations," *NYT*, Oct. 29, 1938.
2. Jüdisches Museum Berlin, "Polenaktion 1938," at https://www.jmberlin.de/en/topic-polenaktion1938#:~:text=On%209%20October%201938%2C%20the,plans%20to%20expel%20foreign%20Jews; Sybil Milton, "The Expulsion of Polish Jews from Germany October 1938 to July 1939: A Documentation," *Leo Baeck Institute Year Book* 29, no. 1 (1984): 169–99; "Zbaszyn," United States Holocaust Memorial Museum, https://encyclopedia.ushmm.org/content/en/gallery/zbaszyn; "Nazi Guns Forced Jews into Poland," *NYT*, Nov. 1, 1938; "6,000 Deported Jews Still in Polish Fields," *NYT*, Nov. 7, 1938.
3. This summary relies on Ian Kershaw, *Hitler: Nemesis*, 131–38. The U.S. Holocaust Memorial Museum suggests hundreds may have been killed: https://encyclopedia.ushmm.org/content/en/article/kristallnacht. The journalist Jimmy Sheean published a detailed account, accompanied by shocking photographs, after doing his own reporting in Germany: Vincent Sheean, "The Persecution Is Total," *Redbook*, Feb. 1939.
4. "Reich Embassy Aide in Paris Shot to Avenge Expulsions by the Nazis," *NYT*, Nov. 8, 1938; "Nazi Diplomat Shot in Paris by Exile, 17," *WP*, Nov. 8, 1938; "Hitler Speech Blames Jews," *LAT*, Nov. 9, 1938; "Germans Attack Jews to Avenge Paris Shooting," *CT*, Nov. 9, 1938; "Nazis Ask Reprisals in Attack on Envoy," *NYT*, Nov. 9, 1938; "Berlin Raids Reply to Death of Envoy," *NYT*, Nov. 10, 1938; "Mobs Wreck Jewish Stores in Berlin," *CT*, Nov. 10, 1938; "Nazis Burn Synagogues as Rath

Dies," *WP*, Nov. 10, 1938; "Germans Storm Jews!," *San Francisco Chronicle*, Nov. 10, 1938; "Nazi Mobs Riot in Wild Orgy," *LAT*, Nov. 11, 1938; Otto Tolischus, "Bands Rove Cities," *NYT*, Nov. 11, 1938; Sigrid Schultz, "Hitler Seizes 20,000 Jews," *CT*, Nov. 11, 1938; "Nazi Secret Police Herd Jews to Jail," *LAT*, Nov. 12, 1938; "Goebbels Calls Halt," *WP*, Nov. 11, 1938. *Life* magazine ran a dozen photographs of the damage done: "For a Diplomat's Murder Nazi Germany Takes an Awful Revenge," *Life*, Nov. 28, 1939.

5. "Great Germany," *NYT* editorial, Nov. 11, 1938; Anne O'Hare McCormick, "Nazi Day of Terror a Threat to All Civilization," *NYT*, Nov. 12, 1938; Sigrid Schultz, "Germany Puts Hundreds of Jews in Camps," *CT*, Nov. 12, 1938; Dorothy Thompson, "To a Jewish Friend," *NYHT*, Nov. 14, 1938.
6. "U.S. Newspapers Assail Nazi Raids," *NYT*, Nov. 13, 1938; "Protest Swells in U.S. over Reich Terror," *WP*, Nov. 13, 1938; "Nazi Cruelties Rouse America," *LAT*, Nov. 14, 1938; "Hoover Protests Brutality in Reich," *NYT*, Nov. 14, 1938; "Pastors Protest Nazi Persecution," *NYT*, Nov. 14, 1938; "Hoover, Landon, Ickes, Condemn Horrors," *LAT*, Nov. 15, 1938; "Texts of Protests by Leaders in U.S. Against Reich Persecution," *NYT*, Nov. 15, 1938; "Dorothy Thompson Urges Boy Who Shot Diplomat Be Spared," *WP*, Nov. 15, 1938; "Thousands in U.S. Offer to Help Assassin," *NYT*, Nov. 16, 1938. In her column, Dorothy Thompson said she received three thousand telegrams of support and money after her first radio broadcast about the cause. "Give a Man a Chance," *NYHT*, Nov. 16, 1938. She also organized a rally to raise money: "20,000 Jam Garden in Protest," *NYT*, Nov. 22, 1938. Some of the difficulties in hiring the well-known and high-priced defense lawyer Vincent de Moro-Giafferi can be seen in letters from Edgar Mowrer, Jan. 20 and July 25, 1939, Dorothy Thompson Papers, box 20, Syracuse University. By February 1939, her fund had swelled to $39,500 (nearly $1 million today), as she told Hamilton Fish Armstrong, letter of Feb. 16, 1939, in Armstrong Papers, box 62, Seeley Mudd Library, Princeton University.
7. "No Regret Voiced," *NYT*, Nov. 12, 1938; Sigrid Schultz, "Nazis Fine Jews 400 Million," *CT*, Nov. 13, 1938.
8. "Berlin Raids Reply to Death of Envoy," *NYT*, Nov. 10, 1938; Wilson to State Department, Nov. 10, 1938, and Benjamin Cohen to Missy LeHand enclosing a brief message from Dr. Wise, Nov. 10, 1938, both in *DHFDRP*, vol. 12, 327–29; Press conference, Nov. 11, 1938, FDRL.
9. Press conference, Nov. 15, 1938, FDRL; "U.S. Envoy Summoned Home as Nazi Rebuke," *LAT*, Nov. 15, 1938; "Wilson to Return," *WP*, Nov. 15, 1938. The decision to recall Wilson may have been hastened by a searing memorandum from George Messersmith to Hull on Nov. 14, in which he "strongly" urged this measure as statement of U.S. disapproval. Messersmith to Hull, Nov. 14, 1938, in *DHFDRP*, vol. 12, 334–37; "Nazis Assailed by Roosevelt," *LAT*, Nov. 16, 1938; "President Says U.S. Is 'Shocked' by War on Jews," *WP*, Nov. 16, 1938; "Statement Sharp," *NYT*, Nov. 16, 1938; "President Rips into Nazis for Harassing Jews," *CT*, Nov. 16, 1938; Press conference, Nov. 15, 1938, FDRL.
10. Press conference transcript, Nov. 18, 1938, FDRL; "The Cabinet," *Time*, Jan. 2, 1939. FDR supported Ickes despite the diplomatic furor the speech caused. See Ickes, *Secret Diary*, vol. 2, 532–34. The Welles exchange with Thomsen, German Chargé d'Affaires, was released to the press: "Summary of U.S.-German Conversation," *NYT*, Dec. 23, 1938.
11. On Corcoran and Cohen, see Joseph P. Lash, *Dealers and Dreamers: A New Look at the New Deal* (Doubleday, 1988), 383. The two men made the cover of *Time* magazine and were the subject of a long article: "National Affairs: The Janizariat," *Time*, Sept. 12, 1938. Also Rosenman, *Working with Roosevelt*, 181–84.
12. Text of the reading copy of the Jan. 4, 1939, address to Congress is in Master Speech File, box 43, FDRL. A handwritten note by Roosevelt pinned to a draft indicates Corcoran and Cohen as the assistants who helped draft the speech. On the film, see FDR White House calendar for Dec. 28, 1938. For details of the scene in Congress, "On the Union: FDR Makes His Report Slowly and Seriously," *NYT*, Jan. 8, 1939.
13. "Congress Divided on the Message," *NYT*, Jan. 5, 1938. Remarkably, the press printed not only FDR's budget message but the charts and tables of expenditures it proposed. "Text of Defense Message Asking for 552 Million," *CT*, Jan. 13, 1939; "Congress Clears Decks for Action on Defense Bill," *WP*, Jan. 13, 1939; on the overall cost of the military program, see "Text of Roosevelt's Message to Congress on Budget Estimates," *WP*, Jan. 6, 1939: the "total for military purposes estimated at 1.3 billion."
14. "French Airman Dies in Crash," AP story in *The Olympian* (Olympia, Washington), Jan. 24, 1939; "Bomber Pilot Killed in Coast Plane Crash," *NYT*, Jan. 24, 1939.

15. John McVickar Haight Jr., *American Aid to France, 1938–1940* (Atheneum, 1970), 23–102.
16. Blum, *Morgenthau Diaries: Years of Urgency, 1938–1941*, 64– 78.
17. U.S. Senate, *Hearings Before the Committee on Military Affairs*, 76th Congress, First Session on H.R. 3791 (Government Printing Office, 1939), 61–89. Arnold testified about the matter on January 25 and 26, 1939.
18. Press Conference, Jan. 27, 1939, FDRL; Morgenthau testimony, Jan. 27, 1939, in *Hearings*, 91–115; Blum, *Morgenthau Diaries*, 76–77.
19. "Spurs Air Works," *NYT*, Jan. 28, 1939; "Gift of Air Secrets Bared," *CT*, Jan. 28, 1939; "Link U.S. in Secret War Pact," *CT*, Jan. 29, 1939; "Sale of Planes Defended as Military Need," *WP*, Jan. 29, 1939.
20. Otto Tolischus, "Backs Rome in War," and "Excerpts from the Official Translation of Hitler's Speech Before the Reichstag," *NYT*, Jan. 31, 1939.
21. A complete transcription was made of the meeting: "Extra Confidential: Conference with the Senate Military Affairs Committee," Jan. 31, 1939, President's Personal File, PPF 1-P, box 118, FDRL.
22. Chesly Manly, "Bare Roosevelt War Aims," *CT*, Feb. 1, 1939; "War Fears Voiced," *NYT*, Feb. 2, 1939.
23. Press conferences, Feb. 3 and 17, 1939, FDRL; Wayne Cole, *Roosevelt and the Isolationists*, 297–309.
24. "The Doctor Dilutes His Prescription," *Nation*, Feb. 11, 1939.
25. For FDR's strategy, see Richard W. Steele, "Franklin D. Roosevelt and His Foreign Policy Critics," *Political Science Quarterly* 94, 1 (1979): 15–32.
26. On the Bund and its evolution after 1936, see Susan Canedy, *America's Nazis: A Democratic Dilemma* (Markgraf, 1990), 109–72; Sander A. Diamond, *The Nazi Movement in the United States, 1924–1941* (Cornell University Press, 1974), 179–304; Bradley W. Hart, *Hitler's American Friends: The Third Reich's Supporters in the United States* (St. Martin's Press, 2018), 23–48. Details of the Bund's structure and organization are in documents seized by the Justice Department: NARA, RG 131, Department of Justice / Office of Alien Property, General Records Seized from the German American Bund, box 9.
27. "25,000 Hear Critics of Nazis Assailed," *NYT*, Aug. 30, 1937; "Inquiry into Nazis Urged," *LAT*, Sept. 10, 1937; "Nazi Putsch Here Is Quickly Denied," *NYT*, Sept. 10, 1937. On Metcalfe: "Nazis: A Tabloid Scoop," *Newsweek*, Sept. 20, 1937. On the initial Justice Department inquiry: "Hoover Reports on Kuhn and Bund," *NYT*, Jan. 6, 1938; "Cummings Weighs 1,000-Page Study of Nazi Activities," *WP*, Jan. 6, 1938; "Says Nazi Bund Here Obeys Federal Laws," *NYT*, Jan. 13, 1938; "Germans Again Warned Not to Join Bund in U.S.," *CT*, Mar. 1, 1938.
28. J. Edgar Hoover, "Personal and Confidential," memo to Col. E. R. Warner McCabe, War Department, May 5, 1938, transmitting 150-page "Report of Special Agent Leon Turrou, April 27, 1938," in ProQuest, History Vault: *U.S. Military Intelligence Reports, 1911–1944*. The history of the spy ring has been well-documented in Rhodri Jeffreys-Jones, *The Nazi Spy Ring in America: Hitler's Agents, the FBI, and the Case that Stirred the Nation* (Georgetown University Press, 2020); and Bradley W. Hart, *Hitler's American Friends: The Third Reich's Supporters in the United States* (St. Martin's Press, 2018), 188–208. The term "brown scare" was coined by Leo Ribuffo in *The Old Christian Right*, 178–224.
29. *Hearings Before a Special Committee on Un-American Activities*, House of Representatives, 75th Congress, August 12, 1938 (Government Printing Office, 1938), 5, 25; "Bund Head Links Jews with Reds and U.S. Enemies," *CT*, June 24, 1938; "American Nazi Plot Charged," *LAT*, Aug. 13, 1938; "Declare Pro-Nazis Map War Sabotage," *NYT*, Aug. 13, 1938; "Dies Reveals U.S. Nazi Plot for Sabotage," *WP*, Aug. 13, 1938; "Hitler Rules Bund, Says Dies Witness," *NYT*, Sept. 29, 1938; "Huge Sabotage Machine Laid at Bund's Door," *LAT*, Sept. 29, 1938; "Says Kuhn Claims Power in Berlin," *NYT*, Sept. 30, 1938; "Dieckhoff Denies Any Link to Bund," *NYT*, Oct. 1, 1938; "Says Bund Seeks to Unite Fascists," *NYT*, Oct. 6, 1938; Attorney General Frank Murphy to FDR, Jan. 5, 1939, *DHFDRP*, vol. 32, 1–2.
30. "20,000 Jam Madison Square Garden as Throng Battles Police Outside; Dorothy Thompson's Jibes Irk Nazis," *WP*, Feb. 21 1939; "Fight Nazis in Big NY Rally," *CT*, Feb. 21, 1939; "Many Injured in Bund Riots," *LAT*, Feb. 21, 1939. The text of the speeches made that evening were reprinted in "Speeches of the German-American Bund: Madison Square Garden, February 20, 1939," available in Gale Primary Sources, *Political Extremism and Radicalism* collection.
31. Dorothy Thompson, "To the Intolerant!," *NYHT*, Feb. 22, 1939; and "The Facts of Life," *NYHT*, Apr. 14, 1939.

32. Sumner Welles to William Bullitt, Mar. 11, 1939, Bullitt Papers, box 88, Sterling Library, Yale University.
33. FDR's order is dated Sept. 6, 1939, in "Directives: June 26, 1939–June 9, 1962," Official and Confidential Files of FBI Director J. Edgar Hoover 60⁄3, Federal Bureau of Investigation Library, available in Gale Primary Sources, *Archives Unbound*: Official and Confidential Files of FBI Director J. Edgar Hoover; see also Aathan Theoharis, *The FBI and American Democracy* (University Press of Kansas, 2004), 53–54.
34. "German Americans! Stand Up Against Persecution!" Fundraising flyer for Kuhn's legal bills, undated, mid-1939, RG 131, Department of Justice / Office of Alien Property, General Records Seized from the German American Bund, box 1, NARA. For FDR and the expansion of the FBI after 1938, see Beverly Gage, *G-Man*, 204–16; Athan Theoharis, *Spying on Americans: Political Surveillance from Hoover to the Huston Plan* (Temple University Press, 1978), 66–76; Athan G. Theoharis, *The FBI and American Democracy: A Brief Critical History* (University Press of Kansas, 2004), 44-64.
35. "Religion: Coughlin Silenced," *Time*, Oct. 18, 1937; "Father Coughlin on 60 Stations!" *Social Justice*, Jan. 3, 1938. His themes at the start of 1938 are summed up in "Together We Stand to Remake America," *Social Justice*, Jan. 17, 1938. "Coughlin Is Seen Regaining Power," *NYT*, Apr. 3, 1938. The final issue of *Social Justice* newspaper was Feb. 21, 1938, after which it moved to a color weekly. The first issue of the new format, Feb. 28, 1938, had a large portrait on Coughlin on the cover. Issues of *Social Justice* in Coughlin Collection, box 15, National Museum of American History.
36. "Spain's Corporative State," *Social Justice*, Mar. 21, 1938; Anthony Ashley, "What Is Fascism?" *Social Justice*, June 20, 1938. On Mussolini: "The Man of the Week: Benito Mussolini," *Social Justice*, May 23, 1938. Coughlin Collection, box 15, NMAH.
37. Coughlin's opposition to the reorganization bill: "Coughlin Warns Senate of Revolt," *NYT*, Mar. 28, 1938. On the telegram flood: "Coughlin Is Seen Regaining Power," *NYT*, Apr. 3, 1938. On Perkins: "The Mother of All," *Social Justice*, May 23, 1938; "Memorial Day," *Social Justice*, May 30, 1938. Coughlin Collection, box 15, NMAH.
38. "Father Coughlin's Paper Features 'Protocols of Zion,'" *Jewish Exponent*, July 22, 1938; "Repudiated 'Protocols' Used by Father Coughlin to Fight the New Deal," *American Israelite*, July 28, 1938; "Egregious Protocols," *Time*, Nov. 14, 1938.
39. "Persecution—Jewish and Christian," sermon of Nov. 20, 1938, Coughlin Collection, box 1, NMAH.
40. "Let Us Consider the Record," sermon, Nov. 27, 1938, Coughlin Collection, box 1, NMAH; "Not Anti-Semitic but Anti-Communist," sermon, Dec. 4, 1938, Coughlin Collection, box 2, NMAH; "WMCA Contradicts Coughlin on Jews," *NYT*, Nov. 21, 1938; "Telling the Facts about Communism," *Jewish Advocate*, Nov. 25, 1938; "Coughlin in New Attack on the Jews," *Jewish Advocate*, Nov. 25, 1938; "Coughlin Unable to Meet WMCA Rule," *NYT*, Nov. 26, 1938; "Nazi Papers Come to Aid of Coughlin," *WP*, Nov. 27, 1938; "Father Coughlin Barred from Air by 3 Stations," *CT*, Nov. 28, 1938; "Coughlin Defends Address on Jews," *NYT*, Nov. 28, 1938; "Slap," *Time*, Nov. 28, 1938; Philip S. Bernstein, "Some Facts about Jews," *Harper's*, Dec. 1, 1938; "Father Coughlin at It Again," *Jewish Exponent*, Dec. 2, 1938.
41. "Catholics in America Rise Up in Protest Against Fr. Coughlin's Anti-Semitism," *Jewish Advocate*, Dec. 9, 1938; "Cardinal Issues Stern Rebuke to Father Coughlin," *CT*, Dec. 12, 1938; "Mundelein Denies Views of Coughlin Represent Church," *NYT*, Dec. 12, 1938; William C. Kernan, "Coughlin, the Jews, and Communism," *Nation*, Dec. 17, 1938; "Not Authorized," *Time*, Dec. 19, 1938; "Nazi Sources of Coughlin's Talk Now Proven," *Jewish Advocate*, Dec. 23, 1938; "The Coughlin Broadcasts," *Contemporary Jewish Record*, Jan. 1, 1939, 51–53; "Fr. Coughlin's Coincidence: Goebbels Ought to Sue Him for Plagiarism," *Jewish Advocate*, Jan. 6, 1939; "What Did Fr. Coughlin Say When He was Shown This?" *Jewish Advocate*, Jan. 13, 1939. Kernan's own account of taking on Coughlin is in William C. Kernan, *My Road to Certainty* (David McKay, 1953), 119–25.
42. "6,000 Here Cheer Coughlin's Name," *NYT*, Dec. 16, 1938; "Coughlin Plea Spurs Wires to Congress," *NYT*, Jan. 16, 1939; "2,000 Meeting Here Cheer Franco's Gains," *NYT*, Jan. 26, 1939; "Boycott on Hatred Urged by Coughlin," *NYT*, Jan. 30, 1939; "Coughlin Hits Aiding Britain and France," *NYT*, Feb. 6, 1939; "Coughlin Lays Woes to 'Internationalism,'" *NYT*, Feb. 20, 1939; "10,000 Rally Here for Franco Cause," *NYT*, Feb. 20, 1939. Coughlin's sermon was "Internationalism—or No Foreign Entanglements," Feb. 19, 1939, Coughlin Collection, box 1, NMAH.

43. Dorothy Thompson, "Cassandra Speaking," *NYHT*, March 17, 1939. On the politics and diplomacy behind the invasion, see D. C. Watt, *How War Came: The Immediate Origins of the Second World War, 1938–1939* (Pantheon, 1989), 141-61.
44. On the death toll and postwar executions: Hugh Thomas, *The Spanish Civil War* (Hamish Hamilton, 1977), 919–27. Contemporary reports claimed a huge number of arrests: "100,000 Arrested by Franco Regime," *NYT*, Mar. 31, 1939; "Last of Spanish Cities Surrender to Franco," *LAT*, Mar. 30, 1939.
45. Shirer, *Berlin Diary*, 162; Gellhorn to Eleanor Roosevelt, Feb. 5, 1939, Mar. 18, 1939, and undated (Fall 1939), in Somerville, ed., *Yours, for Probably Always*, 229–30, 230–31, 235–36.
46. Bowers, *My Mission to Spain*, 381, 418. Writing in 1944, with the benefit of hindsight and in the glow of an imminent allied victory over Nazism, Sumner Welles stated that America's failure to support the Spanish government was "the greatest error in the foreign policy of this country" since Hitler's rise to power. A damning indictment, though far too late to matter. Sumner Welles, *The Time for Decision* (Harper & Brothers, 1944), 306.
47. The first stage of treaty revision is well-covered in Divine, *Illusion of Neutrality*, 229–85. On FDR's desire to repeal the act, see FDR to Hull, in *FDR: His Personal Letters*, vol. 2, 873. For polls, see Cantrill, *Public Opinion*, 1157.
48. "Text of Mr. Stimson's Statement to Senators on Neutrality," *NYT*, Apr. 6, 1939; the ensuing discussion with Stimson is reprinted in *Neutrality, Peace Legislation, and Our Foreign Policy: Hearings before the Committee on Foreign Relations*, U.S. Senate, 76th Congress (Government Printing Office, 1939), 2–39; "Ex-Secretary Stimson's Letter on Foreign Relations," *NYT*, Mar. 7, 1939.
49. Thompson testimony of Apr. 26, 1939, 322–28; and Dorothy Thompson Papers, box 104, Syracuse University. Statement of Louise Leonard Wright, Apr. 13, 1939, *Neutrality, Peace Legislation*, 83–120; similar arguments were made for neutrality revision by Professor Charles G. Fenwick of the Committee for Concerned Peace Efforts, Apr. 17, 1939, 161–209.
50. The shift in British policy is brilliantly analyzed by Watt, *How War Came*, 156–87.
51. FDRL, press conference, Apr. 11, 1939. The next day, the press summarized FDR as believing that American involvement in any future European war was "inevitable" and that the United States should stand "shoulder to shoulder with Great Britain and France." In fact, he said no such thing. "Roosevelt Sees America Involved," *NYT*, Apr. 12, 1939.
52. FDR, "Address to the Governing Board of the Pan American Union," Apr. 14, 1939, at APP.
53. FDRL, press conferences, Apr. 15, 1939. The text of the Apr. 14 letter is in *FRUS 1939*, vol. 1, 130–33. Historian D. C. Watt was especially scathing about FDR's letter-writing in *How War Came*, 260–61.
54. "Peace Group Seeks Aggressor Curbs," *NYT*, Dec. 3, 1938; "Experts Propose Neutrality Shift," *NYT*, Jan. 28, 1939; "New Peace Group Is Organized Here," *NYT*, Mar.16, 1939; "Session Called for Discussion of U.S. Foreign Policy," *WP*, Apr. 8, 1939; "U.S. Has the Power to Curb Conquest, Congress Is Told," *NYT*, Apr. 13, 1939; "100 Peace Leaders Here Urge U.S. Boycott of Aggressors," *WP*, Apr. 17, 1939; "Back Neutrality Change," *NYT*, May 3, 1939; "Roper, Minton Offer Formula for Peace," *WP*, May 4, 1939. For profiles of these activists, see Johnstone, *Against Immediate Evil*, 36–50.
55. "Senators Delay Discussions of Neutrality Bill," *CT*, July 6, 1939.
56. "Senate Committee Votes For Delay on Neutrality; Roosevelt Will Fight On," *NYT*, July 12, 1939; Divine, *Illusion*, 276–78.
57. On FDR's anger at the isolationists, see Freidel, *Rendezvous*, 315; "Roosevelt and Hull Statements on Neutrality," *NYT*, July 15, 1939; "Roosevelt Asks Congress to Change Neutrality Act," *NYT*, July 15, 1939; "First Lady Urges Action," *NYT*, July 16, 1939.
58. "Night Parley Convinces Roosevelt He Must Wait," *WP*, July 19, 1939; "Neutrality Debate Now Goes to the Country," WP, July 23, 1939; Divine, *Illusion*, 281; Hull, *Memoirs*, vol. I, 649–50.
59. Dorothy Thompson, "American Foreign Policy," *NYHT*, Aug. 16, 1939. For a laudatory assessment of FDR's tactics, see William L. Langer and S. Everett Gleason, *The Challenge to Isolation, 1937–1940* (Harper & Brothers, 1952), 75–90. Wayne Cole, *FDR and the Isolationists*, 314–19, suggests FDR was simply stymied by a dozen senators, and did not want to engage in a bloody fight over the issue. Dallek stresses FDR's powerlessness in the summer of 1939, *FDR and American Foreign Policy*, 192.
60. For the critical view: James MacGregor Burns, *Roosevelt: Lion and the Fox*, 398, 403; Divine, *Illusion*, 285. Robert Dallek believes "a more vigorous effort by the president" would not have succeeded. *FDR and American Foreign Policy*, 190.

61. "Mrs. FDR Quits DAR," *BAA*, Mar. 4, 1939. For Eleanor Roosevelt's role, and her work with African Americans in 1939, see Jill Watts, *The Black Cabinet: The Untold Story of African Americans and Politics During the Age of Roosevelt* (Grove Press, 2020), 259–73.
62. David Michaelis, *Eleanor* (Simon & Schuster, 2020), 348–51; Ickes, *Secret Diary*, vol. 2, 612–15; Ralph Matthews, "National Anthem Rings True for Easter Throng," *BAA*, Apr. 15, 1939; details also in "Marian Anderson Sings to 75,000 in Open Air Recital," *CD*, Apr. 15, 1939.
63. "Telecast of President at the World's Fair to Start Wheels of New Industry," *NYT*, Apr. 30, 1939; "President Hails Record of Peace at Fair Opening," *CT*, May 1, 1939; "Mrs. Roosevelt Heads Day's Throng of Visitors at the World's Fair," *NYT*, May 16, 1939; "Miss Anderson Sets 2 Records," *NYAN*, June 3, 1939; "World Fair Throng Acclaims Marian Anderson," *PC*, June 3, 1939.
64. Marcia Winn, "Their Majesties Dine in Splendor with Roosevelt," *CT*, June 9, 1939; "Their Majesties: A Democratic Turnout for British Royal Visitors," *NYT*, June 11, 1939. Further details and documents available at "The British Royal Visit," https://www.fdrlibrary.org/royal-visit. Ambassador Bullitt was tasked with sending details on the personal needs of the royal visitors. See Bullitt to FDR, Mar. 23, 1939, in Orville Bullitt, ed., *For the President*, 327–30.
65. "Fight On; We Are Winning," *BAA*, June 3, 1939; "England's King, Queen Greet Marian Anderson," *CD*, June 17, 1939; "American Songs Are Played and Sung for King and Queen," *NYT*, June 9, 1939; "King and Queen Hear Marian, Carolina Singers, Others at White House Musicale," *PC*, June 17, 1939.
66. "Refugee Ship," *NYT*, June 8, 1939. The story is concisely told in Daniel Greene and Edward Phillips, eds., *Americans and the Holocaust: A Reader* (Rutgers University Press, 2022), 77-90; a detailed account that seeks to insulate Roosevelt from any blame is in Breitman and Lichtman, *FDR and the Jews*, 135–39.
67. "Coughlin Denounces Mongerers of War," *NYT*, March 27, 1939; "Coughlin Attacks 'War Control' Plans," *NYT*, May 1, 1939; "Coughlin Sees Drive to Enmesh US in War," *NYT*, May 8, 1939; "Coughlin Links King's Visit to Clash Abroad," *NYT*, June 12, 1939; "War Up to Us, Priest Says," *NYT*, June 19, 1939.
68. "'Patriotic' Rally Has Anti-Semitic Tinge," *NYT*, May 25, 1939; James Wechsler, "The Coughlin Terror," *Nation*, July 22, 1939; "Crowd Battles Police in Bronx," *NYT*, Aug. 14, 1939.
69. "Coughlin Tells Need for 'Christian Front,'" *NYT*, Aug. 21, 1939; William A. Mueller, "Coughlin and the Nazi Bund," *Look*, Sept. 26, 1939.
70. "800 Groups Linked to Anti-Semitism," *NYT*, Dec. 14, 1938; "Friends of Democracy to Reach Every Hamlet, Rev. Birkhead Reports," *American Israelite*, Feb. 16, 1939; "Calls Coughlin National Menace," *NYT*, Feb. 26, 1939; "Two Catholic Leaders Rap Fr. Coughlin," *Jewish Advocate*, March 3, 1939; "Coughlin Renews Isolation Appeal," *NYT*, April 24, 1939; "Coughlin Will Bring Fascism," *Jewish Advocate*, April 28, 1939; William C. Kernan, *My Road to Certainty* (Philadelphia: David McKay, 1953), 123–27. "My fight for human rights," Kernan wrote later, "against the manifestations of Nazism in America had assumed in my mind the proportions of a crusade on behalf of Christian social justice," 129.
71. "Rabbi Sees Waking of Fascism's Foes," *NYT*, April 2, 1939; "U.S. Rabbis Denounce Fr. Coughlin," *WP*, June 17, 1939; "Coughlin is Assailed," *NYT*, June 29, 1939. "Banquet to be Held in Honor of Rabbi Wise," *CT*, June 4, 1939.
72. Walter Lippmann, "The American Destiny," *Life*, June 5, 1939.

Chapter 14: The Awakening

1. Moffat, *Moffat Papers*, 245, 249, 255.
2. Chamberlain to Ida, Apr. 9, 1939, and Chamberlain to Hilda, Apr. 29, 1939, in Self, ed., *Neville Chamberlain Diary Letters*, 404, 411–12. He confessed his "deep suspicions of Soviet aims" on May 28 in a letter to Hilda, p. 418. Kennedy to Hull, July 20, 1939, *FRUS 1939*, vol. 1, 287–88. For Chamberlain's decision to guarantee Poland and reluctantly explore a Soviet alliance, see Richard Overy and Andrew Wheatcroft, *The Road to War* (Macmillan, 1989), 97–98; Bouverie, *Appeasement*, 326, 334–37.
3. Bouverie, *Appeasement*, 341; Kennedy to Hull, July 20, 1939, *FRUS 1939*, vol. 1, 287–88.
4. On the origins of the Nazi-Soviet Pact of August 1939, see Stephen Kotkin, *Stalin: Waiting for Hitler, 1929–1941* (Penguin Press, 2017), 642–67; Roger Moorhouse, *The Devil's Alliance: Hitler's Pact with Stalin, 1939–1941* (Basic Books, 2014), 1–29; Steiner, *Triumph of the Dark*, 867–909.

5. The documentary record of the German-Soviet rapprochement is extensive. See Raymond James Sontag and James Stuart Beddie, *Nazi-Soviet Relations, 1939–1941: Documents from the Archives of the German Foreign Office* (Department of State, 1948); the full text of the Treaty of Nonaggression, Aug. 23, 1939, with its secret protocol is on pp. 76–78. See also *Documents On German Foreign Policy, 1918–1945*, series 1, vols. 6 and 7 (Government Printing Office, 1949).
6. Chamberlain to Hilda, Aug. 13, 1939, in Self, ed., *Chamberlain Diary Letters*, 439. For the trial commentary from Davies, see the long letter he wrote to the State Department on the Trotsky-Radek trial, which concluded that for all the propaganda, the trial was fair and defendants clearly guilty. Davies to Bullitt, Feb. 19, 1937, Bullitt Papers, box 24, Sterling Library, Yale University.
7. Steinhardt to Hull, Aug. 16, 1939, *FRUS 1939*, vol. 1, 334–35.
8. These quotations come from two speeches Hitler gave on Aug. 22 to his military chiefs. See Office of U.S. Chief Counsel, Nuremberg International Military Tribunal, translation of Document PS-1014, "Second Speech by the Führer on 22 Aug. 1939," available through Nuremberg Trials Project, Harvard Law School Library, https://nuremberg.law.harvard.edu/documents/452263-speech-to-the-military?mode=image; and Nuremberg International Military Tribunal, Office of U.S. Chief Counsel, translation of Document PS-798, "The Fuehrer's speech to the Commanders in Chief on 22 August 1939," Nuremberg Trials Project, Harvard Law School Library, https://nuremberg.law.harvard.edu/documents/450863-address-to-the-commanding?mode=image.
9. Steinhardt to Hull, Aug. 24 and Aug. 31, 1939, *FRUS 1939*, vol. 1, 342–43; 346–47.
10. Text of FDR's letter in Welles to Phillips, Aug. 23, 1939, *FRUS 1939*, vol. 1, 351–52. FDR's calendar in FDR Day by Day. Transcript of FDR press conference, Aug. 25, 1939, FDRL.
11. Chamberlain to Hilda, Aug. 27, 1939, in Self, ed., *Chamberlain Diary Letters*, 440–42. For the detailed twists of these days, see Richard Overy, *1939: Countdown to War* (Penguin Books, 2009), 19–41.
12. FDR recounted the early morning phone call in his Sept. 1, 1939, press conference, transcript, FDRL.
13. Sigrid Schultz, "Germany Takes Danzig; Navy Blockades Gdynia," *CT*, Sept. 1, 1939; "Hitler Tells Reichstag 'Bomb Will Be Met by Bomb,'" *NYT*, Sept. 1, 1939; "War on Poland Begun, Hitler Tells Nation," *CT*, Sept. 1, 1939; "Text of Hitler's Reichstag Address on Reasons for War," *LAT*, Sept. 1, 1939.
14. The scene is painted in Joseph Alsop and Robert Kintner, *American White Paper* (Simon & Schuster, 1940), 58–66. For the determination of the British and French, Bullitt to Hull, Sept. 1, 1939, *FRUS 1939*, vol. 1, 403–4; Kennedy to Hull, Sept. 1, 1939, *FRUS 1939*, vol. 1, 405.
15. Fireside chat, Sept. 3, 1939, at APP.
16. Praetorian Guard comment in Dorothy Thompson's column, "Écrasez l'Infâme," *NYHT*, Aug. 30, 1939; radio address, Sept. 1, 1939, NBC radio, transcript in Dorothy Thompson Papers, box 111, Syracuse University.
17. "One Man's Responsibility," *LAT*, Sept. 2, 1939; "Is Neutrality Possible?," *WP*, Sept. 2, 1939; "What Hitler Has Done in Six Years," *NYT*, Sept. 3, 1939; Harold Callender, "Who Started the War?," *NYT*, Sept. 3, 1939; "One U.S. Eye Kept on Europe, Other on Our Neutrality Act," *Newsweek*, Sept. 4, 1939.
18. William Jones, "What Will Adolf Hitler Do to Us?," *BAA*, Sept. 9, 1939; "War Has Come," *BAA*, Sept. 9, 1939; "Harlem Picks Allies to Win," *NYAN*, Sept. 9, 1939; "War's Affect on Race Weighed," *New Journal and Guide*, Sept. 9, 1939; Charles P. Howard, *Atlanta Daily World*, Sept. 21, 1939.
19. "The Sword Unsheathed," *NYT*, Sept. 4, 1939. See also editorials "Tragedy in Europe" and "The Attack on Poland," equally critical of Germany, *NYT*, Sept. 2 and 3, 1939.
20. "British Mobilize Army and Fleet," *LAT*, Sept. 1, 1939; "British Begin Evacuation of 3,000,000 from London," *WP*, Sept. 1, 1939; "Cheering Commons Backs Chamberlain," *NYT*, Sept. 2, 1939; John Gunther, "Hitler's Tactics Stiffen British," *NYT*, Sept. 3, 1939; Frederick Birchall, "'Better Get it Over,' Londoners Say," *NYT*, Sept. 3, 1939.
21. "Text of Chamberlain Address," *NYT*, Sept. 3, 1939; Winston S. Churchill, *The Second World War, vol. 1: The Gathering Storm* (Houghton Mifflin, 1948), 409; and Winston Churchill, House of Commons, Sept. 3, 1939, at https://www.nationalchurchillmuseum.org/war-speech.html. Thompson, NBC radio address, Sept. 3, 1939, transcript in Dorothy Thompson Papers, box 111, Syracuse University.

22. Bullitt to Hull, Sept. 2, 1939, *FRUS 1939*, vol. 1, 408–11; "Text of Premier Daladier's Address Before the Chamber of Deputies," *NYT*, Sept. 3, 1939. Two classic accounts on French diplomacy in the late 1930s, well-founded on documentary evidence, are Anthony Adamthwaite, *France and the Coming of the Second World War, 1936–1939* (Frank Cass, 1977), and Jean-Baptiste Duroselle, *France and the Nazi Threat: The Collapse of French Diplomacy, 1932–1939* (Enigma Books, 2004).
23. A brisk narrative of the invasion is Roger Moorhouse, *Poland 1939: The Outbreak of World War II* (Basic Books, 2020); also Steve Zaloga and W. Victor Madej, The Polish Campaign, 1939 (Hippocrene Books, 1985); and Alexander B. Rossino, *Hitler Strikes Poland: Blitzkrieg, Ideology, and Atrocity* (University Press of Kansas, 2003); Roberts, *Storm of War*, 21. For contemporary news reports: "Allies Ready to Enter War," *LAT*, Sept. 2, 1939; "Nazis Report Gains," *NYT*, Sept. 3, 1939; "Fires in Warsaw," *NYT*, Sept. 5, 1939; "Germans Report Control of Silesia," *NYT*, Sept. 6, 1939; "Nazis Press Poles," *NYT*, Sept. 8, 1939; "Nazis Say Warsaw Entered," *LAT*, Sept. 9, 1939.
24. Otto Tolischus, "Poles Unprepared for Blow So Hard," *NYT*, Sept. 12, 1939; for Soviet statement, Steinhardt to Hull, Sept. 17, 1939, *FRUS 1939*, vol. 1, 428–29; Berle, ed., *Navigating the Rapids, Papers of Adolf A. Berle*, entry of Sept. 13, 1939, 254.
25. FDR press conference of Aug. 29 and Sept. 8, 1939, transcript, FDRL; FDR to John J. Cochran, Aug. 30, 1939, in *FDR: His Personal Letters*, vol. 2, 914–15; "Proclamation 2352—Proclaiming a National Emergency," text at APP. Stephen Early to FDR, Sept. 7, 1939, in *FDR: His Personal Letters*, vol. 2, 918; FDR to Neville Chamberlain, Sept. 11, 1939, in *FDR: His Personal Letters*, vol. 2, 919.
26. "U.S. Voters Favor Poland in Survey," *NYT*, Sept. 1, 1939; George Gallup, "Hitler Danzig Claim Opposed by Americans," *LAT*, Sept. 1, 1939; George Gallup, "The Gallup Poll," *WP*, Sept. 8, 1939; polling tables of Sept. 1939 polls in Hadley Cantril, ed., *Public Opinion, 1935–1946* (Princeton University Press, 1951), 1157–58. "Congress Called to Meet Sept. 21 on Embargo Issue," *NYT*, Sept. 14, 1939. A roundup of editorial opinion from regional newspapers across the country found a similar shift in favor of lifting the embargo: "America Stirred by New War but Set on Staying Neutral," *Newsweek*, Sept. 11, 1939.
27. "Borah Reviews Huge Losses Inevitable If America Enters War," *CT*, Sept. 11, 1939; Turner Catledge, "Borah Opens Fight Against Revision of Neutrality Act," *NYT*, Sept. 12, 1939; Turner Catledge, "Step Toward War Pictured by Borah If We End Embargo," *NYT*, Sept. 15, 1939; Chesly Manly, "Borah Warns of Road to War," *CT*, Sept. 15, 1939; "Text of Borah Speech," *CT*, Sept. 15, 1939; "Arms Embargo Repeal Hostile Act, Says Borah," *WP*, Sept. 15, 1939.
28. "Isolationists Map 'Vigilante' Drive," *NYT*, Sept. 23, 1939. Coughlin sermon, "If Cash-and-Carry, Then War within a Year," Sept. 17, 1939, Coughlin Collection, box 1, NMAH; "Coughlin Asks March," *NYT*, Sept. 18, 1939. The Friends of Democracy alleged that Coughlin was trying to start a civil war and asked the Federal Communications Commission to ban him from radio.
29. *Wartime Journals*, diary entries of Apr. 2, June 30, Aug. 23, Aug. 27, 173, 218, 245, 247.
30. *Wartime Journals*, diary entries of Aug. 30, Sept. 7, Sept. 14, Sept. 15, 248, 252, 254, 257.
31. Text of radio speech, "America and European Wars," Sept. 15, 1939, available at http://www.charleslindbergh.com/pdf/9_15_39.pdf; Frank Kluckhohn, "Lindbergh Urges We Shun the War," *NYT*, Sept. 16, 1939.
32. Dorothy Thompson, "On the Record: Col. Lindbergh and Propaganda," *WP*, Sept. 20, 1939.
33. On administration efforts, see Stephen Early to FDR, Sept. 14, 1939, in *FDR: Personal Letters*, vol. 2, 921, mentioning Alf Landon, Frank Knox, Henry Stimson, James Bryant Conant as allies who were prepared to speak up in favor of revision. Harold Ickes reports the White House request to Knox: Ickes, *Secret Diary*, vol. 3, 8. Walter Lippmann, "Today and Tomorrow: Specific Question Raised by Borah Is Dangerous," *WP*, Sept. 19, 1939; "Plea By Stimson," with text of his statement, *NYT*, Sept. 16, 1939; "Lift Embargo, Avoid War, Stimson Urges," *WP*, Sept. 16, 1939; "Mr. Borah's Argument," *NYT*, Sept. 15, 1939; "U.S. Neutrality Fight Turns on What Is Best for Country," *Newsweek*, Sept. 25, 1939; "Stimson Attacks Foolish Embargo," *NYT*, Oct. 6, 1939; "Stimson Says Repeal Means U.S. Security," *WP*, Oct. 6, 1939. The full text of Stimson's October 5 address, "Preserve American Security by Repealing the Embargo," may be found in Herbert Feis Papers, box 26, LOC.
34. Transcript of meeting with congressional leaders, Sept. 20, 1939, in "Special Conferences: President and Congressional Leaders on Neutrality," PPF 1P, box 118, FDRL.
35. "The President's Address," *NYT*, Sept. 22, 1939. On the drafting, see Berle diary, *Navigating the Rapids*, Sept. 19, 1939, 256–57; and Rosenman, *Working with Roosevelt*, 189–91.

36. Eleanor Roosevelt, "My Day," Sept. 19, 1939, at https://www2.gwu.edu/~erpapers/myday/displaydoc.cfm?_y=1939&_f=md055375.
37. "Cannot Be Neutral, Frankfurter Holds," *NYT*, Sept. 22, 1939; "Manning Assails Reich and Russia," *NYT*, Sept. 25, 1939, and "Manning Asks Aid for Allies in War," *NYT*, Oct. 2, 1939; "Smith Makes Plea to Lift Arms Ban," *NYT*, Oct. 2, 1939; "Our 'Neutrality' Act," *CD*, Sept. 23, 1939.
38. "Borah Sees Allies 'Pulling Punches,'" *NYT*, Sept. 19, 1939; Berle diary, *Navigating the Rapids*, Sept. 29, 1939, 258, and Sept. 30, 1939, 259; FDR to Lord Tweedsmuir, Oct. 5, 1939, in *FDR: Personal Letters*, vol. 2, 934. Tweedsmuir is better remembered as the novelist John Buchan, a Scot and author of the 1915 adventure tale *The Thirty-Nine Steps*, among other fiction.
39. "Neutrality," *Life*, Sept. 25, 1939. The masked figure was on the cover of *Life* on Sept. 18, 1939, with the headline "Britain Goes to War." For maps, essays, and photos, see *Life*, Sept. 4, Sept. 11, Oct. 2, and Oct. 9, 1939.
40. "Nazis Hint 'Purge' of Jews in Poland," *NYT*, Sept. 13, 1939; "Is Poland Dead—Again?" *LAT*, Sept. 28, 1939; "Nazis in Warsaw: City Still on Fire," *NYT*, Oct. 3, 1939; "Hitler, in Warsaw, Cites It as a Warning," *NYT*, Oct. 6, 1939; "Sees Ruins of Warsaw," *CT*, Oct. 6, 1939; "Folly to Resist, Hitler Boasts at Warsaw," *WP*, Oct. 6, 1939.
41. "Chamberlain Rejects Peace Deal With Hitler," *LAT*, Oct. 4, 1939; "Herr Hitler's Reichstag Speech in Full," *MG*, Oct. 7, 1939; "Peace Drive: Hitler's Last Statement," *NYT*, Oct. 8, 1939; "1,500,000 Jews in Poland Face Death by Hunger," *CT*, Nov. 6, 1939.
42. Walter Johnson, *The Battle Against Isolation* (University of Chicago Press, 1944), 31–54, White quoted on 38; and Johnstone, *Against Immediate Evil*, 54–62.
43. Johnson, *Battle*, 41-3, 51. Examples of the appeals made by White can be seen in White's telegram of Oct. 3 and letter of Oct. 28, 1939, to Robert Sherwood, in Robert Sherwood Papers, box 11, Houghton Library, Harvard University.
44. William Allen White, "The Hour Is Striking," CBS radio broadcast, Oct. 15, 1939.
45. On Coughlin's troublesome ties to the Christian Front, "Evil Acts Charged to Christian Front," *NYT*, Nov. 16, 1939; "Christian Front Faces New Attack," *NYT*, Dec. 6, 1939; Herbert Hoover, "We Must Stay Out," *SEP*, Oct. 28, 1939. On Hoover and Lindbergh contacts, see Lindbergh, *Wartime Journals*, Oct. 2, and Oct. 7, 1939, 267, 270–72; on contacts with Borah, Oct. 11, 1939, 274–75.
46. Lindbergh's October 13 speech can be seen at https://teachingamericanhistory.org/document/neutrality-and-war/; "Aviation, Geography, and Race," *Reader's Digest*, Nov. 1939, 35. On the speech, see his entry of Oct. 13, *Wartime Journals*, 275; on seeing Henry Ford, see Dec. 28, 1939, *Wartime Journals*, 300–301; he sent the draft of the Reader's Digest article to the editor on September 18, 1939, *Wartime Journals*, 259; Shirer, *Berlin Diary*, 211, 220, 241. Dorothy Thompson put out a three-part series on Lindbergh's October speech: *WP*, Oct. 18, 20, and 23, 1939.
47. Ickes, *Secret Diary*, vol. 3, 57; Cole, *Roosevelt and the Isolationists*, 310.
48. Divine, *Illusion of Neutrality*, 334. FDR was speaking to a three-day symposium on world affairs organized by the *New York Herald Tribune*. "Roosevelt's Address to Forum Here," *NYT*, Oct. 27, 1939; "Roosevelt Scores 'Fake' Talk of U.S. Getting Into War," *NYT*, Oct. 27, 1939.
49. "Text of Molotoff Broadcast," *NYT*, Nov. 30, 1939. "Reds Invade Finland," *CT*, Nov. 30, 1939.
50. "Identical Evils," *WP* editorial, Dec. 15, 1939; for an explanation of U.S. public outrage: "Finland's Fate Shocks USA," *Observer* (London), Dec. 3, 1939. An excellent military history is Gordon F. Sander, *The Hundred Day Winter War: Finland's Gallant Stand against the Soviet Army* (University Press of Kansas, 2013); and William R. Trotter, *The Russo-Finnish Winter War of 1939–1940* (Algonquin Books, 1991).
51. "3 Raids on Helsinki Leave City Ablaze," *NYT*, Dec. 1, 1939; "Soviet Blow Heavy," *NYT*, Dec. 1, 1939; "Roosevelt Calls Invasion 'Wanton,'" *WP*, Dec. 2, 1939; "President Is Stern," *NYT*, Dec. 1, 1939; "Hoover Calls Attack on Finns 'Butchery,'" *NYT*, Dec. 1, 1939; "Russia Strikes," *LAT* editorial, Dec. 1, 1939; Walter Lippmann, "Dangerous to Abandon Finns," *WP*, Dec. 5, 1939. See also "Finland: Soviet Russia Crowds Nation of Democrats," *Life*, Oct. 30, 1939.
52. Anne O'Hare McCormick, "Finland Fights Alone, but on the Side of the Angels," *NYT*, Dec. 2, 1939; "Finns Defend Civilization, Says Premier," *WP*, Dec. 2, 1939; "The Defense of Liberty," *NYT* editorial, Dec. 5, 1939; "The Finnish Outpost," *WP* editorial, Dec. 3, 1939.
53. "The Reds Start West," *WP*, Dec. 1, 1939; "Manners in Moscow," *NYT*, Dec. 6, 1939; "Reds vs. Finns," *Newsweek*, Dec. 4, 1939; "Red Steam-Roller?" *Life*, Dec. 25, 1939; "The Finns Prove Themselves the Best Winter Soldiers in the World," *Life*, Jan. 22, 1940; "*Life's* Photo Reporter in Finland Covers War in Winter," *Life*, Jan. 29, 1940.

54. "The Asiatic Barbarian in Europe," *CT* editorial, Dec. 4, 1939; Dorothy Thompson, "The Isolationist's Dilemma," *WP*, Dec. 6, 1939.
55. "The Last Agony of Fighting Is Wrapped in the Beauty of Snow," *Life*, Mar. 11, 1940.
56. "15,000 at Rally for Aid to Finland Cheer as Hoover Pays Tribute," *NYT*, Dec. 21, 1939; "U.S. Helps the Finns," *Life*, Feb. 19, 1940.
57. "America's Stake in the Present War and the Future World Order," *Fortune*, Jan. 1940, 70–84.
58. Alonso, *Robert E. Sherwood*, 167–203; "Movie of the Week: 'Abe Lincoln in Illinois,'" *Life*, Feb. 12, 1940.
59. Alonso, *Sherwood*, 206–13; Robert E. Sherwood, *There Shall be No Night* (Charles Scribner's Sons, 1941), scene III, 100; review, *Life*, May 13, 1940.
60. Brooks Atkinson, "The Play in Review," *NYT*, Apr. 30, 1940; Frankfurter to Sherwood, Apr. 23, 1940, Sherwood Papers, box 4, Houghton Library, Harvard University; and Eleanor Roosevelt to Sherwood, June 5, 1940, in Sherwood Papers, box 8, Houghton Library, Harvard University.
61. Chaplin later acknowledged that his aim in the picture was to lampoon the "mystic bilge" of Nazism. "Hitler must be laughed at," he wrote. But he had regrets: "Had I known of the actual horrors of the German concentration camps I could not have made *The Great Dictator*." Charlie Chaplin, *My Autobiography* (Simon & Schuster, 1964), 392.
62. Noah Isenberg, *We'll Always Have Casablanca: The Life, Legend, and Afterlife of Hollywood's Most Beloved Movie* (Norton, 2017), 1–41.

Chapter 15: Stop Hitler Now!

1. FDR to Bullitt, Nov. 23, 1939, in *FDR: His Personal Letters*, vol. 2, 959–60; Haight Jr., *American Aid*, 156–59.
2. For periodic reports on foreign purchase requests, see War—Reports: Foreign Inquiries for Production of Munitions, 1939–1940, PSF, box 85, FDRL; Haight, *American Aid*, 178–79.
3. FDR to White, Dec. 14, 1939, and FDR to Knox, Dec. 29, 1939, in *FDR: Personal Letters*, vol. 2, 967–68, and 975–76.
4. Annual Message to Congress, Jan. 3, 1940, at https://www.presidency.ucsb.edu/documents/annual-message-the-congress; Rosenman, *Working with Roosevelt*, 191–92. "Dies Presents Proof of Reds' Dictator Plot," *CT*, Jan. 4, 1940; "Dies Report Finds Red 'Tinge' in CIO," *NYT*, Jan. 4, 1940.
5. "18 Seized in Plot to Overthrow U.S.; Arms Found Here," *NYT*, Jan. 15, 1940; "The Coughlin Terror," *Nation*, Jan. 20, 1940; "Coughlin Supports Christian Front," *NYT*, Jan. 22, 1940; Theodore Irwin, "Inside the Christian Front," *Forum and Century*, Mar. 1940.
6. FDR to Arthur Murray, Mar. 4, 1940, PSF, box 38, Murray, Arthur, 1940–44, FDRL.
7. The battle over aircraft sales can be followed in Haight, *American Aid*, 187–231; Blum, *Morgenthau Diaries: Years of Urgency, 1938–1941*, 111–19; Mark Skinner Watson, *United States Army in World War II: The War Department, Chief of Staff, Prewar Plans and Preparations* (Government Printing Office, 1950), 299–305; John W. Huston, ed., *American Airpower Comes of Age: General Henry H. "Hap" Arnold's World War II Diaries*, vol. 1 (Air University Press, 2002), 94–101. Much of the valuable documents are in Diaries of Henry Morgenthau Jr., vols. 232–248, FDRL. "Allies to Spend Billion in U.S. on New Planes," *NYT*, Feb. 24, 1940; "The Aircraft Boom," *Fortune*, Mar. 1940, 69–112; "Allied Purchasing," *Fortune*, Apr. 1940, 68–137; Press conference, Mar. 19, 1940, FDRL; "Government Policy on Aircraft Foreign Sales," dated Mar. 25, 1940, in War—Reports: Foreign Inquiries for Production of Munitions, 1939–1940, PSF, box 85, FDRL.
8. FDR later explained his thinking to Harold Ickes. See Ickes, *Secret Diary*, vol. 3, 220. Polls done by Elmo Roper for *Fortune* magazine showed Roosevelt with a wide lead over any rival. "Fortune Survey," May 1940, 76–77. For two careful studies, see John W. Jeffries, *A Third Term for FDR: The Election of 1940* (University Press of Kansas, 2017); and Richard Moe, *Roosevelt's Second Act: The Election of 1940 and the Politics of War* (Oxford University Press, 2013).
9. Steven Lomazow, *FDR Unmasked: 73 Years of Medical Cover-Ups That Rewrote History* (Kugler, 2024), 117–26.
10. On Kennedy and the Roosevelt dictatorship, see Hearst's columns, "In the News," *SFE*, Mar. 12 and May 11, 1940.
11. Press conference, Feb. 9, 1940, FDRL.
12. Chamberlain to Lord Lothian, British Ambassador, undated, *FRUS 1940*, vol. 1, 1–4; Michael Fullilove, *Rendezvous with Destiny: How Franklin D. Roosevelt and Five Extraordinary Men Took America into the War and into the World* (Penguin, 2013), 26–33.

13. Fullilove, *Rendezvous,* 370, note 41; Langer and Gleason, *The Challenge to Isolation*, 361–75; Dallek, *Franklin D. Roosevelt and American Foreign Policy*, 216–18; Stanley E. Hilton, "The Welles Mission to Europe, February–March 1940: Illusion or Realism?" *Journal of American History* 58, no. 1 (1971): 93–120.
14. The relationship is thoroughly explored in Irwin Gellman, *Secret Affairs: Roosevelt, Cordell Hull, and Sumner Welles* (Johns Hopkins University Press, 1995).
15. The Welles report of Mar. 29, 1940, is published in full in *FRUS 1940*, vol. 1, 21–117. A slightly altered version forms chapter 3 of Sumner Welles, *Time for Decision* (Harper & Brothers, 1944), 73–147.
16. Gerhard Weinberg, *A World at Arms: A Global History of World War II* (Cambridge University Press, 1994), 117, and for an overview of the campaign, 113–21. Equally savage is Max Hastings, *Inferno: The World at War, 1939–1945* (Alfred A. Knopf, 2011), 43–52; and Peter Calvocoressi, Guy Wint, and John Pritchard, *The Penguin History of the Second World War* (Penguin, 1989), 120–27.
17. Press conference of April 9, 1940, and text of remarks to American Society of Newspaper Editors, April 18, 1940, in press conference files, FDRL.
18. Press conference, April 9, 1940, FDRL. These details on the Norway debate are gleaned from contemporary press accounts: "Britons Assail War Chiefs for Slips in Norway," *CT*, May 1, 1940; "Allies Withdraw from South of Trondheim," *MG*, May 3, 1940; "Premier Explains," *NYT*, May 3, 1940; "Chamberlain Faces Growing Criticism," *NYT*, May 4, 1940; "Chamberlain Foes Pressing Attacks," *NYT*, May 5, 1940; "Nazis Win Spectacular Victory in Norway as Allies Withdraw," *WP*, May 5, 1940; "War Hero Rips Chamberlain," *CT*, May 8, 1940; "House is Hostile," *NYT*, May 8, 1940; "Text of Attlee's Speech in Commons," *NYT*, May 8, 1940; "Churchill Takes Full Blame for Norway Defeat," *CT*, May 9, 1940; "Save Chamberlain, 281–200," *CT*, May 9, 1940; "Resignation," *NYT*, May 12, 1940. For a detailed account of these days and the maneuvering to replace Chamberlain, see Andrew Roberts, *Churchill: Walking with Destiny* (Viking, 2018), 494–514. Churchill passage from Winston Churchill, *The Second World War, vol. 1: The Gathering Storm* (Houghton Mifflin, 1948), 667.
19. Some of the contingency of these days in captured in Reynolds, *The Creation of the Anglo-American Alliance*, 95–113. Naturally, many writers have examined this period in depth. For a rich, anecdote-filled account, see Joseph Lash, *Roosevelt and Churchill, 1939–1941: The Partnership That Saved the West* (Norton, 1976), especially 93–167; and Jon Meacham, *Franklin and Winston: An Intimate Portrait of an Epic Friendship* (Random House, 2003), 39–81.
20. Kansas City speech, Nov. 6, 1939, Dorothy Thompson Papers, box 103, Syracuse University.
21. Ickes, *Secret Diary*, vol. 3, 174–76.
22. "President's Talk to Science Congress." *NYT*, May 11, 1940; "President Says Americas Will Defend Liberty," *CT*, May 11, 1940; "Our Feeling Voiced," *NYT*, May 12, 1940; "Mr. Roosevelt and the Nazi Challenge," *MG*, May 12, 1940.
23. Blum, *From the Morgenthau Diaries*, vol. 2, 139.
24. Churchill speech, May 13, 1940, at https://winstonchurchill.org/resources/speeches/1940-the-finest-hour/blood-toil-tears-sweat/. For press coverage, see "Unanimous Confidence Vote," *MG*, May 14, 1940; Andrew Roberts, *Churchill: Walking with Destiny* (Viking, 2018), 527–28.
25. Bullitt telegram to State Department, May 14, 1940, in Bullitt, ed., *For the President*, 415–18.
26. Churchill to FDR, May 15, 1940, in Warren Kimball, ed., *Churchill and Roosevelt: The Complete Correspondence*, vol. 1 (Princeton University Press, 1984), 37–8; Winston Churchill, *The Second World War, vol. 2: Their Finest Hour* (Houghton Mifflin, 1948), 42, 46–47.
27. FDR to Churchill, May 16, 1940, in *Churchill and Roosevelt*, 38–9; on Marshall, see Forrest C. Pogue, *George C. Marshall: Ordeal and Hope* (Viking, 1965), 29–32.
28. "Message to Congress on Appropriations for National Defense," May 16, 1940, at APP.
29. Frankfurter letter, May 16, 1940, in *Roosevelt and Frankfurter*, 522. The text of Lindbergh's May 19, 1940 speech is available at http://www.charleslindbergh.com/pdf/TheAirDefenseofAmerica.pdf. FDR's comment to Morgenthau about Lindbergh is typed up as a separate document, dated May 20, 1940, in the Diaries of Henry Morgenthau Jr., Presidential Diaries Series, vol. 3, 563; FDR letter to Stimson, May 21, 1940, PSF, box 84, FDRL.
30. Churchill to Roosevelt, May 18, 1940, Kimball, ed., *Churchill and Roosevelt*, 39; Bullitt to Roosevelt, May 18, 1940, *FRUS 1940*, vol. 1, 228–30; Churchill radio address on the BBC, May 19, 1940, at https://winstonchurchill.org/resources/speeches/1940-the-finest-hour/be-ye-men-of-valour/.
31. Churchill to Roosevelt, May 20, 1940, Kimball, ed., *Churchill and Roosevelt*, 40.

32. Memorandum of Conversation by Welles, May 23, 1940, *FRUS 1940*, vol. 3, 3–5.
33. Press conference, FDRL, May 23, 1940; Rosenman, *Working with Roosevelt*, 195–98; Ickes, *Secret Diary*, vol. 3, 188.
34. Text of Fireside Chat of May 26, 1940, Master Speech File, box 51, FDRL; Bullitt to Roosevelt, May 17, 1940, *FRUS 1940*, vol. 1, 226–27. The directive on wiretapping is quoted in a letter by Attorney General Tom C. Clark to President Harry Truman, July 17, 1946, in "Directives, June 26, 1939–June 9, 1962," Official and Confidential Files of FBI Director J. Edgar Hoover 60/3, in Federal Bureau of Investigation Library, Gale Primary Sources, Archives Unbound. For a careful analysis of the May 21, 1940, wiretap message, and a copy of the original order to Attorney General Robert Jackson, see Neal Katyal and Richard Caplan, "The Surprisingly Strong Case for the Legality of the NSA Surveillance Program: The FDR Precedent," *Stanford Law Review* 60, no. 4 (2008): 1023–78.
35. Bullitt to Roosevelt, May 28, 1940, *FRUS 1940*, vol. 1, 233–34; Churchill, *Finest Hour*, 99.
36. On the turning point, John Lukacs, *Five Days in London: May 1940* (Yale University Press, 1999), 2; Churchill, *Finest Hour*, 100.
37. FDR to Anna Roosevelt Boettiger, June 1, 1940, in *FDR: His Personal Letters*, vol. 2, 1035.
38. Churchill speech, June 4, 1940, available at https://winstonchurchill.org/resources/speeches/1940-the-finest-hour/we-shall-fight-on-the-beaches/.
39. For the figures and history of the U.S. arms effort in June, see H. Duncan Hall, *North American Supply* (Her Majesty's Stationery Office, 1955), 124–38, quotation on 134; Churchill, *Finest Hour*, 143.
40. Press conference, June 7, 1940, FDRL; "To Defend America," *NYT*, June 7, 1940.
41. The audio tape of the June 10, 1940, speech can be heard at https://www.fdrlibrary.org/utterancesfdr.
42. The text of the speech, with various additions in FDR's hand, can be seen at http://www.fdrlibrary.marist.edu/_resources/images/msf/msf01330. On the background and impact of the speech, see Rosenman, *Working with Roosevelt*, 198. Luce to FDR, June 11, 1940, in President's Personal File, 200B, box 62, FDRL. "The Presidency: Tenth of June," *Time*, June 17, 1940. Felix Frankfurter to FDR, June 10, 1940, in *Roosevelt and Frankfurter*, 528. Henry Stimson confided to his diary that Sumner Welles objected to the "stab in the back" phrase, but FDR insisted on it, writing the words back into the speech in his own hand. See Stimson Diaries, vol. 32, Dec 1940–Jan 1941, 63–64, entry of Dec. 29, 1940, in Stimson Diaries in the Yale University Library, digitized through Center for Research Libraries, available at https://dds.crl.edu/crldelivery/18100. Stephen Early, FDR's press officer, wrote that "perhaps more than any other address the President has made in recent years, the reaction to the Charlottesville speech revealed a virtual unanimity of opinion." Early to J. Edgar Hoover, June 12, 1940, President's Personal File, 200B, box 62, FDRL. This box also contains a huge number of incoming telegrams to the White House that showed near unanimous approval. The *Washington Post* editorial page, acclaiming the speech, took the opportunity to chastise the "stupidity, folly, and lack of foresight" of those who embraced neutrality through the decade of the 1930s. "At Charlottesville," *WP*, June 11, 1940.
43. The figures for spending were reported in numerous articles in the summer of 1940. "Big Steps to Be Taken to Build Up Defenses," *NYT*, June 9, 1940;"Cost of National Defense," *Wall Street Journal*, June 10, 1940; "Army Supply Bill Passed by House," *WP*, June 11, 1940; "Congress Leaders Push Completion of Defense Bills," *Wall Street Journal*, June 11, 1940; "House Votes Defense Funds over 5 Billions," *CT* June 13, 1940; "84 More Warships Asked in Congress," *NYT*, June 18, 1940.
44. "8 1/2 Billion Is Voted for 1,500 Warships," *NYT*, June 19, 1940;"Huge U.S. Navy, National Service Planned," *NYT*, June 19, 1940; "Naval Expansion Program Tripled; 200 Ships Added," *Wall Street Journal*, June 19, 1940; "Defense Costs up 3 Billions Since May 15," *CT*, June 20, 1940; "$5,377,552,058 Voted for Defense This Year," *NYT*, June 23, 1940; "Five Billion More Weighed for Army," *NYT*, June 28, 1940; "2-Ocean Navy Bill Passed by Senate," *NYT*, July 11, 1940; "House Approves Army-Navy Bill for 5 Billions," *CT*, Sept. 6, 1940; "U.S. Plane Orders: Allocation to Industry Total 13,000 Aircraft," *Wall Street Journal*, Sept. 6, 1940; "Congress Sends 5 1/4 Billion Bill to White House," *CT*, Sept. 7, 1940; "Defense Progress Shown in Survey," *NYT*, Sept. 7, 1940; "200 New Vessels," *Wall Street Journal*, Sept. 10, 1940; "Navy Signs Orders to Build 201 Ships for 2-Ocean Fleet," *NYT*, Sept. 10, 1940; "Roosevelt Signs 5 Billion Arms Bill," *NYT*, Sept. 10, 1940.

45. "Army and Navy Orders Close to 7 Billions," *CT*, Sept. 22, 1940; "Tremendous Spending Marks 76th Congress," *NYT*, Sept. 22, 1940; "House Passes a New Bill for War Spending," *CT*, Sept. 27, 1940. For the $12.1 billion figure: "House Votes Fund for Army of $1,474,000,000," *WP*, Sept. 27, 1940. Another *Post* article figured FDR got more than $15 billion in defense spending: "FDR Gets Everything He Asks to Implement Defense," *WP*, Sept. 15, 1940. The *Chicago Tribune* estimated the total outlays by this session of Congress at $16.7 billion: "House Passes a New Bill for War Spending," *CT*, Sept. 27, 1940.
46. Sherwood, *Roosevelt and Hopkins*, 118, 120.
47. For an introduction to the kind of cross-party public-private alliances that emerged in the New Deal, despite the intense partisanship of the era, see Brian Balogh, *The Associational State: American Governance in the Twentieth Century* (University of Pennsylvania Press, 2015), ch. 5, "Meeting the State Halfway: Governing America, 1930–1950," 139–71.
48. Thompson penned an astonishing number of columns and essays in mid-1940; the ones referred to here, all syndicated in the *Washington Post*, are: "Heading For Europe," Apr. 1, 1940; "Hitler's One Way to Win," May 10, 1940; "Roosevelt was Right," May 15, 1940, in which she proposed an FDR-Willkie ticket; "Revising Our Concepts: Defense No Longer Enough," May 20, 1940; "If the Allies Lose," May 24, 1940; "Unearned Increment," June 3, 1940; "The Choice," June 14, 1940; "Opportunity in Crisis: Thoughts After the Fall of Paris," June 17, 1940; and "Lessons from France," June 19, 1940. FDR scoffed at Thompson's idea of a bipartisan ticket, writing to a common friend, "Do try to get this silly business of Wendell Willkie out of her head." Letter to Morris Ernst, May 18, 1940, in *FDR: His Personal Letters*, vol. 2, 1026. Her letter to FDR is undated, but from late June 1940, in Harry Hopkins Papers, Sherwood Collection, Book 2, box 302, FDRL.
49. Walter Lippmann column, "Today and Tomorrow," as reprinted in *WP*, dated June 1, June 4, June 11, June 15, 1940; and Walter Lippmann, "America and the World," *Life*, June 3, 1940.
50. Walter Lippmann, "Today and Tomorrow: The Generation that was Duped," *WP*, June 15, 1940.
51. Archibald MacLeish, "Postwar Writers and Prewar Readers," *New Republic*, June 10, 1940. *Life* magazine published a series of tart rebuttals of MacLeish's essay in "War Writers on Democracy," *Life*, June 24, 1940. For further background, see Eleanor M. Sickels, "Archibald MacLeish and American Democracy," American Literature 15, no. 3 (1943), 223–37; and Scott Donaldson, *Archibald MacLeish: An American Life* (Houghton Mifflin, 1992), 333–38. MacLeish to FDR, June 14, 1940, in PPF, container 4, 1820 Speech Materials and Suggestions, 1939–1940, FDRL.
52. Eleanor Roosevelt, "My Day," May 10, May 13, July 18, 1940.
53. Eleanor Roosevelt, "My Day," May 17, June 27, July 18, 1940. The Thompson column she referred to was "The Facts of Life," *WP*, June 26, 1940.
54. "War and Peace: General Advance," *Time*, June 17, 1940; "30 Leaders Sign Petition Urging U.S. to Declare War on the Reich," *WP*, June 10, 1940. The text of Henry Luce's June 1, 1940, radio speech is in Hamilton Fish Armstrong Papers, box 41, Seeley Mudd Library, Princeton University. The letter of thirty leading citizens was drafted by Francis P. Miller of Virginia and was the first effort in what would soon become the Fight for Freedom organization. For the drafting of that statement, called "A Summons to Speak Out," see the correspondence in the file of Francis P. Miller, Armstrong papers, box 44.
55. Press release, May 20, 1940, CDAAA Papers, box 36, Seeley Mudd Library, Princeton University; "Objectives of the CDAAA," pamphlet dated July 1940, Harry Hopkins Papers, book 2, box 302, Sherwood Collection, FDRL; Robert Sherwood to William Allen White, released to the press on May 22, 1940, in CDAAA Papers, box 36. By June 1, 53 CDAAA chapters had been formed; by July 3, that number rose to 300 and hit 633 by the end of August. At its peak, over 800 chapters of CDAAA had been formed. For the earliest policy papers, see William Allen White Papers, box 13, LOC.
56. The ad ran in the *New York Post*, June 10, 1940. For more, see Alonso, *Robert E. Sherwood*, 214–15.
57. Press conference of June 11, 1940, FDRL; "Stop Hitler Now Poster Approved by Mr. Roosevelt," *MG*, June 12, 1940; "Roosevelt Praises 'Stop Hitler' Ad," *NYT*, June 12, 1940; "'Stop Hitler' Drive in America Ridiculed by Press in Germany," *CT*, June 14, 1940.
58. "Stop Hitler Now—The Negro Must Help," Ralph Bunche for the CDAAA, June 1940, available at https://oac.cdlib.org/ark:/13030/hb2r29n9z2/?order=1&brand=oac4&doc.view=mets; "The War Concerns All of Us," *BAA*, June 1, 1940; Charles P. Howard, "Not for Democracy but for Self-Preservation," *Atlanta Daily World*, June 27, 1940.
59. Henry L. Stimson and McGeorge Bundy, *On Active Service in Peace and War* (Harper & Brothers, 1947), 318–20.

60. "Cabinet Changes Stun Senate," *NYT*, June 21, 1940; "GOP Reads Knox, Stimson Out of Party," *WP*, June 21, 1940; "Bitter Debate Rages in Senate but Confirmation Is Expected," *WP*, June 21, 1940; "Statements of Stimson and Knox Before Senate Groups," *NYT*, July 3, 1940; "Mr. Stimson and Mr. Knox," *NYT*, July 3, 1940; "The Gallup Poll: Naming of Knox and Stimson to Cabinet Approved by Large Vote," *WP*, July 5, 1940; "Stimson Approved by Vote of 56–28," *NYT*, July 10, 1940; "Senate Seats Knox by Vote of 66 to 16," *WP*, July 11, 1940. Grenville Clark as well as Felix Frankfurter had been pushing for Stimson for some months. See Freedman, ed., *Roosevelt and Frankfurter*, 521, 524–25, 530.
61. Speech to Veterans of Foreign Wars, June 19, 1940, in Larry Bland, ed., *The Papers of George Catlett Marshall*, vol. 2 (Johns Hopkins University Press, 1986), 247–49. On Marshall's worries about conscription, see Pogue, *Ordeal and Hope*, 568.
62. "Plattsburg Group Asks Conscription," *NYT*, May 23, 1940; "Asks for Training Here for 3,000,000 Men," *NYT*, May 26, 1940; "Drive Is Started for Conscription," *NYT*, June 4, 1940.
63. FDR's May 18, 1940, letter to Clark is in *FDR: His Personal Letters*, vol. 2, 1026. "Giant Army Is Aim," *NYT*, June 21, 1940; "Senate Gets Compulsory Military Service Bill," *WP*, June 21, 1940; "Senators Warn That War Bluff May Be Called," *CT*, June 13, 1940; "Explains Reasons for Training Bill," *NYT*, July 21, 1940; "Charges Slush Fund Raising to Promote Draft," *CT*, Aug. 7, 1940; "Norris Smashes at Draft; Warns of Dictatorship," *CT*, Aug. 13, 1940. The definitive work on this subject is J. Garry Clifford and Samuel R. Spencer, Jr., *The First Peacetime Draft* (University Press of Kansas, 1986).
64. On Hearst, see "America Should Adopt Swiss Plan for Training Youth," *SFE*, June 9, 1940, and his numerous later columns. "Dr. Butler Warns of Threat to U.S.," *NYT*, Jan. 23, 1940; "Dr. Butler Sees U.S. As World Leader," *NYT*, Mar. 11, 1940; "Harvard Men See Vast U.S. Changes," *NYT*, May 18, 1940. Yale president Charles Seymour lent his support, too: "Open Aid to Allies Urged by Seymour," *NYT*, June 5, 1940; "Yale Head Urges U.S. Aid," *WP*, June 5, 1940; "Columbia Moves to Aid U.S. Defense," *NYT*, July 4, 1940; "Dr. Butler Warns His Faculty Not to Abuse Academic Freedom," *NYT*, Oct. 4, 1940. On the poll numbers, see Langer and Gleason, *The Challenge to Isolation*, 680.
65. "U.S. Must Aid Allies at Once, Conant Says," *WP*, May 30, 1940; "College Drive Due for Preparedness," *NYT*, June 7, 1940; "Dr. Conant Urges Universal Service," *NYT*, June 13, 1940; "Pershing, Conant Back Training Bill," *NYT*, July 4, 1940; "Gen. Pershing, Conant Urge Citizen Army," *WP*, July 4, 1940; "For Military Training," *NYT* editorial, July 5, 1940. For a detailed study, see J. Garry Clifford and Samuel R. Spencer Jr., *The First Peacetime Draft* (University Press of Kansas, 1986).
66. Cantril, *Public Opinion*, polls of June 11, Sept. 17, and Nov. 19, 1940, 971–73.
67. Walter Lippmann, "The Economic Consequences of a German Victory," *Life*, July 22, 1940; Robert Sherwood, "Rush All Possible Aid to Britain," *Reader's Digest*, Sept. 1940, CDAAA Papers, box 35, Seeley Mudd Library, Princeton University.
68. Rosenman, *Working with Roosevelt*, 193; Joseph Lash, *Roosevelt and Churchill, 1939–1941* (Norton, 1976), 168; Ickes, *Secret Diary*, vol. 3, 222.
69. On the various Republican aspirants and Willkie's path to the nomination, see Jeffries, *A Third Term for FDR*, 39–77. For a thoughtful and lively assessment, see David Levering Lewis, *The Improbable Wendell Willkie* (Liveright, 2018).
70. Ickes, *Secret Diary*, vol. 3, 221, 268, 290; Kirchwey, "Willkie and Appeasement," *Nation*, Sept. 14, 1940.
71. Excerpts from the Press Conference in Hyde Park, New York, July 5, 1940, at APP.
72. The text of the July 18 radio address to the convention is at APP. The description of the hall during the speech is in Sidney M. Shalett, "But Silence Came as the Leader Spoke," *NYT*, July 19, 1940. The story of the convention itself, with the prolonged and bitter dispute over putting Wallace on the ticket, can be followed in James MacGregor Burns, *Roosevelt: Lion and the Fox*, 422–30; Jeffries, *A Third Term for FDR*, 78–120; Moe, *Roosevelt's Second Act*, 212–46; Smith, *FDR*, 456-63; Rosenman, *Working with Roosevelt*, 200–21; Goodwin, *No Ordinary Time*, 106–36. The memos that MacLeish and Frankfurter sent can be seen in *Roosevelt and Frankfurter*, 530–35.
73. Kimball, ed., *Churchill and Roosevelt*, Churchill messages of June 11, 1940 and June 15, 1940, 43, 49–51. For careful examination of Anglo-American diplomacy around the destroyers issue, see Reynolds, *The Creation of the Anglo-American Alliance*, 114–32.
74. Churchill to Roosevelt, July 31, 1940, in Kimball, ed., *Churchill and Roosevelt*, 56–57.

75. *FDR: His Personal Letters*, vol. 2, memorandum of Aug. 2, 1940, 1050–51; Ickes, *Secret Diary*, vol. 3, 288–93.
76. The press releases, pamphlets, and speeches of summer 1940 on behalf of White's committee can be found in CDAAA Papers, boxes 34, 35, and 36, Seeley Mudd Library, Princeton University; "Pershing Urges Naval Craft Be Sold to British," *CT*, Aug. 5, 1940. White's speech, "Destroyers for Britain," Aug. 22, 1940, and Kirchwey's speech, "The Traitor in Our Midst," Aug. 29, 1940, both in CDAAA Papers, box 35. On various signatories, see CDAA press release of Sept. 10, and on MacArthur, see press release of Sept. 15, 1940, CDAAA papers, box 36.
77. Stimson, *On Active Service*, 356–58.; "No Legal Bar Seen to Transfer of Destroyers," *NYT*, Aug. 11, 1940.
78. On the origins of the Century Group and its role, see Mark Lincoln Chadwin, *The Hawks of World War II* (University of North Carolina Press, 1968), 43–108; Johnstone, *Against Immediate Evil*, 90–109.
79. "U.S. War a Certainty," *SFE*, Aug. 8, 1940; Stimson, *On Active Service*, 358–59; Churchill, *Their Finest Hour*, 404; "The U.S. and the World," *Fortune*, Sept. 1940, 42.
80. "Willkie Drive 'Lagging' as Washington Sees it," *NYT*, Sept. 8, 1940; Ernest K. Lindley, "An Apparent Decline: What's Wrong with Willkie?" *WP*, Sept. 11, 1940. For the flip-flop on the ships, "Willkie Condemns Destroyers Trade," *NYT*, Sept. 7, 1940; "Willkie Calls Destroyer Deal 'Dictatorial,'" *WP*, Sept. 7, 1940; "Willkie Brands Destroyer Deal a Dictator's Act," *CT*, Sept. 7, 1940. On the appeasement charge, "Willkie Says That Roosevelt 'Promoted' the Munich Pact," *NYT*, Sept. 15, 1940; "Willkie Calls Roosevelt 'Appeaser,'" *WP*, Sept. 15, 1940.
81. "No Clear-Cut Issues," *WP*, Sept. 2, 1940; "Elections Opinions Shift," *NYT*, Sept. 13, 1940; "Roosevelt Passes Willkie in Survey," *NYT*, Sept. 20, 1940; "Willkie Predicts Dictatorship Here If Roosevelt Wins," *NYT*, Sept. 17, 1940; "Willkie Train Stoned in Michigan," *NYT*, Oct. 2, 1940; "Willkie Urges Aid to Britain Even If It Means 'Sacrifice,'" *WP*, Oct. 3, 1940. La Guardia's quip is in "Reuters Poll Sees Roosevelt Victory," *NYT*, Oct. 20, 1940.
82. "The Press vs. the Public," *New Republic*, Sept. 23, 1940; Dorothy Thompson, "The Presidential Election," *WP*, Oct. 9, 1940.
83. Drew Middleton, "Fiery Glow Turns London into Fantastic Dreamworld," *WP*, Sept. 8, 1940. Jimmy Sheean also reported from London: "London Raid Havoc Awes Witnesses," *NYT*, Sept. 9, 1940.
84. Edward R. Murrow, broadcasts of Sept. 10 and 25, 1940, in *This is London* (Simon & Schuster, 1941), 163, 188.
85. "West End's Shops in London Bombed," *NYT*, Sept. 18, 1940; "British Beat Off Seven Day Raids; Many Fire Bombs Fall on Capital," *WP*, Sept. 19, 1940; "Heavy Bombs Blast London in Worst Raid," *WP*, Sept. 25, 1940; "A Diary of the War," *MG*, Oct. 1, 1940; "Nazis Attack London Every Ten Minutes," *WP*, Oct. 8, 1940; "War's Worst Raid," *WP*, Oct. 9, 1940; "Nazis Hit 63 Areas," *NYT*, Oct. 15, 1940; "Evacuee Ship: Torpedoed Liner the City of Benares, *MG*, Sept. 25, 1940; "The Story of the City of Benares," *NYT*, March 8, 1942. On Fred Morley, see Claire Holland, "Face to Face with Yesterday's Heroes," *Financial Times*, Aug. 8, 2007.
86. "Roosevelt Moves," *NYT*, Sept. 27, 1940; and see William L. Langer and S. Everett Gleason, *The Undeclared War: 1940–1941* (Harper & Brothers, 1953), 23–32. The text of the Tripartite Pact directed at America was as follows: "Germany, Italy and Japan agree to . . . assist one another with all political, economic and military means when one of the three contracting powers is attacked by a power at present not involved in the European war or in the Chinese-Japanese conflict." For the documents on the export controls, see "Regulations Governing the Exportation of Articles and Materials Designated in the President's Proclamation of July 2, 1940," July 26, 1940, *FRUS Japan, 1931–1941,* vol. 2, 216–18; press release dated Sept. 26, 1940, *FRUS Japan, 1931–1941,* vol. 2, 222-23; and "Regulations Governing the Exportation of Articles and Materials Designated in the President's Proclamation of July 26, 1940," Sept. 30, 1940, *FRUS Japan, 1931–1941,* vol. 2, 223.
87. "Address on Hemisphere Defense," Oct. 12, 1940, in *PP&A*, 1940, 460–67; "Our Help-Britain Policy in a More Active Phase," *NYT*, Oct. 20, 1940; "Public Favors Firmer Stand on Japan," *WP*, Oct. 20, 1940. The Oct. 6 rally at the World's Fair site was called "American Defenders Day." For Lehman's speech there, see CDAAA Papers, box 36.
88. "The Gallup Poll," *WP*, Oct. 18, 1940; "3d Term, War Issues Indicate Close Election," *CT*, Oct. 20, 1940; "Roosevelt to Make Political Tour, with 5 Major Speeches," *NYT*, Oct. 18, 1940.
89. Rosenman, *Working with Roosevelt*, 232, 234; FDR speech, "Statement on Columbus Day," available at APP.

90. Jeffries, *A Third Term*, 156–65; "Texts of President Roosevelt's Speeches at the Garden Rally and During His City Tour," *NYT*, Oct. 29, 1940; Churchill to Roosevelt, Oct. 27, 1940, in Kimball, ed., *Churchill and Roosevelt*, 79–80; "Campaign Address at Boston, Massachusetts," Oct. 30, 1940, at APP.
91. Rosenman, *Working for Roosevelt*, 247–48. Thompson's contribution can be assessed by comparing her notes to the text FDR actually read. See her memo of Nov. 1, 1940, to Harry Hopkins in Papers of Harry L. Hopkins Papers, box 123, President's Speeches and Speech Material, 1940 Campaign, FDRL.
92. Speech of Nov. 2, 1940, FDR's reading copy in Master Speech File, box 56, FDRL.

Chapter 16: Everywhere in the World

1. FDR to Sam Rosenman, Nov. 13, 1940, in *FDR: Private Letters*, vol. 2, 1078.
2. On Roosevelt's discomfort throughout the 1940 election, see Sherwood, *Roosevelt and Hopkins*, 246–47.
3. The key works in the anti-FDR catalogue are Charles Beard, *President Roosevelt and the Coming of the War, 1941* (Yale University Press, 1948); and Charles C. Tansill, *Back Door to War: The Roosevelt Foreign Policy, 1933–1941* (Henry Regnery, 1952). Both authors were acerbic critics of the New Deal and FDR generally; Tansill's publisher, Regnery, became the home of many right-wing authors including Russell Kirk, William F. Buckley, James Burnham, and Robert Welch, the founder of the John Birch Society. The "back door to war" thesis, refined by additional research and shorn of its ideological dimension, still has its defenders. See John M. Schuessler, "The Deception Dividend: FDR's Undeclared War," *International Security* 34, no. 4 (2010): 133–65; Marc Trachtenberg, "Developing an Interpretation Through Textual Analysis: The 1941 Case," ch. 4, in *The Craft of International History* (Princeton University Press, 2006), 79–139; and his long contribution, titled "Dan Reiter and America's Road to War in 1941," in an online roundtable, "Democracy, Deception, and Entry into War," H-Diplo, May 17, 2013, at https://issforum.org/roundtables/5-4-democracy-deception-war. Warren Kimball, who studied the subject as thoroughly as anyone, concluded: "No evidence has surfaced to demonstrate that Roosevelt lied actively and consistently to the American people about his ultimate intentions, and there are good reasons to conclude that he wishfully hoped that the United States could (or would have to) fight a limited war with only naval and air forces engaged against the Germans." Kimball, "Franklin D. Roosevelt and World War II," *Presidential Studies Quarterly* 34, no. 1 (2004): 83–99. For a well-researched account of the two years before the outbreak of war, see David Kaiser, *No End Save Victory: How FDR Led the Nation into War* (Basic Books, 2014). Another careful study is Waldo Heinrichs, *Threshold of War: Franklin D. Roosevelt and American Entry into World War II* (Oxford University Press, 1988); though chronologically limited to the months between March and December 1941, Heinrich's work is global in scope. An earlier investigation that drew heavily from the Morgenthau and Stimson diaries to illuminate FDR's slow and improvisational rearmament strategy, is William L. Langer and S. Everett Gleason, *The Undeclared War, 1940–1941* (Harper & Brothers, 1953). A well-crafted summary of the main lines of great power diplomacy in 1940–1941 is in Brendan Simms and Charlie Laderman, *Hitler's American Gamble: Pearl Harbor and Germany's March to Global War* (Basic Books, 2021), 1–86.
4. Stimson to Roosevelt, "Preliminary Report of Generals [George] Strong and [Carelton] Emmons," Oct. 9, 1940, PSF, box 84, War—Stimson, 1940–41, FDRL.
5. Churchill to Roosevelt, Oct. 27 and Nov. 6, 1940, in Kimball, ed., *Churchill and Roosevelt*, 79–81.
6. Press conference, Nov. 8, 1940, FDRL; Ickes, *Secret Diary*, vol. 3, 367.
7. "Memorandum for the Secretary," Nov. 4, 1940, box 59, Navy—Nov.–Dec. 1940, FDRL. The final version, dated Nov. 12, 1940, was referred to as the Plan Dog memorandum. (Because options A, B, and C were considered and rejected, Stark chose D; hence Dog.) PSF, box 4, Navy Department, "Plan Dog," FDRL.
8. "White Requests Aid for Britain on Wider Basis," *NYHT*, Nov. 17, 1940; "Conant Urges U.S. to Clarify Its War Stand," *NYHT*, Nov. 21, 1940. The full texts of their speeches are in Papers of the CDAAA, box 38, Seeley Mudd Library, Princeton University.
9. "All U.S. Resources for Britain Urged," *NYT*, Nov. 26, 1940.
10. Press conference, Nov. 22, 1940, FDRL; Harold Ickes, *Secret Diary*, vol. 3, 375. Data on aircraft production and deliveries: "Progress Report on National Defense Program, March 31, 1941," PSF, box 94, Bureau of the Budget, FDRL.

11. Stimson Diary, vol. 32, Dec. 3, 1940, 10–12.
12. "Meeting re British Purchasing Program," Dec. 3, 1940, Morgenthau Diary, vol. 335, 97–136, FDRL.
13. The December 7, 1940, telegram is in Kimball, ed., *Churchill and Roosevelt*, 102–9. According to the U.S. State Department, "This message was sent as a telegram from London on December 7, 1940, to the British Ambassador in Washington, who was instructed to transmit it to the Department with the request that the message be forwarded by plane to President Roosevelt, who was on a cruise in the Caribbean." Churchill to Roosevelt, *FRUS 1940*, vol. 3, footnote 27, 18–19. Warren Kimball points out that the impact of this telegram has been "somewhat exaggerated," since FDR already knew about Britain's financial predicament and had already told his cabinet to work on a solution. *Churchill and Roosevelt*, 88. Still, the memo brilliantly summarized the global implications of Britain's desperate position in late 1940.
14. Sherwood, *Roosevelt and Hopkins*, 224.
15. Press conference, Dec. 17, 1940, FDRL. The Ickes letter, dated Aug. 2, 1940, is in Interior—Ickes, Aug.–Dec. 1940, PSF, box 55, FDRL. Ickes wrote that America was like a "householder who refuses to lend or sell his fire extinguishers to help put out the fire in the house that is right next door, although that house is all ablaze and the wind is blowing from that direction." The foundational work on Lend-Lease remains Warren F. Kimball, *The Most Unsordid Act: Lend-lease, 1939–1941* (Johns Hopkins Press, 1969).
16. Stimson Diary, Dec. 16, 17, 18, and 19, 1940, vol. 32, 32–43, 46–47. "Hillman, Stimson and Knox Also Named to Office of Production: Knudsen Appointed Armament Chief 4-Man Board to Have Full Authority over Defense Production," *WP*, Dec. 21, 1940.
17. Sherwood, *Roosevelt and Hopkins*, 226; Rosenman, *Working with Roosevelt*, 256–62; Fireside Chat, Dec. 29, 1940, APP.
18. "Roosevelt Calls for Greater Aid to Britain," *NYT*, Dec. 30, 1940; "Press Hails Outline of American Policies," *LAT*, Dec. 30, 1940; "Crisis 'Serious as War Itself,' Confronts Nation," *WP*, Dec. 30, 1940.
19. "Tells Story of Biggest London Fire since 1666," *CT*, Dec. 31, 1940; also "London 'City' Ravaged, Bombs Destroy Guildhall," *NYHT*, Dec. 31, 1940. Murrow, *This is London*, Dec. 29 and 31, 1940, 224–28.
20. Rosenman on the dictation of the Four Freedoms, *Working with Roosevelt*, 262–63; the text of the speech, "Annual Message to Congress on the State of the Union [Four Freedoms Speech]," Jan. 6, 1941, is at APP.
21. H.R. 1776, Mar. 11, 1941, "An Act to Promote the Defense of the United States," 55 Stat. 31 (Pub. Law 77-11), 77th Congress, 1st Session, 31–33.
22. Wood circulated in booklet form a statement by the AFC on foreign policy: Robert E. Wood, "Our Foreign Policy," speech delivered to the Council on Foreign Relations, Oct. 4, 1940, America First Committee, 1940.The essential works on the America First Committee include Justus D. Doenecke, ed., *In Danger Undaunted: The Anti-Interventionist Movement of 1940–1941 as Revealed in the Papers of the America First Committee* (Hoover Institution Press, 1990), and his *Storm on the Horizon*; and Wayne S. Cole, *America First: The Battle Against Isolation, 1940–1941* (University of Wisconsin Press, 1953). A more recent narrative of the debate over intervention is H. W. Brands, *America First: Roosevelt vs. Lindbergh in the Shadow of War* (Doubleday, 2024). For Hearst's support, see "America First," editorial in *SFE*, Sept. 21, 1941.
23. *Lend-Lease Bill: Hearings before the United States House Committee on Foreign Affairs*, Seventy-Seventh Congress, First Session, on H.R. 1776, Jan. 15–18, 21–25, 29, 1941 (Government Printing Office, 1941), Testimony of Henry Stimson, Jan. 16, 1941, 85–155; and Stimson, *On Active Service*, 362. For the coordinating of testimony, see Stimson Diary, vol. 32, Dec. 1940–Jan. 1941, 105.
24. *Lend-Lease Bill*, Testimony of Charles Lindbergh, Jan. 23, 1941, 371–436; and "Lindbergh Praised by Reich Official," *NYT*, Jan. 25, 1941; "Lindbergh Says Britain Can't Beat Hitler Even with U.S. Aid Unless Nazis Collapse," *NYHT*, Jan. 24, 1941; "Urges Neutrality," *NYT*, Jan. 24, 1941.
25. *Lend-Lease Bill*, Testimony of Dorothy Thompson, Jan. 25, 1941, 644–57. For a brief summary of the hearings, Langer and Gleason, *Undeclared War*, 253–81.
26. *To Promote the Defense of the United States: Hearings before the Committee on Foreign Relations, United States Senate*, Seventy-Seventh Congress, First Session on S. 275 (Government Printing Office, 1941), Testimony of Reinhold Niebuhr, 169–75.
27. *To Promote the Defense*, Testimony of Robert McCormick and Kingman Brewster, 477–89, 612–21. On "war dictatorship bill," Arthur Sears Henning, "Sees Next Nazi Blow Thru Bulgaria," *CT*, Feb. 10, 1941.

28. *To Promote the Defense*, Testimony of Robert Wood and Hanford MacNider, 342–98; 560–67.
29. *To Promote the Defense*, Testimony of Charles Lindbergh, 490–560; "Lindbergh Talks Again," *LAT*, Feb. 7, 1941; "Lindbergh Says Fall of England Is Last Thing He Wants to See," *NYHT*, Feb. 7, 1941; "Social Leaders Attend Lend-Lease Hearings," *WP*, Feb. 6, 1941.
30. Press conference, Jan. 14, 1941, FDRL; "Wheeler Accuses President of Trying to Discredit Him," *LAT*, Feb. 2, 1941; "Senator Says President Wages Slanderous Campaign on Him," *NYHT*, Feb. 2, 1941; "President Clashes with Wheeler," *LAT*, Feb. 5, 1941; "Wheeler Jousts with President," *NYT*, Feb. 5, 1941; "Allies Credited in Spurt of U.S. Plane Facilities," *NYT*, Feb. 7, 1941.
31. "Senators Attack Lend-Lease Bill," *NYT*, Feb. 2, 1941; "Aid will Put Us in War, Senate Critics Say," *WP*, Feb. 19, 1941; "Nye: 30 Senators for War," *CT*, Feb. 21, 1941; "Warns Dictator Bill Will Leave Us One Word: Ja!" *CT*, Feb. 25, 1941.
32. On Dilling, see Glen Jeansonne, *Women of the Far Right: The Mothers' Movement and World War II* (University of Chicago Press, 1996). The press coverage was extensive. "Seek Petticoat Brigade to Fight Dictator Bill," *CT*, Feb. 7, 1941; "Women on Knees at Capitol to Halt War Bill," *CT*, Feb. 20, 1941; "Capital Police Seize Effigy of Woman Writer," *CT*, Feb. 24, 1941; "Glass Asks FBI Inquiry on 'Sit-Down' by Women," *LAT*, Mar. 1, 1941; "Two Women Are Fined for Senate Disorder," *NYT*, Mar. 7, 1941; "Seek to Inject Anti-Semitism into Hearings on Lend-Lease Bill," *Jewish Advocate*, Mar. 14, 1941.
33. "Nye: 30 Senators for War," *CT*, Feb. 21, 1941; "Wheeler Asserts Aid Bill Seeks War and Dictatorship," *NYT*, Mar. 1, 1941. On Wheeler's antisemitic remarks: "Strange Company," American Israelite, Mar. 6, 1941; "Statesmen—Or Rabble Rousers," American Israelite, Mar. 13, 1941. On McWilliams, see Robert Lewis Taylor, "The Kampf of Joe McWilliams," *New Yorker*, Aug. 16, 1940.
34. "Senate Hears 'Fight If We Must!'" *LAT*, Feb. 18, 1941; "Bailey Backs Aid Even If Axis Sees Act of War by U.S.," *NYT*, Feb. 20, 1941; "Senate Poll Shows 52 Members Back Aid-to-Britain," *NYT*, Feb. 23, 1941.
35. "Lindbergh and Coughlin Called Fascist Spark Plugs by Ickes," *LAT*, Nov. 21, 1940; "Ickes Warns of Propagandists," *NYT*, Nov. 21, 1940; "Ickes Says U.S. Contains Many Potential Lavals," *NYHT*, Dec. 18, 1940; Herbert Agar, "Who Are the Appeasers," *Nation*, Mar. 22, 1941; *Des Moines Register*, Mar. 22, 1941, Fight for Freedom Papers, box 55, Seeley Mudd Library, Princeton University.
36. Dorothy Thompson, "On the Record: Foreign Policy and Native Fascism," *NYHT*, Feb. 17, 1941.
37. The essay appeared in *Life* on Feb. 17, 1941; for a reprint, see "The American Century," *Diplomatic History* 23, no. 2 (1999): 159–71. On the reception of the piece, see Alan Brinkley, *The Publisher: Henry Luce and the American Century* (Random House, 2010), 267–73.
38. FDR to Churchill, Jan. 20, 1941, in Kimball, ed., *Churchill and Roosevelt*, 131; "President Cordial," *NYT*, Jan 20, 1941; "Willkie Pays Visit to Coventry's Ruins," *NYT*, Feb. 3, 1941.
39. "Willkie Rallies Republican Party to Fight for Cause of Freedom," *NYHT*, Feb. 13, 1941; "Willkie's Speech at Lincoln Day Dinner," *NYHT*, Feb. 13, 1941; "Willkie Appeal Widely Praised in Party Ranks," *NYHT*, Feb. 14, 1941.
40. "Lend-Lease Bill Passes Senate, 60-31," *NYHT*, Mar. 9, 1941; "Every Curb Beaten, Roosevelt Gets All Powers He Sought," *WP*, Mar. 9, 1941; "Final Step Swift," *NYT*, Mar. 12, 1941; "War-Aid Bill Signed and Put into Effect," *LAT*, Mar. 12, 1941.
41. "Address at the Annual Dinner of White House Correspondents' Association," Mar. 15, 1941, APP.
42. White wrote to CDAAA board member Lew Douglas, explaining his position and offering to resign, White to Douglas, Dec. 28, 1940, William Allen White Papers, box 14, LOC. The CDAAA rushed out a statement denying a schism and restating its position on aid to Britain: "Statement Adopted by the Advisory Policy Committee," Dec. 30, 1940, "Miscellaneous Letters and Publications of the CDAAA," University of Virgina Special Collections Library. The press covered the shakeup widely: "White's Group to Restate Aim of Aid to British," *NYHT*, Dec. 30, 1940; "White Gives Up Chairmanship, Stays on Aid-for-Allies Board, *NYT*, Jan. 3, 1941; "White Charges War Activity in Aid Allies Body," *CT*, Jan. 6, 1941.
43. Thompson to Helen Rogers Reid, Nov. 10, 1940, Jan. 8, 1941, and Jan. 23, 1941, Reid Family Papers, D254, LOC. Her note of Jan. 29, 1941, to Eleanor Roosevelt is in Dorothy Thompson Papers, box 35, Syracuse University.
44. News release, Apr. 19, 1941, Fight for Freedom Papers, box 56, Seeley Mudd Library, Princeton University.

45. Fight for Freedom press release, Apr. 20, 1941, Fight for Freedom Papers, box 56, Seeley G. Mudd Library, Princeton University.
46. "Wheeler: Quit War Meddling," *CT*, Apr. 16, 1941; "Unite for Peace! Wheeler Urges," *CT*, Apr. 17, 1941; "Lindbergh Is Criticized," *NYT*, Apr. 20, 1941. On the extensive British propaganda campaign in the U.S., see Jennet Conant, *The Irregulars: Roald Dahl and the British Spy Ring in Wartime Washington* (Simon & Schuster, 2008), and Thomas E. Mahl, *Desperate Deception: British Covert Operations in the United States, 1939–44* (Brassey's, 1998).
47. "Lindbergh's Anti-War Plea Draws 25,000," *NYHT*, Apr. 24, 1941; "Crowd Beats Lindbergh's Detractors," *WP*, Apr. 24, 1941; "Text of Col. Lindbergh's Address at Rally of America First," *NYT*, Apr. 24, 1941.
48. Press conference of Apr. 25, 1941, FDRL; "Roosevelt Compares Lindbergh to 'Copperheads' of Civil War," *NYHT*, Apr. 26, 1941; "President Defines Lindbergh's Niche," *NYT*, Apr. 26, 1941.
49. "Lindbergh Quits Air Corps; Sees His Loyalty Questioned," *NYT*, Apr. 29, 1941; "Wheeler Assails 'Copperhead' as Lindbergh Tag," *NYHT*, Apr. 28, 1941. Hearst's San Francisco Examiner printed banner headlines about FDR's "attack." "2 Senators Score Roosevelt Attack on Lindbergh," *SFE*, Apr. 30, 1941.
50. "Lindbergh, Wheeler Call for Leadership," *WP*, May 24, 1941; "Texts of the Address by Lindbergh and Wheeler," *NYT*, May 24, 194; "Our Way of Life at Stake," *SFE*, May 24, 1941; "Lindbergh Says World Power Is Roosevelt's Aim, Not Hitler's," *NYHT*, May 30, 1941; "Administration Leading U.S. Toward War with Empty Gun, Lindbergh Warns Nation," *WP*, June 16, 1941.
51. As Robert Sherwood pointed out, "One has only to read Henry Stimson's record of his own profound dissatisfaction in this spring of 1941 to know how sorely Roosevelt tried the tempers of those trusted advisers who were urging him that the time had passed when 'all aid short of war' was enough." *Roosevelt and Hopkins*, 230. Stimson Diary, Dec. 29, 1940, and Jan. 22, 1941, vol. 32, Dec 1940–Jan 1941; Diary, Mar. 24 and Apr. 9, 1941, vol. 33, Feb.–April 1941; and Stimson, *On Active Service*, 366–71.
52. Walter Lippmann, "The President," *NYHT*, Apr. 19, 1941.
53. Ickes, *Secret Diary*, vol. 3, 458–59, 466, 470, 485, 506–7, 511; "fire the first shot," 523. Stimson deplored FDR's attitude of waiting for the Germans to make a mistake, triggering war. He wanted a firmer declaration of principles. Stimson Diary, vol. 34, May–June 1941, May 23 and 24, 1941.
54. Public Opinion Polls—Subject File, PSF, box 175, FDRL; George Gallup, "Gallup Polls April–October 1941," at Teaching American History, https://teachingamericanhistory.org/document/gallup-polls-april-october-1941; "The Fortune Survey," *Fortune*, April 1941, 102–4.
55. "Radio Address Announcing an Unlimited National Emergency," May 27, 1941, APP.
56. Stimson diary, vol. 34, May–July 1941, May 27 and 29, 1941; Ickes, *Secret Diary*, vol. 3, 526–27.
57. "The Fight for Freedom," *Fortune*, June 1941, 58–59; Walter Lippmann, "America's Greatest Mistake," *Life*, July 21, 1941, 74–80.
58. For a damning investigation of the aircraft industry, see the pamphlet circulated by the National Negro Congress, Los Angeles Council, "Jim Crow in National Defense," (1941), in Gale digital collection *Political Extremism and Radicalism.*
59. "'Defense Rotten'—Randolph," *PC*, Jan. 25, 1941. See the biographical sketch in "A. Philip Randolph: Who Is This Man?" *NYAN*, July 5, 1941. Also David Lucander, *Winning the War for Democracy: The March on Washington Movement, 1941–1946* (University of Illinois Press, 2014); and Cornelius L. Bynum, *A. Philip Randolph and the Struggle for Civil Rights* (University of Illinois Press, 2010).
60. A. Philip Randolph, "The Negro Faces the Future," *NYAN*, Feb. 8, 1941, and "England's Fight Our Cause," *PC*, Feb. 8, 1941; "Mrs. Bethune Urges All-Out Aid to Britain," *New Journal and Guide*, Feb. 15, 1941. "Communists Not Wanted in March to Washington, Declares Randolph," *NYAN*, June 21, 1941. John P. Davis of the Communist-led National Negro Congress opposed Lend-Lease and any cooperation in defense of imperialism and Jim Crow. "David Decries U.S. Bias at Negro Congress Meet," *CD*, Mar. 15, 1941. The issue divided African American intellectuals. See Daniel W. Aldridge III, "A War for the Colored Races: Anti-Interventionism and the African American Intelligentsia, 1939–1941," *Diplomatic History* 28, no. 3 (2004): 321–52.
61. A. Philip Randolph, "Defense Rotten," *PC*, Jan. 25, 1941; "Plans Made for 50,000 to March on Washington," *New Journal and Guide*, May 17, 1941; "March on Washington Drive Draws Nationwide Response," *NYAN*, June 7, 1941; "Industry's Failure to Use Negro Labor Held Defect in U.S. Defense," *New Journal and Guide*, June 14, 1941.

62. A. Philip Randolph to Eleanor Roosevelt, June 5, 1941; ER to Randolph, June 10, 1941, in Selected Digitized Correspondence of Eleanor Roosevelt, 1933–1945, FDRL. ER's letter was published in the press: "Administration Seeks to Curb D.C. March," *Atlanta Daily World*, June 18, 1941.
63. For a detailed account of the meeting with FDR, see "Pres. Roosevelt Opposes March," *Atlanta Daily World*, June 24, 1941. A survey of this topic is given in Kevin M. Burke, Robert Heinrich, and Steven J. Niven, "The Roosevelts and African American Civil Rights Leaders," a report of the Hutchins Center for African and African American Research at Harvard University, and part of the exhibition at the Roosevelt Presidential Library, *Black Civil Rights Leaders and the Roosevelts*.
64. "President Orders an Even Break for Minorities in Defense Jobs," *NYT*, June 26, 1941; "Executive Act Halts March of 100,000 to Capital," *NYAN*, June 28, 1941. For the text of the order: "Executive Order 8802 (1941)," in C. E. Cortés, ed., *Multicultural America: A Multimedia Encyclopedia*, vol. 4 (SAGE, 2013): 852–53.
65. "Yarnell Asks U.S. to Enter War Now," *NYT*, June 8, 1941; "Cornell Record Set with Class of 1,001 Seniors," *NYHT*, June 17, 1941.
66. "Chase Sees Fight for Human Spirit," *NYT*, June 12, 1941.
67. "Jackson Says a Hitler Victory Would Mean Sad Future for U.S.," *NYHT*, June 6, 1941; "Radcliffe Class Hears Address by Frankfurter," *NYHT*, June 19, 1941.
68. "Stimson's Address at West Point," *NYT*, June 12, 1941.
69. Charles Bolté, "Letter to President Roosevelt," *Dartmouth Alumni Magazine*, June 1941, 24–25. On Bolté's postwar work, see "The New Veteran," *Life*, Dec. 10, 1945.
70. Stimson diary, vol. 34, May–July 1941, June 22 and 23, 1941; Knox to Roosevelt, June 23, 1941, PSF, box 62, Navy-Know, Frank, 1939–1941, FDRL.
71. Roosevelt to Admiral William Leahy, then ambassador to Vichy France, June 26, 1941, PSF, box 29, France-1941, FDRL.
72. Memo on FDR conversation with Ambassador Konstantin Umansky, July 10, 1941, *FRUS 1941*, vol. 1, 788–89. Report on Lindbergh's speech in *SFE*, July 2, 1941; "U.S. Aid to Red Barbarism Hit by Lindbergh," *CT*, July 2, 1941. Press conference, June 24, 1941, FDRL; Memo by Sumner Welles, Acting Secretary of State, June 26, 1941, *FRUS 1941*, vol. 1, 769–72; Steinhardt to Welles, June 29, 1941, *FRUS 1941*, vol. 1, 774–75. For the Lend-Lease debate on Russia, see Kimball, *Most Unsordid Act*, 200, 216.
73. "Lindbergh Called a Nazi Tool by Ickes," *NYT*, July 15, 1941; "Ostriches Named for Isolationists at Patriotic Rally," *NYHT*, July 14, 1941.
74. "The Presidency," *Time*, July 14, 1941; "Landing of American Troops in Iceland," Roosevelt to Congress, July 7, 1941, *PP&A, 1941*, 255–64.
75. FDR's address to the nation, July 4, 1941, at https://www.nationalww2museum.org/war/articles/july-4-1941-fdrs-address-nation; "President Roosevelt's Radio Speech," *WP*, July 5, 1951.
76. "Capitol Hill Is Pressed to Hold Draftees," *NYHT*, July 16, 1941; "General Marshall's Testimony," *NYT*, July 16, 1941; "Marshall Asks Emergency Law," *NYT*, July 18, 1941; "President Is Grave," *NYT*, July 22, 1941; "Marshall Sways Group on Army's Danger," *NYT*, July 24, 1941; "Bill Wins by 45–30," *NYT*, Aug. 8, 1941; "House 203–202 Extends Service of All in Army by Year and a Half," *NYHT*, Aug. 13, 1941.
77. Akira Iriye, *The Origins of the Second World War in Asia and the Pacific* (Longman, 1987), 146–50; Frank, *Tower of Skulls*, 184–98.
78. Sherwood, *Roosevelt and Hopkins*, 319, and for the story of Hopkins's visit to Britain, 308–22; "Hopkins Pledges to Help Russians," *NYT*, July 28, 1941.
79. Details on the trip to Moscow in Sherwood, *Roosevelt and Hopkins*, 323–48.
80. Hopkins memorandums for the State Department, dated Sept. 5, 1941, of the meetings on July 30 and 31, 1941, *FRUS 1941*, vol. 1, 802–14. For Hopkins's description of Stalin: Sherwood, *Roosevelt and Hopkins*, 343–44.
81. Sherwood, *Roosevelt and Hopkins*, 351.
82. Details on the meeting are in Theodore A. Wilson, *The First Summit: Roosevelt and Churchill at Placentia Bay, 1941* (University of Kansas Press, 1991); Warren Kimball, *The Juggler: Franklin Roosevelt as Wartime Statesman* (Princeton University Press, 1991), 53–55, 132–39; Heinrichs, *Threshold of War*, 144–61. For an important effort to connect the Atlantic Charter to the New Deal, see Elizabeth Borgwardt, *A New Deal for the World: America's Vision for Human Rights* (Harvard University Press, 2007).
83. Documents on the Atlantic Conference are in *FRUS 1941*, vol. 1, 341–72.

84. "The Meeting with President Roosevelt," Aug. 24, 1941, radio broadcast, in Charles Eade, ed., *The War Speeches of the Rt. Hon. Winston S. Churchill*, vol. 2 (Cassell, 1952), 59–66.
85. "President Roosevelt's Message to Congress on the Atlantic Charter," Aug. 21, 1941, Avalon Project, Yale Law School, https://avalon.law.yale.edu/wwii/atcmess.asp.
86. "Joint Statement of President Roosevelt and Prime Minister Churchill," Aug. 14, 1941, *FRUS 1941*, vol. 1, 367–69.

BIBLIOGRAPHY

MANUSCRIPT SOURCES

Brandeis University Library

Rabbi Stephen Wise Papers (microfilm)

Columbia University Library Oral History Collection

Adolph A. Berle
Anna Roosevelt Halsted
Florence Jaffray Harriman
Walter Lippmann
Frances Perkins
Samuel Rosenman
Rexford G. Tugwell
James P. Warburg

Franklin D. Roosevelt Library (FDRL), Hyde Park, NY

Eleanor Roosevelt Selected Correspondence, 1933–1945
Master Speech File
Presidential Press Conferences
President's Official File (OF)
President's Personal File (PPF)
President's Secretary's Files (PSF)
Personal Papers at FDRL:
Adolph A. Berle Papers
Democratic National Committee Papers
Harry L. Hopkins Papers
R. Walton Moore Papers
Henry Morgenthau Jr. Diaries
Myron Taylor Papers
Rexford G. Tugwell Papers
Sumner Welles Papers

Houghton Library, Harvard University

Pierrepont Moffat Papers
William Phillips Papers
Robert Sherwood Papers

Library of Congress, Washington, D.C.

Joseph Alsop Papers
Robert Bingham Papers
Raymond Clapper Papers
Benjamin V. Cohen Papers
Thomas G. Corcoran Papers
Joseph Davies Papers
Norman H. Davis Papers

William Dodd Papers
James Farley Papers
Herbert Feis Papers
Felix Frankfurter Papers
Breckinridge Long Papers
Henry R. Luce Papers
Archibald MacLeish Papers
Edgar Mowrer Papers
Helen Rogers Reid Papers
Donald Richberg Papers
Raymond Swing Papers
William Allen White Papers

National Archives and Records Administration, College Park, MD

RG 131 Office of Alien Property, General Records Seized from the German-American Bund, 1916–1942

Seeley G. Mudd Library, Princeton University

Hamilton Fish Armstrong Papers
Committee to Defend America by Aiding the Allies
Fight for Freedom
Louis Fischer Papers
George Kennan Papers

Smithsonian National Museum of American History

Father Charles E. Coughlin Collection

Syracuse University, Bird Library, Special Collections

Dorothy Thompson Papers

Yale University, Manuscripts and Archives, Sterling Library, New Haven, CT

William C. Bullitt Papers
Committee to Defend America Papers

University of Delaware Library, Special Collections, Newark, Delaware.

George S. Messersmith Papers

University of Virginia, Special Collections Library, Charlottesville, VA

Committee to Defend America Materials
Homer S. Cummings Papers
John Dos Passos Papers
Carter Glass Papers

PUBLISHED AND DIGITIZED DOCUMENTS

Bland, Larry I., ed. *The Papers of George Catlett Marshall.* Vols 1–6. Johns Hopkins University Press, 1981.

Cantril, Hadley. *Public Opinion, 1935–1946.* Princeton University Press, 1951.

Documentary History of the Franklin D. Roosevelt Presidency [abbr. *DHFDRP*], 40 vols., edited by George McJimsey (LexisNexis, 2001-06).

Documents on British Foreign Policy, 1919–1939. 2nd Series, vol. XXI. Her Majesty's Stationery Office, 1984.

Gale Primary Sources, Archives Unbound (digital collections).

———. *African America, Communists, and the National Negro Congress.*

———. *European Colonialism in the Early 20th Century: Italian Colonies in North Africa and Aggression in East Africa, 1930–1939.*

———. *FBI File on America First Committee.*

———. *Official and Confidential Files of FBI Director J. Edgar Hoover.*
———. *Political Extremism and Radicalism.*
Germany, Auswärtiges Amt. *Documents on German Foreign Policy, 1918–1945: Series C (1933–1937), the Third Reich, First Phase.* U.S. Government Printing Office, 1957.
Germany, Auswärtiges Amt., and Raymond J. Sontag, eds. *Nazi-Soviet Relations, 1939–1941: Documents from the Archives of the German Foreign Office.* Dept. of State, 1948.
Goeschel, Christian, Nikolaus Wachsmann, and Ewald Osers. *The Nazi Concentration Camps, 1933–1939: A Documentary History.* University of Nebraska Press, 2012.
Great Britain Foreign Office. *Documents on British Foreign Policy, 1919–1939.* Vols. 1–63. H. M. Stationery Office, 1946.
Hitler, Adolf, and Max Domarus. *Speeches and Proclamations, 1932–1945.* Bolchazy-Carducci, 1990.
Hoover, Herbert. *Campaign Speeches of 1932.* Doubleday, Doran, 1933.
Kimball, Warren, ed. *Churchill and Roosevelt: The Complete Correspondence.* Vol. 1. Princeton University Press, 1984.
Lester, Robert, and Dale Reynolds. *U.S. Military Intelligence Reports, Germany, 1919–1941.* University Publications of America, 1983 (microfilm).
McDonald, James G., and Karen J. Greenberg. *The James G. McDonald Papers.* Garland, 1990.
ProQuest, History Vault: *American Jewish Congress Records*: Administrative and Executive Committee, Governing Council, National Conventions, and Executive Director Files.
———. *Papers of the NAACP*, Part 07: The Anti-Lynching Campaign, 1912–1955.
———. *U.S. Military Intelligence Reports, 1911–1944.*
Roosevelt, Elliott, ed. *F.D.R. His Personal Letters.* 4 vols. Duell, Sloan, and Pearce, 1947–1950.
Roosevelt, Franklin D. *Nothing to Fear: The Selected Addresses of Franklin Delano Roosevelt, 1932–1945.* Books for Libraries Press, 1970.
Roosevelt, Franklin D., Edgar B. Nixon, ed., and Donald B. Schewe, ed. *Franklin D. Roosevelt and Foreign Affairs* [FDR&FA]. 17 vols. Belknap Press of Harvard University Press, 1969.
Roosevelt, Franklin D., and Samuel I. Rosenman, ed. *The Public Papers and Addresses of Franklin D. Roosevelt* [PP&A]. 9 vols. Random House, 1938–1950.
United States Commission on the Ukraine Famine. *Investigation of the Ukrainian Famine, 1932–1933: Report to Congress.* U.S. Government Printing Office, 1988.
United States Department of State. *Foreign Relations of the United States.* U.S. Government Printing Office.

MEMOIRS, DIARIES, LETTERS, AND CONTEMPORARY ACCOUNTS

Agar, Herbert. *A Time for Greatness.* Little, Brown, 1942.
Alsop, Joseph, and Robert Kintner. *Men Around the President.* Doubleday, Doran, 1939.
———. *American White Paper: The Story of American Diplomacy and the Second World War.* Simon & Schuster, 1940.
Armstrong, Hamilton Fish. *Peace and Counterpeace: From Wilson to Hitler: Memoirs of Hamilton Fish Armstrong.* Harper & Row, 1971.
Baker, Carlos, ed. *Ernest Hemingway: Selected Letters, 1917–1961.* Scribner, 1981.
Berg, A. Scott. *Lindbergh.* G.P. Putnam's Sons, 1998.
Berle, Adolf A., Jr. *Navigating the Rapids, 1918–1971: From the Papers of Adolf A. Berle.* Harcourt Brace Jovanovich, 1973.
Biddle, Anthony Joseph Drexel. *Poland and the Coming of the Second World War: The Diplomatic Papers of A. J. Drexel Biddle, Jr., United States Ambassador to Poland, 1937–1939.* Ohio State University, 1976.
Borkenau, Franz. *The Spanish Cockpit.* Faber & Faber, 1937.
Bowers, Claude G. *My Mission to Spain: Watching the Rehearsal for World War II.* Simon & Schuster, 1954.
Breitman, Richard, Barbara McDonald Stewart, and Severin Hochberg. *Advocate for the Doomed: The Diaries and Papers of James G. McDonald, 1932–1935.* Indiana University Press, 2007.
———. *Refugees and Rescue: The Diaries and Papers of James G. McDonald, 1935–1945.* Indiana University Press, 2009.
Buell, Raymond Leslie. *The Dangerous Year.* Foreign Policy Association, 1936.
———. *Isolated America.* Alfred A. Knopf, 1940.
Bullitt, Orville, ed. *For the President, Personal and Secret: Correspondence Between Franklin D. Roosevelt and William C. Bullitt.* Houghton Mifflin, 1972.

Bullitt, William C. *The Bullitt Mission to Russia*. B. W. Huebsch, 1919.

———. *The Great Globe Itself: A Preface to World Affairs*. Charles Scribner's Sons, 1946.

Chamberlain, Neville, and Robert C. Self. *The Neville Chamberlain Diary Letters*. Ashgate, 2000.

Ciano, Galeazzo. *Ciano's Diplomatic Papers*. Odhams Press, 1948.

Cowles, Virginia. *Looking for Trouble*. Harper & Brothers, 1941.

Davies, Joseph Edward. *Mission to Moscow*. Garden City, 1943.

Dennis, Lawrence. *The Coming American Fascism*. Harper, 1936.

Detzer, Dorothy. *Appointment on the Hill*. Henry Holt, 1948.

Deuel, Wallace Rankin. *People Under Hitler*. Harcourt, Brace, 1942.

Dodd, Martha. *Through Embassy Eyes*. Garden City, 1940.

Dodd, William E., and Martha Dodd. *Ambassador Dodd's Diary, 1933–1938*. Harcourt, Brace, 1941.

Dulles, Allen, and Hamilton Fish Armstrong. *Can We Be Neutral?* Harper & Brothers for Council on Foreign Relations, Inc., 1936.

Earle, Edward Mead. *Against This Torrent*. Princeton University Press, 1941.

Eden, Anthony, Earl of Avon. *Facing the Dictators: The Memoirs of Anthony Eden, Earl of Avon*. Houghton Mifflin, 1962.

Engelbrecht, Helmuth Carol, and Frank Cleary Hanighen. *Merchants of Death: A Study of the International Armament Industry*. Dodd, Mead, 1934.

Farley, James A. *Jim Farley's Story: The Roosevelt Years*. McGraw Hill, 1948.

François-Poncet, André. *The Fateful Years*. Gollancz, 1949.

Freedman, Max, ed. *Roosevelt and Frankfurter: Their Correspondence, 1928–1945*. Little, Brown, 1967.

Goebbels, Joseph. *Die Tagebücher von Joseph Goebbels*. 17 vols. K. G. Saur, 1998–2006.

Gorodetsky, Gabriel, ed. *The Maisky Diaries: Red Ambassador to the Court of St. James, 1932–1943*. Yale University Press, 2015.

Grew, Joseph C. *Ten Years in Japan: A Contemporary Record Drawn from the Diaries and Private and Official Papers of Joseph C. Grew, United States Ambassador to Japan, 1932–1942*. Simon & Schuster, 1944.

———. *Turbulent Era: A Diplomatic Record of Forty Years, 1904–1945*. Houghton Mifflin, 1952.

Guilfoyle, James H. *On the Trail of the Forgotten Man: A Journal of the Roosevelt Presidential Campaign*. Peabody Master Printers, 1933.

Gunther, John. *Inside Europe*. Harper & Brothers, 1936.

Hanfstaengl, Ernst. *Hitler: The Memoir of a Nazi Insider Who Turned Against the Führer*. Arcade, 2020.

Harvey, Oliver. *The Diplomatic Diaries of Oliver Harvey, 1937–1940*. St. Martin's Press, 1970.

Heald, Morrell, ed. *Journalist at the Brink: Louis P. Lochner in Berlin, 1922–1942*. Xlibris, 2007.

Hickok, Lorena A., Richard Lowitt, and Maurine Hoffman Beasley, eds. *One Third of a Nation: Lorena Hickok Reports on the Great Depression*. University of Illinois Press, 1981.

Hull, Cordell. *The Memoirs of Cordell Hull*. Macmillan, 1948.

Ickes, Harold L. *The Secret Diary of Harold L. Ickes*. 3 vols. Simon & Schuster, 1953–1954.

Johnson, Gerald W. *Roosevelt: Dictator or Democrat?* Harper & Brothers, 1941.

Johnson, Hugh S. *The Blue Eagle, from Egg to Earth*. Doubleday, Doran, 1935.

Kennedy, Joseph P., and Amanda Smith. *Hostage to Fortune: The Letters of Joseph P. Kennedy*. Viking Press, 2001.

Kernan, William C. *My Road to Certainty*. David McKay, 1953.

———. *The Ghost of Royal Oak*. Free Speech Forum, 1940.

Knickerbocker, H. R. *The Soviet Five-Year Plan and Its Effect on World Trade*. Bodley Head, 1931.

Lindbergh, Anne Morrow. *The Flower and the Nettle: Diaries and Letters of Anne Morrow Lindbergh, 1936–1939*. Harcourt Brace Jovanovich, 1976.

Lindbergh, Charles A. *The Wartime Journals of Charles A. Lindbergh*. Harcourt, Brace, Jovanovich, 1970.

Lindley, Ernest Kidder. *Franklin D. Roosevelt: A Career in Progressive Democracy*. Blue Ribbon Books, 1934.

———. *The Roosevelt Revolution, First Phase*. Viking Press, 1933.

Lippmann, Walter, and Allan Nevins, eds. *Interpretations, 1931–1932*. Macmillan, 1932.

Lippmann, Walter, and John Morton Blum. *Public Philosopher: Selected Letters of Walter Lippmann*. Ticknor & Fields, 1985.

Luce, Henry R., and John Knox Jessup. *The Ideas of Henry Luce*. Atheneum, 1969.

Lyons, Eugene. *Assignment in Utopia*. Harcourt, Brace, 1937.

Matthews, Herbert Lionel. *The Education of a Correspondent*. Harcourt, Brace, 1946.
———. *Two Wars and More to Come*. Carrick & Evans, 1938.
McIntire, Ross T., and George Creel. *White House Physician*. Putnam's Sons, 1946.
Moley, Raymond. *The First New Deal*. Harcourt, Brace, 1966.
Moorehead, Caroline, ed. *Selected Letters of Martha Gellhorn*. Henry Holt, 2006.
Mowrer, Edgar Ansel. *Germany Puts the Clock Back*. William Morrow, 1939.
———. *Triumph and Turmoil: A Personal History of Our Time*. Weybright and Talley, 1968.
Mowrer, Lilian Thomson. *Journalist's Wife*. Grosset & Dunlap, 1940.
Muggeridge, Malcolm, ed. *Ciano's Diplomatic Papers*. Oldham's Press, 1948.
Ottley, Roi. *New World A-Coming: Inside Black America*. Houghton Mifflin, 1943.
Perkins, Frances. *The Roosevelt I Knew*. Viking Press, 1946.
Phillips, William. *Ventures in Diplomacy*. Beacon Press, 1952.
Roosevelt, Eleanor. *This I Remember*. Greenwood Press, 1975.
Roosevelt, Elliott, and James Brough. *An Untold Story: The Roosevelts of Hyde Park*. Putnam, 1973.
Roosevelt, Franklin D. *On Our Way*. John Day, 1934.
Roosevelt, James, and Sidney Shalett. *Affectionately, F.D.R.: A Son's Story of a Lonely Man*. Harcourt, Brace, 1959.
Rosenman, Samuel I. *Working with Roosevelt*. Harper & Brothers, 1952.
Schuschnigg, Kurt. *My Austria*. Alfred A. Knopf, 1938.
Sheean, Vincent. *Dorothy and Red*. Houghton Mifflin, 1963.
———. *Not Peace but a Sword*. Doubleday, Doran, 1939.
———. *Personal History*. Modern Library, 1940.
Shirer, William. *Berlin Diary, 1934–1941*. Alfred A. Knopf, 1941.
———. *"This is Berlin": Radio Broadcasts from Nazi Germany*. Overlook Press, 1999.
———. *Twentieth Century Journey, Vol. 2: The Nightmare Years, 1930–1940*. Little, Brown, 1984.
Somerville, Janet, ed. *Yours, for Probably Always: Martha Gellhorn's Letters of Love and War*. Firefly Books, 2019.
Steer, G. L. *The Tree of Gernika: A Field Study of Modern War*. Hodder & Stoughton, 1938.
Stimson, Henry L. Diaries. Yale University Library. Digitized through Center for Research Libraries. Available at https://dds.crl.edu/crldelivery/18100.
Stimson, Henry L., and McGeorge Bundy. *On Active Service in Peace and War*. Harper & Brothers, 1947.
Strong, Anna Louise. *The Soviets Conquer Wheat*. Henry Holt, 1931.
———. *This Soviet World*. Henry Holt, 1936.
Swing, Raymond. *Forerunners of American Fascism*. Books for Libraries Press, 1969.
———. *How War Came*. W. W. Norton, 1939.
Thayer, Charles W. *Bears in the Caviar*. J. B. Lippincott, 1951.
Thompson, Dorothy. *Dorothy Thompson's Political Guide: A Study of American Liberalism and Its Relationship to Modern Totalitarian States*. Stackpole Sons, 1938.
———. *Let the Record Speak*. Houghton Mifflin, 1939.
Thompson, Dorothy, Rose Wilder Lane, and William V. Holtz. *Dorothy Thompson and Rose Wilder Lane: Forty Years of Friendship: Letters, 1920–1960*. University of Missouri Press, 1991.
Tugwell, Rexford G. *The Battle for Democracy*. Columbia University Press, 1935.
———. *The Brains Trust*. Viking Press, 1968.
———. *The Democratic Roosevelt: A Biography of Franklin D. Roosevelt*. Penguin Books, 1969.
Tugwell, Rexford G., and Michael V. Namorato. *The Diary of Rexford G. Tugwell: The New Deal, 1932–1935*. Greenwood Press, 1992.
Turrou, Leon G. *Nazi Spies in America*. Random House, 1938.
Vautrin, Minnie, and Suping Lu. *Terror in Minnie Vautrin's Nanjing: Diaries and Correspondence, 1937–38*. University of Illinois Press, 2008.
Wehle, Louis B. *Hidden Threads of History: Wilson through Roosevelt*. Macmillan, 1953.
Welles, Sumner. *Seven Decisions That Shaped History*. Harper & Brothers, 1951.
———. *The Time for Decision*. Harper & Brothers, 1944.
White, William Allen, ed. *Defense for America*. Macmillan, 1940.
———. *The Autobiography of William Allen White*. Macmillan, 1946.
Wise, James Waterman. *Swastika: The Nazi Terror*. H. Smith and R. Haas, 1933.
Wise, Stephen S. *Challenging Years: The Autobiography of Stephen Wise*. Putnam's Sons, 1949.

World Committee for the Victims of German Fascism. *The Brown Book of the Hitler Terror and the Burning of the Reichstag.* Alfred A. Knopf, 1933.

BOOKS AND ARTICLES

Adamthwaite, Anthony P. *France and the Coming of the Second World War, 1936–1939.* Cass, 1977.

Adler, Cyrus, Aaron Margalith, and American Jewish Committee. *With Firmness in the Right: American Diplomatic Action Affecting Jews, 1840–1945.* American Jewish Committee, 1946.

Adlon, Hedda. *Hotel Adlon: The Life and Death of a Great Hotel.* Horizon Press, 1960.

Alexander, Martin S. *The Republic in Danger: General Maurice Gamelin and the Politics of French Defence, 1933–1940.* Cambridge University Press, 1992.

Alexander, Martin S., and William James Philpott. *Anglo-French Defence Relations Between the Wars.* Palgrave Macmillan, 2002.

Allport, Alan. *Britain at Bay: The Epic Story of the Second World War, 1938–1941.* Alfred A. Knopf, 2020.

Alpern, Sara. *Freda Kirchwey: A Woman of the Nation.* Harvard University Press, 1987.

Alpers, Benjamin. *Dictators, Democracy, and American Public Culture: Envisioning the Totalitarian Enemy, 1920s–1950s.* University of North Carolina Press, 2003.

Alpert, Michael. *A New International History of the Spanish Civil War.* Macmillan, 1994.

Applebaum, Anne. *Red Famine: Stalin's War on Ukraine.* Anchor Books, 2017.

Alter, Jonathan. *The Defining Moment: FDR's First Hundred Days and the Triumph of Hope.* Simon & Schuster, 2006.

Bailey, Fred Arthur. *William Edward Dodd: The South's Yeoman Scholar.* University Press of Virginia, 1997.

Balfour, Sebastian, and Paul Preston. *Spain and the Great Powers in the Twentieth Century.* Routledge, 1999.

Bassow, Whitman. *The Moscow Correspondents: Reporting on Russia from the Revolution to Glasnost.* William Morrow, 1988.

Becker, Josef, and Ruth Becker. *Hitlers Machtergreifung 1933: Vom Machtantritt Hitlers 30. Januar 1933 Bis Zur Besiegelung Des Einparteinstaates 14. Juli 1933.* Deutscher Taschenbuch Verlag, 1983.

Beevor, Antony. *The Battle for Spain: The Spanish Civil War, 1936–1939.* Penguin, 2006.

Bell, P. M. H. *The Origins of the Second World War in Europe.* Longman, 1986.

Bellush, Bernard. *Franklin D. Roosevelt as Governor of New York.* AMS Press, 1968.

Bennett, David H. *Demagogues in the Depression: American Radicals and the Union Party, 1932–1936.* Rutgers University Press, 1969.

———. *The Party of Fear: From Nativist Movements to the New Right in American History.* University of North Carolina Press, 1988.

Bernstein, Arnie. *Swastika Nation: Fritz Kuhn and the Rise and Fall of the German-American Bund.* St. Martin's Press, 2013.

Beschloss, Michael R. *Kennedy and Roosevelt: The Uneasy Alliance.* Harper & Row, 1980.

Billings, Richard N., and Will Brownell. *So Close to Greatness: A Biography of William C. Bullitt.* Macmillan, 1987.

Bischoff, Günter, et al., eds. *The Dollfuss/Schuschnigg Era in Austria: A Reassessment.* Transaction, 2003.

Blum, John Morton. *From the Morgenthau Diaries.* 3 vols. Houghton Mifflin, 1959–1967.

Borg, Dorothy. *The United States and the Far Eastern Crisis of 1933–1938.* Harvard University Press, 1964.

Borgwardt, Elizabeth. *A New Deal for the World: America's Vision for Human Rights.* Harvard University Press, 2005.

Bosworth, R. J. B. *Mussolini's Italy: Life Under the Fascist Dictatorship, 1915–1945.* Penguin, 2005.

Bouverie, Tim. *Appeasement: Chamberlain, Hitler, Churchill, and the Road to War.* Tim Duggan, 2019.

Boyce, Robert, and Joseph A. Maiolo, eds. *The Origins of World War Two: The Debate Continues.* Palgrave Macmillan, 2003.

Boyce, Robert W. D., and Esmonde M. Robertson. *Paths to War: New Essays on the Origins of the Second World War.* St. Martin's Press, 1989.

Boyle, Peter G. *American-Soviet Relations: From the Russian Revolution to the Fall of Communism.* Routledge, 1993.

Brands, H. W. *America First: Roosevelt vs. Lindbergh in the Shadow of War.* Doubleday, 2024.

———. *Traitor to His Class: The Privileged Life and Radical Presidency of Franklin Delano Roosevelt.* Doubleday, 2008.

Breitman, Richard. *The Berlin Mission: The American Who Resisted Nazi Germany from Within*. Public Affairs, 2019.

Breitman, Richard, and Alan M. Kraut. *American Refugee Policy and European Jewry, 1933–1945*. Indiana University Press, 1987.

Breitman, Richard, and Allan J. Lichtman. *FDR and the Jews*. Harvard University Press, 2013.

Brenan, Gerald. *The Spanish Labyrinth: An Account of the Social and Political Background of the Civil War.* 2d ed. Cambridge University Press, 1950.

Brinkley, Alan. *The End of Reform: New Deal Liberalism in Recession and War*. Alfred A. Knopf, 1995.

———. *Voices of Protest: Huey Long, Father Coughlin, and the Great Depression*. Vintage, 1983.

Brown, John Mason. *The Worlds of Robert E. Sherwood: Mirror to His Times, 1896–1939*. Greenwood Press, 1979.

Burke, Bernard V. *Ambassador Frederic Sackett and the Collapse of the Weimar Republic, 1930–1933: The United States and Hitler's Rise to Power.* Cambridge University Press, 1994.

Burns, James MacGregor. *Roosevelt: The Lion and the Fox*. Harcourt, Brace, 1956.

Bussey, Gertrude, and Margaret Tims. *Pioneers for Peace: Women's International League for Peace and Freedom, 1915–1965*. Allen and Unwin, 1965.

Canedy, Susan. *America's Nazis: A Democratic Dilemma: A History of the German American Bund.* Markgraf, 1990.

Carew, Michael G. *The Power to Persuade: FDR, the Newsmagazines, and Going to War, 1939–1941.* University Press of America, 2005.

Casey, Steven. *Cautious Crusade: Franklin D. Roosevelt, American Public Opinion, and the War against Nazi Germany*. Oxford University Press, 2001.

Cassella-Blackburn, Michael. *The Donkey, the Carrot, and the Club: William C. Bullitt and Soviet-American Relations, 1917–1948*. Praeger, 2004.

Casto, William R. *Advising the President: Attorney General Robert H. Jackson and Franklin D. Roosevelt*. University Press of Kansas, 2018.

Chadwin, Mark Lincoln. *The Hawks of World War II*. University of North Carolina Press, 1968.

Chapman, Michael E. *Arguing Americanism: Franco Lobbyists, Roosevelt's Foreign Policy, and the Spanish Civil War*. Kent State University Press, 2011.

Charles, Douglas M. *J. Edgar Hoover and the Anti-interventionists: FBI Political Surveillance and the Rise of the Domestic Security State, 1939–1945*. Ohio State University Press, 2007.

Chatfield, Charles, ed. *Peace Movements in America*. Schocken Books, 1973.

Childers, Thomas. *The Third Reich: A History of Nazi Germany*. Simon & Schuster, 2017.

Chukumba, Stephen U. *The Big Powers Against Ethiopia: Anglo-Franco-American Diplomatic Maneuvers During the Italo-Ethiopian Dispute, 1934–1938*. University Press of America, 1979.

Churchwell, Sarah. *Behold, America: The Entangled History of "America First" and "The American Dream."* Basic Books, 2018.

Clavin, Patricia. *The Great Depression in Europe, 1929–1939*. Macmillan Press, 2000.

Clifford, J. Garry, and Samuel R. Spencer Jr. *The First Peacetime Draft*. University Press of Kansas, 1986.

Cole, Wayne S. *Charles A. Lindbergh and the Battle Against American Intervention in World War II.* Harcourt Brace Jovanovich, 1974.

———. *Roosevelt & the Isolationists, 1932–45*. University of Nebraska Press, 1983.

Conant, Jennet. *The Irregulars: Roald Dahl and the British Spy Ring in Wartime Washington*. Simon & Schuster, 2008.

Conquest, Robert. *The Great Terror: A Reassessment*. Oxford University Press, 1990.

———. *The Harvest of Sorrow: Soviet Collectivization and the Terror-Famine*. Oxford University Press, 1986.

Cook, Blanche Wiesen. *Eleanor Roosevelt*. 3 vols. Penguin, 1992–2017.

Costigliola, Frank. *Roosevelt's Lost Alliances: How Personal Politics Helped Start the Cold War*. Princeton University Press, 2012.

Cott, Nancy F. *Fighting Words: The Bold American Journalists Who Brought the World Home Between the Wars*. Basic Books, 2020.

Coulter, Matthew Ware. *The Senate Munitions Inquiry of the 1930s*. Greenwood Press, 1997.

Craig, Douglas B. *After Wilson: The Struggle for the Democratic Party, 1920–1934*. University of North Carolina Press, 1992.

Crowl, James William. *Angels in Paradise: Western Reporters in Soviet Russia, 1917–1937*. University Press of America, 1982.

Cull, Nicholas John. *Selling War: The British Propaganda Campaign Against American "Neutrality" in World War II*. Oxford University Press, 1995.

Dallek, Robert. *Democrat and Diplomat: The Life of William E. Dodd*. Oxford University Press, 1968.

———. *Franklin D. Roosevelt: A Political Life*. Penguin, 2017.

———. *Franklin D. Roosevelt and American Foreign Policy, 1932–1945*. Oxford University Press, 1995.

Daniels, Jonathan. *The End of Innocence*. Da Capo Press, 1954.

Davies, R. W., and Stephen G. Wheatcroft. *The Years of Hunger: Soviet Agriculture, 1931–1933*. Palgrave Macmillan, 2004.

Davis, Kenneth S. *FDR: The Beckoning of Destiny, 188--1928*. Putnam, 1972.

———. *F.D.R.: The New York Years, 1928–1933*. Random House, 1985.

———. *F.D.R.: The New Deal Years, 1933–1937*. Random House, 1986.

———. *F.D.R.: Into the Storm, 1937–1940*. Random House, 1993.

———. *F.D.R.: The War President, 1940–1943*. Random House, 2000.

De Bedts, Ralph F. *Ambassador Joseph Kennedy, 1938–1940: An Anatomy of Appeasement*. P. Lang, 1985.

Diamond, Sander A. *The Nazi Movement in the United States, 1924–1941*. Cornell University Press, 1974.

Divine, Robert *Second Chance: The Triumph of Internationalism in America During World War II*. Atheneum, 1967.

———. *The Illusion of Neutrality*. University of Chicago Press, 1962.

———. *The Reluctant Belligerent: American Entry into World War II*. Wiley, 1965.

Dobson, Alan P. *U.S. Wartime Aid to Britain, 1940–1946*. Croom Helm, 1986.

Doenecke, Justus D. *In Danger Undaunted: The Anti-interventionist Movement of 1940–1941 as Revealed in the Papers of the America First Committee*. Hoover Institution Press, 1990.

———. *Storm on the Horizon: The Challenge to American Intervention, 1939–1941*. Rowman & Littlefield, 2000.

Domeier, Norman. *American Journalists in Hitler's Germany*. Boydell & Brewer, 2025.

Donaldson, Scott. *Archibald MacLeish: An American Life*. Houghton Mifflin, 1992.

Drummond, Donald F. *The Passing of American Neutrality, 1937–1941*. University of Michigan Press, 1955.

Dunn, Dennis J. *Caught Between Roosevelt and Stalin: America's Ambassadors to Moscow*. University Press of Kentucky, 1998.

Dunn, Susan. *A Blueprint for War: FDR and the Hundred Days That Mobilized America*. Yale University Press, 2018.

———. *1940: FDR, Willkie, Lindbergh, Hitler—the Election Amid the Storm*. Yale University Press, 2013.

Durgan, Andrew. *The Spanish Civil War*. Palgrave Macmillan, 2007.

Duroselle, Jean-Baptiste. *France and the Nazi Threat: The Collapse of French Diplomacy, 1932–1939*. Enigma Books, 2004.

Eichengreen, Barry J. *Golden Fetters: The Gold Standard and the Great Depression, 1919–1939*. Oxford University Press, 1992.

Engerman, David C. *Modernization from the Other Shore: American Intellectuals and the Romance of Russian Development*. Harvard University Press, 2003.

Etkind, Alexander. *Roads Not Taken: An Intellectual Biography of William C. Bullitt*. University of Pittsburgh Press, 2017.

Evans, Richard J. *Hitler's People: The Faces of the Third Reich*. Penguin, 2024.

———. *The Coming of the Third Reich*. Penguin, 2003.

———. *The Third Reich in Power*. Penguin, 2005.

Farnham, Barbara Rearden. *Roosevelt and the Munich Crisis: A Study of Political Decision-Making*. Princeton University Press, 1997.

Farnsworth, Beatrice. *William C. Bullitt and the Soviet Union*. Indiana University Press, 1967.

Feis, Herbert. *1933: Characters in Crisis*. Little, Brown, 1966.

———. *The Diplomacy of the Dollar, 1919–1932*. Norton, 1966.

———. *The Road to Pearl Harbor: The Coming of the War Between the United States and Japan*. Princeton University Press, 1950.

Fischer, Heinz Dietrich. *Outstanding International Press Reporting: Pulitzer Prize Winning Articles in Foreign Correspondence*. W. de Gruyter, 1984.

Foglesong, David S. *America's Secret War Against Bolshevism*. University of North Carolina Press, 1995.

Foster, Carrie A. *The Women and the Warriors: The U.S. Section of the Women's International League for Peace and Freedom, 1915–1946*. Syracuse University Press, 1995.
Foster, Catherine. *Women for All Seasons: The Story of the Women's International League for Peace and Freedom*. University of Georgia Press, 1989.
Frank, Richard B. *Tower of Skulls: A History of the Asia-Pacific War*. Vol. 1. Norton, 2019.
Frank, Robert. *Le Prix Du réarmement Français, 1935–1939*. Publications de la Sorbonne, 1982.
Fraser, Steve, and Gary Gerstle. *The Rise and Fall of the New Deal Order, 1930–1980*. Princeton University Press, 1989.
Freidel, Frank. *Franklin D. Roosevelt*. 4 vols. Little, Brown, 1952.
———. *Franklin D. Roosevelt: A Rendezvous with Destiny*. Little, Brown, 1990.
Fronczak, Joseph. *Everything Is Possible: Antifascism and the Left in the Age of Fascism*. Yale University Press, 2023.
Fullilove, Michael. *Rendezvous with Destiny: How Franklin D. Roosevelt and Five Extraordinary Men Took America into the War and into the World*. Penguin, 2013.
Fusfeld, Daniel R. *The Economic Thought of Franklin D. Roosevelt and the Origins of the New Deal*. Columbia University Press, 1954.
Gage, Beverly. *G-Man: J. Edgar Hoover and the Making of the American Century*. Penguin, 2022.
Galbraith, John Kenneth. *The Great Crash, 1929*. 3rd ed. Houghton Mifflin, 1972.
Gamache, Ray. *Gareth Jones: Eyewitness to the Holodomor*. Welsh Academic Press, 2018.
Gelb, Michael, ed. *An American Engineer in Stalin's Russia: The Memoirs of Zara Witkin, 1932–1934*. University of California Press, 1991.
Gelfand, Lawrence E., ed. *The New Deal, Viewed from Fifty Years*. Center for the Study of the Recent History of the United States, 1983.
Gerassi, John. *The Premature Antifascists: North American Volunteers in the Spanish Civil War, 1936–39: An Oral History*. Praeger, 1986.
Glantz, Mary E. *FDR and the Soviet Union: The President's Battles over Foreign Policy*. University Press of Kansas, 2005.
Goodwin, Doris Kearns. *No Ordinary Time: Franklin and Eleanor Roosevelt—The Home Front in World War II*. Simon & Schuster, 1994.
Gordon, Linda. *The Second Coming of the KKK*. Norton, 2017.
Greene, Daniel, and Edward Phillips. *Americans and the Holocaust*. Rutgers University Press, 2022.
Greer, Thomas H. *What Roosevelt Thought: The Social and Political Ideas of Franklin D. Roosevelt*. Michigan State University Press, 1958.
Guttmann, Allen. *The Wound in the Heart: America and the Spanish Civil War*. Free Press of Glencoe, 1962.
Haight, John McVickar. *American Aid to France, 1938–1940*. Atheneum, 1970.
Hall, H. Duncan. *North American Supply*. H. M. Stationery Office, 1955.
Hamby, Alonzo. *For the Survival of Democracy: Franklin Roosevelt and the World Crisis of the 1930s*. Free Press, 2004.
———. *Man of Destiny: FDR and the Making of the American Century*. Basic Books, 2015.
Hanebrink, Paul. *A Specter Haunting Europe: The Myth of Judeo-Bolshevism*. Harvard University Press, 2018.
Harper, John Lamberton. *American Visions of Europe: Franklin D. Roosevelt, George F. Kennan, and Dean G. Acheson*. Cambridge University Press, 1994.
Harris, Brice, Jr. *The United States and the Ethiopian Crisis*. Stanford University Press, 1964.
Hart, Bradley W. *Hitler's American Friends: The Third Reich's Supporters in the United States*. St. Martin's Press, 2018.
Hartshorn, Peter. *I Have Seen the Future: Life of Lincoln Steffens*. Counterpoint Press, 2011.
Haslam, Jonathan. *Soviet Foreign Policy, 1930–1933*. Macmillan, 1983.
———. *The Soviet Union and the Struggle for Collective Security in Europe, 1933–39*. St. Martin's Press, 1984.
Hastings, Max. *Inferno: The Second World War, 1939–1945*. Alfred A. Knopf, 2011.
Hathaway, Oona, and Scott J. Shapiro. *The Internationalists: How a Radical Plan to Outlaw War Remade the World*. Simon & Schuster, 2017.
Heald, Morrell. *Transatlantic Vistas: American Journalists in Europe, 1900–1940*. Kent State University Press, 1988.
Hearden, Patrick J. *Roosevelt Confronts Hitler: America's Entry into World War II*. Northern Illinois University Press, 1987.

Heinrichs, Waldo H. *Threshold of War: Franklin D. Roosevelt and American Entry into World War II.* Oxford University Press, 1988.
Hett, Benjamin Carter. *The Death of Democracy: Hitler's Rise to Power and the Downfall of the Weimar Republic.* St. Martin's Press, 2018.
———. *The Nazi Menace: Hitler, Churchill, Roosevelt, Stalin, and the Road to War.* Henry Holt, 2020.
Hertog, Susan. *Dangerous Ambition: Dorothy Thompson and Rebecca West: New Women in Search of Love and Power.* Ballantine Books, 2011.
Hibbert, Christopher. *Mussolini: The Rise and Fall of Il Duce.* Little, Brown, 1962.
Hochschild, Adam. *Spain in Our Hearts: Americans in the Spanish Civil War, 1936–1939.* Houghton Mifflin, 2016.
Hoff, Joan. *Herbert Hoover, Forgotten Progressive.* Little, Brown, 1975.
Hofstadter, Richard. *The American Political Tradition and the Men Who Made It.* Alfred A. Knopf, 1973.
Hönicke Moore, Michaela. *Know Your Enemy: The American Debate on Nazism, 1933–1945.* Cambridge University Press, 2010.
Hotta, Eri. *Japan 1941: Countdown to Infamy.* Alfred A. Knopf, 2013.
Hull, Katy. *The Machine Has a Soul: American Sympathy with Fascism.* Princeton University Press, 2021.
Iriye, Akira. *The Origins of the Second World War in Asia and the Pacific.* Longman, 1987.
Jeffreys-Jones, Rhodri. *The Nazi Spy Ring: Hitler's Agents, the FBI, and the Case that Stirred the Nation.* Georgetown University Press, 2020.
Johnson, Robert David. *The Peace Progressives and American Foreign Relations.* Harvard University Press, 1995.
Johnson, Walter. *The Battle Against Isolation.* University of Chicago Press, 1944.
Johnstone, Andrew. *Against Immediate Evil: American Internationalists and the Four Freedoms on the Eve of World War II.* Cornell University Press, 2014.
Kagan, Robert. *The Ghost at the Feast: America and the Collapse of World Order, 1900–1941.* Alfred A. Knopf, 2023.
Kaiser, David. *No End Save Victory: How FDR Led the Nation into War.* Basic Books, 2014.
Katznelson, Ira. *Fear Itself: The New Deal and the Origins of Our Time.* Norton, 2013.
Kelly, Tom. *The Imperial Post: The Meyers, the Grahams, and the Paper That Rules Washington.* William Morrow, 1983.
Kennedy, David. *Freedom from Fear: The American People in Depression and War, 1929–1945.* Oxford University Press, 1999.
Kershaw, Ian. *Hitler, 1889–1936: Hubris.* Norton, 1998.
———. *Hitler, 1936–1945: Nemesis.* Norton, 2000.
Keylin, Arleen. *The Depression Years: As Reported by* The New York Times. Arno Press, 1976.
Kimball, Warren F. *Forged in War: Roosevelt, Churchill, and the Second World War.* William Morrow, 1997.
———. *The Juggler: Franklin Roosevelt as Wartime Statesman.* Princeton University Press, 1991.
———. *The Most Unsordid Act: Lend-lease, 1939–1941.* Johns Hopkins University Press, 1969.
Kindleberger, Charles P. *The World in Depression, 1929–1939.* University of California Press, 1986.
King, David. *The Trial of Adolf Hitler.* Norton, 2017.
Kinsella, William E. *Leadership in Isolation: FDR and the Origins of the Second World War.* G. K. Hall, 1978.
Klein, Maury. *Rainbow's End: The Crash of 1929.* Oxford University Press, 2001.
Kotkin, Stephen. *Stalin: Waiting for Hitler, 1929–1941.* Penguin Press, 2017.
Kurth, Peter. *American Cassandra: The Life of Dorothy Thompson.* Little, Brown, 1990.
Lacey, Jim. *The Washington War: FDR's Inner Circle and the Politics of Power That Won World War II.* Bantam Books, 2019.
Langer, William L., and S. Everett Gleason. *The Challenge to Isolation, 1937–1940.* Harper & Row, 1952.
Larson, Erik. *In the Garden of Beasts: Love, Terror, and an American Family in Hitler's Berlin.* Random House, 2011.
Lash, Joseph P. *Dealers and Dreamers: A New Look at the New Deal.* Doubleday, 1988.
———. *Roosevelt and Churchill, 1939–1941: The Partnership That Saved the West.* Norton, 1976.
Lee, Alfred McClung, and Elizabeth Briant Lee, eds. *The Fine Art of Propaganda: A Study of Father Coughlin's Speeches.* Harcourt, Brace, 1939.
Leffler, Melvyn P. *The Elusive Quest: America's Pursuit of European Stability and French Security, 1919–1933.* University of North Carolina Press, 1979.

Leigh, Michael. *Mobilizing Consent: Public Opinion and American Foreign Policy, 1937–1947*. Greenwood Press, 1976.
Leuchtenburg, William E. *Franklin D. Roosevelt and the New Deal*. Harper & Row, 1963.
Lewis, David Levering. *The Improbable Wendell Willkie*. Norton, 2018.
———. *W. E. B. Du Bois: The Fight for Equality and the American Century, 1919–1963*. Henry Holt, 2000.
Lifka, Thomas E. *The Concept "Totalitarianism" and American Foreign Policy, 1933–1949*. 2 vols. Garland, 1988.
Lipstadt, Deborah E. *Beyond Belief: The American Press and the Coming of the Holocaust, 1933–1945*. Free Press, 1986.
Low, Alfred D. *The Anschluss Movement, 1931–1938, and the Great Powers*. Columbia University Press, 1985.
Lubrich, Oliver. *Travels in the Reich, 1933–1945: Foreign Authors Report from Germany*. University of Chicago Press, 2010.
MacDonald, C. A. *The United States, Britain, and Appeasement, 1936–1939*. Macmillan, 1981.
MacDonnell, Francis. *Insidious Foes: The Axis Fifth Column and the American Home Front*. Oxford University Press, 1995.
Mahl, Thomas E. *Desperate Deception: British Covert Operations in the United States, 1939–44*. Brassey's, 1998.
Maiolo, Joseph. *Cry Havoc: How the Arms Race Drove the World to War, 1931–1941*. Basic Books, 2010.
Mallet, Robert. *Mussolini and the Origins of the Second World War, 1933–1940*. Palgrave Macmillan, 2003.
———. *Mussolini in Ethiopia, 1919–1935*. Cambridge University Press, 2015.
Marcus, Sheldon. *Father Coughlin: The Tumultuous Life of the Priest of the Little Flower*. Little, Brown, 1973.
Marolda, Edward J. *FDR and the U.S. Navy*. St. Martin's Press, 1998.
Matthews, Jeffrey J. *Alanson B. Houghton: Ambassador of the New Era*. SR Books, 2004.
Mayers, David Allan. *The Ambassadors and America's Soviet Policy*. Oxford University Press, 1995.
Meacham, Jon. *Franklin and Winston*. Random House, 2004.
Medoff, Rafael. *The Jews Should Keep Quiet: Franklin D. Roosevelt, Rabbi Stephen S. Wise, and the Holocaust*. University of Nebraska Press, 2019.
Merkes, Manfred. *Die Deutsche Politik Im Spanischen Bürgerkrieg*. Röhrscheid, 1969.
Michaelis, David. *Eleanor*. Simon & Schuster, 2020.
Michaelis, Meir. *Mussolini and the Jews: German, Italian Relations and the Jewish Question in Italy, 1922–1945*. Clarendon Press, 1978.
Mitter, Rana. *Forgotten Ally: China's World War II, 1937–1945*. Houghton Mifflin, 2013.
Montefiore, Simon Sebag. *Stalin: The Court of the Red Tsar*. Alfred A. Knopf, 2003.
Moorehead, Caroline. *Gellhorn: A Twentieth Century Life*. Henry Holt, 2003.
Morgan, Ted. *FDR: A Biography*. Simon & Schuster, 1985.
Morris, M. Wayne. *Stalin's Famine and Roosevelt's Recognition of Russia*. University Press of America, 1994.
Mulder, Nicholas. *The Economic Weapon: The Rise of Sanctions as a Tool of Modern War*. Yale University Press, 2022.
Nagorski, Andrew. *Hitlerland: American Eyewitnesses to the Nazi Rise to Power*. Simon & Schuster, 2012.
Nasaw, David. *The Chief: The Life of William Randolph Hearst*. Houghton Mifflin, 2000.
———. *The Patriarch: The Remarkable Life and Turbulent Times of Joseph P. Kennedy*. Penguin, 2013.
Neal, Steve. *Happy Days Are Here Again: The 1932 Democratic Convention, the Emergence of FDR—and How America Was Changed Forever*. William Morrow, 2004.
Offner, Arnold A. *American Appeasement: United States Foreign Policy and Germany, 1933–1938*. Harvard University Press, 1969.
Ohl, John Kennedy. *Hugh S. Johnson and the New Deal*. Northern Illinois University Press, 1985.
Olson, Lynne. *Those Angry Days: Roosevelt, Lindbergh, and America's Fight over World War II, 1939–1941*. Random House, 2013.
Overy, Richard, and Andrew Wheatcroft. *The Road to War*. Random House, 1989.
Paananen, Eloise, and Lauri Paananen. *The Winter War: The Russo-Finnish Conflict, 1939–40*. Scribner, 1973.

Paine, S. C. M. *The Wars for Asia, 1911–1949*. Cambridge University Press, 2012.

Paxton, Robert. *The Anatomy of Fascism*. Alfred A. Knopf, 2004.

Pedersen, William D. *A Companion to Franklin D. Roosevelt*. Wiley-Blackwell, 2011.

Peel, Roy V., and Thomas C. Donnelly. *The 1932 Campaign: An Analysis*. Da Capo Press, 1935.

Pells, Richard H. *Radical Visions and American Dreams: Culture and Social Thought in the Depression Years*. University of Illinois Press, 1998.

Pogue, Forrest C. *George C. Marshall*. Viking Press, 1963.

Preston, Andrew. *Total Defense: The New Deal and the Invention of National Security*. Harvard University Press, 2025.

Preston, Paul. *The Spanish Holocaust: Inquisition and Extermination in Twentieth-Century Spain*. Norton, 2012.

———. *The Spanish Civil War: Reaction, Revolution, and Revenge*. William Collins, 2016.

———. *We Saw Spain Die: Foreign Correspondents in the Spanish Civil War*. Constable, 2008.

Radosh, Ronald, Mary R. Habeck, and G. N. Sevostianov. *Spain Betrayed: The Soviet Union in the Spanish Civil War*. Yale University Press, 2001.

Range, Peter Ross. *1924: The Year That Made Hitler*. Little, Brown, 2016.

Rankin, Nicholas. *Telegram from Guernica: The Extraordinary Life of George Steer, War Correspondent*. Faber & Faber, 2003.

Rappleye, Charles. *Herbert Hoover in the White House: The Ordeal of the Presidency*. Simon & Schuster, 2016.

Rauchway, Eric. *The Great Depression & the New Deal: A Very Short Introduction*. Oxford University Press, 2008.

———. *Winter War: Hoover, Roosevelt, and the First Clash over the New Deal*. Basic Books, 2018.

Reynolds, David. *From Munich to Pearl Harbor: Roosevelt's America and the Origins of the Second World War*. Ivan R. Dee, 2001.

———. *The Creation of the Anglo-American Alliance, 1937–41: A Study in Competitive Co-operation*. University of North Carolina Press, 1981.

Ritchie, Donald A. *Electing FDR: The New Deal Campaign of 1932*. University Press of Kansas, 2007.

Roberts, Andrew. *The Holy Fox: The Life of Lord Halifax*. Weidenfeld & Nicolson, 1991.

———. *The Storm of War*. HarperCollins, 2011.

Roberts, Chalmers M. *The Washington Post: The First 100 Years*. Houghton Mifflin, 1977.

Rock, William R. *Chamberlain and Roosevelt: British Foreign Policy and the United States, 1937–1940*. Ohio State University Press, 1988.

Rogge, O. John. *The Official German Report: Nazi Penetration, 1924–1942, Pan-Arabism, 1939–Today*. T. Yoseloff, 1961.

Roll, David L. *The Hopkins Touch: Harry Hopkins and the Forging of the Alliance to Defeat Hitler*. Oxford University Press, 2013.

Rollins, Alfred B., Jr. *Roosevelt and Howe*. Alfred A. Knopf, 1962.

Romasco, Albert U. *The Poverty of Abundance: Hoover, the Nation, the Depression*. Oxford University Press, 1965.

Rosenstone, Robert A. *Crusade of the Left: The Lincoln Battalion in the Spanish Civil War*. Pegasus, 1969.

Rudin, A. James. *Pillar of Fire: A Biography of Rabbi Stephen S. Wise*. Texas Tech University Press, 2015.

Ryback, Timothy W. *Takeover: Hitler's Final Rise to Power*. Alfred A. Knopf, 2024.

Sander, Gordon F. *The Hundred Day Winter War: Finland's Gallant Stand Against the Soviet Army*. University Press of Kansas, 2013.

Sanders, Marion K. *Dorothy Thompson: A Legend in Her Time*. Houghton Mifflin, 1973.

Sarles, Ruth, and Bill Kauffman. *A Story of America First: The Men and Women Who Opposed U.S. Intervention in World War II*. Praeger, 2003.

Sbacchi, Alberto. *Legacy of Bitterness: Ethiopia and Fascist Italy, 1935–1941*. Red Sea Press, 1997.

Schacht, John N., ed. *Three Faces of Midwestern Isolationism*. Center for the Study of the Recent History of the United States, 1981.

Schivelbusch, Wolfgang. *Three New Deals: Reflections on Roosevelt's America, Mussolini's Italy, and Hitler's Germany, 1933–1939*. Metropolitan Books, 2006.

Schlesinger, Arthur M., Jr. *The Age of Roosevelt*. 3 vols. Houghton, Mifflin, 1957–1960.

Schmitz, David F. *The Sailor: Franklin D. Roosevelt and the Transformation of American Foreign Policy*. University of Kentucky Press, 2012.

———. *The Triumph of Internationalism: Franklin D. Roosevelt and a World in Crisis, 1933–1941*. Potomac Books, 2007.
Schott, Linda K. *Reconstructing Women's Thoughts: The Women's International League for Peace and Freedom Before World War II*. Stanford University Press, 1997.
Schwarz, Jordan A. *The Interregnum of Despair: Hoover, Congress, and the Depression*. University of Illinois Press, 1970.
Scott, William R. *The Sons of Sheba's Race: African Americans and the Italo-Ethiopian War, 1935–1941*. Indiana University Press, 1993.
Service, Robert. *A History of Twentieth Century Russia*. Harvard University Press, 1997.
Sherwood, Robert E. *Roosevelt and Hopkins: An Intimate History*. Harper & Brothers, 1950.
Shirer, William. *The Rise and Fall of the Third Reich: A History of Nazi Germany*. Simon & Schuster, 1960.
Silverman, Dan P. *Hitler's Economy: Nazi Work Creation Programs, 1933–1936*. Harvard University Press, 1998.
Simms, Brendan, and Charlie Laderman. *Hitler's American Gamble: Pearl Harbor and Germany's March to Global War*. Basic Books, 2021.
Skidelsky, Robert. *Oswald Mosley*. Macmillan, 1975.
Smith, Geoffrey S. *To Save a Nation: American Countersubversives, the New Deal, and the Coming of World War II*. Basic Books, 1973.
Smith, Jean Edward. *FDR*. Random House, 2008.
Smith, Richard Norton. *The Colonel: The Life and Legend of Robert R. McCormick, 1880–1955*. Houghton Mifflin, 1997.
Steel, Ronald. *Walter Lippmann and the American Century*. Little, Brown, 1980.
Steele, Richard W. *Free Speech in the Good War*. St. Martin's Press, 1999.
———. *Propaganda in an Open Society: The Roosevelt Administration and the Media, 1933–1941*. Greenwood Press, 1985.
Steiner, Zara. *The Lights That Failed: European International History, 1919–1933*. Oxford University Press, 2005.
———. *The Triumph of the Dark: European International History, 1933–1939*. Oxford University Press, 2011.
Stewart, Barbara McDonald. *United States Government Policy on Refugees from Nazism, 1933–1940*. Garland, 1982.
Stiller, Jesse H. *George S. Messersmith, Diplomat of Democracy*. University of North Carolina Press, 1987.
Strong, Tracy B., and Helene Keyssar. *Right in Her Soul: The Life of Anna Louise Strong*. Random House, 1983.
Stuckey, Mary E. *Voting Deliberatively: FDR and the 1936 Presidential Campaign*. Penn State University Press, 2015.
Swing, Raymond Gram. *Forerunners of American Fascism*. Books for Libraries Press, 1935.
Taylor, F. Jay. *The United States and the Spanish Civil War*. Bookman Associates, 1956.
Taylor, Sally J. *Stalin's Apologist: Walter Duranty: The* New York Times*'s Man in Moscow*. Oxford University Press, 1990.
Taylor, Telford. *Munich: The Price of Peace*. Doubleday, 1979.
Theoharis, Athan G. *Spying on Americans: Political Surveillance from Hoover to the Huston Plan*. Temple University Press, 1978.
———. *The FBI and American Democracy: A Brief Critical History*. University Press of Kansas, 2004.
Theoharis, Athan G., and John Stuart Cox. *The Boss: J. Edgar Hoover and the Great American Inquisition*. Temple University Press, 1988.
Thomas, Hugh. *The Spanish Civil War*. Hamish Hamilton, 1977.
Thompson, John A. *A Sense of Power: The Roots of America's Global Role*. Cornell University Press, 2015.
Thomson, James Claude. *While China Faced West: American Reformers in Nationalist China, 1928–1937*. Harvard University Press, 1969.
Tierney, Dominic. *FDR and the Spanish Civil War: Neutrality and Commitment in the Struggle That Divided America*. Duke University Press, 2007.
Tooze, Adam. *The Deluge: The Great War, America, and the Remaking of the Global Order, 1916–1931*. Penguin, 2014.
Traina, Richard P. *American Diplomacy and the Spanish Civil War*. Indiana University Press, 1968.

Trotter, William R. *A Frozen Hell: The Russo-Finnish Winter War of 1939–1940*. Algonquin Books, 1991.
Tucker, Robert C. *Stalin in Power: The Revolution from Above, 1928–1941*. Norton, 1990.
Tull, Charles J. *Father Coughlin and the New Deal*. Syracuse University Press, 1965.
Turner, Henry Ashby, Jr. *Hitler's Thirty Days to Power: January 1933*. Addison-Wesley, 1996.
Ullrich, Volker. *Hitler: Ascent, 1889–1939*. Alfred A. Knopf, 2017.
———. *Hitler: Downfall, 1939–1945*. Alfred A. Knopf, 2020.
Urofsky, Melvin I. *A Voice That Spoke for Justice: The Life and Times of Stephen S. Wise*. State University of New York Press, 1982.
Vials, Chris. *Haunted by Hitler: Liberals, the Left, and the Fight Against Fascism in the United States*. University of Massachusetts Press, 2014.
Viola, Lynn, et al., eds. *The War Against the Peasantry, 1927–1930: The Tragedy of the Soviet Countryside*. Yale University Press, 2005.
Wakabayashi, Bob Tadashi. *The Nanking Atrocity, 1937–38: Complicating the Picture*. Berghahn Books, 2007.
Ward, Geoffrey. *A First-Class Temperament: The Emergence of Franklin Roosevelt, 1905–1928*. Harper & Row, 1989.
Ward, Geoffrey, ed. *Closest Companion: The Unknown Story of the Intimate Friendship Between Franklin Roosevelt and Margaret Suckley*. Simon & Schuster, 1995.
Watt, D. C. *How War Came: The Immediate Origins of the Second World War, 1938–1939*. Pantheon Books, 1989.
Watts, Jill. *The Black Cabinet: The Untold Story of African Americans and Politics During the Age of Roosevelt*. Grove Atlantic, 2020.
Weinberg, Gerhard L. *The Foreign Policy of Hitler's Germany: Diplomatic Revolution in Europe, 1933–36*. University of Chicago Press, 1970.
White, Graham J. *FDR and the Press*. University of Chicago Press, 1979.
Whitman, James Q. *Hitler's American Model: The United States and the Making of Nazi Race Law*. Princeton University Press, 2017.
Williams, Mason B. *City of Ambition: FDR, La Guardia, and the Making of Modern New York*. W. W. Norton, 2013.
Wilz, John Edward. *From Isolation to War, 1931–1941*. Crowell, 1968.
Winkler, Allan M. *Franklin D. Roosevelt and the Making of Modern America*. Pearson/Longman, 2006.
Witcover, Jules. *Party of the People: A History of the Democrats*. Random House, 2003.
Wyman, David S. *Paper Walls: America and the Refugee Crisis, 1938–1941*. Pantheon Books, 1985.
Zalampas, Michael. *Adolf Hitler and the Third Reich in American Magazines, 1923–1939*. Bowling Green State University Press, 1989.

INDEX

NOTE: "FDR" refers to Franklin D. Roosevelt. Page numbers in *italics* refer to photographs.

ABOUT THE AUTHOR

WILLIAM I. HITCHCOCK is the James Madison Professor of History at the University of Virginia. He received his BA degree from Kenyon College and his PhD from Yale University. He has been a Fulbright Scholar, a fellow of the Nobel Institute in Oslo, the holder of the Henry Kissinger Chair at the Library of Congress, and a Berlin Prize fellow at the American Academy in Berlin. His books include *The Age of Eisenhower: America and the World in the 1950s*, which was a *New York Times* bestseller, and *The Bitter Road to Freedom: A New History of the Liberation of Europe*, which was a finalist for the Pulitzer Prize and a winner of the George Louis Beer Prize from the American Historical Association. He is married to the historian Elizabeth R. Varon and lives in Charlottesville, Virginia.